THE CAMBRIDGE HISTORY OF EIGHTEENTH-CENTURY PHILOSOPHY

More than thirty eminent scholars from nine different countries have contributed to *The Cambridge History of Eighteenth-Century Philosophy* – the most comprehensive and up-to-date history of the subject available in English.

In contrast with most histories of philosophy and in keeping with preceding Cambridge volumes in the series, the subject is treated systematically by topic, not by individual thinker, school, or movement, thus enabling a much more historically nuanced picture of the period to be painted. As in previous titles in the series, the volume has extensive biographical and bibliographical research materials.

During the eighteenth century, the dominant concept in philosophy was human nature, and so it is around this concept that the present work is centered. This allows the contributors to offer both detailed explorations of the epistemological, metaphysical, and ethical themes that continue to stand at the forefront of philosophy and to voice a critical attitude toward the historiography behind this emphasis in philosophical thought. At the same time, due attention is paid to historical context, with particular emphasis on the connections among philosophy, science, and theology.

This judiciously balanced, systematic, and comprehensive account of the whole of Western philosophy during the period will be an invaluable resource for philosophers, intellectual historians, theologians, political theorists, historians of science, and literary scholars.

Knud Haakonssen is Professor of Intellectual History at the University of Sussex.

The Cambridge History of Eighteenth-Century Philosophy

Volume II

EDITED BY
KNUD HAAKONSSEN
University of Sussex

CAMBRIDGE
UNIVERSITY PRESS

CAMBRIDGE UNIVERSITY PRESS
Cambridge, New York, Melbourne, Madrid, Cape Town, Singapore, São Paulo

Cambridge University Press
40 West 20th Street, New York, NY 10011-4211, USA

www.cambridge.org
Information on this title: www.cambridge.org/9780521418546

First published 2006

Printed in the United States of America

A catalog record for this publication is available from the British Library.

Library of Congress Cataloging in Publication Data
The Cambridge history of eighteenth-century philosophy / edited by Knud Haakonssen.
p. cm.
Includes bibliographical references and index.
ISBN 0-521-41854-2 (alk. paper)
1. Philosophy – History – 18th century. I. Haakonssen, Knud, 1947–
B802.C24 2005
190′.9′033–dc22 2004054878

Volume II ISBN-13 978-0-521-86743-6
Volume II ISBN-10 0-521-86742-8

Available only as a set: ISBN-13 978-0-521-41854-6 hardback
Available only as a set: ISBN-10 0-521-41854-2 hardback

CONTENTS

VOLUME I

VOLUME II

III: Philosophy and Theology

IV: Natural Philosophy

V: Moral Philosophy

III

PHILOSOPHY AND THEOLOGY

21

NATURAL AND REVEALED RELIGION

B. A. GERRISH

The importance of the eighteenth century for interpreting religion is commonly recognised; but how its importance is perceived depends on where one sees its outcome. It was a time of intense disagreement about the nature and worth of religion. A student at Cambridge in the early years of the following century – say, around 1810 – would have been confident that the redoubtable Archdeacon Paley had finally vindicated religion, both natural and revealed, against a hundred years of criticisms. The doors of the church and the academy were still open for business as usual. Today's admirer of the Enlightenment is more likely to find the representative figure in the sceptical David Hume or the acid Voltaire, their exposure of frail arguments and pious absurdities being taken as the final antidote to conventional religion. Yet others may think that at the end of the eighteenth century the meagre religious insights of the Enlightenment, such as they were, were taken up in various ways into the grander visions of Herder, Goethe, Schleiermacher, and Hegel. Still, there would be general agreement that the eighteenth century raised good questions about religion, whoever is held to have come up with the best answers.

Old theological controversies endured; frequently, they became entangled in domestic politics. But the main interest of the period for religious thought arises out of questions brought to the forum of public debate by the Deists. The participants in the debate, including both the defenders and the critics of religion, held overconfident opinions that time would prove to be much more parochial than they imagined. On all sides, limited perceptions of the essence, benefits, and defects of religion were naively universalised, and obstinate stereotypes of a complex and elusive mode of human behaviour were bequeathed to future generations. But, for all that, the contestants opened up *approaches* to religion that were characteristically modern. One part of their legacy was what we would call today a non-theological approach, and another was the transformation of theology itself.

An enormous body of literature was generated by the eighteenth-century debates on religion. A few attempts have been made to put together anthologies of representative selections. But much of the literature is accessible today only in research libraries; little more than a small fragment exists in modern reprints or critical editions. The field of eighteenth-century religious studies is currently receiving unprecedented scholarly attention, partly from scholars in search of the roots of the philosophy of religion and the science (or history) of religion as distinctively modern disciplines. (The theologians are usually more interested in the nineteenth century, especially the first three decades, a time when Christian theology enjoyed in Germany one of the most creative periods of its entire history.) It is hardly possible to present a comprehensive survey of the field here. All that is attempted is to place together in context the more important issues and thinkers, some of which are the subjects of individual treatment in subsequent chapters. From the theological point of view (as from others), the century is open-ended both at its beginning and at its close. However, one might roughly identify a period that runs from John Locke's *A Vindication of the Reasonableness of Christianity* (1695) to Friedrich Schleiermacher's *Reden über die Religion an die Gebildeten unter ihren Verächtern* (1799), which clearly marks the transition from the old Christian apologetics to the new. Interest falls naturally on two main themes: the Deist controversy in England and new theological beginnings in Germany.

I. THE THEOLOGICAL SITUATION

The sixteenth-century struggle for reform of the Western church ended in the creation of new churches. After years of appalling armed conflict, the existence of separate churches or 'confessions' could only be an acknowledged fact. In Germany, where the Reformation had begun, the refinement and defence of confessional traditions engaged much of the theologians' energies throughout the seventeenth century. But by the eighteenth century theological disagreements ceased to shape the international situation, and the churches largely assumed the role of supports for the political establishments of their respective lands. The very plurality of churches and the existence of dissenting minorities within them encouraged the spirit of toleration that had been provoked by revulsion against dogmatism and religious wars. A liberal religious tradition emerged. It held the promise of fresh theological directions, transcending the old party lines, even if it sometimes sank into a dry formalism, against which more passionate varieties of religiousness protested. And the extraordinary expansion of knowledge about the human species, other lands, and the wider cosmos further encouraged the openness of the liberal spirit. There was no warfare of science and religion, but there was a crisis of authority in both religion and science.

1. *The 'men of moderation'*

Toleration of dissenting minorities did not come easily or quickly. By the Edict of Nantes (1598), Henry IV ended the French wars of religion and granted the Huguenots the right to free exercise of the Reformed or Calvinist religion in designated locations. But Bourbon hostility to the Huguenots led to further armed conflict, and in 1685 the edict was revoked by Louis XIV, in whose reign the Huguenot exodus from France began. In the German Empire, the pattern of accommodation between the churches was foreshadowed by the Peace of Augsburg (1555), which acknowledged the right of every Lutheran or Roman Catholic ruler to determine the religion of his own domain. The Calvinists were not included in the settlement, and dissenters were confronted with a harsh choice: either to conform or to sell everything and migrate. Only in the imperial free cities could Lutherans and Roman Catholics expect to live together. But 'territorialism', rather than strict toleration, was still the solution that brought the Thirty Years' War to an end (Peace of Westphalia, 1648). This time, the rights of the Calvinists were recognised, but the Anabaptists had no acknowledged homeland.

In the English-speaking world, toleration came sooner in two of the American colonies than in the motherland. Founded by Lord Baltimore as a refuge for English Catholics (1634), Maryland extended its welcome to Protestants as well; and Rhode Island's history began when Puritan separatist Roger Williams bought land from the Indians at 'Providence' (1636) and pledged religious freedom to 'those distressed for cause of conscience'. In England itself, Oliver Cromwell's dream of an inclusive church settlement, which would have given equal recognition to a variety of religious viewpoints and have left the rest alone, did not survive him. With the restoration of the monarchy (1660) came the return of the episcopal establishment, and the Act of Uniformity (1662) deprived an estimated 1,800 Puritan clergy of their pastoral charges. The accession of William and Mary and the Toleration Act (1689) removed some of the more severe penalties of the law from most nonconformists, but not from Roman Catholics or Unitarians.

The antithesis of 'establishment' and 'nonconformity' was never overcome, but the course of theological reflection in the Anglican church did reinforce the legal requirement of toleration. During the fearful religious conflicts of seventeenth-century England, a third stream of religious thought can be identified, self-consciously disowning the dogmatism of the high churchmen and the dogmatism of their Puritan adversaries. Called in derision Latitudinarians, or 'men of moderation', the advocates of a third way were minimalists in their creed and urged modesty and open-mindedness in the pursuit of uncertain questions.

Immensely important though they were for the course of religious thought in the eighteenth century, it is arguable that they won the cause of moderation only at a price: religion came to be widely understood as a private matter for the individual conscience, faith as free assent to a minimum of morally useful beliefs, and churches as voluntary associations for the propagation of beliefs and the promotion of virtue.

This, indeed, was the position John Locke spoke for in his *Letter concerning Toleration*[1], published in the same year as the Act of Toleration. Religion, he held, is an inward persuasion of the mind. Neither the civil power nor bishops and presbyters can force anyone to accept a particular religion, since the nature of the understanding is that it cannot be compelled to believe. A church is a free and voluntary society, which a man is as free to leave as he was to enter, according to the way he judges its doctrine and worship. For Locke, it was plainly doctrine that came first – religious beliefs to which free intellectual assent could be given. And there were not very many of them. In *The Reasonableness of Christianity*, he assures us that the only faith and obedience God requires of us are belief that Jesus is the Messiah and a sincere endeavour after righteousness. It is true that other great doctrines are 'dropt here and there' in the New Testament Epistles, but they are not fundamental articles of faith and must not be thought necessary to salvation. Locke's religion was for plain, labouring men – suited to vulgar capacities and unencumbered with the niceties of the schools.

While it simplified religion, perhaps too drastically, the liberal or latitudinarian mentality cultivated the spirit of free inquiry. The thesis that Puritan ideals gave a strong impetus to the scientific revolution continues to be widely debated, for and against, but some historians of science argue that latitudinarian attitudes must have been much more propitious to the scientific enterprise. In Restoration Cambridge, after the publication of Isaac Newton's *Philosophiæ naturalis principia mathematica* (1687), a 'holy alliance' between moderate churchmanship and Newtonian natural philosophy fostered a buoyant rational theology, and Newton's eminent disciple, Samuel Clarke, was firmly persuaded that the new science left the atheists with no place to hide.

In at least one respect, however, theological discourse in the Age of Reason was to take a turn that the seventeenth-century Latitudinarians did not anticipate. Whereas they wanted to calm theological rancour by reducing the number of essential Christian beliefs, others, more radical than they, decided that the entire inner-Christian quarrel was hopelessly parochial, the real problem being how to relate Christianity itself and all other religions to a presumed universal essence of religion. Whether God wills the church to be presbyterian or episcopalian fades into triviality beside the question whether he has chosen to reveal himself only to contentious Christians. This is the question already raised in the seventeenth century by Lord Herbert of Cherbury, sometimes called the father of Deism.

In the enlarged edition (1633) of his epistemological study *De veritate* (1624), Herbert inserted a discussion of religion and revelation in which he argued that the only doctrines known to be true are those that command universal consent: 'common notions' that God has given in all times and places to all people.[2] Every religion has some portion of the truth, but corrupted by error, so that we have to separate the truth by applying Herbert's method. We discover the common notions by surveying all the religions of the world comparatively, or, more expeditiously, by examining the contents of our own minds. Herbert's five religious notions are that there is a Supreme Deity; that this Sovereign Deity ought to be worshipped; that the best part of divine worship is virtue conjoined with piety; that all vices and crimes should be expiated by repentance; and that there are rewards and punishments after this life. The true Catholic Church, outside of which there is indeed no salvation, is constituted by these common notions, and it embraces people of all times and places. Every particular church's truth depends on how far it is separated from this one. A similar belief in a normative, universally accessible essence of religion is what Matthew Tindal defended in the Deist controversy.

A second variety of radical religious thought also led beyond the Latitudinarians by inquiring into the psychology, rather than the epistemology, of religious belief. An interest in the emotional sources of belief had been sparked by Thomas Hobbes's treatment of the subject in his *Leviathan*. Hobbes endorsed the opinion of the Roman poet Statius (though not by name) that fear first made the gods – 'in the ignorance of causes', Hobbes adds.[3] But he acknowledged that monotheism, at least, had a rational impulse behind it: precisely the desire to know the causes of things. The coincidence of religious fanaticism and early studies of physiology in the seventeenth century invited a further possibility: that religion, or at least 'enthusiasm', is a sickness. In John Trenchard's *Natural History of Superstition* we find a clinical scrutiny of enthusiasm as an emotional disorder with a physiological base. One suspects that despite the cautious title of his work, Trenchard would be willing to include the orthodox zealots in his diagnosis along with the enthusiasts: the cause of their unyielding temper, too, is perhaps an intoxication with 'Vapours ascending from the lower Regions of [the] Body'.[4] Hume, at any rate, who thought such a matter worthy of a philosopher's attention, titled his own venture into the field, quite simply, *The Natural History of Religion*.[5] But is it really a matter for philosophy – or theology – at all?

2. *Theology, natural and revealed*

In our day, theology, the philosophy of religion, the history of religions, and the scientific study of religion have become separate disciplines. Sometimes they are perceived as mutually antagonistic. It would be an anachronism to read these terminological distinctions back into the eighteenth century, even though it was then that the material differences began to emerge. A hint of the need for new nomenclature can be discerned in the Deists' revival of a very ancient Stoic distinction, which they attributed to Varro, between three kinds of theology: mythical, natural or rational, and civil or political. It might also strike us as conceptually tidier to distinguish theology from religion, and science from philosophy. But that, too, would be to impose more order on the sources than they display. Francis Bacon, it is true, began the drive to detach the natural sciences from sacred theology; but he called science 'natural philosophy', as did Newton still, a century later. And if we consult Dr. Johnson's *Dictionary*, we discover that theology itself was, or was thought to be, a science. He equates 'theology' with 'divinity' and illustrates his meaning from Richard Hooker: 'Theologie, what is it but the Science of things Divine?'[6] Properly speaking, it may be that 'religion' denotes a mode of human behaviour, 'theology' one of the intellectual disciplines (sciences) that concern themselves with religion. But no such clarification was current in the eighteenth century.

In the seventeenth-century schools of divinity, the word *theology* was sometimes applied (as *theologia archetypa*) to God's knowledge of himself. But as human knowledge of God (*theologia ectypa*), theology was 'discourse about God and divine things' – a definition warranted, according to the Lutheran Johann Andreas Quenstedt, by the etymology of the word. The general field of theological study was broken down into several sub-disciplines: Johann Friedrich Koenig, for example, another Lutheran divine, distinguished exegetic, didactic (systematic), polemical, homiletic, casuistic, and ecclesiastical theology. Such divisions persist throughout the eighteenth century. But they barely hint at the new distinctions that were to emerge; rather, they betray the clerical connection of theological study, and it must be remembered that the universities, including Oxford and Cambridge, still remained seminaries of the established churches.

Much more important philosophically was the contrast commonly drawn between natural and revealed theology, or natural and revealed religion. Against the Socinian view that the soul is a tabula rasa at birth, the orthodox divines of the seventeenth century affirmed the existence of an innate notion of God, closely connected with the voice of conscience. They further held that the innate notion of God assumed determinate characteristics through observation of nature, understood as a *general revelation*, and in particular through meditation on human nature (the microcosm, or world in miniature). But they deemed all knowledge of God derived from nature insufficient for salvation, because the good pleasure of God cannot be firmly grasped apart from God's self-communication in Scripture, which is *special revelation*. Reason, untouched by grace, is not a neutral instrument of inquiry: it is biased and blinded by the vested interests of the sinful will and must not be regarded as the criterion of what is true in religion. The truths of revelation cannot be conceived by reason. But reason, when enlightened by grace and revelation, has the ability to apprehend these truths and the duty to defend them by proving that revelation has in fact occurred.

There is room in this scheme for rational explication of natural, as well as revealed, religion, and there are a few mixed articles that are accessible in part to philosophy as well as to theology. In practice, however, the distinction between natural and revealed theology required only a perfunctory treatment of the former in a prolegomenon to theology proper. Moreover, theology was taken to be, like medicine, pre-eminently a practical discipline. Just as the goal of medicine was not knowledge of the body but health, so theology was directed to the worship of God and human blessedness. Indeed, as Quenstedt pointed out, theology was a *discipline* only in a secondary sense: in its primary sense, it was a *disposition* (a 'habit') of the mind.[7] It is easy to see why the orthodox divines could use the words *theology* and *religion* interchangeably. Theology was not disinterested academic inquiry; it belonged to the practice of piety. It is also easy to understand that the critics of divinity wondered if it was not, after all, the 'enlightened' reason of the divines that was at the disposal of self-interest – the self-interest of piety.

Purists may insist that 'natural theology' and 'natural religion' are not synonymous concepts. The idea of a natural theology goes back to Plato's attempt to show that certain truths about God can be strictly demonstrated; and it plays, of course, a significant role in medieval scholasticism, notably in the 'five ways' by which Thomas Aquinas sought to prove the existence of God. Natural religion, by contrast, is rooted in Stoic thought. Here the claim is that buried under the various doctrines and practices of the rival religions are a few beliefs held in common by all; and that these alone are the essentials of religion, all else being accidental accretions. It is this Stoic concept that is primary in the Deist controversy, but it is not sharply differentiated from the Platonic concept.[8] The organ by which natural religion comes into existence was held to be reason. And it was an understandable step to add that reason, as ratiocination, could prove at least some of the propositions of natural religion. In practice, the terms were used indifferently. Hume's celebrated work is *Dialogues concerning Natural Religion* (1779). But the dialogues themselves belong to the argumentative genre of the theistic proofs, and they do in fact speak expressly of 'natural and revealed theology' as well as 'natural religion', the terms not being clearly distinguished. Hume's other investigation into the origin of religion in human nature (his *Natural History of Religion*), certainly owes a great deal to eighteenth-century preoccupation with nature and natural explanations. But it is an enterprise that would in due course be transferred from natural theology to the social sciences.

The eighteenth century did not invent the contrast between natural and revealed theology, but in the course of the Deist controversy the inherited priority was reversed. The insufficiency of the light of nature had formerly been the basis of the Protestant appeal to Scripture: reason was unambiguously subordinated to revelation. Nor did the mainline theologians expect to discover beyond Christianity anything but superstition and idolatry. Indeed, that is what the Puritans found in Roman Catholicism and even, in smaller measure, in Anglicanism. They agreed with John Calvin's verdict, that human nature is a 'perpetual factory of idols', and that only Scripture can clarify 'the otherwise confused knowledge of God in our minds', much as a pair of spectacles enables a person with poor eyesight to read. Perhaps the weak link in the argument was the enlistment of reason to prove that revelation had indeed occurred, despite the caution with which Calvin tried to make the case.[9] The Deists, at any rate, wanted to give reason this task – without caution – and more.

II. THE DEIST CONTROVERSY

Persistent questions of revealed theology continued to occupy church divines in the eighteenth century. They debated ecclesiastical authority, the doctrines of the Trinity and the person of Christ, original sin, election and free will, efficacious grace, the Eucharist, and so on. The Jansenist controversy in France, originally about the Augustinian doctrine of grace, became endlessly entangled in the party politics of church and state, not least because the Jansenists took up the ancient demand of Gallicanism for limitation of papal sovereignty over the French church. In England, the incursions of anti-Trinitarianism stirred up continual debates about the deity of Christ. Even establishment theologians such as Samuel Clarke were suspected of Arianism, as, more forgivably, was Sir Isaac Newton. Presbyterians became unitarian by droves, and they found an able leader in the chemist-theologian Joseph Priestley. In Reformed Geneva, Voltaire discovered that all the leading ministers were Socinian.

The Trinitarian debate was plainly connected with the drastic simplification of religion that the age demanded. Other ecclesiastical controversies, too, were by no means cut off from the main trends of secular thought. Hobbesians and Calvinists, for instance, invoked similar psychological arguments to refute *free will* (as commonly understood). Jonathan Edwards, possibly the greatest Reformed theologian of the eighteenth century, certainly the greatest in the English-speaking world, was equally at home in Christian doctrine and philosophical argument. He had been 'entertained and delighted' with Locke's *Essay concerning Human Understanding* at the age of fourteen, and he undertook his great treatise on free will not only as a refutation of the insidious perils of Arminianism, but also as a philosophical study of moral agency. The liveliness of the debates about the Trinity, free will, and other perennial issues in Christian theology did not diminish. But Deism forced other, newer questions on the attention of the theologians, and they were much more radical questions, raising doubts about the truth of Christianity.

Deism was an international phenomenon: the list of representative names includes, among others, John Toland and Matthew Tindal in England, Voltaire in France, Hermann Samuel Reimarus in Germany, and Thomas Paine in America. Unfortunately, however, the description 'Deist', like so many others in the history of ideas, turns out to be elusive. In present-day usage, a deist is someone who believes in an absentee deity: that is, in a God who fashioned the intricate machinery of the universe, then left it to run by its own immanent laws. It is far from clear that all the Deists were deists in this sense, although the mechanistic world-picture of Newtonian science unquestionably pushed theistic thinking in that direction. At any rate, the term *deists*, as used by philosophers of religion today, does not give the defining characteristic of the historical group as a whole. Better, perhaps, is the description often associated with it: 'freethinkers', those who refuse to submit their thoughts – even on religion – to ecclesiastical authorities. It is more convenient to use the expression 'Deist controversy' simply to refer to two constantly recurring *quaestiones disputatae* that moved to the forefront of theological reflection in England during the first half of the eighteenth century. Both questions had to do with the claims of Christian revelation: the first was whether any such revelation was needed; the second, whether, as a matter of fact, a revelation had occurred.

The twofold problem of revelation lies already, just beneath the surface, in the work of John Locke, who in this respect is a transitional figure between orthodoxy and Deism. The chapter on enthusiasm that he added to the fourth edition (1700) of *An Essay concerning Human Understanding*[10] does not depart radically from the orthodox divines, but it underscores the duties of reason just enough to be the harbinger of something new. The mark of a sincere lover of truth is 'not entertaining any Proposition with greater assurance than the Proofs it is built upon will warrant' (IV.xix.1). This, to be sure, means that '*Reason* must be our last Judge and Guide in every Thing' (IV.xix.14). But Locke implies no opposition between reason and revelation. Reason is natural revelation; revelation is natural reason enlarged by a new set of divinely communicated discoveries. Reason may not reject a supposedly revealed proposition simply on the grounds that its truth would never be 'made out by natural Principles' (IV.xix.14.). Its task, rather, is to determine whether in truth the proposition comes from God. And how does reason do that? By noting the miraculous signs that attest a genuine revelation. Even where these are presently lacking, we still have the revelation of Scripture (which has already been attested) and the common dictates of right reason to guide us.

It is precisely the assumptions of this confident argument against enthusiasm (that is, against the vain assurance of immediate, unauthenticated revelation) that the Deist controversy opened to objection. If reason is able to judge revelation, are there really any new discoveries that revelation can bring to us? And is it in fact the case that the Christian Scriptures have been sufficiently attested as divine revelation? The two objections, obviously, belong together. But we may say that the first was acutely raised by Toland and Tindal; the second, by Anthony Collins, Thomas Woolston, Conyers Middleton, and others. The often caustic, always subversive arguments of the Deists provoked an astonishing quantity of orthodox replies. (There were around one hundred fifty refutations of Tindal alone.) But in retrospect one is bound to view the entire controversy as a mere pause on the way from orthodox Christian faith to thoroughgoing scepticism. Correspondingly, the defence moves from detailed counterargument to a weary – or indignant – fideism.

1. The critique of revelation

Toland's anonymously published *Christianity Not Mysterious* is commonly identified as the spark that fired the Deist controversy, albeit Toland denied he was a Deist. (He preferred to represent himself as simply a good Anglican.) Revelation, he argued, is not mysterious; on the contrary, reason is given us as the instrument for comprehending it. When the New Testament speaks of 'mysteries', it means things that were mysterious before they were revealed, but are not mysterious any more. Reason is the candle, the guide, the judge that God has lodged within every man who comes into the world. With its aid, even the vulgar can understand the gospel of Christ: what they cannot understand is the wilful mystification of the gospel by clergymen who want to keep them in subjection. 'The uncorrupted Doctrines of *Christianity* are not above their Reach or Comprehension, but the Gibberish of your *Divinity Schools* they understand not'.[11]

It is easy to surmise what the next step in the controversy is likely to be, but Toland shows himself reluctant to take it. 'Others will say', he writes, 'that this Notion of *Faith* makes *Revelation* useless. But, pray, how so? for the Question is not, whether we could discover all the Objects of our *Faith* by Ratiocination. . . . But I assert, that what is once reveal'd we must as well understand as any other Matter in the World' (§66). The step from which Toland held back was firmly taken in Tindal's *Christianity as Old as the Creation*, often referred to as 'the Deists' Bible'.[12] For Tindal, the question was exactly what Toland said it was not: whether we could discover the objects of our faith without a revelation. To be sure, Tindal proceeded cautiously. He styled himself a Christian Deist and placed on his title page a quotation from an esteemed churchman, Thomas Sherlock, then Bishop of Bangor: 'The Religion of the Gospel, is the true original Religion of Reason and Nature. – And its Precepts declarative of that original Religion, which was as old as the Creation'. Tindal's book, written in the form of a dialogue, is an extended commentary on this assertion in fourteen chapters, the last of which is a response to Samuel Clarke. The core of the argument is evident already in Tindal's subtitle: the gospel is simply a republication of natural religion.

Whether or not an orthodox construction could be placed on the bishop's words, Tindal's argument is plainly designed to make one wonder whether the alleged republication of natural religion was necessary, or even a good idea. He takes his departure from the complaint of the clergy that the people have become cool to the speculative points of Christianity and are being misled by the low-church advocates of natural religion into magnifying mere sincerity, which places all religions on the same level. Tindal's response is that natural religion and revealed are actually the same in content, but the 'Ecclesiasticks' have made revelation into an instrument of control and a cause of dissension. Rightly understood, everyone is perfectly capable of knowing the law of reason, or the religion of nature. The difficulty is that throughout Christian history the leaders of the church have done more to obscure natural religion than to promote it. The Scriptures themselves are partly to blame, because they confuse us with their obscurity; indeed, if taken literally, they mislead us with an imperfect morality, and virtue, after all, is what true religion is about. They even record mistakes. And if the Apostles were wrong about Christ's speedy return, how can we be sure they were not wrong about other matters, too?

Tindal concludes his book with an interesting threefold distinction, which points toward Kant's *Religion innerhalb der Grenzen der bloßen Vernunft*. First, there are 'Things, which, by their internal Excellency, shew themselves to be the Will of an infinitely wise, and good God'. Second, there are 'Things, which have no Worth in themselves; yet because those that have, can't many Times be perform'd without them, these are to be consider'd as Means to an End'. Finally, there are things which are neither ends nor means, but mere superstitions. The second class of things is, of course, the most intriguing. While Tindal thought a great deal of organised religion was designed only to impose on a credulous laity, he was willing to concede an instrumental value to at least some outward forms of ecclesiastical piety. The important thing is not to forget what they are for: to promote the inward religion of the things in the first class. It is then possible to treat them as useful but mutable – to be varied according to human discretion. 'He that carries these Distinctions in his Mind, will have a truer Notion of Religion, than if he had read all the *Schoolmen, Fathers*, and *Councils*' (ch. 14, 431).

By the time we reach Tindal, the appeal to reason has taken a drastic turn. No longer the organ for understanding revelation, reason is the actual source of whatever religious truth we have, and therefore the critical instrument by which we determine just how much truth any 'instituted Religion' may fairly claim for itself. The Christian Deist confesses that Christianity contains the true religion of reason. But he must also admit that the Scriptures sometimes get in the way of the very religion that they are supposed to 'republish'. The reversal of the old dogmatic superordination of Scripture to reason is complete, and it invites a thoroughgoing critical reappraisal of the Bible.

Reappraisal took the form, at least in part, of a direct assault on what had been the two main weapons in the Christian apologetic arsenal ever since the apostolic preaching recorded in the Acts of the Apostles: the fulfilment of prophecy and the performance of miracles. (See, for example, Peter's sermon on the Day of Pentecost: Acts 2:14–36). But it is not possible here to follow the case of Anthony Collins against the literal fulfillment of Old Testament prophecies in Jesus, or the case of Thomas Woolston against a literal interpretation of Jesus' miracles and resurrection from death. The importance of their subversive labours lies generally in their attempt to specify the fundamental principles of historical understanding. (The same holds for Conyers Middleton's work on post-canonical miracle stories.) The single most fundamental principle of all had been laid down already by John Toland: that there is no different rule to be followed in the interpretation of Scripture than is common to all other books.

2. *The defence of revelation*

There was no shortage of replies to the scandalous Deist literature. Apologists rose up by dozens – partly, it is said, because publication held out the hope of ecclesiastical preferment. Only a fraction of the countertreatises is read any more. But much of it was widely acclaimed in its own time, and some, at least, has the marks of enduring wisdom. The apologists adopted many different strategies. Even before the century began, Charles Leslie brought out *A Short and Easie Method with the Deists* (1698), which disposed of the trouble-makers with four rules as to the truth of matters of fact done before our time: a matter attested must have been (1) sensible and (2) public, and (3) must have resulted in monuments and observances that (4) go back to the time when it was done. Thomas Sherlock won renown for works defending the fulfillment of prophecy and the historicity of Jesus' resurrection. But Soame Jenyns, later in the century, wisely conceded that miracles could no longer bear the weight Christian apologists had formerly placed on them. The marvels recorded in the New Testament must have been convincing proofs to those who witnessed them. But today, they will be most credible to someone who is convinced already of the religion they were at first intended to support. Hence we should begin by showing the internal marks of divinity stamped on the Christian religion, and in particular the personal character of its Author.[13]

Some of the brightest luminaries of the English church were drawn into the fray, including Samuel Clarke, George Berkeley, and Joseph Butler. Clarke despised the Deists as closet atheists, who, under the pretence of deism, ridiculed all that was truly excellent even in natural religion. In the introduction to his second series of Boyle Lectures, *The Unchangeable Obligations of Natural Religion*, Clarke insisted that an honest Deist would be well disposed to receive revelation when offered. But the 'loose, vain, and frothy Discourses' of the pretended deists, and above all their 'vitious and immoral Lives', proved them to be mere atheists, incapable of judging the truth of Christianity. Nevertheless, Clarke did stoop to answer Charles Blount's argument against revelation, wherein 'all the Deniers of Revelation agree with him': that what is not equally made known to *all* cannot be needful for *any*.[14] Clarke's undaunted answer is that all, as a matter of fact, are not equal. Even the truths of natural religion, though discoverable by reason, are not accessible to those whose reasoning ability is deficient; and though reason inclines us to expect a revelation, God is not obliged to give it to everyone, or even to give it at all.

A sprightly reply to the 'free-thinkers' was Bishop Berkeley's *Alciphron: Or, The Minute Philosopher*, written in Newport, Rhode Island, as he awaited news of his projected interracial college in Bermuda. The longest of his writings, it has been undeservedly neglected. In seven dialogues, Berkeley pays back the freethinkers in kind – with as much mischievous wit and acute argument as they had mustered against the establishment. They are teased as 'minute philosophers' (an expression borrowed from Cicero) because they 'diminish all the most valuable things, the thoughts, views, and hopes of men'.[15] But their arguments are dealt with seriously. Bernard Mandeville's cynical libertarianism and the Earl of Shaftesbury's notion of moral sense are fairly stated (in the persons of Lysicles and Alciphron) in entire dialogues they receive to themselves (Dials. 2, 3). The fourth dialogue introduces the divine 'Visual Language' proof of God's existence:[16] the totality of our experience consists of nothing but signs by which the Author of Nature speaks to us. And 'this Visual Language proves, not a Creator merely [deism], but a provident Governor, actually and intimately present' (Dial. 4, §14). The last three dialogues defend the utility and truth of Christianity against a wide range of current objections, including objections to the claim that the Scriptures are a divine revelation (Dial. 6).

Berkeley's *Alciphron* anticipates the two main points in the apologetic work that came to eclipse it. He ('Crito') remarks that 'probable arguments are a sufficient ground of faith', and goes on to say: 'And it will be sufficient if such analogy appears between the dispensations of grace and nature as may make it probable (although much should be unaccountable in both) to suppose them derived from the same Author, and the workmanship of one and the same Hand' (Dialogue 6, §31). This is exactly the line Joseph Butler takes in his *Analogy of Religion*, by far the most famous book to come out of the Deist controversy. Taking his cue from a remark by Origen of Alexandria, Butler argues that if Scripture comes from the Author of Nature, we can expect to find difficulties in revelation similar to those observed in the constitution and course of nature.[17] Indeed, what we now know about nature yields instructive analogies to religion both natural and revealed. Biological transformations, such as the change of worms into flies, convince us that the future state affirmed by natural religion is entirely in accord with the analogy of nature (I.i.§2). Similarly, the objection to revelation – that it is not given to all – ignores the plain evidence of nature that God does not in fact bestow the same favours on everyone. If we find problematic the idea of a special revelation disseminated but slowly over an infinite number of ages, at least it is in harmony with what we observe in the operations of nature (II.vi.§§6–9; II.ix).

Butler's tentative tone and grave style are in striking contrast to the optimistic flow of Samuel Clarke's discourse. 'To us,' as his famous aphorism affirms, 'probability is the very guide of life' (*Analogy*, Intro. §4). That is to say: probability, which is all we can hope for, is also as much as we need to get on with the business of living. Similarly, Berkeley asked the rhetorical question: 'Who ever supposed that scientifical proofs are necessary to make a Christian?' (*Alciphron*, Dialogue 6, §31, 280). Well, Clarke supposed they were at least possible: his method of arguing, he claimed, was 'as near to Mathematical as the Nature of such a Discourse would allow'. He was confident that the new science was wholly on God's side. Fresh discoveries in anatomy, physiology, and astronomy had left atheism 'utterly ashamed to show its Head'.[18] The shift from 'mathematical' to 'probable' arguments is significant. Indeed, Butler's case is avowedly ad hominem: he does not try to show what the Deists (publicly, at least) do not deny, that there is an Author of Nature. Many of his contemporaries could greet his book as the final blow to Deism. But, on another reading of the situation, we might judge that the Deist controversy ended when it was superseded by a more radical scepticism – and by the obverse of scepticism, which is fideism.

3. Scepticism and fideism

The Deist controversy was about revelation, the contestants on both sides 'taking for proved, that there is an intelligent Author of Nature, and *natural* Governor of the world' (Butler, *Analogy*, Intro.). The question was whether or not the Author of Nature had favoured some with a special revelation. Butler invoked his principle of analogy, not to prove that revelation had occurred, but to deflate objections to it. He recognised however, that his method of reasoning invited a more negative conclusion: Anyone who, considering the difficulties in Scripture, denies that it comes from God might, on similar grounds, deny that the world was formed by God. This was the road taken by a few in the second half of the century, notably the Baron d'Holbach. But atheism in the strict sense – denial of the existence of a god or gods – was not characteristic of the time. Many more, unpersuaded by the endless marshalling of arguments, chose the path either to scepticism or to fideism. What they had in common was that they took more seriously than Butler himself his remark that probable evidence is 'relative only to beings of limited capacities'. For them, the question was about the limits of reason.

Best known and most read of the eighteenth-century philosophers in Britain is today, of course, David Hume. His contributions to religious thought are misrepresented when he is read out of context, but preferential treatment of him is fully justified: taken together, his writings on religion make up a comprehensive philosophy of religion. This is not the place to enter into the many lively debates on his individual contributions, but precisely to see him, more broadly, in historical context. On the surface, at least, his *Natural History of Religion* seems to place him with those (such as Hobbes and Trenchard) who made a distinction between genuine or pure theism and the crude religion of the uninstructed masses. The springs of the one are reflective; and of the other, emotional. 'The whole frame of nature bespeaks an intelligent author; and no rational enquirer can, after serious reflexion, suspend his belief a moment with regard to the primary principles of genuine Theism and Religion'.[19] But there are hints here and there that this testimony should be taken with a grain of salt, and in the *Dialogues concerning Natural Religion*, Hume submits the foundation of theism in reason to a thorough critique, foreshadowed in section XI of the *Enquiry*.[20]

The sceptical Philo in the *Dialogues* is not insensitive to the power of the cosmic image suggested by Newtonian science: the world as one great machine. The image invites the inference that the cause of order in the universe must be analogous to a human intelligence. But the analogy is very imperfect, and observation actually discloses 'an infinite Number of Springs and Principles' in nature (II, 169). 'What peculiar Privilege has this little Agitation of the Brain which we call *Thought*, that we must thus make it the Model of the whole Universe?' (II, 68; itals. added). Such force as the evidence of rational order retains after these reflections does not permit us to think of nature's ultimate cause as either transcendent or benevolent. Nature may itself be 'the necessarily existent Being' (IX, 216), and her purpose seems to extend no further than the preservation and propagation of species (X, 227). She is blind, 'pouring forth from her Lap, without Discernment or parental Care, her maim'd and abortive Children' (XI, 241). Hence, to worship this Nature-God is wholly inappropriate. '*To know God*, says Seneca, *is to worship him*. All other Worship is indeed absurd, superstitious, and even impious' (XII, 259).

Natural theology, as Hume sees it, is an attempt to carry our thoughts beyond the capacities of human understanding (*Enquiry* 7.1.24–5, SBN 72–3). But he knew that the failure of argument to provide a satisfactory answer to ultimate questions would give rise to 'Contempt of human Reason' and a longing for revelation (*Dialogues*, XII, 260) – in short, to seeking all that religion requires in 'Faith alone' (X, 231). Philo's parting word is this: 'To be a philosophical Sceptic is, in a man of Letters, the first and most essential Step towards being a sound, believing Christian,' (XII, 261). No doubt, we must allow for some irony, as in the famous conclusion to Hume's essay on miracles: that the Christian religion can be believed only by the miracle of faith, mere reason being 'insufficient to convince us of its veracity' (*Enquiry* 10.2.41, SBN 131). Sometimes it is difficult to judge whether a contemporary of Hume's, when appealing to faith against reason, is being ironical, or not. Henry Dodwell's anonymous treatise *Christianity not Founded on Argument* (1741) is a masterpiece of ambiguity, and how his readers took it tells as much about them as about the author. However, there were those who affirmed the insufficiency of reason and the need for faith without irony or embarrassment.

In the eyes of many, the eighteenth century was afflicted by a surfeit of reason. It was not merely that the never-ending clash of argument and counterargument became tedious; it tended, besides, to give a false impression of what religion is all about. The disagreement between the Deists and the orthodox was trivial compared to their common assumption that religion is a matter of truths to be demonstrated, partly by showing that they are socially beneficial – making better Englishmen than free thought could. William Law's response to Tindal in *The Case of Reason* was to put reason on trial, and his verdict was in effect a return to the old orthodox view that autonomous reason is incompetent to pass judgment on 'the fitness and reasonableness of God's proceedings with mankind'.[21] Law exercised a strong influence on John Wesley, who found the chief evidence of Christianity's truth in the experience of 'those who were blind, but now see . . . who were miserable, but now are happy'. In Wesley's sermons we do not hear about the probability or improbability of 'the religious hypothesis', as Cleanthes calls it in Hume's *Dialogues*, but rather about God's free grace, the new birth, and a faith that is not the cool assent of the head so much as the resting of the heart on Christ for salvation.[22]

And yet, neither Hume nor Wesley spoke the last word. The classic English works of Christian apologetics were written after Hume's classic refutations of the entire enterprise. Undismayed by 'Mr. Hume's' objections, William Paley energetically defended miracles in *A View of the Evidences of Christianity*.[23] The argument that no testimony for a miraculous happening can ever be believed against our common experience begs the question, Paley thinks, since a miracle is by definition an exception to common experience. The sole pertinent question is the reliability of the witnesses. And is it likely that anyone would suffer martyrdom for a fabricated story? The defence of miracles was followed by the well-known argument of Paley's *Natural Theology*. The remarkable adaptation of parts to ends in nature bespeaks an intelligent contriver, as a watch requires a watchmaker. Even if the watch sometimes goes wrong, and even if we cannot see how every part conduces to the general effect, that does not invalidate our persuasion that a watch is a contrivance with a purpose. But Paley, of course, did not have the last word either. Charles Darwin read him at Cambridge with deep respect, but later wrote: 'The old argument of design in nature, as given by Paley, which formerly seemed to me so conclusive, fails, now that the law of natural selection has been discovered.'[24]

III. NEW BEGINNINGS IN THEOLOGY

Initially, both France and Germany were debtors to England for the new questions about religion. But Paris became the capital of the Enlightenment, and the great *Encyclopédie* launched by Denis Diderot was in some ways its most characteristic product.[25] Voltaire, more than anyone else, became the spokesman of the Age of Reason. Though he styled himself a 'theist', he did not believe that the Creator troubles himself with human affairs, or that the meaning of human existence turns around the expectation of an afterlife. Whereas Paley thought the main point of revelation was to furnish 'authorised assurances' of a life to come, Voltaire's outlook was concisely stated in the closing words of *Candide*: the tiresome explanations of Dr. Pangloss about the way everything is ordered for the best are all very well, 'but we must cultivate our garden'.[26] Immensely influential though he was, Voltaire was not a greatly original thinker. Indeed, he tried to pass off the anonymous first edition of his *Dictionnaire philosophique* (1764) as largely a compilation of sentiments from English authors. Neither did his writings spark an open exchange of arguments like the Deist controversy in England, partly because the leaders of the French church preferred repression to argument.

In the Profession of Faith of a Priest of Savoy in *Émile*, Rousseau portrayed the conflict between deistic sympathies and the teaching of the Roman Catholic Church as an inward struggle of conscience.[27] A justly celebrated manifesto, it also documents Rousseau's growing apprehension of a critique of religion more radical than his own – the critique that carried Diderot himself from deism to materialism. The priest of Savoy trusts his heart more than the arguments of the philosophers, and in this respect Rousseau hints at the coming revolt against Enlightenment rationalism. But it is the standard natural religion of the Deists – the religion of reason – that provides the content of the priest's confession. Though he conforms outwardly to the church and scrupulously performs the duties assigned to him, the only truths he acknowledges are the moral truths of which his conscience tells him: and they provide the measure by which he determines what is essential in Christianity, or in any other religion. He simply does not trouble himself with dogmas that are without benefit to morality. At the same time, like Voltaire, Rousseau's priest is appalled by the new materialist or naturalist understanding of humanity (la Mettrie, Helvétius, d'Holbach), which means a total rejection of his own deistic faith along with the ecclesiastical faith he himself subjects to criticism. Many have seen in the dogmatic atheism of d'Holbach's *Système de la nature* (1770), which passes beyond the scepticism of Pierre Bayle or even David Hume, the final outcome of the French Enlightenment, perhaps of the Enlightenment in general.[28]

In Germany, it was different: there the scattering of English ideas generated something new and positive in the understanding of religion. For one thing, the religious climate was more benign. The protest of Pietism against the dry intellectualism of orthodoxy had created a religious environment that nurtured a surprisingly large number of Germany's leading thinkers. Most of them saw themselves also as the heirs of Martin Luther: his name was reverently invoked to underwrite a variety of mutually exclusive causes – including orthodoxy, the pietism that rebelled against its formalism, and the rationalism that was critical of them both. Further, the course of the Enlightenment in Germany was decisively shaped by the teleological system of Leibniz, whose watchword that we live in 'the best of all possible worlds' was mercilessly ridiculed in Voltaire's *Candide*. The characteristic products of 'enlightened' religious thought in Germany were not anticlericalism or scepticism, although undercurrents of both were certainly present. More representative in the earlier phase were further ventures in natural theology, or rational theism, notably the attempt of Christian Wolff, Leibniz's most distinguished follower, to reconcile mechanism and teleology, making room for God in his grand system of 'rational philosophy'.[29]

In the later phase of Enlightenment theology in Germany (from around the mid-century), the questions of natural theology and natural religion yielded first place to a church reform programme that came to be called 'neology' (the 'new doctrine'). For their part, the followers of Wolff, whether or not they engaged directly in the explication of church doctrines, were convinced that he had shown the way to harmonise reason and revelation as mutually supplemental sources of theological information. They had no thought of revising orthodoxy. For neologists such as August Friedrich Wilhelm Sack, Johann Friedrich Wilhelm Jerusalem, Johann Joachim Spalding, and others, by contrast, a revision of dogma was among the most urgent tasks of the day. They did not question the concept of revelation but asked how far the official dogmas of the church succeeded in conveying the truths of revelation. Intricate doctrines such as the Trinity, which posed no great intellectual difficulties for the Wolffians, were now judged morally barren, if not logically incoherent; others, such as original sin, were admitted to be an actual hindrance to spiritual improvement, as unbelievers had already noticed. The neologists were eminently practical men, many of them active churchmen rather than academic theologians. They called for a drastic simplification of ecclesiastical dogma in the interests of actual Christian experience. But some of them (notably Johann Salomo Semler, who is usually classed with the neologists) undertook the critique of dogma partly in recognition of the historicity of all the concrete expressions of religion in thought and language. Neither dogma nor the Bible itself can be exempted from the relativities of time and place. Hence a free, 'scientific' inquiry into the Christian tradition is entirely legitimate as well as needful to piety. It is here, rather than in the defence of a natural religion, that neology owed its principal debt to the English Deists.

Besides the neologists, others such as Lessing and Reimarus took up the Deist enterprise of a 'free investigation' of the Scriptures. For Christian theologians, the historical-critical approach to the Bible was to prove more important, in the long run, than rational theism, which is naturally more intriguing to philosophers. True, one early impulse to critical study of Scripture had come from a philosopher, Spinoza, whose aim of distinguishing a philosophical from a theological doctrine of God was set out in his anonymously published *Tractatus theologico-politicus* (1670). But the new historical studies made a division within theology itself, programmatically formulated in J. P. Gabler's academic address (1787) on the proper distinction between biblical and dogmatic theology.[30] The ideal, at least, had come to be a descriptive study of biblical ideas that would be free from external presuppositions, philosophical as well as ecclesiastical. How well the ideal was realised may be open to doubt; Gabler himself *presupposed* that linguistic, literary, and historical examination of the individual books of the Bible would uncover a uniform, timeless biblical truth. But precisely because pure description of historical data was the goal, the emergence of a historical-critical theology is of less philosophical interest than the fate of natural theology and natural religion at the hands of Immanuel Kant and Friedrich Schleiermacher.

1. *Kant's moral theology*

Kant's strictures on rational theology in the transcendental dialectic of the *Kritik der reinen Vernunft* arise from the application of his theory of knowledge to the idea of God.[31] The Kantian categories are strictly categories of *thought*, by which the mind organises sense experience. But there is a persistent tendency of the mind to assume that its structure must be the structure of *being*: it projects the categories on to things-in-themselves. The logic of the mind is then transformed into a metaphysic of reality, and this is illusion. The same holds good for those ideas by which the mind seeks to unify the experience ordered by the categories, including the idea (or ideal) of God as the ultimate unifying ground of everything there is. After dismantling the proofs by which theists have tried to establish the existence of God, Kant concludes that for theoretical reasons the concept of God is a 'mere idea', justified not by its supposed reference to an actual object but by its usefulness in inspiring the quest for a single system of empirical knowledge (A 670–1/B 698–9). However, he drops a hint that there is more to be said: 'consequently, if one did not ground [theology] on moral laws or use them as guides, there could be no theology of reason at all' (A 636/B 664).

What this means becomes clearer in several of Kant's later writings. We may point, by way of example, to his *Lectures on the Philosophical Doctrine of Religion*, probably delivered in the winter semester 1783–84 and published posthumously. The lectures show Kant's familiarity with Hume's *Dialogues*, but his constant conversation partner is the Wolffian philosopher A. G. Baumgarten, whose natural theology he adopted as his main textbook.[32] Defining theology broadly as 'the system of our cognition of the highest being' (Ak 28: 995), he confines his attention to rational theology (the 'theology of reason'), which sets out to see how far reason can get in the knowledge of God without any help from revelation. Rational theology, so understood, falls into two parts. *Transcendental theology* (part one) is organised according to the three traditional proofs of God's existence into onto-, cosmo-, and physicotheology. In adding *moral theology* (part two), Kant believed he was coining a new name for a field that had not previously been correctly distinguished. To be sure, the content of his moral theology was not without antecedents: Butler's writings, for instance, contain at least a suggestion of a natural theology grounded in moral experience. But Kant's claim to originality was largely justified.

Transcendental theology is not only parsimonious in what it can permit us to say about God, seeing that talk of God is of no use in explaining natural phenomena. It also tends to mislead us into forgetting that the question of God is a practical one, which has to do, above all, with the strength of our moral dispositions. Our morality, not our cosmology, needs the idea of God. In this way, Kant makes theology a theory of religion rather than a branch of metaphysics. Indeed, he can say forthrightly: 'religion is nothing but the application of theology to morality' (Ak 28: 997). Our experience of nature ('natural theology' in Kant's narrow sense) does not produce the God that religion requires; it can only stir up fear of a very powerful being. But by way of moral experience, reason furnishes the concept of God as the holy, just, and benevolent ruler of the world. 'God', in short, is 'a *moral* concept, the *practically necessary*' (28: 1071).

Just how and why morality needs the idea of God is spelled out in the doctrine of the three postulates of practical reason – freedom, immortality, and the existence of God – in the second *Kritik*.[33] The argument is a delicate one, since it must not be taken to imply that morality *rests on* belief in God or the prospect of rewards in an afterlife. Moral obligation depends on nothing outside itself. But precisely because we ought to promote the highest good in the world, we necessarily presuppose its possibility, and we can only conceive of this possibility if we assume the existence of a supreme cause whose causality is appropriate to the nature of the moral life: which must mean, a highest intelligence (Ak 5: 125–6). Kant concludes that by this route our knowledge really is extended. But we must not claim to know the nature of the Supreme Being, whom we cannot experience as we experience objects in space and time. Theoretical reason can only *assume* that the concept of God has an object, or a possible object, even if the first *Kritik* has shown that the traditional proofs failed to *demonstrate* it (5: 133–6).

Kant returns to his 'moral proof' in his third *Kritik*. Man's moral nature, which raises him above the rest of nature as its ultimate goal (*Endzweck*), requires us to represent the supreme cause as moral, and this alone can give us a teleological principle – a final intention (*Endabsicht*) – adequate to ground a theology. The consequent definition of religion as '*the recognition of our duties as divine commands*'[34] is taken up again in *Die Religion innerhalb der Grenzen der bloßen Vernunft*, which earned Kant a royal rebuke from Friedrich Wilhelm II. There Kant indulges in some standard Enlightenment anticlericalism. But he argues that the radical evil in humanity requires a collective remedy, and he grants that a church may be the vehicle of the ethical commonwealth at which the pure religion of reason aims. Reason, however, must submit every ecclesiastical belief and practice to critical scrutiny, if their moral core is not to be lost in idle superstition. Hence Kant not only transformed natural theology into moral theology: he also, in effect, implemented Tindal's programme for making natural religion, or the religion of reason, a critical standard for judging the instrumental worth of so-called revealed religion. In short, he was able to view revealed religion as 'a *wider* sphere of faith that includes the other, a *narrower* one [sc. the pure religion of reason] within itself (not as two circles external to one another but as concentric circles)'.[35]

2. *Schleiermacher's theology of consciousness*

Kant's *Religion within Limits* already moves beyond 'enlightened' thinking in some respects (for instance, in his emphasis on radical evil). Much further removed from the Enlightenment than Kant was Friedrich Schleiermacher, whose *Reden über die Religion* appeared anonymously at the close of the century. He wrote this, his first book, in the shadow of the Atheism controversy (1798–99), in which Kantian critical philosophy provided the initial terms of debate. But he himself stood in the stream of ideas that flowed out of the earlier Pantheism or Spinozist controversy, started in 1785 by the quarrel between Friedrich Heinrich Jacobi and Moses Mendelssohn over the religious opinions of Lessing, who died in 1781. Renewed interest in Spinoza led many to abandon the image of God as a mind outside a machine and to re-conceive of deity as the ultimate animating force of nature. Goethe wrote to Jacobi (9 June 1785): '[Spinoza] does not prove the existence of God; existence is God.' And Herder equated God, the primal force, with the luminous rational order discovered in nature by scientific inquiry: the divine activity is not arbitrary but necessary, identical with the law-governed course of nature.[36] The world of this 'neo-Spinozism' was the young Schleiermacher's world. He also shared with Herder the conviction that religion is not correct belief, nor correct behaviour either, but the poetic expression of lively feeling.

True, *Reden über die Religion* could hardly have been written in an earlier century. Schleiermacher's question in the first two speeches is not about the soundest variety of Christian doctrine, but about the nature of religion.[37] Not until the fifth and last speech does he try to show how religion, generically understood, is suitably manifested in Christianity. The defence of Christian faith is launched, not by arguing at the outset for a special revelation, but by insisting that religion generally is rooted in human nature, which is diminished when religion is despised or neglected. But the religion that Schleiermacher finds in humanity is not the *prisca theologia* ('original theology') of which some of the Deists spoke – the cluster of minimal beliefs that all thinking men have held since the beginning of history. With most of his friends, he shared Rousseau's and

Hamann's protest against the abstract intellectualism of the Enlightenment: the whole person is more than thinking, understanding, arguing; and religion is not theology (19–22/14–16). Even if it were necessary to round off the system of our knowledge by setting God at the apex, this would have nothing to do with the religious way of having God. Neither is religion to be justified by the support it allegedly brings to morals. For it surrenders any claim to whatever belongs to the domain either of science or of ethics. What is it, then? Religion, or 'piety', is the sense of the Infinite that surrounds and pervades us: the Infinite, not as the mere sum total of finite things, but as the underlying unity that conditions the whole of which we are a part (46–9/35–8; 136–7/105–6). It matters little whether the imagination moves us to conceptualize this 'feeling' in theistic or in pantheistic terms (120–30/92–9).

Clearly, Schleiermacher thought that the enterprise of rational or natural theology was of no help to anyone who wanted to understand religion. The essence of religion is an elemental 'feeling' or 'intuition', and our access to it is by observing the structure of consciousness – in the final analysis, our own consciousness. Do we then have, by result, the natural *religion* that the Deists sought in all the 'positive' religions? Schleiermacher's answer in the fifth speech is a firm no. To understand religion in its actual manifestations, we must surrender the vain wish for a single religion. Precisely because the essence of religion is not a quantity of common beliefs that can be extracted from the positive religions, everything particular being disdained as superfluous, Schleiermacher had no sympathy with the concept of natural religion or the use to which it had been put. It is an armchair construct: there is little of real religion in it, and it cannot exist on its own. Only in the positive religions is a genuine individual cultivation of the religious capacity possible (242–7/213–17). With this conclusion, Schleiermacher helped to shape the agenda for a future philosophy of religions (plural) and for a Christian theology that would accept religious pluralism as part of the legacy of the eighteenth century.

NOTES

1 John Locke, *Epistola de tolerantia/Letter concerning Toleration* (Gouda, 1689), trans. W. Popple, ed. M. Montuori (The Hague, 1963).

2 Edward, Lord Herbert of Cherbury, *De Veritate*, trans. and ed. M. H. Carré (Bristol, 1937), chs. 9–10, 289–313.

3 Thomas Hobbes, *Leviathan*, ed. R. Tuck (Cambridge, 1991), 76.

4 John Trenchard, *The Natural History of Superstition* (London, 1709), 50.

5 David Hume, *The Natural History of Religion*, ed. A.W Colver, and *Dialogues concerning Natural Religion*, ed. J. V. Price (Oxford, 1976). *Natural History* was first published in *Four Dissertations* (1757).

6 Richard Hooker, *Of the Laws of Ecclesiastical Polity*, 8 bks. (1593–1662), III.viii.11. See also OED.

7 Johann Andreas Quenstedt, cited in Heinrich Schmid, *The Doctrinal Theology of the Evangelical Lutheran Church*, trans. C. A. Hay and H. E. Jacobs (Philadelphia, PA, 1899), Introd., ch. 1, para. 2 [4], 19.
8 See David Cairns, 'Natural Theology', in *A Handbook of Christian Theology*, eds. M. Halverson and A. A. Cohen (New York, 1958), 249–56.
9 John Calvin, *Institutio christianæ religionis*, 1559; translated as *Institutes of the Christian Religion*, trans. F. L. Battles, ed. J. T. McNeill, 2 vols. (London, 1961), I.xi.8; I.vi.1; I.viii.
10 John Locke, *An Essay concerning Human Understanding*, ed. P. H. Nidditch, in the *Clarendon Edition* (1975), IV.xix.
11 John Toland, *Christianity Not Mysterious* (London, 1696), III.4, §67.
12 Matthew Tindal, *Christianity as Old as the Creation: or, The Gospel, a Republication of the Religion of Nature* (London, 1730).
13 For the passage from Charles Leslie, see *Religious Thought in the Eighteenth Century, Illustrated from Writers of the Period*, eds. J. M. Creed and J. S. Boys Smith (Cambridge, 1934), 53–4. This volume also contains representative selections from Thomas Sherlock, Soame Jenyns, Henry Dodwell, and William Law. See also *Deism and Natural Religion: A Source Book*, ed. E. G. Waring (New York, 1967).
14 Samuel Clarke, *A Discourse concerning the Unchangeable Obligations of Natural Religion and the Truth and Certainty of the Christian Revelation* (Boyle Lectures) (London, 1706), Introduction and Prop. VII.§4, 260.
15 George Berkeley, *Alciphron: or The Minute Philosopher*, in *Works*, Dial. 1, §10, 3: 46.
16 Berkeley, *Alciphron*, Dial. 4, §§14–15, 3: 159–61.
17 Joseph Butler, *The Analogy of Religion, Natural and Revealed, to the Constitution and Course of Nature* (1736), in *Works*, ed. W. E. Gladstone, 2 vols. (Oxford, 1896), Introduction, §8.
18 Clarke, *A Demonstration of the Being and Attributes of God* (Boyle Lectures) cf. n. 14 (London, 1704), Preface and Prop. XI, 232.
19 Hume, *The Natural History of Religion*, p. 25.
20 Hume, *An Enquiry concerning Human Understanding* (1748), ed. T. L. Beauchamp, in the *Clarendon Edition* (2000).
21 William Law, *The Case of Reason, or Natural Religion, Fairly and Fully Stated* (London, 1731), ch. 2, heading.
22 John Wesley, 'A Letter to the Reverend Conyers Middleton, Occasioned by His Late "Free Enquiry"' (4–24 Jan. 1748–9), in *Works*, 14 vols. (London, 1872), 10: 1–79 at 78; Sermon I: 'Salvation by Faith', *Works* 5: 7–16.
23 William Paley, *A View of the Evidences of Christianity*, 3 vols. (London, 1794), 'Preparatory Considerations', 1: 1–17.
24 Paley, *Natural Theology* (London, 1802), chs. 1–2; *The Autobiography of Charles Darwin 1809–82*, ed. N. Barlow (London, 1958), 87; see also 59.
25 Denis Diderot and Jean le Rond d'Alembert, *Encyclopédie ou Dictionnaire Raisonné des sciences, des arts et des métiers*, 35 vols. (Paris/Amsterdam, 1751–80).
26 Paley, *Evidences*, Pt. II, ch. 2, in vol. 2, p. 96; François Marie Arouet de Voltaire, *Candide ou L'optimisme* (Paris and Geneva, 1759), ch. 30 (final words).
27 Jean-Jacques Rousseau, *Émile ou De l'éducation* (1762), in *Oeuvres*, 4: 565–635; translated as *Émile, or On Education*, trans. and ed. A. Bloom (Harmondsworth, 1991), 266–313.
28 Paul Henri Thiry d'Holbach, *Système de la nature, ou Des loix du monde physique et du monde moral* [1770], ed. D. Diderot, 2 vols. (Paris, 1821).
29 Christian Wolff, *Theologia naturalis methodo scientifica pertractata*, in *Werke*, II.7–8, ed. J. École (1978–81).
30 Johann Philipp Gabler, 'De iusto discrimine theologiae biblicae et dogmaticae . . . Oratio 1787', in vol. II, *Opuscula Academica*, eds. T. A. Gabler and J. G. Gabler (Ulm, 1831).

31 Immanuel Kant, *Kritik der reinen Vernunft*, in Ak 3 (2nd edn.) and 4 (1st edn.), hereafter B and A, respectively; translated as *Critique of Pure Reason*, trans. and eds. P. Guyer and A. W. Wood, in *Works* (1998).

32 Kant, *Philosophische Religionslehre* (1817; 2nd edn., 1830), Ak 28: 993–1126; translated as *Lectures on the Philosophical Doctrine of Religion* by A. W. Wood, in Kant, *Works/Religion and Rational Theology*, trans. and eds. A. W. Wood and G. di Giovanni (1992). Alexander Gottlieb Baumgarten, *Metaphysica* (1739), translated as *Metaphysik* by G. F. Meier (Halle, 1766), Pt. 3.

33 Kant, *Kritik der praktischen Vernunft*, in Ak 5: 1–163; translated as *Critique of Practical Reason*, in *Works/Practical Philosophy*, trans. and ed. M. J. Gregor (1996).

34 Kant, *Kritik der Urtheilskraft*, in Ak 5, Pt. 2: Kritik der teleologischen Urtheilskraft, 'Allgemeine Anmerkung zur Teleologie', 5: 475–85 at 481; translated as *Critique of the Power of Judgment* in *Works/Critique of the Power of Judgment*, trans. P. Guyer and E. Matthews, ed. P. Guyer (2000).

35 Kant, *Die Religion innerhalb der Grenzen der bloßen Vernunft*, Preface to the 2nd edn., Ak 6: 12; translated as *Religion within the Boundaries of Mere Reason*, trans. and eds. A. Wood and G. di Giovanni, in *Works/Religion and Rational Theology*.

36 Johann Wolfgang von Goethe, *Briefwechsel zwischen Goethe und F. H. Jacobi*, ed. M. Jacobi (Leipzig, 1846), 85; author's trans. Johann Gottfried von Herder, *Gott: einige Gespräche* (1787), in *Sämmtliche Werke*, ed. B. Suphan, 33 vols. (Berlin, 1877–1913), 16: 401–580, at 486–8, 493, 497, 500, 519.

37 Friedrich Schleiermacher, *Reden über die Religion* (1799), in *Friedrich Schleiermacher's Reden über die Religion*, ed. G. C. B. Pünjer (Brunswick, 1879); translated as *On Religion: Speeches to Its Cultured Despisers*, trans. J. Oman, ed. R. Otto (New York, 1958). Page numbers refer to the critical edition by Pünjer followed by those of the translated edition.

22

REVEALED RELIGION: THE CONTINENTAL EUROPEAN DEBATE

MARIA ROSA ANTOGNAZZA

The two extremes of eighteenth-century reflection on the foundations of revealed religion are marked in continental Europe by two major German philosophers: Gottfried Wilhelm Leibniz and Georg Wilhelm Friedrich Hegel. The beginning of the century saw the last, productive years of Leibniz's life – years in which doctrines already present in his youth, matured and refined during the course of many decades, were finally committed to paper in such works as the *Nouveaux essais* (1703–1705), the *Théodicée* (1710), the *Monadologie* (1714) and the *Principes de la nature et de la grace* (1714). The end of the century saw the appearance of the early writings of Hegel, known as his *Theologische Jugendschriften* (1793–1800) – writings which disclose the origins of Hegel's dialectic and exhibit in a graphic way, through the consideration of the figure of Jesus, the shift from the Enlightenment-Kantian interpretive paradigm of Christian religion to the new dialectical paradigm. The change of perspective during the intervening century regarding the philosophical justification of revealed (or, as it would increasingly be called, positive) religion could hardly have been more radical. Leibniz summarised the debate on the relationship between faith and reason inherited from an ancient tradition and renewed in the sixteenth and seventeenth centuries in all its urgency by the Protestant Reformation, and he gave the thesis of the conformity between the two perhaps its most coherent expression. Hegel opened the door to the nineteenth century with a new set of philosophical issues regarding the value and foundations of revealed religion. The interval of time which separated the two philosophers was marked by a great ferment of ideas and lively discussions: the explosion and propagation of Deism especially among the French exponents of the Enlightenment who, drawing heavily on English sources, rejected revealed religion altogether in favour of natural religion; the influence in Germany of Pietism, with its stress on morality and the practice of Christianity rather than doctrinal faith and its aversion to the aridly scholastic intellectualisation of Christianity by Protestant orthodoxy; the tendency, on the other hand, of some of the defenders of Christian religion progressively to 'rationalise' the revelation they were attempting to defend (Christian Wolff, the

German Neologists); the relationship between history and religion proposed by Gotthold Ephraim Lessing on the basis of the distinction of the contingent truths of history from the necessary truths of reason; the perspective of Kant's criticism (followed in his religious thought by the young Fichte) which asserted the priority of practical reason, and the fundamental consequences of this for the knowledge of God and religion in general. We shall consider each of these issues in turn.

I. THE PHILOSOPHICAL JUSTIFICATION OF TRUTHS 'ABOVE REASON'

The issue of the foundations of revealed religion was passed on by Leibniz to the eighteenth century as a question of how to provide philosophical justification for a class of truths which are above reason. Leibniz embraced the traditional scholastic distinction between 'contrary to' and 'above' reason. Truth can never be contrary to reason: it can never imply a contradiction. The very possibility of reaching truth is based, for Leibniz, on the principle of non-contradiction as the ultimate criterion of distinguishing between truth and falsity. If the principle of non-contradiction did not hold in the supernatural realm – if this principle did not have absolute validity – the very possibility of speaking of truth and falsehood would be lost. A first consequence of this position for the epistemological status of revealed doctrines is that, insofar as they are true, they can never be contrary to reason, or, in other words, they can never imply a contradiction. There can, however, be truths which are above reason or, more precisely, above the limited ability of human reason to comprehend. This is exactly the position traditionally assigned to revealed truths such as the mysteries of the Trinity and the Incarnation: doctrines which insofar as they are 'mysteries' are by definition incomprehensible and above human reason, but insofar as they are 'truths' cannot (according to Leibniz and a long tradition stretching back to Thomas Aquinas) be against reason. The only possibility of revelation (and in particular Christian revelation) being regarded as true for Leibniz is, accordingly, the philosophical justification of a class of truths which are 'above' but not 'contrary' to reason. The first problem to be addressed by such a justification was posed by, among others, Pierre Bayle: how can human reason judge concerning the contradictoriness or non-contradictoriness of something which is by definition above its ability to comprehend?[1] If such a judgement is precluded to human reason, that is to say, if it is impossible for us to find out whether a doctrine presented as above reason contains a contradiction or not, it is *eo ipso* futile to distinguish between 'above' and 'contrary' to reason.

Two alternative solutions were offered to this problem. The first one was defended (at least ostensibly) by Bayle, by some controversial and influential Lutheran theologians (such as Matthias Flacius Illyrius and Daniel Hofmann), by the so-called enthusiasts, by some strands of Pietism, and even by a few 'scholastic authors'.[2] This is the thesis of the complete separation and incommensurability of faith and reason, which ultimately issues in fideism. According to this view, human reason is an imperfect and weak instrument, constitutionally unable to reach truth in the supernatural domain, in which the logical and metaphysical principles of the finite world do not apply. We must therefore acknowledge its limits, recognise that there is a double truth – one philosophical, the other theological – and believe by faith even what for human reason implies a contradiction.[3] In other words, we must accept as truths above reason even things which are contrary to reason.

The opposite alternative is the one embraced by theological rationalism of a Socinian kind. Since there must be conformity between faith and reason, given their common origin from God, this view argues that we ought to reject as contradictory and therefore false whatever human reason cannot comprehend – for example, the mystery of the Trinity. It is true that moderate Socinianism still acknowledged in theory the existence of truths above reason. These are not, however, truths structurally incomprehensible for human reason, but merely truths which need a divine revelation in order to be known. Once they have been revealed, they can be grasped by human reason and cease therefore in a strict sense to be *supra rationem*.[4] In other words, what is in the last analysis irreducibly above reason is also contrary to reason.

Both alternatives – theological fideism and theological rationalism – blur and ultimately erase the distinction between above and contrary to reason. As for the specific issue of a philosophical justification of revealed religion, in both cases, for opposite reasons, this issue is ultimately eliminated altogether. For theological fideism, since faith and reason belong to two completely separate spheres, philosophy as such does not have anything to say in the realm of revelation. For theological rationalism of a Socinian kind, since revealed truths are within the limits of human reason, the necessity or even the utility of revelation is progressively undermined until it is completely denied by the Deists. Furthermore, this denial eliminates the need for a philosophical foundation for any revelation which is now useless or, still worse, intrinsically misleading.

Leibniz, however, believed that he had a different answer: an answer which justified the epistemological status of revealed propositions as above but not contrary to reason, avoiding, on one hand, the submission of reason to faith; on the other, that of faith to reason. There is a difference, he pointed out, between judging a given proposition non-contradictory and demonstrating the truth of it. The fact that the mysteries are above our ability to comprehend precludes the possibility of a demonstration of their truth, but not the possibility of judging about their non-contradictoriness. This judgement is, however, subjected to an important qualification: it is not a positive demonstration of the possibility (that is non-contradictoriness) of the mysteries, but a demonstration that their impossibility (that is contradictoriness) has not so far been proved. A positive demonstration of their possibility would in fact require, in the last instance, the comprehension of the mysteries, that is to say, the resolution of the notion which expresses a mystery in its last elements, something which is excluded by definition, given the epistemological status claimed for the mysteries as truths above reason. It should here be pointed out that Leibniz in his *Meditationes de cognitione, veritate et ideis* (1684) distinguished two means of knowing the possibility of something: a priori and a posteriori. We know something a priori when we resolve the concept into its necessary elements or into other concepts the possibility of which is known. If we have carried our analysis to the end and no contradiction has appeared, the possibility of this concept is demonstrated. We know something a posteriori when we experience the actual existence of the thing, for what actually exists or has existed is in any case possible (Akademie-Ausgabe, IV.4: 589–90). As nature contains no example which adequately corresponds to what is indicated by the mysteries, an a posteriori positive demonstration of their possibility is ruled out as well.[5]

The proposed negative procedure, however, allows Leibniz to maintain the non-contradictoriness of revealed propositions without losing their status as supra-rational truths. With a proposition which has not yet been demonstrated to be true, or, still more, whose truth cannot be demonstrated, one can invoke a 'presumption of truth' which holds as long as the contrary has not been proved.[6] This is precisely what Leibniz claims for the mysteries handed down as divine revelation by the ancient tradition of what he calls the 'universal Church'. Thanks to the appeal to the 'presumption of truth', it is assumed as a starting point that the mysteries are true (and therefore non-contradictory) although they cannot be comprehended. As long as their contradictoriness is not positively proved, we are justified in believing them as truths above reason. In other words, the 'burden of proof' falls on the attacker and not on the defender of a thesis.[7] The defender merely has to show that the contradictoriness of his thesis has not yet been proved. He is not required to provide a positive proof of the truth of the thesis defended – a proof that by definition cannot be given in the case of revealed propositions claimed to be above reason. Once this general strategy has been established, the task of the defender of the mysteries was to win an indefinite series of single battles in the defence of the mysteries by showing time after time that their contradictoriness has not yet been proved.

II. THE IDENTIFICATION OF 'ABOVE' AND 'CONTRARY' TO REASON

No matter how good the strategy and how many battles Leibniz may have won in rejecting Socinian charges of contradiction against the mysteries, he did not win the war. Socinianism and its English expression, Unitarianism, although fiercely persecuted during the seventeenth century, established roots and bore fruit throughout Europe. It prepared the ground for Deism: first for the reduction of revealed religion to natural religion in the name of reason, and then for the acrimonious battle against revelation as such. With Deism the identification between 'above reason' and 'contrary to reason' was consummated. Abandoning the attempt to maintain the concept of *supra rationem*,[8] the more radical late exponents of Socinianism had already drawn the obvious conclusion of ascribing to reason the last word in determining what is acceptable as true revelation. In his *De judice et norma controversiarum fidei Libri II* (1644), Joachim Stegmann the Elder stated that there is nothing above reason in the original Christian revelation. John Toland followed in the same line, stigmatising in the very title of perhaps his most influential work the identification of 'above' and 'contrary' to reason – a title which, according to Leibniz, for this reason went 'much farther than it is proper':[9] *Christianity not Mysterious: Or, a Treatise Shewing, that there is Nothing in the Gospel Contrary to Reason, nor above it: And that no Christian Doctrine Can Be properly Call'd a Mystery* (1696). All the alleged incomprehensible mysteries are simply absurdities introduced later on by the clergy. Matthew Tindal took this thesis to its extreme consequences, accomplishing with his *Christianity as old as the Creation* (1730) the reduction of Christian religion to natural religion. The article 'Foi' in Voltaire's *Dictionnaire philosophique* (1764) well represented the end of the trajectory of this line of reasoning. Cutting short the complex sixteenth- and seventeenth-century discussions about the difference between 'above' and 'against' reason, the equivalence of faith and irrationality was presented as matter of fact. 'Impossible' and 'incomprehensible' – two concepts which Leibniz carefully distinguished, building his defence of the supra-rational domain precisely on their difference – were now used as interchangeable terms. 'Faith' said Voltaire speaking through the person of Pico della Mirandola 'consists in believing things because they are impossible'. And you, continued 'Pico' addressing Pope Alexander VI, 'oblige me to believe in even more incomprehensible mysteries' than the fact that the grandson of the pope should be regarded as the child of an impotent man. As for the central tenet of religion – 'that there is a necessary, eternal, supreme, intelligent being' – this is not 'a matter of faith, but of reason'.[10]

If Socinian rationalism fed directly into the rejection of revealed religion, the official fideism of Bayle was transformed by Deism into its converse. As

Leibniz saw well in advance, Bayle wanted to silence reason after it had already spoken too much.[11] Bayle's abundant arguments showing the conflict between faith and reason and the lack of any rational justification for belief in revelation proved to be the best weapons in the hands of the Deists. They endorsed Bayle's arguments for the irrationality of Christian mysteries and beliefs, but left the fideistic conclusion aside. In one of the ironic twists of history, on the basis of Bayle's supposedly irrefutable demonstration of the absurdity of the mysteries, Deism drew the logical conclusion of what Leibniz himself wrote in 1705 to Lady Damaris Masham (albeit with a very different target than the Deists in mind): 'one must keep as a maxim that to be irrational is a mark of falsehood in Theology just as it is in Philosophy'.[12] If the supposed revealed truths which are not reducible to the truths of natural religion are irrational – in virtue of the fact that they cannot be comprehended by reason – this means *eo ipso* that they are false. Therefore, Voltaire concluded, 'faith consists in believing, not what appears to be true, but what appears to our understanding to be false' (208). The gap between this view and that of the tradition represented by Leibniz, according to whom faith is 'verum putare',[13] was at this point unbridgeable.

At the beginning of the eighteenth century, the influence in France of English Deism and of theological rationalism in general was emblematically represented by Voltaire's *Lettres Philosophiques ou Lettres sur les anglaises* (1734). It echoed also in the works of many other eminent representatives of the French Enlightenment, as well as in some well-known manuscripts: the famous and controversial *Livre des trois Imposteurs* (Moses, Christ, and Mohammed),[14] *Le Militaire philosophe*,[15] and the *Examen de la religion*.[16] The common feature of these works is their trust in the rational analysis of religion. Reason has the task of determining what is or is not acceptable and of rejecting as superstition, prejudice, and ignorance all those elements of revealed religion which are prodigious or incomprehensible – in short, all those elements that, being 'above reason', are *ipso facto* 'contrary to reason' and therefore false. The war against the mysterious and miraculous aspects of revealed religion was no longer conducted, as it had been during the previous century, primarily with sophisticated logical reasoning and painstaking biblical exegesis to prove the irrationality of this or that mystery. It was rather the weapon of irony and sarcasm which was used to ridicule as blatantly absurd much of the teaching of revealed religion. The first and most important target was certainly the Christian revelation, although sometimes this was hidden behind the criticism of superstition in pagan or ancient religions, as in Fontenelle's *Histoire des oracles* (1687) and *De l'origine des fables* (1724), or of Judaism, as in Voltaire's *Dictionnaire philosophique*. Montesquieu, for instance, in his *Lettres persanes* (1721) liquidated in a few witty lines the Trinity and transubstantiation – the two very mysteries around which endless complicated theological and philosophical discussions had flourished in the sixteenth and seventeenth centuries: 'there is another magician called the Pope. He will make . . . believe that three are only one, or else that the bread one eats is not bread, or that the wine one drinks is not wine, and a thousand other things of the same kind'.[17]

The teaching of this kind of absurdities, Rousseau stressed in the 'Profession de Foi du Vicaire Savoyard', is detrimental to social life and offensive to God:

> The greatest ideas of the divinity come to us from reason alone. View the spectacle of nature; hear the inner voice. Has God not told everything to our eyes, to our conscience, to our judgement? What more will men tell us? Their revelations have only the effect of degrading God by giving Him human passions. I see that particular dogmas, far from clarifying the notions of the great Being, confuse them; that far from ennobling them, they debase them; that to the inconceivable mysteries surrounding the great Being they add absurd contradictions; that they make man proud, intolerant, and cruel; that, instead of establishing peace on earth, they bring sword and fire to it.[18]

The attacks against revealed religion multiplied. In writings such as Diderot's *Pensées philosophiques* (1746), the foundations of revealed religion were undermined through the criticism of miracles and of the divine inspiration of Scriptures. It was once again Voltaire who dealt some of the most devastating blows against the claim of Christian religion to be founded on a supernatural revelation by levelling trenchant criticism against the classical proofs called in its support: prophecies, miracles, martyrdom. His arguments relied heavily on English sources,[19] as well as Bayle's *Pensées diverses sur la comète* (1682) and *Dictionaire historique et critique* (1697), Spinoza's *Tractatus theologicus-politicus* (1670), and Fontenelle's *Histoire* and *Origine*.[20]

According to Voltaire, prophecies, once they have been interpreted literally as they should be, are clearly not applicable to Jesus. Even if they referred to him, they would not attest to his divinity but to his identity with the worldly Messiah expected by the Hebrews. Miracles should also be rejected as proofs of a divine revelation. First of all, given our imperfect knowledge of the very complex laws of nature, we can never be certain that an extraordinary event is a violation of a physical law, instead of being simply the natural result of a set of conditions never observed before.[21] Moreover, the very definition of miracle as 'the violation of the divine, immutable, eternal laws of mathematics . . . is a contradiction in terms', because 'a law cannot be at once immutable and violated'. In any case it is absurd and impossible that God, a being infinitely wise, should 'have made laws in order to violate them' or 'would invert the eternal play of the immense engines which move the entire universe' for the sake of human beings – 'three or four hundred ants on this little heap of mud'.[22] Finally, miracles are based on testimony, but, disregarding the possibility of illusion, hallucination, or deformed reports, testimony can be reliable only if the witnesses do not have any vested interest in the facts they are recounting. This key condition is, however, never fulfilled in the case of miracles, since they are always reported in support of a vested interest, namely the alleged revelation itself. But even if we were to discover one authentic miracle, this would not prove anything: Scripture itself attests that impostors can perform miracles.[23] As for the testimony given by martyrs, were these not simply intolerant fanatics?[24] Deprived of its claim to superiority over other historical religions on the basis of a privileged revelation, the Christian religion has a value only insofar as it is a historical manifestation of theism, the only universally valid religion.

A similar agenda was pursued in Germany by Hermann Samuel Reimarus. The publication by Lessing between 1774 and 1778 of seven fragments from Reimarus's *Apologie oder Schutzschrift für die vernünftigen Vereher Gottes* stirred a violent debate. The key thesis was one typical of Deism: the rejection of revealed religion in favour of natural religion. According to Reimarus, the original teaching of Jesus coincided with this purely rational universal religion. Its transformation into a positive religion was the work of Jesus' disciples, who claimed divinity for him after his death. The force of the reaction which followed the appearance of these fragments reflected the complex intellectual situation of eighteenth-century Germany. Protestant *Schulphilosophie*, Pietism, Wolffianism, Neology: all of these, with their different attempts to rescue revelation, contributed to give to the German Enlightenment a peculiar character.

III. THE 'RADICALISATION' VERSUS THE 'RATIONALISATION' OF THE REALM 'ABOVE REASON'

Whereas the Enlightenment in England and France displayed a strong bias against revelation, the same cannot be said for Germany. Answering Bayle's question on how human reason can judge about the contradictoriness or non-contradictoriness of something which is by definition above its ability to comprehend, English and French Deists picked up the tread of Socinian rationalism and stretched it to its extreme logical consequences: what is irreducibly above reason (that is to say, the mysterious and incomprehensible element of revelation) is also contrary to reason and therefore false. On the opposite side, a strand of German Pietism pursued the alternative answer to Bayle's question, a pursuit, it was claimed, originating in the teaching of Luther himself and, for this reason, boldly defended by some bellicose Lutheran theologians of the previous generation.[25] Since revealed truths are above reason, this line of argument maintained, they must be withdrawn from the judgement of human reason. This brought about a 'radicalisation' of the realm 'above reason'. To be 'above' reason was taken in its strictest and literal sense: the sphere of faith, which is in turn the realm of grace, was separated from the incommensurably inferior sphere of reason. Although it would be deeply misleading to portray such a complex phenomenon as a monolithic entity, Pietism did have a distinctive common feature in the stress it put upon the practice of Christianity rather than knowledge and doctrine; this was clearly present already in the work that conventionally marks the movement's beginning, the *Pia desideria* (1675) of Philipp Jakob Spener. The emphasis was on personal faith and inwardness aiming at the love of God and neighbour. Love, not abstract doctrine, is the guide of the Christian, the new creature reborn from grace. From an intellectual point of view the consequence of this approach was a tendency to remove religion from the sphere of philosophical inquiry, in open polemic against the so-called *Schulphilosophie*, which was charged with distorting Christianity with its excessive intellectualisation. Reason has its place in the purely human sphere, but when the order of faith and grace is entered it is the 'heart' which should be followed. Christianity is concerned with action, active love of fellow human beings, and not with contemplation of truth for its own sake.

A good representative of this tendency, at least in one stage of his intellectual development, was Christian Thomasius with whom the first phase of the German Enlightenment opened. Following the teaching of Samuel Pufendorf, Thomasius separated jurisprudence from revealed theology: our knowledge of natural law is independent of revelation. Although jurisprudence shares with theology the task of promoting human happiness, it is sharply distinguished from theology in being concerned solely with the temporal dimension. In the *Institutiones iurisprudentiae divinae* (1688) Thomasius embraced Pufendorfian voluntarism: natural law does not come before the divine will, and no act is in itself right or wrong before the imposition of the law. As in jurisprudence, so in theology, this voluntarism led directly to history. If rational criteria cannot be applied to revelation, then revelation has to be treated as a historical phenomenon. As for the specific task of reason, in the *Vernunftlehre* (1691)[26] Thomasius maintained that instead of being involved in useless metaphysical speculations, reason should be employed for a practical goal: the advancement of the good of man. Since philosophy has little or nothing to say in the sphere of faith, it should not be concerned with abstract theological discussions but with ethical questions. Its aim is utility, in the sense of promoting the common good through rational love.

The hostility toward metaphysics, shared by Thomasius and Pietism, was not a feature of the German Enlightenment in general. The other face of the *Aufklärung*, represented by Christian Wolff and his school, valued metaphysics and conceived the relationship between reason and revelation in a very different way than did the Pietists. If Pietism generally was a 'radicalisation' of the sphere 'above reason', Wolff and his school offered a 'rationalisation' of that sphere – however paradoxical such an endeavour might be. Wolff followed in the footsteps of Leibniz and the scholastic tradition in maintaining the distinction between 'above' and 'contrary' to reason: revealed truths can be supra-rational but never irrational. The space 'above' reason, although recognised in theory, nevertheless tended in practice to shrink dramatically, being progressively overtaken by reason per se. How limited a genuine sphere 'above' reason became in the context of the rationalistic and systematic approach of Wolff to theology (as to every other field) is apparent in his own words:

> I always wanted to see whether it would be possible to present the truth of theology in such a distinct way as to exclude every contradiction. And when I heard of the fact that mathematicians demonstrate things with so much certainty that everyone is forced to recognise them as true, I wished to learn mathematics for its method, to devote myself to the task of taking theology to incontrovertible certainty.[27]

In order to reach correct demonstrations, he argued, it is necessary to reduce the words of Scripture to distinct notions and propositions which can be employed to build a scientific system. This scientific method of interpreting Scripture would provide infallible criteria for recognising the authenticity of an immediate revelation. Against the Deists in particular, Wolff proposed a rational proof of the necessity of revelation.

This process of progressive 'rationalisation' of the sphere 'above' reason was carried on and completed by the movement of 'Neology', represented by thinkers such as Johann Salomo Semler, Johann Joachim Spalding, Johann Gottlieb Töllner, and Johann August Eberhard. Although Neology accepted in theory both the concept of a divine revelation and its necessity, in practice it tended to resolve the content of revealed theology into rational truths by means of a philosophical, historical, and philological analysis and reinterpretation of traditional Christian doctrine. To be sure, the starting point of Neology was distinct from that of Deism insofar as its agenda was not a criticism or a rejection of revelation as such; but its end point was nevertheless substantially the same. The outcome of the neological reinterpretation of Christianity was in fact the final dissolution of the distinctive dogmas of Christian revelation: emptied of its specific content, what remained of Christianity was identical with the basic truths of natural religion. With Neology, as with Deism, the circle from revelation to a purely rational religion was closed – but only to be reopened by Lessing's attempt to go beyond Deism and against Neology with his new account of the foundations of revelation.

IV. NEW DIRECTIONS

The early period of Lessing's religious and philosophical thought was still under the aegis of Deism. In *Über die Entstehung der geoffenbarten Religion*, a brief fragment probably written during the Breslau years (1760–5), Lessing stated in typically deistic tones that 'the best revealed or positive religion is that which contains the least of conventional additions to natural religion and limits as little as possible the good effects of natural religion'. So, 'all positive and revealed religions are . . . equally true and equally false'[28] – they are true insofar as they present the key tenets of natural religion, false insofar as they add conventional and positive elements to the purity and simplicity of natural religion. After 1770, however, Lessing's views began to change, indicating a new direction toward a possible revaluation of revealed religion. In a series of publications culminating with the edition of Reimarus's controversial fragments, mentioned above, Lessing both attacked Neology and abandoned Deism. With biting sarcasm he denounced the incoherence of the neological claim to preserve the value and necessity of revelation once it had been entirely emptied of every supernatural element and had been reduced to a purely rational doctrine. This was a complete depletion of the concept of faith itself: why should we speak of 'believing' if every revealed doctrine can be rationally proved? Commenting on Leibniz's defence of the Trinity against the Socinian Andreas Wissowatius, Lessing exclaimed:

> He [Leibniz] *believed*! If only I still knew what is meant by this word. I must confess that in the mouth of so many new theologians it is for me a true enigma. In the last twenty or thirty years these people have made such great steps forward in the knowledge of religion, that when I compare them with an old dogmatist I have the impression of being in an entirely foreign territory. They have at hand so many cogent foundations of belief, so many incontrovertible proofs for the truth of the Christian religion, that I can never be sufficiently surprised by the fact that anyone could be so short-sighted as to hold belief in this truth for a supernatural effect of grace.[29]

On the other hand, Deism itself was no longer seen as giving a satisfactory account of revealed religion.[30] The various revealed religions were now regarded as historical processes presenting different degrees of insight which were adequate to the community in which they evolved. As explained in *Die Erziehung des Menschengeschlechts*, revelation is analogous to education: its aim is to facilitate the development of human potentialities,[31] progressing through different phases in accord with the degree of development of the subjects to which it is directed. In his departure from Deism in favour of a re-assessment of revelation, Lessing went as far as to conjecture that revealed religion could teach more accurate ideas of the divine being in the form of historical truths than human reason could ever reach on its own.[32] In this way he indicated a possible solution to the crucial problem raised by himself in *Über den Beweis des Geistes und der Kraft* (1777): how to pass from one class of truths – the truths of history – to a completely different class – the truths of reason. Revelation is founded on historical proofs, in particular prophecies and miracles. Lessing followed Leibniz's distinction between truths of fact and truths of reason and asked how we on contingent truths of history, such as Christ's resurrection, can build necessary truths of reason, such as the consubstantiality of Christ with God.[33] In *Die Erziehung des Menschengeschlechts* he seemed to suggest that in reality we are not dealing with two completely opposed kinds of knowledge: truths of reason are initially communicated as revealed truths as part of a unitary process of education conducted by God.

Lessing thus indicated a new possible way of justifying the value of revelation. Kant in turn reached the most striking and consistent expression of a general tendency of the Enlightenment concerning the relationship between philosophy and theology: the shift of the philosophical point of reference of theology from metaphysics and ontology to morality.[34] The priority of practical reason consecrated by Kant's second *Kritik* had its natural complement in the purely moral conception of religion presented by *Die Religion innerhalb der Grenzen der bloßen Vernunft* (1793): '*Religion* is (subjectively regarded) the recognition of all duties as divine commands'.[35] There is only one true Church: the invisible Church constituted by all human beings who follow the universal moral law. It is however very difficult for human beings to reach purely moral concepts without external help and support. In order to be convinced that it is their duty to follow the moral law, that law needs to be presented as a positive divine command, historically contained in Scripture. The passage from rational or natural religion to revealed or positive religion is the passage from a religion in which something is known as a duty before it is accepted as a divine command, to a religion in which something must first be known as a divine command in order to be recognised as a duty (see 6:153). In short, revealed religion is a necessary means for bringing the majority of human beings to follow moral precepts. The worth of positive religion is not therefore in any way dependent upon its being a truly divine revelation, but upon its conformity with the universal moral law. This is the case with the Christian religion which was regarded by Kant as the only positive religion that can be reduced to a pure natural religion. Its value and justification rests therefore in the last instance on mere (*bloße*) reason.

On the Kantian distinction between speculative and practical reason the young Fichte built his *Versuch einer Kritik aller Offenbarung* (1792).[36] This distinction indicated to him the way to overcome the contradiction into which Deism inevitably fell: wanting to give religion an exclusively rational support, Deism ended up destroying the very nature of religion as faith. In the light of

Kantian philosophy, Fichte saw the possibility of providing a rational foundation for religion which preserved at the same time its specific character. God cannot be known by theoretical reason. If therefore a speculative consideration of God must be ruled out, a philosophical enquiry about religion remains possible before the tribunal of practical reason.[37] The idea of God is in fact founded on practical reason and on respect for the moral law. Religion represents God as moral legislator and just judge, offering a motive to follow the law when the pure respect for the law itself is not strong enough to effect obedience. Pure rational religion corresponds to an ideal state in which man is freed from his sensible nature and his will is not determined by a positive command of God but by the pure moral law. The same will to obey the moral law alone is characteristic of natural religion as well, but in this case a complete freedom from sensible inclinations is still lacking. Revealed religion is necessary in order to overcome this intrinsic weakness of human nature before the pure moral law. It exercises a direct influence on the will, representing the moral law as a positive divine law (I.1: 37, 53–54).[38] Like Lessing, Fichte had by now left behind Deism's corrosive contempt for revelation and recognised the important pedagogical task of revelation.

This reappraisal of the place and significance of revelation was pushed still further by Georg Wilhelm Friedrich Hegel. Hegel proposed in many respects a new foundation for revealed religion which superseded not only the attacks of Deism but also the Kantian-Fichtian moral model. In the very first fragment of Hegel's early theological writings, there is already a remarkable distance from Kant.[39] Although Hegel shared Kant's depreciation of positive religion, the alternative he proposed was not a purely rational natural religion but a national religion (*Volksreligion*). Such a religion that has a real impact on the life of a nation cannot be founded on mere (*bloße*) reason: it must appeal to 'heart' and 'imagination' and can form itself only in the context of the life of an authentic nation. The real contrast is not between natural and revealed religion but between national and private religion. Of the latter, Christianity is a much criticised example: the moral teaching of Jesus can guide the life of single individuals, but not that of a people as a whole. Hegel preferred the religion of the ancient Greeks; as an alternative to the model of Christ he proposed that of Socrates. Although he would soon change his views on the matter, the interest of this initial position rests upon its stress on history: from the very beginning history was at the heart of Hegel's philosophical reflection. The young Hegel was already pointing to what he would later call 'objective Spirit', the collective experience with its social and cultural institutions. Religion, and in particular revealed religion, had to be seen as one manifestation of objective Spirit. Arising from the unfolding of the Spirit in the concrete life of the nations, it presented rational (philosophical) truths in an imaginative and emotional form. It is true that *Das Leben Jesu* – a text composed only a few months after the last fragment of *Volksreligion und Christentum*[40] – still depicted a truly Kantian Jesus (that is to say, a mere moral teacher, presenting the Gospel in the terms of Kantian morality). Likewise *Die Positivität der christlichen Religion* (1795–6) was still under the shadow of a typical Enlightenment and Kantian contempt for positive religion. But *Der Geist des Christentums und sein Schicksal* (1798–1800) and the second draft of *Die Positivität der christlichen Religion* (1800) displayed the definitive departure of the young Hegel from this Enlightenment-Kantian interpretive paradigm and a clear change of direction toward his mature dialectic. The Jewish religion, the Old Testament, is now seen as the 'objective' that is the opposite of the 'I', the 'subject'. Jewish religion is slavery to the 'other', namely to the law.[41] In the same way, also the Kantian moral law is 'objective': being against instincts and sensibility, it is against part of the 'subject' intended as the concrete human being:

> For the particular – impulses, inclinations, pathological love, sensuous experience, or whatever else it is called – the universal is necessarily and always something alien and objective. There remains a residuum of indestructible positivity[.] (*Werke*, 1: 323; Nohl, 266; tr., 211)

The real difference between the follower of positive religion and the follower of natural religion is that for the former the master is outside, for the latter inside. Neither of them however is free. 'The positivity' (intended by Hegel as equivalent to 'objectivity') 'is only partially taken away' by Kantian natural religion (*Werke*, 1: 323; Nohl, 265–6; tr., 211). The 'positivity' can be sublated (*Aufhebt*) only by the reconciliation of the opposites indicated by the Christian concept of 'love'. Christian love is the reconciliation between the universal (the moral law) and the particular (the concrete individual), between law and inclinations. The particular is no longer opposed to the universal, because love compels the same actions ordered by the law but not as a commandment opposed to the inclinations. The 'content' is the same, the 'form' is different:

> The correspondence of inclination with law is such that law and inclination are no longer different. . . . In the 'fulfilment' of both the laws and duty, their concomitant, however, the moral disposition, etc., ceases to be universal, opposed to inclination, and inclination ceases to be particular, opposed to the law, and therefore this correspondence of law and inclination is life and, as the relation of differents to one another, love[.] (*Werke*, 1: 326–7; Nohl, 268; tr., 214–15)

Far from being summarily dismissed, revelation and its concept of Christian love is now seen as a necessary moment in the unfolding of the Spirit which produces a synthesis superior to the initial position of the abstract moral law. Religion (and in particular revealed religion) is nevertheless only a stage in this unfolding process: as expressed in the famous triad of absolute Spirit, the final synthesis which embodies thesis (art) and antithesis (religion) in a superior unity is philosophy. Only upon attaining the final synthesis in philosophy does the Spirit become fully conscious of itself. In the end the battle between reason and 'above' reason which had raged throughout the eighteenth century was won by reason, and a uniquely strong assertion of it: Hegelian absolute knowledge.

NOTES

1 See Gottfried Wilhelm Leibniz, *Essais de théodicée*, 'Discourse preliminaire de la conformité de la Foy avec la Raison', §§72–3, where Leibniz quoted from Bayle's *Dictionaire historique et critique* (2nd edn., Rotterdam, 1702), 3140 ('Eclaircissement sur les Manichéens'); in *Phil. Schriften*, 6: 92. Commenting on Leibniz's *Defensio trinitatis*, P. Leyser expressed a similar view: *Apparatus literarius singularia nova anecdota rariora ex omnis generis eruditione depromens studio Societatis Colligentium*, Collectio I. (Wittenberg, 1717), 210–11. Translations are by the author unless other source is given.

2 See Leibniz, *Remarques sur le Livre d'un Antitrinitaire Anglois*, in Maria Rosa Antognazza, 'Inediti leibniziani sulle polemiche trinitarie', *Rivista di Filosofia neo-scolastica* 83, (1991): 525–50 at 547. Leibniz seems to be referring in particular to the Jesuit Honorato Fabri. See *Nouveaux essais*, IVxviii.9, in Akademie-Ausgabe, VI.6: 498; and *De non violando principio contradictionis in Divinis contra Honoratum Fabri* (c. 1685), Akademie-Ausgabe, VI.4: 2340–2.

3 See for instance Leibniz's account of this position in *Dialogus inter theologum et misosophum* (c. 1678–1679), Akademie-Ausgabe, VI.4: 2212–9 and his forceful rejection, in the 'Discourse preliminaire' of the *Théodicée*, of Bayle's thesis of the opposition between faith and reason.

4 See Zbigniew Ogonowski, 'Le 'Christianisme sans mystères' selon John Toland et les sociniens', *Archiwum Historii Filozofii i Myśli Spolecznej*, 12 (1966): 205–23; and 'Leibniz und die Sozinianer', in *Theatrum Europaeum*, ed. R. Brinkmann (Munich, 1982), 385–408, especially 391–3.

5 See Maria Rosa Antognazza, 'The Defence of the Mysteries of the Trinity and the Incarnation: an Example of Leibniz's "Other" Reason', *British Journal for the History of Philosophy* 9, (2001): 283–309, especially 288.

6 See the following texts by Leibniz: *Defensio trinitatis contra Wissowatium* (c. 1669), Akademie-Ausgabe, VI.1: 520, 522; *Elementa juris naturalis* (c. 1670–1), VI.2: 567; *Raisons que M. Jaquelot m'a envoyées pour justifier l'Argument contesté de des-Cartes qui doit prouver l'existence de Dieu, avec mes reponses* (20 November 1702), *Phil Schriften*, 3:444; *Nouveaux essais*, IV.xiv.4, 457; *Théodicée*, 'Discourse preliminaire', §33, 69.

7 See Leibniz, *Raisons que M. Jaquelot . . .* (444); also *Defensio trinitatis* (521). Compare, Ignacio Angelelli, 'The Techniques of Disputation in the History of Logic', *The Journal of Philosophy*, 67 (1970): 800–15.

8 See for instance Andreas Wissowatius, *Religio rationalis seu de rationis judicio, in controversiis etiam theologicis, ac religiosis, adhibendo, tractatus* ([Amsterdam], 1685) and Stephen Nye, *Considerations on the Explications of the Doctrine of the Trinity, By Dr. Wallis, Dr. Sherlock, Dr. S[ou]th, Dr. Cudworth, and Mr. Hooker; as also on the Account given by those that say, the Trinity is an Unconceivable and Inexplicable Mystery* (London, 1693), especially p. 30.

9 See Leibniz, *Annotatiunculae subitaneae ad Tolandi librum de Christianismo Mysteriis carente* (8 August 1701), in *Opera omnia*, ed. L. Dutens, 6 vols. (Geneva, 1768), 5: 142–3.
10 Voltaire, *Dictionnaire philosophique*, in *Oeuvres complètes*, ed. L. Moland, 52 vols. (Paris, 1877–85), vol. 17; translated as *Philosophical Dictionary*, trans. and ed. T. Besterman (Harmondsworth, 1971), here at 207 and 208.
11 See Leibniz, *Théodicée*, 'Preface', 39.
12 *Phil. Schriften*, 3: 367.
13 Leibniz, *Commentatiuncula de judice controversiarum* (c. 1669–70), Akademie-Ausgabe, VI.1: 550.
14 See for instance the manuscript copy, *Le livre des trois Imposteurs*, held by the British Library (Add. Mss. 12064). This work, although published in Amsterdam in 1719, continued to circulate as a manuscript under different titles such as *L'esprit de Spinoza, Traité des trois imposteurs*, and *De tribus impostoribus*. On this clandestine literature, see Ira O. Wade, *The Clandestine Organization and Diffusion of Philosophic Ideas in France from 1700 to 1750* (Princeton, NJ, 1938); Mario Sina, 'L'illuminismo francese', in *Storia della Filosofia Moderna*, ed. S. Vanni Rovighi (Brescia, 1981); 382–6, Robert Darnton, *The Corpus of Clandestine Literature in France, 1769–1789* (New York, NY, 1995), and chapter 5, sect. ii, this volume.
15 The circle of Paul-Henri Thiry d'Holbach published an abridged version of this text under the title *Le militaire philosophe, ou, Difficultés sur la religion proposées au R. P. Malebranche, prêtre de l'Oratoire, par un ancien officier* (London [in fact, Amsterdam], 1768).
16 See for instance the manuscript held by the British Library (Lansdowne 414). The *Examen de la religion* was published in 1764 in *L'evangile de la raison* (London, [in fact, Netherlands]).
17 Charles de Secondat de Montesquieu, *Lettres persanes* (Amsterdam, 1721); Letter 24; translated as *Persian Letters*, trans. and ed. C. J. Betts (Harmondsworth, 1973). Other representative examples are the articles 'Antitrinitaires' and 'Transsubstantiation' in Voltaire's *Dictionnaire*.
18 Jean-Jacques Rousseau, *Émile, ou De l'education* (1762), in *Oeuvres*, 4: 607; translated as *Émile*, trans. A. Bloom (New York, NY, 1979), 295.
19 See Peter Annet, *David, ou l'histoire de l'homme selon le coeur de Dieu*, trans. by P.-H. T. d'Holbach (London [in fact, Amsterdam], 1768); Anthony Collins, *A Discourse of the Grounds and Reasons of the Christian Religion* (London, 1724) and *Scheme of Literal Profecy considered* (London, 1726); Conyers Middleton, *A Free Inquiry into the Miraculous Powers, which are Supposed to have Subsisted in the Christian Church* (London, 1749); Matthew Tindal, *The Rights of the Christian Church Asserted* (London, 1706) and *Christianity as old as the Creation: The Gospel a Republication of the Religion of Nature* (London, 1730); Thomas Woolston, *A Discourse on the Miracles of Our Saviour* (London, 1727).
20 See Haydn Trevor Mason, *Pierre Bayle and Voltaire* (London, 1963); Mario Sina, *L' 'Anti-Pascal' di Voltaire* (Milan, 1970); René Pomeau, *La religion de Voltaire*, (Paris, 1969).
21 On this point see Jean-Raoul Carré, *Réflexions sur l'anti-Pascal de Voltaire* (Paris, 1935), 74–5.
22 See 'Miracles' in Voltaire, *Dictionnaire*.
23 See the additions of 1771 to the article 'Miracles' of Voltaire's *Dictionnaire*.
24 See Voltaire, *Traité sur la tolerance* (1763), ed. J. Renwick in *Les oeuvres complètes/The Complete Works*, ed. T. Besterman (Geneva, 1968–), vol. 56C (Oxford, 2000), ch. 9, 'Des martyrs'; translated as *Treatise on Tolerance*, trans. B. Masters, ed. S. Harvey (Cambridge, 2000).
25 In particular the above mentioned Matthias Flacius Illyrius and Daniel Hofmann.
26 The *Vernunftlehre* is composed of two parts, both published in Halle in 1691: the *Einleitung zu der Vernunfft-Lehre* and the *Ausübung der Vernunfft-Lehre*.
27 *Christian Wolffs eigene Lebensbeschreibung*, ed. by H. Wuttke (Leipzig, 1841), 121.
28 See, Lessing, *Werke*, eds. K. Eibl and H. G. Göpfert, 8 vols. (Munich, 1970–9), vol. 7: *Theologiekritische Schriften I und II* (1976), 283.

29 See *Des Andreas Wissowatius Einwürfe wider die Dreieinigkeit*, in Lessing, *Werke*, 7: 223.

30 See in particular Lessing's 'antithesis' to the arguments presented by Reimarus in his fragments ('Gegensätze des Herausgeber', in Lessing, *Werke*, 7: 457–91).

31 See *Die Erziehung des Menschengeschlechts*, §4, in Lessing, *Werke*, 7: 477. The first 53 paragraphs were published in 1777 as part of the comment on Reimarus's fragment; a second group of paragraphs appeared in 1780.

32 See *Die Erziehung*, §77, *Werke*, vol. 8: *Theologiekritische Schriften III; Philosophische Schriften* (1979), 507.

33 Leibniz, *Über den Beweis des Geistes und der Kraft*, in *Werke*, 8: 13.

34 See Max Wundt, *Die deutsche Schulphilosophie in Zeitalter der Aufklärung* (Tübingen, 1945), 277; and Graziella Rotta, *La 'Idea Dio': Il pensiero religioso di Fichte fino all'Atheismusstreit* (Genoa, 1995), 24.

35 Immanuel Kant, *Die Religion innerhalb der grenzen der bloßen Vernunft*, Ak 6: 153; translated as *Religion within the Boundaries of mere Reason*, in *Works/Religion and Rational Theology*, trans. and eds. A. W. Wood and G. di Giovanni (1996).

36 See Rotta, 79–94.

37 Johann Gottlieb Fichte, *Versuch einer Kritik aller Offenbarung*, in *Gesamtausgabe*, I.1: 114.

38 Compare Fichte, *Versuch einer Kritik aller Offenbarung* (I.1: 37, 53–4).

39 The bulk of Hegel's early writings was published by Herman Nohl in 1907 as *Hegels Theologische Jugendschriften* (Tübingen, 1907); hereafter 'Nohl'. Nohl collected under the title of *Volksreligion und Christentum* a series of fragments written between 1793 and 1795.

40 Hegel wrote *Das Leben Jesu* in Bern between 9 May and 24 July 1795.

41 Hegel, *Der Geist des Christentums und sein Schicksal*, in *Werke*, eds E. Moldenhauer and K. M. Michel, 20 vols. (Frankfurt am Main, 1969–72), vol. 1: *Frühe Schriften* (1971), 298 (Nohl, 386).

23

REVEALED RELIGION: THE BRITISH DEBATE

M. A. STEWART

The distinction that is now drawn between natural and revealed theology evolved gradually. In its eighteenth-century form it is traceable to a debate that started with the Reformation but took a recognizably modern shape only in the seventeenth century. That reason and experience offer a route to some degree of religious belief or knowledge has been a common assumption for as long as philosophy has served the interests of the Church, the Synagogue, or the Mosque; but historically it was a route that was not sharply differentiated from revelation. The evidence of the world was one kind of revelation and that of conscience another. Verbal revelation as a third kind has always had an important role in institutional religion. Different modes of revelation suited the knowledge and mental capacities of different believers and were considered compatible.

In the eyes of the Reformers, however, the institutions of religion had become corrupted over the centuries and had corrupted in turn both the spirit and the letter of the message they purported to preserve. The Catholic Church took refuge in the longevity and solidity of its tradition, including a continuity of biblical and doctrinal interpretation and of what were taken to be miraculous occurrences that identified it uniquely with the original Church from the days of the Apostles. Protestants sought to discredit Catholic miracles while safeguarding those of the Bible and to portray themselves as the rediscoverers and true heirs of the first Church. In this contest, the nature and basis of institutional authority and historical evidence, and the role of reason in general and individual reason in particular, were all up for review. By the seventeenth century, secular knowledge too was in flux and philosophical horizons were changing. Theology had long been considered the highest form of *scientia*, so that the new notions of science that developed in Britain during that century had a direct impact on theological debate and apologetics. Political dissention, however, divided the Protestant cause.

Responding to the ferment of ideas, Protestants were keen to show that their position was not a merely negative one, and that they had a self-contained system of belief based on sound foundations. In Britain, the Anglican Church was ahead of the field, staking out its territory in opposition not only to the Church of Rome, but to infidels, real or imaginary, and to Calvinists and sectaries. There was a Calvinist residue within Anglicanism, but the influence was stronger among the Dissenting denominations. Calvinists thought reason too fallible to be the arbiter of the rule of faith, and traditional religious structures too much the work of priestcraft. By embracing the new rational mood, Anglican leaders laid themselves open to counterattack not only from the Calvinist side, but from theological and philosophical freethinkers. By the beginning of the eighteenth century, the integrated package of natural and revealed religion was starting to look a little less secure, as the interpretation of revelation became increasingly contested, and as the strategy of testing the biblical documents as historical artefacts backfired in the face of unflattering analyses by deist critics. Orthodox and heterodox Protestants alike relied on the Bible as the authority for their differences. The defence of the documents was by now a study in its own right, as deist writers contended for the possibility of a rationally founded religion without them.

The standard form of the conventional package, whose prototype was Edward Stillingfleet's influential *Origines sacrae*, was to start with familiar arguments for the being and attributes of God to show the grounds for monotheism. The next steps were to defend the need for identifiable communication between the Creator and the intelligent creation, and to argue the soundness of the Mosaic and Gospel histories in comparison with other histories. This soundness being established, the miracles and prophecies reported in the Bible served to validate the theological doctrines and moral injunctions it contained, and from these followed practical consequences for life here and hereafter.[1] The strategy required the development of a historical methodology, establishing quasi-legal models to appraise the testimony of friendly and hostile witnesses. The tactic was in part to show that biblical history is as reliable as any ancient history and more reliable than most; in part to discredit reports from rival religions. The practice of rubbishing the competition had been a stock-in-trade of Christian apologists for as long as alternative belief systems were known. Within the Christian tradition, Catholics were victims of the same technique at the hands of Protestant critics; and by a natural progression, the Protestant dependence on a smaller corpus of miraculous events was targeted in turn as the deist movement gained in confidence. It is a mistake to credit deism itself – a movement that paid a sometimes ambivalent lip service to theism without embracing revelation – with the original collection of comparative data from other religions.

It was a commonplace of the anti-deist literature to bewail the baneful influence of Hobbes and Spinoza, whose metaphysics seemed incompatible with any meaningful theism. The seventeenth-century freethinker who cast the longest shadow over the British debate in the following century, however, was Charles Blount, whose youthful follower, the Edinburgh student Thomas Aikenhead, was hanged after a show trial in 1697. Blount wrote extensively on religious beliefs and practices, always from the viewpoint of a historian of politics and human psychology, often emphasizing the connection between religion and politics and the political management of belief. His *Miracles no Violations of the Laws of Nature* is typical of his output.[2] While never formally impugning Christianity or denying its supernatural origin, Blount concentrates on phenomena that other religions share with Christianity and explains them naturalistically. The Irish religious controversialist Charles Leslie took up the challenge in *A Short and Easie Method with the Deists*, a rather facile work which sets out the distinctive rules of evidence that Christianity is said to meet: that it appeals to matters of fact open to sensory tests, that the tests were public at the time they were made, and that memorials and public observances associated with the facts have survived to the present.[3] More sophisticated writers, however, from Henry More to John Wilkins, had long emphasized the importance of such factors as the number, skill, and objectivity of the ancient witnesses.[4]

I. THE LEGACY OF LOCKE

The most important theoretician for the early eighteenth-century debate, from the side of Christian belief, is John Locke. Locke may have derived his basic logic of historical evidence from earlier writers, including the Port-Royal *Logic*, but he gives it new clarity in his *Essay concerning Human Understanding*. In discussing our confidence in facts for which we are reliant on the testimony of others, Locke distinguishes the grounds of probability that lie in 'the conformity of any thing with our own Knowledge, Observation, and Experience' from those grounds that lie in 'the Testimony of others, vouching their Observation and Experience'. The latter include the number, integrity, and expertise of the witnesses, 'the Design of the Author, where it is a Testimony out of a Book cited', and 'the Consistency of the Parts, and Circumstances of the Relation'. As important as any of these is the contrary testimony, which can be similarly appraised.[5]

We attain the highest degree of probability in respect of particular matters of fact 'when the general consent of all Men, in all Ages, as far as it can be known, concurrs with a Man's constant and never-failing Experience in like cases'. Locke associates this near-certainty with the uniform course of nature, as detected in the observable order. 'For what our own and other Men's constant Observation has found always to be after the same manner, that we with reason conclude to be the Effects of steady and regular Causes, though they come not within the reach of our Knowledge.' The next degree of probability arises from the evidence of history and experience that things of the given kind 'are, for the most part, so'. Here too, and in purely indifferent matters 'when any particular matter of fact is vouched by the concurrent Testimony of unsuspected Witnesses', belief follows naturally upon the testimony (*Essay*, IV.xvi.6–8).

Where testimonies conflict with 'common Experience' and 'the ordinary course of Nature', or with each other, however, the proof is diminished and we must 'proportion' our assent. The degree of disparity with experience will lead us to an appropriately graduated response: 'such different Entertainment, as we call *Belief, Conjecture, Guess, Doubt, Wavering, Distrust, Disbelief,* etc.' Reports of reports are subject to diminishing returns. 'Passion, Interest, Inadvertency, Mistake of his Meaning, and a thousand odd Reasons, or Caprichio's, Men's Minds are acted by, (impossible to be discovered,) may make one Man quote another Man's Words or Meaning wrong.' And in matters that lie beyond any literal testimony, we can think only by analogy (IV.xvi.9–12).

Miracles are, nevertheless, an exception, 'wherein the strangeness of the Fact lessens not the Assent to a fair Testimony given of it', and furthermore gives 'Credit' to 'other Truths, which need such Confirmation'. God is a free agent and we cannot circumscribe his actions or purposes or the actions and purposes in which he aids his agents. '[W]here such supernatural Events are suitable to ends aim'd at by him, who has the Power to change the course of Nature, there, under such Circumstances, they may be the fitter to procure Belief, by how much the more they are beyond, or contrary to ordinary Observation' (IV.xvi.13).

Furthermore, where the testimony is not another person's report, but the direct declaration of God himself, it is infallible; but as such, it cannot conflict with the clear 'evidence of Reason' (IV.xvi.14). To believe in something that does so conflict is to yield to 'Fancies' and 'natural Superstition', which are a source of 'Follies' and 'extravagant Practices in Religion', so reason must still be the judge of what is and is not a revelation (IV.xviii.5, 8, 11). To believe in something which, though not contrary to reason, exceeds all evidence, is no better. That is a sign of enthusiasm, when 'all that surplusage of assurance is owing to some other Affection, and not to the Love of Truth'. It is to yield to our 'Passions or Interests'. The 'Ease and Glory it is to be inspired and be above the common and natural ways of Knowledge' flatters our 'Laziness, Ignorance, and Vanity'. Those who had a mission to communicate their revelation to the world, unlike modern enthusiasts, had it verified by a divine miracle (IV.xix.1, 7, 15; this chapter added in 1700). Thus revelation and the validation of miracles are interlinked.

The point is repeated in Locke's posthumous *Discourse on Miracles*,[6] where he finally addresses the question of how we identify a divine intervention in which it is appropriate for us to override the usual criteria for assessing testimony. The testimony is accepted at face value, and one has to believe that Locke thinks that the witnesses have met the tests of 'a fair Testimony given of it'. The problem is that it is confronted with the contrary evidence of experience. A different calculation is involved. Now it becomes a matter of weighing the *power* needed to achieve a truly divine work against the known inferior power needed to bring about lesser marvels. He stresses the 'numbers, variety and greatness' not of the witnesses but of the miracles wrought in confirmation of Christianity. This goes along with a curiously subjective definition of a miracle as 'a sensible Operation, which being above the comprehension of the Spectator, and in his Opinion contrary to the establish'd Course of Nature, is taken by him to be Divine', but the definition is not doing the main work in his argument. The substantive question remains that of showing 'what shall be a sufficient inducement' to take the phenomenon as 'wrought by God himself for the attestation of a Revelation from him'. The degree of power involved is one of the standard tests employed throughout eighteenth-century apologetics; that is to say, a miracle involves an action that it is beyond the unaided power of humankind to achieve. Whereas Locke, however, rested his main case on this, most other writers make altogether heavier use of Locke's witness tests.

Those tests are among Locke's measures of probability, and a revelation that has met the tests of reason is the object of 'faith'. Locke avoids talking about knowledge, but sometimes admits certainty, at least in the early editions of the *Essay*; and that for him is interchangeable with knowledge. He says, however, that revelation commands 'the highest degree of our Assent' and there is uncertainty as to whether this means more than belief or judgement. He was assailed on this from across the theological spectrum, for not admitting divine faith as a form of knowledge and revelation as the highest certainty. It was one of the themes of the pamphlet war with Stillingfleet in Locke's lifetime, and of the Scots Calvinist, Thomas Halyburton's (1674–1712) posthumous *Essay concerning the Reason of Faith* in 1714. In response to Stillingfleet, Locke permitted himself still to speak of the certainty of revelation. This is hard to square with the seemingly probabilistic character of any assessment of the confirming signs. It is important to remember, however, that for Locke certainty comes through reflection. It is possible that in his own mind he thought that the kind of biblical analysis that he pursued in a work like *The Reasonableness of Christianity* did present him with a kind of 'perception of the agreement and disagreement of ideas' that he equated with knowledge. If so, he was not so far removed from the Calvinist view that the Bible carried its authority on every page, but he did at least think that the question could be, and had to be, investigated without incurring a charge of blasphemy.

The English Dissenter Isaac Watts (1674–1748), who promoted Halyburton's works in the wider market, adapted Locke's epistemology to the needs of orthodox, if unsophisticated, belief in his influential *Logick* (1724). The 'absolute and infallible Assurance' of 'supernatural Certainty' comes by direct inspiration to a chosen prophet, who 'is under a superior heavenly Impression, Light and Evidence, whereby he is assured that God reveals it'. It is, however, 'hard to make out this Inspiration to others, and to convince them of it' except by 'some antecedent or consequent Prophecies or Miracles, or some publick Appearances more than human'. The faith of the 'common Christian' who 'believes any Proposition which God has revealed in the Bible upon this account, because *God has said it*' presupposes a 'Train of Reasonings' that falls short of this. But Watts was writing for common Christians, not prophets and their audiences, and like many preachers thought the Resurrection the best attested event in history; there was therefore nothing *more* certain than the Christian revelation.[7]

II. THE DEIST DEBATE

In the period between Locke and Hume, there was much the same kind of continuous outpouring of ephemeral pamphlets on the subject of revealed religion as there was on natural religion. The period is significant, however, for a small group of high-profile deist writings, and a smaller group of writings that genuinely respond to the deist challenge and re-write the case for traditional belief. 'Deism' is here used in a general sense, of any system of belief that purports to accept natural religion but restricts the role of revelation and of the evidences of revelation; it discounts doctrines that rest on revelation alone and is frequently silent on the subject of an afterlife. Deism is not always anti-clerical, just as anti-clericalism is not always anti-religious; but it is critical of the disciplinary power exercised by ecclesiastical agencies, and the tendency of clerical and political authority to work to each other's benefit. It is possible that in some cases the deist façade is a disguise for more radical views,[8] and likely that some writers varied in the extent of their freethinking in the course of their literary careers. The religion of the established churches was still protected by law, so that dissent had to be circumspect; a number of deist writers wrote in dialogue or adopted some other form of literary cover.

Anthony Ashley Cooper, third earl of Shaftesbury, and Bernard Mandeville were more significant as writers on morals, Shaftesbury for his optimistic view and Mandeville for his cynical view of human nature and motivation. Both, however, challenged the place of ecclesiastical structures in the maintenance and enforcement of moral standards. Such attacks on received modes of moral direction were read, not least by the clergy themselves, as a challenge to Church teaching, so that an assault on the institutions that imparted Christian instruction merged into a critique of the authority of the revelation on which the instruction was based. Shaftesbury had travelled widely on the Continent and, under the pretext of identifying Catholic excesses, used his learning and experience to demonstrate how far Christian institutions had been grafted onto older pagan superstitions; but his main message was that religion is open to moral tests and cannot of itself be a moral arbiter.[9] It is therefore fruitless to seek physical signs of revelation. Miracles are a proof of power, not of rectitude.[10] Whether in Shaftesbury's view there have ever been true miracles is never discussed at a theoretical level. As for Mandeville, he leaves the case against miracles as strongly defended as the case for. His attitude to Christianity is ambivalent: at times it appears to be a highly moral religion, but most of its practitioners come across as hypocritical.[11]

John Toland and Anthony Collins to some degree compromised Locke's reputation by seeking to inherit his philosophical mantle. Toland in his classic *Christianity not Mysterious*, and Collins in *An Essay concerning the Use of Reason* responding to Toland's early critics, used the epistemology of Book IV of Locke's *Essay* to argue that there can be no assent to mysteries and that therefore there is no room for anything 'above reason' in religion. On the surface, this entails that there is nothing above reason in Christianity; but it can be read as challenging Christianity precisely for clinging to mysteries and as challenging Protestantism for not recognizing that doctrines such as the Trinity are as contrary to reason as the Catholics' transubstantiation.[12] Both authors require that the scriptures must satisfy logical tests, while conceding that some of the more anthropomorphic descriptions of deity may be read allegorically. Toland traces the mysteries of the creeds to early priestcraft and ridicules the Church's creation of a worldly hierarchy,[13] while Collins draws on the Anglican divine John Tillotson to argue that no testimony to divine authority can validate a doctrine inconsistent with natural religion.[14] Toland allows a role for miracles considered simply as the exercise of superhuman power in doing something that is in itself intelligible and possible, provided that it occurs in the public validation of an intelligible doctrine. Both Toland and Collins were well informed in biblical scholarship, but Toland became increasingly idiosyncratic in textual interpretation and in his metaphysical views, coming to distinguish the secret meaning of a text from that intended for popular understanding.[15] This seems nothing better than priestly mysteries secularized. If his Latin *Pantheisticon* of 1720 represents his mature stance, this was not pantheism in the established sense, even though Toland invented the term *pantheist*.[16] It was a religious attitude that floated free of all established sects, drawing ideas from any and all sources; it was centrally concerned with the idea of an ethical society, and far removed from the aggressive rationalism of his early career.

Collins, who never acknowledged the authorship of any of his works, maintained a more consistent stand, though not without its ambiguities. His defences of materialism and determinism set him on a collision course with established theological opinion, but not with Joseph Priestley's later brand of theism; *A Vindication of the Divine Attributes* is an attack on the evasions in William King's sermon of 1709 on predestination and divine foreknowledge.[17] Collins's better known *Discourse of Free-Thinking* compares King unfavourably with Tillotson: whereas Tillotson discounts revelation only in respect of the literal ascription to God of parts and passions, King leaves him also without any comprehensible 'understanding, wisdom, will, mercy, holiness, goodness, or truth' that we might be expected to emulate. All religions have their scriptures and the 'free thinker' needs to know why the officers of one religion have a better insight into the superiority of their own sacred documents than those of another, particularly when they disagree among themselves on matters of interpretation:

> The Popish Priests contend that the Text of Scripture is so corrupted, precarious, and unintelligible, that we are to depend on the Authority of their Church for the true Particulars of the Christian Religion. Others who contend for a greater Perfection in the Text of Scripture, differ about the inspiration of those Books; some contending that every Thought and Word are inspir'd; some that the Thoughts are inspir'd, and not the Words; some that those Thoughts only are inspir'd, which relate to Fundamentals; and others that the Books were written by honest Men with great Care and Faithfulness, without any Inspiration either with respect to the Thoughts or Words.[18]

Every attempt to resolve these differences is seen to be special pleading; but the disagreements are healthier for society than the abrogation of rational judgement that is implied in enforced conformity. Collins further challenges the guardians of revelation in an early pamphlet defending natural religion against the encroachment of the Anglican Articles, and in his last work, *A Discourse of the Grounds and Reasons of the Christian Religion*, where he lambasts the Old Testament as a set of fables, the Jewish religion as a superstition, and the Fathers of the early Church as fraudsters. His main target, however, is the attempts to vindicate the life of Christ and the rise of the Christian religion as the fulfilment of Old Testament prophecies. Too many prophecies are unspecific and must be read symbolically, but this becomes an interpreter's free-for-all. Where they are specific, they were either fulfilled independently of the life of Jesus, or there is no conclusive evidence of their being fulfilled at all.[19]

Matthew Tindal was another who had been an early admirer of Locke. In middle age in the 1690s he became involved in the Unitarian controversy; and in two political works, one of them contemporary with Locke's writings on toleration, he argued that because there is no right in a state of nature to enforce uniformity of conscience, no such right has been communicated by society to the magistrate, and no such right can be delegated by the magistrate to any ecclesiastical authority. The clergy who enforce such uniformity have no moral basis for it and are motivated only by interest.[20] Later, he responded to a pastoral letter from Edmund Gibson, bishop of London, on infidelity, continuing his attack on the *ultra vires* role of the clergy. If the propriety of a religious doctrine is not evident to reason, it cannot be successfully attested as divine. At seventy-three he published his best known work, *Christianity as Old as the Creation*, an attempt to show that the kind of rationalist ethic developed by Samuel Clarke can be free-standing without the biblical teaching that Clarke considered an essential complement to it.[21]

The Christianity of Tindal's title is the humanitarian ethic of the New Testament, shorn of its basis in revelation but with no disrespect to the biblical personages who promoted it. Tindal believes that it can be derived from the same principles of natural religion as establish the existence of a deity and that deity's moral attributes. Being already infinitely happy, God seeks nothing from his human creation beyond their own good, which he has given them the rational means to attain.

> It unavoidably follows, nothing can be a part of the divine Law, but what tends to promote the common Interest, and mutual Happiness of his rational Creatures; and every thing that does so, must be a part of it. (ch. 2, 12)

A study of the relationship between the Creator and the creation, and the nature and relations of things within the creation, is sufficient to determine our duties, if we will but observe the dictates of nature implanted in us. This is a more extensive guide than 'external Revelation', which offers too few rules to meet all circumstances.

> And to suppose any thing can be true by Revelation, which is false by Reason, is not to support that thing, but to undermine Revelation; because nothing unreasonable, nay, what is not highly reasonable, can come from a God of unlimited, universal, and eternal Reason. (ch. 12, 158)

Religious rites and ceremonies are a distraction from moral living and due to priestcraft (ch. 11). Laws such as those that revelation aims to supply need interpreters, but the distinction between an interpreter and a lawmaker is but a verbal one, and once again the priests interpose an improper authority (ch. 13). In his hostility to church establishments Tindal does not discuss in any detail the traditional historical basis of revelation.

Two more extravagant writers faced civil punishment for their writings: Thomas Woolston and Peter Annet. Woolston, who qualified as a divine, believed that the biblical documents were fully allegorical and that only as allegory did the Old Testament prefigure the New. The Bible was not history, and the miracles and prophecies portrayed in it are spiritual events to be understood figuratively. To read them literally is to be deceived by false prophets. After developing this thesis in a number of minor works, he published between 1727 and 1729 a series consisting of *A Discourse on the Miracles of our Saviour* and five numbered sequels; in response to a conviction for blasphemy he also issued a *Defence of his Discourses on the Miracles of our Saviour.*[22] Tindal's response to Gibson was a defence of Woolston's integrity. Woolston's work has an internal logic, however perverse, but is best known for its rumbustious condemnation of various Gospel miracles on a literal reading and of the inadequacy of the documentation in their support. For example, to make sense of the story of the Gadarene swine, we need to know why so many possessed people were not locked up or otherwise taken care of, and what swine were doing in a country where no one ate pork; but those are small problems compared with the 'Injury done to the Proprietors' by the wanton destruction of a farmer's livestock. If we are to take seriously the notion of physical cures as proof of divine authority, we shall need adequate case histories of individual patients to be sure that the work was supernatural, but no such records are provided by the evangelists. Why would anyone of sense curse a fig tree for not having fruit out of season, when the failing was their own for not having laid proper lunch plans? By these and other challenges Woolston claimed to save Christianity from unsustainable trappings, but he had to redefine the product in the process and thereby undermined the established institutions and their agents.

Annet (1693–1769), another former preacher and later a schoolteacher, supports freedom of enquiry in the spirit of Collins, and an ethic founded in natural religion in the spirit of Tindal. His opposition to revelation is based on scepticism about miracles, because he believes in the universal application of the laws of nature as the foundation of natural religion. Even competent theologians – he has particularly in mind John Jackson – see miracles as part of the course of nature, expedited by the power and will of a superior agent. Annet, however, stumbles at this: we do not in fact know how purported miracles are brought about, but if they do indeed occur as part of the course of nature we would expect them to recur. We do not know how to distinguish a newfound human skill from one conferred by God; and whatever skills humans exercise, they do so with a consistency of cause and effect from which nature never deviates. The problem is not just insoluble at a practical level; it points also to a theoretical impossibility. It is inconsistent with the divine attributes for God to vary what he has settled by his wisdom and power. If the laws change, so does the lawgiver, and God's immutability is destroyed; so is the putative perfection of the original creation, if reason is found to change it, while the foundation of all certainty is lost. There is also a moral argument against interfering with the course of nature, if that is considered a means to reform humankind; for it is better that our hearts and actions are guided by clear reason than by a momentary response to a surprise. If the mind is not repaired, the heart will not be. But the mind cannot detect a miracle. Our senses are not proof against deception; even less is the testimony of others, particularly if they are strangers whose interests and biases are unknown to us.[23]

This is a sufficient sample of the range of views that come under the deist rubric.[24] Each author attracted many responses, varied in their way, but springing few surprises. Clerics defended their profession, and a few prominent laymen added their support.[25] Shaftesbury and Mandeville together provoked one of the greatest thinkers of the age – George Berkeley – but Berkeley's defence of revealed religion in *Alciphron* (1732) is superficial. He responds to the sniping rather than to the substance of the debate. Collins and Tindal provided the occasion for a small flurry of anti-deist literature by Scottish thinkers – in particular, George Turnbull's argument that Christ's miracles, by evincing 'proper samples' of his power to cure the sick and raise the dead, validate his teaching about immortality and the rewards of virtue.[26] The most powerful riposte to Tindal came from the English evangelical writer, William Law (1686–1761), a convinced believer in the depravity of human nature who made short work of Tindal's attempts to pit human against divine reason. But Tindal posed too weak a challenge to Law's absolute conviction that the miracles and prophecies of the Bible give overriding authority to its moral injunctions; as a result, Law's attack was better argued than his defence.[27] Woolston's aspersions particularly on the Resurrection prompted Thomas Sherlock (1678–1761) to publish *The Tryal of the Witnesses of the Resurrection of Jesus* (1729) in which he set up a contest between two advocates over whether the Apostles gave false evidence in respect of the Resurrection. Against certain unprovable generalities about the state of knowledge and expectation among the Jews of antiquity, counsel for the revelation argues for the harmony of the evidence drawn from diverse sources, for the willingness of the witnesses to suffer for their testimony, and for the fact that the evidence of sense can prove that something is possible but can never prove that it is impossible. The form rather than the substance is the only thing that is original in Sherlock's argument, and Annet came back to challenge his uncritical use of sources. Edmund Law's *Considerations on the State of the World with Regard to the Theory of Religion* (1745) was a response in part to Thomas Morgan and to the common objection about the primitive state of knowledge in

New Testament times. Law depicts it, on the contrary, as a period of great awakening. Both natural and revealed religion need mental maturity. God chose a time when the seed could be sown – when there was a spiritual need, a growth of reason, and a spirit of enquiry abroad. But these are broad generalizations about the ancient world, with no proven relevance to the immediate context in biblical Palestine.

Two writers are worth noting briefly for an attempt to shift the ground of the debate: Arthur Ashley Sykes (1684?–1756) and Conyers Middleton. They are willing to make concessions to deism without feeling that revelation is in jeopardy, and are important as reminders that theological opinion can move as well as the opposition – and has indeed moved since the eighteenth century. Sykes, an active member of the liberal theological group around Benjamin Hoadly, personally accepts all the standard testimonial evidence, but he also sees that the deist criticisms have force. Gullible, ignorant, and superstitious people do fall for miracle stories, especially when their peers do so too; passion and partiality are a constant problem; perfectly honest people can impose on themselves in describing what they have witnessed; and we can lose track of the lapse of time since an event was originally observed. Let us then concede that these considerations *may* have been true of New Testament times. That does not show that the Apostles actually got it wrong, but it means we have to be more critical in picking our evidence. Sykes thinks there is one domain in which later evidence with all the certainty of sense-perception is possible, and that is prophecy. He is not concerned with the traditional debate as to whether events in the New Testament are the fulfilment of prophecies in the Old, but with prophecies of future idolatry, apostacy, persecution, and superstition in the Church itself. The eighteenth century was considered particularly ripe for the fulfilment of prophecies, as many believers thought they foresaw the millennium, and Sykes found in the Catholic Church of his day all the corruption that Christ himself had foreseen. This falls foul of the usual complaint against prophecy – that it is too unspecific. But Sykes has useful things to say in restricting the events that should count as genuinely miraculous, and he is conscious that the class will shrink with increasing knowledge. He agrees that the supernatural phenomena reported at the tomb of the Abbé François de Pâris in 1734 are exceptionally well attested and that something unusual went on there, but he knows it was not a miracle: there was no observable agent and nothing was done to confirm a mission or validate a doctrine.[28]

Middleton, a Cambridge don, likewise finds the modern reports abundantly confirmed, yet not credible. The reports were all collected after the wonders ceased, and they show the effect of a blind deference to authority; since no other wonders in the history of the Church have been so well attested, the credibility of the rest is less. Earlier in his career Middleton had debated with Daniel Waterland on the Genesis account of the fall of man. Waterland took it literally; Middleton read it allegorically, while not denying that there was a historical reality within the allegory. On miracles, too, his ideas are relatively progressive. The strategy is to try to insulate the miracles of biblical times and show that they are in a different category from those alleged since the end of the Apostolic age. He caused offence not by belittling those reported by the Catholic Church, but by denying the need to believe in any of those reported in the grey period between the death of the Apostles and the rise of the Catholic Church. Indeed Middleton believes he is able to show that with the death of the Apostles the reports cease, so that the Apostolic era is indeed truly insulated. What happens is that retrospective tales start to develop only later, in conjunction with reports of occurrences in those later periods. But by then the need to establish the original revelation has passed and the new phenomena must be considered suspect. The Church, having increased in power, is in a position to excite and reward false pretensions to help advance the faith. The early Fathers are coy about the evidence: no names and no particular incidents are identified, but the agents are reputed to have been common people. The Fathers consistently fail to come up to the standards of 'sound judgement and strict veracity' in reporting quackery and imposture. Middleton has a stronger sense of why later tales are uncompelling than of why the New Testament reports are credible, but he draws attention to what he believes to be the studiously sparing exercise of miraculous powers in New Testament times for a high purpose.[29]

None of the leading supporters of miracles addresses the seemingly decisive indictment of their enterprise by Halyburton and other evangelical writers earlier in the century – namely, that if one reads the texts it is simply *not true* that the biblical miracles were worked to verify a revelation; they had other functions, and the proof of revelation has to be something more instinctive.[30]

III. HUME'S CRITIQUE

Hume's critique of the credentials of revealed religion is to be found in Section X of *An Enquiry concerning Human Understanding* (1748), entitled 'Of miracles'.[31] In the eleven editions prepared by Hume, 'Of miracles' underwent more substantial changes than any other section of the *Enquiry*.[32] As in the Protestant debate that preceded him, the credentials under review are historical. The dispute is about the reliability of others' testimony, not about how Hume himself or his readers would react to a personal experience of something wholly abnormal. There are two parts to the discussion. Part I concentrates on the theoretical issues: what criteria must a miracle report meet to be credible to a reasonable person? The substance of the argument goes back to the time when Hume was working on *A Treatise of Human Nature* in his French retreat at La Flèche in the 1730s; he draws on the philosophy of probability developed in Book I, Part III of that work, where he establishes the basis of our beliefs in matters of fact that lie outside immediately present experience. Part II of 'Of miracles' concerns the practical side of the debate: have the criteria ever been met? This has affinities with his treatment of religious phenomena and of the institutions of religion in some of his essays and in the *History of England*, and with his discussion of literary authenticity in the posthumous essay on Ossian. If the whole discussion meshes well, therefore, with other parts of Hume's own writing, it also draws from, or is much of a pattern with, other writing of the previous half-century from both Britain and France.[33]

Hume appears to take from Locke the view that probability questions arise according to the degree of uniformity or otherwise of previous history and of our personal experience; knowledge both of the type of fact involved and of the informant's reliability are equally relevant in assessing a report. Where experience and report conflict, we weigh the evidence and lean towards the stronger, discounting factors such as passion and interest that typically distort people's testimony. Hume, however, does not make the exception for miracles that Locke does, and he questions whether the exception can legitimately be made. He defines a miracle as 'a transgression of a law of nature by a particular volition of the Deity, or by the interposition of some invisible agent'. Hume's discussion of 'particular volition' in his essay 'Of suicide' is relevant here: 'Every action, every motion of a man innovates in the order of some parts of matter, and diverts, from their ordinary course, the general laws of motion.' The laws are what operate in the absence of any intervention. With God, however, 'if general laws be ever broke by particular volitions of the deity, 'tis after a manner which entirely escapes human observation'.[34] What is at issue in the discussion of miracles is their detectability, and Hume's conclusion in the *Enquiry* is that they can 'never be proved, so as to be the foundation of a system of religion' (10.2.36, SBN 127).

The problem is epistemological. We need all the evidence of history and experience, all the uniformities we can detect, to understand the laws of nature. (In Section VIII of the *Enquiry*, he admits that these may operate at the microscopic rather than the macroscopic level, and be sometimes undetectable.) This gives us what Hume calls 'proof' on the one side. 'And as a uniform experience amounts to a proof, there is here a direct and full *proof*, from the nature of the fact, against the existence of any miracle' (10.1.12, SBN 115). If, however, a contrary event (a putative miracle) shows up in the evidence, it automatically corrupts the evidence and we cannot successfully proceed. This obstacle is averted by counting it not as a contrary incident, but as contrary testimony, isolated from historical events:

> The very same principle of experience, which gives us a certain degree of assurance in the testimony of witnesses, gives us also, in this case, another degree of assurance against the fact, which they endeavour to establish; from which contradiction there necessarily arises a counterpoise, and mutual destruction of belief and authority. (10.1.8, SBN 113)

This is standard sceptical imagery, but Hume's scepticism is selectively applied. He edits the historical evidence that is heavily dependent on testimony, assuming that he can already tell fact from fiction. He will discount or explain away seeming anomalies and what he considers ignorant testimony, but he fails to account adequately for this process, pretending that it is only a problem for the superstitious. He assumes the law of nature has been proved by actual observation, then mounts against it the testimony in favour of what has become a merely hypothetical counterexample. The case for the counterexample would be established where the witnesses, having met all the tests, provide a contrary 'proof' that exceeds the evidence for the uniformity:

> [I]n that case, there is proof against proof, of which the strongest must prevail, but still with a diminution of its force, in proportion to that of its antagonist. (10.1.11, SBN 114)

What he has done is to set up and follow through Locke's worst-case scenario, where there is a disproportionate discrepancy between the evidence of experience on one side and a group of 'fair' witnesses on the other. Both of them speak of 'weighing' the results, but Hume takes the quantitative comparison more literally:

> In all cases, we must balance the opposite experiments, where they are opposite, and deduct the smaller number from the greater, in order to know the exact force of the superior evidence. (10.1.4, SBN 111)

This is the same philosophy that Hume developed in Book II of the *Treatise* when discussing the degree of uniformity in human behaviour:

> When any phaenomena are constantly and invariably conjoin'd together, they acquire such a connexion in the imagination, that it passes from one to the other, without any doubt or hesitation. But below this there are many inferior degrees of evidence and probability, nor does one single contrariety of experiment entirely destroy all our reasoning. The mind ballances the contrary experiments, and deducting the inferior from the superior, proceeds with that degree of assurance or evidence, which remains.[35]

The strength of belief that ensues is for Hume a direct function of the quantity of experience, and it is important to realize that Hume is engaged in a psychological exercise and not a calculus of chances. For Locke, on the other hand, and most others, the issue in the appraisal of testimony is not directly a contest of quantities, but of quantity against quality.

In Part II of 'Of miracles', Hume shows that the arithmetical exercise that he has just proposed will never work to the advantage of miracles in practice, because witnesses of the required calibre do not exist. Once again he seems to have Lockean criteria in mind, although he could have found them in any recent writer on the subject, where they dogmatically assert what Hume dogmatically denies:

> [T]here is not to be found, in all history, any miracle attested by a sufficient number of men, of such unquestioned good sense, education, and learning, as to secure us against all delusion in themselves; of such undoubted integrity, as to place them beyond all suspicion of any design to deceive others; of such credit and reputation in the eyes of mankind, as to have a great deal to lose in case of their being detected in any falsehood; and at the same time, attesting facts, performed in such a public manner, and in so celebrated a part of the world, as to render the detection unavoidable. (10.2.15, SBN 116–17)

Hume proposes a particularly destructive form of his quantitative test, arguing that a miracle of any given religion has the combined testimony to the miracles of all rival religions throughout history against it, a counterweight that he considers to be 'infinite'. Hume considers the psychological and social factors that have induced belief and the primitiveness of the societies in which such beliefs originate. Though he adapts the account to his own philosophy of human nature, he is following the conventional deist strategy. He picks examples from pagan religion, and from Catholic (Jansenist) history that he knows will carry no credit with his readers. More dangerously, he gives a secular parody of the Resurrection story, transferring it to an English historical context where it would have no weight, and he challenges the Old Testament stories considered by the standards of historical narrative. Supporters of the Christian religion are thrown the lifeline of a resort to faith:

> And whoever is moved by *Faith* to assent to it, is conscious of a continued miracle in his own person, which subverts all the principles of his understanding, and gives him a determination to believe what is most contrary to custom and experience. (10.2.41, SBN 131)

IV. AFTER HUME

The first responses to Hume came from Anglican writers.[36] Philip Skelton (1707–87), an Irish cleric in the tradition of William King and Peter Browne, believed in the mysteries of religion and scorned the rationalizing tendencies of the age. The new trends, among which he included Francis Hutcheson's

Christianized reading of Shaftesbury as well as writings that made reason the sole arbiter of truth, gave respectability to deism, which in turn gave cover to atheism. He tried to show this in a set of dialogues entitled *Ophiomaches*. But, for all Skelton's objections to the trend, his own spokesman in the work repeats the then standard 'rational' defence of the biblical record:

> Those believers, whose faith is to rely on the truth of the Christian history, rest their assent on a written report, made by eye-witnesses; which report the various Churches and Sects, jealous of one another, took care to preserve genuine and uncorrupted, at least in all material points, and all the religious writers in every age since have amply attested. That the first spreaders of this report were competent witnesses, can hardly be questioned, when it is considered, that, in respect to facts, they only reported what they saw; in doing which they were so far from having any interest, that they forfeited every comfort and pleasure of life, and life itself, for the sake of gaining followers to a better. In the case of ordinary facts, indifferent witnesses may suffice; but, when miracles were to be recorded, Providence, for the satisfaction of distant places and ages, gave witnesses, who embraced the terrors of death to confirm their testimony, who, if I may be allowed the expression, were sworn on their own blood to the truth of the evidence.[37]

When this assessment is repeated in Dialogue V, the most abrasive of Skelton's characters cites Hume's a priori argument against it. After seeing what it should be – a weighing of 'the improbability of the facts against the credibility of the witnesses' – he follows Hume in converting it into an arithmetical calculation. Skelton's persona replies with a leaf from Hume's own book: it implies no contradiction to say that the sun will not rise tomorrow, for the contrary of any matter of fact is possible; a resurrection or other miracle is therefore possible. Whether it is probable is not to be measured against the normal course of nature, but against an understanding of the corruption of ancient times and of what it would take for God to reveal and fulfil his benevolent purpose. Skelton's prior religious commitments always lead the argument.

Thomas Rutherforth of Cambridge published a sermon in which he argued that there are other forms of knowledge that compete with experience.[38] Experience generates the degrees of probability that Locke enunciated; but since, prior to any consideration of miracles, we have demonstrative knowledge of the existence of a being with power over nature, experience cannot set limits to the exercise of such power, or establish that it has not been exercised. The New Testament miracles invoke this power, whereas 'pagan histories and popish legends', in Rutherforth's view, do not. He has not fully appreciated the role of laws of nature in Hume's argument and thinks the testimony of the evangelists has been so far vindicated by others that he does not need to address it.

William Adams (1706–89) of Oxford notes Hume's tendency to subsume testimony under the general heading of 'experience' and his willingness to detect an inclination to truth in human nature.[39] He finds this hard to square with an opposite pull in Hume's argument, where there is an opposition between experience and testimony, and lack of experience of a phenomenon is portrayed by Hume as the 'contrary' of testimony to it. On such lack of experience rests Hume's 'proof' against a miracle. Since the proof fails, it is a legitimate question whether an unexampled event may occur by divine intervention. That is a matter of assessing the evidence, on which firsthand experience alone is an inadequate guide. We depend on the objectivity and conviction of others and, in the case of miracles, on the superhuman power involved and the demonstrable consequences and beneficial effects of the event. The Gospel records meet Hume's tests, and his data testifying to the credulity of humankind cannot constitute a blanket indictment of all such records.

Anthony Ellys (1690–1761), a future bishop, argues that fear of divine punishment makes people tell the truth, a fear that would have been equally felt by those who reported the Gospel miracles. He is not using revelation to vindicate revelation, but rather assuming an argument from natural theology:

> Every one who reflects at all, must be sensible that God was the Author of our Faculty of Speech, and that he gave it, in order to the Benefit and Improvement that Men might receive by imparting their Thoughts and Dispositions to each other. For which Purpose, it is necessary that their Words should express their Thoughts as they really are; because if they did otherwise, their Speech would produce frequently Distrust, Ill-Will and Disturbance among them. On which Account we may justly conclude, from Reason itself, that God has strictly obliged each Person to speak the Truth.[40]

Against the general reliability of ancient testimony Ellys sets a somewhat relative picture of the laws of nature. The uniformity of Hume's own experience cannot show that the laws of nature are 'unalterably' fixed; and he cannot claim as he does a uniform 'Experience against Miracles', since a lack of experience is not experience of the contrary. All Hume's method can establish is that there have been no miracles in our own time, something that suits Ellys's Protestant instincts. But we can all come to learn on reliable evidence that phenomena have occurred of a kind that we have had no experience of, and that explanations of these phenomena are possible. Ellys's best move is against the logic of the 'contrary miracles' argument under which all religions in combination undermine each other's evidences, an argument found both in some of the deist writers and in Hume. Hume's a priori number game here gets out of hand. If the evidences of different religions are genuinely incompatible, which Hume has not in fact demonstrated, then they cannot *combine* to defeat another. Considered individually, they must vary considerably in quality, and Hume has made no attempt to assess the strength of the different cases; but the evidence of one counts against the evidence of another only when there is some individual who has knowledge of both and is in a position to compare them.

The first Dissenter of significance to join the debate was John Leland of Dublin. He sought to defend Christianity, on broadly non-sectarian grounds, on two fronts: an exposition and critique of the principal deist writers, and a historical defence of revelation. In the active part of his career he published tracts directed at individual deists such as Tindal, Morgan, and Bolingbroke; he was particularly keen to answer Bolingbroke's aspersions on the credibility of scriptural history, even citing the unsavoury detail of many Old Testament stories as evidence of the chroniclers' objectivity. He then worked on a more systematic and comprehensive *View of the Principal Deistical Writers*.[41] Despite the conventionality of his own views and his disproportionate attention to Bolingbroke, whom later scholars no longer see as a canonical figure, Leland's work shaped perceptions of deist aims and techniques, and of early eighteenth-century thought more generally, well into the following century. He identified what he took to be the deists' dishonest way of proceeding, without seeing the grounds on which deists might retort the charge. Not only can they not agree over natural religion, but in pursuing it to the exclusion of revelation, they tend to caricature what they cannot refute. This for Leland is tacitly to concede the strength of revealed religion, a strength that lies in the soundness of its evidences (well-authenticated miracles and prophecies), the superiority of its moral teaching, and the coherence of its doctrine. Adding Hume to his targets in 1755, he mostly follows the criticisms of Adams while making an honest effort to understand Hume's position on miracles in the context of his overall philosophy; but Leland has made up his mind that contradiction is the hallmark of an infidel writer and finds contradictions in Hume where they do not exist. The failure of the rational thinkers of the ancient and modern worlds to agree on the principles of natural religion and on their consequences for human living is for Leland proof that even among cultured nations, revelation is in practice essential, a thesis that he carries further in his last major work.[42] While broad principles of natural religion and morals may be derived from the intelligent study of nature and can to that degree be known to the heathen, he accepts the common Christian view that revelation offers a more precise and reliable presentation.

The leading Scottish writer on the subject, George Campbell of Aberdeen, was the most successful of Hume's critics. While picking the best of previous criticisms – for example, that we cannot discountenance testimony simply by citing against it the experienced course of nature, since that experience incorporates other testimony – and highlighting Hume's careless use of sources, he helped put the subject in a new perspective as one of the pioneers of the 'common sense' philosophy. The success of that philosophy, the succinct organization of Campbell's critique, and his leading role in Scottish theology for over a third of a century ensured a long life for his *Dissertation on Miracles*. Campbell is the classic exponent of the view that testimony has 'a natural and original influence on belief', moderated by experience rather than derived from it.[43] The burden of proof rests with those who wish to resist this tendency, and then the weight of contrary testimony on the particular occasion is more relevant than the abnormality of the event. An untested witness to a river disaster does not lose credit because no disaster has occurred there previously, but only from a proven record of unreliability. Campbell developed this position in partnership with his contemporaries Thomas Reid and Alexander Gerard, and for the full strength of the Aberdeen response to Hume it is important also to read Gerard's *Dissertations*, a work which raises more penetrating issues about historical evidence. Both Campbell and Gerard support the orthodox position that monotheism originated in revelation rather than reason, but Gerard makes more of the distinction between evidence and argument. 'Evidence perceived is the immediate cause of belief; reasoning is but one mean of bringing men to perceive the evidence.'[44]

Hume's leading critic among the English Dissenters was Richard Price, with whom he later established a friendship, as a result of which Price modified the second edition of his 'Dissertation' on historical evidence and miracles. While seeking to deflate the high-flown rhetoric of much of the preceding debate, he offers a useful overview of it; but his main target is Hume. Price, a skilled mathematician and practised actuary, first introduced Bayes's theorem to the world, and by attacking the mathematical basis of Hume's attempts to calculate the antecedent probability of untoward events, opened up the whole debate on the nature of Hume's enterprise. Playing what he takes to be Hume's game, Price shows it will not work:

> In many cases of particular histories which are immediately believed upon the slightest testimony, there would have appeared to us, previously to this testimony, an improbability of almost infinity to one against their reality, as any one must perceive, who will think how sure he is of the falsehood of all facts that have *no* evidence to support them, or which he has only *imagined* to himself. It is then very common for the slightest testimony to overcome an almost infinite improbability.[45]

Hume was naively trying to quantify degrees of belief in terms of expectation born of experience, but for Price this is not where causality is detected, and true belief is proportional to our ability to understand the workings of providence. For this, neither experience nor natural philosophy is a complete guide, and he defends revelation as an essential source of information bearing on our highest needs.

Price was not alone in criticizing Hume's account of the operation of probability. George Gleig thought he could meet Hume's challenge to show that the Apostles' combined false testimony to Christ's miracles would be a more improbable deviation from a law of nature than the miracles themselves.[46] The Irish natural philosopher, Richard Kirwan (1733–1812), who trained as a lawyer, devoted five chapters of his *Logick* to logical and epistemological issues relating to testimony. In respect of miracles, the 'natural' impossibility of the event must be offset by the 'certainty' of the testimony and he believes that moral certainty, of a kind admitted in law, is attainable in this context.

> The method recommended by Mr. Hume . . . for comparing and balancing contradictory testimonies, consists in deducting the *inferior* credibility from the superior; the remainder, he says, will show, how much the superior is weakened. If so, this absurdity would follow, that the credit of the most respectable witness would be destroyed by the opposition of one whose credibility is doubtful; for, suppose the credibility of the one to be $9/10$, and of the other only $5/10$, then $(9-5)/10 = 4/10$, which being below $1/2$, denotes improbability, or incredibility.[47]

The only end-of-the-century writer on the subject who had any considerable following, however, was William Paley.[48] In *A View of the Evidences*, he answered Hume in his 'Preparatory Considerations', starting from assumptions that he thinks cannot be dismissed – God exists, we stand in need of a revelation, in the historic state of humankind a revelation is not improbable, and miracles must be the means of authenticating it. It is in this frame of mind that we must test for evidence appropriate to the situation. 'We assert only, that in miracles adduced in support of revelation, there is not any such antecedent improbability as no testimony can ever surmount'. He finds, not unfairly, that Hume equivocates in the concepts of experience and of contrariety and contradiction. The problems generated by our lack of experience of miraculous events are spurious: 'the improbability which arises from the want (for this properly is a want, not a contradiction) of experience, is only equal to the probability there is, that, if the thing were true, we should experience things similar to it, or that such things would be generally experienced'. But there is no probability, let alone certainty, in this requirement. Paley offers a solid restatement of the orthodox position, discussing a wide range of examples and counterexamples; and he does, by his own lights, employ tests for the authenticity of the general historical record that will minimize the risk of fraud or misrepresentation.

Thus at the end of the century the prevailing view was not significantly different from what it was at the start. One irreversible change, however, is that, from the 1750s on and for at least a hundred years, every significant theological writer in Britain, and many insignificant ones, writing on the evidences of Christianity, found Hume's challenge unavoidable. But one figure, Alexander Geddes, deserves recognition for heralding a shift that otherwise only began to take root among any defined group of religious believers in Britain in the following century. Geddes, a Scots Catholic priest, was one of the great literary and biblical scholars of his day. He knew the Aberdeen philosophical community and received an honorary doctorate from Marischal College. It is thus likely that either through Campbell or through his own reading he was aware of Hume's work, but he makes no mention of it. In working on a new translation of the Bible, which he left unfinished after the appearance of two controversial volumes and a volume of commentary, Geddes came to view the biblical sources as works of primitive ignorance. His criticisms would be indistinguishable from deism but for one thing. He never lost his devotion to the religion of Jesus he found in the New Testament, despite all the 'taudry cumbersome load of exotic ornaments' and 'ungainly meretricious garb' with which Judaism and paganism had encumbered it. He repudiated the 'loads of hay and stubble which have been blended with its precious gems' in every Christian tradition.[49] He thus considered that the message could offer itself for acceptability on its own terms.

Geddes thought the Hebrew scriptures very beautiful, but the histories in them exhibit 'no intrinsic evidence of inspiration, or any thing like inspiration'. They emanated from a 'grossly carnal people' and were 'human compositions, written in a rude age, by rude and unpolished writers, in a poor uncultivated language'. Indeed, there is no reason why *history* should be inspired: Christians do not think that the records of Constantine or Charlemagne are inspired. It is not difficult to discover internal inconsistencies. About one, he says: 'The Jewish historians, both here and in many other places, put in the mouth of the LORD words, which he never spoke; and assign to him views and motives, which he never had'. The writers are like Homer, exercising poetic licence, 'continually blending real facts with fanciful mythology, ascribing natural events to supernatural causes, and introducing a divine agency on every extraordinary occurrence'.[50]

Where, then, does this leave religious belief? For the mass of people, 'religion is the fruit of unenlightened credulity'. But neither the Bible nor the institutions of the Church are a crutch for people who will not think. Reason alone, applied to the evidence of experience, scripture, history and tradition, can establish a religion free of the 'vain and useless trapping, and tinsel decoration' of superstition at the one extreme and 'the sacrilegious fangs of gloomy fanaticism' at the other. In the contest between Christianity and Judaism, 'Shall I disbelieve the pretended miracles, the spurious deeds, the forged charters, the lying legends of the one, and give full credit to those of the other?' And in the contest between Catholicism and Protestantism, it is irresponsible to believe in an infallibility, whether of the Church or of the Bible, whose basis we do not understand, just because the ministers on one side or the other impress it on us. Geddes is always evenhanded in his condemnations. 'I cannot revere metaphysical unintelligible creeds, nor blasphemous confessions of faith.' 'I cannot revere any system of religion, that, for divine doctrines, teacheth the dictates of men.'[51] This, paradoxically, is why he never abandoned the Catholic Church although sections of it abandoned him: the other side was no better, and whatever is sound in Christianity can be preached and practised anywhere.

NOTES

1 Edward Stillingfleet, *Origines sacrae* (London, 1662; many subsequent editions). Stillingfleet continued the argument in *A Letter to a Deist, in Answer to Several Objections against the Truth and Authority of the Scriptures* (London, 1677), arguing that deism is a rejection of moral authority and a cover for depravity.

2 Charles Blount, *Miracles no Violations of the Laws of Nature* (London, 1683). Other writings include *Anima mundi: or An Historical Narration of the Opinions of the Ancients concerning Mans Soul after this Life, according to Unenlightened Nature* (Amsterdam, 1678); *Great is Diana of the Ephesians: or The Original of Priestcraft and Idolatry, and of the Sacrifices of the Gentiles* (London, 1680); an annotated edition of Philostratus (London, 1680); and an edited miscellany, *The Oracles of Reason* (London, 1693).

3 Charles Leslie, *A Short and Easie Method with the Deists* (London, 1698). Other anti-deist literature of the period includes William Stephens, *An Account of the Growth of Deism in England* (London, 1696); Charles Gildon, *The Deist's Manual: or A Rational Enquiry into the Christian Religion* (London, 1705).

4 For additional background, see M. A. Stewart, 'Hume's Historical View of Miracles', in *Hume and Hume's Connexions*, eds. M. A. Stewart and John P. Wright (Edinburgh, 1994), 171–200, and sources cited there.

5 John Locke, *An Essay concerning Human Understanding* [1690], ed. P. H. Nidditch in *The Clarendon Edition* (1975), IV.xv.4–6.

6 John Locke, *Writings on Religion*, ed. V. Nuovo (Oxford, 2002), 44–50. Locke's *Discourse* was a brief reflection on William Fleetwood's *An Essay on Miracles* (London, 1701) and an anonymous response to it. Fleetwood defended the view that miracles verify a divine mission. Locke's account of the nature of miracles in his *Discourse* is criticized by the prominent English Dissenter Samuel Chandler, in *A Vindication of the Christian Religion, in Two Parts* (London, 1725), Part I, chapter 1.

7 Isaac Watts, *Logick: or, The Right Use of Reason in the Enquiry after Truth* (London, 1725), II.ii.9; see iv.6, v.5–6. On the primacy of the Christian evidences, see also Francis Gastrell, *The Certainty of the Christian Revelation, and the Necessity of Believing it, Established* (London, 1699).

8 David Berman, 'Deism, Immortality, and the Art of Theological Lying', in *Deism, Masonry, and the Enlightenment: Essays honoring Alfred Owen Aldridge*, ed. J. A. L. Lemay (Newark, DE, 1987), 61–78, 'Disclaimers as Offence Mechanisms in Charles Blount and John Toland', in *Atheism from the Reformation to the Enlightenment*, eds. M. Hunter and D. Wootton (Oxford, 1992), 255–72. See also James A. Herrick, *The Radical Rhetoric of the English Deists: The*

Discourse of Skepticism, 1680–1750 (Columbia, SC, 1997). For traditional interpretations, see Leslie Stephen, *History of English Thought in the Eighteenth Century* [1876], 3rd edn., 2 vols. (London, 1902); Peter Gay, *Deism: An Anthology* (Princeton, NJ, 1968). For a recent appraisal, see Isabel Rivers, *Reason, Grace, and Sentiment: A Study of the Language of Religion and Ethics in England 1660–1780*, 2 vols. (Cambridge, 1991–2000), vol. 2, ch. 1.

9 [Anthony, Earl of Shaftesbury], 'Soliloquy: or Advice to an Author', III.i, 'An Inquiry concerning Virtue, or Merit', I.iii.2; both in *Characteristicks of Men, Manners, Opinions, Times* (n.p., 1711; 2nd edn., 3 vols., London, 1714, acknowledging authorship). For an excellent account of Shaftesbury's literary method and multiple levels of meaning, and of the responses of different constituencies of readers, see Rivers, *Reason, Grace, and Sentiment*, vol. 2, chs. 2–3.

10 [Anthony, Earl of Shaftesbury], 'The Moralists: A Philosophical Rhapsody', II.v, 'Miscellaneous Reflections', II.iii; both in *Characteristicks*.

11 Bernard Mandeville, *The Fable of the Bees*, ed. F. B. Kaye, 2 vols. (Oxford, 1924), 2: 21–2, note. 2, 205–6, 309–18. See also his *Free Thoughts on Religion, the Church, and National Happiness* (London, 1720) and *An Enquiry into the Origin of Honour, and the Usefulness of Christianity in War* (London, 1732).

12 [John Toland], *Christianity not Mysterious: or, A Treatise shewing, that there is Nothing in the Gospel contrary to Reason, nor above it: and that no Christian Doctrine can be properly call'd a Mystery* (London, 1696; 2nd edn., acknowledging authorship, 1696); [Anthony Collins], *An Essay concerning the Use of Reason in Propositions, the Evidence whereof depends upon Human Testimony* (London, 1707). For a recent set of studies on Toland, see the edition of *Christianity not Mysterious* edited by P. McGuinness, A. Harrison, and R. Kearney (Dublin, 1997). On Collins, see James O'Higgins, *Anthony Collins, the Man and his Works* (The Hague, 1970); David Berman, 'Anthony Collins: Aspects of his Thought and Writings', *Hermathena*, 119 (1975): 49–70.

13 A critique developed further in *Nazarenus: or Jewish, Gentile and Mahometan Christianity* (London, 1718); new edition, ed. J. Champion (Oxford, 1999).

14 'I can have no assurance that that is from God, which if it were true, I should be uncertain whether there was a God or not.' John Tillotson, *Works*, ed. Ralph Barker, 4th edn., 3 vols. (London, 1728), 3: 504.

15 Of the four tracts of Toland's *Tetradymus* (London, 1720), the first, 'Hodegus', denies the miraculous nature of 'the Pillar of Cloud and Fire, that Guided the Israelites in the Wilderness'; the second, 'Clidophorus; or of the Exoteric and Esoteric Philosophy', goes back to the distinction between external and internal doctrine that he finds characteristic of ancient paganism.

16 There was a posthumous translation, *Pantheisticon: or, The Form of Celebrating the Socratic Society* (London, 1751).

17 [Collins], *A Philosophical Inquiry concerning Human Liberty* (London, 1717), republished with introduction by Joseph Priestley (Birmingham, 1790); *A Vindication of the Divine Attributes, in some Remarks on his Grace the Archbishop of Dublin's Sermon intituled Divine Predestination and Foreknowledg consistent with the Freedom of Man's Will* (London, 1710). Collins's side in the pamphlet debate with Samuel Clarke in 1707–8 is reproduced in volume 3 of Clarke's *Works*, ed. B. Hoadly, 4 vols. (London, 1738).

18 [Collins], *A Discourse of Free-Thinking, occasion'd by the Rise and Growth of a Sect call'd Free-Thinkers* (London, 1713), 55 (Gay, *Deism*, 90–1).

19 [Collins], *Priestcraft in Perfection* (London, 1710); *A Discourse of the Grounds and Reasons of the Christian Religion* (London, 1724). Collins was answered by Chandler in Part II of *A Vindication of the Christian Religion*. Although he found the tone of Collins's *Discourse* reprehensible, Chandler played down the significance of prophecy for Christian belief, and sided with

Collins in defending liberty of speech. He thought it absurd that Christianity should be specially protected by the magistrate, as if it could not hold its own in open and rational debate.

20 Matthew Tindal, *A Letter to the Reverend Clergy of both Universities concerning the Trinity and the Athanasian Creed* (London, 1694); *The Reflections on the XXVIII Propositions touching the Doctrine of the Trinity, in A Letter to the Clergy, &c.* (n.p., 1695); *An Essay concerning the Power of the Magistrate, and the Rights of Mankind, in Matters of Religion* (London, 1697); *The Rights of the Christian Church Asserted, against the Romish and all other Priests who claim an independent Power over it*, Part I only published (London, 1706).

21 Tindal, *An Address to the Inhabitants of the two Great Cities of London and Westminster; in relation to a pastoral Letter said to have been written by the Bishop of London to the People of his Diocese* (London, 1729); *Christianity as Old as the Creation; or the Gospel a Republication of the Religion of Nature*, vol. 1 only published (London, 1730).

22 Thomas Woolston, *A Discourse on the Miracles of our Saviour, in view of the Present Controversy between Infidels and Apostates* (London, 1727); *A Second Discourse on the Miracles of our Saviour, in view of the Present Controversy between Infidels and Apostates* (London, 1727), [etc.]; *Mr. Woolston's Defence of his Discourses on the Miracles of our Saviour. Against the Bishops of St. David's and London, and his other Adversaries*, 2 parts (London, 1729–30). For commentary see William H. Trapnell, *Thomas Woolston: Madman and Deist* (Bristol, 1994).

23 These themes are extracted from Dissertation II of *Supernaturals Examined: in Four Dissertations on three Treatises* (London, n.d.), in which Annet adopts the pseudonym of a 'Moral Philosopher'. It is included in the author's *Collection of the Tracts of a certain Free Enquirer* (ca. 1750) and should be read alongside *The Resurrection of Jesus Considered; in Answer to the Tryal of the Witnesses* (n.d.; 3rd edn., London, 1745), Annet's hard-headed response to Thomas Sherlock in the same collection. Annet was answered by John Jackson, *An Address to Deists, being a Proof of Reveal'd Religion from Miracles and Prophecies. In answer to a book, entitled, The Resurrection of Jesus consider'd by a Moral Philosopher* (London, 1744). The notoriety of Annet's view that miracles are impossible coloured early perceptions of Hume's argument, published a few years later. On Annet, see Ella Twynam, *Peter Annet, 1693–1769* (London, 1938).

24 I have not discussed Thomas Morgan or Lord Bolingbroke, in whom I can find less substance. On Bolingbroke, see D. G. James, *The Life of Reason: Hobbes, Locke, Bolingbroke* (London, 1949), chapter 4. William Wollaston and Thomas Chubb are often classed as deists but this characterization is far from certain.

25 Gilbert West, *Observations on the History and Evidence of the Resurrection of Jesus Christ* (London, 1747); George (later Baron) Lyttelton, *Observations on the Conversion and Apostleship of St. Paul, in a Letter to Gilbert West, Esq.* (London, 1747). West in sections XXII–XXVII defends the authenticity of the record, against Annet. Hume refers to Lyttelton's contrast between Paul and Alexander of Pontus in early editions of *An Enquiry concerning Human Understanding.*

26 [George Turnbull], *A Philosophical Enquiry concerning the Connexion betwixt the Doctrines and Miracles of Jesus Christ* (London, 1731; 3rd edn., 1739), and *Christianity neither False nor Useless, tho' not as Old as the Creation: or, an Essay to prove the Usefulness, Truth, and Excellency of the Christian Religion* (London, 1732); Robert Wallace, *The Regard due to Divine Revelation, and to Pretences to it, Considered* (London, 1731), and *A Reply to a Letter directed to the Minister of Moffat, concerning the Positive Institutions of Christianity* (London, 1732). Between Wallace's two pamphlets appeared, anonymously, *The Necessity of some of the Positive Institutions of Ch——ty consider'd, in a Letter to the Minister of Moffat* (London, 1731). This is ascribed to William Dudgeon, the Scottish deist who owed much of his metaphysics to Berkeley and Samuel Clarke, but whose aversion to Calvinism resulted in *A Catechism Founded upon Experience and Reason: Collected by a Father for the Use of his Children. To which is prefixed, An Introductory*

Epistle to a Friend, concerning Natural Religion (n.p., 1739), reprinted in Dudgeon's *Philosophical Works* (n.p., 1765).

27 William Law, *The Case of Reason, or Natural Religion, Fairly and Fully Stated, in Answer to a Book, entitled, Christianity as Old as the Creation* (London, 1731).

28 Arthur Ashley Sykes, *A Brief Discourse concerning the Credibility of Miracles and Revelation* (London, 1742).

29 Conyers Middleton, *A Free Enquiry into the Miraculous Powers, which are Supposed to have Subsisted in the Christian Church, from the earliest Ages through several successive Centuries* (London, 1749).

30 Thomas Halyburton, *Essay concerning the Reason of Faith*, published and bound with *Natural Religion Insufficient; and Reveal'd Necessary to Man's Happiness in his Present State: or, A Rational Enquiry into the Principles of the Modern Deists* (Edinburgh, 1714). A similar stance is found in James Hog, *A Letter to a Gentleman concerning the Interest of Reason in Religion* (Edinburgh, 1716); Archibald Campbell, *The Necessity of Revelation* (London, 1739). Some concession to this view is made later in the century by Soame Jenyns.

31 For a judicious account and appraisal, see J. Houston, *Reported Miracles: A Critique of Hume* (Cambridge, 1994).

32 David Hume, *An Enquiry concerning Human Understanding* (critical edition), ed. T. L. Beauchamp, in *The Clarendon Edition* (2000), editorial appendix, 257–63.

33 R. M. Burns, *The Great Debate on Miracles* (Lewisburg, PA, 1981); David Wootton, 'Hume's "Of Miracles"', in *Studies in the Philosophy of the Scottish Enlightenment*, ed. M. A. Stewart (Oxford, 1990), 191–229; M. A. Stewart, 'Hume's Historical View of Miracles'.

34 Hume, *Essays Moral, Political and Literary*, ed. E. F. Miller (Indianapolis, IN, 1987), 581–2.

35 Hume, *A Treatise of Human Nature*, eds. D. F. Norton and M. J. Norton, in *The Clarendon Edition* (2006), 2.3.1.12, SBN 403. See also, more generally, 1.3.12–13, SBN 130–55.

36 Many of the writings cited in this section are reproduced in whole or part in *Early Responses to Hume's Writings on Religion*, ed. J. Fieser, 2 vols. (Bristol, 2001). I have not attempted to discuss all the authors that Fieser reproduces.

37 Philip Skelton, *Ophiomaches, or Deism Revealed*, 2 vols. (London, 1749), 1: 30–1. The second edition (1751) was entitled simply *Deism Revealed*. Skelton's biographer reported on Skelton's authority that Hume had served as a publisher's reader for the work; but since Skelton bore the expense, it is of little significance. Samuel Burdy, *The Life of the late Reverend Philip Skelton, with some curious Anecdotes* [1792], ed. N. Moore (Oxford, 1914), 100.

38 Thomas Rutherforth, *The Credibility of Miracles Defended against the Author of Philosophical Essays* (Cambridge, 1751).

39 William Adams, *An Essay on Mr. Hume's Essay on Miracles* (London, 1752; with additions, 1754).

40 [Anthony Ellys], *Remarks on an Essay concerning Miracles, published by David Hume, Esq; amongst his Philosophical Essays* (London, [1752]), 7–8 (Fieser, 1: 97–8).

41 John Leland, *A View of the Principal Deistical Writers that have Appeared in England in the last and present Century*, 2 vols. and suppl. (London, 1754–6); 3rd edn., 2 vols. (1757).

42 Leland, *The Advantage and Necessity of the Christian Revelation shewn from the State of Religion in the Ancient Heathen World: especially with respect to the Knowledge and Worship of the one true God: a Rule of Moral Duty: and a State of Future Rewards and Punishments*, 2 vols. (London, 1764).

43 George Campbell, *A Dissertation on Miracles* (Edinburgh, 1762; many subsequent editions), 14. On Campbell, see Jeffrey M. Suderman, *Orthodoxy and Enlightenment: George Campbell in the Eighteenth Century* (Montreal and Kingston, 2001). Materials belonging to the rest of his theological output are in Campbell, *Lectures, Sermons and Dissertations*, ed. D. Sonheim, 3 vols. (Bristol, 2001).

44 Alexander Gerard, *Dissertations on Subjects relating to the Genius and the Evidences of Christianity* (Edinburgh, 1766), 43. Reid's views on religious testimony are buried in his manuscripts and an inadequate student transcription of his logic lectures. See M. A. Stewart, 'Rational Religion and Common Sense', in *Thomas Reid: Context, Influence and Significance*, ed. J. Houston (Edinburgh, 2004): 123–60.

45 Richard Price, 'Dissertation IV. On the Importance of Christianity, the Nature of Historical Evidence, and Miracles', in *Four Dissertations* [1767], 2nd edn. (London, 1768), 406.

46 *Encyclopaedia Britannica*, 3rd edn., 15 vols. (Edinburgh, 1788–97), article 'Miracle'.

47 Richard Kirwan, *Logick; or, An Essay on the Elements, Principles, and different Modes of Reasoning* (London, 1807), 332; see also 'Remarks on some Sceptical Positions in Hume's *Enquiry concerning Human Understanding* and his *Treatise of Human Nature*', *Transactions of the Royal Irish Academy* 8 (1801), 157–201.

48 William Paley, *Horae Paulinae, or, The Truth of the Scripture History of St. Paul Evinced, by a Comparison of the Epistles which bear his Name, with the Acts of the Apostles, and with one another* (London, 1790); *A View of the Evidences of Christianity*, 3 vols. (London, 1794).

49 Alexander Geddes, *Critical Remarks on the Hebrew Scriptures: corresponding with a new Translation of the Bible*, vol. 1 only published (London, 1800), vi, vii. On Geddes, see Reginald C. Fuller, *Alexander Geddes 1737–1802: Pioneer of Biblical Criticism* (Sheffield, 1984).

50 *The Holy Bible, or the Books accounted Sacred by Jews and Christians*, translated with notes and critical remarks by Alexander Geddes, 2 vols. only published (London, 1792–7), 2: v, xiii, iii, and xii.

51 *Critical Remarks*, v, vi.

24

ARGUMENTS FOR THE EXISTENCE OF GOD: THE BRITISH DEBATE

M. A. STEWART

In eighteenth-century Britain, rational religion was much in vogue, and every year saw works of no great originality rolling off the presses. They embraced a wide spectrum of theological opinion. The majority considered that both theistic belief in general and belief in the Christian revelation in particular were founded on solid reasoning, even though the revelation itself was subject to significantly different interpretations among Athanasians, Arians, Arminians, and others. Some, while sharing the view that reason was the only possible foundation, set stringent limits to what was believable, but they normally conceded enough of the initial principles of theism to make it difficult for critics to pin on to them any firmly sustainable charge of atheism. Hume's subversive *Dialogues concerning Natural Religion*, written in the 1750s but published only posthumously in 1779, challenged this culture of reason and has had a lasting influence on subsequent debate; but it was not through this work, whose literary form presents a frequently ambiguous message, that he had his main impact at the time.[1] His sceptical philosophy, particularly in more accessible writings such as *An Enquiry concerning Human Understanding* (1748), challenged what had hitherto seemed to be basic certainties across a wide front. The implications for religious certainties were clear enough, even without the provocation of his gentle irony, but they could not easily be answered without addressing a whole philosophy.

In the longer term, nevertheless, Hume's *Dialogues* have shaped modern debate in an important way, giving currency to the idea that the arguments for God's existence are a distinct subject of enquiry, a semi-autonomous offshoot from epistemology. For most of his educated contemporaries, religious belief was so interwoven with the rest of their belief that it neither had, nor was expected to have, the independent rigour that Hume found lacking in it. In the Bible-founded Protestant tradition, natural theology had been less developed than in Catholic apologetics, and how far it was expressed as *argument* varied. Most Protestant writers accepted the possibility of natural religion, considered as assent to certain evident truths about deity on the authority of reason and experience, and as an attitude of awe and worship directly inspired by that experience.

Experience was as important as reasoning, not just because of lingering theological doubts among evangelical writers about the efficacy of unaided reason, but because of scruples about the propriety of an intellectual exercise that could seem to be testing God rather than humanity. Caution was strongest among Calvinist writers,[2] but even someone as committed to humanity's rational potential as John Locke had accepted that most of humankind were at best polytheists and the victims of priestcraft, and that the monotheistic belief that he judged capable of rational proof had *de facto* come about largely through revelation.[3] Nevertheless, despite Locke's endorsement of the evidence,[4] there remained massive resistance to travellers' tales about the existence of whole communities lacking a sense of deity.

Although natural religion has its origins in antiquity – a point exploited by many who wanted to show that it is in some way instinctive to human nature – and although its later representation in argument owes much to a tradition continued from medieval Arabic, Jewish, and Catholic thought, the British debate in the eighteenth century is best seen in relation to specific developments of the previous century.[5] One influence was Hugo Grotius's *De veritate religionis Christianae* (1627), translated into English as *The Truth of the Christian Religion* by Simon Patrick in 1680 and by John Clarke, brother of Samuel Clarke, in 1711. Grotius devoted less space to natural theology than to revelation, but his importance lies in what he was trying to do. The work originated in a Dutch poem he wrote so that merchant sailors might function as missionaries. The Christianity they were encouraged to present was a simple religion, intended to be free of sectarian biases, although that in due course became a sectarian stance in its turn. The exercise is founded on the conviction that, barring individual perversions, there are no atheists, and the fact that there are not is itself one of the confirmations of theism. The arguments of natural religion are essentially impressionistic, to show pagans that at a fundamental level they *share the same ground* as the Christian; the missionary task is to convince them that Christians have the best map of that ground. By inducing reflection on the divine nature and on human dependency, however, the arguments also impress upon believers a deeper appreciation of their faith. In seventeenth-century England, supporters of this strategy tried to extend it, moving from a different common ground, that between Protestant and Catholic, to establish a different superiority, that of the Protestant position. This involved the development of a new epistemological armoury, which is found in religious apologists like John Wilkins and Edward Stillingfleet.[6]

Natural religion alone is not religion: it normally lacks doctrinal content, although among the Boyle Lecturers – those contributing to an annual series of lectures for proving the Christian religion against infidels, established under the will of Robert Boyle at his death in 1691 – one can occasionally find seemingly a priori arguments justifying belief in original sin and the atonement. By reflecting on the relationship between God's attributes and his works in the creation, some writers would go further to deduce a system of morals that ran parallel to revelation. In the early eighteenth century, such purely natural religion – that is, deism – was something of an intellectual fashion in England, but one that had scarcely advanced in half a century. Most of those who thought it too weakly founded did not challenge its philosophical basis, but its omission of revelation. Those, like Hume, who sharply separated the foundations of natural and revealed religion, assessing each in isolation, deliberately rejected the possibility of their providing mutual support.

This summary is sufficient to show that natural theology has traditionally been concerned with more than the *existence* of deity. The narrowing of the subject is a twentieth-century shift reflected in changing conventions in teaching and text-book writing. In earlier periods the emphasis is always jointly on what came to be called 'the being and attributes', which in traditional thought are as much two sides of one coin as are natural religion and revelation. The logical impasse implied in trying to discuss the existence of deity without any notion of what is under consideration rarely arises. The inscrutability of the divine 'nature' sets limits to the debate, but it does not automatically block discussion of the attributes derived from that nature, any more than the inscrutability of substance blocks discussion of the mundane world. The task is to consider the existence of something under some description and to determine on the evidence what further descriptions are possible to us if the existence is proved. Such a discussion will normally have some ethical dimension, so that the problem of the existence of both natural and moral evil cannot be avoided.[7] No significant eighteenth-century thinker is unaware of these issues, but those who pursue them are generally doing nothing more than choosing their way through a well-charted field.

The ontological argument is not significant in the British debate. Anselm was scarcely known. Descartes's argument, which is inferior to Anselm's, had been promoted in the seventeenth century by writers like Henry More and Stillingfleet, but interest had peaked by the century's end and both Locke and Samuel Clarke expressed scepticism about his argument. Although the ontological argument is one among several deployed by Richard Fiddes (1671–1725) in *A Body of Divinity* in 1718, some of the detail duplicates that of his cosmological argument, and in minor writers the two arguments are occasionally confused.[8] In the relevant form of the cosmological argument, God's perfections are inferred from his status as a necessary being; in the ontological argument, his necessary being is inferred from the perfections by which he is defined. Fiddes, an Anglican controversialist, rejects any sort of Leibnizian requirement that a perfect being must first be proved possible, arguing that possibility relates only to contingent things, but he muddies the issue in insisting that a perfect being has all 'possible' perfections.[9]

I. THE COSMOLOGICAL ARGUMENT

The cosmological argument provides one main tradition in this period, and the design or teleological argument another. The argument from universal consent still has followers, but after Locke's critique of innate ideas it is less consistently an argument about God's leaving an imprint of the divine handiwork in the human mind. By appealing to a supposed universality in our experience of and response to the world, it comes to look like another version of the design argument.

The cosmological argument is at root an argument about what constitutes a satisfactory explanation, on the assumption that an *explanans* is ineffective if it repeats the features of the *explanandum*; an explanation must identify something whose characteristics are in salient respects complementary to those of the phenomenon to be explained. In the eighteenth century the argument follows two main directions. The first gives priority to the causal relation, tracing a sequence of dependent causes to an independent or uncaused cause. The causality is agent causation, whose output is 'works'. Locke's formulation is frequently cited.[10] A few authors express it in terms of an unmoved mover, notably the Scottish thinker Andrew Baxter (1686–1750), for whom the immaterial source of motion in matter is the central plank of his metaphysics.[11] The other form of the argument emphasizes the notion of a necessary being. For this, Samuel Clarke's first series of Boyle Lectures is most often cited; William King's formulation in *De origine mali*, which precipitated a significant controversy through the subsequent critical commentary of its translator, can, however, claim priority.[12]

Locke was thought to have established that the argument has the force of demonstration, but a modern reader is more likely to see in it the suppressed assumptions of the period. Because it is a demonstration, every step must be intuitively obvious, beginning from the acknowledgement by all individuals that they have a knowledge of their own existence. This establishes, empirically but self-evidently, a 'real being' which has not been eternal. The second step is the intuitive recognition that 'nothing can . . . produce any real being', or 'what had a Beginning, must be produced by something else'. Production, or a principle of causation, is thus taken for granted. From the two steps together Locke infers 'that from Eternity there has been something', read as meaning that there is something that has been from eternity. The minimum attributes of such a being are inferred from the characteristics of some of the derived beings, on certain assumptions about what bare matter in itself is capable of; so for a second time Locke draws on empirical information that he considers self-evident.[13] Sensing that the argument has been too quick, he restates it, and some of the assumptions are elaborated and explored to show that if from eternity there had been nothing but unintelligence, intelligence could never have emerged within the system later. (If there is an external source of intelligence, then *it* could theoretically have added intelligence to matter; but that is not the same thing.) Thus from the fact of intelligence now, we can infer the existence of intelligence from eternity. It is unclear whether Locke has the resources to show (he says it 'must be') that the same eternal source is the source of all other attributes to which a similar argument applies, so that there is a single eternal being, or that something in whose nature it is to exist from eternity must perforce continue to eternity.[14] Locke expanded on the argument in correspondence with Philippus van Limborch in 1697–8, which became public in 1708. Limborch, writing on behalf of Johannes Hudde, burgomaster of Amsterdam, asked him to demonstrate the singleness of the eternal, self-existent being. Locke claims to do this by establishing an infinite being, from which nothing can be removed and to which nothing can be added; it therefore cannot be divided or be more than one.[15]

Samuel Clarke's formulation in terms of a necessary being went through six lifetime editions, each running to over a hundred pages.[16] The demonstrative nature of the argument is emphasized and efforts are made to show the absurdity in challenging it at any stage. In calling his procedure 'a priori', Clarke means that he proceeds, as the scholastics expressed it, 'from cause to effect' in deducing the attributes. The argument is constructed round a graduated series of propositions: 'Something has existed from Eternity'; 'There has existed from Eternity, some one Immutable and Independent Being'; 'That Immutable and Independent Being, which has Existed from Eternity without any external Cause of its Existence, must be Self-Existent, that is, Necessarily-Existing'; 'What the Substance or Essence of that Being, which is Self-Existent or Necessarily-Existent, is, we have no Idea'; 'Though the Substance or Essence of the Self-Existent Being is itself absolutely incomprehensible to us, yet many of the Essential Attributes of his Nature are strictly Demonstrable'; etc.[17] To speak of necessary existence is to say that there is an internal ground or reason of existence which is conceptually and 'in nature', but not temporally, prior to the thing itself. The meat of the book lies less in these numbered propositions than in their extensive defences. For example, in defending the existence from eternity of 'some one Immutable and Independent Being' (he means at least one, and postpones till later the demonstration that it is at most one), he creates a characteristic dilemma. Either there has always been an 'Unchangeable and *Independent* Being' or there has been 'an infinite Succession of changeable and *dependent* Beings'. The latter is defeated by showing that the succession cannot have an external cause if every possible cause is contained within the series; nor has it an internal reason of existence that renders it self-subsistent, since no member of the series is self-subsistent. As it is not necessary, it has a cause, and yet there is nothing in the hypothesis of an eternal succession to explain why there is something rather than nothing.

Clarke proceeds to derive the divine attributes, distinguishing natural from moral. Natural attributes belong to a self-existing being in its own nature; moral attributes derive from a freely chosen relationship with the sentient creation. Clarke seeks to show that a self-existent being must be eternal, simple, unchangeable, incorruptible, boundless, and single; these are attributes that the design argument alone cannot establish. However, in turning in his eighth proposition to the divine powers, he changes tack. Power can only be demonstrated a posteriori from the nature of the world engendered by that power. Like Locke, he appeals to the existence of intelligence in humans, and the impossibility of deriving this from the attributes of matter, to argue its eternal existence in a (or, by now, the) self-existent being; but he also supports it with appeal to 'the excellent *Variety, Order, Beauty*, and *Wonderful Contrivance*, and *Fitness of all Things in the World, to their proper and respective Ends*'. With cosmic intelligence finally in place, he feels able to deduce God's infinite agency, liberty, wisdom, and – since a being so endowed must have full knowledge of the eternal fitnesses of things and the means and ability to maintain them – moral attributes. The a priori deduction of the attributes pre-empts the problem of evil, which is transformed into one of seeing the total economy of nature in perspective and recognizing the risks that are for good reason endemic in human liberty. Clarke's recognition of the need for the cosmological and design arguments to harmonize was of more lasting influence than his particular formulation of the cosmological argument and addressed the problem that the design argument on its own, though better adapted to ordinary intelligences, was merely probabilistic. His tactic might be seen as arising from the same considerations that later led Kant to suggest that the 'physico-theological' and other arguments could not attain their target without the ontological argument, with its own idiosyncratic (and, as Kant considered, invalid) conception of a necessary being.

By seemingly avoiding probabilistic reasoning, which to traditionalists was offensive in this context, Clarke's argument offered a way in which they could be comfortable in embracing the rational spirit of the age. It brought him extensive mail from young thinkers who thought him misguided. Two exchanges – with Joseph Butler and John Bulkeley, and with excerpts from other correspondence – were published and posthumously included in Clarke's collected works, after which a third exchange, thought to be with Anthony Atkey, was identified and published.[18] Correspondence with two Scots, Henry Home (later Lord Kames) and Walter Bowman, survives in manuscript;[19] an exchange with Francis Hutcheson is lost. Published reaction began as early as 1705, and in 1718

Samuel Colliber published a work that modified the Clarkean line, seeing necessity of nature not as the ground of God's existence but as the consequence of his eternity.[20] A former Cambridge don, Phillips Gretton (1678?–1746), in 1726 found in Clarke a notion of 'antecedent' necessity that would accord divine status to only one member of the Trinity, a charge that would subsequently confront Clarke's staunch Glasgow admirer, John Simson.[21] The 1730s and 1740s saw an escalation of critical interest in Clarke's work after his death, his supporters including the clerics Henry Stebbing, Samuel Clarke's nephew John Clarke of Corpus Christi College, Cambridge (not to be confused with Samuel's brother), John Jackson, and the laymen Phillips Glover and Benjamin Heath.[22] Opponents included Edmund Law, Daniel Waterland, Joseph Clarke, and Thomas Knowles, all of them members of Cambridge colleges.[23] Law, who was influenced by Colliber, became an immediate target for Clarke's followers, and, with Joseph Clarke and Knowles, targeted those followers in turn. The commonest points of contention are the obscurity in Clarke's concept of necessity and its unattractive associations, the difficult notion that God's nature is somehow prior to his eternal existence, and the inclusion of spatial and temporal infinity among the attributes. While they appear to impugn the a priori pretensions of the argument, all critics resolutely defend a more Lockean form of the demonstration, although Law accepts and is fairly nonchalant about a merely 'moral' certainty for the divine omniscience, singleness and moral attributes. Clarke's defenders, on the other hand, believe that his emphasis on necessity is his great strength. It points to the ground or foundation and not just the manner of God's existence, and they stress the importance of Clarke's order of exposition – for example, that self-existence is proof of eternity, not the reverse.

Independently of the main contest, others pursued the cosmological argument on their own terms.[24] The most engaging is William Wollaston, whose *Religion of Nature Delineated* shows a novel disproof of the possibility of an endless succession. If W moves X, X moves Y, and Y moves Z, then X, Y, and Z are but 'one moved' relative to W, and so on regardless of the length of the series until an 'original' and 'independent' power is traced. But there cannot be such a 'moved' without a mover. Let the series be infinite: then that is an infinite body moved, and the cause must be proportional.

Suppose a *chain* hung down out of the heavens from an *unknown* height, and tho every link of it gravitated toward the earth, and what it hung upon was not visible, yet it did not descend, but kept its situation; and upon this a question should arise, *What supported or kept up this chain*: would it be a sufficient answer to say, that the *first* (or lowest) link hung upon the second (or that next above it), the *second* or rather the *first and second together* upon the *third*, and so on *ad infinitum?* For what holds up the *whole*? A *chain* of *ten* links would fall down, unless something able to bear it hinderd: one of *twenty*, if not staid by something of a yet greater strength, in proportion to the increase of weight: and therefore one of *infinite* links certainly, if not sustained by something *infinitely* strong, and capable to bear up an infinite weight. And thus it is in a *chain* of causes and effects tending, or as it were gravitating, towards some end.[25]

II. THE DESIGN ARGUMENT

The design argument, the other common approach to natural religion in this period, had gained popularity in the late seventeenth century under the impetus of the Scientific Revolution. Boyle's writings typify the way in which the science fed the argument, which provided the motive for further intensifying the science and a sense of historical mission that came from confidence in a providential order.[26] Knowledge had expanded so far that it was no longer credible to stress only human folly. The task became one of accepting and interpreting the evidence and ensuring that the implications were not misconstrued by the weak-minded. A favourite bogey is 'Epicureanism' or 'Hobbism', a target too elastic to have any clear content, but frequently associated with a mechanistic worldview more developed in France than Britain.

Like the cosmological argument, the design argument in Britain has two possible slants. One tradition emphasizes biological and botanical research, stressing the intricate structure in which parts fulfil precise functions within larger wholes. Those who investigate these functions feel naturally attracted to the use of purposive language, without any very profound analysis of the analogy between organism and artefact that this implies. The commonest expression of the analogy is in terms of a mathematical comparison between the complex organization of organic parts and the intelligent disposal of letters on a written page, but the methodology of analogy itself is explored only in relation to the question of how God's attributes are to be understood.[27] The substantial empirical work started with the research of John Ray and Nehemiah Grew on plants and animals in the seventeenth century and received added support from developments, including continental developments, in microscopy. On the other hand, a more specialist tradition, given most weight by Newton, emphasizes meteorological and astronomical phenomena in those sciences whose primary tools are mathematics and the telescope. The purpose is to show the extent to which nature is subject to mathematical description, and that its organization is the work of an omnicompetent mathematician. In Newton's hands this belief has a special force: he thinks it possible to demonstrate, against Descartes, that matter left to its own laws could never have constituted the world as we know it – one instance he makes much of is planetary motions – and that there are 'harmonies' in the system that are proof of the close involvement of a governing being, exercising dominion.[28] His account of this dominion relies heavily, however, on the concepts (of eternity and infinity) of the cosmological argument and it is in that form that it occurs in some popularizations.[29] Other more sophisticated popularizations of the Newtonian argument did not preserve the sharp distinction between the mathematical and life sciences. The Boyle Lectures of Richard Bentley and William Derham went through many editions, Derham's undergoing several foreign translations.[30] Here cosmology and terrestrial studies are combined. Another influential synthesis was that of the Dutch natural philosopher, Bernard Nieuwentijt.[31] George Cheyne promoted the image of the world as a set of machines within machines, picked up by Hume in Part II of his *Dialogues*, but this is not a narrowly mechanistic image, since Cheyne, a physician, was convinced that mechanism alone is of limited use.[32] His view of the world is organic, and a machine (*mechane*) is any kind of structured device. Later, Colin MacLaurin could move in a brief space from the anatomy of the eye to cosmic motion, by way of a first cause. In a famous passage that later influenced Hume's characterization of Cleanthes in the *Dialogues*, MacLaurin illustrates the kind of evangelical fervour that often did duty for formal reasoning: 'There is no need of nice or subtle reasonings in this matter: a manifest contrivance immediately suggests a contriver. It strikes us like a sensation; and artful reasonings against it may puzzle us, but it is without shaking our belief.'[33] Among those writing for a popular public, like Joseph Addison in *The Spectator* and in his famous hymns, the presentation rarely reached any higher level.

A few authors manage to give the argument a distinctive twist. These include Francis Hutcheson and the circle associated with him. Hutcheson's *Inquiry into Beauty* may be a study in aesthetic analysis, but it reaches its climax in an encomium on the providential ordering of our sense of beauty in rendering so attractive in nature what is also so beneficial to the well-ordering of human life; a similar encomium attends his account of the design data in his classroom textbook *Synopsis metaphysicae*, where he also presents the cosmological argument in a non-Clarkean form, drawing on both to deduce a traditional list of the communicable and incommunicable attributes of deity.[34] The theology of his aesthetics is developed by John Abernethy (1680–1740), the leading Irish dissenter of the day, who uses Hutcheson's criteria of beauty to show more fully how the 'variety' in nature is inconsistent with its being the work of necessity and its 'uniformity' is inconsistent with its being the work of chance, the only alternatives they can envisage to intelligent creation.[35] Abernethy believes the coherence of nature is sufficient to demonstrate the singleness of the deity, but makes explicit or implicit use of the cosmological argument to justify the ascription of eternity and immensity.

Another interesting variant is provided by George Berkeley. Berkeley in much of his writing is a design theorist, appealing to the constancy, order, and magnificence of nature as the effects or signs of a mind greater than we already recognize in fellow humans; the difference is that he uses it to support a broader metaphysics – immaterialism – than theism pure and simple. He gives more shape to the argument than most writers, seeing in it a special application of what later philosophy would see as the 'other minds' problem;[36] indeed, the fact that the two topics mature together is historically significant. But in *Alciphron* he changes the nature of the argument. An unsympathetic character in his dialogue refuses to acknowledge that the world bears the same obvious signs of design as the creations of human intelligence. It is suggested that we recognize intelligence in others not by their products but by their speech. So Berkeley's persona redescribes our experience of the world in terms of a 'language of nature', in which experiences 'suggest' other experiences with all the order of a syntax and consistency of a semantics. An image that earlier in Berkeley's career assumed the existence of God is now used to prove it.[37]

Taken on its own the design argument became a useful vehicle of popular science, but it rarely consists in more than an accumulation of favourable data, seeking to convince by the quantity or 'weight' of the evidence. That the evidence is psychologically weighty is read as evidence that it is logically weighty too, but this is rarely logic in the sense of a fully articulated argument; and when authors bring hard argument to bear on it, it is often the reasoning of the cosmological argument. Most eighteenth-century exponents take a sufficiently optimistic view of the benefits of the world order to humanity, and of the favoured place of humans within that order, to infer God's beneficence and to shrug off the problem of evil; but this left the door open to deism. Matthew Tindal accepted the optimistic worldview as the basis for a divinely sanctioned form of utilitarian ethic, but he saw this running sufficiently counter to the biblical account of God's acts and commands to call into question the authenticity of at least some purported revelation and the authority of religious institutions; he thus sows doubts about the biblical deity without directly addressing the theistic proofs.[38] William Dudgeon (1706–43) combines similar doubts with acceptance of those proofs:

> The ideas of order, administration, and a God, naturally spring up in the mind of man, as his understanding opens; and all God's works proclaim his being; their passiveness and independence infer his self-existence and independence; their beauty, order and happiness prove his goodness, wisdom and power.[39]

Dudgeon's reading of the design evidence causes him to deny the existence of evil, while his parallel support for Clarke's argument precipitates a correspondence with John Jackson (1686–1783) in which he contends that God's self-existent infinite substance excludes other substances from the universe, rendering the rest of nature mere modes and dependencies.[40] Lord Bolingbroke, in his posthumous literary remains, goes further on the ethical front than Tindal or Dudgeon, condemning Clarke's apriorism as sophistry, supporting the design argument only as far as the intellectual attributes, and rejecting the ascription to God of moral attributes in any sense intelligible to humans.[41]

III. HUME AND HIS CRITICS

Hume's lack of sympathy for institutional religion and those employed to uphold it put him in the same camp in the eyes of his opponents, and some critics dismiss him as merely Bolingbroke's shadow. In fact Hume is more critical than Bolingbroke and the deists of the design argument, but the argument he criticizes is not the argument his contemporaries knew. He does not directly discuss the customary barrage of design evidence, but searches for an underlying logic that he finds more clearly in the ancient models from which the argument originally derived. While his discussion in the *Enquiry*, in which he projects the debate back into a classical past, attracted notice and comment, many readers were disoriented by it.

> When we infer any particular cause from an effect, we must proportion the one to the other, and can never be allowed to ascribe to the cause any qualities, but what are exactly sufficient to produce the effect. . . . Allowing, therefore, the gods to be the authors of the existence or order of the universe; it follows, that they possess that precise degree of power, intelligence, and benevolence, which appears in their workmanship; but nothing farther can ever be proved, except we call in the assistance of exaggeration and flattery to supply the defects of argument and reasoning.[42]

Early critics like John Leland were unclear whether Hume had left room in his philosophy for the causal relation,[43] and thus for causal reasoning at all, but those who took him at his word considered this position plainly exaggerated. Towards the end of the section Hume himself allows that we sometimes draw on collateral knowledge to infer more than the evidence in isolation warrants: if we are on the seashore when the tide is in close, we may judge that a two-footed individual has passed by even though the prints of only one foot remain. For two Scottish critics, George Anderson (1677–1756) and later Archibald Arthur (1744–97), this is the typical rather than the untypical case.[44] When we see a painting, says Anderson, we properly assume in the painter a greater range of skills than was needed for the painting, while Arthur sees Hume as a too facile judge of character. There is some force in the objections where the inference is to intelligent causes since intelligence virtually entails versatility, but Hume must be right in sounding a general caution against inflation of the data as they pass through the argument: he is particularly troubled that a world that to simple observation contains both good and bad can so quickly be transformed into one where the bad is explained away. He has not seen, however, that the design argument is typically not self-standing and that the inflation arises from assumptions drawn from the perceived prerequisites of a first cause. This for his opponents is a metaphysical issue and cannot be settled from experience.

A second criticism that he appears to level at theistic proof in this section of the *Enquiry* concerns the uniqueness of the universe and the impossibility of inferring a cause where two 'species of objects' have not been regularly experienced to co-occur. The point is about our ability to reason: he is not suggesting that there cannot *be* a uniquely caused object. That the universe is indeed unique, rather than a diversity of multifarious phenomena, is something an interlocutor will contest in Part IX of the *Dialogues*, but it was the common view at the time. Hume's criticism, however, can be read as an instruction to rework the argument so as to find strong enough resemblances with other effects, which the design theorist will believe can be done.

The most sympathetic of Hume's early critics, Lord Kames, was seen by many contemporaries to concede too much to his kinsman's freethinking. In *Essays on the Principles of Morality and Natural Religion*, he agrees with all Hume's strictures against reasoning that goes beyond experience, and even agrees that we cannot rule out a priori either that the world, or a succession of intelligent beings, has existed from eternity.[45] But he has a different view of experience in which he includes an internal or instinctual 'feeling'. This includes the feeling of power operating between a cause and any effect exhibiting contrivance or design, or an aptitude for some end. We learn to identify the cause as intelligence in human works and we extend the application to the works of nature. Reasoning is not involved: merely a development of our perceptual faculty. Kames does appear to employ reasoning to conclude the existence of a first cause, but even this he puts down to feeling, abjuring any thought either of a Clarkean demonstration or of a rational understanding of the principle on which our knowledge of cause and effect actually rests. His derivation of the attributes is less precise than that of most other authors.

At the time Kames was writing, Hume was preparing the *Dialogues* in which he presses further the arguments of the *Enquiry*, as well as others that he had been working on since early in his career, but had not published. These show that the reason the great body of empirical evidence is missing from Hume's debate is that no one expects to contest it. His characters all grant that there is an adaptation of means to ends in nature. The question is, what follows from that? They all grant that there is a first cause, meaning that the search for an ultimate point in the scheme of explanation does stop somewhere, but the question is, what is its character? Hume can find no basis in experience from which to pursue these questions. The only form of the cosmological argument that his characters test is Clarke's, the structure and premises of whose argument he travesties.[46] Nor does he understand the kind of 'demonstration' that the cosmological argument attempted – a demonstration from intuitive premises, not from logically necessary ones.

Although he sets up the design argument virtually in isolation, the moves Hume makes through the person of Philo show why he and his opponents talked past each other. His most important theme is that experience cannot establish the priority of ordering mind over ordered matter, but implicitly this is a challenge to the priority accorded to agent causation in the metaphysics of the day. Given the assumption on both sides that the essence of matter and of mind is equally unknown, Hume is prepared to think the unthinkable – that mind itself is explainable through natural causes (Parts IV, VIII).

As for the order and arrangement that we find in nature, we do not have the cosmic perspective that might give evidence of overall design. We must limit our inferences to the kinds of cases we know from experience; order and arrangement are not, of themselves, kinds of cases. But if it is requisite that the manifestations of design are recognizably analogous to those in human creations, we both limit the evidence and risk ascribing human characteristics to divinity (Part V). There is another way of reading the restrictions of the evidence. Experience reveals many 'springs and principles' in nature, and different kinds of order. There is an absurdity in taking any singly as the model for all nature. If we must generalize, we have no worse reason to see the world as an ordered animal, or vegetable, than to see it as an artefact; and even a disordered world must have its parts so structured that they would in due course establish some sustainable pattern (Parts II, VI–VIII).

The topic to which Hume devotes more space than any other is the problem of evil.[47] Here, uniquely, he does proceed by the accumulation of examples, weighting the evidence firmly on the side of the calamities of human and animal life. The hedonism underlying the discussion is at times naive; there is no recognition of Joseph Butler's point that moral attributes are to be judged not by the delivery of pleasure or pain as such, but by whether it is merited and by the function it serves in the development of character.[48] In this case, however, Hume does acknowledge that the committed theist can accommodate the problem, a tacit admission of the role of the cosmological argument.

IV. AFTER HUME

Hume's *Dialogues* attracted relatively little immediate notice, and what there was was largely directed at the moral issues – the problem of evil and divine benevolence.[49] Joseph Priestley was dismissive of all the main arguments of the *Enquiry* and *Dialogues* in Part I of his *Letters to a Philosophical Unbeliever*, a work which restates the conventional views that Hume had contested. Priestley's position is already clear in an earlier work, *Institutes of Natural and Revealed Religion*, published without direct reference to Hume's views on natural religion.[50] It presents a consolidated cosmological and design argument in a way that forestalls one of Hume's objections and shows how the consolidation actually works. In section I of the *Institutes*, Priestley concedes the possibility of an intermediate designer who is not the first cause; in that case its existence and powers are derived, and the argument is still traced back to an original, superior cause. He also devotes considerable space to the moral issues, in particular trying to show that nature's system of animal predacity maximizes rather than minimizes the available happiness. Priestley's defences of theism are less significant in themselves than they are for provoking a critic into making the first avowed admission of atheism in English print. It is, however, a pretty odd atheism, as Priestley shows in a supplement added to the second edition of his *Letters*. The critic, believed to be Matthew Turner (dates unknown), a Liverpool physician and chemist known to Priestley, still traces the world to a designing will distinct from it, and yet believes this to be internal, not external to matter and its organization.[51]

Others writing with knowledge of Hume include the Irish episcopalian Hugh Hamilton (1729–1805), who reviews the history of the cosmological argument and gives a new presentation.[52] There must be at least one being whose non-existence is impossible, because there has to be something that forever determines whether there is something or nothing. It is free of all limitations, because limitation involves causal dependence. Two or more such beings would be either incompatible or indistinguishable, and therefore there is only one. Hamilton sides with those who include happiness among the a priori attributes and makes it the key to deriving the moral attributes, whereby a being, infinitely happy in its infinite sufficiency, wills to maintain the well-being of its creation. Hamilton's purpose is to counter the impact of Hume's *Dialogues*. Hume, he explains in his introduction, has handled natural religion with too much levity, and has demeaned the cosmological argument by putting it in the mouth of 'a silly character', Demea. Insinuating as he does that the material world may be self-sufficient and contain the source of all the changes that occur within it, Hume has no original arguments; he is restating objections to theism that have long been answered in the literature. Another Irishman, Richard Kirwan (1733–1812), an eminent scientist who was familiar with Hamilton's work, was both a Berkeleyan metaphysican and a dissenting friend of Priestley. He argues a priori for the existence of at least one and, in due course, at most one being that has always existed and is a necessary being, but a posteriori for the limitless power, intelligence, and wisdom of this being, including an appeal to Berkeley's argument from the language of nature. Much of the detail of his discussion of the attributes is nevertheless more a priori than a posteriori and involves a substantial treatment of the problem of evil.[53] Further defence comes from the Scots episcopalian George Gleig (1753–1840), writing in the third edition of the *Encyclopaedia Britannica*.[54] Gleig reworks the argument for a necessary being, devoting special attention to the impossibility of an infinite series (because even in an infinite series, he argues, *every* item was once a future item, so the problem of explaining the whole series remains), and the kind of necessity involved in a non-dependent being. He criticizes Clarke on detail, and has probably read Law, sharing Law's view that there could in principle be more than one necessary being in the totality of things; but as one is necessary and sufficient to explain any particular existence, no other can have meaning for *us*. Following the now familiar pattern of blending a priori and a posteriori reasoning, he sees unity as an a posteriori attribute, to be inferred from the overall unity of the natural system; however, he considers the moral attributes to be deducible a priori.

The Scottish 'common sense' philosophers employ the customary data to support the design inference on intuitive principles somewhat like those of Kames, but they keep the cosmological argument in reserve, primarily to establish the unity of the divine being. They so often have Hume in their philosophical sights that it is surprising they say relatively little in print about his critique of natural religion – their lectures on this subject were never developed into separate treatises – and what they do say continues to be directed mostly at his earlier writing. They can afford to be dismissive because they see Hume's scruples about religious belief as undermining all belief. Since they consider that they can answer him on the broader front, they see no separate threat to religion. Thomas Reid's view, which is clearer in his lectures than in his published work, is that the cosmological and design arguments work together; the recognition of design in the phenomena of nature is intuitive, a feature of our mental constitution that needs no 'other minds' argument of the kind that Berkeley attempted, but the buildup of the data to support belief in a *unitary* designer with the requisite attributes is the work of reason.[55] Dugald Stewart is the first in this tradition to address some of the difficulties raised by Hume in the *Dialogues*.[56] He supports Hume's view that the design inference is based neither on a process of reasoning nor on experience, but sees the signs of divine creation as analogous to the signs of habitation one might leave in a remote place to signal that there had once been human life there.

In the short term, the 'weight' of evidence amassed by supporters of the design argument won, over Hume's logical scruples, but it would be unfair to suggest that the argument survived only through public inertia. There may be only one direct reference to the *Dialogues* in William Paley's *Natural Theology*, but it is enough to show that he knew that work.[57] Paley's combination of updated though derivative science with a far stronger logical structure and attention to the philosophical argument gave reassurance to a new generation of readers, and it was only after Darwinism opened up the possibility of alternative approaches to the study of nature that Hume attracted a following. Paley did more than revitalize the argument. He did it in a way calculated to evade Hume's critique. His opening chapter, 'State of the Argument', is a summary of Humean moves and of the counter-moves that Paley will develop *seriatim* in the ensuing chapters. He begins with the example of a watch found on a walk – a standard example but one allowed by Hume himself in section IV of the *Enquiry* – and interpreted as a product of design just as Hume interpreted it. Paley then goes on to consider and reject a number of potentially captious objections. It is immaterial that we have never seen a watch made and have no idea how the manufacture is achieved. 'Ignorance of this kind exalts our opinion of the unseen and unknown artist's skill, if he be unseen and unknown, but raises no doubt in our minds of the existence of such an artist, at some former time, and in some place or other.' It is immaterial that the watch sometimes, even often, goes wrong. 'It is not necessary that a machine be perfect, in order to show with what design it was made: still less necessary, where the only question is, whether it were made with any design at all.' It is immaterial that we do not understand the relevance of all the parts. No one would think the arrangement of the parts sufficiently accounted for by being told that they were necessarily in some order or another, or think that anything was gained by talking about a 'principle of order' (a phrase of Hume's in Parts II, IV, VI and XII). Principles cannot make watches. Nor will a selective scepticism avail: 'This point being known, his ignorance of other points, his doubts concerning other points, affect not the certainty of his reasoning.' In chapter 2, Paley turns from an everyday to a fictional scenario and considers the watch to be capable of generating further watches: a parody of Cleanthes's vegetating library in Part III, but with the same message. Then, in chapter 3, he draws the implications for the design argument, being very careful not to contemplate the universe as a whole, which Hume has ruled out, but a single phenomenon open to everyone's observation: the anatomy of the eye. Until there was an equally good hypothesis available to explain that, Paley was seen to trump Hume at each move. Those who, early in the nineteenth century, detected the weaknesses in his presentation, such as John Ballantyne, Alexander Crombie, and Lord Brougham,[58] did not come to Hume's defence, but rather sought to rebuild Paley's.

NOTES

1 On Hume's reception, see Isabel Rivers, 'Responses to Hume on Religion by Anglicans and Dissenters', *Journal of Ecclesiastical History*, 52 (2001): 675–95; M. A. Stewart, 'Religion and Rational Theology', in *The Cambridge Companion to the Scottish Enlightenment*, ed. A. Broadie (Cambridge, 2003), 31–59. Representative texts are in *Early Responses to Hume's Writings on Religion*, ed. J. Fieser, 2 vols. (Bristol, 2001).

2 Typical are Thomas Halyburton, *Natural Religion Insufficient and Reveal'd Necessary to Man's Happiness in his Present State: or, A Rational Enquiry into the Principles of the Modern Deists* (Edinburgh, 1714), *Memoirs of the Life of the Reverend Mr. Thomas Halyburton* (Edinburgh, 1714); and James Hog, *Memoirs ... Written by himself, in a Testamentary Memorial* (posthumous, Edinburgh et al., 1798), 9–16.

3 John Locke, *The Reasonableness of Christianity* [1695], ed. J. C. Higgins-Biddle, in *The Clarendon Edition* (1999), 143–7.

4 Locke, *An Essay concerning Human Understanding* [1690], ed. P. H. Nidditch, in *The Clarendon Edition* (1975), I.iv.8.

5 For other approaches to this context, see Robin Attfield, *God and the Secular: A Philosophical Assessment of Secular Reasoning from Bacon to Kant* (Cardiff, 1978); John H. Brooke, *Science and Religion: Some Historical Perspectives* (Cambridge, 1991).

6 For illustrations of this debate over what has come to be called 'the rule of faith controversy', see M. A. Stewart, 'Stillingfleet and the Way of Ideas', and Beverley C. Southgate, '"Beating down Scepticism": The Solid Philosophy of John Sergeant', chapters 8 and 9 of *English Philosophy in the Age of Locke*, ed. M. A. Stewart (Oxford, 2000).

7 For a typical working out of the relationship, see Henry Grove, *Wisdom the First Spring of Action in the Deity. A Discourse in which among other things, the Absurdity of God's being Acted upon by Natural Inclinations, and of an Unbounded Liberty, is Shewn. The Moral Attributes of God are Explain'd. The Origin of Evil is Consider'd. The fundamental Duties of Natural Religion are Shewn to be Reasonable, &c.* (London, 1734). Grove debates with Hutcheson whether the deity is motivated by kind affections, or by the intrinsic beauty and merit of his actions (18–19).

8 For example, George Anderson, *A Remonstrance against Lord Viscount Bolingbroke's Philosophical Religion* (Edinburgh, 1756), section VI.

9 Richard Fiddes, *Theologia Speculativa: or, The First Part of a Body of Divinity under that Title. Wherein are Explain'd the Principles of Natural and Reveal'd Religion* (London, 1718), I.i.9; see also I.i.2. Leibniz, *Principes de la philosophie ou Monadologie* in *Principes de la nature et de la grace fondés en raison et Principes de la philosophie ou Monadologie*, ed. A. Robinet (Paris, 1954), section 45; translated as *The Principles of Philosophy, or, the Monadology*, in *Philosophical Essays*, eds. R. Ariew and D. Garber (Indianapolis, IN, 1989).

10 Locke, *Essay*, IV.x. For Locke's likely debt to Pierre Nicole and the contemporary reception of his argument, see Wolfgang von Leyden, 'Locke and Nicole: Their Proofs of the Existence of God and their Attitude towards Descartes', *Sophia* [Padua], 16 (1948): 41–55.

11 Andrew Baxter, *An Enquiry into the Nature of the Human Soul; wherein the Immateriality of the Soul is Evinced from the Principles of Reason and Philosophy* (Edinburgh, 1733; 2nd edn. in 2 vols., London, 1737), 1: section II.

12 Samuel Clarke, *A Demonstration of the Being and Attributes of God: More Particularly in Answer to Mr. Hobbs, Spinoza, and their Followers* (London, 1705; five further editions to 1725); William King, *De origine mali* (Dublin, 1702), translated as *An Essay on the Origin of Evil* by Edmund Law (Cambridge, 1731; four further editions with updated commentary to 1781), chapter 1, sections 2–3.

13 Locke, *Essay*, IV.x.2–6.

14 For a modern critique, see J. J. MacIntosh, 'Locke and Boyle on Miracles and God's Existence', in *Robert Boyle Reconsidered*, ed. M. Hunter (Cambridge, 1994), chapter 12.

15 *The Correspondence of John Locke*, ed. E. S. de Beer, 9 vols., in progress (Oxford, 1976–), letter 2443. See 2318, 2352, 2410, 2432, 2460, 2485 (Limborch), 2340, 2395, 2413, 2498 (Locke).

16 For fuller discussion, see J. P. Ferguson, *The Philosophy of Dr. Samuel Clarke and its Critics* (New York, NY, 1974); Ezio Vailati, Introduction to Clarke, *A Demonstration of the Being and Attributes of God* (Cambridge, 1998). For a technical analysis, see William L. Rowe, *The Cosmological Argument* (Princeton, NJ, 1975).

17 *A Demonstration*, Propositions I–V.

18 *Several Letters to the Reverend Dr. Clarke, from a Gentleman in Glocestershire, relating to the First Volume of the Sermons Preached at Mr. Boyle's Lecture; with the Dr.'s Answers Thereunto* (London, 1716); 'Letters to Dr. Clarke concerning Liberty and Necessity, from a Gentleman of the University of Cambridge, with the Doctor's Answers to them', appended to *A Collection of Papers, which Passed between the late Learned Mr. Leibniz and Dr. Clarke in the Years 1715 and 1716: relating to the Principles of Natural Philosophy and Religion* (London, 1717); *Letters Written, in MDCCXXV, to the Rev. Dr. Samuel Clarke, relating to an Argument Advanced by the Doctor, in his Demonstration of the Being and Attributes of God, in Proof of the Unity of the Deity: with the Doctor's Answers* (London, 1745). Clarke's *Works*, in four volumes, were posthumously edited by Benjamin Hoadly (London, 1738).

19 Kames's papers are in the National Archives of Scotland (GD24/1/548), Bowman's in the National Library at Florence (N. A. 1197).

20 [William Carroll?], *Remarks upon Mr. Clarke's Sermons, Preached at St. Paul's against Hobbs, Spinoza, and Other Atheists* (London, 1705); S[amuel] C[olliber], *An Impartial Enquiry into the Existence and Nature of God* (London, 1718; third edition, 'with considerable Additions and Improvements, made partly with Regard to some Objections of the Reverend Mr. Jackson', 1735). Colliber's argument, particularly as it relates to spatial attributes and infinity, was subjected to detailed criticism by Philip Doddridge, *A Course of Lectures on the Principal Subjects in Pneumatology, Ethics, and Divinity* (London, 1763), Part II. Doddridge is helpful for identifying more voices in these debates than there is room to discuss here. See also Thomas Johnson, *Quaestiones philosophicae* (Cambridge, 1734; 2nd edn. 1735; posthumous 3rd edn. 1741), X.iii.

21 Phillips Gretton, *A Review of the Argument a Priori, in Relation to the Being and Attributes of God: In Reply to Dr. Clarke's Answer to a Seventh Letter concerning that Argument, Printed at the End of the Last Edition of his Boyleian Lectures* (London, 1726); John Dundas, *State of the Processes Depending against Mr. John Simson Professor of Divinity in the University of Glasgow; Setting forth the Proceedings of the Presbytery of Glasgow, General Assembly, and Committees thereof* (Edinburgh, 1728).

22 Henry Stebbing, *A Defence of Dr. Clarke's Evidence of Natural and Revealed Religion* (London, 1731); [John Clarke, d. 1741], *A Defence of Dr. Clarke's Demonstration of the Being and Attributes of God, wherein is particularly Consider'd the Nature of Space, Duration, and Necessary Existence* (London, 1732), *A Second Defence of Dr. Clarke's Demonstration of the Being and Attributes of God* (London, 1733), *A Third Defence of Dr. Clarke's Demonstration of the Being and Attributes of God, being a Vindication of the Two Former Defences* (London, 1734); John Jackson, *Calumny no Conviction; or, A Vindication of the Plea for Human Reason* (London, 1731), *The Existence and Unity of God; Proved from his Nature and Attributes. Being a Vindication of Dr. Clarke's Demonstration of the Being and Attributes of God* (London, 1734), *A Defense of a Book entitled The Existence and Unity of God; Prov'd from his Nature and Attributes. Being a farther Vindication of Dr. Clarke's Demonstration of the Being and Attributes of God* (London, 1735); [Phillips Glover], *The Argument A Priori concerning the Existence and Perfections of God, and its Importance to Virtue and true Religion, Stated and Consider'd* (London, 1737); Benjamin Heath, *An Essay Towards a Demonstrative Proof of the Divine Existence, Unity and Attributes: To Which is Premised a Short Defence of the Argument Commonly Called A Priori* (London, 1740). Heath aimed to revise Clarke's argument so as to make it less liable to criticism. See also an anonymous tract, *Some Thoughts Concerning the Argument à Priori; Occasion'd by Mr. Knowles's Discourse Entitled the 'Existence and Attributes of God not Demonstrable à Priori'* (London, 1748).

23 King, *An Essay on the Origin of Evil*, translated with notes by Edmund Law; Edmund Law, *An Enquiry into the Ideas of Space, Time, Immensity, and Eternity* (Cambridge, 1734); [Daniel Waterland], 'A Dissertation upon the Argument a Priori for Proving the Existence of a First Cause. In a Letter to Mr. Law', appended to Law's *Enquiry*; Joseph Clarke, *Dr. Clarke's Notions of Space Examin'd. In Vindication of the Translator of Archbishop King's 'Origin of Evil'* (London, 1733), and *A Farther Examination of Dr. Clarke's Notions of Space; with Some Considerations on the Possibility of Eternal Creation* (Cambridge, 1734); Thomas Knowles, *The Existence and Attributes of God not Demonstrable a Priori; in Answer to the Arguments of the Learned Dr. Clarke, and his Followers* (Cambridge, 1746); *The Scripture-Doctrine, of the Existence and Attributes of God, As Manifested by the Works of Creation and Providence: In Twelve Sermons, to Which is Prefixed a Preface, In Answer to a Late Pamphlet, Intitled, 'Some Thoughts concerning the Argument à Priori'* (Cambridge, 1750). On Law and his circle, see John Stephens, 'Edmund Law and his Circle at Cambridge', in *The Philosophical Canon in the 17th and 18th Centuries*, eds. G. A. J. Rogers and S. Tomaselli (Rochester, NY, 1996), 163–73.

24 For example, the Boyle Lecturer Thomas Burnet, in *A Demonstration of True Religion*, 2 vols. (London, 1726), and the English dissenters Henry Grove, in *Wisdom the First Spring of Action in the Deity*, Moses Lowman, in *An Argument to Prove the Unity and Perfections of God a Priori* (London, 1735), and Jeremiah Hunt, in *Sermons*, 4 vols. (London, 1748).

25 William Wollaston, *The Religion of Nature Delineated* (privately published, 1722; commercially marketed, London, 1724), section V. Quotation from the posthumous 6th edition (London, 1738), with life of the author.

26 Brooke, *Science and Religion*, especially chapter 2; Margaret G. Cook, 'Divine Artifice and Natural Mechanism: Robert Boyle's Mechanical Philosophy of Nature', *Osiris*, 2nd series, 16 (2001): 133–50; Jan Wocjik, *Robert Boyle and the Limits of Reason* (Cambridge, 1997).

27 See Peter Browne, *Things Divine and Supernatural Conceived by Analogy with Things Natural and Human* (London, 1733), and other writings.

28 Isaac Newton, *The Mathematical Principles of Natural Philosophy*, trans. A. Motte (London, 1729), Book III, General Scholium; *Four Letters from Sir Isaac Newton to Doctor Bentley; containing some Arguments in Proof of a Deity* (London, 1756). Newton admits the relevance of terrestrial science, including the life sciences, in *Opticks: or, A Treatise of the Reflections, Refractions, Inflections and Colours of Light*, 4th edn. (London, 1730), Book III, Part I, query 31.

29 Ephraim Chambers, *Cyclopaedia: or An Universal Dictionary of Arts and Sciences*, 2 vols. (London, 1728), article 'God', citing John Maxwell's *Discourse concerning God; Wherein the Meaning of His Name, His Providence, the Nature and Measure of His Dominion are consider'd. To which is subjoined a translation of Sir Isaac Newton's General Scholium* (London, 1715).

30 Richard Bentley, *The Folly and Unreasonableness of Atheism* (London, 1693), combining eight lectures separately published under various titles; William Derham, *Physico-Theology: or, A Demonstration of the Being and Attributes of God, from the Works of Creation* (London, 1713).

31 Bernard Nieuwentyt, *The Religious Philosopher: or, The Right Use of Contemplating the Works of the Creator*, trans. J. Chamberlayne (London, 1718–19; three further editions to 1730).

32 George Cheyne, *Philosophical Principles of Religion, Natural and Revealed* (London, 1715; 5th edn., 1736).

33 Colin MacLaurin, *An Account of Sir Isaac Newton's Philosophical Discoveries* (London, 1748), IV.ix.6–14. Quotation from p. 381.

34 Francis Hutcheson, *An Inquiry in to the Original of our Ideas of Beauty and Virtue; in Two Treatises* (London and Dublin, 1725; three further lifetime editions), section V, *Synopsis metaphysicae*, 2nd edn. ([Glasgow], 1744), Part III, chapters 1–3.

35 John Abernethy, *Discourses concerning the Being and Natural Perfections of God* (Dublin, 1740). See also his *Discourses concerning the Perfections of God; in which his Holiness, Goodness, and Other Moral Attributes, are Explained and Proved* (Dublin, 1742). In later British editions these are published as a two-volume set without a common title.

36 George Berkeley, *A Treatise concerning the Principles of Human Knowledge*, in *Works*, 2: sections 140, 145–49.

37 George Berkeley, *Alciphron*, in *Works*, 3: dialogue IV, sections 5–12. The significance of this argument was identified by Andrew Kippis, *Biographia Britannica*, 2nd edn. (London, 1780), entry 'Berkeley'; for later appraisal, see Edward A. Sillem, *George Berkeley and the Proofs of the Existence of God* (London, 1957), chapter 6.

38 Matthew Tindal, *Christianity as Old as the Creation: or, The Gospel, a Republication of the Religion of Nature* (London, 1730).

39 William Dudgeon, *A Catechism Founded upon Experience and Reason: Collected by a Father for the Sake of his Children* (n.p., 1739), reprinted in *Philosophical Works* (n.p., 1765), 181.

40 *Philosophical Works*, 231–90.

41 Henry St. John, Viscount Bolingbroke, 'Fragments or Minutes of Essays', *Works*, ed. D. Malet, 5 vols. (London, 1754), vol. 5.

42 David Hume, *An Enquiry concerning Human Understanding*, ed. T. L. Beauchamp, in *The Clarendon Edition* (2000), 11.12 and 14; SBN 136–7.

43 John Leland, *A View of the Principal Deistical Writers that have Appeared in England in the Last and Present Century*, 2 vols. and suppt. (London, 1754–6), vol. 2, letters I–II, renumbered in 3rd edn. (1757) and subsequent editions XVI–XVII.

44 [George Anderson], *An Estimate of the Profit and Loss of Religion, Personally and Publicly Stated* (Edinburgh, 1753), section VI; Archibald Arthur, *Discourses of Theological and Literary Subjects* (Glasgow, 1803), discourse III, section II.

45 Henry Home, Lord Kames, *Essays on the Principles of Morality and Natural Religion* (Edinburgh, 1751; 2nd edn., 1758), Part II, essay VII.

46 *Dialogues concerning Natural Religion*, Part IX.

47 *Dialogues*, Parts X–XI. See also M. A. Stewart, 'An Early Fragment on Evil', in *Hume and Hume's Connexions*, ed. M. A. Stewart and J. P. Wright (Edinburgh, 1994), 160–70.

48 Joseph Butler, *The Analogy of Religion, Natural and Revealed, to the Constitution and Course of Nature*, 2nd edn. (London, 1736), Part I, chapters 2–3.

49 Thomas Hayter, *Remarks on Mr. Hume's Dialogues concerning Natural Religion* (Cambridge, 1780). Another writer, Thomas Balguy, *Divine Benevolence Asserted; and Vindicated from the Objections of Ancient and Modern Sceptics* (London, 1781), does not discuss Hume.
50 Joseph Priestley, *Letters to a Philosophical Unbeliever*, Part I (Bath and London, 1780; 2nd edn. Birmingham and London, 1787), *Institutes of Natural and Revealed Religion*, 3 vols. (London, 1772–74), vol. 1, 'containing the Elements of Natural Religion'.
51 [Matthew Turner], *Answer to Dr. Priestley's Letters to a Philosophical Unbeliever* (London, 1782). Preface and postscript are presented as the work of 'William Hammon', whom Priestley judged fictitious. See further David Berman, *A History of Atheism in Britain: From Hobbes to Russell* (London, 1988), chapter 5.
52 Hugh Hamilton, *An Attempt to Prove the Existence and Absolute Perfection of the Supreme Unoriginated Being, in a Demonstrative Manner* (Dublin, 1784); a revised text, with an additional essay, 'Of the Permission of Evil', is in his posthumous *Works*, 2 vols. (London, 1809), vol. 2.
53 Richard Kirwan, *Metaphysical Essays, containing the Principles and Fundamental Objects of that Science* (London, 1809), essay III.
54 *Encyclopaedia Britannica*, 3rd edn., 15 vols. (Edinburgh, 1788–97), article 'Metaphysics', Part III, chapter 6, 'Of the Being and Attributes of God'.
55 M. A. Stewart, 'Rational Religion and Common Sense', in *Thomas Reid: Context, Influence and Significance*, ed. J. Houston (Edinburgh, 2004): 123–60. For Reid's published views, see Thomas Reid, *Essays on the Intellectual Powers of Man* (Edinburgh, 1785), VI.vi.6. For Reid's lectures and those of Alexander Gerard, see Thomas Reid, *Lectures on Natural Theology (1780)*, ed. E. H. Duncan (Washington, DC, 1981), an imperfect transcription of an imperfect student copy; Alexander and Gilbert Gerard, *A Compendious View of the Evidences of Natural and Revealed Religion* (London, 1828).
56 Dugald Stewart, *The Philosophy of the Active and Moral Powers of Man* (Edinburgh, 1828), Book III, chapter 2.
57 William Paley, *Natural Theology* (London, 1802), chapter 26, citing Hume, *Dialogues*, Part XI, on indolence as the primary cause of evil.
58 John Ballantyne, 'On the Being of a God', in *Theological Tracts*, ed. J. Brown, 3 vols. (Edinburgh, 1853–4), 2: 37–53; Alexander Crombie, *Natural Theology*, 2 vols. (London, 1829); Henry, Lord Brougham, *A Discourse of Natural Theology* (London, 1835).

25

ARGUMENTS FOR THE EXISTENCE OF GOD: THE CONTINENTAL EUROPEAN DEBATE

MARIA ROSA ANTOGNAZZA

Natural or rational theology, as opposed to revealed theology, is concerned with the knowledge of God which can be attained by human reason without the help of revelation. Traditionally, a central part of natural theology is devoted to the arguments for the existence of God, that is, to rational demonstration of the existence of God through the light of unaided natural reason. Not surprisingly, therefore, philosophical arguments for the existence of God (intended as first cause or first principle) pre-date Christianity. Yet they became an integral part of traditional Christian theology from the patristic period onward as preamble to the specifically Christian revelation by providing arguments which are valid for every human being on purely rational grounds. To be sure, different thinkers held different and often opposite views regarding the way in which human reason can lead to God – notably whether human reason can prove the existence of God a priori (that is to say, according to scholastic terminology, from the cause to the effect or, according to modern terminology, independently of experience) or a posteriori (from the effect to the cause, or, in the modern sense, starting from experience). But despite these important differences, both camps agreed that unaided human reason could prove God's existence. The outbreak of the Protestant Reformation in the sixteenth century undermined this Christian consensus by raising a question preliminary to that of whether the way of human reason to God is a priori or a posteriori. Following in the footsteps of Martin Luther and Jean Calvin, Protestant theologians asked: is natural theology even possible? In other words, is a true knowledge of God available to human reason after the Fall and before revelation? More specifically, is it at all possible for unaided natural reason to prove the existence of God? This general question of principle gained new prominence and had to be addressed before entering the discussion of specific proofs of His existence.

I. THE PROVABILITY OF GOD'S EXISTENCE

At least ostensibly a Calvinist, Pierre Bayle did much to develop a negative answer to this question. His lack of confidence in the proofs derived not so much from an accumulation of individual faults as from a pervasive suspicion about reason's power to settle so great an issue. Reason is by its deepest nature weak and indecisive. It can prove one thing, but it can just as easily prove the contrary;[1] and so finally it is able to prove nothing. The role of reason in religion is critical, not constitutive.[2] It can show what cannot be known, but if more than that is expected from reason, it leads astray and stands in need of correction by tradition or revelation.[3] On its own, reason leads to perplexity and doubt about God; scepticism, however, can lead to faith in God.[4] True religion is grounded in revelation, not reason.[5]

By taking at face value what Bayle said on faith and reason, it is possible to read him as a 'sceptical fideist'. But Bayle was not always taken at face value. Even his traditional Calvinist emphasis upon the authority of revelation and the insufficiency of reason was regularly presumed by Dutch Protestants and French *philosophes* alike, albeit from very different motives, to be little more than a subterfuge for the *Dictionaire historique et critique*'s covert strategy of undermining belief in the God of Abraham, Isaac, and Jean Calvin. To be sure, Bayle was not an atheist; but his claims, (1) that on purely rational grounds there is little to choose between opposing views and, (2) that atheism or Manichaeism appear equal to Christianity,[6] helped create a new climate of opinion in which atheism gradually gained cultural credibility. Orthodox theologians and heterodox *philosophes* recognised the importance of Bayle's concession that atheism was intellectually possible. In addition, his composite picture of virtuous atheists in distant lands played a key role in establishing the moral possibility of atheism in an era when it was conventionally presumed to be not only irrational but also immoral. Whether intentionally or not, Bayle's *Pensées diverses* (1682) and *Commentaire philosophique* (1686) as well as his more popular *Dictionaire* hastened the demise of the venerable *argumentum e consensu gentium* underlying the presumption of theism. In the absence (advocated by Bayle) of decisive rational evidence for or against the existence of God, one could not appeal (as had usually been done by scholastic philosophers and their heirs) to the presumption of theism on the ground that atheism was contrary to the consensus of humanity in general. This argument may in fact have been undermined by the progressive discovery of apparently atheistic cultures in remote countries.

Like Descartes, Bayle insisted on the necessity of evidence (that is, rigorous conditions of cognitive certainty),[7] but, unlike Descartes, he concluded that human reason was unable to attain such evidence, especially concerning God.

In this way Bayle paved the way – intentionally or otherwise – for the most radical fringe of the French Enlightenment which consciously pursued the project of undermining not just Christianity, but theism all together.

While the 'Calvinist' Bayle's stated motives in developing the fideistic approach to theism and Christianity can themselves be regarded sceptically, the same does not apply to another even more influential voice inside the Protestant world: Pietism. Undoubtedly guided by a sincere desire to be faithful to the Christian God in general and to Martin Luther's views of Him in particular, Pietism was more a devotional than an intellectual movement, though it had direct and indirect influence on philosophical debate through its opposition to rationalism and its insistence on the primacy of the will. Pietism initially represented a reaction against the over-intellectualization of religion in scholastic orthodoxy and a rediscovery of spiritual disciplines, personal piety, and morality. The Pietists spread outward from Frankfurt through local *collegia pietatis* encouraged by Philipp Jakob Spener (1635–1705). The importance of the movement for the history of philosophy arises from the suspicion it created about the capacity of reason to ground religious certainties and from the prominence it gave to inner experience and moral rectitude. Prominent German philosophers – including Immanuel Kant (1724–1804), Friedrich Heinrich Jacobi (1743–1819), Friedrich Schleiermacher (1768–1834) and Georg Wilhelm Friedrich Hegel (1770–1831) – emerged out of Pietist backgrounds, and this may have had an effect on their approach to some philosophical issues, including whether the proofs of God's existence are foundational for the knowledge of God's being. At a time when he still offered a version of the a priori argument, the 'pre-critical' Kant could also write: 'It is absolutely necessary that one should convince oneself that God exists; that His existence should be demonstrated, however, is not so necessary.'[8] True to his Pietist upbringing, Jacobi grounded religious certainty in the immediacy of feeling (*Gefühl*), not rational argument. In harmony with Hume and Kant, he held it impossible for reason to take knowledge beyond sense experience. That which lies beyond our senses can be known only insofar as it is given to us.[9] There is no way from nature to God[10] and the Cartesian proofs are dismissed as 'Hocuspocus'.[11] The only God who might be proved by demonstration would be a fatalistic, monistic God lacking in intelligence, feeling, and will.[12] For his part, Schleiermacher, the self-styled 'Pietist of a higher order', had no need for rational proofs to add certainty to what was already a matter of immediate self-consciousness.[13]

These views were not unusual in German Protestant circles. Among orthodox, rationalist, and pietist Protestants alike, there were lower expectations for the proofs of God than there were in the thought of their Catholic contemporaries. A version of the 'sceptical fideist' approach nevertheless found advocates in the

Roman Catholic world as well. The Jansenists – followers of the Augustinian doctrine as reasserted by the Flemish bishop, Cornelius Jansen (1585–1638) – were equally determined to halt what they saw, in both the new rationalism of the Cartesians and the old Aristotelian scholasticism of the Jesuits, as an over-dependence on philosophy instead of enlisting the resources of faith in explaining the mysteries of Christianity. Their entry into debate with Catholic co-religionists helped consolidate the case against the provability of God's existence in eighteenth-century French philosophy. Nicolas l'Herminier (1657–1735), a Sorbonne Jesuit sympathetic to the Jansenist cause, warned that feeble arguments can do great damage to faith and strengthen unbelief, while insisting that neither the Cartesian nor the scholastic proofs of God were in the least convincing. Using the scholastic refutation of Cartesian proofs and the Cartesian refutation of scholastic proofs, he insisted that all a priori proofs of God were circular and that no a posteriori proof can arrive at the supremely perfect Being or God.[14] Claude-François Houtteville (1686–1742) and Claude Buffier (1661–1737) similarly argued that neither set of arguments could demonstrate what they claimed.[15] The mutual refutation of the Cartesian and scholastic positions was taken by all of them as a healthy reminder of the frailty of reason and of our dependence upon faith (l'Herminier) or sentiment (Buffier) or Pascal-like reasons of the heart (Houtteville) in averting the destructive consequences of scepticism.

This three-sided warfare between Jesuits, Cartesians, and Jansenists produced arguments which, in other hands, would be made to support the very atheism they had been constructed to refute. With tongue firmly in cheek, Paul-Henri Thiry d'Holbach (1723–89) later recorded in his entertaining *Théologie portative* that the harmony that reigned supreme among the Christian theologians was the most compelling argument for the truth of that religion.[16] In *Christianisme dévoilé* (1756), he made much of the fact that Christians agreed among themselves neither about the proofs of God's existence, nor about the soundness of particular proofs, nor even about God's provability in principle. The cause of this discord, d'Holbach argued, was to be found in the incoherence of the very concept of God. For this reason, the criticisms leveled by all three parties against their opponents were generally correct, though their own positive arguments were always untenable. Whatever the starting-point – be it Aristotelian or Cartesian or Jansenist – atheism followed necessarily.

The urbane *philosophe* d'Holbach was not the first person to come to this view. An obscure village *curé* from the Champagne named Jean Meslier (1664–1729) had done so some thirty years before in a remarkable *Testament* in which he repudiated not only the Christian religion and its Triune God but also natural religion and its generic God.[17] He too derived his case against God from books that had been written in the Deity's defence in the debate between Jesuits, Cartesians, and Jansenists. Their inability to agree on a single proof for God's existence became for Meslier a good reason to presume that there is no compelling ground for belief in God. In effect, he embraced the scepticism of the Jansenists, but not their fideism. The significance of Meslier's rejection of God did not lie in the originality of his arguments (for all of them were derivative) but in the fact that he was able to derive his case against God entirely out of the works of orthodox theologians such as the pro-Cartesian Archbishop François Fénelon (1651–1715), the learned Scholastic Jesuit René Joseph Tournemine (1661–1739), and the pro-Jansenist Nicolas l'Herminier.[18]

II. A PRIORI ARGUMENTS

Firmly convinced that the existence of God can be proved by natural reason with mathematical certainty and that to abdicate it would be equivalent to giving up the most effective weapon against incipient atheism, Leibniz saw that the first step of reason on its way to God was to refute the kind of 'fideist scepticism' particularly pervasive within Protestantism. Although a Lutheran himself, he rejected the idea that human reason was totally corrupted by the Fall. As he claimed in a direct clash with Bayle, even after original sin, a natural light remains in human beings which is God's gift and which conforms to His supreme and universal reason. However limited, this natural light can reach truth.[19] Having thus maintained in principle the soundness of human reason, Leibniz could move on to a positive demonstration of the existence of God. Alongside other arguments, he proposed a more rigorous version of the traditional a priori argument.[20]

The a priori or (following the terminology adopted by Kant) 'ontological' argument is so called because it starts from the consideration of the essence of God as it is represented in the idea that we have of Him, independent of our experience of existing entities. According to the famous presentation of this argument in the *Proslogion* of Anselm of Canterbury (1033–1109), the idea that we have of God is the idea of 'something than which nothing greater can be conceived' (*aliquid quo nihil maius cogitari possit*). But if 'that than which a greater cannot be conceived' (hereafter IQM = *id quo maius cogitari nequit*) existed only in the intellect and not in reality, it would not be IQM, because the IQM existing in reality would be greater than the IQM existing only in the intellect. Therefore the IQM must necessarily exist in reality.[21] In short, the concept of God implies real existence.

Anselm's proof was reformulated by Descartes in the Fifth Meditation:

> the idea of God, or a supremely perfect being, is one which I find within me just as surely as the idea of any shape or number. And my understanding that it belongs to his nature that he always exists is no less clear and distinct than is the case when I prove of any shape or number that some property belongs to its nature.[22]

The existence of God is constitutive of His own essence or nature just as to have three angles equal two right angles is constitutive of the essence of a triangle.[23]

According to Leibniz, however, this proof as presented by Anselm and reformulated by Descartes is incomplete because it demonstrates only that if God is possible, then He must exist, but not that God *is* possible. The a priori proof holds only if it has first been proven that 'this idea of a wholly great or wholly perfect being is possible', that is, 'does not imply a contradiction'.[24] Now, argued Leibniz in the *Monadologie*, 'perfection' is

> nothing but the quantity of positive reality taken strictly, when we put aside the limits or bounds in the things which are limited. But where there are no bounds, that is, in God, perfection is absolutely infinite.[25]

The *ens perfectissimum* is the *pure positivum*, the being which does not participate of any negation. Since 'nothing can prevent the possibility of that which is without any limits, without any negation, and consequently without any contradiction', God must be possible. This alone, concluded Leibniz, 'suffices to know the existence of God a priori', because only God 'has the privilege of necessarily existing if he is possible' (*Monadologie*, §45, 614/647).

Leibniz added straightaway, however, that 'we have proved it also through the reality of eternal truths.' In fact, he gave another argument a priori which starts from possibility and arrives at the existence of God.[26] Following this time in the tradition of the Augustinian argument *ex veritatibus aeternis*,[27] he claimed that if there is a reality in the essence or possibility of things or in the necessary truths, this reality must be 'founded on something existent and actual, and therefore in the existence of a necessary being' (§44, 614/647). Possibility presupposes actuality. If something is true (or possible), there must be (exist) something by virtue of which it is true (or possible). If there is a reality in the possibility of things, there must be something actual, something really existing, because 'every reality must be grounded in something existent' (*Théodicée*, §184; Adams 178). This something is God as the 'root of possibility', as the ultimate foundation of the essence or nature of things on which their possibility depends.[28]

A similar argument claiming that God's existence is required to account for the reality of possibilities was endorsed by the pre-critical Kant in *Der einzig mögliche Beweisgrund*. In this work Kant refuted the Cartesian-Leibnizian proof a priori on grounds that are virtually identical to those that survive in his refutation of the ontological argument in the *Kritik der reinen Vernunft* (1781).[29] Existence can never be derived from a concept. It is not a real predicate, but merely the positing of a thing as existing in itself (See Ak 2: 75; A 598/B 626). As he explained in a famous example,

> a hundred real actual dollars do not contain the least bit more than a hundred possible ones. For since the latter signifies the concept and the former its object and its positing in itself, then, in case the former contained more than the latter, my concept would not express the entire object and thus would not be the suitable concept of it. But in my financial condition there is more with a hundred actual dollars than with the mere concept of them . . . yet the hundred dollars themselves that I am thinking of are not in the least increased through this being outside my concept. (A 599/B 627)

That appears to be the end of the matter in the first *Kritik*, but in the 1763 monograph, Kant used his new *Beweisgrund* to show how the traditional proofs a priori and a posteriori could be reformulated as sound arguments. Even if 'existence' is a grammatical and not a real predicate and the reality of something cannot be inferred from its concept, some version of the a priori argument may still be sound. Kant's proposed transcendental proof runs as follows:

All possibility presupposes something actual in and through which all that can be thought is given. Accordingly, there is a certain reality, the cancellation of which would itself cancel all internal possibility whatever. But that which eradicates all possibility if it is cancelled is absolutely necessary.

In other words, it is impossible that nothing is possible. However, if nothing exists, nothing would be possible. 'Therefore', concluded Kant, 'something exists absolutely necessarily' (*Beweisgrund*, Ak 2: 83).[30] From this first attribute (necessity) he then deduced the others (unity, simplicity, immutability and eternity, highest reality, spirituality), arriving at the conclusion that the necessary being is God (Ak 2: 83–9). The *Beweisgrund* – as well as Leibniz's argument from the reality of eternal truths – arrives at God as the 'ultimate ground of the possibility of all other beings' (Ak 2: 83). It is a proof which Kant never repudiated – not even in the *Kritik der reinen Vernunft*, where his early refutation of the Cartesian proof a priori was repeated with little alteration.

III. A POSTERIORI ARGUMENTS

Unlike Kant, Leibniz maintained that it is possible to demonstrate the existence of God a posteriori as well. The general scheme of the a posteriori arguments can be presented as follows. The arguments start from a certain given experience and then infer the conditions of the possibility of that experience. Their tacit presupposition is the intelligibility (rationality) of reality, or, the validity of the principle of non-contradiction. The experience under consideration would be unintelligible – irrational, contradictory, impossible – if it were not given a certain reality which is the condition of possibility of that experience. Depending then on the kind of experience which is considered (change, to be caused or beginning to be, corruptibility, degrees of perfection, or the pre-ordination to an end of certain beings which lack intelligence), the arguments conclude to a different specific condition of possibility of that experience (the existence of an unchanged changer, of a first cause which is not caused, of a necessary being, of a *maxime bonum* and *maxime ens*, of an intelligent being which orders natural things to their ends). These 'conditions of possibility' represent one or another of the attributes which are proper only of the Being traditionally called 'God'. The most famous and influential formulation of the a posteriori arguments are Thomas Aquinas's five ways. The kind of experience considered by them corresponds respectively to five different 'signs' of contingency given in our experience of the world. Following in the Thomistic tradition, Leibniz reduced the five ways to their general 'scheme', applying to the experience of contingency the principle of sufficient reason:

> we have also proved [the existence of God] a posteriori, since contingent beings exist, and their final or sufficient reason can be discovered only in a necessary being which has its reason for its existence in itself. (*Monadologie*, §45, 614/647; see also §32,612/645)

Despite his merciless ridicule of Leibniz in *Candide* (1759), Voltaire (1694–1778) adopted the Leibnizian proof from contingency as one of two arguments for the existence of God endorsed in his *Homélies* (1767). The other argument employed there was the so-called design argument.[31] This argument took different forms corresponding to the different kinds of 'design' or 'order' discovered in nature. Broadly speaking, it is possible to distinguish two main streams. The first one stressed purposefulness or finalism in nature; hence the alternative name, the 'teleological argument'. A version of it was the Thomist fifth way which presupposed Aristotelian finalism ascertainable not in the universe as a whole, but in a certain kind of being.[32] A different version was seventeenth- and eighteenth-century physico-theology which, following in the footsteps of Newton, recognised a 'design' in the laws of movement governing the universe as a whole.[33] Although Aristotelian finalism was replaced by a mechanistic conception of the universe, a form of teleology or purposefulness still held. The second main stream of design arguments stressed regularity. Both main forms – from purpose and from regularity – can be found in Voltaire's *Homélies*. Voltaire took over from English authors, particularly from the Newtonian Samuel Clarke (1675–1729),[34] the argument from regularity in nature. In the course of upholding the design argument and in order to defend teleology in the natural order, Voltaire found it necessary to refute the materialism proposed by La Méttrie.[35] On none of these fronts did he make an original contribution to philosophy, but Voltaire's writings – filled as they were with witty anecdotes and biting humour – did much to popularise the issues raised in the debate about God.

A similar position regarding the arguments for the existence of God is to be found in Jean-Jacques Rousseau's (1712–78) most eloquent statement of his religious convictions – the famous 'Profession de foi du vicaire savoyard' in book IV of *Émile*. Just as Voltaire favoured the argument from contingency and the design argument, Rousseau thought that the two arguments for God's existence which can withstand sceptical doubts and materialist claims are (1) the argument from causality (corresponding to the second sign of contingency in the world identified by Thomas Aquinas) and (2) the argument from order (that is, one of the versions of the design argument).

In order to understand the place of these arguments in Rousseau's strategy, it is necessary first to note his inversion of the Cartesian method of enquiry.[36] Descartes had assumed nothing to be true except that which was absolutely known to be true, but Rousseau assumed everything to be true except that which was the subject of real doubt. Descartes subjected his deepest intuitions to sceptical doubt and rational proof, whereas Rousseau tested sceptical arguments by his most deeply held intuitions, which he regarded as stronger and more reliable than rational proof.[37] This strategic difference preserved for Rousseau the presumption of theism. It also eased the requirements for any successful proof of God and tightened up the requirement for any putative 'disproof' of God. The burden of proof was shifted dramatically from believer to sceptic. In these circumstances, believers needed only to show that their imaginative intuitions of God were not contrary to reason and experience, whereas sceptics must demonstrate the truth of what were for Rousseau entirely counter-intuitive claims. The evidence produced by sceptical proofs must be sufficient to persuade him against his will to abandon his inner feelings and intuitions. Rousseau reckoned the odds of this occurring as being infinitesimal.

The structure of Rousseau's argument remained the Thomistic way *ex parte motus*, except that it moved directly into a design argument stressing the orderliness rather than the purposefulness of the universe. From both arguments, Rousseau concluded that materialism was incoherent and that no good reason had been found that would lead him to question his original intuitions. Indeed, everything he had found confirmed the inner feeling that the universe is governed by a wise and powerful will, appropriately called God, even if the nature and purposes of that Being remained unknowable to humankind (576–81).

The same consideration of the laws governing the universe led to opposite conclusions in two other prominent exponents of the French enlightenment: Denis Diderot (1713–84) and the baron d'Holbach. Both were confident that the scientific evidence proved movement to be essential to matter, which is both active and self-regulating, so that there is no need in the universe for a substance of a different kind to explain motion and the organisation of matter.

Diderot seems to have been converted to atheism slowly and even reluctantly, but eventually he accepted it without reservation. By the time he penned the *Pensées sur l'interpretation de la nature* (1753) he was overcome by the 'great revolution in the sciences' and no longer required a God to explain order in the universe. Philosophy herself would by experiment and reason lift the veil and discover nature's hidden Truth. In struggling toward an immanent explanation of the unity, movement, and order of the universe, Diderot in effect reinterpreted Spinoza's phrase '*Deus sive natura*' as expressing disjunction, $a \vee b$, and not logical equivalence, $a = b$. For Diderot, the naturalistic disproof of God would run: *Deus sive natura; non Deus; ergo natura.*[38] Nature's force is itself endlessly creative and eternally in motion, without recourse to transcendent cause or to immanent spirit. From this point onward, Diderot had no need of God as an explanatory principle.

D'Holbach was even more resolute in his rejection of God. The idea of God as an independent, spiritual being was for him incoherent and incredible. God is Nature, the cause of all that is. The worship of God is misplaced wonder before Nature. The attributes of God are misattributed qualities of Nature, which lead to paradoxes when predicated of a single being but not when predicated of Nature as a whole. The proofs of God can likewise be subverted as proofs of Nature – not as proofs of the 'existence' of Nature, for that is simply a fact, but as proofs of the attributes of Nature insofar as they can be known. Clarke had used Newton-like proofs from causality and order to demonstrate the metaphysical and moral attributes of God. In his *Systême de la nature* (1770), d'Holbach mimicked those theistic proofs in order to show that the metaphysical attributes were right but the subject wrong and that the moral attributes applied neither to God nor to Nature itself but emerged out of Nature.[39] Throughout the *Systême de la nature*, arguments set up by Clarke to refute materialism were inverted by d'Holbach in its defence. He did, however, resist the temptation to anthropomorphise Nature in the manner that all theists and some deists use to project essentially human qualities onto their God. For instance, Nature does not 'think' but it produces through an unceasing chain of causes and effects the organisation of matter from which intelligence emerges.

Toward the end of the century the debate about God was in remission in France, but it continued in Britain – where scientists exhibited far more positive support for God and the established religion of the land. Indeed, the argument from design was never more popular than it was in Great Britain long after leading French intellectuals had come to regard the word 'God' as no more than an anthropomorphic way of talking about Nature.

In Germany the situation was quite different. The most eager (if not the most trustworthy) interpreter of Leibniz – Christian Wolff (1679–1754) – shaped the framework of the debate on the proofs of God's existence, even though he had little of originality and substance to contribute. Wolff invented no new proof of God. He did invent a new taxonomy of the branches of philosophy, however, and achieved a new clarity on the place of the existing proofs within them. Through the widespread use of his *Theologia naturalis* as a textbook in faculties of both philosophy and theology, Wolff's account of the arguments for the existence of God became a template to be copied by followers and opponents alike.[40] Moreover, his taxonomy of philosophical disciplines and his designation of theology's place within them provided essential ingredients for the taxonomy Kant would later use in his critique of rational theology.

In line with Wolff's conception of philosophy as the science of possibles,[41] natural theology was declared the science of those things that are possible *per Deum*, for and through God (*Theologia*, Pt 1, §§1ff; *Discursus*, §57). In Wolff's scheme of things, natural theology is not a free-standing activity, capable of generating all its own principles. It depends, rather, on the other branches of metaphysics (ontology, cosmology, and psychology) for its necessary principles (*Theologia*, Pt 1, §11; *Discursus*, §96). Implicit in the account of ontology, cosmology, and teleology (as a sub-branch of physics) in Wolff's *Discursus praeliminaris de philosophia in genere* are links to the three proofs of God discussed in his writings: the a priori proof from possible being, the a posteriori proof from the contingency of the world, and a 'teleological' proof from order and purpose in the world. Although he did not explicitly identify the three proofs with ontology, cosmology, and teleology, he did in effect associate each proof with the principles generated by each of those branches.

Wolff's way of classifying the arguments for the existence of God were taken over by other philosophers, including Moses Mendelssohn (1729–86) and Kant. It was Kant, however, who gave names to the arguments that are derived from Wolff's classification of philosophy's branches: onto-theology (ontological argument), cosmo-theology (cosmological argument), and physico-theology (physico-theological argument) – a minor, terminological landmark in the history of ideas.[42] Furthermore, it was Kant who first recognized and exploited the implications of Wolff's account of the necessary dependency of physics and cosmology on ontology for the proofs of God that are associated with each: physico-theology and cosmo-theology both depend finally for their success on principles secured by onto-theology. Since, according to Kant, the ontological argument fails, the other two arguments necessarily fail as well.

The cosmological argument (corresponding to the general scheme of the a posteriori argument and explicitly identified with the Leibnizian argument *ex contingentia mundi*) was so called by Kant because it deals with 'the object of all possible experience', that is, the world (*Kritik*, A 604–5/B 632–3). It has two steps: (1) from experience of existence in general (for instance, my own existence) to the existence of an absolutely necessary being; (2) from the existence of an absolutely necessary being to the existence of the *ens realissimum* (the most perfect being, the *ens perfectissimum*).[43] But, asked Kant, how is the claim justified that the necessary being is the *ens realissimum*? The experience from which the existence of the necessary being has been concluded (the first step of the proof) cannot tell us what properties this necessary being might have. Necessary existence is attributed to the *ens realissimum* in virtue of 'an old argument . . . disguised . . . as a new one', the old argument being the ontological proof. It is in fact presupposed that only the concept of *ens realissimum* 'contains within itself the required conditions (*requisita*) for an absolute necessity' (A 606–7/B 634–5). Kant therefore concluded that

> it is clear that here one presupposes that the concept of a being of the highest reality completely suffices for the concept of an absolute necessity in existence, i.e., that from the former [the *ens realissimum*] the latter [necessary existence] may be inferred – a proposition the ontological proof asserted, which one thus assumes in the cosmological proof and takes as one's ground. (A 607/B 635)

So the cosmological argument presupposes the ontological argument and therefore collapses with it.

The third and last possible way of proving the existence of God was, according to Kant, the physico-theological argument. Unlike the cosmological argument which 'abstracts from every particular property of objects of experience through which this world might differ from any other possible world', the physico-theological argument 'uses observations about the particular constitution of this sensible world of ours for its grounds of proof' (A 605/B 633). What Kant had in mind here was, broadly speaking, the design argument. Now, 'the proof could at most establish a highest *architect* of the world . . . not a *creator*' (A 627/B 655). In order to move from the existence of an architect to that of a creator, this argument must appeal to the cosmological argument and is therefore in the last instance invalid (A 629/B 657).

IV. NEW DIRECTIONS

Kant's general conclusion was that reason, in its merely speculative employment, cannot demonstrate the existence of a supreme being (*Kritik*, A 639/B 667).

There is, however, another way of reason to God: the way of morality. Where speculative reason fails, practical reason succeeds.

The primacy of practical reason over speculative reason in philosophy, including rational theology, is already clear in Kant's lectures on metaphysics of 1773–4 (see, for instance, Ak 5.1: 301). We live within the boundaries of our experience of this world, marked off *a parte ante* by God and *a parte post* by the world to come. Since these things lie beyond the limits of possible experience, however, we cannot actually know them. Yet a belief in a creator of this world and a hope for a future life arise in us naturally as knowledge of possible objects of human experience. Indeed, belief in a Creator and Governor of the world is necessary for us in order to make sense of our intuitions, of our experience, and of the moral law's demands on us. The existence of such a being can be no more than a presumption – which Kant, like Leibniz, held to be rational while the presumption of atheism was irrational – but the concept of God is a necessary hypothesis or presupposition of pure, empirical, and practical reason (Ak 5.1: 304, 322). The traditional proofs of God are thereby transformed by Kant from abortive efforts at demonstrating the existence of such a being into viable aids in constructing a concept of God sufficient to the needs of reason, experience, and morality.

Kant's earlier argument a priori survives explicitly in the lectures on metaphysics, and implicitly in the first *Kritik*, not as a transcendental proof of God's existence, but as a necessary presupposition of pure reason able to give practical certainty to our natural belief in what he would later term the 'transcendental ideal' (*Kritik*, A 571–84/B 599–612). The earlier argument's continued presence in the first *Kritik* is sometimes overlooked because it did not appear in the account of rational theology, which had been simplified to make sharper the critique of any possible proof that employed reason speculatively and not practically.

Paradoxically, however, the traditional arguments for the existence of God became necessary for Kant as postulates of practical reason in a way they never had been for Kant as demonstrations (*Beweisgrund*, Ak 2: 163). They took on the function of regulating or correcting false and impure concepts of God (Ak 5.1: 307). Kant's critical philosophy was the first major attempt to construct a rational theology grounded neither in the truths of revelation nor in the truths of speculative reason. This was managed by making theoretical reason serve the needs of practical reason, so that moral certainty was all that would be required to sustain a rational belief in God (Ak 5.1: 304). Kant made no effort to show that the God who was a natural and necessary postulate of reason was also the God of Abraham, Isaac, and Jacob. His purified God was the God of the philosophers *par excellence*.

Johann Gottlieb Fichte (1762–1814) showed essential agreement with Kant that morality is the *Hauptsache*, that practical reason is the ground of metaphysics and of religion as well. In the *Versuch einer Kritik aller Offenbarung* (1792), his most parasitically Kantian production, Fichte adopted the transcendental mode in order to deduce the idea of revelation by the principles of practical reason. Religion is understood not as belief in the existence of a being called 'God', but as belief in the moral law as divine, with the divine attributes adding to its authority in our lives.[44] To arrive at the idea of revelation from principles of practical reason, without recourse to the revelatory claims of any particular religion, however, Fichte made unconventional use of the shadowy proofs of God, understood with Kant as necessary postulates of reason.[45]

Fichte gathered around him a circle of keen philosophy students, whose development he oversaw. Among those he encouraged was Friedrich C. Forberg (1770–1848), whose essay on the 'Entwicklung des Begriffes der Religion' ('Development of the Concept of Religion') was published with Fichte's 'Über den Grund unseres Glaubens an eine göttliche Weltregierung' ('On the Ground of Our Belief in a Divine Government of the World') in the *Philosophisches Journal* (1798), co-edited by Fichte. This unwittingly initiated the so-called *Atheismusstreit* that occasioned his unwilling and probably avoidable resignation from Jena in 1799.[46] Fichte and Forberg concluded that the Kantian critique of natural theology and the Kantian elevation of practical reason to primacy affected not just the way we postulate God, but also the God that is postulated (*Werke*, 5: 267ff). The God that is a necessary postulate of pure practical reason is not a being (*ein Seyn*) who may or may not exist; the God that is necessary is pure act (*ein reines Handeln*) (5: 261, 267). God is the striving after the triumph of good over evil; to speak of God is to speak of the sovereignty of the moral law (5: 185, 186, 187f). Whether God as an independent being exists or not has no practical consequences, but whether or not we work for the triumph of good does matter supremely. What is it then to be an atheist? The 'true atheist', Fichte pleaded, is not the person who denies that God has independent existence, but the person who fails to follow the sovereign moral principle in his life, the person who thinks that evil means can achieve the good (5: 188, 185). A person believes in God, according to Fichte, insofar as a striving toward the moral good is sovereign in that person's life. Is this statement a criterion or a definition of belief in God? Although the texts are not unambiguous, both Forberg and Fichte seemed inclined to the latter view. God is the moral order; to follow the moral law is to believe in God.

Kant's critique of all theology was not finally effective, however, in disposing of every possible argument for the existence of God by undermining confidence in the so-called ontological argument. His critique could not cover every type of a priori argument, including perhaps the one he himself formulated as a young man. The hydra-headed argument a priori would not in fact be defeated so easily. Even if Moses Mendelssohn's version were not itself finally victorious, the proof a priori did gain new devotees in Germany.[47] A prominent example is the unashamed endorsement of that proof by Kant's erstwhile but disaffected pupil Johann Gottfried Herder (1744–1803) in *Gott: Einige Gespräche* (1787), a second edition of which appeared in 1800 as *Einige Gespräche über Spinozas System*. Notwithstanding Kant's strictures on the powers of reason and his objections to the ontological argument, Herder had his spokesman in the dialogues confidently speaking of God as the necessary condition for the possibility of rationality itself, so that if there were no God, there could be no rationality.[48]

Finally, a transformed ontological argument was soon given new life by Hegel as part of a speculative project the boldness of which Kant could scarcely have imagined possible. According to Hegel, the ontological argument infers Being from 'the *abstractum* of Thought'. The chief objection against this procedure is the Kantian contention that 'Being cannot be deduced from the notion by any analysis.'[49] The uniformly favourable reception and acceptance of this objection, Hegel continued, was undoubtedly due to the example of the hundred dollars used by Kant to explain the difference between thought and being, and one would have thought that such a basic distinction would not have escaped philosophers. The truth of the matter is, however, that this distinction holds only in the case of such finite objects as the hundred dollars:

It is in fact this and this alone which marks everything finite: – its being in time and space is discrepant from its notion. God, on the contrary, expressly has to be what can only be 'thought as existing'; His notion involves being. It is this unity of the notion and being that constitutes the notion of God. (108)

The key point on which Hegel's re-proposition of the ontological argument rests is that for him, as opposed to Kant, thought is not just the finite activity of a finite thinking subject. On the contrary, the principle of 'idealism' is that 'reason is consciousness' certainty of being all reality'.[50] Authentic 'thinking' (*denken*) does not coincide with mere 'representing' (*vorstellen*); 'concept' (*Begriff*) is not mere 'representation' (*Vorstellung*). It is as 'represented' that the object of thinking is not real. On the other hand, the concept (*Begriff*) grasps (*begriffen*) the object in its reality (*Logic*, 211). As Hegel put it in his *Vorlesungen über die Philosophie der Religion* (1832), the problem with Kant's example of the hundred dollars is precisely that he confused 'concept' and 'representation':

[I]n ordinary life we do indeed call a representation of a hundred dollars a concept. It is not a concept, however, but only a content-determination of my consciousness; an abstract sensible representation such as 'blue', or a determinacy of the understanding that is within my head, can of course lack being. This sort of thing however, is not to be called a concept. We must take the concept as such, we must take the absolute concept in its consummate form or the concept in and for itself, the concept of God – and this concept contains being as a determinacy.[51]

The concept, taken 'in and for itself', by its very nature coincides with being: 'that the notion, in its most abstract terms, involves being is plain' (*Logic*, 108). Being is indeed the 'very poorest and most abstract' of all categories – the minimum of reality – and 'certainly it would be strange if the notion, the very inmost of mind . . . , or above all, the concrete totality we call God, were not rich enough to include so poor a category as being' (108–9). In short, strictly speaking, it is not the concept of God which implies being, but the concept as such. On the other hand, this latter is for Hegel nothing else than the concept of God – a God which 'becomes', starting from the poorest content of the concept (being) until becoming spirit.[52] As his striking phrase in the *Vorlesungen über die Philosophie der Religion* reads, 'this is the concept as such, the concept of God, the absolute concept; this is just what God is.'[53] With the great German idealist, one of the constantly recurring topics of natural theology – Anselm's widely celebrated and not less fiercely criticised a priori argument for the existence of God – had been completely transfigured to serve the purposes of an immanent vision of reality as far removed as possible from that of the medieval thinker.

NOTES

1 See Pierre Bayle, *Dictionaire historique et critique* (1697), 3 vols. (Rotterdam, 1702), 'Bunel', E.; 'Hipparchia', D.; *et passim*.

2 See Bayle, *Dictionaire*, 'Acosta', G.

3 See Bayle, *Dictionaire*, 'Simonides', F.

4 See Bayle, *Dictionaire*, 'Pyrrho', C.

5 See Bayle, *Dictionaire*, 'Bunel', E.

6 See Bayle, *Dictionaire*, entries on China, Japan, and the 'Manichaeans'.

7 Bayle's early attraction to Descartes is apparent in his exposition of Cartesian metaphysics in the *Système de philosophie*, written in Sedan between 1675 and 1677, and in his *Dissertation* (1680) in defence of 'quelques Cartésiens' (Claude Clerselier, Jacques Rohault, and Nicolas Malebranche) against the Jesuit Louis de Valois (*Oeuvres diverses* (The Hague, 1727–31), ed. E. Labrousse, 5 vols. (Hildesheim, 1964–2001), 4: 479ff.; 109ff.). The method of enquiry followed in his *Dictionaire* was a development or 'transposition' of the Cartesian method. See Elisabeth Labrousse, *Pierre Bayle*, 2 vols. (The Hague, 1963–4), vol. 2: *Hétérodoxie et rigorisme* (1964), 39ff.

8 Immanuel Kant, *Der einzig mögliche Beweisgrund zu einer Demonstration des Daseins Gottes* (1763), in Ak 2: 63–163 (*Beweisgrund*); translated as *The Only Possible Argument in Support of a Demonstration of the Existence of God*, in *Works/Theoretical Philosophy, 1755–1770*, trans. and eds. D. Walford and R. Meerbote (1992); here at 163.

9 Friedrich Heinrich Jacobi, *Werke*, eds. F. Roth and F. Köppen, 6 vols. (Leipzig, 1812–25), 4.2: 155.

10 Jacobi, *Werke*, 4.1: xli *et passim*.
11 Jacobi, *Briefwechsel*, eds. M. Brüggen, S. Sudhof, et al. (Stuttgart, 1981–), 1.1: 160–1.
12 Jacobi, *Werke*, 4.1: 223; 4.2: 125ff.
13 See Friedrich Schleiermacher, *Der christliche Glaube* (Berlin, 1821–2).
14 Nicolas l'Herminier, *Summa theologiae*, 8 vols. (Paris, 1718–19), 1: 24ff.
15 Claude-François Houtteville, *La vérité de la religion chrétienne prouvée par les faits* (Paris, 1722); Claude Buffier, *Traité des premières véritez et de la source de nos jugements* (Paris, 1724), and *Elémens de métaphysique* (Paris, 1725).
16 Paul-Henri Thiry d'Holbach, *Théologie portative ou dictionnaire abrégé de la Religion Chrétienne* (London [in fact, Amsterdam], 1768), 'Concorde'.
17 Jean Meslier, *Oeuvres complètes*, eds. J. Deprun, R. Desné, and A. Soboul, 3 vols. (Paris, 1970–2), 2: 149–525.
18 See Meslier's notes in the margins of Fénelon's *Démonstration de l'existence de Dieu* and of Tournemine's *Réflexions sur l'athéisme*, ed. J. Deprun and printed in Meslier, *Oeuvres*, 3: 209–388. Though direct evidence is less strong, it has been suggested that Meslier's case was developed in close dependence on l'Herminier's critique of the proofs of God in his *Summa theologiae*. See A. C. Kors, *Atheism in France, 1650–1729* (Princeton, NJ, 1990), 374, note 60.
19 See Gottfried Wilhelm Leibniz, *Essais de théodicée* (1710), 'Discours preliminaire de la conformité de la Foy avec la Raison', §61, in *Phil. Schriften*, vol. 6.
20 For a detailed discussion of Leibniz's version of the ontological argument, see Robert M. Adams, *Leibniz. Determinist, Theist, Idealist* (Oxford, 1994), 134–56.
21 See Anselm of Canterbury, *Proslogion*, ch. 2, in *Patrologia Latina*, ed. J.-P. Migne, 158: 227–8.
22 René Descartes, *Meditations on First Philosophy*, in *Descartes: Selected Philosophical Writings*, trans. J. Cottingham, R. Stoothoff, and D. Murdoch (Cambridge, 1988), 106–7. See *Oeuvres*, 7: 65.
23 See Descartes's Fifth Meditation.
24 See Gottfried Wilhelm Leibniz, *Nouveaux essais* (1703–1705), IV.x.7, in Akademie-Ausgabe, VI.6: 437–8; translated as *New Essays on Human Understanding*, trans. and eds. P. Remnant and J. Bennett (Cambridge, 1981).
25 Leibniz, *Monadologie* (1714), §41 in *Phil. Schriften*, 6: 613; translated in *Philosophical Papers and Letters*, by L.E. Loemker (Dordrecht, 1969), 646–7. The first set of page numbers refer to vol. 6 of *Phil. Schriften*, the second set to the translation.
26 See Adams, *Leibniz*, 177–91.
27 See Augustine, *De libero arbitrio*, in *Patrologia Latina*, 32: 1243ff.
28 See Leibniz, *Specimen inventorum de admirandis naturae Generalis arcanis* in *Phil. Schriften*, 7: 311.
29 Ak 2: 72ff; and *Kritik der reinen Vernunft*, 1st edn. 1781 (Ak 4), hereafter 'A'; 2nd edn. 1787 (Ak 3), hereafter 'B', A 592ff/B 620ff.; translated as *Critique of Pure Reason*, trans. and eds. P. Guyer and A.W. Wood in *Works* (1988). See Adams, *Leibniz*, 182–3.
30 See Gordon Treash's 'Introduction' in the parallel edition of *Beweisgrund/The One Possible Basis for a Demonstration of the Existence of God*, trans. G. Treash (Lincoln, NE, 1994); and A.W. Wood, *Kant's Rational Theology* (Ithaca, NY, 1978), 64–79.
31 On the importance of the design argument in the British context see 24, this volume chapter.
32 The fifth way appeals to *aliqua quae cognitione carent* (some things which lack the capacity to know).
33 A typical example is the General Scholium added by Newton to the second edition of his *Philosophiae naturalis principia mathematica* (Cambridge, 1713).
34 See p. 672 in chapter 22.
35 See also 'Fin, causes finales' in Voltaire, *Dictionnaire philosophique* (London [in fact, Geneva], 1764).

36 See Jean-Jacques Rousseau, *Émile, ou De l'education* (Amsterdam, 1762), in *Oeuvres*, 4: 567ff.

37 See Rousseau, *Émile*, 570. The imperative to trust one's 'inner light' is a *Leitmotif* that runs through *Émile*.

38 Denis Diderot, *Oeuvres philosophiques*, ed. P. Vernière (Paris, 1964), 224ff.

39 See d'Holbach, *Systême de la nature, ou, Des loix du monde physique & du monde moral*, 2 vols. (London [in fact, Amsterdam], 1770), vol. 2.ii.

40 See Christian Wolff, *Theologia naturalis, methodo scientifica pertractata* (Frankfurt and Leipzig, 1736–7) in *Werke*, II.7–8.

41 See Wolff, *Discursus praeliminaris de philosophia in genere* (Frankfurt and Leipzig, 1728), §29.

42 See Kant, *Beweisgrund*, Ak 2: 160 and 116f.

43 Kant, *Kritik*, A 590–1/B 618–19; A 604–6/B 632–4. See also Sofia Vanni Rovighi, *La filosofia e il problema di Dio* (Milan, 1986), 142.

44 See Johann Gottlieb Fichte, *Werke*, 5: 39ff.

45 Fichte made novel use of the proof a priori (*Versuch* 79ff.), the proof a posteriori (84ff.) and the 'physical' or teleological proof (106ff.).

46 The main primary texts of the controversy are available in two editions: *Fichte und Forberg: Die philosophischen Schriften zum Atheismusstreit*, ed. F. Medicus (Leipzig, 1910); *Die Schriften zu J.G. Fichte's Atheismus-Streit*, ed. H. Linday (Munich, 1912). The material by Fichte, published and unpublished, is included in Fichte, *Werke*, 5: 175–396.

47 In the final chapter of his *Morgenstunden oder Vorlesungen über das Daseyn Gottes* (Berlin, 1785), Moses Mendelssohn attempted to defend a modified version of his proof a priori against Kantian objections.

48 See Johann Gottfried Herder, *Gott: Einige Gespräche* in *Sämmtliche Werke*, ed. B. Suphan, 33 vols. (Berlin, 1877–1913), vol. 16; translated as *God: Some Conversations*, by F. H. Burkhardt (Indianapolis, IN, 1940), 149ff.

49 *Die Wissenschaft der Logik* is the first part of Hegel's *Enzyklopädie der philosophischen Wissenschaften im Grundrisse* (Heidelberg, 1817; 2nd edn. 1827; 3rd edn. 1830), §51. Page references are to the translation, *The Logic of Hegel*, trans. W. Wallace, 2nd edn. (Oxford, 1892), 107.

50 *Phänomenologie des Geistes*, ed. J. Hoffmeister (Hamburg, 1952), 176, 178. Quoted from Quentin Lauer, *Hegel's Concept of God* (Albany, NY, 1982), 207.

51 Georg Wilhelm Friedrich Hegel, *Lectures on the Philosophy of Religion*, trans. by R. F. Brown, P. C. Hodgson, and J. M. Stewart (Berkeley, CA, 1984), 1: 436.

52 See Vanni Rovighi, *La filosofia e il problema di Dio*, 159.

53 Hegel, *Lectures on the Philosophy of Religion*, 1: 436–7. The most detailed treatment by Hegel of the proofs of the existence of God is to be found in his *Vorlesungen über die Beweise vom Dasein Gottes* (1829), ed. G. Lasson (Leipzig, 1930).

26

THE PROBLEM OF THEODICY

LUCA FONNESU

It is not difficult to agree with the scholars who maintain that the eighteenth century saw the end of philosophical theodicy, or at least of an important chapter in its history.[1] The decisive attack on rational theodicy (and theology) was by Pierre Bayle at the end of the seventeenth century. Much of his work is intended to illustrate the impossibility of a rational, hence philosophical, solution to the question of evil in the world. The Christian conscience, on his view, has to choose between reason (that is, scepticism and ultimately atheism) and fideist religion.

The most important response to Bayle is Leibniz's *Théodicée*, which is, on the one hand, an attempt to revive old categories already destroyed by Bayle and, on the other, an original metaphysical construction, which yet does not fulfil its aim of justifying evil. Leibniz's philosophy, still rooted in the metaphysical framework of the seventeenth century, was one of the main topics of European philosophical discussion in the first half of the eighteenth century. With regard to the question of evil, the so-called optimism of the German philosopher was discussed, defended or condemned, sometimes trivialised and equated with the naive optimism of Alexander Pope.

The question of the human condition and its capabilities became central in mid-century when the crisis in the great metaphysical systems of the past became clear. Worries and doubts that might undermine an optimistic view of the universe and human existence are highlighted in the writings of Samuel Johnson and particularly in Voltaire's literary and philosophical works. Voltaire's very ambiguity toward religion is an excellent key to understanding the multiplicity of attitudes in the century, including its characteristic anxiety. In Germany, where intellectual life did not adopt a polemical attitude to metaphysics and religion, significant thinkers investigated the question of the human condition and the problem of man's destiny, while renouncing the rigid framework of the scholastic tradition.

The writings which, following Bayle, show the *collapse* of rational theodicy date from around 1750: Hume's *Dialogues concerning Natural Religion* (1779) again prove the contradictory position of rationalist theology and describe human reason as faced with a choice between atheism and fideism. From this it is a short step to use the same arguments against the existence of God. What Bayle wrote against idolatry was now directed by d'Holbach against Christianity itself. Kant and Rousseau, on the other hand, consider the question in new ways. Kant, disputing the possibility of a philosophical theodicy, at the same time indicates, through his concept of practical reason, a new way of looking at a particular aspect of it. Rousseau views the question of evil in the context of the social and historical formation of modern humankind.

The question of the relationship between faith and reason in Leibniz's response to Bayle is discussed in Section I. Section II considers Leibniz's theodicy and the debate on optimism. Section III focuses on the central problem of the human condition in Johnson, Voltaire, and the idea of the destiny of man current in the German *Spätaufklärung*. Section IV shows the collapse of theodicy in Hume's *Dialogues* and d'Holbach's explicit atheism, and Section V analyses the new approaches offered by Kant and Rousseau.

I. FAITH AND REASON

The term *theodicy* first appears in philosophical language with the publication of Gottfried Wilhelm Leibniz's *Essais de théodicée sur la bonté de Dieu, la liberté de l'homme et l'origine du mal* (1710).[2] The introduction shows how aware the writer was of the danger of Bayle's attack on rational theodicy: his answer must begin with proof of the 'conformity of faith to reason'. But even the title of his book recalls Bayle: God's goodness is to be defended here, at least programmatically, and it is this very goodness which for Bayle is the most important and puzzling attribute of the Deity. In his *Dictionnaire historique et critique* (1697) Bayle recalls the question of Epicurus: God, says Epicurus, is either willing to remove evil, but cannot; or he can but is not willing; or he neither can nor will; or else he both can and will. If the first, he must be weak, which cannot be true of God; if the second, he must be envious, which is likewise contrary to his nature. If the third, he must be both envious and weak and cannot be God; if the last, which alone agrees with notions of God, whence then comes evil?[3]

In this famous passage it is not difficult to identify Bayle's strategy in attacking rational views of the Christian God. His attributes are pitted against each other, to show the contradictory view of God in *every* form of Christian thought, particularly when this God is faced with the problem of evil. Strangely, our reason is fated to see that Manichaeans can better explain the facts of experience than can orthodox thinkers, though, as Bayle ironically adds, the former start from an absurd and contradictory hypothesis and the latter from a right, necessary, and true supposition ('Pauliciens', as above). The old Augustinian answers to the Manichaeans cannot convince Bayle. The idea that evil is not something positive but just a *privation of being* which characterises finite creatures – the so-called metaphysical evil – is contrary to all evidence of actual suffering and crime on earth. Moreover, why imperfection should imply suffering is incomprehensible ('Marcionites', n. F, 711) and still more so is the idea that suffering is a punishment for human sin and crime. A good and all-powerful God should rather have created Adam without a tendency to evil ('Manichéens', n. D, 704). Bayle concludes that human reason is too weak for this task: the only solution that remains is the submission of reason to Christian faith, the only weapon divine revelation ('Pauliciens', n. E, 858). In his *Éclaircissement sur les Pyrrhoniens* Bayle sets out his main thesis clearly. We must choose between philosophy (that is, reason) and the gospel: whichever we choose, we must abandon the other.

Like John Toland in *Christianity not Mysterious* (1696), Bayle maintains that the fictitious distinction between what is *above* and what *against* reason cannot be helpful.[4] In the *Reponse aux questions d'un provincial* (1703–6) he explains that the distinction is fictitious if by reason we mean God's reason, because mysteries are neither above nor against God's reason, and equally so if we mean human reason, as our reason can explain neither what is above nor what is against it. Throughout the century most defenders of divine justice, such as Leibniz, Jaquelot, Le Clerc, or later, Crousaz and Houtteville,[5] were to preserve this distinction, while Anthony Collins, in this too, was a follower of Toland. A peculiar position was that adopted by such a pious thinker as Pierre Poiret who, at the end of his life, finally convinced of the frailty of reason, refused the distinction and accepted the fideist solution offered by his old adversary from Rotterdam.[6]

Leibniz's revival of the distinction rejected by Bayle must be considered within the rationalist project of the *Théodicée*. He understands that the conflict of faith and reason is actually a conflict between two gifts of God and thus a dangerous attack on the concept of God.[7] This is why he urges the validity of the distinction, both for asserting a rationalistic theology and for defending particular aspects of the Christian faith, such as the Trinity.[8] For Leibniz, real contradiction is only proved of propositions that contradict eternal, that is, mathematical truths, not of those that merely contradict contingent truths or truths of fact (*Discours*, §§2, 23). In the former case we must choose between articles of faith and reason, and Leibniz thinks that in this case we must choose the rational solution, abandoning the article of faith (§39; *Théodicée*, §294), but this is a borderline case. In principle, his point is that mysteries can contradict contingent laws of nature – be *above* reason – but not necessary truths, be *against* reason (§3, 51/75 and §22, 63/87).

Leibniz's argument on how far human beings can understand God's reason and actions is directed against two positions that for him are, though opposed, equally dangerous. On the one hand, philosophy has to prove, against Bayle, its ability to speak rationally of the concept and attributes of God, demonstrating his goodness and justice. On the other, he thinks a voluntarist conception of God no less dangerous to rational theology, a danger arising in connection with the complex question of eternal truths. For the question of evil, the problem is crucial. If God's rules are completely different from ours, if his power has no limits at all, we can pretend neither to judge the existence of evil in the world nor to justify it. Therefore Leibniz criticises the voluntarist concept of God suggested, on his view, by Descartes and some Cartesians. It is a new version of the old dispute between theological voluntarism and theological rationalism and here Leibniz unhesitatingly agrees with Bayle: the rules of divine justice are the same as ours.[9] Leibniz's philosophical construct is, in fact, founded on the qualitative analogy of man's and God's reason. God's perfections are not different from ours, though they are without limits, and our *lumière naturelle* differs from God's reason 'as a drop of water from the ocean', that is, our reason is based on the same principles, being just a gift of God (*Théodicée*, Préface, 27/51; *Discours*, §61, 84/107; §4, 41/75).

II. THEODICIES

1. *Leibniz*

The revival of the distinction between what is above reason and what against it is not the only traditional argument in Leibniz's *Theodicée*, most of which is, on the contrary, a learned review of the long debate about evil. We can identify three main threads in his argument, only one of which is new and original. His first traditional line of argument is the minimisation of evil in the world from both a physical and a moral point of view. He has in mind the pessimistic view of the human condition and human nature so often expressed by Bayle: humankind is evil and wretched and everyone is aware of this truth.[10] Leibniz counters this with a decidedly positive view of human existence and moral nature (*Théodicée*, §§13, 148, 251, pp. 109, 198, 266/130, 216, 281). Although our vices outnumber our virtues, the vicious nature of human beings must not be overstressed, he writes, because this judgement could be used to criticise Providence.[11] Perhaps he realises the frailty of the minimisation-of-evil argument, because he tries to defend a positive view of reality even against the argument that life on earth is not really very good, an argument that gained currency after the publication of Fontenelle's *Entretiens sur la pluralité des mondes* (1686). This argument was also used apologetically by Ralph Cudworth and in the works of King, Jaquelot, and Le Clerc as a defence against Bayle's pessimism. Happiness and virtue, if not in this world, would, unknown to us, prevail in other worlds of God's universe (*Théodicée*, §§19, 123, 129, 221, pp. 114, 177–8, 248–9, 250/134–5, 197, 264, 265–6).

The most important traditional themes in the *Théodicée* are Neoplatonic in origin. Apart from themes like the necessity of particular evil for the good of the whole or the image of a 'great chain of being', Leibniz's second traditional argument is the tripartition of evil into the metaphysical, the moral, and the physical.[12] He thus reintroduces the concept of evil as privation, the result of the original imperfection of human beings, a notion rejected by both Bayle and Malebranche.[13] Following the Christian tradition, physical evil is seen mainly as a punishment for sin and crime, though sometimes as a means to greater good and a better enjoyment of it (*Théodicée*, §241, p. 261/276; §17, p. 111/132; §23, p. 116/137). But the *Théodicée* clearly states that it is metaphysical evil which is the foundation of all other forms of evil (*Théodicée*, §156, p. 203/221; §288, p. 288/302–3).

Leibniz was not the first to revive the concept of metaphysical evil after its refutation by Malebranche and Bayle. A few years before the appearance of the *Théodicée* the Anglican bishop William King published in London his *De origine mali* (1702).[14] This book was very influential throughout the century, particularly after the publication of the English translation, and was to be the main source for the entry 'mal' in the *Encyclopédie*.[15] The importance of King's work is evidenced by Leibniz's discussion of it in an appendix to the *Théodicée*, 'Remarques sur le livre du l'origine du mal . . . ' (*Théodicée*, pp. 400–36/405–42). There are several points in common between Leibniz and King. Both seek to defend divine justice from Bayle's attack, using the whole arsenal of traditional arguments, such as the great chain of being and the variety of the universe, and both criticise the alleged anthropomorphism of Bayle's position. But the most important feature they share is the use of the concept of metaphysical evil.

King's chapter on the definition of evil starts from the classical tripartition and here too metaphysical evil plays the chief role.[16] Though Leibniz agrees with most of King's work, he cannot agree with the conception of God's and man's free will that he finds in *De origine mali*. This is the theory of free will as *libertas indifferentiae*, freedom in the absolute sense, without any determination, which Leibniz thinks neither possible nor adequate for the exercise of reason by either God or man, and for which he reproaches Descartes and his followers.[17] For him, the *libertas indifferentiae* implies the nullification of one of the two founding principles of his philosophy, that of sufficient reason, which determines all events and actions of the universe, including the actions of God and men. (The other principle is that of contradiction.) This principle, as we shall see, is the central point of his most original theory in the *Théodicée*, that of the best possible world. *Libertas indifferentiae* for God would imply an arbitrary Deity, while for human beings it would imply that their decisions were casual. Altogether, the presence of absolute freedom in any form whatever would eliminate one of the main features of Leibniz's universe, the rational, well-grounded connection of all things.

The idea of freedom is central to King's view. He believes that the defence of God's absolute freedom, in the moral sense alone, not including the realm of eternal truths, is the only means of preserving his power. With regard to man, a determined will, as in Leibniz's conception, would imply a determinist universe (*Origin of Evil*, V.1.ii, §1, 229). Moreover, human freedom is similar in quality to God's, though not infinite, because it is a gift from God to us. With this view of human freedom King can finally distinguish between moral and physical evil. The most interesting aspect of Leibniz's *Théodicée*, however, is not the revival of traditional themes like the minimisation of evil or evil as privation of being. A strong a priori thesis underlies the whole construct of God's justice: that this world is the best possible. Unlike most eighteenth-century apologetics, this is probably the only one after Bayle to propose a new theoretical approach to the problem of theodicy: in this sense, Leibniz's is the last philosophical theodicy.[18]

For Leibniz God's understanding is not identical with his will. The former contains the whole realm of possibility (that which is not contradictory) and the act of creation is God's deliberate choice of one combination of possibilities. To become real, each possibility has to be compossible[19] with other elements of a combination, that is, of a world; God chooses this as the best possible combination. Leibniz thinks that God requires a sufficient reason for creating the world and this is that there can be a *best* possible world, and only one. If there had not been such a world God would have created nothing (*Théodicée*, §8, 107/128). This is Leibniz's answer to the question running through Western philosophy until Heidegger: why is there something rather than nothing.[20]

The theory of the best possible world is a separate strand in the context of Leibniz's theodicy. The preponderance of good over evil, in both a natural and a moral sense, and the emphasis on the imperfections of created beings are not directly implied by it. They are rather signs of Leibniz's apologetic position, and the theory of the best possible world may be interpreted as pessimistic. The world is certainly not good but cannot be different and so must be accepted as it is.[21]

Leibniz starts his a priori thesis from a factual position, that there is a world. Since this is so and God can also be shown to exist, God must have acted for reasons that we can understand. But for him the creation of the best possible world is the only possible reason for acting. In spite of all the limitations of evil, this argument becomes the central one as Leibniz admits:

> It is true that one may imagine possible worlds without sin and without wretchedness . . . but these same worlds again would be very inferior to ours in goodness. I cannot show you this in detail. For how can I know and can I present infinities to you and compare them together? But you must judge with me *ab effectu* since God has chosen this world as it is (*Théodicée*, §10, p. 108/129).

Later in the text Leibniz again says that it is too difficult to show the origin of evil 'in detail' and that Bayle asks too much in wanting a detailed account of how evil is bound up with the best of all possible worlds (§145. p. 196/214). We, however, may feel that Bayle is right and that the origin of evil is impenetrable.

2. *After Leibniz*

Leibniz's theodicy is the main focus for the discussion of evil in the first half of the eighteenth century, a discussion that offers no new or original solutions.[22] With it we move slowly into a different philosophical context where learned arguments about the attributes of God become less important. The Leibnizian thesis found few defenders outside the circle of followers such as Christian Wolff and the Wolffians. Wolff's review of the *Théodicée* appeared in *Acta Eruditorum* (1711) and he later defended the best possible world thesis in his *Theologia naturalis* (1736). Bilfinger and Gottsched also supported it and Baumgarten, the most important and influential Wolffian, devoted several sections of his *Metaphysica* (1739) to it.[23] Among partial defenders of the thesis Albrecht von Haller took a peculiar position with the publication of his poem 'Über den Ursprung des Übels' (On the Origin of Evil, 1734).[24] Though there have been many attempts to identify its philosophical sources (Bayle, Leibniz, King, and others)[25], it may more reasonably be seen as an example of philosophical eclecticism. It offers a rather pessimistic view of humankind's moral condition, combined with faith in Providence and God's goodness. A God choosing the best available possibility certainly comes from Leibniz but the centrality of sin and moral evil is more probably from King.

The influential Jesuit journal, *Mémoires de Trévoux*, published in 1713 a review of the *Théodicée* by Father Tournemine, praising Leibniz's defence of divine justice against Bayle, though he could not accept the determinist conception.[26] Father Castel's longer and more detailed review of the second edition (1734) in the same journal is quite different in tone (1737; 5–36, 197–241, 444–71, 953–91). Much of the discussion is devoted to optimism, a neologism probably making its first appearance here (207). Castel reproaches Leibniz for his extreme rationalism, a kind of Spinozism. God too is just a sort of machine whose choice is illusory (203, 209, 209–11, 448). Castel is even more scandalised by the idea of a best possible world that includes evil and sin: 'How could a Christian . . . think that a world in which evil and sin exist is the best that God can create?' (214). Even Pope and Voltaire are mentioned as optimists (221–2).

On the Protestant side, Johann Franz Budde, a Pietist follower of Thomasius, began the attack in his work on the origin of evil (1712).[27] This excludes any minimisation, as a negative view of humankind was characteristic of the Pietist tradition. For Budde only that being or thing is *optimus* which contains no evil, whether physical or moral, and that is not to be found in this world (4–6). In his view, original sin, with all its dramatic consequences, is at the centre of human history: weakness of reason, physical evil as *malum poenae*, dependence on a future life for just reward (2, 23). After sin, the world became a place where evil triumphs over good (25, 81). This negative view of life appears even in the idea that we must praise, not censure, works that speak of human misery.[28]

Christian August Crusius, the most important thinker in the Thomasian-Pietist tradition, offers another critique of *mundus optimus*.[29] For him the crucial point in the philosophy of Leibniz and Wolff is the principle of sufficient reason. He cannot accept the idea that actions as well as events are determined by a sufficient reason. The concept of an ever-determined will implies Spinozism, determinism, the end of religion and morality. Four paragraphs of Crusius's metaphysical work, *Entwurf der nothwendigen Vernunft-Wahrheiten* (1745) are devoted to the concept of the best world and here and in other works is also the critique of the principle of sufficient (or, as Crusius prefers, determinant) reason, together with his defence of free will as *libertas indifferentiae*.[30] According to Crusius, Leibniz's God is not truly free since his will is and must be determined by a 'reason'. For Crusius, too, Leibniz's 'possible' worlds are improbable and unprovable (*Entwurf*, §338, 749, 751); the existence of *one* best possible world, which has to be proved, is presupposed by both Leibniz and Wolff. Leibniz's theory destroys the freedom of both God and man. He pretends to defend God's perfection but takes away his most important quality, the (true) freedom of the will. For Crusius, however, the world created by God is not the best possible but only very good (§389, 753), and the whole responsibility for moral evil is humankind's, whose freedom again must be absolute, a *libertas indifferentiae*.

Besides Crusius the most important opponent of Leibniz and Wolff was Maupertuis. He was president of the Academy of Sciences in Berlin from 1746 to 1759 and during this time wrote his most significant philosophical essays: *Essai de philosophie morale* (1749) and *Essai de cosmologie* (1750).[31] Maupertuis is well known for his pessimistic view of human life. Only the prospect of a future life makes present pains and evils bearable.[32] Suicide would be the only reasonable solution if we did not believe in immortality, which is in fact the Christian answer to our wish for happiness.[33] In ordinary life, the sum of evils outweighs that of goods, and were it not for the idea of immortality, it would be better not to exist (203, 227). Religious faith is thus the result of our frailty and our search for happiness (252).

Maupertuis's *Essai de cosmologie* offers human beings no easy consolation. The system of nature is enough to convince us of God's existence but the individual parts of reality offer no proofs.[34] Like Voltaire, Maupertuis criticises the excessive use of finalist considerations as in physico-theology but is still convinced that it is impossible to banish final causes from our observation of nature (7, 12, 13ff). Natural teleology should rather be sought in the general laws and the simplicity of nature.[35] General laws even provide a solution to the problem of evil, and that points strongly to the influence of Malebranche. It is no accident that God's most revered attribute is wisdom and the most important feature of the world is order. Maupertuis cites several solutions to the problem of evil (Malebranche, Leibniz, Pope) but only in the case of Pope does he indicate strong disagreement. To say 'that there is no evil at all in nature' is a pure act of faith if God is presupposed, and a total error if he is not.[36]

In 1753 the Academy of Sciences in Berlin offered a prize for a dissertation on optimism.[37] This was (a) to show the plausibility of Pope's system (whatever is, is right); (b) to compare that system with that of 'optimism or of the choice of the best'; and (c) to offer arguments for or against the system. Clearly the coupling of Leibniz and Pope was designed to trivialise the best possible world theory and indirectly its author. Moses Mendelssohn wrote an important essay against this tendentious interpretation: 'Pope ein Metaphysiker!' (1755); and even Gottsched criticised the terms of the prize in his *De optimismi macula diserte nuper Alexandro Popio . . .* (1753). The prize went to A. F. Reinhard, a disciple of Crusius.[38] The competition popularised a supposed affinity between Leibniz and Pope, much talked of in the first half of the century. The idea of the best of all possible worlds seemed similar to Pope's 'Whatever is, is right'.[39]

The afore-mentioned Father Castel was not alone in criticising optimism. Jean-Pierre Crousaz, a severe critic of scepticism, characterised Leibniz as the source of Pope's views and accused both of Spinozism.[40] William Warburton counter-attacked, maintaining that though Leibniz was a Spinozist, Pope had nothing to do with him, having found his own middle way between bigots and freethinkers.[41] Crousaz's attack also provoked Emerich de Vattel to his *Défense du système Leibnitien* (1741) against the charge of fatalism. The real problem, in Vattel's eyes, was that the critics read the commentators, not Leibniz himself. Most critics did not examine Leibniz's philosophical system closely but only its ethical and theological consequences in the context of the old debate on predestination.[42] In fact, the two ideas share only the traditional Neo-Platonist ancestry. Pope's sources are more probably the English Platonist tradition through its most influential thinker Shaftesbury, who both directly and through Bolingbroke influenced early eighteenth-century literature.[43]

Universal harmony, order, beauty, and goodness are central concepts in Shaftesbury's worldview. In the dialogue 'The Moralists', written between 1704 and 1709, we find an aristocratic sensibility which praises harmony in both nature and man. Shaftesbury knew and appreciated Bayle personally and this certainly influenced his thought.[44] Scepticism, in the person of Philocles, is present throughout the dialogue. Shaftesbury, however, cannot accept the conflict of faith and reason; he explicitly defends the deistic rational view of religion. The ideas of goodness and beauty are part of the same harmony, by virtue of which we can understand the presence of God.[45] Shaftesbury's rationalism is even expressed in the idea that God's principles are the same as ours, that religion has its roots in morality: 'How can supreme goodness be intelligible to those who know not what goodness itself is?' (267). God speaks to human reason, not against it, and his most important quality is goodness (333–4). In this harmonious context, the problem of the existence of evil has to be explained and removed. Against the Manichaean thesis, Shaftesbury maintains that evil is merely apparent (362ff), just one of many Neo-Platonist themes in his writings of which Leibniz approved.[46] The part is not the whole, human reason has its own limits, evil can be a means to a greater good or even part of a variety which has its own value.

Among English philosophers of the early eighteenth century, Joseph Butler made the question of the relationship of nature and religion central to his thought in *The Analogy of Religion* (1736), citing Shaftesbury as one of his main sources.[47] Butler's aim is not to convince atheists and freethinkers; in fact, the existence of God is explicitly presupposed, and trust in the truthfulness of the voice of God is also manifest here (Introd. §§9, 11, 13, pp. 10, 12, 14–15). The problems surrounding an alleged contradiction between nature and religion must be set aside; incomprehensibility exists in both nature and religion, and analogies may be observed between them. In Butler's view, arguments concerning God and religion cannot have a proper demonstrative status, and probability plays an important role here. Thus it is much more probable that if we are alive now we are destined also to live after death, by analogy with nature's continuous transformations (I.i. §1, 19ff), and that we shall be punished or rewarded according to rules similar to ours (I.ii. §1, 47ff, and I.iii. §1, 63ff). One chapter of the book is devoted specifically to 'The government of God, considered as a scheme or constitution, imperfectly comprehended' (160–76), and it is through this idea of imperfect human comprehension that the question of evil is approached.

Butler does not accept the idea that a world full of vice and suffering is the best possible world (I.vii. §§16–17, 160–70). He thinks rather that the key to the question of evil lies in human ignorance, in the limits of human reason. We cannot actually 'give the whole account of any one thing whatever' (I.vii. §6, 163), still less judge a whole composed of infinite relations: 'it is most evident, that we are not competent judges of this scheme, from the small parts of it which come within our view in the present life: and therefore no objections against any of these parts can be insisted upon by reasonable men' (I.vii. §9, 165). Butler uses even the argument of the general laws of nature, in which 'irregular interpositions' could have worse effects (I.vii. §19, 171–2). His peculiarity consists mainly in awareness of the difficulties of a naive optimism. The anxiety of the human condition is not, for him, only a way of celebrating the beauty and harmony of nature, but a genuine expression of the awareness of the 'little scene of human life': 'we are placed, as one may speak, in the middle of a scheme, not a fixed but a progressive one, every way incomprehensible: incomprehensible, in a manner equally, with respect to what has been, what now is, and what shall be hereafter' (I.viii. §1, 176).

III. THE HUMAN CONDITION

Leibniz's metaphysics was in several respects the last system originating in post-Cartesian discussion. It is well known that the crisis in metaphysical systems was particularly marked in countries like France and England, where philosophy had become empiricist in content and informal in style. But even where metaphysics was still systematically organised, as in Germany with the Wolffian school and its traditions, there were new approaches to philosophical problems.[48] While Crusius's opposition to 'dogmatic' metaphysics had a mainly ethical and religious emphasis, the *Spätaufklärung* was characterised by a 'popular philosophy' which could not be expressed in rigid scholastic language.

An awareness of the limits of human reason[49], which found its deepest and most significant expression in Kant's *Kritik der reinen Vernunft*, led many thinkers to an inquiry centred on human existence, including suffering and crime, instead of the discussion of traditional metaphysical or theological questions. D'Alembert's short entry on 'Optimisme' in the *Encyclopédie* demonstrates this increasing separation from metaphysical questions.[50] Perhaps one of the last significant discussions of the question was Robinet's *De la nature* (1763–6), in which he criticises Leibniz's theory of the best of possible worlds and maintains that every possibility comes into existence. In nature, evil is necessarily joined with good in a perfect balance. The difference between this and the Manichaean view is that this balance of good and evil does not touch God, being just an element of the natural world.[51]

In general, the great metaphysical systems of Descartes, Malebranche, and Leibniz became a reservoir of individual philosophical themes and concepts, since the defence of or attack on systems as dogmatic wholes was no longer the prime concern. At the same time, Spinoza was a formidable weapon in the materialist armoury, providing arguments for a coherent monistic explanation of the universe. Spinozistic materialism solves the question of evil by eliminating it. For thinkers like Diderot, La Mettrie, and Fréret[52], the problem of evil is just a human way of perceiving events which are qualitatively not different from one another, being all the result of the necessary interrelation of things. Although, in Diderot's *Pensées philosophiques*, the atheist raises the question of evil, the consequence of the Spinozist affiliation is that the old question of Epicurus becomes 'a childish difficulty' for Diderot, the alleged evil being the result of necessary laws of nature.[53]

1. *England and France*

An anti-metaphysical disposition and a deep concern for the human condition are to be found in the work of Samuel Johnson. In a long review he strongly criticises and satirises the Popian optimism of Soame Jenyns's *Free Enquiry into the Nature and Origin of Evil* (1757).[54] He discusses the traditional themes of theodicy, showing their inadequacy when confronted by human questions and doubts (38). In particular he criticises the concept of the chain of being which is based on the alleged continuity of natural forms (30). The inconsistency of this idea lies for Johnson in the fact that the notion of imperfection cannot explain suffering: 'That *imperfection implies Evil, and Evil suffering*, is by no means evident. Imperfection may imply privative Evil, or the absence of some good, but this privation produces no suffering' (38). For him it is no answer at all to consider the pains of individuals as necessary means for an incomprehensible happiness elsewhere or belonging to the whole (44–6). Just as unfounded is the connection between moral evil and man's suffering, which Johnson describes as a paradox: 'pain is necessary to the good of the universe; and the pain of one order of beings extending its salutary influence to innumerable orders above and below, it was necessary that man should suffer; but because it is not suitable to justice that pain should be inflicted on innocence, it was necessary that man should be criminal' (57–8).

In the travels of Rasselas, the Abyssinian prince and protagonist of Johnson's novel, the legitimacy of the human perspective and scepticism about the possibility of answering fundamental existential questions go together with man's search for happiness.[55] The novel is nearly contemporary with the review of Jenyns and was published in the same year as the surprisingly similar history of *Candide* (1759) by Voltaire. Rasselas's journeys bring increasing disillusionment regarding the possibility of human happiness on earth. The events of daily life constantly contradict his optimism, bringing him back finally to the dull but happy Abyssinia from which he originally escaped.

Voltaire presents the most brilliant and disenchanted eighteenth-century analysis of the human condition. Here are described, in masterly fashion, both an awareness of the loss of an anthropocentric universe and the impossibility of escaping the question of the meaning of human existence. Here the question of evil plays a central role, though with some modifications and variations. Even the main crisis in Voltaire's intellectual history, in the decade 1750–60, is marked by the question of evil. One of the permanent elements – the anti-anthropocentric view of the world and reality – changes its meaning at different points. In the first 'optimistic' stage, the polemic against anthropocentrism has several affinities with the arguments of traditional apologetics, used by Pope among others. The exaggeration of evil in the world arises from a narrow anthropocentric view. The end of optimism, brought about by the death of Mme du Châtelet and the Lisbon earthquake, means the loss of even a partial answer to the question of evil and suffering and a deep anxiety provoked by observation of the actuality of evil.[56] This is behind the painful questioning of the *Poème sur le désastre de Lisbonne*: 'What am I, where am I, where am I going and where do I come from?' After 1750 the fact of evil, the misery of the human condition, and the inadequacy of theoretical answers were ever-present themes in Voltaire's writing: 'This is among the most difficult and important questions, as it concerns all human existence. It would be far more important to find a remedy for our evils but there is none, and we are reduced to a sorry investigation of their origins'.[57] In practice, the only possible answer, from a metaphysical and existential, not a political point of view, is Candide's garden which must be cultivated. Theoretically, since all philosophical explanations have failed, it makes no sense to try to understand evil, though it is impossible not to. If the Manichaean thesis is nonsense, the contradictory character of the Christian idea of God has already been demonstrated by Bayle: 'If we ignore revelation, which makes everything credible, Christian scholars offer no better an explanation of the origin of good and evil than the followers of Zoroaster'.[58]

Voltaire has no alternative solution for the problem of the origin of evil but is convinced of the weakness of traditional arguments for rational theodicy. First, any minimisation is an offence against those who suffer in the world, as he shows in *Candide* or the *Poème sur le désastre de Lisbonne*. Second, other traditional arguments are either inadequate or paradoxical. The idea that the good of the whole may be achieved by evil in the part is ridiculous[59] and the idea of a chain of being is strongly criticised both in the Lisbon poem and in the different versions of the *Dictionnaire philosophique*.[60] His position on the question of God's moral principles is unclear. It has been argued that Voltaire adopts contrary positions on this, even in the same chapter of his *Traité de métaphysique*, proving again his difficulties with the problem of evil.[61] The rationalist, anti-voluntarist position is more in tune with his deism, as it maintains that 'eternal truths', both moral and mathematical, are the same for God as for us: 'People say that God's justice is not ours. I would rather they said that two times two equals four is not the same for God as for me'.[62] Voltaire understands the destructive character of the critique of theodicy and the insistence on God's goodness that characterises Bayle. In *Éléments de la philosophie de Newton* he writes: 'This is the great refuge of the atheist. If I admit the existence of a God, he says, this God must be goodness itself. He who gives me existence owes me well-being. But I see nothing in humankind but disorder and calamity.' Voltaire's reply is still 'optimistic': 'Our answer to this atheist is that "good" and "well-being" are equivocal terms. Something which is bad for you may be good in the general scheme of things'.[63]

Much of Voltaire's life was spent in fighting two opposing views, defined by their attitude to the question of evil: pessimistic atheism and optimistic metaphysics. Toward the end of his life he was increasingly obsessed with the dangers of atheism. His faith in a supreme Being and partial acceptance of a teleological universe – though with Maupertuis he criticised the exaggerations of physico-theology[64] – became with time not simply the reasonable residue of a critique of positive religion but the value that had to be defended against the dangers of atheism. Moreover, the less than enlightened idea that religion is a useful means of social control must be seen in the context of the struggle against atheism. Two lines of criticism, from opposing sides, illuminate Voltaire's ambiguous attitude to religion.[65] On the one hand, Rousseau, continuing his battle for Providence after the famous letter of 18 August 1756, writes in his *Confessions*: 'While always appearing to believe in God, Voltaire really never believed in anything but the Devil; since his so-called God is nothing but a maleficient being who according to him takes pleasure only in harming'.[66] On the other, materialistic side, d'Holbach reproaches Voltaire for not having drawn the obvious conclusion that a genuinely disenchanted view of evil in the world would suggest that God does not exist.[67]

2. *Germany*

In Germany the theologian Johann Joachim Spalding provides an interesting example of an approach to the problem of theodicy which linked human existence to the idea of development in a religious context. In 1748, in answer to La Mettrie's *L'homme machine* (1748), he published a short book, *Betrachtung über die Bestimmung des Menschen*, which went through thirteen editions. Spalding, the German translator of Butler and Shaftesbury, was also a representative of the rationalist theological movement known as neology.[68] For him the only solution for the Christian conscience seeking the true meaning of life lay in the idea of the destiny of humankind.[69] Through a *phenomenology of the soul*, man progresses through life by a moral dissatisfaction with the qualities of each stage as it is achieved: natural and intellectual pleasures, virtue, natural harmony, and religion itself. Faced with the problem of the destiny of virtuous man, conscience sees only the suppression of virtue and triumph of vice. Spalding's solution is immortality, the infinite extension of the soul, but not simply in the traditional Christian interpretation. For him immortality is the infinite *development* of conscience, an endless perfecting of our own qualities and faculties. This, as later with Mendelssohn and Lessing, is understood as a continuation of our earthly task and thus shows a strong anthropological element in the religious thought of these authors. Apart from the interesting idea that religion arises in the context of our own moral experience, which anticipates Kant, the notion of development puts the question of evil in a new light: evil may be part of a process whose end result is the disappearance of evil (27–8).

The theme of the destiny of humankind is central to the ethical and religious discussion of the German *Aufklärung*. It is no accident that Thomas Abbt, in his *Zweifel über die Bestimmung des Menschen*, invokes the name of Bayle, underlining the inadequacy of moral need and conviction in solving the question of man's anxiety. But Moses Mendelssohn, in his answer to Abbt, *Orakel, die Bestimmung des Menschen betreffend* (1763), bases his doctrine of subjectivity, immortality, and progress on the idea of the destiny of man. His most famous work, *Phädon, oder über die Unsterblichkeit der Seele* (1767), develops the discussion with Abbt and attempts to expound a new concept of man in the framework of Plato's dialogue.[70]

Mendelssohn is interesting because he was influenced by the wider European discussion. He admired Shaftesbury, Hutcheson, and Locke's theory of human understanding but was also strongly influenced by the Leibniz-Wolff tradition. In addition, his interest in aesthetic problems led him to consider psychological and anthropological questions in greater depth. Moreover, his theory of the striving for perfection was directed against Rousseau's idea that perfectibility (a Rousseauan neologism) and society are the source of human corruption.[71] For him the highest good was not a Rousseauan balance between needs and satisfactions but rather the continuing pursuit of perfection.[72] We are also led to seeking perfection by the need to exert ourselves, the process by which nature (or its providential constitution) moves us to action and reflection. This process does not cease with death and it is on this basis that our immortality is asserted in *Phädon*. Human death, as Mendelssohn wrote on the death of

Lessing, means only that perfection can be pursued no further here on earth.[73] This is a complete reversal of the traditional idea of damnation: imperfection and evil necessitate a striving for perfection and it is this that is our human destiny. Belief in universal harmony and strong providential tendencies are Mendelssohn's characteristics. The process of creation has a final end, the same moral world or realm of grace that we find at the end of Leibniz's *Monadologie* as of Kant's *Kritik der Urtheilskraft*.[74]

Mendelssohn's *Reich der Geister*, spiritual realm, should not be interpreted as a collective being. Humankind is not a being (*Wesen*) at all; only individuals are real beings. If the individual is destined to be united with supreme perfection, this is certainly not true of the human race.[75] Indeed the cyclical movement of history is necessary for individual perfection. But progress and perfection of humankind as a whole can be only a contingent fact, not a continuous process.[76] If humanity were making a continuous progress, individuals of later generations would not be able to make the same progress as their predecessors – 'What then can our children do?' (66).[77] With regard to the problem of evil, Mendelssohn's idea has one central result. Earthly imperfections are necessary to individual perfection and must not be eliminated because they are at once the condition and the object of humanity's infinite search for perfection.

In his political work *Jerusalem* (1783) Mendelssohn criticises the idea of collective progress by his friend Lessing in *Die Erziehung des Menschengeschlechts* (1780). After a lifetime's reflection on theological questions, Lessing here gives a definite if not definitive account of his ideas on the human search for perfection.[78] He agrees with Spalding's and Mendelssohn's transfer of the problem of evil and imperfection to a temporal scale but not with the individualistic interpretation of this process. In his eschatology, the history of humankind is the history of the slow but certain advance of human reason and moral character, both in the race as a whole and in individuals. The opposition between good and evil is solved by the idea of development. Both individuals and humanity in general must undergo the same process and each individual must develop his subjectivity in the same degree as the race as a whole, since there is an exact parallel between the formation of the individual through education and the formation of humankind through a revelation that must develop a pure rational content. This is the 'new eternal gospel' prematurely proclaimed by Joachim of Fiore.[79] The infinite approach to a perfectly rational human race corresponds to the eternal transmigration of souls. If every individual has to undergo the same process of perfection, no one can be lost – not even in the cause of the perfecting of humanity – but each must return to earth as often as necessary for his complete subjective development.[80] In Lessing's view, that is, evil is progressively eliminated by the infinite search for perfection. It will increasingly become a residual part of human existence, even if never completely eliminated.

IV. THE COLLAPSE OF THEODICY

The most thorough deployment of Bayle's conceptual arsenal against theodicy is David Hume's *Dialogues concerning Natural Religion*. Even the characters evoke a Baylean atmosphere: Philo, the sceptic; Cleanthes, the rational theologian; and Demea, the fideist. In the text, the most frequent alliance is between scepticism and fideism. As Bayle said, they are the only genuine possibilities for the human mind. Cleanthes puts it clearly: 'How do you *Mystics*, who maintain the absolute Incomprehensibility of the Deity, differ from Sceptics or Atheists, who assert, that the first Cause of All is unknown and unintelligible?'[81]

Hume several times repeats that the question concerns the *nature* of God, not his *existence* (144–5, 159–60); if we – prudently – suppose that God definitely exists, the real problem is how to describe him and his attributes rationally. In his essay 'Of Miracles' in the *Enquiry concerning Human Understanding* Hume had already maintained the centrality of faith, not reason, for the Christian religion and the discussion of providence clearly states his position on the inadequacy of human reason and philosophy when faced with the question of evil: 'all the fruitless industry to account for the ill appearances of nature, and save the honour of the gods; while we must acknowledge the reality of that evil and disorder, with which the world so much abounds'.[82]

In the *Dialogues* Cleanthes advances the so-called design argument in favour of God's existence, consisting of two sub-arguments, one centred on the idea of order and regularity (the nomological argument), and the other (teleological argument) centred on the idea of purpose.[83] Cleanthes's main methodological argument is the analogy between God and man and the allegedly 'finalist' constitution of nature. Philo and Demea, on the other hand, maintain the weakness of the analogy and radically criticise an anthropomorphic conception according to which signs of God's wise providence may be found everywhere. In actual fact man cannot speak about things of which he has no direct experience (*Dialogues*, V, 188–94 and *passim*).

Cleanthes is alone in defending the possibility of a rational conception of God's nature. The alliance between scepticism and fideism is even clearer in Parts X and XI of the *Dialogues*, devoted specifically to the problem of evil. For Philo and Demea human misery and suffering are, despite the denials by Leibniz and King, simple matters of observation by ordinary people as well as the learned (X, 220). In the face of strong opposition from both of them, Cleanthes is a decided supporter of the minimisation of evil (228). But even imagining, against the facts, that there is more of good than of evil in life, 'why is there any Misery at all in the World?' (230). Everything proves that '*Epicurus's* old Questions are yet unanswer'd', as Hume says, using the argument from Bayle's *Dictionnaire* (226). In Part XI Hume confronts four questions about natural evil, showing the impossibility of answering them and thus proving, once more, a sort of anti-teleology. Why must we be urged to action by suffering and not just by the search for pleasure? (XI, 234–5). Why can general laws of nature with bad results not simply be broken, given that many events are indeed uncertain? Hume writes, 'A Being, therefore, who knows the secret Springs of the Universe, might easily, by particular Volitions, turn all these Accidents to the Good of Mankind, and render the whole World happy' (235). Moreover, we are called upon to observe 'the great Frugality, with which all Powers and Faculties are distributed to every particular Being', while 'an indulgent Parent wou'd have bestow'd a large Stock, in order to guard against Accidents, and secure the Happiness and Welfare of the Creature' (236–7). Finally, it would be easy to show parts which have certainly some function in the natural economy but 'none of these Parts or Principles, however useful, are so accurately adjusted, as to keep precisely within those Bounds, in which their Utility consists. . . . One wou'd imagine that this grand Production had not receiv'd the last hand of the Maker' (239). Philo's pessimistic account frightens Demea himself with the consequences of the irrationality of faith (242–3).

Hume's criticism stops short of questioning God's existence and considers only his nature and attributes. Philo's aim is not explicitly to deny God's existence on the grounds of human misery or the contradictions in nature concerning human needs, but to deny that observation of man and nature proves that existence (X, 221). Disorder and Deity may be compatible but in ways beyond our understanding.

The further step of arguing that the existence of evil is incompatible with the idea of a good and wise God and therefore a proof of his non-existence had already been taken earlier. This non-Spinozistic atheism was formulated by Jean Meslier in his *Mémoire*, a clandestine text from ca. 1720 which was published in expurgated form by Voltaire as *Extraits des sentiments de Jean Meslier* (1762).[84] It was another radical interpreter of Bayle's arguments, however, namely d'Holbach, who popularized the critique of theodicy as a premise for atheism.[85]

D'Holbach does not retain the fideistic solution to the problem of theodicy but further develops the argument, already present in Bayle and Hume, of the impossibility of a rational theology. Among the many similarities between his work and Hume's, d'Holbach stresses the contradictory character of the idea of God and emphasises that we must not renounce reason, our only guide through the fear and ignorance which produce religion. These themes first appear in his *Système de la nature* (1770), but are treated in greater depth in his *Le bon sens*, for long attributed to Meslier.[86] Evil is d'Holbach's main justification for criticising all forms of theology. In *Le bon sens* he denounces the irrationality of a discipline whose objects are 'only incomprehensible things . . . this science is theology and this theology is a continual insult to human reason' (29).[87]

Confused ideas about God are those that deny positive qualities and offer a negative definition of God based on ideas of infinity, eternity, immutability, and immateriality (*Système*, II.459–60). But the greatest problems stem from the attempt to define a more human God with moral attributes, notably his *goodness* and justice. For d'Holbach this is clearly absurd when human existence is full of misery and crime. His pessimistic view of the human condition informs *Le bon sens*, in which a critique of anthropocentrism does not imply the illegitimacy of a human perspective (chs. 51, 94, pp. 61, 111–13). One does not, however, need to start from an extreme pessimism since even minor evil is a crucial objection to providence (ch. 52, pp. 62–4). At all events, his description of human life, indeed of all sentient beings, is a negative one, and the idea of the chain of being is seen as a dream contradicted by experience (ch. 54, pp. 65–6; ch. 58, p. 70).

For d'Holbach, the concept of the impenetrability of God's decisions is another absurdity: how can one speak of the attributes of an unknowable God (*Système*, 459–60)? He pits the rationalist and voluntarist conceptions of God against each other. If the theory of the best of all possible worlds or Pope's 'whatever is, is right' limit God's power, still less convincing is the idea that God, having it in his power to create a better world, created such a bad one, a notion that merely confirms God as evil (*Le bon sens*, ch. 87, pp. 102–3). Thus the attempt to defend God's freedom becomes a new argument against rational theology. The final attack is against the possibility of rational *deism* (but d'Holbach actually speaks of 'theists' as opposed to the orthodoxy of 'theologians'), that is, against Voltaire: the mystery of evil is no more irrational or incomprehensible than the mystery of incarnation and its aporetic character demonstrates the impossibility of preserving both the orthodox God of the theologians and the allegedly rational *Être Suprême* of Voltaire (ch. 118, pp. 142–4).[88]

V. OTHER WAYS

Official declaration of the failure of philosophical theodicy came late in the century, in a short work by Kant significantly entitled *Über das Miszlingen aller philosophischen Versuche in der Theodicee* (1791). The theme of the limits of human reason found in Kant its profoundest and most significant expression in the history of Western philosophy. This is at once the main presupposition and the key to the solution in Kant's consideration of theodicy. Here he uses a traditional argument of the opponents of theodicy – the impossibility of the rational justification of evil – but inserts it in his own conception of reason and of the centrality of moral experience for the discussion of religious questions. He introduces his essay with a definition of the problem: 'By "theodicy" we understand the defense of the highest wisdom of the creator against the charge which reason brings against it for whatever is counterpurposive in the world'.[89] Early in the paper Kant speaks of a reason that does not accept its own limits. Moreover, the defenders of rational theodicy have an obligation to present their arguments to the court of reason (Ak 8: 256).

The forms of evil by means of which Kant demonstrates the impossibility of rational theodicy are forms of *Zweckwidrigkeit* (that which is contrary to purpose) and the exact opposite of a term central to the argument of the second part of the *Kritik der Urtheilskraft, Zweckmässigkeit* (purposiveness). Evil is the most important example of anti-teleology and he recognises three forms of it. They are not those of Leibniz or King but, rather moral evil (the absolutely counter-purposive), which is most important; physical evil (the conditionally counter-purposive), which cannot be an end but may be a means; and the disproportion between crime and punishment in the world, the old problem of equitable retribution (Ak 8: 256).

Rational theodicy has solved none of these problems; the holiness, goodness, and justice of God cannot be rationally maintained when faced with the objection of evil. The recognition of holiness as the most important attribute of God agrees with the Kantian conception of ethical religion: holiness characterises a morally perfect being for whom the moral law is not an imperative but the actual law of his willing and acting. It would be impossible for Kant to choose goodness as a central quality of God since this would imply a eudaemonic conception of the relationship of God and man and eudaemonism is, for Kant, the worst ethical position. His ethical rationalism and anti-voluntarism are evident in the narrow bounds set for God's power.

One of the most important themes in Kant is his contempt for the idea of a voluntarist God, according to which moral crimes are nothing but definitions of human convention or law which might be adequate means to particular or general good. This defence, according to Kant, is worse than the original charge (see Ak 8: 258). The justification that moral evil is actually something else, based on man's finitude (or metaphysical evil), simply means that moral evil does not exist and there can therefore be no responsibility for it.

Regarding natural evil, Kant rejects any attempt to minimise the misery of the human condition, a view already evident in the third *Kritik*: as humans are natural beings, their destiny is no different from that of other natural beings. Even immortality is insufficient as a rational argument; the idea of a future happiness 'can indeed be pretended but in no way can there be insight into it' (Ak 8: 260) because we cannot understand why our whole life should not be happy. Still less convincing for Kant are the disparities between people's actions and their reward or punishment (260–2). From this survey of the defence of God, he can only conclude: 'Every previous theodicy has not performed what it promised, namely the vindication of the moral wisdom of the world-government against the doubts raised against it on the basis of what the experience of this world teaches' (263).

These words mark publicly the end of the history of rational theodicy. But in Kantian thought we find another view of the question or of one aspect of it: that of divine rewards for moral men. This is made possible by the Kantian distinction between theoretical and practical reason. In the essay on theodicy, Kant singles out Job as the best example of authentic theodicy based on the principle of the 'unconditional divine decision' (Ak 8: 265). This, however, does not imply agreement with the voluntarist view of God, for nothing is further from Kantian ethics, as we have seen. Kant's purpose here, and in the whole essay, is to show the impossibility of confronting, far less answering, theological questions by use of theoretical reason.

In his so-called pre-critical period, Kant more than once defended the idea of the best of all possible worlds and with it the idea that God's will is determined by a principle of creation. This position is clearly asserted in the *Nova dilucidatio* as also in the reflections on optimism and the short but significant *Versuch einiger Betrachtungen über den Optimismus* (1759),[90] and we can then follow, through the *Vorlesungen über Metaphysik und Rationaltheologie* (1770–80), the gradual transformation of the Leibnizian idea of the best of all possible worlds into the new Kantian concept of *highest good*.[91]

This new perspective of critical philosophy has important consequences for the concept of God and the idea of religion.[92] Theoretical reason can know neither God nor his attributes and therefore cannot justify evil in the world. At this level there is no analogy between God and man; intuition, for example, can be only sensible, never intellectual.[93] Therefore our only way of knowing things is the discursive way. The situation, if viewed from the practical perspective of ethics, is different. God's principles are in this view the same as ours because the moral law is valid for *every rational being*; the difference between God and men is that law for humankind is an imperative, a prescriptive proposition, while for God it is the immanent (descriptive) law of the will. Rationalist theology has been transposed from the theoretical to the ethical level. Only from the practical point of view can we know the central characteristics of God and to some degree the principles of creation. In the dialectic of the *Kritik der praktischen*

Vernunft, the concept of God is the result of our moral constitution because it is, like immortality, a postulate of practical reason. Because of them we can at least hope that in a future life morality and happiness will fairly correspond. The highest good, that is the union of morality and happiness, is the answer of practical reason to our hope for a just reward for our morality.[94] It is morally impossible that creation has no regard for the happiness of just men and so the creator has to be actuated by the principle of fair retribution. Thus the antinomy of practical reason originates in the idea of happiness, which proves how important the concept is, even for Kant, the thinker who, more than any other, argues against an eudaemonistic foundation of ethics.[95]

The role of society and history in the questions that torment the modern world is most deeply and clearly analysed by Rousseau.[96] For him the question of evil arises as a result of historical and social development whose origins we can understand and for which we may perhaps even discover some remedies. The most important and novel aspect of Rousseau's philosophy is perhaps his concept of the original goodness of human nature. He is one of the few to maintain that humankind was originally good and that its actual moral vices are not innate, thus changing the idea of original sin into its opposite. This anthropological optimism, furthermore, has an existential manifestation. In his *Discours sur l'origine et les fondements de l'inégalité* (1755), discussing Maupertuis's thesis that evil prevails over good in human life, Rousseau argues that Maupertuis is confounding civilised man with natural man: it is civilisation that has brought about our alienated unhappy existence.[97] And in the well-known letter to Voltaire of August 1756, occasioned by the latter's *Poème sur le désastre de Lisbonne*, Rousseau several times asserts his positive view of human life; he speaks of the 'sweet sentiment of existence, independent of any other sensation', which is forgotten by philosophers, writes of his preference for existing rather than not, and ironically remarks that 'however ingenious we may be in exacerbating our miseries by dint of ever fancier institutions, we have as yet not been able to perfect ourselves to the point of generally making life a burden to ourselves and preferring nothingness to our existence' (1062). The defence of providence and optimism is not conducted with new arguments but some lines reveal a new approach: 'I do not see that one can seek the source of moral evil anywhere but in man, free, perfected, hence corrupted; and as for physical evils, if, as it seems to me, it is a contradiction for matter to be both sentient and insentient, they are inevitable in any system of which man is a part' (1061). It is important to note that physical evil is not considered a central question; it is rather the result of natural laws, though natural evils are often provoked by human societies, as Lisbon's earthquake proves.[98]

The most important passage is that of man 'free, perfected, hence corrupted'; the new notion of perfectibility, which Mendelssohn used in a positive sense to describe the infinite development of individuality, signifies for Rousseau the negative factor which initiates the process of corruption. Perfectibility, freedom, society are not in themselves negative factors but only in their historical realisation and misuse. The real villain here is not the individual person; Rousseau's theodicy is unusual in defending both man and God and placing responsibility elsewhere. When, at the beginning of *Émile*, he writes, 'Everything is good as it leaves the hands of the Author of things; everything degenerates in the hands of man'[99], he is not talking of human nature but of human society and history. Here is the origin of the real evil, moral evil. Moral corruption is a social and political fact which needs to be explained and thus morality and politics cannot be examined separately (524/235). Only through this connection is it possible to see the genesis of corruption. '[S]ermonizers perceived the evil, and I lay bare its causes and above all I point out something highly consoling and useful by showing that all these vices belong not so much to man, as to man badly governed'.[100]

The *Discours sur les sciences et les arts* was the first description of the corruption of Western societies; the *Discours sur l'origine de l'inégalité* shows Rousseau's awareness of the need for a genetic analysis of society. For some societies, if not for over-civilised European ones, evil (that is, moral corruption) may be remedied by a new political order, such as that described in the *Contrat social*. In thus transposing the question of evil into social and historical analysis of the human race, Rousseau was the most important precursor of the dominant trend of nineteenth-century inquiry.

NOTES

1 See Karl Löwith, 'Die beste aller Welten und das radikal Böse im Menschen', in *Wissen, Glaube und Skepsis: zur Kritik von Religion und Theologie, Sämtliche Schriften*, eds. K. Stichweh and M. B. de Launay, 9 vols. (Stuttgart, 1981–8), 3: 275–97; Paul Hazard, 'Le problème du mal dans la conscience européenne du dix-huitième siècle', *Romanic Revue* 32 (1941), 147–70. For the background to eighteenth-century discussion of theodicy, Descartes to Leibniz, see Sergio Landucci, *La teodicea nell'età cartesiana* (Naples, 1986). For a recent analytical overview, see *The Problem of Evil*, eds. M. M. Adams and R. M. Adams (Oxford, 1990).

2 G. W. Leibniz, *Phil. Schriften*, 6: 21–462; translated as *Theodicy: Essays on the Goodness of God, the Freedom of Man and the Origin of Evil*, trans. E. M. Huggard, ed. A. Farrer (London, 1951). References are to paragraphs, followed by pages in the French text in *Phil. Schriften*, followed by pages in the translation: §13, 109/130. 'Theodicy' occurs already in a note of 1695; see Leibniz, *Textes inédits*, ed. G. Grua, 2 vols. (Paris, 1948), 370–1. The basic work on Leibniz's theodicy remains Gaston Grua, *Jurisprudence universelle et théodicée selon Leibniz* (Paris, 1953).

3 See the entry 'Pauliciens' in Pierre Bayle, *Choix d'articles tirés du Dictionnaire historique et critique* (5th edn., Leiden, 1740), in *Oeuvres diverses*, ed. E. Labrousse, 5 vols. (Hildesheim, 1964–2001), suppl. vol. I.2: 858 (the source is Lactantius, *De ira Dei*, ch. 13). The in-text refs. that follow are to this edn. A survey of discussions of Bayle's thought, from Jurieu (1706)

to the present day, is Gianluca Mori, *Introduzione a Bayle* (Rome, 1996), 155–80, with a comprehensive bibliography, 183–219, used in Elisabeth Labrousse, *Pierre Bayle* (1963–4), 2 vols., vol. 2: *Pierre Bayle: Hétérodoxie et rigorisme* (2nd edn., Paris, 1996), 633–44. See also G. Mori, *Bayle philosophe* (Paris, 1999); Stefalno Brogi, *Teologia senza verità. Bayle contro i 'rationaux'* (Milan, 1998); Pierre Rétat, *Le Dictionnaire de Bayle et la lutte philosophique au XVIIIe siècle* (Paris, 1971); C. Louise Thijssen Schoute, 'La diffusion européenne des idées de Bayle' in *Pierre Bayle, le philosophie de Rotterdam*, ed. P. Dibon (Paris, 1959), 150–95; Gerhard Sauder, 'Bayle-Rezeption in der deutschen Aufklärung', with bibliographical supplement, in *Deutsche Vierteljahresschrift für Literaturwissenschaft und Geistesgeschichte*, Sonderheft (1975), 83–104; Erich Lichtenstein, *Gottscheds Ausgabe von Bayles Dictionnaire* (Heidelberg, 1915).

4 For discussion of this point in seventeenth- and eighteenth-century England, see Mario Sina, *L'avvento della ragione. 'Reason' e 'above reason' dal razionalismo teologico inglese al deismo* (Milan, 1976).

5 See Rétat, *Dictionnaire de Bayle*, 22, 24, 159–60, 181.

6 See G. Mori, *Tra Descartes a Bayle. Poiret e la teodicea* (Bologna, 1990), 247–55.

7 Leibniz, *Théodicée, Discours préliminaire* (hereafter, *Discours*), §39, 49–101, at 73/96. Leibniz specifically mentions Toland as 'The English author of a book which is ingenious but has met with disapproval', §60, 83/106.

8 See Marcelo Dascal, 'La razon y los mysterios de la fe segun Leibniz', *Revista Latinoamericana de Filosofia*, 1 (1975): 193–226; Maria–Rosa Antognazza, 'Die Rolle der Trinitäts- und Menschenwürdigungsdiskussion für die Entstehung von Leibniz Denken', *Studia Leibnitiana*, 26 (1994): 56–75; same, 'Inediti leibniziani sulle polemiche trinitarie', *Rivista di filosofia neoscolastica*, 83 (1991): 525–50 (with documents of importance in Leibniz's treatment of the problem of the Trinity in the light of Socinian criticism); same, *Trinità e Incarnazione: il rapporto tra filosofia e teologia rivelata nel pensiero di Leibniz* (Milan, 1999). Bayle had challenged the Protestant distinction between the dogmas of the Trinity and transubstantiation.

9 For Leibniz on Bayle, see *Théodicée*, §180, 221/239. On justice, see *Discours* §37, 71–2/95; see also §§35, 37, pp. 70, 71–2/93–4, 95; Théodicée §§167, 176–80, pp. 210, 219–22/228, 236–40; Préface, pp. 29, 34–5/53–4, 58–9.

10 See the entry 'Manichéens', n. d., in *Bayle, Choix d'articles*, I.2: 704.

11 Leibniz, *Théodicée*, §259, p. 270/285. See also §§15, 57, 148, 221, pp. 110, 134, 198, 250/131, 154, 216–17, 265–6. Note the assertion (§26, p. 118/138) that moral evil is not a great evil as such, but because 'it is a source of physical evils'.

12 See Arthur O. Lovejoy, *The Great Chain of Being: A Study of the History of an Idea* (Cambridge, MA, 1936), ch. 5.

13 Leibniz, *Théodicée*, Préface, 37/61; §21, p. 115/136. Leibniz specifically mentions Augustine, §29, 378, pp. 119, 340/140, 352.

14 William King, *De origine mali* (Dublin, 1702); translated as *An Essay on the Origin of Evil*, trans. Edmund Law (London, 1731), with King's replies to his critics. See *A Great Archbishop of Dublin, William King, D. D., 1650–1729*, ed. C. S. King (London, 1906), and Lovejoy, *Great Chain of Being*, ch. 6.

15 Jean le Rond d'Alembert and Denis Diderot, *Encyclopédie ou Dictionnaire raisonné des sciences, des arts et des métiers*, 5 vols. (New York, NY, 1969), article 'Mal', 9: 916–19. The author is Jaucourt.

16 King, *Origin of Evil*, II.1, 73. For the physical evil founded upon the metaphysical, see IV.4, §7, p. 116; IV.9, §2, pp. 143–4; V.5.i, §1, pp. 226–7. For moral evil equally founded on the metaphysical, see V.5.ii, §14; V.5.vi, §7

17 Leibniz, 'Initia et Specimina Scientiæ Generalis', in *Phil. Schriften*, 7: 57–123 at 109.

18 See Heinrich Schepers, 'Zum Problem der Kontingenz bei Leibniz. Die beste der möglichen Welten', in *Collegium Philosophicum. Studien Joachim Ritter zum 60. Geburtstag*, ed. E.-W. Böckenförde (Basel, 1965), 326–50; George Gale, 'On what God Chose: Perfection and

God's Freedom', *Studia Leibnitiana*, 8 (1976): 69–87; Wolfgang Hübener, 'Sinn und Grenzen des Leibnizschen Optimismus', *Studia Leibnitiana*, 10 (1978): 222–46; Gino Roncaglia, 'Cum Deus Calculat – God's Evaluation of Possible Worlds and Logical Calculus', *Topoi*, 9.1 (1990): 83–90; *Leibniz: Le meilleur des mondes: Table ronde 1990*, eds. A. Heinekamp and A. Robinet, *Studia Leibnitiana* Sonderheft 21 (Stuttgart, 1992).

19 Leibniz, *De rerum originatione radicali*, in *Phil. Schriften*, 7: 302–8; and *Théodicée*, §201, 236/252–3. See David Blumenfeld, 'Leibniz's Theory of the Striving Possibles', *Studia Leibnitiana*, 5 (1973): 163–73. The compossibility cannot be understood by human minds: see Leibniz, *Opuscules et fragments inédits*, ed. L. Couturat (Paris, 1903), 522.

20 Leibniz, *Principes de la nature et de la grace fondés en raison*, in *Phil. Schriften*, 7: 598–606 at 602; see D. Goldstick, 'Why Is There Something Rather than Nothing?' *Philosophy and Phenomenological Research*, 40 (1979–80): 265–71.

21 Albert Heinekamp, *Gottfried Wilhelm Leibniz*, 2 vols. (Munich, 1992), 1: 274–320 at 278.

22 An interesting contemporary survey is Friedrich Christian Baumeister, *Historia doctrinae recentius controversiae de mundo optimo exposit* (Leipzig, 1741). See Fonnesu, 'Der Optimismus und seine Kritiker im Zeitalter der Aufklärung', *Studia Leibnitiana*, 26 (1994): 131–62; W. H. Barber, *Leibniz in France from Arnauld to Voltaire: A Study in French Reactions to Leibnizianism 1670–1760* (Oxford, 1955); Stefan Lorenz, *De mundo optimo. Zu Leibniz' Theodizee und ihrer Rezeption in Deutschland, 1710–1791, Studia Leibnitiana* Suppl., 31 (Stuttgart, 1997).

23 *Acta Eruditorum* 1711, March, 110–21, and April, 159–68, unsigned review. Christian Wolff, *Theologia naturalis*, ed. J. École, in *Werke*, II.7–8 (1978–81), Pt. 1; in 7.1: §§325ff., pp. 322ff. Georg Bernhard Bilfinger, *Dilucidationes philosophicae de Deo, anima humana, mundo* (Frankfurt, 1737), §§431ff., 228, 490–91, pp. 124–5, 59–60, 142; Johann Christoph Gottsched, *Erste Gründe der gesammten Weltweisheit* (Leipzig, 1756), §§341, 429, pp. 244–5, 272; Alexander G. Baumgarten, *Metaphysica*, 4th edn. (Halle, 1757), §§436–47.

24 Albrecht von Haller, 'Über den Ursprung des Übels', in *Gedichte*, ed. L. Hirzel (Frauenfeld, 1882), 118–42.

25 See Giorgio Tonelli, *Poesia a pensiero in Albrecht von Haller* (Turin, 1961), 63ff.; Karl S. Guthke, 'Zur Religionsphilosophie des jungen Albrecht von Haller', *Filosofia*, 17 (1966): 638–49.

26 Anon., *Mémoires pour l'histoire des sciences et des beaux-arts* (*Mémoires de Trévoux*) (Trévoux, 1701–67), July 1713, 1178–99. See Alfred R. Desautels, *Les mémoires de Trévoux et le mouvement des idées au XVIIIe siècle, 1701–1734* (Rome, 1956).

27 Budde, Johann Franz, *Doctrinæ orthodoxæ de origine mali contra recentiorum quorundam hypotheses modesta assertio* (Jena, 1712).

28 Budde, 82. For the contrary view, see Leibniz, *Théodicée*, §15, p. 110/83.

29 See Sonia Carboncini, 'Die thomasianisch-pietistische Tradition und ihre Fortsetzung durch Christian August Crusius' in *Christian Thomasius, 1655–1728: Interpretationen zu Werk und Wirkung*, ed. W. Schneiders (Hamburg, 1989), 287–304.

30 Christian August Crusius, *Entwurf der nothwendigen Vernunft-Wahrheiten*, 'Kosmologie', ch. 1, §§385–9, in *Die philosophischen Hauptwerke*, eds. G. Tonelli, S. Carboncini and R. Finster (Hildesheim, 1964–), 2: 741–56. For a critique of the principle of sufficient reason see *Dissertatio philosophica de usu et limitibus principii rationis determinantis, vulgo sufficientis*, and *Epistola ad Jo. Ern. L. B. ab Hardenberg de summis, rationis principiis, speciatim de principio rationis determinantis*, in *Hauptwerke*, 4.1: 182–324, 327–444.

31 Pierre-Louis Moreau de Maupertuis, *Oeuvres*, 4 vols. (Lyon, 1768), vol. 1. See also Giorgio Tonelli, *La Pensée philosophique de Maupertuis: son milieu et ses sources*, ed. C. Cesa (Hildesheim, 1987).

32 Maupertuis, *Essai de philosophie morale*, in *Oeuvres*, 1: 171–252, Préface, 189.

33 *Philosophie morale*, 189, 228–9; 232. See Lester G. Crocker, 'The Discussion of Suicide in the Eighteenth Century', *Journal of the History of Ideas*, 13 (1952): 47–72.

34 Maupertuis, *Essai de cosmologie*, in *Oeuvres*, 1: 1–78; see also 'Avant-propos', xviii–xix.

35 *Essai de cosmologie*, 21–4. On the question of general laws see Giorgio Tonelli, 'La necessité des lois de la nature au XVIIIe siècle et chez Kant en 1762', *Revue d'histoire des sciences et leurs applications*, 12 (1959): 225–41.

36 *Essai de cosmologie*, 16–19.

37 See Adolf von Harnack, *Geschichte der Königlich-Preussischen Akademie der Wissenschaften zu Berlin*, 3 vols. in 4 (Berlin, 1900), 1.i: 404ff.; Cornelia Buschmann, 'Die philosophischen Preisfragen und Preisschriften der Berliner Akademie der Wissenschaften im 18. Jahrhundert', in *Aufklärung in Berlin*, ed. W. Förster (Berlin, 1989), 165–228.

38 See Mendelsohn's *Gesammelte Schriften*, Jubiläumsausgabe, eds. F. Bamberger and A. Altmann (Stuttgart-Bad Cannstatt, 1971–), vol. 2: *Schriften zur Philosophie und Ästhetik*, eds. F. Bamberger and L. Strauss (1972), 43–80. Adolf F. Reinhard, 'Le sistème de Pope sur la perfection du monde comparé avec celui de Mr. Leibnitz, avec un examen de l'optimisme . . . ', published with three others in *Dissertations sur l'optimisme* (Berlin, 1755). On the ensuing discussion, see *Sammlung der Streitschriften ueber die Lehre von der besten Welt und verschiedene damit verknuepfte wichtige Wahrheiten, welche zwischen dem Verfasser der im Jahre 1755 von der Akademie zu Berlin gekroenten Schrift vom Optimismus, und einigen beruehmten Gelehrten gewechselt worden*, ed. C. Ziegra (Rostock-Wismar, 1759); *Wieland und Martin und Regula Künzli: ungedruckte Briefe*, ed. L. Hirzel (Leipzig, 1891).

39 Alexander Pope, *An Essay on Man* (1733) in *Poetical Works*, ed. H. Davis (Oxford, 1966), I.289–94.

40 See Jean-Pierre de Crousaz, *Examen du pyrrhonisme ancien et moderne* (The Hague, 1733); *Examen de 'l'Essai de M. Pope sur l'Homme'* (Lausanne, 1737); *Commentaire sur la traduction en vers de M. l'abbé du Resnel de l'Essai de M. Pope sur l'homme* (Geneva, 1738). Resnel's translation appeared in 1737; there were others around that time.

41 William Warburton, *A Vindication of Mr. Pope's Essay on Man, from the Misrepresentations of Mr. de Crousaz . . . in six letters* (London, 1740).

42 Emerich de Vattel, *Défense du système Leibnitien contre les objections et les imputations de Mr. De Crousaz, contenues dans l'Examens de L'Essai sur l'Homme de Mr. Pope: où l'on a joint la Réponse aux objections de Mr. Roques* (Leyden, 1741), Préface.

43 See Ernst Cassirer, *The Platonic Renaissance in England*, trans. J. P. Pettegrove (Austin, TX, 1953), ch. 6; C. A. Moore, 'Shaftesbury and the Ethical Poets in England, 1700–1760', *Proceedings of the Modern Language Association*, 31 (1916): 264–325.

44 See Shaftesbury's letter of 21 January 1706 to Basnage de Beauval, in *The Life, Unpublished Letters, and Philosophical Regimen of Anthony, Earl of Shaftesbury*, ed. B. Rand (London, 1900), 372–7.

45 Anthony Ashley Cooper, Earl of Shaftesbury, 'The Moralists: A Philosophical Rhapsody' (1709), in his *Characteristicks of Men, Manners, Opinions, Times, etc.*, 3 vols. (London, 1711), 2: 181–443, at 399.

46 Leibniz, *Jugement sur les œuvres de M. le comte de Shaftsbury*, in *Opera omnia*, ed. L. Dutens, 6 vols. (Geneva, 1768), 5: 45. See Armand Bacharach, *Shaftesburys Optimismus und sein Verhältnis zum Leibnizschen* (Thann, 1912); Yvon Belaval, *Études leibniziennes: de Leibniz à Hegel* (Paris, 1976), 86–105: 'L'harmonie'.

47 Joseph Butler, *The Analogy of Religion, Natural and Revealed, to the Constitution and Course of Nature*, in *Works*, ed. W. E. Gladstone, 2 vols. (Oxford, 1896), vol. 1. On Shaftesbury, see *Works*, 2: 52 n.1–6.

48 See Max Wundt, *Die deutsche Schulphilosophie im Zeitalter der Aufklärung* (Tübingen, 1945), ch. 3.i, at 265ff.

49 See Giorgio Tonelli, 'La question des bornes de l'entendement humain au XVIIIe siècle et la genèse du criticisme kantien, particulièrement par rapport au problème de l'infini', *Revue*

de métaphysique et de morale (1959): 396–427; same, 'The "Weakness" of Reason in the Age of Enlightenment', *Diderot Studies*, 14 (1971): 217–44.

50 Diderot, *Encyclopédie*, 11: 517.

51 Jean-Baptiste-René Robinet, *De la nature*, 3 vols. (Amsterdam, 1763–6), 3: 181 and 183. See Hazard, 'Le problème du mal', 163–6.

52 Nicolas Fréret, *Lettre de Thrasybule à Leucippe*, ed. S. Landucci (Florence, 1986). This is among the most important clandestine manuscripts. See Paul Vernière, *Spinoza et la pensée française avant la révolution*, 2 vols. (Paris, 1954); Ira O. Wade, *The Clandestine Organization and Diffusion of Philosophic Ideas in France from 1700 to 1750* (Princeton, NJ, 1938); *Le matérialisme du XVIIIe siècle et la littérature clandestine*, ed. O. Bloch (Paris, 1982); and Ann Thomson in ch. 6 in this volume.

53 Diderot, *Pensées philosophiques*, XV, in *Oeuvres philosophiques*, ed. P. Vernière (Paris, 1956), 16; and *Introduction aux grandes principes, ou Réception d'un philosophie*, in *Oeuvres complètes*, ed. J. Assézat, 20 vols. (Paris, 1875–7), 2: 71–99 at 85fns.

54 Samuel Johnson, *A Review of A Free Enquiry into the Nature and Origin of Evil*, in *Works*, ed. A. Murphy, 12 vols. (London, 1792), 8: 23–61.

55 Johnson, *Rasselas, Prince of Abyssinia* (1759) in *Works*, 3: 299–442.

56 See Wilhelm Lütgert, *Die Erschütterung des Optimismus durch das Erdbeben von Lissabon 1755* (Gütersloh, 1901); Theodore Besterman, 'Voltaire et le désastre de Lisbonne: ou, La mort de l'optimisme', *Studies on Voltaire and the Eighteenth Century*, 2 (1956): 7–24; Harald Weinrich, 'Literaturgeschichte eines Weltereignisses: Das Erdbeben von Lissabon', in his *Literatur für Leser: Essays und Aufsätze zur Literaturswissenschaft* (Munich, 1986), 74–90; George R. Havens, 'The conclusion of Voltaire's *Poème sur le désastre de Lisbonne*' *Modern Language Notes*, 56 (1941): 422–6; same, 'Voltaire's pessimistic revision of the conclusion of his *Poème sur le désastre de Lisbonne*', *Modern Language Notes*, 44 (1929): 489–92.

57 F. M. A. de Voltaire, *Poèmes sur la religion naturelle, et sur la destruction de Lisbonne* (Paris, 1756); 'Bien. Du bien et du mal, physique et moral', from *Dictionnaire philosophique* (1764), in *Oeuvres complètes*, ed. L. Moland, 52 vols. (Paris, 1877–85), 17: 576.

58 Voltaire, 'Bien', 577. See Haydn T. Mason, 'Voltaire and Manichean Dualism', *Studies on Voltaire and the Eighteenth Century*, 26 (1963): 1143–60.

59 Voltaire, Letter to Élie Bertrand, 18 February 1756, in his *Correspondence*, ed. T. Besterman, 107 vols. (Geneva, 1953–65), 17: 72–3.

60 Voltaire, 'Chaine des êtres créés', *Dictionnaire philosophique* (vol. 2), in *Oeuvres complètes*, 18: 123–5.

61 Voltaire, *Traité de métaphysique* (1734), in *Oeuvres complètes*, 22: 189–230 at 197, 200–1. See H. T. Mason, *Pierre Bayle and Voltaire* (London, 1963), 66.

62 Voltaire, *Homélie sur l'athéisme* (1767), in *Oeuvres complètes*, 25: 315–29 at 321.

63 Voltaire, *Éléments de la philosophie de Newton*, Pt. 1, ch. 1, in *Oeuvres complètes*, 22: 403–7 at 406.

64 Voltaire, 'Causes finales', *Dictionnaire philosophique* (vol. 2), 28: 97–106.

65 See René Pomeau, *La religion de Voltaire*, (Paris, 1969).

66 Jean-Jacques Rousseau, *Les confessions*, Bk. 9, in *Oeuvres*, 1: 1–656 at 429, as translated in *The Confessions and Correspondence*, trans. C. Kelly, eds. C. Kelly, R. D. Masters, and P. G. Stillman in *Collected Writings of Rousseau*, eds. C. Kelly and R. D. Masters (Hanover, NH and London, 1992), 5: 360.

67 See Section IV of this chapter.

68 See Jonathan Schollmeier, *Johann Joachim Spalding. Ein Beitrag zur Theologie der Aufklärung*, (Gütersloh, 1967); Christian F. Weiser, *Shaftesbury und das deutsche Geistesleben* (Leipzig, 1916). On neology, see Karl Aner, *Die Theologie der Lessingzeit* (Halle/Saale, 1929); Bruno Bianco, "Vernünftiges Christentum': Aspects et problèmes d'interpretation de la néologie

allemande du XVIIIe siècle', *Archives de philosophie*, 46 (1983): 179–218; and chs. 21 and 22 in this volume.

69 Johann Joachim Spalding, *Spaldings Bestimmung des Menschen (1748) und Wert der Andacht (1755)*, ed. H. Stephan (Giessen, 1908), 15.

70 See Thomas Abbt, *Zweifel über die Bestimmung des Menschen* and Moses Mendelssohn, *Orakel, die Bestimmung des Menschen betreffend*, both publ. 1764, in Mendelssohn's *Gesammelte Schriften*, vol 6.i (1981), 7–25. For the two men's discussion of Spalding's work see Alexander Altmann, 'Die Entstehung von Moses Mendelssohns Phädon' in his *Die trostvolle Aufklärung, Studien zur Metaphysik und politischen Theorie Moses Mendelssohns* (Stuttgart-Bad Cannstatt, 1982), 84–108; Stefan Lorenz, 'Skeptizismus und natürliche Religion. Thomas Abbt und Moses Mendelssohn in ihrer Debatte über Johann Joachim Spaldings *Bestimmung des Menschen*' in *Moses Mendelssohn und die Kreise seiner Wirksamkeit*, eds. M. Albrecht, E. J. Engel, and N. Hinske (Tübingen, 1994), 113–33.

71 See Frederic C. Tubach, 'Perfectibilité: der zweite Diskurs Rousseaus und die deutsche Aufklärung', *Études germaniques*, 15 (1960): 144–51; Gottfried Hornig. 'Perfektibilität. Eine Untersuchung zur Geschichte und Bedeutung dieses Begriffs in der deutschsprachigen Literatur', *Archiv für Begriffsgeschichte*, 24 (1980): 221–57.

72 See Mendelssohn, 'Zu Rousseaus *Discours sur l'origine et les fondements de l'inégalité parmi les hommes*'; 'Sendschreiben an Lessing, 2. Jenner 1756' ; 'Betrachtung über die Ungleichheit und Geselligkeit der Menschen', in *Gesammelte Schriften*, 2: 7–8; 83–96; and 133–40 at 134–6.

73 Mendelssohn, 'Brief an Karl Gotthelf Lessing, Februar 1781' in *Gesammelte Schriften*, 13: 6–7; see his *Anmerkungen zu Abbts freundschaftlicher Correspondenz* (1782) in *Gesammelte Schriften*, 6.i: 27–65 at 41.

74 See Mendelssohn, 'Orakel, die Bestimmung des Menschen betreffend', 22–3; 'Abbts Korrespondenz', 46–7, 55; *Phädon oder über die Unsterblichkeit der Seele* (1767), *Gesammelte Schriften*, 2: 5–128, *passim*. See Leibniz, *Philosophische Abhandlungen*, IX, *Philosophische Schriften*, 6: 607–23 at 621–3, and Immanuel Kant, *Kritik der Urtheilskraft*, §§83–4, in Ak 5: 165–485 at 429–36.

75 Mendelssohn, *Abbts Correspondenz*, 48.

76 Mendelssohn, 'Brief an August Hennings, June 1782', in *Gesammelte Schriften*, 13: 64–7.

77 The theme of the decline of civilisation occurs in the essay, *Ueber die Frage: was heiszt aufklären?* (1784), written, like Kant's famous essay, for the prize offered by the Berlin Academy of Sciences (*Gesammelte Schriften*, 6.i: 113–9). See also Norbert Hinske, 'Mendelssohns Beantwortung der Frage: Was ist Aufklärung? oder Über die Aktualität Mendelssohns', in *Ich handle mit Vernunft... Moses Mendelssohn und die europäische Aufklärung*, ed. N. Hinske (Hamburg, 1981), 85–117.

78 Mendelssohn, *Jerusalem*, in *Gesammelte Schriften*, 8: 99–204 at 162. Gotthold Ephraim Lessing, *Die Erziehung des Menschengeschlechts* in *Sämtliche Schriften*, eds. K. Lachmann and F. Muncker, 23 vols. (Leipzig, 1886–1924), 13: 413–36. See Walther von Loewenich, *Luther und Lessing* (Tübingen, 1960); Georges Pons, *Gotthold Ephraim Lessing et le christianisme* (Paris, 1964); Wilhelm Totok, 'Theodizee bei Leibniz und Lessing', in *Beiträge zur Wirkungs- und Rezeptionsgeschichte von Gottfried Wilhelm Leibniz*, ed. A. Heinekamp (Stuttgart, 1986), 177–87.

79 Lessing, *Erziehung des Menschengeschlechts*, §§86–7, pp. 433–4.

80 §§94–100, pp. 435–6. See Alexander Altmann, 'Lessings Glaube an die Seelenwanderung' in his *Die trostvolle Aufklärung*, 109–34.

81 David Hume, *Dialogues concerning Natural Religion*, ed. J. V. Price, in *The Natural History of Religion and Dialogues concerning Natural Religion*, eds. A. W. Colver and J. V. Price (Oxford, 1976), 181.

82 Hume, *An Enquiry concerning Human Understanding*, ed. T. L. Beauchamp, in the *Clarendon Edition* (2000), 11.17, SBN 138; see also 10.2.40, SBN 130.

83 Hume, *Dialogues*, II, 161–2. See J. C. A. Gaskin, *Hume's Philosophy of Religion* (London, 1988), 13; Robert H. Hurlbutt, *Hume, Newton and the Design Argument* (Lincoln, NE, 1965); R. G. Swinburne, 'The Argument from Design', *Philosophy*, 43 (1968): 199–212.

84 Jean Meslier, *Mémoire des pensées et sentiments*, in *Oeuvres complètes*, eds. J. Deprun, R. Desné, and A. Soboul, 3 vols. (Paris, 1970–72), vol. 1. On Meslier's critique of God's goodness, see *Oeuvres*, 1: 492–7. See also Jean Deprun, 'Meslier philosophe', *Oeuvres*, 1: lxxxi–c; Pierre Rétat, 'Meslier et Bayle: un dialogue cartésien et occasionaliste autour de l'athéisme', in *Le curé Meslier et la vie intellectuelle, religieuse et sociale à la fin du 17e et au début du 18e siècle*, ed. R. Desné (Reims, 1980), 497–516.

85 See Anna Minerbi Belgrado, *Paura e ignoranza: studi sulla teoria della religione in d'Holbach* (Florence, 1983); Rétat, *Le Dictionnaire de Bayle*, 419–30.

86 Paul-Henri-Thiry d'Holbach, *Système de la nature ou Des loix du monde physique et du monde morale*, ed. D. Diderot, 2 vols. (Paris 1821); same, *Le bon sens du curé Meslier, suivi de son Testament* (Paris, 1833).

87 See also *Système de la nature*, 2: ch. 19, 458–62, and the final section of ch. 18, 'On mythology and theology', 456–7.

88 Voltaire was impressed by *Le bon sens*; see his *Remarques sur Le bon sens ou Idées naturelles opposées aux idées surnaturelles* (1774) in *Oeuvres complètes*, 31: 151–60, and his comment in a letter to d'Alembert, 29 July 1775, *Correspondence*, 42: 110–11.

89 Immanuel Kant, *Über das Miszlingen aller philosophischen Versuche in der Theodicee*, Ak 8: 255–71 at 255; translated as *On the Miscarriage of all Philosophical Trials in Theodicy* by G. di Giovanni, in *Works/Religion and Rational Theology*, trans. and eds. A. W. Wood and G. di Giovanni (1996).

90 Kant, *Principiorum primorum cognitionis metaphysicae nova dilucidatio*, Ak 1: 387–416; translated as *A New Elucidation of the First Principles of Metaphysical Cognition* in *Works/Theoretical Philosophy 1755–1770*, trans. and eds. D. Walford and R. Meerbote (1992); Kant, *Versuch einiger Betrachtungen über den Optimismus*, Ak 2: 27–35; and *Reflexionen zur Optimismus*, nos. 3703–5, Ak 17: 229–39; translated as *An Attempt at Some Reflections on Optimism* and 'Appendix: Three Manuscript Reflections on Optimism' in *Theoretical Philosophy 1755–1770*.

91 Kant, *Vorlesungen über Metaphysik und Rationaltheologie*, Ak 28.ii.2: 1071–99, 1181–1201, 1286–1302. See Kurt Hildebrandt, 'Kant's Verhältnis zu Leibniz in der vorkritischen Periode', *Zeitschrift für philosophische Forschung*, 8 (1954): 3–29.

92 See Robert Theis, *Gott, Untersuchung zur Entwicklung des theologischen Diskurses in Kants Schriften zur theoretischen Philosophie bis hin zum Erscheinen der Kritik der reinen Vernunft* (Stuttgart-Bad Cannstatt, 1994); Giovanni B. Sala, *Kant und die Frage nach Gott, Gottesbeweise und Gottesbeweiskritik in dem Schriften Kants* (Berlin, 1990).

93 Kant, *Kritik der reinen Vernunft*, B 72; translated as *Works/Critique of Pure Reason*, trans. and eds. P. Guyer and A. W. Wood (1998).

94 See John R. Silber, 'Kant's Conception of the Highest Good as Immanent and Transcendent', *Philosophical Review*, 68 (1959): 469–92; Klaus Düsing, 'Das Problem des höchsten Gutes in Kants praktischer Philosophie', *Kant-Studien*, 62 (1971): 5–42; Giovanni B. Sala, 'Wohlerhalten und Wohlergehen', *Theologie und Philosophie*, 68 (1993): 182–207, 368–98.

95 Kant, *Kritik der praktischen Vernunft*, Ak 5: 113–14, as translated in *Works/Practical Philosophy*, trans. and ed. M. J. Gregor (1996). See Michael Albrecht, *Kants Antinomie der praktischen Vernunft* (Hildesheim, 1978); Klaus Düsing, 'Kant und Epikur', *Allgemeine Zeitschrift für Philosophie* (1976), 39–58; Norbert Hinske, 'Zwischen fortuna und felicitas. Glücksvorstellungen im Wandel der Zeiten', *Philosophisches Jahrbuch*, 85 (1975): 317–30; Manfred Sommer, 'Kant

und die Frage nach dem Glück' in *Die Frage nach dem Glück*, ed. G. Bien (Stuttgart-Bad Cannstatt, 1978), 131–45; Emil Angehrn, 'Der Begriff des Glücks und die Frage der Ethik', *Philosophisches Jahrbuch*, 92 (1985): 35–52.

96 See especially Ernst Cassirer, *The Question of Jean-Jacques Rousseau*, trans. P. Gay (New Haven, CT, 1989); same, *The Philosophy of the Enlightenment*, trans. F. C. A. Koelln and J. P. Pettegrove (Princeton, NJ, 1951), esp. 153ff. and 258–274.

97 Rousseau, *Discours sur l'origine et les fondements de l'inégalité*, in *Oeuvres*, 3: 109–223 at 202; translated as *Discourse on the Origin and Foundation of Inequality among Men*, in Rousseau, *The Discourses and Other Early Political Writings*, trans. and ed. V. Gourevitch (Cambridge, 1997), 113–222, at 197.

98 Rousseau, *Lettre de J. J. Rousseau a Monsieur de Voltaire*, in *Oeuvres*, 4: 1059–75, at 1061–3; translated as *Letter from J. J. Rousseau to M. de Voltaire* in *The Discourses*, 232–46, at 234–5. See Luigi Luporini, *L'ottimismo di Jean-Jacques Rousseau* (Florence, 1982).

99 Rousseau, *Émile ou De l'éducation*, in *Oeuvres*, 4: 239–868 at 245; translated as *Émile, or On Education*, trans. and ed. A. Bloom (Harmondsworth, 1991), 37.

100 Rousseau, Préface to *Narcisse*, in *Oeuvres*, 2: 957–1018 at 969; translated as 'Preface to *Narcissus*' in *The Discourses*, 92–106, at 101. See *Confessions*, Bk. 9, p. 404; trans. 340.

27

RELIGION AND SOCIETY

SIMONE ZURBUCHEN

After the French Revolution, optimistic radical reformers expected a new society to emerge, one in which the conflicts between different religious denominations, which provoked the intolerant policy of the Old Regime, would be overcome. Most philosophers demanding the separation of religion and society identified the moral beliefs on which the new society would be built with the rational core of true Christianity, pessimistic conservatives, however, suggested that the Revolution was the result of the decidedly anti-Christian tendencies of the Enlightenment. These conflicting notions of the relationship between the Enlightenment and the Christian religion represent two tendencies of eighteenth-century philosophy, which among other things directed attempts to re-define the role of religion in society. On the one hand, most philosophers were convinced that the order of human society was based on a belief in God as provider of moral law and thus they tried to harmonise the tensions between the other-worldly oriented Christian religion and secular society. On the other hand, philosophers attacked the Christian religion, since they perceived institutionalised Christianity as a form of intolerant superstition or fanaticism.

Two wholly different ways of harmonising the tensions between religion and society are depicted in Sections 1 and 4. The first can generally be characterised by the tendency to separate religious issues from social or political ones. Eighteenth-century concepts of toleration proceeded on the assumption that the care of religion did not belong among the duties of the state because religious faith was the purely personal concern of the individual. Among the main arguments used to reject the pretensions of church and state to control religious belief was the assertion of a right to private judgment in religious matters. The demand for legal protection of this individual right finally led to the abandonment of the notion of toleration and the demand for constitutional reform. The second way is marked by a critical account of the other-worldly orientation of the Christian religion. Since religion was, nonetheless, within the tradition of republicanism, considered as an essential factor in guaranteeing social stability, the criticism of Christian values as contradicting worldly interests led to the conception of a new kind of religion which sought to replace Christianity in its role as a civil or public religion.

Sections 2 and 3 focus on those theories which were labelled dangerous for society, since they would, through their attack on the Christian religion, undermine the moral foundations of society. Section 2 deals with philosophical atheism, which was seen as lurking everywhere, although in fact only a few thinkers openly avowed it and even then only relatively late in the century. Section 3 describes the results of some of the new theories of society, in which religion was treated as a social phenomenon, subject to scientific investigation. As these theories discussed the social utility of religions independent of their truth, they could be used to support the claim for toleration of religious nonconformity while demonstrating both the irrational origin of religion and its distorting effects on society. In this way they provided a basis for attacking the conviction that social order was ultimately based on religious belief.

I. FROM TOLERATION TO RELIGIOUS LIBERTY

Toleration represents one of the central ideas of eighteenth-century intellectual life. Not only was it one of the most debated issues, it was also linked with the notion of enlightenment itself. When Kant, in his *Beantwortung der Frage: Was ist Aufklärung?*, stresses 'freedom to make public use of one's reason', he focuses on the principle which governs both philosophical speculation and religious dissent.[1] In the first decades of the century philosophers who advocated the 'right to think freely also in matters of religion' (Collins), or who demanded '*libertas philosophandi*' and '*libertas cogitandi*' (Thomasius) were also attacking the view that heresy was a crime.[2] In the second half of the century, when the best-known writings on toleration such as Voltaire's *Traité sur la tolérance*, Lessing's *Nathan der Weise*, and Mendelssohn's *Jerusalem* were published, the alliance between enlightenment and dissent found expression in growing public awareness of the contradiction between the progress of reason on the one hand and the continuing intolerance toward philosophers and religious nonconformists on the other.[3]

In spite of the intrinsic relation between enlightenment and toleration, by the end of the century the idea of toleration was already considered outdated. After the American and French Revolutions some of the most prominent advocates of religious liberty wished to abolish toleration in the name of universal rights of conscience. Thomas Paine's remarks best exemplify this kind of criticism:

> The French constitution hath abolished or renounced *toleration*, and *intoleration* also, and hath established *universal right of conscience*.
>
> Toleration is not the *opposite* of intoleration, but the *counterfeit* of it. Both are despotisms. The one assumes to itself the rights of withholding liberty of conscience, and the other

of granting it. The one is the pope, armed with fire and faggot, and the other is the pope selling or granting indulgences. The former is church and state, and the latter is church and traffic.[4]

Toleration is to be replaced with the 'universal right of conscience' because 'liberty of conscience' belongs to the 'natural and imprescriptible rights of man' (141), which can be preserved, according to Paine, only in the republican system. As he identifies the union of church and state as an arbitrary power threatening liberty of conscience, the legal protection of the right of conscience presupposes the abolition of any religion established and maintained by the state. Paine's advocacy of a universal right of conscience illustrates the convergence of religious and political principles, a convergence which also characterises the political theories of radical Dissenters such as Richard Price and Joseph Priestley. Although they still used the term *toleration,* they recognised, like Paine, an indissoluble link between religious and civil liberty, which 'must be enjoyed as a right', and demanded the separation of church and state.[5] The radicalisation of the claim for toleration can thus be seen as a shift from toleration to religious liberty.

The following overview aims less at elaborating the concepts of toleration than at exploring the reasons which motivated them. First, I will investigate how the idea of toleration was linked to the defence of a 'right of conscience' or a 'right of private judgment in matters of religion'. This link was made early in the eighteenth century and later served as a necessary presupposition for the concept of a right of conscience as one of the rights of men. Secondly, I will trace the origins of the notion that the abolition of all religion established and maintained by the state is a precondition for the legal protection of religious liberty.

1. *Toleration and conscience*

Eighteenth-century concepts of toleration were greatly indebted to the new theory of the state as it was developed within Protestant natural-law theory. Both Samuel Pufendorf and John Locke[6] had advocated the separation of state and religion on the grounds that each serves wholly different ends. Whereas it is the duty of the state to secure the things belonging to this life, religion is concerned with the care of souls and the question of eternal welfare. Since both Pufendorf and Locke explained religious faith as the spiritual relation between the individual and God, they concluded that the care of religion did not belong to the duties of the state, which is concerned with the outward control of actions. The concept of toleration was thus based on an individualistic concept of religion as well as on the limitation of the purposes of the state. Both these arguments were adapted and developed in the eighteenth century.

Before proceeding, the following two points should be mentioned as they show why it is impossible to present a clear-cut account of toleration in the eighteenth century. First, although the Protestant tradition enjoyed priority in advocating toleration, representatives of the Catholic Enlightenment helped to secure public acceptance of a tolerant reform policy by promoting the idea of Christian toleration.[7] Second, the meaning of toleration varies in different contexts.[8] In Great Britain, discussions focused on the provisions of the Toleration Act of 1689. As the act only lifted the penalties of some laws on which the former discrimination against Dissent was based, the Test and Corporation Acts still left 'orthodox' Protestant Dissenters (Presbyterians, Independents, Baptists) in a politically inferior position; the Toleration Act omitted all others.[9] In France, intervention in favour of toleration were directed at the provisions of the Revocation of the Edict of Nantes (the Edict of Fontainebleau) and related pieces of legislation by which all the rights earlier granted to the Huguenots were revoked, all forms of public worship in the Reformed rite were suppressed, and severe punishments were meted out to those who sought refuge abroad. Until well after mid-century toleration had nothing to do with freedom of worship or freedom of thought, but meant the recognition of the civil status of the Calvinists, that is, the validation of their births and marriages.[10] In the German Empire the term *toleration* had been used to define the arrangements between Protestants and Roman Catholics in the Treaty of Westphalia, which granted legal recognition to Catholics, Lutherans, and Reformed Church members, but excluded all others. As its provisions gave the territorial princes power over the church (*jus reformandi*), toleration, in the eighteenth century, was considered a matter of absolutist reform policy, which tended to grant latitude to religious minorities in the territories and privileges to immigrants.[11]

Protestant accounts of the nature of religion can generally be characterised, first, by a tendency to spiritualise religion and thus to stress the difference between inward conviction and outward behaviour, and secondly, by a tendency to see religious faith as purely the personal concern of the individual seeking to become acceptable to God. As religious reformers such as the Pietists in the Lutheran parts of Germany and sects such as the Baptists in America supported this tendency, they contributed, each on different grounds, to the religious justification of toleration.[12] Like Pierre Bayle in his extensive plea for toleration, certain philosophers questioned especially the doctrine of the erring conscience, which the established churches had used to legitimise their control of individual consciences; Jean Barbeyrac adapted Locke's theory of conscience;

and conscience played a role in the ideas of toleration of such important German thinkers as Justus Henning Boehmer and Christoph Matthäus Pfaff.[13] An often mentioned ideal was the notion of an 'invisible church', which represents the Kingdom of Christ as 'wholly not of this world'.[14]

A link was established between the nature of religion and a secular concept of toleration by examining what the purpose of a state should be. Since Locke had determined the aims of a state in terms of the natural rights of men, his theory could be used to develop a new argument in defence of toleration.[15] The rights-based doctrines of toleration, however, were not, as many Dissenters claimed, adaptations of Locke's concept of toleration to the religio-political questions discussed in the eighteenth century; they were rather new interpretations of it, which go beyond Locke's main argument for toleration. This is best shown when Locke's position on the question of toleration is depicted as a negative one.[16] For Locke aims, in his *Letter on Toleration*, to demonstrate that it is irrational to use coercive means to alter a person's religious belief. Toleration is thus understood as the absence of force in matters of religion. He does not mention religion as one of the natural rights of men.

The lead in this re-interpretation of Locke's theory was taken by Dissenters and philosophers in Great Britain. In the first extensive discussion between the attackers and defenders of the Test and Corporation Acts, the Bangorian Controversy, the debate already centered on different conceptions of natural rights.[17] In France and the German Empire, toleration was not linked to the idea of natural rights until, under the influence of the ideas of the American Revolution, natural rights were labelled inalienable human rights.

There were two ways of relating toleration to the idea of natural rights. The first is based on the correlation between the duty to obey God and the right of private judgment. The rights-based argumentation is fully developed in Philip Furneaux's *Essay on Toleration*,[18] where he claims that the right of private judgment is a right belonging to every man 'as a rational and moral agent' (sect. I: 364). Furneaux links this right, which is understood as a right 'without the control of others' (I: 346), to the duty to obey God. The 'right of private judgment' is one of the 'original, primary rights' (II: 367); it is, according to Furneaux, 'essential to our nature' (I: 364). 'Religious liberty' contains not only the 'right of private judgment' but also the right to overt acts (III: 370) and 'the right of public instruction in matters of religion' (III: 375), which is a consequence of the former. These rights 'should never lie at the mercy of any; but on the contrary, should have every protection and ground of security, which law, and the policy of free states, can give them'.[19] The same argument is developed by Madison, who was probably the first to advocate a change in terminology. He recommended altering article XVI of the Virginia

Declaration of Rights of 1776, which demanded 'the fullest toleration in the exercise of religion' to the affirmation that 'all men are equally entitled to the free exercise of it [religion], according to the dictates of Conscience'.[20] The *Memorial and Remonstrance against Religious Assessments* of 1785 in some way provides a comment on article XVI of the Virginia Bill of Rights, to which Madison refers several times. Here Madison derives the 'unalienable right' to exercise religion from the 'duty which we owe to our Creator', which 'is precedent, both in order of time and in degree of obligation, to the claims of Civil Society'.[21]

The correlation between religious duties which belong to the responsibilities of the individual and a natural right to freedom of worship is also invoked by the Unitarian Dissenters Joseph Priestley and Richard Price. However, they surpass moderate Dissenters such as Furneaux in their adaptation of Locke's political theory in two directions. First, they develop, each on a different basis, a comprehensive theory of civil liberty, as distinct from political liberty to which Price, unlike Priestley, gives priority, meaning by political liberty 'self-government' or 'self-direction'. Civil liberty comprises not only the right to freedom of worship but all natural rights.[22] Priestley declares, in the *Essay on the First Principles of Government*, that 'the *civil liberty* of the state' depends on the question 'whether a people enjoy more or fewer of their natural rights' (sect. III: 29). Second, they argue that the legal protection of natural rights depends on the self-government of the people, that is, their participation in representative institutions by which they can exercise control over their government. For, as Price states, civil liberty 'changes its nature, and becomes a species of slavery' 'if there is any human power which is considered as giving it, on which it depends, and which can invade or recall it at pleasure'.[23] As the legal protection of religious as well as civil liberty presupposes a republican government, according to Priestley and Price, toleration is achieved by constitutional reforms.[24]

The other direction in which Locke's theory of natural rights was developed took its departure from his notion of the right to self-preservation. Compared to other rights this one has an exceptional position because Locke claims that it was 'planted in him [Man] as a Principle of Action by God himself'.[25] Whereas Locke seems to restrict this right to physical preservation, Thomas Jefferson, in his preamble to the Bill for Establishing Religious Freedom, stresses that God is the Lord 'both of body and mind'.[26] He thus links the claim for religious liberty to the belief that 'Almighty God hath created the mind free, and manifested his supreme will that free it shall remain by making it altogether insusceptible of restraint'. Similar interpretations of the right to preservation were developed by Moses Mendelssohn and Peter Winkopp. Although in the German Empire debates on civil liberty within the context of modern constitutionalism did not arise until after the French Revolution, the idea of inalienable rights, expressed as the rights of humanity, the rights of mankind or the rights of human nature, was of growing importance in the debates after 1770.[27] The most important works treating questions of toleration, such as Christian Wilhelm Dohm's *Über die bürgerliche Verbesserung der Juden* and Moses Mendelssohn's *Jerusalem*, are marked by reception of the new ideas. Both Dohm and Mendelssohn advocate Jewish emancipation in the name of the rights of mankind.[28] Whereas Dohm still draws on earlier debates about naturalizing the Jews and thus points to their political and economic utility, Mendelssohn justifies his demand for the toleration of Jews in terms of the doctrine of natural law. Although Mendelssohn is largely indebted to Christian Wolff's theory of the state, he combines German natural-law theory with considerations drawn from Locke's theory of property. In his preface to the German translation of Manasseh Ben Israel's *Rettung der Juden* he defends a right to investigate and examine beliefs by reason, of which he declares: 'This right is inseparable from the person and can, by its very nature, be no more alienated or granted to others than the right to still our hunger or to breathe'. As our belief is, according to Mendelssohn, 'unmovable and also inalienable property', it cannot be delegated in a social contract to the civil magistrate (20). By declaring the right to believe to be a person's property, Mendelssohn is obviously adapting Locke's right to property, which Locke had derived from the right to preservation, to the problem of toleration. Following in the tradition of German natural-law theory he also resorts, in *Jerusalem*, to the distinction between perfect and imperfect duties and rights when he argues that men have a perfect right to develop their own faculties, the physical as well as the mental (114–23). A similar argument was developed by Peter Winkopp, who, in an anonymously published tract, criticised Joseph II's Edict of Toleration because it did not apply to the deists. He claims freedom of thought not as a favour, but as a duty of the magistrate (sect. III: 3–6) and reminds Austrian admirers of the Edict of Toleration that such toleration should not depend on the will of the monarch (37). Laws concerning freedom of thought and religion ought to be deduced from the purpose of civil society (46–49), which he defines, in the tradition of Christian Wolff's natural-law theory, as happiness (sect. IV: 50–1). Winkopp criticises Pufendorf and Locke for having incompletely described the ends of civil society[29] and claims that the satisfaction not only of physical needs (life, liberty, and property) but also of mental ones ought to be considered as essential to men's happiness (50–2). As freedom of thought and religion are mental needs, Winkopp concludes that every member of society has a complete right (54) to them and that the state must protect them just as much as physical needs.

The depiction of a similar development of the idea of toleration in France seems problematic. In spite of Jean Barbeyrac's reference to Locke's theory of rights in his influential French translation of Pufendorf's *De jure naturae et gentium*, Locke's ideas were rarely adapted to the problem of toleration. French intellectuals, with few exceptions, had welcomed the Revocation of the Edict of Nantes.[30] Even the Calvinists living in France and those in the 'Refuge' were not interested in radical ideas; they were more concerned with demonstrating their loyalty to the Catholic king since they had laboured, from the sixteenth century, under suspicion of defending republican ideas.[31] It was only after 1760 that a radical change took place in the perception of the Calvinists' situation, as a result of the Calas affair and the Franco-American Alliance. Voltaire's public involvement in defence of Calvinist civil rights, of which the *Traité sur la tolérance* was but one result, proved decisive in effecting a change in the national consciousness.[32] He denounces the collaboration between the judicial power of the state and fanatical Catholicism, which had led to the assassination of the innocent Calvinist, Jean Calas. The juridical assistance thus provided is labelled barbarian, conflicting with natural law, the foundation of all human law.[33]

More significant than Voltaire's criticism of fanaticism was the discussion in connection with the numerous drafts of human rights for which the different American declarations provided the model. Anne-Robert-Jacques Turgot, who was the first French philosopher to demand the abolition of a religion protected by the state, and Jean-Antoine-Nicolas Caritat, marquis de Condorcet, pointed to the exemplary character of liberty cherished by the American people. Its admirers also included Honoré Gabriel Riquetti, comte de Mirabeau, who later played an important role during the debates on religious toleration in the National Assembly, where he recommended the abolition of the concept of toleration in favour of religious liberty.[34]

Both ways of re-interpreting Locke's theory of toleration rested originally on the view that human authority should not interfere with God's relationship to the individual. Since they depended on a religious presupposition, it is not at first sight evident how these arguments could be used to defend free-thinking in matters of religion. Free-thinkers, however, far from wishing to abolish Christian values, believed that philosophical reasoning would confirm the essential practical doctrines of the Christian religion and thus could safely be tolerated by the state. This was consistent with the argument from the progress of truth.

This argument was fully developed in the second half of the century when it was linked to the idea of human perfectibility through reason and truth. As advances in arts and sciences suggested that reasoning and truth would always defeat error, many philosophers, especially under the influence of the French Revolution, concluded that vices and moral weakness are not invincible. Since freedom of thought was conceived as a necessary presupposition to improve human powers, the idea of the progress of truth could be used to justify full liberty of thought.[35] Priestley's and Kant's theories of the perfectibility of mankind show clearly how the idea of moral progress could be adapted to modify opposition between natural religion, accessible to reason, and revealed religion, whose content was fixed within the dogmas of the established churches. Priestley, in the *Essay on the First Principles of Government*, depicts the progress of humankind as guided by Divine Providence, which intended 'to lead mankind to happiness in a progressive, which is the surest, though the slowest, method' (sect. X: 124), that is, through self-thought or self-instruction. Since establishments, and more specifically religious establishments, 'be they ever so excellent, still fix things somewhere' (125), they contradict the intention of Divine Providence. Religious establishments should therefore be abolished and full religious liberty granted to allow the reform of religion. Unlike Priestley, whose optimism is nourished by the conviction that reason will soon predominate and that the end of this world 'will be glorious and paradisiacal' (sect. I: 9), Kant conceives of moral progress as a process which can never be completed. In his *Religion innerhalb der Grenzen der bloßen Vernunft*, taking up Lessing's idea of moral progress, he distinguishes between pure moral religion, founded on reason, and statutory or historical faith, founded on revelation.[36] Although the factual transition to a pure religion of reason corresponds to the moral condition of reasonable beings, it is, according to Kant, infinitely distant. The unification of the religion of reason, which corresponds to full liberty of religion, and of statutory faith in a universal visible church is an idea of reason which serves merely as a regulative practical principle. Kant thus rejects the idea of a revolution and advocates a steady process of reform to realise the idea of a religion of reason and liberty in matters of religion (Ak 6: 123n).

2. *Church and state*

The main opponents of toleration in the eighteenth century were the theologians who were convinced that non-conformity and philosophy, which questioned the prerogatives of the established churches, were endangering the stability of the old order. They persisted in the opinion that non-conformity was a schism and therefore a crime and resorted to the doctrine of the divine right of the church. In Great Britain this position was defended by Henry Sacheverell and later in the century by William Blackstone, who was attacked by Dissenters such as Furneaux and Priestley.[37] Reacting to attacks on the position of the church in society, William Warburton developed new arguments to defend its prerogatives. His *Alliance between Church and State*, which was also well known in Germany and France, is the most important tract defending the prerogatives of a national church.[38] It not only aimed at rejecting the Dissenters' claim for dispensation from the Test and Corporation Acts, but also developed the main arguments for not extending toleration to the philosophers, who claimed a right to think freely in religious matters. Unlike High Church representatives, who were still guided by the former Anglican concept of an indissoluble religious link between church and monarchy, Warburton accepted the Toleration Act as part of the Revolutionary settlement. Since he did not question the political principles of the Revolution his moderate orthodox theory was also used by conservative minded Whigs, who wanted to uphold a state church protected by Test Laws.

Warburton develops a concept of limited toleration which he claims to derive from Locke's theory of toleration.[39] Civil society and church are, according to Warburton, sovereign and independent societies (Bk II, sect. V: 248). If the magistrate wishes to improve the influence of religion 'by human Art and Contrivance', he has to seek a Union or Alliance with the church, which can be produced only 'by free Convention and mutual Compact' (248). Such an alliance produces a 'Religion by Law established' (242, 258). Warburton mentions three motives for the state to enter into this alliance (248–56). First, it allows the magistrate to control the clerics. Secondly, it lends to the church 'a coactive power', by which it is enabled to enforce 'duties of imperfect Obligation', that is, moral duties, which civil laws cannot enforce. Thirdly, the alliance prevents conflicts between different religious denominations and sects as well as their vying with each other for 'influence in the public Administration'. The last point furnished Warburton with the main argument justifying the Test and Corporation Acts. He concluded that the alliance was 'the most effectual Remedy' to these dangers (256). That he thought it necessary to exclude the free-thinkers from toleration is obvious, because he considered them dangerous to public peace and security. He charged them with the abuse of natural rights, which he recognised only in name, not in spirit (Dedication, xxxi–xlvii).

Since restrictions on religious liberty and freedom of thought were justified as necessary means to protect the alliance between church and state, any future claim for legal protection of a 'right to private judgment in matters of religion' had to include the demand for the abolition of all established religion. With regard to the latter, developments in America were, once more, of particular relevance.[40] The American model was at first, for most Anglicans and Dissenters, one of moderation. It served the Dissenters, who were still ready to acknowledge an established church, as a demonstration that the state's interests could be congruent with granting individual rights. However, radical Dissenters such as Priestley and Price used the model to argue for a total disestablishment of all religion, interpreting the union between church and state as the origin of the abuse of power infringing on the natural rights of men. Madison's arguments best show the link between the advocacy of an unalienable right to exercise religion and the criticism of an established church. In the second part of the *Memorial* Madison complains that the civil magistrate's use of religion 'as an engine of civil policy' is nothing but 'an unhallowed perversion of the means of salvation' (301). Established religion would serve neither to maintain the purity and efficacy of religion nor to support the civil government, because in the past it served only to uphold 'the thrones of political tyranny'. Established religions were never, according to Madison, 'the guardians of the liberties of the people' (302).

The radical Dissenters' attacks on any form of established church as well as their demands for constitutional reform provoked strong reactions. Thus Edmund Burke, for example, changed his attitude toward the Dissenters, whose claim for toleration he had previously supported. When he published his *Reflections on the Revolution in France* he was still ready to extend toleration even to Catholics, Jews, Muslims, and pagans.[41] Burke's hostility toward the Dissenters, therefore, was not motivated by his attitude toward a right of conscience, but was the result of his aversion to atheism, which he believed to have inspired the French Revolution. As he judged atheism to be intimately related to political radicalism, he suspected the Dissenters, who demanded the abolition of the religious establishment, of being infidels whom he considered 'outlaws of the Constitution; not of this country, but of the human race'.[42] Burke's conviction that Dissenters had turned to support atheism, which for him was linked with republican principles, had its counterpart in France, where, after the French Revolution, the Protestants were suspected of being in league with the *philosophes* (and sometimes with the Jansenists and the Freemasons), in a conspiracy which aimed to destroy the monarchy and the Catholic Church.[43]

II. ATHEISM

Atheism in the eighteenth century was marked by numerous paradoxes. It may at first seem somewhat surprising that, with the exception of Priestley, no philosopher of note was ready to extend toleration to atheism, and this in spite of the tendency discussed above to separate religious from social or political issues.[44] In fact, the danger of atheism was widely conjured up, not only by religious orthodoxy but also by philosophers like Voltaire, himself famous for his anti-Christian polemics. This did not, however, prevent many prominent philosophers from being themselves charged with atheism. The accusation or even the mere suspicion of atheism proved among the most effective means of intimidation or suppression, since atheism was punishable even in a relatively free country like England.[45] In Germany, during the 'atheism controversy' (*Atheismusstreit*) in the closing years of the century, Johann Gottlieb Fichte and Friedrich Karl Forberg were charged with atheism and the controversy ended in Fichte's dismissal by the University of Jena.[46] Yet more paradoxical, in spite of the extended attacks on atheism, especially in the early part of the century when several works aiming to refute atheism took on encyclopedic proportions,[47] only a small minority of thinkers openly avowed it and then only relatively late in the century. The first clear public proclamation of atheism, Paul-Henry Thiry d'Holbach's *Système de la nature*, dates from 1770; in the first half of the century antireligious opinions circulated in clandestine manuscripts or were cautiously published under the mask of feigned orthodoxy.[48]

What then was atheism and on what grounds was it considered dangerous to society? These questions are difficult to answer because generally in eighteenth-century culture behavioral and conceptual atheism were conflated and very often no distinction was made 'between denying the 'true' God and denying that there was a Supreme Being at all'.[49] The one distinction which was commonly made in the eighteenth century was the one between speculative and practical atheism, the former designating the intellectual conviction that there is no God, the latter referring to the behaviour of the ignorant.[50] As both David Berman and Alan Charles Kors have convincingly shown, an important claim in polemical literature throughout the century was that there could be no sincere atheistic belief, since '*being an atheist* . . . was a function solely of the will, while *thinking as an atheist* obviously referred in some essential way to a function of the mind'.[51] With the claim that it was impossible to think as an atheist, an atheist was presented as an ignorant person aiming at an intellectual justification of an immoral life by denying God's existence. In spite of the denial that speculative atheism was possible, this position was nevertheless acknowledged as one to refute, and thinkers such as Samuel Clarke or Johann Franz Budde seem to have assumed in their arguments against atheism that reasoning or philosophical atheists did actually exist.[52]

There are three recent suggestions for dealing with the paradox that atheists in the eighteenth century were seen everywhere although in reality they hardly existed. One is Kors's proposal that hypothetical atheism, as conceived in the apologetic literature of the late seventeenth century, constituted one of the main sources of eighteenth-century atheism. Alternative accounts are presented by Berman and David Wootton.[53] The former has interpreted the common insistence on the non-existence of reasoning atheists as a strategy used both by those who wanted to suppress atheism and by those who intended to defend their own philosophical positions against the charge of atheism. Berman explains his theory of the double strategic use by pointing to examples of how the respective opponents of such strategic uses exposed them for what they were. Whereas David Hume in his *Enquiry* ridiculed those religious philosophers who, while denying the existence of speculative atheism, nevertheless argue against it, Richard Bentley had claimed to uncover the subversive tendencies of those hiding atheism 'under the mask and shadow of a Deity'. Hume's own denials of the existence of atheists are interpreted by Berman as a strategy of defence, as an attempt to eliminate the word *atheism*, with which his philosophy was charged. An example of a theoretical account of the kinds of strategy described by Berman is provided by John Toland who, taking up the ancient distinction between esoteric and exoteric philosophy, sees the place of pure esoteric teaching in secret societies as described in the *Pantheisticon*.[54] Exoteric teaching, on the other hand, consists in what Berman calls 'the Art of Theological Lying', a kind of writing between the lines, which will seem innocuous to the uninitiated observer.[55]

Toland's esoteric-exoteric distinction also provides evidence for Wootton's claim that a *History of Atheism* has to investigate the lines of a distinguished tradition of antireligious thought, for Toland was a member of a secret society of French Protestant refugees in The Hague, the Knights of Jubilation. Since one of its members had published an important clandestine manuscript, it provides a model for other groups of philosophers which secretly organised the distribution of atheist tracts: the Boulainvilliers' connection and the 'coterie d'Holbach'.[56]

The question of why and how atheism was considered dangerous to society is best discussed by examining the question of whether atheists were seen as valuable members of society. It was Pierre Bayle who, in his reflections on the problem, set up the terms in which the impact of atheism on society was discussed throughout the eighteenth century. Bayle was the first to claim that a society of atheists was perfectly viable on the grounds that moral actions were independent of religious beliefs. He conceived of a society governed by laws related to men's inclinations and habits, laws which made the fear of God superfluous as a foundation of society. The observation that men's theoretical beliefs have no effect on their behaviour led Bayle to state his paradox that atheism was less dangerous to society than superstition. He did not, however, intend the paradox as a defence of atheism, of which, incidentally, he was accused by his contemporaries, for he did not wish to abolish a rigoristic outlook on morality as it was included in 'true' Christianity. Bayle's ambivalence toward atheism is also evident in his interpretation of Spinoza's philosophy in the *Dictionary*. Although he transmitted the myth of the 'virtuous atheist' Spinoza to the eighteenth century, he himself advanced the main arguments for rejecting

Spinoza's 'systematical atheism' as dangerous philosophical speculation which would make ethics meaningless.[57]

The following three issues, all raised by Bayle, constituted the main points of the eighteenth-century debate on the social implications of atheism. (a) Bayle's suggestion of separating immorality from atheism was echoed by those defending atheism as a philosophical position. (b) The question of whether atheism or superstition was more dangerous to society led to a self-definition of philosophy as the reasonable middle way between the two 'monsters'. (c) The association of atheism with Spinozism dominated the controversies about the compatibility of rational speculation with the requirements of a moral and political order.

The terms in which the danger of atheism was discussed by theologians and philosophers were taken up by those philosophers who indirectly or openly professed atheism. Julien Offray de La Mettrie defends philosophers who were labelled as dangerous atheists (Hobbes, Spinoza, Bayle) and declares that the religious fanaticism of the priests represents the true danger to society, whereas philosophical atheism and a moral life are wholly compatible.[58] In the *Answer to Dr. Priestley's Letters* (1782) atheism is presented as a philosophical position resulting from 'free thought upon the subject'.[59] D'Holbach, in his *Système de la Nature*, takes up the distinction between atheism and immorality by clearly dissociating his speculative atheism from simple irreligion and libertinism.[60]

This distinction, however, had no part in the so-called atheistical clubs in Britain in the early part of the century, clubs in whose rituals atheism was associated with a new type of libertinism. Most notable among these groups were the so-called hellfire clubs, famous for religious blasphemy and debauchery.[61] The Marquis de Sade, who characterised himself as a disciple of d'Holbach's atheism, was the main eighteenth-century theoretician of libertinism. Unlike d'Holbach and most of the French materialists who defended the compatibility of atheism and sociability, de Sade depicts immorality and sexual deviance as the result of his materialistic hedonism.[62]

By presenting true religion as the middle way between the two monsters of atheism and superstition, Budde followed the Aristotelian doctrine of virtue as 'mesotes'. Budde mentions Toland as the author of the metaphor, though he rejects the suggestion of atheism in Toland's talk of the middle way between the Scylla of atheism and the Charybdis of superstition (in order to defend Livy against the reproach of superstition). Considering the social consequences of atheism and superstition, he also rejects Bayle's preference for atheism. Although superstition affects more people than atheism and leads to the chimera of witchcraft, religious fanaticism, and the like, it is not as dangerous as atheism. For atheists deny God as a superior moral law-giver and therefore as guarantor of the social contract. Their inclinations remain wholly without restrictions and thus make individual happiness impossible and endanger society.[63]

The metaphor of the middle way as used by Budde dominated eighteenth-century moral and political philosophy. It was adopted at the beginning of the century and was still influential in the time of Immanuel Kant.[64] An Anglican cleric such as William Warburton, a rational metaphysician such as Christian Wolff and a fervent critic of priestcraft such as Voltaire all attempted to harmonise religious belief with the worldly interests of society on the basis of a rational idea of God as provider of moral law. A delicate balance is struck by Warburton and Wolff, who still feel compelled to reject the paradox of the virtuous atheist and thus cannot conceive that moral obligation can be independent of God's will.[65] While acknowledging – although on different grounds – the rational foundation of natural law, they feel constrained to relate it to God's will for a complete account of obligation. Wolff, having drawn the conclusion that an atheist, provided he is a rational person, would act as morally as a Christian, yet tries to repudiate the moral value of atheism.

Even though the French *philosophes*, with the exception of Rousseau, displayed radical tendencies, represented by their anti-clericalism, anti-Christianity, and hostility to metaphysical systems, the tendency to maintain a middle way between atheism and superstition is manifest in Voltaire's opposition to the militant atheism of d'Holbach and his friends. Voltaire wholly supported the anticlericalism of the atheist philosophers, directed not only against the clergy of the Roman Catholic Church but, after the scandal surrounding d'Alembert's article 'Genève' in the *Encyclopédie*, also against the Genevan Calvinists.[66] From 1759 on he concentrated, in his publications, on combating *l'infâme*, by which he envisaged not just the Catholic Church but all forms of institutionalised Christianity. Once they attain power, according to Voltaire, Lutheranism, Calvinism, and Catholicism all tend inherently toward fanaticism and intolerance.[67] To characterise this tendency he uses medical metaphors: Fanaticism is an 'epidemic disease . . . like the plague', it is a 'mental disorder'.[68] The fanaticism of the Christian religion can still subsist, despite the acknowledged progress of reason, because it is based on people's stupidity, their liability to prejudices and superstitions, which are preserved by the practice of rituals and ceremonies. Despite his scathing criticism of Christianity, Voltaire is nevertheless not ready to conceive of a society without religion. Although he recognises that atheism 'in the quiet apathy of private life' does not oppose social virtues, he rejects the 'treacherous, graceless, slanderous, criminal, bloodthirsty atheist' as a danger to public life. Voltaire advocates reason against atheism and superstition: 'Atheists in power would be just as disastrous to the human race as the superstitious.

Between these two monsters reason offers a saving hand'. He did, however, consider fanaticism to be more dangerous to society than atheism, for atheism, unlike superstition, is curable.[69]

These arguments for excluding atheists from society on the grounds of their immorality were attacked by those who claimed that atheism rather than religion can promote morality and happiness. Although d'Holbach and Naigeon, 'the two foremost proselytizers for materialistic atheism among the *philosophes*', explained materialistic naturalism as a philosophical system based on sensationalist empiricism 'their justifications of their philosophical positions were, in the final analysis, utilitarian', for they stated that matter and motion are the cause and agent of all phenomena.[70] As human nature is subject to the invariable laws of cause and effect, which direct nature, men are constrained to seek their survival, well-being, and the diminution of suffering. Religion, relying on men's fear of nature, which presents itself in catastrophes, is understood as being in conflict with the natural tendencies, depriving men of the satisfaction of needs and of the diminution of pain. Atheistic materialism is defended on the grounds of the possible benefits to humanity that would accrue through a progressive, cumulative knowledge of nature.[71]

A similar tendency to defend its moral value is characteristic of British atheism at the end of the century. In the anonymous *Investigation of the Essence of the Deity*, atheism is presented as the result of the progress of truth, the atheist as 'a man, who destroyeth chimeras prejudicial to the human species, in order to reconduct men back to nature, to experience, and to reason'.[72] The main opponents to the progress of truth are the priests, who are forced by interest to support a futile and failing system, attributing the operations of nature to a supernatural power.

As a result of Bayle's article on Spinoza in the *Dictionaire*, Spinozism – later associated with pantheism, materialism, or fatalism – belonged to the most often used synonyms of atheism. Philosophers entertaining sympathies for Spinoza tended to keep them secret. The complicated history of the adaptation and transmission of Spinoza's thought by eighteenth-century philosophers is beyond the scope of the questions investigated here. It is sufficient to note that Spinozism was one of the monsters to be eradicated, because Spinoza's philosophy proved – from Toland through the clandestine literature of the French and German Enlightenment to Naigeon and d'Holbach – to be one of the main starting points for developing materialistic positions, marked by their denial of God as creator of the world and provider of moral law.[73]

It is therefore remarkable that a new variant of Spinozism emerged in the second half of the century, which dealt mainly with speculative questions and which later gave rise to the systems of German Idealism. It was in the so-called *pantheism controversy* that the two opposing types of Spinozism confronted each other. In 1785 Friedrich Heinrich Jacobi published *Über die Lehre des Spinoza*,[74] his private correspondence with Moses Mendelssohn concerning Lessing's reported Spinozism. Jacobi used this occasion to direct the reproaches of Spinozism, fatalism, and atheism against the religious rationalism of the Berlin Enlightenment, of which Mendelssohn was the chief representative. According to Jacobi, Lessing deplored Spinoza's being 'treated like a dead dog' (32–3) and this provoked Jacobi to refute Spinozism by declaring himself an adherent of Spinoza's philosophy, accepting it as fatalism, the result of a consistent determinism. Jacobi declared himself unable to refute Spinozism by arguments and proposed instead a *salto mortale*, 'that from fatalism I directly conclude against fatalism, and against everything connected with it'. Jacobi's *salto mortale* refers to the transition from knowledge to belief, the belief 'in a rational, personal cause of the world', a personal deity (26). The implications of his report, namely his attack on the Berlin Enlightenment, are apparent in passages where he refers to Mendelssohn's understanding of Spinozism as presented in the *Gespräche*.[75] In the *Morgenstunden*, where Mendelssohn reacts to Jacobi's report of Lessing's Spinozism, he explains the idea of a 'purified pantheism' as able to coexist with the truths of religion and ethics. According to Mendelssohn, 'purified Spinozism' represents the reasonable middle way between the atheism and superstition which result from misunderstandings of Spinoza's philosophy.[76]

III. RELIGION AND SOCIAL UTILITY

In his *Spirit of the Laws*, Montesquieu claimed to speak, not as a theologian but as a political writer who, in surveying the different religions of the world, examines 'the good which they contribute to the civil state' rather than their truth.[77] To treat religion as a social phenomenon, subject to scientific investigation, is characteristic of some of the new theories of society. Montesquieu's examination of religions demonstrates how considerations of their social or political utility could be used to promote the integration of different religions or of different religious denominations into society. To persuade political leaders to grant toleration to minorities suspected of being disloyal to the state because of their religious convictions, the social or political utility of different denominations or of religious diversity was invoked. Utility arguments were, however, also used to justify doubts about the possibility of harmonising Christianity with human nature and worldly affairs. Where Christianity was analysed as a kind of superstition, enthusiasm or fanaticism, as by Bernard Mandeville and David Hume, its traditional role as guarantor of social and political stability was questioned.

1. *Montesquieu*

In *De l'esprit des lois* (*Spirit of the Laws*) Montesquieu discusses the paradox of the virtuous atheist (24.2–18: 715–28), criticising Bayle's conclusion that superstition is worse than atheism as a case of fallacious reasoning, on the grounds that although religion does not always prevent immorality one should not conclude that it never does so. Religion has positive as well as negative effects on society. Montesquieu claims that Bayle misrepresented the nature of religious directives. By distinguishing between human law and religious advice, the former directed by the idea of the good, the latter by the idea of the perfect, he shows how religious and secular duties coexist to the advantage of a society (24.8: 719).

Montesquieu's remarks on the spirit of Christianity do, however, differ radically from his critical examination of institutionalised Christianity (24.6),[78] which he attacks very much as Bayle does. In the *Lettres persanes* (*Persian Letters*) he describes the high costs of intolerance, arising from the fact that suppressed minorities emigrate, taking their wealth with them, and from depopulation, which has its cause in Catholic celibacy and the prohibition of divorce and which also leads to a decline in commerce and thus in wealth. In this respect Protestantism is favourable to public utility, because everybody is allowed to have children.[79]

By examining the possible impact of religions and religious sects on national welfare, Montesquieu resorted to one of the standard arguments used in debates on toleration and naturalisation. Although political and economic considerations had always provided influential arguments in such debates, in the eighteenth century they took on a new character, as they were used to attack traditional prejudice and to oppose the conservative arguments of the clergy.[80] The innovative character of utility arguments is best seen in the debates on the naturalisation of the Jews. Unlike Justus Henning Boehmer who, in an adaptation of the idea of natural law, argued for toleration of the Jews on the basis of the duties owed to them as human beings, John Toland and Christian Wilhelm Dohm argued for their full integration into Christian society on utilitarian grounds, which were used to attack traditional prejudice against the political and, above all, economic harm attributed to them.[81] In this respect Toland's *Reasons for Naturalizing the Jews in Great Britain and Ireland* anticipates the arguments later used by Dohm. Toland is concerned with 'a Defence of the Jews against all vulgar Prejudices in all countries',[82] analysing the characteristics of the Jews not as 'from Nature', but 'from Accident' (60). He insists on the 'benefit and safety of naturalizing them' (92), as it is in the state's interest to increase its population and does not contradict its interest in peace and prosperity (52–8).

2. *Mandeville and Hume*

Bayle's sceptical reflections on harmonising the moral principles of 'true' Christianity and worldly interests served as a basis for Mandeville and Hume in developing new concepts of religion and society. Mandeville was among the first to adapt Bayle's paradox of the virtuous atheist in order to develop a new kind of political philosophy, which was based on the idea of manipulating selfish human passions instead of on moral beliefs. In the *Fable of the Bees* he applies two different standards in assessing the morality of actions, one rigoristic, judging the motives of individuals' behaviour, the other empirical or utilitarian, judging the social consequences of such behaviour. This double standard also underlies his analysis of the Christian religion in *Free Thoughts* and the *Enquiry*.[83] He states that 'real religion' (*Free Thoughts*, 16) consists in 'inward religion' and 'spiritual Devotion' (131), which corresponds to the 'universal Church' (132) of Christ, whose kingdom 'was not of this world' (151). Christian religion in this true sense demands 'strictest Morality' (150), 'the avoiding of Sin for the love of God' (11). The strict morality of the Christian religion, which is required for the eternal welfare of the individual, stands, however, in contradiction not only to the 'worldly Interest of the whole Society' (12), but also to human nature, which means passions and lusts (8). For this reason Mandeville explains men's actual religious behaviour in terms of selfish passions. Christianity in its different forms of worldly organisation, the visible church (132) with its outward signs of devotion, rites, and ceremonies is judged by the second, utilitarian standard. Outward religion is explained as the result of men's incapacity to overcome their appetites and to curb their passions (138–42), contradicting thereby 'the chief Duty' of 'real Religion' (16). Mandeville does not, however, conclude that a society would be better off without any religion. For, as he explains, religion might be used by a ruler 'to make Men tractable and obedient' by informing himself 'of those Sentiments that are the natural Result of the Passions and Frailties which every Human Creature is born with' (20), provided the clergy, responsible for schism and intolerance, is subordinated to the government and controlled by the laity (214–51).[84]

Mandeville's adaptation of Bayle's paradox represents a shift to a secular view of religion and its role in society. Whereas Bayle responded to the paradoxical results of philosophical investigation by a return to faith,[85] Mandeville's assessment of rigoristic religious principles does not seem to imply any inward commitment or religious belief, but is used as a critical standard to evaluate the impact of Christianity as a worldly institution.

Hume's 'Essay of Superstition and Enthusiasm' and his *Natural History* mark, in a way, the end of an evolution begun by Mandeville's treatment of religion as a public phenomenon, subject to an investigation of its origins in human nature and of its effects on society.[86] Whereas Mandeville's explanation of 'true' religion is based on a Protestant understanding of the 'invisible church of Christ',[87] Hume contents himself with mere hints in this direction. In his 'Essay' he distinguishes between true religion and corruptions of it (46). In the *Natural History* he mentions 'the notion of a perfect being, the creator of the world', which corresponds to 'the principles of reason and true philosophy' (330), and contrasts it with theism, which he labels vulgar superstition (331). The main object of Hume's investigation is restricted to what Mandeville had called outward religion. Religion is depicted as endangering society, since it is based on men's irrational passions which directly influence their behaviour. In 'Of Superstition and Enthusiasm' Hume distinguishes between 'two species of false religion' (46), superstition and enthusiasm. By a comparison of their effects he develops a classification of the religious confessions and sects of his own time. As superstition grows out of an attempt to appease imaginary enemies by practices like 'ceremonies, observances, mortifications, sacrifices, presents', it invents priests to this end. Enthusiasm, on the other hand, originated in the imagined 'immediate inspiration' of the Divine Being, 'thinks itself sufficiently qualified to *approach* the Divinity' and therefore neglects outward ceremonies. Whereas enthusiasm 'produces the most cruel disorders in human society', superstition 'steals in gradually and insensibly'. It becomes a 'tyrant and disturber of human society' only when the power of the priests is established (46–9). The *Natural History*, explaining polytheism and theism as the two subsequent religions of mankind, is directed at a critical apprehension of the detrimental social effects of theism, a kind of popular superstition (330). Monotheists, not allowing the veneration of other gods, get into sectarian disputes and nurture persecuting zeal (sect. IX). Theism has further pernicious and distorting effects on morality by preaching submission and degradation, represented in the virtues of the monks (sect. X). It advances the corruption of reason, abusing it in endless disputes about contradictions and absurdities, directed at the extermination of heretics and critical philosophers (sect. XI).

As John Passmore has stated, it is hard to be confident about Hume's idea of true religion, as it sometimes 'functions as nothing more than a line of defence behind which Hume can retreat when he is accused of attacking religion'.[88] But it is certain that, unlike Bayle and Mandeville, he no longer identifies true religion with Christianity. Instead, it is depicted as a rational account of God and morality by the philosopher, who, Hume concludes, can safely be tolerated by the state.

It would, however, be misleading to conclude that utility arguments were, toward the end of the century, merely used to demonstrate that religious belief was of no value in a flourishing society. As Crimmins has pointed out in connection with his analysis of William Paley's moral philosophy, they could also be used to 'claim that for the sake of the well-being of the community the privileged position of the clergy as the guardian of the nation's morals should be protected by the state'.[89]

IV. RELIGION AND CIVIC VIRTUE

Political considerations of religion did not always lead to the rejection of religion as an element guaranteeing social stability. This is best evidenced by the numerous efforts designed to replace institutionalised Christianity with a religion reduced to the moral principles on which all humankind agrees. Ideas of civil religion were also developed by representatives of the natural law tradition who tried to establish natural religion as a kind of moderate and liberal Christianity.[90] I shall concentrate here on the most influential concept of such a religion, a notion developed within the republican tradition. Compared to the large number of studies dealing with the renewal of classical republicanism or civic humanism in eighteenth-century political thought, relatively little attention has been paid to the republican outlook on religion and on church-state relations.[91] The idea of religion in republican thought was not bound up with any one specific term. Rousseau was the only one to use the expression civil religion; others spoke of public religion, national religion, and the like. The key to understanding the role which, according to this tradition, religion ought to play in a tolerant and flourishing society, lies in the idea of civic virtue, one of the distinctive features of republican theory. It was a commonly accepted idea in republicanism up to the end of the eighteenth century that the stability and prosperity of the state required the citizens to be willing to grant priority to the interests of the community over their own particular interests. Politics, therefore, had to do not just with the formal arrangements of institutions, but required the promotion of the citizens' virtue. Religion was thus considered an important ally in politics.

Although republican conceptions of religion exercised an extensive influence in the second half of the century, especially in France, they can be traced to the very beginning of the Enlightenment in England. The failure of comprehension provoked an intellectual confrontation between the defenders and the attackers of the position of the church in society. One result was the free-thinkers' attack on the authority of the church. Those re-articulating James Harrington's republican thought had abandoned the idea of an institutional and political revolution. Their aim was the abolition not of the monarchy but of arbitrary power. In these reforms religion played an important role as a political means to maintain social and political stability.[92]

The key element of a republican theory of religion is the duality of public and private religion, of which the *locus classicus* is Harrington's *Oceana*. Walter Moyle's *Essay on the Roman Government*, which transmitted the classical tradition to the eighteenth century, took up Harrington's dualism and further stressed the prerogatives of a national religion – reduced to the common principles of religion on which all humankind agrees – against the clericalism of the Church of England.[93]

The most important free-thinker to contribute to this religious current was John Toland. He planned a complete, annotated edition of Cicero, *Cicero illustratus* (1712), for which, however, only a prospectus exists; and he made an edition of Harrington's works.[94] In addition to conveying republicanism to the eighteenth century, he also further developed and applied the notion of the dualism of public and private religion, declaring that

> as the conviction of a man's private Conscience, produces his private Religion; so the conviction of the national Conscience, or of the majority, must every where produce a National Religion. . . . A National Religion must not be *a Publick Driving*, but *a Publick Leading*, says *Harrington*, to whom every man is oblig'd who writes on this subject.[95]

In his *State-Anatomy* as well as in *Anglia Libera*, where he deals with the political questions of post-revolutionary England, he adopts the formula 'civil liberty and a national church' in order to define the concept of toleration. The expression demands full liberty of conscience for the sects, without political discrimination, and an established church, subordinated to the authority of the magistrate.[96] Although Toland never elaborated his concept of public religion, leaving us to uncertain reconstruction, there is nevertheless evidence that he, unlike Rousseau, deemed Protestantism adequate to play the role of a public religion. Reduced to its true core, Protestantism, thanks to its abhorrence of the idolatry and tyranny of the Roman Catholic clergy, proves to be 'the most accommodated' to the civil government of England. Protestantism and civil liberty are the main instruments for securing general peace, order, and happiness (*Anglia Libera*, 14: 97). But Toland, 'a Protestant for political reasons' (Jacob), also developed a far more radical private religion by elaborating the philosophical doctrine of the pantheists. Thus in the esoteric *Pantheisticon* he invents a new religious vision with a new ritual, based on pantheistic materialism, as an alternative to Christianity. In view of Toland's engagement as a public and as a private philosopher, Sullivan's assessment that 'Toland's practice realized Harrington's theory'[97] seems accurate.

The duality of public and private religion reappears in Rousseau's *Contrat social*. For civil religion is not conceived as 'exclusive national religion' but as a kind of political supplement to Christianity, which for Rousseau plays the role of private religion.[98] Christian religion, which Rousseau terms religion of man, consists of the 'inner veneration of the Supreme God' and the 'eternal moral duties' (464). Although it is true religion, it does not serve the political interests of the state, as it is wholly not of this world. Rousseau's position thus lies between that of Bayle, who reportedly claimed that no religion was useful to political societies, and that of Warburton, who defended the political utility of Christianity (464). To counteract the lack of political usefulness of Christianity, Rousseau develops the idea of civil religion, which has its paradigm in the 'religion of the citizen' of the ancient republics, where religion was, according to him, exclusively bound to the laws of the state (461–2). Divine worship aimed at the love of these laws and the veneration of one's country (464–5). To avoid the tendency toward superstition and intolerance evidently inherent in heathen religion (465), Rousseau restricts the domain of the dogmas of civil religion to those opinions which pertain to the interests of the community (468–9).

Although civil religion is neither exclusive nor intolerant, present-day scholars have criticised it as a new form of intolerance. For Rousseau wished to allow the state to banish all those who did not believe in civil religion and to punish by death all those who acted contrary to established dogma (468). As Leigh rightly observes, Rousseau's exclusion of atheists as men without morals was shared by most advocates of toleration.[99] An evaluation of Rousseau's idea of civil religion should not, however, be carried out within the context of eighteenth-century debates on toleration, but rather within the context of the renewal of republican ideals in his political philosophy. As civil religion is not religion in a proper sense, but a 'sentiment of sociability' (468) characterising good citizens and loyal subjects, it serves the state's interest by promoting civic virtue, which in turn guarantees the stability of the political order. Unlike Montesquieu, who 'set the terms in which republicanism was to be discussed' in the eighteenth century,[100] Rousseau locates the proper constitution of the state not in institutional arrangements, but in the hearts of the citizens, in their habits, customs, and opinions (394). To delay the natural tendency of states to decay, it is therefore necessary to guide the opinions of the citizens so as to prevent their private interests from dominating the public interest (428–9). One way of sustaining the required moral constitution of men (381–2) is the state's establishment of a civil religion. An important characteristic of the idea of a civil religion is therefore the new alliance between religion and patriotism. For civil religion consists mainly of a love of law and of the readiness to sacrifice one's life in the performance of one's duty (468). Rousseau intends to use the 'great passion' animating fanaticism for political ends. In view of this it is not surprising that he wishes to combat the atheism of the *philosophes*, for they reduce men's affections to a secret egoism, which contradicts virtue.[101]

Rousseau's justification of the required total alienation (360) of the citizens from their own individual interests in favour of the community is based on what has been called the paradox of freedom.[102] As civil liberty, according to Rousseau, depends on the prevailing manners and opinions of the citizens, it is necessary to restrict natural liberty, that is, the right of the individual to do what he desires. Since for Rousseau the only free society was an ordered and virtuous one, he completely subordinated the interests of the individual to those of the state (364–5).

The idea of liberty modelled on the virtuous citizen of Sparta is generally recognised as typical of the French Enlightenment. James E. Crimmins has, however, demonstrated, in his analysis of John Brown's idea of 'a science of politics based on manners', that a tendency to base political stability mainly on the citizens' patriotic spirit also emerged – as an atypical variation – in English republican thought.[103] Brown, who was influenced by Machiavelli and Montesquieu, may be classified as a representative of the idea of civil religion in the broad sense of civic religiosity, entailing a fusion of patriotic and religious sentiments.

The impact of religious values on developing American nationalism has chiefly been discussed in the United States. According to Robert N. Bellah, the idea of civic loyalty, which emerged during the political crisis of the revolutionary period, became the expression of a common American religion, of which the belief in America as the chosen nation was characteristic.[104] Whereas some interpreters concentrate on the emergence of nationalism within the movement for independence, others have stressed the continuity between the millennial thought of the Awakening and of the revolutionary period.[105] The American discussion of civil religion, however, concentrates on religious convictions as they were expressed in the political culture of the day rather than on coherent theories.

Another variation of the fusion of religion and patriotism was proposed in a very different context by a representative of the Berlin Enlightenment, Thomas Abbt, who was the first to claim that patriotism, which had formerly been identified as the public virtue of a republic, could be linked with monarchy. By his appeal for Prussian patriotism he provoked a scandal, as he suggested that the clergy should become preachers of enthusiastic patriotism. Emphasising the secular components of a cleric's duties, he supported the already existing widespread tendency for theologians to redefine 'the pastoral role to meet the needs of the modern sovereign state'.[106]

The idea of civil religion, however, remained a characteristic property of Rousseau and his followers, among them the abbé de Mably.[107] One practical consequence of this emerged during the French Revolution, when Robespierre, in his speech of *18 floréal An II*, repeated many of the arguments of the French republican tradition, urging that 'all must change in the moral and political order' (114). In his quest for peace and stability he suggests Rousseau's idea of a legislator who would immediately create a sense of social duty by means of public education and the institution of a national festival. As a supplement to this 'immediate instinct' which directs men to good actions, he proposes a 'religious sentiment', implanting the idea of sanctions into men's hearts (123). As a result of this speech a decree was passed establishing national holidays, among them the 'festival of the Supreme Being', to confirm the cult of reason begun by the de-Christianisation movement.

New philosophical reflections on the relationship between public religion and civic virtue are contained in Georg Wilhelm Friedrich Hegel's early manuscripts, written in Bern and Frankfurt. They are situated in the context of an ongoing progressive critical discussion of Kant's concept of morality, a discussion which provides the starting point for Hegel's later distinction between morality and ethical life.[108] Hegel introduces the idea of a folk religion (*Volksreligion*) as a public religion, which practically influences thoughts and actions and also shapes a national spirit.[109] In contrast to objective religion, a matter of understanding and memory with which theologians are concerned, folk religion is understood as subjective religion, a matter of the heart, influencing the determinations of the will (27–35). As the state is interested in civic morality, which can neither be enforced by law nor be produced through an enlightenment of the understanding (35), it can use folk religion as a superior means to this end (248). This religion aims at producing enthusiasm, which Hegel, unlike Kant, considers a necessary prerequisite for leading a moral life. According to Hegel, the pure motive of duty, abstracted from human desires and interests cannot produce good actions (43–4). The manuscripts Hegel wrote in Bern are influenced by Kant's idea of a pure moral religion of reason.[110] The doctrines of folk religion are thus based on reason, but directed at influencing the imagination, the heart, and sensibility. In *Der Geist des Christentums und sein Schicksal* (*The Spirit of Christianity and its Fate*) (447–580), written in Frankfurt 1798–1800, Hegel conceives of religion as transcending Kant's concept of moral law and concentrating instead on the morality of love as contained in the Sermon on the Mount and in the conduct of Jesus. He criticises as authoritarian and heteronomous both the Judaic concept of law, set out in earlier manuscripts, and Kant's conception of moral law, reproaching Kant for merely internalising, not abolishing, the heteronomous law, which thus remains external to human desires and interests (478–80). Hegel confronts the idea of general laws and duties, based on reason, with the idea of virtues, whose principle is love (491–2, 578–20), but he also identifies a certain tension between love and the economy of modern societies (489–91, 557–61). It is thus not love, but ethical life which is later regarded as the cement of a modern society.

The relationship between folk religion and Christianity has been interpreted in two different ways. One interpretation, represented by Georg Lukacs, focuses on Hegel's interest in the French Revolution and depicts him as a radical republican, defending a classical concept of politics in opposition to an otherworldly oriented Christianity. The other, taking Hegel's Protestant background of Old-Württemberg into consideration, acknowledges the continuity between his reform projects and Pietist attempts 'to ethicize public life in the name of applied Christian theology'.[111]

NOTES

1 Immanuel Kant, *Beantwortung der Frage: Was ist Aufklärung? (Answer to the Question: What is Enlightenment?)*, in Ak 8: 33–42 at 36. See Mark Philp, 'Enlightenment, Toleration and Liberty', *Enlightenment and Dissent*, 9 (1990): 47–62.

2 Anthony Collins, *A Discourse of Free-Thinking, Occasion'd by The Rise and Growth of a Sect call'd Free-Thinkers* (1713), with parallel German trans., ed. G. Gawlick (Stuttgart-Bad Cannstatt, 1965), sect. II, 97–9. Thomasius, *Erörterung der Juristischen Frage: Ob Ketzerey ein straffbares Verbrechen sey?*, in *Auserlesene deutsche Schriften*, vols. 23–4 of *Ausgewählte Werke*, ed. W. Schneiders (Hildesheim, 1994), 23: 210–307; Thomasius, *Discours von der Freyheit der itzigen Zeiten gegen die vorigen*, in *Aus der Frühzeit der deutschen Aufklärung: Christian Thomasius und Christian Weise*, ed. F. Brüggemann (Leipzig, 1938), 19–29. See Günter Gawlick, 'Die ersten deutschen Reaktionen auf A. Collins' "Discourse of Free-Thinking" von 1713', in *Eklektik, Selbstdenken, Mündigkeit*, ed. N. Hinske (Hamburg, 1986), 11–25; Zurbuchen, 'Gewissensfreiheit und Toleranz: Zur Pufendorf-Rezeption bei Christian Thomasius', in *Samuel Pufendorf und die europäische Frühaufklärung*, eds F. Palladini and G. Hartung (Berlin, 1996), 169–80.

3 Voltaire, *Traité sur la tolérance* (1763), critical edn., ed. J. Renwick, in *Les Oeuvres complètes / The complete works*, ed. T. Besterman (Geneva, 1968–), vol. 56C (Oxford, 2000); Gotthold Ephraim Lessing, *Nathan der Weise* in *Werke*, ed. K. Balser, 5 vols. (Berlin, 1975), 2: 5–158. Moses Mendelssohn, *Jerusalem oder über religiöse Macht und Judentum* (1783), in *Gesammelte Schriften, Jubiläumsausg*, ed. F. Bamberger and A. Altmann (Stuttgart-Bad Cannstatt, 1971–), vol. 8: *Schriften zum Judentum II*, ed. A. Altmann (1983), 99–204.

4 Thomas Paine, *The Rights of Man, Part I* (1791), in *Political Writings*, ed. B. Kuklick (Cambridge, 1989), 49–143 at 94.

5 Richard Price, 'Additional Observations on the Nature and Value of Civil Liberty, and the War with America' (1777) in *Political Writings*, ed. D. O. Thomas (Cambridge, 1991), 77; Price, 'Observations on the Nature of Civil Liberty' (1776), *Two Tracts on Civil Liberty, the War with America, and the Debts and Finances of the Kingdom* (1778), in *Political Writings*, 22.

Joseph Priestley, *An Essay on the First Principles of Government, and on the Nature of Political, Civil, and Religious Liberty* (2nd edn., 1771), in *The Theological and Miscellaneous Works*, ed. J. T. Rutt, 25 vols. in 26 (London, 1817–32), 22: 3–144.

6 Samuel Pufendorf, *De habitu religionis christianae ad vitam civilem*, (Bremen, 1687); translated as *Of the Nature and Qualification of Religion in Reference to Civil Society*, trans. J. Crull [1698], ed. S. Zurbuchen (Indianapolis, IN, 2002). John Locke, *Epistola de Tolerantia – A Letter on Toleration*, ed. R. Klibansky, trans. and ed. J. W. Gough (Oxford, 1968). See Christoph Link, *Herrschaftsordnung und bürgerliche Freiheit. Grenzen der Staatsgewalt in der älteren deutschen Staatslehre* (Vienna, 1979); Zurbuchen, 'Samuel Pufendorf's Concept of Toleration', in *Difference and Dissent, Theories of Tolerance in Medieval and Early Modern Europe*, eds. C. J. Nederman and J. C. Laursen (Lanham, 1996), 163–84.

7 See Charles O'Brien, 'Ideas of Religious Toleration in the Time of Joseph II: A Study of the Enlightenment among Catholics in Austria', *Transactions of the American Philosophical Society*, 59.7 (1969): 5–76; and 'Jansenists and Civil Toleration in France, 1775–1778: Le Paige, Guidi and Robert de Saint-Vincent', in *La tolérance civile*, ed. R. Crahay (Brussel, 1982), 183–93; Daniele Menozzi, 'Il dibattito sulla tolleranza nella chiesa italiana della seconda metà del Settecento', in same, 161–79.

8 See *Toleration in Enlightenment Europe*, eds. O. P. Grell and R. Porter (Cambridge, 2000).

9 For Anglican reactions to the Toleration Act, see Geoffrey Holmes, *The Trial of Dr. Sacheverell* (London, 1973), 21–47. See also Richard Burgess Barlow, *Citizenship and Conscience: A Study in the Theory and Practice of Religious Toleration in England during the Eighteenth Century* (Philadelphia, PA, 1962); Ursula Henriques, *Religious Toleration in England 1787–1833* (London, 1961), 1–135.

10 See Geoffrey Adams, *The Huguenots and French Opinion, 1685–1787: The Enlightenment Debate on Toleration* (Waterloo, Ont., 1991); Burdette C. Poland, *French Protestantism and the French Revolution: A Study in Church and State, Thought and Religion, 1685–1815* (Princeton, NJ, 1957); Gisela Schlüter, *Die französische Toleranzdebatte in Zeitalter der Aufklärung. Materiale und formale Aspekte* (Tübingen, 1992); Catherine Bergeal, *Protestantisme et tolérance en France au XVIIIe siècle. De la Révocation à la Révolution, 1685–1789* (Carrières-sous-Poissy, 1988), a collection of documents.

11 See 'Toleranz' in *Geschichtliche Grundbegriffe. Historisches Lexikon zur politisch-sozialen Sprache in Deutschland*, ed. O. Brunner, W. Conze, and R. Koselleck, 8 vols. (Stuttgart, 1972–97), esp. §§XI, XIII, XIV, 495–510, 520–64. A bibliography of German writings on toleration is provided by Harald Schultze, *Lessings Toleranzbegriff. Eine theologische Studie* (Göttingen, 1969), 128–72. See also Walter Grossmann, 'Religious toleration in Germany, 1684–1750', *Studies on Voltaire and the Eighteenth Century*, 201 (1982): 115–41; Günter Birtsch, 'Religions- und Gewissensfreiheit in Preussen von 1780 bis 1817', *Zeitschrift für Historische Forschung*, 11 (1984): 177–204.

12 For Germany, see Grossmann, 'Religious toleration in Germany', 127–31; Klaus Deppermann, *Der hallesche Pietismus und der preussische Staat unter Friedrich III. (I.)* (Göttingen, 1961); Carl Hinrichs, *Preußentum und Pietismus. Der Pietismus in Brandenburg-Preußen als religiös-soziale Reformbewegung* (Göttingen, 1971); Martin Pott, 'Thomasius' philosophischer Glaube', in *Christian Thomasius, 1655–1728. Interpretationen zu Werk und Wirkung*, ed. W. Schneiders (Hamburg, 1989), 223–47; Stephan Buchholz, 'Christian Thomasius: Zwischen Orthodoxie und Pietismus – Religionskonflikte und ihre literarische Verarbeitung', in same, 248–55. For America, see Mark Valeri, 'Church and State in America from the Great Awakening to the American Revolution', in *Church and State in America, a Bibliographical Guide: The Colonial and Early National Periods*, ed. J. F. Wilson (New York, NY, 1986), ch. 4, 115–50.

13 Pierre Bayle, *Commentaire philosophique sur ces paroles de Jesus-Christ, Contrain-les d'entrer; où l'on prouve . . . qu'il n'y a rien de plus abominable que de faire des Conversions par la Contrainte* in *Oeuvres diverses* (The Hague, 1727–31 edn.), ed. E. Labrousse, 5 vols. in 6 (Hildesheim, 1964–8), 2: 355–496; in part translated as *Pierre Bayle's Philosophical Commentary*, by A. G. Tannenbaum (New York, NY, 1987). See Walter Rex, *Essays on Pierre Bayle and Religious Controversy* (The Hague, 1965); John Kilcullen, *Sincerity and Truth: Essays on Arnauld, Bayle, and Toleration* (Oxford, 1988), 54–105; Sally L. Jenkinson, 'Two Concepts of Tolerance: Why Bayle Is not Locke', *The Journal of Political Philosophy*, 4:4 (1996): 302–22; T. J. Hochstrasser, 'Conscience and Reason: The Natural Law Theory of Jean Barbeyrac', *Historical Journal*, 32 (1993): 289–308; Alexander Altmann, 'Gewissensfreiheit und Toleranz. Eine begriffsgeschichtliche Untersuchung', in his *Die trostvolle Aufklärung. Studien zur Metaphysik und politischen Theorie Moses Mendelssohns* (Stuttgart-Bad Cannstatt, 1982), 245–75.

14 Benjamin Hoadly, *The Nature of the Kingdom, or Church, of Christ. A Sermon Preach'd Before the King at the Royal Chapel at St. James's, on Sunday March 31, 1717*, in *The Reception of Locke's Politics*, ed. M. Goldie, 6 vols. (London, 1999), 5: 145–55; Bernard Mandeville, *Free Thoughts on Religion, the Church, and National Happiness*, (London, 1729 edn., Stuttgart-Bad Cannstatt, 1969), ch. VI, 129–61; Kant, *Die Religion innerhalb der Grenzen der bloßen Vernunft*, Ak 6: 136.

15 Locke, *Letter on Toleration*, 64–7.

16 Jeremy Waldron, 'Locke: Toleration and the Rationality of Persecution', *A Letter concerning Toleration in Focus*, eds. J. Horton and S. Mendus (London, 1991), 98–124; Gordon J. Schochet, 'John Locke and Religious Toleration', in *The Revolution of 1688: Changing Perspectives*, ed. L. G. Schwoerer (Cambridge, 1992), 147–64.

17 Henry Stebbing, *An Essay concerning Civil Government, Consider'd as It Stands Related to Religion, wherein the Magistrate's Right to Support and Encourage True Religion by Human Laws is Asserted, against the Modern Pleaders of an Absolute, Unrestrained Toleration* (London, 1724), ch. II, 43–57; Thomas Sherlock, *Arguments against a Repeal of the Corporation and Test Acts, wherein Most of the Pleas Advanced in a Paper now Circulating, Styled the Case of Protestant Dissenters . . . Are Discussed* (London, 1787), 18, 19; Benjamin Hoadly, *Refutation of Bishop Sherlock's Arguments against a Repeal of the Test and Corporation Acts, wherein the Justice and Reasonableness of such a Repeal are Clearly Evidenced* (London, 1787).

18 Philip Furneaux, *An Essay on Toleration. With a Particular View to the Late Application of the Protestant Dissenting Ministers to Parliament* (London, 1773), in *The Reception of Locke's Politics*, ed. Goldie, 5: 355–85; see also his *Letters to the Honourable Mr. Justice Blackstone, Concerning his Exposition of the Act of Toleration, and Some Positions relative to Religious Liberty, in his celebrated Commentaries on the Laws of England*, (2nd edn., 1773), in *The Palladium of Conscience, or the Foundation of Religious Liberty displayed, asserted, and established, agreeable to its true and genuine Principles* (Philadelphia, PA, 1774).

19 Furneaux, *Letters to Blackstone*, xi.

20 *Declaration of Rights and Form of Government of Virginia*, in *The Papers of James Madison*, eds. W. T. Hutchinson and W. M. E. Rachal, 17 vols. (Chicago, IL, 1962–91), 1: 173f.

21 James Madison, *Memorial and Remonstrance against Religious Assessments*, in *Papers*, 8: 298–304 at 299.

22 Priestley, *An Essay on the First Principles of Government*, sect. I, 11 and sect. III, 29; Price, *Observations*, Pt. I, sect. I, 2–5; *Additional Observations*, Pt. I, sect. I, 4. See D. O. Thomas, *The Honest Mind. The Thought and Work of Richard Price* (Oxford, 1977), chs. 6, 8, 9. Jenny Graham, 'Revolutionary Philosopher: The Political Ideas of Joseph Priestley (1733–1804)', *Enlightenment and Dissent*, 8 (1989): 43–68; 9 (1990), 14–46.

23 Price, *Additional Observations*, Pt. I, sect. I, 4.

24 Price, *Observations*, Pt. I, sect. II; Priestley, *Essay on the First Principles of Government*, sect. II.

25 Locke, *Two Treatises of Government*, First Treatise, §86, in *Works*, 10 vols. (London, 1823 edn.; Aalen, 1963), 5: 207–485.

26 Thomas Jefferson, *A Bill for Establishing Religious Freedom* in *The Portable Thomas Jefferson*, ed. M. D. Peterson (New York, NY, 1975), 251–3.

27 See Horst Dippel, *Germany and the American Revolution, 1770–1800: A Sociohistorical Investigation of Late Eighteenth-Century Political Thinking*, trans. B. A. Uhlendorf (Wiesbaden, 1978); Diethelm Klippel, 'Naturrecht als politische Theorie. Zur politischen Bedeutung des deutschen Naturrechts im 18. und 19. Jahrhundert', in *Aufklärung als Politisierung – Politisierung der Aufklärung*, eds. H. E. Bödeker and U. Herrmann (Hamburg, 1987), 267–93. See Bödeker, ''Menschenrechte' im deutschen publizistischen Diskurs vor 1789', in *Grund- und Freiheitsrechte von der ständischen zur spätbürgerlichen Gesellschaft*, ed. G. Birtsch (Göttingen, 1987), 392–433.

28 Christian Wilhelm von Dohm, *Über die bürgerliche Verbesserung der Juden*, 2 vols. (Berlin, 1781–3). Mendelssohn's preface to his German translation (1782) of Menasseh Ben Israel, *Rettung der Juden* (1656), in *Schriften zum Judentum II*, 3–25 at 3, 11. See Klaus L. Berghahn, *Grenzen der Toleranz. Juden und Christen im Zeitalter der Aufklärung* (Vienna, 2000), 127–49, 150–82.

29 [Peter A. Winkopp], *Geschichte der Böhmischen Deisten nebst freimüthigen Bemerkungen über die Grundsäzze und Duldung der Deisten* (Leipzig, 1785).

30 Samuel Pufendorf, *Le droit de la nature et des gens, ou Système général des principes les plus importans de la morale, de la jurisprudence, et de la politique*, trans. J. Barbeyrac, 2 vols. (Amsterdam, 1712), Bk. VII, ch. 4, §11, note 2, 2: 264–5. See Adams, *The Huguenots*, Pt. I, ch. 2.

31 See Poland, *French Protestantism*, ch. 2, 57–64.

32 See the collection of Voltaire's writings on toleration in *L'Affaire Calas*, ed. van den Heuvel; and Valérie Van Crugten-André, *Le 'Traité sur la tolérance de Voltaire': Un champion des Lumières contre le fanatisme* (Paris, 1999).

33 Voltaire, *Traité sur la tolérance*, ch. 6.

34 Anne-Robert-Jacques Turgot, baron de Lauine, *Lettre au Docteur Price sur les constitutions américaines*, in *Oeuvres*, ed. G. Schelle, 5 vols. (Paris, 1913–23), 5: 532–40; *Première lettre à un grand vicaire* (1753) in *Oeuvres*, 1: 387–91. Marie Jean Antoine Nicolas de Caritat, marquis de Condorcet, *De l'Influence de la révolution de l'Amérique sur l'Europe*, in *Oeuvres*, eds. A. C. O'Connor and F. Arago, 12 vols. (Paris, 1847–9), 8: 1–113; *Lettres d'un citoyen des Etats-Unis à un Français sur les affaires présentes* in *Oeuvres*, 9: 95–123. Honoré Gabriel Riquetti, comte de Mirabeau, *De la monarchie prussienne sous Frédéric le Grand*, 7 vols. (London, 1788); *Aux Bataves sur le Stathoudérat* ([Amsterdam], 1788). See Jürgen Sandweg, *Rationales Naturrecht als revolutionäre Praxis. Untersuchungen zur 'Erklärung der Menschen- und Bürgerrechte' von 1789* (Berlin, 1972), ch. 1.1, 29–35; Poland, *French Protestantism*, ch. 3; Adams, *The Huguenots*, chs. 16, 17.

35 See Martin Fitzpatrick, 'Toleration and Truth', *Enlightenment and Dissent*, 1 (1982), 3–31.

36 Kant, *Religion*, Ak 6: 109–14.

37 See Holmes, *The Trial of Doctor Sacheverell; Palladium of Conscience;* William Blackstone, *Commentaries on the Laws of England*, 4 vols. (London, 1765–9), 4: IV.iii. In the German territories the structure of opposition with regard to the church's position in society was different; see Klaus Schlaich, 'Der rationale Territorialismus. Die Kirche unter dem staatsrechtlichen Absolutismus um die Wende vom 17. zum 18. Jahrhundert', *Zeitschrift der Savigny-Stiftung für Rechtsgeschichte*, 85 (1968): Kanonistische Abt., 269–340; John Stroup, *The Struggle for Identity in the Clerical Estate: Northwest German Protestant Opposition to Absolutist Policy in the Eighteenth Century* (Leiden, 1984), Introduction; *Der Josephinismus. Bedeutung, Einflüsse*

und Wirkungen, ed. H. Reinalter (Frankfurt am Main, 1993); Jochim Whaley, 'A Tolerant Society? Religious Toleration in the Holy Roman Empire, 1648–1806', in *Toleration in Enlightenment Europe*, eds. Grell and Porter, 175–95.

38 William Warburton, *The Alliance between Church and State, or, The Necessity and Equity of an Established Religion and a Test-Law demonstrated* (London, 1736), in *The Reception of Locke's Politics*, ed. Goldie, 5: 179–279. A summary is contained in his *The Divine Legation of Moses demonstrated, on the Principles of a Religious Deist, From the Omission of the Doctrine of a Future State of Reward and Punishment in the Jewish Dispensation*, 2 vols. in 3 (London, 1738–42); see Arthur William Evans, *Warburton and the Warburtonians: A Study in Some Eighteenth-Century Controversies* (London, 1932).

39 Warburton, *Divine Legation of Moses*, 'Dedication to the Free-Thinkers', xxv–xxvi.

40 See Colin Bonwick, *English Radicals and the American Revolution* (Chapel Hill, NC, 1977), ch. 7; James E. Bradley, *Religion, Revolution, and English Radicalism: Nonconformity in Eighteenth-Century Politics and Society* (Cambridge, 1990), ch. 4.

41 Edmund Burke, *Reflections on the Revolution in France* (1790), in *The Writings and Speeches of Edmund Burke*, ed. P. Langford, vol. 8: *The French Revolution*, ed. L. G. Mitchell (Oxford, 1989).

42 See Michael Freeman, *Edmund Burke and the Critique of Political Radicalism* (Oxford, 1980), 141–2.

43 See Poland, *French Protestantism*, 141–92.

44 Priestley, *Essay on the First Principles of Government*, 60–1 with critical discussion of Locke 63–4 and note.

45 For an interpretation of the 1697 Act for the Effectual Suppressing of Blasphemy and Profaneness see David Berman, *A History of Atheism in Britain: From Hobbes to Russell* (London, 1990), 35–6.

46 See *Appellation an das Publikum: Dokumente zum Atheismusstreit um Fichte, Forberg, Niethammer, Jena 1798/99*, ed. W. Röhr (Leipzig, 1987).

47 For example Johann Franz Budde's, *Theses theologicae de atheismo et superstitione variis observationibus illustratae et in usum recitationum academicarum editae* (Jena, 1717); Jakob Friedrich Reimmann, *Historia universalis atheismi et atheorum falso et merito suspectorum . . .* (Hildesheim, 1725). See Hans-Martin Barth, *Atheismus und Orthodoxie. Analysen und Modelle christlicher Apologetik im 17. Jahrhundert* (Göttingen, 1971); Martin Pott, *Aufklärung und Aberglaube. Die deutsche Frühaufklärung im Spiegel ihrer Aberglaubenskritik* (Tübingen, 1992), 171–7; Alan Charles Kors, *Atheism in France, 1650–1729* (Princeton, NJ, 1990–), vol. 1: *The Orthodox Sources of Disbelief*, 46–7, 231–44.

48 Paul-Henry Thiry d'Holbach, *Système de la nature ou Des lois du monde physique et du monde moral*, ed. D. Diderot; facsim. repr. of Paris, 1821 edn., ed. Y. Belaval, 2 vols. (Hildesheim, 1966). See Winfried Schröder, *Ursprünge des Atheismus. Untersuchungen zur Metaphysik- und Religionskritik des 17. und 18. Jahrhunderts* (Stuttgart-Bad Cannstatt, 1998).

49 Kors, *Atheism in France*, 1: 12.

50 See Berman, 'The theoretical/practical distinction as applied to the Existence of God from Locke to Kant', *Trivium*, 12 (1977): 92–108.

51 Kors, *Atheism in France*, 1: 17.

52 See Samuel Clarke, *A Demonstration of the Being and Attributes of God: More Particularly in Answer to Mr. Hobbs, Spinoza, and their Followers* (London 1705), 1–5; Budde, *Lehrsätze von der Atheisterey und dem Aberglauben mit gelehrten Anmerckungen erläutert . . . in lateinischer Sprache hrsg. [Theses theologicae] ins Teutsche übersetzet* (Jena, 1717), ch. 2, §1, p. 184; §§6–10, pp. 198–215.

53 Kors, 'The Atheism of d'Holbach and Naigeon', in *Atheism from the Reformation to the Enlightenment*, eds. M. Hunter and D. Wootton (Oxford, 1992), 273–300; same, 'Skepticism and the Problem of Atheism in Early-Modern France', in *Scepticism and Irreligion in the Seventeenth and Eighteenth Centuries*, eds. R. H. Popkin and A. Vanderjagt (Leiden, 1993), 185–215; Berman, *History of Atheism*. Wootton, 'New Histories of Atheism', in *Atheism from the Reformation to the Enlightenment*, 13–53. See also Michael J. Buckley, *At the Origins of Modern Atheism* (New Haven, CT, 1987).

54 David Hume, *An Enquiry Concerning Human Understanding* (1777), ed. T. L. Beauchamp, in *The Clarendon Edition* (2000), 12.1.1, SBN 149; Richard Bentley, *The Folly and Unreasonableness of Atheism Demonstrated* (London, 1693), First Sermon, 10; Berman, *History of Atheism*, 101–5; and 'David Hume and the Suppression of "Atheism"', *Journal of the History of Philosophy*, 21 (1983): 375–87; see also J. C. A. Gaskin's critical comment in 'Hume's Attenuated Deism', *Archiv für Geschichte der Philosophie*, 65 (1983): 160–73. John Toland, 'Clidophorus, or, Of the Exoteric and Esoteric Philosophy', in *Tetradymus* (London, 1720). Toland, *Pantheisticon* [1720], translated as *Pantheisticon: Or, the Form of Celebrating the Socratic-Society* (London, 1751), 9–62. See Gavina Cherchi, *Pantheisticon. Eterodossia e dissimulazione nella filosofia di John Toland* (Pisa, 1990).

55 Berman, 'Disclaimers as Offence Mechanisms in Charles Blount and John Toland', in *Atheism from the Reformation to the Enlightenment*, eds. Hunter and Wootton, 255–72 at 259–60; John Redwood, *Reason, Ridicule and Religion: The Age of Enlightenment in England 1660–1750* (London, 1976).

56 Wootton, 'New Histories of Atheism'; Margaret C. Jacob, *The Radical Enlightenment: Pantheists, Freemasons and Republicans* (London, 1981), 142–81; Silvia Berti, 'The First Edition of the *Traité des trois imposteurs* and Its Debt to Spinoza's *Ethics*', in *Atheism from the Reformation to the Enlightenment*, eds. Hunter and Wootton, 182–220. Ira O. Wade, *The Clandestine Organization and Diffusion of Philosophic Ideas in France from 1700 to 1750* (Princeton, NJ, 1938), 97–123; A. C. Kors, *D'Holbachs Coterie. An Enlightenment in Paris* (Princeton, NJ, 1976).

57 Pierre Bayle, *Pensées diverses écrites à un docteur de Sorbonne a l'occasion de la comète Qui parut au mois de Décembre M.DC.LXXX*, §§139–43, 149, 161, 172, 177, in *Oeuvres diverses*, 3: 89–93, 95–6, 97–9, 113–14. Article 'Spinoza', in *Choix d'articles tirés du Dictionnaire historique et critique* (The Hague, 1740 edn.), in *Oeuvres diverses*, suppl. vols., ed. E. Labrousse, 2 vols. in 3 (Hildesheim, 1982), 1.2: 1069–87. See Bayle, *Ecrits sur Spinoza*, eds. F. Charles-Daubert and P.-F. Moreau (Paris, 1983); Elisabeth Labrousse, *Pierre Bayle*, 2 vols. (The Hague, 1963–4); Harry M. Bracken, 'Bayle's Attack on Natural Theology: The Case of Christian Pyrrhonism', in *Scepticism and Irreligion*, eds. Popkin and Vanderjagt, 254–66.

58 Julien Offray de La Mettrie, *Discours préliminaire* in *Oeuvres philosophiques*, 3 vols. (Amsterdam, 1774), 1: 1–61 at 29.

59 *Answer to Dr. Priestley's Letters to a Philosophical Unbeliever*, (London 1782), x. Authorship was first ascribed to William Hammon, later to Matthew Turner: see Berman, *History of Atheism*, 112–16.

60 D'Holbach, *Système de la nature*, 2: 357–404.

61 See Donald McCormick, *The Hell-Fire Club: The Story of the Amorous Knights of Wycombe* (London, 1958); Shearer West, 'Libertinism and the Ideology of Male Friendship in the Portraits of the Society of Dilettanti', *Eighteenth-Century Life*, 16 (May 1992): 76–104; Betty Kemp, *Sir Francis Dashwood: An Eighteenth-Century Independent* (London, 1967), 101–36; James G. Turner, 'The Properties of Libertinism', in *'Tis Nature's Fault: Unauthorized Sexuality during the Enlightenment*, ed. R. P. Maccubbin (Cambridge, 1987), 75–87.

62 See Jean Deprun, 'Sade philosophe', in Donatien Alphonse François, marquis de Sade, *Oeuvres*, ed. M. Delon (Paris, 1990–), 1: lix–lxix; 'Sade et le rationalisme des Lumières', *Raison présente* 55, (1980): 17–29; Josué V. Harari, 'D'une raison à l'autre: le dispositif Sade', in *Studies on Voltaire and the Eighteenth Century*, 230 (1985): 273–82. Pierre Klossowski, 'Sade, or the Philosopher-Villain', *Sub-stance* 50, (1986): 5–25.

63 Budde, *Lehr-Sätze*, ch. 8, §2, 590–1; ch. 10, §2, 711–17; John Toland, *Adeisidaemon, sive Titus Livius, a Superstitione vindicatus* (The Hague, 1709), 79. See also Pott, *Aufklärung und Aberglaube*, 171–7; Kors, *Atheism in France*, 239–44.

64 Zurbuchen, *Naturrecht und natürliche Religion. Zur Geschichte des Toleranzbegriffs von Samuel Pufendorf bis Jean-Jacques Rousseau* (Würzburg, 1991), 82–3, 133–5; Kant, *Kritik der reinen Vernunft* (2nd edn., 1787), Ak 3: 20–1.

65 Warburton, *Divine Legation of Moses*, Bk. I, sects. IV and V, and sect. IV, 36–7. See Pierre Rétat, *Le Dictionnaire de Bayle et la lutte philosophique au XVIIIe siècle* (Paris, 1971), 162–7; Christian Wolff, *Vernünfftige Gedancken von der Menschen Thun und Lassen, zur Beförderung ihrer Glückseligkeit* (Deutsche Ethik), ed. H. W. Arndt, *Werke*, I.4.1 (1976), ch. 1, §§20–22, 29–32; *Theologia naturalis Pars II*, ed. J. Ecole, *Werke*, II.8 (1980), sect. II. See Thomas P. Saine, 'Who's Afraid of Christian Wolff?' in *Anticipations of the Enlightenment in England, France, and Germany*, eds. A. C. Kors and P. J. Korshin (Philadelphia, PA, 1987), 102–33.

66 *Encyclopédie ou Dictionnaire raisonné des Sciences des Arts et des Métiers*, eds. Diderot and d'Alembert, 35 vols. (Paris and Amsterdam, 1751–80), 7: 574b–578b; René Pomeau, *La religion de Voltaire* (Paris, 1969), 314–16.

67 Voltaire, *Traité sur la tolérance*; *Avis public sur les parricides imputés aux Calas et aux Sirven*, in *Oeuvres*, 38: 400–34; articles 'Athée', 'Athéisme', 'Dieu' 'Fanatisme', in *Dictionnaire philosophique, Oeuvres*, vols. 52, 54, and 55; 'Première Homélie sur l'athéisme', in *Homélies prononcées à Londres en 1765*, in *Oeuvres*, 43: 331–57; *Histoire de Jenni, ou le sage et l'athée*, chs. VIII–X, in *Oeuvres*, 60: 277–31. See Roland Mortier, 'L'athéisme en France au XVIIIe siècle: progrès et résistances', *Problèmes d'Histoire du Christianisme*, 16 (1986): 45–62.

68 Voltaire, *Avis public*, 429; *Traité sur la tolérance*, ch. 5, 165.

69 Voltaire, *Avis public*, 411–14; 'Première sur l'atheisme', in *Oeuvres*, 43: 347, 356–7, 1128, 1134; Article 'Athée', in *Oeuvres*, 52: 285–98 at 291.

70 Kors, 'The Atheism of d'Holbach and Naigeon', 273, 275.

71 D'Holbach, *Système de la nature*, vol. 2, ch. 11, 321–2.

72 Scepticus Britannicus, *An Investigation of the Essence of the Deity; with a word or two by way of Postscript, to the Professors of Deism, in Refutation of their Doctrine, that the Bible is not the word of God* (London, 1797), 40–1. This definition of the atheist refers to d'Holbach, *Système de la nature*, 2: ch. 11. See Berman, *A History of Atheism*, 126.

73 See Schröder, *Ursprünge des Atheismus*, 321–42.

74 Friedrich Heinrich Jacobi, *Über die Lehre des Spinoza in Briefen an den Herrn Moses Mendelssohn*, ed. M. Lauschke (Hamburg, 2000); see also *Jacobis Spinoza Büchlein nebst Replik und Duplik*, ed. F. Mauthner (Munich, 1912). See Sylvain Zac, *Spinoza en Allemagne: Mendelssohn, Lessing et Jacobi* (Paris, 1989); Kurt Christ, *Jacobi und Mendelssohn. Eine Analyse des Spinozastreits* (Würzburg, 1988); Rüdiger Otto, *Studien zur Spinozarezeption in Deutschland im 18. Jahrhundert* (Frankfurt am Main, 1994), 172–346; Susan Neiman, *The Unity of Reason. Rereading Kant* (Oxford, 1994), 147–56.

75 Mendelssohn, *Philosophische Gespräche* (1755), in *Gesammelte Schriften*, vol. 1, ed. F. Bamberger (1971), 3–39.

76 Mendelssohn, *Morgenstunden oder Vorlesungen über das Daseyn Gottes* (1785), in *Gesammelte Schriften*, vol. 3.2, ed. L. Strauss (1974), 1–175, here at 114 and 123–4. See *An die Freunde*

Lessings. Ein Anhang zu Herrn Jacobi, Briefwechsel über die Lehre des Spinoza (1786), in *Gesammelte Schriften*, 3.2: 179–218.

77 Charles Louis de Secondat, baron de Montesquieu, *De l'esprit des lois ou Du rapport que les lois doivent avoir avec la constitution de chaque gouvernement, les moeurs, le climat, la religion, le commerce etc*, Bk. 24, ch. 1, in *Oeuvres complètes*, ed. R. Caillois, 2 vols. (Paris, 1949–51), 2: 714, quoted hereafter by book, chapter, and page.

78 See Richard Myers, 'Christianity and Politics in Montesquieu's "Greatness and Decline of the Romans"', *Interpretation* 17.2, (1989–90): 223–38.

79 Montesquieu, *Lettres persanes*, Letter 85, 114–17, in *Oeuvres*, 1: 258–60, 299–307. See Pauline Kra, *Religion in Montesquieu's 'Lettres persanes'* (Geneva, 1970).

80 See Erich Hassinger, 'Wirtschaftliche Motive und Argumente für religiöse Duldsamkeit im 16. und 17. Jahrhundert', *Archiv für Reformationsgeschichte*, 49 (1958): 226–45. For examples of how utility arguments conflicted with popular prejudice, see Adams, *The Huguenots*, 87–98, on public debate concerning the civil status of Calvinists in France; John Toland, *Reasons for Naturalizing the Jews in Great Britain and Ireland/ Gründe für die Einbürgerung der Juden in Großbritannien und Ireland*; English text with German trans. and introd. by H. Mainusch (Stuttgart, 1965), Einleitung, 19–20, on the naturalisation of Protestants in Great Britain; Barlow, *Citizenship and Conscience*, 203–13, on the toleration of Catholics in Ireland, England, and Scotland; and Thomas W. Perry, *Public Opinion, Propaganda and Politics in Eighteenth-Century England. A Study of the Jew Bill of 1753* (Cambridge, MA, 1962), on the naturalisation of Jews in England.

81 Justus Henning Boehmer, *praeses*, *Dissertatio iuridica de cauta Iudaeorum tolerantia*, Joannes Andreas Bastineller, respondent (Halle, 1723: orig. publ. 1708), §XI; Dohm, *Über die bürgerliche Verbesserung der Juden*, 1: 3–16. See Leonore Loft, 'J.-P. Brissot and the Problem of Jewish Emancipation', in *Studies on Voltaire and the Eighteenth Century*, 278 (1990): 465–75; Pierre Aubery, 'Montesquieu et les Juifs', in *Studies on Voltaire and the Eighteenth Century* 87, (1972): 87–99; and Arthur Hertzberg, *The French Enlightenment and the Jews* (New York, NY, 1968), 273–80.

82 See Justin Champion, 'Toleration and Citizenship in Enlightenment England: John Toland and the Naturalization of the Jews, 1714–1753', in *Toleration in Enlightenment Europe*, eds. Grell and Porter, 133–56.

83 Bayle, *Pensées diverses*, §141, in *Oeuvres*, 3: 90–1; Bernard Mandeville, *Free Thoughts*, 7–11; Mandeville, *An Enquiry into the Origin of Honour, and the Usefulness of Christianity in War* (London, 1732). See M. R. Jack, 'Religion and Ethics in Mandeville', in *Mandeville Studies: New Studies in the Art and Thought of Dr. Bernard Mandeville (1670–1733)*, ed. I. Primer (The Hague, 1975), 35; E. D. James, 'Faith, Sincerity and Morality: Mandeville and Bayle', in *Mandeville Studies*, 43–65; Shelley Burtt, *Virtue Transformed: Political Argument in England, 1688–1740* (Cambridge, 1992), ch. 7.

84 The third Dialogue of the *Enquiry* discusses the question, raised by Bayle of whether Christians would be good soldiers. See Jonathan I. Israel, *Radical Enlightenment. Philosophy and the Making of Modernity 1650–1750* (Oxford, 2001), 623–7.

85 See Bracken, 'Bayle's attack on natural theology', in *Scepticism and Irreligion*, eds. Popkin and Vanderjagt, 254–66.

86 David Hume, 'Of Superstition and Enthusiasm', in his *Political Essays*, ed. K. Haakonssen (Cambridge, 1994), 46–50; *The Natural History of Religion*, in *Works*, 4: 309–63; *The History of England from the Invasion of Julius Caesar to the Revolution in 1688*, 8 vols. (London, 1778). See Rudolf Lüthe, *David Hume. Historiker und Philosoph* (Freiburg, 1991), 141–65; J. C. A. Gaskin, *Hume's Philosophy of Religion* (London, 1988), ch. 9.

87 See Hoadly, *The Nature of the Kingdom, or Church, of Christ.*

88 John Passmore, 'Enthusiasm, Fanaticism and David Hume', in *The 'Science of Man' in the Scottish Enlightenment. Hume, Reid and Their Contemporaries*, ed. P. Jones (Edinburgh, 1989), 86.

89 James E. Crimmins, 'Religion, Utility and Politics: Bentham versus Paley', in *Religion, Secularization and Political Thought. Thomas Hobbes to J. S. Mill*, ed. J. E. Crimmins (London, 1989), 137; and 'John Brown and the Theological Tradition of Utilitarian Ethics', *History of Political Thought*, 14 (1983): 523–50.

90 For other such efforts, see James Fulton Maclear, 'Isaac Watts and the Idea of Public Religion', in *Journal of the History of Ideas*, 53 (1992): 25–45; Alfred Owen Aldridge, *Benjamin Franklin and Nature's God* (Durham, NC, 1967), 207–21; Stroup, *The Struggle for Identity*, 99–105; Pierre-André Bois, 'Engagement maçonnique et engagement révolutionnaire: Les droits de l'homme comme 'Religion de l'humanité' d'après Knigge', *Francia*, 16 (1989): 99–113.

91 Two exceptions are Justin Champion, *The Pillars of Priestcraft Shaken: The Church of England and Its Enemies, 1660–1730* (Cambridge, 1992), and Burtt, *Virtue Transformed*. See also Zurbuchen, 'Republicanism and Toleration', in *Republicanism: A Shared European Heritage*, eds. M. van Gelderen and Q. Skinner, 2 vols. (Cambridge, 2002), 2: 47–71.

92 Champion, *Pillars*, 8–20 and 170–3.

93 James Harrington, *The Commonwealth of Oceana* (1656), in *The Political Works*, ed. J. G. A. Pocock (Cambridge, 1977), 155–359; Walter Moyle, *An Essay upon the Constitution of the Roman Government*, in *Works*, 2 vols. (London, 1726), 1: 12–23. See Mark Goldie, 'The Civil Religion of James Harrington', in *Languages of Political Theory in Early Modern Europe*, ed. A. Pagden (Cambridge, 1987), 197–222; Champion, *Pillars*, 186–91.

94 See Günter Gawlick, 'Cicero and the Enlightenment', in *Studies on Voltaire and the Eighteenth Century*, 25 (1963): 657–82; Pocock, Introduction to Harrington, *Political Works*, xi–xiii.

95 Toland, *The State-Anatomy of Great Britain. Containing a Particular Account of Its Several Interests and Parties, their Bent and Genius* (Pt. 1, 4th edn.; Pt. 2, 2nd edn., London, 1717), Pt. 1, 28.

96 Toland, *Anglia Libera: or The Limitation and Succession of the Crown of England Explain'd and Asserted* (London, 1701); *State-Anatomy*, 19–32. See Robert Rees Evans, *Pantheisticon: The Career of John Toland* (New York, NY, 1991), chs. 1, 2.

97 Toland, *Pantheisticon*, 93–110; Jacob, *Radical Enlightenment*, 153; Robert E. Sullivan, *John Toland and the Deist Controversy: A Study in Adaptations* (Cambridge, MA, 1982), 169.

98 Jean-Jacques Rousseau, *Du contrat social ou Principes du droit politique*, Bk. 4, ch. 8, in *Oeuvres*, 3: 469.

99 R. A. Leigh, *Rousseau and the Problem of Tolerance in the Eighteenth Century. A Lecture Delivered in the Taylor Institution Oxford* (Oxford, 1979), 23–6.

100 Judith Shklar, 'Montesquieu and the New Republicanism', in *Machiavelli and Republicanism*, eds. G. Bock, Q. Skinner, and M. Viroli (Cambridge, 1990), 265–79 at 265.

101 Rousseau, *Émile ou De l'éducation*, in *Oeuvres*, 4: 632–3.

102 James E. Crimmins, "The Study of True Politics': John Brown on Manners and Liberty', in *Studies on Voltaire and the Eighteenth Century*, 241 (1986): 65–86 at 84.

103 Crimmins, 'Study of True Politics'. See also Martin Fitzpatrick, 'Reflections on a Footnote: Richard Price and Love of Country', *Enlightenment and Dissent*, 6 (1987): 41–58.

104 Robert N. Bellah, 'The Revolution and Civil Religion', in *Religion and the American Revolution*, ed. J. C. Brauer (Philadelphia, PA, 1976), 55–73.

105 An overview is provided in *Church and State in America*, ed. J. F. Wilson, chs. 4 and 5. See Elise Marienstras, *Nous, le peuple: les origines du nationalisme américain* (Paris, 1988).

106 Stroup, *Struggle for Identity*, 97. Thomas Abbt, *Vom Tode für das Vaterland* (1761), in *Vermischte Werke*, 6 vols. (Berlin and Stettin, 1772–81), 1: Pt. 2. See also Dagobert de Levie, 'Patriotism and Clerical Office: Germany 1761–1773', *Journal of the History of Ideas*, 14 (1953): 622–27.

107 Gabriel Bonnot de Mably, *De la législation ou Principes des lois, Collection complète des oeuvres*, 15 vols. (Paris 1794–95), 9: 385–423. For the following, see Jean-Philippe Domecq, 'La Fête de l'Etre suprême et son interprétation', *Esprit*, 154:9 (1989): 91–125, referring to Maximilien de Robespierre, *Sur les rapports des idées religieuses et morales avec les principes républicains, et sur les fêtes nationales*, in *Oeuvres*, 11 vols. (Paris, 1910–67), 10: 442–65.

108 For Hegel's distinction between 'morality' (*Moralität*) and 'ethical life' (*Sittlichkeit*), see Allen W. Wood, *Hegel's Ethical Thought* (Cambridge, 1990), 127–39.

109 Georg Wilhelm Friedrich Hegel, *Fragmente über Volksreligion und Christentum* (1793–4), in his *Frühe Studien und Entwürfe, 1787–1800*, ed. I. Gellert (Berlin, 1991), 23–128 at 26 and 56. All subsequent references are to this edition unless otherwise indicated.

110 Kant, *Die Religion innerhalb der Grenzen der bloßen Vernunft*.

111 Laurence Dickey, *Hegel: Religion, Economics, and the Politics of Spirit, 1770–1807* (Cambridge, 1987), 144.

IV

NATURAL PHILOSOPHY

28

ARTIFICE AND THE NATURAL WORLD: MATHEMATICS, LOGIC, TECHNOLOGY

JAMES FRANKLIN

If Tahiti suggested to theorists comfortably at home in Europe thoughts of noble savages without clothes, those who paid for and went on voyages there were in pursuit of a quite opposite human ideal. Cook's voyage to observe the transit of Venus in 1769 symbolises the eighteenth century's commitment to numbers and accuracy, and its willingness to spend a lot of public money on acquiring them. The state supported the organisation of quantitative researches, employing surveyors and collecting statistics to compute its power.[1] People volunteered to become more numerate;[2] even those who did not had the numerical rationality of the metric system imposed on them.[3] There was an increase of two orders of magnitude or so in the accuracy of measuring instruments and the known values of physical constants.[4] The graphical display of quantitative information made it more readily available and comprehensible.[5] On the research front, mathematics continued its advance, even if with notably less speed than in the two adjoining centuries. The methods of the calculus proved successful in more and more problems in mechanics, both celestial and terrestrial. Elasticity and fluid dynamics became mathematically tractable for the first time.[6] The central limit theorem brought many chance phenomena within the purview of reason.

These successes proved of interest for 'low philosophy', or philosophy-as-propaganda, as practised by the natural theologians and the *Encyclopédistes*. Both had their uses for scientific breakthroughs, though sometimes not much interest in the details. For 'high philosophy', as constituted by the great names, mathematics and science had a different importance. A feature common to the biographies of all the well-known philosophers of the eighteenth century is a mathematical youth. Wolff began as a professor of mathematics, and it was in that subject that he first made the contributions to the intellectual vocabulary and style of German for which he is so universally loathed. Kant taught mathematics, and his Prize Essay begins with an analysis of the mathematical method. D'Alembert, Condorcet, Lambert, even Diderot in a smaller way (and of course Leibniz earlier) made serious mathematical contributions. Reid also taught mathematics, and his first published work was on quantity. Paley was

Senior Wrangler in the Cambridge Mathematical Tripos. Berkeley's *Analyst* is one of the most successful interventions ever by a philosopher into mathematics. Hume and Vico, though no mathematicians, used mathematical examples as the first illustrations of their theories. Adam Smith's 'invisible hand' and Malthus's model of population growth both belong to what is now called dynamical systems theory.

Naturally, these philosophers did not all draw the same lessons from their mathematical experience. But philosophers have one thing in common in their attitude toward mathematics, in this last century before the surprise of non-Euclidean geometry undermined the pretensions of mathematics to infallibility. It is envy. What is envied, in particular, is the 'mathematical method', which apparently produced what philosophy wished it could but had been unable to: certain truths, agreed to by all, delivered by pure thought.

I. THE 'MATHEMATICAL METHOD' PRAISED

The eighteenth century was the last to accept, fundamentally without question, certain approved opinions of the ancients concerning the method and content of mathematics. The ideas were largely Aristotelian in origin but had survived the demise of scholasticism by being accepted almost in full by the Cartesians and Newton. The much admired 'mathematical method' is the deriving of truths by syllogisms from self-evident first principles; the method was believed to be instantiated by Euclid's *Elements*. As to the content, mathematics is the science of 'quantity', which is 'whatever is capable of increase, or diminution'.[7] Numbers arise from considering the ratio of quantities to an arbitrarily chosen unit. Quantity is of two kinds: discrete (studied by arithmetic) and continuous (studied by geometry). However, geometry is also the study of 'extension', or real space. Quantity in the abstract is studied by pure mathematics, while 'magnitude as subsisting in material bodies'[8] is the object of mixed or applied mathematics, which includes optics, astronomy, mechanics, navigation, and the like. Tendencies to regard mathematics as about some abstraction of reality did exist but were generally resisted. Euler, for example, says that in geometry one does not deal with an ideal or abstract triangle but with triangles in general, and that generality in mathematics is no different from generality elsewhere;[9] to the same purpose, d'Alembert defends an approximation theory, whereby the perfect circles of geometry allow us to 'approach' the truth, 'if not rigorously, at least to a degree sufficient for our use'.[10]

There are several philosophical problems with this complex of opinions, which are sufficiently obvious to keep surfacing in one form or another again and again:

- Why is the mathematical method found in *mathematics*?
- Why are the first principles in mathematics necessary, and how are they known?
- Is the reasoning in Euclid in fact all syllogisms? (in the strict sense, that is, of the form: All A are B, All B are C, so All A are C). If not, what kind of reasoning is it?

1. *Wolff*

Wolff at least had answers to these questions. The mathematical method, he thinks, is applicable everywhere; and there is no problem about the self-evidence of the first principles because there is only one of them, and it is the principle of non-contradiction. Geometrical demonstrations can all be resolved into formal syllogisms, and discoveries in mathematics are made exclusively by syllogistic means.[11] His central place in eighteenth-century philosophy results from his attempt to derive all philosophical truths from the principle of non-contradiction, by the 'mathematical method'.[12] A look at how he actually proposes to *prove* that everything has a sufficient reason, using only the principle of non-contradiction, reveals why Wolff's 'method' achieved less than universal agreement:

> Let us suppose A to be without a sufficient reason why it is rather than is not. Therefore nothing is supposed by which it can be understood why A is. Thus A is admitted to be, on the basis of an assumed nothing; but since this is absurd, nothing is without a sufficient reason.[13]

Wolff's ideal differs from those of others essentially in lacking anything like Plato's dialectic, or Aristotle's induction, or Kant's analysis: the roundabout discussion and sorting of experience which allows the intellect to come to an insight into first principles. It is unnecessary in Wolff's system because the principle of non-contradiction is the sole starting point. Any tendency to regard brute facts as contingent and outside the scope of explanation by necessary reasons is suppressed, in Wolff, by his acceptance of Leibniz's Best of All Possible Worlds theory. According to that theory, everything, however particular, has an explanation in principle.

2. *Mathematics as philosophical propaganda*

Mathematics, because of its immense prestige, is always destined to be used in support of various philosophical positions. It was a natural as a prop for the Enlightenment motif that there should be more Reason all round. The *Encyclopédie* says: 'M. Wolff . . . made it clear in theory, and especially in practice, and in the composition of all his works, that the mathematical method belongs to all the sciences, is natural to the human spirit, and leads to discoveries of truths of all kinds.'[14] Not that the French needed Wolff to tell them this, given the Cartesian ideals expressed by, for example, Fontenelle:

> The geometrical spirit is not so attached to geometry that it cannot be carried over to other knowledge as well. A work of ethics, of politics, of criticism, perhaps even of eloquence will be better, all things else being equal, if it is made by the hand of a mathematician. The order, clarity, precision and exactitude which have reigned in the better works recently, can well have had their first source in this geometrical spirit which extends itself more than ever and which in some fashion communicates itself even to those who have no knowledge of geometry.[15]

Of course, there were counter-currents. There were the complaints common in all centuries from self-proclaimed 'practical men' like Frederick the Great and Jefferson,[16] who regarded the higher abstractions of mathematics as useless, and from humanists like Vico and Gibbon, who abhorred the 'habit of rigid demonstration, so destructive of the finer feelings of moral evidence'.[17]

Mathematics was also called to the aid of more particular philosophical theses. On the one side, there was the support allegedly given to natural theology by the various 'principles of least action'. On the other, the success of prediction in astronomy could be a support to determinism. It was found that many phenomena in physics could be derived from 'methods of maxima and minima', or 'principles of least action', such as the one stating that the path of light from one point to another is the one which minimises the time of travel (even if the path is not straight, because of reflection or refraction). Maupertuis and Euler take this to be evidence of final causes, and for the existence of God.[18] Their idea owes something to the more general claim of Leibniz's *Theodicée* that everything is the necessary result of a maximum principle, namely, that the goodness of this world is the best possible. D'Alembert, to the contrary, warns of the danger of 'regarding as a primitive law of nature what is only a purely mathematical consequence of some formulae'.[19] He believes the best hope for the countries of Europe oppressed by superstition is to begin studying geometry, which will lead to sound philosophy.[20] Laplace also, in an image that haunts philosophy still, invites mathematics to assist an anti-religious worldview:

> Given for one instant an intelligence which could comprehend all the forces by which nature is animated and the respective situation of the beings who compose it . . . it would embrace in the same formula the movements of the greatest bodies of the universe and those of the lightest atom.[21]

History would thus be a subfield of the theory of differential equations.

3. D'Alembert versus Diderot

Wolff's ant-like progress through a farrago of equivocations and circularities is merely dispiriting and only brings rationalism into disrepute. D'Alembert is not so easily dismissed when he argues for essentially the same conclusions. His immediate claim, is not, indeed, that *all* subjects are entirely amenable to the geometric method, only that mechanics is. But mechanics is very inclusive, on a typical eighteenth-century view. If La Mettrie and d'Holbach were right about the nature of man, for example, psychology would be a sub-branch of mechanics. D'Alembert argues, more convincingly than Descartes, that mechanics is a branch of mathematics, based like arithmetic on absolutely necessary first principles. In a kind of mathematical version of Hume's scepticism about causes, he regards forces as 'beings obscure and metaphysical': 'All we see distinctly in the movement of a body is that it crosses a certain space and that it employs a certain time to cross it.'[22] Hence collisions are to be explained in terms of impenetrability, and the density of a body is merely 'the ratio of its mass (that is, the space it would occupy if it were absolutely without pores) to its volume, that is, to the space it actually occupies'.[23] It might seem that there is no hope of demonstrating the conservation of momentum purely geometrically:

> However, if we consider the matter carefully, we shall see that there is one case in which equilibrium manifests itself clearly and distinctly; that is where the masses of the two bodies are equal, and their velocities equal and opposite.[24]

The *Encyclopédie* article 'Expérimentale', which one expects to be along Baconian lines, is in fact used by d'Alembert to propagate his extreme anti-experimental views. He regards collecting facts as a rather medieval exercise, superseded by Newton's introduction of geometry into physics. The laws of colliding bodies are demonstrable: nature could not be any other way. But there is an admission that how fast a body falls under gravity, and what the weight of a fluid is, must be measured; only after that do the relevant sciences become 'entirely or almost entirely mathematical':

> No theory could have allowed us to find the law that heavy bodies follow in their vertical fall, but once this law is found through experience, all that belongs to the movement of heavy bodies, whether rectilinear or curvilinear, whether inclined or vertical, is found entirely by theory.[25]

While these cases appear as unfortunate weakenings of his original wish for purely deductive science, d'Alembert's comments here are perhaps his most solid achievement. In the more mathematical sciences, experience does appear only in support of a few easily checkable symmetry principles and simple laws, while most of the weight of explanation rests on the difficult mathematical derivations of more subtle phenomena from these. And, as Leibniz points out,[26] a symmetry principle has a special logical status, being an application of the principle of (in)sufficient reason: in d'Alembert's example, if two bodies have equal and opposite velocities, their momenta must balance, as there is no reason why one should overcome the other. D'Alembert was widely thought to have succeeded in showing that the principles of mechanics had 'a necessity as rigorous as the first elementary truths of geometry'.[27] Kant concurred in d'Alembert's unlikely conclusion.[28] Lagrange's *Mécanique analytique* of 1788 confirmed further that mechanics could look like a deductive system, managing almost to conceal the existence of forces.[29]

Of one mind on the iniquity of priestcraft, the inevitable progress of mankind, and other such Enlightenment staples, the two prime movers of the *Encyclopédie* fell out over mathematics. Diderot believed mathematics had reached its highest point and was now in decline.[30] He preferred sciences full of life and ferment, like chemistry and biology, criticising mathematics as abstract and over-simple.[31] D'Alembert, on the other hand, held that an abundance of experiential 'principles' is 'an effect of our very poverty'.[32] Diderot's attack is not all invective; he has a philosophical argument to undermine rationalist pretensions about mathematics which is the same as the contention of twentieth-century empiricists and positivists that mathematics is essentially trivial. Geometrical truths are merely identities, saying the same thing in a thousand different ways without generating any new facts.[33] D'Alembert allowed this argument to appear in the *Discours préliminaire* to the *Encyclopédie*, but replied that it just showed how powerful mathematics was to be able to get so much from so little.[34]

II. THE 'MATHEMATICAL METHOD' DOUBTED

As in the twentieth century, the success of science and mathematics attracted from professional philosophers not praise, but complaints, to the effect that they, the philosophers, could not see how so much knowledge could possibly be achievable. While very few were prepared to go as far as Diderot, much argument was undertaken to show that the claims of mathematical proof were not all they seemed. The argument mostly centred on geometry. The problem at its simplest, as Gauss put it, is, 'if number is entirely a product of our own minds, space has a reality outside of our minds and we cannot prescribe its laws *a priori*'.[35] The century inherited what could be called the Euclid-Newton view of space and time. The essential features are these: Space and time are infinite in extent in all directions, homogeneous, flat, and infinitely divisible. Truths about space and time may be proved with absolute certainty, in the style of Euclid. After two thousand years of success, the facade seemed unbreakable. This prevented two developments which, at various times during the eighteenth century, seemed on the point of happening. The first is the discovery of non-Euclidean geometry. The second is the adoption of the philosophical opinion that knowledge of space, which is something real outside the mind, must be empirical and fallible. The problem with the Euclidean claims is that it is difficult to see how they could be known, if true. Without the scholastic magic of an intellect equipped with a natural aptitude for truth, and with epistemological worries becoming more central to philosophy, empiricism and rationalism were in equal but opposite quandaries. For the empiricist, the infinitely large and the infinitely small are not available for inspection, so where is knowledge of them to come from? Hume will pursue this thought to its limit. For the rationalist, the certainty of the deliverances of reason on space and time will suggest a dependence of those concepts on the mind. Kant will pursue this idea to, or beyond, its limits.

1. *Bayle and Saccheri: doubts on the foundations of geometry*

The problem as it appeared at the beginning of the century can be seen in two widely known semi-philosophical works: Bayle's *Dictionary* (1697) and Saccheri's *Euclid Cleansed from All Spot* (1733). Bayle remarks that the certainty of the mathematical method is not all it is claimed to be, since there are disputes even among mathematicians, for example, over infinitesimals.[36] He argues that space can consist neither of mathematical points nor of Epicurean extended atoms, nor can it be infinitely divisible. He takes this to exhaust all the possibilities, and concludes, in a remark that contains seeds of both Hume and Kant, that the attempted geometrical proofs that space is infinitely divisible 'serve no other use but to show that extension exists only in our understanding'.[37]

An essential claim of admirers of the 'mathematical method' was that Euclid's axioms were self-evident. But how true is this? Somewhere, Euclidean geometry must claim that space is infinite, which seems a claim beyond the capacity of experience to know. Euclid's Fifth Postulate, in particular, asserts something that seems to require an intuition about arbitrarily distant space:

> That if a straight line falling on two straight lines makes the interior angles on the same side less than two right angles, the two straight lines, if produced indefinitely, meet on that side on which are the angles less than the two right angles.

Saccheri undertook to derive the fifth postulate from the others by showing that the first four postulates, plus the negation of the fifth, led to a contradiction. This is in fact impossible to show. If true, it would have removed all doubts about the self-evidence of Euclid's axioms. He proceeds well for some time, demonstrating what would later be called theorems in hyperbolic geometry, the non-Euclidean geometry in which the sum of the angles in any triangle is less than 180 degrees. Then he derives a 'contradiction', but it is unconvincing, as it involves common perpendiculars to two straight lines 'at infinity'. He makes another attempt and again claims success, but there is a mistake. He hints that the result is not as clear as it might be, and publication of his book was withheld in his lifetime (possibly entitling him to a footnote in the history of ethics).[38]

The problem became well-known: d'Alembert called it the 'scandal of the elements of geometry'. G. S. Klügel's dissertation of 1763 reviewed twenty-eight attempts to prove the fifth postulate, concluding that they were all deficient. He gave his opinion that the postulate was not provable, its truth thus resting on the judgment of the senses.[39] Kant's only serious attempt to do work of his own in mathematics was an attempt to prove the fifth postulate.

Lambert came closest to thinking in terms of an actual alternative geometry, writing, 'I should almost conclude that the third hypothesis [of angle sum less than 180 degrees] holds on an imaginary sphere'.[40] Nevertheless, like Saccheri, he incorrectly claims to derive a contradiction, and the genuine possibility of a non-Euclidean geometry was not recognised until well after 1800. The philosophical commitment to the self-evidence of Euclid certainly stimulated important mathematical work but at the same time delayed the discovery of the correct answer, which was not that desired by philosophy.

2. *Berkeley's* Analyst: *calculus and infinitesimals*

Berkeley's general philosophy of mathematics shows intellectual independence, to say the least. Rejecting completely views that mathematics is about either quantity or abstractions, he is the first formalist philosopher of arithmetic, maintaining that there is only the manipulation of symbols according to rules.[41] Geometry, he believes, can only be about perceived extension. He is thus led to reject the infinite divisibility of space; like Hume after him (and this is where Hume's and Berkeley's philosophies come closest) he denies the meaningfulness of any talk about lengths less than the *minimum visibile or minimum tangibile*.[42]

Prepared by these non-standard speculations, Berkeley, in his *Analyst* of 1734, attacked the mathematicians' understanding of the foundations of the calculus as hopelessly confused and contradictory. The episode has a special place in the history of philosophy, as one of the very few cases where a technical field eventually admitted that philosophy strictly so-called had won a victory over the technical practitioners. Berkeley intended the argument to serve a purpose in the philosophy of religion, by showing that there were mysteries as incomprehensible as those of religion even in the paradigm of reason, mathematics.[43] The argument itself, however, is quite independent of its purpose.

At issue is the meaning of a derivative, or rate of change of a variable quantity – the 'fluxion' of a 'fluent', in Newton's terminology. If we wish to measure the speed of a moving object, that is, the rate of change of distance, we use a unit like miles per hour. To find the numerical value of an object's speed, therefore, we divide the distance it travels in any time interval by the length of the interval. If the speed is constant, no problems arise: the answer is the same whatever interval is taken: 12 miles divided by 3 hours gives the same answer as 8 miles divided by 2 hours, namely 4 miles per hour. But if the speed is itself variable, conceptual problems arise in trying to explain what the instantaneous speed is, at any given instant. For the speed calculated from dividing any finite distance traversed by the finite time taken to do so is not an instantaneous speed but the average speed over the interval. It is natural to approximate the speed at an instant more closely by taking smaller and smaller intervals including that instant, but the problem remains that an instantaneous speed and an average speed are different, both conceptually and numerically. Newton used such doubtfully intelligible language as

> Fluxions are very nearly as the augments of the fluents generated in equal, but very small, particles of time; and, to speak accurately, they are in the *first ratio* of the nascent augments . . .[44]

In calculating the speed if the distance travelled in time x is x^n, he first finds the distance travelled in the time between x and $x + o$, divides it by the 'augment' of time o, and finally claims that when the augment o vanishes, their 'ultimate ratio' is as nx^{n-1} to 1. Berkeley's criticism is perfectly correct:

> For when it is said, let the increments vanish, or let there be no increments, the former supposition that the increments were something, or that there were increments, is destroyed, and yet a consequence of that supposition, *i.e.*, an expression got by virtue thereof, is retained.[45]

Indeed, the division by o to find the average speed requires that o not be zero, while later o is taken to be zero. It is no use maintaining that o is small, since as Berkeley again says, 'the minutest errors are not to be neglected in mathematics'. Newton's attempts to speak of the augments as 'nascent' and 'evanescent', and the ratios as 'first' and 'ultimate' attracts Berkeley's most famous piece of ridicule: 'And what are these same evanescent increments? They are neither finite quantities, nor quantities infinitely small, nor yet nothing. May we not call them the ghosts of departed quantities?'(§35, 4: 89). Berkeley also attacks with justice other parts of Newton's calculus, notably the higher derivatives. A speed is itself a variable quantity, so it has a fluxion, or rate at which it is changing, the acceleration. If it is hard to explain a first derivative in terms of the ratios of 'evanescent' quantities, it is doubly so to explain in such terms what a second or third derivative is:

> The incipient celerity of an incipient celerity, the nascent augment of a nascent augment, *i.e.*, of a thing which hath no magnitude, – take it in what light you please, the clear conception of it will, if I mistake not, be found impossible. (§4, 4: 67)

Bad answers to Berkeley began with his own,[46] and a flood of them appeared from as far away as America.[47]

There are other possible ways of expressing what it is of which ratios are being taken. On the continent, it was common to speak in terms of 'infinitesimals'. These were conceived of as quantities smaller than any finite quantities, yet not zero. An instantaneous speed might then be regarded as exactly the ratio of infinitesimal augments, though only approximately the ratio of any finite augments.[48] 'The clear conception of them' proved no easier to achieve than that of fluxions.

One of the more serious attempts to resolve the problems was Maclaurin's *Treatise of Fluxions* of 1742. It attempts to show that fluxions are a generalisation of the 'geometry of the antients', by using Archimedes' method of exhaustion to replace infinitesimals, of which he complains, 'From geometry the infinities and infinitesimals passed into philosophy, carrying with them the obscurity and perplexity which cannot fail to accompany them'.[49] His idea is in principle the same as the modern treatment using limits, but Maclaurin retains kinematic notions which would later be regarded as inadequate. In particular, he defines a fluxion obscurely in terms of a counterfactual: 'the increment or decrement that would be generated in a given time by this notion, if it was continued uniformly.'[50] D'Alembert and L'Huilier tried to base calculus on limits, in a way that was essentially correct, but still lacked the precision achieved in the next century by the use of multiple quantifiers.[51] Lazare Carnot's *Réflexions sur la métaphysique du calcul infinitésimal*, of 1797, achieved much greater popular success, by repeating all the worst excesses of infinitesimals.[52] The debates over whether infinitesimals are zero or not, whether they can be conceived, and whether a limit is or is not actually attained often read more like a Kantian antinomy than the real thing.

3. Hume on mathematics

Hume's philosophy of mathematics is a natural outgrowth of his combining the usual 'science of quantity and extension' view with his requirement that all concepts be explained in terms of impressions and ideas. In the division of truths between relations of ideas and matters of fact, mathematics falls entirely on the side of ideas. But whereas relations of ideas like resemblance and contrariety are 'discoverable at first sight', this is not so with '*proportions of quantity or number*'. Though not different in kind from resemblance, because of their complexity 'their relations become intricate and involved', so that coming to know them may need some 'abstract reasoning and reflexion', or demonstration (unless 'the difference is very great and remarkable'). The relations treated in arithmetic and algebra are the best known, because of their 'perfect precision and exactness'. For example, two numbers may be infallibly pronounced equal when 'the one always has an unite answering to every unite of the other', since this is something directly checkable.[53] Such complicated mathematical facts as that a number is divisible by nine if the sum of its digits is also divisible by nine may at first appear due to chance or design, but reasoning shows they result from 'the nature of these numbers'.[54] Hume thus does not agree that mathematics is syllogistic, or in any other way 'analytic' in any trivial or vacuous sense. But he does hold that mathematical truths are known by subjecting ideas (of quantity) to some kind of purely conceptual 'analysis' (not Hume's word).[55]

Even demonstrated mathematical knowledge is in practice fallible, however. For the certainty that results from discovering the relations is only an 'in principle' one, since an actual reasoner can make mistakes. 'The rules are certain and infallible; but when we apply them, our fallible and uncertain faculties are very apt to depart from them.'[56]

Geometry has less certainty than algebra and arithmetic, because it deals with continuous quantities, which cannot be measured exactly. The result is that Hume becomes, with Berkeley, one of the few philosophers in history to reject the infinite divisibility of space. The topic belongs more properly to his philosophy of space than to his philosophy of mathematics – even granted that the distinction is anachronistic. But his replies to the alleged *mathematical* demonstrations of the infinite divisibility of space, approved by such good authorities as the Port-Royal *Logic* and Isaac Barrow,[57] are of some worth. The mathematical arguments simply consist in extracting the assumption of infinite divisibility that is contained implicitly in Euclid, and cannot determine whether actual space is infinitely divisible. Hume goes some way toward exposing this flaw when he doubts the exact correspondence between the axioms of geometry and our ideas of space: 'none of these demonstrations can have sufficient weight to establish such a principle, as this of infinite divisibility; and that because with regard to such minute objects, they are not properly demonstrations, being built on ideas, which are not exact.'[58] There is no way to be sure, for example, that two straight lines with a small angle between them meet in only one point (1.3.1.4, SBN 71).

But the errors of geometry 'are never considerable'. It would seem that Hume has been substantially vindicated by subsequent developments, which have revealed that deciding whether space is exactly Euclidean is an empirical question, although it is obviously approximately Euclidean in our region.

An aspect of Hume and Berkeley's writing on geometry that is central but that some commentators have found odd is their talk of 'parts of ideas'. They discuss, for example, into how many indivisible parts an idea of extension 'as conceived by the imagination' can be divided.[59] If one takes this seriously, it would appear that ideas or imagination themselves have a quasi-spatial quality. Hume does not develop this notion further, but Reid does, and goes so far as to say what exactly is the spatial structure of the 'geometry of visibles'. It is the geometry of the surface of a sphere.[60]

4. *Kant*

The key to Kant's views on mathematics, and much else, is the notion of *construction* in geometry. In Euclid, there are postulates, such as 'To draw a straight line from any point to any point', which assert that certain things exist, or may be constructed. The first thing Euclid proves is that an equilateral triangle may be *constructed* on any line. In learning how to prove in geometry, as of course all educated eighteenth-century persons did, one must spend a good deal of time deciding which lines to prolong, when to draw a new circle, and so on. From the point of view of modern formal logic, this can be regarded as a defect in Euclid's treatment of geometry, but from an earlier point of view it reinforces two convictions: that Euclidean geometry is not purely syllogistic, and that it is about real space.

A fascination with construction had already been evident in Vico. The first statement of his *verum-factum* theory is in the context of geometry: 'We demonstrate geometrical things because we make them.'[61] Even when his 'New Science' of human things is fully developed and its contrast with the natural sciences emphasised, its links with geometry are retained. Both construct the world they study.[62] It was realised that constructions did not fit well into the Wolffian view of sciences as demonstrating truths about universals from their definitions. Wolff was prepared to assert that the drawing of a straight line between two points flowed from the definition of a line, but this is not plausible. Andreas Rüdiger alleges that the Wolffian 'mathematical method' is a travesty of real mathematics, by recalling the inspection of particulars in geometrical constructions and in counting.[63] Johann Heinrich Lambert describes the experience of reading Euclid after Wolff and recognising that Euclid is nothing like Wolff says he should be. He notes that Euclid does not derive things from the definition of space, but starts with lines as simples, and exhibits first the possibility of an equilateral triangle.[64]

So, when the Berlin Academy posed the question, whether metaphysical truth could be equated with mathematical truth, Kant in his 'Prize Essay' replied: mathematics has construction, or synthesis, while metaphysics does not.[65] In Kant, construction in geometry is used to fill out the vaguer notions of the previous one hundred and fifty years along the lines that the possible is what can be clearly and distinctly conceived (in the 'imagination', conceived as a mental visualisation facility). Kantian 'intuition' is, like the scholastics' 'intelligible matter', a medium in which can be drawn not just a few simple ideas to be compared with one another, in the style of Locke, but whole geometrical diagrams. What can be so drawn is more restricted than what merely does not contain a logical contradiction. For example, there is no contradiction in the concept of two straight lines meeting in two points and enclosing a figure; nevertheless, no such figure is possible, since it cannot be constructed: 'That between two points there is only one straight line . . . can[not] be derived from some universal concept of space; [it] can only be *apprehended* concretely, so to speak, in space itself.'[66] Similarly, that there is a plane passing through any three given points is evident because the intuition constructs the figure 'immediately'.[67] These necessities and possibilities are 'synthetic', in the sense that they do not follow simply from formal logical principles, and also in the sense that they involve 'synthesis', or construction. These truths are also a priori, since Kant is not prepared to compromise the absolute certainty of mathematics. So Leibniz, he thinks, cannot be right about space arising out of relations between real objects because that would make geometry empirical, and there might be a non-Euclidean space, which Kant takes to be impossible.[68] It is his own theory, that space is imposed by the mind, that is needed to ensure the certainty of geometry: 'Assuredly, had not the concept of space been given originally by the nature of the mind . . . then the use of geometry in natural philosophy would be far from safe' (§15E, Ak 2: 404–5).

It is clear then how Kant's synthetic a priori, on which so much in his philosophy depends, is the result of combining three pre-existing ideas: Euclidean construction, the reduction of concepts to ideas in 'imagination' or 'intuition', and the certainty of geometry.

Kant finds construction also in arithmetic, in the thinking of how many times a unit is contained in a quantity: 'this how-many-times is grounded on successive repetition, thus on time and the synthesis (of the homogeneous) in it' (*Kritik* B 300). The concept of number is one which 'in itself, indeed, belongs to the understanding but of which the actualisation in the concrete requires the auxiliary notions of time and space (by successively adding a number of things and setting them simultaneously side by side)' (*De mundi*, §12, Ak 2: 397). In the famous passage of the *Kritik der reinen Vernunft* explaining why the proposition '7 + 5 = 12' is synthetic, Kant writes:

> The concept of twelve is by no means already thought merely by my thinking of that unification of seven and five, and no matter how long I analyze my concept of such a possible sum I will still not find twelve in it. . . . For I take first the number 7, and, as I take the fingers of my hand as an intuition for assistance with the concept of 5, to that image of mine I now add the units that I have previously taken together in order to constitute the number 5 one after another to the number 7, and thus see the number 12 arise. (B 15–16, see also B 205 and B 299)

The construction here is with real fingers, not 'in the imagination', but Kant means exactly to assimilate the mind's structuring of experience while perceiving fingers to construction in the imagination: 'this very same formative synthesis, by means of which we construct a figure in imagination is entirely identical with that which we exercise in the apprehension of an appearance, in order to make a concept of experience of it' (B 271). Kant emphasises that he does not just mean reading off results from a picture; there is an intellectual operation involved, which is responsible for the necessity of the truth. Large numbers, for example, obviously cannot be counted by an immediate glance; what is important is the 'schema' of successive addition of units that allows the aggregate to be synthesised, that is, counted (B 16, B 179–81). The essentials of this discovery, that the necessity in mathematical knowledge comes from assimilating an image or experience to construction or synthesis according to some rule, Kant attributes to the earliest Greek geometers (B xii).

Kant brings the same ideas to the problems of the infinite. How those problems appeared to mathematicians in Kant's time is apparent from the terms of the prize set by the Berlin Academy of Sciences (Mathematical Section) for 1786:

> *There is needed a clear and precise theory of what is called Infinite in Mathematics* . . . certain eminent modern analysts admit that the phrase *infinite magnitude* is a contradiction in terms. The Academy, therefore, desires an explanation of how it is that so many correct theorems have been deduced from a contradictory supposition, together with enunciation of a sure, a clear, in short a truly mathematical principle that may be substituted for that of the *infinite*.[69]

Kant sees this problem too in terms of construction or synthesis: 'Since *unrepresentable* and *impossible* are commonly treated as having the same meaning, the concepts both of the *continuous* and of the *infinite* are frequently rejected' (*De mundi* §1, Ak 2: 388). So the notion of a completed infinity contains no contradiction, but since it 'can never be completed through a successive synthesis' (*Kritik*, B 454), it is not the object of any possible experience, intuition, or construction. But, on the other hand, there seems no limit to space or time either; for example, 'the beginning always presupposes a preceding time' (B 515). So to the question, 'But what is the magnitude of the world we live in, finite or infinite?', Kant replies: neither; to demand an answer is to assume 'that the world (the whole series of appearances) is a thing in itself. For the world remains, even though I may rule out the infinite or the finite regress in the series of its appearances'.[70]

Many of the same considerations apply to the infinitely small. To see the problems about the continuity of space in terms of 'infinite divisibility' already plays into Kant's hands. Division is a human act, suggesting to Kant that the act of constructing a line by a continuous flowing motion comes first, followed by the construction of its parts by a further act of division (rather than the parts coming first and together forming space).[71]

The demand for constructibility is, it appears, at the bottom of such central Kantian themes as the ideality of the world. Also of the noumenon, unreachable by experience, of which the infinite is, so to speak, the first example. Lest it seem that the problem of construction is an artifact of the eighteenth century's primitive view of geometry, it may be noted that the problem recurs in the modern foundations of mathematics. There, one normally proves the consistency of a concept by constructing it out of sets, but to do so requires an 'axiom of infinity', which ensures that sufficiently many sets 'exist', in particular, that a completed infinity of them exists.

III. NEW OBJECTS OF MATHEMATICS

1. *Algebra*

Algebra tended to take over more and more of mathematics in the eighteenth century. Where Newton had recast his reasoning in geometrical form for public consumption, Joseph-Louis de Lagrange's *Mécanique analytique* of 1788 says:

> No drawings are to be found in this work. The methods which I present require neither constructions nor geometrical or mechanical arguments, but only algebraic operations, subject to a regular and uniform progression.[72]

Condorcet says that Euler

> sensed that algebraic analysis was the most extensive and certain instrument one can employ in all sciences, and he sought to render its usage universal. This revolution... earned him the honour, unique so far, of having as many disciples as Europe has mathematicians.[73]

And in a rare moment of agreement with Euler, d'Alembert says algebra

> is the foundation of all possible discoveries concerning quantity. . . . This science is the farthest outpost to which the contemplation of the properties of matter can lead us, and we would not be able to go further without leaving the material universe altogether. (*Oeuvres* 1: 26, see also 30–31; transl. 20 and 26)

But, having established that algebra is a good thing, what exactly is it? Originally, it was a method of solving problems by making letters stand for unknown quantities, and manipulating the letters as if they were numbers. Even on this narrow view, algebra had philosophical significance, as it was a method for discovering answers, and thus seemed on the side of 'analysis', as opposed to the 'synthetic' deriving of known truths from axioms in the style of Euclid.[74] But by 1700 it seemed more than that. Noting that the letters could stand for geometrical quantities as easily as for numerical ones, various thinkers proclaimed algebra to be the science of quantity in general, that is, virtually the whole of mathematics.[75] Even if that were agreed, many things remained unclear. For example, what could the letters represent – complex numbers? Infinities? Infinitesimals? And if algebra was a general mathematics, where were its axioms?[76] Another view of algebra was that of Wolff, who saw it as part of Leibniz's universal characteristic, that is, as a general method of reasoning symbolically.[77] In the same vein, Condillac's idea of the mathematical method that ought to be imposed on philosophy was not so much Euclid as the solving of equations, manipulating known and unknown quantities until the knowns appeared by themselves.

> *Equations*, *propositions* and *judgements* are basically the same thing, and . . . consequently one reasons in the same manner in all the sciences . . . we have seen that, just as the equations $x - 1 = y + 1$, and $x + 1 = 2y - 2$, pass through different transformations to become $y = 5$ and $x = 7$, sensation passes equally through different transformations to become the understanding.[78]

Regarding French as a language lacking taste and precision, Condillac proposed to reform it on the basis of the grammar of algebra.[79] Kant says that algebra proceeds by manipulating uninterpreted symbols 'until eventually, when the conclusion is drawn, the meaning of the symbolic conclusion is deciphered'. The simple pushing around of symbols is what gives 'the degree of assurance characteristic of seeing something with one's own eyes' (whereas with philosophy one must keep the meanings in mind all the time).[80] These are the same claims made around 1900 for formal logic. The possibility of manipulating symbols without attending to their meaning is not without problems. One may end up with conclusions that do not mean anything either. Euler is famous for his lack of rigour in calculating with infinite series without worrying about their convergence; it is typical not only of him but of the century to conduct long 'philosophical' debates about the true sum of the series:

$$1 - 1 + 1 - 1 + 1 - \ldots$$ [81]

The case is even worse when manipulating symbols that are explicitly stated to have no meaning, such as those denoting the square roots of negative numbers. Though necessary for calculations, they do not satisfy the definition of quantities as being 'capable of increase and decrease', as they cannot be less than or greater than one another. Euler describes them as 'impossible', but proceeds to calculate extensively with them.[82]

Euler played a crucial role in emphasising the centrality of the notion of *function* in mathematics (its significance is indicated by the fact that about half of modern pure mathematics is 'functional analysis'). His aim was to replace vague geometrical notions and dynamical metaphors of 'fluents' with something more precise and amenable to calculation. He initially defined a function in algebraic terms as an *expression* involving variables: 'A function of a variable quantity is an analytic expression composed in any way whatsoever of the variable quantity and numbers or constant quantities.' For example, $az + \sqrt{a^2 - z^2}$ is a function of z (where a is a constant).[83] But later, his debate with d'Alembert over the vibrating string convinced him this notion was too narrow, because of the need to consider more irregular functions, which might not be expressible by an algebraic formula. He had little success in explaining what this notion should be.[84] Lagrange also attempted a purely algebraic notion of function and tried to use it as a foundation for the calculus 'independent of all metaphysics'. He claimed to prove that every differentiable function could be expressed as a power series, that is, represented algebraically (except perhaps at isolated points).[85] This is false, as Cauchy soon showed. When the best mathematicians in the world begin claiming to have proved what is false – a rare event, much to the credit of mathematics – it is time to conclude that rigour is not a luxury. The nineteenth century drew the correct conclusion, leading to the correct foundations of calculus, and to set theory.

Just visible in the work of Lagrange are the beginnings of modern abstract algebra. This is the subject that perhaps most obviously deals not with quantity but with certain kinds of abstract structure. Lagrange, inquiring why it had not been possible to find formulas for solving equations of degree 5 or higher, considers functions of the roots of the equation which do not change if the roots are permuted, or interchanged. He understands that some permutations may be 'independent' of others, thus thinking of the permutations as themselves entities with interrelationships. These permutations form the first of a new kind of subject matter of mathematics, later the object of modern group theory.[86] Paolo Ruffini's work of 1799 goes further, considering the totality of permutations (a group, in modern terms) and their composition.[87]

Any or all of these developments in mathematics might have provided the philosophers of the eighteenth century with perfect examples of the advancement of knowledge through the analysis of ideas, had they informed themselves about them.

2. *Experimental evidence in mathematics*

While the eighteenth century admired the rigour of Euclid, its own mathematics is famous for a lack of rigour. It may be that the philosophical emphasis on ideas as against formal logic contributed to a disregard of formal rigour.[88] In any case, if mathematical conclusions are to be supported by anything less than complete formal demonstration, there is a need to consider how there can be a less than deductive logical support. Euler was the first, among either philosophers or mathematicians, to argue explicitly for the use of experimental, or probable, reasoning in mathematics.

> It will seem not a little paradoxical to ascribe a great importance to observations in that part of the mathematical sciences which is usually called Pure Mathematics, since the current opinion is that observations are restricted to physical objects that make impression on the senses. As we must refer the numbers to the pure intellect alone, we can hardly understand how observations and quasi-experiments can be of use in investigating the nature of the numbers. Yet, in fact, as I shall show here with very good reasons, the properties of the numbers known today have been mostly discovered by observation, and discovered long before their truth has been confirmed by rigid demonstrations. There are even many properties of the numbers with which we are well acquainted, but which we are not yet able to prove; only observations have led us to their knowledge.[89]

Euler's works contain a number of examples of how to reason probabilistically in mathematics. He used, for example, some daring and obviously far from rigorous methods to conclude that the infinite sum $1 + \frac{1}{4} + \frac{1}{9} + \frac{1}{16} + \frac{1}{25} + \ldots$ (where the numbers on the bottom of the fractions are the successive squares of whole numbers) is equal to the prima facie unlikely value $\pi^2/6$. Finding that the two expressions agreed to seven decimal places, and that a similar argument led to the already proved result $1 - \frac{1}{3} + \frac{1}{5} - \frac{1}{7} + \frac{1}{9} - \frac{1}{11} + \ldots = \frac{\pi}{4}$, Euler concluded, 'For our method, which may appear to some as not reliable enough, a great confirmation comes here to light. Therefore we shall not doubt at all of the other things which are revealed by the same method.'[90]

Laplace and Gauss, who were in a position to know, agreed casually that such reasoning was central to mathematics.[91] Even Wolff writes that 'examples of hypotheses are also found in arithmetic, which first influenced me to look upon philosophical hypotheses more favourably'. What he has in mind is the calculation of answers by successive approximation, the initial guess being the hypothesis.[92] Yet philosophers pronouncing on mathematics since have rarely given it a place.

A different connection between probability and pure mathematics was discovered by Lambert. He understands that a series of digits produced by a random process, like throwing a die, will be disordered or patternless, but that the same can be said of the digits of π or of $\sqrt{2}$, which are completely determined. He is prepared to say that the probability of the hundredth digit of $\sqrt{2}$ being five is $1/10$.[93] Whether a notion of probability can be applied in such a deterministic case is still a crucial issue in the philosophy of probability.

3. Topology

Topology provided the clearest example of an object of mathematics that would not fit under the old rubric, 'the science of quantity'. The citizens of Königsberg noticed that it seemed to be impossible to walk over all seven of the bridges connecting the two banks of the River Pregel and its islands, without walking over at least one of them twice. Euler proved they were right. This is a problem in the area now called the topology of networks. There is no quantity involved in the problem, only the *arrangement* of the system of bridges and land areas. Euler writes:

> The branch of geometry that deals with magnitudes has been zealously studied throughout the past, but there is another branch that has been almost unknown up to now; Leibniz spoke of it first, calling it the 'geometry of position'. This branch of geometry deals with relations dependent on position alone, and investigates the properties of position; it does not take magnitudes into consideration, nor does it involve calculation with quantities. But as yet no satisfactory definition has been given of the problems that belong to this geometry of position.[94]

What Leibniz said about the 'geometry of position' was both short and extremely vague,[95] but Euler was not the only one to find it suggestive. Buffon relates it briefly to the folding of seeds and to symmetry in plaiting, and remarks that 'the art of knowing the relations that result from the position of things would be as useful as and perhaps more necessary than that which has the magnitude of things only for its object'.[96] Kant sees a connection between it and his ideas on incongruent counterparts.[97] The subject was given some more definite content by Vandermonde, who first drew a graph, in the modern sense of a system of nodes connected by lines. He used it to solve the problem of the knight's tour in chess, 'using numbers which do not represent quantities at all, but regions in space'.[98]

4. Social mathematics and moral algebra

If ideas have parts, perhaps one should count them, or maybe weigh them, if they differ in their force. There would result a 'moral arithmetic', or 'moral physics'. Naturally, there are measurement problems: how are psychological units to be measured and compared, or even identified? Hume suggests that the size of the smallest impression can be found from measuring the least visible dot (*Treatise*, 1.2.1.4, SBN 27–8); such measurements of the threshold of visibility were carried out in Hume's lifetime.[99] Buffon suggests regarding the probability of sudden death in the next twenty-four hours, for one in the prime of life, as a standard unit of 'moral impossibility', to which the reasonable man gives no serious thought.[100] Maupertuis reduces morality to prudence, and prudence to a hedonistic calculus: 'The estimation of happy and unhappy moments is the product of the intensity of the pleasure or pain by the duration.' Measurement of intensities may be difficult, but Maupertuis invites introspection on the inevitability of comparing, for example, the pain of an operation for the stone with the longer but lesser pain of forgoing the operation.[101] The problem is urgent for economics, which can hardly avoid being quantitative, when explaining prices, but seems to rely on a subjective 'utility' whose measurement is as dubious as that of pleasure and pain. Adam Smith achieves the trick, so useful in these matters, of claiming the right to speak quantitatively, while avoiding the responsibility of commitment to any actual quantities or formulas. He writes that the value of any wealth to its owners 'is precisely equal to the quantity of labour which it can enable them to purchase or command. . . . Equal quantities of labour, at all times and places, may be said to be of equal value to the labourer', but he undercuts the apparent accuracy of his measure by adding:

> It is often difficult to ascertain the proportion between two different quantities of labour. The time spent in two different sorts of work will not always alone determine this proportion. The different degrees of hardship endured, and of ingenuity exercised, must likewise be taken into account. There may be more labour in an hour's hard work than in two hours easy business.[102]

He appeals to the market to coordinate different people's measures, but 'not by any accurate measure'.

Benjamin Franklin advises, in cases of perplexity about a decision, the listing of the reasons for and against in two columns:

> When I have thus got them all together in one View, I endeavour to estimate their respective Weights; and where I find two, one on each side, that seem equal, I strike

them both out: If I find a Reason *pro* equal to some two Reasons *con*, I strike out the three . . . and thus proceeding I find at length where the Ballance lies. . . . And tho' the Weight of Reasons cannot be taken with the Precision of Algebraic Quantities . . . in fact I have found great Advantage from this kind of Equation, in what may be called *Moral or Prudential Algebra*.[103]

The special difficulties of measurement in the social and mental realm suggested to Condorcet that social mathematics should rely chiefly on the theory of probability.[104] There, the equality of the beliefs one should have that a die will fall on any side is inferred from symmetry, or 'insufficient reason': there is no reason to prefer any side to any other. He believed he had proved, using probability, that decisions taken by majority vote were perfect for achieving the truth.[105] Before being hounded to death by a regime that exalted Equality over Liberty and Fraternity, Condorcet had the opportunity to reconsider the assumptions of his proof, and wonder if perhaps he did not mean that those voting had to reach some standard of Reason.[106]

As long as there has been 'social mathematics', there have been explanations of why it fails to work, or at least lacks anything like the success of mathematics as applied to physics. The suggestion that lack of exact measurement is the problem was anticipated, and argued against, as the quotations above indicate. Another idea was that of Reid, who thought the problem lay in the definition of quantity as 'whatever has increase or diminution'. This is too wide, he says, as it allows in pleasure and pain, which admit of degrees but cannot be measured in units.[107]

Mathematical modelling of social, as opposed to introspective, phenomena was attempted qualitatively in Hume's and Adam Smith's conception of the economy as a self-regulating system,[108] but the most successful quantitative project was that of Malthus, whose conclusions about the poor laws are intended to follow from a purely mathematical fact:

Population, when unchecked, increases in a geometrical ratio. Subsistence increases only in arithmetical ratio. A slight acquaintance with numbers will shew the immensity of the first power in comparison with the second.[109]

He takes these ratios to be evident and feels no need to support them with empirical evidence. This kind of a priori fitting of formulas has particularly afflicted economics, so it is interesting to see Condorcet criticising Verri's mathematical economics on just this ground. It is true, Condorcet says, that more buyers mean a higher price, but what justification is there for Verri's assumption of a *direct* proportion between the two, if no empirical data are considered?[110] A remedy is to fit formulas to actual social statistical data. This is not a strong point of eighteenth-century mathematics, but Lambert had some understanding of how to do it.[111]

IV. LOGIC

1. *Textbook logic*

Eighteenth-century writing on 'logic' is extensive,[112] but neither the school of traditional Aristotelian logic nor their opponents, the 'men of ideas', produced much that has commanded respect since.

As systems of thought go, Aristotelian logic was one of the great survivors. For several centuries, it was attacked vigorously, in almost identical terms, by almost all the thinkers remembered by history. It was defended by nonentities. In each generation, when the dust settled, it was found to be still in control of the field (that is, of the undergraduate syllabus). This was true in 1700, just after Locke had renewed the attacks of Bacon and Descartes. It was equally true in 1800, when Aristotelian logic was about to undergo a revival in Britain. Its contents are the traditional logic of terms, judgments, and inference by syllogism, largely unchanged since the logic textbooks of the thirteenth century.

The English representative of the old school was Henry Aldrich's *Artis Logicae Compendium*, the standard Oxford textbook for the whole century. First published in 1691, it appeared in many editions, epitomes, and expansions until the mid-nineteenth century, including an English translation by John Wesley.[113] On the continent, Wolff found traditional logic satisfactory – so much so that he in effect tried, as we saw, to incorporate the rest of philosophy into it. It is a little more surprising to find Kant largely on the side of the syllogism. He has some minor criticisms of traditional arrangements of the four figures, which he thinks over-elaborate,[114] but he accepts that the syllogism is not intended to be a method of discovery, and on the whole his logic teaching agrees with tradition. He is clear about, and opposed to, psychologism in logic.[115]

2. *'Facultative' logic and Hume's 'psychologism'*

The opposing school produced voluminous works of 'logic', but they are full of what would now be called cognitive psychology, epistemology, semiotics, philosophy of logic, and introspection. They are full also of invective, against 'scholastic headpieces', full indeed of everything except logic, in the modern sense of formal logic. It is not that logic was confused with (not yet existent) disciplines like psychology. On the contrary, the scholastics had been clear about formal logic, and it was in deliberate opposition to them that the followers of the 'way of ideas' identified logic with 'psychologistic' notions instead.

Bacon, Descartes, and Locke, between them, had convinced most that the syllogism, and formal logic generally, was of no use or interest.[116] The essence of Locke's attack was that the syllogism was not useful for the *discovery* of truths, and that it concealed the fact that inference consisted in the 'agreement or disagreement' or 'connexion' of ideas.[117] Traditional logic had certainly opened the way to such criticisms by holding that logic is about 'thought' or 'judgment', and by concentrating on a single argument form, the syllogism, which has an air of being analytic and trivial. Whatever the justice of the Lockean criticisms, they failed to issue in anything better, either in new logical ideas or in textbooks. If adherence to the syllogism restricts logic, the 'agreement and disagreement of ideas' is if anything an even worse straitjacket. It does nothing to encourage the discovery of logical structure, and instead diverts logic into vapidity. It is all very well to offer advice like, 'Enlarge your general Acquaintance with Things daily, in order to attain a rich Furniture of Topics or middle Terms'[118], but how do you examine that? The logics of Crousaz, Duncan, and Watts followed the Port-Royal *Logic* in including enough of the traditional classifications, distinctions, and so on to provide some content, and in simply adding critical observations in the style of Bacon and Descartes.[119] At the end of the century, however, Reid and Campbell revert to a purely negative approach, speaking as if they have just discovered that the syllogism is not a logic of discovery.[120] But neither they nor any of their school have a replacement to offer. Campbell ventures the opinion that mathematical demonstrations are not syllogisms but does not suggest what their form is, if not syllogistic. Reid is closer to the truth in holding that mathematical reasoning cannot usually be syllogistic, as it deals with *relations* of quantities, and the syllogism is not applicable to relations.

Hume takes to its extreme the 'psychologising' of logic, and so exhibits most dramatically the problems in doing so. Plainly, there are tensions in 'naturalising' logic by reducing it to manipulations the mind happens to perform on ideas, while relying on logic as normative for argument. Hume applies general principles, such as, '*like objects, plac'd in like circumstances, will always produce the same effects*', to particular cases, without apparently noticing that he is using a formal logical principle of instantiation. Much the same could be said of his use of 'not'.[121] Hume exacerbates these difficulties by adding a sceptical project to his naturalising one. What he is sceptical about is the *logical* force of common inferences: causal inferences, inferences from 'is' to 'ought', and so on.[122] It is odd, certainly, to say that causal inference is not logically cogent but only an unavoidable habit, at the same time maintaining that all logical inference is only an unavoidable habit.

Hume's views on *inference* are seen to better advantage if they are thought of not in terms of formal logic, or even introspection, but as a research proposal to be implemented in, say, silicon chips. Modern Artificial Intelligence, like most eighteenth-century writing, is concerned with the *implementation* of a system of inference, not just the formal structure of the system itself. From that point of view, it is necessary to answer questions that do not arise in formal logic, such as how the symbols become attached to the things they mean. One must consider, in short, the 'natural history of the understanding'. It is then a matter for debate whether the syllogism needs to be explicitly represented internally, and whether one can replace an explicit generality with exemplars linked by 'custom', so that when one individual is activated, the linked ones 'immediately crowd in upon us' (*Treatise*, 1.1.7.7–8, SBN 20–1). The links between the exemplars are to be induced by the resemblance, constant conjunction, and like relations that hold between them. Hume's claim for his rules about causes that 'Here is all the LOGIC I think proper to employ in my reasoning' (1.3.15.11, SBN 175) is then a claim that can be investigated empirically: will a mechanism equipped with only the principles of association Hume names be able to reason adequately?

Logic's place at the centre of the curriculum makes certain wider effects of eighteenth-century logic more interesting than the subject itself. One student of logic who took the natural undergraduate reaction against the subject to an extreme was Swift, whose inversion of the stock logical examples, 'Man is a rational animal; a horse is a whinnying animal' led to the satire of the Yahoos and Houyhnhnms.[123] Another who used its rhetoric to good effect was Thomas Jefferson.[124] The claim of the Declaration of Independence, 'We hold these truths to be self-evident, that all men are created equal', combines the logical theme of self-evidence with the mathematical one of deriving such self-evidence from a symmetry principle. A true logician will ask why, if a principle is indeed self-evident, it is necessary to 'hold' it to be so. The French were clearer that Equality is not a given but a goal.

The discrediting of logic in England had consequences in education that are still felt. While tradition-bound, High Church Oxford took no notice of the problem and continued to teach logic, in Latin from Aldrich's text, and examined by disputation,[125] Whig Cambridge did the opposite. It replaced logic by the only credible alternative, mathematics, and produced the ancestor of the modern written examination system, the Mathematical Tripos. By a happy feedback effect, mathematics permitted an ever finer objective grading of candidates, leading to ever more concentration on mathematics. Since mathematics was a substitute logic, however, the matter examined was confined largely to geometry, continental innovations like algebra being considered unpatriotic.[126] Geometry is also more amenable to being considered in terms of 'ideas' than the formal manipulations of algebra.[127]

3. Symbolic logic and logic diagrams

Leibniz's vision of a universal characteristic, allowing logical inference by calculation, inspired some, but resulted in little of significance. The logical symbolism of Segner, Ploucquet, Holland, Maimon, and Castillon does not need much reinterpretation to yield various theorems in propositional and predicate calculus, but only the simplest ones.[128]

Euler developed the traditional theory of the syllogism in a popular work, illustrating it with diagrams similar to the later Venn diagrams. Particular (existential) propositions have always posed problems for such diagrams, as there needs to be some way of indicating which of the regions are non-empty. Euler distinguishes between 'Some A is B' and 'Some A is not B' as follows:

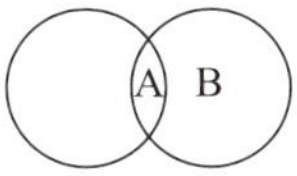

Some A is B

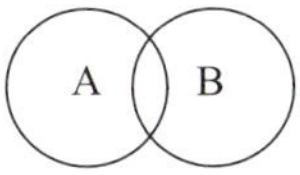

Some A is not B[129]

If one believes that it is a good thing for logic to become extensionalist, then logic diagrams will appear one of the century's few advances in logic. Euler himself does not mean to be taken this way. He uses only intentional vocabulary, such as 'If the notion C is entirely contained in the notion A . . . ' He takes no notice whatsoever of two centuries of criticism of the syllogism, and goes so far as to maintain that all truth arises from it.

A similar idea, but using lines instead of circles, appears in Lambert.[130] But this is only a small part of a larger project for the mathematising of logic. He proposes to give some precision to the analysis of concepts into simple ideas, thus doing for quality what geometers had done for quantity, and deducing everything from a firm basis.[131] An aspect of the project was a symbolic logic of concepts; one analyses a concept $a\gamma$ into its genus a and differentia $a\delta$; the equation

$$a\gamma = a - a\delta$$

then means that the genus of a is the result of abstracting the differentia from a. Lambert is sometimes misled by false analogies to ordinary algebra, to the extent of considering the square root of a relation.[132] In another attempt to bring logic and mathematics together, he considers the valid argument:[133]

$$\frac{3}{4} \text{ of } A \text{ are } B, \ \frac{2}{3} \text{ of } A \text{ are } C, \text{ so some } B \text{ are } C.$$

Few logicians since have cared to follow him into such numerical territory.

V. TECHNOLOGY

The subtitle of the *Encyclopédie* is *Dictionnaire raisonné des sciences, des arts, et des métiers*. The prominence given to the 'arts and trades' is due to Diderot, who writes:

> Let some man go out from the academies and down into the workshops, and gather material on the arts to explain them in a work which will persuade artisans to read, philosophers to think usefully, and the great to make at last some worthwhile use of their authority and wealth.[134]

'Useful science', as an idea, is Baconian, but science as an accepted route to profit, military superiority, and progress is really an eighteenth-century development. While the French government and the Royal Navy were among the largest investors in research, the practical orientation of research was especially evident in peripheral regions, where abstract thought, including philosophy, survived at all only on the promise of its practicality. Boundless confidence in the usefulness of science was as characteristic of the America of Franklin and Jefferson[135] as it was of Russia, where Euler and Lomonosov worked assiduously on 'improvements'. In England, the Industrial Revolution was associated less with London than with the provincial cities that were the homes of 'Philosophical Societies' devoted to practical science.[136]

Diderot found a significant fact about practical knowledge: it could not be written down adequately in text. Asking the practitioners to clarify it produced simply a garbled mass of unintelligibilities and inconsistencies. It proved essential to ask the tradesmen to *show* what they were doing and present the result in pictures. Hence the *Encyclopédie* has eleven volumes of plates (compared to seventeen of text).[137] Though there were no large-scale encyclopedic projects in England, their place was to some extent taken by public lectures on science, especially useful science. The famous London lectures of John Desaguliers taught by showing working machines. Science thus became accessible to those lacking mathematics; the Newtonian philosophy, Desaguliers says, 'tho' its truth is supported by Mathematicks, yet its Physical Discourses may be communicated without. The great Mr Locke was the first who became a Newtonian Philosopher without the help of Geometry'.[138] Inventions like the steam engine, the lightning rod and balloons were certainly spectacular and capable of conveying a message without the need for supporting captions.

But what message? The relation of machines to abstract thought was a vexed one. The formula for gravity is not much use, while the textile and steam engines were mostly invented by practical engineers, not scientists. Still, inventions are 'efforts of the mind and understanding which are calculated to produce new effects from the varied applications of the same cause, and the endless changes producible by different combinations and proportions',[139] that is, intellectual products. Adam Smith, who recognises the importance of machine inventions in improving productivity (though he tends to subordinate it to his *idée fixe* of division of labour), speaks of 'philosophers or men of speculation, whose trade it is, not to do anything, but to observe every thing; and who, upon that account, are often capable of combining together the powers of the most distant and dissimilar objects'.[140] The description is exactly true of James Watt, mathematical instrument maker to the University of Glasgow, who analysed the heat losses in Newcomen's steam engine and realised that the condensation was a separable process that could be better situated somewhere else.[141] The skills involved are cognitive, but they are not so much the formal geometry of Euclid as the draughtsmanship or design of the engineer – Diderot's 'experiential and manipulative mathematics', or the 'practical geometry' which Swift's Laputans 'despise as vulgar and mechanic'. And it was the eighteenth century's advances in cast iron and steel making that meant any shape could be made cheaply and durably. The availability of arbitrary rigid shapes, cheap, long-lasting, and reliably resistant to high pressures, stimulated imaginations to fashion intricate geometries of interacting parts. The iron machines are concrete realisations, so to speak, of several philosophical projects at once: Bacon's useful science, Kant's constructions, Vico's 'maker's knowledge', and Descartes's dream of explaining the world as the effect of interactions of rigid bodies.

There was some opposition to the idea of the beneficence of 'useful' science. Swift's satire attacked scientific research as either divorced from reality or productive of inventions that did not actually work.[142] But in general, technology had a positive glow, like mathematics, sufficient to tempt philosophers of most persuasions to claim it as on their side. Derham's *Physico-theology*, for example, saw the advances in mechanical inventions as evidence for God's providence.[143] *L'homme machine* may have seemed an idea of obviously atheist consequence in Paris, but Paley knew a good deal more about machines than La Mettrie, and convinced most, at least in the short term, that the teleological aspect of machines supported a theist interpretation of the man-machine analogy. 'Watches, telescopes, stocking-mills, steam-engines, &c.' are not the kind of things that can arise by chance – not even chance followed by selection.[144]

The consequences for political philosophy of Diderot's praise of artisans are generally left implicit in the *Encyclopédie*, but Hume's essay *Of Refinement in the Arts* supplies the gap:

> We cannot reasonably expect, that a piece of woollen cloth will be wrought to perfection in a nation, which is ignorant of astronomy, or where ethics are neglected. . . . Can we expect, that a government will be well modelled by a people, who know not how to make a spinning-wheel, or to employ a loom to advantage? . . . a progress in the arts is rather favourable to liberty, and has a natural tendency to preserve, if not produce a free government.[145]

The idea that machines create progress autonomously has remained an attractive one for the Enlightened. Citizen Gateau, administrator of military provisions, writes of the machine that has come to be most associated with Liberty:

> Saint Guillotine is most wonderfully active, and the beneficent terror accomplishes in our midst, as though by a miracle, what a century or more of philosophy and reason could not hope to produce.[146]

NOTES

1 Ian Hacking, *The Taming of Chance* (Cambridge, 1990), ch. 3.

2 Patricia C. Cohen, *A Calculating People: The Spread of Numeracy in Early America* (Chicago, IL, 1982).

3 J. L. Heilbron, 'The Measure of Enlightenment', in *The Quantifying Spirit in the 18th Century*, eds. T. Frängsmyr, J. L. Heilbron, and R. E. Rider (Berkeley, CA, 1990), 207–42; Ronald Edward Zupko, *Revolution in Measurement: Western European Weights and Measures Since the Age of Science* (Philadelphia, PA, 1990), chs. 4–5.

4 Heilbron, 'Introductory Essay', in *The Quantifying Spirit*, eds. Frängsmyr et al., 1–23; Maurice Daumas, 'Precision of Measurement and Physical and Chemical Research in the Eighteenth Century', in *Scientific Change: Historical Studies in the Intellectual, Social and Technical Conditions for Scientific Discovery and Technical Invention, from Antiquity to the Present*, ed. A. C. Crombie (London, 1963), 418–30.

5 L. Tilling, 'Early Experimental Graphs', *British Journal for the History of Science*, 8 (1975): 193–213.

6 H. J. M. Bos, 'Mathematics and Rational Mechanics', in *The Ferment of Knowledge: Studies in the Historiography of Eighteenth-Century Science*, eds. G. S. Rousseau and R. Porter (Cambridge, 1980), ch. 8. John L. Greenberg, *The Problem of the Earth's Shape from Newton to Clairaut: The Rise of Mathematical Science in the Eighteenth Century and the Fall of 'Normal' Science* (Cambridge, 1995).

7 Leonhard Euler, *Vollständige Anleitung zur Algebra mit den Zusätzen von Joseph Louis Lagrange*, ed. H. Weber, *Opera omnia*, I.1 (Leipzig, 1911–), Pt. I, Sect. I, ch. 1, p. 9; translated as *Elements of Algebra* (London, 1797), 1. See also Jean Le Rond d'Alembert, 'Explication détaillée du système des connaissances humaines', appended to his *Discours préliminaire de l'Encyclopédie*, in *Oeuvres*, 5 vols. (Paris, 1821–2), 1: 99–114 at 105–7; as translated in *Preliminary Discourse to the Encyclopedia of Diderot*, trans. R. N. Schwab and W. E. Rex (Indianapolis,

IN, 1963), 152–4; article 'Algebra', in *Encyclopaedia Britannica*, 3 vols. (Edinburgh, 1771), 1: 80.

8 Article 'Mathematics', in *Encyclopaedia Britannica*, 3: 30.

9 Euler, *Lettres à une Princesse d'Allemagne sur divers sujets de physique & de philosophie* (1768), I, letter 122, 25 April 1761, in *Opera omnia*, III.11: 289; translated as *Letters of Euler on Different Subjects in Natural Philosophy. Addressed to a German Princess*, [trans. H. Hunter], eds. D. Brewster and J. Griscom (facsim. of 1833 edn.), 2 vols. in 1 (New York, NY, 1975), 2: 33; see W. A. Suchting, 'Euler's "Reflections on Space and Time"', *Scientia*, 104 (1969): 270–8.

10 Article 'Géometrie', in *Encyclopédie, ou Dictionnaire raisonné des sciences, des arts, et des métiers*, eds. D. Diderot and J. d'Alembert, 17 vols. (Paris, 1751–65), 7: 629–38, at 632.

11 Christian Wolff, *Vernünfftige Gedancken von den Kräfften des menschlichen Verstandes und ihrem richtigen Gebrauche in Erkänntnis der Wahrheit* (1713), *Werke*, I.1 (1965), ch. 4, §22, 173; as translated in *Logic, or Rational Thoughts on the Powers of the Human Understanding, with their Use and Application in the Knowledge and Search of Truth* (London, 1770), 94; *Der Anfangsgründe aller Mathematischen Wissenschaften erster Theil, welcher einen Unterricht von der Mathematischen Lehr-Art, die Rechenkunst, Geometrie, Trigonometrie und Bau-Kunst in sich enthält* (1710), esp. the 'Kurtzer Unterricht von der mathematischen Methode oder Lehr-Art', prefaced to this work, in which Wolff sets out his programme, *Werke*, I.12 (1973). See also Gottfried Wilhelm Leibniz, *Second letter to Clarke*, in *The Leibniz-Clarke Correspondence, together with Extracts from Newton's Principia and Opticks*, ed. H. G. Alexander (Manchester, 1956), 15; W. Jentsch, 'Christian Wolff und die Mathematik seiner Zeit', in *Christian Wolff als Philosoph der Aufklärung in Deutschland*, eds. H.-M. Gerlach, G. Schenk, and B. Thaler (Halle, 1980), 173–80; Hans-Jürgen Engfer, *Philosophie als Analysis: Studien zur Entwicklung philosophischer Analysiskonzeptionen unter dem Einfluss mathematischer Methodenmodelle im 17. und frühen 18. Jahrhundert* (Stuttgart-Bad Cannstatt, 1982).

12 Tore Frängsmyr, 'The Mathematical Philosophy', in *The Quantifying Spirit*, eds. Frängsmyr et al., 27–44; see esp. Wolff, *Discursus præliminaris de philosophia in genere*, Pt. I of his *Philosophia rationalis sive logica*, ed. J. École, in *Werke*, II.1.1 (1983), ch. 4, 53–71, esp. §139. See also *Preliminary Discourse on Philosophy in General*, trans. R. J. Blackwell (Indianapolis, IN, 1963), 76–7.

13 Wolff, *Philosophia prima sive ontologia*, ed. J. École, in *Werke*, II.3 (1962), §70, 47.

14 Article 'Méthode (logique)', in *Encyclopédie*, 10: 445–6.

15 Bernard Le Bovier de Fontenelle, *Préface sur l'utilité des mathématiques et de la physique et sur les travaux de l'Académie des Sciences* (1699), in *Oeuvres*, ed. G.-B. Depping, 3 vols. (Geneva, 1968), 1: 30–8 at 34; see Noel M. Swerdlow, 'Montucla's Legacy: The History of the Exact Sciences', *Journal of the History of Ideas*, 54 (1993): 299–328.

16 Floridan Cajori, 'Frederick the Great on Mathematics and Mathematicians', *American Mathematical Monthly*, 34 (1927): 122–30; Thomas Jefferson, letter of 1799, quoted in David Eugene Smith and Jekuthiel Ginsburg, *History of Mathematics in America Before 1900* (Chicago, IL, 1934), 62.

17 Edward Gibbon, *Memoirs of My Life*, ed. B. Radice (London, 1984, repr. 1990), ch. IV, 99; Giambattista Vico, *Autobiografia* in *Opere*, vol. 5; translated as *The Autobiography of Giambattista Vico*, trans. M. H. Fisch and T. G. Bergin (Ithaca, NY, 1944), 123–5.

18 Euler, *Methodus inveniendi lineas curvas* (1744), Additamenta I and II; *Opera omnia*, I.24: 231–2, 298. The second passage is translated in Herman Heine Goldstine, *A History of the Calculus of Variations from the 17th through the 19th Century* (New York, NY, 1980), 106; See also Suzanne Bachelard, *Les polémiques concernant le principe de moindre action au XVIII*ᵉ *siècle* (Paris, 1961); Pierre Brunet, *Maupertuis*, 2 vols. (Paris, 1929), 2: ch. 5; Joachim Otto

Fleckenstein, Introduction, in Euler, *Opera omnia*, III.5; Helmut Pulte, *Das Prinzip der kleinsten Wirkung und die Kraftkonzeptionen der rationalen Mechanik* (Stuttgart, 1989).

19 D'Alembert, 'Introduction au *Traité de dynamique*', in *Oeuvres*, 1: 391–406 at 404.

20 Article 'Géometre', in *Encyclopédie*, 7: 627–9.

21 Pierre Simon, marquis de Laplace, *Essai philosophique sur les probabilités*, translated as *Philosophical Essay on Probabilities*, trans. F. W. Truscott and F. L. Emory (New York, NY, 1951), ch. 2, p. 4.

22 D'Alembert, 'Introduction', 398; Thomas L. Hankins, *Jean d'Alembert: Science and the Enlightenment* (Oxford, 1970), 179–85; see Jean G. Dhombres and Patricia Radelet-de Grave, 'Contingence et nécessité en mécanique', *Physis*, 28 (1991): 35–114; Veronique le Ru, *Jean le Rond d'Alembert philosophe* (Paris, 1994).

23 Article 'Densité', in *Encyclopédie*, 4: 833.

24 D'Alembert, 'Introduction', 398.

25 Article 'Expérimentale', in *Encyclopédie*, 4: 300; see Thomas Christensen, 'Music Theory as Scientific Propaganda: The Case of d'Alembert's *Elémens de musique*', *Journal of the History of Ideas*, 50.3 (1989): 409–27.

26 *Leibniz–Clarke Correspondence*, 18; Herbert Breger, 'Symmetry in Leibnizian Physics', in *The Leibniz Renaissance: International Workshop . . . 1986* (Florence, 1989), 23–42.

27 Jean Étienne Montucla, *Histoire des mathématiques*, ed. J. de la Lande, 4 vols. (Paris, 1799–1802), 3: 628.

28 Immanuel Kant, *Kritik der reinen Vernunft* (2nd edn., 1787, referred to as 'B'), in Ak 3: 'Einleitung', B 17–18; translated as *Critique of Pure Reason*, trans. and eds. P. Guyer and A. W. Wood in *Works* (1998); Giorgio Tonelli, 'La necessité des lois de la nature au XVIIIe siècle et chez Kant en 1762', *Revue d'histoire des sciences*, 12 (1959): 225–41.

29 Clifford A. Truesdell, 'A Program toward Rediscovering the Rational Mechanics of the Age of Reason', *Archive for History of Exact Sciences*, 1 (1960/2): 3–36, esp. sections 14–15.

30 Denis Diderot, *De l'Interpretation de la nature* (1753), in *Oeuvres philosophiques*, ed. P. Vernière (Paris, 1956), §4, 180–1; see trans. by D. Coltman in *Diderot's Selected Writings*, ed. L. G. Crocker (New York, NY, 1966), 71.

31 Hankins, *Jean d'Alembert*, 74–5.

32 D'Alembert, *Preliminary Discourse*, 29 (*Oeuvres*, 1: 33).

33 Diderot, *Lettre sur les aveugles* (1749), in *Oeuvres philosophiques*, 146; see Diderot's *Early Philosophical Works*, trans. and ed. M. Jourdain (Chicago, IL, 1916), 141. See also Johann Gottfried Herder, *Verstand und Erfahrung. Eine Metakritik zur Kritik der reinen Vernunft*, Pt 1 (1799), in *Sämmtliche Werke*, ed. B. L. Suphan, 33 vols (Berlin, 1877–1913), 21: 36.

34 D'Alembert, *Preliminary Discourse*, 28–9 (*Oeuvres*, 1: 32).

35 Gauss, Brief an Bessel, 9 April 1830, in Carl Friedrich Gauss, *Werke*, 12 vols. (Göttingen, 1863–1929), 8: 200–1; selection translated in *The History of Mathematics: A Reader*, eds. J. Fauvel and J. J. Gray (Basingstoke, 1987), 499.

36 Article 'Zenon [de Sidon]', remark D, in Pierre Bayle, *Dictionnaire historique et critique* (1696); translated in *Historical and Critical Dictionary: Selections*, trans. and ed. R. H. Popkin (Indianapolis, IN, 1965), 389–94.

37 Article 'Zeno d'Elée', in Bayle, *Dictionary*, 359–72 at 366.

38 Girolamo Saccheri, *Euclides vindicatus*, trans. and ed. G. B. Halstead, parallel Latin-English text (Chicago, IL, 1920); Richard J. Trudeau, *The Non-Euclidean Revolution* (Boston, MA, 1987), 131–47; Boris Abramovic Rosenfeld, *A History of Non-Euclidean Geometry: Evolution of the Concept of a Geometric Space*, trans. A. Shenitzer (New York, NY, 1988), 98–9; Jeremy Gray, *Ideas of Space: Euclidean, Non-Euclidean and Relativistic*, 2nd edn. (Oxford, 1989), ch. 4.

39 Trudeau, *Non-Euclidean Revolution*, 154.

40 Johann Heinrich Lambert, 'Theorie der Parallellinien', in F. Engel and P. Stäckel, *Die Theorie der Parallellinien von Euklid bis auf Gauss* (Leipzig, 1895), 152–207; Rosenfeld, *Non-Euclidean Geometry*, 100–1; Gray, *Ideas of Space*, ch. 5; W. S. Peters, 'Johann Heinrich Lamberts Konzeption einer Geometrie auf einer imaginären Kugel', *Kant-Studien*, 53 (1961): 51–67.

41 Douglas M. Jesseph, *Berkeley's Philosophy of Mathematics* (Chicago, IL, 1993), ch. 3.

42 Jesseph, ch. 2; Robert J. Fogelin, 'Hume and Berkeley on the Proofs of Infinite Divisibility', *Philosophical Review*, 97 (1988), 47–69.

43 Geoffrey Cantor, 'Berkeley's *The Analyst* revisited', *Isis*, 75 (1984): 668–83.

44 From Isaac Newton, *Quadratura curvarum*, in David Eugene Smith, *A Source Book in Mathematics* (New York, NY, 1929), 614–18 at 614. The work was published in Newton's *Opticks, or A Treatise of... Light, Also Two Treatises of the Species and Magnitude of Curvilinear Figures* (London, 1704), 165–211. The translation is slightly modified from that of John Stewart (London, 1745).

45 George Berkeley, *The Analyst*, §13, in *Works*, 4: 72.

46 Berkeley, *Analyst*, §§20–5 in *Works*, 4: 76–81; Jesseph, *Berkeley's Philosophy of Mathematics*, chs. 4–7; Ivor Grattan-Guinness, 'Berkeley's Criticism of the Calculus as a Study in the Theory of Limits', *Janus*, 56 (1969): 215–27.

47 G. C. Smith, 'Thomas Bayes and Fluxions', *Historia Mathematica*, 7 (1980): 379–88; Roy N. Lokken, 'Discussions of Newton's Infinitesimals in Eighteenth-Century Anglo-America', *Historia Mathematica*, 7 (1980): 141–55.

48 H. J. M. Bos, 'Differentials, Higher-Order Differentials and the Derivative in the Leibnizian Calculus', *Archive for History of Exact Sciences*, 14 (1974): 1–90; Hidé Ishiguro, *Leibniz's Philosophy of Logic and Language* (Cambridge, 1990), ch. 5.

49 Colin Maclaurin, *A Treatise of Fluxions* (Edinburgh, 1742), 39; see Niccolò Guicciardini, *The Development of Newtonian Calculus in Britain, 1700–1800* (Cambridge, 1989), ch. 3.

50 Maclaurin, *Treatise of Fluxions*, 57.

51 Carl B. Boyer, *The History of the Calculus and Its Conceptual Development: The Concepts of the Calculus* (New York, NY, 1959), ch. 6.

52 Charles C. Gillispie, *Lazare Carnot, Savant: A Monograph Treating Carnot's Scientific Work* (Princeton, NJ, 1971), ch. 5.

53 David Hume, *A Treatise of Human Nature*, eds. D. F. Norton and M. J. Norton, in the *Clarendon Edition* (2006), 1.3.1.2–5, SBN 69–71; Hume, *An Enquiry Concerning Human Understanding*, ed. T. L. Beauchamp, in the *Clarendon Edition* (2000), 7.1, SBN 60–73 and 12.3, SBN 161–5; R. F. Atkinson, 'Hume on Mathematics', *Philosophical Quarterly*, 10 (1960): 127–37; Farhang Zabeeh, *Hume, Precursor of Modern Empiricism: An Analysis of His Opinions on Meaning, Metaphysics, Logic and Mathematics* (The Hague, 1960), 128–37.

54 David Hume, *Dialogues Concerning Natural Religion*, Pt. 9, in *The Natural History of Religion and Dialogues Concerning Natural Religion*, eds. A. W. Colver and J. V. Price (Oxford, 1976), 218.

55 Donald Gotterbarn, 'Kant, Hume and Analyticity', *Kant-Studien*, 65 (1974): 274–83; Dorothy P. Coleman, 'Is Mathematics for Hume Synthetic *a priori*?', *Southwestern Journal of Philosophy* 10.2 (1979): 113–26.

56 Hume, *Treatise*, 1.4.1.1, SBN 180; W. E. Morris, 'Hume's Scepticism about Reason', *Hume Studies*, 15 (1989): 39–60.

57 R. J. Fogelin, 'Hume and Berkeley on the Proofs of Infinite Divisibility', *Philosophical Review*, 87 (1988): 47–69; James Franklin, 'Achievements and Fallacies in Hume's Account of Infinite Divisibility', *Hume Studies*, 20 (1994): 85–101.

58 Hume, *Treatise*, 1.2.4.17, SBN 44–5; Rosemary Newman, 'Hume on Space and Geometry', *Hume Studies*, 7 (1981): 1–31.

59 Hume, *Treatise*, 1.2.2.1–2, SBN 29–30; Berkeley, *A Treatise Concerning the Principles of Human Knowledge* (1710), §124, in *Works*, 2: 1–113 at 98–9.

60 Thomas Reid, *An Inquiry into the Human Mind* (1764), ed. D. R. Brookes (Edinburgh, 1997), VI.9, 122–5; Norman Daniels, *Thomas Reid's 'Inquiry': The Geometry of Visibles and the Case for Realism* (Stanford, CA, 1989); see Berkeley, *An Essay towards a New Theory of Vision* (1709), §156 in *Works*, 1: 141–239 at 234.

61 Vico, *De nostri temporis studiorum ratione* (1709) in *Opere*, 1: ch. 4, translated as *On Method in Contemporary Fields of Study* in *Selected Writings*, trans. and ed. L. Pompa (Cambridge, 1982), 40–1; see *On the Ancient Wisdom of the Italians* (*De antiquissima Italorum sapientia*, 1710), Bk. 1, ch. 1, §2, and ch. 3 in *Selected Writings*, 54–5 and 64–5; see also Georges-Louis Leclerc, comte de Buffon, *Histoire naturelle*, 'Premier discours: de la manière d'étudier et de traiter l'Histoire naturelle', in *Oeuvres philosophiques*, ed. J. Piveteau (Paris, 1954), 23–5; this selection gives references to the Imprimerie Royale edn. of *Oeuvres complètes*, 44 vols. (Paris, 1749–1804); see 1: 3–62.

62 Vico, *The Third New Science* (*Scienza nuova*, 3rd edn., 1744), §349, in *Selected Writings*, 206; see *Second New Science* (*Scienza nuova*, 1730), §1133, in *Selected Writings*, 269.

63 Andreas Rüdiger, *De sensu veri et falsi*, 2nd edn. (Leipzig, 1722), §§8–12, see Lewis White Beck, *Early German Philosophy: Kant and His Predecessors* (Cambridge, MA, 1969), 299; Engfer, 'Zur Bedeutung Wolffs für die Methoden-diskussion der deutschen Aufklärungsphilosophie. Analytische und synthetische Methode bei Wolff und beim vorkritischen Kant', in *Christian Wolff 1679–1754. Interpretationen zu seiner Philosophie und deren Wirkung*, ed. W. Schneiders (Hamburg, 1983), 48–65; Raffaele Ciafardone, 'Von der Kritik an Wolff zum vorkritischen Kant: Wolff-Kritik bei Rüdiger und Crusius', in Schneiders, 289–305; David Rapport Lachterman, *The Ethics of Geometry* (New York, NY, 1989), ch. 2, Pt. 4.

64 Lambert, *Abhandlungen vom Criterium veritatis*, ed. K. Bopp, *Kantstudien* 36 (1915); see letter to Kant, 3 February 1766, in Kant, *Works/Correspondence*, ed. A. Zweig (1999), 84–7.

65 Kant, *Untersuchung über die Deutlichkeit der Gründsätze der natürlichen Theologie und der Moral* (1764), First Reflection, §1, Ak 2: 276–8, translated as *Inquiry concerning the Distinctness of the Principles of Natural Theology and Morality*, in *Works/Theoretical Philosophy, 1755–1770*, trans. and eds. D. Walford and R. Meerbote (1992); *Kritik der reinen Vernunft*, B 741; see Michael Friedman, *Kant and the Exact Sciences* (Cambridge, MA, 1992), ch. 1; Tonelli, 'Der Streit über die mathematischen Methode in der Philosophie in der ersten Hälfte des 18. Jahrhunderts und die Entstehung von Kants Schrift über die "Deutlichkeit"', *Archiv für Philosophie* 9 (1959): 37–66; Ted B. Humphreys, 'The Historical and Conceptual Relations between Kant's Metaphysics of Space and Philosophy of Geometry', *Journal of the History of Philosophy*, 11 (1973): 483–512, Sect. 1; Gregor Büchel, *Geometrie und Philosophie* (Berlin, 1987), ch. 1; W. R. De Jong, 'How Is Metaphysics as a Science Possible? Kant on the Distinction between Philosophical and Mathematical Method', *Review of Metaphysics* 49 (1995): 235–74.

66 Kant, *De mundi sensibilis atque intelligibilis forma et principiis* (1770), §15C, Ak 2: 402–3, translated as *On the Form and Principles of the Sensible and the Intelligible World* [*Inaugural Dissertation*] [1770], in *Works/Theoretical Philosophy 1755–1770*; see *Kritik der reinen Vernunft*, B 268.

67 Kant, *Kritik der reinen Vernunft*, Ak 3: 480; Friedman, *Kant and the Exact Sciences*, ch. 2, §1; Introduction and several papers in *Kant's Philosophy of Mathematics: Modern Essays*, ed. Carl J. Posy (Dordrecht, 1992); Jaakko Hintikka, 'Kant's Theory of Mathematics Revisited', in *Essays on Kant's Critique of Pure Reason*, eds. J. N. Mohanty and R. W. Shahan (Norman, OK, 1982), 201–15; Robert E. Butts, 'Rules, Examples and Constructions: Kant's Theory of Mathematics', *Synthese* 47 (1981): 257–88; Alfredo Ferrarin, 'Construction and

Mathematical Schematism: Kant on the Exhibition of a Concept in Intuition', *Kant-Studien* 86 (1995): 131–74.

68 Kant, *De mundi*, §15D, Ak 2: 403–4.

69 A. P. Youschkevitch, 'Lazare Carnot and the Competition of the Berlin Academy in 1786 on the Mathematical Theory of the Infinite', in Gillispie, *Lazare Carnot, Savant*, 149–68.

70 *Kritik*, B 532; Anthony Winterbourne, *The Ideal and the Real: An Outline of Kant's Theory of Space, Time and Mathematical Construction* (Dordrecht, 1988), 79–89.

71 Arthur Melnick, *Space, Time, and Thought in Kant* (Dordrecht, 1989), 5–20, 189–98; Friedman, *Kant and the Exact Sciences*, 74–9.

72 Joseph-Louis de Lagrange, *Mécanique analytique* (1788), 'Avertissement', in *Oeuvres*, eds. J.-A. Serret and G. Darboux, 14 vols. (Paris, 1867–92), 11: xi–xii.

73 Marie Jean Antoine Nicolas de Caritat, marquis de Condorcet, 'Discours sur les sciences mathématiques', in *Oeuvres*, eds. A. C. O'Connor and F. Arago, 12 vols. (Paris, 1847–9), 1: 453–81 at 467.

74 Thomas L. Hankins, *Science and the Enlightenment* (Cambridge, 1985), ch. 2.

75 Euler, *Anleitung zur Algebra*, Pt. I, Sect. 1, ch. 1, in *Opera omnia*, I.1: 10; d'Alembert, *Essai sur les éléments de philosophie . . . avec les éclaircissemens* (1759–67), Pt. 14, §11 in *Oeuvres complètes*, 1: 263; Kant, *Kritik der reinen Vernunft*, B 745; see R. E. Rider, *Mathematics in the Enlightenment: A Study of Algebra, 1685–1800*, PhD thesis, Univ. California, Berkeley, 1980.

76 Lubos Nový, *Origins of Modern Algebra*, trans. J. Tauer (Leiden, 1973), ch. 2.

77 Wolff, *Psychologia empirica* (1738), in *Werke*, II.5, Pt. 1, Sect. 3, ch. 2, §294, 208.

78 Étienne Bonnot de Condillac, *La Logique* (1780), Pt. 2, ch. 8, in *Oeuvres philosophiques*, ed. G. Le Roy, 3 vols. (Paris, 1947–51), 2: 410, 411, see *La Logique-Logic*, trans. and ed. W. R. Albury, with parallel French facsim. repr. (New York, NY, 1980), 311, 315.

79 Condillac, *La langue des calculs* (1798), in *Oeuvres philosophiques*, 2: 421–558, at 429; Isabel F. Knight, *The Geometric Spirit: The Abbé de Condillac and the French Enlightenment* (New Haven, CT, 1968), 171–5.

80 Kant, *Untersuchung über die Deutlichkeit der Grundsätze*, First Reflection, §2, and Third Reflection, §1 (Ak 2: 278, 291).

81 M. Kline, 'Euler and Infinite Series', *Mathematics Magazine*, 56 (1983): 307–14.

82 Euler, *Vollständige Anleitung zur Algebra*, Pt. 1, Sect. 1, ch. 13, in *Opera*, I.6: 55; Nový, *Modern Algebra*, 95–7, 112–14; see also J. Playfair, 'On the Arithmetic of Impossible Quantities', *Philosophical Transactions of the Royal Society of London*, 68 (1778): 318–43, on which D. Sherry, 'The Logic of Impossible Quantities', *Studies in History and Philosophy of Science*, 22 (1991): 37–62.

83 Euler, *Introductio in analysin infinitorum*, Bk. I, ch. 1, §4 in *Opera*, I.8: 18; translated as *Introduction to Analysis of the Infinite*, Bk I, trans. J. D. Blanton (New York, NY, 1988), 3.

84 J. Lützen, 'Euler's Vision of a General Partial Differential Calculus for a Generalized Kind of Function', *Mathematics Magazine*, 56 (1983): 299–306; C. Truesdell, Introduction, to Euler, *Rational Mechanics*, in *Opera*, II.11, Sect. 2, especially 244–50.

85 Lagrange, *Théorie des fonctions analytiques* (Paris, 1797), 2, 7–8, 12; a later edn. is included in vol. 5 of the *Oeuvres*. See also Judith V. Grabiner, *The Calculus as Algebra: J.-L. Lagrange, 1736–1813* (New York, NY, 1990); Ivor Grattan-Guinness, *The Development of the Foundations of Mathematical Analysis from Euler to Riemann* (Cambridge, MA, 1970), ch. 1.

86 Lagrange, 'Réflexions sur la résolution algébrique des équations' (1770/1), in *Oeuvres*, 203–421; Hans Wussing, *The Genesis of the Abstract Group Concept: A Contribution to the History of the Origin of Abstract Group Theory*, trans. A. Shenitzer (Cambridge, MA, 1984).

87 Paolo Ruffini, *Teoria generale delle equazioni in cui si dimostra impossibile la soluzione algebraica delle equazioni generali di grado superiore al quarto* (Bologna, 1799); Wussing, 80–4;

R. Bryce, 'Paolo Ruffini and the Quintic Equation', *Symposia Mathematica*, 27 (1986): 169–85.

88 Mary Tiles, *Mathematics and the Image of Reason* (London, 1991), 10–24.

89 Euler, *Specimen de usu observationum in mathesi pura* (1761), in *Opera*, I.2: 459–92 at 459; as translated in George Polya, *Mathematics and Plausible Reasoning*, 2 vols. (Princeton, NJ, 1954), 1: 3.

90 Polya, 1: 18–21, see also 91–8.

91 Laplace, *Philosophical Essay*, ch. 1, 1; Gauss, *Werke*, 2: 3.

92 Wolff, *Discursus preliminaris*, §127, trans. 68.

93 Lambert, *Anlage zur Architectonic, oder Theorie des Einfachen und des Ersten in der philosophischen und mathematischen Erkenntnis*, 2 vols. (Riga, 1771), Pt. 2, ch. 11, §§315–27, facsim. repr. in *Philosophische Schriften*, ed. H. W. Arndt, 10 vols. (Hildesheim, 1965), 3: 306–19; O. B. Sheynin, 'On the Prehistory of Probability', *Archive for History of Exact Sciences*, 12 (1974): 97–141 at 136–7.

94 Euler, 'Solutio problematis ad geometriam situs pertinentis', *Opera*, I.7: 1–10; translated as 'The Koenigsberg Bridges' in *Scientific American* 189.1 (1953): 66–70, repr. in *The World of Mathematics*, ed. J. R. Newman, 4 vols. (New York, NY, 1956), 1: 573–80; see H. Sachs, M. Stiebitz, and R. J. Wilson, 'An Historical Note: Euler's Königsberg Letters', *Journal of Graph Theory* 12 (1988): 133–9.

95 Gottfried Wilhelm, Freiherr von Leibniz, *Philosophical Papers and Letters: A Selection*, trans. and ed. L. E. Loemker, 2 vols. (Chicago, IL, 1956), 1: 381–96.

96 Buffon, *Histoire naturelle*, ch. 11 'Histoire générale des animaux: Histoire naturelle de l'homme', in Impr. Royale edn., 2: 373.

97 Kant, *Von dem ersten Grunde des Unterschiedes der Gegenden im Raume* (1768), in Ak 2: 375–83 at 377; translated as *Concerning the Ultimate Ground of the Differentiation of Directions in Space*, in *Works/Theoretical Philosophy, 1755–1770*.

98 A.-T. Vandermonde, 'Remarques sur les problèmes de situation', *Histoire de l'Académie Royale des Sciences*, 1771 (Paris, 1774), 566–74, translated in Norman L. Biggs, E. Keith Lloyd, and Robin J. Wilson, *Graph Theory 1736–1936* (Oxford, 1976), 22–6.

99 O. J. Grüsser, 'Quantitative Visual Psychophysics during the Period of European Enlightenment', *Documenta Ophthalmologica*, 71 (1989): 93–111.

100 Buffon, 'Essai d'arithmétique morale', §8, in *Oeuvres philosophiques*, 459; see *Histoire naturelle: Supplément*, IV, in Impr. Royale edn. 2: 46–148, at 56; Lorraine Daston, *Classical Probability in the Enlightenment* (Princeton, NJ, 1988), 91–3.

101 Pierre-Louis Moreau de Maupertuis, *Essai de philosophie morale* (1749), ch. 1, in *Oeuvres* (Lyons 1768 and Berlin 1758 edns.), ed. G. Tonelli, 2 vols. (Hildesheim, 1974), 1: 171–252 at 195.

102 Adam Smith, *An Inquiry into the Nature and Causes of the Wealth of Nations*, eds. R. H. Campbell, A. S. Skinner, and W. B. Todd, 2 vols., in *Works* (1976), I.v at 1: 48, 50 and 48; see Condorcet, 'Tableau général de la science qui a pour objet l'application du calcul aux sciences politiques et morales' (1793), in *Oeuvres*, 1: 539–73, at 558.

103 Benjamin Franklin, Letter to Joseph Priestley, 19 September 1772, in *Papers*, ed. L. W. Labaree and W. J. Bell (New Haven, CT, 1959–), 19: 299–300.

104 Condorcet, 'Tableau', *Oeuvres*, 1: 541; Daston, *Classical Probability*, 217–18.

105 Condorcet, *Essai sur l'application de l'analyse a la probabilité des décisions rendues à la pluralité des voix* (Paris, 1785); Keith M. Baker, *Condorcet: From Natural Philosophy to Social Mathematics* (Chicago, IL, 1975), 225–44; Daston, *Classical Probability*, 345–55; R. Rashed, *Condorcet: Mathématique et société* (Paris, 1974).

106 Baker, *Condorcet*, 340–1.

107 Thomas Reid, *An Essay on Quantity* (1748), in *Philosophical Works*, ed. W. Hamilton, 2 vols. in 1 (Edinburgh, 1895), 715–19.

108 Otto Mayr, 'Adam Smith and the Concept of the Feedback System', *Technology and Culture*, 12 (1977): 1–22.

109 Thomas Robert Malthus, *An Essay on the Principle of Population*, 1st edn. (London, 1798), 13; the *Essay* was substantially rewritten for the influential edn. of 1803.

110 'Condorcet au comte Pierre Verri, 7 novembre 1771', in *Oeuvres*, 1: 281–5 at 283–4; Baker, *Condorcet*, 337–8.

111 O. B. Sheynin, 'J. H. Lambert's Work on Probability', *Archive for History of Exact Sciences*, 7 (1970/1): 244–56, Sect. 2.

112 Wilhelm Risse, *Bibliographia logica*, 4 vols. (Hildesheim, 1965), 1: 180–235; Risse, *Die Logik der Neuzeit*, 2 vols. (Stuttgart-Bad Cannstatt, 1964–70), vol. 2; Anton Dumitriu, *History of Logic*, 4 vols. (Tunbridge Wells, 1977), 3: 150–62; I. H. Anellis, 'Theology against Logic: The Origins of Logic in Old Russia', *History and Philosophy of Logic* 13 (1992): 15–42.

113 Wilbur Samuel Howell, *Eighteenth-Century British Logic and Rhetoric* (Princeton, NJ, 1971), ch. 2, §5; see M. Feingold, 'The Ultimate Pedagogue: Franco Petri Burgersdijk and the English Speaking Academic Learning', in *Franco Burgersdijk (1590–1635): Neo-Aristotelianism in Leiden*, eds. E. P. Bos and H. A. Krop (Amsterdam, 1993), 151–65.

114 Kant, *Die falsche Spitzfindigkeit der vier syllogistischen Figuren erwiesen von M. Immanuel Kant* (1762), §5, in Ak 2: 45–61 at 55–7, translated as *The False Subtlety of the Four Syllogistic Figures demonstrated by M. Immanuel Kant* in *Works/Theoretical Philosophy 1755–1770*.

115 Kant, *Jäsche Logik*, 'Einleitung', Sect. 1 (Ak 9: 1–150 at 14); as translated in *Works/Lectures on Logic*, trans. and ed. J. M. Young (1992), 529; *Kritik der reinen Vernunft*, 'Vorrede', B viii.

116 J. G. Buickerood, 'The Natural History of the Understanding: Locke and the Rise of Facultative Logic in the Eighteenth Century', *History and Philosophy of Logic*, 6 (1985): 157–90; John Passmore, 'Descartes, the British Empiricists and Formal Logic', *Philosophical Review*, 62 (1953): 545–53.

117 John Locke, *An Essay Concerning Human Understanding*, ed. P. H. Nidditch (Oxford, 1975), IV.xvii, esp. 670–6; Howell, *Logic and Rhetoric*, ch. 5, §2.

118 Isaac Watts, *Logick: or, The Right Use of Reason in the Enquiry after Truth* (London, 1725), Pt. 3, ch. 4, (II Rule), 492.

119 Howell, *Logic and Rhetoric*, ch. 5, §3.

120 Reid, *A Brief Account of Aristotle's Logic* (1774), ch. IV, Sect. 5, in *Philosophical Works*, 681–714 at 701–2; George Campbell, *The Philosophy of Rhetoric*, 2 vols. (London, 1776), esp. Bk. I, ch. 6; see Howell, ch. 5, §4.

121 Hume, *Treatise*, 1.3.8.14, SBN 105; John Passmore, *Hume's Intentions*, 2nd edn. (Cambridge, 1968), ch. 2, 'The Critic of Formal Logic'; Zabeeh, *Hume*, 106–11; P. M. Longley, *Hume's Logic: Ideas and Inference*, PhD thesis, Univ. of Minnesota, 1968.

122 D. C. Stove, 'The Nature of Hume's Skepticism', *McGill Hume Studies*, eds. D. F. Norton, N. Capaldi, and W. L. Robison (San Diego, CA, 1979), 203–25.

123 R. S. Crane, 'The Houyhnhnms, the Yahoos and the History of Ideas', in *Reason and the Imagination: Studies in the History of Ideas 1600–1800*, ed. J. A. Mazzeo (New York, NY, 1962), 231–53.

124 Howell, 'The Declaration of Independence and Eighteenth-Century Logic', *William and Mary Quarterly*, 3rd ser., 18 (1961): 463–84.

125 John W. Yolton, 'Schoolmen, Logic and Philosophy', in *The History of the University of Oxford, vol. V: The Eighteenth Century*, eds. L. S. Sutherland and L. G. Mitchell (Oxford, 1986), 565–91.

126 John Gascoigne, 'Mathematics and Meritocracy: The Emergence of the Cambridge Mathematical Tripos', *Social Studies of Science*, 14 (1984): 547–84.
127 R. G. Olson, 'Scottish Philosophy and Mathematics 1750–1830', *Journal of the History of Ideas*, 32 (1971): 29–44.
128 N. I. Styazhkin, *History of Mathematical Logic from Leibniz to Peano* (Cambridge, MA, 1969), ch. 3.
129 Euler, *Lettres à une Princesse*, I, letter 103, 17 Feb. 1761, in *Opera*, III.11: 233, trans. 340–1.
130 Gereon Wolters, *Basis und Deduktion: Studien zur Entstehung und Bedeutung der Theorie der axiomatischen Methode bei J. H. Lambert (1728–1777)* (Berlin, 1980), ch. 4; John Venn, *Symbolic Logic*, 2nd edn. rev. (London, 1894), ch. 20, 517–20.
131 Lambert, *Anlage zur Architectonic*, Pt. 1, ch. 1, §10, in *Philosophische Schriften*, 3: 8; Wolters, ch. 3.
132 C. I. Lewis, *A Survey of Symbolic Logic*, 2nd corr. edn. (New York, NY, 1960), 19–29; Styazhkin, *Mathematical Logic*, 112–27; Karl Dürr, *Die Logistik J. H. Lamberts* (Zürich, 1945).
133 Lambert, *Neues Organon*, 2 vols. (Leipzig, 1764) 2: 355; Styazhkin, 123.
134 Diderot, article 'Art', in *Encyclopédie*, 1: 713–19.
135 I. Bernard Cohen, *Benjamin Franklin's Science* (Cambridge, MA, 1990), ch. 3; Silvio A. Bedini, *Thomas Jefferson, Statesman of Science* (New York, NY, 1990); Meyer Reinhold, 'The Quest for "Useful Knowledge" in Eighteenth-Century America', *Proceedings of the American Philosophical Society*, 119 (1975): 108–32.
136 R. E. Schofield, 'The Industrial Orientation of Science in the Lunar Society of Birmingham', in *Science, Technology and Economic Growth in the Eighteenth Century*, ed. A. E. Musson (London, 1972), 136–47; Roy Porter, 'Science, Provincial Culture and Public Opinion in Enlightenment England', *British Journal for Eighteenth Century Studies*, 3 (1980): 20–46.
137 *A Diderot Pictorial Encyclopedia of Trades and Industry*, ed. C. C. Gillispie, 2 vols. (New York, NY, 1959); Gillispie, *Science and Polity in France at the End of the Old Regime* (Princeton, NJ, 1980), 337–56.
138 John Desaguliers, *A Course of Experimental Philosophy*, 2 vols. (London, 1734–44), Preface; Larry Stewart, *The Rise of Public Science: Rhetoric, Technology and Natural Philosophy in Newtonian Britain, 1660–1750* (Cambridge, 1992), ch. 7; Simon Schaffer, 'Natural Philosophy and Public Spectacle in Eighteenth-Century Science', *History of Science* 21 (1983): 1–43; Margaret C. Jacob, 'Scientific Culture in the early English Enlightenment', in *Anticipations of the Enlightenment in England, France and Germany*, eds. A. C. Kors and P. J. Korshin (Philadelphia, PA, 1987), ch. 6; Barbara Maria Stafford, *Artful Science: Enlightenment, Entertainment and the Eclipse of Visual Science* (Cambridge, MA, 1994).
139 Joseph Bramah, *A Letter to the Rt. Hon. Sir James Eyre* (London, 1797), quoted and discussed in Christine MacLeod, *Inventing the Industrial Revolution: The English Patent System, 1600–1800* (Cambridge, 1988), 220.
140 A. Smith, *Wealth of Nations*, Bk. I, ch. I, 1: 21.
141 D. S. L. Cardwell, 'Science, Technology and Industry', in *The Ferment of Knowledge: Studies in the Historiography of Eighteenth-Century Science*, eds. G. S. Rousseau and R. Porter (Cambridge, 1980), ch. 12; Richard L. Hills, *Power from Steam: A History of the Stationary Steam Engine* (Cambridge, 1989), ch. 4.
142 Marjorie Nicolson with N. M. Mohler, 'The Scientific Background to Swift's *Voyage to Laputa*', in Marjorie Nicolson, *Science and Imagination* (Ithaca, NY, 1956), 110–54; Richard G. Olson, 'Tory-High Church Opposition to Science and Scientism in the Eighteenth Century: The Works of John Arbuthnot, Jonathan Swift, and Samuel Johnson', in *The Uses of Science in the Age of Newton*, ed. J. G. Burke (Berkeley, CA, 1983), 171–204.

143 William Derham, *Physico-Theology, or, A Demonstration of the Being and Attributes of God* (London, 1713), Bk. 5, ch. 1; W. Coleman, 'Providence, Capitalism and Environmental Degradation', *Journal of the History of Ideas* 37 (1976): 27–44.

144 William Paley, *Natural Theology*, ch. 5, in *Works*, a new edn., 7 vols. (London, 1825), 5: 39–52 at 46; N. C. Gillespie, 'Divine Design and the Industrial Revolution', *Isis* 81 (1990): 214–29.

145 Hume, 'Of Refinement in the Arts', in *Political Essays*, ed. K. Haakonssen (Cambridge, 1994), 105–14 at 107, 109, 111.

146 Quoted in Hector Fleischmann, *La Guillotine en 1793* (Paris, 1908), 255.

29

THE STUDY OF NATURE

JOHN GASCOIGNE

On the map of knowledge which the eighteenth century inherited from long centuries of scholastic instruction and debate, natural philosophy or 'physics' occupied a large and prominent place. The university culture of the High Middle Ages had absorbed much of the Aristotelian canon into four main compartments: metaphysics – the study of being as such; 'physics' – the study of being as qualified; logic; and ethics. Thus a form of education was created whose imprint was still evident at the beginning of the eighteenth century despite the great intellectual upheavals of the seventeenth century. At most universities the arts students (including those who subsequently undertook postgraduate education in medicine, law, or theology) were exposed to a curriculum which – despite some modifications prompted by Renaissance humanism – was still very largely dominated by such philosophical canons. Moreover, as confidence waned in the possibility of the unaided human intellect to arrive at worthwhile conclusions in the fields of ethics or metaphysics – particularly in Protestant cultures with their emphasis on the fallibility of the human mind – the study of natural philosophy waxed in importance.

The weight of tradition, then, accorded natural philosophy an important place in the mental furniture of the elite, and the domain accorded to it was extremely broad. Natural philosophy in the scholastic tradition embraced the study of all natural things both organic and inorganic. Aristotle and his innumerable scholastic commentators and disputants had sought to provide a priori, qualitative explanations about such fundamental concepts as form, matter, cause, and motion which could be used to explain all natural phenomena.[1] Such an inclusive view of the extent of natural philosophy is reflected in the definition of '*Physicks* or Natural Philosophy' – for the two terms were used interchangeably – given by John Harris at the beginning of the eighteenth century in his widely used *Lexicon Technicum* (1704) as being the 'Speculative Knowledge of all Natural Bodies'.[2]

From the late seventeenth to the beginning of the nineteenth century, however, natural philosophy was to be transformed from this wide-ranging attempt to arrive at a knowledge of nature as a whole by largely qualitative, 'speculative', methods to a collection of increasingly separate disciplines no longer united by a common philosophical endeavour. The major developments in bringing about this transformation were first, the increasing attention paid by natural philosophers to empirical information, thus weakening the traditionally a priori character of natural philosophy; secondly, the growing emphasis on experiment which was to accelerate the growth of different disciplines which had once found a common intellectual home under the rubric of natural philosophy; and thirdly, the increasing mathematisation of natural philosophy which undermined its qualitative character. After a discussion of the changing nature and scope of the term 'natural philosophy' over the course of the eighteenth century, this chapter considers each of these major developments in turn before concluding with an analysis of the chief characteristics of the eighteenth-century scientific community.

I. THE SCOPE OF EIGHTEENTH-CENTURY NATURAL PHILOSOPHY: CONTINUITY AND CHANGE

The natural philosophy which had been fostered by the universities of Europe since the High Middle Ages constituted an attempt to arrive at the basic causes of natural phenomena by the methods of close reasoning and debate. It took as its starting point the Aristotelian canon; but over the centuries it had assimilated many varying philosophical strands, and by the late seventeenth century scholastic natural philosophy was something of an intellectual patchwork quilt.[3] In some universities there was even an attempt to absorb the new wine of the Scientific Revolution into the old scholastic bottles, though the resulting fermentation hastened the disintegration of both scholastic natural philosophy and the scholastic framework of studies more generally. Scholastic natural philosophy represented a major pillar of the larger scholastic order, and as it crumbled, so, too, the overall philosophical system with which it was inextricably linked began to collapse. For the great attraction of the scholastic curriculum from both a pedagogical point of view and from the natural human desire for intellectual coherence was that all its branches, including natural philosophy, shared a common set of philosophical presuppositions and methods. Much of the appeal of Cartesianism was that it also provided a similarly, all-embracing, integrated philosophical *schema* in which natural philosophy played a prominent part. Consequently, for many individuals and institutions, Cartesianism with its reassuringly familiar all-embracing deductive structure provided a means of weaning themselves away from the traditional scholastic natural philosophy. Some institutions and textbook writers even attempted to square the circle by combining scholastic natural philosophy with Cartesianism.[4]

At the beginning of the eighteenth century, then, scholastic natural philosophy was in rapid decay throughout the universities of Europe as it disintegrated in the wake of attempts to combine its methods with the achievements of the Scientific Revolution or was replaced by some variant of Cartesianism. Nonetheless, the long scholastic heritage continued to leave its mark on what the eighteenth century still called natural philosophy. First, the subject retained the Schoolmen's preoccupation with the search for the basic causes of natural phenomena even if the eighteenth century increasingly abandoned the scholastics' *methods* of arriving at knowledge of such causes. In particular, natural philosophy continued to remain centred on the causes of motion, reflecting the Aristotelian legacy which had defined physics as the study of 'the first principles of things *qua* in motion' – motion here being understood to embrace all forms of change.[5]

Early eighteenth-century definitions of natural philosophy, even by such self-consciously modernising followers of Newton as Desaguliers, still reflected the traditional view that the task of natural philosophy was to arrive at an understanding of the basic causes of change (for to Aristotle the link between motion and change was unbreakable). 'Natural Philosophy', wrote Desaguliers in *A System of Experimental Philosophy* (1719), 'is that Science which gives the reasons and Causes of the Effects and Changes which naturally happen in Bodies'. He did add, however, an aside that underlined his rejection of the methods of the Schools that lest we 'be deceived by false Notions which we have embraced without Examining, or that we have received upon the Authority of others; we ought to call in Question all such Things as have an Appearance of Falsehood; that by a new Examen we may be led to the Truth'.[6] 's Gravesande, Newton's first major disciple in the Netherlands, defined natural philosophy similarly as that study which 'explains Natural Phaenomena, that is, treats of their causes'.[7] His colleague and fellow Newtonian populariser, Musschenbroek, was even more explicit in defining natural philosophy as an enquiry into the philosophical bases of our understanding of nature focussing above all, as Aristotle had, on the problem of motion or change. 'The objects of Physics', wrote Musschenbroek, 'are Body, Space and Motion', adding that 'motion is the principal object of Physicks'.[8] Even at the end of the eighteenth century, the *Encyclopaedia Britannica* (1797), in the article on 'Physics' by John Robison, insisted that 'The disquisitions of natural philosophy must therefore begin with the considerations of motion'.[9] This view, that it was the province of natural philosophy to arrive at knowledge of causes, limited the growth of scientific disciplines which emerged out of areas other than those traditionally traversed by natural philosophy. This applied particularly to those, such as the future discipline of biology, linked with natural history[10] – an issue which will be considered at greater length in the next section of this chapter.

Secondly, the lingering scholastic imprint on eighteenth-century natural philosophy remained evident in the way in which the domain of natural philosophy was classified and subdivided – the use of categories and classifications being a basic characteristic of the scholastic mind. Like the scholastics, eighteenth-century natural philosophers continued to use the basic division of 'natural philosophy' or 'physics' – for the terms continued to be largely interchangeable – into 'general and particular physics'. Within the universities the distinction between general and particular physics was used in much the same way as it had been for centuries. Thus the definitions given in a Dutch natural philosophy textbook of 1786 would not have been out of place in a scholastic manual: 'General physics is that part of natural philosophy, which explains the properties, forces, and actions of body considered in general'; 'Particular physics', by contrast, 'explains the nature, qualities, and forces of single bodies, which exist in nature'.[11] This distinction was also employed by d'Alembert in the 'Discourse préliminaire' to the *Encyclopédie* in which he defines 'General Physics' in terms which again reflect the traditional linkage between natural philosophy and the study of the basic philosophical presuppositions of our understanding of nature. 'Intellectual speculation', he wrote, 'is related to General Physics, which is properly speaking, simply the metaphysics of bodies'. Particular physics he defines as that 'which studies the bodies in themselves and whose sole object is individual things'; it is on this which he concentrates in his 'Explication détaillée du systeme des connoissances humaines', subsequent to the *Discours* and with a table which, in the manner of scholastic natural philosophy, embraced both the organic and inorganic worlds.[12]

D'Alembert also emulated the scholastics in dividing the map of knowledge into neat and orderly subdivisions, reflecting the continuing belief that ultimately all branches of learning were interrelated. It followed that knowledge in one field could illuminate that in another, a view brought out, for example, in an early seventeenth-century scholastic textbook of natural philosophy in which physics is linked to theology. 'From Physics', wrote Keckermann in this work, 'the first three chapters of Genesis are known and explained. . . . In the other books of Moses, whatever is said about the gems, metals and foods cannot be understood without Physics'.[13] In the eighteenth century, too, there remained residues of this belief that the findings of natural philosophy could be relevant to other areas of philosophy and learning more generally. Maupertuis, for example, believed that the 'principle of least action' in rational mechanics proved the existence of God, while Madame du Châtelet took the view that the Leibnizian theory of mechanics supported a philosophical belief in free will.[14]

Though the possibility was receding of neatly integrating all branches of philosophy into a consistent system in the manner of the scholastics or the Cartesians, eighteenth-century natural philosophers continued to relate their discipline to the larger purposes of philosophy. In his *Elementa physicae* Musschenbroek began by providing a definition of philosophy in general which made evident the primary importance and utility of natural philosophy. 'Philosophy', he wrote, 'is the knowledge of all things both divine and human, and of their properties, operations, causes, and effects; which may be known by the understanding, the senses, reason, or by any way whatever. It's [sic] end is to promote the real happiness of mankind, as far as may be attained in this life'.[15] The *Encyclopaedia Britannica* of 1797 also attempted to draw natural philosophy (or physics) within the larger sphere of philosophy by writing in Baconian terms that 'The principal objects of philosophy are, God, nature, and man. That part of it which treats of God is called *theology*; that which treats of nature, physics and metaphysics; and that which treats of man, *logic* and *ethics*'. In the first edition of 1771, the *Encyclopaedia* had attempted, too, to draw parallels between the method employed by both the natural and moral philosopher, writing that 'Moral Philosophy has this in common with Natural Philosophy, that it appeals to nature or fact; depends on observation; and builds its reasonings on plain uncontroverted experiments, or upon the fullest indication of particulars, of which the subject will admit'.[16]

The tenor of this last quotation – with its emphasis on the Baconian methods of observation, experiment, and induction – is an indication of how far natural philosophy had become the exemplar of the philosophical method more generally. No longer was natural philosophy but one branch of philosophy; increasingly its methods and successes were regarded as establishing goals which other branches of philosophy should emulate. It was becoming the exemplar of the most fruitful path that the human mind could follow. In his famous 'Epistle to the Reader' in his *Essay concerning Human Understanding* Locke had set the tone for much of the philosophical discourse of the eighteenth century by deferring to such 'Master-Builders' as Boyle, Sydenham, Huygens, and Newton 'whose mighty Designs, in advancing the Sciences, will leave lasting Monuments to the Admiration of Posterity'. For his own work Locke had simply claimed the humble dignity of acting as 'an Under-Labourer in clearing Ground a little, and removing some of the Rubbish, that lies in the way of Knowledge'.[17] Hume's attempt to develop a 'Science of Man' in his significantly entitled *A Treatise of Human Nature: Being an Attempt to Introduce the Experimental Method of Reasoning into Moral Subjects* was prefaced by an obvious appeal to the standards of proof demanded by natural philosophy arguing that 'the only solid foundation we can give to this science itself must be laid on experience and observation. 'Tis no astonishing reflection to consider that the application of experimental philosophy to moral subjects shou'd come after that to natural at the distance of above a whole century'.[18] Natural philosophy, then, became more and more the pre-eminent branch of philosophy defining the methods and extent of other branches of philosophy. As a consequence, disciplines such as metaphysics which did not conform readily to the methods of experiment and observation employed by the eighteenth-century natural philosophers faded in their significance and standing over the course of the century.

II. OBSERVATION AND NATURAL HISTORY

Scholastic natural philosophy had grown out of a university culture which deferred to the authority of texts, whether the seminal works of Aristotle or the dense thicket of commentaries, whether supportive or critical of his principles, which had accumulated over the centuries. From this long and tenacious habit of subservience to the written text there also grew the tradition of attempting to arrive at explanations by means of logical argument – for, if the texts were regarded as authoritative, it followed that it was possible to extend their conclusions by logical deduction. Though the scholastic tradition never entirely ignored the fruits of firsthand observation and experiment, the canons of debate tended to give privileged status to those positions which could be maintained by recourse to the textual authorities rather than to empirical data. Thus the growth of natural history (the study of the animal, vegetable, and mineral kingdoms) and, with it, an increasing wealth of firsthand observations of the natural world was a major factor in the transition from the scholastic natural philosophy which still predominated in the seventeenth century to the form that natural philosophy took in the eighteenth century. As well as diminishing the speculative character of natural philosophy, the growth of natural history was eventually to assist in limiting natural philosophy to more manageable proportions: the study of nature was now divided between two fields – natural philosophy and natural history – and, by the end of the eighteenth century, natural history was more and more to lay claim to the living world.

This division of labour in the study of nature between natural philosophy and natural history was already established before the eighteenth century, having been programmatically developed by Francis Bacon in his *Advancement of Learning*. In this work Bacon argued that human knowledge was the outcome of what he considered were the three major faculties of the human mind: memory, imagination, and reason. History, whether it be a record of things past or of the study of nature, was the province of memory, poetry of imagination, while philosophy was the offspring of reason. Such a re-charting of the map of human knowledge challenged the scholastic practice of studying nature in an a priori manner, for the student of nature was henceforth expected to combine the fruits of natural history, culled from its patient record of firsthand observations and the reasoning faculties that belonged to philosophy. This need to ground explanations of the workings of nature on firsthand observation became a cliché of eighteenth-century natural philosophy: in his course of lectures at Leyden on Newtonian natural philosophy, for example, 's Gravesande insisted that 'The laws of nature cannot be obtained but from an Examination of Natural Phaenomena'.[19] It was a development particularly associated with Francis Bacon who, as Zedler put it in his *Grosses vollständiges Universal-Lexikon*, combined reason and observation in an unprecedented manner.[20]

But even in Bacon's *schema*, philosophy and, in particular, natural philosophy retained much of its traditional pre-eminence, for the task of the natural historian was that of the under-labourer collecting data which the philosopher would then incorporate into a schematic understanding of the workings of nature, an intellectually more demanding task. For in *Advancement of Learning* Bacon described the division of intellectual labour in these terms: 'natural history describeth the variety of things; physique [physics], the causes, but variable or respective causes'. He also added that to metaphysics fell the task of describing 'the fixed and constant causes',[21] but as the status of metaphysics declined in the eighteenth century this more and more left physics or natural philosophy in the superior position of being the discipline concerned with the most intellectually and prestigious mission of describing the basic causes of nature's behaviour. Such a division of labour between the natural historian as the collector of the raw data and the natural philosopher who worked with it was to become part of the accepted map of knowledge in the eighteenth century. In Britain it was perpetuated by the long shadow cast by Bacon's work. When, in 1765–6, James Scott defined natural history in his *General Dictionary of Arts and Sciences*, he termed it 'a description of the productions of the earth, air, water, &c' in contrast to natural philosophy which 'considers the powers and properties of natural bodies, and their mutual actions on one another'. Scott added, in good Baconian fashion, that natural philosophy should be firmly based on observation – that 'this science [cannot] be acquired otherwise than by observing, by means of our senses, all the objects which the author of nature has made cognizeable thereto'.[22]

The Baconian view was succinctly put by Lord Kames at the end of the eighteenth century when he remarked that 'Natural History is confined to effects, leaving causes to Natural Philosophy';[23] it was incorporated by Kames's Scottish compatriots into the structure of the third edition of the *Encyclopaedia Britannica*. With a bow to Bacon the author of the article on 'Philosophy' wrote that 'classification and arrangement is called NATURAL HISTORY; and must be considered as the only foundation of any extensive knowledge of nature'. The natural historian had a threefold task: '1. To observe with care, and describe with accuracy, the various objects of the universe. 2. To determine and enumerate all the great classes of objects. . . . 3. To determine with certainty the particular group to which any proposed INDIVIDUAL belongs'. It followed that 'DESCRIPTION therefore, ARRANGEMENT, and REFERENCE, constitute the whole of his employment; and in this consists all his science'. With such a secure empirical foundation the natural philosopher could, then, pursue his goal of 'the discovery of the laws of nature', a mission which, the article made it abundantly clear, was intellectually superior to that of the natural historian:

> There is no question that this view of the universe is incomparably more interesting and important than that which is taken by the natural historian; contemplating every thing that is of value to us, and, in short, the whole life and movement of the universe. This study, therefore, has been dignified with the name of PHILOSOPHY and of SCIENCE; and natural history has been considered as of importance only in so far as it was conducive to the successful prosecution of philosophy.[24]

On the Continent, too, the Baconian division between the natural historian who collects the empirical information on which the natural philosopher draws was entrenched by means of an even more influential encyclopedia, that of Diderot and d'Alembert. For, as an enthusiastic advocate of Bacon's method, d'Alembert incorporated into the 'Explication détaillée du systeme des connoissances humaines', which prefaced the great work, the distinction between natural history as a product of memory and philosophy (including 'The Science of Nature') as a product of reason. Nonetheless, Daubenton, an associate of Buffon and the author of the article on natural history, indicated the increasing popularity and stature that natural history was coming to enjoy in the second half of the eighteenth century: 'In the present century', he wrote, 'the science of natural history is more cultivated than it has ever been . . . at present natural history occupies the public more than experimental physics or any other science'.[25] This increasing popularity of natural history may help to explain the assertive tone of late eighteenth-century French apologists for natural philosophy such as Joseph-Aignan Sigaud de La Fond who, in his textbook on physics of 1777, reaffirmed the Baconian division between the role of the natural historian as the collector of facts and the natural philosopher as the discerner of basic causes:

> More extended than natural history, of which the sole aim is to describe the products of our globe, their varieties and their virtues . . . physics encompasses the knowledge of all material things: it not only sets out to discover the properties and qualities, but also the laws which bind them, their behaviour, and the causes which produce this.

Physics, he concluded, 'therefore encompasses all the knowledge which belongs to natural history'.[26]

Sigaud de La Fond's rather combative attitude to natural history can perhaps be explained not only by the fact that natural history was growing in importance but also because it was claiming greater intellectual stature. In the 'Initial Discourse' of his great *Histoire Naturelle* (1759), for example, Buffon urged that natural historians should rise above their traditional role of collectors of data and aspire to provide generalisations about the workings of nature: 'it is not necessary', he wrote 'to imagine even today that, in the study of natural history, one ought to limit oneself solely to the making of exact descriptions and the ascertaining of particular facts'. The task of the natural historian was now a larger one: 'we must try to raise ourselves to something greater and still more worthy of our efforts, namely: the combination of observations, the generalization of facts, linking them together by the power of analogies, and the effort to arrive at a high degree of knowledge'. By so doing, he continued, 'we are able to open new routes for the further perfection of the various branches of natural philosophy'.[27]

This increasing self-confidence of natural history owed much to the diffusion of rigorous systems of classification – and above all that of Linnaeus – which lifted natural history out of the intellectually lowly position of a collector of miscellanea to that of a science capable of bringing order to bear on the seemingly random products of the animal, vegetable, and mineral kingdoms. One symptom of the changing image of natural history was that in the first (1771) edition of the *Encyclopaedia Britannica* natural history was defined as 'that science which not only gives compleat descriptions of natural productions in general, but also teaches the method of arranging them into Classes, Orders, Genera, and Species'.[28] Since animals, plants, and, to a lesser extent, minerals were particularly suited to such classificatory methods the scope of natural history, which had once encompassed the whole of nature, became more and more associated with the study of living things. By thus rendering nature more orderly and more amenable to human needs, natural history could provide the theoretical foundation for the improvement of everyday life through the more effective exploitation of nature – a goal basic to the *Encyclopédie* and to the Enlightenment more generally. Thus, when in his *A Preliminary Discourse on the Study of Natural Philosophy* (1830) John Herschel came to define natural history, he first gave the traditional Baconian description of it 'as a collection of facts and objects presented by nature ... from which ... all sciences arise' but then added that it was, secondly, 'an assemblage of phenomena to be explained ... and of materials prepared to our hands, for the application of our principles to useful purposes'.[29]

But though the standing of natural history rose, both as a result of its increasing utility and of the greater rigour made possible by effective systems of classification, its status as a science was still limited by the traditional allocation of the investigation of causes to the realm of natural philosophy. Thus in his 'Explication détaillée du systeme des connoissances humaines' d'Alembert allocated subjects such as zoology, botany, and mineralogy to the sphere of particular physics. By the late eighteenth century, however, a number of developments help to explain why the division of effects to natural history and causes to natural philosophy was beginning to break down, enabling the emergence of a science of biology specifically concerned with the causes of the behaviour of living things. First, as confidence in the all-pervading mechanical model of the workings of nature diminished, it became possible to argue that living things needed to be explained by principles and causes other than those that applied to the inanimate world.[30] Secondly, natural historians came to argue that it was possible to arrive at patterns of causation based on historical development rather than the familiar patterns of causation based on a static worldview of particles in motion. Such a change of outlook was epitomised by Kant when, in 1775, he distinguished between the description of nature ('Naturbeschreibung') and the understanding of nature in its historical development ('Naturgeschichte').[31] It followed, then, that less and less could natural history be regarded as a preliminary to natural philosophy but rather that both were *sui generis* pursuing different goals by different routes. Such a re-conceptualisation of the role of natural history was slower to take place in Britain with its long Baconian tradition than on the Continent. It is not surprising, then, that the word 'biology' appears to have been first used in Germany by Reinhold and, subsequently, by Lamarck in France in 1802 and not to have been employed in Britain (by Stanfield) until 1813.[32]

The increasing need to take account of the fruits of the ever-widening scope of observation which was fostered by natural history helped to transform natural philosophy in a number of important ways. First, in the seventeenth and early eighteenth centuries it undermined the textually based natural philosophy of the Schools. This insistence that natural philosophy be tested against observed reality fostered the attitude summarised by Rutherforth in a mid-eighteenth-century Cambridge textbook: 'In explaining the appearance of nature, that alone can be called true philosophy, which is deduced from fact and experience'.[33] Secondly, as natural history grew in sophistication with the adoption of widely diffused systems of classification, it drew the study of animate nature – which lent itself to such a system – more and more out of the span of natural philosophy, thus limiting it (or its traditional synonym, 'physics') to a more limited and manageable range of phenomena. Last, by the end of the century, natural history began to cross the traditional divide into the realm of causation which had traditionally been reserved for natural philosophy, thus opening the way for the discipline of biology and further weakening the view that natural philosophy should take as its domain all of nature. Furthermore, the growth of biology, together with other fields such as chemistry and geology, meant that natural philosophy began to move toward the status of one discipline among others rather than an all-encompassing field of human knowledge – in short, natural philosophy was becoming metamorphosed into 'physics' in the modern sense.

III. THE GROWTH OF EXPERIMENT

Closely allied with the growing emphasis on observation was that on experiment. In Bacon's scheme of things the two were sides of one coin – the former being the study of '*nature* in *course*' and the latter 'of *nature altered* or wrought'.[34] Even more than observation, experimental evidence challenged the reliance on textual authorities and the a priori methods of deduction of scholastic natural philosophy. In the article on 'Experimental Philosophy', Chambers's encyclopedia of 1786–8 asserted that 'the great advantages the modern physics have above the ancient, is chiefly owing to this; that we have a great many more *experiments*, and that we make more use of the *experiments* we have. Their way of philosophizing was, to begin with the course of things, and argue to the effects and phenomena; ours, on the contrary proceeds from *experiments* and observations alone'. 'In effect', it continued, '*experiments*, within the last century, are come into such a vogue that nothing will pass in philosophy but what is founded on, or confirmed by, *experiment*, so that the new philosophy is almost altogether *experimental*'.[35] Another late eighteenth-century encyclopedia also used its article on 'Experimental Philosophy' to advance the view that the distinguishing difference between modern natural philosophy and that of the scholastics was the use of 'sensible experiments and observations' thanks to which 'the true physics was brought to light; it was drawn from the obscurity of the schools'.[36]

More and more, then, the scope of natural philosophy or 'physics' came to be defined by the possible range of experiments. As early as 1728, Christian Wolff in his *Discursus prœliminaris de philosophia in genere* argued that such was the importance of experiment that it was necessary 'to distinguish the science which we previously called physics from experimental physics' terming the former 'dogmatic physics'. Moreover, 'Experimental physics must precede dogmatic physics'.[37] A mid-eighteenth-century reviewer of Jean-Antoine Nollet's *Leçons de physique expérimentale* (1743–8) went further, writing that 'Apart from a few general principles . . . the entire study of physics today reduces to the study of experimental physics'.[38] An encyclopedia from the beginning of the nineteenth century made the same point even more forcibly: 'Our knowledge of nature being now found to result entirely from well-conducted experiments, the term natural philosophy has been latterly compounded with that of experimental philosophy, and indeed they seem nearly to mean the same thing'.[39] Consequently, subjects such as those connected with natural history which were less amenable to laboratory experimentation came to be pushed further to the fringes of natural philosophy.

Chemistry which drew on the methods and subject matter of both natural history and natural philosophy developed an experimental style of its own based on the analysis of substances which, by the second half of the eighteenth century, helped to give it the standing of a separate discipline. An entry on chemistry in the first *Encyclopaedia Britannica* emphasised both its experimental character and its distinctive method:

> The object and chief end of chemistry is to separate the different substances that enter into the composition of bodies; to examine each of them apart; to discover their properties and relations; to decompose those very substances, if possible; to compose them together, and combine them with others, to reunite them again into one body, so as to reproduce the original compound with all its properties. (2: 66)

By adopting such procedures, chemistry distinguished itself not only from natural philosophy but also from natural history. As Daubenton stated in his article on natural history in the *Encyclopédie*, chemistry 'begins at the point where natural history ends' for the chemist 'decomposes every natural production'. This was for Daubenton an instance of the way in which natural history was giving birth to new disciplines as the scale and intensity of the study of nature increased: 'Happy the century in which the sciences have risen to such a high point of perfection that each of the parts of natural history has become the object of other sciences which all contribute to the happiness of mankind'.[40] Thus the emphasis on experimentation which increased over the course of the eighteenth century – partly because of the increasing number and sophistication of scientific instruments – changed the scope of natural philosophy. Being less suited to the laboratory methods of the eighteenth century, the study of the living world tended to be left in the hands of the natural historians and, eventually, their scientifically more prestigious offspring, the biologists. Chemistry, the experimental discipline *par excellence*, was, by the end of the eighteenth century, growing so rapidly thanks to a set of distinctive laboratory practices that it more and more inhabited a scientific world of its own.

Experiment also was corrosive of a unified body of theory, whether Newtonian or Cartesian, which in the late seventeenth and much of the eighteenth centuries linked together the study of nature in all its different guises. The work at Leyden of the great Dutch experimentalists and teachers, 's Gravesande and Musschenbroek, did much to popularise and promote the use of experimental methods;[41] these men were, in practice, for all their avowed allegiance to

Newton, eclectic in their use of experimental methods drawing on both the Cartesian and Newtonian traditions. As Brunet stresses, in the pursuit of experimental data, the Dutch physicists were willing 'to turn their back on all metaphysical discussions or demonstrations' and 'to see in hypotheses no more than suggestions essentially provisional and precarious'.[42] The increasing emphasis on experiment, then, allowed greater room for a plurality of positions in relation to such philosophical fundamentals as the nature of matter or attraction. As a consequence, separate scientific disciplines such as chemistry or biology could emerge without being inhibited, as in the past, by the attempt to explain all natural phenomena by a set of scientifically consistent principles.

By the end of the eighteenth century, then, natural philosophy had been more and more reduced to a core of subjects which were linked by the fact that they could still be largely explained in terms of a mechanical model as well as being particularly amenable to being investigated by experiment. The *Encyclopaedia Britannica* of 1797 defined natural philosophy, in true mechanical fashion, as the 'science which considers the powers and properties of natural bodies, and their mutual actions on one another'. The four major parts of natural philosophy it defined as 'Mechanics, Hydrostatics, Optics, and Astronomy', all subjects open to experimental investigation with the notable exception of astronomy which retained its place within the fold of natural philosophy by right of tradition and because of its primacy within the mechanical model of the workings of the universe. To these four, it continued, there should now be added as a result of 'Modern discoveries' (that is, experiments) the fields of 'magnetism and electricity' (12: 670). In short, by the end of the eighteenth century the study of natural philosophy was beginning to assume the character of physics as it was to be understood in the nineteenth century. Physics was no longer the study of *all* natural phenomena; it had become one discipline among an increasing number of other scientific disciplines – a change which weakened that confidence in the fundamental unity of all the sciences which the seventeenth century had bequeathed to the eighteenth.[43]

IV. MATHEMATICS

Along with observation and experiment, the mathematisation of the study of nature was the third major development in undermining scholastic natural philosophy and in shaping the forms of natural philosophy which emerged over the course of the seventeenth century to dominate the eighteenth. The growth of experiment and the growth of a mathematically based natural philosophy were linked, since experimental evidence of a numerical kind was, by its nature, suited to mathematical treatment. Before mathematics can be used in physics it is necessary to have measurements of physical quantities. But making measurements was, like doing experiments, an unphilosophical activity alien to the scholastic tradition. Thus the use of experiment and of mathematics was frequently coupled, particularly by those advocating change in the traditional scholastic curriculum. When Gershom Carmichael reshaped the course in natural philosophy at the University of Glasgow at the end of the seventeenth century, he stressed the need to take account of 'ye two great Hinges of Naturall Philosophy, or rather ye constituent parts of it... Mathematicall Demonstration & Experiment'.[44] The increasing sophistication of measuring instruments over the course of the eighteenth century made this marriage between experiment and mathematics even more fruitful as translating experimental data into mathematical terms became more and more possible.[45] It was an association on which Matthew Young remarked in 1800 in a Trinity College Dublin textbook on natural philosophy when surveying 'The obstacles which impeded the Ancients in founding a rational system of Physics', namely, 'First, the want of many instruments discovered by the moderns. Secondly, their not having recourse to Mathematical reasoning. Thirdly the influence of the Aristotelic Philosophy'.[46]

Young's last point – 'the influence of the Aristotelic Philosophy' – was of particular relevance to the association between natural philosophy and mathematics since in the traditional scholastic scheme of things the two areas of knowledge had been separated and frequently taught by different professors, thus further strengthening the institutional divide. Scholastic physics was concerned with extended being insofar as it was qualified not quantified; conversely, in the traditional curriculum, mathematics concentrated on being insofar as it was quantified and regarded changes in quality (such as motion) as beyond its realm.[47] This legacy cast a long shadow, leaving its mark on even some of the most vehement critics of scholastic natural philosophy. Bacon, for example, continued to separate mathematics from natural philosophy arguing that 'it [was] more agreeable to the nature of things and to the light of order to place it as a branch of Metaphysique'.[48] In France, the Cartesian tradition, in which mathematics was less integrated into the structure of natural philosophy than in the Newtonian tradition, helped to reinforce this ancient divide. Thus in his 'Explication détaillée du systeme des connoissances humaines', d'Alembert, influenced both by Bacon and Descartes, separated mathematics and its applications from particular physics. Moreover, his article in the *Encyclopédie* on 'Expérimental' accorded mathematics a privileged position over and above experimental evidence. For d'Alembert advanced the view that the laws of motion could be derived almost solely from 'geometry' (that is, mathematics), relegating experiment simply to the role of providing a check on such mathematically derived theory. Such views led his friend the Abbé Bossut to comment that d'Alembert 'had little respect for simple observers, practical mechanics'.[49]

But resistance to consummating fully the marriage between mathematics and experiment faded as the fruitfulness of such a coupling became ever more evident. The origins of mathematisation of nature derived from Galileo, but it was Newton's example which, over the course of the eighteenth century, did most to extinguish the last vestiges of the traditional view that natural philosophy and mathematics inhabited different intellectual domains. At the end of the eighteenth century the English *New Royal Encyclopaedia* could look back with native pride (in its article on philosophy) on the way in which England's most famous scientific son had established the true path of philosophy:

> The present method of philosophising, established by Sir Isaac Newton, is to find out the laws of nature by experiments and observations. To this, with a proper application of geometry, is owing the great advantage the present system of philosophy has over all the preceding ones, and the vast improvements it has received within the last age.

The application of geometry, the author insisted, was of particular significance for without it 'we can never be certain whether the causes we assign be adequate to the effects we would explain, as the various systems of philosophy, built on other foundations, evidently shew'.[50]

Important as Newton's example was, the coupling of mathematics with experiment owed much to other sources, notably the Dutch universities; most of these institutions were relatively new, compared to many European universities, and more open to institutional innovations such as the merging of the teaching of mathematics and natural philosophy. At Leyden, as early as 1682, the chair of natural philosophy was combined with mathematics, an innovation marked by an address decrying the scientifically deleterious effects of the long separation of the two disciplines and commending the advances in the science of motion which had been achieved by an alliance between these two fields.[51] This tradition of fruitfully combining the study of mathematics and natural philosophy continued at Leyden, strengthened by the introduction of Newtonian natural philosophy by Musschenbroek and 's Gravesande in the early eighteenth century. Though, as we have seen, both men actively promoted the application of experiments in natural philosophy, they also took the view that the proper outcome of experimentation was a more rigorous mathematisation of the study of natural philosophy.[52] Significantly, an edition of 's Gravesande's lectures was entitled *Physices elementa mathematica, experimentis confirmata* (Mathematical Elements of Natural Philosophy, confirmed by Experiments). In this work 's Gravesande went so far as to argue that 'Physics belongs to Mixed Mathematics. The Properties of Bodies and the Laws of Nature, are the Foundations of Mathematical

Reasonings'. Experimental evidence should, of course, provide the foundation for any study of physics, but the further elaboration of such experimentally derived data belonged to the realm of mathematics. 'In Physics then we are to discover the Laws of Nature by the Phaenomena, then by Induction prove them to be general Laws; all the rest is to be handled Mathematically'.[53] For Musschenbroek, as for 's Gravesande, such a combination of experiment and mathematics served to act as a check on the philosophical speculation that had for so long been a source of debate and division among students of natural philosophy. Unbridled quests for hypotheses, declared Musschenbroek in his *Elementa physicae*, had at last been overcome 'and in their place have come proper geometric demonstrations, careful observations, and purposeful experiments'.[54]

By the end of the century the equation of natural philosophy or physics with the mathematical treatment of experimentally derived data had become widely accepted. In the system of classification adopted by the Koninklijke Maatschappij der Wetenschappen in 1807, 'physics' was included under the heading of 'experimental and mathematical sciences'. A nineteenth-century English encyclopaedia acknowledged that the term 'physics' was used both to describe 'the application of mathematics to material phenomena' and 'the science of experiment'.[55]

The increasing reliance on experimental evidence in the study of natural philosophy and the increasing rigour of the mathematical treatment of the data thus acquired combined to narrow the traditional span of natural philosophy. Both factors restricted the range of subjects that the natural philosopher could study, since eighteenth-century methods of experiment and, *a fortiori*, of mathematical reasoning were of little use in accounting for the behaviour of animate nature. The increasingly complex character of mathematics also brought in its wake growing specialisation as the different areas of natural philosophy became the domain of a few experts.[56] Like the impact of experiment, then, the mathematisation of natural philosophy hastened its transition to physics in its modern sense. By the nineteenth century less and less could natural philosophy lay claim to its traditional function of providing explanation for all natural phenomena as its subject matter shrank to mathematically and experimentally manageable proportions. But what natural philosophy had lost in breadth it had gained in depth, and in its new disciplinary guise of physics it was to show the continuing potency of the Galilean programme for the mathematisation of nature.[57]

NOTES

1 Thomas Hankins, *Science and the Enlightenment* (Cambridge, 1985), 46.

2 John Harris, *Lexicon Technicum: or, An Universal English Dictionary of Arts and Sciences*, 2 vols., (London, 1704–10) vol. 1, s.v. 'Physicks'.

3 Charles Schmitt, 'Towards a Reassessment of Renaissance Aristotelianism', *History of Science* 11(1973), 159–93; and William Wallace, 'Traditional Natural Philosophy' in *The Cambridge History of Renaissance Philosophy*, eds. C. Schmitt, Q. Skinner, and E. Kessler (Cambridge, 1988), 201–35.
4 John Gascoigne, 'A Reappraisal of the Role of the Universities in the Scientific Revolution', in *Reappraisals of the Scientific Revolution*, eds. D. C. Lindberg and R. S. Westman (Cambridge, 1990) 251–20.
5 William T. Costello, *The Scholastic Curriculum at Early Seventeenth-Century Cambridge* (Cambridge, MA, 1958), 83.
6 John Desaguliers, *A System of Experimental Philosophy Prov'd by Mechanicks* (London, 1719), 1–2.
7 Willem van 's Gravesande, *Philosophiae Newtonianae institutiones, in usus academicos* (Leiden, 1723); translated as *An Explanation of the Newtonian Philosophy in Lectures read to the Youth of the University of Leyden*, trans. E. Stone (London, 1741), 2.
8 Petrus van Musschenbroek, *Elementa physicae* (Leiden, 1734); translated as *The Elements of Natural Philosophy*, trans. J. Colson (London, 1744), 3, 5.
9 *Encyclopaedia Britannica*, 18 vols. (Edinburgh, 1797), 14: 647.
10 Hankins, *Science and the Enlightenment*, 113.
11 Jan van Swinden, *Positiones physicae*, 2 vols. (Harderwijk, 1786), 2: 2. On scholastic definitions for these terms see Mary Reif, 'Natural Philosophy in Some Early-Seventeenth-Century Scholastic Textbooks' (unpublished PhD dissertation: St. Louis University, 1962), 75.
12 Jean le Rond d'Alembert, 'Discours préliminaire', in *Encyclopédie*, 1: xvii; translated as *Preliminary Discourse to the Encyclopedia of Diderot*, trans. R. N. Schwab and W. E. Rex (Indianapolis, IN, 1963), 54. The article on 'Natur-Lehre, Natur-Kunde, Natur-Wissenschaft, Physick' in Johann Heinrich Zedler's *Grosses vollständiges Universal-Lexikon aller Wissenschaften und Künsten*, 64 vols. (Leipzig and Halle, 1732–54), 23: 1155, also divides the subject into general and particular physics.
13 Reif, 'Natural Philosophy', 54.
14 Hankins, *Science and the Enlightenment*, 11–12.
15 Musschenbroek, *Elementa physicae*; trans. 1.
16 *Encyclopaedia Britannica*, 3 vols. (Edinburgh, 1771), 2: 270.
17 John Locke, *An Essay Concerning Human Understanding*, ed. P. H. Nidditch, in the *Clarendon Edition* (1975), 9–10.
18 David Hume, *A Treatise of Human Nature*, eds. D. F. Norton and M. J. Norton, in the *Clarendon Edition* (2006), Intro 7, SBN xvi.
19 's Gravesande, *An Explanation of the Newtonian Philosophy*, 2.
20 Zedler, *Grosses vollständiges Universal-Lexikon*, s.v. 'Natur-Lehre', 23: 1162.
21 Francis Bacon, *Of the Advancement of Learning* (1605), Bk. 1, in *Works*, eds. J. Spedding, R. L. Ellis, and D. D. Heath, 14 vols. (London, 1857–74), 3: 354.
22 James Scott, *General Dictionary of Arts and Sciences*, 2 vols. (London, 1765–6), s.v. 'Natural History'.
23 Henry Home, Lord Kames, *The Gentleman Farmer* (1776; 4th ed. Edinburgh, 1798), 1
24 *Encyclopaedia Britannica* (1797), 14: 582.
25 Louis-Jean-Marie Daubenton, 'Histoire Naturelle' in *Encyclopédie*, 8: 228.
26 Joseph-Aignan Sigaud de La Fond, ed. *Élémens de physique théorique et expérimentale*, 4 vols. (Paris, 1777), 1: 1–2.
27 Georges-Louis Leclerc comte de Buffon, in *From Natural History to the History of Nature: Readings from Buffon and His Critics*, trans. and eds. J. Lyon and P. R. Sloan (Notre Dame, 1981), 121.

28 *Encyclopaedia Britannica* (1771), 2: 362.
29 John Herschel, *A Preliminary Discourse on the Study of Natural Philosophy*, facsimile of the 1830 edn., ed. M. Partridge (New York, NY, 1966), 221.
30 Hankins, *Science and the Enlightenment*, 117, Philip C. Ritterbush, *Overtures to Biology. The Speculations of Eighteenth-Century Naturalists* (New Haven, CT, 1964), 6, 186, 189.
31 'Von den verschiedenen Racen der Menschen' [1775], in *Ak*, 2, 427–43, at 434 note; translated as 'Of the Different Human Races', trans. J. M. Mikkelsen, in *The Idea of Race*, eds. R. Bernasconi and T. Lott (Indianapolis, IN, 2000), 8–26.
32 *Oxford English Dictionary*, s.v. 'biology'.
33 Thomas Rutherforth, *A System of Natural Philosophy, being a Course of Lectures in Mechanics, Optics, Hydrostatics and Astronomy*, 2 vols. (Cambridge, 1748), [i].
34 Bacon, *Advancement of Learning*, Bk. 2, in *Works*, 3: 330.
35 Ephraim Chambers, *Cyclopaedia; or, an Universal Dictionary of Arts and Sciences . . . With the Supplement and Modern Improvements Incorporated in One Alphabet* by Abraham Rees, 5 vols. (London, 1786–8), 2: s.v. 'experimental philosophy'.
36 William Hall, *The New Royal Encyclopedia*, 3 vols. (London, [1788]), 1: s.v. 'Experimental Philosophy'.
37 Christian Wolff, *Discursus prœliminaris de philosophia in genere* (Frankfurt and Leipzig, 1728); translated as *Preliminary Discourse on Philosophy in General*, trans. R. J. Blackwell (Indianapolis, IN, 1963), 54.
38 John L. Heilbron, *Electricity in the 17th & 18th Centuries: A Study of Early Modern Physics* (Berkeley, CA, 1979), 15.
39 George Gregory, *A Dictionary of Arts and Sciences*, 2 vols. (London, 1806–7), 2: 255.
40 Louis-Jean-Marie Daubenton, 'Histoire Naturelle' in *Encyclopédie*, 8 : 228.
41 Heilbron, *Electricity in the 17th & 18th Centuries*, 14.
42 Pierre Brunet, *Les physiciens Hollandais et la méthode expérimentale en France au XVIIIe siecle* (Paris, 1926), 99.
43 Hankins, *Jean d'Alembert: Science and the Enlightenment* (Oxford, 1970), 104.
44 'Gershom Carmichael's Account of His Teaching Method (1712)', MS GUL 43170, in *Natural Rights on the Threshold of the Scottish Enlightenment: The Writings of Gershom Carmichael*, trans. M. Silverthorne, eds. J. Moore and M. Silverthorne (Indianapolis, IN, 2002), 386–7.
45 A. Lundgren, 'The Changing Role of Numbers in Eighteenth-Century Chemistry' in *The Quantifying Spirit in the Eighteenth Century*, eds. T. Frängsmyr, J. L. Heilbron, and R. E. Rider (Berkeley, CA, 1990), 256–66, and Maurice Daumas, 'Precision of Measurement and Physical and Chemical Research in the Eighteenth Century' in *Scientific Change. Historical Studies in the Intellectual, Social and Technical Conditions for Scientific Discovery and Technical Invention, From Antiquity to the Present*, ed. A. C. Crombie (London, 1963), 418–30.
46 Matthew Young, *An Analysis of the Principles of Natural Philosophy* (Dublin, 1800), 3–4.
47 Costello, *The Scholastic Curriculum*, 70.
48 Bacon, *Advancement of Learning*, 98.
49 Hankins, *Jean D'Alembert*, 94–6.
50 George S. Howard, *The New Royal Cyclopaedia, and Encyclopaedia or Complete, Modern and Universal Dictionary of Arts and Science*, 3 vols. (London, 1796–1802), 3: 1589.
51 Edward G. Ruestow, *Physics at Seventeenth- and Eighteenth-Century Leiden: Philosophy and the New Science in the University* (The Hague, 1973), 108.
52 Brunet, *Les physiciens Hollandais*, 100.
53 Willem van 's Gravesande, *Physices elementa mathematica, experimentis confirmata. Sive, Introductio ad philosophiam newtonianam* (Leiden, 1720–1); translated as *Mathematical Elements of Natural*

Philosophy, confirmed by Experiments (1720–1), 2 vols., trans. J. Desaguliers, 6th edn. (London, 1747), ix, xvi.

54 Ruestow, *Physics*, 31.

55 *The English Cyclopaedia*, ed. C. Knight, 27 vols. (London, 1854–72), Div. IV, Arts and Sciences, vol. 6, s.v. 'Physics'.

56 David Miller, 'The Revival of the Physical Sciences in Britain, 1815–1840', *Osiris*, 2nd series, 2 (1986), 107–34; Crosbie Smith, '"Mechanical Philosophy" and the Emergence of Physics in Britain: 1800–1850', *Annals of Science* 33 (1976), 3–29; Michael Shortland, '"On the Connexion of the Physical Sciences": Classification and Organization in Early, Nineteenth-Century Science', *Historia Scientiarum* 41 (1990), 545–73.

57 For an analysis of the social composition of the eighteenth-century scientific community, see J. Gascoigne, 'The Eighteenth-Century Scientific Community: A Prosopographical Study', *Social Studies of Science* 25 (1995), 575–81.

30

NATURAL PHILOSOPHY

PIERRE KERSZBERG

I. NEWTON AND BEYOND

In the preface to his work on the metaphysical foundations of Newton's science, Kant wrote that 'since in any doctrine of nature there is only as much proper science as there is *a priori* knowledge therein, a doctrine of nature will contain only as much proper science as there is mathematics capable of application there'.[1] Precisely because it is so radically uncompromising, Kant's statement echoes much of the whole orientation of eighteenth-century natural philosophy.[2] The Newtonian scheme of thought was proving a perfect instrument for research because something more fundamental and more general than Newton's laws of motion had been discovered by means of mathematical exposition which was of greater universality than that employed by Newton himself. The successful outcome of such an ambitious enterprise was so significant that Kant went on to exclude chemistry from the realm of science proper on the grounds that, contrary to mathematical physics, the principles of chemistry 'are merely empirical, and allow of no *a priori* presentation in intuition . . . they do not in the least make the principles of chemical appearances conceivable with respect to their possibility, for they are not receptive to the application of mathematics' (Ak 4: 471). Kant seems not to have realised soon enough the significance of Lavoisier's work in the 1770s, which practically founded chemistry on its present basis; after Lavoisier, chemical science had only to wait for the atomic theory in the next century. However in his later, post-critical work, Kant embarked on the ambitious project of including chemical phenomena in a wider metaphysical concept. This development reflects a movement of thought characteristic of the whole of eighteenth-century science: an application and extension of Newtonian principles, which to a large extent complied with Newton's own hopes that the mode of explanation of gravity could be extended to other phenomena (electricity, magnetism, chemistry, etc.), but which finally paved the way to a synthesis that bore little resemblance to Newton's original project. D'Alembert had a perceptive anticipation of this peculiar situation, when he wrote as early as 1759 in his *Eléments de philosophie* that the remarkable discoveries of the previous century had bequeathed enthusiasm and elevation of spirit to scientists and philosophers, but ultimately this 'lively ferment, as was entirely natural, swamped all that stood against it with the violence of a river that has burst its banks.'[3] In 1767, Joseph Priestley was even more radical when he suggested that by 'pursuing this new light' offered by investigations in electricity, light, chemistry, and so on, 'new worlds may open to our view, and the glory of the great Sir Isaac Newton himself, and all his contemporaries, be eclipsed, by a new set of philosophers, in quite a new field of speculation'.[4]

The eighteenth century witnessed the rise of this wave of ideas which were needed in the following century in order to formulate a general law of conservation of energy. It was not until the middle of the nineteenth century that the final extension of the concept of energy to problems involving heat was achieved. Historically, much of the work that led to this final extension was done by the end of the eighteenth century: this is the work that clarified and brought together the several separate energy concepts, and so made possible the first general law of conservation. In many ways, this work constituted a reformulation of the rights of elementary intuitions about the world – those rights which had formed the basis of Aristotle's physics or the natural philosophy of the ancient Greek atomists. Galileo and Newton had shown that in order for the motion of bodies to be described accurately, the path of projectiles or the orbits of the planets (as well as the forces needed to account for such motions) to be analysed correctly, immediately felt experiences are deceptive and must be corrected by the proper use of the mathematical method. But when Aristotle had stated that a body should move when it is somehow pushed or pulled by an agent in direct contact, he had implicitly given plausible reasons as to *why* a body could not continue in motion in the absence of net forces or of any material agency in immediate contact with the body. Within a context of growing evidence supporting the correctness of Newton's mechanics, the formulation of the laws of conservation of mass and of momentum was an attempt to satisfy the remaining needs of basic common sense. Several old issues, such as the distinction between primary and secondary qualities, which had apparently been settled by the very successes of Newtonian science, were resurrected in the new framework.

On the other hand, the eighteenth century also saw the rise of experimental physics (in areas such as heat and electricity), where the significance of mathematics was debated. Some, like Diderot, Buffon, and Franklin, believed that the excessive use of mathematics in physics leads the scientist away from nature.[5] Diderot, in particular, argued that mathematics is always circular because it deals with its own concepts, and therefore it has no direct access to empirical reality; a new ideal must be advocated for physics, which is purely descriptive and not axiomatic. Against this view, d'Alembert argued in the 'Discours préliminaire' to the *Encyclopédie* that mathematics was basic for all physics because the relationship between properties of bodies 'is almost always the only object we are permitted to attain'.[6] A good illustration of this ambiguity is provided by the work of the Dutch physicist W. J. 'sGravesande: even though he emphasized the importance of mathematics in experimental physics, it turned out to play only a minor role in his actual work. 'sGravesande is one of those Dutch Newtonians who still attached particular significance to the Aristotelian elements. In fact, the scientific world in the eighteenth century generally did accept a whole set of imponderables and ethers that bore a striking resemblance to scholastic categories. Not until late in the century did physicists undertake to quantify concepts such as temperature, specific heat, and charge, much as Newton had discovered that he could describe the phenomena of gravity mathematically without supposing any ether or any other occult quality.

The whole century is dominated by one philosophical figure, Immanuel Kant, who was able to adjust the rationalism of the previous century to the conditions and limits of scientific experience. The sections of this essay are organized in such a way that the Kantian interpretation emerges as pivotal for the intelligibility of the progress of science in the eighteenth century. However, it must be pointed out that certain areas of science (such as electricity), which came to be fully developed only in the following century, are atypical because they fail to fall within the range of metaphysics. In these areas, which are theologically and cosmologically neutral, new instruments, not metaphysical commitments, gave the main impulse to the development of theory.

II. MECHANICS

Newton had thought of matter as inert, in the sense that it has an innate tendency to resist movement; its inertial force is a passive principle, whereby it acts only when acted upon from outside. Gravitation was one of those active principles which would supply the necessary action. In the eighteenth century, both Newtonians and anti-Newtonians shared a fundamental problem-situation: Should or could one describe the universe in terms of discrete particles with forces acting between them; can force act through a vacuum; are forces essential properties of matter? Despite their disagreement over the foundation and ultimate meaning of physical theory, in practice the Newtonian experimental philosophers thought in much the same way as their Cartesian counterparts. Ether was to the Newtonian what subtle matter was to the Cartesian; each side thought highly of experimentation and the need to achieve quantification.

Thus, Maupertuis was soon followed by many other scientists and philosophers when he called attention to the fact that the Newtonian force of attraction is no less intelligible than the Cartesian impulsion, for we have no conception of the true cause of either. At the level of the foundation of physical theory, however, the concept of force remains as foreign to the Cartesians as it is inseparable from the Newtonian viewpoint. Accordingly, Cartesian mathematical rationalists aimed at developing mechanics as a branch of mathematics. For the Cartesians, matter was inert in the sense that it has only geometrical qualities, so that action comes from collisions between bodies. The entire physical universe imagined by Descartes was likened to a clockwork mechanism. In order to ensure that the world machine would not run down, Descartes argued, there must be a principle of conservation of the quantity of motion, defined as the product of mass times the speed of an object. The total quantity of motion of all the parts in the world, or in any isolated system, must then be constant at all times, even though transfers of motion from one body to another occur constantly by collisions.

As it turned out, two flaws undermined the proposed law. First, the law is not sufficient to determine the outcome of a collision. Secondly, speed is a scalar quantity, whereas experiments indicated that the outcome of a collision depends also on the directions of motion. In the second half of the seventeenth century, Huygens and others had redefined the law: what is conserved is the total momentum of a system, where momentum is defined by the product mass times vector velocity. However, unless all collisions of objects are completely elastic (as, for example, when two objects bounce back with the same speeds as before the collision, but in opposite directions), the total momentum of the world machine will continually decrease, indicating the possibility that eventually it will come to a halt. Huygens had already proposed that in the special case of perfectly elastic collisions, another scalar quantity must be conserved in addition to momentum: the product mass times the square of velocity. This quantity, which became known as *vis viva* ('living force', or kinetic energy), provided a means for determining the outcome of a collision if the initial masses and velocities are known. While Newton operated with four fundamental notions (space, time, mass, and force), for Leibniz, too, the concept of force was fundamental, but its conservation was at the core of his scientific metaphysics. The *vis viva* was thought by Leibniz to be the only dynamic quantity that was actually conserved in the universe, and in the eighteenth century, arguments were proposed as to whether it corresponded to any real thing.[7] A fairly common assumption of the time was that the law of inertia, and hence the existence of absolute space and absolute time, could be demonstrated by means of the Leibnizian principle of sufficient reason. Thus Euler argued in his *Réflexions sur l'espace et le temps* that for the determination of motion to be possible, 'both absolute space and time, as conceived by the mathematicians, had to be real things that exist also outside our imagination.'[8] Yet, in trying to make the concept of inertia intelligible, Euler's Leibnizian spirit led him to refuse to grant Newtonian inertia the status of a force: inertia is the essence of passivity, whereas force is the essence of activity. He suggested that inertia should rather be called 'Standhaftigkeit', perseverance. His key notion is that of power, which is the force that sets in motion a body at rest, or which alters the motion of a body.[9] Just as Newton had distinguished between absolute and relative space and time, Euler argued that power could be either absolute or relative. While the latter acts in accordance with whether a body is at rest or in motion, the former acts always in the same way: such is the force of gravitation.

The Leibnizian approach tallied with the theory of monads and a mode of explanation in terms of internal principles: in inelastic collisions, where the *vis viva* seemed to disappear, it was supposed to be transferred to the invisible particles making up bodies. The question thus became: is mv or mv^2 the true quantity of motion? At the centre of the debate was the career of the Marquise du Châtelet, who in 1733 became Voltaire's companion in the study of science and literature. Much to Voltaire's dismay, her early commitment to Newton was shaken by exposure to Leibniz's thought in 1736. In 1740, she published the *Institutions de physique*, which was instrumental in spreading Leibniz's philosophy in France.[10] Early experiments by 'sGravesande about 1720 had seemed to favour kinetic energy. The dents left in clay by a body falling into it were proportional to the kinetic energy, not the momentum. In the second edition of his *Traité de dynamique* in 1758, d'Alembert put an end to the dispute and showed that it was merely about words. Indeed, he demonstrated that the conservation of *vis viva* is not a principle at all, but merely a theorem which can be deduced from the laws of dynamics. The living force corresponds to a work: for a falling body, work is the product of the weight of the body and the height from which it falls, that is (using Galileo's law), velocity squared. Thus, d'Alembert was the first to free mechanics from the bond of metaphysical considerations. His programme was that all that can be theorized in physics must be reduced to the smallest number of fundamental principles, which are the more fruitful as they are general. In 1743, d'Alembert gave his name to a principle which reduces all motions of a system of solid bodies acting upon one another through any kind of interaction to Newton's three fundamental laws of mechanics. By means of Newton's laws, any motion of bodies interacting within a system could be reduced to the equilibrium resulting from the interactions.

Newton's laws of motion, in their original formulation, were applicable only to particles, that is, to pieces of matter which were small enough to be treated as points, and so could have definite positions, velocities, and accelerations unambiguously assigned to them. Every body is of course made up of particles, so that in principle, one can deduce its motion from Newton's laws, but the passage from the general principles to the solution of a particular problem may be long and difficult. There was an obvious need to find general methods for effecting this passage.

The decisive advance was made by Lagrange, who transformed Newton's laws so that they were applicable to the most general system of bodies imaginable. However complicated a system may be, its configuration can always be described by a sufficient number of generalized coordinates, the changes of which tell us all about its motion. Lagrange showed how to obtain this knowledge by purely routine methods. The other great gain he achieved stemmed from an attempt to unify the principles of mechanics and optics. He demonstrated that the laws of propagation of light and the laws of the motion of material bodies are similar in form; in each case a certain quantity assumes its minimum value. Already in antiquity Hero of Alexandria had shown that a ray of light always followed a path of minimum length, and this is true even if the ray is reflected by one or more mirrors. As light always travels at the same speed in air, a path of minimum length is also a path of minimum time. In the seventeenth century, the law of refraction of light (known as Snell's law, though it is normally attributed to Descartes) was discovered, following which Fermat showed that refracted light conformed to this same principle of minimum time, provided that the speed of light depended on the substance through which it was travelling. In his *Essai de cosmologie* of 1751, Maupertuis then conjectured that *all* natural phenomena must conform to some similar principle. His reasons were theological and metaphysical rather than scientific, because he thought that final causes had to be rehabilitated in natural philosophy. The perfection of the universe demanded a certain economy in nature which would be opposed to any needless expenditure of activity, so that the natural motions must be such as to make some quantity a minimum; it was the kind of general principle that was to pave the way for the various syntheses successfully achieved a century later. The main difficulty, however, was to find the quantity in question. It could no longer be the time, since to make this a minimum all objects would have to dash through space at the highest speeds of which they were capable. Maupertuis introduced a quantity which he called the 'action' of motion. It was the time of the movement multiplied by the average value of the *vis viva* throughout this time, and he thought that this quantity ought to assume a minimum value when bodies moved in their natural way; he called this the principle of least action. Leibniz had already spoken of a 'principe de la route la plus facile', but this implied that the speed increased with the resistance of the medium. Even though Maupertuis restricted his investigation to the deduction of the laws of propagation of light from his own principle of least action, he postulated the validity of the principle for all the motions and operations of nature. While Euler had advanced arguments in support of the principle, Lagrange, in his *Mécanique analytique* of 1788, produced positive proof that the action would be a minimum if objects moved in accordance with Newtonian mechanics; in other words, the principle of least action was simply a transformation of the Newtonian laws of motion. This new principle did not involve any explicit reference to generalized coordinates; these had formed merely a useful scaffolding in establishing the principle, but they were removed before the principle was exhibited in its final form.

The principle of least action reduced every problem of dynamics to a problem of algebra. In the preface to his treatise on analytical mechanics, Lagrange explained that the plan of his treatise was entirely new, because the solution of any problem in mechanics was now reduced to the simple development of general formulae. These methods required neither geometrical nor mechanical construction or reasoning but only algebraic operations.

III. DYNAMIC ASTRONOMY

The first science to benefit from Lagrange's revolution was astronomy. Newton had obtained his principal results by using simplifying assumptions, avoiding the intricacy of the actual motions found in the solar system. Thus he treated the planets as perfect spheres, or even as points, and had usually assumed that they moved under the influence only of the sun's attraction, the moon only under that of the earth, and so on. Laplace, sometimes known as the French Newton, set himself the task of refining this analysis, hoping (as he put it in his *Exposition du système du monde* of 1796) to offer a complete solution of the great mechanical problem presented by the solar system. This amounted to bringing theory to coincide so closely with observation that empirical equations would no longer find a place in astronomical tables; all celestial movements would become no more than arbitrary constants in a general problem of mechanics, so that even the discovery of a new heavenly body would necessarily conform to Newtonian principles.[11] Among the many problems Laplace treated (the tides of the oceans, the flattened shapes of the earth and other planets, etc.), two in particular are worth mentioning.

The first figured in Laplace's earliest scientific paper, which he contributed to the Académie des Sciences in 1773.[12] The planets do not move round the sun in the perfect ellipses we should expect if the sun alone controlled their movements. The other planets act on them as well and continually drag their orbits out of shape; these orbits can be imagined so greatly altered that, for instance, the earth might ultimately become uninhabitable. Laplace attempted to show that there is no ground for such fears. This result was in direct opposition to the ideas of Newton, who had thought that the mutual action of planets and comets on one another would produce irregularities 'which will be apt to increase, till this system wants a Reformation' at the hand of its Creator.[13] The instability which Newton had predicted could not occur, as Laplace was able to demonstrate that these interactions would simply cause the average distances between the planets and the sun to oscillate periodically within finite limits. Newton's laws by themselves guaranteed the stability of the solar system over indefinitely large periods of time, both past and future; God is not needed.

The second example comes from the *Systême du monde*. Laplace remarked that the planets all move in the same direction around the sun, and that their satellites all move in this same direction round their planets. In Query 31, Newton had already commented on this regularity and suggested that 'blind Fate could never make all the Planets move one and the same way in Orb concentrick' (378). Again, he attributed the regularity to an order which had been introduced by God, such that occasional re-establishment at His hand would be compatible with it; such order could not arise out of chaos by the mere laws of nature. Even though Laplace rejected mere chance, he held a different view of the origin of the regularity in the solar system. In his famous nebular hypothesis as to the origin of the planets, he considered that the natural causes which had produced the planets could also produce the regularity; the hypothesis of God was simply unnecessary. At the time of its appearance, and for many years after, Laplace's model was widely accepted as a plausible and interesting conjecture. According to this model, the sun had begun as a nebulous mass of hot gas in a state of rotation. It gradually cooled, and as it cooled it shrank. Using Newtonian mechanics, it was possible to show that the mass would rotate ever faster and faster as it shrank. Since Laplace had already shown that the oval-shaped flattening of the earth and planets resulted from their rotations – the faster the planet rotated, the flatter it would become – he went on to suppose that as the sun rotated ever faster, its shape became ever flatter until it assumed a disk-like shape. At the point where it could flatten no further, it broke into pieces by shedding successive rings of matter from its protruding equator. These rings of matter could either condense into a planet, disintegrate into the group of asteroids discovered between Mars and Jupiter in the nineteenth century, or even form the rings circling Saturn. The planets, too, would start as masses of hot rotating gas and would go through the same series of changes as their parent sun before them; they too would cool, shrink, flatten in shape, and finally throw off rings of matter which would in time condense, thus forming the satellites of the planets. This was a plausible explanation of why the planets and satellites were all revolving and rotating in the same direction: the direction was that in which the primeval sun had rotated.

Until the publication of James Hutton's epoch-making *Theory of the Earth* (1785; 2nd ed. 1795), virtually all scientists and philosophers had found good reasons for believing that the earth was originally formed in a hot, molten state and had subsequently cooled down, solidifying at least on the outside. One indication was provided by the presence of rocks on the surface of the earth which appeared to have been formed by the action of fire. Jean Sylvain Bailly in *Histoire de l'astronomie* (1775–87) then further conjectured that all the planets must have an internal heat and were now at some particular stage of cooling; all bodies in the universe were cooling off and would eventually reach a final state of equilibrium with no motion, so that they became too cold to support life. While Hutton accepted the hypothesis that the inside of the earth was now much hotter than the surface, he did not believe that there had been any cooling during past epochs. Basing himself on the continuing existence of subterranean fire, he proposed a cyclic view of the earth's history, with periods of erosion and denudation leading to destruction of mountains and possibly entire continents, followed by consolidation of sediments and uplifting of new continents. The Huttonian system was thus reminiscent of the kind of periodical variations discovered by Laplace in the solar system. Contrary to Newton's opinion, the laws of nature do not carry in themselves the elements of their own destruction. Ironically enough, although the successes of Newtonian planetary theory seemed to vindicate the view of the world as a machine, speculations about the earth's interior sowed the seeds for another approach. Early in the nineteenth century, Fourier was to develop a theory of heat conduction in solids which helped solve quantitatively the problem of terrestrial temperatures. But Fourier's heat conduction equation, unlike Newton's laws of motion, is irreversible with respect to time.

IV. OBSERVATIONAL ASTRONOMY AND THEORETICAL COSMOLOGY

The two principal contributors to observational astronomy are James Bradley and William Herschel. Bradley measured the positions of a number of stars with unheard-of accuracy, and used his discovery of the aberration of light to prove that light travelled with finite speed. Herschel is best known for his discovery of the planet Uranus in 1781, which made a great sensation at the time, since only five planets had been known from ancient times. Herschel established beyond doubt that the sun is a member of a great system of stars which is isolated in space and bounded by the stars of the Milky Way. His studies suggested that the entire system is in motion, shaped like a wheel or a millstone. Furthermore, he studied double and binary stars, and calculated that many such pairs consisted of stars revolving around one another in just the kinds of orbits that the Newtonian law of gravitation required.[14]

The case of binary stars is a remarkable extension of Newton's law of gravitation, which proves that it is not merely a local effect but extends throughout space. This seems to make possible a way out of a logical dilemma at the basis of Newtonian science. Newton had shown that gravitation extends to great distances, and by the middle of the eighteenth century there were three spectacular confirmations of this. Alexis Claude Clairaut and Euler announced a discrepancy between the inverse square law and the motion of the moon, but a few years later admitted their own error of calculation;[15] expeditions to Peru and Lapland showed that the shape of the earth was flattened at the poles, which tallied with Newton's prediction (where Descartes could hardly make one); and in 1759 Halley's comet returned almost on time and in the orbit predicted by Newton.[16] But when all is said and done, is it really true that everything attracts everything else? Is it possible to make a direct test and not just wait to see whether the planets, or other heavenly bodies yet to be discovered, attract each other? A direct test was made by Henry Cavendish, who called his experiment 'weighing the earth'. The idea was to hang by a very fine fibre a rod with two balls. Because of the attraction of the balls there would be a slight twist to the fibre, and the gravitational force between ordinary things, even if very tiny, could be measured.[17] Cavendish's results, and all the more accurate ones since, have shown that the constant of gravitation has indeed the same value, no matter what the composition of the two masses. From then on, it could safely be argued, in the absence of evidence to the contrary, that all materials in the world, including sun, planets, and satellites, obey the same law of gravitation. Thus, Herschel's discovery of Uranus, in widening the ancient horizon, proved empirically the heuristic value of Newton's gravitational theory at the large-scale level of the heavens. He had patiently looked at and re-examined every corner of the heavens, finding new stars, nebulae, and comets. Herschel discovered Uranus one night in 1781 when he found a celestial object, hitherto uncatalogued and of 'uncommon appearance'. By that time, astronomers knew how to compute the elliptic orbit of a planet from a few widely separated observations of its varying positions. Also, the expected small deviations from the true ellipse owing to the perturbing force of the other planets were accurately predictable on the basis of Newton's law of gravitation. Uranus's orbit was mapped out by calculation. Herschel was also convinced that not every nebulosity in the sky could be resolved by increased telescopic power. In Laplace's scheme, some nebulae could serve as a point of attraction for the formation of stars and planetary systems.

Thus, in addition to the first systematic typology of nebulae, Herschel speculated on what he called 'the great laboratories of nature', that is, those seats of physico-chemical transformations in which entire cosmic processes of condensation and fragmentation could be generated or modified. In so doing, he was probably echoing the eighteenth-century search for a Newtonian active principle in the universe.[18] In fact, the achievements of Laplace and Herschel are quite typical of the turn of the nineteenth century. Cosmological theory and observation began to be systematic, based on the self-sufficiency of Newtonian gravitation and the use of probabilities in accounting for the emergence of physical structures; they no longer rested on a priori arguments or on narrowly selected facts.

Before this work could be achieved, cosmology in the first half of the eighteenth century was dominated by attempts to reconcile Newtonian principles and the Cartesian cosmogonical model based on the vortex theory of motion.[19] The fusion was never successful because Descartes did not allow for an interplanetary void – and it was precisely this void that, in the Newtonian system, allowed interpenetrating but seemingly independent orbits such as those of the planets and the comets. These attempts culminated in Daniel Bernoulli's model of the 1730s, in which the emergence of planets and comets was accounted for in terms of an extended solar atmosphere. This atmosphere, however, was so tenuous that it really bore little resemblance to Descartes's original model. Earlier, Jean Bernoulli had already suggested the existence of an ether with negligible inertia, which would explain both gravity by contact and the free motion of comets. One advantage of the vortex theory was that it gave a physical, not a supernatural, explanation of the fact that planetary orbits, however random their initial distributions may be, all move close to the plane of the solar equator. In Bernoulli's model, the density of the vortex decreases with the distance, which explains why comets can move so far apart from the plane of the solar equator. On the other hand, all planets should be dragged exactly in the plane after an infinite time.

The merit of this model was to throw light on the need to conceive of the solar system as an evolutionary system – an idea quite alien to Newton's original law of gravitation. When Laplace proposed his nebular hypothesis, he said that he knew of no one except Buffon who had given any thought to the matter of the origin of the solar system; Buffon's theory was quite different, since it argued that the planets had resulted from some astronomical object (a comet) crashing into the sun and splashing out planets. Laplace was probably unaware that Kant, in an early work of 1755 (*Allegemeine Naturgeschichte und Theorie des Himmels*), had already propounded a model of the origin of the solar system which has some striking resemblances to his own. Kant is more speculative and less plausible scientifically.[20] For instance, Kant argued that the sun had acquired its rotation through shrinkage: this was the basis of an attempt to account for the very origin of motion in the universe. But it turns out to be a mathematical impossibility, because such a model violates the law of conservation of angular momentum. (Bear in mind, however, that only with Euler in 1775 was the relationship between force and acceleration as we know it today fully spelled out, and it is from this formulation that the law of conservation followed.[21]) Laplace started with a proto-sun already in a state of slow rotation, because the solar system could not generate its own angular momentum from nothing. Kant, however, had made another astronomical speculation which soon became recognized. In 1742, in his *Discours sur les différentes figures des astres*, Maupertuis had described nebulae, which are faint fuzzy-looking objects, of which only very few can be seen without powerful telescopic aid. Since they are small luminous patches of very feeble light, having in common shapes that are more or less open ellipses, Maupertuis conjectured that they might be immense suns, flattened by rotation. Kant, on the other hand, was bold enough to speculate that a nebula is not a solitary sun, but a very remote system of stars which appear crowded, because of their distance, into a space so limited that their light combines to a give a pale lustre. In other words, the many nebulae scattered throughout the universe testified to the existence of a multitude of Milky Ways. This interpretation became known as the island universe theory, which has stood the test of time. Kant was inspired by Thomas Wright who had conjectured that not just the earth but the sun itself should lose its privileged central position, by proposing a Milky-Way-like model for the entire system of stars.[22] Kant's early speculations were highly distinctive, although he later dismissed the absolute validity of any rational cosmology. His model was a dynamic one, derived from the concept of the simplest possible conditions prevailing at the moment of creation. The very existence of an attractive force at a central point (endowed with a sort of transgeometric function) was derived from an infinite diversity of specific densities among the primitive particles; the production of organized material entities would follow from the instability of primeval chaos. In this universe, a sphere of ever more highly organized systems is continually expanding from the point of highest specific density. By identifying creation and organization in this way, Kant wanted to prove that the material powers of the world can only exhibit a divine, pre-established harmony.

Halley in 1721 and Jean de Chéseaux in 1744 investigated the paradox according to which stars distributed uniformly throughout an infinite universe should result in a sky ablaze with light. When in the nineteenth century this became known as Olbers's paradox, it was sometimes argued that a kind of specific spacing between the stars or the galaxies could annihilate the paradox. In fact, in 1761, Johann Friedrich Lambert, who thought the Milky Way was only one member in a chain of similarly structured systems of stars, proposed in his *Kosmologische Briefe über die Einrichtung des Weltbaues*[23] the first-known hierarchical model of the universe with stars forming galaxies, galaxies forming clusters, clusters becoming superclusters, and so on.

V. THE CRITIQUE OF SCIENTIFIC REASON

In the *Kritik der reinen Vernunft*, Kant was concerned with the conditions of possibility of the knowledge of nature in general.[24] In the celebrated preface to the second edition (1787), he described that dual character of spectators of nature who are at the same time active (through experimentation) and passive (which they must be if nature is to teach them anything at all): he referred to the work of Galileo or Torricelli in terms of reason which 'has insight only into what it itself produces according to its own design; . . . it must . . . compel nature to answer its questions'.[25] This formulation enabled Kant to identify the supposed basis of any possible natural science with the total possibilities of experience, which is a far cry from positing some sort of suprasensible prototype of experience. These total possibilities were expressed in transcendental principles of understanding, which supply the formal structure of thought (combinations of mind-dependent categories) without which no objective experience could be given. These principles are judgments which have the peculiarity of being both synthetic (material) and a priori (conceptual), whereas in pre-critical philosophy, a priori conceptual knowledge would be analytical knowledge of the purely intelligible world, not the world of sense experience. According to Kant, the discovery of the transcendental principles of understanding was made possible thanks to their similarity with the propositions of mathematics, which he took to be synthetic a priori as well, and not merely analytical. In his *Metaphysische Anfangsgründe der Naturwissenschaft*, he went on to argue that no genuine science of nature, dealing with determinate things (not nature in a formal sense), could rest on merely empirical foundations. What, then, is its a priori basis?

Newton's works were always for Kant the paradigmatic model of any science. He considered universal gravity to be an a priori truth, that is, the highest expression of all synthetic a priori judgments. Yet, in *Metaphysische Anfangsgründe*, where he treats the general conception of matter as such, interesting differences occur.[26] In accordance with his view that a general science of nature cannot be built up in disregard of the transcendental principles of understanding and experience, Kant proposes to analyse the concept of matter under the four headings of his table of categories – quantity, quality, relation, and modality. The progressive explication of the concept of matter is supposed to provide a complete analysis of it, thereby justifying the application of mathematics to the knowledge of material bodies. The work thus divides into four sections. Each section is to consider the concept of matter in one of its aspects and each is said to add a new determination to it. In defining matter in its basic sense, Kant states that motion is fundamental, and all other predicates of matter are said to find their ground in it. 'Das Bewegliche' means something which is capable of moving or of being moved; it embraces both the fact of the motion and a 'that which' moves. The subject-matter of the four sections is determined accordingly. The definition of matter according to the Phoronomy (what we today would call kinematics) states that matter is the movable in space (pure quantum of motion); this is the purely geometrical aspect of motion. The definition according to the Dynamics states that matter is the movable inasmuch as it fills a space: it has the quality of an original power of motion, since this filling contains the fundamental forces which reside in matter. In the Mechanics, matter is considered as having a moving force as a consequence of the motion of material bodies and their mutual actions. In the Phenomenology, matter is seen as having motion or rest relative to a mode of representation, that is, as appearance of outer sense.

The Phoronomy contains the principles of the application of the category of quantity to matter in motion. Under what conditions does matter in motion fall within the requirements of an extensive magnitude, according to which several parts of a given whole can be juxtaposed? What are the minimum conditions of possibility for the composition of the smallest number of parts, that is, any two motions? Kant's answer is that this composition requires two spaces moving in opposite directions, one absolute and one relative. By absolute motion, however, he understands a motion which refers to a non-material space, which cannot be subjected to experience. An absolute space is therefore a relative space which can always be thought of as beyond any given space; as an Idea of Reason, it has a merely regulative, not constitutive, role in the systematic organization of experience. Kant poses as an axiom the classical formulation of the principle of relativity. He does this by showing how the principle can be applied to the motion of a body in order for it to become an object of experience: 'Every motion, as object of a possible experience, can be viewed arbitrarily as motion of the body in a space at rest, or else as rest of the body, and, instead, as motion of the space in the opposite direction with the same speed' (Ak 4: 487). But from a dynamical point of view, where the *effects* of motion with respect to space become significant, *true* motion (in particular the earth's motion) cannot be viewed as *absolute* motion. True motion in the dynamic sense is relative, that is, it is the relation to one another of the parts of the movable body. The only thinkable absolute motion in a consistent Newtonian theory would be the motion of the whole universe in empty space (which can never become an object of experience), because then true motion would seem to be irrespective of other matter (Ak 4: 562–3). In one of his pre-critical works, however, Kant had produced a remarkable argument in favour of the existence of absolute space.[27] The intrinsic relations among the individual parts of our left hand with regard to each other are the same as in our right hand, and yet it is a matter of intuition that one hand cannot be substituted for the other. Therefore, if such a fundamental difference cannot be explained in terms of a difference in the order of the parts with respect to each other, it can be accounted for only by the assumption of a different disposition with respect to absolute space. This discovery that immediate intuition rather than conceptual cognition lies at the basis of geometry put Kant on the track of transcendental philosophy, where, as forms of any sensible intuition, space and time are said to be both empirically real (they have an objective validity with respect to objects given to the senses) and transcendentally ideal (they are nothing if abstracted from the subjective conditions of sensible intuition).

Under the heading of Dynamics, matter is analysed as pure quality of motion or power. The concept of a filling of space is one of the distinctive features of Kant's theory; Hegel was later to write that this chapter gave the momentum to modern 'Naturphilosophie'. The origin of this view can be traced back to Euler and Ruggero Giuseppe Boscovich. As followers of Leibniz, they considered that the essential properties of matter are impenetrability and force. Euler thought of impenetrability as fundamental in the sense that all other properties could be derived from it; any force was an effect of impenetrability. For Boscovich, in his *Theoria philosophiae naturalis* (1758),[28] the essence of matter was force, and impenetrability was its effect. As a result, for Euler all action was by impact, while for Boscovich all action was due to forces acting at a distance. In Kant's own argument, to fill a space means the power to resist penetration, and is to be distinguished from the occupancy of space by a body, which means the capacity of that body to alter – obstruct or redirect – the motion of another body. Matter is thus a cause of motion in the sense of being able to alter motion by occupying space with intensity. Kant calls the cause of motion 'moving force' and holds that this property and not mere occupancy of space defines what we mean by matter filling a space. Kant is, in fact, arguing against certain of his contemporaries who held that according to the principle of contradiction, it is inconsistent for the same space to be occupied by two different things at the same time. But the principle of contradiction falls short of questions of material content: the principle does not exclude any material which approaches and seeks to penetrate a space in which something is already to be found. Only complete penetration would be contradictory (except in chemistry). Kant goes on to analyse other aspects of the occupancy of space by matter – repulsion, elasticity, and so on – in terms of his dynamic conception, and finds that impenetrability, and indeed force in general, is subject to degrees, no matter how small; the notion of void becomes superfluous. He thus goes beyond Euler, who had argued that impenetrability is fundamental to matter because, as a metaphysical concept, it is not measurable and it has no degrees. But by itself the property of impenetrability is insufficient to account for a material object. Another force is required: the force of attraction. In so far as matter consists in or maintains itself through repelling other forces, in the absence of attraction it would have no cohesion; it would be infinitely scattered and the consistency of matter occupying a given space could not be explained. If repulsion were the only force, space would be empty of matter: for matter to be possible, it must have, as an original property, a force of attraction, which Kant calls fundamental because it cannot be derived from reversed repulsion. For Newton, on the contrary, attraction could not be an essential property of matter.[29] Even though they are both fundamental, a difference exists between repulsion and attraction at the level of the possibility of experience of matter. While the property of filling a space is apprehended immediately, attraction is assigned the status of an inference: we have no immediate sensation of it. The difference enables Kant to deduce a priori a certain number of characters of these forces, in particular that repulsion is action by contact whereas attraction always operates at a distance.

The chief problem with Kant's work is that the parallel drawn between attraction and repulsion is quite deceiving. His investigation of repulsion is, in fact, a study of impacts, which cannot be extended to a physics of central forces. In the final page of *Metaphysische Anfangsgründe*, Kant returns to the possibility that attraction might be merely apparent, not original. He gives the name 'ether' to any matter below the threshold of perception (Ak 4: 563–4). It would be scattered continuously over all cosmic spaces, and it would exert a compression such that space is always full by virtue of the sole expansive force of matter. These speculations announce the *Opus postumum*, Kant's last, post-critical project which remained unfinished. Kant proposed to add *physical* principles to the mathematico-metaphysical principles of natural science. They would no longer be moving forces, but rather 'forces which would never be present in matter without an external moving cause'.[30] This external cause is nothing other than the ether, which Kant now explicitly identified with attraction, whereas the Dynamics had identified it with repulsion. The concepts of this new physics can no longer be simply given by reason or experience. Rather, they are 'fabricated' quite on purpose, as it were, in order to make possible the search for the principles of nature.[31] As a result of the fabrication, any partitioning of the appearances of the world in terms of categories is to be dropped; Kant speaks of a filling of space which can be either extensive or intensive. From this bringing together emerges a new concept, or 'third thing', the matter of which is the ether. Kant defines this ether as 'continual . . . agitation, by attraction and repulsion'.[32] As a third term, the ether corresponds to the transcendental schematism in the cognitive faculties. The transition (or *Übergang*) from mathematics and metaphysics to physics is thus something like the working out of the schematism of nature itself, disclosing what Kant called the possibility of the possibility of experience.

The ether is one of the sources of the concept of field which was to be developed in the following century. Another source is Boscovich, who had noticed that attractions and repulsions became more intelligible if primitive particles were conceived as points. Any pair of points would interact according to the same spherically symmetric, multi-valued law of force. When the distance is infinitely small, the law is infinitely repulsive, which accounts for impenetrability. At a certain distance, this repulsion vanishes, to be followed by an attraction; a second repulsion sets in at a further distance, so that after several oscillations the law settles down to the usual gravitational attraction. This provided the basis of an original notion of matter as a set of 'indivisible points, that are non-extended, endowed with a force of inertia, & also mutual forces represented by a simple continuous curve . . . defined by an algebraic equation'.[33] Even though no one had really any idea of how to find the form of the law, Boscovich thought that the merit of his theory was that it explained everything, including the exchange of motions in collision, by means of continuity.

VI. CHEMISTRY AND THE INNER STRUCTURE OF MATTER

In d'Alembert's principle, which paved the way for Lagrange's general equations of mechanics, no mention is found of the word 'force'. D'Alembert insisted that the concept of force must be banished from mechanics, the foundation of which rests upon the sole concept of motion. This attitude went too far, because it led d'Alembert to ignore physical phenomena which seemed impossible to reduce to motion. Thus, he thought that any explanation concerning what he called the 'intimate structure of bodies' (such as the transformation of motion into heat in the case of inelastic collisions) would resurrect the spectre of alchemy and the old metaphysics. When Daniel Bernoulli published his *Hydrodynamica* (1738), which was the first kinetic model for gases,[34] d'Alembert rejected it as the kind of hypothesis about which no certainty could ever be expected. Bernoulli thought of a gas in terms of a practically infinite number of minute corpuscles. In their rapid motion these corpuscles collide with one another; these collisions can be assumed to be perfectly elastic, meaning the kinetic energy of the particles is conserved. Bernoulli calculated the increase in pressure exerted on the walls of a closed vessel where the volume is made smaller and found that it corresponded to a well-defined numerical relationship found experimentally by Boyle. At the time his work was generally neglected, even though the line of reasoning and the result are all similar to the work which more than a century later finally clarified the main problems of the nature of gases, heat, and chemistry. Indeed, from a methodological viewpoint, Bernoulli's direct equivalence of heat and internal molecular motion is so striking because it ignores interactions with any putative ether.

Thus, whereas *vis viva* and least action were two particular issues that generated philosophical controversy within the scope of what was explicable by Newton's laws, gas theory was an example of the vast range of natural phenomena which simply escaped explanation by Newton's laws. Were new principles needed to understand light, sound, heat, electricity, and so on, and if so should they be formed somehow on the model of Newton's investigations or not?[35] The hallmark of Newtonianism was the attempt to quantify the chemical forces and calculate tables of affinity, that is, comparative tables of forces of affinity between the various elements and their 'mixts' and compounds. In the anti-Newtonian camp (represented by Boscovich, Georg Ernst Stahl, and some of the Scottish speculative philosophers), chemical phenomena were explained on the basis of the internal structure of matter. Interactions between ultimate particles were explained in terms of principles inherent to matter, not in terms of forces spreading between material bodies. When, at the turn of the century, John Dalton established the starting point of modern chemical atomic theory, he abandoned the reduction of chemistry to forces of affinity, and returned to solid, spherical atoms combining in accordance with simple mechanical considerations.[36]

A hundred years separate Newton's *Principia* from the work that provided the final and explicit proof that the quantity of matter in a given system or, practically speaking, the weight of some material in a closed container, does not change during chemical transformations. This was achieved in memoirs on calcination and the text *Traité élémentaire de chimie* by Lavoisier, often called the father of modern chemistry.[37] The obstacles that had to be overcome in the interval between Newton and Lavoisier can now be so stated as to make them sound almost trivial. Lavoisier was one of the first to show conclusively that the most familiar of all chemical transformations, combustion of matter, is generally oxidation, that is, the combination of the material with that part of the ambient air to which he gave the name oxygen and that therefore the gas taken from the atmosphere has to be taken into account. Before Lavoisier's time, neither the nature of gases nor that of the combustion process itself was clear enough; there was therefore little reason or facility for working with carefully measured quantities of gases, or even for carrying out reactions in closed vessels, isolated from the rest of the chemical universe. Instead of a general law of conservation of all participating matter during chemical processes, clear but obstinate and confusing facts impressed themselves on the scientific mind: that on combustion in the open some materials, like wood, would lose weight, whereas others, like phosphorus, would conspicuously gain weight. In modern terms, we should now say that in the case of loss, more gases are given off than are taken on by oxidation, whereas in the case of gain, more oxygen is fixed than vapours given up. During the reverse type of reaction, now called reduction, in which oxygen may be given up, a similar variety of changes would occur.

Chemistry before Lavoisier was much like mechanics before the revolution brought about by Galileo and Newton. Chemical theories tended to deal with concepts derived simply and directly from the most conspicuous aspects of the phenomena. The fundamental conceptual scheme of eighteenth-century chemistry centred on *phlogiston*. Heating ores with charcoal produces metals; heating the metals in air often produces a 'calx', a kind of artificial ore, which on being heated with charcoal yields the metal again. According to the phlogiston theory that became standard around 1700, phlogiston is a substance in the charcoal that is transferred to the ore to make it into a metal. That a candle in an enclosed jar would soon stop burning was explained by the air's becoming saturated with phlogiston. More generally, phlogiston was regarded as a substance or 'principle' whose migration into or out of the transforming bodies was to account for a large number of diverse observations on combustion, including the change in the physical structure and chemical nature of the burning object, the presence of heat and of flames, the changes in the quality of the surrounding air, even the diverse changes of weight. Stahl and the phlogistonians emphasized that not forces but rather primary principles, which are present in finite quantities and which obey conservation laws (like the principles of heat, electricity, chemical affinity, etc.), are the ultimate entities to which all phenomena have to be reduced. Yet the Stahlians who rejected Newtonian forces endorsed the Newtonian empirical attitude. An anomaly of the phlogiston theory was always reasonably well known: the calx (which is supposed to be simple) resulting from combustion weighs slightly more than the original metal. Probably influenced by the Russian poet and scientist Mikhail Lomonosov, Lavoisier proved essentially that the concept of phlogiston is unnecessary. He began the overthrow of the theory by showing that burning phosphorus in an enclosed jar results in a calx of greater weight, with a reduction in the amount of air. He described other similar experiments, involving all types of reactions then known, such as the combustion of iron in which the air is found diminished in weight exactly by the amount that the iron has gained. He concluded that something had disappeared from the air and combined with the metal. Thus, by the incontrovertible evidence of the balance, he could show that shifting one's attention to the total quantity of matter undergoing a chemical reaction (including the gases and vapours) would lead to a rigorous law of conservation of matter. In reactions within a closed system, the gain experienced by any one part of the system exactly counterbalances the loss to the rest of the system, that is, the total quantity of matter within the system remains constant.

The phlogiston theory died a decade or so after Lavoisier's attack on it, precisely because the concept of phlogiston had tried to explain so large a range of phenomena that it failed to achieve a quantitative focus and became self-contradictory.[38] The power of Lavoisier's conceptual scheme of combustion and reduction is that it follows a principle of explanation already used successfully in seventeenth-century mechanics. A great many observations, such as the presence of flames or the change in appearance of the material, are now declared to be secondary and inessential to the actual phenomenon. On the other hand, it cannot be denied that Lavoisier's synthesis translates into the certainty of numerical predictions a fundamentally intuitive idea about the conservation of everything now existing in the universe. The continual existence in the past, present, and future of that which exists now, despite changes of position, shape, phase, chemical composition, and so forth, is one of the earliest hints of a profound general principle of science; it was already found in the Roman poet Lucretius, according to whom all appearances and their changes had to be explained in terms of rearrangements of atoms in the void. Conservation of matter had been stated explicitly by Lomonosov, but most of his works remained unknown to the West. Lavoisier did not really formulate a law of conservation of matter but simply assumed it as an 'incontestable axiom'.

At the end of the eighteenth century, despite Lavoisier's emphatic statement of the true universality of the conservation law, there was still room for doubt. For example, Priestley was able to maintain a revised phlogiston theory. One idea was to assign phlogiston negative weight, but the suggestion was generally regarded as implausible, presumably on metaphysical grounds. The discovery that water was a compound of hydrogen and oxygen suggested that hydrogen was the long-sought phlogiston, and a slight complication of the theory was able along these lines to account for the greater weight of calces. To be sure, Priestley put forward some experimental results which Lavoisier was never able to explain, but ultimately these results relied on using impure substances and misidentifying two gases. Priestley's rear-guard attempt to defend the modified phlogiston theory shows an interesting fact of the history of science, namely, that it is possible to save a theory by adding new auxiliary hypotheses to a conceptual scheme – at least temporarily.

The general philosophical significance of chemistry has to be assessed against the background of the model provided by physics. Whereas physics deals with the gross, external characteristics of bodies, chemistry actually penetrates the essence of bodies. In chemistry, the theory may be approximate, but the fit with natural facts is exact; it could be viewed as Cartesianism stripped of geometry and clear ideas.

Thinkers such as Priestley and Hutton came to reject the validity of the distinction between primary (absolute) and secondary (relational and mind-dependent) qualities with respect to theories of matter.[39] They denied that qualities such as extension and solidity defined the essence of matter and argued that such qualities were the effects of certain powers; the essential qualities were now to be found in the seventeenth century domain of secondary qualities. The notion of power as part of the intrinsic nature of material bodies was borrowed from Locke, who had spoken of powers as 'imputed' properties of matter – causes which, for instance, produce the idea of colour in the mind, instead of matter having such property. This conception of matter was developed in the context of the rejection of the primary-secondary distinction by Berkeley and Hume. For Berkeley, the idea of power cannot be obtained from experience; ideas are passive and can reveal neither activity nor power. Drawing on his argument that activity is not a necessary character of a physical thing's continuing in existence, Hume rejected the notion that we have an idea of power at all. But Thomas Reid replied that we derive the idea of power from an instinctive disposition to see nature as uniform with respect to change and from attention to the operations of the mind, though we perceive the change only, not the agent or the power.[40] Priestley's account of the origin of the concept of power was similar to Reid's; his theory of matter as powers of attraction and repulsion reflected Newton's view on the paucity of solid matter in the world. Like Priestley, Hutton denied that solidity was the essence of substance, but he went further in holding that power alone, considered as first cause, characterised matter.[41]

VII. HEAT

Throughout the seventeenth and far into the eighteenth century, two views of the nature of heat were in competition, though neither became firmly established. Both can be traced back to the qualitative accounts of the phenomenon given by the ancient Greeks. A commonsense and intuitively clear explanation, maintained by the Greek atomists, is that observed differences in the temperature of bodies compel us to picture heat as a special, not directly perceptible, substance, atomic in structure like all the others, quick to diffuse through bodies, and presumably possessing some weight. The picture, chiefly defended by Herman Boerhaave and other Dutch Newtonians, became that of heat as a tenuous imponderable fluid, free to pass in and out of the smallest pores of materials without any apparent change in mass, the amount of which determines temperature.

In fact, the subtle fluid of heat was related to the Aristotelian element of fire; its volatility made it suitable to account for combustion, fermentation, and evaporation. The other view, which has its roots in Galileo, Descartes, and Newton, claimed that heat was not a substance but merely the motion of parts of bodies. It tended to the general though not yet clearly defined representation of heat as a vibration or similar small-scale motion of the atomic particles of heated bodies. As evidence for this view, there was the experience of friction between two bodies, which is a case of heat being generated by motion.

In the meantime the subtle fluid theory proved superior in the sense that it had the advantage of lending itself to measurement. Forces of gravity could be measured, as Newton had demonstrated, but forces acting between atoms could not. However, once satisfactory quantification was achieved, the theory of subtle fluid itself ceased to be of much value. The great advance in the theory was made when Joseph Black (1760) introduced the distinction between temperature and 'quantity of heat'.[42] According to Black, heat must be regarded as fluid (named caloric by Lavoisier in 1787) which is as indestructible as matter. Accumulation of caloric would mean heating, loss of caloric would mean cooling. In experiments on mixtures, where bodies of varying temperature are brought together, heat turns out to be neither destroyed nor created. No matter how diverse the redistribution of heat among the different bodies in mixtures, the total amount of heat remains constant; it is proportional to the temperature, the mass, and what became known as the specific heat of the object. The specific heat was thus a constant of proportionality giving the amount of heat required to raise the temperature of a unit mass of a given substance one degree. Interestingly enough, the conservation of heat thus seems closely allied to the conservation of matter. From the 1760s on, other properties were assigned to the caloric. Thus, the particles of the caloric, unlike those of ordinary matter, repel one another even though they are attracted to the corpuscles of ordinary matter. However, two assumptions of the theory finally proved fatal to it. Direct experimentation showed, after much controversy, that the caloric material cannot possess any weight. Another assumption was that the caloric fluid is conserved in all processes involving heat. But in one of the most famous set of experiments ever performed, Rumford showed that heat cannot be a substance, since the motion of boring a cannon can produce an indefinitely large amount of heat. Indeed, experiments with the metallic chips, and comparison with the bulk metal of the cannons themselves, showed Rumford that their specific heat had not changed, which revealed as unwarranted the supposition according to which the mechanical treatment of metals in boring might decrease the capacity for holding caloric in the metal. As Rumford argued in a paper of 1798,

> anything which any *insulated* body, or system of bodies, can continue to furnish *without limitation*, cannot possibly be *a material substance*, and it appears to me to be extremely

difficult, if not quite impossible, to form any distinct idea of anything capable of being excited or communicated in the manner the Heat was excited and communicated in these experiments, except it be MOTION.[43]

The actual significance of Rumford's conclusion that heat is motion, which appeared a half-century later, is that heat is in fact a form of energy – the kinetic energy associated with the constant motions of the atoms and molecules comprising all matter. What we call kinetic energy was then called *vis viva*, which brings attention to the connection between mechanics and theories of heat. Already in 1780 Lavoisier and Laplace, in their *Mémoire sur la chaleur*, pointed out that heat is the *vis viva* resulting from the insensible movements of the particles of a body. It could be conceived as the sum of the products of the mass of each particle by the square of its velocity. On balance, Lavoisier and Laplace seem to have thought of the two explanations of heat – fluid versus motion – as somewhat complementary to each other.

However, the caloric theory was still most practical and plausible in a great region of other physical and chemical phenomena. One of the most convincing arguments against Rumford's theory was the phenomenon of radiant heat. The fact that heat could travel across empty space (for example, from the sun to the earth) was thought to indicate that heat was a substance, not a mode of motion of matter. The downfall of caloric in the early nineteenth century did not come from work on heat as such, but rather from research on the properties of light, which was thought to be qualitatively identical to radiant heat. On the other hand, those scientists who adopted the caloric theory in the eighteenth century also favoured a conception of the nature of gases which differs from the above-mentioned impact theory of gas pressure proposed by Bernoulli. Heating a gas meant pouring in some caloric, expanding the atmospheres surrounding each atom, and thereby intensifying the repulsive forces supposed to exist between gas particles. This seemed to be incompatible with Bernoulli's hypothesis that heat is nothing but the motion of particles.

VIII. LIGHT AND ELECTRICITY

The development and reception of Newton's optical work revealed fundamental changes in early modern science. In his mechanistic philosophy, Descartes had retained an element of Aristotelian philosophy when he argued that the colours produced by a prism or by the surface of a body are modifications of white light; the refraction of light was explained in terms of the rotations of ether particles. Based on well-controlled experiments, Newton had introduced the concept of white light as being an aggregate of different rays of different colours. This is the view that is now generally accepted. In the early eighteenth century, a series of replications of his experiments was made, which led philosophers such as Malebranche in France or Wolff in Germany to accept his conclusions. In particular, Malebranche denied Newton the title of 'physicist' because he thought Newton had reached his results without mingling his experimental propositions with a metaphysical, global picture of the world.

However, in the Queries that he added to subsequent editions of his *Opticks* (from 1704 to 1718), Newton went on to propound new views concerning the assessment of physical claims. The emphasis was on description and prediction rather than on guessing at the causes of things. In connection with the nature of light, in contrast to his colour theory, Newton used no controlled experiments; most of his suggestions were sketchy and in some cases contradictory. The emerging picture was something like this.[44] Rejecting a wave theory of light, Newton argued that the production of colours in refraction could be explained in terms of the hypothesis of a light ray as a stream of small particles; each light particle was assigned a specific size. Against the wave theory of light, Newton argued that light travels in straight lines, whereas waves would bend around corners, by analogy with water and sound waves. But the argument was mathematically imprecise and lacked strong empirical evidence. Furthermore, Newton also introduced a ubiquitous ether composed of very small particles which had repulsive short-range forces. This view was dangerously close to the Cartesian theory of light, which counted advocates among French natural philosophers of the time, according to which light is a pressure to motion in the universal ether. This wave theory was represented by Christiaan Huygens, who argued in his *Traité de la lumière* (1690) that every point on a luminous body disturbs the ubiquitous ether because it experiences agitated motion. Among the optical writers who were partisans of Newton's emission theory of light, an extraordinary variety of interpretations prevailed well into the nineteenth century. Quite typical in this respect is a comparison between two influential textbooks in the 1720s and 1730s. Whereas 'sGravesande treated the refractive force as existing, but in need of further explanation, Musschenbroek regarded it as an inherent property of matter. Both attitudes stemmed from devout Newtonianism, yet each was equally understandable.[45] In 1746, in his *Nova theoria lucis et colorum*, Euler developed a fairly complete wave theory of light, which soon became essential to those who opposed the emission theory. Euler proposed that each particle of a luminous body oscillates like a stretched string setting the neighbouring ether particles into oscillation, so that a wave spreads from the source. Yet, Euler did not rely on any detailed experiments either, and preferred to draw a close analogy between sound and light. The disconnection between experiment and theory, or mathematical exactness and philosophical hypotheses, was thus quite apparent in the writings of virtually all optical writers in the eighteenth century. It was not until the early nineteenth century that mathematics, experimentation, and explanation were successfully integrated.

The development of electrical theory reflects this methodological separation. In 1730 Charles-François de Cisternai Dufay tried to explain the well-known electrical phenomena of attractions and repulsions on the supposition that all substances contained two kinds of electric fluid. These were usually present in equal quantities, and then they neutralized one another; for this reason he called them positive and negative electricity. Benjamin Franklin suggested in 1747 that the attractions and repulsions were better explained by supposing that a single 'electric fire' or 'electric fluid' existed in all bodies. A body which had more than its normal share of the fluid was said to be plus, or positively, charged, while one with a subnormal share was minus or negatively charged.[46] This one fluid explanation of electric phenomena prevailed for more than a century, but ultimately it turned out that the older two-fluid explanation fits the phenomena better.

Following the development of techniques for handling and storing electricity (the Leyden jar, Franklin's 'lightning conductors', etc.), Priestley found in the 1760s that there was no charge in the interior of an electrified conductor. Comparing this with a mathematical theorem of Newton, which said that there is no gravitational force in the interior of a hollow sphere, Priestley concluded that the law of force between electric charges must be the same law as for gravitational force, namely, that of the inverse square of the distance. Charles Augustin de Coulomb confirmed the law in 1785 by directly measuring the forces required to keep two small electrified pith balls at a series of measured distances apart. On the basis of this result, Coulomb proceeded to build up a mathematical theory of electric force. By the end of the eighteenth century the science of electric charges at rest – electrostatics, as we now call it – had attained pretty nearly to its present form. But new territory was being opened in the latter part of the eighteenth century by the discovery of the electric current – electric charges in motion. The starting point was Luigi Galvani's investigation of phenomena associated with muscular contraction. In 1800 Allesandro Volta showed that electric activity could stimulate the organs of touch, taste, and sight, and thus produce a variety of bodily sensations. Volta was deeply imbued with the method of Newton's *Principia* and the research programme of Boscovich. As for the cause and continuance of the electricity generated by the contact of dissimilar conductors, he adopted a rather simple-minded version of Newtonian methodology. The mechanism did not matter, in the sense that an exact description lacking clear physical foundations was preferred to any qualitative model. The early eighteenth century had still witnessed a dubious association between optics and theology: one of Newton's disciples, George

Cheyne, had conjectured the existence of a correspondence between physical and spiritual light. To the light emitted by the sun, Cheyne associated '*the Sun of Righteousness* . . . [who] sends forth his enlightning and enlivening Beams on all the *System* of created intelligent Beings'.[47]

IX. FACTS AND METHODS: ON SCIENTIFIC PROGRESS

'Facts are what the physicist must seek mainly to learn about; he cannot gather too many of them'. This sentence from d'Alembert's *Eléments de philosophie* enables us to see in the natural philosophy of the eighteenth century the triumphant march of the analytical mode of investigation of nature.[48] For d'Alembert and the other Encyclopedists, this mode represents the victory of Newton over Descartes. The latter must be rejected because he has introduced in physics what d'Alembert calls 'cette fureur d'expliquer tout'. Thus Voltaire, following Newton and Locke, argued that there is no knowledge of first principles; nothing absolutely original can ever be known adequately. The absolute is not opposed to the relative, but contains it. The phenomena, not the ultimate principles, are given; the principles must be found from within the sheer proliferation of phenomena. Nature dissolves into independent phenomena connected by mechanical laws only, the study of which depends on several distinct procedures of thought. In the *Encyclopédie*, nature is said to be a vague term, precisely because it has lost any character in itself. At most, it is a condensed representation of the mutual action of bodies. Deprived of ontological unity, nature retrieves its unity via the mathematical laws themselves; the explanation of the latter is found in God, whose function is limited to the initial impulse to the world. At the end of the century, Laplace even went so far as to cut the world from an extrinsic will.

First with Locke, and later with Condillac and Hume, the conception of human beings as mere particular cases of a universal mechanics was to gain ground. Following Locke, human consciousness was reduced to internal perception – a mechanics of sensation. Taking physics as model, Locke treated the mind on the analogy with Newtonian matter. Elementary ideas, identical in origin with elementary sensations, led to an atomistic view of consciousness in which the association of ideas was thought to be the counterpart of universal attraction. Condillac radicalized this conception when he claimed that as the nature of things is unknowable, we can only know their operations with certainty. We think through the medium of words, the exemplar of language being analytical mathematics because it is both a language and a method. A proposition is scientific in the measure that it is analytical.

Since the facts are prior to the method, no method can set in advance the kind of connection between the facts that the scientists discover. Thus Euler advocated a methodology of physical science such that whether we proceed by the direct method of minima and maxima from efficient causes, or by the indirect method from final causes (i.e., from a priori principles), we must reach the same conclusions; the choice of method depends on the circumstances.[49] These are the first hints of a view according to which knowledge does not grow simply by accumulation. As d'Alembert puts it, what makes progress intelligible is that error is not opposed to truth but is rather the historical condition of truth.

If first principles cannot be accepted as a starting point, because they are too general, one cannot evade the sceptical objection (which was formulated rigorously by Hume) that our actual starting point will always remain arbitrary to some extent. The emphasis on facts and observations leads to the logical problem of how to relate univocally our own statements about facts to the facts themselves. Kant's search for ultimate foundations of science, which led him from the transcendental to the metaphysical, and on to the physical level, was motivated by the desire to overcome the sceptical objection. Kant rehabilitated the superiority of synthesis over analysis when he took mathematical propositions to be the prototype of synthetic judgments that we make prior to sensible experience itself. In the realm of transcendental knowledge, Kant began by acknowledging that principles cannot have their reason of being in themselves. Any transcendental proof is based on the idea that principles draw their only possible truth and certainty from that which they ground, that is, the phenomena.[50] Whether or not Kant succeeded in establishing general and necessary principles of any possible natural science, it is noteworthy that a notion of universality limited by the character of phenomena remains the most significant achievement that modern metaphysics has borrowed from the scientific revolution.

NOTES

1 Immanuel Kant, *Metaphysische Anfangsgründe der Naturwissenschaft* (1786) in Ak 4: 470; translated as *Metaphysical Foundations of Natural Science* by M. Friedman in *Works/Theoretical Philosophy after 1781*, trans. G. Hatfield, et al., eds. H. Allison and P. Heath (2002).

2 For general background, see J. L. Heilbron, *Elements of Early Modern Physics* (Berkeley, CA, 1984); *The Ferment of Knowledge*, eds. G. S. Rousseau and R. Porter (Cambridge, 1980).

3 Jean le Rond d'Alembert, *Essai sur les éléments de philosophie, ou Sur les principes des connaissances humaines* (1759), ed. C. Kintzler (Paris, 1986), 11.

4 Joseph Priestley, *The History and Present State of Electricity with Original Experiments* (London, 1767), xiii. On the conflicting images of Newton in the eighteenth century, see Henry Guerlac, 'Where the Statue Stood: Divergent Loyalties to Newton in the Eighteenth

Century', in *Aspects of the Eighteenth Century*, ed. E. R. Wasserman (Baltimore, MD, 1965), 317–34. See also Guerlac, *Newton on the Continent* (Ithaca, NY, 1981).

5 See I. Bernard Cohen, *Franklin and Newton* (Philadelphia, PA, 1956).

6 d'Alembert, 'Discours préliminaire', in *Encyclopédie*, 1: i–xlv, at vi; translated as *Preliminary Discourse to the Encyclopedia of Diderot*, trans. R. Schwab and W. E. Rex (Indianapolis, IN, 1963), 22.

7 Thomas L. Hankins, 'Eighteenth-Century Attempts to Resolve the *Vis Viva* Controversy', *Isis* 56 (1965), 281–97.

8 [Leonhard Euler], *Histoire de l'Académie Royale des Sciences et des Belles-Lettres*, 1748 (Berlin, 1750), 324.

9 Euler, *Mechanica sive motus scientia analytice exposita*, 2 vols. (St. Petersburg, 1736).

10 K. Kawashima, 'La participation de Madame du Châtelet à la querelle sur les forces vives', *Historia Scientiarum* 40 (1990), 9–28.

11 Pierre Simon, marquis de Laplace, *Exposition du systême du monde*, 2nd edn. (Paris, 1796), 341–2 and 349–51; see his *Oeuvres complètes*, 14 vols. (Paris, 1878–1912), 4: Bk. 5, ch. 6, 474–5 and 483–6. See Jacques Merleau-Ponty, 'Situation et rôle de l'hypothèse cosmogonique dans la pensée cosmologique de Laplace', *Revue d'histoire des sciences* 29 (1976), 21–49.

12 Laplace, 'Sur le principe de la gravitation universelle et sur les inégalités séculaires des planètes qui en dépendent', in *Oeuvres*, 8:203–75.

13 Isaac Newton, *Opticks: or, A Treatise of the Reflections and Refractions, Inflections and Colours of Light*, 2nd edn. (London, 1718), Query 31, 378.

14 Michael Anthony Hoskin, *William Herschel and the Construction of the Heavens* (London, 1963).

15 See D. B. Meli, 'The Emergence of Reference Frames and the Transformation of Mechanics in the Enlightenment', *Historical Studies in the Physical and Biological Sciences* 23.2 (1993), 301–35 at 301.

16 See Philip Stewart, 'Science and Superstition: Comets and the French Public in the Eighteenth Century', *American Journal of Physics* 54 (1986), 16–24.

17 Henry Cavendish, 'Experiments to determine the Density of the Earth', in *Philosophical Transactions of the Royal Society of London* (1798): 469–526.

18 Simon Schaffer, ' "The Great Laboratories of the Universe": William Herschel on Matter Theory and Planetary Life', *Journal for the History of Astronomy* 11 (1980), 81–111.

19 Eric John Aiton, *The Vortex Theory of Planetary Motions* (London, 1972), 152ff.

20 Kant, *Allegemeine Naturgeschichte und Theorie des Himmels*, Ak 1: 215–368; translated as *Universal Natural History and Theory of the Heavens*, trans. and ed. S. L. Jaki (Edinburgh, 1981); see K. G. Jones, 'The Observational Basis for Kant's *Cosmogony*', *Journal for the History of Astronomy* 2 (1971), 29–34.

21 Clifford A. Truesdell, 'Whence the Law of Momentum?', in *Mélanges Alexandre Koyré*, 2 vols. (Paris, 1964), vol. 1: *L'aventure de la science*, 588–612.

22 Thomas Wright, of Durham, *An Original Theory or New Hypothesis of the Universe, Founded upon the Laws of Nature* 1750 edn. facsim., ed. M. A. Hoskin (London, 1971).

23 Augsburg 1761; translated as *Cosmological Letters on the Arrangement of the World Edifice*, trans. S. L. Jaki (Edinburgh, 1976).

24 See Michael Friedman, *Kant and the Exact Sciences* (Cambridge, MA, 1992).

25 Kant, *Kritik der reinen Vernunft*, Ak 3: B xii–xiii; translated as *Critique of Pure Reason*, trans. and eds. P. Guyer and A. W. Wood, in *Works* (1998).

26 Kant, *Metaphysische Anfangsgründe*, preface, Ak 4: 467–79;.

27 Kant, *Von dem ersten Grunde des Unterschiedes der Gegenden im Raume* (1768), Ak 2: 377–83; translated as *Concerning the Ultimate Ground of the Differentiation of Directions in Space*, in *Works/Theoretical Philosophy, 1755–1770*, trans. and eds. D. Walford and R. Meerbote (1992).

28 Roger Joseph Boscovich, *A Theory of Natural Philosophy*, Latin-English text from the Venice 1763 edn., trans. J. M. Child (Chicago, IL, 1922).
29 Kant, *Metaphysische Anfangsgründe*, Ak 4: 514–5.
30 Kant,'Eintheilung der bewegenden Kräfte der Materie', *Opus postumum*, Ak 21: 355–6 at 356 (author's translation); translated as *Works/Opus postumum*, trans. E. Förster and M. Rosen, ed. E. Förster (1993), the quoted passage is not in this translation.
31 Kant, 'Anmerkungen', in *Opus postumum*, Ak 21: 358.
32 Kant, 'Von der *Qualität* der Materie', *Opus postumum*, Ak 22: 211–13.
33 Boscovich, *A Theory of Natural Philosophy*, §516, 365. See also *Roger Joseph Boscovich, SJ, FRS, 1711–1787: Studies of his life and work on the 250th anniversary of his birth*, ed. L. L. Whyte (London, 1961).
34 Clifford A. Truesdell, 'Early Kinetic Theories of Gases', in his *Essays in the History of Mechanics* (Berlin, 1968), 272–304.
35 See Robert E. Schofield, *Mechanism and Materialism: British Natural Philosophy in an Age of Reason* (Princeton, NJ, 1970); Arnold Thackray, *Atoms and Powers: An Essay on Newtonian Matter Theory and the Development of Chemistry* (Cambridge, MA, 1970).
36 John Dalton, *A New System of Chemical Philosophy*, 2 vols. in 3 parts (Manchester, 1808, 1810, 1827), 1.
37 Antoine Lavoisier, *Traité élémentaire de chimie*, 2 vols. (Paris, 1789). See also James B. Conant, *Science and Common Sense* (New Haven, CT, 1951), ch. 7; Henry Guerlac, *Antoine-Laurent Lavoisier: Chemist and Revolutionary* (New York, NY, 1975).
38 See J. B. Conant, 'The Overthrow of the Phlogiston Theory: The Chemical Revolution of 1775–89', in *Harvard Case Histories in Experimental Science*, ed. J. B. Conant (Cambridge, MA, 1966), 67–115.
39 J. E. McGuire, 'Force, Active Principles and Newton's Invisible Realm', *Ambix*, 15 (1986), 154–208; P. M. Heimann and J. E. McGuire, 'Newtonian Forces and Lockean Powers: Concepts of Matter in Eighteenth-Century Thought', *Historical Studies in the Physical Sciences* 3 (1971), 233–306.
40 Thomas Reid, *Essays on the Active Powers of the Human Mind* (1788), in *The Philosophical Works*, ed. Sir W. Hamilton, 2 vols. in 1 (Edinburgh, 1895), Essay 1.
41 Joseph Priestley, *Disquisitions Relating to Matter and Spirit* (London, 1777) and *A Free Discussion of the Doctrines of Materialism and Philosophical Necessity . . . to which are added . . . Introduction . . . and Letters . . . on his Disquisitions Relating to Matter and Spirit* (London, 1778). See Reid, *Thomas Reid on the Animate Creation: Papers on the Life Sciences*, ed. P. B. Wood (Edinburgh, 1995).
42 See Joseph Black, *Lectures on the Elements of Chemistry, Delivered in the University of Edinburgh*, ed. J. Robison, 2 vols. (Edinburgh, 1803), 1: pt. 1. See R. Fox, *The Caloric Theory of Heat* (Oxford, 1971); D. Roller, 'The Early Development of the Concepts of Temperature and Heat', in *Harvard Case Histories in Experimental Science*, ed. Conant, 119–214.
43 Benjamin Thompson, Count Rumford, 'An Inquiry Concerning the Source of Heat which Is Excited by Friction', *Philosophical Transactions of the Royal Society* 88 (1798), 80–102. See Sanborn C. Brown, *Count Rumford on the Nature of Heat* (New York, NY, 1967), 52–73.
44 Caspar Hakfoort, 'Newton's Optics: The Changing Spectrum of Science', in *Let Newton Be!*, eds. J. Fauvel et al. (Oxford, 1988), 81–99; Geoffrey N. Cantor, *Optics after Newton: Theories of Light in Britain and Ireland, 1704–1840* (Manchester, 1983).
45 Edward G. Ruestow, *Physics at Seventeenth- and Eighteenth-Century Leiden: Philosophy and the New Science in the University* (The Hague, 1973), ch. 7.
46 Benjamin Franklin, *Experiments and Observations on Electricity*, 3 vols. (London, 1751–54).

47 George Cheyne, *Philosophical Principles of Religion: Natural and Reveal'd*, Pt. 1 (London, 1715), Pt. 1 (2nd edn.) and Pt. 2 (1716), Pt. 2, 112.

48 D'Alembert, *Essai sur les éléments de philosophie*, 184.

49 L. Euler, *De curvis elasticis* (Lausanne and Geneva, 1774), Introduction; translated as 'Leonard Euler's Elastic Curves', by W. A. Oldfather, C. A. Ellis, and D. M. Brown, in *Isis* 20 (1933), 72–160 at 77.

50 Kant, *Kritik der reinen Vernunft*, A 736–7/B 764–5.

31

NATURAL HISTORY

PHILLIP R. SLOAN

Eighteenth-century natural history comprised a complex body of investigations that included local studies of botany and zoology, collection of natural artifacts, geographical and meteorological descriptions, geological study, landscape and gardening design, and other forms of inquiry conducted by an international group of practitioners.[1] Deriving inspiration from the researches and speculations of Aristotle, Dioscorides, Theophrastus, Pliny, and Vergil in Antiquity, natural historians of the period could also draw upon important Renaissance transformations of the field inspired by such naturalists and herbalists as Otto Brunfels (1488–1534), Conrad Gesner (1516–65), Guillaume Rondelet (1507–66), Andrea Cesalpino (1519–1603), and Ulysses Aldrovandi (1522–1605) who created the tradition of 'emblematic' natural history.[2] Institutionally, natural history developed in the seventeenth century in different forms of association with medical schools, in courts of the nobility, and in association with the new scientific academies inspired by the societies of London and Paris. Less elite forms of natural history were practiced by pharmacists, farmers, country clergy, and 'local' naturalists who created in the early modern period, particularly in the British Isles, the tradition of 'chorographic' natural history. This had originated in the works of William Lambarde and William Camden in the Elizabethan period and was developed by Gerard Boate and Joshua Childrey in the middle seventeenth century. It was exemplified for the early Enlightenment by Robert Plot's *The Natural History of Oxfordshire* of 1677 (Oxford).[3]

Each of these complex strands of development has a separable historical analysis and each feeds into the formation of eighteenth-century natural history. For the purposes of this chapter and this volume, the primary focus will be upon a select set of cognitive questions and will concentrate on an elite tradition of European naturalists, recognizing that a full understanding of the topic in this period requires analysis on several levels.[4]

I shall argue that it supplied for many natural philosophers an alternative form of scientific investigation to that represented by the physical and mathematical natural philosophy of the period. For a complete understanding of the sciences in the eighteenth century, the era must be seen as much as an 'age of Linnæus and Buffon' as an 'age of Newton'. During the course of the century, natural history developed its own institutional structures, novel epistemologies, and modes of inquiry. Evolutionism, historical geology, and the development of 'Humboldtian' sciences – quantitative meteorology, comparative ethnography, biogeography – in the nineteenth century manifested some of the consequences of these eighteenth-century developments. Romanticism and German *Naturphilosophie* also drew heavily upon these developments. This chapter seek to characterize this alternative natural philosophy.

The theoretical reflections that were to transform the original meaning and content of 'natural history' in the eighteenth century will be analysed by sub-periodisations. The first phase, running from approximately 1690 to the 1740s, represents the development of the great classification systems. The second period will be characterized in terms of the 'Buffonian' revolution of mid century. The third phase will deal with the 'vitalist' revolution of the late Enlightenment and its impact on the development of dynamic and constructive dimensions of natural history. The final section will deal with the extension of natural history into anthropology at the close of the century.

I. THE SEARCH FOR THE SYSTEM OF NATURE

1. *Institutionalising natural history*

A review of the *Eighteenth Century Short Title Catalogue* reveals some of the range and diversity of this domain. Of the numerous works published between 1701 and 1800 that have 'natural history', 'historia naturalis', 'histoire naturelle', 'Historie der Natur', or 'Naturgeschichte' in their titles, one finds treatises on the passions, religion, medicine, local geography, psychology, music, printing, exploratory voyages, arboriculture, natural theology, travel guides, and almanacs along with the anticipated descriptive treatises on animals, plants, geological phenomena, and minerals.[5] This displays the way in which 'natural history' characterized inquiries into a wide range of issues defined primarily by their distinction from mathematical physics, astronomy, and experimental science. A more positive definition requires attention to institutional developments and the nature of networks of interacting individuals whose work gave a more specific meaning to the subject.

In Francis Bacon's influential classification of the sciences in his *Parasceve ad historiam naturalem et experimentalum*, appended to the *Novum organon* of 1620, a classification drawn upon by d'Alembert and Diderot in the *Encyclopédie*, natural history was conceived as a 'preparatory' inquiry to natural philosophy:

It treats of the *liberty* of nature, or the *errors* of nature, or the *bonds* of nature; so that we may fairly distribute it into history of *Generations*, of *Pretergenerations*, and of *Arts*; which last I also call *Mechanical* or *Experimental* history.[6]

In the course of the century, however, natural history acquired the character of an autonomous scientific discipline. To understand this development requires initial attention to strategically located individuals occupying primary positions within eighteenth-century institutions pursuing specific aspects of a more broadly defined natural history. The teaching and research dimensions of these institutions made possible a considerable focus of inquiry and gave direction to speculative reflections that could be pursued by identifiable networks of inquirers. If these researches lacked the specificity and focus suggested by Thomas Kuhn's notion of paradigm-governed normal science, we can nonetheless speak of distinctive 'styles' of scientific inquiry, resulting in rival research programmes and competing groups of workers at these centres of inquiry.[7]

Natural history as a discipline was primarily practised within five main forms of institutional organization, all operative in the eighteenth century. Authors of major works were typically associated with at least one of these institutions, and each social body created networks of individuals. Many practitioners belonged to more than one of these institutional forms, but as a means of livelihood, typically only one of these constituted the primary means of support for a given individual.

A traditional institutional home for natural history since the sixteenth century had been the medical faculties of major universities.[8] Beginning with the Italian universities, medical schools often included botanical gardens and, on occasion, substantial anatomical museums where fossils, comparative anatomical preparations, and specimens from wide ranges of animals and plants were displayed and studied by workers. Curators and demonstrators were required by these institutions to arrange collections and conduct teaching. Students were taught to recognize the medicinally important plants and might also study the comparative anatomy of animals at such locations. The botanical gardens in particular raised practical issues concerning the systems of classification by which such gardens were planted and by means of which the properties of plants could be remembered and taught. Important eighteenth-century natural historians associated with such medical teaching gardens and museums included Hermann Boerhaave (1668–1738) in Leiden, Carl von Linné (1707–78) in Uppsala, Albrecht von Haller (1708–77) and Johann Blumenbach (1752–1840) in Göttingen, and François Boissier de Sauvages (1706–67) and Antoine Gouan (1733–1821) in Montpellier. In this same tradition can be placed the Demonstrator of plants at the Physic Garden of the Society of Apothecaries in London.[9] In the American Colonies, the American natural historian Benjamin Smith Barton (1766–1815) was associated with the University of Pennsylvania.

The arts faculties of universities involved with teaching responsibilities in natural philosophy also provided a non-medical context for the prosecution of various aspects of natural history studies. Here can be mentioned Lazzaro Spallanzani (1729–99) at Pavia, Louis Bourguet (1678–1742) at Neûchatel, Nicolas-Joseph Jacquin (1727–1817) at Vienna, and Joseph Gottlieb Kölreuter (1733–1806) at Karlsruhe. In the British Isles, John Walker (1731–1803) became the first holder of the Chair of Natural History at the University of Edinburgh. Johann Jacob Dillenius (1684–1747) was named the first professor of botany at Oxford. Investigators in these positions were able to carry out inquiries into animal and plant physiology, chemistry, comparative anatomy, geology, and animal and plant geography.

Patronized academies, organized on the French or Italian models, formed a third means of support for many professional natural historians.[10] René Antoine Réaumur (1683–1757), Michel Adanson (1727–1806), and the Jussieu dynasty – Antoine (1686–1758), Bernard (1699–1777), Joseph (1704–79), and Antoine Laurent (1748–1836) – were all *pensionnaires* of the Paris Académie Royale des Sciences. Joseph Gärtner (1732–91), Jacob Theodor Klein (1685–1759), and Peter Simon Pallas (1741–1811) constituted an important group at the St. Petersburg Academy. Smaller academies supported important individuals such as John Turberville Needham (1713–81) at Brussels. Privately employed individuals associated with other important smaller academies included such workers as Jean Sénebier (1742–1809), Abraham Trembley (1710–84), and Charles Bonnet (1720–93), all active members of the Genevan academy of sciences. In the American Colonies William Bartram (1739–1823) was associated with the American Philosophical Society. The Edinburgh Philosophical Society had associated with it such individuals as James Hutton (1726–97), the early historian of the earth. However supported, these investigators were able to explore theoretical issues in considerable detail on a wide range of topics.

In contrast to the French model, the main British scientific association, the Royal Society of London, lacked pensioned positions. Much of the work in British natural history was carried out by members of metropolitan natural history societies that can be dated from the founding of the Temple House Botanic Club (1689). These reached their most illustrious expression in the founding of the Linnean Society of London in 1788, created to consolidate the many metropolitan and provincial inquiries into plants and animals.[11]

Separate from the academies, if often overlapping them in membership, were the private natural history museums, private collections, and *cabinets d'histoire naturelle* established in European contexts primarily by the nobility.[12] The foremost institution of this character was the Jardin du Roi in Paris, which by the late eighteenth century had acquired a remarkable physical facility and attained the considerable financial support of Europe's most powerful monarchy. Associated with this institution were Joseph Pitton de Tournefort (1656–1708), Sébastien Vaillant (1669–1722), Charles-François de Cisternay du Fay (1698–1739), Bernard de Jussieu, Georges Louis Le Clerc, comte de Buffon (1707–88), Louis Jean-Marie Daubenton (1716–1800), Michel Adanson (1727–1806), the Jussieu family, Jean Baptiste de Monet, Chevalier de Lamarck (1744–1829), and Bernard de Lacépède (1756–1825), to name only the most prominent members. Smaller cabinets and museums in Göttingen, Leiden, Zürich, and Bologna also employed important natural historians.

The British Museum, originating in 1753 from the enormous private collection of Sir Hans Sloane (1660–1753), provided support for a few individuals interested in natural history, most notably Joseph Banks (1743–1820), the naturalist who accompanied James Cook's first voyage, and also for Linnæus's disciple Daniel Solander (1736–82). But the looser forms of scientific organization in the British Isles also encouraged the development of natural history in the private medical and anatomical schools, widespread in London in the latter half of the century. Subscription courses in natural history and animal anatomy were commonly delivered at such private institutions. Representative of this tradition is the London surgeon John Hunter (1728–93), who delivered private natural history and comparative anatomy lectures at his sumptuous house in Leicester Square that included an anatomical museum of more than 13,000 preparations, forming by the 1790s one of the largest collections of fossils, animal specimens, skulls, and anatomical parts in the world. Hunter's collection was to form the basis for the great Hunterian Museum of comparative anatomy of the Royal College of Surgeons, established by Royal Charter in 1799 and officially opened in new quarters in 1813.

These institutions of natural history created major depositories of materials in Uppsala, London, Paris, Edinburgh, Philadelphia, and Leiden, where specimens obtained from exploratory expeditions to the interior of the Americas, Africa, and the South Pacific could be assembled and reviewed. Individuals in these cities were able to survey large collections of plants and animals from all over the world in a single location, and work in conjunction with cartographers and artists to analyse these in rational catalogues. By this process, the complexity of the geographical and biological space of the planet was reduced to the first bio-geographical maps and worldwide systematisations. The 'natural historian' in such contexts gained rational control of the world not only by personal visits to remote regions but also by systematisation and the mathematics of the cartographer.

Natural history cannot be considered a purely passive subject under this conception. The natural historian could intervene and manipulate the natural world, if not by experiment, at least by the systematising and revisions of classificatory systems in the great collections. The transportation to Europe of living exotic organisms for public display, or in the case of plants, as seeds and sprouts to be sown in hothouses, also allowed a wider public to participate in the encounter with the unusual dimensions of the natural world and made it possible for specialists to conduct experiments at centralized locations.[13] The emergence of the first national zoological garden with the founding in 1794 of the *Ménagerie* at the Paris Muséum national d'histoire naturelle, the Revolutionary successor to the Jardin du Roi, provided a model for public display that was followed in the nineteenth century by all major European nations. These displays also included the exhibition of man-like apes and aboriginal peoples, confronting a wider public with the complexities of defining human existence in European terms.[14]

2. *The ideal of the natural system*

Efforts to reduce the complexity of objects of the natural world to manageable tables, maps, classifications, and systems, initiated by Renaissance herbalists and encyclopedists, formed an important backdrop to the work of the eighteenth-century naturalists. The systematisation of organisms constituted a search for a truly 'natural' system of arrangement, one that reflected the objective structure of the world rather than human convenience or utility. How this was to be attained with any epistemic certainty was a more difficult problem.

An influential Renaissance solution to this question was offered by the Pisan professor of medicine and pharmacology, Andrea Cesalpino, who developed his conclusions on the framework of the Aristotelian theory of the soul in his *De plantis libri xvi* (Florence, 1583). Those parts associated with the primary vegetative functions of nutrition and reproduction, defined by Aristotle (*De Anima* Bk. ii, 414b 1–5) to be central to plant existence, were considered by Cesalpino to be the key to this natural system.[15] Although significant debates over Cesalpino's principle of the *fundamentum fructificationis* were to take place in the late seventeenth century, its axiomatic character was accepted by Joseph Pitton de Tournefort in his landmark *Elémens de botanique* of 1694, and subsequently by the Swedish physician and naturalist Carl von Linné (or Linnæus) (1707–78) in his fundamental works of the 1730s and 1740s as the rational basis of natural and artificial plant classification.

Less explicitly developed on Aristotelian theoretical foundations, but still in keeping with Aristotle's definition of the functions of 'animate' existence, a similar principle formed the basis of the important arrangement of the quadrupeds, birds, and fishes by the English divine and Fellow of the Royal Society, John Ray (1627–1705) in association with Francis Willughby (1635–72).[16] In these important works, the structures associated with circulation and locomotion furnished the primary grounds for classifying animals in a rational subordination of groups that presumably reflected their 'natural' relationships.

With the significant work of Tournefort, Ray, and especially Cesalpino as his principal sources, Linnæus opened up a new era in systematic natural history in a form that was to create much of the enthusiasm for the subject during the Enlightenment. Prior to his work – the point must be emphasized – there was no similar attempt to connect plants, animals, and minerals in a comprehensive system that openly claimed to be the key to the order of created nature. Furthermore, Linnaeus revolutionized anthropology by including human beings in his classification of the animals, including them with the apes and sloths.[17] Published at Leiden in 1735 in thirteen folio pages, the first edition of the *Systema naturae, sive, regna tria naturae systematice proposita per classes, ordines, genera, & species* organized the main genera of all three kingdoms into a system of subordinated Kingdoms, Orders, Classes, Genera, and Species. Although highly schematic in form, using brief characterizations by genera and essential differentiae, it suggested the kind of rational control possible over the objects of the natural world. Supplying a new nomenclature for the higher groups (Orders, Classes, Kingdoms) and taking in all natural forms in its purview, Linnæan natural history presented a bold, programmatic enterprise that was subsequently prosecuted by an expanding network of workers at numerous museums, academies, and cabinets.[18]

The importance of Linnæan science as an *alternative* eighteenth-century scientific programme to Cartesian-Newtonian natural philosophy has rarely been appreciated.[19] In terms of the familiar categories of eighteenth-century natural philosophy – experimental method, quantitative idealization, belief in an underlying mathematical structure of reality, primary-secondary qualities distinction, mechanistic and reductive explanations – Linnæan science presented almost a point by point contrast. Pervaded by a direct epistemological realism, in which the object of true science was 'to know things in themselves', Linnæan science was qualitative, non-experimental, and descriptive. It denied a radical subject-object dichotomy; it admitted no 'problem of knowledge' that troubled over epistemological scepticism and problems of sensation. It was theocentric, teleological, and more in touch with classical sources (Roman Stoicism, Scholastic logic) and Renaissance nature-philosophy than with the science of Descartes or

Newton. The natural world, as it was experienced by the interested layman in all its colours, shapes, even in its anthropomorphic analogies, took precedence over material and mathematical analysis. Represented not only in the familiar classificatory works and expositions of Linnæan systematics – *Systema naturae* (13 eds., 1735–1788); *Genera plantarum* (1737); *Species plantarum* (1753); *Fundamenta botanica* (1736); *Philosophia botanica* (1751) – but also in the important orations and dissertations carried out under Linnæus's direction during his forty-year tenure at the University of Uppsala,[20] Linnæan natural history formed a broad tradition of inquiry, pursued throughout much of the world by a cadre of devoted disciples and popularised in works by such influential authors as Jean-Jacques Rousseau.[21] In spite of these efforts, the larger Linnæan project of discovering and cataloguing the unique natural system of arrangement of plants remained an unachieved ideal for Linnæus, with his speculations left as fragments bequeathed to his disciples for completion.[22]

The original Linnæan systematisations – simply schematic tables in the first edition of the *Systema naturae* – formed a structure within which the explosive expansion of eighteenth-century knowledge of the natural world could be assimilated. With the invention of the accurate marine chronometer in the middle decades of the century, the persistent problem of longitudinal location had finally been solved.[23] Eighteenth-century naturalists were able to grasp for the first time an accurate view of the extent and contours of the world's surface. With this went the remarkable eighteenth-century encounters with exotic South-Sea islanders, romanticised in Louis Bougainville's circumglobal voyage (1766–69). Mapping of the west coast of the Americas was completed. The encounter with New Zealand and Australia, and James Cook's three famous voyages (1768–71; 1772–75; 1776–80), which included the European contact with the Hawaiian Islands, all contributed to the remarkable expansion of knowledge of new plants, animals, and human varieties in the century.[24] Expeditions to Siberia, the Bering Straits, and Kamchatka mapped the contours of the northern Pacific and brought back exotic creatures, including remains of frozen extinct mammoths, to European museums.

In some respects the data from these explorations presented a greater rational challenge to eighteenth-century European assumptions than the residual issues surrounding the Columbian encounters of the fifteenth and sixteenth centuries. The existence in the Americas of human beings and animal and plant life similar to European forms ceased to be the problem it had originally appeared, once the possibility of migrations across Siberia and North America became tenable solutions following the extended exploration of the upper Pacific rim by the 1760s. But the discovery of exotic human beings and novel organisms on remote islands of the Pacific, thousands of miles from the nearest land mass, presented new questions about origins that were not easily answered by nomadic migrations. The possibility of multiple and autonomous 'centres of creation', even implying different creations of human beings, seemed to many the only solution to these questions.[25]

Although Linnæus's best-known works were primarily descriptive, he had also turned his attention to problems of historical development and the distribution of organisms in his early oration of 1743, the *Oratio de telluris habitabilis incremento* (published 1744). In this he proposed an imaginative hypothesis of an original equatorial island in a primeval circumglobal ocean, on which an original pair of each primary species had been created. From this Edenic site, the plants and animals were able to spread as more land emerged, with species intermixing to form additional species. This historical thesis, reconciling natural and sacred history, suggested a means by which the problems of distribution might be explored by his successors in terms of migrations from primeval sources of origin.[26] It suggested one route by which historical questions might be combined with issues of systematisation.

Linnæus's theories had some remote similarities to hypotheses of species transformism suggested in such works as Benoît de Maillet's (1656–1738) *Telliamed* (1748), which had been circulated in manuscript since 1720. Nevertheless it would be incorrect to view Linnæus as putting forth 'evolutionary' views by such speculations. He never questioned the 'essentiality' of species, and his hybridization theory meant no more than a combining of these essential natures. Nor was he a strong advocate of the continuity of the *scala natura* or 'chain of beings', as developed by his contemporary Charles Bonnet.

II. THE BUFFONIAN REVOLUTION

Theoretical conflicts developed within natural history at mid century between Linnæus and his growing band of disciples and the French naturalist George Louis Le Clerc, comte de Buffon, the powerful *Intendant* of the King's garden and natural history collection in Paris after 1739. These conflicts display the tensions between two rival conceptions of the discipline that profoundly affected the aims and practices of the science. The dynamic interplay between these alternative research programmes forced naturalists to come to terms with the claims and consequences of both scientific styles. Neither programme could be pursued to the exclusion of the other. Their effective combination set the agenda for the disciplinary professionalisation of natural history in the nineteenth century.

In contrast to Linnæan natural history, the Buffonian tradition can be characterized as concerned with a causal, secular, and historical science of nature, a set of inquiries which by the end of the century was often designated as a 'history of nature' to distinguish it from natural history of the more traditional form. Aspects of this re-conceptualization represent a revival, after a significant historical hiatus, of the lines of speculation initiated by Réné Descartes in parts three and four of his *Principiæ philosophiæ* of 1644.

Descartes had developed the implications of his theory of matter as *res extensa* by sketching out the first modern hypothetical account of the formation of the solar system and the earth by the simple transference of an initial quantity of motion to an extended plenum by God acting by means of the Cartesian rules of contact action and the three Cartesian laws of nature. In this system, the earth was formed by the consolidation and cooling of a star. By a drying and fissuring of the crust, the surface was broken and by violent processes, the 'mountains, plains, oceans' were created through natural causes.[27] This quasi-historical account – formally non-literal because it is presented as a counterfactual hypothesis[28] – supplied an influential model for subsequent speculations on 'theories of the earth'. Revised in the late seventeenth century by the Danish natural philosopher Niels Stensen (Steno) (1638–86), and given its most influential expression by the English divine Thomas Burnet (1635?–1715) in his *Sacred Theory of the Earth* (*Telluris theoria sacras*, 1681), Cartesian genetic history of the earth was transformed into literal history by its reconciliation with traditional Mosaic cosmology.[29]

Natural philosophers of the eighteenth century confronted a significant problem with reference to these issues in the wake of Newton's revolution. A few disciples of Newton – most notably William Whiston (1667–1752) – continued Burnet's efforts to reconcile a history of the earth with Mosaic genesis, employing Newtonian, rather than Cartesian, mechanics.[30] Newton, however, explicitly rejected these efforts in his published works. Emphasizing the mathematical analysis of the motions of bodies according to the established synchronously acting laws of nature, which he distinguished from speculations about the first origins of this world order, Newton's planetary system was functionally non-historical, if not strictly eternalist.[31] His disciple John Keill (1671–1721) directly attacked the hypothetical character of Descartes's and Burnet's 'world building' in both its Newtonian and Cartesian variants in his *An Examination of Dr. Burnet's Theory of the Earth, Together with Some Remarks on Mr. Whiston's New Theory of the Earth* (Oxford, 1698), suggesting that rejection of such speculation was an important means of distinguishing Cartesian and Newtonian natural philosophies. Although some notable efforts to continue a tradition of speculation about the 'theory of the earth' as it was commonly termed in the early eighteenth century can be cited,[32] the paucity of literature dealing with these questions in the early decades of the century suggests that these Newtonian criticisms formed an important block to the development of historical cosmology and geology until the middle decades of the century.[33]

In this context Buffon played a primary, if not exclusive, role in the eighteenth-century revival of historical cosmology and theories of the world, subsuming this under a broadened and altered conception of natural history that eventually resulted in a synthesis of cosmological, geological, historical, and biological questions.

Buffon's emergence as the foremost architect of this new 'natural history' in several respects resulted from an unusual intellectual biography. Important dimensions of his intellectual formation connect him with the standard picture of a Newton-Locke-empiricist tradition in eighteenth-century thought. Nonetheless, this chapter takes the position that Buffon's thought also departed in important ways from this philosophical axis, and it is in this divergence that his novelty is to be understood.[34] His reformulation of the character and directions of natural history involved on the one hand an important revival of Aristotelianism, and on the other the construction of a complex synthesis of Cartesian and Leibnizian natural philosophies that Newton's hegemony had served to check. It also involved his formulation of a novel epistemology for natural history that departed from the assumptions of mathematical physics.

First admitted to the prestigious Académie royale des sciences in 1734 for his work in probability theory, Buffon's interest in the life sciences was evidently sparked by his first published work, a translation, with his own introduction, of Stephen Hales's Newton-inspired *Vegetable Staticks and Analysis of the Air* (1727), an important work dealing both with the physiology of plants and with the chemical analysis of gases.[35] In the same year that Linnæus had publicly entered the field of botany with the *Systema naturæ*, Buffon had established his early reputation in the Académie as an advocate of Newtonian experimental methods applied to the organic realm. The diametric opposition of methodologies and conceptions of scientific inquiry that were to divide Buffon and Linnæus only deepened from this date.

In 1739 Buffon was named the successor to Charles-François de Cisternay du Fay as *Intendant* of the Jardin du Roi in Paris, both a botanical garden and the repository for the extensive zoological, anthropological, and geological specimens gathered by French investigators from at home and in the colonies. Through his administrative skills and political finesse, over the next forty-nine years he was able to transform the Jardin into the century's foremost research institution in natural history, with workers dedicated to botany, various branches of zoology, animal and human anatomy, mineralogy, chemistry, and bio-geographical studies.

The development of Buffon's thought between 1739 and 1749, the date of publication of the first three volumes of his *Histoire naturelle générale et particulière, avec la description du cabinet du Roy* (HN), remains one of the main interpretive issues in Buffon scholarship.[36] Spanning this period, his published works include an important translation of and introduction to Newton's work on the calculus (1740),[37] and a series of articles in the *Mémoires de l'Académie royale des sciences* dealing with such subjects as the strength of wood, the construction of large-scale burning-mirrors, a series of exchanges with Alexis-Claude Clairaut (1713–65) on the interpretation of Newton's inverse-square law of universal gravitation, and a paper dealing with the claimed microscopic discovery of spermatic bodies in female mammals.[38] Little in this immediately suggests strong interests in the traditional domain of natural history as it was understood in this period. Taking shape in the background, however, was an ambitious project that was only to emerge to public view in 1749.

Buffon's unusual career qualified him to engage several of the fundamental questions of Enlightenment philosophy at issue in the 1730s and 1740s as he prepared for his entry into natural history. His early writings display his awareness of the debates on the foundations of Newtonianism initiated by the Leibniz-Clarke dispute (1717). Contacts with Genevan mathematicians and natural philosophers acquainted him with the efforts of members of the Genevan Academy to reconcile aspects of Cartesian, Newtonian, and Leibnizian natural philosophies.[39] His early concern with probability mathematics engaged him with the combination of epistemological and mathematical questions that lay at the foundations of this mathematics of certitude.[40] Able to read English writers at an early age, Buffon was conversant with British natural philosophy and with British philosophical works, including those of Locke and Berkeley. He displays familiarity with the debates on the relation of mind, world, and sensation brought into focus by authors such as Etienne Bonnot de Mably de Condillac (1715–80). On the other hand, his direct study of the biological writings of Aristotle and of biological thinkers influenced by Aristotelian theories of the organism, such as William Harvey (1578–1657), also contributed significantly to his thinking.[41] All these factors play a role in the formation of Buffon's novel 'relational' epistemology, developed at greatest length in the 'De la manière d'étudier et de traiter l'histoire naturelle', which prefaced the first volume of the *Histoire naturelle* (1749), and also in the long 'Discours sur la nature des animaux' opening volume four (1753).[42]

Buffon's contact with the Leibniz-Wolff philosophy, diffused in French circles in the 1730s and 1740s, has significance for his revolution on three fronts.[43] First, the Leibnizian philosophy offered a fundamental systematic critique of the Newtonian conceptions of absolute time and space, offering in their place an immanent conception of time and space that intimately connected the existence of time with the material succession of the empirical world. Second, Leibnizianism grounded a substantive conception of 'nature' that conceived it as an autonomous, teleological system developing in relation to the unfolding of immanent time and space. Finally, it provided a philosophical foundation for re-establishing a genetic theory of the earth in a form that seemed to escape the Newtonian critique of 'world-building'. These will be elaborated briefly.

1. *Time in nature*

The complexities of the Leibnizian philosophy of time and space were rendered more systematic, concrete, and empirically applicable for a Francophone audience in the 1740s by their reformulations in the writings of the Halle professor of philosophy Christian Wolff (1679–1754). These restatements allowed the highly metaphysical discussions of Leibniz himself, only incompletely accessible during most of the century, to be given popular expositions that could also be applied to specific issues in the sciences. The concept of time is one primary example of how these views were assimilated by French enthusiasts for the Leibnizian philosophy.

Isaac Newton's definitions of absolute time and space, most clearly stated in the scholium to Definition Eight of the *Principia mathematica*, defined 'true mathematical' time and space as absolutes standing independent of any empirical instantiation or measurement of these quantities. Furthermore, these two absolute infinities, identified in the 'General Scholium' to the second edition of the *Principia* (1713) with attributes of God, were conceptually unconnected with the history or origin of the material world order. Time and space are dimensionalities within which world or cosmic history transpires. But in Newton's philosophy of nature no intimate connection exists between the absolute infinity of time, for example, and the history of the cosmic system or the world. Consequently, Newton conceived the age of the universe in terms reasonably consistent with accepted biblical chronologies. The planetary system is a nearly steady-state system, created within relatively recent time, undergoing a slow historical decay of motion.

In his critique of the foundations of Newtonian natural philosophy in the series of letter exchanges with Newton's proxy Samuel Clarke, published jointly in French and English in 1717, Leibniz had challenged this Newtonian independence of time and space along with several other components of the Newtonian system. In its place he offered a purely relational definition of time and space in which neither entity was considered conceivable apart from the relations of substances.[44]

Christian Wolff's refashioning of Leibniz's fragmentary and complex ideas into a systematic textbook tradition was particularly important in making these notions applicable in scientifically practical ways. Expounding these views in systematic Latin treatises, which were made available to a Francophone readership in the early 1740s in popular expositions,[45] Wolff reshaped Leibnizianism into a concrete philosophy, pruned of the more abstruse metaphysical dimensions of Leibniz's monad theory. Even before these French expositions of the Wolffian interpretation of Leibniz were available, Buffon's circle of associates was made aware of the importance and novelty of the Leibnizian-Wolffian philosophy through the substantial contacts that had developed between French intellectuals, most notably Buffon's friend Pierre de Maupertuis (1698–1759), and the Berlin Academy of Sciences. Also important was the anonymously published exposition of Wolffian principles, the *Institutions de physique* (Paris, 1740; 2nd ed. 1742) by Gabrielle-Émilie le Tonnelier de Breteuil, marquise du Châtelet (1709–49). This work attempted to synthesize Newtonian mechanics with Leibniz-Wolffian metaphysics. Buffon is known to have read this work late in 1740.[46] Prefaced by a long introductory exposition of the essentials of Wolff's philosophy as it had been taught to her personally by Wolff's disciple Samuel Koenig (1712–57),[47] du Châtelet defended Leibnizian relational interpretations of time and space against the Newtonian absolutes that she, along with Wolff, considered mere abstractions. Time, she writes,

> is therefore in reality nothing else than the order of successive beings [*Etres*]; and one forms the idea of it only in so far as one considers it as the order of their succession. Thus there is no time without true beings successively arranged in a continuous series, and there is time as soon as such beings exist.[48]

In these terms, temporality and historicity are intrinsically imbedded in the structure of existent things. Furthermore, this development of temporality is concretely realised by the unfolding of a succession of entities in a connected series. Very similar notions were subsequently to reappear as an important feature of Buffon's biological and geological reflections.

2. *The idea of nature*

A second important component of the Leibniz-Wolff philosophy that seems formative for Buffon's views is the dynamic and substantive conception of nature found within this tradition. For the primary seventeenth-century natural philosophers enamoured with mechanical philosophy, nature functioned primarily as a passive, inert, created order of things.[49] This passive, nominalist conception of nature of seventeenth-century mechanism was to undergo important transformations in the eighteenth century under the complex impact of the natural philosophies of Newton, Leibniz, Spinoza, and the Cambridge Platonists.[50] Re-established was the concept of nature as a substantive, causal agency, either as an intermediary between God and matter, as advocated by the Cambridge Platonists, or as the inherent principle of action underlying the dynamic force (*vis*) of matter, the view of Leibniz.[51] Restated by du Châtelet in her *Institutions*, this Leibnizian-Wolffian conception of 'nature' was defined as

> an internal principle of changes that occur in the world; thus, it is not a little God distinct from the world, who has governance over this machine. It is only the motive force joined to the other properties [of matter] which together with it compose the essence of bodies.[52]

Nature in this sense provided a metaphysical object for a science concerned generally with the inner system of forces and dynamic actions and relations immanent in matter itself. Again, it is in terms closely similar to these Leibniz-Wolff formulations that the concept of nature will be encountered in Buffon's writings.

3. Reviving the theory of the earth

The immanent nature of time in the Leibniz-Wolff philosophy suggests at least one important reason that it is within the writings of those in close contact with the Leibnizian tradition in the eighteenth century that we perceive a willingness to revive the historical cosmology and theory of the earth which had seemingly been discredited by the epistemic strictures of Newtonian science. Historicity is a necessary, and not simply a contingent and accidental, dimension of Leibnizian natural philosophy. Nature is a dynamic, unfolding system, manifested through the inner powers of matter in which time itself cannot be separated from this successional unfolding of phenomena. The principle of sufficient reason renders the order of this unfolding reality a unique system with an inherent rationality, autonomous and without need of miraculous interventions. Leibniz's own effort at developing a genetic history of the world, the *Protogaea*, available only as a short prospectus until 1749 but circulated in manuscript before then, opened with the claim that 'if one wishes to return to the most remote origin of our land, one must say something about the first configuration of the earth [*terrarum*], the nature of the soil and that which it contains'.[53] Although Leibniz himself does not attempt an epistemological justification of the knowledge claims involved in such discussions of origins – the point at issue with the Newtonians – once again Wolff was to supply this in a form readily accessible to a wide audience. Defining 'Cosmology' as a science that applied the principles of his comprehensive metaphysical system to empirical nature, Wolff related the issue of the origin of beings and the origin of the universe to the succession of time. The empirical reality of the world is to be understood as a chain of connections in a causal relationship, either contemporaneously in space, or diachronically in time.[54] The earth, for example, is related causally to the sun, and changes in one are related to changes in the other.[55]

Although Wolff did not himself enter into specific discussion of various theories of the formation of the world, it is particularly through the writings of individuals in some contact with this Leibnizian-Wolffian tradition that one encounters a revival of the defunct theory of the earth.[56] One example is the Swiss polymath Louis Bourguet (1678–1742), who proposed the outlines of a 'théorie de la terre' in a treatise of 1729 that was to influence Buffon's views.[57] These three contributions of Leibniz-Wolff philosophy outlined above form important components of Buffon's new conception of natural history.

4. *Buffonian history of nature*

The publication in 1749 by the Imprimerie royale of the first three volumes of Buffon's *Histoire naturelle* presented the eighteenth century with its principal alternative to the Linnæan conception of natural history. Voluminous in form, elegantly written, and discursive rather than analytical and classificatory in style, it presented a marked contrast to Linnæan natural history in its immediate presentation. Opening with a lengthy 'discourse on method' reminiscent of Descartes's famous treatise, Buffon set out a programmatic agenda for his new approach to natural history.

Opposition to Linnæan natural history forms a central focus of his opening discourse. Linnæus's Latin style, his crabbed classificatory presentations, and his system-building mentality were in marked contrast to Buffon's approach. Buffon's discourse also advocated the restoration of metaphysics to science, and as part of this he sought to provide natural history with epistemic foundations that could overcome sceptical critiques of historical knowledge. In the discussion of truth closing the discourse, the impact of the Leibniz-Wolff notion of physical truth was prominent.[58] Buffon made the attainment of the truth in the physical world a consequence of understanding natural objects and phenomena in terms of relations of connected and temporal succession.[59] On these grounds, he surprisingly denied a central claim of seventeenth-century natural philosophy – namely that abstract mathematical idealisation provided the privileged means to acquire this physical truth. On the contrary, mathematics yielded only abstract truth, grounded on the relations of ideas rather than on the successional relations of real things. For this reason it was inferior to the natural knowledge founded on the observation of a succession of events:

There are several kinds of truths, and customarily placed in the first order are mathematical truths, which are, however, only truths of definition. . . . Physical truths, to the contrary, are in no way arbitrary, and do not depend on us. Instead of being founded on suppositions that we have made, they are only grounded upon facts. A series of similar facts or, if you prefer, a frequent repetition and uninterrupted succession of the same events constitutes the essence of physical truth. What is called physical truth is thus only a probability, but a probability so great that it is equivalent to certitude.... One goes [*va*] from definition to definition in the abstract sciences, but one proceeds [*marche*] from observation to observation in the sciences of the real. In the first case one arrives at evidence, in the latter at certainty.[60]

In this discussion, Buffon effectively reversed the conclusions of his contemporary David Hume (1711–76) on the relationship of analytic and synthetic truths. Only a year previously, Hume had made this distinction in his *Enquiry Concerning Human Understanding*, and from this had drawn sceptical conclusions about the certitude of empirical knowledge.[61] To the contrary, for Buffon this distinction of analytic and synthetic truths implied that the latter, if understood in terms of a physical succession of phenomena, offered a greater epistemic certitude than that available through the mere abstract relations of ideas. This unusual epistemology – a 'realism' seen by the late Professor Jacques Roger as Buffon's most revolutionary concept – forms the unifying theme of his new conception of natural history.[62] It implied that the knowledge to be gained through natural history was superior to the abstractions of mathematical physics. This premise also supplied the grounds for his attack on Linnæan systematics set forth in the 'First Discourse.'

The new directions implied by these principles are immediately evident in the plan and content of the *Histoire naturelle*. Claiming that Linnæan classification is a mere abstract arrangement of forms without connection to their true physical relations, Buffon returned to Aristotle's suggestion in the *Historia animalium* (491a 20) that organisms were to be classified in terms of their relation to human beings. This implied for Buffon the novel conclusion that the forms closest to human beings were the domestic animals rather than the apes and monkeys, rejecting the Linnaean classification of humans in the *Systema*. The expository arrangement of the *Histoire naturelle* was to pursue this novel anthropocentric system as its basic plan of organization through the initial series of the work, the *Histoire naturelle des quadrupèdes* (1753–67).

The rest of the three original volumes of the *Histoire naturelle* display further dimensions of Buffon's concern with temporal succession and material relation. In the first of the two long discourses that complete the first volume, he offered a secular account of the slow, causal agencies – in this case the action of water – that have given shape to the earth and formed the mountains, sea basins, and continents. Technically rejecting the earlier speculations of Thomas Burnet, John Woodward, and William Whiston because they required catastrophic causes outside ordinary purview, Buffon's initial account was not intended as a theory of first origins, but as a secular explanation of the immediate formative causes of the world as it currently exists. To this degree he apparently accepted Newtonian epistemic restrictions on world building.[63]

In a second discourse, however, Buffon did consider the issue of first origins. In the long article 'Proofs of the theory of the earth', which forms the conclusion of the first volume, he returned to the question of the origins of the solar system itself, offering a secular account that postulated the collision of a passing comet with the sun. This is assumed to have resulted in the ejection into space of masses of molten material that have consolidated into the planets as they cooled. Proof of this theory is offered in the form of mathematical calculations based on the orbital velocity of the planets. However, Buffon makes no effort to unite this catastrophic theory of planetary origin with the history of the earth. Only later would this integration take place.

The themes of the second and third volumes of the *Histoire naturelle* display again the character of Buffon's divergence from the reigning Linnæan programme. His treatment of organic beings adopts a functional, rather than a classificatory approach, opening with a long discussion of the process of generation. In this discourse he offers an explanation of embryological formation and the maintenance of form through sexual reproduction, offering an ambitious theory of organic molecules organized by immanent force-fields, the 'internal moulds'. The developmental history of man forms the topic of the latter part of the second volume, and the third volume deals with the natural history of the human species, accompanied by the detailed anatomical descriptions by his collaborator Louis Daubenton, offering the eighteenth century the longest treatise hitherto on this subject. In these discussions of the human species Buffon characterized the various stages of human life, the function of the senses, and then summarized the physical differences, habits, and geographical distributions of the main varieties of the human species.

In contrast to Linnæus's creationist, classificatory natural history, Buffon's science makes no effort to synthesise his natural history accounts with biblical history. Nature is related to a divine order only in the establishment of the laws of motion and the creation of the first internal moulds of each species. But in company with the Leibnizian tradition, Buffon's nature is neither a separate demiurge nor merely a mechanical order of things. As he was later to define the concept of nature in an influential discourse, it is 'an immense, living force, which embraces all things, which animates all, and which subordinated to that [power] of the first Being, commenced its action only by his order, and acts still only by his concourse or consent'.[64]

5. *Degenerating species*

In his analysis of the quadruped animals commencing with the fourth volume of the *Histoire naturelle* (1753), Buffon's emphasis was geographical, ecological, and relational rather than classificatory. This emphasis is displayed strikingly in his re-definition of organic species, most explicitly presented in the article on the Ass (1753). Arguing that the traditional notion of a species as a logical class of similar individuals did not meet the criterion of a properly physical definition, Buffon introduced into the literature a revolutionary conception of organic species defining it as a 'constant succession and uninterrupted renewal of the individuals constituting it'.[65] Such species were to be recognized empirically by reproductive compatibility rather than by morphological characteristics. This novel definition, given wider circulation by Diderot's *Encyclopédie*,[66] supplied a substantive ontology for the concept of biological species that deeply affected the subsequent history of the life sciences. This novel redefinition of 'species' as a successional lineage of organisms, rather than as a universal of logic, opened up a discourse about species in which naturalists could discuss the birth, death, geographical distribution, and variation of organic species as ontological entities.

The integration of this functional, historical, and ecological approach to organisms with the physical history of the earth was a topic that slowly developed in Buffon's natural history over a forty-year period. As his survey of natural history encountered the issue of geographical variation, an issue necessarily forced into the foreground by his physical conception of organic species, the unusual arrangement of the *Histoire naturelle* first raised this issue with respect to the geographical variation of domestic animals.[67] In 1756, as he expanded his review to include the wild animals, Buffon suggested a causal mechanism responsible for this change of species. The differences created by climatic variations in the constituent organic molecules making up every living being presumably produced slight, heritable, and cumulative effects on the transmitted internal moulds that were transmitted to subsequent generations.[68] These reflections were considerably expanded in the ninth volume of the *Histoire naturelle* (1761), when Buffon finally treated the complex problem of the relations of the Old and New World quadrupeds. In these discussions he developed his theory of a historical degeneration of species over time to account for these geographical variations. By the middle 1760s, Buffon's theory of degeneration allowed him to carry out a considerable collapsing of mammalian forms into a few original stem-species that had altered into the other groups as they migrated from an originating site in northern Europe.[69]

6. *Buffon and evolution*

An older historiographic tradition has often discussed Buffon's concept of species degeneration in the light of later evolutionary reflections of nineteenth-century naturalists. It is indeed the case that the degeneration theory and the historical conception of species expounded in Buffon's immensely popular work raised to prominence a thesis of the gradual alteration of forms in history under the action of purely secular forces. Furthermore, Buffon's impact upon early French species transformists – Jean Baptiste de Lamarck (1744–1829), and Etienne Geoffroy St. Hilaire (1772–1844) – who succeeded him at the Muséum national d'histoire naturelle, the Revolutionary successor to the Jardin, illustrates lines of development from some of Buffon's ideas.[70] But to designate Buffon's species degeneration as an 'evolutionary' view is misleading and historically inaccurate. The changes of species, in spite of the significant breadth Buffon allowed species degeneration in his writings by 1766, was always an ontologically limited change, confined within the limits defined by the organizing internal mould. Primordial cat, canine, or bovine stem-species might fragment into the plurality of existing geographical variants, creating *genres physiques* or *familles* in his technical parlance, but never new kinds of creatures.

Buffon's theory of species degeneration was indebted to his growing awareness of the extent of geographical variation of forms. Located at the centre of Parisian natural history, he was in an ideal position to consider the expanding body of new information in the 1760s and 1770s from scientific expeditions to the New World, South Pacific, East Indies, and the northlands by French explorers and other European inquirers.[71] The full complexity of the issues raised by this material could only partially be considered by Buffon in his last published works – the *Histoire naturelle des oiseaux* (1770–83) which was part 2 of *Histoire naturelle*, and the supplementary volumes to the latter (1774–89). This new information expanded the problem of accounting for the geographical distribution of forms and forced to the foreground the problem of the origin of forms on the remote islands and continents of the South Seas. New information from the Old and New Worlds on the apparent extinction of large mammals related to the elephants and hippopotami, and further collections of remains of woolly mammoths from Siberia and America, required explanation.[72] Buffon's emphasis on historical processes and the physical connectedness of forms was to stimulate further bio-geographical analyses. The great bio-geographers of the late Enlightenment – Johann Reinhold Forster (1729–98), Eberhard Zimmermann (1743–1815), and Alexander von Humboldt (1769–1859) – if often critical of Buffon, all drew in important respects on his work.[73]

Buffon's most powerful synthesis of cosmological, geological, and biological issues was published in 1779, the year following the death of his rival Linnæus, in the fifth supplementary volume to the *Histoire naturelle* as *Des Époques de la nature*.[74] In this work, Buffon drew together his reflections on the history of the cosmos, the physical formation of the earth, the history of life, and the theory of climatic and geographical degeneration of organic beings. Claiming that natural and human history formed a single historical scheme, Buffon suggested a model of analysis that was expounded in more developed form by several others in succeeding decades.

Utilizing for his chronological scale the results of experiments on the cooling of various molten materials conducted at his forge in Montbard in the 1760s, Buffon presented a secular Genesis story divided into seven long historical epochs encompassing in the published edition 75,000 years from first formation of the earth from the sun to the present. The first of these epochs described the cometary collision with the sun and the consolidation of the planetary bodies, a sequence requiring 2,936 years. The second epoch, lasting 32,064 years, encompassed the history of the earth from its molten state through the consolidation of various minerals and strata, the formation of mountains, and the cooling of the surface of the earth to the point where water could remain in a non-vaporized state. The third epoch of 15,000 years' duration described a primeval ocean covering the globe in which the first aquatic animals and plants arose. In the fourth epoch, lasting until approximately 60,000 years from the first origins, the waters retreated and land emerged, with a period of vulcanism resulting from the central heat created by electrical matter in the earth. Epoch five (to 65,000 years) encompassed the origins of the larger land quadrupeds in the northern latitudes, arising from the clumping together by natural forces of the organic molecules into the first forms of each of the main species. This period was followed by a sixth epoch (to 70,000 years) in which the continents separated and the contemporary geography of the earth assumed its present shape, with migrations of animals to the tropical zones. Extinction of large quadrupeds also occurred in this period. It is in this epoch that the first humans appeared in Siberia, 'in the pure state of nature, without clothes, religion, or society except among widely dispersed families . . .'[75] Spreading and diversifying, these humans form the various geographical races as they cover the habitable world. The final epoch moves to the domain of recorded human (and biblical) history, the organization of society, and the progress of the arts and sciences. The continued cooling of the earth was extrapolated to an end of all life at 168,000 years from the first origins of the world.

Although these estimates would seem, by nineteenth-century chronologies at least, unduly limited, Buffon speculated much more freely in the manuscripts, estimating in one version at least 2,993,280 years to the present with an end of life at 7,000,000 years.[76] By eighteenth-century standards, these figures involved an enormous expansion of the accepted time scale, and they were supported by the first plausible empirical estimates of the age of the Earth.

The range of this first modern integrated scientific story of the origins of the world order and its contained inhabitants, connecting natural and human history to a general history of nature, suggests the conceptual scope of Buffon's version of natural history. Outrageous to many, the *Epoques* was, like his 1749 treatise, censured by the theologians of the Sorbonne. But in its unified, comprehensive, naturalistic analysis, it supplied a framework upon which his successors could develop more complex integrations of cosmology, geology, and the subsequent history of life.

III. FROM DEGENERATION TO THE DEVELOPMENT OF NATURE

Buffon's history of nature, in spite of its ambitious historicising intentions, was nonetheless framed within a degenerating model of history. Buffon's world system, no longer open to Newton's intermittent divine repairs, was necessarily running down, gradually cooling to the state that life would no longer be possible. In this same framework, species lose coherence, organisms become smaller, and life itself wears out. Human beings, through their arts and sciences, can resist this decay for a period, but even the human species must eventually lose in this conflict with the course of nature. In this important respect, Buffon remained more a Newtonian than a Leibnizian. Nature and its immanent forces governing matter lacked constructive, teleological directedness. It is on this theoretical point that his successors were to revise Buffon's insights. Rather than a degeneration of nature, the end of the century was to see the emergence of speculative histories of nature that postulated dynamic progress and development. It is in this framework that the first genuine transformist theories were proposed.

This change in the late eighteenth century from degenerating or steady-state to progressivist histories of nature was considerably indebted to the revival of vitalistic conceptions of life. This 'vitalist' revolution of the late Enlightenment was profound in its implications. It marked the crucial transition from the assumptions of the 'mechanical' philosophy to those of nineteenth-century philosophies of nature.[77]

The conception of the organism as governed by dynamic and constructive forces, challenged but never fully eliminated from medical discourse by the hegemony of the animal-machine theory of Descartes, had been continued into the eighteenth century through philosophical programs, such as the revived nature philosophy of Ralph Cudworth (1618–77), and also on the Continent in the medical 'animism' of University of Halle theoretician of medicine, Georg Ernst Stahl (1660–1774). Aspects of Stahlianism were incorporated in select centres of medical training – Halle, Montpellier, and Göttingen. British vitalism, derived from the medical theories of William Cullen at the University of Edinburgh and John Hunter in London, provided additional sources of these ideas. Although differing widely in specifics, these medical theories were united by the conclusion that the inert conception of matter assumed by Cartesian, and some versions of Newtonian, natural philosophies, was inadequate to account for important areas of biological function.[78] In place of mechanical models of the organism, living beings were re-conceptualized as governed by new powers within matter – *vis essentialis* (Caspar Friedrich Wolff); *Lebenskraft* (Friedrich Casimir Medicus, 1736–1808); *Bildungstrieb* (Johann Blumenbach); *sensibilité* (Théophile Bordeu, Paul Joseph Barthez); and 'matter of life' (John Hunter). This new reliance on vital powers became a prominent feature of the biomedical and philosophical literature of the late Enlightenment. The total effect of the vitalist revival was to reconstitute medical theory on vitalistic rather than mechanistic grounds. Living beings now constituted a metaphysically distinct domain, governed by special dynamic forces or principles that served to explain their primary biological functions. Methodologically, this appeal to vital forces took many different forms. Johann Blumenbach, for example, defended his notion of the *Bildungstrieb* on Newtonian methodological grounds, justified by abductive inference from phenomena. Marie-François Xavier Bichat (1771–1802) emphasised a phenomenological, rather than a realistic, conception of vital agencies. The primacy of force over matter in the Leibnizian and later Kantian tradition enabled some versions of these theories to escape the charge that they involved inserting occult forces into passive matter. Disseminated at mid century through the medical articles of Diderot's and d'Alembert's *Encyclopédie*, and through other writings of medically oriented *philosophes*, vitalism in its many forms was able to enter the literature of natural history in prominent ways by the end of the century.

Particularly in the Germanies, the link that developed between the concept of a developmental history of nature and the assumption that life is governed by inherent vital forces had important consequences. An influential application of vital forces in 1759 to account for embryological development by stages (epigenesis) by Caspar Friedrich Wolff (1733–94) marked an important break with the reigning eighteenth-century mechanistic theory of embryological formation (pre-existence theory),[79] This conception of embryological development under the action of vital forces was then extended to nature and to history by the end of the century, most generally in a broader philosophical statement by Johann Gottfried von Herder (1744–1803). In his massive *Ideen zur Philosophie der Geschichte der Menschheit* (1784–91), Herder synthesised the historical cosmology of Kant and Lambert with Buffon's epochal history of nature into a dynamic developmental history progressing, rather than degenerating, under the action of an inherent vital genetic force (*genetische Kraft*), modeled on Caspar Wolff's embryological force. In his integration of cosmology, natural history, and human history into one grand schema, Herder envisaged a slowly advancing naturalistic system leading progressively to contemporary European society.[80] This raised a critical discussion within German philosophy over the epistemic status of vital forces and their relation to a developmental history of nature that was to pit Kant against Herder and his disciples in a conflict that in important respects opposed Linnæan and Buffonian conceptions of natural history against one another. It also raised questions over the limits of reason that had been brought into prominence by Kant's project for a 'critical' metaphysics.

The concept of nature as a system of interconnected processes and entities with a history developing with some kind of purposive plan under the action of teleological forces forms a prominent feature of natural history at the end of the century. The speculative, vitalistic developmentalism of Herder represented one form of this turn of events. The systematic, rational philosophy of nature set forth particularly by Friederich Schelling (1775–1854) and his disciples formed another.[81] In opposition to both stood the critical history of nature of Immanuel Kant (1724–1804).

1. *History or description of nature?*

Kant's entry into the field of natural history and his concern with functional questions of biology were a direct outgrowth of his annual academic lectures on physical geography and anthropology, offered regularly from 1757 until 1798.[82] In these lectures he had evidently treated the 'theories of the earth' of Burnet and Woodward, the *De telluris* of Linnæus, the *Protogaea* of Leibniz, and Buffon's *Histoire naturelle*. He also was aware of other biological issues being debated in his time that were to have implications for his larger epistemology.[83] The continuation of these lectures before and through the critical period provides a framework for reading Kant's statements on natural history and the classification of the sciences in his better known philosophical treatises. Tracing the impact of these inquiries on the development of Kant's thought as he moved from his earlier standpoint in *Popularphilosophie* to the critical perspectives of his mature philosophy forms a topic of current research.[84]

As Kant's scientific reflections developed alongside his mature philosophy, he made an effort to reconcile his analysis of physical-geographic and natural-historical questions with the more general structure of his critical philosophy. Beginning with his 1775 summer lectures in anthropology, Kant introduced into his writings a technical distinction between a genetic history of nature that sought a causal connection between the situation at the present and events in the past (*Naturgeschichte*), exemplified particularly by Buffon's speculations and earlier 'theories of the earth,' and the Linnæan a-temporal classificatory description of natural objects (*Naturbeschreibung*).[85] In the wake of the conflicts with Herder and certain of his *Sturm und Drang* followers in the mid-1780s,[86] Kant developed these reflections further in important essays of the late 1780s, and in the *Kritik der Urtheilskraft* (1790). Herder's speculative synthesis was attacked by Kant severely in a series of reviews in 1785, and this critique was further elaborated in the conflict with Herder's admirer, the natural historian and ethnographer Johann Georg Forster (1754–94). In these controversies, Kant denied the status of a genuine science (*Wissenschaft*) to the 'history' of nature, to some extent agreeing with Newton, but on different conceptual grounds. *Naturgeschichte* was only an inquiry of Reason (*Vernunft*) in its speculative function, organized by a regulative idea of nature as a teleological system developing in time toward the final goal of human culture and moral freedom.[87] As Kant wrote in an important essay of 1788 generated by this controversy:

> This distinction [of history and description of nature] lies in the nature of things [der *Sachen Beschaffenheit*], and I demand nothing new, but merely the careful separation of one line of inquiry from the other. Because they are wholly heterogeneous, and if the one (description of nature [*Naturbeschreibung*]) appears as a science [*Wissenschaft*] in the full glory of a great system, the other (history of nature [*Naturgeschichte*]) can exhibit only fragments [*Bruchstücke*] or shaky [*wankende*] hypotheses. Through this distinction and presentation of the second as a separate science, even if for the present (and perhaps forever) it only can be realized in outline (and most questions perhaps only be answered with a blank), I hope to make sure that one does not accept a presumed insight into something in the one that simply belongs to the other.[88]

Within the restrictions of the critical philosophy, the conception of nature as a causal developing system creating changes over historical time, unifying geological and biological developments in the manner of Buffon and Herder, could only be an ideal construct, a guide into the classification, description, and mechanistic analysis of life. It could not be claimed to be a true story of the past in itself.[89]

In spite of these careful restrictions on the claims that could be made for such speculative organizing views, however, Kant's impact on the ensuing discussion was ambiguous. Some readers, typically dropping the purely regulative status of his formulations, read him through Herder's lenses, seeing Kant providing the framework for a comprehensive program for synthesising natural history and historical inquiry into a genuine science (*Naturwissenschaft*).[90] Others, more convinced of the epistemic limits placed upon historical knowledge of nature by

Kantian epistemology, confined their attention to a description of nature.[91] This emphasis on physiographic over physiogonic inquiry, and the conclusion that genuine scientific knowledge was to be confined to the analysis of empirically ascertainable patterns of distribution, rather than speculations about historical processes, was to be an important feature of the bio-geographical researches of Eberhard Zimmermann in his landmark *Geographische Geschichte des Menschen und der allgemeinen verbreiteten vierfüssigen Thiere* (1778–83).[92]

The project of Schelling's *Naturphilosophie*, first sketched out in his *Ideen für eine Philosophie der Natur* (1797) and his *Erster Entwurf eines System der Naturphilosophie* (1799), suggested, on the other hand, a more systematic combination of the description and history of nature. This tradition can be followed into British contexts through the writings of Samuel Taylor Coleridge and his medical disciple Joseph Henry Green (1791–1863).[93]

2. *French transformism*

The most direct development from Buffon's natural history to the theory of transformism took place at the Paris Muséum national d'histoire naturelle. This displayed a different form of interaction between the classificatory insights of Linnæus and his followers and the speculative, historical views of Buffon. Restored to a position of prominence in French life science at the Revolution, Linnæan methods and theories were even proclaimed as triumphant over the *ancien régime* natural history of Buffon in some quarters.[94] Sensing the necessity of rational systems but convinced of the value of the historical and bio-geographical insights of Buffon, many French naturalists made efforts to combine the two programmes.[95] Some chose to pursue the more speculative insights of the history of nature in this tradition. Exemplary among this group is Jean Baptiste de Lamarck. Originally encouraged to work in natural history by Buffon, Lamarck's first inquiries were in botany, exemplified by his *Flore françois* of 1778. In this work Lamarck sought to work out a true natural system of botanical arrangement.

Lamarck viewed the natural system in botany as an arrangement of plants in a continuous series, beginning with the least complex mosses and lichens, and ending in the complex flowering plants. This insight was then transferred to the zoological realm in part as the result of the radical reorganization of the Jardin du Roi into the Muséum National in 1793. Lamarck shifted career directions at this time from the study of plants to the study of the complex bloodless animals, which he proceeded to define on anatomical grounds as the 'animals without backbones'. Applying to these forms the same principle of the natural system he had developed in botany, he set forth in his lectures at the reorganized Paris

Muséum the presentation of the invertebrates as a natural sequence of forms arranged from the simplest polyps to the most complex squid and octopi. In his Muséum lectures of 1800 he first proposed that this natural order was also a dynamic historical order of genetic development of lower into higher forms, a thesis expanded in print in his *Considérations du corps organiques* (1802), the *Philosophie zoologique* (1809), and in a revised form in his major work, the *Histoire naturelle des animaux sans vertèbres* (1815–22). Drawing on contemporary French medical vitalism and his own work in phlogistic chemistry, Lamarck explained the ascending system of increasing complexity through the causation of the constructive powers of chemical and electrical fluids. These were able to create life spontaneously from matter and also were able to supply the efficient cause for the progress of life to greater degrees of organization. In these first truly transformist reflections, Lamarck denied the traditional fixity of organic species and proposed a general evolutionary picture of life that was to influence the nineteenth-century reflections in several important ways. Lamarck's Muséum colleague Etienne Geoffroy St. Hilaire developed somewhat similar reflections in laying out the evidence for a great 'unity of plan' uniting the vertebrates and invertebrates.

Developing matters in a different direction, Lamarck's fellow botanist at the Muséum, Antoine Laurent de Jussieu, proposed a 'natural' arrangement of plants that recognized their distribution into distinct natural groups, within which species could be arranged by a subordination of characters.[96] This principle was applied to zoology by the young Alsatian naturalist Georges Cuvier (1769–1832), who joined the Paris Muséum staff in 1795. Cuvier undertook a novel reclassification of the animal kingdom, dividing animals into discrete, disconnected major *embranchements* – molluscs, radiates, articulates, vertebrates – within which forms were arranged on the basis of the principle of the subordination of parts. Although generally critical of the speculative transformism of Lamarck and Geoffroy St. Hilaire,[97] Cuvier reflected his contact with the Buffonian tradition through his theory of the historical revolutions of the globe, developed in the preliminary discourse to his *Recherches sur les ossemens fossiles de quadrupèdes* (1812). As in Buffon's epochs, life displays a historical sequence, separated by major geological events, resulting in the extinctions of forms and different arrangements of fauna and flora at different historical epochs.

The end of the century also saw a growing emphasis upon more limited, professionalised inquiries. The quantity of materials available to workers at the major museums demanded specialized expertise and division of labour. The reorganization of the Paris Muséum at the Revolution into twelve professorships, each with responsibility for a separate domain of natural history, formed a new disciplinary model of organization of the inquiries which had traditionally constituted natural history, setting the stage for a wider disciplinary fragmentation of the subject.[98]

The change of focus from the natural history of the opening of the century to the botany, zoology, geology, comparative anatomy, and physiology at its end represented the triumph, at least within the professional organizations of science, of the more narrowly conceived experimental work of Kölreuter, Gärtner, and Spallanzani, the detailed inquiries into microscopic structure by Réaumur and Bonnet, the comparative anatomy of Daubenton, the ornithological studies of Mathurin Jacques Brisson (1723–1806), and the detailed local faunal studies of Eberhard Zimmerman, over the more speculative and theoretical tradition represented by Buffon.[99]

IV. FROM NATURAL HISTORY TO ANTHROPOLOGY

In terms of its general philosophical impact, the speculative tradition of natural history was important and even transformative for some prominent lines of philosophical reflection of the late Enlightenment. The willingness of natural historians and philosophers conversant with natural history – Herder, Kant, Rousseau, Monboddo, and Kames – to discuss the philosophy of the human sciences in relation to the work of the great philosophical natural historians of the century carried with it profound implications. No other area of inquiry more seriously threatened to undermine the philosophical project of Enlightenment philosophers, exemplified by David Hume's programme of 1739[100] to develop a secular 'science of man' that was to be built upon the concept of a uniform human nature presumed to serve as a secular foundation for politics and ethics. To this enterprise was opposed the evidence for the great variety of types, customs, beliefs, and geographical variations within the human species revealed by the expansion of natural history, employing the very process of empirical inquiry Hume had recommended.[101] The redefinition of 'anthropology' and the refocus of attention on the questions related to the 'natural history of man' in the latter part of the Enlightenment reflect this new level of concern. Kant, for example, inaugurated his own lectures on anthropology in 1772, splitting these off his lectures on physical geography. Furthermore, he was concerned to distance his project of a transcendental and 'moral' anthropology from the growing ethnographic and physical approach generated by the work of the philosophical physicians and natural historians.[102] His former student Johann Herder, on the other hand, openly sought to replace formal philosophical treatment of human beings with a cultural and historical anthropology and ethnography, explicitly developing on the reflections of Buffon, Rousseau, and the philosophical physicians.[103]

The impact of natural history on these philosophical developments in the human sciences can be followed through an examination of the question of the unity of the human species. Linnæus's struggles in the major revisions of the *Systema naturae* of 1744, 1748, 1758 and 1766, generated by the welter of reports of man-like apes, aborigines, feral children, and curious man-like creatures with tails living in the woods or in underground caves, revealed the issues besetting a classificatory approach to the question.[104] The massive quantity of new information on the geographical variations of the human species, summarized in the reports of naturalists accompanying major voyages of exploration in the latter half of the century, further complicated the assumed unity of human nature. If novel animals and plants seemed to form distinct species confined to distinctive fauna regions, could not human beings also be considered to form the same plurality of species? More closely in touch with the conclusions of the natural history of the day than Hume, Jean-Jacques Rousseau saw the solution to the great philosophical questions of ethics and politics in a 'conjectural history', describing the development of human beings to the state of civilization from more primitive 'men of the woods', apparently constructing his account of the original state of humanity upon the contemporary reports of the orang-outang of Borneo.[105] Whether Rousseau intended his treatise as a literal 'historical' account of the rise of human beings is a major interpretive issue in the text itself. For those who read Rousseau in a literal sense, it was not the discovery of a constant human nature that supplied the key to the moral and political questions of his age. Rather, the solution lay in a historical transformation of human nature, accompanied by a parallel physical transformism, in which man-like apes were changed over time into civilized humans. This historical account, claimed Rousseau, promised to resolve 'an infinity of moral and political problems which the philosophers cannot resolve'.[106]

For those unwilling to countenance Rousseau's slow transformation of human nature, the discoveries in natural history of the end of the century challenged the unity of the human species itself. Growing immediately from the efforts by naturalists to discriminate specific faunal and floral regions in response to the new bio-geographical data of the second half of the century, the period was presented with two competing interpretations that vied for acceptance. One interpretation, following Buffon's views, defended the unity and essential identity of the human species over time but admitted the possibility of permanent historical 'degenerations' within the species under the impact of differing climatic conditions, resulting in the production of permanent historical varieties within the human species. This concept underlay the concept of 'race' developed explicitly by Kant and Johann Blumenbach in the 1770s.[107] The other possibility, given its most influential scientific statement by the French naturalist

Jules Joseph Virey (1775–1847) in 1800, concluded that human beings formed distinct species, either created independently or derived separately by historical transformation from apes.[108] Although polygenism – the thesis of multiple species of human beings – was a venerable theory, dating particularly from the Pre-Adamite theory of Isaac de la Peyrère in the seventeenth century,[109] the new polygenism of the end of the century was developed on new grounds. It now claimed strong empirical warrant, and it was supported by the arguments of important natural historians. The 'anthropology' of the new century was forced as a result to deal with a wide range of issues generated by these speculations of the natural historians.

By the close of the century, natural history had clearly been transformed from a propaedeutic discipline, located among the sciences of memory in Bacon's classification of the sciences, into a dynamic programme of related researches, pursued at major scientific institutions and prosecuted with narrowing focus on detailed areas. It had also developed its own methodologies and forms of analysis distinct from those of the physical sciences. In this form it deeply affected the nineteenth century in both scientific and philosophical dimensions.

NOTES

1 See *The Cultures of Natural History*, eds. N. Jardine, J. Secord, and E. Spary (Cambridge, 1996).
2 William Ashworth, 'Emblematic Natural History of the Renaissance', in *The Cultures of Natural History*, eds. Jardine et al., 17–37; 'Natural History and the Emblematic World View', in *Reappraisals of the Scientific Revolution*, eds. D. C. Lindberg and R. S. Westman (Cambridge, 1990), 303–32.
3 See Vladimir Jankovic, *Reading the Skies: A Cultural History of English Weather, 1650–1820* (Chicago, IL, 2000), chs. 4–5. See also Lesley B. Cormack, '"Good Fences Make Good Neighbors": Geography as Self-Definition in Early Modern England', *Isis* 82 (1991), 639–61; David Elliston Allen, *The Naturalist in Britain: A Social History* (London, 1976), esp. ch. 1.
4 See Allen, 'Natural History in Britain in the Eighteenth Century', *Archives of Natural History* 20 (1993), 333–47, for an overview of the social history dimensions. See also W. P. Jones, 'The Vogue of Natural History in England, 1750–1770', *Annals of Science* 2 (1937), 332–56.
5 A primary title citation list generated by computer gives 685 works with these terms in the title, including duplicates and new editions.
6 Francis Bacon, *Preparative Towards a Natural and Experimental History: Aphorisms on the Composition of the Primary History*, in *Works*, eds. J. Spedding, R. L. Ellis, and D. D. Heath, 14 vols. (London, 1857–74), 4: 253.
7 On the concept of 'style' in science, see symposium in *Science in Context* 4 (1991), 223–447.
8 Harold Cook, 'Physicians and Natural History', *Cultures of Natural History*, eds. Jardine et al., 91–105; Andrew Cunningham, 'The Culture of Gardens', in same, 38–56; Karen M. Reeds, *Botany in Medieval and Renaissance Universities* (New York, NY and London, 1991).
9 Allen, *The Naturalist in Britain*, ch.1.

10 Daniel Roche, 'Natural History in the Academies', in *Cultures of Natural History*, eds. Jardine et al., 127–44; Alice Stroup, *A Company of Scientists: Botany, Patronage, and Community at the Seventeenth-century Parisian Royal Academy of Sciences* (Berkeley, CA, 1990), esp. ch. 6.

11 Allen, *Naturalist in Britain*, ch. 1: 'Natural History in Britain'.

12 See Paula Finlen, 'Courting Nature', in *Cultures of Natural History*, eds. Jardine et al., 57–74, for the early background of this tradition.

13 On this notion of the natural history museum as a centre of geographical control, see Bruno Latour, *Science in Action* (Cambridge, MA, 1987), ch. 6, and Emma Spary, *Utopia's Garden: French Natural History from Old Regime to Revolution* (Chicago, IL, 2000), ch. 2.

14 Christopher Fox, 'How to Prepare a Noble Savage: The Spectacle of Human Science', in *Inventing Human Science: Eighteenth Century Domains*, eds. C. Fox, R. Porter, and R. Wokler (Berkeley and Los Angeles, CA, 1995), 1–30.

15 Scott Atran, *Cognitive Foundations of Natural History* (Cambridge, 1990), chs. 6–7; James L. Larson, *Reason and Experience: The Representation of Natural Order in the Work of Carl von Linné* (Berkeley, CA, 1971), ch. 1; and Phillip R. Sloan, 'John Locke, John Ray and the Problem of the Natural System', *Journal of the History of Biology* 5 (1972), 1–53.

16 John Ray, *Synopsis methodica animalium quadrupedum et serpentini generis* (London, 1693) 53, 60; *Synopsis methodica avium & piscium*, ed. W. Derham (London, 1713).

17 Gunnar Broberg, '*Homo sapiens*: Linnaeus's Classification of Man', in *Linnaeus: The Man and His Work*, ed. T. Frängsmyr (Berkeley, CA, 1983), 156–94, and P. R. Sloan, 'The Gaze of Natural History', in *Inventing Human Science*, eds. Fox et al., 112–51.

18 On the spread of linnæanism, see Frans Stafleu, *Linnaeus and the Linnaeans: The Spreading of Their Ideas in Systematic Botany, 1735–1789* (Utrecht, 1971); Allen, 'Natural History in Britain,' esp. 342–3; Lisbet Koerner, 'Carl Linnaeus in His Time and Place', in *Cultures of Natural History*, eds. Jardine et al., 145–62.

19 For an exception see J. L. Larson, 'An Alternative Science, Linnæan Natural History in Germany, 1770–1790', *Janus* 66 (1979), 267–83.

20 The most theoretically interesting of these are Linnæus's *Oratio de telluris habitabilis incremento* (Leyden, 1744); and the dissertations of Isac J. Biberg, *De Oeconomia naturæ* (Uppsala, 1749); H. C. D. Wilcke, *De Politia naturae* (Uppsala, 1760); and Christian Hoppius, *Anthropomorpha* (Uppsala, 1760). Linnæus is estimated by Stafleu to have had over 186 pupils under his immediate supervision during his teaching career at Uppsala between 1741 and 1776 (Stafleu, *Linnaeus and Linnaeans*, 143).

21 Jean-Jacques Rousseau, *Lettres élémentaires sur la botanique* (Paris, 1789), first appearing as letters in J. J. Rousseau, *Collection complète des oeuvres de J. J. Rousseau* (Geneva, 1782). The first publication as a separate monograph is in the English version edited by Thomas Martyn as *Letters on the Elements of Botany, Addressed to a Lady* (London, 1785), to which had been added twenty-four additional letters by Martyn explaining the Linnæan system.

22 Carl von Linné, *Praelectiones in ordines naturales plantarum*, eds. J. C. Fabricius and P. D. Giseke (Hamburg, 1792).

23 J. C. Beaglehole, 'Eighteenth Century Science and the Voyages of Discovery', *New Zealand Journal of History* 3 (1969), 107–23. On the work of Harrison and longitude, see *The Quest for Longitude*, ed. W. J. H. Andrewes (Cambridge, MA, 1996).

24 See Michèle Duchet, *Anthropologie et histoire au siècle des lumières* (Paris, 1995), chs. 2–3; Alan Frost, 'The Pacific Ocean: The Eighteenth Century's "New World"', *Studies on Voltaire and the Eighteenth Century* 152 (1976), 779–822; Sloan, 'The Gaze of Natural History,' esp. 133–9.

25 On the concept of centres of creation, see Larson, *Interpreting Nature: the Science of Living Form from Linnaeus to Kant* (Baltimore, MD, 1994), 27.

26 See Janet Browne, *The Secular Ark: Studies in the History of Biogeography* (New Haven, CT, 1983), chs. 1–3.
27 René Descartes, *Principles of Philosophy*, trans. V. R. Miller and R. P. Miller (Dordrecht, 1983), Pt. 4, princ. 44, p. 203.
28 Descartes, *Principles*, Pt. 3, princ. 45, pp. 105–6.
29 Paolo Rossi, *The Dark Abyss of Time: The History of the Earth & the History of Nations from Hooke to Vico*, trans. L. G. Cochrane (Chicago, IL, 1984), ch. 7.
30 William Whiston, *A New Theory of the Earth, From its Original, to the Consummation of All Things* (London, 1696).
31 Isaac Newton, *Opticks: or, A Treatise of the Reflections, Refractions, Inflections and Colours of Light*, 3rd edn. (London, 1721), Qu. 31, 350–82. See Rossi, *Dark Abyss*, ch. 8, 41–49. See also David Kubrin, 'Providence and the Mechanical Philosophy: The Creation and Dissolution of the World in Newtonian Thought. A Study of the Relations of Science and Religion in Seventeenth Century England' (unpublished PhD dissertation, Cornell University, 1968), chs. 8–11.
32 Important eighteenth-century works on the theory of the earth in the period before Buffon's writings include John Woodward's influential, *An Essay toward a Natural History of the Earth and Terrestrial Bodies* (London, 1695; 2nd edn., 1702; Latin, 1714; 3rd English edn., 1723; French edn., Amsterdam 1735); Leibniz's 1693 prospectus of his later *Protogaea* in *Histoire de l'Académie Royale des Sciences*, Année MDCCVI . . . (Paris, 1707), 10–11; Louis Bourguet's 'Mémoire sur la théorie de la terre', in his *Lettres philosophiques sur la formation des sels et des cristaux* (Amsterdam, 1729); and Henri Gautier's *Nouvelles conjectures sur le globe de la terre* (Paris, 1721). On the general character of the pre-Buffonian context see François Ellenberger, 'Les sciences de la terre avant Buffon: bref coup d'oeil historique', in *Buffon 88: Actes du Colloque international 1988*, ed. J. Gayon (Paris, 1992), ch. 21, 327–42; Gabriel Gohau, 'La "Théorie de la terre", de 1749', in the same, ch. 22, 343–520, and François Ellenberger, 'A l'aube de la géologie moderne: Henri Gautier (1660–1737),' Pt. 1, *Histoire et nature* 7 (1975), 3–58; Pt. 2, *Histoire et nature* 9–10 (1976–7), 3–142.
33 I emphasize that my concern here is with the genetic history of the earth, and not with actualist theories of geology as they were developed by Gautier and others.
34 For an alternative view, see Paolo Casini, 'Buffon et Newton', in *Buffon 88*, ed. Gayon, ch. 19, 299–308.
35 Stephen Hales, *La Statique des végétaux et l'analyse de l'air*, trans. G.-L. L. Buffon (Paris, 1735).
36 Roger, *Buffon*, chs. 5–6; and Lesley Hanks, *Buffon avant l'Histoire naturelle* (Paris, 1966).
37 Isaac Newton, *La Méthode des fluxions, et des suites infinies* [trans. G.-L. L. Buffon.] (Paris, 1740).
38 A complete listing of these papers is to be found in 'Bibliographie de Buffon', compiled by E. Genet-Varcin and Jacques Roger, in Buffon, *Oeuvres philosophiques*, ed. J. Piveteau (Paris, 1954), 513–75.
39 See Michael Heyd, *Between Orthodoxy and the Enlightenment: Jean-Robert Chouet and the Introduction of Cartesian Science in the Academy of Geneva* (The Hague, 1983), esp. ch. 7.
40 Lorraine J. Daston, *Classical Probability in the Enlightenment* (Princeton, NJ, 1988).
41 Jacques Roger, *Buffon: A Life in Natural History*, trans. S. L. Bonnefoi (Ithaca and London, 1997), ch. 6. See also Sloan, 'From Logical Universals to Historical Individuals: Buffon's Conception of Biological Species', in *Histoire du concept d'espèce dans les sciences de la vie*, eds. J. Roger and J.-L. Fischer (Paris, 1987), 101–40 at 109–18.
42 Roger, *Buffon*, ch. 9.
43 See William H. Barber, *Leibniz in France, from Arnauld to Voltaire; a Study in French Reactions to Leibnizianism, 1670–1760* (Oxford, 1955). See also Sloan, 'L'hypothétisme de Buffon: sa

place dans la philosophie des sciences du dix-huitième siècle', in *Buffon 88*, ed. Gayon, 207–22.

44 Gottfried Wilhelm Leibniz, 'Third Paper' and 'Fifth Paper', in *The Leibniz-Clarke Correspondence*, ed. H. G. Alexander (Manchester, 1956), 25–6, 90.

45 Jean-Henri-Samuel Formey, *La belle Wolfienne* (The Hague, 1741); Emerich de Vattel, *Défense du Système leibnitien contre les objections et les imputations de Mr. de Crousaz. . . .* (Leiden, 1741); and especially Jean des Champs, *Cours abrégé de la philosophie wolffienne, en forme de lettres*, 2 vols. (Amsterdam and Leipzig, 1743–7).

46 Letter of Claude Hélvetius to Mme du Châtelet, December, 1740, as quoted in *Les Lettres de la Marquise du Châtelet*, ed. T. Besterman, 2 vols. (Geneva, 1958), 2: 36n.

47 Linda G. Janik, 'Searching for the Metaphysics of Science: The Structure and Composition of Madame Du Châtelet's *Institutions de Physique*, 1737–1740', *Studies on Voltaire and the Eighteenth Century* 201 (1982), 85–113.

48 Du Châtelet, *Institutions de physique* (Paris, 1740), ch. 6, §102, p. 119.

49 Descartes, *Le monde de René Descartes ou traité de la lumière*, in *Oeuvres*, eds. C. Adam and P. Tannery, 11 vols. (Paris, 1897–1910), 11: 36–7. See James E. McGuire, 'Boyle's Conception of Nature', *Journal of the History of Ideas* 33 (1972), 523–42; and Jean Ehrard, *L'idée de nature en France dans la première moitié du XVIII siècle* (Paris, 1970), ch. 2: 'Le mécanisme universel'.

50 Ehrard, *L'idée*, ch. 3: 'Impulsion ou attraction?' On the revival of the nature philosophy of the Cambridge Platonists in the early decades of the century, see Roger, *The Life Sciences in Eighteenth-Century French Thought*, ed. K. R. Benson, trans. R. Ellrich (Stanford, 1997), 336–53.

51 Gottfried W. Leibniz, 'On Nature Itself, or On the Inherent Force and Actions of Created Things', *Acta eruditorum*, Sept. 1698, as trans. by L. E. Loemker in Leibniz, *Philosophical Papers and Letters*, 2nd edn. (Dordrecht, 1969), 498–508.

52 Du Châtelet, *Institutions*, ch. 7, §161, 174. Compare this definition to that in Buffon's 'De la nature, première vue', *Histoire naturelle, générale et particulière avec la description du cabinet du roi*, 14 vols. (Paris, 1749–67), 12: iii–xvi (1764), reprinted in *Oeuvres phil.*, 31–35 at 31.

53 Leibniz, *Protogaea: De l'aspect primitif de la terre et des traces d'une histoire très ancienne que renferment les monuments mêmes de la nature* (Latin and French text), trans. B. de Saint-Germain, ed. J.-M. Barrande (Toulouse, 1993), 13.

54 See, for example, des Champs, *Cours abrégé*, letter 20, 1: 235–77 at 236–7.

55 Des Champs, letter 19, 1: 232.

56 An important exception to this is Benoît de Maillet's Epicurean-inspired *Telliamed, ou Entretiens d'un philosophe indien avec un missionaire françois sur la diminution de la mer* (Amsterdam, 1748), written between 1698 and 1718 and circulated in manuscript. On the history of the text see Albert V. Carozzi, 'Introduction' to *Telliamed or Conversations Between an Indian Philosopher and a French Missionary on the Diminution of the Sea*, trans. and ed. A. V. Carozzi (Urbana, IL, 1968), esp. 5–24.

57 Bourguet, 'Memoire sur la theorie de la terre,' *Lettres philosophiques*, 177–220. On Bourguet see François Ellenberger, 'Louis Bourguet', *Dictionary of Scientific Biography*, ed. C. C. Gillispie (New York, NY, 1970–80): *Supplement* (1978) 15: 52–9. On Buffon's relation to Bourguet, see Roger, *Buffon*, 99–103.

58 Many of Buffon's distinctions on these issues are closely similar to those in des Champs, *Cours abrégé*, letter 21, 1: 248–61 at 248–51. See also letter 19, 1: 223–34.

59 Buffon, 'Premier discours (2): de la manière d'étudier et de traiter l'histoire naturelle', *Histoire naturelle* 1, 3–62 (repr. in *Oeuvres phil.*, 7–26 at 23–5); translated as *From Natural History to the History of Nature: Readings from Buffon and His Critics*, trans. and eds. J. Lyon and P. R. Sloan (Notre Dame, IN, 1981), 89–128. For discussion see Roger, *Buffon*, ch. 2.

60 Buffon, 'Premier discours', in *Oeuvres phil.*, 23–4.

61 Hume, *Enquiry Concerning Human Understanding* (1748), ed. T. L. Beauchamp in the *Clarendon Edition* (2000), especially Pt. 3. There is no direct evidence that Buffon had read either this treatise or the *Treatise on Human Nature* of 1739–40.

62 Roger, *Buffon*, 426.

63 On Buffon's 'actualism' in this period see Gohau, 'La 'Théorie de la terre' en 1749', in *Buffon 88*, ed. Gayon, 348–51.

64 Buffon, 'De la nature: première vue', *Histoire naturelle* 12 (in *Oeuvres phil.*, 31).

65 Buffon, 'L'Asne', *Histoire naturelle* 4 (1753) (in *Oeuvres phil.*, 353–8 at 355). See also the earlier 'De la Reproduction en général', *Histoire naturelle* 2 (1749) (in *Oeuvres phil.*, 238–64 at 238). On Buffon's species concept, see Sloan 'From Logical Universals,' 101–40; Jean Gayon, 'L'individualité de l'espèce: une thèse transformiste?' in *Buffon 88*, ed. Gayon, 475–89; and Paul L. Farber, 'Buffon's Concept of Species', *Journal of the History of Biology* 5 (1972), 259–84.

66 'Espèce: histoire naturelle', in *Encyclopédie*, 5: 956–7.

67 Buffon, 'La Brebis' and 'La Chèvre', *Histoire naturelle* 5 (1755); see *Oeuvres phil.*, 359.

68 Buffon, 'Le Cerf', *Histoire naturelle* 6 (1756).

69 Buffon, 'De la dégéneration des animaux', *Histoire naturelle* 14 (1766); see *Oeuvres phil.*, 394.

70 See especially Pietro Corsi, *The Age of Lamarck*, trans. J. Mandelbaum (Berkeley, CA, 1988), esp. ch. 1.

71 Buffon's source for much of this information was Antoine François Prévost d'Exiles, *Histoire générale des voyages, ou, Nouvelle collection de toutes les relations de voyages qui ont été publiées jusqu'à présent*, 20 vols. (Paris, 1746–70), a work appearing almost in parallel to the *Histoire naturelle*.

72 Claudine Cohen, *Le destin du mammouth* (Paris, 1994), chs. 4–5; John L. Greene, *The Death of Adam: Evolution and Its Impact on Western Thought* (Ames, IA, 1959), ch. 4.

73 See Larson, *Interpreting Nature*, ch. 4, and also, 'Not without a Plan: Geography and Natural History in the Late Eighteenth Century', *Journal of the History of Biology* 19 (1986), 447–88.

74 Buffon, *Des Époques de la Nature* in *Histoire naturelle*: Supplément vol. 5 (Paris, 1778), as in Buffon, *Les époques de la nature* (critical edn.), ed. J. Roger (Paris, 1962), 2–3, (reissued Paris, 1988), 4. See also *Oeuvres phil.*, 117–229 at 117–8. The work actually was published in 1779.

75 Buffon, *Époques*, Sixième époque, 212 (Roger edn., 192; *Oeuvres phil.*, 183).

76 See the exhaustive discussion of these chronologies in the introduction to the Roger edition of *Époques*, lx–lxvii.

77 I am deeply indebted for some of these insights to Peter Hanns Reill's *Vitalizing Nature in the Enlightenment* (University of California Press, 2005), although we disagree on the degree to which Buffon can be classed as a 'vitalist'. See also John Zammito, *Kant, Herder, and the Birth of Anthropology* (Chicago, IL, 2002), ch. 8; François Duchesneau, *La Physiologie des lumières: empirisme,modèles et theories* (The Hague, 1982), chs. 8–10; and Roger, *Life Science*, 336–53.

78 On the distinction between 'mechanistic' and 'materialistic' Newtonianism, see Robert E. Schofield, *Mechanism and Materialism: British Natural Philosophy in an Age of Reason* (Princeton, NJ, 1970).

79 See Shirley A. Roe, *Matter, Life and Generation: Eighteenth-Century Embryology and the Haller-Wolff Debate* (Cambridge, 1981).

80 See Zammito, *Kant, Herder, and the Genesis of Kant's Critique of Judgment* (Chicago, IL, 1992) ch. 9; Owsei Temkin, 'German Concepts of Ontogeny and History around 1800', *Bulletin of the History of Medicine* 24 (1950), 227–46; Reill, 'The History of Science, the Enlightenment

and the History of "Historical Science" in Germany', in *Beiträge zur Geschichtskultur* 5 (1991), 214–31, esp. 222–28.

81 On the distinctions between these two programmes, I am particularly indebted to Peter Reill's *Vitalizing Nature in the Enlightenment* (see note 77).

82 Kant's anthropology lectures were separated from the physical geography lectures in 1772–3.

83 On Kant's sources see Erich Adickes, *Kants Ansichten über Geschichte und Bau der Erde* (Tübingen, 1911). For a recent analysis of Kant's relations to Buffon, see Jean Ferrari, 'Kant, lecteur de Buffon', in *Buffon 88*, ed. Gayon, 155–63.

84 Zammito, *Kant and Herder*, esp. chs. 3, 7. See also my 'Preforming the Categories: Eighteenth-Century Generation Theory and the Biological Roots of Kant's *A-Priori*,' *Journal of the History of Philosophy* 40 (2002), 229–253.

85 Kant, 'Von den verschiedenen Racen der Menschen', in Ak 2: 429–43. An English translation of the revised 1777 version of this prospectus is given in 'Immanuel Kant, "Of the Different Human Races"', trans. J. M. Mikkelsen, in *The Idea of Race*, eds. R. Bernasconi and T. Lott (Indianapolis, IN, 2000), 8–26.

86 On the Herder conflict, see Zammito, *Genesis*, chs. 8–9.

87 See Rudolf A. Makkreel, 'Kant and the Interpretation of Nature and History', *Philosophical Forum* 21 (1989–90), 169–81.

88 Kant, 'Über den Gebrauch teleologischer Principien in der Philosophie'(1788), in Ak 8: 157–84 at 162, translation my own. The first full English translation of this text is found in 'On the Use of Teleological Principles in Philosophy', in *Race*, ed. R. Bernasconi (Malden, MA, and Oxford, 2001), 37–56.

89 See esp. Kant, *Kritik der Urtheilskraft*, Pt. 2, §80 (Ak 5: 417–22); translated as *Critique of the Power of Judgment*, trans. P. Guyer and E. Matthews, ed. P. Guyer, in *Works* (2000).

90 See, for example, Christoph Girtanner, *Ueber das Kantische Prinzip für die Naturgeschichte: ein Versuch diese Wissenschaft philosophisch zu behandeln* (Göttingen, 1796).

91 This seems to be important for understanding the primarily physiographic approach of Alexander von Humboldt. On this see J. A. May, *Kant's Concept of Geography and Its Relation to Recent Geographical Thought* (Toronto, 1970), 75–9. However, others have seen Humboldt as deeply interested in the integration of description and history of nature. See on this Michael Dettlebach, 'Introduction' to Alexander von Humboldt, *Cosmos*, trans. E. C. Otté (Baltimore, MD, 1997), 2: (esp.) xxix–xxxviii.

92 See Larson, *Interpreting Nature*, ch. 4.

93 See discussion and relevant Green texts in Richard Owen, *The Hunterian Lectures in Comparative Anatomy, May–June 1837*, ed. P. R. Sloan (Chicago, IL and London, 1992), 307–21.

94 Pietro Corsi, *The Age of Lamarck*, ch. 1; Spary, *Utopia's Garden*, ch. 5. Linnæus's botanical system had already been established in practice at the Jardin in the 1770s, but was most deeply influential on the provincial academies until the Revolution. See Pascal Duris, *Linné et la France, 1780–1850* (Geneva, 1993).

95 See Georges Cuvier, 'Prospectus', *Dictionnaire des sciences naturelles . . . par plusieurs professeurs du Jardin du Roi*, 60 vols. (Strasbourg and Paris, 1816–30), 1: vii. On the complex history of this text, first issued in part in 1804–5, see Corsi, *Age of Lamarck*, 220–1.

96 Antoine-Laurent de Jussieu, *Genera plantarum . . . secundum ordines naturales disposita . . .* (Paris, 1789).

97 Toby Appel, *The Cuvier-Geoffroy Debate: French Biology in the Decades before Darwin* (New York, NY, 1987).

98 See Appel, *Cuvier-Geoffroy Debate*, 13–19 and 'Appendix A,' 238–40; On the history of the Muséum, see symposium *Le Muséum au premier siècle de son histoire*, eds. C. Blanckaert et al. (Paris, 1997).

99 Larson, *Interpreting Nature*, ch. 3.

100 David Hume, *A Treatise of Human Nature* (1739–40), eds. D. F. Norton and M. J. Norton (Oxford, 2006), Introduction, 4–6 (SBN xx). On Hume's subsequent struggles with polygenecism, see John Immerwahr, 'Hume's Revised Racism', *Journal of the History of Ideas* 53 (1992), 481–6. See also Zammito, *Kant, Herder*, ch. 5.

101 See Peter J. Marshall and Glyndwr Williams, *The Great Map of Mankind: Perceptions of New Worlds in the Age of Enlightenment* (Cambridge, MA, 1982), ch. 9.

102 Zammito, *Kant, Herder*, esp. 292–307.

103 Zammito, *Kant, Herder*, ch. 8.

104 See Sloan, 'The Gaze of Natural History,' 121–6. Linnæus first proposed his new species *Homo troglodytes* in the tenth edition of the *Systema naturae* of 1758.

105 See Rousseau, *Discours sur l'origine et les fondemens de l'inégalité parmi les hommes*, in *Oeuvres*, 3: Note X, 208–14. See also Francis Moran, 'Pongos and Men in Rousseau's *Discourse on Inequality*', *Review of Politics* 57 (1995), 641–64; and R. Wokler, 'Anthropology and Conjectural History in the Enlightenment', *Inventing Human Science*, eds. Fox et al., 31–52.

106 Rousseau, *Discours*, 192.

107 See Robert Bernasconi, 'Who Invented the Concept of Race? Kant's Role in the Enlightenment Construction of Race,' *Race*, ed. Bernasconi, 11–36.

108 Julien-Joseph Virey, *Histoire naturelle de genre humain, ou, recherches sur les principaux fondements physiques et moraux, precedées d'un discours sur la nature des êtres organiques*, 2 vols. (Paris, 1801), 1: 91. On Virey, see especially C. Blanckaert, 'J. J. Virey, observateur de l'homme (1800–1825)', in *Julien-Joseph Virey: naturaliste et anthropologue*, eds. C. Benichou and C. Blanckaert (Paris, 1988), 97–182.

109 Richard H. Popkin, *Isaac la Peyrère (1596–1676): His Life, Work and Influence*, (Leiden, 1987), ch. 9.

V

MORAL PHILOSOPHY

32

THE FOUNDATIONS OF MORALITY

DAVID FATE NORTON AND MANFRED KUEHN

I. BRITAIN

1. *Introduction*

In the seventh and final part of his *Theory of Moral Sentiments*, Adam Smith reviews 'the most celebrated and remarkable of the different theories which have been given concerning the nature and origin of our moral sentiments'. Nearly all earlier theories agree, he suggests, in one important respect: 'they are all of them . . . *founded* upon natural principles'. He then adds that, in analysing moral theories, we should consider their answers to two questions: (1) 'wherein does virtue consist?' and (2) 'by what power or faculty of mind is it that virtue is recommended to us?'[1]

In the course of his review of answers to the first of these questions, Smith discusses four different theories: the theory that traces morality to *propriety*; that which traces it to *prudence*; and that which traces it to *benevolence*. He then compares these three theories with a fourth, or what he calls the 'licentious system'. He describes this fourth system as a theory that has its 'real foundation' in a misguided understanding of popular asceticism. The proponents of this system, he says, attempted 'to prove that there was no real virtue' and that 'what pretended to be [virtue], was a mere cheat and imposition upon mankind'. But however 'groundless' this licentious theory really is, Smith argues, it 'must have had some foundation', even a 'foundation in nature'; otherwise its fraudulent character would immediately have been perceived by everyone (VII.ii.4.12 and 14).

In answer to the second question, that concerning the power or faculty of mind that recommends virtue to us, Smith notes that three different principles have been suggested: self-love, sentiment, and reason. Hobbes and his followers – the egoists, as we now call them – adopt the first of these principles, and suggest that the ground of approbation or disapprobation is simply a consideration of the tendency of our actions to our own happiness or disadvantage. In direct opposition to the egoists, Francis Hutcheson 'had been at great pains to prove that the principle of approbation [is] not founded on self-love', but is instead 'founded upon a sentiment of a peculiar nature, upon a particular power of perception exerted by the mind at the view of certain actions or affections (VII.iii.3.2 and 4).[2] And, whereas Ralph Cudworth and others had claimed that it is reason that enables us to 'distinguish between what is fit and unfit', or moral and immoral, in our actions and passions, Hutcheson 'had the merit of being the first who distinguished with any degree of precision in what respect all moral distinctions may be said to arise from reason, and in what respect they are founded upon immediate sense and feeling'. In fact, Smith argues that Hutcheson had 'demonstrated' that our moral assessments 'could not arise from any operation of reason'. Although he does not agree with Hutcheson on some details, Smith is convinced that moral assessment is founded on sentiment, and that there is no room for further dispute about this particular issue (VII.iii.intro.2, VII.iii.2.9, VII.iii.3.4).

Smith's open concern with the foundations of morality is not unusual for his time. Twenty years earlier, in his *A Treatise of Human Nature* (1739–40), David Hume had remarked on a controversy that had in 'late years . . . so much excited the curiosity of the public, [namely] *Whether these moral distinctions be founded on natural and original principles, or arise from interest and education*'. Those who adopted the second of these views – those who traced the alleged distinction between virtue and vice to self-interest and education – had claimed, as Hume puts it, that morality itself has 'no foundation in nature', but is, rather, founded merely on the pain or pleasure that arises from considerations of self-interest. In contrast, those who aligned themselves on the other side of this issue – those who said that moral distinctions are founded on what Hume thinks of as '*natural and original principles*' – claimed that 'morality is something real, essential, and founded on nature'.[3]

Hume does not say what he means by 'late years'. He may have been thinking only of the more recent past, in which case he will have had in mind the debate that raged following the appearance in 1723 of an expanded edition of Bernard Mandeville's *Fable of the Bees*, a work that claims, to use Hume's terms, that morality is entirely dependent on interest and education.[4] In response, one writer after another entered the debate about moral foundations. In 1723, Robert Burrow published *Civil Society and Government Vindicated from the Charge of being Founded on, and Preserv'd by, Dishonest Arts*. In 1724 Richard Fiddes added *A General Treatise of Morality, Form'd upon the Principles of Natural Reason only . . . in Answer to two Essays lately Published in The Fable of the Bees. . . .* In 1725, Hutcheson joined the battle with his *An Inquiry into the Original of our Ideas of Beauty and Virtue* and some shorter contributions to periodicals. John Clarke's *The Foundation of Morality in Theory and Practice Considered* appeared in 1726.

Archibald Campbell's *Enquiry into the Original of Moral Virtue* appeared in 1728, as did the first part of John Balguy's *The Foundation of Moral Goodness: or A further Inquiry into the Original of our Idea of Virtue* in 1728; the second part of this work followed in 1729. Thomas Bott's *Morality, Founded in the Reason of Things, and the Ground of Revelation* appeared in 1730. John Gay's *Preliminary Dissertation concerning the Fundamental Principle of Virtue or Morality* was published in 1731, as was John Jackson's *Calumny no Conviction . . . wherein is Consider'd the Ground and Obligation of Morality*. Thomas Mole's *The Foundation of Moral Virtue Consider'd* appeared in 1732; his *The Foundation of Moral Virtue Re-consider'd* in 1733. Joseph Forster's *Two Essays: the One on . . . the Foundation of Morality* appeared in 1734. In 1735, an exchange of letters between Gilbert Burnet and Hutcheson was republished in book form as *Letters . . . concerning the True Foundation of Virtue*. Joseph Butler's brief *Of the Nature of Virtue* appeared in 1736. Catherine Trotter's *Remarks upon . . . the Controversy concerning the Foundations of Moral Duty* was written in 1737.

Hume himself, in addition to drawing attention to this debate about foundations, contributed to it. His earliest discussion of justice, found in Book 3 of the *Treatise* (1740), concludes with the claim that the distinction between justice and injustice has 'two different foundations, *viz.* that of *self-interest* . . . and that of *morality*' (3.2.6.11, SBN 533), while in the opening section of his later *An Enquiry concerning the Principles of Morals* (1751) he tells us that there 'has been a controversy started of late, much better worth examination, concerning the general foundation of MORALS'. The issue, he suggests in this later work, can be put in two ways. We can ask what appears to be an epistemological question: Do we attain our knowledge of morals 'by a chain of argument and induction, or by an immediate feeling and finer internal sense'? Or we can phrase the same question so that it raises ontological issues: Are moral judgements, 'like all sound judgment of truth and falsehood . . . the same to every rational intelligent being', or are they, 'like the perception of beauty and deformity . . . founded entirely on the particular fabric and constitution of the human species'?[5]

It is obvious, then, that the *foundations problem* continued to be of central importance well after 1740. Additional works that can be seen to contribute to the controversy include Thomas Rutherforth's *An Essay on the Nature and Obligations of Virtue* (1744), and Trotter's reply to this work, *Remarks upon the Principles and Reasonings of Dr. Rutherforth's Essay on the Nature and Obligations of Virtue: in Vindication of the Contrary Principles and Reasonings* (1747). Thomas Chubb's *The Ground and Foundation of Morality Considered* appeared in 1745; James Balfour's response to Hume, *A Delineation of the Nature and Obligation of Morality*, in 1753. Richard Price's important *A Review of the Principal Questions and Difficulties in Morals; Particularly those Relating to . . . its Nature and Foundation* was published in 1758, while Smith's *The Theory of Moral Sentiments* followed a year later.

One must be careful not to overstate the extent to which the participants in this debate were genuinely engaged with one another and with a set of univocal questions. More often than not they seem to have been talking past one another. To put the point differently and more generally, the foundations debate was not as straightforward as Smith intimates. From his vantage point it may have seemed helpful to suggest that the debate over the foundations of morality was focused on the answers to the two questions he mentions: 'Wherein does virtue consist?' and 'By what power or faculty of mind is it that virtue is recommended to us?'. In the heat of actual debate the situation looked very different. To those debating the issue, it routinely appeared that there were additional and even more fundamental questions. One of these questions was, clearly, 'Does morality have a secure foundation in the nature of things?' Less explicitly, the debate also focused on answers to the question, 'What is the proper characterisation of morality?' Some philosophers characterised morality as a distinctive phenomenon and concluded that moral differences are both 'real' and in some sense unique. These writers supposed that one could give a foundational account of morality only if one could trace such real and unique moral differences to some set of objective and unique ontological differences adequate to ground moral differences in a nonreductive way. Then, supposing themselves successful in this enterprise, these same writers manifested a marked tendency to suppose that they and they alone had shown that morality is something 'real', and that they and they alone had offered an account of the foundations of morality. Moreover, those who told a different story about the foundations of morality were typically alleged to have denied that morality has a foundation, and were, often enough, characterised as moral sceptics. As a consequence, writers who had good reason to suppose that they had provided an account of the foundations of morality were attacked as moral sceptics who denied that morality has a foundation in the nature of things.

To illustrate: Despite what were clearly substantial differences of opinion, every participant in the foundations debate appears to believe that there is a phenomenon of morality to explain. No participant, for example, appears to deny that there exists a range of moral terms (in English, *good, evil, virtue, vice, right, wrong, just, unjust*), nor does anyone appear to deny that ordinary individuals, as much as moral theorists, are able to use these terms competently (i.e., to use them in the appropriate contexts and intelligibly). Consequently, one might suppose that the controversy about the foundations of morality is to be understood as a relatively straightforward disagreement regarding those features of the world that underlie such facts as the competent, intelligible use of these terms. To some degree, such a supposition would be correct. Even Hobbes and Mandeville, two of those widely attacked for denying that morality has a foundation in nature, assume that it is to humans or human actions that this set of terms applies, and suppose that ordinary humans do so apply them without making what we would think of as egregious category errors.[6] Both also provide a relatively detailed account of how this feature of our experience has arisen. Both trace it to settled features of human nature. But despite this obvious effort to trace morality to its source in human nature, Hobbes and Mandeville were typically perceived to be moral sceptics denying that morality has a foundation in the nature of things.

To illustrate further: Francis Hutcheson was one of the moralists who criticized Hobbes and Mandeville for denying that morality is something real with a secure foundation in the nature of things. To rectify the damage done by such sceptical moralists, Hutcheson undertook to show that virtue and vice are real and well founded. But another group of moralists, despite what were clearly substantial agreements with Hutcheson (including in particular a concern to refute the allegedly dangerous views of Hobbes and Mandeville) criticised him for denying that morality is something real with a secure foundation in the nature of things. Hutcheson was thus accused of making exactly the same mistake that Hobbes and Mandeville had made. To these philosophers, as a moralist Hutcheson was in certain ways an improvement on Hobbes and Mandeville (he was at least a 'friend of virtue'), but at the most fundamental level he was no improvement at all. This leads us to suggest that although the foundations debate was ostensibly about the foundations of morality, it was equally a highly polemical contest to determine which moral theorists could justifiably claim to be 'moral realists' (as we might now say) and be taken to have offered a reliable guide to the understanding of morality.

The present part of this chapter focuses on some of the principal eighteenth-century participants in the foundations debate and emphasises the polemical nature of the debate in which these participants engaged. We are, in other words, as much concerned with the nature of the debate as with the foundations that were offered, for the debate shaped, and continues to shape, philosophical views about what constitutes a valid account of morality. We note, however, that it is clearly artificial and possibly misleading to begin an account of this debate with discussions of early eighteenth-century figures. The foundations issue is a coherent theme running through the writings of Montaigne, Grotius, Hobbes, Pufendorf, Cudworth, and Bayle, to mention only some of the principal luminaries of the late sixteenth- and seventeenth-century controversy.[7] On the other hand, our central thesis may stand out more sharply when we see that the well-known epistemological features of the eighteenth-century debate have a significant ontological dimension.

2. *Shaftesbury and Samuel Clarke*

The two turn-of-century writers who did the most to ensure that the foundations debate continued into the eighteenth century were probably Anthony Ashley Cooper, the third Earl of Shaftesbury (1671–1713), and Samuel Clarke (1675–1729). Although both have been represented as concerned principally with an epistemological issue, that is, specifying which faculty, reason, or sense enables us to grasp moral distinctions, each is equally concerned with an ontological issue, that is, specifying those features of reality that underlie and correspond to, and thus give substance and reality to, the moral differences we experience.

Shaftesbury, at the outset of his *Inquiry concerning Virtue or Merit*, notes that religion and virtue seem so closely related as to appear inseparable.[8] But he supposes it necessary to examine this relationship, to ask (with, clearly, Pierre Bayle's claim that there could be a society of atheists in mind) what 'virtue is, considered by itself, and in what manner it is influenced by religion; how far religion necessarily implies virtue; and whether it be a true saying that it is impossible for an atheist to be virtuous' (1: 238).

Shaftesbury's view of atheism is typical of a period in which atheism was not restricted to those who explicitly denied the existence of a Deity. There were few who were willing to take so dangerous a step. For Shaftesbury the 'perfect Atheist' is one who believes that nature was formed merely by chance and thus without any design or purpose (1: 240). He might also have noted that the atheists of the period included those who granted that there might be a Deity, but claimed that He takes no interest in human affairs, as well as those who believed there is no life after death. In other words, the label 'atheist' was at this time applied to those who denied to morality the traditional assistances it had been provided by religious belief: the assistance of understanding the world as having been designed and created to serve some higher purpose, of believing the course of this world as under the continuous care and guidance of a concerned Deity, and of believing there is a future state in which we can expect divine rewards and punishments to be meted out.[9] In raising the question of the relationship of religion and virtue, Shaftesbury was asking if morality is dependent on the assistance provided by belief in a Deity who continuously monitors our thoughts and actions, and who rewards or punishes us as we conform or fail to conform to divine rules.

To know how virtue relates to religion we must know, as Shaftesbury puts it, 'what virtue is, considered by itself'. To this end, he draws our attention to what he calls the frame or system of nature. Although there is much we do not know about nature, and particularly about the role some species are intended to play in the larger scheme of things, there is also much that we do know. We know, for example, that each creature is better off in some conditions than in others, and hence that 'there is in reality a right and a wrong state of every creature' and 'a certain end, to which every thing in his constitution must naturally refer'. We can see, too, that what is good for individuals is good for their species, and thus that what we might call antisocial behaviour is against the interest of each individual. We can also see that, as the wing of the fly is suited to the web of the spider, so are many species suited to the existence and well-being of other, very different species. In consequence of many such perceived interdependencies, it is reasonable to conclude not only that all animals form a system, but also that everything found in the universe is part of a general system. It is also reasonable to conclude that whatever contributes positively to this system is good, and whatever is destructive of it is ill or bad. The terms *good* and *ill*, in other words, can be used to refer to real or objective differences between possible states of affairs (1: 238, 243–6).

We do not, however, consider a creature virtuous merely because it contributes positively to the good of itself, its species, or the universe in general. To be virtuous, this creature must also satisfy other requirements. She must first be a sensible, reflective creature who is aware of what she does. That is, she must not act merely from instinct as would a thoughtless and unreasoning automaton. She must also have a notion of the public interest and a sense of right or wrong – she must grasp the moral character of situations and of what she does. Finally, she must act from a self-determined motive to do good or avoid evil. A creature who lacks self-consciousness or the ability to grasp the moral character of situations cannot be virtuous. A person who unavoidably does ill (because of constraint or irreparable physical debility, for example) is not counted among the vicious. Likewise, a person who contributes to the public good merely as a consequence of selfish motives is not counted among the virtuous (1: 247–58).

The virtuous individual, then, is the individual who, aware of what contributes to or detracts from the public good, undertakes, by conscious intent or from settled character, to add to the store of good, or to avoid increasing the supply of evil. This established, we can return to the issue of the relationship of religion and virtue. It is clear, Shaftesbury argues, that neither virtue nor what comes to the same thing, the practice of virtue, is dependent on religion. It is true that belief in a providential, judging Deity and a future state of reward or punishment may provide an additional incentive to act in ways that are consistent with virtue, an incentive that atheism cannot provide. And yet virtuous behaviour does not depend on holding religious beliefs, and may even be hindered by such beliefs. Many religions teach that 'treachery, ingratitude, or cruelty' have been given a divine sanction, or call on their followers to persecute friends, to offer human sacrifices, or to abuse and torment themselves out of religious zeal. But nothing, Shaftesbury insists, not even religion, can justify brutality or barbarity or make them beneficial. Nothing, not custom, law, or religion, can ever 'alter the eternal measures, and immutable independent nature of worth and virtue' (1: 255).

Moral differences, according to Shaftesbury, derive from the different motives available to rational agents. That he supposes this distinction of motives an effective, practical foundation of morality is made clear in his attacks on what he took to be the moral scepticism of Hobbes and Locke. Shaftesbury knew, of course, that both of these philosophers had offered positive, even dogmatic, moral theories. He nonetheless supposes they are moral sceptics because, in one-sidedly insisting on a favourite explanatory hypothesis, they in effect doubt or deny the reality of important aspects of human experience.[10] Hobbes attempted to explain every human act by the one principle of self-interest, an explanation that has the important consequence of making our apparent moral distinctions meaningless. If Hobbes is right, then *friendship, love, public interest* – all those words that appear to make reference to altruistic acts or motives – have ultimately the same meaning as their apparent opposites. There are no differences in motivation. If Hobbes is right, then there is 'no such thing in reality as virtue'. To Shaftesbury, who alludes to himself as a 'realist in morality', reducing all motivations to selfish ones is to introduce what he explicitly calls a 'general scepticism' about morality – a scepticism that denies that there is such a thing as real good or real virtue or natural justice (*Characteristicks*, 1: 61–5, 79; 2: 53; *Life* 37–8). Privately, Shaftesbury argued that Locke, because he is more subtle, is even worse than Hobbes. Locke tells us that our moral ideas are mere inventions, constructs without real models, and he credulously repeats stories of cultures that have no idea of virtue, and thus concludes that 'virtue . . . has no other measure, law, or rule, than fashion and custom; morality, justice, equity, depend only on law and will . . . And thus neither right nor wrong, virtue nor vice, are anything in themselves; nor is there any trace or idea of them naturally imprinted on human minds' (*Life* 403–5).

Shaftesbury took these views to be dangerous, despite the fact that they are merely one-sided speculations. Because Hobbes and Locke explicitly deny that moral distinctions either are real, observer-independent distinctions, or that they derive from real differences in the nature of things (Shaftesbury finds no practical difference between these two hypotheses), these views encourage individuals to disregard moral considerations and thus threaten to undermine morality. To counter this danger, Shaftesbury eschews the speculative and a priori in favour of an observationally based study of human nature, a study that leads him to conclude that humans are inherently moral and inherently capable of recognising moral distinctions. Just as animals have instincts that enable them not only to survive, but even to thrive, so too do humans have the features or dispositions they need. We see that humans cannot survive without society, and we find that certain ideas, the ideas of benevolence or the general good, for example, although perhaps not strictly innate, naturally arise in individuals as they mature. We find that humans not only have these ideas, but also have an interest in what they represent. We find that humans are motivated not only by the gross selfishness Hobbes describes, but also by public spirit or a concern for the general good. We find that we are able to distinguish benevolence from indifference or malice. We find, to sum up, that we humans have a kind of moral instinct, a natural 'moral sense' that enables us to be just the kind of creature Hobbes says we never are, and that provides in human motivation archetypes for those moral ideas that Locke says are only arbitrary constructs. To show that morality is not founded on religion, Shaftesbury argues that it is founded in the distinctions of motive available to rational agents. To show that those who deny that morality has any real foundation are mistaken, he argues for this same conclusion and insists that we as moral creatures are equipped with a moral sense that enables us to act morally and to distinguish virtue from vice.

Samuel Clarke pursues a different path to much the same end. In the first of two linked discourses published in 1705–06, Clarke argues that there must necessarily have existed from eternity a unified, unchangeable, and self-existing Being who is not only infinite, omnipotent, and the cause of everything, but also possesses infinite goodness and justice and any other moral perfections suited to being the supreme governor and judge of the world.[11] In the second of these discourses, he goes on to argue that there are eternal and necessary differences between created things, and that these differences are alone sufficient to make it morally appropriate and right ('fit and reasonable') that creatures should act in some ways, and morally inappropriate and wrong that they should act in other ways.

Clarke argues that Hobbes and the voluntarists generally fail to take into account the fact that in even the most primitive state of existence there are individual beings of a distinct character and between whom there are unchangeable relationships. Even in the primitive state postulated by Hobbes there was an infinite and omnificent Deity and a set of finite and dependent human beings. Given that there is such a being as this Deity, it is clearly more appropriate that He should be supreme governor and direct the course of events toward the regular and rational ends He perceives to be best for the whole of creation, than that He allow things to run on at random. Given that there is such a Deity and such creatures as we humans are, it is clearly more appropriate that we should honour, imitate, and obey Him, than that we should do the contrary. Given that there is a set of humans, it is 'undeniably more Fit, absolutely and in the Nature of the thing itself, that all Men should endeavour to promote the universal good and welfare of All, than that all Men should be continually contriving the ruin and destruction of All'.[12] Prior to any command of the Deity (save His command that we should exist) and prior to any convention or positive law, there are, in the very nature of things themselves, characteristics and relationships (and especially differences) that translate immediately into real moral differences. Because there are, as Clarke puts it, 'certain necessary and eternal differences of things', we can see that moral differences are 'founded unchangeably in the nature and reason of things, and unavoidably [arise] from the differences of the things themselves', and that 'Some things are in their own nature Good and Reasonable and Fit to be done' (2: 611–12).

That Clarke means to say that these real and enduring factual differences provide both a necessary and a sufficient ground for morality is confirmed by what he has to say about moral knowing and moral obligation. The differences and relationships he is speaking of are, he argues, absolutely fixed and unalterable, and no more open to wilful change than are the differences between 'Light and Darkness . . . Sweet and Bitter . . . Pleasure and Pain', or 'Mathematical or Arithmetical Truths' (2: 626). Furthermore, the differences that constitute morality are known in just the way these other differences are known: immediately or intuitively. For any rational being to deny that there are such differences would be equivalent to denying, while seeing the sun, that there is such a thing as light, or to denying that twice two is equal to four or that the whole is larger than any of its constituent parts (2: 609, 613).

Clarke grants that there is one notable difference between our response to these nonmoral ('speculative') truths and our response to perceived moral differences. Perception of a speculative truth forces our minds to assent to that truth, leaving us with no choice but to assent. In contrast, the perception of a moral truth still leaves us free to act contrary to what we have perceived (2: 615). But, he argues, acting in this contrary way is not only absurd, but also immoral. We are said to perceive, for example, that there is an infinite Deity and that we are finite creatures dependent on Him. Where there is such a difference, we also perceive that we as lesser creatures ought to honour, imitate, and obey the vastly superior One, the Deity. To fail to act consistently with these perceptions is absurd because it is in effect to deny the very truths we have perceived; it is absurd in the same sense that it is absurd to deny that twice two is four. And, to fail to act consistently with these perceptions is at the same time blameworthy. Once we have seen that we as creatures ought to honour the Deity, it then obviously follows that any failure to honour Him is nothing more than insolence or a 'wilful wickedness and perversion of Right'. Once we have seen the real and eternal differences of things, our minds, of their own accord, are 'compelled to own and acknowledge' that there really are such obligations unavoidably binding us to a particular course of action (2: 613–14; see 618). The recognition of this obligation can no more be avoided than our recognition of light when standing in bright sunshine or our recognition that twice two is four. The 'original Obligations of Morality', as Clarke calls them, follow immediately from our recognition of 'the necessary and eternal' relationships of things themselves. For him, then, the ground or foundation of morality is nothing more than a set of real and perceivable relationships between existing things, relationships the mere perception of which is sufficient to inform us of what is right and wrong, and to oblige us to the right or virtuous course of action (2: 630).

3. Mandeville and Hutcheson

The decade following the appearance of Shaftesbury's *Characteristicks* was a relatively quiet one for the foundations debate, but the publication, in 1723, of an expanded version of Bernard Mandeville's *The Fable of the Bees* changed that. Mandeville (1670–1733) took direct aim at Shaftesbury, and particularly at the latter's optimistic view of human nature and his account of the foundation of the moral distinctions we find ourselves making. But Mandeville's challenge may easily be misunderstood. He does not challenge Shaftesbury's claim that a real and significant moral difference would follow from actions consciously motivated by a concern for public interest, in contrast to actions motivated by a concern for private interest. In one sense, Mandeville accepts exactly Shaftesbury's account of the foundations of morality. But he in effect insists that this account is only hypothetically correct: it would be correct if there were distinctions of motive of the sort Shaftesbury hypothesises, but Mandeville then argues that there are in fact no such differences of motive. Humans are motivated only by selfish interest. Mandeville sees that we do call some persons or actions virtuous, and others vicious, but insists that Shaftesbury's explanation of this fact about our moral practice cannot be correct. An alternative explanation is needed, and this Mandeville was ready to supply.

Shaftesbury had traced morality to distinctions of motive, arguing that virtuous individuals are those and only those who consciously act from other-regarding motives. Mandeville, although the fact is seldom noticed, accepts this conclusion.[13] At least he agrees that genuinely virtuous individuals are those and only those who consciously act from other-regarding motives. He denies, however, that anyone acts from such motives, and then goes on to give an altogether different account of morality as practised. Seen as premises and conclusions, Mandeville's argument looks like this:

- Genuinely virtuous individuals are those and only those who act from other-regarding motives.
- No individuals act from benevolent or other-regarding motives.

- Therefore, there are no genuinely virtuous individuals.[14]
- Therefore, what is called *virtue* is not really virtue, but only the appearance of virtue, an invention without foundation in nature.

Whether Mandeville accepted the first of these premises because he genuinely agreed with it, or simply because doing so made it easier for him to demonstrate that selfishness and hypocrisy are all-prevailing, is a question we need not attempt to answer here. It is clear that the view constituting this premise, the claim that moral distinctions are founded on genuine and significant differences of motivation, was the view of many. And it is clear that Mandeville accepted precisely this view: it is, he says, 'impossible to judge of a Man's Performance, unless we are thoroughly acquainted with the Principle and Motive from which he acts'.[15] But Mandeville's critics heard only the balance of his argument, heard only his shocking attack on human nature and his outrageous suggestion that what we call morality is nothing more than deception and hypocrisy.

The significance of the first premise is revealed by the second, for this tells us that humans never act from benevolent or other-regarding motives. Humans act only from selfish or self-regarding motives. As Mandeville puts it at the beginning of his "Enquiry into the Origin of Moral Virtue," animals, including humans, 'are only solicitous of pleasing themselves, and naturally follow the bent of their own Inclinations, without considering the good or harm that from their being pleased will accrue to others' (1: 41). Granted we may appear to witness contrary phenomena, but we are in fact mistaken. A closer examination shows that actions that are *apparently* other-regarding (and hence genuinely virtuous) are in fact self-regarding and hence lacking all moral merit. Close examination shows that even an act that *seems* to be done from pure kindness is in fact done from self-interest. Pity, says Mandeville, 'is the most gentle and the least mischievous of all our Passions', but it is still as much a passion as 'Anger, Pride, or Fear'. As a consequence, he goes on, whoever acts from pity, no matter how much good he does,

> has nothing to boast of but that he has indulged a Passion that has happened to be beneficial to the Publick. There is no Merit in saving an innocent Babe ready to drop into the Fire: The Action is neither good nor bad, and what Benefit soever the Infant received, we only obliged our selves; for to have seen it fall, and not strove to hinder it, would have caused a Pain, which Self-preservation compell'd us to prevent. (1: 56)

Given such findings, Mandeville's first conclusion is inescapable. If virtue is the product of other-interested motivation, and if such motivation is impossible, it follows that virtue is nonexistent, and the distinction between virtue and vice is only an apparent distinction. Yes, we obviously do talk about virtue and vice, and we act as though virtue and vice are real qualities that can be attributed to, or experienced in, moral subjects, but we are sadly deceived. At bottom, neither motivations nor actions are morally distinct, and consequently there are neither virtuous nor vicious individuals. We do see, however, that we do *appear* to make moral distinctions. We see individuals praised as virtuous, as good or generous, and honest or courageous; we also see them, even the same individuals, censured as evil or selfish, dishonest or cowardly. Mandeville does not shy from accounting for this fact. The 'Moral Virtues', he argues, 'are the Political Offspring which Flattery begot upon Pride' (1: 51). We do appear to make moral distinctions, but these are entirely without foundation in reality; they are mere inventions of the imagination.

Mandeville's account of the invention of morality takes the form of what we might call *the inventor's story*, a kind of antihero version of the myth of Prometheus. No animal, Mandeville tells us, is so headstrong, selfish, cunning, and difficult to govern as the human being. So difficult are humans to govern that, if we are to be governed, it will never be by force alone. From this beginning Mandeville goes on to explain that humans have become governable through the invention of morality. Those who have undertaken to establish society (an ordered accumulation of humans) have been engaged, according to this story, in a massive and long-standing deceit. Knowing that humans are all selfish and self-willed, these inventors nonetheless consistently inform us that we will each be better off if each controls his or her appetite, and sacrifices personal interests to the good of the public in general.

In Mandeville's view this claim that self-interest is best served by sublimating it to the general good is nothing more than an outright lie. For this lie to be effective, it had to be attractively circumstanced. That is, if this lie was to serve the end for which it was (and is) told, those who pattern their behaviour on it – those who have diverted their naturally self-regarding inclinations – must be rewarded, while those who fail to divert their selfish inclinations must be punished. The rewards offered include tangible benefits, but have not been limited to such tangible items. There are not, for one thing, enough tangible goods to satisfy everyone, and, even if there were enough, there would be constraints on their dispersal.

As it happens, the most important of the nontangible rewards has been found to be moral praise, or, to use Mandeville's preferred and deflating term, *flattery*. Having found flattery to be an effective and 'bewitching Engine' of morality, the moral inventors managed to convince the balance of humankind of their superiority to other animals. Moreover, they convinced the individuals making up one part of our species that they were superior to those making up another, merely animal-like group. That is, some of us were made to feel morally superior to those 'low-minded' types who, 'always hunting after immediate

Enjoyment ... yielded without Resistance to every gross desire, and made no use of their Rational Faculties but to heighten their Sensual Pleasure'. Characteristically, individuals of the 'superior Class', supposing themselves of a loftier sort altogether, make war on themselves (they fight against their natural but allegedly irrational inclinations) and seek nothing less than the general good through the 'Conquest of their own Passion'. In short, these individuals were conned by their own pride and the machinations of the inventors, and this induced a number of them, especially

> the fiercest, most resolute, and best among them, to endure a thousand Inconveniences, and undergo as many Hardships, that they may have the pleasure of counting themselves Men of the second [that is, superior] Class, and consequently appropriating to themselves all the Excellences they have heard of it. (1: 43–5)

It was in this fashion that 'Savage Man was broke' (1: 46). In the course of time, even the sensual class was also brought under control by the moral inventors or lawgivers. Even these unpretentious individuals came to believe that a reciprocal moderation would work to individual advantage, or that their individual self-interests would best be served by moderation. Taken generally, the story leads one to the conclusion that morality is indeed 'the Political Offspring which Flattery begot upon Pride'.

The *Inquiry into the Original of our Ideas of Beauty and Virtue* of Francis Hutcheson (1694–1746) was first published in 1725. Although this work contained no essay entitled, as Hutcheson had projected, "An Essay upon the Foundations of Morality, according to the Principles of the Ancients",[16] there can be little doubt of his interest in the foundations debate. A lengthy subtitle describes the *Inquiry* as a defense of Shaftesbury's principles '*against the Author of the Fable of the Bees*', while the Preface explained that the author aimed to show that '*Human Nature* was not left quite indifferent in the Affair of Virtue',[17] and nearly every section of the work reverberated with explicit concern with moral foundations. Noting that we distinguish between moral good and evil, Hutcheson asks 'what general Foundation there is in Nature for this Difference'. After he examines 'the springs of the Actions which we call virtuous, as far as it is necessary to settle the general Foundation of the Moral Sense', he finds that neither esteem nor benevolence is 'founded on Self-Love, or Views of Interest', and he devotes an entire section to the proposition that the 'Sense of Virtue, and the various Opinions about it, [are] reducible to one general Foundation', namely, benevolence. More precisely, Hutcheson seeks to show 'that the universal Foundation of our Sense of moral Good' is benevolence, while the foundation of our sense of moral evil is 'Malice, or even Indolence, and Unconcernedness about ... manifest publick Evil'.[18]

Hutcheson's efforts to find in human nature a foundation for genuine moral differences were clearly a response to the claim, found in Mandeville and others, that we humans are motivated only by self-interest. Seen as a set of premises and conclusions that correspond to those of Mandeville, Hutcheson's argument took this form:

- Genuinely virtuous individuals are those and only those who act from other-regarding motives.
- Individuals do regularly, although not invariably, act from benevolent or other-regarding motives.
- Therefore, there are genuinely virtuous individuals.[19]
- Therefore, what is called *virtue* is something *real*.[20]

Given his intention to defend the view of Shaftesbury, Hutcheson's association of virtue and other-regarding motives comes as no surprise. And given that Mandeville had also accepted this principle, it is clear that he and Hutcheson reach their significantly different conclusions about the reality of virtue because they affirm contrary second premises. Or because, in other words, their views regarding certain crucial factual matters are diametrically different. Mandeville's survey of human behaviour had led him to the view that individuals never do act from benevolent or other-regarding motives. Hutcheson counters with a more detailed survey that attempts to show that this cynical conclusion is mistaken. This new survey shows that at least some actions are performed from other-regarding motives. As a result, Hutcheson validly concludes that there are genuinely virtuous individuals or acts, and hence that virtue is something real – something, that is, that has a distinctive foundation in the nature of things.

Hutcheson's conclusion depends heavily on the results of his new and, he argues, more careful survey of our moral approvals or disapprovals or of the circumstances in which we say individuals are virtuous or vicious. This survey reveals, for example,

- that of many long-dead individuals who can no longer contribute to our interests or pleasure, some are morally approved and others are morally disapproved (about some we remain morally indifferent).
- that although the generous acts of an agent and a fruitful field may equally serve our interests and gain our approval, it is only the agent that is called *virtuous*; although the fraudulent acts of a partner and a falling beam may both injure us, it is only the partner that is called *vicious*.
- that if two individuals contribute in similar ways to our well-being, the one from benevolent motives with an intent to benefit us, the other from purely self-interested motives, we count as virtuous only the individual who was benevolently motivated. Moreover, because we consider the motives from which individuals act, we may morally disapprove an agent whose behaviour causes no actual injury to

others, and morally approve agents whose behaviour has happened to cause harm to others.

- that while we can be bribed to perform an action which we think to be morally wrong, we cannot be bribed to feel that this same action is right or that we are right to undertake it. More generally, we find that we cannot by any act of our will alter our moral approvals and disapprovals. Thus while we can bribe an enemy to betray his country and benefit ours, thus furthering our self-interest, we nonetheless feel moral disapproval and brand this person a traitor (*Inquiry* 111–15, 123–7).

Facts of this sort, Hutcheson concludes, establish beyond doubt that Mandeville and the other egoists are mistaken. These facts show that there are natural or unlearned differences in our responses to actions or events, differences that would not arise if these moralists are right about human nature. But they are not right. The egoists badly misdescribe our approbative experience. When we look more carefully at that experience, we see that our approvals and disapprovals are more subtle than they have thought. More particularly, we find that we quite naturally make some important distinctions: Without training or indoctrination we distinguish, for example, between *natural* and *moral* goods and between moral *good* or *virtue* and moral *evil* or *vice*.

Moral good, Hutcheson argues, is a characteristic of, or at least attributable to, only rational agents *qua* agents, while *natural good* may be a characteristic of many different classes of things. Hutcheson's crucially important claim is that we recognize this distinction, and show that we recognize it because we respond in one way to the honesty, kindness, or generosity of an agent, and in another substantially different way to the beneficial qualities of an inanimate object, or even to the wealth, houses, lands, health, sagacity, or strength of human beings. We necessarily esteem those who possess such qualities as generosity, but we may very well envy or hold in disesteem those who possess wealth or power, and we simply do not take fields and houses or clothes and horses to have *moral* characteristics. In addition, our idea of *moral good* is the 'Idea of some Quality apprehended in Actions', a quality that produces 'Approbation, attended with Desire of the Agent's Happiness', while our idea of *moral evil* is of a quality that produces disapprobation, and is attended with a desire for the agent's misery. He goes on to suggest that *approbation* and *disapprobation* probably cannot be explained further because they are simple or primitive ideas, and even these descriptions of moral good and evil are here offered provisionally. They are the best we can do until we find out whether we really do have such ideas and what general and natural *foundation* there is for this distinction between the morally good and the morally evil (*Inquiry* 105–6).

We have been reviewing Hutcheson's attempt to show, contra Mandeville, that some actions are performed from other-regarding motives, and thus that there is a real, well-founded distinction between virtue and vice. Assuming that Hutcheson's description of our approbative experience is accurate, it appears that he is on track to accomplish his goal. If it is true that we consistently respond differently not only to different kinds of goods but also to different kinds of actions, and if it is true that what constitutes the relevant differences between these actions is a difference in the motivations that give rise to them (so that we feel a special kind of approbation only in response to other-regarding actions), then it is clear that some actions are the result of other-regarding motives. The facts of approbative experience are significantly more complex than Mandeville has supposed. Given these facts, it follows, contra Mandeville, that there are genuinely virtuous individuals, and that *virtue* and *vice* are real and founded in the nature of things.

Given these important facts, the question becomes, as Hutcheson typically frames it, What feature of human nature is presupposed by the fact that we can and do make these distinctions? Elaborating on the suggestion made by Shaftesbury, Hutcheson devotes an entire section to showing that we have 'implanted in our nature' a complex moral disposition, a moral sense, whose presence and operation provide a foundation for morality.[21] This the moral sense does by making it possible for us to be moral agents and moral observers. But even before he reaches this part of his account, Hutcheson has argued that the moral sense comprises both an inherent benevolence able 'to direct our Actions' and an innate 'disinterested ultimate Desire of the Happiness of others' (129, 152). It is this aspect of the moral sense that motivates us to participate in society, to pursue the public good, and to take pleasure in the realisation of that good. Had we lacked this disposition we might have developed an abstract or speculative idea of virtue, but our concern for our own interest would have caused us, contrary to fact, to be concerned only with this interest and to approve only those agents and actions that serve this interest.

The moral sense is also comprised of an inherent cognitive power that enables us to respond differently to benevolence and self-interest. The human mind is formed in such a way that it can and often does approve or condemn actions or agents without concern for its own pleasure or interest. Thus if two individuals contribute in similar ways to our well-being, but one acts 'from an ultimate Desire of our Happiness, or Good-will toward us; and the other from Views of Self-Interest, or by Constraint', we respond differently (113). In response to the first one we feel gratitude and approbation; to the other we are indifferent. Or, if we know that an individual has benevolent dispositions, but has been prevented from exercising these, we approve of her and count her as morally good even though she has not been able to act, even though she has done nothing to benefit us. The nature and complexity of these responses show that we must have a perceptual power, a sense of moral discrimination, for without such a sense we would assess fields and agents or patriots and traitors all in the same way and only with regard to our own interests and well-being.

Because Hutcheson held that the moral sense discriminates between virtue and vice by means of feelings of approval and disapproval, some of his critics supposed that he meant to reduce virtue and vice to these feelings or sentiments. Hutcheson explicitly denied such a reductivist intent. The moral sense relies on feelings to distinguish virtue or vice, but moral qualities are themselves independent of the observer who feels approbation or disapprobation of them. The 'admired Quality', he says, is a quality of the agent judged, and entirely distinct from the approbation or pleasure of either the approving observer or the agent, and the moral perceptions (the idea or concept) involved 'plainly represents something quite distinct from this Pleasure'.[22] Feelings play a cognitive and a motivating role, but virtue is constituted by the benevolent disposition that gives rise to approbation, and vice by the malevolent or sometimes indifferent dispositions that give rise to disapprobation. Virtue and vice, although known through the feelings they arouse, are real and observer-independent qualities of agents, and thus morality can be seen to have a foundation in human nature.

4. *Hutcheson, Burnet, and Balguy*

Soon after the publication of the first edition of Hutcheson's *Inquiry*, Gilbert Burnet the Younger (1690–1726) and Hutcheson published an exchange of letters in the *London Journal*. Burnet readily granted that he was impressed by Hutcheson's effort to find 'one plain and simple Principle of Nature' as the source of morality.[23] But, although Hutcheson's conclusions are 'generally *True* and *Right* in themselves', he was later to write, they lack 'a sufficient Foundation'. Hutcheson got the conclusion right – virtue and vice have a real foundation – but he got the argument wrong. Consequently, Burnet urged him to carry out a 'further and deeper Search into the very Bottom of Virtue, in order to discover the true and solid Foundation of it'.[24]

Burnet's fundamental complaint is that Hutcheson's account of moral good and evil explains these notions only relatively – only as good or evil things relate to us or affect us – and gives us no guarantee that these relationships are fixed by any immutable principle. In Burnet's terms, Hutcheson's account fails to establish that 'the Ideas of Moral Good and Evil must be immutably fixed' in 'the divine Mind'. Moral Good cannot mean merely that which is approved by humans or even by the Deity. If we do not know why the Deity approves, if we cannot say that He approves of the thing because it is good and because He is a being of moral perfection, then what He approves today He may disapprove tomorrow.

In that event what is morally good today will be morally evil tomorrow. But, assuming it is absurd to think that good and evil can, as it were, 'change Places', then it follows 'that Moral Good and Evil have an immutable foundation in the Nature of Things; as immutable as the Truths of Geometry . . . which even the divine Mind cannot be conceived to alter' (*Works* 7:[8]–[9]).

John Balguy's response to Hutcheson is in many ways similar to Burnet's. Balguy (1686–1748) begins with praise for this 'ingenious Author' whose work is 'written . . . with so good a Design, is every where so instructive, or entertaining, and discovers upon all Occasions such a Fund of Good-Nature, as well as Good Sense' that he only reluctantly points out 'some Particulars wherein I apprehend he [Hutcheson] has erred'. But because these mistakes appear to be of 'the utmost Consequence', because they 'lie at the Foundations of Morality, and like Failures in Ground-work, affect the whole Building', they must be mentioned.[25]

Balguy approves of Hutcheson's rejection of the egoist's view that all human actions are motivated by self-interest. Hutcheson is right in his claim that this theory 'can never account for the Principal Actions of human Life; such as the Offices of Friendship, Gratitude, natural Affection, Generosity, publick Spirit, Compassion'. Balguy also accepts Hutcheson's claim that humans have implanted in them benevolent affections; experience shows this to be true. And he grants that these affections were given to us to 'engage, assist, and quicken us in a Course of virtuous Actions'. They are important auxiliaries in the battle to be virtuous. But Hutcheson treats these affections or instincts as more than mere auxiliaries. He treats them as 'the true Ground and Foundation of [Virtue]. He makes Virtue entirely to consist in [this ground], or flow from it'.[26]

This last Hutchesonian position is, Balguy argues, mistaken. To rest moral goodness on the 'two Instincts of Affection and Moral Sense' will undermine its beauty and dignity. 'I am', he says, as unwilling as Hutcheson 'that Virtue should be looked upon as wholly artificial'. It is right to try to represent virtue as something natural to us, as something that flows 'unalterably from the Nature of Men and Things'. But, contra Hutcheson, 'Virtue has a natural Right and Authority, antecedently to every Instinct, and every Affection', and 'Truth and Right Reason' are its ultimate grounds (7–8).

Of the five objections Balguy makes to Hutcheson, two are especially interesting here. He objects, first, that Hutcheson appears to turn virtue into something 'of an arbitrary and positive Nature; [as something] entirely depending upon Instincts, that might originally have been otherwise, or even contrary to what they now are; and may at any time be alter'd, or inverted, if the Creator pleases'. Assuming that our instincts or affections constitute the good of morality, it is reasonable 'to ask, what it was that determined the Deity to plant in us these Affections rather than any other'? Hutcheson's answer, that the Deity acted on a 'certain Disposition' essential to his nature and 'corresponding to the Affections he has given us', appears to miss the point. Is this disposition one of the Deity's perfections? If not, it is presumptuous to ascribe it to Him. But if it is, it appears that goodness or virtue (in the form of the Deity's perfection) existed prior to our affections, and hence that virtue is grounded in something prior to these affections. It is not the moral sense, but Reason, the Deity's grounds for acting as He has, that provides the foundation of morality. On the other hand, if virtue does depend on the moral sense and the Deity is in fact amoral, then we can have no security that the Deity will not alter our constitution, and in doing so, alter the constitution of good and evil. In short, Hutcheson is charged with ethical voluntarism and the arbitrary, antirealist conception of virtue associated with that view (8–10).

Balguy's final complaint is that, in Hutcheson's hands, 'Virtue is depreciated and dishonoured' by being described as a mere instinct, and not as something rational and of a higher nature. Moreover, if virtue proves to be merely instinctive we will be led to doubt that there is any genuine merit in what we call *virtue*. If we are excited to what we *call* virtuous acts by an instinctive necessity, of what moral merit are the resulting actions? It seems, says Balguy, 'utterly impossible to reconcile Virtue with any kind of Necessity'. Should Hutcheson reply that these instincts do not 'force the Mind, but only incline it', then, says Balguy, just in so far as the mind is not forced, there will be room for reason to work. And just to the extent that there is liberty to use reason, there will be virtue (20–1).

Hutcheson found none of these objections insuperable. To the claim that his theory of the moral sense made morality dependent on the arbitrary actions of an amoral deity, he replied briefly in his second letter to the *London Journal*, and then again in his *Illustrations on the Moral Sense*, the second part of his second major work.[27] To Burnet he said, in effect, that we simply cannot conceive of the creative activity of the Deity having any motive more fundamental than some feature of the divine nature that is analogous to 'our Kindness and Sweetest Affections'. So far as any *justifying* reasons of divine action are concerned, when we humans judge these we must do so by means of our moral sense. This leads us to approve of the beneficent nature we have been given, and of the agent who gave it. On the other hand, did we not have a moral sense, we would have no moral ideas at all, neither about the Deity nor about ourselves. This would not prevent the Deity from judging His own actions in whatever way he does now judge them, but humans would be amoral (*Works* 7: 64). To put the matter differently, Hutcheson modestly professes to know nothing about the Deity but that which is known by a study of His effects. The relevant effect in this case is the fact that He has given us a moral sense. This sense requires us to think about the Deity in certain ways, but neither it nor any other human faculty can provide us with certain knowledge of the principles by which the Deity acts or judges.

In the *Illustrations* Hutcheson sees Balguy's first objection as the suggestion that, prior to the creation of the moral sense, all moral constitutions would have seemed morally equal, which would mean that the choice actually made was morally arbitrary. To this he replies that, if the Deity had no disposition analogous to our kindest affections and best moral nature, then He would have had no exciting or motivating reason to form us as He has. On the other hand, if we grant that the Deity does have such a disposition, then we see that this disposition could well have served as the motivating reason of the choice He did make.[28] In other words, by arguing from effects to causes Hutcheson attempts to give an a posteriori proof, or an argument from moral design, showing that he has not made morality arbitrary or a mere positive creation.

To the objection that making what is called 'virtue' flow from instincts robs it of all merit – and, by consequence, of all reality – Hutcheson devotes the whole of Section V of his *Illustrations*. The key to his response is a distinction between kinds of instincts. On the one hand there are 'bodily Powers' that 'determine us without Knowledge or Intention of any End'. These instincts cannot be a source of virtue. On the other hand, the mind may include powers that lead us to the 'Approbation of certain Tempers and Affections, and to the Desire of certain Events when it has an Idea of' these things. Perhaps *instincts* is not the correct term, but, whatever these affections are called, they are no more destructive of morality than is the 'Determination to pursue Fitness' that characterizes, according to his opponents, the divine will. To make a long story short, Hutcheson argues 'that Virtue may have whatever is meant by [moral] Merit; and be rewardable upon the Supposition, that it is perceived by a Sense, and elected from Affection or Instinct' (*Essay* 290–2).

Hutcheson's critics were not, of course, satisfied with these replies. Burnet's 'Preface', cited earlier, sums up his view: Hutcheson's theory is a well-intended failure. Balguy read Hutcheson's *Illustrations* and responded with the second part of his *Foundations*, a work itself intended to illustrate and defend his own rationalist perspective on the foundations of morality, and one that clearly reveals his continuing dissatisfaction with Hutcheson's account.[29] Nearly 30 years later Richard Price was to again argue that Hutcheson had treated morality as the product of 'an *implanted* and *arbitrary* principle' that reduces morality to 'an affair of taste' and that explains right and wrong as mere 'qualities of our *minds*'. In contrast, Price undertook to show that virtue has 'a foundation in the *nature* of its object' and that right and wrong 'are real characters of *actions*'.[30] In short, notwithstanding Hutcheson's avowed moral realism, Burnet, Balguy, and Price insisted that his moral sense theory had the effect of undermining the foundations of morality – of finding in those foundations an element of uncertainty in the form of contingency. However good his intentions, Hutcheson had fostered, as Price put it, a 'monstrous scepticism' about morality (44). This is by no means a surprising outcome. The debate about the foundations of morality was nothing if not polemical, and participants liked nothing better than to argue that their opponents' views were sceptical. Thus while virtually every participant, including even Montaigne, gives some positive account of the foundations of morality, we find that any philosopher who dared to suggest that morality is anything less than eternal and immutable and constraining even of the Deity Himself came eventually to be branded a moral sceptic by some platonically inclined rationalist critic.

5. *David Hume and the Two-Foundations Theory*

As we have already seen, David Hume took note of the controversy over the foundations of morals. Are, he asked, moral distinctions '*founded on natural and original principles, or*' do they '*arise from interest and education*'? As Hume describes the issue, those who had traced the distinction between virtue and vice to self-interest and education had claimed that morality itself has 'no foundation in nature' and, consequently, that it is, despite its real effects, something merely conventional. In contrast, those who suppose that moral distinctions are founded on certain 'natural and original principles' conclude that 'morality is something real, essential, and founded on nature' (*Treatise* 2.1.7.2–5, SBN 295–6).

Having brought up this issue in the second book of the *Treatise*, Hume ostensibly postpones its examination to the third and final book. But in fact, Hume's account of the foundation of morality runs through the *Treatise* from beginning to end. In the Introduction to this long work he tells us that all the sciences, especially human sciences such as morals and politics, depend on the new science he undertakes to establish, that is, the science of human nature. There is, he argues, no important issue whose solution is not linked to an understanding of human nature itself, that is, to an understanding of the operation of the mind and of the formation and effects of our ideas, passions, or sentiments. Consequently, we can expect Hume's account of morality to be a part of his new and 'compleat system of the sciences' (Intro 4–6, SBN xv–xvi).

This expectation is fulfilled. Hume says that Book 3 of the *Treatise* can be understood without reviewing Books 1 and 2 if we remember that by the term *impression* he means our stronger, original perceptions, and by *idea* he refers to the copies of these found in the memory or imagination. He also reminds us that 'nothing is ever present to the mind but its perceptions', and that these are of only two kinds, impressions and ideas. From this simple beginning he goes on to tell us that well-formed enquiry into the foundation of morals can begin with a single and very precise question: Is it by means of ideas or of impressions that we mark the difference between virtue and vice, such that we call one action virtuous and another vicious?[31] We find, however, that the ensuing analysis depends substantially on conclusions reached earlier: that we learn about natures and causal connections only by experience; that we have a tendency to form and follow general rules; that reason and ideas are inert, unable to influence directly our passions and actions; that our responses to the actions of agents are fundamentally determined by the motives that give rise to those actions; and that, unless there is a causal link between agents and their choices and actions, agents could not be held responsible for these choices and actions, and morality would collapse.

In addition, Hume's account of the foundations of morality presupposes a comprehensive picture or understanding of morality as practised, of common-sense morality. This picture underlies and motivates Hume's discussion of the fundamental issues he addresses, but is never presented whole, and thus we need to fit together the pieces that make up this picture. For a start, Hume was clearly impressed with the fact that we use moral language competently. Our languages include terms such as '*honourable* or *dishonourable, praise-worthy* or *blameable*', and ordinary speakers of these languages, as much as the intellectual and political elite, use these terms to indicate which actions and characters are acceptable, and which unacceptable (*Treatise* 3.2.2.25, see also 3.3.1.11; SBN 500, 579). Such usage is highly significant. It is nothing less than the public face of a complex process of moral discrimination, a process more complex than many other moralists had indicated.

This fact is brought home to us when we begin to see just how many constraints there are on our moral assessments. We do not, for example, morally condemn or blame those who make what we take to be mistakes of fact. Neither do we blame individuals for merely thinking of a vicious act. We do not blame inanimate objects or other animals, not even when their behaviour seems exactly parallel to human behaviour that is blamed. We do not blame humans who fail to act for the good because of circumstances beyond their control. We do not blame those who injure us without intent to do so. We do blame those who, although they fail to injure us, intend to do so. We find that there are degrees of moral turpitude, that some moral defects or failings are worse than others. We find that morality is a practical affair, and that every moral judgement has an influence on our passions and actions. We find that we may despise an enemy for the harm he does our country, and yet recognise him to be virtuous. We find that Brutus, although he collaborated in the assassination of his friend

Julius Caesar, is taken to have been virtuous, and even a paradigm of virtue. We find that the seemingly inflexible demands of justice or allegiance would have been significantly different had human nature and circumstances been different, and that these demands may in some circumstances be overruled because of a concern for the public good. We find that the range of our moral approval is broad: we approve not only qualities that are pleasing or beneficial to ourselves, but also those that are pleasing and beneficial only to those who possess them or to others affected by them. And we find that we give moral approval to what appear to be merely natural abilities.[32]

Hume's effort to account for these features of common-sense morality has both a critical and a constructive side. He argues that alternative theories regarding the foundation of morality are unable to account for crucial aspects of our moral practice, while at the same time offering a theory that can account for this practice. It is in response to the rationalists (to those who trace morality to eternal and immutable relationships between ideas) that Hume notes that morality is practical and that all moral judgements have a practical import, something that would not be the case if they depended on reason, which he had shown to be inert. It is in response to the rationalists that he draws attention to the fact that our moral assessments are limited to the motives and actions of human beings, a limitation that would be missing if morality depended on reason and the relationships between ideas. And it is in response to the rationalists that he points out that the rules of justice, although inflexible in their demands, depend so much on contingent features of human nature and the human situation that certain substantial changes in those features would eliminate either the need or the possibility of justice.

As we have seen, Mandeville and others claimed that our apparent moral distinctions are ultimately unfounded because, although the distinction between virtue and vice depends on distinctions of motive, there are no such distinctions of motive. Our actions are motivated by self-interest, and only by self-interest, and the moral distinctions we appear to make are a sham and an illusion foisted on us by a clever, self-serving elite. In response, Hume points out that we give moral approval not only to actions that fail to benefit us, but also to actions (some of the actions conforming to the rules of justice, for example) that we know to harm us, something we could not do were we unable to control and eventually to overcome an admittedly powerful tendency always to put private interest first. And it is in response to the egoists that he points out that we competently use a moral vocabulary, something we could not do had we no deep-seated, natural disposition to recognize fundamental differences of motive. In short, because both egoists and rationalists ignore crucial features of our moral practices, they then go on to offer vastly oversimplified accounts of the foundations of morality.

In contrast, Hume's account is a complex one. Given that there are only two kinds of perceptions, and that moral distinctions are not dependent on ideas and their relationships, it obviously follows that these distinctions depend on impressions. Given that Hume has argued that all ideas derive from impressions, it may seem that this conclusion was entirely predictable. His claim, however, is that moral distinctions depend on certain secondary impressions, on certain impressions or sentiments that themselves derive from prior impressions and ideas of sensation.

Suppose, says Hume, we observe (see and hear) an action, the intentional killing of another human being, for example, that we take to be morally wrong. Suppose then we review our ideas of this action to determine why we have taken it to be wrong. No matter how attentively we observed the sequence of events making up this action, and no matter how many times we replay, so to speak, the ideas derived from our initial impressions of it, no perceptible moral quality, no *matter of fact*, reveals itself to us. If, however, we consider our response to this action, we do find something of interest. This action arouses in us a sentiment of disapprobation, a feeling of disapproval. This feeling and only this feeling enables us to designate as vicious the action observed. In one sense, then, the judgement that an action is immoral must be understood as nothing more than the report of a sentiment of disapprobation felt by an observer of some action.

If Hume had said no more than this he might justifiably be supposed to have been the champion of some form of moral subjectivism, and to have come far short of explaining common-sense morality. In fact, his claim that moral judgements are reports of observers' feelings is heavily qualified.

Hume goes on to argue that the moral approbation and disapprobation of which he is speaking are unique responses to unique causes, and that they derive from fundamental features of the human condition. The sentiment of approbation, he says, is not merely an agreeable impression, but the most satisfying of all pleasures, while that of disapprobation is the most abhorrent of all pains. He also argues that there are fundamental differences between the pleasures aroused by inanimate objects and animals and those aroused by human actions or character. We who can discriminate between the pleasures produced by a good bottle of wine and those produced by a fine piece of music can also readily distinguish the fundamentally different – the unique – feelings produced by the actions of a fellow human being. That we can and do make this further distinction is shown by the fact that we do not attribute moral qualities to inanimate objects and animals, or to their activities. Hume also notes that we do not attribute virtue or vice to every action or character that causes pleasure or pain. We somehow realize that the distinctive moral sentiments are felt only when we have abstracted from our own interests. An enemy of our country, *qua* enemy, may cause intense pain and anger, and yet still be taken to be a virtuous person. It is a particular quality of the moral sentiment, and not the strength or generally pleasant character of our feelings, that enables us to distinguish virtue from vice. Nonmoral feelings may prevent us from feeling or noticing approbation or disapprobation, but it does not follow that these other feelings usurp the role of the moral sentiments.

Satisfied that we make moral distinctions by means of a set of unique moral sentiments, or that morality is founded on sentiment, Hume immediately asks after the foundation of this foundation. Why and how do actions and characters arouse these moral sentiments? His answer in the most general terms is that actions and characters have this effect because of deep-seated features of human nature, but that actions are, after all, considerably less important than has so far been supposed. Throughout much of *Treatise* 3.1 Hume was content to suppose that moral judgements are directed toward actions – toward parricide, murder, and theft, for example. But in *Treatise* 3.2 he argues that actions themselves are not the true object of moral assessments. Although we appear to attach moral praise or blame to certain actions, Hume argues that such actions are in fact only signs or outward manifestations of the motives (of certain durable principles of 'mind or temper') found in the acting agent. Because we cannot look directly at these inner principles or motivations, we tend to focus our attention on the actions we suppose them to have produced. 'The external performance has no merit.... the ultimate object of our praise and approbation, is the motive, that produc'd them' (*Treatise* 3.2.1.2, SBN 477). We are left, then, to determine which durable principles or motives arouse the moral sentiments, and how they do so.

Hume's answer to this question is presented as a theory of virtue or, more accurately, a theory about the kinds of virtue. As we have seen, Hume initially suggested that the debate about the foundation of morality revolves around the question, Are the moral distinctions we make founded on natural and original principles, or on interest and education? When he comes to answer this question, he in effect tells us that it is ill formed or at least misleading. He sees that there are two distinct foundations of virtue and hence two fundamentally different kinds of virtue: *natural* and *artificial*. The former are founded on principles embedded in human nature itself, and thus these virtues are practised by even the most primitive humans. In contrast, the artificial virtues are in effect conventions developed over time. The contrast is only partial, however, for the artificial virtues, although not practised in humanity's original condition, do derive from natural or inherent human features and are thus in another sense natural.[33]

Viewed as features of agents, the natural virtues are certain original, inherent dispositions of agents to act in ways that benefit others or themselves. Generosity, humanity, and compassion, for example, are three of the several qualities of human nature that motivate agents to act for the good of others. Prudence, frugality, and temperance are among the qualities that motivate agents to act for the good of themselves. Viewed from the perspective of observers, the natural virtues are those dispositions which, if they function as we expect them to function (if they do actually motivate unconstrained agents to act as we expect them to act), cause observers to feel the unique sentiment of approbation and moral praise. If these same dispositions fail to have their normal or natural effect (if they fail to motivate unconstrained agents to act as we expect them to act), then the observance of these omissions gives rise to the unique sentiment of disapprobation and moral blame.[34]

Several clarifications are in order. First, because moral sentiments are, ultimately, responses to motives rather than to actions, we will praise an individual who has the appropriate motivation, but who is prevented from acting as she is inclined to act. The benevolently motivated individual who is prevented from acting is nonetheless a virtuous person.[35] Secondly, we should note that Hume's theory tells against the egoists in two ways. If we have natural dispositions to act for the benefit of others, then the egoists are obviously wrong to claim that all acts are self-interested and that there are in consequence no genuine moral distinctions. Again, it will be obvious that the egoists are mistaken if we as observers are able to approve motives and actions that in no way benefit us. And this is exactly what we find ourselves doing. We hear of individuals whose generosity and humanity benefited those who came in contact with them; we observe other individuals whose prudence and frugality were of great benefit to themselves. These individuals are all, we know, long dead and we are absolutely certain that none them can do the least thing to benefit us now. Nonetheless, what they have done arouses approbation in us: the pleasure they have produced in others or in themselves produces pleasure in us.

It is the principle of sympathy that makes this vicarious and disinterested pleasure possible. For Hume, sympathy is not a particular feeling, but a principle of 'communication' that, through the use of quite ordinary impressions and ideas, enables one person to feel as his or her own the sentiments and opinions of others. It is this principle that accounts for the fact that we as observers feel approbation when an agent's character and actions are useful or pleasing to herself alone, or useful or pleasing to those affected by her. In these circumstances the agent or those around her feel the sentiment of approbation, and then this sentiment is communicated to us by sympathy. If this communication did not take place, we would be able to approve or disapprove the character and actions of others only insofar as they have a real or imagined effect on us ourselves, a thesis championed by the egoists, but rejected by Hume. Sympathy is, then, 'the chief source of moral distinctions', for without it we would be unconcerned about the happiness of others, and our moral approvals and disapprovals would lack that important element of disinterestedness that they have and require.[36]

The artificial virtues also depend on sympathy, but, in comparison to the natural virtues, there is a complex story to tell about their development. Initially absent from human experience, the artificial virtues gradually developed on the basis of human nature as humans interacted with one another and their environment. It is Hume's view that even the most primitive people, organized into the smallest viable social unit, the family, could have been and were moved to act generously toward one another, but that such peoples, in such units, had no need for the artificial virtues – no need, for example, for the rules of justice. In Hume's system, justice is concerned entirely with property arrangements. When the social unit was the family, there was no more need for a system governing private property than there is for 'mine' and 'thine' between husband and wife. It was only as societies grew larger and more complex, and as certain goods came to be in short supply, that a system of justice was developed.[37]

How is it, Hume asks, that '*the rules of justice are establish'd by the artifice of men*'? In response to his own question he emphasizes humanity's naturally perilous condition: 'Of all the animals, with which this globe is peopled, there is none towards whom nature seems, at first sight, to have exercis'd more cruelty than towards man . . . '. It is only by banding together in societies that humanity was able to overcome these natural disadvantages: society enables those in it to increase their force, their abilities, and their safety. Hume goes on to suggest that while society (a social unit governed by the rules of justice) itself was not entirely natural – society was not an original feature of the human condition – its development, fortunately, was natural. Certain features of human nature and of our environment have led us beyond the most primitive social unit, the extended family, to the larger units of true societies (*Treatise* 3.2.2.1–3, SBN 484–5).

If nature led the way to this development, there were nonetheless natural obstacles to it. There was first the natural human disposition toward a disruptive selfishness. There is the further fact that possessions acquired by industry or good fortune can be stripped from us and are in such short supply that violent dispossessions are a likely feature of our primitive state. We need society in order to increase our abilities, strength, and safety, yet in this primitive state, no such rule-governed society was to be found. The abstract idea of justice 'wou'd never have been dream'd of' among the rude and savage, for their conduct was ruled by natural partiality. The remedy came when even these earliest humans could see that their private interests could be served by cooperating with other humans. Eventually, this kind of practical cooperation led to the development of conventions that had the effect of curbing their heedless natural partiality, thereby bestowing a beneficial stability of possession to scarce external goods. In time, this insight was developed to the point that enlightened self-interest was able to bring heedless self-interest under control. From these beginnings, justice was founded.[38]

This story is complicated by the fact that Hume is committed to the view that it is not actions per se, but the motives from which they are done, that are virtuous or vicious. But if distinctions of motive underlie moral distinctions, and if the conventions and practice of justice derive originally from self-interested motives, what real moral distinction can there be between justice and injustice? Hume shows that he is well aware of this difficulty when he goes on to consider a second question about justice: What, he asks, are '*the reasons, which determine us to attribute to the observance or neglect of these rules [of justice] a moral beauty and deformity*', or, as he also puts it, why do '*we annex the idea of virtue to justice, and of vice to injustice*'? (3.2.2.1, 3.2.2.23; SBN 484, 498). In answering this second question Hume tells us, in effect, how justice is moralised. He explains how we come to attach *moral* significance to what is apparently a self-interested concern that the rules of justice be maintained – or how observations of just or unjust actions give rise to the unique moral sentiments.

In the normal and slowly developing course of events, Hume tells us, the societies that were made possible after heedless self-interest was brought under the control of enlightened self-interest increased in size. As they did so it became more difficult for individuals to see how their private interests were being served by adherence to the established rules of justice. As a consequence, some individuals broke these rules (they acted unjustly), perhaps without even realising that they were doing so. Other individuals, however, invariably noticed when these rules were broken and they themselves were thereby harmed – just as we now notice the harmful effects of such transgressions. Moreover, even when the injustices perpetrated by others are so remote as not to harm us or to affect our interest, we are nonetheless displeased because, by the operation of sympathy, we find the rule-breaking behaviour 'prejudicial to human society, and pernicious to every one that approaches the person guilty of it' (3.2.2.24, SBN 499). In short, what began as a purely self-interested concern that the rules of justice be maintained became an other-regarding concern that these rules be followed. Indeed, this additional concern develops to the extent that individuals who contravene the rules of justice feel disapprobation in response to their very own contraventions and are thus led to declare even themselves vicious.

According to Hume, two features of human nature make this development possible. The first is our tendency to establish general rules, and to give to these rules an inflexibility that can withstand even the pressures of self-interest. Once we have established rules that are to govern the possession and exchange of property, we find our sentiments are influenced by these rules even when their use is contrary to our self-interest. Rules with that kind of continuing force exercise at least a partial check on self-interest. The second feature is sympathy. Were this principle not to play its part, we would feel no approbation for characters and actions that enhance the public good while yet, as may sometimes be the case, thwarting our own private interests. Furthermore, any individual act of justice may even be contrary to the public good, so that it is only our acceptance of a general system of justice that benefits the public good, but sympathy is equal to this difficulty. Unaffected by our narrowly selfish interests, sympathy causes us to feel approbation in response to actions that maintain the system of justice and, by extension, the public interest, and disapprobation in response to those that fail to give such support: it is because sympathy causes us to share the approbation or uneasiness of others that 'the sense of moral good and evil follows upon justice and injustice . . . *self-interest* is the original motive to the *establishment* of justice: But a *sympathy* with *public* interest is the source of the *moral* approbation, which attends that virtue' (3.2.2.24; SBN 499–500, 670). The net result is that justice, because it comes to have a second foundation in human nature, does eventually evolve into a full-fledged moral virtue. In Hume's own words:

Upon the whole, then, we are to consider this distinction betwixt justice and injustice, as having two different foundations, *viz.* that of *self-interest*, when men observe, that 'tis impossible to live in society without restraining themselves by certain rules; and that of *morality*, when this interest is once observ'd to be common to all mankind, and men receive a pleasure from the view of such actions as tend to the peace of society, and an uneasiness from such as are contrary to it. 'Tis the voluntary convention and artifice of men, which makes the first interest take place; and therefore those laws of justice are so far to be consider'd as *artificial*. After that interest is once establish'd and acknowledg'd, the sense of morality in the observance of these rules follows *naturally*, and of itself. . . . [39]

The reception accorded Hume's efforts to settle the foundations question was even more hostile than that to Hutcheson. Indeed, Hutcheson himself was apparently highly suspicious of Hume's claim that justice and other virtues are not natural but *artificial*. In response, Hume clarified his position by pointing out that there is a perfectly good sense in which justice is natural:

as no principle of the human mind is more natural than a sense of virtue; so no virtue is more natural than justice. Mankind is an inventive species; and where an invention is obvious and absolutely necessary, it may as properly be said to be natural as any thing that proceeds immediately from original principles, without the intervention of thought or reflection. Tho' the rules of justice be *artificial*, they are not *arbitrary*.

(3.2.1.19, SBN 484)

On the whole, this clarification fell on deaf ears. In 1745, Hume, then a candidate for the Chair of Moral Philosophy in the University of Edinburgh, was charged with

sapping the Foundations of Morality, by denying the natural and essential Difference between Right and Wrong, Good and Evil, Justice and Injustice; making the Difference only artificial, and to arise from human Conventions and Compacts.[40]

Six years later, Henry Home (later Lord Kames) argued that Hume mistakenly claims 'that justice, so far from being one of the primary virtues, is not even a natural virtue, but [is] established in society by a sort of tacit convention'.[41] James Balfour responded to Hume's *Enquiry concerning the Principles of Morals* with the complaint that Hume appears to have used his obvious philosophical talents to 'confound', rather than clarify, moral distinctions, and that he has undermined the distinction between justice and injustice by tracing it to private interest. As a result, Hume leaves us without the 'slightest foundation' for any antipathy toward acts of injustice.[42] Richard Price, although he directed his attack more explicitly toward the alleged moral scepticism of Hutcheson, made it clear that he found Hume's theory equally inadequate. Regrettably, Price's dogmatic and outmoded platonism still appears to provide the standard by which many evaluate moral theories.[43]

II. THE CONTINENT

Although the discussion 'concerning the nature and origin of our moral sentiments', or perhaps better: concerning the 'foundations of morality' continued in Britain even after Hume's subtle contribution to it, the really significant new developments took place in Germany. But, if only because of their different philosophical background, the Germans changed the problem. If the original contributors to the discussion had often talked past one another, the Germans were not really interested in engaging in a discussion with philosophers such as Smith and Hume. Rather they were trying to solve problems inherent in their own philosophical position. They remained basically Wolffians in their answer to the question, 'Wherein does virtue consist?' But in their attempts at answering the question, which power of the mind recommends virtue to us, most of these philosophers were trying to find a middle road between the principles of reason and sentiment at least until Immanuel Kant argued that this was just as impossible as was Hume's two-foundations theory.

Until the second part of the eighteenth century, the discussion of the foundations of morality had not played an important role on the continent. Neither German nor French philosophers were greatly interested in the question of moral foundations per se. Though for different reasons, philosophers in both countries were more concerned with fostering a certain kind of morality than with the analysis of foundational questions. This is especially clear in Germany, where the discussion of every philosophical subject was largely defined by the opposition between the adherents of the religious movement of Pietism and the followers of Christian Wolff, also called the Leibnizian–Wolffian school of philosophy. At the beginning of the century, the philosophical position most prevalent at German universities was still Aristotelianism, which was favoured by the orthodox Protestant theologians. Early in the century, however, Aristotelianism came under attack by Pietists and by Wolff.

Pietism constituted a 'religion of the heart', very much opposed to intellectualism.[44] Pietists emphasised the importance of independent Bible study, personal devotion, the priesthood of the laity, and a practical faith issuing in acts of charity.[45] They believed that salvation could be found only after one had undergone a so-called a 'struggle of repentance' that led to a 'conversion' and 'awakening'. In this struggle the 'old self' was, through the grace of God, replaced by a 'new self'. The 'child of the world' became a 'child of God'. This rebirth was, however, only the first step on a long road. The living faith of the converted had to be reconfirmed every day by 'acts of obedience to God's commandments [which] included prayer, Bible reading, and renunciation of sinful diversions and service to one's neighbor through acts of charity'.[46] That the Pietists rejected not just Aristotelianism, but all of philosophy, was not surprising. Reason, corrupted by the Fall, could only lead people astray. It need not be pointed out that such a view did nothing to further questions about the foundation of morality. Indeed, the presence of these Pietists in the philosophical debate in Germany during much of the first half of the eighteenth century was – at least in part – responsible for the mediocrity of that debate.

The best philosophers among those closely affiliated with Pietism were Christian Thomasius and Christian August Crusius, neither of whom contributed much that was new to the discussion of the foundations of morality.[47] Thomasius was really more interested in practical issues and his views changed repeatedly. There is no doubt, however, that Thomasius was important in the natural law tradition. Indeed, that is where his merits can be found. He began as an adherent of Pufendorf, then adopted a position that had a heavy dose of utilitarianism, only to abandon it in favor of a more Pietistic doctrine. He was also heavily influenced by Baltasar Gracian's *Oráculo manual y arte de prudencia* (*Hand Oracle and The Art of Worldly Wisdom*) (1647). Although he always endorsed an ethics of love, during the years of his Pietistic crisis, he increasingly emphasised the corruption of reason by an evil will. While, disillusioned with Pietism, he returned to a more worldly view during his last years, one would look in vain to Thomasius for consistent answers to Smith's question, 'Wherein does virtue consist?' Propriety, prudence, and benevolence (or 'reasonable love', as he would have put it) were all involved. But the faculty responsible for virtue (or rather the lack thereof) was for him the will. Self-love, sentiment, and reason were all expressions of the will. Furthermore, 'the recognition of the incapacity (*Unvermögen*) of the natural faculties is the first contact with divine grace and the light of nature'.[48]

Crusius was, if anything, even more sceptical about reason than was Thomasius. His Lutheran position on morality, in which everything became a question of how our will, corrupted by the Fall, can become good, was similar to that found in Thomasius's *Ausübung der Sittenlehre*. Not surprisingly, the problem of the freedom of the will was for him most central in morality. Crusius's main work in ethics, the *Anweisung Vernünftig zu leben* (*Instructions for Living Rationally*) (1744), was characterised by the view that ethics is founded not on reason, but on God's will.[49] Virtue was for him nothing but the agreement of the human will with the divine laws: 'Do what is in accordance with the perfection of God and your relations to him, and further what accords with the essential perfection of human nature, and omit the opposite'.[50] A moral act cannot be performed in order to obtain happiness. It must have been done to fulfill the duties that have been imposed on us by God. We must follow our conscience. The only true foundation of morality consists in divine laws or in God's choices and these are inscrutable to us. Accordingly, Crusius gives a theological foundation of morality, explicitly renouncing that it has any foundation in nature.[51]

Wolff and his followers, although constantly criticised and attacked by the Pietists, dominated the philosophical discussion between 1720 and 1750. Wolffians pursued ethics as *Philosophia practica universalis methodo mathematica conscripta*, or as a universal practical philosophy drawn up in accordance with the mathematical method.[52] This was, in effect, a form of neo-Stoicism wherein the basic principle was: 'Do what makes you and your condition, or that of others, more perfect; omit what makes it less perfect'. Every rational person can know this principle and therefore is in no need of another law. Through reason every man is 'a law unto himself'.[53] Thus the faculty by which 'virtue is recommended to us' is reason. Wolff appears to have viewed this feature of his moral philosophy as properly basic, and thus did not provide any arguments for it. So, for him virtue consisted of some sort of propriety and the principle of approbation was nothing but reason. Although there are many interesting aspects of Wolff, and although he was important for the further philosophical development in Germany, he too failed to present any new ideas about the foundations of morality.[54]

In France, there was a similar lack of concern with the foundations of morals, although for very different reasons. For the French philosophers, the discussion of moral issues was closely bound up with materialism and thus with what Smith called the 'licentious system'. Rejecting any attempt at a religious foundation of morality, most of the French were interested in showing that egoism and self-interest did not preclude interest in the well-being of our fellow creatures. Although there were great differences between such thinkers as La Mettrie, Helvetius, d'Holbach, Diderot, D'Alembert, and Voltaire, they all remained ultimately within the framework of the ideas of Hobbes and Mandeville. They were following the lead of British egoists, and they cannot be said to have contributed anything substantially original to the discussion of the foundations of morality.[55] Furthermore, to an even greater extent than the early Thomasius and Wolff, the French moralists were working to bring about the enlightenment of humanity and thus to make a practical contribution to our cultural advancement. With this as their goal, they often eclectically took what they considered the best moral insights from wherever they could find them. Thus it should come as no surprise that they also made use of ideas from Shaftesbury, Hutcheson, and Hume – but none of them made an original and decisive contribution to what we have called the Foundations of Morality Debate. They left things more or less as they found them.

If there was an exception to this rule, it was Jean-Jacques Rousseau. In his *Discours sur l'origine et les fondements de l'inégalité parmi les hommes* (*Discourse on the Origin of Inequality*) (1755), Rousseau challenged many of the central notions of his fellow enlightened thinkers. His central idea was that of a 'state of nature'. But Rousseau's 'original man' was different from that of Hobbes. Rousseau's original was innocent and characterised by 'a feeling of pity', freedom, and perfectibility. He contrasts this picture to the artificial and harmful 'civil state' in which the corrupting influence of 'society' had perverted the good nature of human beings. Rousseau meant to subvert the project of those who hoped to better the world by 'enlightenment', but his idea was also an original contribution to the discussion of moral philosophy.

This was how Adam Smith saw it. In a letter to the editor of the *Edinburgh Review* of 1756, he argued that Rousseau's idea is 'English philosophy transported into France'. And he compared the *Discourse* favorably to Mandeville's *Fable of the Bees*, which, he claimed, had given rise to Rousseau's work. In 'Mr. Rousseau . . . the principles of the English author are softened, improved, and embellished, and stript of all that tendency to corruption and licentiousness which has disgraced them in their original author'.[56] In other words, from the perspective of one of the best philosophers acquainted with the Foundations of Morality Debate, it appeared that there was nothing new here either. Though turned on its head, softened, improved, and embellished, it was still the 'licentious system'.

Perhaps this was too harsh a judgement. If Rousseau was right that man 'in his savage . . . and . . . in his civilized state, differ[s] so essentially in [his] passions and inclinations', then any attempt to found morality on 'natural and original principles' would be far more complicated than Hume and Smith had ever believed (253). Neither the language nor the moral feelings of civilised men would be reliable guides to those natural and original feelings. But, of course, it would be a difficulty only if Rousseau was right about the state of nature and the state of civil society. It is at the very least doubtful this could be shown empirically. But however that may be, Rousseau's theory was most fundamentally a form of naturalism. He insisted that moral issues needed to be discussed in terms of human nature and the principles operative at different stages of its development. And that was not fundamentally at odds with Hume's view. If Rousseau's view was the 'licentious system', softened, improved, and embellished, then how was that of Hume significantly different?[57]

Smith in the same letter also makes an interesting observation on German philosophy: the 'Germans have never cultivated their own language; and while the learned accustom themselves to think and write in a language different from their own, it is scarce possible that they should either think or write on any delicate or nice subject, with happiness and precision'. They may be fairly good at tasks that 'require only plain judgement joined to labour and assiduity, without demanding a great deal of what is called either taste or genius', but this does not include philosophy. Just as Smith was writing this, the situation in Germany was changing. Not long after the middle of the eighteenth century, Leibnizian–Wolffian philosophy rapidly declined in influence and German philosophers began to take greater care in writing German. Furthermore, foreign, especially British, authors began to exert an increasing influence on German thought and culture. These Germans found that the works of Locke, Shaftesbury, Hutcheson, Hume, Smith, and others were full of problems that needed to be solved. Most of them seemed to have to do with the analysis of sensation in theoretical, moral, and aesthetic contexts, and the question became how British 'observations' could be incorporated into a comprehensive theory of thinking and sensation. Moses Mendelssohn proposed a division of labor in which the neighbors of the Germans 'observed' and the Germans 'explained'. This would lead to a 'complete theory of sensation'.[58]

Mendelssohn and other Germans, such as Johann August Eberhard, had rather definite ideas about the general approach to be followed. It had to be shown that the phenomena observed by British philosophers and traced by them to a special sense were fundamentally rational. Thus it is wrong, he argued, to speak of a special 'moral sense'. Although the moral sense may appear to be an independent faculty of the mind, it is in the end reducible to reason. This reduction to reason may appear difficult in the case of moral judgements, for as these 'present themselves in the soul [they] are completely different from the effects of distinct rational principles', but that does not mean that moral judgements cannot be analysed into rational and distinct principles.[59] Our moral sentiments are 'phenomena which are related to rational principles in the same way as colors are related to the angles of refraction of light. They are apparently of a completely different nature, yet they are basically one and the same'

(2: 184). Moral phenomena are phenomena in the Leibnizian sense, but they are also '*phenomena bene fundatum*' because they are ultimately founded in something rational. The task of showing how the 'moral sense' could be reduced to 'rational principles' became a central concern of German moral philosophers during the second half of the eighteenth century.[60]

Johann Georg Heinrich Feder, somewhat more sceptical than his predecessors, characterised the moral sense as a human capacity 'of very mixed relations'. It was for him an effect of 'education and our own reason, that is, of concepts and principles resulting from experience and thinking'.[61] Jurisprudence, religion, political laws, and considerations of utility were all seen as playing a role in the development of the moral sentiments, but ultimately it was sympathy that was the cause of our approval of the good. Like most Germans, Feder argued that we do not have to postulate a special sense in order to account for our moral approval and disapproval. Although we are not usually aware of the multiple causes of our moral convictions, we can become aware of them. And 'in so far as we commonly and not always quite properly . . . call "sense" or "feeling" any species of knowledge of whose origin in other representations we are unconscious, and especially when it is connected with emotions and passions, we can say that man has a moral feeling or a moral sense in this sense'.[62]

In this way Mendelssohn, Eberhard, Feder, and many other German thinkers were able to accept much of what Shaftesbury, Hutcheson, and Hume said about the nature of moral phenomena but without having to renounce the basic tenets of Wolffian morality. One may doubt whether these Germans contributed anything of lasting significance to the debate about the foundations of morality. Their reduction of moral phenomena to rational principles remained unconvincing, and therefore their claim that morality seemed to be based only on sense while in fact it was rational rings somewhat hollow even if it was an interesting idea. Furthermore, for these German thinkers the problem concerning 'moral sense' was not an isolated issue. It was one important part of the broader problem concerning the relation of sensibility and reason in general. How could one unified theory be given of sensation and reason? It is also interesting to note that for these people sensations and thoughts formed part of a continuum. Some emphasised the sensitive part of this continuum as basic (though no one went as far as Hume). Most, however, thought that the intellectual part was most important.

Immanuel Kant (1724–1804) was just as much interested in the foundations of morals as were the British and German predecessors discussed here. Indeed, in an influential paper Dieter Henrich has claimed that 'Kant became aware of the general situation of ethics at the middle of the eighteenth century through the opposition between Wolff's *philosophia practica universalis* and Hutcheson's moral philosophy, and his first independent formulation of an ethical theory resulted from a critique of these two philosophers'.[63] Although it is misleading to suggest that there was such opposition, given that everyone was busy trying to show how the two approaches were compatible, it is true that the German approach (as evidenced in Wolff and Crusius) and the British approach (as found in Hutcheson and Hume) did define the parameters of Kant's early discussion of these issues.

During the sixties and perhaps even into the early eighties of the eighteenth century Kant followed an approach not at all unlike that of his German predecessors. Thus, in his so-called 'Prize Essay' of 1764, *Untersuchung über die Deutlichkeit der Grundsätze der natürlichen Theologie und Moral*, he not only endorsed a recent distinction between 'the faculty of representing the true' (or cognition) and that of 'experiencing the good' (or feeling) – by arguing that the two must not be confused – but he also pointed out that Hutcheson and others had 'under the name of moral feeling, provided . . . some excellent observations' relevant for the discussion of the fundamental principles of morals. He accepted Hutcheson's views that what is good 'is never encountered in a thing absolutely but only relatively to a being endowed with sensibility', and that there are 'simple feelings of the good', which give rise to 'an indemonstrable material principle of obligation'.[64] In *M. Immanuel Kants Nachricht von der Einrichtung seiner Vorlesungen in dem Winterhalbenjahre von 1765–1766* (*M. Immanuel Kant's Announcement of the Programme of His Lectures for the Winter Semester 1765–1766*), he said that he would try to supplement and clarify 'the attempts of *Shaftesbury, Hutcheson* and *Hume*, which, although incomplete and defective, have nonetheless penetrated furthest in the search for the fundamental principles of all morality'. Claiming that he would 'always begin by considering historically and philosophically what *happens* before specifying what *ought to happen*', and that he would clarify the method according to which human beings should be studied, he argues that we should not concentrate only on their changing forms, which are the result of their environment, but rather on 'the unchanging *nature* of man, and his distinctive position within the creation'. This, he thought, would tell us how we should act while seeking the highest physical and moral perfection (Ak 2: 311). However, Kant was sceptical even then. In the last section of this *Untersuchung* he observed that, to obtain

> the highest degree of philosophical certainty in the fundamental principles of morality, nonetheless the ultimate fundamental concepts of obligation need first of all to be determined more reliably . . . for it has yet to be determined whether it is merely the faculty of cognition, or whether it is feeling . . . which decides its first principles. (Ak 2: 300)

We take this to be directed against Mendelssohn and others who were confident that the principles of moral philosophy were decided *simply* by the cognitive faculty, and that feeling could be reduced to rational principles. Kant argued that this is not as clear as Mendelssohn made it out to be, and that perhaps judgements concerned with moral good cannot be made distinct. However, this disagreement between Mendelssohn and Kant takes place against the background of a fundamental agreement on a related matter. Both appear to believe that there is a certain continuity between rational representations and sensible representations. At the basis of the confused representations that characterise morality we may very well find clear and distinct concepts of reason, although, as a matter of fact, it may also be impossible for us to accomplish the task of analysis. Both accept what may be called the continuity thesis. The most abstract concepts are ultimately nothing more than clarified observations or sensations. This is the reason why we must start with the objects of sensations and feelings in theoretical philosophy as well as in ethics.

It appears that for the next 20 years Kant struggled with this problem: Was it reason or was it feeling that decides the basic principles of morality? Should he follow Hutcheson, Hume, and Smith, or should he follow his German contemporaries? As it happens, Kant finally answered this question concerning the ultimate foundation of morality in a way radically different from that of any of his predecessors. Indeed, Kant's mature work in ethics represented a radical break with both the Wolffian and the moral sense tradition, so that his *Grundlegung zur Metaphysik der Sitten* (1785) and *Kritik der praktischen Vernunft* (1788) changed the discussion of the foundations of morals forever.[65]

This break is apparent in four fundamental aspects of Kant's metaphysics of morals. First, his position represents 'a complete abandonment of any form of eudaemonism'.[66] For Kant, morality per se no longer had anything to do with happiness or pleasure. Any view that suggests that there is a close connection between morality and happiness – be it our own or that of others – was for him not merely wrong, but a serious perversion of true morality.[67] We are not meant to be happy, but we are meant to be moral – or so Kant claimed. Secondly, morality is not in any sense 'founded upon natural principles' (Smith, TMS VII.i.2). While Smith, whose work Kant knew well and appreciated highly (at least during the early seventies), thought that each of the several views regarding moral foundations had at least partial truth insofar as each of them supposed that there was a natural foundation of morals, Kant argued that each of the views was wrong precisely in so far as each maintained some form of naturalism.

The third, more positive aspect of Kant's position was that the foundations of morals had to be found in rational and absolutely a priori principles of reason. Indeed, Kant argued that the 'basic principles' of morality 'must have their source entirely and completely a priori' (*Grundlegung*, Ak 4: 425–6). This insistence on the purely a priori and rational character of morals was closely connected with a fourth and most fundamental point on which he broke with tradition: according to Kant, we are morally autonomous. Although the Stoics had also considered 'autonomy' a fundamental moral concept, Kant had a rather different understanding of it. 'Autonomy' was for him another word for freedom, freedom in a *positive* sense. To be moral or autonomous for Kant meant precisely *not* to submit to nature in any sense, but to assert a rationality not bound by nature.[68] He claimed that we freely legislate moral laws and that morality has its only source in us as rational agents. Indeed, only insofar as we are autonomous in this sense are we, for Kant, moral.

Like Thomasius, Wolff, and Crusius, Kant emphasised the will. Morality had to do with mastering our will, or, as Kant said, with transforming our will into a 'good will': '. . . reason is nevertheless given to us as a practical faculty, that is, as one that is to influence the *will*. . . This will need not. . . be the sole and complete good, but it must still be the highest good and the condition of every other. . . ' (Ak 4: 396). This meant that we must think and act in the right way. Only acts done from duty have any moral worth. This is the source of our dignity and also, perhaps, of tragedy. The most fundamental concept of Kant's ethical theory is accordingly duty, not virtue. Virtue is nothing but the result of acts done from duty. Kant also argued that an action will fail to have moral worth if we act merely in accordance with duty. We must act from the realisation that it is our duty. The criterion of such dutiful acts is his well-known categorical imperative, which states that we should act in such a way that the maxim of our action can become a universal law (of nature), that we should never treat ourselves or other rational beings *simply* as a means, and that we should look at ourselves as legislating moral laws for all rational beings. Morality can never be understood as something that is given to us in nature. Morality is never an object of empirical inquiry, as Hutcheson and Hume had believed. It is an ideal that we need to realise. We must try to act morally even if 'the world has perhaps so far given no example' of a moral act (Ak 4: 408).

Kant argued that all philosophers before him had failed to appreciate the autonomous nature of morality and that they therefore had based morality on 'heteronomous principles', which was for him just another way of saying that these philosophers were wrong. In a highly revealing passage of the *Grundlegung*, Kant classifies 'All Possible Principles of Morality Taken from Heteronomy Assumed as the Basic Concept' (Ak 4: 441). These appear to exhaust the principles of morality that had been advanced before him (but perhaps do not). These principles, which are all characterised by their failure to recognise the fundamental importance of autonomy for the foundations of the metaphysics of morals, fall into one of two categories, rational or empirical (4: 441–5). In the empirical category he differentiated further between principles based on self-regarding considerations (or happiness) and principles based on a moral sense. Insofar as these two positions are empirical, he rejected them both. But he did grant that the moral sense 'remains closer to morality and its dignity' than is the other principle, that of self-regard (4: 442). He also saw the rational principles as of two types, namely, the theological conception 'which derives morality from a most divine, all-perfect will' and the ontological conception of perfection as a possible result of our moral actions (4: 443). The ontological conception of perfection seemed better to Kant than the theological conception. Indeed, it appears that Kant ordered these principles in accordance with his view of morality and dignity. Egoism is the lowest form of a moral principle in this scheme; the altruistic moral sense is better, but both are less perfect than the two rational principles. The theological concept was better, according to Kant, than either of the empirical principles. But the ontological concept of perfection is the best of all of these principles.

In *Kritik der praktischen Vernunft* Kant has an even more elaborate table of what he calls there the 'practical material determining grounds in the principle of morality' (Ak 5: 40). All of these 'grounds' fall into eight categories. Four of these are subjective, and four are objective. Both the subjective and objective principles are either external or internal. Under the subjective external principles Kant lists 'education' as found in Montaigne and 'civil constitution' as advocated by Mandeville. The subjective internal ones are 'physical feeling' (Epicurus) and 'moral feeling' (Hutcheson). Internal objective grounds are represented by 'perfection' (Wolff and the Stoics), while the external one is 'the will of God' (Crusius and other theological moralists). Again, it is clear that the objective principles are superior to the subjective principles and that the internal principles are superior to the external ones. And the highest form of the material principles is again perfection. Although Crusius insists that it is our conscience that tells us what these duties are, ultimately they are supported by something 'in heaven', and they are therefore heteronomously based. Wolff's ethical theory, which is more decisively rationalistic and is characterised by a certain kind of secularism, is heteronomous for a different reason. The view that moral goodness is constituted by what increases our perfection (and evil by what decreases it) is for Kant dependent on the situation in which we find ourselves in this world. It presupposes that certain ends are already given independently from reason. Furthermore, Wolff, although a rationalist, failed to understand the essential nature of reason as a spontaneous faculty radically different from sensibility. However, this does not rule out Wolff's crucial importance for understanding his project. In fact, in the Preface to the *Grundlegung* Kant finds it necessary to forestall the criticism that Wolff has already done what he himself proposes to do in that work and that he therefore does not open 'an entirely new field' (Ak 4: 390).

The philosopher closest to Kant in his rejection of any form of naturalism was Plato. And there are many passages (especially in reflections that were not published during Kant's lifetime) that suggest that Plato, as someone who based morality on a rational *ideal*, was not only viewed by Kant as close to his own view, but also helped him in formulating it. Although he belittled Plato as being too 'enthusiastic' and as having a too fantastic conception of reason, Kant appreciated Plato's rejection of any empirical principles and in the *Kritik der reinen Vernunft* specifically noted that Plato provided 'principles which are indeed excellent for the practical [i.e., moral]'.[69] These principles were those of the theory of ideas that allow us to impose on the world an 'architectonic connection according to ends, i.e., ideas', an enterprise, Kant says, that 'deserves respect and imitation' (A 318/B 375).

Indeed, Kant's moral philosophy has a somewhat Platonic outlook; but there are also fundamental differences. Whereas Plato claimed to know ultimate truth, Kant argued only for beliefs. Ideas, for him, were not 'archetypes of things themselves', but 'necessary' concepts of reason 'to which no congruent object can be given in the senses' (A 313/B 370, A 327/ B 383). And for him there were only three such ideas, namely freedom, God, and immortality (B 395). In his speculative philosophy these three ideas were nothing but expressions of a subjective need to give an ultimate order and unity to our knowledge. There they remained ultimately unjustifiable and defensible only as ordering principles which are convenient and required by a complete rational account of the world, but which may have to be given up if we are challenged by sceptics. However, in the context of moral considerations these ideas could not only be justified, but also turned out to be foundational. We must believe in the reality of these ideas in order to be consistent moral agents.

Kant's revolutionary emphasis on the absolute autonomy of the moral agent and the corresponding glorification of 'freedom' undoubtedly would have struck earlier eighteenth-century philosophers as blasphemous, overly enthusiastic, or even dangerous. Hume would have rejected it as not being based on 'a true delineation or description of human nature'.[70] Such objections were in fact made by Kant's contemporaries. Kant understood these complaints, but explained that he was formulating an 'ideal', something to be believed in, and not something that already existed or that could easily be achieved. And he tried to show that it was a noble ideal, an ideal that could guide us on our way toward an ideal state. He also argued that these ideals came from pure reason itself, though he insisted that they are supported by 'nothing in heaven or on earth' (*Grundlegung*, Ak 4: 425).

In other words, moral principles were neither theological nor natural. Neither God, nor nature (human or otherwise), nor convention, nor anything else could provide a foundation for morals. In his own way, Kant substituted faith for knowledge.

It may be doubted whether Kant would have succeeded in convincing his predecessors that such an idealistic foundation of morality was possible or even amounted to a foundation. But it is a fact that he had a profound effect on the members of the younger generation whose view of the world and philosophy was formed more by the developments connected with the American and French Revolutions and who themselves craved freedom from oppressive authority. While many of the older generation saw Kant's attempt at a foundation of the metaphysics of morals (and indeed his entire philosophy) as a form of scepticism, the younger generation found its effects liberating. Thus Moses Mendelssohn felt it wise to ignore, at least in public, the works of the 'all-crushing' Kant, while Karl Leonhard Reinhold, whose *Briefe über die kantische Philosophie* (1786–7) was instrumental in popularizing the Kantian view, celebrated Kant's moral philosophy and its consequences for religion.[71]

NOTES

1 Adam Smith, *The Theory of Moral Sentiments*, eds. D. D. Raphael and A. L. Macfie, in *Works* (1976), VII.i.2; italics added. This work was first published in 1759.

2 Hutcheson had been Smith's teacher at the University of Glasgow.

3 David Hume, *A Treatise of Human Nature*, eds. D. F. Norton and M. J. Norton, in the *Clarendon Edition* (2006), 2.1.7.2–5, SBN 295–6.

4 Bernard Mandeville, *The Fable of the Bees: or, Private Vices, Publick Benefits*, 2nd edn. (London, 1723); first published in 1714.

5 Hume, *An Enquiry concerning the Principles of Morals*, ed. T. L. Beauchamp in the *Clarendon Edition* (1998), 1.3, SBN 170.

6 This is not to say that Hume failed to recognise that moral terms are sometimes used in extended or metaphorical senses. We may, he notes, speak of the virtues (or powers) of inanimate objects, but when we do so we are not making moral assessments; see *Enquiry*, 5.1.1n, SBN 213n.

7 For a sketch of this development, see D. F. Norton, 'Hume, Human Nature, and the Foundations of Morality', in *The Cambridge Companion to Hume*, ed. D. F. Norton (Cambridge, 1993), 148–81.

8 Anthony Ashley Cooper, Earl of Shaftesbury's *Inquiry* was first printed from an 'Imperfect Copy' in 1699. The work was reprinted in 1711 as a part of *Characteristics of Men, Manners, Opinions, Times*, and is here quoted from the edition of this work edited by John Robertson, 2 vols. (London, 1900).

9 On this point, see Norton, 'Hume, Atheism, and the Autonomy of Morals,' in *Hume's Philosophy of Religion*, ed. M. Hester (Winston-Salem, NC, 1986), 108–10.

10 See Shaftesbury, *The Life, Unpublished Letters, and Philosophical Regimen of Anthony, Earl of Shaftesbury*, ed. B. Rand (London, 1900), 37–8.

11 Samuel Clarke, *A Demonstration of the Being and Attributes of God: More Particularly in Answer to Mr. Hobbs, Spinoza, and their Followers* (London, 1705) and *A Discourse concerning the Being and Attributes of God, the Obligations of Natural Religion, and the Truth and Certainty of the Christian Revelation* (London, 1706).

12 Clarke, *Discourse*, in *Works*, ed. B. Hoadly, 4 vols. (London, 1737), 2: 609; see also 641. Clarke's plentiful italics have been deleted.
13 Smith, as we have seen in Section I, does notice this fact.
14 We can restate this much of Mandeville's argument in a more familiar form: If there are virtuous individuals or acts, then there are other-regarding motives. There are no other-regarding motives. Consequently, there are no virtuous individuals or acts.
15 Mandeville, 'An Enquiry into the Origin of Moral Virtue,' *The Fable of the Bees: or, Private Vices, Publick Benefits*, ed. F. B. Kaye, 2 vols. (Oxford, 1924), 1: 56.
16 In a letter to *The London Journal* (No. 277, London, 1724), Hutcheson says that his *Inquiry into the Original of our Ideas of Beauty and Virtue* will contain an essay of this title. This letter is reprinted as 'Reflections on the Common Systems of Morality' in *On Human Nature: Reflections on our Common Systems of Morality and On the Social Nature of Man*, ed. T. Mautner (Cambridge, 1993), 96–106.
17 Francis Hutcheson, *An Inquiry into the Original of our Ideas of Beauty and Virtue*, 4th edn. (London, 1738), xiii.
18 *Inquiry*, 105, 132, 154, 166, 172. Hutcheson's plentiful italics have been deleted.
19 This argument can also be restated in a more familiar form: If there are other-regarding motives, then there are virtuous individuals. There are other-regarding motives. Therefore there are virtuous individuals.
20 For Hutcheson's concern to prove 'the *Reality of Virtue*' and to show that we only give moral approvals to actions in which we perceive 'some really good moral Quality', see *Inquiry*, xi, 201.
21 *Inquiry*, title to Part II, Section V, 218.
22 *Inquiry*, 130–31. Hutcheson added this comment to the third edition of the *Inquiry* (1729) in order to prevent what he took to be misunderstandings of his position.
23 Hutcheson, *Letters . . . concerning the True Foundation of Virtue and Moral Goodness* (London, 1735), in *Works*, 7 vols. (Hildesheim, 1971), 7: [19]. As the title of this collection indicates, the issue of the 'true foundation' of morality is discussed throughout these letters.
24 Gilbert Burnet, in Hutcheson, *Works*, 7: [5]–[6]. Burnet composed his Preface sometime after the exchange of letters ended and before his death in 1726.
25 John Balguy, *The Foundation of Moral Goodness: or A further Inquiry into the Original of our Idea of Virtue* (London, 1728), 3–4. As noted above, the second part of this work appeared in 1729.
26 Balguy, *Foundation*, 5–7. Balguy's plentiful italics have been deleted.
27 Hutcheson, *An Essay on the Nature and Conduct of the Passions and Affections: With Illustrations on the Moral Sense* (London, 1728). References to this work in this chapter are to the third edition (London, 1742).
28 Hutchson, *Essay*, 243. Hutcheson explicitly refers to Balguy's argument in *Foundation*, 9–10.
29 Balguy, *Foundation of Moral Goodness*, Pt. 2, 38–52, 57–64.
30 Richard Price, *A Review of the Principal Questions in Morals*, ed. D. D. Raphael (Oxford, 1974), 15. The *Review* was first published in 1758.
31 Hume, *Treatise*, Bk 3, Advertisement and 3.1.1.1–3, SBN [454]–6. Generally speaking, Hume's *Treatise* explains how certain important ideas and impressions arise in the human mind. Book 1 provides a genetic account of our ideas of space and time, causal connection, external existence, and the self. Book 2 provides a similar account of such passions as pride, love, desire and fear, and of the feeling of volition. Book 3 provides a genetic account of our moral perceptions. The *Treatise* is an attempt, that is, to explain how a mind, acquainted originally only with impressions of sensation, comes to have and to use moral ideas – to have and to use, for example, the ideas of virtue and vice, duty and blame, justice and injustice, or benevolence. Thus for Hume the issue of moral foundations resolves itself into questions

of the sort that Hutcheson had asked in his *Inquiry*, namely, what is the original of our idea of virtue?

32 See, for example, *Treatise*, 3.1.1–2, 2.2.3, 2.3.2.7, 3.3.1.18–19, 3.2.6.6, 3.3.1, 3.3.4; SBN 457–72, 348–9, 412. 584, 528–29, 575–91, 606–17; *Enquiry*, 3.1.7–14, SBN 185–8; For Hume's clearest assessment of Brutus, see *The Letters of David Hume*, ed. J. Y. T. Greig, 2 vols. (Oxford, 1932), 1: 35, letter of 17 September, 1739, to Hutcheson.

33 For Hume's important discussions of several different senses of natural, see *Treatise*, 3.1.2.6–11, 3.2.1.19; SBN 473–6, 484.

34 See, for example, *Treatise*, 3.2.1.4–5, SBN 478.

35 See, for example, *Treatise*, 3.2.1.3, SBN 477–8.

36 *Treatise*, 2.3.6.8, 3.3.6.1; SBN 427, 618; on sympathy more generally, see 2.1.11.1–8, 3.3.1.7–31; SBN 316–20, 575–91.

37 Hume's account of the development of justice is found first in the *Treatise*, 3.2.2, 3.2.6; SBN 484–501, 526–34, and then again, with minor modifications, in the *Enquiry*, 2.1–3.2, App 3; SBN 176–204, 303–311.

38 *Treatise*, 3.2.2.7–9, SBN 488–9. Hume, attempting to distinguish himself from Locke and other contract theorists, argues that such cooperation does not depend on a promise or covenant: 'Two men, who pull the oars of a boat, do it by an agreement or convention, tho' they have never given promises to each other.' (*Treatise*, 3.2.2.10, SBN 490).

39 *Treatise*, 3.2.6.11, SBN 533. Hume adds that this artifice is augmented by 'the public instructions of politicians, and the private education of parents', but he twice (3.2.3.25, 3.3.1.11; SBN 500, 578–9) criticises Mandeville and others who have exaggerated the effect of politicians. All such artifices, he suggests, are dependent on the foundation provided by human nature.

40 Hume, *A Letter from a Gentleman to his Friend in Edinburgh* (1745), eds. E. C. Mossner and J. V. Price (Edinburgh, 1967), 18.

41 Henry Home, Lord Kames, *Essays on the Principles of Morality and Natural Religion* (Edinburgh, 1751), 103.

42 James Balfour, *A Delineation of the Nature and Obligation of Morality* (Edinburgh, 1753), 45, 53, 58.

43 Price, *Review of the Principal Questions in Morals*, 56, 63.

44 Its most important source of inspiration was Philipp Jakob Spener's *Pia desideria* of 1675. The subtitle of this work speaks of the 'heartfelt desire for the improvement of the true evangelical Church that is approved by God, together with some Christian suggestions, designed to lead towards it.' Another important proponent of this view was August Hermann Francke (1663–1727), who taught at the University of Halle.

45 For useful introductions, see Albrecht Ritschl, *Geschichte des Pietismus*, 3 vols. (Bonn, 1880–96) and Emanuel Hirsch, *Geschichte der neuern evangelischen Theologie*, 2nd edn., 2 vols. (Gütersloh, 1960), 2: 91–43. See also Max Weber, *The Protestant Ethics and the Spirit of Capitalism*, trans. T. Parsons (New York, NY, 1958), 128–39. For a short collection of writings by Pietists, see *Pietists: Selected Writings*, ed. Peter C. Erb (New York, NY, 1983). For Francke and the Halle School see especially 97–215. Pietism was a highly evangelical movement, and it usually involved an insistence on a *personal* experience of radical conversion or rebirth, and an abrogation of worldly success. Pietism remains influential in Germany today. It also had significant effects outside of Germany; see F. E. Stoeffler, *The Rise of Evangelical Pietism*, 2nd edn. (Leiden, 1971).

46 Richard L. Gawthrop, *Pietism and the Making of Eighteenth-Century Prussia* (Cambridge, 1993), 141.

47 See also J. B. Schneewind, *The Invention of Autonomy: A History of Modern Moral Philosophy* (Cambridge, 1998), 442–4 (A Note on Pietism), 159–66 (on Thomasius), and 445–56. It

would have been helpful if Schneewind had pointed out how closely the views of Thomasius and Crusius are connected with Pietistic doctrine. While neither of them can be properly understood without this background, Thomasius's conflict with Pietism is especially interesting. See, for instance, Werner Schneiders, *Naturrecht und Liebesethik: Zur Geschichte der praktischen Philosophie im Hinblick auf Christian Thomasius* (Hildesheim, 1971), 226–39.

48 Christian Thomasius, *Ausübung der Sittenlehre* (Halle, 1696), §532. The full title translates as, *On the Medicine against Irrational Love and the Necessary Prior Knowledge of Self. Or: Execution of the Moral Doctrine. Together with a conclusion in which the Author shows the manifold Use of His Moral Doctrine and Honestly Confesses His Christian Concept of Moral Doctrine.*

49 There is a translation of a short selection from this text in *Moral Philosophy from Montaigne to Kant*, ed. J. B. Schneewind, 2 vols. (Cambridge, 1990), 2: 565–85. For a discussion of Crusius's relation to Kant see especially Dieter Henrich, 'Hutcheson und Kant', *Kant-Studien* 49 (1957–8), 49–69; and his 'Über Kants früheste Ethik', *Kant-Studien* 54 (1963), 404–31. These papers are, of course, also important for the relation of Kant to Hutcheson.

50 Schneewind, *Moral Philosophy*, 2: 576; compare 451. Crusius is influenced by Wolff in his formulation of this 'universal rule of action'. But he insists it is given by God.

51 It is perhaps of interest to note that these theological views have more in common with Smith's licentious system than with any positive account of the foundations of morality.

52 This is the title of Wolff's so-called 'German Ethics' of 1736 and 1739. There is a translation of short selections in Schneewind, *Moral Philosophy*, 1: 333–48.

53 Schneewind, *Moral Philosophy*, 1: 336.

54 Furthermore, insofar as the relationship of theology and morality was concerned, the Pietists and the Wolffians were not as far apart as it might appear. For Wolff agreed that the demands of reason could also be understood as commands of God.

55 Compare Schneewind, *Moral Philosophy*, 2: 416.

56 Adam Smith, *Essays on Philosophical Subjects*, eds. W. P. D. Wightman and J. C. Bryce, in *Works* (1980), 249.

57 Indeed, it did appear to be the same to some philosophers – Thomas Reid, for instance. But this means, Reid explains, that morality has been reduced to the agreeable and the useful, to the '*dulce* and the *utile*'. There is thus no room left for any essentially moral quality, and in particular there is no longer any room for moral worth or what Reid calls with Cicero '*honestum*'. This makes Hume, in Reid's eyes, essentially an Epicurean. Pleasure remains ultimately the only end 'that is good in itself, and desirable for its own sake; and virtue derives all its merit from its tendency to produce pleasure'. See Thomas Reid, *Philosophical Works*, ed. Sir W. Hamilton, 2 vols. (Hildesheim, 1983), 2: 651.

58 Moses Mendelssohn in a review of Edmund Burke's *A Philosophical Enquiry into the Origin of our Ideas of the Sublime and Beautiful*, which appeared in the *Bibliothek der schönen Wissenschaften und der freyen Künste* II, 2 (1759), quoted in accordance with the 2nd edn. of 1762, 290–1.

59 Moses Mendelssohn, *Gesammelte Schriften: Jubiläumsausgabe*, eds. F. Bamberger and A. Altmann (Stuttgart-Bad Canstatt, 1971–), 2: 183.

60 Johann August Eberhard, *Allgemeine Theorie des Denkens und Empfindens* (Berlin, 1776), 186f. See M. Kuehn, *Scottish Common Sense in Germany, 1768–1800: A Contribution to the History of Critical Philosophy* (Kingston and Montreal, 1987), 103–4.

61 Johann Georg Heinrich Feder, *Untersuchungen über den menschlichen Willen*, 2 vols. (Göttingen, 1779–82), 1: 391. Feder admitted that 'in the first development and ordering of [his] concepts' Hume's second *Enquiry* was more important to him than any other book, and that he had learned much from Smith's account of sympathy.

62 Feder, *Über den menschlichen Willen*, 1: 385.

63 Dieter Henrich, 'The Concept of Moral Insight', trans. M. Kuehn, in Henrich, *The Unity of Reason. Essays on Kant's Philosophy*, ed. R. Velkley (Cambridge, MA, 1994), 70.

64 Immanuel Kant, *Untersuchung über die Deutlichkeit der Grundsätze der natürlichen Theologie und Moral* (1764), in Ak, 2: 273–301 at 299–300; translated as *Inquiry concerning the Distinctness of the Principles of Natural Theology and Morality*, in *Works/Theoretical Philosophy, 1755–1770*, trans. and eds. D. Walford and R. Meerbote (1992).

65 Kant, *Grundlegung zur Metaphysik der Sitten* (Ak 4: 385–463); translated as *Groundwork of The Metaphysics of Morals*; *Kritik der praktischen Vernunft* (Ak 5: 1–163); translated as *Critique of Practical Reason*. Both can be found in *Works/Practical Philosophy*, trans. and ed. M. J. Gregor (1996).

66 Sir David Ross, *Kant's Ethical Theory: A Commentary on the Grundlegung zur Metaphysik der Sitten* (Oxford, 1954), 92.

67 This point notwithstanding, Kant is willing to say that to 'assure one's own happiness is a duty (at least indirectly)' (*Grundlegung*, Ak 4: 399). However, it is important to understand that it is just that, namely a duty; and only an indirect one as well as one among many.

68 The Stoic maxim was, of course, 'Follow nature'.

69 Kant, *Kritik der reinen Vernunft*, A 472/B 500; translated as *Critique of Pure Reason*, trans. and eds. P. Guyer and A. W. Wood, in *Works* (1998).

70 The phrase is Hume's, *An Enquiry concerning the Principles of Morals*, App 2.13, SBN 302. I have no doubt that he would have included Kant's among those philosophies that are 'more like a satyr' and 'a good foundation for paradoxical wit and raillery'.

71 Karl Leonhard Reinhold, *Briefe über die kantische Philosophie*, first published in *Teutscher Merkur*, then in 2 vols. separately in 1790, 1792 (Leipzig).

33

NORM AND NORMATIVITY

STEPHEN DARWALL

'Obligation' and its cognates have had several different uses in the history of ethical thought. The oldest refers to a tie or bond one person can have to another, either by virtue of some action (an oath or the receipt of some service, for example) or just because of the relationships in which they stand (say, parent to child or superior to inferior).[1] Obligation here is personal; one person is bound *to another*. Thought of in this way, obligations cement individuals together into families, groups, and societies.

A second use points to a different way persons might compose larger wholes or orders, not by being glued part to part (even to a single 'ruling' part), but through rules, norms, or laws that govern all. Here 'obligation' conveys a prescriptivity or requiredness that is part of the very idea of a rule or norm. Naturally enough, therefore, when philosophers in the seventeenth and eighteenth centuries came to argue for the existence of universally binding norms of conduct ('laws of nature' or a 'moral law'), they used the language of obligation to express their idea. Conceived in this way, the bond inherent in obligation is not a tie to others, but a constraint operating impersonally on all. Indeed, it is possible to think, as increasingly it was in the modern period, that personal obligations can have genuine moral or normative force only if they ultimately derive from impersonal ones of this sort. If, for example, parents really owe special obligations to their children, that must be because of some norm or law requiring special care – not a positive law, but one of universal morality or 'nature'.

However, a person may be within the scope of a norm's intended application, and it may still sensibly be asked why or whether she must comply. After all, rules of parlour games bind in the trivial sense that they state requirements on players. But that does not mean they create obligations of any serious interest for ethics. A third, philosophically more important way early modern thinkers used the concept of obligation was to raise questions of just this sort. What ought we to

I am indebted to the National Endowment for the Humanities for support from a Fellowship for University Teachers during the time this was written, and to William Frankena, David Fate Norton, J. B. Schneewind, and Knud Haakonssen for helpful comments on earlier drafts.

do or must we do *really*? What, if anything, is genuinely binding on us? And what is the source of the power to obligate? In what does this normativity consist?

Questions concerning the 'roots of oughtness' preoccupied early modern moral philosophy, and this brought the language of obligation into the foreground during this period in an unprecedented way. With thinkers who were concerned to advance universal ethics of duty, from Grotius and the other seventeenth-century natural lawyers through to Kant and Bentham at the end of the eighteenth, this will hardly seem surprising. But sharp critics of the legal model in ethics – including such champions of virtue ethics as Shaftesbury, Leibniz, Hutcheson, and Hume – felt compelled to use the language of obligation as well. In part, they were seeking to reinterpret this language for their own philosophical aims. But also they simply could not avoid it in confronting the issues of fundamental justification it had been used to raise.

In what follows we shall survey eighteenth-century views of norms and the normative. Overall, two phenomena are pre-eminently noteworthy. One is the development of competing *systematic normative theories* of conduct on a model not dissimilar to that of theory in modern science. Just as Boyle and Newton sought to explain particular natural occurrences by universal laws, so, increasingly, did eighteenth-century moral philosophers seek to uncover universal moral laws or norms of conduct. This was inspired partly by a desire to bring the same systematicity to comprehending the moral realm that had yielded such impressive results in understanding the natural and, frequently, by a desire to base ethics on the latter and thereby make it 'scientific'. But equally important was the emergence of an ideal of a *public* (and potentially democratic) moral philosophy. This brought a significant part of ethics closer to law, inspiring similar demands for systematicity and for the formulation of publicly criticisable principles. To this period we owe the development of utilitarianism as a systematic theory of right along with its major competitors, intuitionism and Kantianism.

The second phenomenon is the one I mentioned. Never before had philosophers thought with such focus and effect about the nature of obligation (normativity) itself. Increasingly, they viewed the problem as that of explaining how agents can be bound *internally*, within deliberative practical reasoning. This led to much fruitful philosophy concerning the relationships between obligation, autonomy, agency, and the will.

The agenda for these developments in the eighteenth century was largely set by thinkers in the seventeenth known as the modern natural lawyers. Beginning with Grotius's *De iure belli ac pacis* (1625), and including Pufendorf's *De jure naturæ et gentium* (1672) and Cumberland's *De legibus naturæ disguisito philosophica* (1672) – as well as, more generally, the ethical thought of Hobbes and Locke – the modern tradition of natural law sought to describe a set of universal norms necessary to regulate and co-ordinate human conduct and to ground these in a philosophical account of their obligatory force. To understand what was novel about this agenda, we must first survey briefly the classical theory of natural law deriving from St. Thomas against which the modern tradition of the seventeenth century was reacting.

I. THE CLASSICAL THEORY OF NATURAL LAW

The idea that there are norms or laws to which all rational human beings are subject goes back as far as the Stoics. But it was not until the work of Thomas Aquinas in the thirteenth century that it was developed systematically. For Aquinas, natural law is a formulation of 'eternal law', God's ideal or archetype for all of nature – 'the exemplar of divine wisdom as directing the motions and acts of all things'.[2] Eternal law specifies the distinctive perfection or ideal state of every natural thing. But although all things are 'regulated and measured' by this, rational beings are subject to law in a distinctive way, since they join in and make their own the Eternal Reason'. They are bound by what Aquinas calls 'natural law': eternal law as applied and made accessible to rational creatures (I.ii.91.2).

Aquinas's theory of good was perfectionist: the good of each being is its perfection.[3] It followed that individual human beings can realise their respective goods only if they function properly in the overall scheme specified by eternal law. Any genuine conflict between individuals' interests is thus ruled out metaphysically – harmony is guaranteed by perfectionist-teleological metaphysics. It followed also that, for each, following natural law is necessary to achieving his greatest good. For the question of human law and governance, Aquinas recognises that important issues of conflict arise. Although these could be raised well enough in terms of conflicting *beliefs* about the good, and consistently with the doctrines concerning the relationship between eternal law and good already cited, Aquinas does speak here about conflicting interests.[4]

Aquinas's picture of natural law requires a teleological metaphysics to make sense, since that both guarantees coincidence between duty and interest and gives natural law its normativity. Inherent in every natural being's nature, including that of every human being, is an ideal that exists *as end*: what that being *should be*. Normativity is thus 'built into' what we are.

II. THE MODERN, SEVENTEENTH-CENTURY THEORY OF NATURAL LAW

By the early seventeenth century, Aristotelian teleology was hardly the orthodoxy it had been in preceding centuries.[5] With the early successes of modern science, the best explanations of natural phenomena seemed likelier to proceed in terms of value-free natural mechanisms than by reference to intrinsic ends or 'final causes'. In quite a different way than for Aristotle and Aquinas, value and normativity played no essential role in the world of the emerging science and, once metaphysical teleology was given up, it was guaranteed neither that human interests are necessarily harmonised nor that human nature has any direct normative implications.

Both consequences provided important background for the seventeenth-century natural law tradition. Grotius, indeed, begins his founding work of modern natural law, *De iure belli ac pacis* (1625), by discussing a fundamental sceptical objection that simply could not have arisen on the traditional view: '[T]here is no law of nature, because all creatures, men as well as animals, are impelled by nature towards ends advantageous to themselves . . . consequently, there is no justice, or, if such there be, it is supreme folly, since one does violence to his own interests if he consults the advantage of others.'[6] This objection can arise only if it is possible for individuals' interests to conflict with the requirements of natural law. On the classical theory, it could not get off the ground.

For modern natural lawyers, natural law does not direct individuals to their own good, naturally harmonised with that of others. On the contrary, according to them, it is the possibility of genuine conflicts of interest that creates the need for natural law in the first place. Natural law is necessary to solve what is currently called the 'problem of collective action': How can interaction be structured to mutual advantage in view of the fact that the unrestrained pursuit of self-interest can be mutually disadvantageous?[7] Roughly, 'modern' natural laws are norms that, if universally accepted and followed, make everyone better off than each would be were everyone to pursue his or her individual good. But though everyone benefits from universal conformity (relative to universal nonconformity), individuals may sometimes do even better if they violate with impunity natural laws that others are following.

The problem for modern natural lawyers was *how* natural law could bring collective benefit. Partly this was a psychological question of motivation: How can human beings act on these norms when they limit self-interest? For psychological egoists, such as Locke, this issue was especially pressing. In addition, however, there was also a fundamental issue of moral philosophy: Why *should* individuals act on such norms? What makes them obligatory? Or, as we might also say, what makes them *laws* for us?

Ultimately, modern natural lawyers and their successors came to see that these two questions cannot be entirely separated, that any satisfying account of obligation must be integrated with a convincing theory of moral motivation and practical reason. Indeed, one of the most exciting developments in fundamental moral philosophy of the seventeenth and eighteenth centuries was the working out of the idea that all genuine obligation is *internal*, binding through rational motive – a view that found both an empirical naturalist interpretation in Hutcheson and Hume and a rationalist one in Kant's doctrine that the moral law is self-legislated in the practical reasoning of free rational agents. But to work toward such 'internalist' theories of obligation, or any others, it was necessary first to achieve some focus on the issue of normativity itself.

Particularly important here was Pufendorf, whose influential distinction between 'physical' and 'moral' entities highlighted the rejection of classical teleological metaphysics and focused moral philosophy squarely on the issue of obligation.[8] Pufendorf claimed that moral aspects of situations (those concerning what agents *should* do) are distinct and underivative from 'the intrinsic nature of the physical properties of things'. The latter compose a realm of entities 'already existent and physically complete', to which the moral realm is entirely additional. Physical things are distinguished by their varying capacities directly 'to produce any physical motion or change', but the 'active force' of moral entities consists 'only in this, that it is made clear to men along what line they should govern their liberty of action' (I.i.4). Pufendorf accepted what I have identified as the distinctively modern conception of morality: individuals can 'secure a certain orderliness and decorum in civilized life' only if moral ideas 'direct and temper the freedom' of their voluntary action (I.i.3).

Once 'moral entities' are thus distinguished, the question of the nature and source of obligation may be faced directly. What makes it the case that someone *should* govern his liberty of acting in some way or other? Pufendorf's own view was that obligation consists in a 'moral necessity', that, unlike natural necessity which operates in the physical realm, is created by the *imposition* of a superior authority. His model was that of law. Without the declared will of some superior with authority over others, no obligations can exist. The obligation of natural law derives from the authority of its source.

This became the reigning paradigm of seventeenth-century natural law. In addition to Pufendorf, it can be found in some form or other in Cumberland, Selden, Locke, and even, it has been argued, in Hobbes. It continued to reverberate in the eighteenth century, especially in the theological utilitarianism of Gay, Berkeley, and Paley.

The obvious question for theological voluntarism of this sort is, What does *authority* consist in? Without some satisfactory answer to that question, it is hard to see how any advance is made; obligations to obey specific commands (laws of nature) seem to be explained only by a yet unexplained general obligation to obey God's commands. Pufendorf and Locke agreed, as against Hobbes, that God's authority is different from His power. God's sanctions give us motives to obey, but these do not obligate. Obligation requires additionally, they held, that His sanctions be *justified* because He has the authority to impose them. But again, whence comes this authority?

Here Pufendorf and Locke gave versions of the same answer, that God is the source of all that is good in our lives – Locke stressing our utter dependence on God and Pufendorf something like a debt of gratitude. But, as Cudworth argued against Ockhamites and Calvinists, and as Leibniz would later object to Pufendorf himself, voluntarism of this sort apparently assumes a background 'moral fact'. Now, the voluntarist cannot say that the requisite moral fact (say, that we ought to obey a Being on whom we are totally dependent) itself derives from God's will, since it is necessary to give God's will authority in the first place. So the question arises, In what does this moral fact consist? And why suppose that it is the only 'ought' or obligation-fact, every other deriving from God's will by virtue of it?[9]

Voluntarist attempts to ground the obligation of natural law in our relation to its (personal) source in effect derive impersonal obligation (the second – and third – ideas of obligation mentioned at the outset) from the more traditional notion of obligation as a debt owed by one individual to a particular other individual or group. But a version of Cudworth's point applies here also. With respect to any personal debt, we can ask the substantive normative question: Ought we pay this debt? If the answer is yes, then that apparently assumes some background moral fact (say, that we ought to discharge our personal debts). And the question will again arise, What is the nature and source of this fact?

As we shall better appreciate later, these problems combined with others concerning the relationship between the voluntarists' theories of obligation, rational motivation, and the will to stimulate a significant reorientation of natural law thinking about obligation in the last 30 years of the seventeenth century. The natural lawyers wanted to understand obligation as a bond or necessity operating on (or in) the will. But while Pufendorf defined moral ideas by their capacity to 'direct' voluntary action, theological voluntarisms like his and Locke's apparently gave them no intrinsic power to do so. On the one hand, Pufendorf says, 'whatever we do from an obligation is understood to come from an intrinsic impulse of the mind' (III.vi.6); on the other hand, he also says that 'nothing can constrain the human mind, as it deliberates on the future, to do or avoid anything, except reflections on the good and evil which will befall others and ourselves from what we do' (I.iv.5).

III. EARLY EIGHTEENTH-CENTURY CRITIQUES OF NATURAL LAW: SHAFTESBURY, LEIBNIZ, AND THE ETHICS OF VIRTUE

Pufendorf and Locke made morality *external* to the moral agent in various ways that came to be sharply criticised, provoking an alternative, virtue-based approach in modern moral philosophy, as well as a significant reinterpretation of the natural law tradition itself. Most obviously, for Locke and Pufendorf, morality concerned primarily what critics came to call 'external' or 'outward' actions, rather than a person's character or motives.[10] Second, as we have just noted, Locke and Pufendorf took moral obligation to rest on features outside the moral agent also, specifically, on external authority. Third, both resisted any attempt to understand the idea of authority in terms intrinsic to moral agency – for example, in terms of motives agents have to obey. Finally, both held that externally imposed sanctions, rather than anything arising naturally within moral agents, is the form moral motivation distinctively takes.

Two critics who rejected all four of these tenets of voluntarist natural law and who were most influential in developing an alternative ethics of virtue at the beginning of the eighteenth century were Shaftesbury and Leibniz. Neither shared the modern natural lawyers' fundamental concern with obligation, but what they did say about it is revealing both of basic differences with the natural law tradition and of ways in which that tradition had already come to be reinterpreted by the century's turn.

1. Shaftesbury

Shaftesbury's 'An Inquiry concerning Virtue or Merit' is an especially interesting case study. In the course of arguing that there is an 'obligation . . . to virtue', Shaftesbury evidently assumes he can use 'obligation' without special explanation to refer to a rationally conclusive motive of self-interest for leading a virtuous life.[11] How he could have thought such a thing is initially puzzling because the modern natural law tradition by and large followed Suárez's distinction between advice or counsel and obligating precept, holding that whether agents have reason to be moral is one thing, and whether they have an obligation is another.[12] Nevertheless, even Locke and Pufendorf had held that obligation is not really intelligible without the authoritative creation of motives to obey. Otherwise, Locke thought, God's commands would be vain, while, Pufendorf added, we would lack 'fear mingled with reverence', the mark of obligation, on realising that unless we obey we would justifiably suffer sanctions (*De iure naturae*, I.vi.9).

But this was still far from what Shaftesbury had in mind, as he clearly assumed that the motive of self-interest can be regarded as obligating whether or not it comes from imposed sanctions. The 'missing links' to this idea were provided, implicitly, by Hobbes and, explicitly, by Richard Cumberland. Although he accepted the distinction between command and counsel, Hobbes also wrote that natural laws are called 'Lawes, but improperly'. All they really are are 'Theoremes concerning what conduceth to' ends all human beings seek by natural necessity: peace and self-preservation.[13] This made the normative force of natural law depend entirely on instrumental rationality, on its necessity from an agent's deliberative perspective in achieving contingently inescapable ends.

Cumberland was more explicit. If obligation is to be a necessity operating upon the will, he held, it can be nothing other than an inescapably conclusive reason or motive. The 'received' definition of obligation, he remarks, is 'somewhat *obscure* from Metaphors; for the *Mind* of Man is not properly '*tied with bonds*'', and '[n]othing . . . can superinduce a *Necessity* of doing or forbearing any thing, upon a Human Mind deliberating upon a thing future', he continues, 'except Thoughts or *Propositions* promising Good or Evil, to ourselves or others, consequent upon what we are about to do'. He concludes that an action can be '*necessary to a rational Agent*', only '*when it is certainly one of the Causes necessarily requir'd to that Happiness, which he naturally, and consequently necessarily, desires*'.[14]

Cumberland's theory of obligation resulted from a systematic empiricist reductionism about which he was no less explicit. All ethics, he proposes, can be 'resolv'd' into 'conclusions of true *Natural Philosophy*' (ch. 1, §3). In particular, 'practical propositions' may be expressed in various ways. We may say that an alternative before an agent is necessary to achieve an end that, given her natural makeup, she cannot avoid having. Or we may say ('in the *Form* of a *Gerund*') that 'Such an Action ought to be done'. Or we may express the same thing as a 'command': 'Let that Action . . . be exerted.' 'In my Opinion', Cumberland declares, '*these several Forms* of Speech, relating to the Law of Nature, mean the *same thing*' (ch. 4, §1).

Shaftesbury's discussion of the obligation to virtue is only one mark of how influential this approach came to be. In the first half of the eighteenth century, it became very common for writers to refer to the motive of self-interest as obligating. John Gay was an especially clear example, holding that 'obligation is the necessity of doing or omitting any Action in order to be happy'.[15] Shaftesbury, repelled as he was by Locke's picture of people cowed into morality by a superior's threats, must have welcomed the trend Cumberland began. The voluntarists, he charged, make 'war . . . on virtue itself'.[16] Shaftesbury's indictment included several interrelated charges. First, voluntarism portrayed virtue no differently from the 'tame and gentle carriage' of a beast cowed by 'fear of his keeper' ('Inquiry', I.ii.2). Secondly, by making 'outward action' the focus of ethics, voluntarists reversed the true order of ethical ideas. Character, not acts, is what ethics is fundamentally concerned with (I.ii.3). Finally, Shaftesbury opposed voluntarism on a fundamental issue of the metaphysics of ethics. The idea that moral properties are (in Pufendorf's terms) 'imposed' by superior will and thereby 'superadded' to the physical world of nature amounted, Shaftesbury believed, to a kind of nihilism or moral scepticism. But how could a modern avoid this consequence of Pufendorf's distinction between the moral and the physical without lapsing into teleological metaphysics? Shaftesbury's answer, to which we shall return below, was found in his doctrine of the moral sense, an idea pregnant with philosophical possibilities, leading both to the empiricist sentimentalism of Hutcheson and Hume and the 'constructivist' rationalism of Kant's Copernican revolution in moral philosophy.

Shaftesbury's example of the intimidated beast illustrates five important themes in his virtue ethics. First, and most obviously, fear is not a pleasing but an ugly motive to contemplate. True virtues, however, are amiable. Indeed, Shaftesbury believes, that is what *makes* them virtues. They are objects of a disinterested reflective 'affection', moral sense ('Inquiry', I.ii.3, I.iii.1).

Human passions and affections form a system or 'economy', both within an individual person and in the natural interrelation and reciprocation of human psyches into larger wholes, including the species. These economies may be balanced, ordered, and harmonious when psychic items are properly adapted, or out of balance when they are not. Shaftesburean moral sense is a natural (although cultivated) aesthetic sensibility that responds to contemplated order and disorder in the psychic economy. Fear is a destabilising, hence unlovely, emotion. Consequently, it is a vice.

Secondly, fear makes no intrinsic contribution to the value of a human life. The most important virtues – love, for example – are, however, intrinsic to the good of all brought into relation through them. Thirdly, fear masks the real nature of those motivated by it. Worse, it corrupts intrinsically good motives and sentiments, including moral sense, especially when its object is a 'God whose character it is to be captious and of high resentment' ('Inquiry', I.iii.2, II.ii.2, II.ii.3). Fourthly, fear of authority is ignobly servile (I.iii.3). Were fear the distinctive moral motive, morality would be beneath human dignity.

What our dignity derives from, fifthly, is the human ability to give shape to and thereby 'author' our lives. Whereas 'only good fortune or [a trainer's] right management' can control a savage beast, moral agents can control themselves. By self-reflecting, they can gain critical distance on their motives and, through moral sense, endorse or reject them, making those on which they subsequently act *their own* and not just causes to which they are simply subject. Shaftesbury describes at some length a process of self-critical deliberation or 'self-converse', through which individuals can become their own masters.[17]

This last, proto-Kantian theme combined in Shaftesbury's thought with another anticipating Kant's doctrine that moral worth can be achieved only by actions undertaken for self-consciously moral motives. The 'mere goodness' of such motives as pity or kindness, which 'lies within the reach and capacity of all sensible creatures', contrasts with 'virtue or merit', which can be achieved only by beings who can determine themselves through moral sense ('Inquiry', I.ii.3).

Actually, 'moral sense' is misleading terminology here, as Shaftesbury's whole point is that, unlike the senses for which we have organs, moral sense depends on how an agent critically 'frames' its object in thought. A person cannot appropriately be held responsible for visual defects, but she can, he thinks, for failure to determine herself adequately through moral sense (I.ii.3). In connecting moral subjecthood to self-determining agency in this way, Shaftesbury gave expression to an idea that was to play an important role in the thinking of a number of eighteenth-century moralists, including the British rational intuitionists and Butler, Rousseau, and Kant. It would be the central element in Kant's 'autonomist internalist' theory of obligation as self-legislated in autonomous practical reasoning.[18]

Although he found voluntarism nihilistic, Shaftesbury could have accepted Pufendorf's contrast between the moral and the physical, as he thought there would still be an important sense in which moral distinctions are natural and real. 'If there be no real amiableness or deformity in moral acts, there is at least an imaginary one of full force. Although perhaps the thing itself should not be allowed in Nature, the imagination or fancy of it must be allowed to be from Nature alone' ('Inquiry', I.iii.1). Unlike the physical, the moral properties' 'way of being' is through moral sense, and so long as disinterested reflection leads to a convergent response, this will adequately fund judgements of vice and virtue.

What ensures convergence in Shaftesbury's scheme is not always clear. For his empiricist followers, Hutcheson and Hume, convergence in moral judgement derives from contingent universal features of the human condition. But though it has become customary to view Shaftesbury retrospectively, through the lens of his founding influence on the empiricist sentimentalism of Hutcheson, Hume, and Adam Smith, it is more accurate to understand him as carrying forward a tradition deriving from the seventeenth-century rationalists known as the Cambridge Platonists, including Cudworth and Whichcote.[19] For Shaftesbury and these earlier writers, moral goodness is ultimately grounded in creative, practical aspects held to be essential to mind or reason. Moral sense is guaranteed to approve beautiful psychic order, because both contemplating and contemplated are aspects of creative mind. This amounts to a kind of rationalism that has in common with Kant's the idea that reason is itself practical, creating the ethical realm as an object of its own knowledge. For Shaftesbury, however, it is an order whose organising ideals are aesthetic rather than legal and constitutional.

2. *Leibniz*

Much of Shaftesbury's critique of voluntarism and alternative ethics of virtue is repeated in Leibniz. More than Shaftesbury, however, Leibniz turned these ideas in the direction of what would come to be called utilitarianism. Moreover, within Leibniz's distinctive metaphysics, his virtue ethics became a metaphysically realist perfectionism, lacking anything like Shaftesbury's doctrine of the moral sense and, as well, any attempt to ground the ethical in autonomous moral agency as a realm of freedom.

Leibniz's critique of voluntarism is contained primarily in his *Opinion on the Principles of Pufendorf*.[20] The morally good person, Leibniz objects, is not one who simply performs certain 'external acts'. Moral conduct proceeds from an internal goodness, from the goodness of the good person's motives, and these are not fear of sanction, nor even hope for reward, but a core 'inclination of his soul' (72, 73). After all, both Pufendorf and Locke held God to have motives, intrinsic to His benevolent nature, for commanding us as He does. They just thought, as well, that these cannot *obligate*; that requires authoritative command. But Leibniz points out that Pufendorf effectively credits God's benevolence as the source of His authority, since he holds that obedience is grateful reciprocation of God's goodness towards us. This already suggests a doctrine of moral goodness and virtue, so why should human moral goodness not also consist in benevolence, 'imitating, in a certain way, as a man, divine justice' (72). God's reasons are no less valid for us than for Him, Leibniz argues, so we must have good reason to follow the collectively beneficial rules He wishes us to follow, regardless of any reward or sanction (74–5). Indeed, it appears we would have this reason even if God did not exist, although there are complications here we must consider below.

Obligation is, Leibniz agreed, a moral necessity. But the requisite constraint must be understood to operate *within* the will, not by external imposition. Even without recognising a superior, a person is constrained by necessity, because 'the very nature of things and care for one's own happiness and safety . . . have their own requirements' (*Opinion on Pufendorf*, 73). By moral necessity Leibniz meant 'that which is equivalent to "natural" for a good man', where 'a good man is one who loves everybody, in so far as reason permits'[21] Moral necessity is thus natural necessity for the good person. What one ought to do in a given situation is whatever act would be determined by good (benevolent) nature – what a good person would do in that situation, or what one would do oneself were one good.

Like the classical natural law view, Leibniz's position required a metaphysical guarantee of various harmonies and coincidences, both within morality and between morality and self-interest. Within morality, Leibniz's perfectionism led him ultimately to identify all justice, enlightened benevolence, wisdom, virtue, and happiness. Justice is 'the charity of the wise man', so whatever an enlightened love of all leads to is just (*Political Writings*, 171). Nor are wisdom and benevolence really distinct, for Leibniz. Every being's good is its perfection, and though the good life is pleasurable, that is not because pleasure is intrinsically good. Rather, 'pleasure is a knowledge or feeling of perfection, not only in ourselves, but also in others'. This ensures that knowledge of (the prospect of) good (perfection) in *anyone* will lead to a desire for it for its own sake. Indeed, it apparently follows that this knowledge itself *is* either pleasure in or a desire for the good of others, depending, presumably, on whether the latter is actual or envisaged as a possibility in prospect. Since wisdom includes knowledge of perfection, virtue (benevolence) may also be described as 'the habit of acting according to wisdom'.[22]

Leibniz's identification of moral goodness (and justice) with universal benevolence led him to assert a version of the greatest happiness principle, for perhaps the first time in the history of ethical thought. 'To act in accordance with supreme reason', he wrote, 'is to act in such a manner that the greatest quantity of good available is obtained for the greatest multitude possible and that as much felicity is diffused as the reason of things can bear'.[23] The utilitarians were to reject Leibniz's perfectionism, but they followed him in drawing the same formal, maximising consequences of an equal concern for the good of all.

Despite Leibniz's stress on benevolence, however, he ultimately agreed with Shaftesbury that *obligation* operates through 'care for one's own happiness' owing to the intrinsic contribution to the agent's good made by actively furthering that of others'. 'If God did not exist,' he writes, 'wise men would have no more cause to be benevolent than such as would be required for their own welfare'. This may seem puzzling, but Leibniz's point must be that, through an eternal community of all spirits made possible by the immortality of the soul, God 'ensures that every good act will be beneficial, and every bad one harmful, to the agent'. Not even someone who 'endures torture and death for the public good can be regarded as an idiot', he says.[24] God ensures a harmony between the eternal interests of all members of the 'Universal Republic of Spirits' or 'Realm of Grace', guaranteeing for each a coincidence between virtue and good.[25]

3. Followers of Shaftesbury and Leibniz: Hutcheson, Hume, and Wolff

Shaftesbury's main successors developed his ideas primarily within the framework of empiricist naturalism. For Hutcheson, the doctrine of moral sense followed from the Lockean thesis that all ideas come from experience together with the fact, confirmable by introspection, that moral approbation and disapprobation involve distinctive, irreducible ideas. That human beings have a moral sense thus amounted to the thesis that (as a contingent fact of human nature) the contemplation of motive and character gives rise to these distinctive ideas.

Moreover, moral sense 'obeys' a simple, contingent natural law: human beings disinterestedly approve characters and motives in proportion to the degree of benevolence that is manifested in them. As Leibniz had before, Hutcheson drew the proto-utilitarian conclusion that the action 'that accomplishes the greatest happiness of the greatest numbers' is always the morally best choice.[26] But whereas Leibniz thought this followed necessarily on metaphysical grounds, Hutcheson regarded it as part of an empirically confirmed theory of (contingent) human nature. This, together with his hedonism, brought his formulation far closer to the form the greatest happiness principle would take in the utilitarian tradition of Bentham and his followers.

Hutcheson also diverged from Shaftesbury in another important way. Shaftesbury's argument for the 'obligation to virtue' assumed that self-interest is the uniquely final rational motive, but Hutcheson argued that universal benevolence is no less rational in the only sense that, by empiricist lights, any motive can ever deserve the title. The comprehensive use of theoretical reason – informing ourselves perfectly in a way that allows us to respond equally to all we know – leads (again, contingently) to *two* ultimate desires, not just one – self-love *and* universal benevolence.[27] Hutcheson also rejected what he took to be Shaftesbury's position that self-love is the only source of obligation. Surprisingly, however, he identified a distinctively moral obligation not with benevolence, but with the approbation and disapprobation of moral sense, which according to his psychology can never be a direct motive.

Hume followed Hutcheson's distinction between 'interested' and 'moral' obligation (as Hume called them). For our purposes, his main departure was his rejection of Hutcheson's monistic theory of virtue. There are many virtues other than benevolence, Hume believed, as moral sense approves by sympathy any trait or motive that is either immediately agreeable *or* useful to either the agent or others.[28] Most significantly, Hume argued that among the most useful traits are various forms of *justice*, and he stressed that these virtues are 'artificial' in the sense that they involve *regulation* by conventional, collectively beneficial *rules*, even when these call for sacrifice of self-interest *or* the public good. Justice, Hume emphasised, is a distinct virtue from any desire for the good or form of love. Indeed, it can conflict with any of these.

With his theory of justice and of the obligation to be just, Hume took an important step away from the kind of virtue ethics, founded entirely on love, that had been advanced by Shaftesbury, Hutcheson, and Leibniz. Under the usual conditions of human life, Hume argued, love simply cannot provide an adequate basis for social order. A notion of justice that is distinct from any form of love is required: governance by mutually advantageous rules (*Treatise*, 3.2). This evidenced and helped further to stimulate a renewed interest in what had earlier energised the seventeenth-century tradition of natural law – the idea of a regime of norms or laws relating (and obligating) individuals who cannot expect to be loved by others as each loves himself, or even as each loves his family, neighbours, or those with whom he shares the same confession. This, while Hume did not notice it, also insinuated a substantially different theory of the will, as we shall see.

Unlike Shaftesbury's, Leibniz's followers remained steadfastly rationalist. The major one was Christian Wolff, who provided the authoritative version of rational perfectionism for German philosophy of the first half of the eighteenth century. What might be called the Leibniz/Wolff view was virtual academic orthodoxy in Germany during this period. Echoing Leibniz, Wolff identified obligation with 'whatever gives a motive'.[29] Also, like Leibniz, he assumed a harmony of goods (perfections) to be metaphysically guaranteed and concluded that each person is obligated to promote the greatest perfection of all. In so acting, each simultaneously promotes his own greatest good (perfection) and, so much as it is in his power, that of every other person as well.

As the eighteenth century progressed, however, the metaphysical picture required to sustain rational perfectionism seemed irredeemably in conflict with the world-view of modern science, much as that assumed by classical natural law had seemed in the seventeenth century. At the same time, various philosophical (and political) incentives that had driven the early interest in modern natural law had either remained or increased. An ethics of virtue, whether empiricist or rationalist, appeared ill suited to structure an acceptable conception of moral order, at least under the social and political conditions of life in eighteenth-century Europe. More and more, what seemed to be wanted was some conception of norms to which individuals could appropriately be held accountable, and whose power to obligate could be explained, without appeal to controversial metaphysical conceptions of value, debatable views about the objective significance of different forms of human activity, or even, indeed, on the grounds that conformance always made sense in terms of goods the agent herself endorsed. As Hume had shown, a norm could be mutually advantageous even though (indeed, partly because) its dictates occasionally conflicted with either the agent's or the public good. If, consequently, an account of the norm's obligatory force were to spring from, or somehow otherwise ensure, a rational motive for conformance, it would apparently have to draw on motives distinct from any form of love, whether self-love *or* benevolence.

IV. RATIONAL INTUITIONIST ETHICS OF DUTY

The early eighteenth-century virtue ethicists such as Leibniz and Shaftesbury saw theological voluntarism as failing to capture what they considered to be morality's intrinsic importance as an area of human concern. The voluntarists, they thought, made morality out to be something like magnetism, with human beings playing the role of iron filings to God's lodestone. Take away the magnet and there would be no morality.

To a significant extent, this line of criticism was turned back against empiricist virtue ethics by a number of writers who sought to defend a rationalist ethics of duty, most importantly John Balguy, Richard Price, Thomas Reid, and, before them, Samuel Clarke; for most purposes, Bishop Butler might also be included within this group. The doctrine of moral sense, they argued, founded morality on a contingent, posited, and arbitrary sense in something like the way the voluntarists had based morality on posited will. And although they applauded Hutcheson's thesis that a motive to morality exists other than '*the Prospect of private Happiness*', they objected that, for the empiricists, moral sense and benevolence were but 'Instincts' or 'Affections', making virtue 'of an arbitrary and positive Nature . . . entirely depending upon *Instincts*, that might originally have been otherwise'.[30]

The idea of necessity entered the rationalist critique in several different ways. First, as against the notion that moral qualities depend upon the approval of a contingent moral sense, the rationalists were concerned to argue that morality is, in Cudworth's phrase, 'eternal and immutable'. Hutcheson and Hume were roughly agreed that virtue and vice 'may be compar'd to sounds, colours, heat and cold, which, according to modern philosophy, are not qualities in objects, but perceptions in the mind' (Hume, *Treatise*, 3.1.1.26, SBN 469; Hutcheson, *Illustrations*, Sect. 4). And since it is no more necessary that we have the moral sense we do than that we have our actual colour sense, it must be similarly contingent that, say, benevolence is morally good, and malevolence morally evil, rather than vice versa. The rationalists objected, however, that such fundamental moral truths could not be altered by a change in human sentiment, nor indeed, by a change in *anything*, because they depend only on the intrinsic natures of benevolence and moral goodness and these are unalterable. Care is required as Hutcheson would certainly have held, at any rate, that, because God is benevolent, it is no accident we have the moral sense we do, and neither is it an accident that God is benevolent.

Secondly, the empiricists held that any motivation to be moral is also contingent. But 'Moral Goodness', Balguy objected, 'no more depends originally on *Affections* and *Dispositions*, than it does on [positive] *Laws*' (*Foundation*, 11). Had 'we found in our Hearts no kind Instinct towards our Benefactors', we would nonetheless be able to recognise an obligation to return good offices, and, in that recognition, an adequate motive to do so (12). For the rationalists, it is a necessary truth that moral agents can be virtuous. Whatever moral agency consists in, whatever makes us subject to morality, must ensure we can be moral.

Thirdly, according to the empiricists, nothing guarantees that moral considerations will be conclusive in practical reasoning, and hence, that moral conduct is *rationally* necessary. As it happens, Hutcheson believed, the thorough use of theoretical reason leads simultaneously to universal benevolence and to calm self-love, and God has further orchestrated their coincidence. But nothing in the natures of morality and moral agency themselves entails that to go against morality is to go against practical reason.

This conclusion results, the rationalists argued, from an impoverished conception of agency and from a mistaken view of the relationship between practical reason and the will. Agency, for the empiricists, emerges from the combination of belief and desire. A person desires a state of affairs, believes something within her power will achieve that, and those two internal states cause her to act. The role of reason in this picture is wholly theoretical, informing agents of facts about means to satisfy desires and, perhaps, as Hutcheson held, facts that cause modifications of desires as well. The rationalists, however, distinguish between 'mere' intelligent goal-seeking of this sort and genuine agency. Distinctively, agents act *for reasons*; they undertake conduct on account of considerations they regard as justifying (or tending to justify) what they do. Whereas an intelligent goal-seeker need have no end beyond the various goals he seeks, an agent has, they believe, a defining aim: to do what (in his view) the best reasons recommend. As Balguy put it: 'The *End* of Rational Actions, and Rational Agents, consider'd as such, is *Reason* or Moral *Good*' (48). Bishop Butler's famous thesis of the 'authority of conscience' amounted to the same thing. Without a 'Principle of Reflection or Conscience' – in this context, a conception of what one *should* do – a being is not an agent capable of having reasons to act.[31]

The rationalists believed that agency requires having *principles* in addition to beliefs and desires. 'Principle' here had a distinctive sense that contrasted with the seventeenth- and eighteenth-century use to refer to any spring of action. It denoted some articulable rationale for acting that, at its deepest level, applied universally to all rational agents. In doing something for a reason, an agent aims not merely to satisfy some desire she has only as a matter of contingent fact. Her governing aim is rather to do what she has the best reasons for doing, what a person like her should do in a situation like hers. To put it another way, she is governed by principles of rational or reasonable conduct (alternatively, norms or rules of conduct) which she accepts.

Although we shall not be able to appreciate its full significance until we come to Kant, we should note here the sea change this view of agency represents from the traditional theory of the will as rational appetite or desire. According to the orthodox theory, accepted in the main by both classical and modern natural lawyers as well as by the virtue theorists, voluntary action invariably aims at a desired good – will is *appetitus rationalis* (rational desire). Usually, the good in question is held to be the agent's, but not always. Cumberland and Hutcheson insist that rational action can have any good as object, whether the agent's or someone else's.

As against this, the central thrust of the rationalist account was that rational will (as such) aims at conforming to *norms of conduct* – doing what one ought to do (in this context, what it would be rational, reasonable, or justified for a person to do). We might call theirs a *normative theory of the will.* It is consistent with this, of course, that what one ought to do is to promote one's own good, or the greatest good of all. But, according to the rationalists, rational agents act on principles, and this is different from being caused to act by the desire for any good, even if the relevant principle counsels promoting that very good.

The rationalists agreed with Shaftesbury's proto-Kantian thesis (as against Hutcheson and, to a considerable extent, Hume), that genuine virtue is realised only by moral agents who govern themselves in acting by their own moral convictions. Only if 'Virtue consists in a *Rational Determination*, and not in a blind Pursuit of the *Instinct*', Balguy argued, is it rightly attributed to a *person* as opposed to some aspect of or in her (21).

Although they often treated this issue as identical to the metaphysical problem of free will and determinism, the contrast to which the rationalists were really pointing is better seen as that between autonomy and heteronomy, between self-determination and determination by something other than the self. A moral agent, Butler argued, must have a conscience, the capacity to govern himself by normative convictions he accepts; this makes the moral agent a 'Law to himself' (*Sermons*, 36). 'Virtue', added Price, 'supposes determination, and determination supposes a determiner; and a determiner that determines not himself, is a palpable contradiction'.[32]

The rationalists' claim that moral conduct is *rationally* necessary (or required) thus went hand in hand with their belief that it is, in a different sense, not necessary but *free*, as they believed that acting on a (correct) judgement that an action is required by reasons is what genuine (self-determining) agency is. Important as these two claims were to prove in Kant's elaboration of the idea that moral norms are self-legislated by agents in autonomous practical reasoning, they were connected in the thought of Balguy, Clarke, and Price to an intuitionist epistemology and a metaphysical realism that were, in fact, farther from Kant's Copernican revolution than either rationalist or empiricist theories of moral sense.[33]

The intuitionists shared the modern natural lawyers' contention that there are universal norms of conduct that obligate all rational persons. The problem, recall, was to say how these norms obligate (or, alternatively, what makes them norms). Accepting the rationalists' claim that agents determine themselves by a judgement of what they should do (a normative judgement) still leaves the following substantial philosophical problems: What can make such a judgement true? And how can we know whether it is? Furthermore, it is unexceptionable that self-determining rational action aims at moral goodness (Balguy) or requires a consciousness of rectitude (Price) only if these latter terms are taken broadly to refer to whatever a person should do. Once we specify these formal ideas, for example, with a conception of morality as mutually advantageous norms, exception may reasonably be taken unless we can be convinced that moral norms, *so* understood, really do obligate.

Clarke, Balguy, and Price were united in the belief that we neither need nor can have any argument to convince us of the most fundamental moral norms; they are (and must be) self-evident. Nor is there any use for a theory that aims to say what normativity consists in; that notion is fundamental and irreducible (Price, ch. 6). Attempts such as the theological voluntarists' derive whatever plausibility they may be thought to have from simply assuming a fundamental, irreducible moral fact in the background.[34]

The intuitionists' preferred analogy was to another area where truths can seem to hold necessarily and self-evidently: mathematics. In Clarke's version, facts about what a person should do concern which action would be most *fitting*, and he thought it no less evident that acts are related to situations as fit or unfit as 'that one *magnitude* or *number* is greater, equal to, or smaller than another'.[35] We can no more say what makes it the case that, say, gratitude is a fitting response to benevolence (one of Clarke's favourite examples) than we can further say why it is true that two plus three equals five. Both facts just are. We may here compare Clarke's view of our moral relationship to God with that of the Cambridge Platonists, Shaftesbury, and Leibniz, who held that perfect reason (God) has a practical bent (love or benevolence), and that this determines moral goodness. For Clarke, it is God's knowledge of the eternal truths of fitness and unfitness, which are entirely independent of Him, that determines His will, making it morally good (*Discourse*, Prop. XII).

What, then, did the rationalists consider to be the self-evident norms of conduct? Prominent among them was a principle of *reciprocity* or 'equity', as Clarke called it, which he and Balguy explicitly distinguished from benevolence or love. Even if we lack any concern for the good of others, Balguy wrote, we can see that it is reasonable to do unto them 'as we would be done unto' (12). Love, Clarke added, leads us 'to promote . . . the welfare and happiness of all men', while equity requires that we 'deal with every Man, as in like Circumstances we could reasonably expect he should deal with Us'.[36]

When we recall the problematic of modern natural law, we can see why equity or reciprocity might appear a more promising source of the normativity of moral norms than self-love or disinterested benevolence. Mutually advantageous norms sometimes require sacrifice. But what obligates an agent to make such sacrifices? If the norms are mutually advantageous, we might say that since the agent would want others to conform in similar situations, with roles reversed, it is reasonable for him to conform here. Such a rationale does not require that the agent should be able to care about others for their own sakes. It depends rather on an ideal of reciprocal or reasonable treatment that is independent of fellow-feeling, and so may be better suited to ground a conception of normative order among individuals (and groups) who cannot expect each other's love. Moreover, as a number of eighteenth-century writers came to recognise, collectively beneficial norms will sometimes require conduct that also conflicts with the general good, and so conflict with benevolence, in any case.

Now if norms of conduct are to bind agents' wills, it would seem they must be able to operate somehow *within* deliberative practical reasoning and actually govern agents' decisions. The rationalists honoured this idea, but it proved difficult to explain on their theory. Balguy, for example, used 'internal obligation' to refer to an intrinsically motivating '*State of the Mind into which it is brought by the Perception of a plain Reason for acting*'.[37] But, as Price was careful to make explicit, the intuitionists did not believe motivation has anything to do with what makes it true that an agent ought to act. Motivation is a consequence of *perceiving* the fact of obligation, not part of obligation itself (Balguy, 31; Price, 114).

But what then explains why, knowing 'that an action is fit to be done or that it ought to be done, it is not conceivable that we can remain *uninfluenced* or want a *motive* to action'? (Price, 186). For the rationalists, the faculty of normative knowledge (for Price, 'the understanding') is no different from that through which we know other facts without intrinsic motivational influence, those of mathematics, for example. If motivation then has, as Price insisted, nothing to do with normative facts themselves, what guarantees that anyone who is aware of them will necessarily be moved? Practical reason, for the intuitionists, is nothing but theoretical reason in contact with practically normative fact. In a famous passage of the *Treatise*, Hume challenged the rationalists to exhibit any relationship between the ideas of an action and circumstances, awareness of which 'wou'd be universally forcible and obligatory' 'on every rational mind' (3.1.1.23 and 22; SBN 466, 465). How this demand could be met continued to seem a mystery to all but convinced intuitionists.

V. MANDEVILLE AND THE 'ECONOMIC' CRITIQUE OF VIRTUE

An almost diametrically opposite criticism of the ethics of virtue was presented by Bernard Mandeville in *The Fable of the Bees*, first published in 1706 as a poem, 'The Grumbling Hive; or Knaves Turned Honest', and later supplemented with clarifying essays. Its subtitle, 'Private Vices, Publick Benefits', indicated Mandeville's main theme that the unintended effect of widespread individual vice, taken in the aggregate, is net public good. Correlatively, widespread virtue, in the aggregate, is publicly harmful. By virtue, Mandeville meant the attempt to surmount (natural) selfish impulses in order to benefit others, by vice, gratifying such impulses when to do so could, in the individual case, be socially disadvantageous.[38] The actual, if unintended, effect if everyone tries to help others at his own cost, Mandeville argued, is significant public harm.

The intrinsic moral goodness of benevolence had been fundamental for all moralists of virtue but Hume. Although Leibniz and Hutcheson held there to be a derivative sense in which the morally best choice is whichever actually has the best consequences, that was because they thought this is what a benevolent (hence, morally good) person aims at, not because it matters morally that these good consequences should actually be realised. But what if disinterested benevolence in the aggregate is not publicly useful? The virtue ethicists believed it was, so they were able to avoid the issue. Mandeville, however, provided a vivid picture of the contrary possibility, showing persuasively what might in some ways be the actual situation of eighteenth-century life.

A hive of vain, self-serving and, to some extent, dishonest creatures, 'endeavouring to supply each other's lust and vanity' ('The Grumbling Hive', I: 18), creates great wealth, the fruits of which all enjoy. When, however, they grumble about the wicked avarice dishonesty, and luxury in their midst, God makes them all honest. The results are catastrophic. With no desire for luxuries, avarice, or vanity, the engine of their productive activity is stilled, and they are left in poverty.

The importance of Mandeville's thesis of unintended perverse effects is obvious for modern economics from Adam Smith on, but it also had a powerful influence on eighteenth-century moral philosophy. Most apparent was its role in the development of utilitarianism after Hutcheson. Once it was seriously envisaged that the effects of widespread benevolence might diverge from those intended by the benevolent, the question of the relative importance for morality of motive and consequence became crucial. Increasingly, those attracted by utilitarian ideas rejected Hutcheson's position in favour of one, like Bentham's, that saw good consequences as basic requirements. Since *The Fable of the Bees* appeared two decades before Hutcheson's *Inquiry*, one may wonder why he did not assimilate such of Mandeville's ideas as became staples of the utilitarian tradition after him. Much as Hobbes in the seventeenth century, Mandeville was at first almost universally regarded as an atheistic moral sceptic, who delighted in making fun of moralists and should therefore be repudiated. Hutcheson characterises his *Inquiry* as a defence of Shaftesbury against 'the author of *The Fable of the Bees*'.

Mandeville's major and lasting contribution was to highlight how subtle and complex the relationships between intended and actual effects can be. For example, it underlies Butler, Berkeley, and Hume's insistence that rules strictly regulating the pursuit of an overall good can lead to a greater good than could be achieved by individuals each trying to promote the good themselves.[39] Mandeville's insistence on the malleability of moral sensibility and moral education also suggested to an emerging consequentialist tradition how these might be shaped in ways that are socially useful. This idea, in particular, was to prove central to Helvétius's thought. 'Moral Virtues', Mandeville famously proclaimed, are 'the Political Offspring which Flattery begot upon Pride' (*Fable*, 1: 51).

Finally, for this tradition, Mandeville showed how the relationships between socially useful practices, motivation, and consequences admit of significant complexity, putting in question any intrinsic connection between moral obligation and the will. He insisted he did not mean to advocate vice, even while saying that economic health is impossible without a good deal of it. That a level of vice is useful does not mean that it should not be criticised. The best consequences of all may come from some complex mix as when, say, a speed limit is publicly promulgated but a degree of speeding is tacitly tolerated though not publicly condoned. This may help to explain why the question of an intrinsic connection between moral obligation and rational motive, so important for other thinkers of the seventeenth and eighteenth centuries, is not significant for Bentham and his followers.

VI. THEOLOGICAL UTILITARIANISM

Yet another critical perspective on Shaftesbury and his successors (directed, at some points, against rational intuitionism as well) was provided by theological utilitarianism. This was a largely British phenomenon, which combined a utilitarian theory of norms with a theological voluntarist theory of normativity, and it included such thinkers as Berkeley, John Gay, and William Paley. Although some of their arguments recalled the seventeenth-century voluntarisms of Pufendorf and Locke, the theological utilitarians also departed from these in fascinating ways that pointed towards an ambition distinctive of the last half of the eighteenth century: the desire to formulate *public* norms to structure a liberal (and potentially democratic) society, underwritten by an account of their normativity. Ironically, the form of systematic moral philosophy that this ultimately inspired became thoroughly secular.

Berkeley's attack on Shaftesbury in *Alciphron* is especially interesting, for two reasons.[40] First, he argues that the adequacy of a moral conception can be judged only by looking to the consequences of its general promulgation, and that Shaftesbury's ethics fail this test. Secondly, he bases on this a *political* critique of virtue ethics. The former echoes Locke's objection to ancient virtue ethics that, without connection to authority and sanction, morality lacks adequate 'force'.[41] Individuals rationally seek to promote their own interest ('he's a fool that acts on any other Principle') and for most people the beauty of virtue is an utterly insufficient motive.[42] The widespread acceptance of Shaftesbury's and Leibniz's philosophy will thus have disastrous consequences. Morality's collective benefits can be secured only through *conscience*, which 'supposeth the being of a God' (*Alciphron*, I, §12; 3: 52) who constantly reminds us of the eternal personal benefits and costs of our own morality and immorality, respectively.

To this Lockean line, Berkeley added a political twist. Even were moral sense natural, only the wealthy few can be Shaftesburian virtuosi, cultivating a sense finely tuned to moral beauty. Therefore publicly to disseminate such a conception of virtue will, in the name of 'making men heroically virtuous', end up by destroying 'the means of making them reasonably and humanly so'. The consequences will be calamitous, especially for the poor and the vulnerable. An ethics of virtue such as Shaftesbury's recommends 'morals on the same foot with manners', as what is 'agreeable and polite'. At best, it confirms virtue only for an elite's 'conceited mind, which will ever be its own object, and contemplate mankind in its own mirror', and which cares little for the consequences to the lower classes of a general acceptance of its views (*Alciphron*, III, §13; 3: 132–3).

Class analysis runs through the whole of *Alciphron*. Shaftesbury is portrayed as 'of a rank above most men's ambition, and a fortune equal to his rank' (III, §13; 3: 132), and Berkeley suggests that his views are smugly class centred, out of touch with the great mass of humanity. He pits the 'ingenious men' and 'people of fashion' against 'the middle sort' and the poor, who pay the cost of public promulgation of the ethical and philosophical views of their economic betters (§3; 3: 69). Berkeley believed, for example, that the speculative South Sea Bubble, whose bursting was so disastrous for the middle class and the poor, was attributable in large measure to the prevalence of gentlemanly ethics.[43] Only a moral order that credibly promises reward and threatens punishment can protect the innocent and the weak, and that is possible, Berkeley believed, only on the assumption that these are divinely ordained and executed.

Towards the century's end, a similar line was taken by William Paley. Paley repeated the associationist arguments of Gay, David Hartley, and others against moral sense – namely, that intrinsically pleasant approvals and unpleasant disapprovals can be explained as arising by psychological association with their respectively pleasurable and painful effects, and, therefore, that no hypothesis of a moral sense is required.[44] But he also argued that even were such a sense to be admitted it would remain to establish its 'authority' and power to obligate. Although the disapproval of moral sense is painful, this may not provide adequate rational motive, since if a sinner 'finds the pleasure of the sin exceed the remorse of conscience . . . the moral-instinct-man, so far as I can understand, has nothing more to offer' (12).

Like Berkeley, Paley lampooned the intuitively held 'Law of Honour' of 'people of fashion', which is 'calculated to facilitate their intercourse with one another; and for no other purpose'. Through such class-centred ideals, 'cruelty to servants, rigorous treatment of tenants or other dependants, want of charity to the poor; [and] injuries done to tradesmen by insolvency or delay of payment', are rationalised, since these render a gentlemen 'not a less agreeable companion' (*Principles*, 1–2). The only antidote to such oppression, Paley believed, is a universal public code of conduct by which all are bound by motives adequate to determine the will. The only things sufficiently strong to guarantee such motives are eternal rewards and punishments deriving from God's will.

The idea that inescapable, eternal sanctions are a necessary condition for the very possibility of mutually advantageous moral order had already been present in Locke. And, in truth, Locke had also described a 'law of opinion or reputation' consisting in the intuitive 'approbation or dislike, praise or blame, which by a secret and tacit consent establishes it self in the several Societies, Tribes, and Clubs of Men in the World', and by which 'Vertue and Vice are Names pretended . . . every where to stand for actions in their own nature right and wrong'.[45] But Berkeley and Paley made clearer the ways in which economic interest and social status can stand behind the invocation of a moral sense (or, for that matter, a claim to an intuition of reason). Moral philosophy must be conceived, in Paley's words, as a '*science which teaches men their duty and the reasons of it*' (*Principles*, 1). It should seek by empirical, and so universally available, methods to uncover a law of conduct going beyond human laws and to show the reasons of this law by connecting it to God's will and eternal sanction. In the process, it will ground the law of duty in propositions that (a) can be confirmed uncontroversially without any esoteric faculty appropriated by 'men of fashion' to oppress their inferiors and (b) thereby give all agents sufficient reason/cause to follow the law independently of these mischievous 'prejudices'.

The goal of a *scientific ethics*, so important to secular forms of utilitarianism, thus sprang not just from the empirical naturalist desire to locate morality as part of nature. It derived also from the idea that because only empirical methods are both universally available and uncontroversial, they provide the unique basis for unprejudicial public justification.

What made Berkeley, Gay, and Paley theological *utilitarians* was the connection they drew between God's sanctions and His benevolence. Berkeley was the most interesting here. Obligation, he argued, is based on the solely rational human end, and this is self-happiness.[46] It is empirically evident that the universe is the work of an omniscient and omnibenevolent God 'who alone can make us for ever happy, or for ever miserable'. So conformity to His will must be the 'sole rule whereby every man who acts up to the principles of reason must govern and square his actions' (§6; 6: 20). Because God is omnibenevolent, *His* governing end is the greatest well-being of all. There are, then, two possibilities. One is that we are enjoined 'upon each particular occasion to consult the public good'. The second is that we should follow 'some determinate, established laws, which, if universally practised, have, from the nature of things, an essential fitness to procure the well-being of mankind; though in their particular application they are sometimes . . . the occasions of great sufferings and misfortunes . . . to very many good men' (*Passive Obedience*, §8; 6: 21).

With this contrast Berkeley crisply formulated, perhaps for the first time in the history of ethical thought, the distinction between act-utilitarianism and rule-utilitarianism. Moreover, he came down squarely on the rule-utilitarian side. Individuals attempting unaided to promote the general welfare will produce a disastrous lack of co-ordination, owing to ignorance of 'all the hidden circumstances and consequences of an action' (*Passive Obedience*, §9; 6: 21). It is evident, therefore, that God wills us to follow maximally beneficial rules, even on those occasions when to do so will have less than maximally beneficial consequences.

VII. SECULAR (PUBLIC) UTILITARIANISM: HELVÉTIUS, D'HOLBACH, AND BENTHAM

While it was evidently possible in Britain to advance a conception of moral philosophy as an empirically based public critique within a fundamentally religious or theological framework, this was hardly a live option in France. There writers such as the Baron d'Holbach and Claude Helvétius put it forward as a secular antidote to the theological ethics of established clerical power.[47] D'Holbach's *Système de la nature* (1770) contrasted theological ethics, which he characterised as a 'superstitious' morality promulgated by the establishment to confirm its own power, which actually causes widespread ignorance and vice, with a 'natural morality', grounded in empirical knowledge of the objective conditions of life, that is the liberating instrument of human happiness.[48] In his *Morale universelle*, he defined morality as the 'science of the relations among men and of the duties that flow from these relations', or, alternatively as 'the knowledge of what must necessarily be done or avoided by intelligent and reasonable beings who wish to preserve themselves and to live happily in society'.[49]

Earlier, Claude Helvétius had defended a broadly similar outlook in *De l'esprit* which, while less direct in its criticisms of the church, was more philosophically sophisticated in its defence of secular utilitarian morality. A moral system, he argued, should be experimental, founded on empirical study of the human condition, rather than speculative or theological. The key to understanding morality, as well as to making people moral, is nothing supernatural or metaphysical, but only interest. The moral universe is no less subject to the 'laws' of interest than the physical universe is 'subject to the laws of motion'.[50] Religious moralists, especially, make the mistake of supposing that people are good or evil, either inherently or as a matter of acquired character. Like Mandeville, Helvétius held that it is simply self-interest that drives both human behaviour and moral evaluation. People act well seen from the standpoint of others only when they have the appropriate incentives. There are no evil people, only conditions that breed antisocial behaviour. To change people for the good, moralists must substitute 'the soft language of interest' for 'the peremptory clamour of invective'.[51]

To advance human happiness, morality must be demystified and those who promulgate superstition unmasked as 'protectors of ignorance' and 'the most cruel enemies of human beings' (*De l'esprit*, II.xxiv; trans., 425). In fact, Helvétius argued, everyone 'calls Probity in another only the habitude of actions which are useful to him' (II.ii; trans., 416). It follows that to have a common, public moral discourse individuals must somehow unify the perspectives from which they make their respective judgements. This is possible, Helvétius believes, only if individuals are knit together politically into a genuine public with which they *identify* – publicly affirming common interests, including an interest in how they are regarded, and how they regard themselves, from this perspective. Thus, even though it is self-interest that ultimately drives attributions of virtue, under such conditions *public welfare* becomes 'the object of virtue' and all 'form the same idea of it' (II.xiii; trans., 421).

The same combination of empirical naturalism and desire for a public moral philosophy without illusions stood also behind the first genuinely systematic work of secular utilitarianism, Bentham's *An Introduction to the Principles of Morals and Legislation*. Any moral theory deserving 'the name of Science' must begin with definitions, Bentham asserted.[52] Because ordinary moral and legal thinking are especially rife with 'fictitious entities', a kind of definition is required here that makes clear what natural and perceptible features ('real entities') give real, verifiable content to its concepts and propositions.

'Obligation' was a prime example for Bentham. Echoing Cumberland's complaint that standard definitions are 'obscure from metaphors' (and Hutcheson's reference to 'ought' as an 'unlucky word in morals'), Bentham remarks that while we fictitiously *imagine* obligation to be a kind of constraint – like 'a heavy body pressing upon' a person, preventing action in any manner other than 'the direction or manner in question' – this 'fictitious entity' has a 'real source' in a 'real entity', namely, the sensation of *pain* or loss of pleasure. If 'obligation' is to have literal meaning, therefore, it should be defined as follows: 'an obligation . . . is incumbent on a man (*i.e.*, is spoken of as incumbent on a man) in so far as, in the event of his failing to conduct himself in that manner, pain, or loss of pleasure is considered as about to be experienced by him'.[53]

This definition is so easily satisfied that it is hard to avoid the impression that obligation as a constraint on *individual* practical reasoning had become far less important for Bentham than it had been for most seventeenth- and eighteenth-century thinkers. In fact, Bentham was less concerned with this than with understanding morality as a social and *public* form of discourse.

The signal merit of the principle of utility, Bentham argues at the beginning of the *Principles*, is that it provides an 'extrinsic ground' or 'external standard' for approving of conduct in the confirmable fact that an act will promote the happiness of affected parties. His point is that because the consequences of an action for people's happiness are open to empirical investigation, they can be agreed on by people who hold sharply conflicting moral views. The problem with both the doctrine of moral sense and rational intuitionism is that in claiming self-evidence for their fundamental moral positions, they reject the demand to provide an external ground, and so prevail 'upon the reader to accept of the author's sentiment or opinion as a reason . . . for itself' (25–6). They engage in what Bentham later called '*ipse-dixitism*': 'it is so, because I say it's so'. 'The mischief common to all these ways of thinking and arguing . . . ', Bentham writes, 'is their serving as a cloak, and pretence, and aliment, to despotism' (28). Why despotism? Public moral discourse aims to direct collective power, and to attempt to do so without appealing to 'extrinsic grounds' is to require others to acquiesce without giving them any reason they can be expected to accept without already agreeing with controverted moral opinion in the first place.

Now it may seem puzzling to say that Bentham argues for the principle of utility on what are essentially liberal grounds, but consider what he says. He allows that 'our notions of right and wrong' may actually derive from sources other than a view of utility and he even admits that moral sentiments might 'be actually persisted in and justified' on other grounds 'by a person reflecting within himself'. But whether these are so, he says, are relatively unimportant 'questions of speculation'. There is, however, another question, the answer to which 'is of as much importance as that of any can be', and that is, 'whether *in point of right* it [a moral opinion] can properly be justified on any other ground, by a person *addressing himself to the community*' (28, emphases added).

The principle of utility is uniquely suitable as a basis for noncoercive public moral debate because it is empirically confirmable, and thus morally uncontroversial, and because it concerns 'the two sovereign masters' of human motivation, pleasure and pain (*Principles*, 11). If someone will propose some principle other than utility, Bentham says, 'let him say whether there is any such thing as a *motive* that a man can have to pursue the dictates of it' (16). Moral debate can be both public and non-coercive only if all parties attempt to justify their moral positions to others by considerations with which anyone can reasonably be expected to agree and in which all will take an interest. The principle of utility, Bentham concluded, is the only principle that satisfies these two conditions. In view of Bentham's famous remark that the idea of natural rights is 'nonsense on stilts', it may reasonably be wondered how he thought liberal constraints on public moral discourse might themselves be justified. We should note, however, that he apparently thought this question did not itself arise in practical public moral discourse.

VIII. PUBLIC MORAL DISCOURSE AND MORAL THEORY

Bentham's ambition was a common one in the latter half of the eighteenth century. Increasingly, philosophers sought a conception of normative order that could be justified publicly to individuals, independently of their conflicting attachments to family, community, sect, or class. For the secular utilitarians, the basis for the principle of utility was no assumption of universal benevolence or love, but rather their contention that that principle is uniquely suited for a public morality that can structure reasonable co-operation between equals with conflicting ideals and attachments.

The project of articulating *principles* of conduct – in the sense of norms or standards that can be formulated in a public language – is likely to be part and parcel of any public discourse about how individuals or groups should act, when they cannot expect each other to share the same intuitive judgements (whether these be thought of as sentiments or rational cognitions) and when they accept the burden of justifying their views in terms that others can be expected to accept as moral equals. It is no accident, therefore, that as the 'century of revolution' advanced, and liberal and egalitarian values came to be represented in an underlying conception of public normative order, moral philosophers came increasingly to participate in a public practice of articulating principles of conduct and comprehending them together as a systematic whole. To this period we owe the ideal of (publicly articulable) systematic normative moral theory that has come to be such an important part of moral philosophical practice ever since.[54] It is what lies behind Paley's idea of a 'science which teaches men their duty and the reasons of it', and, many years later, Mill's complaint that in over two thousand years so 'little progress' had been made in formulating 'the criterion of right and wrong'.[55]

The formulation of utilitarian moral theory, in both its act-utilitarian (Bentham) and rule-utilitarian (Berkeley) versions, dates from the eighteenth century. So also do some of the most familiar lines of objection to utilitarianism. Butler argued, for example, that moral common sense includes principles prohibiting lying, assault, and injustice, quite independently of their consequences in the individual case (*Dissertation of Virtue*, 8). Hume's theory of justice, that it is mutually advantageous that individuals regulate themselves by specific, publicly articulable rules of property and promise, even when these require private or public sacrifice, showed that this was not merely common sense. And the rational intuitionists, such as Price and Reid, argued that, in addition to a principle of beneficence, an adequate account of moral duty must also include principles of gratitude, veracity, prudence, and justice, among others.

IX. ROUSSEAU, KANT, AND THE ETHICS OF FREEDOM

Important as these developments were, they left the problem of obligation pretty much where it had been. Even if individuals can be brought to accept a common conception of public morality together with its justification, there is still the question of why (or whether) each should actually follow it. What, if anything, makes such norms obligatory for individual agents? In what does their normativity consist?

We should do well at this point to recall briefly the early modern responses to the problem of obligation we have canvassed thus far. We may distinguish between those in which the idea of law or norm is fundamental and those in which the good is basic. Clearly on the law side are theological voluntarism and rational intuitionism. On the other, we can place the various eighteenth-century ethics of virtue, all of which agreed on the proposition that the virtuous life is obligatory for moral agents at least partly because it is good for them. Theological and secular utilitarians fall on different sides of the line for different purposes. Both stressed the importance of the idea of law (whether divine or secular) in capturing a notion of obligation that is internal to morality. But both held also that the reason why agents really (and not just morally) ought to follow morality is that incentives mean that this is for their good.

The legal approaches, both voluntarist and intuitionist, share an outstanding problem: they do not so much explain normativity as assert it. To be sure, both Pufendorf and Locke aimed to explain the normativity of *morality* (natural law) in particular – but they did this by relying on a normative fact as background: that we ought to obey the commands of any being related to us in the way God is. Nor did they offer any explanation of what might make this normative fact true. The same is true for the basic norms the rational intuitionists claimed to be self-evident to reason.

The good-based approaches face problems of their own. Unlike those of voluntarists and intuitionists, they do offer a philosophical theory of obligation, namely, as an inescapably conclusive motive for an agent 'deliberating upon a thing future', in Cumberland's phrase. Their problem, however, is how such a theory can provide a convincing account of *moral* obligation. If the only 'obligation to virtue' is, as Shaftesbury held, the motive of self-interest, then it may be objected that this fails to support morality in its own terms – the motive to virtue is not itself virtuous. Faced with this prospect, Hutcheson and Hume identified moral obligation, not with a motive, but with the approving or disapproving sentiments of a disinterested spectator. This, however, cannot explain how moral obligation binds the will. What is more, the rejoinder to that problem most congenial to Hutcheson – that universal benevolence is simultaneously the distinctively moral, *and* a conclusive rational, motive – faces two significant problems of its own. First, it is doubtful that even fully informed benevolence and self-love coincide, as Hutcheson and Leibniz assumed. Secondly, there is the problem that inspired Hume's theory of justice, namely, that in the circumstances of normal human life, the public interest is served by agents regulating their conduct, not by desires for the good (private *or* public), but by their acceptance of specific norms that structure mutually advantageous practices, such as property and promise.

As we noted earlier, an important feature of Hume's theory of justice was its reliance on the idea of agents governing themselves by norms.[56] This notion also played a central role in the rational intuitionists' general theories of agency and the will. The intuitionists thought, however, that nothing could be said about what earns something the status of a norm, and hence, about normative force. If something has it, that is simply self-evident.

There is, however, another dialectical possibility. If guidance by norms is essential to agency, then maybe the validity of norms – normativity itself – can somehow be explained by this very fact. This was the possibility seized upon, first in broad outline, by Rousseau, and then, in systematic detail, by Kant. It amounted to a synthesis of the two approaches we have distinguished. Like the good-based approaches, it sought an explanation of the normative in an understanding of the practical reasoning of deliberating agents. But unlike these, and like the rational intuitionists, it brought the *idea* of the normative into that very understanding. An autonomous agent must act on a 'conception of law', in Kant's phrase. What it is for him actually to be obligated by laws, then, is, very roughly, for it to be the case that he would prescribe them to himself in autonomous practical reasoning.

Of course, the utilitarians had also combined the two approaches, using law for *moral* obligation, and a good-based approach for genuine normativity. But this had the consequence that morality is no more than extrinsically normative, contingent on the appropriate sanctions. Kant's project, however, was to establish morality's intrinsic normativity, to exhibit its norms as categorical imperatives. A genuine synthesis was needed.

1. *Rousseau*

Rousseau's contribution was to propose a connection between autonomous agency and regulation by self-prescribed law, and to maintain that the latter requires the capacity to govern oneself by universal laws one can prescribe for all from a standpoint one can occupy in common with others – for Rousseau, the common standpoint of a social collective.

Rousseau's primary focus, of course, was the philosophy of politics rather than morals. But the way he framed the problem of political association had important implications for fundamental moral philosophy: 'To find a form of association . . . by means of which each, uniting with all, nevertheless obey only himself and remain as free as before.' 'This', Rousseau wrote, 'is the fundamental problem to which the social contract provides the solution'.[57] To think of the problem of political obligation in this way encourages the thought that moral obligation may be approached similarly.

Like the rationalists, Rousseau distinguished autonomous agency ('moral liberty') from other forms of intelligent activity. In the state of nature, individuals can act intelligently to satisfy their appetites, but this is not yet autonomy. To be his own master, a person must escape the slavery of appetite and obey a law he gives himself (*Social Contract*, 53–4). Rousseau believed this to be possible only in the civil state, because it requires direction by universal prescriptions that a person issues from a standpoint she shares in common with others, effectively instituting the state through the social contract.

There are two contrasts between individual and general at play in Rousseau's thought, one concerning the *subject* of autonomous will and the other, its *object*. The former is Rousseau's distinction between 'private will' and 'general will', depending on whether a person prescribes from her own 'private' perspective or, as part of a 'we', from a standpoint she shares in common with others. In the social contract, '*each of us puts his person and his full power in common under the supreme direction of the general will*' (50). The second is a distinction between prescribing for a particular person and prescribing universally, for all persons, and hence, for oneself as one person among others.

Rousseau's position was that autonomy involves obeying a prescription that is general in both senses. Its point of origin is the first-person-plural perspective of the general will, and its object is also general, because it prescribes law, and 'law considers the subjects . . . and their actions in the abstract, never any man as an individual or a particular action'. It is the universal character of law, indeed, that leads to the thought that governance by self-prescribed law involves regulation by general will, since general will is uniquely directed to the universal (*Social Contract*, 67).

Like the rationalists', Rousseau's picture of self-determining agency crucially included regulation by universal norms. The difference is that the rationalists held that the validity of norms does not itself depend on agency in any way. Normative facts are metaphysically independent and given self-evidently to reason, which can then govern action by them. This leaves it mysterious both what such an independent metaphysical order might consist in, and how it could bind the will. The central Rousseauan move was to hold that laws could bind (in the political realm, anyway) only if they expressed the general will, that is, the will of everyone they bound as such. This amounted to a Copernican revolution in political philosophy. The normative order of civil society cannot be given by an external authority; it must be self-legislated.

2. *Kant*

Such a political philosophy is, however, compatible with different views about normativity's ultimate source. Rousseau held that persons are independent, no one having authority over any other. Consequently a person is obligated by the laws of civil society if, and only if, he can consent to them as a matter of (his own) general will. But what is the source of this normative truth? One might hold, with the rationalists, that it has no further source; it is simply a fact given self-evidently to reason. Such a position would be the analogue of theological voluntarism about morality with the general will playing the role of God's command. And it would leave the rationalists' two mysteries unanswered: What can such a normative fact *be*? And how can it bind the will?

A different possibility would be to project Rousseau's political philosophical Copernican revolution into fundamental moral philosophy, to hold that normativity must itself ultimately be rooted in self-determining practical reason – that binding norms are, so to say, self-legislated 'all the way down'. This was the central thesis of Kant's critical ethics: the moral law is a 'law of freedom'.

Philosophical orthodoxy in Germany when Kant began to think these issues through was the Leibniz/Wolff view, according to which will invariably aims at the good (perfection) and obligation consists in such necessarily operative motives. Against this view, Christian August Crusius had objected in his *Anweisung vernünftig zu leben* (1744) that such a picture was inconsistent with genuine freedom and that moral obligation must involve determination by norms or laws.[58] Crusius agreed with the British rationalists that morality is a law *for* free agents. Only agents who can determine themselves by norms can be moral subjects.

He also agreed with them that such norms or laws are independent of agents and given to them, not, as the rationalists believed, self-evidently, but by God's command.

Kant was influenced by Crusius in his early thinking, but he came to believe that no demand could have its source outside the moral agent and be genuinely obligating. That would be heteronomy, not autonomy. Morality, Kant concluded, must consist of laws *of* freedom: norms an agent prescribes for herself in her own free deliberative activity. Such 'positive freedom', he maintained, can be realised only by following morality's fundamental principle, the categorical imperative: act only on principles on which you can will that everyone act. The normativity of moral obligation, Kant concluded, consists in self-imposition in the free practical reasoning of a moral agent.

Kant tried to lead his readers to these ideas by inviting them to take seriously various aspects of their own moral thought and experience. When we do so, he claimed, we shall see the centrality to our moral convictions of the ideas of universal law and freedom. Reflection on the 'common Idea of duty' reveals, he argued, that we are committed to thinking that moral obligation depends on universal laws grounded 'a priori simply in concepts of pure reason'.[59] Suppose we believe, for example, that it is morally obligatory not to lie for our own advantage, other things being equal. If we push on this idea, Kant thought we will find that we do not think this obligation falls on us because we happen to be members of any local community, or because a prescription against lying is part of the general will of an established civic association to which we belong, or even because we are members of *Homo sapiens*. Rather, Kant held, we will find we think that the moral obligation not to lie for advantage would fall equally on *any* rational moral agents who, perhaps, are among others with the same vulnerabilities to deception that make it wrong, other things equal, for us to lie for gain.[60]

Ordinary moral thought is committed to moral obligations being 'categorical imperatives', in Kant's famous phrase. This includes at least three different ideas. First, moral oughts derive from universal laws binding all rational agents. Secondly, unlike hypothetical imperatives, which tell an agent what she must do to accomplish an adopted end, the bindingness of a categorical imperative is independent of any optional end. Thirdly, categorical imperatives are laws of practical reason. So moral obligation is not *merely* internal to morality (in the way requiredness is trivially intrinsic to any rule). To violate a moral ought is to violate practical reason.

It is one thing to prove that ordinary moral thought is staked on the thesis that moral oughts are categorical imperatives, and another to vindicate that thesis. Kant's vindication had two major prongs. The first was analytical, continuing his examination of implications internal to moral thought. Here Kant argued that the source of moral norms is in the universal *form* of the moral agent's practical reasoning and will. The fundamental principle of morality is the categorical imperative. This made explicit the claim to be vindicated: a requirement to act only on principles on which one can will all to act is binding on all rational agents.

Unlike the first, Kant's second prong did not take morality as a given. It sought an understanding, rather, of free agency, argued that this is possible only if the will can be a 'law to itself' and then that that requires determination by the categorical imperative. It follows, Kant concluded, that treating the fundamental principle of morality as binding is a necessary condition of the possibility of autonomous practical reason. Moral obligation is self-imposed in autonomous deliberation, and this vindicates the conviction, to which we are committed by the deepest strands of our moral thinking, that the moral ought is necessary a priori.

Kant began the first prong by arguing that morality is committed to the existence of a distinctive value that can be realised only in moral agency and actions. This is noteworthy in itself. Ultimately, Kant wanted to derive from these claims about moral character and agency a fundamental principle of conduct that would then be able to ground specific moral duties. His ethics is frequently described as an ethics of duty, but although the idea of duty undoubtedly plays a central role in his thought, his approach is actually closer in spirit to the virtue ethics of Hutcheson and Shaftesbury than to the duty ethics of either the modern natural lawyers or the rationalists. For Kant, moral obligations are not given to moral agents, either self-evidently to our reason or by the commands of a superior. On the contrary, his starting place is the distinctive and, he says, unqualified, goodness of the morally good will and the distinctive worth of actions that express it. As with Shaftesbury and Hutcheson, the right emerges from the morally good.

Moral common sense, Kant believed, is deeply committed to the thesis that good will has a value that is both intrinsic and unqualified. Kant agreed with the modern natural lawyers and the rationalists that morality is a regime of law according to which moral agents are responsible for determining their conduct. But he also agreed with another deep strain in both natural law and rationalist thought that obligation requires a free agent 'capable of a Law'.[61] And this, he thought, puts the primary emphasis not on 'external acts', but on the determination of the will. The evaluation that is distinctive of morality is of agents' wills – of their exercise of a responsibility to determine themselves by the moral law – not of their talents, temperament, or 'gifts of fortune'. Even such virtues as moderation, self-control, and 'calm reflexion' are only conditionally valuable, considered morally, since, Kant argues, 'without the basic principles of a good will they can become extremely evil'. Only good will – not 'mere wish', but 'the summoning of all means insofar as they are in our control' to govern ourselves by the moral law – is unqualifiedly good (*Grundlegung*, Ak 4: 394).

Action that expresses good will manifests this distinctive moral value. In Kant's terms, it has *moral worth*. Moral worth is thus a quality, not of an 'external act', but of action *as willed* and actions have moral worth precisely as the agent is determined, in so acting, by the moral law. Unless an agent's action is governed by the moral law, conforming to the law will be accidental from her deliberative standpoint.

The virtue ethicists would have agreed that actions have moral value only as they express virtuous character. But most would have objected that virtue is love, not dutifulness. Kant, however, argues that this possibility is inconsistent with morality as an expression of free agency. Any affection such as love, no matter how universal in the human species, cannot be assumed to be intrinsic to rational agency as such. How, then, can morality universally bind free rational agents if the moral motive is one they might lack? Actions can express the distinctive value of morality only if they are determined in a way for which all rational agents can be held responsible.

But if actions have moral worth only if they are determined by the moral law, how does a morally good will discover what the moral law is? Kant begins an utterly remarkable paragraph in the *Grundlegung* with this very question: 'But what kind of law can that be, the representation of which must determine the will, even without regard for the effect expected from it, in order for the will to be called good absolutely and without limitation?' 'Nothing is left', he argues, 'but the conformity of actions as such with universal law, *which alone is to serve the will as its principle*'. He then concludes with the *Grundlegung*'s first formulation of the categorical imperative, remarking: 'Here mere conformity to law as such, without having as its basis some law determined for certain actions, is what serves the will as its principle, and must so serve it, if duty is not to be everywhere an empty delusion and a chimerical concept' (Ak 4: 402, emphasis added).

Having ruled out the possibilities that either a desire for some substantive end or an externally given moral law 'determined for certain actions' might ultimately ground the determination of a morally good will, Kant believed no further possibility remained than that the good will guides itself by the formal idea of conformity to universal law itself. This requires, he thought, that it be governed by the categorical imperative, that it not act on any principle it cannot will *as* universal law, willing its own acting on that principle as a consequence of willing that all do.

This may sustain conviction *within morality* that duty is not a 'chimerical concept', but so far its only force is internal to assumptions of the moral sphere. Nothing yet said rules out the possibility that, although it is essential to our moral thinking that moral imperatives purport to be categorical and genuinely binding on all rational agents, they are not so in fact. Eliminating this possibility was the task of the second prong of Kant's vindicating argument, which aimed to exhibit a deep connection between the categorical imperative and freedom.

For Kant, as for the rationalists, genuine action is always freely undertaken for some reason of the agent. While all natural occurrences can be explained in terms of reasons ('Everything in nature works in accordance with laws' (*Grundlegung*, Ak 4: 412), actions, uniquely, are explained by citing *the agent's reasons*. An agent's reasons for action are considerations that, in her own view, were (normative or justifying) reasons for her so to have acted (and *on which* she acted). In acting for a reason, therefore, agents commit themselves to normative propositions. And because one can hardly believe that one has reason to do something as an individual without seeing one's situation in terms that would give a similar reason to any relevantly similar agent, Kant believed that action involves commitment to universal normative principles, to a conception of universal practical law. 'Only a rational being has the capacity to act *in accordance with the representation* of laws, that is, in accordance with principles, or has a *will*' (4: 412).

But just as we cannot act except under a conception of the normative, so also action is possible only under the idea of freedom (4: 448). Desires, emotions, passions, and other motivational sources give rise to an action only when an agent freely incorporates them into a principle on which she acts, since for a deliberating agent, the question remains open what to do given their existence.[62] An agent may of course decide that, given her desire, she should act to satisfy it. But, strictly speaking, what she acts on, Kant believed, is not the bare desire, but the normative principle that incorporates it, which she freely adopts.

If action requires the agent's commitment to universal practical law, how is an agent to determine what universal law is? This problem is structurally identical to the one we considered earlier involving the good will and the moral law. There Kant argued that the freedom of the moral agent and the necessity of the moral law together entail that only universal legislative form can serve the will as governing principle, and thus, that moral agents are ultimately bound by the categorical imperative – the requirement that they not act on any principle on which they cannot will that they all act. Kant confronts the problem in its present, not explicitly moral form in *Kritik der praktischen Vernunft*: 'Supposing that a will is *free*: to find the law that alone is competent to determine it necessarily.' And he draws the same conclusion: '. . . lawgiving form, insofar as this is contained in the maxim, is therefore the only thing that can constitute a determining ground of the will.' Again, from this he draws the categorical imperative as a consequence.[63] Agents' commitment to the categorical imperative is a necessary condition for the very possibility of free action.

If this line of thought can succeed, then Kant may have a fair claim to have solved the problem of moral obligation as it had been posed in the modern period. The distinctively modern conception of morality, I have said, is that of a set of mutually advantageous norms, and the modern problem of moral obligation has been, Why should a person follow these, especially when it will be personally disadvantageous for him to do so? If, however, the fundamental law of practical reason is the categorical imperative, and if no one would prescribe that some violate mutually advantageous norms which others are following when their own conformance requires sacrifice, then no one can regard his own advantageous violation as rationally justified. Morality derives its normative force from laws an agent prescribes in autonomous practical reasoning.

It can reasonably be argued that this solution was available only to someone who could view the range of seventeenth- and eighteenth-century attempts to account for morality's normativity. Kant's problematic and conceptual frameworks were set by the modern natural law tradition, but his theory of action and views about the centrality of normative conviction to rational conduct followed Crusius and the rationalists. When, however, it came to the relationship between conduct and character, Kant parted company with both natural lawyers and rationalists, and embraced the virtue ethicist's premise that norms of conduct derive from an ideal of character. Finally, although modern thought had been working towards the idea of autonomous agency, it was Kant's genius to see how the Rousseauan idea of self-prescribed law could be made the foundation of an account of the normative as 'laws of freedom', and thus vindicate the categorical bindingness on which he believed morality to be staked.

NOTES

1 See *Oxford English Dictionary of English Etymology* (Oxford, 1966), 620. Also *Oxford English Dictionary*.

2 Thomas Aquinas, *Summa theologiae*, Blackfriars edn., 61 vols. (New York, NY and London, 1964–81), 28: Pt I.ii.93.1.

3 Aquinas, *Summa contra gentiles*, III.xvi.

4 See, for instance, *De regimine principum ad regem Cypri* (1265–6), I.i.

5 For a more extended discussion of the seventeenth-century natural law tradition, see Knud Haakonssen, 'Divine/Natural Law Theories in Ethics', in *The Cambridge History of Seventeenth-Century Philosophy*, eds. D. Garber and M. Ayers, 2 vols. (Cambridge, 1998), 2: 1317–57.

6 Hugo Grotius, *De iure belli ac pacis* (*On the Law of War and Peace*), facsim. of 1646 edn. with translation by F. W. Kelsey, 2 vols. (Oxford, 1925), Prolegomena §5, 2: 10–11. For

a discussion of Grotius as responding to the sceptical challenges posed by Montaigne and Charron, see Richard Tuck, 'Grotius, Carneades, and Hobbes', *Grotiana*, 4 (1983): 43–62, and 'The "Modern" Theory of Natural Law', in *The Languages of Political Theory in Early-Modern Europe*, ed. A. Pagden (Cambridge, 1987), 99–119. Tuck argues that Grotius's response foreshadows Hobbes. For a different view see Robert Shaver, 'Grotius on Scepticism and Self-Interest', *Archiv für Geschichte der Philosophie*, 78 (1996): 27–47.

7 Mancur Olson, *The Logic of Collective Action: Public Goods and the Theory of Groups* (Cambridge, MA, 1971).

8 Samuel Pufendorf, *De jure naturae et gentium libri octo*, facsim. repr. of 1688 edn., trans. and eds. C. H. Oldfather and W. A. Oldfather, 2 vols. (Oxford, 1934), I.i.2–23.

9 Ralph Cudworth, *A Treatise concerning Eternal and Immutable Morality* (London, 1731), I.ii; Gottfried Wilhelm Leibniz, *Opinion on the Principles of Pufendorf* (1706) in *Political Writings*, trans. and ed. P. Riley, 2nd edn. (Cambridge, 1988), 64–75 at 70–75.

10 Leibniz, *Opinion on Pufendorf*, 68; see David Hume, *A Treatise of Human Nature* (1739–40), eds. D. F. Norton and M. J. Norton, in the *Clarendon Edition* (2006), 2.3.1–2, SBN 399–412; [Anthony Ashley Cooper, 3rd Earl of Shaftesbury] Preface to Benjamin Whichcote, *Select Sermons* (London, 1698).

11 Shaftesbury, 'An Inquiry concerning Virtue or Merit' (hereafter 'Inquiry'), II.i. Originally published in an unauthorised edn. in 1699; a revised version was included as Treatise IV in his *Characteristicks of Men, Manners, Opinions, Times, etc.* (London, 1711). See the edn. by J. M. Robertson, 2 vols. (London, 1900), 1: 235ff.

12 Francisco Suárez, *De legibus ac Deo legislatore* (1612), in *Selections from Three Works*, trans. G. L. Williams, A. Brown, and J. Waldron, 2 vols. (Oxford, 1944), I.i.1.

13 Thomas Hobbes, *Leviathan*, ed. R. Tuck (Cambridge, 1991), 1.xv, 111.

14 Richard Cumberland, *De legibus naturae disquisitio philosophica* (1672); translated as *A Treatise of the Laws of Nature*, trans. J. Maxwell (London, 1727), ch. 5, §27 at 232–3. Actually Cumberland has two strains of argument, corresponding to the two aspects of his claim that only thoughts of good to self *or* others can bind an agent. I discuss these in *The British Moralists and the Internal 'Ought': 1640–1740* (Cambridge, 1995), ch. 4.

15 [John Gay] *A Dissertation concerning the Fundamental Principle of Virtue or Morality*, prefixed to William King, *An Essay on the Origin of Evil*, trans. E. Law (London, 1731), Sect. II.

16 Shaftesbury, Preface to Whichcote, *Select Sermons*.

17 See 'Soliloquy, or Advice to an Author', Treatise III in the *Characteristicks*, and the Stoic-inspired notebooks, in part in *The Life, Unpublished Letters, and Philosophical Regimen of Anthony, Earl of Shaftesbury*, ed. B. Rand (London, 1900).

18 I discuss autonomist internalism of the thought of the seventeenth- and eighteenth-century British moralists, including Cudworth, Shaftesbury, and Butler, in *British Moralists*.

19 Sidgwick treats Shaftesbury as the first moralist to make the empirical study of mental phenomena the basis of ethics: Henry Sidgwick, *Outlines of the History of Ethics for English Readers* (London, 1886), 184–91.

20 See note 9 above.

21 Leibniz, *Textes inédits d'après les manuscrits de la Bibliothèque provinciale de Hanovre*, ed. G. Grua, 2 vols. (Paris, 1948), 607, 706, as quoted in John Hostler, *Leibniz's Moral Philosophy* (London, 1975), 68, 66. The second passage, from *Codex juris gentium* (1693), Praefatio, is included in Leibniz, *Political Writings*, 165–76 at 171.

22 Leibniz, *Felicity* (ca. 1694–8?) in *Political Writings*, 83.

23 'Observationes de principio juris', in *Monathlicher Auszug Aus allerhand neu-heraus-gegebenen nützlichen und artigen Büchern*, 1700, 371ff. at 378; quoted in Joachim Hruschka, 'The Greatest Happiness Principle and Other Early German Anticipations of Utilitarian Theory', *Utilitas*, 3, (1991): 165–77 at 166, 172.

24 *Rechtsphilosophisches aus Leibnizens ungedruckten Schriften*, ed. G. Mollat (Leipzig, 1885); trans. Hostler in *Leibniz's Moral Philosophy*, 59.
25 Leibniz, *Phil. Schriften*, 2: 125, quoted in Hostler, *Leibniz's Moral Philosophy*, 16–17.
26 Francis Hutcheson, *An Inquiry into the Original of our Ideas of Beauty and Virtue*, ed. W. Leidhold (Indianapolis, IN, 2004), VIII.iii. Hruschka argues that Hutcheson's formulation derives from Leibniz: see 'The Greatest Happiness Principle', 168–72.
27 Hutcheson, *An Essay on the Nature and Conduct of the Passions and Affections, With Illustrations on the Moral Sense* (1728), ed. A. Garrett (Indianapolis, IN, 2002), Sect. 2.
28 Hume, *An Enquiry concerning Human Understanding* [1748], ed. T. L. Beauchamp, in the *Clarendon Edition* (2000), 9.2; *Treatise* 3.3.1.
29 Christian Wolff, *Vernünfftige Gedancken von der Menschen Thun und Lassen, zur Beförderung ihrer Glückseligkeit*, 4th edn., 1733; ed. H. W. Arndt, in *Werke*, I.4 (1976), Pt 1, ch. 1, §8, pp. 8–9.
30 [John Balguy] *The Foundation of Moral Goodness* (London, 1728), 5, 8–9.
31 Joseph Butler, *Fifteen Sermons Preached at the Rolls Chapel* (London, 1726), in *The Works of Bishop Butler*, ed. J. H. Bernard (London, 1900), Preface, 14–29; I.8; II.4–17; III.1–5 (by paragraphs).
32 Richard Price, *A Review of the Principal Questions and Difficulties in Morals* (1758), ed. from 3rd edn., 1787, by D. D. Raphael (Oxford, 1974), 181.
33 Ralph Cudworth is frequently represented as a precursor to this line of thought. In *British Moralists* I argue that this is a mistake and that he is better seen as forerunner of the creative rationalism of Shaftesbury and the constructive rationalism of Kant.
34 Samuel Clarke, *A Demonstration of the Being and Attributes of God: More Particularly in Answer to Mr. Hobbs, Spinoza, and their Followers* (1705), in *A Discourse concerning the Being and Attributes of God, the Obligations of Natural Religion, and the Truth and Certainty of the Christian Revelation* (1706), 10th edn. (London, 1749), Prop. XII, 114ff.; Price, *Review of Morals*, ch. 6.
35 Clarke, *Discourse*, Prop. 1, §1, 176; see *Moral Philosophy from Montaigne to Kant*, ed. J. B. Schneewind, 2 vols. (Cambridge, 1990), 1: 295.
36 Clarke, *Discourse*, Prop. I, §4, 205, 201; see Schneewind, *Moral Philosophy*, 303.
37 Similarly, Clarke: 'the Judgement and Conscience of Man's own Mind, concerning the Reasonableness and Fitness of the thing, that his Actions should be conformed to such or such a Rule or Law; is the truest and formallest *obligation*' (*Discourse*, Prop. I, §2, 190–1).
38 Bernard Mandeville, *The Fable of the Bees: or, Private Vices, Publick Benefits* (1732 edn.), ed. F. B. Kaye, 2 vols. (Oxford, 1924), 1: 48.
39 Butler, *Fifteen Sermons*, Sermon 12, §4, 248–51; Butler, *Three Sermons upon Human Nature, with A Dissertation on the Nature of Virtue* (Cambridge, 1834), 60–3; Berkeley, *Passive Obedience* (1712), §8, in *Works*, 6: 21; Hume, *Treatise*, 3.3.1.12, SBN 579–80.
40 Berkeley, *Alciphron, or the Minute Philosopher* (1732), Dialogue III, in *Works*, 3: 112–40.
41 John Locke, 'Of Ethick in General', in Peter King, *The Life of John Locke, with Extracts from His Correspondence, Journals, and Commonplace Books*, 2 vols. (London, 1830), 2: 129–30.
42 Berkeley, *Philosophical Commentaries*, Notebook A, in *Works*, 1: 68.
43 Berkeley, *An Essay towards Preventing the Ruin of Great Britain* (1721), in *Works*, 6: 69–85, at 71.
44 William Paley, *The Principles of Moral and Political Philosophy* (1785), ed. D. L. Le Mahieu (Indianapolis, IN, 2002), Bk 1, ch. 5.
45 Locke, *An Essay Concerning Human Understanding*, ed. P. H. Nidditch, in the *Clarendon Edition* (1975), II.xxviii.10, 353.
46 George Berkeley, *Passive Obedience*, §5, in *Works*, 6: 19.
47 See Jacques Domenech, *L'Éthique des lumières: les fondements de la morale dans la philosophie française du XVIII*[e] *siècle* (Paris, 1989), especially the Introduction.

48 Paul-Henri Thiry, baron d'Holbach, *Système de la nature, ou Des loix du monde physique et du monde morale*, 2 vols. (London, 1770). See, for example, vol. 1, ch. 9 and translated selections in Schneewind, *Moral Philosophy* 2: 437–45.

49 d'Holbach, *La morale universelle, ou les devoirs de l'homme fondés sur sa nature*, 3 vols. (Paris, 1795–6), ch. 1; trans., Schneewind 2: 432.

50 Helvétius, *De l'esprit* (Paris, 1758), Essay II, ch. ii; trans., Schneewind 2: 418.

51 Helvétius, *De l'esprit*, II.xv; trans., 2: 422. For a discussion of how this 'doux commerce' idea figured in this period more generally, see Albert O. Hirschman, *The Passions and the Interests: Political Arguments for Capitalism before Its Triumph* (Princeton, NJ, 1977).

52 Jeremy Bentham, *An Introduction to the Principles of Morals and Legislation* (1789), eds. J. H. Burns and H. L. A. Hart, *Collected Works* (London, 1970); *A Comment on the Commentaries and A Fragment of Government*, eds. J. H. Burns and H. L. A. Hart, *Collected Works* (London, 1977), Appendix F, 347.

53 Bentham, *Essay on Logic*, in *Works*, ed. J. Bowring, 11 vols. (Edinburgh, 1843), 8: 247.

54 For present-day defences of moral theory along similar lines, see Peter Railton, 'Pluralism, Determinacy, and Dilemma', *Ethics*, 102 (1992): 720–42, and Samuel Scheffler, *Human Morality* (Oxford, 1992), 9–16.

55 John Stuart Mill, *Utilitarianism*, ed. R. Crisp (Oxford, 1999), 49.

56 I discuss this at length in 'Obligation and Motive in Hume's Ethics', *Nous*, 27 (1993): 415–48.

57 Jean-Jacques Rousseau, *Du contrat social ou Principes du droit politique* (1762). See *The Social Contract and Other Later Political Writings*, trans. and ed. V. Gourevitch (Cambridge, 1997), 49–50.

58 Christian August Crusius, *Anweisung vernünftig zu leben* facsim. of Leipzig, 1744 edn., ed. G. Tonelli (Hildesheim, 1969); selections translated as *Guide to Rational Living* in Schneewind, *Moral Philosophy*, 2: 568–85.

59 Immanuel Kant, *Grundlegung zür Metaphysik der Sitten* (1785) in Ak 4: 385–462, at 389; translated as *Groundwork of The Metaphysics of Morals*, trans. and ed. M. J. Gregor, in *Works/Practical Philosophy* (1996).

60 Kant, *Grundlegung*, 4: 402–3. Famously, Kant thought that it is always wrong to lie, but it helps to see his idea here, if we put it in this more cautious way.

61 Locke, *Essay*, I.iii.14, 76.

62 Kant, *Die Religion innerhalb der Grenzen der bloßen Vernunft* (1793), Ak 6: 17–202 at 68–9; translated as *Religion within the Boundaries of mere Reason*, trans. and eds. A. Wood and G. di Giovanni, in *Works/Religion and Rational Theology* (1996).

63 Kant, *Kritik der praktischen Vernunft* (1788), Ak 5: 29–30; translated as *Critique of Practical Reason*, trans. and ed. M. J. Gregor, in *Works/Practical Philosophy* (1996).

34

POLITICS

WOLFGANG KERSTING

The fundamental methodological controversy of the eighteenth century also affected the philosophical treatment of political problems, and two major currents, one rationalist and one empiricist, may be distinguished in the many-sided political philosophy of the period. Each of these traditions is of course considerably heterogeneous in itself and includes quite different thinkers who are, however, connected by characteristic family resemblances so that it is permissible to assign them to a single theoretical conception. Rationalist political philosophy is based either on a sort of natural law theory or on a conception of human rights and organises its justificatory arguments within the conceptual framework of contractarianism.[1] Rousseau and Kant are the great protagonists of eighteenth-century contractual political philosophy, but it also includes the political philosophy of early and late German natural law theory,[2] which has to be taken into account as an exceedingly interesting variant of modern contractarianism. Empiricist political philosophy, on the other hand, rejects both the justificatory constructs of the natural state and the normative presuppositions of natural law and human rights theories. Its basic arguments are founded on human interests and needs, on history, on prudence, and on the most profitable development of society. Elements of an empiricist political philosophy may be found in Montesquieu, the father of the modern theory of the separation of powers. The centre of empiricist political philosophy, however, is in Britain; its first great representative was Bernard Mandeville but Shaftesbury and Hutcheson, the inventor of the utilitarian formula of the greatest happiness of the greatest number, also belong to this tradition. Its philosophically most significant figures are the two great names of the Scottish Enlightenment, David Hume and Adam Smith. Its most influential expression came at the end of the century in the works of Jeremy Bentham, the founder of utilitarianism.

I. THE POLITICAL PHILOSOPHY OF ENLIGHTENED ABSOLUTISM

While the contractualist conceptions of Kantianism and in certain respects also Rousseau's social contract theory, as well as the empiricist political philosophies of Hume, Smith, and Bentham, may be regarded as manifestations of political modernity, this is not true of German natural law theory. This political philosophy, the most influential in Germany until the 1780s, was the theory of enlightened absolutism, which, however, did not survive the rise of the competitive market economy, the French Revolution, and American and European constitutionalism, either politically or philosophically. As these revolutionary events began to influence German political thought, the absolutist doctrines of the natural law tradition were forgotten. No contemporary political theory refers to Wolff, Thomasius, or Pufendorf.

The political philosophy of enlightened absolutism rests on a natural law theory inaugurated by Grotius, systematically developed by Pufendorf, and further elaborated by Thomasius and Wolff. Characteristic of this philosophy is the theory of the double contract, which divides the single contract of Hobbes, Locke, Rousseau, and Kant into two or more contracts, of social union and political subjection, and so modifies the revolutionary idea of contractarianism that it can be used to legitimate Enlightenment absolutism. Also typical is a pre-modern model of society which, in spite of a comprehensive contractualist hermeneutics defining every social formation from the family to the state, the *societas maxima*, on the pattern of the contract between individuals, remains committed to the Aristotelian conception of the early European household and shows almost no signs of the modern market society. Society is here conceived as consisting of family units rather than associations of individuals. The social and political radicalism of the individualist contract paradigm could not develop freely because of these teleological dregs of Aristotelianism. Clearly, this contractually tinged Aristotelianism is an adequate conceptual picture of a contradictory social reality: by comparison with the economic, social, and political modernisation of contemporary Britain, enlightened absolutism was reactionary. A third feature of this philosophy is political paternalism: the state is introduced as a necessary means of achieving presumed natural goals and ethical ends. It is entrusted with the task of promoting happiness, improving morals, and perfecting human nature.

One might possibly agree with the second part of Leibniz's well-known and dismissive judgement on Pufendorf, that he was 'vir parum Jurisconsultus, et minime Philosophus',[3] when comparing his natural law theory with Hobbes's political philosophy, in respect of methodological rigour, brilliance of argument, intellectual radicalism, and originality. It is hard, however, to agree with the first part of this assessment. Pufendorf was the leading natural lawyer for the entire century. His *De jure naturæ et gentium libri octo* (1672) was, until the emergence of legal positivism, regarded by all European natural lawyers as the systematic ideal and reliable model of presentation. Moreover, natural law of the Pufendorfian style functioned unchallenged as the political philosophy of welfare-state absolutism until the age of the Kantian law of reason.[4] Committed to the typically modern consensual concept of legitimation, it made use of contractual terminology while at the same time modifying the harshness resulting from the Hobbesian individualist and physicalist theoretical framework with the help of a residual Aristotelian idea of natural sociality. Furthermore it recommended itself to those in power by a notable resistance to the human-rights individualism of Lockean liberalism.

Pufendorf's natural law theory, based on Grotius and developed in critical dialogue with Hobbes, is social and not individualist in character.[5] It rests on an empirical view of human nature, unconditionally dominated by 'socialitas'. Human beings are dependent on cooperation and ordered coexistence with one another, not only to satisfy their basic needs but also to achieve happiness and fully realise their abilities. This partly empirical and naturalistic, partly teleological bias of human nature towards sociality is reflected in the fundamental natural law principle that determines the conditions of prosperous social existence, prohibits antisocial and uncooperative behaviour, and lays down rules of action that promote and further social life. Pufendorfian natural law, like all eighteenth-century natural law, is a theory of duties, not of rights. Its basic premise is a reciprocal obligation to sociality; on this is grounded a series of absolute duties with corresponding rights, which, however, have no determining function. They remain secondary. Although in natural law all individuals are equal before the law and the natural law order is characterised by symmetry and reciprocity, Pufendorf must not be viewed as a theorist of human rights and the basic rights of the individual. In his theory there are no traces of either human-rights egalitarianism or of liberalism. The law is not the normative starting point but the reflex of a pre-existing natural obligation to sociality on the part of all. Human beings have rights because they have duties; they have these, first because they possess a distinct contingent nature and, secondly, because God has imposed these obligations on us. If human beings are to live according to the fundamental natural law principle of socialitas they must join together in societies and protect their social cooperation by means of a political sovereign authority. Pufendorf interprets this process of socialisation and politicisation through the conceptual means of modern contractual theory.

Whereas the great modern political philosophers recognise only a single contract, Pufendorfian natural law works with a two-stage concept of contract, which temporally and conceptually strictly distinguishes between a social contract and one of political authority. Moreover, the latter often includes an additional constitutional contract interposed between the *pactum unionis* and the *pactum subjectionis*. Pufendorf, and all the German natural law school with him, followed not the Hobbesian tradition but that of Althusius.[6] This conception of a double and a triple contract, by its internal logic, leads to an evolutionary interpretation of society which relates the individual contracts to significant social, legal, and administrative stages of development. No wonder then if the further development of Pufendorfian natural law gives rise to theories which, through a suitably differentiated account of social evolution and consequent increase in legal proceedings, produce yet more contracts.

The recurrent argument underlying German natural law contractarianism runs as follows. Through a contractual association of families in the natural state

> there is constituted a supreme power, an authority, which always depends upon a free nation and never ceases, because it is the foundation of all power in the state. But, since the nation as a whole is hardly qualified to exercise this united strength itself it is necessary to determine how, in what manner and by whom the combined power of the state should be exerted and used. This is how the properly so-called supreme power in the state originates and develops.[7]

This contract theory begins with the doctrine of the natural condition but the methodological status of the latter is ambivalent. Whereas Pufendorf and his followers stress the supposedly ahistorical character of the *status naturalis*, Carl Gottlieb Svarez collects biblical references and 'Citations from secular writers' to support a historical view of the natural condition. The strategic significance of this doctrine, however, remains the same: history, experience, and reason alike

> teach us that the state of natural freedom and independence is not one in which the human race can realise its happiness, the purpose of its existence, and that people, in order more nearly to achieve this aim, must come together in those great civil associations under a common supreme authority, which we term states.[8]

Pufendorf does not adopt Aristotle's metaphysical teleology but naturalises the Aristotelian *zoon politikon*, changing its political nature into a social nature and transforming a metaphysical definition of being into a natural disposition supported by a wide range of empirical evidence. But he retains enough residual teleological Aristotelianism to revise the decidedly anti-Aristotelian premises of Hobbes's political philosophy. The latter's characteristic opposition of nature and society gives way to a harmonious cooperative relationship between human nature and social form; the natural condition is no longer represented as an extremely isolated atomistic individualism but assumes the character of a sociable condition. The newly discovered individual of Hobbesian theory relinquishes his position as protagonist to the earlier European household, politically and legally represented by the *oikodespotes*, the *pater familias* or head of the family. In this way the radicalism of Hobbesian legitimation theory is moderated. Natural freedom is made part of humanity's social nature and thereby loses its role as the norm by which political power is legitimated.

There are exceptions of course. Thomasius, for one, is less ready to dress up the natural condition in Aristotelian political philosophy.[9] By replacing Pufendorf's and Grotius's communally oriented principle of sociality with the principle of the happiness of the individual, that is, exchanging a political and collective teleology for a strictly individual one, he distances himself significantly from the traditional natural law conceptions. His avowed purpose is to steer a middle course 'between the Hobbesians and the scholastico-Aristotelians',[10] that is, the orthodox Lutheran Aristotelians of the Alberti-type who, by the way, were strongly fought by Pufendorf in his *Eris Scandica* (1686) as well. But this fundamental change of position from the social to the individual has no normative or political consequences. Thomasius's political theory remains absolutist, requiring absolute obedience from the subject and giving the prince unlimited power and authority to define and carry out political ends. Politics is the business of the masters alone; ordinary citizens with their more limited understanding are fit only to deal with civic administration, to manage their petty and readily comprehensible daily affairs cleverly and decently, and to remain respectable and pursue their own small pleasures.

The earlier German natural law theory of the state of nature differs from the Hobbesian concept of the *status naturalis* not only in a communitarian anthropology but also with regard to the normative constitution of pre-state existence. From Pufendorf to Wolff the state of nature is understood as the state of natural law, as the sphere controlled by natural law norms, which cannot be reduced to measures of prudence or expediency, and by the legal connections based on these. It is, according to Wolff, 'either the original state (*originarius*), in so far as it is determined solely by innate rights and obligations, or an adventitious one (*adventitius*), in so far as it is determined by incurred obligations and acquired rights, according to natural law'.[11]

The state of nature is thus a state governed by natural law principles, a highly complex legal structure, combining innate legal relationships together with those reached by consensus. But on the question of the validity of natural law itself Pufendorf and Wolff differ considerably. Whereas Wolff, a rationalist, is a value cognitivist, understanding the validity of natural law principles as a rational predicate, independent of any divine imposition, Pufendorf is a legal voluntarist, who can allow full legal force to natural law principles (in this anticipating the positivist command theory of law in a natural law guise) only when they are accepted as divine commands and directions. In his basic natural law philosophy Wolff combines the *socialitas* tradition with that of *perfectio*: human nature is characterised by sociability and perfectibility and determined by the ultimate goal of perfection. Whereas for Pufendorf God, the source of all obligation, requires socially conforming behaviour which promotes community and cooperation, for Wolff, the rationalist metaphysician, an obvious natural law obliges us to do our utmost to promote the perfectibility of humankind and to abstain from all that would hinder this. The teleological character of Wolffian natural law sets the goal of perfection and the means of achieving it at the centre of the normative system. Consequently for Wolff too the concept of duty takes precedence over that of right: 'right originates in the duties and responsibilities of humankind'.[12] Duty precedes right, both logically and teleologically. We have rights only because we have duties; they are rights to actions by means of which we may fulfil our duty to promote perfection. It is, in fact, a common dogma of eighteenth-century natural law theorists that rights must be derivative from the higher moral standard of teleological natural law and therefore functionally dependent on the natural duty to promote the common good.[13] Only at the end of the century, first in Kant's philosophy of right, did the obligation-based natural law give way to the new doctrine of the rights of man that inverted the logical dependency between rights and duties and founded the latter on the former.[14]

The aims of government in the political philosophy of enlightened absolutism are modelled on Aristotelian theory. They comprise a moral teleology which goes far beyond pure self-preservation. Just as in Aristotle political association exists for the sake of the good life, the *eu zen*, so in German natural law people did not abandon the natural condition simply to ensure survival but essentially to realise the natural end of human existence, happiness and the perfecting of their natural and moral talents. The achievement of this aim is a public, not a private matter. It concerns the protection of the *salus publica*, the *bonum commune* and has nothing to do with the protection of individual rights or autonomy. The political theory of earlier German natural law is a substantive teleology of the good, not a formal teleology of right. It is decidedly antiliberal.

People forsake the state of nature and join together in a social group, an 'association of families'.[15] The basis for this is the realisation that only through cooperation can the moral quality of communal life be improved. The *bonum commune* achieved by such cooperation is generally understood in accordance with traditional moral theory. Towards the end of the century it was occasionally, as for example by Schlözer, interpreted in terms of rational self-interest and distributive gain, and then the social state assumes the form of market-economic cooperation.

Each could subsist without the other: but . . . they hope for a better way of life by this means. *Salus publica* does not mean the benefit of the majority but is the sum total of all benefits for each and every individual. All either cooperate with others in order to achieve an immediate profit or they do something for another, but only as an advance, expecting similar services in return. (64)[16]

What is interesting in Schlözer's political theory is that it does contain elements of a liberal conception of society, which, however, is not translated into political terms. This liberalism is evidenced in a change of the state's purpose; the concept of an ethical welfare state is replaced by that of a state guaranteeing an institutional foundation for organised self-interest. All traces of sociality and perfection have disappeared from human nature: for Schlözer the individual has become a creature of interests. But this modernisation of anthropology and natural law has no political consequences, nor does it correct the Aristotelian view of society. Schlözer pours his new anthropological wine into the old wineskins of enlightened absolutism. He clings to the contractarian combination of socialisation and subjection, and a political emancipation of citizens is the last thing he thinks of. His conception of the state is just as much based on absolute sovereignty as that of Pufendorf or Wolff. He sees it as a sort of 'fire insurance office' but the manager of the office remains the same absolutist sovereign prince (3).

The first contract of natural law contractarianism is one of cooperation, a 'pactum unionis virium' (65). It means: 'When a state is founded, the individual citizens commit themselves to promote the common weal and the community as a whole commits itself to ensure the welfare, peace and security of all.'[17] The partners who thus contractually combine their powers, abilities, and efforts are not the asocial individuals of the Hobbesian natural condition but the 'patres familias segreges',[18] the Aristotelian *oikodespotes*. The natural state is a social state or, as Schlözer puts it, a 'family state',[19] its social constitution determined by the household community of early Europe. Pufendorf expressly reserves the status of citizen to the contracting male heads of families and classifies women, children, servants, and hired labourers as members of the society in need of its care and protection. The deciding criterion is independence; the socially and economically independent head of the family is master of his own, but the members of the household are not and have no independent wills: 'Their wills were . . . included in the Wills of their domestical Governor'.[20] In order not to lose the advantages of cooperation resulting from the social contract, systems will have to be devised to secure them. 'Experience and philosophy will . . . lead to ways of making society, so essential for human happiness, lasting and as useful as possible, of buttressing collapsing structures and of enjoying the benefits of fire without suffering from the smoke' (Schlözer, 64). A contractual foundation for the state is required. The first step is a constitutional decree, a *decretum circa forma regiminis*, as Pufendorf calls it; others speak of a *pactum ordinationis civilis* or a constitutional contract. This will establish the fundamental laws of society, the *leges fundamentales*, which will determine the exercise of power. A contract of subjection is linked to this, creating a relationship of sovereign authority within the agreed constitutional framework and on the basis of natural law theory concerning the purposes of government. 'The supreme authority promises to exert all its power and its efforts to promote the general welfare and security by appropriate measures and the necessary institutions: in return the subjects promise willingly to perform all that it considers beneficial.'[21]

The contract of subjection is a *pactum unionis voluntatum* and allows of the effective combination of the powers of all and the concentration of the many distinct individual wills in a single directing supreme will. This anthropological metaphor recalls the famous copper engraving on the title page of the first edition of *Leviathan* in 1651 in which the political state is represented as *makros anthropos*, man writ large, illustrating this contractual union of powers and wills. The *pactum unionis virium* constitutes the gigantic body of society, covered with scales in human form, while the *pactum unionis voluntatum* provides this mighty social frame with a head capable of effective political direction.[22]

The social contract is at the same time a contract for the body politic as a powerful concentration of forces. But little is gained by this combination of forces if a single strong will able to accomplish its purposes is not in control, directing these forces to one goal, and if a single intelligence is not planning and formulating these aims to which the efforts of society as a whole are to be directed. A society constituted by contractual union is of course prepared to employ the abilities of all for the general good but it cannot reach agreement on the goals and ends to be pursued. It is lacking in decisiveness and the ability to act. It is crippled politically by a multiplicity of contradictory opinions and divergent wills. The second contract deals with this political immobility in society and provides the intelligence and willpower needed, by subjecting the people to the will of a prince who will put an end to indecisiveness and will inspire them to rational resolve and effective action. 'The *pactum unionis virium* was inadequate as long as it did not include *unio voluntatum* and the latter could only be achieved through the *pactum subjectionis*' (Schlözer, 76).

The bifurcation of the Hobbesian contract into a *pactum unionis* and a *pactum submissionis* leads to a legal revaluation of the people. In contrast to Hobbes, early German natural law does not legally annul the contractually united people but preserves it as a legal subject. The idea of the double contract entails that the people continues as a legal identity from the social contract to that of subjugation. Through the contract of individuals, the people becomes a legal entity that contracts with the prince and retains a legal identity under the prince. Contrary to Hobbes, it is not as individuals but as a contractual union that the people institutes governance. However, this difference should not be overrated.

Pufendorf's criticism of Hobbes was an academic dispute among friends of absolutism. The people's political lot is clearly not eased by conceiving absolutist rule as a direct contractual relationship. The surrender of power is not a loan, and contractual surrender is still surrender. Such a contract entails imperfectly mutual obligation, for the surrender is total; the citizens have no power left to enforce their interpretations of the contract and they have no right left to recover their power by force if they think the contract has been violated by the ruler.

This was an undeniable principle of early German natural law, which recognised no fundamental safeguard for the individual against state interference in his private life. In the political philosophy of enlightened absolutism the social and state contract has no emancipatory functions.[23] Indeed, no politically progressive role for contractarianism should be inferred from the fundamental anti-traditionalism of the consensual justificatory contract. Pufendorfian contractarianism demonstrates this very conformity of the contractual model to existing conditions and the political effectiveness of justificatory contractarianism, since it engenders an absolute princely rule and unqualified duty of obedience. Or, in Schlözer's words:

> The nation as a whole and every individual owes the ruler obedience, even blind obedience; that is, the ruler's commands must always be assumed to be valid and useful, even though the reasons for them may not be understood or indeed the opposite may be firmly believed. The citizen must calmly obey all orders; when he has committed a crime he must quietly submit to whatever punishment the ruler ordains, even if it be the death penalty. This is the fundamental law of the state and the citizen's highest duty, if he wants to avoid the horrors of anarchy. All willful disobedience to any command of the ruler or his subordinates is high treason. (104)

If one carefully considers the position of power which earlier German natural law allotted to the prince, there is scarcely any difference between that and the absolute power of Hobbes's *Leviathan*. On closer examination, the criticism of Hobbes by Pufendorf and others turns out to be empty natural law rhetoric. German natural law is just as much a justification of absolutism as Hobbes's constructive contractarianism. In it, too, there is no restriction of rule, whether on natural law, human rights, or contractual grounds, nor is there any constitutional limitation of the ruler's authority.[24] The prince is above all laws; he is not legally bound by contract and even stands above the law itself and can do whatever he thinks right for the welfare of the state and the maintenance of his rule.

> The dispute as to whether the legislator can issue decrees contrary to natural law is in the end just hot air. All admit that he can command, permit, or forbid whatever is for the common weal and whatever will prevent a greater evil, whether it be a matter of indifference to, forbidden, or permitted by natural law.[25]

For the natural law theorist, who has thrown away his best weapons by devaluing the catalogue of human rights he himself drew up, nothing remains but to appeal to the prince's monopoly of wisdom and offer himself as political adviser. It is very common for natural law theorists to offer their systems for the ethical education of rulers.[26] In the tradition of the moralist Mirrors for Princes, they hope to see these accepted as rational programmes for princely rule and hope to enlighten absolutism through natural law, replacing reasons of state as the sole end of government by natural law goals of civil security, social satisfaction, concern for the happiness and morality of citizens, and care for human perfection. Thus the political philosophy of enlightened absolutism confronts a twofold task: on the one hand it hopes to make absolutism unassailable through natural law and contractual legitimation, while on the other hand it seeks to modify the absolute sovereignty so justified by ethical and natural law education. Rights-based constitutionalism is replaced by natural law ethics. This view of a natural law education for princes, of cooperation between the *philosophus regnans* and the *rex philosophans* is particularly marked in Wolff. He considers his natural law system alone suitable for political instruction: 'But it is much easier and quicker [by comparison with all previous systems] to acquire the ideas of good government through a coherent philosophy developed on our plan.'[27]

II. FEUERBACH, HUMBOLDT, AND LATER GERMAN NATURAL LAW

In early German natural law the contract of subjection seals the alliance between eudæmonism and absolutism. In Kant's view it is a paternalistic contract, beneath human dignity and contradicting the innate human right of freedom; it legally incapacitates the individual and it contradicts the principle of the sovereignty of the people, according to which sovereignty belongs to the contractually united community alone and is essentially inalienable. A régime based on such a pact and established on 'the principle of benevolence toward the people like that of a *father* toward his children' is 'the greatest *despotism* thinkable'.[28] Kant's philosophy of pure practical reason rejects the normative teleological orientation of traditional natural law doctrines of happiness. Just as moral eudæmonism must give way to the grandeur of the autonomy of reason, so political eudæmonism, the justificatory ideology of paternalist absolutism, must yield to the nobility of the innate and inalienable right to freedom. Human beings should not be subjected to authoritarian disposal of their happiness. The moralistic *cura promovendi salutis* of the welfare state insults human dignity.

No one can coerce me to be happy in his way (as he thinks of the welfare of other human beings); instead, each may seek his happiness in the way that seems good to him, provided he does not infringe upon that freedom of others to strive for a like end which can coexist with the freedom of everyone in accordance with a possible universal law (i.e., does not infringe upon this right of another). (Ak 8: 290)

Later German natural law joins Kant in opposing welfare absolutism and the eudæmonist preference for happiness over right, and it joins Fichte in declaring 'unremitting war on that poisonous source of all our wretchedness, the phrase, that it is the task of the prince to watch over our happiness.'[29] It was thus forced to recognise 'how far the idea of the common weal could be stretched in restricting freedom'.[30] In this matter, an impetus came from the American and French declarations of human rights, on the one hand, and on the other, from John Locke's liberalism, Rousseau's *Contrat social*, and, not least, Kant's revolution of practical philosophy through the concept of the autonomy of reason. Under these influences, a political philosophy was formulated in Germany during the last two decades of the eighteenth century which was based on the idea of human rights and the concept of the rule of law. Although the later natural lawyers, including Kant and Fichte, held on to the traditional natural law vocabulary, their arguments are no longer based on natural teleology and man's essential predispositions. Nature has given way to reason; the common good has been replaced with the individual right of freedom; welfare absolutism has given way to the rule of law; and happiness, virtue, and human flourishing are transformed from concerns of public interest and political responsibility to matters of private interest. The new theory is centred on individual rights which determine aim, form, and limit of rule; shape the constitution; and define legitimacy in philosophical theory and political praxis.

In this later natural law theory, the contract must reinforce the innate, precontractual legal position of individuals as norm and limit of government activity in civil affairs. As a justificatory theory of government, contractarianism offers a reconstruction of the development of government authority from the original rights of man, using only legal steps consonant with the natural right to freedom. Under the aegis of this right the expansive goals of the enthusiastically regulatory government of natural law tradition declines to a concern with safeguarding coexistence, protecting freedom, and guaranteeing rights. As the Sophists once proclaimed, so later German natural law too argues that 'the state is not a system of education but an insurance company governed by laws to be implemented by force'.[31] It is a specific, typically German version of liberalism, which is interested only in the proper purpose of the state and the appropriate limits of its activities and considers of minor importance questions of the form of government and its implementation, and participation by the citizens. Generally, German liberalism is no champion of democracy. It believes that guarantees of rights can be secured under any form of government and that absolute rule does not necessarily thwart liberal aims or politically debase its subjects. It sees no constitutive connection between the liberal purpose of a state and its form of government and cannot adopt the Rousseauan thesis of a necessary link between the individual right of freedom, general laws, and democratic rule.

The theories of later German natural law are usually compromises, which forge links with political modernism while clinging to the conceptual patterns of Enlightenment absolutist political theory. Undoubtedly, the liberal goal of preserving freedom and guaranteeing rights is central to their conception of the state: their anthropological starting point is no longer Aristotelian or teleological but concerned with the individual and with human rights. Their determination of the links of government is based on liberal ideas. But they still cling to Pufendorf's model of two or three contracts and choke off the democratic consequences of the human rights starting point with a concept of absolute sovereignty. Paul Johann Anselm Feuerbach is a typical representative of this German compromise between liberal and absolutist aims in government. In his *Anti-Hobbes* he considers the task of political philosophy from a Rousseauan angle: it must solve the problem of 'finding a condition in which human freedom is assured, or, in other words, a state of security in which human beings are as free as they should be, in accordance with their rational nature'.[32] Influenced by Kant, Feuerbach outlines the state of nature as one of 'complete external lawlessness', which will be abandoned on the way to a union through social contract, whereby all 'relinquish their previously unlimited right to dispose of their freedom' and vow 'to use all their powers to fulfil this pledge and to do everything possible in order that the demand of the general will . . . for freedom as the ultimate goal of society may be completely satisfied' (17, 23).

As everyone is still the 'interpreter of his civil contract', the aim of socialisation has not yet been achieved: 'An organising will must be present if the purpose of civil contracts is to be achieved, a will which as interpreter of the social contract directs the wills of the members of society for the welfare of all' (25, 26–7). This interpreter for the general public is created by the contract of subjection and provided with all the characteristic features of sovereignty. Because the 'sort of effectiveness' of this role is still indeterminate, a constitutional contract is also necessary (34). Feuerbach's contract of subjection is still very much the *pactum subiectionis* of Pufendorfian tradition. It is a true bilateral contract and 'an unconditional contract, that is, it gives the ruler the right of unconditional and fully effective choice of means for the purposes of the state' (57). The limitation of power, which Feuerbach, in his title *Anti-Hobbes*, explicitly made the programme of his work, follows on from the goal of power as determined by the social contract and the legal conditions of its creation: the condition

> that . . . the will of the ruler shall be determined and restricted by the general will is one which derives inevitably from the nature of the enterprise, from the idea of the civil contract and of the general will, without requiring any express declaration by the people, and cannot even be limited or revoked by the will of the people unless it intends to dissolve civil society. (112)

To avoid all similarity to Hobbes's 'privilege for robbers and hangmen . . . and slave-drivers', Feuerbach gives the *pactum submissionis*, essential for law enforcement and requiring the nomination of a ruler as empirical representative of the general will, the honorary title of 'civil contract of subjection', without apparently realising the paradoxical character of this combination of ideas (103, 145). On closer examination, Feuerbach's contractarianism is revealed as a distorted compromise, which uses the Rousseauan–Kantian concepts of the right of freedom and of the general will as weapons against traditional welfare absolutism while simultaneously seeking to eliminate popular sovereignty through the same traditional *pactum submissionis*. He does, of course, adopt normative individualism and, like the great philosophical contractarians, teaches the inalienability of the basic right of freedom of the individual, but at the same time he refuses to recognise the political implications of this right or to elevate contractually constituted civil society to the position of ruler.

One of the most convincing exponents of the liberal conception of the state in the last years of the eighteenth century was Wilhelm von Humboldt who in 1793 completed, in his *Ideen zu einem Versuch, die Grenzen der Wirksamkeit des Staats zu bestimmen*, a sort of manifesto of early German liberalism.[33] Apart from Kant, he was the only German liberal philosopher to play an important role in the development of liberalism outside Germany. But Humboldt too saw no necessary connection between the purposes of state and the power structure; he opposed eudæmonism and a state system of moral education. He designed a liberal programme for the state but was no adherent of democracy. He was convinced that liberal purposes could be achieved independently of democracy and that neither the safeguarding of basic rights nor the rule of law necessarily called for democracy. He feared that democracy might degenerate into mob tyranny and thought that a monarchy or aristocracy would be better guardians of liberty and the rule of law. A further peculiarity of his liberalism is that he links the goal of protecting rights and freedom to an ethical teleology. It is not merely the right to freedom that determines the limits of state action, but also the duty to develop and cultivate human abilities. It is a sort of teleological humanism requiring the state not only to provide space for individual development but also to prove itself as an institution for the development of humanity. Humboldt is a liberal perfectionist; he replaces the eudæmonist teleology of enlightened absolutism with a teleology of human perfectibility. Like Kant he fought against the ethical and political paternalism of the absolutist state and against political theorists who saw the welfare of its citizens as the ultimate end of the state. But he failed to recognise the dangerous paternalism closely connected with his vision of a state dedicated to the perfection of humankind.

Humboldt is not the only German thinker of this decade who sought to develop a humanist political philosophy based on an ethic of self-realisation and the perfection of the characteristic powers of the human race; it was an ideal widely shared by theorists and poets of the time. Because such a philosophy lays more stress on ethical and educational questions than on constitutional problems, it can all too easily turn into a compensatory activity obscuring political powerlessness. The thought of one of the most radical figures in late eighteenth-century political philosophy shows the limitations of this thesis. Georg Forster, although representative of this perfectionist humanism, was one of the few German friends of the French Revolution because he believed that a political order founded on liberty, equality, and self-determination was the best guarantee for the development of humanity.

> I am still of the opinion that a republican constitution deserves to be supported and maintained, not because it produces more happiness than any other, but because it gives a new turn, development and direction to our mental powers. Experience and action are the great schools of humanity; the more someone has done and suffered, the more perfect he is in the use of his powers and his knowledge of himself. . . . It seems to me that opportunities for the general education of most people under our present monarchy have almost disappeared. . . . But in a republic a wide field is open to all.[34]

III. KANT'S STATE OF REASON

The outstanding philosopher in later German natural law is Immanuel Kant.[35] His foundation of political philosophy in rational law offers the most ambitious theoretical account of a national and international community of law. His philosophy is in stark contrast to the eudæmonistic ethical absolutism of the eighteenth century, linking up with the tradition of the great theories of political modernity represented by Hobbes, Locke, and Rousseau. It ends the contractarianism of the seventeenth and eighteenth centuries while at the same time bringing about its greatest philosophical maturity.

Kant shares the conviction, common to all variants of natural law theory, that there is an objective, eternally valid and universally binding principle of right, which is accessible to human knowledge and comprehends the criterion by which the normative correctness of human actions and the justice of human social and political orders are judged. What distinguishes him from all his predecessors, however, is that in determining the concept and principle of right he appeals neither to empirical human conditions nor to the teleological nature of the traditional metaphysical world-view but solely to pure practical, legislative reason. In the previous history of political philosophy, foundations and first principles had been sought in objective ideas, in a normative cosmic constitution, in the will of God, the nature of man, or prudent self-interest, but Kant was convinced that these were without exception inadequate as the basis of unconditional practical laws and that human reason would acknowledge absolute practical necessity and obligation only in norms arising from its own legislation. We are subject to the laws of reason alone: with this revolutionary new ground of validity Kant frees us from domination by theological absolutism and the bonds of teleological natural law, as well as elevating us above the prosaic banalities of prudential theory. Human beings may and must obey only their own reason.

Because human beings share their lives in space and time with others of their kind, enter into external relationships with them, and influence their actions through their own, they are subject to the rational law of right. Kant sees this as a universal formal law of freedom of action. Indifferent to all questions of the content of human actions, it is directed solely to the formal compatibility of one individual's external freedom with that of others and so limits individual action within the boundaries of its possible universalisation. Just as the moral law brings inner freedom into harmony with itself and promotes the consistency of the inner world by excluding all non-universal maxims, so the law of right brings external freedom into harmony with itself and promotes the consistency of the external world by opposing all non-universalisable uses of freedom of action. The world of pure right, the fundamental order of human rights, is a strictly symmetrical, reciprocally structured web of external relationships between free and equal individuals.

This ethically filtered world of pure right, however, is unattainable, but not because men behave like wild beasts to one another. Even if all men were lambs they could not live in such a world. This is simply because a rational law of freedom, on account of its indeterminacy and lack of selectivity, cannot serve as a reliable basis on which to judge conflicting claims. In a situation governed solely by rational law, the necessary coordination of the actions of individuals cannot be achieved. It is an awkward situation, governed by a competing multiplicity of subjective and a priori irreconcilable representations of right. Owing to the absence of generally accepted and sufficiently selective laws and of a competent judge accepted by all parties, the affair is likely to lead to violence. To obviate this, reason devises the 'postulate of public right'.[36] Behind this rational command is the philosophically significant argument of an inherently necessary and rationally required positive determination of the pure principles of justice and of a concrete expression of rational law through legislation resulting from the united will of the whole body of citizens. The state of nature has to be replaced by conditions in which the violence arising from the imprecision of the juridical principles of pure practical reason is eliminated by legislative determination of the rational law, whereby the competing private interpretations of 'just' and 'unjust' will be replaced by an authoritative public system of distributive justice. In such a system the rational principles of right will be given concrete form by a publicly approved legislature and controversial legal cases will be decided by the public administration of justice.

There are two ways of achieving this transformation. The first, the arbiter model of peace, is that adopted by Hobbes. The second, the justice model, is a special version of the first; it offers a morally proven order, combining security and justice, because the basic structure of the legal state, which guarantees these by establishing procedures for decision-making and arbitration and, in Hobbes's phrase, a common power to keep them all in awe, has been molded in accordance with Kantian principles of natural law. Kant terms such a political order a republic. This, more specifically, includes the following characteristics: a constitutional law based on the inalienable human rights of freedom and equality, the reliable administration of justice through the rule of law, democratic procedures regulating political decision-making, a legislature deriving its authority from the will of the citizens, institutional control of the exercise of authority through the separation of powers, and the whole empowered by the deliberative community of its citizens.

Because Kant regards the transition from the state of nature to the civil state as legally necessary and required by the law of pure practical reason, he distances himself from the contractualist decision of modern times to ground the state in the arbitrariness of the individual and to legitimise state rule by appealing to individual freedom which is contractually binding. This voluntaristic justification of the state becomes impossible against the background of a categorical obligation on all to join the state and the complementary right of enforcing membership of the state. Kant's anti-voluntarism, derived from his metaphysics of pure practical reason, no longer requires the contract for purposes of legitimation. He finds a new and revolutionary use for it, as a fundamental norm of legislative justice and political ethics. Stripped of all connotations of voluntarism and empiricism, the contract is viewed as an essential principle of reason, as the constitutional form of the rational state, 'that is, of *the state in idea*, as it ought to be in accordance with pure principles of right. This idea serves as a norm (*norma*) for every actual union into a commonwealth' (Ak 6: 313). Kant transforms the contractual basis of state rule into a principle of rational law, functioning normatively as a principle of political justice.

The idea of contract, however, is not merely an adjunct of political justice but also a principle of action, absolutely binding on every historical ruler. The legislator is a priori obliged to 'give his laws in such a way that they *could* have arisen from the united will of a whole people'.[37] Consequently he must consider himself as the representative of the contractually united will of the people and as exercising power on their behalf. Above all, he can enact only laws which will obtain general consent. This last condition does not, however, require the legislature to investigate the actual will of the society. Kant's criterion for guaranteeing justice, or rather excluding injustice, is a logical one requiring only an intellectual operation of the type familiar from his process of universalisation. The activation of the contract provides the logical basis for contractual democracy. The legislator must consider whether every citizen can be co-legislator of any given law, whether he is logically conceivable in this role, and where the watershed between just and unjust laws lies. Public legislation will run counter to the contractual norm when it violates the conditions constitutive for the contractual community, when it establishes legal conditions lacking the formal properties of equality, liberty, and reciprocity.

The contract alone offers a constitutional form of sovereignty consistent with pure practical reason. Only laws approved by the general will are consonant with human rights and they are just simply because each participating legislator is voting on his own behalf. Also, and uniquely, any limitation of freedom imposed by them has been approved by those affected by it. Such laws are not merely just, they are necessarily just; consequently the legislating will of the contract, the sovereign of the rational state, is necessarily infallible. Hobbes describes the state depicted in *Leviathan* as a mortal god, combining, like the immortal God, the characteristics of omnipotence and infallibility. Because the laws of the state originally determined what was just and what unjust and because normative rules cannot apply to themselves, state injustice is impossible for simple logical reasons: on conceptual grounds the Hobbesian state can commit injustice as little as God can sin. Rousseau and Kant took over this combination of sovereignty and infallibility from Hobbes, but with a difference. Hobbes derives infallibility from the concept of sovereignty: it is an essential characteristic of his absolute lawgiver. In the context of his legal positivism it is an analytical predicate of general legislative activity. Rousseau and Kant, however, reverse the argument, deriving the concept of sovereignty from the normative concept of infallibility. The role of sovereign can be assumed only by someone who fulfils the condition of infallibility, who necessarily promulgates just laws simply by following the *volonté générale*, the united will of the people. This argument is possible because both Rousseau and Kant support procedural concepts of justice – a first in the history of political or legal philosophy. It is not agreement with the material norms of natural law that characterises a law as just, but the nature and manner of its generation. We have before us a legislative method which guarantees justice when law is produced by democratic procedures. For Kant and Rousseau the concepts of sovereignty, justice, and democracy are clearly interconnected systematically; the justice of a régime and the political participation of its citizens are mutually interdependent.

The significant difference between Kant and Rousseau is that, for the former, the democratic method of legislation can be simulated. Just as the sovereign under rational law can be represented by any empirical ruler, the plebiscitary procedure of lawmaking can always, without any restriction of legal obligation, be replaced by a simple thought experiment applying the criterion of the people's decision. The empirical representative of the normative ideal sovereign is acting in exact agreement with legal reason when his use of power is informed by the clear logic of asking himself whether the law in question imposes an equal burden on all, disadvantages or discriminates against none, and does not create privileges. Typical Kantian strategy allows the general will to realise itself independently of a true democratic system of state sovereignty. It also relieves Kant's political philosophy from embarrassing demands for immediate political insurrection, replacing the German autocracies of the day with revolutionary democracy of the French kind. Rousseau, on the other hand, recognises only a plebiscitary, direct democracy as legitimate. Even a representative system established under a democratic form of sovereignty offends, on his view, against the inalienable right of self-determination. For him, the *volonté générale* can be manifested only in the assembly of members of the civil union, the ensemble of the empirical wills of all citizens. Kant, in transforming truly democratic legislative procedure into a principle of legislative justice, separates the empirical democracy of the *volonté de tous* from the *volonté générale*, the general united will, and so is able to combine the latter with all forms of sovereignty. By thus freeing it from the Rousseauan tie to the democratic assembly, the united will of the people, as a lawgiving maxim directing every form of sovereignty in the path of justice, has been rendered much more effective politically.

The tolerance by Kantian contractarianism of nondemocratic régimes must disappear if the right of legislation is considered an integral part of human rights, for this renders it inalienable and Kantianism Jacobinical.[38] This is not to say that radicalised Kantianism is the only path to German Jacobinism. The few political theorists of this time who ally themselves with the French Jacobins are not usually Kantians. However, some of Kant's disciples rejected his lukewarm political attitudes and radicalised the political implications of the foundations of rational law. Johann Adam Bergk, one of the better-known and more distinguished of the young *enragés*, considered such a politicisation of human rights and taught that juridically considered human being, private individual, and citizen are a unity. For him only a 'democratic republic' is compatible with human rights;[39] the *status naturalis*, rendered normative by the law of reason, defines a free system, guaranteed legally and institutionally by the democratic constitution. The democratic republic is the empirical and temporal form of contract: '[I]t is the symbol of justice' (94). Bergk is aware, of course, that the history of states shows us 'fraud, cunning and violence on one side and stupidity, cowardice and weakness on the other in their founders', but reason insists that legal justification of the state alone should be the permanent principle directing the empirical political development of informed opinion and that the contract, viewed empirically and restricted by no normative handicaps, should be seen as the means to this end (83).[40] Bergk's democratic republic is the institutionalised form of contract in which true consensus is regarded as more rational.[41] Whereas for Kant the contract serves as the basic element in anti-revolutionary and progressive legal reform, Bergk once more releases its revolutionary dynamic. The political–ethical norm of tolerant practical rule is replaced by the normative pattern of a democratic republic. Thereby the contractual legislative norm is reduced to a contractual norm of the organisation of power. By the end of the eighteenth century, German natural law contractarianism, which in its earlier Pufendorfian version had been the core of welfare absolutism, had reached, in Bergk's left-wing Kantianism, the level of political emancipation resulting from the French Revolution.

IV. KANT ON REVOLUTION AND REFORM

Kant's political philosophy is faced with a twofold task. As a metaphysics of right, it derives the purely rational principles of political coexistence from the universal law of rational right. Freedom, equality, and contract are shown to be the principles on which an ideal state is founded, and which determine the political status of citizens and the organisation of a just and rational rule. But his political philosophy is not merely a metaphysics of right, a normative theory of rational law. It also reflects the problem of the historical actualisation of rational legal principles and in this context becomes a philosophy of compromise and reform. As such it forms a pragmatic synthesis of Hobbesian political reality and Rousseauan democratic justice. It does not banish reason to a suprahistorical utopia nor does it identify it with current political realities. Kant understands that right, freedom, and reason can be achieved only under the conditions of the historical world. A normative political philosophy with practical concerns must engage the existing power relationships to find a starting point for nonviolent change, to make them republican and reform them according to the principles of rational right. The politics of reform is always a compromise of transition, and a political philosophy of reform must be both firm in principle and pragmatically prudent.

Compromise and reform go together. A compromising republicanism results in a strange republic, a simulation of democracy and contract in the government of states which have arisen out of violence and have no democratic justification. True republican rule means legislation authorised by an assembly representing the united will of all citizens, and authority based on a division of powers. Kant's concept of republicanism unites experience, prudence, and hope. It gives the citizens the benefits of a republic while leaving power to the autocrats. At the same time it assumes that illegitimate domination arising from force and violence cannot in the long term withstand the spirit of republicanism and that it will one day freely yield to true republicanism and the rule of law. But where the ruler refuses to reform or listen to criticism from the public and intellectuals, sometimes even stifling adverse criticism by censorship, Kant can only advise citizens whose right to freedom is so restricted to hope and wait for better times. Revolution and resistance by force are not part of his philosophy.

Although Kant welcomes the improvement of state policy on rights, he does not recognise the rights of revolution, insurrection, or resistance. Injustice condoned by law and an absence of civil rights do not, for him, justify political disobedience. The legal justification of resistance and rebellion is impossible, the traditional right of resistance a contradiction in terms. On the one hand it makes the people judges of their own cause, contrary to the logic of political jurisdiction, while on the other it implies a return to the lawlessness of the natural condition. Any form of resistance, be it insurrection, mutiny, or revolution, threatens the order of the state, which guarantees the possibility of peaceful coexistence. Revolution in particular – for obvious reasons the empirical background to Kant's remarks – is the supreme sin against the rightful state and the citizens' right to live in peace. For him, progressive violence is unthinkable. The revolutionaries who argue that 'when constitutions are bad it is up to the people to reshape them by force and to be unjust once and for all so that afterwards they can establish legal justice all the more securely and make it flourish' may be driven by the highest motives but their actions cannot be justified.[42] Right can be improved only by methods that are themselves right, that is, by reform and republicanisation.

V. KANT ON PERPETUAL PEACE

No account of Kant's political philosophy is complete that does not take account of his theory of the highest political good, perpetual peace.[43] The central theme of his philosophy of right is the transition from a situation allowing only provisional and insecure legal relationships to one providing human rights in conditions of security and general acceptance. These are imperative requirements for a realisation of the juridical order dictated by pure practical reason; they share the categorical obligatory force of natural law and must not be confused with instrumentalities or useful institutions. We are absolutely obliged to support the establishment and maintenance of these conditions which secure our rights. We owe them to one another by virtue of our natural right of freedom. Just as our freedom of action may be restricted by right through general laws, so we have a right to conditions making possible a lawgiving and law-enforcing authority. Therefore, human beings have a right to a state, a legal system, and a republican constitution. By virtue of their humanity and their shared existence on Earth they also possess a natural right to an international republican order of peace. If every state had an internally just constitution, guaranteeing the natural and acquired rights of its citizens, and if the rights of each state, derived from these, were secured by a just international order, then the transition from provisional rights to absolute rights would be complete and the threat of the lawless state of nature would vanish. No philosopher has ever presented a more ambitious concept of human rights. It far transcends standard liberal theories of individual rights and the civil rights of political participation. It embraces both these and in addition a utopian dimension of legally secure membership of a world community. If natural human right fully realises its normative implications, it will consistently manifest itself in a right to justice within the state and between states, and as a right to global peace. Practical reason, in thus seeking perpetual peace, shows itself to be not dreaming but logically consistent.

Kant's concept of peace is very different from Hobbes's. Kant hopes to control states in their natural condition by law and so achieve peace; Hobbes seeks only to administer the state of nature between nations. His concept of peace makes use of the same elements which support humankind in the state of nature in their struggle for survival, that is, armed distrust and recognition of the need to distrust others. If neutrality is to be established among nations, even inadequate instruments for peace must be brought into play; the key is to make breaches of neutrality so expensive that they profit no one. The central theme here is that of deterrence, in which the logic of distrust drives a spiralling arms race. Kant's vision is not one of mutual paralysis through effective deterrence. His aim is the cooperative management of conflict through established and universally accepted procedures and institutions in a global order of justice. It is not a formal, ethically neutral concept but a substantive and ethically determined one. Its end is not just a state of nonviolence but a secular definition of true peace generated and formed by justice. The first requirement for this is the international acceptance of the rule of law. All conflicts between states must be mediated through an international organisation for justice established for that purpose. Secondly, the position of every state in the international legal order is determined on human rights principles. Each state is legally entitled to act as it wishes, provided that it does not thereby infringe the same right of other states. Here is no social idyll, with wolves and lambs lying down together. Kant was well aware of the social tensions among human beings and their part in the manifold achievements of cultural evolution.

In describing peace as the highest political good Kant lays himself open to pacifist misinterpretation. If a pacifist is one who seeks peace at all costs and totally rejects the use of force, then Kant is no pacifist. Peace is the highest political good not because it has absolute priority over all others but because it offers the best opportunity for realising the political values of freedom and justice. Kant's point is that practical reason should strive for peace, freedom, and justice simultaneously, because they require and complete each other.

VI. THE SOCIAL CONTRACT OF JEAN-JACQUES ROUSSEAU

Despite persistent conservatism, if not because of it, an economic and cultural progressivism existed in eighteenth-century Europe. People were aware that the various processes of economic, social, and cultural modernisation had transformed them into creatures of interests and rationality, without the strict moral code or the social ties of their forebears. They knew that the ethical solidity and security of earlier generations had given way to a fragile morality and shrewd expansionist strategies. They clearly recognised the concomitant problems of social security and integration, but were mostly optimistic in believing that these could be solved by reason and autonomy. They were also proud of modern achievements, especially in technology and economics. They relied on the efficient machinery of state, on the balance of trade, and hoped for similar cultural and ethical advances. They had a positive attitude to modern culture.

Rousseau is the century's great dissident.[44] He opposed this consensus on the achievements of modern civilisation, he took the new liberal politics and the new capitalist economics to task, and he denounced the growing gap between civilisation and nature as waste, decay, and ethical degeneracy. This is the basis for his fame. From his well-known discourses of 1750 and 1755 his contemporaries could learn that modernity has its price and that progress entails ethical and social costs. In thus questioning the experiment of modernity Rousseau provided the script for all later generations of social critics. In his first award-winning *Discours sur les sciences et les arts* Rousseau argues that advances in science and the arts have destroyed social cohesion and increased competitiveness. This modern combination of technological progress, artistic refinement, economic capitalism, and the morality of rational self-interest, which 'all our Writers regard [as] the crowning achievement of our century's politics', corrupts human nature. It teaches men to consider avarice and ambition as natural and to satisfy those selfish passions and interests by serving the needs of others, thus thickening the social web of commerce and reciprocal dependence.[45] The modern competitive market society is characterised by being nonpolitical and amoral. There are no longer citizens but only bourgeois, partners in an exchange of goods and abilities, private individuals making use of one another. In his second *Discours sur l'origine et les fondements de l'inégalité parmi les hommes*, Rousseau develops a negative philosophy of history, interpreting social development and the socialisation of humanity as a falling away from nature and as moral degeneration. He views contemporary contractarianism as the ideology of an unjust, unpolitical society, reinforcing inequality and quite incapable of the formation of a genuine common will. For him Locke's compact is a contract of illusion and deception used by the wealthy as an efficient instrument for promoting their interests. The poor, who obviously are not in the least interested in perpetuating a system of social and economic inequality which deprives them of all rights, are misled by a deliberately false representation of the interests involved and are used to secure a social and economic order diametrically opposed to their interests. In this Rousseau is anticipating Marx's critique of formal law, which is inevitably always the privilege of the wealthy and propertied classes, a means of perpetuating the class system and ensuring the rule of the *beati possidentes*.

In his *Du contrat social ou Principes du droit politique* Rousseau outlines an alternative to prevailing social and economic conditions.[46] He sketches a society not destroyed by the rivalry and competition of private material interests but comprising a body of virtuous and politically alert citizens, and a state ruled by justice, in which power is exercised not by parties and classes but by the whole body of citizens. Rousseau's political philosophy is concerned with just rule founded on contract. Whereas in the second *Discours* the state of nature is contrasted with contemporary society seen as another Fall of Man, the *Contrat social* shares the view common to all modern theories of contract, that the state of nature must be abandoned and a sociopolitical order must be established. But Rousseau is not happy with the available versions of contract theory. Hobbes's contract seems to him just as unlawful as Pufendorf's dualism of social contract and contract of subjection. He finds even Locke's trust solution unacceptable. All these, in one way or another, violate the fundamental human right of freedom. None has satisfactorily solved the basic political problem of how 'to find a form of association that will defend and protect the person and goods of each associate with the full common force, and by means of which each, uniting with all, nevertheless obey only himself and remain as free as before'.[47]

Freedom requires more than a government decree to protect the contractual rights of individuals by enforcement of general laws. In Rousseau's view people have the right not only to equal freedom and to a life under universal laws; they also have the right to autonomy and self-rule. This significantly increases the legitimate demands made on a political system, for nothing less is required than the establishment of an absolute, universally legislating will, free of all normative restrictions, without dismantling the inalienable right to self-rule of the individual. How can this requirement be met? What conceivable system of government can preserve such a right to material self-determination inviolate?

> The clauses of this contract are so completely determined by the nature of the act that the slightest modification would render them null and void . . .
>
> These clauses, rightly understood, all come down to just one, namely the total alienation of each associate, with all of his rights to the whole community: For, in the first place, since each gives himself entirely, the condition is equal for all, and since the condition is equal for all, no one has any interest in making it burdensome to the rest.
>
> Moreover, since the alienation is made without reservation, the union is as perfect as it can be, and no associate has anything further to claim: For, if individuals were left some rights, then, since there would be no common superior who might adjudicate between them and the public, each, being judge in his own case on some issue, would soon claim to be so on all, the state of nature would subsist . . .
>
> Finally, each, by giving himself to all, gives himself to no one, and since there is no associate over whom one does not acquire the same right as one grants him over oneself, one gains the equivalent of all one loses, and more force to preserve what one has.
>
> If, then, one sets aside everything that is not of the essence of the social compact, one finds that it can be reduced to the following terms: *Each of us puts his person and his full power in common under the supreme direction of the general will; and in a body we receive each member as an indivisible part of the whole.* (3: 360–1)

The act of alienation, for Rousseau as for Hobbes, marks the beginning of authoritarian rule, the birth of sovereignty. It is a legal creation, possessing no legal existence apart from those contractual relationships of individuals which produced it. The distinguishing feature of Rousseau's *Contrat social* is that in it the contracting community itself assumes sovereignty. Through the political chemistry of the social contract the act of alienation transforms the aggregative and distributive community into a collective unity of wills. The sum of the many separate individual wills becomes a political unity with a single general will.

The Rousseauan social contract is the symbol of a democratic self-organisation of society in which every individual shares in both the rights of a ruler and the duties of a subject. Moreover, it is the symbol of a political republican community, integrated both by the modern formal law of equality and by a binding common vision of the good. Its coherence is founded on an equality which does not tolerate the distinctions of liberal society. Through this alienation

> the social pact establishes among the Citizens an equality such that all commit themselves under the same conditions and must all enjoy the same rights. Thus by the nature of the pact every act of sovereignty . . . obligates or favors all Citizens equally, so that the Sovereign knows only the body of the nation and does not single out any one of those who make it up. (3: 374)

Liberal contractarianism assumes that the authoritative model of a well-ordered society can be adequately described in the language of rights. Rousseau, paradoxically, dismissed this premise and enlarged the legal model of rule by including the democratic model, because he was convinced that only a democratic process of legislation, based on the equal participation of all citizens, could guarantee justice. In this way the negative concept of freedom is integrated into a positive concept, based on participation, the internalisation of experienced communal values, and the affective sense of belonging. This complete change of political semantics takes place within the conceptual framework of contract theory. In Rousseau's paradoxical dream republican intuitions are spelt out in the vocabulary of liberal contractarianism.

The sovereignty established by the Rousseauan contract of total alienation has four distinct characteristics: it is inalienable, irreplaceable, indivisible, and infallible. These are direct consequences of the contract which in itself follows from the descriptive and normative requirements of the state of nature. Sovereignty manifests itself in the operation of the general will which alone

> can direct the forces of the State according to the end of its institution, which is the common good: for while the opposition of particular interests made the establishment of societies necessary, it is the agreement of these same interests which made it possible. What these different interests have in common is what forms the social bond, and if there were not some point on which all interests agree, no society could exist. Now it is solely in terms of this common interest that society ought to be governed. (3: 368)

Sovereignty expresses itself in legislation. Only the nation as a whole can decide for the whole nation. Autonomy allows no representation, not even the representation of the whole by the majority. The *volonté générale* is infallible; Rousseau has so designed it that it *must* be infallible. If all share equally in its formation and it appears only in unanimous decisions, it must necessarily promote the general good.

Rousseau's concept of the general will is irritatingly ambiguous, straining the categorical framework of contractarianism. If the republican aspect of life under the general will is stressed, then the contract proves itself a completely unsuitable model of socialisation for it has always been a convincing symbol of modern, individualistic, state-protected, unpolitical society. If the democratic aspect of Rousseau's republic is stressed, then contract seems to be short-hand for a process for guaranteeing justice. In the history of the political philosophy of the social contract, Rousseau opens the chapter of democratic contractarianism. He is the founder of a procedural concept of justice which makes the justice of laws dependent on their democratic origin and elevates free democratic deliberation to guardian of the law. He turned egalitarian contractarianism into a procedure that was constitutive of justice and the rule of law.

Rousseau's political philosophy has many faces. Its idea of contract puts it beside modern liberalism; it no longer recognises a teleological nature but starts from normative individualism and takes its direction from the Hobbesian concept of sovereignty. Its strong emphasis on individual autonomy is one of the ideological foundations of the French Revolution. Its plebiscitary ideal of democracy continues to sustain the critics of politically fossilised and ethically barren liberal democracy. But its heart is republican, not liberal. It carries on the discourse of virtue abandoned by contemporary liberalism. Its understanding of citizenship resembles that of Aristotle or Machiavelli, not of Locke. The liberal fondness for social differentiation is here replaced by support for a high level of social and cultural homogeneity, which fosters identity and coherence. Rousseau replaces liberal individualism with a republican communitarianism which views individuals as social beings and reinforces their community spirit by suitable educational and political measures. Social integration is not enforced from without, as in liberalism, by means of a compulsory legal system and the exchange mechanism of the market, but from within, through virtue, political commitment, and identification with the general will. In the century which saw the rise of liberalism, Rousseau developed the great communitarian, republican alternative. His political philosophy is equally well adapted to inspire and radicalise the democratic tendencies of modern politics and to act as a reactionary opposition to liberalism, casting doubt on the self-assurance of prevailing conceptual forms of political modernism.

VII. MONTESQUIEU'S POLITICAL THEORY

As a young man Montesquieu had emphatically declared himself to be a *cartésien rigide*, but his mature political thought shows him to be strongly influenced methodologically by Aristotle. The rationalism of his time did not impress him and contractarianism was an inappropriate conceptual frame for his sphere of interest. Just as Aristotle, in his *Politics*, combines descriptive and analytical examination of constitutions, institutions, and forms of government with clear evaluations, so, too, Montesquieu's *Esprit des lois* does not deal merely with the political sociology of democracy, aristocracy, and monarchy. It is also a normative treatise on old freedoms, endangered by new absolute monarchies, and their control by a cunning, cleverly thought-out system of checks and balances, influenced by the English constitution, which takes up the classical concept of *regimen mixtum*. By temperament Montesquieu was politically conservative, mistrusting people and their ability to make sensible political changes. The revolutionary approach of the innovator, creator, and planner was contrary to his nature and political experience. His vision of social and political harmony is illuminated and illustrated by physical and mechanistic metaphors and analogies from seventeenth-century thought.

> What is called union in a political body is a very ambiguous thing: true unity is a harmonious union which brings all parties, however opposed to each other they may seem, together for the general good of society, just as dissonances in music combine in the general harmony. Thus there can be union in a state where one would expect only confusion, that is to say, harmony leading to happiness, which alone is true peace. In this it is like the parts of the universe itself, eternally linked by the action of some and the reaction of others.[48]

The structure of political unities is very complex; no one can reliably master the patterns of social harmony. The physics of human and social forces, and their antagonisms and cooperation, is incalculable: 'One can never know what will be the result of any change one makes.'[49] Therefore, '*Bleib im Lande und nähr dich redlich*', or as Montesquieu paraphrases this old German saying, 'The best government of all is ordinarily that under which one lives, and a sensible man should love it; for, as it is impossible to change it without changing manners and customs, I do not see, given the extreme shortness of life, what use it would be for men to abandon in all respects the habits they have adopted' (1: 1153).

It is instructive and illuminating to compare Montesquieu with another, considerably more influential French constitutional theorist, born in 1748, the year when *Esprit des lois* first appeared, who, in his famous satire *Qu'est ce que le Tiers Etat?*, wrote:

> We shall never understand social machinery unless we examine a society as though it were an ordinary machine. It is necessary to consider each part of it separately, and then link them all together in the mind in due order, to see how they fit together and hear the general harmony that necessarily follows. We need not embark on so extensive a task here. But, since one must always be clear, and since one is not clear unless one expounds from first principles, we shall at least ask the reader to distinguish three periods in the making of a political society, and these distinctions will pave the way for such explanation as is necessary.[50]

Although Sieyès, like Montesquieu, calls upon the harmony of the whole and apostrophises political thought as a mereological theory of harmony, whose task is the examination of the proper relationship between the whole and the parts, his conception could scarcely differ more widely from Montesquieu's, for Sieyès opts for principles whereas Montesquieu looks for facts and experience. In Sieyès we find the conviction, so characteristic of revolutionaries, that human communities can be planned and constructed on rational and principled foundations. He espouses a political scientism which sees social policy as a scholarly version of a joint stock company, protecting the interests and liberties of all. On the one hand we have the progressive creator, the student of laws, the political engineer, and on the other the careful guardian, the prudent administrator, who greatly distrusts all a priori thinking, is convinced of the risks of change, and fears the power of accidents and unforeseen circumstances.

In his *Esprit des lois* Montesquieu develops a political sociology which describes the institutions of democracy, aristocracy, and monarchy and considers their stability and the chances of their success or corruption.[51] Montesquieu's concept of law can be reduced neither to positive law nor to constitutional law; it embraces the whole complex chemistry of a democratic, aristocratic, or monarchical society – the specific concatenation of passions, interests, and virtues; of constitutional laws and administrative methods; of customs and morals; history; tradition; and geography. For Montesquieu the central principle of democracy, its moving and integrating force, is virtue, whereas monarchy adopts the modern method of legal regulation.

In monarchies, politics accomplishes great things with as little virtue as it can, just as in the finest machines art employs as few motions, forces, and wheels as possible.

The state continues to exist independently of love of the homeland, desire for true glory, self-renunciation, sacrifice of one's dearest interests, and all those heroic virtues we find in the ancients . . .

The laws replace all these virtues, for which there is no need; the state excuses you from them: here an action done noiselessly is in a way inconsequential.[52]

Montesquieu feared that monarchy would become the political model of the future and that the virtuous political citizen would die out and vanish. Of the citizens of the ancient republics he says that they 'were bound together by all sorts of ties', whereas

today, all this has been abolished . . . each man is isolated. It seems that the natural effect of arbitrary power is to particularise all interests. Yet the links that detach a man from himself and attach him to others lead to noble actions. Without this all is vulgar and all that is left is a base interest which is really just the animal instinct common to all men. (Pensée 604; *Oeuvres* 1: 1130)

He diagnoses the depoliticising effects of modernity and of the growing influence of commerce on human thought and action and thus anticipates fundamental themes in Rousseau's social criticism (Pensée 1228; *Oeuvres* 1: 1306). Unlike Rousseau, however, he does not outline a republican society based on contract, but, as a political realist, devotes himself to present dangers, the danger of a constantly increasing autocratic power, the danger of an absolutist state which would level out and destroy all social and political complexity and would reduce the rich chemistry of society to a flat asymmetry between absolute power and the subject masses.

In his battle against the uniform political monism of the absolute state, Montesquieu anticipates the twentieth-century critique of totalitarianism. His central concern is the preservation of complexity, for only by maintaining a political system can freedom be secured. Despotism with its structural simplicity will suffocate freedom. A complex political system is supported by a moderate government resembling the *regimen mixtum* of the ancients. At the heart of its constitution is a specific form of the separation of powers, which has nothing in common with modern ideas.[53] 'To form a moderate government it is necessary to combine powers, temper them, make them work and regulate them; that is, to provide ballast for one to enable it to withstand another. This is a masterpiece of legislation which chance rarely produces and prudence is seldom given the opportunity to create' (Pensée 1794; *Oeuvres* 1: 1429). Montesquieu develops his famous theory of the separation of powers in *Esprit des lois*, Bk II, ch. 6, where he outlines a complex system of balances between political and social forces.[54] The common people, the nobility, and the king are mutually held in check by an ingenious distribution of responsibilities, so that none can achieve supremacy. His concern is to give all political groups of the corporate society a share in the exercise of power by a distribution of legislative and executive authority and so to commit them to the need for a reconciliation of interests and political compromise. An interconnected system of powers of decision-making and veto produces a high degree of interdependence. It creates a very complex constitutional structure, requiring balance and reconciliation, which works like a filter in the development of a politically informed opinion and allows only decisions taken in common to pass. Montesquieu is a political thinker of the same type as Machiavelli and Tocqueville and not a political philosopher in search of normative principles with eternal validity. His goal is to secure acquired freedoms, to stabilise corporate society in the face of the growing danger of absolute monarchy. His constitutional order is directed against absolute rule, a monarchy striving for limitless power. Its elaborate structure of interconnected responsibilities spreads like a web over the whole of corporate society and allows no single power to acquire the uncontrolled and Leviathan-like authority so destructive of freedom.

VIII. THE FEDERALIST

Publius, that is, the authors of the *Federalist Papers*, deserve a place beside Montesquieu and Rousseau, as representatives of eighteenth-century republicanism.[55] The eighty-five essays on the constitutional proposals of the Philadelphia Convention, written by Alexander Hamilton, John Jay, and James Madison in the post-Revolution years 1787–8, use republican language. They deal with characteristic republican themes, the corruption and prosperity of communities, the disastrous influence of factions and how best to counter it, the passions harmful to society and the virtues that restrain them, and the importance of publicly conducted politics and a committed body of citizens. The Federalist's proposals are not based on natural law principles but on a republican anthropology, a view of human nature described in the republican language of passion and virtue. 'But what is government itself but the greatest of all reflections on human nature?'[56] Republican self-government seems to them a political system fair to humankind, controlling its inherent dangers and strengthening its virtues. Only this system is compatible 'with the genius of the people of America; with the fundamental principles of the Revolution; or with that honourable determination which animates every votary of freedom, to rest all our political experiments on the capacity of mankind for self-government' (Madison, No. 39, p. 190). Nevertheless, outstanding political ability is still required to establish such a political order of self-government and to consolidate it constitutionally. While for Rousseau the legislator was a quasi-divine figure, whose role was to rescue human beings corrupted by modern society, to restore their general and political ability, their moral and virtuous character, through a suitable constitution, appropriate laws, and education, the Federalists undoubtedly saw themselves in the role of lawgiver and *nomothete*. They saw themselves as heirs of the classical legislators, American descendants of Solon and Lycurgus, Theseus, Romulus, and Numa, believing that the American task of self-organization by popular consent parallelled in world history the classical achievement in which alone 'government has been established with deliberation and consent' (No. 38, p. 182).

The most interesting constitutional developments of federal republicanism were a system of checks and balances and various measures designed to tame the ambitions of leaders of factions and to strengthen the virtues of citizens.

> The aim of every political constitution is, or ought to be, first to obtain for rulers men who possess most wisdom to discern, and most virtue to pursue, the common good of the society; and in the next place, to take the most effectual precautions for keeping them virtuous whilst they continue to hold their public trust. The elective mode of obtaining rulers is the characteristic policy of republican government. (No. 57, p. 291)

This leads to a system of representation which, through its qualitative recruiting mechanism, discovers and brings to political responsibility citizens dedicated to the common good. It thus serves 'to refine and enlarge the public views, by passing them through the medium of a chosen body of citizens, whose wisdom may best discern the true interest of their country, and whose patriotism and love of justice will be least likely to sacrifice it to temporary or partial considerations' (No. 10, p. 45).

The political thinking of the *Federalist* resembles a tapestry with varying systematic and historical motifs. There is a strong republican pattern with its unmistakable characteristics, the orientation towards the common good, and the distrust of factions and ambitious partisans, but there is also recognition of the compelling structure of the modern spirit of commerce and its individualising and disruptive effects. What we find is the pattern of modern contractarianism, although the *Federalist* develops no strict contractual argument, which would in any case be inappropriate to the character of the papers. There are, however, clear echoes of the consensual language of the social compact: 'The fabric of American empire ought to rest on the solid basis of THE CONSENT OF THE PEOPLE. The streams of national power ought to flow immediately from the pure, original fountain of all legitimate authority'; the 'genius of republican liberty' demanded both that 'all power should be derived from the people' and that its exercise should be regarded as the discharge of a trust subject to a system of careful checks and controls; here the tones of Locke and Montesquieu are unmistakable.[57]

IX. DAVID HUME, ADAM SMITH, JEREMY BENTHAM, AND EDMUND BURKE

'Whether man in the state of nature is as meek as a lamb or as vicious as a tiger is a question to be decided by the anthropologist. It does not concern the natural lawyer.'[58] He is just as little interested in whether historical states originated in contractual agreements or in acts of violence. Later German natural law, influenced by Kant's methodologically assured philosophy, learned to distinguish *quaestiones facti* from *quaestiones juris*. Before Kant, natural law contractarianism too often confused matters of historical origin with those of legitimacy and validity. Locke and the German natural law contractarians, in particular, always viewed contract theory as a richly descriptive social evolutionary thesis, thus making things very easy for the opponents of contractarianism.[59] The most substantial philosophical critique of eighteenth-century social contract theory was provided in 1748 by David Hume in his famous essay 'Of the Original Contract'. 'We must necessarily allow', given the nearly equal physical and mental equipment of men, 'that nothing but their own consent could, at first, associate them together, and subject them to any authority'.[60] This brings to mind Hobbes who, appealing to the equality of humankind, declared the establishment of a lasting natural system of rule to be an impossibility, thus opening the way for contractual socialisation. Even if, at the beginning of human social history, unforced agreement may have occurred, yet in the growing complexity of social and political conditions, the contract as an instrument of social coordination and political legitimation was increasingly driven out by ruthless power. 'Almost all the governments, which exist at present, or of which there remains any record in story, have been founded originally, either on usurpation or conquest, or both, without any pretence of a fair consent, or voluntary subjection of the people' (471).

The reaction to this irrefutable diagnosis was the makeshift hypothesis that silent acquiescence indicated consent. This was equally unacceptable to Hume: even unspoken consent must contain an element of free will. Agreement must be indicated by a free action: but, faced with the oppressive and inescapable conditions in which most people have always had to live, it is not only logically dubious but also a deplorable exercise in cynicism and counterfeit morality to equate necessity with freedom.

> Can we seriously say, that a poor peasant or artizan has a free choice to leave his country, when he knows no foreign language or manners, and lives from day to day, by the small wages which he acquires? We may as well assert, that a man, by remaining in a vessel, freely consents to the dominion of the master; though he was carried on board while asleep, and must leap into the ocean, and perish, the moment he leaves her. (476)[61]

For Hume 'a more philosophical refutation of this principle of an original contract' is of greater systematic significance.[62] This rests on his empirical theory of duty and obligation, in which duties belonging to the legal sphere are traced back to an empirically demonstrable and comprehensible interest, thus rendering unnecessary the contract as a basis of obligation. Now interest assumes a double role, both in explaining the origins of sociopolitical associations and as basis for the effective and valid interrelationships of rights and duties which operate in them. The philosophical point of Hume's critique of contractarianism is that the contract is unnecessary. The interest which, according to the contractual argument, is the motive for acceding to the contract and influences agreement to its provisions is released from the viselike grip of obligation theory and claimed as the direct authority for the foundation of the state and its institutions. This anti-contractarianism was strengthened further by the first utilitarian systems outlined by John Austin and Jeremy Bentham. Commenting on the contractarianism 'of the newer German philosophy', especially that of Kant and the Kantians, Austin remarks, 'Warmly admiring German literature and profoundly respecting German scholarship, I cannot but regret the proneness of German philosophy to vague and misty abstraction'. And Bentham, who contemptuously dismissed talk of human rights, natural rights, and natural law, considers the original contract as a 'sandy foundation' and a 'fable' invented by 'Whig lawyers'.[63] When utilitarianism penetrated every branch of practical philosophy, contract theory was effectively banished from the English philosophical scene.

Nevertheless, the social contract model was employed by the empiricists for their political theory, but as a metaphor of social coherence and an allegory of the fundamental pattern of social integration rather than as a descriptive claim concerning the origins of states, a norm of rational law, or the normative internal structure of the general will. 'The only true and natural foundations of society are the wants and the fears of individuals' and not any contract between individuals and a particular form of government.

But though society had not it's [sic] formal beginning from any convention of individuals, actuated by their wants and their fears: yet it is the sense of their weakness and imperfection that keeps mankind together; that demonstrates the necessity of this union; and that therefore is the solid and natural foundation, as well as the cement, of society. And this is what we mean by the original contract of society; which, though perhaps in no instance it has ever been formally expressed at the first institution of a state, yet in nature and reason must always be understood and implied, in the very act of associating together: namely, that the whole should protect all it's [sic] parts, and that every part should pay obedience to the will of the whole.[64]

Blackstone here employs the idea of the social contract against the revolutionary intentions of radicalism and apriorism, a conservative application taken up again by Edmund Burke towards the close of the century. In his *Reflections on the Revolution in France*, with the acute awareness of an uneasy conservative, he lays bare the alliance of revolution, human rights, and abstract contractarianism so characteristic of the democratic strain in eighteenth-century thought and, in a strangely distorted apotheosis of contract theory, transforms the voluntary contract based on natural law into an ontological principle of coherence embracing all creation.

Society is indeed a contract. Subordinate contracts for objects of mere occasional interest may be dissolved at pleasure – but the state ought not to be considered as nothing better than a partnership agreement in a trade of pepper and coffee, calico, or tobacco. . . . It is to be looked on with other reverence, because it is not a partnership in things subservient only to the gross animal existence of a temporary and perishable nature. It is a partnership in all science; a partnership in all art; a partnership in every virtue and in all perfection. As the ends of such a partnership cannot be obtained in many generations, it becomes a partnership not only between those who are living, but between those who are living, those who are dead, and those who are to be born. Each contract of each particular state is but a clause in the great primeval contract of eternal society, linking the lower with the higher natures, connecting the visible and invisible world, according to a fixed compact sanctioned by the inviolable oath which holds all physical and all moral natures, each in their appointed place.'[65]

At a time when a contract theory based on natural law was becoming a political reality, Burke takes up the idea and polemically transforms it into a metaphor of cosmological partnership, into an ontological, constitutional principle of an ordered and strictly ordained creation.[66] For modern contractarianism it was in the idea of contract itself that concepts of the state as the work of humankind and of the possibility of rationally creating political relationships were concentrated. Burke, in contrast, integrates contract into a way of thinking which seeks to cancel the boundaries drawn between natural and established order and to engraft the state into a pre-existing and all-embracing order. Against the revolutionary principle of rationally reorganising circumstances, he sets the binding nature of convention and humankind's devotion to tradition.

The German disciples of Burke adopted this line of argument. As advocates of empirically based theory and in agreement with Savigny's historical school of law, they rejected all apriorism and all abstract principles of reason. They regarded Kant's metaphysics of law and its *contractus originarius* as a revolutionary theory. They feared rational contractarianism because it tended to demand realisation through revolution. For them the rationally pure, radical contract was the symbol of democratic revolution, Jacobinism turned into a principle. Advocates of the law of reason were suspected of sympathising with the revolution: 'The philosopher forms systems out of which the mob forges weapons for murder. No sword is more terrible than a general principle in the hands of an ignorant person. . . . A state which uses declarations of rights as instruments of government is arming its subjects against itself.'[67]

While contractarianism is either giving an empirically false account of the origin of human societies, institutions, and systems of government or, in a narrative guise, developing an a priori normative argument based on natural law principles, Hume offers an empirical thesis of social evolution, which, on empirical anthropological grounds, explains the motives of socialisation and highlights its internal structure and dynamics.[68] We thus arrive at a very different type of political philosophy. Instead of contractarianism and natural law we have empirical anthropology and sociology. Arguments concerning the theory of legitimation no longer make use of natural rights and contractual promissory obligations, but talk of the general utility of social and political institutions, especially positive law and political rule. Institutional regulation is seen as a utilitarian invention. Hume's political philosophy outlines a political system entirely inherent in history and whose standards of legitimacy must likewise be developed in a historical context and ultimately be founded on the basic interests of humankind.

No natural or rational norms have eternal validity. For the empiricist such claims, concerning the existence of natural rights, normative principles of pure law-giving reason, and human rights deriving solely from the possession of human nature, are simply 'nonsense upon stilts'.[69] Naturally Hume values individual liberty and the possibilities for its development but he is opposed to the ideas of natural law and human rights. Liberty is for him a basic human interest and as such must be artificially controlled. His political philosophy ascribes great importance to political institutions: indeed it is mainly a theory of institutions, an interest-based constitutionalism which embraces all moral, social, and political institutions. Its foundation is anthropological and epistemological: human beings need institutions and their socialisation can succeed only if it is stabilised by a network of institutions, reconciling competing interests, controlling the forces of egoism, promoting cooperation in society, and limiting and controlling the necessary political power by a system of laws and constitutional regulations.

It must here be asserted, that the commerce and intercourse of mankind, which are of such mighty advantage, can have no security where men pay no regard to their engagements. In like manner, may it be said, that men could not live at all in society, at least in a civilized society, without laws and magistrates and judges, to prevent the encroachments of the strong upon the weak, of the violent upon the just and equitable.[70]

The remedy for men's plight in the world is not derived from nature, but from artifice or, more properly speaking, from inventive prudence. Nature, in judgement and understanding, provides a remedy for what is irregular, troublesome, and dangerous in the affections: institutions are the prudent response to the natural weaknesses of human beings in society.

This institutional structure mirrors human needs, historical experience, and problems, in that it can be altered and improved. Its instrumental rationality can be increased and it can better accommodate the needs of humankind. There is no end to this process of improving these institutional contrivances; it always remains provisory. On this philosophical foundation, with its epistemological basis of scepticism, its rational defeatism and ethical noncognitivism, neither apriorist élan nor revolutionary vision will flourish: it will support only a conservative caution, preserving the well-tried and mistrusting the new.[71]

Did one generation of men go off the stage at once, and another succeed, as is the case with silk-worms and butterflies, the new race, if they had sense enough to choose their government, which surely is never the case with men, might voluntarily, and by general consent, establish their own form of civil polity, without any regard to the laws or precedents, which prevailed among their ancestors. But as human society is in perpetual flux, one man every hour going out of the world, another coming into it, it is necessary, in order to preserve stability in government, that the new brood should conform themselves to the established constitution, and nearly follow the path which their fathers, treading in the footsteps of theirs, had marked out to them.[72]

Enlightened human interest is the absolute guideline for all private and political conduct, the institutional requirement for successful social cooperation with thoughtful interest. This is also the foundation of political authority and the political obedience of all the citizens. 'The general obligation, which binds us to government, is the interest and necessities of society; and this obligation is very strong' (486).

What Kant described as social unsociability also provides the focus of political anthropology for other eighteenth-century thinkers. Man is paradoxically structured, full of tension; in him an 'original desire to please and an original aversion to offend his brethren' oppose one another.[73] Adam Smith, like all empirical theorists, renounces the elaborate arguments of contractarianism; no concept of a state of nature but simple knowledge of human nature provides the necessary reasons for a legal system and a state administration. Since Smith, unlike Rousseau and Kant, is no advocate of human rights apriorism, he must appeal to the fact of human interest as the basis for his outline of a legal theory. Rights are to be socially and politically protected as general human interests; the more basic the interest to be legally protected, the more important, valuable, and significant the right is.[74]

Unlike dogmatic classic liberals, Smith recognizes that law is an insufficient means of social integration, and that the cement of society requires both moral and legal rules. But law is the most important system of norms; without legal precautions 'civil society would become a scene of bloodshed and disorder, every man revenging himself at his own hand whenever he fancied he was injured'.[75] The single most important task of the state is legal protection, ensuring nonviolent competition and guaranteeing compatible ways of life.

The wisdom of every state or commonwealth endeavours, as well as it can, to employ the force of the society to restrain those who are subject to its authority, from hurting or disturbing the happiness of one another. The rules which it establishes for this purpose, constitute the civil and criminal law of each particular state or country. (VI.ii, Introduction).

However, this conception of the rule of law has no a priori basis either, but is founded in anthropology. Without emphasising human rights, it shows how collective reason can intervene in society to further the interests of the social contract. This political theory is entirely empirical and may reasonably be seen as the forerunner of modern political science. Smith gives this scientific enterprise the title of *jurisprudence*. Its function is to produce politically useful knowledge addressed to politicians and so Smith also describes it as the 'science of the statesman or legislator'. The programme embraces, in greater detail,

> the study of politics, of the several systems of civil government, their advantages and disadvantages, of the constitution of our own country, its situation, and interest with regard to foreign nations, its commerce, its defence, the disadvantages it labours under, the dangers to which it may be exposed, how to remove the one, and how to guard against the other. (IV.i.11)[76]

Naturally Smith could not realise such an open-ended program, but the impressive basic features are clear: a realistic political theory for the world in which we actually live, but no value-neutral positivism. The rule of law, based on interest, and liberal welfarism are not called into question but, as a matter of course, retained as normative guidelines. The legislator who is the ideal addressee of Smith's science of politics is no professional power politician, no manipulator of competition, no tyrant or partisan abusing his power to serve his private interests. The ideal legislator is imbued with public spirit, inspired by the values outlined here; in fact he closely resembles the legislators of republican tradition. Like these, he finds his finest hour not in the day-to-day business of politics but at times of crisis and threatening anarchy. In such situations the existential flair of the true statesman will reveal itself.

> He may re-establish and improve the constitution, and from the very doubtful and ambiguous character of the leader of a party, he may assume the greatest and noblest of all characters, that of the reformer and legislator of a great state; and, by the wisdom of his institutions, secure the internal tranquillity and happiness of his fellow-citizens for many succeeding generations. (VI.ii.2.14)

Amazingly, Adam Smith, allegedly a propagandist of unrestricted capitalism, reveals himself as a republican in disguise and gives further proof of the close relationship between early liberalism and late republicanism in the anti-apriorist, empiricist thought of the eighteenth century. This description of the conversion of a party leader into a statesman, solely concerned for the common good and the welfare of all, closely resembles early republican accounts of the great legislator who, in times of crisis, discovered his true political task and left a solid tradition of statecraft as a legacy to his nation.[77]

Francis Hutcheson was the first to formulate the hedonistic principle of the greatest happiness of the greatest number but it was left to Jeremy Bentham to supply a systematic development of utilitarian moral and political philosophy in his *An Introduction to the Principles of Morals and Legislation* (1789). The history of utilitarianism as the great modern standard of moral philosophy begins with Bentham.[78] In his view human behaviour is governed by pleasure and pain and human beings seek to avoid situations and actions causing pain, while pursuing such as give pleasure. The normative reflection of this is the moral precept that pain should be avoided and pleasure promoted. Because there is no reason for supposing the interest and pleasure of one individual to be more valuable than that of another, all separate claims to happiness are of equal worth. Viewed against the background of contemporary feudal society this was a most revolutionary idea. It established a utilitarian normative perspective opposed to the motivational structure of self-interest, and provided moral norms not just for individual behaviour but also for political administration, legislation, and the design of social and political institutions. The utilitarian imperative of the maximisation of benefit was valid for all and all structures should be designed in such a way as to ensure the greatest possible benefit to the greatest possible number of people.

Bentham, when compared to his empiricist forerunners Hume and Smith, manifests a certain scientistic naïveté, akin to that of the utopian communities of the nineteenth century with their faith in science. Bentham, too, was influenced by the idea of utopian communities, scientifically and therefore infallibly directed and mechanical. Utilitarianism thus turns out to be the twin of human rights revolutionary theory. Both are doctrinaire concepts, secular ideologies of salvation, claiming to be able to design scientifically emancipating societies to rescue humanity, without any regard for history or tradition. While revolutionaries, believing in human beings as rational creatures, are guided by a priori normative assumptions, the student of the nature of man is concerned with fundamental human needs. He recognises no fundamental human rights. In Bentham's view, rights are social conventions, political instruments subject to the utilitarian calculus. He acknowledges no natural rights, which might restrict the utilitarian aim of increasing the benefits of the majority and limit the utilitarian dictatorship of that majority. His contemptuous dismissal of natural right discourse in his comment on the *French Declaration of the Rights of Man and of Citizens* is famous: 'Natural rights is simple nonsense: natural and imprescriptible rights, rhetorical nonsense – nonsense upon stilts'.[79]

NOTES

1 See Wolfgang Kersting, 'Die Logik des kontraktualistischen Arguments', in *Der Begriff der Politik*, ed. V. Gerhardt (Stuttgart, 1990), 216–37.

2 See Kersting, 'Der Kontraktualismus im deutschen Naturrecht', in *Das Europäische Naturrecht im ausgehenden 18. Jahrhundert*, eds. D. Klippel and O. Dann (Hamburg, 1994), 90–110. On eighteenth-century contractarianism as a whole see the relevant chapters in Otto Gierke, *Johannes Althusius und die Entwicklung der naturrechtlichen Staatstheorien* (Breslau, 1902); Simone Goyard-Fabre, *L'interminable querelle du contrat social* (Ottawa, 1983); Giuseppe Duso, *Il contratto*

sociale nelle filosofia politica moderna (Milan, 1993); and Kersting, *Die politische Philosophie des Gesellschaftsvertrags* (Darmstadt, 1994).

3 Gottfried Wilhelm Leibniz, *Monita quaedam ad Samuelis Pufendorfii Principia* (*Opera omnia*, ed. L. Dutens, Genf, 1789), IV.3.281: '. . . not much of a legal scholar and no philosopher at all.'

4 See Hans Wenzel, *Naturrecht und materiale Gerechtigkeit* (Göttingen, 1962); Christoph Link, *Herrschaftsordnung und bürgerliche Freiheit* (Vienna, 1979); Diethelm Klippel, *Politische Freiheit und Freiheitsrechte im deutschen Naturrecht des 18. Jahrhunderts* (Paderborn, 1976); Klippel, 'Naturrecht als politische Theorie: Zur politischen Bedeutung des deutschen Naturrechts im 18. und 19. Jahrhundert', in *Aufklärung als Politisierung – Politisierung der Aufklärung*, eds. H. E. Bödecker and U. Herrmann (Hamburg, 1987), 267–93.

5 See Wenzel, *Die socialitas als oberstes Prinzip der Naturrechtslehre Samuel Pufendorfs* (Heidelberg, 1930); Leonard Krieger, *The Politics of Discretion: Pufendorf and the Acceptance of Natural Law* (Chicago, 1965); Horst Denzer, *Moralphilosophie und Naturrecht bei Samuel Pufendorf: Eine geistes- und wissenschaftsgeschichtliche Untersuchung zur Geburt des Naturrechts aus der praktischen Philsophie* (Munich, 1972); Pierre Laurent, *Pufendorf et la loi naturelle* (Paris, 1982); Fiammetta Palladini, *Samuel Pufendorf discepolo di Hobbes: per una reinterpretazione del giusnaturalismo moderno* (Bologna, 1990); Vanda Fiorillo *Tra egoismo e socialità: il giusnaturalismo de Samuel Pufendorf* (Naples, 1992).

6 For Althusius' contractarianism, wrongly taken as the norm by Gierke, who consequently branded Hobbes, Locke, Rousseau, and Kant as dissidents, see Gierke, *Johannes Althusius*; see also Kersting, 'La dottrina del duplice contratto nel diritto naturale Tedesco', in *Filosofia politica*, 8 (1994): 409–37.

7 Johann Heinrich Gottlob von Justi, *Die Natur und das Wesen des Staates als Grundwissenschaft der Staatskunst, der Polizei und aller Regierungswissenschaft* (Berlin, Stettin, Leipzig, 1760), 48.

8 Carl Gottlieb Svarez, *Vorträge über Recht und Staat*, eds. H. Conrad and G. Kleinheyer (Köln, 1960), 461.

9 See Werner Schneiders, *Naturrecht und Liebesethik: Zur Geschichte der praktischen Philosophie im Hinblick auf Christian Thomasius* (Hildesheim, 1971).

10 Christian Thomasius, *Fundamenta juris naturae et gentium* (Halle, 1705), I.6.19–21.

11 Christian, Freiherr von Wolff, *Grundsätze des Natur- und Völckerrechts* (Halle, 1754), ed. M. Thomann, in *Werke*, I.19, §102. Concerning Wolff's natural law theory, see Hanns-Martin Bachmann, *Die naturrechtliche Staatslehre Christian Wolffs* (Berlin, 1977).

12 Wolff, *Jus naturae, methodo scientifica pertractatum*, ed. M. Thomann, in *Werke*, I.17–24, I: 23.

13 See, for example, Jean-Jacques Burlamaqui, *Principes du droit naturel et politique*, 2 vols. (1747–51), translated as The *Principles of Natural and Politic Law*, 2 vols., trans. T. Nugent, 2nd edn. (London, 1763), 1:74.

14 See Knud Haakonssen, 'From Natural Law to the Rights of Man: A European Perspective on American Debates' in *A Culture of Rights. The Bill of Rights in Philosophy, Politics, and Law – 1791 and 1991*, eds. M. J. Lacey and K. Haakonssen (Cambridge and New York, NY, 1991), 19–61.

15 August Ludwig von Schlözer, *Allgemeines StatsRecht und StatsVerfassungsLere* (Göttingen, 1793), 65.

16 See Richard Saage, 'August Ludwig Schlözer als politischer Theoretiker', in *Vertragsdenken und Utopie: Studien zur politischen Theorie und zur Sozialphilosophie der frühen Neuzeit* (Frankfurt am Main, 1989); Merio Scattola, *La nascità della scienze dello stato: August Ludwig Schlözer (1735–1809) e le discipline politiche del settecento tedesco* (Milan, 1994).

17 Wolff, *Jus naturae*, VIII.1.28, in *Werke* I.24; see his *Vernünfftige Gedancken von dem gesellschafftlichen Leben der Menschen* (Frankfurt, Leipzig, 1736), ed. H. W. Arndt, in *Werke*, I.5: 213.

18 Samuel Pufendorf, *De officio hominis et civis* (Lund, 1673), II.1.6.
19 Schlözer, 64: 'Familien Stand.' In spite of his early liberalism, Schlözer follows Pufendorf in describing the partners to the social contract as 'vollbürtige, also freie HausVäter', that is, socially and economically independent men presiding over their houses and exercising a sort of patronage over its members.
20 Pufendorf, *De jure naturae et gentium* (Lund, 1672), translated as *The Law of Nature and Nations*, 5th edn., trans. B. Kennet (London, 1749), VII.2.20.
21 Wolff, *Vernünfftige Gedancken*, 230.
22 See Kersting, *Thomas Hobbes* (Hamburg, 1992), 28–37, 148–59.
23 See Klippel, *Politische Freiheit*, 46.
24 See Kurt Wolzendorff, *Staatsrecht und Naturrecht in der Lehre vom Widerstandsrecht des Volkes gegen rechtswidrige Ausübung der Staatsgewalt. Zugleich ein Beitrag zur Entwicklungsgeschichte des modernen Staatsgedankens* (Breslau, 1916).
25 Ludwig Julius Friedrich Höpfner, *Naturrecht des einzelnen Menschen, der Gesellschaften und der Völker*, 3rd edn. (Giessen, 1785), 168, Anm. 4.
26 See Schneiders, 'Die Philosophie des aufgeklärten Absolutismus', in *Der Staat* 24, (1985): 383–406.
27 Wolff, 'Von den Regenten, die sich der Weltweisheit befleißigen, und von den Weltweisen, die das Regiment führen', in his *Gesammelte kleine philosophische Schriften*, in *Werke*, I.21.1–6; 21.6: §8.
28 Immanuel Kant, 'Über den Gemeinspruch: Das mag in der Theorie richtig sein, taugt aber nicht für die Praxis'; translated as 'On the Common Saying: That May Be Correct in Theory, but It Is of No Use in Practice' in *Works/Practical Philosophy*, trans. and ed. M. J. Gregor, Ak 8: 290–1.
29 Johann Gottlieb Fichte, 'Zurückforderung der Denkfreiheit von den Fürsten Europens', in *Gesamtausgabe*, I.1: 171.
30 Ernst Ferdinand Klein, *Freyheit und Eigenthum* (Berlin, 1790), 77.
31 Johann Adam Bergk, *Untersuchungen aus dem Natur-, Staats- und Völkerrechte* (n.p., 1796), 26.
32 Paul Johann Anselm Feuerbach, *Anti-Hobbes, oder Über die Gränzen der höchsten Gewalt und das Zwangsrecht der Bürger gegen den Oberherrn* (Giessen, 1797), 19–20.
33 See Frederick C. Beiser, *Enlightenment, Revolution and Romanticism: The Genesis of Modern German Political Thought, 1790–1800* (Cambridge, MA, 1992), 111–37.
34 Georg Forster to Therese Forster, 1 August 1793, in Georg Forster, *Werke*, 4 vols. (Frankfurt, 1967–70), 4: 883. See Beiser, *Enlightenment*, 154–88.
35 See Georges Vlachos, *La pensée politique de Kant: Métaphysique de l'ordre et dialectique du progrés* (Paris, 1954); Simone Goyard-Fabre, *Kant e le problème du droit* (Paris, 1971); Susan Meld Shell, *The Rigthts of Reason: A Study of Kant's Philosophy and Politics* (Toronto, 1980); Patrick Riley, *Kant's Political Philosophy* (Totowa, NJ, 1983); Hans-Georg Deggau, *Die Aporien der Rechtslehre Kants* (Stuttgart, 1983); Howard Williams, *Kant's Political Philosophy* (New York, NY, 1983); Kersting, *Wohlgeordnete Freiheit. Immanuel Kants Rechts- und Staatsphilosophie* (Frankfurt am Main, 1993); Leslie A. Mulholland, *Kant's System of Rights* (New York, NY, 1990); Claudia Langer, *Reform nach Prinzipien. Untersuchungen zur politischen Theorie Immanuel Kants* (Stuttgart, 1986); and *Kant's Political Philosophy*, ed. H. Williams (Cardiff, 1992).
36 Kant, *Metaphysik der Sitten*; translated as *The Metaphysics of Morals*, trans. and ed. M. J. Gregor in *Works/Practical Philosophy*, Ak 6: 307.
37 Kant, 'Uber den Gemeinspruch . . . ', Ak, 8: 297.
38 See Jörn Garber, 'Nachwort', in *Revolutionäre Vernunft. Texte zur jakobinischen und liberalen Revolutionsrezeption in Deutschland, 1798–1810*, ed. J. Garber (Kronberg, 1974), 202ff.
39 Bergk, *Untersuchungen*, 95. See Garber, 'Liberaler und demokratischer Republikanismus. Kants Metaphysik der Sitten und ihre radikaldemokratische Kritik durch J. A. Bergk', in

Mitteleuropa im ausgehenden 18. und frühen 19. Jahrhundert, eds. O. Büsch and W. Grab (Berlin, 1980), 250ff.

40 See Bergk, *Briefe über Kants metaphysische Anfangsgründe der Rechtslehre* (Leipzig, Gera, 1797), 176ff, 188.

41 See Friedrich von Schlegel, 'Versuch über den Begriff des Republikanismus' (1796), in *Kritische Friedrich Schlegel-Ausgabe*, ed. E. Behler (Paderborn, 1958–), 7: 11–25.

42 Kant, *Metaphysik der Sitten*, Ak 6: 353.

43 See Georg Cavallar, *Pax Kantiana: Systematisch-historische Untersuchung des Entwurfs 'Zum ewigen Frieden'* (1795) *von Immanuel Kant* (Vienna, 1992); *Immanuel Kant: Zum Ewigen Frieden*, ed. O. Höffe (Berlin, 1995); Volker Gerhardt, *Kants Entwurf 'Zum Ewigen Frieden', Eine Theorie der Politik* (Darmstadt, 1995).

44 See Timothy W. Luke, 'On Nature and Society: Rousseau versus the Enlightenment', in *History of Political Thought*, 5 (1984): 211–44.

45 Rousseau, 'Preface' to *Narcisse*, in *Oeuvres*, 2: 968; translated as 'Preface to *Narcissus*', in *The Discourses and Other Early Political Writings*, trans. and ed. V. Gourevitch (Cambridge, 1997), 100.

46 Rousseau, *Du contrat social ou Principes du droit politique* in *Oeuvres*, 3: 347–470; translated as *The Social Contract or Principles of Political Right* in *The Social Contract and Other Later Political Writings*, trans. and ed. V. Gourevitch (Cambridge, 1997); this translation preserves the pagination of *Oeuvres*. See Roger D. Masters, *The Political Philosophy of Rousseau* (Princeton, NJ, 1968); Judith Shklar, *Men and Citizens: A Study of Rousseau's Social Theory* (Cambridge, 1969); Reinhard Brandt, *Rousseaus Philosophie der Gesellschaft* (Stuttgart, 1973); Victor Goldschmidt, *Anthropologie et politique: Les principes du système de Rousseau* (Paris, 1974); Maximilian Forschner, *Rousseau* (Freiburg, 1977); Iring Fetscher, *Rousseaus politische Philosophie: Zur Geschichte des demokratischen Freheitsbegriffs* (Frankfurt am Main, 1978); Hilail Gildin, *Rousseau's Social Contract. The Design of the Argument* (Chicago, 1983); Jim Miller, *Rousseau: Dreamer of Democracy* (New Haven, CT, 1984); Robert Derathé, *Jean-Jacques Rousseau et la science politique de son temps* (Paris, 1988); Arthur M. Melzer, *The Natural Goodness of Man: On the System of Rousseau's Thought* (Chicago, IL, 1990); and Tracy B. Strong, *Jean Jacques Rousseau: The Politics of the Ordinary* (London, 1994).

47 Rousseau, *Contrat social*, *Oeuvres*, 3: 360.

48 Charles de Secondat, de Montesquieu, *Considérations sur les causes de la grandeur des Romains et de leur décadence*, in *Oeuvres complètes*, ed. R. Caillois, 2 vols. (Paris, 1949–51), 2: 119.

49 Montesquieu, 'Pensée 1918', in *Oeuvres* 1: 1461.

50 Emmanuel Joseph Sieyès, *Qu'est ce que le Tiers Etat?* (Paris, 1789), ch. 5; translated as *What is the Third Estate?*, trans. M. Blondel, ed. S. E. Finer (London, 1963), 120–1.

51 See Louis Althusser, *Montesquieu, la politique et l'histoire* (Paris, 1959) and Thomas L. Pangle, *Montesquieu's Philosophy of Liberalism: A Commentary on the Spirit of the Laws* (Chicago, IL, 1973).

52 Montesquieu, *Esprit des lois* (*Oeuvres*, vol. 2), I.3.5; translated as *The Spirit of the Laws*, trans. and eds. A. M. Cohler, B. C. Miller, and H. S. Stone (Cambridge, 1989), 25.

53 Concerning Montesquieu's conception of *gouvernement modéré*, see Walter Kuhfuss, *Mässigung und Politik. Studien zur politischen Sprache und Theorie Montesquieus* (Munich, 1975). See also Nannerl O. Keohane, *Philosophy and the State in France: the Renaissance to the Enlightenment* (Princeton, NJ, 1980), 392–419.

54 See Ulrich Lange, 'Teilung und Trennung der Gewalten bei Montesquieu', in *Der Staat*, 19 (1980): 213–34.

55 See J. G. A. Pocock, *The Machiavellian Moment* (Princeton, NJ, 1975); Gordon Wood, *The Creation of the American Republic* (Chapel Hill, NC, 1969); Bernard Bailyn, *The Ideological*

Origins of the American Revolution (Cambridge, 1967); Isaac Kramnick, *Republicanism and Bourgeois Radicalism: Political Ideology in Late Eighteenth-Century England and America* (Ithaca, NY, 1990); Morton White, *The Philosophy of the American Revolution* (New York, NY, 1978); John P. Diggins, *The Lost Soul of American Politics. Virtue, Self-Interest, and the Foundations of Liberalism* (Chicago, IL, 1986); M. White, *Philosophy, The Federalist, and the Constitution* (New York, NY, 1987); Thomas L. Pangle, *The Spirit of Modern Republicanism: The Moral Vision of the American Founders and the Philosophy of Locke* (Chicago, IL, 1988); and Richard S. Sinopoli, *The Foundations of American Citizenship. Liberalism, the Constitution, and Civic Virtue* (New York, NY, 1992).

56 Alexander Hamilton, James Madison, and John Jay, *The Federalist, or, The New Constitution* (New York, NY, 1965), No. 51 (by James Madison), 264.

57 Hamilton, No. 22, p. 110; Madison, No. 37, p. 178.

58 Salomon Maimon, 'Über die ersten Gründe des Naturrechts' (1795), in *Gesammelte Werke*, ed. V. Verra, 7 vols. (Hildesheim, 1965–76), 6: 356.

59 On the history of the criticism of social contract theory, see Michael H. Lessnoff, *Social Contract* (Houndmills, 1986), 83–90, 97–122.

60 David Hume, 'Of the Original Contract' (1748), in *Essays Moral, Political and Literary*, ed. E. F. Miller (Indianapolis, IN, 1987), 465–87 at 468.

61 See Adam Smith, *Lectures on Jurisprudence*, eds. R. L. Meek, D. D. Raphael, and P. G. Stein, in *Works* (1978), 403. For Hume's criticism of social contract theory see P. S. Atiyah, *The Rise and Fall of Freedom of Contract* (Oxford, 1979), 52ff, and Jonathan Harrison, *Hume's Theory of Justice* (Oxford, 1981), 190ff.

62 Hume, 'Of the Original Contract', 479.

63 John Austin, *Lectures on Jurisprudence, or The Philosophy of Positive Law*, 5th edn., 2 vols. ed. R. Campbell (London, 1885), 1: 325 fn; see also 280–1, 320–1, 324–5; Jeremy Bentham, *A Fragment on Government* (1776) in *Works*, ed. J. H. Burns (London, 1968–82, Oxford, 1983–), 3: 441, 509.

64 Blackstone, Sir William, *Commentaries on the Laws of England*, 4 vols. (Oxford, 1765–9), 1: 47–8.

65 Burke, Edmund, *Reflections on the Revolution in France* (1790), ed. J. G. A. Pocock (Indianapolis, IN, 1987), 84–5.

66 See Peter J. Stanlis, *Edmund Burke and the Natural Law* (Ann Arbor, MI, 1958); Alfred Cobban, *Edmund Burke and the Revolt against the Eighteenth Century: A Study of the Political and Social Thinking of Burke, Wordsworth, Coleridge, and Southey* (London, 1960) and F. P. Lock, *Burke's Reflections on the Revolution in France* (London, 1985).

67 Friedrich von Gentz, 'Politische Abhandlungen', in *Betrachtungen über die Französische Revolution: Nach dem Englischen des Herrn Burke ... mit einer Einleitung, Anmerkungen, politischen Abhandlungen*, 2 vols. (Berlin, 1793), 2: 113–4, 183.

68 See Duncan Forbes, *Hume's Philosophical Politics* (Cambridge, 1975); Harrison, *Hume's Theory of Justice*; Knud Haakonssen, *The Science of a Legislator. The Natural Jurisprudence of David Hume and Adam Smith* (Cambridge, 1981); David Miller, *Philosophy and Ideology in Hume's Political Thought* (Oxford, 1981); Frederick G. Whelan, *Order and Artifice in Hume's Political Philosophy* (Princeton, NJ, 1985); K. Haakonssen, 'The Structure of Hume's Political Theory', in *The Cambridge Companion to Hume*, ed. D. F. Norton (Cambridge, 1993), 182–221.

69 Bentham, 'Anarchical Fallacies', in *Bentham's Political Thought*, ed. B. Parekh (New York, NY, 1973), 269.

70 Hume, 'Of the Original Contract', 481.

71 See Whelan, *Order and Artifice*.

72 Hume, 'Of the Original Contract', 476.

73 Smith, Adam, *The Theory of Moral Sentiments*, eds. D. D. Raphael and A. L. Macfie, in *Works* (1976), III.ii.6.

74 See Daniel Brühlmeier, *Die Rechts- und Staatslehre von Adam Smith und die Interessentheorie der Verfassung* (Berlin, 1988).

75 Smith, *Theory of Moral Sentiments*, VII.iv.36.

76 See Haakonssen, *The Science of a Legislator* and Donald Winch, *Adam Smith's Politics: An Essay in Historiographic Revision* (Cambridge, 1978).

77 See Kersting, *Niccolò Machiavelli* (Munich, 1988).

78 See Douglas Long, *Jeremy Bentham's Idea of Liberty in Relation to His Utilitarianism* (Toronto, 1977); Ross Harrison, *Bentham* (London, 1983).

79 Bentham, 'Anarchical Fallacies', in *Bentham's Political Thought*, ed. B. Parekh (New York, NY, 1973), 269.

35

SOCIAL SCIENCES

ROBERT BROWN

I. PROGRAMS IN SEARCH OF A SCIENCE

The briefest useful summary of some of the chief topics of eighteenth-century thought concerning the social, or moral, sciences was written by the nineteenth-century entrepreneur of social reform, Robert Owen. The summary forms the long title of one of the many editions of his program for a 'new moral world': '*An Outline of the Rational System of Society, founded on demonstrable Facts developing the Constitution and Laws of Human Nature being the only effective Remedy for the Evils experienced by the Population of the World: the immediate Adoption of which would tranquilize the present agitated State of Society*' (1830). The search for demonstrable facts, and for the true character and laws of human nature, in the interests of immediate social therapy was a characteristic feature of eighteenth-century thought in Europe. It was characteristic because the success of Newtonian physics at the end of the seventeenth century powerfully stimulated interest, early in the eighteenth century, in the development of an analogous science of social topics. Advocacy of the application of the new 'experimental philosophy' of such natural scientists as Hooke, Boyle, and Newton to the problems of society was difficult to resist. Not only were the problems urgent and general, but the benefits might be great. Investigators had only to proceed on the assumption, as Hume later put it in the *Treatise* (1739–40), that there is a close similarity between the uniformity of nature and the 'uniformity of human actions'. For if that is true, then it follows that 'in judging of the actions of men we must proceed upon the same maxims, as when we reason concerning external objects'. The inconstancy of human behaviour is, in Hume's words, 'no more than what happens in the operation of body, nor can we conclude any thing from the one irregularity, which will not follow equally from the other'.[1] On this crucial point people could and did differ, and continue to do so today.

The author gratefully acknowledges the helpful information provided from unpublished papers by Dr. Andrew Vincent. Much of the information about Kant and racism is owed to Dr. Vincent.

However, eighteenth-century expressions of interest in establishing a science of social issues could not of themselves create such a science, and any discussion of that interest must at least refer to the different forms that it took and the differences if any, that each made.[2] We need to begin, then, by distinguishing specific examples of social investigation – studies made during the century of particular social activities, institutions, and events – from general theoretical speculations about the desirability and character of a future social science. Mandeville's pamphlet *Enquiry into the Causes of the Frequent Executions at Tyburn* (1725) on Jonathan Wild, director of a 'Kind of Corporation of Thieves', is an example of reformative journalism; Montesquieu's *Considérations sur les causes de la grandeur des Romains et de leur décadence* (1734) is, in large part, political education by historical means; the *Essai sur la nature du commerce en général* (1755) by Richard Cantillon is a treatise on economic principles as they are exemplified in actual commerce. None of these three works is explicitly concerned with the future character of a new science of society although each contributes something to its formation.

In *The Idea of Progress* (1920) the Cambridge historian J. B. Bury argued that Bacon's enthusiasm for the advancement of natural science, and Descartes's belief in human progress through the 'supremacy of human reason and the discovery of immutable scientific laws', were between them important factors in weakening the 'order and unity' that 'the Christian theory of providential design and final causes' had provided hitherto for the faithful. New principles, said Bury, 'were needed to replace the principles which rationalism had discredited'. Scientific progress had 'depended on the postulate that physical phenomena were subject to invariable laws'. If history was to teach us any lessons, 'some similar postulate as to social phenomena was required'. Bury suggested that three works of the mid-eighteenth century began this task: Montesquieu's *De l'esprit des lois* (1748), Voltaire's *Essai sur les moeurs* (1756), and Turgot's plan for an *Histoire universelle* (1751).[3] However, these are mid-century contributions, and Bury himself pointed out that Montesquieu's 'most striking and important idea' first appears in his *Considérations sur les causes de la grandeur des Romains et de leur décadence*. There, in one paragraph, he dispenses with the rule of chance in history, thus partially disagreeing, we can add, with Machiavelli's remark in *The Prince* (1532) 'that it is probably true that fortune is the arbiter of half the things that we do, leaving the other half or so to be controlled by ourselves'.[4] The same paragraph eliminates, says Bury (146), the influence in history of divine guidance and ends. The passage he refers to is this:

It is not chance that rules the world. Ask the Romans, who had a continuous sequence of successes when they were guided by a certain plan, and an uninterrupted sequence of reverses when they followed another. There are general causes, moral and physical, which act in every monarchy, elevating it, maintaining it, or hurling it to the ground. All accidents are controlled by these causes. And if the chance of one battle – that is a particular cause – has brought a state to ruin, some general cause made it necessary for that state to perish from a single battle. In a word, the main trend draws with it all particular accidents.[5]

Still earlier in the century, there had been many calls for the recognition of the social laws at operation in social life, or alternatively, of the divinely created patterns to be found in human, and indeed earthly, history. These calls varied from general exhortations to study political science, as in the case of the Abbé de Saint-Pierre (1658–1743) and Henri de Boulainvilliers (1658–1722), to detailed treatises of which Vico's *Scienza nuova* (*The New Science*) (1725–44) is now the best known example. In *État de la France* (1737) Boulainvilliers wrote:

[A]ll men agree that there is no science higher than that of Government, nor one in which errors have more dangerous consequences. Therefore, since it is morally impossible that the practice of Government succeed without rule or theory, we must also conclude that there is no other science that should be cultivated by citizens with so much ardor, research, work, and method.[6]

For both Boulainvilliers and Saint-Pierre the political science of the future was to be an applied science. It would generate projects for social and political improvement, and to that extent it would be a science of what ought to be done: 'The highest point in politics', Saint-Pierre said, 'is to find or establish a form of government that will perfect itself independently of any talented or hard-working monarch'[7] – a self-regulating and self-preserving social machine that would require minimum care by the monarch. Its guiding principle would be the need, and thus goal, of every government to maximise the pleasure of its citizens and minimise their pain. Experience, observation, and research would teach educators and rulers how to bring this about in the most efficient way.

In Italy at this time a rather different conception of social studies was being advocated by Vico in his *Scienza nuova.* Virtually unknown outside Italy until almost a century later, Vico claimed that self-examination of our various human natures would reveal the law-governed and evolutionary pattern of historical stages 'which, without human discernment or intent, and often against the designs of men, providence has given . . . the human race'.[8] In brief, God achieves his aims in our history. So by learning what these are we can learn what 'the course of the affairs of the nations' has been in the past and will be in the future. The timeless pattern of human history can be discovered by the educated study of human natures; once we know that pattern we can derive from it the sequence of the cultural development of human beings. Knowing that sequence, we can find it illustrated in the growth and decline of different social institutions, languages, customs, laws, and political arrangements throughout the world. Thus the new science will be based on our knowledge of our own human natures, be guaranteed by our justified belief in divine intervention, and result in the empirical study of the actual products of human cultural activity and the discernment of their pattern.

The advocates, heralds, and enunciators of a future social science commonly found it difficult to distinguish the moral principles of a society from the causal, or other, regularities of its operation. The difficulty arose and flourished because the desire for such a science was essentially practical: knowledge of social causes and regularities was desired for the solution of the problems of government. Hence the science required was to be both descriptive and prescriptive. It would consist in a set of moral precepts that would be obeyed by people because they thought the precepts not only morally correct but also appropriate for human nature – appropriate because the precepts accurately described the properties that human agents required in order to achieve their ideal development. The precepts, then, had a dual character. On the one hand, they were empirical generalisations about the properties that people need for their own full development to occur. On the other hand, the precepts were moral judgements concerning what outcomes are to count as the full and ideal development of human beings. This reliance on the regulation of human society by some kind of universal moral principles based on human nature was a considerable obstacle to those thinkers who wished to create a science of society closely resembling the sciences of nature. For one, the proponents of such a social science first had to detach it from the problems of political philosophy and conjectural history with which it was usually enmeshed. For another, the proponents had to find a field of social studies which could serve as an example of what they hoped to establish more widely. The example of a strict science of society had to be one whose content neither entailed moral and religious statements nor was entailed by them. In the early eighteenth century the only plausible instance of such a field was economics.

The major political philosophers had always discussed economic questions as part of their brief. In this respect neither the sixteenth-century philosophers, such as Bodin, nor their seventeenth-century successors – Hobbes, Pufendorf, and Locke, for example – differed from such early eighteenth-century figures as Mandeville, Montesquieu, and Hume. Yet from the mid sixteenth-century onward there was a long line of theologians and other thinkers who concentrated their attention on economic topics such as the money supply, foreign trade, the just price, the balance of payments, taxes, and agriculture. These thinkers included members of the School of Salamanca – Martinus de Azpilcueta (Navarro),

Domingo de Soto, and Saravia de la Calle – and then elsewhere in Spain, Molina, and the Flemish Lessius. There was also the English contingent of De Malynes, Petty, Misselden, Mun, and North. The work of such economists had resulted in the creation of a body of empirical generalisations; the work had also produced the belief that there existed a self-regulating system of economic transactions, in both domestic and foreign trade, that operated independently of government control and of other social and political influences. This 'circle of commerce' was taken to be a self-maintaining mechanism of interacting causal factors, a mechanism that required description but resisted outside interference. Writing on usury in 1556, Azpilcueta suggested that the determination of the value of a currency by its 'scarcity and need' was apparently 'a law of God and Nature'.[9] In *England's Treasure by Forraign Trade* (1664) Thomas Mun wrote 'that so much treasure only will be brought in or carried out of a Commonwealth as the Forraign Trade doth over or under ballance in value. And this must come to pass by a Necessity beyond all resistance'.[10] At the opening of the century Gerald De Malynes, Assay Master of the English Mint, compared the self-regulating operation of the balance of payments to a causal mechanism: 'We see how one thing driveth or enforceth another, like as in a clocke where there be many wheels, the first wheel being stirred, driveth the next, and that the third, and so forth, till the last that moveth the instrument that strikes the clocke'.[11]

The question raised by these views was how they fitted with the widespread desire – present from the time of Saint-Pierre to that of Bentham – to produce social reforms. Isaiah Berlin has written:

> [T]rue political science is the science not of *what is, but of what ought to be*, said the abbé Sieyès towards the end of the eighteenth century, but he might just as well have said it fifty years earlier, for this is the view of almost all the rational thinkers of the great century. The proper concern of an intelligent man was with science; and science meant not mere description and systematisation, but practical rules designed to change things for the better by the most rapid and effective means.[12]

In principle, it was easy enough to say that social reformers' knowledge of the unalterable laws of society would permit reforms to be scientifically sound, just as the physical laws of optics provided a secure basis for the design of telescopes. In practice, this reply seemed to offer no guidance as to which of the many conflicting political and moral goals that were consistent with social laws ought to be pursued. Knowledge of social regularities would exclude some political proposals, but how could it enable a person, at any specific time or place, to choose from among the indefinitely large remainder? If social laws resembled physical laws, then apparently neither could give moral guidance. If social laws were different and could indicate which moral ends should be pursued, what was the nature of those laws and how were they to be discovered? In his novel *Émile* (1762) Rousseau put forward the view that in order 'to make healthy judgements about existing governments' we need to know what ought to be in order to judge well that which exists.[13] The problem this sort of claim generated once again was whether such a judgement was a purely moral one that somehow followed from the description of 'what ought to be' – or whether the judgement was both moral and factual. In short, the two problems of the nature of moral judgements and the nature of social regularities had become interlaced. Their solutions would help to determine what answer was to be given to the question, 'What form should a future social science take?' If it could serve no reformative purpose, then perhaps this new science had little to offer. Throughout the eighteenth century these two problems remained intertwined in the thought of a large number of philosophers, and they displayed no clear line of progress in dealing with the matter.

The situation, then, was that no genuine science of society could emerge as long as social problems were treated merely as an area for the employment of moral principles. Unless social problems were distinguished from those of social ethics, the question 'Why does this custom exist?' was liable to receive one of two unsatisfactory replies. One was the empty assertion that it was part of God's benevolent design for human nature. The other was to select those factors that seemed to be susceptible to moral control, and to let their apparent utility for that purpose determine the scope of further explanation. A view that apparently combined the advantages of both these replies and yet fostered scientific inquiry was given by Dugald Stewart in his *Elements of the Philosophy of the Human Mind* (1792). In it he suggested that 'When the general laws of our internal frame are attentively examined, they will be found to have for their object the happiness and improvement both of the individual and of society. This is their Final Cause, or the end for which we may presume they were destined by our Maker'. Yet when someone is guided by the 'efficient causes' that produce his behaviour, he is usually unaware 'of the ultimate ends which he is promoting'.[14] Science investigates efficient causes; ethics teaches us final causes. Stewart concludes that the two sorts of causes have a symbiotic relationship:

> In various cases, the consideration of final causes has led to the discovery of some general law of nature; and in almost every case, the discovery of a general law clearly points out some wise and beneficent purposes to which it is subservient. Indeed, it is chiefly the prospect of such applications which renders the investigation of general laws interesting to the mind.[15]

Thus scientific law statements are not ethical judgements, but in fact are indications of the means that God uses to achieve His divine ends. However, the question then recurs: 'How do such laws, including social laws, tell us or point out – the 'wise and beneficent purposes' to which each law is 'subservient'? Can the prospect of identifying them motivate our search if we have no means of recognising the final causes?

II. DETERMINING THE VARIABILITY OF HUMAN NATURE

The problem of which methods should be used for the study of human society was intimately joined to two other problems, and the solution of any one of them required the solution of all three. Those two problems were, first, the character of the laws, if any, that governed human history, and, second, the extent to which human nature varied throughout the world. The latter question engrossed the attention of every major social commentator in the eighteenth century. The constancy of Human Nature, especially the belief in the universality of reason as a property of the soul, was an essential feature of orthodox Christianity. Nevertheless, notions of what human constancy amounted to varied considerably. On the one hand, variation in the character of peoples could not be indefinitely large or they would not all be human. On the other hand, people in different societies displayed qualities and interests, and thus adhered to value judgements, that were often remarkably divergent. The moral character of one society could be incompatible, it seemed, with that of another. What one group cherished an adjoining group despised, and the considerations that led the former to evaluate something favourably led the latter to devalue it without delay. Two hundred years of European expansion in the other continents had revealed an astonishing and unsettling diversity of culture. It was not clear to every educated European, and certainly not to the uneducated, that all these newly discovered people were fully human. Differences of culture might be due to differences of native ability. What was clear to some of the educated was that much evidence on the matter had recently become available. Thus in 1777 Edmund Burke wrote to William Robertson (1721–93), royal chaplain, Principal of Edinburgh University, and historian:

> I have always thought with you, that we possess at this time very great advantages towards the knowledge of human nature. We need no longer go to history to trace it in all its stages and periods. History, from its comparative youth, is but a poor instructor. . . . But now the great map of mankind is unrolld at once; and there is no state or tradition of barbarism, and no mode of refinement which we have not at the same instant under our View.[16]

Having the great map of mankind under his view, Robertson concluded that 'the human mind, whenever it is placed in the same situation, will, in ages the most distant, assume the same form and be distinguished by the same manners'.[17] Conversely, the differences between peoples are the result of the differences in their social and physical environment – differences, for example, in their means of subsistence, their history, their type of government, or in their geographical location and climate. These observable features were only some of a long list of interrelated factors that had been popular for explanatory purposes in earlier centuries. The difficulty was to select from among them the ones at work in any given case. In *Les six livres de la république* (1576) Jean Bodin had remarked that:

> [I]n the same climats the people of the East are found to differ much from them of the West: and in the same latitude and difference from the Equator, the people of the North differ from them of the South: And which is more, in the same climat, latitude, and longitude, and under the same degree, we find a difference betwixt a hilly countrey and the plaines: so as in the same citie, the diversitie of hills and vallies forceth a diversitie of humors and dispositions . . .[18]

Although Bodin's list of causal factors is extensive and includes force of winds, nearness to the sea, and soil fertility, Bodin also makes use of what he believes is the variation of internal body heat between Southern and Northern populations. It is the more intense body heat of the Northerners that causes their 'natural powers' to be greater than those of the Southerners.[19] Bodin also wishes to take account of government, customs, and laws, but his list has become so long that choosing from among its members requires an advanced knowledge of their causal influence, if any. This was a problem that was bequeathed to eighteenth-century thinkers such as Montesquieu and Hume. Their efforts to deal with, and in some cases develop, the hypotheses that they inherited form a significant portion of their century's contribution to the growth of the human sciences.

Robertson and Burke were only two of the numerous people who claimed to believe in the uniformity of human nature. R. V. Sampson has quoted Voltaire as saying: 'Man in general has always been what he is . . . he has always had the same instinct which leads him to feel affection for himself, for the companion of his toils, for his children, and so forth. . . . We all have two instincts which are the basis of society, pity and justice'.[20] Sampson quotes Fontenelle's essay *Sur l'histoire* to the same effect. Anyone who is appropriately educated should be able to discover 'all past history and all the history to come' simply by knowing the qualities which human nature always has displayed – the qualities of ignorance, credulity, vanity, ambition, and wickedness combined with a small amount of good sense (74). In Rousseau's *Discours sur l'origine et les fondements de l'inégalité parmi les hommes* (1755) the distinction between the basic, fixed, and common human nature, on the one hand, and its social accretions, on the other, becomes a matter of historical conjecture concerning the difference between the essential or original human nature and its artificial development over time.

Rousseau asks, '[H]ow shall man hope to see himself as nature made him, across all the changes which the succession of place and time must have produced in his original constitution?' This constitution is then identified by Rousseau as the fundamental nature of humankind. For how, Rousseau continues, can a person 'distinguish what is fundamental in his nature from the changes and additions which his circumstances and the advances he has made have introduced to modify his primitive condition?'[21] A way not available to him, Rousseau says, is the ability to answer two questions: '*What experiments would have to be made, to discover the natural man? And how are those experiments to be made in a state of society?*' (39). Indeed, he has to rely on 'mere conditional and hypothetical reasonings, rather calculated to explain the nature of things, than to ascertain their actual origin; just like the hypotheses which our physicists daily form respecting the formation of the world' (45).

In *An Enquiry concerning Human Understanding* (1748) David Hume, in one of his best remembered remarks, wrote that 'It is universally acknowledged, that there is a great uniformity among the actions of men, in all nations and ages, and that human nature remains still the same, in its principles and operations. The same motives always produce the same actions: The same events follow from the same causes.' A few sentences later Hume added: 'Mankind are so much the same, in all times and places, that history informs us of nothing new or strange in this particular. Its chief use is only to discover the constant and universal principles of human nature, by showing men in all varieties of circumstances and situations. . . .'[22] Hume's view, of human uniformity, like that held by Robertson, Burke, Fontenelle, Voltaire, and Rousseau, was not, it appeared, universally acknowledged. The first two sentences of chapter one of Sir James Steuart's *An Inquiry into the Principles of Political Economy* (1767) seemed to contain an important modification. He wrote that we find mankind

> acting uniformly in all ages, in all countries, and in all climates, from the principles of self-interest, expediency, duty, or passion. In this he is alike, in nothing else.
>
> These motives of human actions produce such a variety of circumstances, that if we consider the several species of animals in the creation, we shall find the individuals of no class so unlike to one another, as man to man.[23]

Diderot, in his *Supplément au Voyage de Bougainville* (1798), gave similarly weak support to the uniformity thesis. He asserted that 'We have no more in common with other human beings at birth than an organic similarity of form, the same need, an attraction to the same pleasures and a shared aversion to the same pains. These are the things which make man what he is. . . .'[24]

In short, where these various authors seemed to agree, they agreed on the most general of human traits and not always on those. Could such attributes as passion, self-interest, pity, a desire for justice, ignorance, credulity, vanity, and a little good sense be the elements of a uniform human nature? Would not the opposites of all those qualities be equally good candidates for that title?

Beneath any agreement on such generalities there lay obvious disagreement on particular issues. Montesquieu wrote that if he had to defend the right that Europeans had to make negroes slaves, he would say that it is impossible for Europeans to assume that negroes are men because Europeans would then have to believe that they themselves were not Christians.[25] Montesquieu had other reasons for criticising slavery, but they are all based on his belief that since 'all men are born equal, one must say that slavery is against nature' (III.v, p. 252). Men born equal have equal right to political liberty and that consists in that personal security 'or, at least, in the opinion one has of one's security' – a security that the practice of slavery destroys (II.ii, p. 188). The chevalier Louis de Jaucourt (1704–1779), the largest single contributor to the 35 volumes of the *Encyclopédie* that was edited by Diderot and d'Alembert from 1747, echoed Montesquieu's views on equality and liberty. 'Since human nature', Jaucourt wrote, 'is the same in every man, it is clear that, according to natural law, every one must regard others as creatures that are naturally equal to him, that is to say, who are men like him.' Because '[s]uch equality is the principle and foundation of liberty',[26] it was possible for Diderot to claim that liberty can neither be exchanged for something else, nor lost, nor sold – as it was in slavery.[27] Yet it was possible, as the cases of Hume and Kant show, to believe in the biological inferiority of some races with respect to certain attributes but to oppose slavery.

In his essay 'On National Characters' David Hume added a footnote on negroes that became widely, and now unfavourably, known. He wrote in his final edition of 1772:

> I am apt to suspect the negroes to be naturally inferior to the whites. There scarcely ever was a civilized nation of that complexion, nor even any individual eminent either in action or speculation. No ingenious manufactures amongst them, no arts, no sciences. On the other hand, the most rude and barbarous of the whites, such as the ancient GERMANS, the present TARTARS, have still something eminent about them, in their valour, form of government, or some other particular. Such a uniform and constant difference could not happen, in so many countries and ages, if nature had not made an original distinction between these breeds of men.[28]

The original 1753 version of this footnote was attacked by James Beattie in *An Essay on the Nature and Immutability of Truth* (1770), on three grounds: (1) even if Hume's assertions were true, they 'would not prove the point in question, except it were also proved, that the Africans and Americans' would not take advantage of arts and sciences even if they were introduced to them; (2) no one could know all the negroes of the world, past and present, so Hume's evidence is insufficient; (3) Hume's claims are false; the empires of Peru and Mexico could not have existed without people of ability and ingenuity. They, like the Africans, 'are known to have many ingenious manufactures and arts'. They lack sciences only because they lack letters.[29] Hume seems to have weakened his earlier remarks in response to Beattie. In contrast to the original, the revised version says nothing about different races being different species; suspects only negroes to be a naturally inferior race; and replaces the words 'There scarcely ever was a civilized nation of any other complexion than white' with the words 'there scarcely ever was a civilized nation of that complexion', that is, black. In drawing attention to these changes John Immerwahr concludes that they show that 'Hume's racism was a considered and deliberate position, rather than an offhand remark'.[30] Immerwahr also says that since Beattie's counterexamples were drawn from the known empires and achievements of the American Indians, the way was left open for Hume to confine his criticism to blacks, and thus to strengthen its force (485).

On the other hand, Hume strongly opposed slavery. His essay 'On the Populousness of Ancient Nations' is chiefly concerned, he says, with 'the influence of slavery on the populousness of a state', but he makes his opinion of slavery quite clear:

> The remains which are found of domestic slavery, in the AMERICAN colonies, and among some EUROPEAN nations, would never surely create a desire of rendering it more universal. The little humanity, commonly observed in persons, accustomed, from their infancy, to exercise so great authority over their fellow-creatures, and to trample upon human nature, were sufficient alone to disgust us with that unbounded dominion. Nor can a more probable reason be assigned for the severe, I might say, barbarous manners of ancient times, than the practice of domestic slavery; by which every man of rank was rendered a petty tyrant, and educated amidst the flattery, submission, and low debasement of his slaves.[31]

Hume's position, then, is that the natural inferiority of the negro race offers no justification for enslaving its members, a position directly opposed to one of the most popular reasons offered by defenders of slavery: that a permanent intellectual inferiority justified a permanent status of moral and political inferiority.

Throughout his life Kant agreed strongly with Hume's view of the moral and intellectual inferiority of blacks. In his *Beobachtungen über das Gefühl des Schönen und Erhabenen* (1764) Kant uses Hume's essay in support of his own beliefs:

> The Negroes of Africa have by nature no feeling that rises above the trifling. Mr Hume challenges anyone to cite a single example in which a Negro has shown talents, and asserts that among the hundreds of thousands of blacks who are transported elsewhere

from their countries, although many of them have even been set free, still not a single one was ever found who presented anything great in art or science or any other praiseworthy quality, even though among the whites some continually rise aloft from the lowest rabble, and through superior gifts early gain respect in the world. So fundamental is the difference between these two races of man, and it appears to be as great in regard to mental capacities as in color.[32]

A few paragraphs later Kant emphasises his unfavourable opinion of blacks by remarking that 'this fellow was quite black from head to foot, a clear proof that what he said was stupid' (trans. 113). Kant believed in the existence of four distinct races of mankind whose permanent properties such as physique, abilities, and predispositions were fixed in the germplasm. However, local geographical and economic conditions could, and did, produce differences of national character, and Kant was able to discover a considerable number of unflattering features in the characters of the French, Spanish, Italians, and English. Between the 1760s and 1790s Kant's initially favourable judgements on the American Indians became increasingly harsh as his sources of information changed. The Indians described in his lectures on physical geography (1775) are no longer frank, honest, and able; they are physically, morally, and intellectually weak.[33] Elsewhere he characterised them as politically incompetent and unlikely to survive. He wrote: 'The Americans insensitive . . . Love of liberty is here mere idle independence. They do not speak, do not love, care about nothing. Mexico and Peru accept no culture.'[34] Although Kant's beliefs about blacks and American Indians were shared by many European observers, including J. F. Blumenbach (1752–1840), the inventor of race classification by means of skull measurements, and Carl von Linné (1707–78), the pioneer of scientific botany, Kant's views were by no means held universally. Nor were they commonly used by such people as Blumenbach and Linné as an argument for slavery.

For his part, Kant's support for the principle of equality before the law forbade the enslavement of citizens. In *Zum ewigen Frieden* (1795–6) Kant referred to the Sugar Islands as 'that place of the cruelest and most calculated slavery', and as the work of 'powers that make much ado of their piety and, while they drink wrongfulness like water, want to be known as the elect in orthodoxy'.[35] A year later in *Metaphysik der Sitten* Kant denied that '*bondage* and its legitimacy [can] be derived from a people's being overcome in war, since for this one would have to admit that a war could be punitive'. Yet this would contradict Kant's claim that war between independent states can never be punitive. 'For punishment occurs only in the relation of a superior (*imperantis*) to those subject to him (*subditum*), and states do not stand in that relation to each other.' The justification of hereditary slavery is less possible still, 'for the guilt of a person's crime cannot be inherited'.[36] On the other hand, Kant limits the application of equality before the law to citizens – to those who accept the legitimacy, and hence rule, of the law. He says that when an unruly crowd or 'rabble unites against the law, it forms a mob (*agere per turbas*) – conduct that excludes its members from the status of citizens'.[37] This suggests that under certain conditions slaves are not citizens. The question whether in those circumstances enslavement is justifiable is not given a clear answer by Kant.

Kant's opinions did not go unchallenged. His former student, Johann Gottfried Herder (1744–1803), disagreed with him about human races. In *Ideen zur Philosophie der Geschichte der Menschheit*(1784–91) Herder wrote 'that in spite of the vast realm of change and diversity, *all mankind is one and the same species upon earth*'.[38] Several paragraphs later, in an obvious reference to Kant's views, Herder wrote:

> Some, for instance, have thought fit to employ the term *races* for four or five divisions, according to regions of origin or complexion. I see no reason for employing this term. Race refers to a difference of origin, which in this case either does not exist or which comprises in each of these regions or complexions the most diverse 'races'.... Complexions run into each other; forms follow the genetic character; and *in toto* they are ... but different shades of the same great picture which extends through all ages and all parts of the earth. (*Ideas*, 284)

Herder also pointed out in detail the accomplishments of non-European peoples and concludes that 'If a man were to compose a book of the arts of various nations, he would find them scattered over the whole Earth, and each flourishing in its proper place'.[39] He elaborated on this point by saying that

> The difference between the so-called enlightened and unenlightened, or between the cultured and uncultured peoples, is not one of kind but merely of degree.... If we take the idea of European culture for our standard, we shall, indeed, only find it applicable to Europe. If, however, we establish arbitrary distinctions between cultures and modes of enlightenment, we are liable to lose ourselves in cloud-cuckoo-land. (*Ideas*, 313–14)

Moreover, it is mere vanity, Herder says, for a European to think himself superior to people elsewhere simply because he lives amidst highly developed arts and sciences. For which of all these has he himself invented? What has he contributed to the techniques and discoveries that help him? He is merely a sponge. Overwhelmed at first by European tools and weapons, the native peoples came to realize that the Europeans were in many respects inferior in ability to themselves, and the individual native discovered that the European's 'techniques were no part of himself'. The European 'sits perched on a lofty edifice erected by the hands of others, by the labours of preceding generations'. Herder believes that primitive peoples, within their narrower spheres, can use their physical and mental abilities with greater skill, understanding, precision, and force than the politically sophisticated Europeans. For the latter can, and do, rely on the achievements of others (*Ideas*, 315–16).

The significance of such arguments about the uniformity of human nature was considerable. Some of the difference in opinion could be reconciled by more accurate information that was already available. Thus William Marsden in his *History of Sumatra* (1783) remarked that historians of man needed

> facts to serve as *data* in their reasonings, which are too often rendered nugatory, and not seldom ridiculous, by assuming as truths, the misconceptions of travellers. The study of our own species is doubtless the most interesting and important that can claim the attention of mankind; and this science, like all others, it is impossible to improve by abstract speculation, merely.[40]

Other disagreements, such as those on the number of races and the origin of specific human traits, required scientific solutions that were still to be developed. The bearing of these arguments on the further issue of which methods were appropriate for the study of society was obvious. Hume had said of history – and the same could be said of politics and economics – that 'Its chief use is only to discover the constant and universal principles of human nature, by showing men in all varieties of circumstances and situations, and furnishing us with materials, from which we may form our observations, and become acquainted with the regular springs of human action and behaviour'.[41] If there were regular springs that could be modified in specific cases by economic and political conditions, by education, custom, character, natural forces, and opinion, then such 'contrary causes' could be taken into account in explaining human behaviour. Moreover, it ought to be possible to use 'conjectural history': that is, to extrapolate from what was known of the nature of current primitive peoples to the nature of early mankind. The evidence available to investigators in the form of living specimens was more reliable and less fragmentary, it seemed, than that contained in ancient texts of dubious quality. However, not only preliterate peoples offered suitable evidence. There were also the innumerable varieties of social conditions, societies, and governments to be found still present in the highly developed areas of the Asian world, and these varieties could be studied from Turkey to China.

Thus by the mid-eighteenth century it was clear that the question whether there was only one human nature or more than one – whether local circumstances acted on one uniform human nature or distinct human natures expressed themselves in different ways – had an important bearing on how social studies should be pursued. Travel and exploration beyond Europe had revealed customs and institutions so diverse that it had become a significant issue whether they were as diverse as they appeared; and if so, how a uniform human nature could have helped to produce them. The answers to those questions had moral and political implications. For if there were genuinely distinct races, and the Europeans were genetically superior in temperament and intellect to others, what treatment, morally and politically, was appropriate to the inferior groups? On the other hand, if all abilities and temperaments were distributed in much the same way throughout the human population, the presumption of inferiority could not be used to justify cruel or unequal treatment. Some reason other than mere political convenience or benefit would have to be found to support it. There was also a methodological implication. If human beings belonged to one uniform race, then a social science would study not only the external and local conditions that caused one group to be different from another but, to a lesser extent, the similarities of behaviour that arose from a common biological and psychological heritage. Both those projects would be different if human beings belonged to races whose biological and psychological differences could in themselves somehow explain the existence of distinct societies and cultures. Social science would then be a purely descriptive activity. It would supply only the details of the various economic, political, and social systems actually existing in the world. The basic explanations for their presence, however, would be biological or neurological. In point of fact, the scope of the term 'basic' was never made clear; nor was the causal relationship, if any, between the biological foundation and the cultural superstructure examined in detail.

In spite of that, one underlying argument accepted, knowingly or not, by many critics of a uniform human nature was simple. It was that because all human beings do not have the same needs, desires, and instincts, they do not share the same set of basic ends. Hence the behaviour of members of distinct races cannot be explained by reference to the same goals. Each race favours different goals because it is subject to its own distinctive needs and instincts and predispositions; those, after all, are what make the races different from each other. An alternative argument was even simpler. It was that all races share the same instincts, needs, and predispositions but that the races vary in their biological and psychological abilities to satisfy their needs and fulfil their instincts. The many variations of customary behaviour and institutions displayed by societies throughout the world express their members' success or failure to achieve the same set of goals – a success ratio that is determined by the particular abilities and temperament of each race.

The answer given to the question 'One human nature or several?' determined, in part, what kinds of factors were taken to be causally active in the structure, maintenance, and development of social life. Since those factors formed the future subject matter of a social science, the view taken of the uniformity of human nature was an important step in deciding the character of that subject matter. In the one case the subject of study would be, for the most part, the causal effects of different economic, political, and social conditions. In the other case, those conditions would be studied as the effects of biological and psychological causes that formed no part of social investigation. However, this distinction between the two alternatives was somewhat blurred by the existence of a third view – promulgated by some of the Italian humanists of the fifteenth and sixteenth centuries – the view that since human beings possess free will they create their own characters. Human nature is indeterminate and has no essential or fixed properties. That is why several centuries later Vico said that the history of human beings is the history of their construction of their own characters. Giovanni Pico della Mirandola (1463–94) in his celebrated *Oratio de hominis dignitate* (1486) let God explain to Adam that He was giving him an indeterminate nature since 'there was left to Him no archetype according to which He might form this new being':

> O Adam, We have given you neither visage nor endowment uniquely your own, so that whatever place, form, or gifts you may select after pondering the matter, you may have and keep through your own judgment and decision. All other creatures have their natures defined and limited by laws which We have established; you, by contrast, unimpeded by any such limits, may, by your own free choice, to whose custody We have assigned you, establish the features of your own nature.[42]

The consequences of such a view for the development of a social science could be diverse. The most familiar and systematic use of some of them was by Vico: that despite the absence of a uniform human nature, all people have the similar social needs within the specifiable social stages through which they are fated to pass. As a result, people everywhere deal in similar ways with similar problems and conditions. The unintended social regularities produced by people's efforts to overcome obstacles are discoverable because they create an historical sequence of identifiable cultural patterns. These can be identified, recovered, and forecast by the methods of interpretation that Vico claims to supply. Vico's alternative science, then, contains elements of the other two. It is partly an investigation of social laws and cultural products, and partly a method of historical interpretation based on assumptions about the basic constitution of human beings.

III. THE CHOICE OF METHOD

Because the problem of the appropriate methods of social investigation was so closely intertwined with that of the nature of social laws, the two problems were usually taken up together, although they will be separated here. The three authorities most commonly referred to in the methodological discussions of the early eighteenth century were Bacon, Descartes, and Newton, although Newton's greatest popularity in this respect came in the nineteenth century. There were two troublesome features of this reliance. The first was that Bacon's views were often misunderstood, misrepresented, or assimilated to those of Newton, whose suggestions were themselves often distorted by enthusiasts. The second difficulty was that the methodological views of all three men dealt with only some of the scientific issues in which social investigators and commentators had an interest. Those issues arose from the use of a motley mixture of explanatory procedures whose chief purpose was to discover, and then employ, the natural laws that controlled human societies. One procedure was modelled on the deductive system of Euclidean geometry: from a small set of postulates and definitions a number of explanatory theorems were drawn and then buttressed as needed with illustrative evidence. Since the choice of axioms, or unproven statements, was often determined by the metaphysical or political views of the system's author, the theorems varied accordingly. It was this procedure that Bacon criticised in *Novum organum* (1620)[43]. He complained that 'the usual method of discovery and proof, by first establishing the most general propositions, then applying and proving the intermediate axioms according to them, is the parent of error and the curse of all science' (Aphorism LXIX). The cautious ascent from sense-experience to abstract general principles that Bacon advocated was the outcome of his attempt to reverse the procedure of the mathematical systematisers, that is, the descent from the most general of axioms to the most specific of instances by means of 'middle axioms'. Instead, he believed that principles were to be suggested by sense-experience in the form of reliable experiments and, in turn, new experiments suggested by the principles already established. This view of the utility of the *axiomata media*, continuously popular among scientists since Bacon first credited it to Plato's *Theaetetus*, was inherited by many thinkers in the eighteenth century.

The previous century had been marked by a continuing controversy over the status of experimental science, and this continued during the eighteenth century. There was widespread agreement among many natural scientists and philosophers that scientific procedure should consist in making probable hypotheses or conjectures whose logical consequences would then be either confirmed or disconfirmed by submitting them to the tests of observation and experiment. However, this general agreement masked a number of different opinions concerning three important issues, all of which reappeared in the nineteenth century in discussions concerning the social sciences. The first issue was how plausible hypotheses are to be chosen; the second was how the discoveries of science are connected to the truths of metaphysics; and the third was how, and to what extent, hypotheses are tested by experience. On all three questions the followers of Descartes had much to say, and in his book *Occult Powers and Hypotheses*

(1989) Desmond Clarke examines their answers. On the important distinction between arbitrary and plausible conjectures, supporters of the Cartesian ideal of science were faced with the task of showing that the conjectures they used were not arbitrary – that the basic principles of Cartesian physics actually entailed the plausible conjectures. For if this entailment did not exist, what other relationship could organise the principles and conjectures into a system that made the latter plausible? Clarke makes it clear that there is no such entailment. The principles of Cartesian physics, he says, merely prohibit nonmechanical models of explanatory ones that are not constrained by Cartesian definitions of matter, motion, force, causality, and the axioms that connect these. Hence the foundations whose absence Descartes deplored in the work of Galileo – for the latter tried to explain only a few 'individual effects' – are also absent in Cartesian science. For Cartesians, the distinction between arbitrary (foundationless) and plausible (entailed) hypotheses simply relies, Clarke suggests, on analogies drawn between microscopic and macroscopic objects, and on the concepts appropriate to discussing mechanical models of physical processes. Neither the analogies nor the concepts offer any more guidance to locating a plausible hypothesis than do the Cartesian physical principles themselves.[44]

The interpretation of complex experimental results by Cartesians was made difficult for them, Clarke says, by the looseness of their physical theory, the vagueness of their empirical hypotheses, and, in consequence, the impossibility of adequate testing. Many explanatory hypotheses were consistent with the same set of observations, and since the physical axioms offered no means of distinguishing between competing hypotheses, recourse was had to their 'relative simplicity'. What this amounted to was consistency with the Cartesian laws of physics – the 'laws of nature' – and reliance on a few additional and independent assumptions. So of competing theories or hypotheses the one most closely adhering to Cartesian laws of nature was to be judged the simplest. The upshot of this confidence was, as Louis de la Forge put the matter in 1664, that proper theory and confirmation could ensure the truth of our hypotheses:

> [T]he hypotheses are not only probable, but they are also *indubitable*, when they explain something very clearly and very easily, when our observations do not oppose them, when reason shows that the thing in question could not be caused otherwise since it is deduced from principles which are certain, and when these hypotheses serve not only to explain one effect but many different effects.[45]

Thus the Cartesians argued that all experimental results required interpretation by means of a theory – a view given wide circulation in our own day by Karl Popper – but left open the question whether the theory used for interpretation must be the same theory on which the experiment was based. It soon became obvious that they can and do differ, for otherwise our theories could not be improved by experiments.

The Cartesians' faith in the utility of an axiomatic system in the sciences was a belief that never lacked critics in the seventeenth century, especially in Britain. Robert Boyle's arguments with Hobbes concerning the behaviour of air in Boyle's air pump have long been recognised as debates between two competing conceptions of scientific procedure. The disagreement was not merely on the question whether the air pump experiments had produced a genuine vacuum inside a glass tube partly filled with mercury. Nor was the difference of view simply a disagreement on whether the air's elasticity or weight or pressure had produced the impressive fall in the height of the mercury column. In *Leviathan and the Air Pump* Stevin Shapin and Simon Schaffer have argued that the disagreement was also a philosophical one.[46] It arose from the definitions and premises adopted by Hobbes in his metaphysical system, and from their consequences for his description of physical properties. One of these consequences, for example, was the logical impossibility of a vacuum in nature. Another was the restriction of genuine knowledge to propositions that are logically derivable from philosophical premises and definitions. Thus Boyle's empirical conclusions, and indeed the entire program of the experimenters, could not for Hobbes, as they could not for Descartes, be contributions to scientific knowledge. The program had no system of philosophical premises and theorems to support it.

Hobbes was an adherent, then, as Boyle was not, of a philosophical system that was so constructed as to provide for the logical entailment of descriptions of natural effects by descriptions of their metaphysical causes. So Hobbes denied Boyle's distinction between the soundness of experimental observations and the soundness of their explanatory hypotheses – between the truth of observation reports and the truth of the theories used to account for them. For Hobbes, the two were joined by logical entailment, not by an empirical and thus contingent relationship. It was a conception that stressed the confirmatory and illustrative functions of experiments but ignored their exploratory and knowledge-seeking uses. Since Hobbes mistakenly believed that his own procedure closely followed the mathematical experimentalism of Galileo, the attack that Hobbes mounted against Boyle's method assumed the truth of what he had yet to show: first, that his definitions of his basic physical terms, such as body, motion, endeavour, fluid, and vacuum, led him to produce confirmed scientific explanations of the behaviour of physical bodies; and, second, that these empirical propositions were logically entailed by his philosophical definitions and principles, and that they, in turn, belonged to a consistent metaphysical system. The first requirement was not in fact met, and the second was logically impossible to fulfil. The methodological contributions of the Newtonian enthusiasts, with their emphasis on the importance of experiments and induction, were intended to be quite different. The Newtonians, who did not include Locke or Hume, and included Berkeley only in some respects, concentrated their attention on a pair of topics: the interpretation of Newton's provocative remark, 'Hypotheses non fingo' ('I do not frame hypotheses') and the proper use of Newton's four philosophical rules, or procedural maxims (*Regulae Philosophandi*). On hypotheses, Newton's views changed, between his earlier and later writings, from acceptance to rejection. He began by using the term in its common meaning of an axiom or first principle. Later he converted its sense to that of a nonempirical, and thus untestable, claim – one that was maintained even when shown to be false if taken to be an empirical proposition. It was this latter usage that he criticised.[47] Instead of employing untestable conjectures, Newton advocated careful generalisation from observations and experiments to general laws, laws that in consequence would be both correct and for all practical purposes certain.

In the fourth edition of the *Opticks*, published posthumously in 1730, Newton gave a concise account of his beliefs concerning scientific method:

> [A]lthough the arguing from Experiments and Observations by Induction be no Demonstration of general Conclusions; yet it is the best way of arguing which the Nature of Things admits of, and may be looked upon as so much the stronger, by how much the Induction is more general. And if no Exception occur from Phenomena, the Conclusion may be pronounced generally. But if at any time afterwards any Exception shall occur from Experiments, it may then begin to be pronounced with such Exceptions as so occur. By this way of Analysis we may proceed from . . . Effects to their Causes, and from particular Causes to more general ones, till the Argument end in the most general.[48]

This is the method promulgated in the thirteenth century by Grosseteste and Albertus Magnus, later passed on to Galileo by his instructors at Padua, and then exemplified in the seventeenth century in the work of such experimentalists as Boyle and Robert Hooke. Nevertheless, in the course of describing how Thomas Reid publicised and enlarged Newton's views on hypotheses, L. L. Laudan has suggested that 'most of the available evidence seems to indicate that Reid was the first major British philosopher to take Newton's opinions on induction, causality, and hypothesis seriously', and thus to introduce Newton 'into the mainstream of British philosophical thought on epistemology and philosophy of science'.[49] Whether or not the available evidence establishes Reid's pride of place, it is certainly true, as Laudan tries to show, that Reid believed 'that a patient and methodical induction coupled with a scrupulous repudiation of all things hypothetical was the panacea for most of the ills besetting philosophy and science'.[50]

Laudan gives a list of Reid's criticisms of hypotheses, and several of these objections are of considerable interest. One is that accepting an hypothesis prejudices us in its favour; the hypothesis becomes the medium through which we interpret our observations. Instead of testing it by means of independent empirical propositions, we adapt those propositions to conform to our hypothesis or conjecture. This is the result of our conjecture relying on unobservable properties, entities, and processes as explanatory causes of the event in question. In brief, for Reid, the antecedent of the hypothetical must be instantiated and thus directly observable or testable. Another objection of his to hypotheses is that they cannot be tested and confirmed even by indirect means. On this point, David Hartley (1705–57), the father of physiological psychology and an early exponent of the doctrine of the association of ideas, was the object of Reid's attack. Hartley had written in his *Observations on Man* (1749): '[L]et us suppose the existence of the aether, with these its properties, to be destitute of all direct evidence, still if it serve to explain and account for a great variety of phaenomena, it will have an indirect evidence in its favour by these means'. This is because 'any hypothesis that has so much plausibility as to explain a considerable number of facts, helps us to digest these facts in proper order, to bring new ones to light, and to make *experimenta crucis* for the sake of future inquirers'.[51] This version of the hypothetico–deductive method drew Reid's reply that as long as we have no other, more direct, proof of the existence of the aether – or of the vibrations in the nerves that Hartley was postulating – 'to build a system' on such a basis was 'building a castle in the air'.[52] For many hypotheses, other than the one under test, could be invented that would account for a great variety of the same phenomena. The fact that we could not think of alternative accounts did not show that the one under test was the correct one. How, therefore, could we construct a complete list of the alternatives and submit each to a crucial test? Reid's conclusion was that hypotheses could properly be used to order facts, and 'suggest experiments, or direct our inquiries; but let just induction alone', he said, 'govern our belief' (82). Yet if hypotheses have these legitimate uses, what is the task of a 'just induction'? Peter Urbach has argued that Bacon took hypotheses or conjectures to be 'doubtful guesses which have, as yet, insufficient support to be committed to the body of accepted ideas, but which nevertheless may be perfectly respectable preliminary theories for scientists to entertain, though in a tentative way'. Urbach notes that 'Bacon himself published a number of such conjectures in the hope that they would eventually be "made good by experience"'.[53] Their scope, according to Bacon, had to extend beyond the data on which they were based; and the new predictions that the conjectures generated would, if substantiated, help to confirm those hypotheses (49). Put in this way, Bacon's conjectures and hypotheses were obviously elements of the hypothetico-deductive method that Reid attacked in Hartley and mistakenly thought that Bacon also rejected. What, then, was left for induction to do once unobservable entities were dealt with satisfactorily? Underlying this question was the more basic one of what criteria Reid depended on to ensure that any generalisation from some members of a class to all its members was legitimate. Reid's answer was to refer the questioner to Newton's four rules of inductive reasoning. However, these maxims of scientific reasoning were themselves subject to many different conflicting interpretations, as their later history shows, and Reid's reliance on Newton's maxims simply exposed him to Hume's strictures on inductive reasoning and the supposed constancy of natural laws. Since Reid responded by arguing that the inductive principle was an instinctive but fallible belief, and thus did not require justification or defence, it appeared that his inductive method was merely the hypothetico–deductive procedure with unobservable entities, in some sense of 'unobservable', excluded from it. 'Induction' was not the name of a distinctive, new, and more reliable, technique for deriving general laws from descriptions of specific details.

Neither, it turned out, was one of Vico's notable contributions, namely what has been variously called imaginative or empathetic insight, intuitive sympathy, fellow-feeling, or Einfühlung. This ability of human beings to feel their way into situations – to know what it is like to feel revenge, to be a rebel, to understand sarcasm, someone's character, a piece of music, a facial expression – was often taken in the later part of the nineteenth century to be an alternative method of learning how other people, including those in remote societies, conceived of their own actions and behaviour. This information would become an essential element in our European attempt to understand that behaviour, and hence in any explanation to be given of it. However, Vico's view, like that of Herder decades later, was rather different. Both thinkers stressed the fact that each person has a participant's knowledge of his or her own actions, motives, intentions, plans, goals, and emotions – a knowledge quite distinct in kind from that which people can obtain of nature and its laws. Yet neither thinker believed that mere introspective awareness of our own thoughts and feelings gave us indisputable causal knowledge of the institutional life of remote peoples or past societies. For Vico the procedure was to be the reverse of this: because God ensures that by self-reflection we can obtain incorrigible empirical knowledge of the natural propensities of human beings and the social life that they create, we can supplement this framework with ordinary empirical propositions and thus produce law-like explanations of particular social events and historical processes. Unfortunately, the supposed necessity of the metaphysical propositions that make up the framework – our knowledge of the basic institutions found everywhere in human societies, that is, marriage, religion, burial – and the fundamental psychological properties of human nature, such as rationality, ambition, and ferocity, was exposed to Hume's argument that every empirical proposition is testable by experience. Until Kant tried to show, in *Kritik der reinen Vernunft*, that some empirical propositions are necessary – are synthetic a priori – Vico's proposals lacked a plausible argument to support them. Moreover, Vico relied inescapably on our human knowledge, by means of self-examination, of the general nature of God's plan. If God does not exist, we have no assurance that our self-examination has correctly revealed the principles that govern the course of human societies. To nonbelievers, Vico could only argue that human history would have been different if the principles that he advanced had been different. Yet how, then, do we avoid being fatalistic about the future? The constraints set by the principles must be broad enough to allow people to affect the future by their actions. In that case, how can human beings know that other principles would have produced different outcomes?

Fifty years after Vico, these same problems were faced by Herder and answered in much the same way. Relying on the assurances of an omniscient God, we can learn the pattern of history-in-general. Human perfectibility is the result of the laws of inevitable human progress; and they, in turn, are based on the permanent features of human nature such as the instinct of self-preservation and that of sympathy. On the latter Herder wrote in *Ideen zur Philosophie der Geschichte der Menschheit* that '[L]ove apart, tender emotions express themselves in the form of sympathy, empathy or participation. Amongst all living creatures, man was chosen by Nature to possess these emotions to the highest degree', for 'he can put himself in the place of almost every creature and share its feelings even at the risk of his own well-being' (*Ideas*, 269). Thirty years earlier Adam Smith had said in the first paragraph of *The Theory of Moral Sentiments*:

> How selfish soever man may be supposed, there are evidently some principles in his nature, which interest him in the fortune of others, and render their happiness necessary to him, though he derives nothing from it except the pleasure of seeing it. Of this kind is pity or compassion, the emotion which we feel for the misery of others, when we either see it, or are made to conceive it in a very lively manner.

Smith immediately went on to say that since we cannot directly experience what other people feel, 'we can form no idea of the manner in which they are affected but by conceiving what we ourselves should feel in the like situation . . . it is by the imagination only that we can form any conception of what are his sensations'.[54] Granted that empathy often seems to enable someone to understand the point or goal of another person's actions, to discover what he or she is suffering, or to predict the psychological outlook of a favourite relative, the question remains how the empathiser knows that the diagnosis is correct. Perhaps empathy is simply a means, at least, of learning something of a person's psychological inclinations and the social rules in which they are embedded. If so, then the scientific laws that govern people's adherence to those rules in a given society have still to be determined. Once the rules have been found by non-empathetic means to be the operative ones, ordinary scientific procedures may tell us which sociological, economic, or other material factors causally affect the existence and maintenance of different sets of rules – and conversely.

In *The Theory of Moral Sentiments*, Smith himself distinguished between an observer identifying by means of imagination alone with the sensations of another person and an observer who is also familiar with the cause of those sensations:

> If the very appearances of grief and joy inspire us with some degree of the like emotions, it is because they suggest to us the general idea of some good or bad fortune that has befallen the person in whom we observe them. . . . The effects of grief and joy . . . do not, like those of resentment, suggest to us the idea of any other person for whom we are concerned, and whose interests are opposite to his. The general idea of good or bad fortune, therefore, creates some concern for the person who has received it. Nature, it seems, teaches us to be more averse to enter into this passion, and till informed of its cause, to be disposed rather to take part against it. (I.i.1.8)

Smith then enlarges on this last point by remarking that our sympathy with grief or joy when we do not know their cause is 'always extremely imperfect'. The sufferer's pains

> create rather a curiosity to inquire into his situation, along with some disposition to sympathize with him, than any actual sympathy that is very sensible. The first question which we ask is, What has befallen you? Till this be answered, though we are uneasy both from the vague idea of his misfortune, and still more from torturing ourselves with conjectures about what it may be, yet our fellow-feeling is not very considerable.
>
> Sympathy, therefore, does not arise so much from the view of the passion, as from that of the situation which excites it. (I.i.1.9–10)

Thus for Smith, as for Vico and Herder, fellow-feeling is an important aid in formulating general explanations of social behaviour, but fellow-feeling is not in itself an adequate example of such explanations. However, its utility is shown, for example, in Smith's attempt to explain 'the origin of ambition' and 'the distinction of ranks'. Because people wish, he says, to be the centre of approbation, societies in which wealth and power attract it are ones in which most people have fellow-feeling 'with all the passions of the rich and powerful'. Upon this is 'founded the distinction of ranks'(I.iii.2.1–3). Here the operative social and psychological 'law' is the desire of people to be the centre of approbation – not the fact that a specific form of the desire spreads by means of sympathy. Given the desire for approbation, sympathy with those people who are approved of in the society will produce a set of graded ranks of esteem. If the desire for approbation does not exist, then sympathy cannot distribute it.

IV. THE SEARCH FOR SOCIAL LAWS

It was the mission of a great many social thinkers in the eighteenth century to discover the laws that regulated the origin, growth, and maintenance of human societies. That there were such laws was very widely believed; that they were discoverable was an opinion that had been much encouraged by the publication and scientific acceptance of Newton's *Principia* with its universal physical laws, for it seemed plausible that social analogues must exist. Nevertheless, it is a long-standing curiosity that the nature of those laws, and the connections among their different kinds, should have received so little discussion until John Stuart Mill provided it in his work, *A System of Logic Ratiocinative and Inductive, Being a Connected View of the Principles of Evidence and the Methods of Scientific Investigation* (1843). It is true that much the same could be said of physical laws. Because there were not a large number of those yet known, the way appeared open for their social analogues to take a variety of forms. The distinction between laws and hypotheses was certainly much discussed, but it was not until J. F. W. Herschel wrote on the nature of physical theories and laws in *A Preliminary Discourse on the Study of Natural Philosophy* (1830) that their character was systematically examined; and it was not until Auguste Comte published his *Cours de philosophie positive* (1830–42) that the distinction between social laws of coexistence and succession was attempted, however unclearly, to be drawn. As a result of this slow development, the kinds of law-candidates enthusiastically put forward by social thinkers during the eighteenth century ranged from impossibly broad to uselessly narrow. In between, there were more plausible nominees.

Late in the century, Herder made use of several explanatory principles – explanatory both of the evolution of the Earth and of human civilisation. One of these 'laws of nature' was this: 'As the storms of the sea occur less frequently than moderate gales, so in the human species nature has benevolently ordered *that fewer destroyers than preservers should be born*'. Predatory animals and ferocious generals have appeared in much smaller numbers than vegetarian animals and 'quiet peaceful monarchs' (*Reflections*, 89). Another example of a law of nature, says Herder, is that '*the progress of arts and inventions puts into the hands of man increasing means of restraining or rendering innocuous, what Nature herself cannot eradicate*'. Thus storms at sea are compensated for by the art of navigation. Again, as mechanical inventions are made use of in warfare, brute human strength increasingly counts for little (93–4). Both these principles, insofar as they have a descriptive content and are not merely claims of faith, are statements of trends – of rather general changes over time – which are assumed to continue in the future. This is an unwarranted assumption that needs to be replaced with some identification of the particular conditions by which the future maintenance of the trend will be determined. A genuine social law would then take the form, 'When conditions of types X, Y, and Z are present so will a trend of type T'. The difficulty for Herder, as for everyone who wishes to treat trends as laws, is that unless we have additional laws that tell us those specific conditions are likely to occur, we cannot count on the future existence of the associated trend. Herder did not face this problem, for his laws of inevitable human progress were supposed to be based on the natural features of human beings given to them in the plan provided by an omniscient God. If these religious assurances are rejected, there is no reason to believe that the laws of human progress will be more than general descriptions of historical changes.

Very different from the mistaking of trends for laws are Hume's proposals for 'universal maxims of politics' and economics. The latter are instances of the habitual connection between certain types of laws, or political institutions, and specific forms of governmental policies or administrative behaviour. One of Hume's examples is this: '[T]hough free governments have been commonly the most happy for those who partake of their freedom; yet they are the most ruinous and oppressive to their provinces'. The reason Hume gives for this claim is that

> When a monarch extends his dominions by conquest, he soon learns to consider his old and his new subjects as on the same footing; because, in reality, all his subjects are to him the same, except the few friends and favourites, with whom he is personally acquainted. He does not, therefore, make any distinction between them in his *general* laws; and, at the same time, is careful to prevent all *particular* acts of oppression on the one as well as on the other.

Free states, Hume goes on to say, are necessarily more oppressive because the victors are legislators who will try to obtain both public and private benefits from the new provinces. Their appointed governors will seek plunder while they are in office; and the citizens of the victorious provinces will tolerate this behaviour since they will share in the booty. Whatever the merits of this maxim, it is open to testing by reference both to historical examples and to future cases. Hume himself gives a number of confirming instances, but not, of course, any disconfirming ones. He takes maxims such as this one to be evidence 'that politics admit of general truths, which are invariable by humour or education either of subject or sovereign'.[55]

In his essay 'On Money', Hume argues 'that, provided the money increase not in the nation, every thing must become much cheaper in times of industry and refinement, than in rude, uncultivated ages'. The reason is that it is almost a self-evident maxim that prices are fixed by 'the proportion between the circulating money and the commodities in the market'. When money becomes the universal measure of exchange, the same national cash has a much greater task to perform since its circulation is increased. The result is that 'the proportion being here lessened on the side of the money, everything must become cheaper, and the prices gradually fall' (291–2). Hume provides further examples of economic maxims and they all share a common feature: they claim that observable changes in one factor are dependent on observable, and sometimes measurable, changes in some other specifiable factor. Because the maxims are put forward as testable, we have some hope of discovering whether the causal relationships they describe are invariable enough for the maxims to be classified as social laws. That Hume was quite clear about the necessity of framing generalizations that could be put to tests is shown by his remarks on parallel cases of psychological hypotheses. In the *Treatise* Hume writes that 'to explain a mental operation, which is common to men and beasts, we must apply the same hypothesis to both; and as every true hypothesis will abide this trial, so . . . no false one will ever be able to endure it.' He then says that he will put his hypothesis on the relation between human and animal reasoning to a decisive trial and thus learn whether the hypothesis will equally well explain both kinds (1.3.16.3, SBN 177). Later in the *Treatise* (2.2.2) Hume discusses at some length eight experiments that will test his views on the nature of four of the indirect passions: humility, pride, love, and hatred. In those experiments, as in his earlier experiment on the indivisibility of our idea of a point, he emphasises his wish to take account of experience, observation, differing degrees of evidence, the difference between fact and theory, law-like regularities, and confirmation by experiment – all features that he had found in the work of Boyle, Hooke, and Newton.

One of the perennial difficulties that faced social theorists of the eighteenth century was that of distinguishing between common social customs and practices and psychological – or sociological – generalisations. Many social regularities are simply the outcome of rule-following and are not examples of causal relationships. However, it was very easy to confound the two sorts of regularities, and Hume sometimes does so. He wavers, as did other writers, between treating generalisations (or maxims) as merely social customs based on no causal necessity, and taking his maxims to be social practices that are exemplifications of psychological, or sociological, laws. In Montesquieu also, the distinction is often obscure, for he has no account of what constitutes an empirical law of social behaviour. On the other hand, he makes constant use of general causal propositions concerning the nature of social life: 'The barrenness of the earth renders men industrious, sober, inured to hardship, courageous, and fit for war. . . . The fertility of a country gives ease, effiminacy, and ascertain fondness for the preservation of life'. Another homely generalisation of this kind is that 'fertile provinces are always of a level surface, where the inhabitants are unable to dispute against a stronger power; they are then obliged to submit; and when they have once submitted, the spirit of liberty cannot return; the wealth of a country is a pledge of their fidelity'.[56] These generalisations are of the pattern made famous by Machiavelli, Guicciardini, and Bodin. As generalisations they do not seem to have benefited in the 1757 edition of *L'Esprit de lois*, from Montesquieu's reading of Hume's 1748 edition of *Essays, Moral and Political*, or of his *Philosophical Essays* – later retitled *Enquiry concerning Human Understanding* – of the same year.

The social thinkers of the eighteenth century discussed, and cast some light on, at least six central topics concerning the nature of social science. One was the uniformity of human nature; a second was the distinction between empirical social laws and moral principles; a third was the use of the hypothetico–deductive method; and a fourth was the difference between empirical social laws and mere social regularities and customs of various kinds. The two remaining topics, yet to be examined, are the idea of an economic system as an autonomous and self-regulatory one, and the attempt to apply the calculus of probability to descriptive statements of social behaviour. The development of the first topic owed most to the physician François Quesnay, one of the central figures of the economic Physiocrats, and to his colleague, the political economist and financial administrator A. R. J. Turgot. The second topic is chiefly the province of the Marquis de Condorcet, mathematician and admirer and friend of Turgot, and in 1792 briefly president of the legislative assembly before being hounded to death by his political opponents.

The Physiocrats whose publications and influence flourished in the period 1756–80, are commonly credited with being not only the first school of systematic economists but the first group to possess the notion of a general and integrated science of society. Their views were first expressed by their leading contributor, Quesnay, who used his medical familiarity with the circulation of blood in animal bodies to extend the idea of this process to the circulation of money and goods in an 'agricultural nation'. In short, he found in society the economic analogue of the circulatory system of the body, for he suggested that goods and money circulate in a law-like way through the three economic classes: the farmers and fishermen; the landed proprietors, nobility, and senior governmental administrators; and the manufacturing and merchandising groups. The only productive class is the first. After they retain what is necessary for their support and reproduction, their remaining production is sold to enable them to obtain manufactured goods, and to pay the proprietors the rent and the government its taxes. The proprietors buy food from the farmers and goods from the manufacturers, thus sending on some of their rent money. In turn, the manufacturers sell to the other two classes and receive goods and services from them. The entire cycle, endlessly repeated, is based on all three classes distributing among their members the agricultural surplus produced by nature. This circulation of wealth takes place according to the morally worthy laws established by God, and for that reason any interference by the government must be strictly limited. Free competition, free trade, freedom of labour, landed property, and single taxation – on land alone – these are God-given 'laws' that must all be preserved. Otherwise the natural stability of the economic system will be jeopardised, for its interlocking regularities allow it to be self-maintaining. Thus Quesnay's economic table, or diagram, of 1758, later published as a *Tableau économique*, was a generalisation to the entire society of the views on the 'circle of commerce' held in the previous century by such English economic writers as Misselden, Mun, and North. Because the Physiocratic system was held to be beneficent, God-created, and self-maintaining, its supporters were as convinced as their seventeenth-century predecessors had been that their respective systems should be kept free of outside interference, especially by the government.

However, it was Turgot and not Quesnay who tried to identify in detail the interlocking regularities of the economic system and some of its social consequences. It was Turgot, for example, who by 1750, like Adam Smith but independently, had formulated the notion that the growth of civilisation has taken place in definite economic stages, and that the different means of subsistence embodied in those stages had important social effects. In his *Plan de deux discours sur l'histoire universelle* (1751) Turgot identifies three successive economic stages: that of hunting and gathering; that of pastoral activities; and that of agriculture. For each stage Turgot describes some of the social and economic consequences of its subsistence techniques. He remarks, for instance, that the agricultural stage would have developed with difficulty from the hunting stage because hunters have no domesticated animals to provide labour and manure. In turn, the agricultural stage yields a surplus product and the unneeded people develop towns and trade and 'all the useful arts and accomplishments'.[57] Stage theories concerning what were thought to be laws of large-scale social development over long periods of time became popular from the mid-century onward – popular because a host of French and Scottish thinkers believed that such laws would explain why some societies had developed at a different rate of progress from other societies. Since 'progress' was a term reserved for the presence of ethically and politically superior forms of social change, the problem was to account for their development from inferior stages. What conditions would have to be met in the two lower stages for them to advance into the highest one? Once again, there was a familiar resistance to distinguishing empirical social laws from moral principles. As a consequence, two sorts of laws had to be discovered. One was that of the law-like sequence of stages. The other was that of the set of law-like connections among the ethical, political, and economic factors, within each stage. Both types were to preoccupy such major nineteenth century figures as Comte and Marx.

In his *Plan de deux discours* Turgot made use of many causal claims of intra-stage connections. In city-republics, he says, 'the spirit of equality cannot be banished because the spirit of commerce rules'. He also states that 'In nations of small size it is impossible for despotic authority to become consolidated; the dominion of a chief can in such a nation rest on nothing but the consent of the people, or on a veneration either for a person or a family' (72). The strength and significance of the causal links with the economic bases of the three stages was stressed not only by Turgot but by many other writers. In their *Philosophie rurale* (1763) Quesnay and the Marquis de Mirabeau made this link explicit: 'It is upon subsistence, upon the means of subsistence, that all the branches of the political order depend. . . . This is the fundamental force to which is due everything which men cultivate, navigate and build'.[58] Like Adam Smith in his Glasgow lectures of 1763, Quesnay and Mirabeau added a fourth stage, that of commerce, to follow that of agriculture. It was commonly agreed that the usual sequence of stages was subject to modification by local conditions. Smith pointed out, for instance, that in North America hunting was succeeded by agriculture, for there was no pastoral stage. Similarly, a good number of authors believed that there were common, but not invariable, connections between the major factors, in particular between forms of property and forms of government. Thus William Robertson (1721–93), the Scottish historian, remarked that hunting tribes, which have hardly any conception of property, will have much simpler institutions concerning it than those in societies where 'the earth is cultivated with regular industry, and a right of property, not only in its productions, but in the soil itself, is completely ascertained'.[59]

Turgot was among the earliest thinkers to note that the entire merchant economy is a set of interacting variables that can reach positions of equilibrium. In 1767 he wrote to David Hume and said that 'A kind of equilibrium or balance is established among the value of all the produce of the land, the consumption of different kinds of goods, and different kinds of products, the number of men employed, and the cost of their wages.' If we change one factor, 'it is impossible that there should not occur in the entire machine a movement which tends to re-establish the former balance or equilibrium'.[60] He went on to suggest that the interest rate on loans in a country is a sort of thermometer because the rate is a mathematical function of the quantity of capital available for loans. In the same year Turgot stated in print the law of diminishing physical returns in agriculture from a specific piece of land. Soil, he said, has a limited fertility so that beyond a certain point of expenditure the product's increase will be less and less until finally no increase of expenditure will add to the product (2: 645).

The mere list of the theoretical notions to which Turgot gave early expression is in itself an impressive epitaph. They include treatment of the economy as a system of interacting and quantifiable variables, some of which co-vary; the belief that the evolution of human society has been through a describable sequence of economic stages on which the growth of the arts and sciences has been based; the claim that law-like connections exist between the cultural superstructure and its economic bases; the opinion that the sequence of the economic stages is simultaneously a sequence of social development of the perfectible human race; and, finally, instances of social laws such as those of the diminishing returns in agriculture and the interest rate on loans.

Turgot's younger friend and admirer, the Marquis de Condorcet, in the introduction to his *Essai sur l'application de l'analyse à la probabilité des décisions rendues à la pluralité des voix* (1785), wrote that Turgot 'was convinced that the truths of the moral and political sciences are susceptible of the same certainty as those forming the system of the physical sciences, even those branches like astronomy which seem to approach mathematical certainty'. This 'led him to the consoling hope that the human race will necessarily progress toward happiness and perfection'.[61] Condorcet tried to advance the claims to mathematical certainty of the science of man by arguing that most of our grounds for belief consist in our experience of 'the constancy of the order of phenomena' – on the probability that our future experience will resemble that of the past. These expectations provide the grounds of our belief in the law-like structure of nature. They allow us to believe rationally that nature is subject to invariable laws that we can discover. That material objects exist is a belief of this kind and so is our belief that tomorrow the sun will rise as usual. The certainty available to us in the natural sciences, in mathematics, and in political and moral sciences is all of this same sort. Because it is based on our experience of regularities, we can investigate the influence of marriage, birth and death ratios, for instance, on moral qualities or bodily size. We can also investigate whether these effects are independent or causally affect each other, and to what extent. The use of the calculus of probabilities will enable us to determine whether a co-variation between factors is a law-like one. Although use of the calculus will not in itself generate laws from observed facts, it will certainly measure the weight of our evidence for a belief and permit us to identify any laws that are present. One of Condorcet's more ambitious suggestions is that we can calculate 'the effect of the destruction of the privileged orders and of feudal rights' (203). The chief obstacle, he thinks, is not theoretical but purely practical: we need to acquire the numerical data to which we can apply our calculations of probability.

V. THE ORIGIN OF THE SUBSPECIES

The second half of the eighteenth century was notable for the efflorescence of political economy – the study of the economic determinants of political life, and conversely. Adam Smith characterised the field in the Introduction to Book IV of *An Inquiry into the Nature and Causes of the Wealth of Nations* (1776):

> Political oeconomy, considered as a branch of the science of a statesman or legislator, proposes two distinct objects; first, to provide a plentiful revenue or subsistence for the people, or more properly to enable them to provide such a revenue or subsistence for themselves; and secondly, to supply the state or commonwealth with a revenue sufficient for the publick services. It proposes to enrich both the people and the sovereign.[62]

These were the practical applications to which the study of political economy could be put. There was also its explanatory role. In *The Wealth of Nations* that role is strikingly large and complex: it includes such topics as the four sources of authority in social life, namely age, personal qualities, wealth, and birth; the origin and importance of government in the protection of property holders; the connection between economic stages and the allocation of social power; and the significance of the pursuit of social esteem. All these, and many more, are in addition to what we should now call purely economic issues such as the price of commodities and the accumulation of capital. Smith's treatment of these economic questions was highly systematic, very detailed, and of great scope. Yet this treatment was accompanied by such discussions as those on the rise and progress of towns and cities, and on the establishment of colonies. In short, *The Wealth of Nations* includes topics drawn from economics, political theory, politics, history, and the study of the nature and determinants of historical change in general. With a scope this broad, it is natural to ask of a compendium of this kind whether it leaves any substantial opening for the independent growth of its components. If economics, politics, political theory, and history are best dealt with as interacting elements of a unified, and thus single, social science, then what useful purpose is served by encouraging their separation and thus independent elaboration? Nevertheless, subdivision of the all-embracing field of political economy is what in fact took place both before and after Smith wrote.

The causes of the independent growth of subdisciplines – or of the failure of a unified social science to maintain itself – arise from a variety of historical, practical, and administrative factors rather than purely intellectual ones. The curricula of such early European universities as Salamanca, Bologna, Vienna, Oxford, Cambridge, and Paris illustrate the way in which the fields of political theory, government, and economics developed as adjuncts of the major disciplines of law, historiography, and theology. Since those disciplines, in turn, drew their support from the special character and preoccupations of medieval European society, the emergence of the subdisciplines bore many traces of those preoccupations. The medieval churchmen's views about interest charges and the barrenness of money, or their debates about the just wage are examples of this. So are the efforts of Bodin in the mid-sixteenth century to strengthen the claims of the French rulers to complete and undivided political power; and of his urging of the need for the laws of France to be redrafted and codified after an examination of the best legal practice in many countries. All these were attempts to solve some urgent practical problems of the period. Both the urgency of those problems and the consequent need for procedural reform encouraged the separate development of the subfields that grew up around such topics. A unified social science might be intellectually desirable, but until the political and economic state of a society revealed to its administrators and its educated class which practical problems demanded remedies, the scope and subject matter of those problems would be obscure. As a result, so would be the scope and benefit of the more general social science that was supposed to embrace them.

Against this it may be argued, as it was by Montesquieu, that we can have better knowledge of the aggregate social tendencies produced by the combination of individual causes than we can have of those causes themselves. Montesquieu wrote that physical

> causes become less arbitrary to the extent that they have a more general effect. Thus we know better what gives a nation its special character than what gives an individual his particular spirit; we know better the characteristics of an entire sex than those of any one person belonging to it; we know better what shapes the genius of societies that have adopted a given way of life than what shapes that of an individual.[63]

This view, discussed critically in Condorcet's *Tableau général de la science qui a pour objet l'application du calcul aux sciences politiques et morales* (A General View of the Science of Social Mathematics) (1793), surfaced again in Mme de Staël's introduction to her volume, *De l'influence des passions sur le bonheur des individus et des nations* (On the Influence of the Passions of the Happiness of Men and Nations) (1796):

> [T]he events which are most dependent on chance are subject to genuine calculation when the cases are many. In the canton of Berne, for example, it has been noticed that in every decade there are approximately the same number of divorces; there are cities in Italy where one can calculate exactly how many murders will be committed regularly each year. Thus events which result from a multitude of diverse combinations have a periodic recurrence, a fixed proportion, when the observations are derived from a large number of cases.[64]

Forty years later, L. A. J. Quetelet in his *Sur l'homme, et le developpement de ses facultés* (1835) was to elaborate, as J. S. Mill was also to do, and as Hume had foreshadowed, the aggregate character of social laws. The significance of this point here is that it seemed to offer the possibility that since only collective behaviour appeared to be subject to law-like regularities, a unified social science might be the most promising project to examine. For although a particular subdiscipline might display no such regularities, some combination of subdisciplines might do so. Despite this apparent benefit, other more urgent and practical considerations ensured the continued development of economics and government as independent fields.

History occupied an anomalous position, for it appeared to have no pattern or theoretical structure capable of explication. The most that could be said for its utility, and was said by Bolingbroke in his *Letters on the Study and Use of History* (1735–6), is that in history there can be found enlightening illustrations of basic moral and political principles – principles drawn from the study of ethics and politics but given dramatic expression in historical examples. The intellectual growth of history as a discipline, therefore, can consist only in the improvement of its methods of exploration and verification, not in the elucidation of its theoretical framework. As a discipline, history has little explanatory, but much admonitory, value and hence is a science only in the most general sense of that term. It was left to Vico to argue the opposite, and for the historical determinists of the nineteenth century, such as Marx and Engels, to find a theory and laws of historical development where there had seemed to be only spectacle.

It is commonly agreed that the eighteenth century ended chronologically before its intellectual effects were fully developed. One of its characteristic projects was Jean-Baptiste Say's attempt in his *Traité d'economie politique* (1803) to describe the methodology and structure of the field of economics as the science of the laws of the 'production, distribution, and consumption of wealth'. Not only was the *Traité* the first systematic treatment of the field, but in it Say discusses at length the role of the political economist as an impartial spectator who, like the physical scientist, describes the inevitable consequences of scientific laws but gives no political advice concerning them. Political economists are equipped only to give government officials purely factual information. What those officials do with it is a matter for their political judgement. Say, like his contemporary Malthus, later became an important academic professor; and like his acquaintance, the stockbroker Ricardo, exerted much influence on the development of scientific economics in the nineteenth century. Say's influence was especially significant in the debate concerning the unity of the social sciences because of his strong advocacy of the view that economics has its own independent laws and theories. He thought that governments are free to make use of them without also having to take into account the many special theories of government or political philosophy. Those latter fields can contribute value judgements and suggested goals, but such factual information as they provide is largely independent of – and so does not affect – the local details of time and place which can be discovered within the constraints set by the general laws of economics.

Philosophical preoccupations are not easily given up. James Mill's 'Essay on Government' (1820) continued into the nineteenth century the long-standing attempt of many thinkers in the previous century to base a science of government on a science of human nature – on general propositions about human behaviour that would allow us to deduce a science of government. For Mill, this science would make possible the achievement of 'the greatest happiness of the greatest number'. For his critic, Thomas Macaulay, there are no such reliable principles of human nature. It is not true, for instance, that people always behave from self-interest. In fact, he says, the nature of human motives cannot be described in true generalisations. On any specific occasion we can be unable to predict the agent's goal or the means he will use to reach it. In brief, Macaulay believes that the feasibility of deducing a science of government depends on the 'absolute and universal truth' of the premises.[65] He does not consider whether a science of government might be founded, but not 'deduced', from tendency statements or statistical generalisations. What this type of controversy shows, however, is that utilitarians such as James Mill and Bentham envisaged the operations of government as subject to certain scientific principles concerning human behaviour; if those could be revealed the process of governing a country could be managed scientifically. Thus well after the end of the eighteenth century, as at its beginning, the search for the 'true laws of human nature' as a basis for a practical science of society – for a science of social therapy – continued with unabated enthusiasm. Saint-Pierre's original desire for the discovery of a form of government that was a self-regulating and self-preserving social machine, one that did not depend on the talents and art of its governors, was far from being forgotten.

NOTES

1 David Hume, *A Treatise of Human Nature*, eds. D. F. Norton and M. J. Norton, in the *Clarendon Edition* (2006), 2.3.1.11–12, SBN 403–4.
2 See David Carrithers, 'The Enlightenment Science of Society' in *Inventing Human Science: Eighteenth-Century Domains*, eds. C. Fox, R. Porter, and R. Wokler (Berkeley, CA, 1995), 232–70.
3 J. B. Bury, *The Idea of Progress* (London, 1921), 145.
4 Nicolo Machiavelli, *The Prince*, trans. G. Bull (Harmondsworth, 1981), 130.
5 Charles de Secondat, Baron de Montesquieu, *Considérations sur les causes de la grandeur des Romains et de leur décadence* (1734); translated as *Considerations on the Causes of the Greatness of the Romans and Their Decline*, trans. D. Lowenthal (Ithaca, NY, 1968).
6 Henri de Boulainvilliers, *État de France* (London, 1727), 76–7. Quoted in N. O. Keohane, *Philosophy and the State in France* (Princeton, NJ, 1980), 363 fn.

7 Charles, Abbé de Saint-Pierre, *Ouvrajes de politique*, 16 vols. (Rotterdam, 1733–41), 12: 202–3. Quoted in Keohane, 371.
8 Giambattista Vico, *Principi di una scienza nuova intorno alla commune natura delle nazioni* (1725); translated as *The New Science* (3rd edn., 1744), trans. T. G. Bergin and M. H. Fisch (Ithaca, NY, 1948), 93.
9 Azpilcueta Navarro, *Comentario resolutorio de usuras* (1556), 80. Quoted in *The School of Salamanca*, ed. M. Grice-Hutchinson (Oxford, 1952), 94.
10 Thomas Mun, *England's Treasure by Forraign Trade* (London, 1664), reprinted in *Early English Tracts on Commerce*, ed. J. R. McCulloch (Cambridge, 1954), 208.
11 Gerald De Malynes, *A Treatise of the Canker of Englands Common Wealth* (London, 1601), 95–6.
12 Isaiah Berlin, 'Montesquieu' in *Against the Current* (London, 1979), 145.
13 Jean-Jacques Rousseau, *Émile ou de l'éducation*, in *Oeuvres*, 4: 239–877; translated as *Emile or On Education*, trans. A. Bloom (Harmondsworth, 1991), 458.
14 Dugald Stewart, *Elements of the Philosophy of the Human Mind*, in *Works*, ed. W. Hamilton, 11 vols. (Edinburgh and London, 1854–60), vols. 2–4, 3: 350.
15 Stewart, *Elements*, in Works, 3: 357.
16 *The Correspondence of Edmund Burke*, ed. T. H. Copeland, 10 vols. (Cambridge, 1958–78); vol. 3 (1961), ed. G. H. Guttridge, 350–1. Quotation in Peter J. Marshall and Glyndwr Williams, *The Great Map of Mankind: Perceptions of New Worlds in the Age of Enlightenment* (London, 1982), 93.
17 William Robertson, *The Progress of Society in Europe*, ed. F. Gilbert (Chicago, IL, 1972), 154. Quoted in Marshall and Williams, 93.
18 Jean Bodin, *Les six livres de la république*; translated as *The Six Books of a Commonweale*, trans. R. Knolles (1606); (Cambridge, 1962), 547.
19 Bodin, *Six Books*, 549.
20 Ronald Victor Sampson, *Progress in the Age of Reason* (London, 1956), 75.
21 Jean-Jacques Rousseau, *Discours sur l'origine et les fondements de l'inégalité parmi les hommes* in *Oeuvres*, 3: 109–223; translated as *A Discourse on the Origin of Inequality* in *The Social Contract and Discourses*, trans. G. D. H. Cole, revised by J. H. Bumfitt and J. C. Hall (London, 1973), 38. Page citations refer to the translation.
22 David Hume, *An Enquiry concerning Human Understanding*, ed. T. L. Beauchamp, in the *Clarendon Edition* (2000), 8.1.7, SBN 83.
23 Sir James Steuart, *An Inquiry into the Principles of Political Oeconomy*, 2 vols., ed. A. S. Skinner (Edinburgh, 1966), 1: 20.
24 Denis Diderot, *Supplément au voyage de Bougainville, ou dialogue entre A. et B.*; translated as *Supplement to the Voyage of Bougainville*, in *Political Writings*, trans. and eds. J. H. Mason and R. Wokler (Cambridge, 1992), 67.
25 Charles de Secondat, Baron de Montesquieu, *L'esprit des lois* in *Oeuvres complètes*, ed. R. Caillois, 2 vols. (Paris, 1949–51), vol. 2; translated as *The Spirit of the Laws*, trans. and eds. A. M. Cohler, B. C. Miller, and H. S. Stone (Cambridge, 1989), Pt 3, ch. 5, p. 250.
26 Louis, Chevalier de Jancourt, 'Egalité' in *Encyclopédie*, vol. 5. Quoted in Claudine Hunting, 'The Philosophes and Black Slavery: 1748–1765' in *Race, Gender, and Rank*, ed. M. C. Horowitz (Rochester, NY, 1992), 17–30, at 24.
27 Diderot, 'Liberté' in *Encyclopédie*, vol. 9. Quoted in Hunting, 23.
28 David Hume, *Political Essays*, ed. K. Haakonssen (Cambridge, 1994), 86 note.
29 James Beattie, *An Essay on the Nature and Immutability of Truth*, ed. J. Fieser (Bristol, 2000), 229.
30 John Immerwahr, 'Hume's Revised Racism' in *Journal of the History of Ideas*, 53 (1992): 481–6.

31 David Hume, *Essays, Moral, Political, and Literary*, ed. E. F. Miller (Indianapolis, IN, 1987), 383–4.
32 Immanuel Kant, *Beobachtungen über das Gefühl des Schönen und Erhabenen*, in Ak 2: 243–56; translated as *Observations on the Feelings of the Beautiful and Sublime*, trans. J. T. Goldthwaite (Berkeley, CA, 1960), 110–11.
33 Arthur O. Lovejoy, 'Kant and Evolution' in *Forerunners of Darwin 1745–1859*, eds. B. Glass, O. Temkin, and W. Strauss Jr. (Baltimore, MD, 1959), 178 (quoting from Kant's 'Von den verschiedenen Racen der Menschen,' Ak 2: 427–43).
34 Kant, Menschenkunde (1781/2) in *Vorlesungen über Anthropologie*, Ak 25.2: 849–1203. Quoted in Antonello Gerbi, *The Dispute of the New World*, trans. J. Moyle (Pittsburgh, PA, 1973), 330 n.14.
35 Kant, *Zum ewigen Frieden* (Ak 8: 341–86), translated as *Toward Perpetual Peace*, trans. M. J. Gregor, in *Works/Practical Philosophy* (1996), 8: 359.
36 Kant, *Metaphysik der Sitten* (*The Metaphysics of Morals*), trans. M. J. Gregor, in *Works/Practical Philosophy* (1996), 6:348–9, 347.
37 Kant, *Anthropologie in pragmatischer Hinsicht* [1798] (Ak 7: 117–333); translated as *Anthropology from a Pragmatic Point of View*, trans. M. J. Gregor (The Hague, 1974), 174.
38 Johann Gottfried Herder, *Ideen zur Philosophie der Geschichte der Menschheit* in *Werke in zehn Bänden*, ed. M. Bollacher, vol. 6 (1989); translated as *Ideas for a Philosophy of the History of Mankind*, in *J. G. Herder on Social and Political Culture*, trans. and ed. F. M. Barnard (Cambridge, 1969), 283.
39 Herder, *Reflections on the Philosophy of History of Mankind*, trans. T. O. Churchill (1800), ed. F. E. Manuel (Chicago, IL, 1968), 52.
40 Quoted in Marshall and Williams, *The Great Map*, 82.
41 Hume, *Enquiry concerning Human Understanding*, 8.1.7, SBN 83.
42 Pico della Mirandola, *Oratio de hominis dignitate*; translated as *Oration on the Dignity of Man* in *Renaissance Philosophy*, trans. and eds. A. B. Fallico and H. Shapiro, 2 vols. (New York, NY, 1967), 1: 143.
43 Francis Bacon, *Novum organum* in *The Physical and Metaphysical Works*, ed. J. Devey (London, 1891).
44 Desmond Clarke, *Occult Powers and Hypotheses* (Oxford, 1989).
45 Louis de la Forge, *L'homme de René Descartes*, 218; cited in Clarke, 218–20.
46 Stevin Shapin and Simon Schaffer, *Leviathan and the Air Pump* (Princeton, NJ, 1985).
47 See I. B. Cohen, *Franklin and Newton: An Inquiry into Speculative Newtonian Experimental Science and Franklin's Work in Electricity as an Example thereof* (Philadelphia, PA, 1956).
48 Isaac Newton, *Opticks*, 4th edn. (London, 1730), Book III, Pt. 1, 404–5.
49 L. L. Laudan, 'Thomas Reid and the Newtonian Turn of British Methodological Thought' in *The Methodological Heritage of Newton*, eds. R. G. Butts and J. W. Davis (Oxford, 1970), 103–31 at 106.
50 Laudan, 'Thomas Reid', 108.
51 David Hartley, *Observations on Man* (1749), 6th edn. (London, 1834), I, ch. 1, prop V, p. 10.
52 Thomas Reid, *Essays on the Intellectual Powers of Man* (1785), eds. D. R. Brookes and K. Haakonssen (Edinburgh, 2002), II.3, 80.
53 Peter Urbach, *Francis Bacon's Philosophy of Science* (La Salle, IL, 1987), 47.
54 Adam Smith, *The Theory of Moral Sentiments* (1759), eds. D. D. Raphael and A. L. Macfie, in *Works* (1976), I.i.1.1.
55 Hume, *Political Essays*, 7.
56 Montesquieu, *Spirit*, 272–3.

57 A. R. J. Turgot, *Plan de deux discours sur l'histoire universelle* in *Works*, 1: 275–323; translated as 'On Universal History' (1751) in *Turgot on Progress, Sociology and Economics*, trans. and ed. R. L. Meek (Cambridge, 1973), 65–9.

58 Francois Quesnay and Victor Riquetti, Marquis de Mirabeau, *Philosophie rurale* (Amsterdam, 1763); trans. in R. L. Meek, *The Economics of Physiocracy: Essays and Translations* (London, 1962), 57.

59 William Robertson, *The History of America*, 2 vols. (Edinburgh, 1777), 1: 324.

60 *Oeuvres de Turgot*, ed. G. Schelle, 5 vols. (Paris, 1913–23), 2: 663–4.

61 Condorcet, *Selected Writings*, ed. K. M. Baker (Indianapolis, IN, 1976), 33.

62 Adam Smith, *An Inquiry into the Nature and Causes of the Wealth of Nations*, eds. R. H. Campbell, A. S. Skinner, and W. B. Todd, 2 vols., in *Works* (1976), 428.

63 Montesquieu, *Essay sur les causes qui peuvent affecter les esprits et les caractères* in *Oeuvres*, 2: 39–68; translated as 'An Essay on the Causes that May Affect Men's Minds and Characters', trans. M. Richter, *Political Theory*, 4.2 (1976): 139–62, at 139.

64 Germaine Necker (baronne de Staël-Holstein, *Oeuvres complètes*, 17 vols. (Geneva, 1967), 1: 108.

65 Thomas Macaulay, 'Mill's Essay on Government: Utilitarian Logic and Politics' (1829); reprinted in *Utilitarian Logic and Politics*, ed. J. Lively and J. Rees (Oxford, 1978), 97–129 at 124–6.

36

PHILOSOPHICAL REFLECTION ON HISTORY

DARIO PERINETTI

The expression 'philosophy of history' was coined by Voltaire, but in the eighteenth century it referred to a specific project that by no means exhausted the scope of philosophical interest in history during the period. We will do better to speak of a *philosophical reflection on history*, both because it is terminologically more appropriate and because this broader term will remind us that a philosophical interest in history affected almost all spheres of philosophy in the period. Philosophical stances on providential history, the stages of history, and the status of historical knowledge played a crucial but often overlooked role in the debates on the foundation of morals and politics, in efforts to produce a science of human nature, and in central epistemological discussions.

The rise of modern science, the impact of Cartesianism and scepticism, and the progress made by concrete historical research in the seventeenth century all helped to undermine any model of knowledge in which providential history could remain the frame of reference for all moral and empirical sciences. In fact the foundation of the different areas of knowledge was an open question, as was their place in the emerging 'science of man', or 'science of human nature'. In that context, a common problem was how to provide a single account of both the factual and the normative sides of history. The challenge was to produce an account of history that revealed the origins of social life without counterfactual speculations. This was not easy, for the development of historical research (essentially the work of antiquarians and philologists) constantly threatened universal histories that wanted to preserve the normative function of history as a 'teacher of life'.

The reflection on history by key eighteenth-century philosophers can be understood in the light of two main concerns. The first was to secure the objectivity of historical knowledge both at the level of describing and explaining historical

I am indebted to comments by David Fate Norton and Knud Haakonssen and to the participants in a seminar on eighteenth-century philosophy of history at McGill University. This work was supported by the Social Sciences and Humanities Research Council of Canada.

facts, the second to secure the possibility of a philosophical reconstruction of universal history. However, a unified 'philosophy of history' was not the aim of philosophers puzzling over history. They thought that solutions to these puzzles would improve understanding of the foundations of empirical knowledge and of morals, both of which were preoccupations of the time. On one hand, the epistemological problems proper to history, relating to justification of knowledge derived from human testimony, were also central to other disciplines. Not only geography, but also many other sciences of the period relied on reports by travellers or found in books, so any serious doubt about the reliability of testimony threatened the scientific enterprise as a whole. On the other hand, the improvement of historical research constantly and rapidly eroded the credibility of sacred history, which was still thought by many to be the ultimate source of moral norms. The prospect of reconstructing universal history on philosophical grounds thus became an attractive option for philosophers attempting a secular understanding of the sources of normativity.

I. HISTORICAL PYRRHONISM AND THE OBJECTIVITY OF HISTORY

The role of early-modern versions of scepticism in informing what we now typically call the modern scientific outlook has been well documented.[1] Much less attention has been given to the role of scepticism about historical knowledge, or historical pyrrhonism. Historical pyrrhonism is difficult to define. Like 'relativism' today, 'historical pyrrhonism' then was widely used to dismiss someone's views and no one claimed to be a historical pyrrhonist. The concept may be approached by listing the usual charges against historical pyrrhonism.

The following activities were likely to be described and denounced as 'historical pyrrhonism'.[2]

1. Undermining the canonical histories, sacred or civil.
2. Denying the possibility of historical knowledge and recommending suspension of judgement about historical facts.
3. Denying *certain* knowledge of history and recommending proportion between our belief in historical facts and available evidence.
4. Claiming that ancient history is unreliable because it confounds historical facts with fables, myths, and oral traditions.
5. Claiming that modern history is unreliable because contemporary historians are biased and do not have the distance required to acquire an impartial point of view.
6. Claiming that the credibility of any history decays as it passes through long chains of testimony.
7. Critical scrutiny of accepted historical facts through rigorous assessment of testimony.

Part of the interest of pyrrhonian arguments about historical knowledge is that they are based, not on doubts about the reliability of sense perception or of reason, but on challenges to the reliability of human testimony. Since the main problem of historical knowledge, as conceived in the eighteenth century, was to assess knowledge derived from human testimony, it is not surprising that historical pyrrhonists borrowed their epistemological tools from legal theory rather than from theories of perception. Historians can rarely observe the facts they discuss and do not treat them as something passively received in perception. Like the 'judges of fact' on a jury, historians see 'facts' as something actively established through the process of weighing testimony. Important philosophers adopted this legal–historical approach to empirical facts, seeing a knower not as a passive observer, but as an active judge. The accuracy of empirical knowledge was to be evaluated in moral terms such as impartiality, honesty, and justice. Accurate knowledge of facts, in the tradition of historical pyrrhonism, entails doing *justice* to the complete empirical situation.[3]

The foremost advocate of historical pyrrhonism was the seventeenth-century French *libertin érudit* François La Mothe le Vayer (1588–1672). From mild worries about historical veracity, La Mothe le Vayer evolved to a radical stance, recommending the total suspension of judgement about knowledge based on historical testimony (point 2 in the preceding list). In *Du peu de certitude qu'il y a dans l'histoire* (1668) he formulated the radical claim characteristic of his historical pyrrhonism: '[T]here is almost no certainty at all in what the most famous past historians have told and it is likely that those that will embrace this profession in the future will not do much better in all their enterprises'.[4] La Mothe le Vayer included both ancient and modern history as guilty of selecting facts according to the personal agenda of the historian. His central claim is that testimony is unreliable because witnesses inevitably are biased by their social, religious, or political perspective.

Another major exponent of historical pyrrhonism and perhaps the most influential for eighteenth-century philosophers and historians is Pierre Bayle. His *Dictionnaire historique et critique*[5] was originally meant to correct the countless errors of Louis Moreri's *Grand Dictionnaire historique*, a compilation of facts about history and historical characters which Bayle devastated with an amazing erudition and a battery of sceptical arguments. Bayle's dictionary is a monumental collection of critically established facts, in the legal–historical sense of that word. It is not a theory about the critical ascertainment of facts but an example of that critical attitude put into practice. It is, in fact, the prime example of strand No. 7 of historical pyrrhonism in the preceding list and one of particular importance here. Bayle's ironic treatment of historians' and other scholars' credulity regarding received facts gave a formidable impetus to the independent attitude towards authority and tradition characteristic of much Enlightenment philosophy.

Unlike La Mothe le Vayer, Bayle did not recommend a suspension of judgement about all historical facts. Although such respected historians as Livy, Plutarch, and Dionysius Halicarnassus made contradictory reports about the same event and most canonical histories were plagued by mistakes, Bayle did not believe the objectivity of historical knowledge thereby to be irredeemably endangered. Bayle suggests, rather, that the flaws of canonical histories are an invitation to train our judgement by making critical assessments of historical facts and thus help us get towards a more accurate representation of history. To the question whether the countless inconsistencies of history demand a radical historical scepticism, Bayle responds by advising 'the reader to make use of these observations to fortify his judgment against the custom of reading without attention, and of believing without examination'.[6]

Although historians and witnesses are always interested actors and a great many flaws of history are due to partisanship this does not mean that all history is hopelessly partial but, rather, that criticism is needed to establish rules for historical practice. The real problem is the lack of objective criteria and institutionalised procedures to justify knowledge claims about historical facts: 'An author ought not to go by particular rules of his own; he must conform to public rules: but, according to the public laws in point of history, what is proved by the testimony of grave authors is admitted: and whatever a modern writer advances concerning antiquity, without taking it from good historians, is rejected as a fable'.[7]

Conceived as a form of mitigated scepticism, historical pyrrhonism played an important role in the discussions about the certainty of nondemonstrative knowledge that were so central to eighteenth-century epistemology. Unlike most seventeenth-century attempts to salvage the certainty of empirical knowledge, historical pyrrhonists did not focus on the reliability of sense perception[8] but were concerned with the reliability of testimony as a source of probable knowledge. This constructive form of historical pyrrhonism took various forms. Some writers held that modern history is unreliable because we lack the distance needed for impartiality (No. 5 in the preceding list). The closer testimonies are to the events, the more probable that they are tainted by partisanship and prejudice or concealed. Thus Voltaire in his foreword to the *Histoire de la guerre de 1741* (*History of the War of 1741*): 'The history of events that occurred two or three centuries ago is often more certain, more faithful, and more complete than a history of recent events'.[9] Voltaire deplores this for the history of past centuries nourishes only our curiosity, while contemporary history directly influences our lives. However, the general public is, alas, utterly misinformed about the major events that will forever influence their own destiny, for the gazettes and newspapers report only the surfaces of events, leaving hidden the deeper causes of wars and revolutions: 'The sources of truth remain concealed. The archives of politics – the secret causes of so many intrigues, the proofs of so many ambitions, of so many stratagems, of so many mistakes, of so many confounded hopes – are hidden away in cabinets'(3).

Voltaire complained that a just perspective on historical facts seemed an ideal too elusive to attain when the interested actors of history are still in the scene. Nonetheless, ancient history remained the preferred target of historical pyrrhonists, if only because uncovering the flaws of what had been for so long considered as canonical histories reinforced the sense of many that they were living in a more enlightened age. This version of historical pyrrhonism, characterised as No. 4 in the preceding list, was a common assumption among many early-modern scholars, but the thesis was particularly clearly formulated by Louis-Jean Lévesque de Pouilly in a paper presented in 1722 to the *Académie royale des inscriptions et belles lettres*, challenging the reliability of the first four centuries of Roman history:

> Most of those who have written the history of remote times have filled it with fictions; either because they intended to flatter their nation; or because, to the simplicity of truth, they have preferred the entertainment of the marvelous; or, finally, because they have been attracted by the vain pleasure of mendacity and of acquiring a kind of superiority over people by deceiving them. However, history so altered loses its value, and the observations drawn from it, by physics, morals, politics, and the law of nations, become suspect and misleading.[10]

Lévesque de Pouilly's paper generated a heated debate within the *Académie des Inscriptions*. Echoes of this debate about the certainty of ancient history resound in the work of such well-known philosopher-historians as Bolingbroke and Hume. Bolingbroke, who corresponded with Lévesque de Pouilly, contended in his *Letters on the Study and Use of History* that the unreliability of oral traditions forces us to cast doubts even on sacred history, particularly the Old Testament, which, although perhaps a solid basis for religious faith, cannot provide the foundations 'for a chronology from the beginning of time, nor for universal history.' Books such as Genesis give only 'bare names, naked of circumstances, without descriptions of countries, or relations of events', they 'furnish matter only for guess and dispute; and even the similitude of them, which is so often used as a clue to lead us to the discovery of historical truth, has notoriously contributed to propagate error, and to increase the perplexity of ancient tradition'.[11]

Bolingbroke recommended the following rules for judging in the reliability of historical narratives:

1. To suspend judgement about histories of which there are no written memorials extant.
2. To suspend judgement when the chain by which testimony is transmitted originated in a single witness.
3. To proportion one's assent according to the number of testimonies when several concur (55).

David Hume was also an historical pyrrhonist on ancient history. He opens the *History of England* explaining that he has excluded the pre-Roman history of the Britons because ancient history is 'so much involved in obscurity, uncertainty, and contradiction'. Those historians who inquire 'beyond the period in which literary monuments are framed or preserved' forget that 'the history of past events is immediately lost or disfigured when entrusted to memory and oral tradition'. But Hume's historical scepticism goes beyond epistemology and stresses also a moral point. He points out that the histories of 'barbarous nations' present scarce moral interest, given that very little can be learned about human nature from actions of barbarians which are 'guided by caprice, and terminate so often in cruelty, that they disgust us by the uniformity of their appearance; and it is rather fortunate for letters that they are buried in silence and oblivion'.[12]

Nicolas Fréret (1688–1749), another prominent member of the *Académie des Inscriptions*, gave perhaps the most interesting answer to the version of historical pyrrhonism advocated by Lévesque de Pouilly. In his 'Réflexions générales sur l'étude des anciennes histoires et sur le degré de certitude des différentes preuves historiques', Fréret held that Lévesque de Pouilly's argument, which left unchallenged contemporary testimony and questions only tradition, was but a veiled form of a much more radical historical pyrrhonism. Except for facts which we directly witness, every past event is known to us only indirectly through testimony and its credibility is open to exactly the same charges as tradition. All history is tradition and even contemporary and well-attested events will become tradition for future generations who will not have the same access to evidence as contemporaries do. Either we embrace radical historical pyrrhonism and reject all history, Fréret suggested, or we should be satisfied with the available means for establishing the credibility of testimony. From this perspective, the only difference between ancient history and modern history is that evidence for the former is scarce and requires more analysis. However, the fact that we have to be more cautious about ancient history does not entail that we should reject it. In all cases 'we must consider all, weigh the various degrees of probability, reject the false and assign to each fact its degree of truth or likelihood; vague and general suspicions should not lead us to indiscriminately reject all, but merely to avoid indiscriminately accepting all'.[13]

Fréret's understanding of historical pyrrhonism (thesis 3 in the preceding list) was the point of view that dominated the discussions of historical objectivity during the eighteenth century. Those upholding a probabilistic approach to knowledge depending on testimony, of which history was paradigmatic, typically addressed two questions:

1. How certain is historical knowledge and how does it compare to demonstrative knowledge or to knowledge derived from sense perception?
2. How do we come to endorse probable beliefs transmitted by human testimony?

Answers to the first question drew on the new understanding of probability that had been taking form since the mid-seventeenth century. However, this conceptual repertoire was not yet stable, and distinctions between subjective and objective probability, between probability as epistemic state or as observed frequency, were not always drawn, at least not clearly.[14] On the one hand, many were tempted by the idea that human testimony could be quantified and taken as a continuum of degrees of probability. On the other hand, admitting that historical beliefs cannot rise above probability conceded too much to the Cartesian claim that without warranty by intuitive evidence such beliefs can never yield certainty and therefore cannot be integrated into a philosophical curriculum of truth-finding disciplines.[15]

To meet that challenge, some argued that, beyond a certain point, the probability of historical testimony amounted to *moral certainty* which was different only in kind, not in degree, from mathematical demonstrations. This view had already been suggested in the seventeenth century by Pierre-Daniel Huet, Nicolas Filleau de la Chaise, and, most significantly, by Antoine Arnauld and Pierre Nicole in the Port-Royal *Logic*. Arnauld and Nicole contend that when there is ample and unanimous testimony attesting a historical matter of fact, our belief in that fact is as certain and indubitable as if it were the product of a mathematical demonstration. The falsity of such a putative event, if not logically impossible, is nevertheless 'morally impossible'. They admit that it is not always easy to establish when testimony attains the high degree of probability equivalent to sense perception and mathematical demonstration and deserving to be called 'certainty'. They insist, nevertheless, that the boundary between 'human certitude' and mere probability can be established.[16]

Hume also argued that historical evidence yields as high a degree of certainty as sense perception and mathematical demonstrations and that the distinction between types of certainty is a distinction in kind, not in level: 'It is common for Philosophers to distinguish the Kinds of Evidence into *intuitive*, *demonstrative*, *sensible* and *moral*; by which they intend *only* to mark a Difference betwixt them, not to denote a Superiority of one above another. *Moral Certainty* may reach as *high* a Degree of Assurance as *Mathematical*'.[17] Likewise he suggested that some commonsense beliefs, for example, 'the sun will rise tomorrow' or 'Caesar was killed in 44 B.C.', despite being founded on mere probable reasoning, yield firmer conviction than some intricate mathematical demonstrations requiring much effort to be followed or understood (*Treatise*, 1.4.1, SBN 180–7).

These attempts to establish the certainty of historical beliefs show that for many the problem of the objectivity and reliability of history was a crucial challenge not only for history, but for any comprehensive account of empirical knowledge. However, contemporary scholarship on the period tends to focus exclusively on how personal experience understood as perceptual information yields knowledge. The relationship between mind and world is thus conceived as one of contemplation and the connection between perception and conceptual capacity is emphasised. But the omnipresence of the problem of historical testimony reveals that many philosophers of the period had a much more nuanced understanding of the relationship between mind and world as one mediated by the social game of giving and receiving testimony. It is from this point of view that accounts of empirical knowledge need to address the second question set out earlier: How do we come to endorse beliefs transmitted by human testimony?

On this topic, the root of the eighteenth-century discussion of testimony was, again, the Port-Royal *Logic*. As a solution to the problem of testimony Arnauld and Nicole suggested that the epistemic force of a belief derived from testimony could be established by considering the *internal* and the *external* 'circumstances' of the fact reported. The former established whether or not the fact reported coheres with our general experience; the latter established the reliability of the witnesses reporting the fact.[18] The credibility of a reported matter of fact results from a prudential weighing of the internal and external circumstances. This leaves open the possibility of accepting a fact which, although conflicting with common experience, is nevertheless endorsed by a great number of reliable testimonies. The latter possibility was essential for the credibility of miracles and the main tenets of revealed religion.

Cautious or sincerely religious philosophers restricted critical examination of testimony almost exclusively to the 'external circumstances', attempting to spell out the conditions in which testimony leads to reliable beliefs, conditions such as:

1. General 'laws' of human nature, for example, a general inclination to veracity.
2. Cognitive dispositions of the witness, such as a reliable memory, a good understanding.
3. Epistemic conditions, such as a witness's level of expertise or knowledge.
4. Moral conditions, such as sincerity, integrity, or impartiality.[19]

Meeting these conditions was not a guarantee of historical knowledge, in the broad sense of testimony-dependent knowledge, for this is always transmitted by complex chains of witnesses which makes it difficult, if not impossible, to reduce its reliability to that of any individual involved in the transmission. A different set of problems arose when historical knowledge was considered as the result of complex social transmissions and validations of knowledge. The problem was not so much how to assess the reliability of a single witness but that of chains of testimony.

Among the first to point out this problem was Locke: '*in traditional Truths, each remove weakens the force of the proof*: And the more hands the Tradition has successively passed through, the less strength and evidence does it receive from them'.[20] The argument was later deepened in an eccentric way by a Scottish mathematician and theologian, John Craig or Craige (1662?–1731). In *Theologiæ Christianæ principia mathematica* (1699) he produced a 'theorem' to calculate the rate of decay in different testimonial scenarios (single successive chains, concurrent chains, oral or written chains), and this revealed that any history is doomed to be buried in disbelief.[21] Craig intended to 'demonstrate' that the historical evidence for the Christian faith will not fade before A.D. 3150, which, according to his interpretation of Luke 18:8, proved that the millenarian expectations of a New Coming were unfounded. Craig's argument was considered as a form of historical pyrrhonism, namely thesis No. 6. Although unanimously rejected or criticised, the argument was nevertheless discussed by a host of serious philosophers and mathematicians: Bayle, Bernoulli, Samuel Clarke, Hume, and Reid.[22] The attention given to this odd endeavour shows that a sensitive chord had been struck.

The main reply to this form of historical pyrrhonism was that historical facts are rarely transmitted from an original testimony through a single chain of successive testimonies. Rather, it was argued that historical knowledge is generally transmitted by way of multiple chains of concurrent testimony. A first answer to Craig by George Hooper pointed out that probability increases with concurrent chains of testimony.[23] Hooper provided a different mathematical treatment of the problem, based on the quantification of the expectation yielded by single witnesses, and arrived at the opposite conclusion that, with multiple and independent chains of testimony attesting a historical fact, the probability of the report increases with the number of testimonies.

In his *Weg zur Gewißheit und Zuverlässigkeit der menschlichen Erkenntniß* (1747), Christian August Crusius gave a number of reasons why in most cases historical credibility increases with the multiplication of testimonies. First, 'proofs grounding historical probability can corroborate one another without going in a circle'.[24] It is rarely the case that the veracity of a fact depends on only a single testimony. As most of historical facts are tied to other facts, credibility results from the mutual support provided by different, but related, facts. Secondly, corroboration results from concurrent testimonies of independent witnesses (1060). Thirdly, Crusius minimised the importance of the number of witnesses in a chain as well as the role of time in the erosion of historical credibility. It was much more important to consider the quality or 'character' (*Beschaffenheit*) of the witnesses than their number, and although time was fatal for some histories, others acquired new force by the discovery of new evidence (1061, 1075).

Hume's essay 'Of Miracles', although not usually related to problems in philosophy of history, stands out for a radical version of the criteria of reliability set by the Port-Royal *Logic*.[25] Most philosophers play ambiguously with the internal and external 'circumstances' so as not to harm the credibility of miracles, but Hume offers a much stricter criterion according to which a reported event that is not just extraordinary but *radically* different from common experience, cannot be rendered credible by any testimony:

> [N]o testimony is sufficient to establish a miracle, unless the testimony be of such a kind, that its falsehood would be more miraculous, than the fact, which it endeavours to establish: And even in that case, there is a mutual destruction of arguments, and the superior only gives us an assurance suitable to that degree of force, which remains, after deducting the inferior. (*Enquiry*, 10.13, SBN 115–16)

Hume has been often interpreted as claiming that testimony is neither a sufficient nor a reliable source of belief and that every testimony ought to be checked against personal experience.[26] This misses Hume's point. Rather than undermine testimony as a good source of belief, Hume intends to protect it from undesirable consequences, such as accepting the credibility of incredible events.

However, in proposing a stricter application of the internal and external criteria, Hume also ventured the final philosophical assault on the citadel of sacred history. Hume's criterion, as many immediately realized, constitutes a serious threat to religions that depend on acceptance of the testimony of those to whom religious truths were revealed. The critical attitude towards historical facts elicited by historical pyrrhonism compromised the credibility of sacred history and undermined the only available account of universal history that could preserve the normative function of history as a 'teacher of life'.

Historical pyrrhonism thus left a problematic legacy. On the one hand, it produced a moralised account of empirical knowledge in which epistemic and semantic notions such as justification, correspondence, and truth are intrinsically tied to morally charged notions such as authority, impartiality, and justice. On the other hand, by developing critical tools for establishing historical facts, historical pyrrhonism disenchanted history, depriving it of its providential meaning and *telos*. It is precisely at this point that some philosophers called for a philosophical approach to history that could protect history from becoming a mere collection of facts.

II. PHILOSOPHICAL HISTORY

The disenchantment of history impinged not only on the credibility of the sacred histories but on historical explanation in general. On the one hand, until the mid-eighteenth century, historians dealing with providential history appealed to final causes to give meaning to historical events. This tradition stemmed from Augustin's *City of God* and was represented in the seventeenth century by Bossuet's *Discours sur l'histoire universelle* (1681).[27] On the other hand, traditional humanist historians explained historical events by reference to the actions or motivations of individuals, in the manner of Polybius or Cicero.

Two factors influenced the development of a new approach to historical explanation. The first was the growing awareness that moral sciences, particularly politics, deal with phenomena not easily reducible to individual actions or motivations. This arose in part from the first statistical tables of mortality which suggested that social phenomena could be observed at a supraindividual level.[28] The second new factor in historical explanation was the impact of the 'experimental approach' developed by natural philosophers, particularly in England. These two factors were linked, for it seemed obvious that if social phenomena displayed statistically measurable regularities, then some form of causal explanation for these phenomena could be sought in ways similar to those used by naturalists.

Two issues facilitated the adoption of experimentalism in history. First, it was important in natural law and political legislation to account for the diversity of national characters. Secondly, closely related to the quarrel between the Ancients and the Moderns, was the question whether there is progress in the 'arts and learning'. These issues turned on whether differences in national character and in level of culture are to be accounted for by *physical* or *moral* causes. 'Physical causes' meant the influence of climatic and geographic factors on social phenomena while 'moral causes' mainly meant the influence of political and social 'climate', that is, forms of government, manners, and customs.

The first influential text in this connection is Abbé Jean-Baptiste Du Bos' *Réflexions critiques sur la poësie et la peinture* (1719). Du Bos wants to understand why arts flourish in some periods of history and decay in others, upholding that physical causes ought to be given a predominant role in explaining these phenomena. While recognising that moral causes play some role, he observes that the flourishing and decline of arts in different countries and in different periods seem to occur irrespective of the moral causes.[29] Du Bos presses the metaphor of flourishing and suggests that the variations in cultural fecundity can be thought of by way of an analogy with agricultural fertility:

> Cannot we maintain [. . .] that there are some countries where men are not endowed at birth with the dispositions required to excel in some professions, as there are some countries where some plants cannot succeed? Cannot we maintain, then, that as the seeds we sow and full-grown trees do not produce every year a fruit equally perfect in the countries where they are more apt to thrive [*où ils se plaisent davantage*], so children brought up under happy climates do not become men equally perfect in all times? (2:14, 249)

In support Du Bos accounts for the influence of the air and climate on human beings.[30] The quality of the air in any region is partly dependent on the composition of the earth because the air is altered by the 'emanations of the earth'. Since air is assimilated by the lungs and distributed in the organs by the blood, it influences the physical constitution as well as the character and inclination of human beings (251–4). National characters too can be explained by reference to climate and other physical causes. For instance, only the difference in air can explain how the Portuguese or the Spanish acquire a different character when they settle in their colonies or how people of different lineage who inhabit the same territory in different periods of history nonetheless exhibit the same national character (266–7, 274–5).

Du Bos' influence may have been reinforced by John Arbuthnot's *Essay Concerning the Effects of Air on Human Bodies* (1733). This medical essay also ventures into morals and politics by supposing that air influences both our physical and moral constitution: 'It seems agreeable to Reason and Experience, that the Air operates sensibly in forming the Constitutions of Mankind, the Specialities of Features, Complexion, Temper, and consequently, the Manners of Mankind, which are found to vary much in different Countries and Climates'. This leads to contentions that must have impressed Montesquieu:

> In countries which do not produce without much Labour, the Land-holder must have Assurance of the Necessaries for his Culture, as his Seed, Granary, domicile Working-tools, etc. This must create some Property, and where there is Property, there must be Laws to secure it: From which I beg leave to draw one Corollary; That despotick Governments, tho' destructive of Mankind in general, are most improper in cold Climates; for where great Labour is necessary, the Workman ought to have a certain Title to the Fruits of it. There are Degrees of Slavery, and, generally speaking, it is most extreme in some hot and fruitful Countries.[31]

From one or the other source, these ideas influenced Montesquieu's and Hume's theses which established an ongoing debate on the relative importance of physical and moral causes in explaining national characters and historical development. In his *Considérations sur les causes de la grandeur des Romains et de leur décadence* (1734), Montesquieu undertook an inquiry into the history of Rome that gave priority to explanations covering wide-ranging social phenomena. This focus on supraindividual factors is made possible by Montesquieu's distinction between moral and physical causes on the one hand, and between 'general' and 'particular causes' on the other hand. In Montesquieu's summary:

It is not chance [*la Fortune*] that rules the world [. . .]. There are general causes, moral and physical, which act in every monarchy, elevating it, maintaining it, or hurling it to the ground. All accidents are controlled by these causes. And if the chance of one battle – that is, a particular cause – has brought a state of ruin, some general cause made it necessary for that state to perish from a single battle. In a word, the main trend draws with it all particular accidents.[32]

Montesquieu's position is not the simple-minded deterministic view of historical causation often ascribed to him. He preserves a role for chance, or the intervention of unpredictable 'particular causes', while insisting that wide-ranging phenomena such as the birth or decline of an empire or a monarchy need to be explained in terms of 'general causes'. Nor does Montesquieu embrace a one-sided view of the relative importance of moral and physical causes. True, he devotes many pages of *L'esprit des lois* (1748) to stress the influence of climate in the formation of national characters and legislation. One of his main contentions is that the human 'spirit' and passions vary significantly according to the various climates and that legislation, instead of struggling to mould all characters to a single universal view of human nature, must be designed according to the natural differences among human beings.[33] In fact, he not only explains a variety of social phenomena such as sexual habits, social inequality, or the rate of suicide in England in terms of physical causes but explicitly contends that 'the empire of climate is the first of all empires' (19.14; trans. 316). Despite this apparent support of climatic reductionism, Montesquieu gives an important role to moral causes in the constitution of national characters, which he calls *ésprit general*, a notion adopted by many during the eighteenth century:

Many things govern men: climate, religion, laws, the maxims of the government, examples of past things, mores, and manners; a general spirit is formed as a result. To the extent that, in each nation, one of these causes acts more forcefully, the others yield to it. Nature and climate almost alone dominate savages; manners govern the Chinese; laws tyrannize Japan; in former times mores set the tone in Lacedaemonia; in Rome it was set by the maxims of government and ancient mores.[34]

Moral and physical causes concur in the formation of the general spirit of a nation and the task is to discover which one is to be ascribed a dominant role – that of a general cause – in the national character of a given nation.

Hume's biting attack on climatic reductionism in 'Of National Characters' (1748) is probably not aimed at Montesquieu but at earlier reductionist versions of the climatic approach such as those of Du Bos or Arbuthnot.[35] Hume disputes that there is any significant influence of physical causes in the formation of natural characters: 'As to *physical causes*, I am inclined to doubt altogether of their operation in this particular; nor do I think, that men owe any thing of their temper or genius to the air, food, or climate'.[36] Hume gives a number of counterexamples to the climatic theory; for example, characters are not only national, also different professions have similar turns of mind. Thus, a soldier and a priest have definite and different characters that remain unchanged 'in all nations, and all ages'. The specific differences of the priest and the soldier are explained by the difference in their respective way of life. Furthermore, the boundaries within which we find a common national character seem to coincide with the political boundaries of the state: the air of the Pyrenees does not differ so much across the border as to justify the differences of character between France and Spain (198–9, 204).

National characters result, for Hume, from a social sympathy or 'contagion of manners' that occurs in any society thanks to the 'imitative nature' of the human mind and facilitated by commerce, politics, and military life. We find a common character in social groups where there is intense social intercourse; a common language and political government support the formation of a national character. However, communities living apart but maintaining intense communication can acquire and maintain a similitude in manners – for instance the Jews, the Armenians, and the Jesuits. On the other hand, communities inhabiting the same place but divided for cultural, linguistic, or religious reasons maintain distinct national characters. And a common character can be shared by neighbouring nations having 'a very close communication together, either by policy, commerce or travelling' (202, 205, 206). Thus, although Hume never completely rules out the influence of physical causes,[37] he maintains that national characters are not given by nature but historically shaped in the context of the cultural, economical, and political interaction of individuals in society.

In 'Of the Rise and Progress of Arts and Sciences' (1742) Hume also supports a distinction between causes and occasions, which he refers to as a distinction between 'causes' and 'chance:' 'What depends upon a few persons is, in a great measure, to be ascribed to chance, or secret and unknown causes: What arises from a great number, may often be accounted for by determinate and known causes'. Historical explanations, in the wide eighteenth-century sense of explanations of 'human affairs', should focus on social phenomena, such as the state of a nation, its manners, commerce, and opinions, rather than on individual action; for the former is 'less subject to accidents, and less influenced by whim and private fancy, than those which operate on a few only' (*Essays*, 112).

The discussion of national characters was the catalyst for a new approach to historical writing that dispensed with final causes, focused on moral and/or physical causes, and was based on a critical examination of facts, in short, philosophical history. In his *Essai sur les mœurs et l'esprit des nations*, Voltaire summed it up. First, we have to consider history independently of any providential plan and 'follow the human spirit abandoned to itself'.[38] Secondly, the writing of history must be based on critically established facts that are explained according to known causes and relate or illuminate problems that are of political, moral, or philosophical interest. Stressing this approach in the preface to the *Essai sur les mœurs*, Voltaire invites the reader to seek in history 'only what deserves to be known [. . .]: the spirit, the mores [*mœurs*] and the manners of the principal nations supported by facts that one cannot afford to ignore' (15.1: 245). Voltaire thinks that Hume's *History of England* is the paradigmatic combination of traditional humanistic historical narrative and philosophical explanations of manners, opinions, commerce, and learning. Hume's *History* is not only 'the best, perhaps that was ever written in any language', but, most fundamentally, Hume has shown 'that the task of writing history belongs to philosophers' (*Oeuvres*, 41.5: 451).

The histories produced by the philosophical historians will reveal the fecundity of the approach to historical and social phenomena delineated in the debate on national characters. Hume's *History of England*, Voltaire's *Siècle de Louis XIV* (1751), and William Robertson's *History of Scotland* (1759) and *History of Charles V* (1769) are important milestones in a tradition attaining its peak in Edward Gibbon's *History of the Decline and Fall of the Roman Empire* (1776–1788).

III. THE EMERGENCE OF PHILOSOPHIES OF HISTORY

Three factors fostered discontinuity between religious and civil history, the critical attitude towards historical facts, the 'experimental' approach to historical explanation, and the political interest in the diversity of human characters. At the same time, philosophers were increasingly aware that the secularisation of history was not without loss. Religious history could account for the origin of basic moral norms and provide an eschatology that facilitated a teleological understanding of human action. These traditional ideas were threatened by the critical and experimental approach to history.

Natural law theory offered a foundation for morals that many saw as neutral with respect to providential history. In the formulation of protestant thinkers such as Grotius, natural law admitted of two foundations, in nature and in the will of God. The sources of moral norms could be investigated either in 'the internal Principles of Man' or in revealed divine laws reported in sacred history.[39] Although Grotius argued that the two were consistent, the formulation was sufficiently ambiguous to inspire many to avoid revealed religion in the foundation of morals.[40] This had the added attraction that it apparently made moral theory independent of uncertain historical data.[41] For instance, for Hobbes it was possible to know the 'fountain of rights' natural to all human beings by stripping away the 'artificial' ornaments of culture and civilisation and depicting people in a state of nature. Eighteenth-century philosophies of history express dissatisfaction with such ahistorical approaches to the study of human nature.

Beginning in the mid-eighteenth century there is a profusion of philosophical attempts to come to terms with universal history. It is notoriously difficult to classify all the different forms of these early philosophies of history and to understand what motivates this new philosophical genre. Although a general feature of the Enlightenment, the philosophies of history are often studied in their national context.[42] These universal histories may of course be seen in the context of emerging national consciousness, but they do have a common background of philosophical problems and sources to which they respond.[43] From a philosophical point of view, philosophies of history respond to what was seen as failed attempts to account for human nature, the origins of government, and moral norms. If philosophies of history are considered as responses to problems in natural law theory, one can group them according to how they link history and the theory of human nature.

First, there were philosophies of history that held that a theory of human nature can be arrived at independently of history. On this approach philosophy of history is derivative of the theory of human nature. History is the progressive unfolding of innate and uniform natural faculties, a process that also enables individuals to gain consciousness of their own nature. An understanding of history is, thus, *derivative* from the metaphysics of human nature.

Secondly, there was the contrary view that a theory of human nature cannot be arrived at independently of history. On this approach the very nature of human beings is subject to evolution and cannot be understood independently of the exertion of human faculties in history. History is, thus, *constitutive* of the metaphysics of human nature.

1. *History derived from human nature*

The first approach to universal history originates in Rousseau's *Discours sur l'origine et les fondements de l'inégalité parmi les hommes* (1755). In the preface, Rousseau expresses dissatisfaction with the natural law theorists' basic tenets about the law of nature. Their common mistake is the attempt to derive human nature from humanity's 'artificial', or cultural, existence. Natural law becomes apparent only in 'natural man', not in 'men as they have made themselves'.[44] Philosophy must think human existence prior to any culture. As neither human records nor Scripture permit a reconstruction of this natural state, we must depart from factual history – for facts 'do not affect the question' – and proceed exclusively by conjecture (132).

In the state of nature, Rousseau sees isolated individuals who meet only to satisfy basic needs, such as reproduction, whose intellectual capacities are reduced to perception and feeling, and who are motivated only by primitive desires. These individuals differ from other animals by the fact that, beyond the basic instinct of self-preservation, they also have a capacity of free choice, a faculty of perfectibility, and a natural sentiment of pity towards fellow human creatures (24–5). If human beings, unlike animals, can evolve as a species (Rousseau of course could not be a Darwinian), it is due to a faculty of perfectibility that is triggered in situations of necessity when people supply their natural weakness with artifices that solve basic problems (25–6). Such artifices toll the bell for the state of nature. The skills developed to overcome threats to survival elicited the exertion of even more complex intellectual functions, and these in turn accelerated the progress of arts and learning (47). Up to this point, the 'savages' lived in small groups and rude dwellings. They lived free, in health, and in a generally happy, childlike state until the development of arts created a situation in which the surplus provisions of some could entice others into the bondage of work for them. In that situation both inequality and property entered the species and gave birth to civil society. Thus began the real misfortunes of humankind because inequality and the accumulation of riches by a minority gave rise to the domination which pervades human societies and destroys the felicity experienced in the state of nature. Although Rousseau in this conjectural approach makes use of historical data and interestingly brings the economic analysis of property to the fore, it remains a highly speculative reconstruction of history.

The passage from childhood to maturity was also the central theme of Lessing's *Die Erziehung des Menschengeschlechts* (1780). Mainly of theological concern, Lessing's little book rests on an analogy between education and revelation: 'What education is for the individual, revelation is for the whole human race'.[45] We can see each of the several books of the Judeo–Christian tradition as a schoolbook (*Elementarbuch*) with a 'pedagogy' adapted to the capacities of each age of humanity. Thus the Old Testament presents moral teachings in the form of '*allusions* and *hints*' (§43; 18) to impress a rude and uncultivated people who can be made to act morally only through rewards and punishments. When humankind is no longer a child and becomes a boy, it is capable of a more rational understanding of moral motivation, namely the teachings of Christ and the New Testament (§55; 47–8). These inculcate the immortality of the soul, a doctrine that presents morality not as the result of fear, but as a desire for a better life. The pedagogy of the first 'schoolbook' was revelation; that of the New Testament is 'preaching' in which reason plays a much more important role – namely, giving Christianity a theological form – and, thus it can be foreseen that a third age is to come in which we will dispense with the New Testament as we did with the Old (§§71–2; 50–1). Against Rousseau's pessimism, Lessing sees in history a long education that, despite reversals, aims at moral perfection in an enlightened society in which human beings will act morally for the sake of the good and not because they fear punishment or expect to be rewarded in a future life. For Lessing as for Kant the end of history is the realisation of the ideal of moral autonomy.

Kant, too, saw history as the unresolved conflict between nature and culture and recognised the necessity of reconciling moral and political life with nature. Only a conjectural approach to universal history could bring about the philosophical *mise en scène* of the historical struggle between nature and culture. While writing *Kritik der reinen Vernunft*, Kant devoted important portions of his lectures on logic to the problems of testimony and historical knowledge, defending the former against unmitigated scepticism. Not only did he grant historical testimony the status of 'knowledge' but he also contended that the entire historical discipline can be given scientific status.[46] Historical facts, like natural facts, admit of systematic presentation: 'a system can be given for historical things, too, namely, by my setting up an idea, in accordance with which the manifold in history is to be ordered' (Ak 24: 891).

Kant was, however, more cautious than Rousseau about the theoretical status of conjectures regarding universal history. In his *Idee zu einer allgemeinen Geschichte in weltbürgerlicher Absicht* (1784)[47] he proposed that a philosophical reconstruction of history was a regulative principle of reason – that is, an 'idea' in Kant's technical sense – and that this could be achieved by the a priori supposition of a purpose in human history. Outlining arguments later developed in the *Kritik der Urtheilskraft* (1790), Kant said that we are justified in using the notion of purpose where we have good reason to believe that events follow regular laws and yet available experience is insufficient to make these laws known to us. This is the case with history; patterns can be observed in past events and causal explanations could be expected because we know that human actions can be rationally motivated. A teleological account not only seems possible, it is also preferable to a representation of history as a purposeless aggregate of events and actions. In postulating a purposive rational order in history we can gain clarity about human affairs, we can answer anxious questions about the future, and we can guide human affairs rationally. This *idea* of history contributes actively to substantiate the very end it postulates and conjectural history can therefore play the normative role which providential history once had. In fact, in an argument similar to Lessing's, Kant in 'Muthmaßlicher Anfang der Menschengeschichte' (1786) suggested that a rational reconstruction of history coincides almost exactly with sacred history as told in *Genesis*.[48]

Reason and free choice entail the insufficiency of a purely naturalistic account of human nature. Whereas the end of the natural faculties of animals is achieved in the life span of the individual, the end of human faculties can be achieved only in the species, not in the individual. The possession of reason and freedom marks a departure from a purely instinctual existence and the necessity of learning by practice and experience.[49] While natural 'norms' – instincts – are sufficient for other species, humans need a social environment in which reason and freedom can find expression. Whereas animals respond to 'norms' that are simply given, human beings need to elaborate and give themselves the norms under which they can fully develop their own faculties. Accordingly, the *end* of history is a social and political environment adapted to the flourishing of human rational faculties.

It follows that Kant cannot share Rousseau's nostalgia for the state of nature. Remaining in that state would be a hindrance to the development of human freedom. Although Kant saw in culture the birth of inequality and oppression, he also thought that the antagonism inherent in culture is essential to achieve the natural ends of humankind. Antagonism, the 'unsocial sociability of men' (*ungesellige Geselligkeit der Menschen*), is the result of two different drives (Ak 8: 20/15). The drive to society explains how individuals gather in groups to overcome their merely natural existence. The selfish drive puts the individual in opposition to the individuals he chooses to live with. Without this unsocial sociability, humankind would never have departed from the Arcadian golden age and embarked on the toilsome path of culture. Thus, the end of human nature can be attained only when the social environment allows individuals the maximum of freedom while preventing them from encroaching on the rights of others. Morals will cease to conflict with nature when 'art will be strong and perfect enough to become second nature' (Ak 8: 117–18/62–3). The central problem of human history is that of achieving a self-governed international community – a League of Nations – assuring equilibrium between freedom and justice for both states and individuals.[50]

The thinkers so far considered show that a 'theory of progress' should not be attributed to Enlightenment philosophies of history without important qualifications. Rousseau considered that technical progress implies moral regress. Lessing saw the education of humankind as an uneven process in which failures occur just as in individual education. Kant considered the prospect of moral perfection in a stable and just League of Nations as a regulative idea, not a factual prediction; furthermore, he suspected that perfect morality may not be entirely reconcilable with human nature. The theory of progress that is often presented appears largely in the work of a few French Enlightenment philosophers.

The leitmotif of the historical theory of progress is set in Turgot's *Plan de deux discours sur l'histoire universelle* (1751).[51] In his first *Discours*, Turgot presented the view of a relentless improvement of humanity. History's apparently anarchic succession of governments and revolutions, of 'upheavals and ravages', was a process in which 'no change took place without bringing about some gain . . . '. Overall, 'the human race as a whole has advanced ceaselessly towards its perfection' (1: 285/72). Condorcet developed this view in his *Esquisse d'un tableau historique des progrès de l'esprit humain* (1795). An understanding of the faculties of human nature, of the 'general facts and constant laws exhibited by the development of these faculties', is the business of metaphysics, and this may be conducted independently of historical considerations.[52] However, when the development of the faculties is considered empirically, in groups of real, historical individuals, we obtain not a metaphysics of human nature but an historical 'picture' (*tableau*) of the actual development of these faculties. Given a metaphysics of human nature – basically a description of the human faculties conjoined with the claim of their perfectibility – it is possible to project human nature into history and thus conjecture about primitive history, give form to the available historical data, and foresee the future course of human affairs. The metaphysics of human nature provides laws that would enable us to make perfect predictions in history, were it not for the fact that we have imperfect knowledge of objects that are independent of human nature. Prediction at this stage can never go beyond probability. But as technical and cultural progress socialises the human environment, the objects of the historical and social sciences become increasingly artificial, or man-made, and their cognition, aided by the development of a universal language, will eventually be as certain as that of the demonstrative sciences (199). Condorcet believes that the perfectibility of human nature coupled with the available historical data authorise belief in an ineluctable progress of human society (4–5). Making humanity aware of its historical progress by giving it a 'picture' of history could only accelerate this evolution.

2. *Human nature derived from history*

Philosophies of history belonging to the second strand sketched earlier claim that human nature cannot be investigated independently of an understanding of human history. Such histories stress how human faculties develop in different fields of activity and contend that the specific cultural and economic activities in different countries and times provide a nuanced and complex account of what constitutes human nature. Philosophy of history thus becomes a central component, not a mere by-product, of metaphysics.

The earliest example of this reconstruction of universal history is the work of the Italian philosopher and jurist Giambattista Vico (1668–1744). Little known during his own time, Vico was rediscovered in the nineteenth century by Jules Michelet who, to his surprise, found in Vico most of the central tenets of nineteenth-century historicism. The reading of Vico as a forerunner of Hegelian idealism was reinforced by Benedetto Croce[53] and remained for long the dominant interpretation until scholars began to consider Vico's philosophy in its own historical context.

Vico's philosophy of history is mainly expounded in his *Principi di una scienza nuova* (1725, substantially revised 1744) but other works are also important, particularly *De antiquissima italorum sapientia* (1710) and *De universi iuris* (1720–21).[54] Vico's new science of the 'common nature of nations' responded to a failure he found in the natural law theories of Grotius, Pufendorf, and Selden. Once the providential foundation of natural law is disregarded, only two avenues are open: claims about human nature rest on either experience, such as reports about the customs of native American peoples, or on philosophical conjectures. The former, taken by the natural lawyers, makes natural law merely 'probable and verisimilar' (*Iuris*, 9). This leaves the door open for endless controversy about the original nature of human beings and for the moral scepticism manifest in Hobbes, Spinoza, and Bayle, among others (*Iuris*, 9; see also *Scienzia*, §135). The second avenue was equally flawed; philosophical conjectures about the origins of humankind are at odds with obvious facts of human history.[55] Vico criticizes philosophical accounts of history that represent it as the progressive development of human faculties. This is an implausible picture of the first human beings as concerned only with survival, limited in their intellectual capacities to sense perception and the apprehension of particular things, and only later evolving to comfort and pleasure in practical life and to the thinking and abstraction typical of intellectual life. These accounts conflict with the fact that primitive peoples indulged in 'poetry' (mythological narratives), that they had religious beliefs about nonsensuous beings, and that they could think and take decisions about their commonwealths, activities that give evidence of relatively abstract thinking (*Iuris*, lxiv).

Vico thought that the nature of things (*cose*) is exhausted by an account of their coming into being or birth (*nascimento*) and that also human nature needs a genetic explanation.[56] However, to produce the history of mankind – of the birth of the human 'things' – a methodological problem has to be solved. On the one hand, a regressive approach, deducing the birth from the present state, would be unsatisfactory as such conjectures are often at odds with available historical data. On the other hand, the attempt to reach the origins of mankind seems to be jeopardised by the lack of reliable evidence about remote history. At this point Vico advanced one of his most original contributions: we do have access to primitive history provided we take seriously the first mythologies and pay attention to the sediments of ancient institutions still present in our language and culture and regularly unearthed by the work of philologists.

Extant mythologies make plain that 'the world of peoples began everywhere with religion'[57]. Philosophical conjectures also ignore this and fail to understand what the proper social and symbolic function of religions is. Poetry and religious mythology emerge from the need to preserve laws, customs, and institutions in social memory. For that reason it is licit to take mythologies as conveying civil truths and as being the first civil histories, however obscured by fable they may have been, a line taken also by thinkers such as Fontenelle and Fréret.[58] The philosophical reconstruction of history becomes a problem of how to give 'scientific' respectability to the vagaries of ancient histories. To see how 'poetry' (which at best gives us probable knowledge based on authority) can play a role in a science of history, one has to understand how such a science would emerge from the interplay of what Vico calls 'poetical sentences' and 'philosophical sentences'.

For Vico, the difference between poetry and philosophy lies in their respective languages, which reflect different mental abilities. In early times imagination, which is a function of memory, and poetical allegories were prevalent. Allegories do not involve the use of full-fledged concepts, as they do not depart from the particularity of the objects or class of objects represented. Allegories get embedded in the 'poetical sentences' by which people in the infancy of humanity try to articulate their proto-concepts into proto-thoughts. Poetic sentences 'are formed by feeling passion and emotion' whereas 'philosophical sentences', that is, full-fledged thoughts using universal concepts, 'are formed by reflection and reasoning' (*Scienza*, §§218–19). Poetic sentences seek to apprehend particulars and when they succeed they can claim to be certain. Philosophical sentences seek to apprehend universals and when they succeed they can claim to be true. Vico's point is that philosophical speculation applied to primitive history, when divorced from any factual evidence, produces 'true', although empty, accounts. An idea of history must arise as a philosophical reflection on what has previously been thought 'poetically'. By reflecting on the 'poetical' sediments in our culture we can reconstitute the history of our origins and achieve a true presentation of human nature. Philosophical sentences without poetical sentences are empty, and poetry without philosophical reflection is blind.

Comparing different mythologies we learn that three basic institutions (*cose*) are common to all nations at all times: religion, marriage, and burials. In all nations religion represents divinities as endowed with freedom. Marriage celebrates and consecrates the social link by securing the role of the family in obliging the members to mutual protection and to transmit religion, language, and customs. Finally, burials reflect belief in transcendence – the immortality of the soul – and constitute, so to speak, a 'compact' between the living and the dead by which the dead will 'clear the way' for the living, rather than rot in cities and fields or wander about haunting them (*Scienza*, §§333–7). Burials serve also to 'socialize' the realm of death by assigning it a fixed place in human space and by structuring this space according to social hierarchy and lineage (*Iuris*, lxix). Vico also finds from a survey of the histories and mythologies of the gentile nations (he excludes the Hebrews because they have been helped by Providence) that these nations all evolve in three stages:

1. An age of gods marked by belief that laws are given by the gods and have to be obeyed blindly. This is the age of theocratic government, which reserves knowledge of law to an elite initiated into a hermetic language (hieroglyphs) based on a physical resemblance to the things signified.
2. An age of heroes characterized by aristocratic government in which law and knowledge are transmitted in a symbolic language with allegoric reference.
3. An age of men in which 'all men recognized themselves as equal in human nature' and governed themselves in popular commonwealths through laws that use a conventional language (*Scienza*, §§31–2).

For Vico, this stadial view of human history suggests that the natural equity ascribed by natural law theorists to primitive societies is something that can be understood only by individuals already endowed with philosophical capacities and living in popular governments. Natural equity is a hard-won result of political and social struggles as well as of the late capacity for philosophical reflection. Although natural equity is implicit in every society, it can be made explicit only in societies that have attained a certain degree of political and intellectual development, particularly ones that can make philosophy perform the tasks hitherto performed by 'poetry'.

Vico's 'new science' will 'describe at the same time an ideal eternal history traversed in time by the history of every nation in its rise, development, maturity, decline, and fall' (*Scienza*, §331). But how can the amalgam of myths and obscure histories unearthed by philology yield a 'science', at least in the Baconian sense which Vico seems to intend? How can merely probable 'poetical sentences' build a 'true' science? The answer lies in Vico's understanding of the nature of facts. Giving a personal twist to the Latin usage of the words *verum* and *factum*, Vico asserts, 'the true is precisely what is made (*verum esse ipsum factum*)', meaning that only that can be perfectly known of which we are the makers (*Sapientia*, 46). The rationale of history can be discovered and given demonstrative force because human beings are the makers of history; for 'the world of civil society has certainly been made by men, and . . . its principles are therefore to be found within the modifications of our own mind' (*Scienza*, §331). History proceeds like geometry, by construction, 'but with a reality greater by just so much as the institutions having to do with human affairs are more real than points, surfaces, and figures are' (§349). For this very reason, Vico also believes that the science of history and human institutions must be given priority over natural science, for whoever reflects on the kind of apodictic certainty obtained in history

> cannot but marvel that the philosophers should have bent their energies to the study of the world of nature, which, since God made it, He alone knows; and that they should have neglected the study of the world of nations . . . which, since men had made it, men could come to know. (§331)

For Vico, reflective consciousness of the universality of right could be achieved only at the end of a historical development beginning with the specific attempt of each nation or culture to conceive the moral bond of the community. Attention was to be given to the cultural specificity of each nation in order to find the common substratum on which natural law theory is to be based. This line of thinking was also predominant in early German historicism which developed particularly in Göttingen. Because of the links between the House of Hanover and the English Crown, Göttingen was at the crossroads of German interest in jurisprudence and theology and English and Scottish inclination towards the natural and the emerging social sciences.[59] German scholars such as Justus Möser, Johann Christoph Gatterer, and August Ludwig von Schlözer were interested in the way legal norms connect with national history. Attention was given to 'customary law' (*Gewohnheitsrecht*) and to the specifics of the German past and national character. This formed the culture-centred approach to history characteristic of German 'cultural history' (*Kulturgeschichte*).[60] This German interest in the implicit normativity of the national past and its customs was the context of Herder's philosophy of history. But Herder bent his interest in national customs and culture to make it conflict with the Enlightenment project of a universal history on a philosophical basis. His *Auch eine Philosophie der Geschichte* (1774) saw in the philosophical reconstructions of history as a 'general and progressive improvement of the world' nothing but incredible novels (*Romane*) unlikely to convince any serious student of history.[61] The price of a philosophical picture (*Bild*) of universal history is pure abstraction which misses the rich concrete forms that nations take in history. Only God is able to see at once the unity of the historical plan and the diversity of historical forms (505). But consideration of an individual historical form, of a nation, is enough for the human perspective. Human nature is not dispersed in the totality of history, but self-contained in the individual national forms (509). So, instead of investigating human nature through total history, Herder invites us to focus on the individuality of each nation's character. This national specificity accounts for the moral boundaries between people.

The second important trend in this type of universal history was Scottish *conjectural history* represented by Lord Kames, John Millar, Adam Ferguson, and John Logan and significantly influenced by David Hume's *Natural History of Religion* and Adam Smith's teaching at the University of Glasgow.[62] The expression 'conjectural history' was coined by Dugald Stewart, who claimed that in 'examining the history of mankind, as well as in examining the phenomena of the material world, when we cannot trace the process by which an event has been produced, it is often of importance to be able to shew how it may have been produced by natural causes.' This approach Stewart proposed to call '*Theoretical* or *Conjectural History*, an expression which coincides pretty nearly in its meaning with that of *Natural History*, as employed by Mr Hume, and with what some French writers have called *Histoire Raisonnée*'.[63] However, the expression fails to capture the specificity of the Scottish project. Unlike other uses of conjecture to complete a philosophical history, such as those of Rousseau, Lessing, or Kant, in the Scottish histories, 'conjecture' signifies naturalistic explanatory hypothesis rather than rational or theological speculation.[64] Ferguson denied that his approach is conjectural at all and saw himself as simply applying the method of natural history to the moral domain. A distinguishing feature of conjectural histories is their stress on the structural link between economic relations, such as modes of production and relations of property, and forms of government.[65] Accordingly, they tended to view universal history as divided into three or four stages. A typical four-stages view of history, as found in Adam Smith's *Lectures on Jurisprudence* or in Millar's *Origin of the Distinction of Ranks*, divides history into ages of hunters, herders, farmers, and commerce.

Perhaps the most important of the Scottish conjectural histories was Ferguson's *An Essay on the History of Civil Society* (1767), not least because it was extremely influential with Kant, Hegel, and Marx. Ferguson criticised the old philosophical enterprise that human nature can be understood by purely philosophical means without empirical investigation. This leads to 'wild suppositions' in the selection of human characteristics which suit the philosophers' own agenda and which they hypostatise as an imaginary 'state of nature'. Ferguson has in mind

Rousseau's procedure of stripping his contemporaries of all the attributes of civilisation in order to discover the natural substratum. Ferguson thinks that in deriving human nature from a conjectural state of nature, 'we overlook what . . . has always appeared within the reach of our own observation, and in the records of history'.[66]

Ferguson believed that the proper method for investigating human nature is that of the natural historian who proceeds not by conjectures but by collecting and assembling facts. Inquiry into the principles of human nature entails an investigation of the human faculties and their development; no a priori access is possible, for human faculties can only be known when they are exerted (30). Furthermore, an investigation of individual minds is insufficient; the proper objects of study are groups and societies, because 'the history of the individual is but a detail of the sentiments and thoughts he has entertained in the view of his species'(10). This entails that the only proper method for understanding human nature is historical: 'If the question be put, What the mind of man could perform, when left to itself, and without the aid of any foreign direction? we are to look for our answer in the history of mankind'(9).

Historical observation shows that human beings have 'always' – as far as historical records reach – been endowed with those qualities that distinguish them from animals. The idea of a 'state of nature' imposes a distinction between nature and culture that cannot be observed at any point in history. The natural history of the species shows humans to be industrious and imaginative beings always embedded in social groups. Art, or the faculty of producing artefacts, is natural to man and so is culture. For that reason, human beings are everywhere and at every time in the 'state of nature'.[67]

Although Ferguson believed that human beings tend to perfect their natural faculties, he did not conclude that we should think of universal history as a narrative of human 'progress'. People in the 'savage state' are by no means thought to be imperfect, childish, or amoral. On the contrary, communities of hunters and fishers, as described by travellers to Canada and Central America, have a communal life with a strong sense of equality because there is among them no private property. Their attachment to equality is not the product of ignorance; for in these 'savage' societies, 'Men are conscious of their equality, and are tenacious of its rights' (83). The 'savages' are not to be considered as infants either; they exert and even excel in the application of their faculties to the extent that they satisfy their needs, those based on a subsistence economy. Their 'rationality' is thus adapted to the pursuit of the relevant goals in such society, goals which do not require the formation of general principles (88). They do not think beyond the immediate necessities and practical needs of everyday life and they 'seem incapable of attending to any distant consequences, beyond those they have experienced in hunting or war' (88). Ferguson adds that all the qualities required for civilisation, viz. love of society, friendship, penetration, eloquence, and courage, can be found in the savage state (93).

The crucial step that makes some societies depart from the savage state is property. Communities of herders are, according to Ferguson, more likely to introduce property and, then, to accept an unequal share in its distribution. When there is an unequal distribution of property Ferguson calls it a 'barbarous state', one characterised by primitive relationships of subordination. Such social subordination is not based on moral obligation but follows mainly from the tribute paid to a chieftain based on admiration of his riches, birth, and military skills, and it can easily be overturned. The basic activity of barbarous nations is rapine; when prosperous they give rise to despotic government. A 'polished' nation is the result of various factors, none of which is entirely intentional or the result of a rational design:

> Like the winds, that come we know not whence, and blow whithersoever they list, the forms of society are derived from an obscure and distant origin; they arise, long before the date of philosophy, from the instincts, not from the speculations, of men. The croud of mankind, are directed in their establishments and measures, by the circumstances in which they are placed; and seldom are turned from their way, to follow the plan of any single projector. (119)

Ferguson singles out three types of causes to explain the passage from the savage to the polished state. First, he contends that climate has an influence on the character of peoples; for both extreme heat and extreme cold – the former because it renders people too 'feverish' and the latter because it makes them 'dull and slow' – hinder the development of mankind's industrious capacities (110). Secondly, nations with greater and more concentrated city-populations are also, and most significantly, driven by the contagion of passions that are easily communicated. As a result, moral and political causes also play an important role in the evolution of 'polished nations'. Thirdly, the progress in mechanical arts, motivated by the love of property, produces a social division of labour ('Separation of Arts and Professions') and a progressive specialisation of the social functions and this, in turn, generates the need for specific social institutions. The general explanation for the passage to more polished social forms consists in a set of related claims. Owing to climatic factors or to the lack of untransformed economical resources, some peoples are more inclined to develop industry and thus to specialise the social functions and generate the need for social institutions. The specialisation of social functions and general prosperity produce significant alterations in the moral life of the nation depending both on physical (climate) and moral (contagion of passions) causes.

The impression that there is progress in history derives from an appreciation of the specialisation of occupations in the commercial states, which is responsible for the improvement of the national capacity. However, Ferguson contends that the latter is not necessarily associated with advance in learning. In fact, he argues, the specialisation of the workers is necessary to the progress of industry and industry works better when people are ignorant (174). Ferguson's phrasing is close to Marx's theory of alienation, although he draws substantially different conclusions. For the Scotsman, progress in manufacture necessarily entails that part of the population becomes so specialised that their ability to share in the rights and duties of citizenship is dramatically diminished. For that reason, he thinks that popular democracies only mask the real inequality of the social relationships and admit into political deliberation sectors of the population that cannot, in fact, exert their political rights with discernment (178).

IV. CONCLUSION

The richness of the philosophical reflection on history reveals its importance for philosophers in the eighteenth century. In the traditional quest for the origins and destiny of the human kind, they asked about the validity of human testimony, the status of mythology as an historical source, the nature of historical explanation, the importance of economic and political factors in the shaping of different historical forms, the status of national characters, and whether there is progress in history. These issues were in general not treated as problems specific to 'philosophy of history'. They were considered as problems of the most central philosophical concern. The nature and reliability of testimony – which was a central component of any empirical science in the period – was crucial in discussions of the foundations of empirical knowledge. The debate about the importance of natural and physical causes in social explanation influenced new conceptions of causality and explanation. The reconstruction of universal history on philosophical grounds was a critique of contractarianism and part of the debate on the foundation of morals. Although insufficiently noticed, reflection on history is a pervasive feature in the work of almost all the major philosophers of the eighteenth century and it sheds new light on many of the central philosophical projects of the period.

NOTES

1 See Richard H. Popkin, *The History of Scepticism from Erasmus to Spinoza* (Berkeley, CA, 1979).

2 For general surveys of historical pyrrhonism see Carlo Borghero, *La certezza e la storia: Cartesianesimo, pirronismo e conoscenza storica* (Milan, 1983); Arnaldo Momigliano, 'Ancient History and the Antiquarian', in *Studies in Historiography* (New York, NY, 1966), 1–39;

Popkin, 'Skepticism and the Study of History', in *David Hume: Philosophical Historian*, eds. D. F. Norton and R. H. Popkin (Indianapolis, IN, 1965), ix–xxxi; Meta Scheele, *Wissen und Glaube in der Geschichtswissenschaft: Studien zum historischen Pyrrhonismus in Frankreich und Deutschland* (Heidelberg, 1930); Paul Hazard, *The European Mind: The Critical Years, 1680–1715* (New Haven, CT, 1953); Markus Völkel, *'Pyrrhonismus Historicus' und 'Fides Historica': Die Entwicklung der deutschen historischen Methodologie unter dem Gesichtpunkt der Skepsis* (Frankfurt am Main, 1987).

3 See Barbara J. Shapiro, *A Culture of Fact: England, 1550–1720* (Ithaca, NY and London, 2000).

4 François La Mothe Le Vayer, *Du peu de certitude qu'il y a dans l'histoire* [1668] in *Oeuvres*, 7 vols. in 14 (Dresden, 1756–9), 5.2: 444, my translation.

5 Pierre Bayle, *Dictionnaire historique et critique* (1697). I refer to the 5th edn., 4 vols. (Amsterdam, 1740), as follows: article title, note, volume number: page number (for example, 'Mariana', note D, 3: 328). English quotations are from *The Dictionary Historical and Critical of Mr. Peter Bayle*, trans. Pierre Des Maizeux, 5. vols. (London, 1734–8), referred to by volume number: page number, separated from the original by a slash.

6 *Dictionnaire*, 'Horace (Publius)', note A, 2: 790; *Dictionary* 3: 485.

7 'Guevara', note D, 2: 632/3: 269. For further reference, see Ruth Whelan, *The Anatomy of Superstition: A Study of the Historical Theory and Practice of Pierre Bayle* (Oxford, 1989), Elisabeth Labrousse, 'La méthode critique chez Pierre Bayle et l'histoire', *Revue Internationale de philosophie de Bruxelles*, 11 (1957): 450–66. The idea that strict rules of criticism can warrant historical objectivity in spite of the fact that historians are themselves interested historical agents was further developed in Germany by Johann Martin Chladenius in *Vernünftige Gedanken von dem Wahrscheinlichen und desselben gefährlichen Missbrauche*, trans. U. G. Thorschmid (Leipzig, 1748) and *Allgemeine Geschichtswissenschaft: worinnen der Grund zu einer neuen Einsicht in allen Arten der Gelahrheit gelegt wird* (Leipzig, 1752). See also Johann Christoph Gatterer, 'Abhandlungen vom Standort und Gesichtpunct des Geschichtsschreibers oder der deutsche Livius', *Allgeimeine historische Bibliothek* 5 (1768), 3–17.

8 For an account of how this sense perception–based form of mitigated scepticism contributed to the development of British natural philosophy, see Henry G. Van Leeuwen, *The Problem of Certainty in English Thought, 1630–1690* (The Hague, 1963).

9 François Marie Arouet de Voltaire, *Histoire de la guerre de 1741* (1756) (Paris, 1971), 3. Author's translations unless otherwise noted.

10 Louis Jean Lévesque de Pouilly, 'Dissertation sur l'incertitude de l'Histoire des quatre premiers siècles de Rome. Par M. de Pouilly', *Mémoires de littérature tirés des registres de l'Académie Royale des inscriptions et belles lettres: Depuis l'année M. DCCXVIII. jusques & compris l'année M. DCCXXV* (Paris, 1729), 14.

11 See Henry St John Bolingbroke, 'The Substance of some Letters, Written Originally in French, about the Year One Thousand Seven Hundred and Twenty, to M. De Pouilly', *The Works of Lord Bolingbroke*, 4 vols. (Philadelphia, PA, 1841), vol. 2; and *Letters on the Study and Use of History*, 2 vols. (London, 1752), vol. 2, here quoted from Bolingbroke, *Historical Writings*, ed. I. Kramnick (Chicago, IL, 1972), 41 and 45.

12 David Hume, *The History of England*, 6 vols. (Indianapolis, IN, 1983), 1: 3–4.

13 Nicolas Fréret, 'Réflexions générales sur l'étude des anciennes histoires et sur le degré de certitude des différentes preuves historiques' (General Reflections on the Study of Ancient Histories and on the Degree of Certitude of Historical Proofs), in *Mémoires académiques* (Paris, 1996), 90.

14 See Ian Hacking, *The Emergence of Probability: A Philosophical Study of Early Ideas about Probability, Induction and Statistical Inference* (London, 1975); Lorraine Daston, *Classical Probability in the Enlightenment* (Princeton, NJ, 1988); Barbara J. Shapiro, *Probability and Certainty in Seventeenth-Century England: A Study of the Relationships between Natural Science, Religion, History, Law, and*

Literature (Princeton, NJ, 1983). Daston and Shapiro highlight the contribution of history and legal theory to the development of probability.

15 See especially the second of René Descartes's, *Regulæ ad directionem ingenii*, in *Oeuvres de Descartes*, eds. C. Adam and P. Tannery, 11 vols. (Paris, 1897–1910), 10: 362.

16 Pierre-Daniel Huet, *Demonstratio evangelica ad serenissimum delphinum* (Paris, 1679). Nicolas Filleau de la Chaise, 'Traité qu'il y a des demonstrations d'une autre espece & aussi certaines que celles de la geometrie', *Pensées de M. Pascal sur la religion et sur quelques autres sujets . . .*, ed. B. Pascal (Amsterdam, 1688). Quotations here from, Antoine Arnauld and Pierre Nicole, *Logic or the Art of Thinking* (The Port-Royal *Logic*), trans. and ed. J. V. Buroker, (Cambridge, 1996), 261. The most important defence of moral certainty in English was Humphry Ditton, *A Discourse Concerning the Resurrection of Jesus Christ* (London, 1712).

17 David Hume, *A Letter from a Gentleman to his Friend in Edinburgh* (1745), eds. E. C. Mossner and J. V. Price (Edinburgh, 1967), 22; see also Hume, *A Treatise of Human Nature*, eds. D. F. Norton and M. J. Norton, in the *Clarendon Edition* (2006), 2.3.1.15, SBN 404–5. See David Fate Norton, *David Hume: Common-Sense Moralist, Sceptical Metaphysician* (Princeton, NJ, 1982), 44 n.34.

18 Arnauld and Nicole, *Logic*, 264.

19 See esp. Christian August Crusius, *Weg zur Gewissheit und Zuverlässigkeit der menschlichen Erkenntniss* (Leipzig, 1747), 1041–78. Hume mentions some of these stipulations: 'Were not the memory tenacious to a certain degree; had not men commonly an inclination to truth and a principle of probity; were they not sensible to shame, when detected in a falsehood: Were not these, I say, discovered by *experience* to be qualities, inherent in human nature, we should never repose the least confidence in human testimony' (*An Enquiry concerning Human Understanding*, ed. T. L. Beauchamp, in the *Clarendon Edition* (2000),10.5, SBN 112). Kant lists the conditions for authoritative testimony, including (a) 'that [the witness] have sufficient skill to obtain experience'; (b) 'that he was in circumstances in which he was able to obtain experience'; and (c) 'that he also has the skill to declare his experiences, so that one can understand his sense well'. (Immanuel Kant, *Wiener Logik* in Ak 24: 898; translated as *The Vienna Logic* in *Works/Lectures on Logic*, trans. and ed. J. M. Young (1992)).

20 John Locke, *An Essay Concerning Human Understanding*, ed. P. H. Nidditch (Oxford, 1975), IV.xvi.10.

21 John Craig, *Theologiae Christianae principia mathematica* (London, 1699). A translation is appended to Richard Nash, *John Craige's Mathematical Principles of Christian Theology* (Carbondale, IL, 1991). Locke was aware of the pyrrhonian implications of his argument: he would 'not be thought . . . to lessen the Credit and use of *History*: 'tis all the light we have in many cases; and we receive from it a great part of the useful Truths we have, with a convincing evidence. . . . But this, Truth it self forces me to say, That no *Probability* can arise higher than its first Original (*Essay*, IV.xiv.11).

22 See Nash, *John Craige's*. . . . Nash, however, does not mention Reid as one of the readers of Craig. See Reid, *Essays on the Intellectual Powers of Man*, eds. D. Brookes and K. Haakonssen (Edinburgh, 2002), 537 and note.

23 [George Hooper], 'A Calculation of the Credibility of Human Testimony', *Philosophical Transactions of the Royal Society of London* 21 (1699), 359–65. The text has previously been attributed to many authors.

24 Crusius, *Weg zur Gewissheit*, 1056.

25 See M. A. Stewart, 'Hume's Historical View of Miracles', in *Hume and Hume's Connexions*, eds. M. A. Stewart and J. P. Wright (Edinburgh, PA, 1994); David Wootton, 'Hume's "Of Miracle": Probability and Irreligion', in *Studies in the Philosophy of the Scottish Enlightenment*, ed. M. A. Stewart (Oxford, 1990), 191–229.

26 This interpretation stems from Hume's 'friendly adversaries', such as Thomas Reid and George Campbell. The latter particularly charges Hume with failing to see that there is no such thing as a purely personal experience. From the moment we begin to learn a language, all our claims to experience are informed by different forms of 'testimony'. Autonomy of judgement results from the differentiation in common social practices. See George Campbell, *A Dissertation on Miracles: Containing an Examination of the Principles Advanced by David Hume, Esq. in An Essay on Miracles* (Edinburgh, 1762). The same reading of Hume on testimony has been more recently advanced by C. A. J. Coady, *Testimony: A Philosophical Study* (Oxford, 1992).

27 Jacques Bénigne Bossuet, *Discours sur l'histoire universelle* (1681) in *Oeuvres de Bossuet*, eds. S.-M. Girardin and H. J. G. Patin, 4 vols. (Paris, 1841), vol. 1, translated as *Discourse on Universal History*, trans. E. Forster, ed. O. Ranum (Chicago, IL, 1976).

28 The interest in demography is evident in natural scientists such as Edmund Halley, 'An Estimate of the Degrees of the Mortality of Mankind, Drawn from Curious Tables of Births and Funerals at the City of Breslaw; With an Attempt to Ascertain the Price of Annuities Upon Lives. By Mr. E. Halley, R.S.S.', *Philosophical Transactions of the Royal Society of London*, 17 (1693): 596–610. For others the scientific approach was to apply the 'mathematical method' to moral phenomena; for example Georges-Louis Leclerc Buffon, *Arithmétique morale* in *Oeuvres complètes de Buffon*, 12 vols. (Paris, 1855), vol. 12; William Petty Knight, 'An Extract of Two Essays in Political Arithmetick concerning the Comparative Magnitudes, etc. of London and Paris by Sr. William Petty Knight. R.S.S.', *Philosophical Transactions*, 16 (1686–92): 152. See also Daston, *Classical Probability*, Stephen M. Stigler, *Statistics on the Table: The History of Statistical Concepts and Methods* (Cambridge, MA, 1999).

29 Jean Baptiste Du Bos, *Réflexions critiques sur la poësie et sur la peinture*, 7th edn., 3 vols. (Paris, 1770), 2: 151–248.

30 For seventeenth- and eighteenth-century scholars, 'climate' was a notion derived from geography: 'a space upon the surface of the terrestrial globe, contained between two parallels, and so far distant from each other, that the longest day in one differs half an hour from the longest day in the other parallel'. *Encyclopaedia Britannica*, 1st edn., 3 vols. (Edinburgh, 1771), 2: 210, 'climate'. See also the entries for climate in the 1694 (1st) and the 1798 (5th) editions of the *Dictionnaire de l'Académie Française*, 2 vols. (Paris); in Ephraim Chambers, *Cyclopaedia: Or, an Universal Dictionary of Arts and Sciences*, 2 vols. (London, 1728); and in *Encyclopédie, ou Dictionnaire raisonné des sciences, arts, et métiers*, eds. D. Diderot and J. le Rond d'Alembert.

31 John Arbuthnot, *An Essay Concerning the Effects of Air on Human Bodies* (London, 1733), 146 and 153. On Arbuthnot and Montesquieu, see Robert Shackleton, *Montesquieu: A Critical Biography* (London, 1961), 307–8. Hume did read Du Bos' *Réflexions* but it is uncertain whether he read Arbuthnot's *Essay*.

32 Charles de Secondat Montesquieu, *Considérations sur les causes de la grandeur des Romains et de leur décadence* (Amsterdam, 1734); translated as *Considerations on the Causes of the Greatness of the Romans and Their Decline*, trans. D. Lowenthal (Ithaca, NY, 1968), 169.

33 Charles de Secondat Montesquieu, *L'esprit des lois* (1748) in *Oeuvres complètes*, ed. R. Caillois, 2 vols. (Paris, 1949–51), vol. 2; translated as *The Spirit of the Laws*, trans. and eds. A. M. Cohler, B. C. Miller, and H. S. Stone (Cambridge, 1989), Bk 14, ch.1; trans., 231.

34 19.4; trans., 310. Robert Shackleton has argued against the view that Montesquieu embraced climatic reductionism. See *Montesquieu*, 316–19. See also Carlo Borghero, 'Dal "Génie" All' "Esprit". Fisico e Morale Nelle *Considérations*', in *Storia e ragione*, ed. A. Postigliola (Naples, 1987), 251–76. For further discussion of Montesquieu's philosophy of history see David

Carrithers, 'Montesquieu's Philosophy of History', *Journal of the History of Ideas*, 47 (1986): 61–80.

35 The common idea that the debate about the respective importance of physical and moral causes is between Hume and Montesquieu arises from the assumption that Montesquieu supports climatic reductionism and from the fact that Hume begins 'Of National Characters' as if the issue were solely a choice between physical and moral explanation. However, it is very unlikely that Montesquieu had read Hume's remarks on national characters in the second book of the *Treatise* (1739) (see *Treatise*, 2.1.11.2, SBN 316–17) and neither *De l'esprit des lois* (1748) nor Montesquieu's earlier essay on national characters, *Essay sur les causes qui peuvent affecter les esprits et les caracteres* (written in 1734 but published only posthumously) were published before the appearance of Hume's essay (1748). P. E. Chamley has argued that Hume may have heard about the argument of *De l'esprit des lois* before its publication, which would explain why some of Hume's arguments seem aimed at Montesquieu. It is simpler to suppose that Hume was acquainted with the literature on climatic influence, particularly Du Bos' *Réflexions* which he mentions in his *Early Memoranda* (1729–40) and cites twice in the essay 'Of the Populousness of Ancient Nations' (1752) (in *Essays, Moral, Political, and Literary*, ed. E. F. Miller, Indianapolis, IN, 1987, 377–464). P. E. Chamley, 'The Conflict between Montesquieu and Hume. A Study of the Origins of Adam Smith's Universalism', in *Essays on Adam Smith*, eds. A. S. Skinner and T. Wilson (Oxford, 1975) and Ernest Campbell Mossner, 'Hume's Early Memoranda, 1729–1740: The Complete Text', *Journal of the History of Philosophy*, 9.4 (1948): 500. See also Roberto Romani, *National Character and Public Spirit in Britain and France, 1750–1914* (Cambridge, 2002).

36 Hume, 'Of National Characters' in *Essays*, 197–215, here 200.

37 In 'Of the Rise and Progress of Arts and Sciences' Hume explains the flourishing of arts and sciences in ancient Greece as a concurrence of many factors including climate and the fertility of the soil, *Essays*, 120.

38 The first edition of the *Essai sur les mœurs* appeared in 1756. When republished as volumes 8–10 (1769) of the *Collection complette des oeuvres de M. de Voltaire*, 30 vols. (Geneva, 1768–77), the *Essai* was issued with an introduction, 'La philosophie de l'histoire' which had first appeared as a separate work in 1756. The *Essai* is volumes 15–18 of *Oeuvres de Voltaire*, 72 vols., ed. A. Beuchot (Paris, 1829–40); here 15.1: 17.

39 Hugo Grotius, *De iure belli ac pacis* (Paris, 1625); translated as *The Rights of War and Peace*, ed. J. Barbeyrac (London, 1738), xix–xx.

40 For a study of the impact of Grotius's ambiguity in the development of moral theory see Knud Haakonssen, *Natural Law and Moral Philosophy: From Grotius to the Scottish Enlightenment* (Cambridge, 1996), and his 'The Moral Conservatism of Natural Rights', in *Natural Law and Civil Sovereignty: Moral Right and State Authority in Early Modern Political Thought*, eds. Ian Hunter and David Saunders (Basingstoke, 2002): 27–42

41 Although this was the inference of many natural law philosophers, it was not made by either Grotius or Pufendorf. See Grotius, *The Rights of War and Peace*, xxxii; see also Stephen Buckle, *Natural Law and the Theory of Property: Grotius to Hume* (Oxford, 1991), 4–7; and, for a brief discussion of Pufendorf's historical writings, Peter Hanns Reill, *The German Enlightenment and the Rise of Historicism* (Berkeley, CA, 1975), 14–22.

42 See Bertrand Binoche, *Les trois sources des philosophies de l'histoire: (1764–1798)* (Paris, 1994). See also Eduard Fueter, *Geschichte der neueren Historiographie* (Munich and Berlin, 1936).

43 Comprehensive discussions of eighteenth-century philosophy of history can also be found in Friedrich Meinecke, *Historism: The Rise of a New Historical Outlook*, trans. J. E. Anderson (London, 1972); R. G. Collingwood, *The Idea of History* (New York, NY, 1956); Donald R. Kelley, *Faces of History: Historical Inquiry from Herodotus to Herder* (New Haven, CT, 1998);

Joseph M. Levine, *The Autonomy of History: Truth and Method from Erasmus to Gibbon* (Chicago, 1999).

44 Jean-Jacques Rousseau, *Discours sur l'origine et les fondements de l'inégalité parmi les hommes* in *Oeuvres*, 3: 109–223; translated as *Discourse on the Origin of Inequality*, in *The Discourses and other Early Political Writings*, trans. and ed. V. Gourevitch (Cambridge, 1997), 127.

45 Gotthold Ephraim Lessing, *Die Erziehung des Menschengeschlechts* (Berlin, 1780); translated as *Education of the Human Race*, trans. J. D. Haney (New York, NY, 1908), §1, 33.

46 'We can see that historical belief can also be knowledge if I ask someone, What is the capital of Spain? and if he would say, *I believe* it is Madrid [;] then I would say, You have to *know* this, not believe it. If one wanted to say that one cannot know it unless one has been there oneself, then I can answer, If I am there myself, I cannot learn it except from what the residents there tell me, and hence I accept it on the testimony of others. The fact that it is testimony does not hinder there being certainty in this matter. For we can just as well accept something on the testimony of others as on our own experience'. Kant, *Wiener Logik*, Ak 24: 896.

47 Kant, *Idee zu einer allgemeinen Geschichte in weltbürgerlicher Absicht*, Ak 8: 17–31; translated as *Idea for a Universal History from a Cosmopolitan Point of View* in *On History*, trans. L. W. Beck (Indianapolis, IN, 1963), 11–26.

48 Kant, 'Muthmaßlicher Anfang der Menschengeschichte', Ak 8: 107–23; translated as 'Conjectural Beginning of Human History', in *On History*, 53–68.

49 In 'Muthmaßlicher Anfang', Kant traces a parallel between 'man's *release* from the womb of nature' and the Fall of Man as is described in Genesis 3: 22–23. Ak 8: 114/trans., 59.

50 See *Zum ewigen Frieden* (1795), Ak 8: 341–86, translated as *Toward Perpetual Peace*, in *Works/Practical Philosophy*, trans. and ed. M. J. Gregor (1996).

51 In Anne-Robert-Jacques Turgot, *Plan de deux discours sur l'histoire universelle*, in *Oeuvres de Turgot*, ed. G. Schelle, 5 vols. (Paris, 1913–23), 1: 275–323; translated as *On Universal History*, in *Turgot on Progress, Sociology and Economics*, trans. and ed. R. L. Meek (London, 1973), 63–118.

52 Jean-Antoine-Nicolas de Caritat, Marquis de Condorcet, *Esquisse d'un tableau historique des progrès de l'esprit humain* (Paris, 1795); translated as *Sketch for a Historical Picture of the Progress of the Human Mind*, trans. J. Barraclough (London, 1955), 3–4. Translation modified.

53 Benedetto Croce's *La filosofia di Giambattista Vico* (Bari, 1911).

54 Giambattista Vico, *Principi di una scienza nuova intorno alla natura delle nazioni per la quale si ritruovano i principi di altro sistema del diritto naturale delle genti*, 3rd edn. (Naples, 1744); translated as *The New Science of Giambattista Vico*, trans. T. G. Bergin and M. H. Fisch (Ithaca, NY, 1984). Vico, *De antiquissima italorum sapientia ex linguae latinae originibus*, 3 vols. (Naples, 1710); translated as *On the Most Ancient Wisdom of the Italians*, trans. L. M. Palmer (Ithaca, NY, 1988). Vico, *De universi iuris: Uno principio, et fine uno* (Naples, 1720–1); translated as *Universal Right*, trans. and eds. G. A. Pinton and M. Diehl (Amsterdam and Atlanta, GA, 2000). Page references are to the translations.

55 Vico wrote before any conjectural history was written. Probably he had Hobbes in mind.

56 Vico, *Scienza*, §§147–8. The English translation gives 'institutions' for *cose*, which is the Italian version of the Latin *res* and preserves its polysemy (thing, event, fact, affair). The translation, 'institutions', reduces too much the scope of Vico's claim. When Vico thinks about institutions he refers to *cose umane* – human 'things'. See, for example, §§10 and 239.

57 *Scienza*, §176. In §§335 and 1110, Vico presses this point against Pierre Bayle's *Pensées diverses sur la comète* (1683), where it is claimed that, as reports on some American nations had shown, peoples can live in justice without having religious beliefs. Vico rejects Bayle's evidence, saying that these 'are travelers' tales, to promote the sale of their books by the narration of portents (§334)'. See Hume's *Natural History of Religion*: '[t]he belief of invisible, intelligent

power has been very generally diffused over the human race, in all places and in all ages; but it has neither perhaps been so universal as to admit of no exception, nor has it been, in any degree, uniform in the ideas, which it has suggested. Some nations have been discovered, who entertained no sentiments of Religion, if travellers and historians may be credited; and no two nations, and scarce any two men, have ever agreed precisely in the same sentiments' in *Works*, 4: 309.

58 *Scienza*, §§201, 198. Bernard Le Bovier de Fontenelle, *De l'origine des fables* (1724) in *Oeuvres Complètes*, ed. G.-B. Depping, 3 vols. (Geneva, 1968), vol. 2; Fréret, 'Réflexions générales sur l'étude des anciennes histoires et sur le degré de certitude des différentes preuves historiques', in *Mémoires académiques*.

59 See Binoche, *Les trois sources*, 157–84.

60 See Reill, *The German Enlightenment*, ch. 2.

61 Johann Gottfried Herder, *Auch eine Philosophie der Geschichte*, in *Herders Sämmtliche Werke*, ed. B. L. Suphan, 33 vols. (Berlin, 1877–1913), 5: 475–593, at 511.

62 Henry Home, Lord Kames, *Sketches of the History of Man* (Edinburgh, 1774); John Millar, *The Origin of the Distinction of Ranks; or, An Inquiry into the Circumstances which Give Rise to Influence and Authority, in the Different Members of Society* (Edinburgh, 1771); for Ferguson, see note 67 below; John Logan, *Elements of the Philosophy of History* (Edinburgh, 1781); for Hume, see note 57 above; Adam Smith, *Lectures on Jurisprudence*, eds. R. L. Meek, D. D. Raphael and P. Stein, in *Works* (1978). The profusion of conjectural histories is typical of the Scottish Enlightenment but important conjectural histories were written also elsewhere. Noteworthy is Isaak Iselin, *Über die Geschichte der Menschheit* (Basel, 1786).

63 Dugald Stewart, 'Account of the Life and Writings of Adam Smith LL.D.', in *The Collected Works of Dugald Stewart*, ed. W. Hamilton, 11 vols. (Edinburgh, 1854–60), 10: 34.

64 See Roger L. Emerson, 'Conjectural History and Scottish Philosophers', *Historical Papers/Communications historiques* (1984), 63–90; Paul Wood, 'The Natural History of Man in the Scottish Enlightenment', *History of Science*, 27 (1989): 89–123; Mark Salber Phillips, *Society and Sentiment: Genres of Historical Writing in Britain 1740–1820* (Princeton, NJ, 2000), 171–89; Binoche, *Les trois sources*, 79–155.

65 This does not make the Scottish approach into proto-Marxist materialism. See Emerson, 'Conjectural History and Scottish Philosophers'; Knud Haakonssen, *The Science of a Legislator: The Natural Jurisprudence of David Hume and Adam Smith* (Cambridge, 1981), 181–5; and Phillips, *Society and Sentiment*, 172–3.

66 Adam Ferguson, *An Essay on the History of Civil Society*, ed. F. Oz-Salzberger (New York, NY, 1995), 8. Later he adds: 'Our method, notwithstanding, too frequently, is to rest the whole on conjecture; to impute every advantage of our nature to those arts which we ourselves possess; and to imagine, that a mere negation of all our virtues is a sufficient description of man in his original state. We are ourselves the supposed standards of politeness and civilization; and where our own features do not appear, we apprehend, that there is nothing which deserves to be known' (75).

67 Ferguson, 14: 'If we admit that man is susceptible of improvement, and has in himself a principle of progression, and a desire of perfection, it appears improper to say, that he has quitted the state of his nature, when he has begun to proceed; or that he finds a station for which he was not intended, while, like other animals, he only follows the disposition, and employs the power that nature has given'.

BIOBIBLIOGRAPHICAL APPENDIX

KNUD HAAKONSSEN AND CONTRIBUTORS

This section contains entries for all of the main figures discussed in this history, along with many others. The first part of each entry contains a brief biographical sketch, including a list of the major works of philosophical significance and the standard edition, if any, of the thinker's works. Other editions that have been referred to in the main text are listed in the Bibliography. The second part of each entry contains a brief selection of secondary literature, beginning with biographical and bibliographical material, if possible and appropriate. These biographical and bibliographical entries are not intended to be comprehensive and complete but to supplement the main text and to provide a starting point for further investigation. The entries were written by authors of chapters in the volume and by: Thomas Ahnert (University of Edinburgh); Daniel Dahlstrom (Boston University); James Schmidt (Boston University); and Åsa Söderman (Boston University).

ABBT, THOMAS b. Ulm, 1738; d. Bückeburg, 1766. Writer and philosopher. Studied theology, then mathematics, history, and philosophy at Halle; Privatdozent there (1760), Extraordinarius at Frankfurt an der Oder (1761), Ordinarius (in mathematics) at Rinteln (1761). Reviewer for Nicolai's *Briefe, die Neueste Litteratur betreffend* and *Allgemeine Deutsche Bibliothek*. Offered positions in mathematics at both Halle and Marburg in 1765; instead entered the service of the Margrave of Schaumburg-Lippe, but died within a year. Influenced by the work of Shaftesbury and Helvétius, he cultivated an accessible style of argument patterned on Ciceronian rhetoric that was greatly admired by Nicolai, Mendelssohn, and Herder. His influential *Vom Tode für das Vaterland* (1761) argued that a well-governed monarchy could foster the civic virtue typically associated with republics; *Vom Verdienste* (1765) pursued the question of civic virtue further. His exchange with Mendelssohn, *Zweifel über die Bestimmung des Menschen* (1764?), recommended philosophical anthropology rather than theology as a basis for morality. Nicolai edited vols. 1–5 of his *Vermischte Werke*, 6 vols. (Berlin and Stettin, 1768–81; fascim. Hildesheim and New York, NY, 1978).

Secondary Sources: H. E. Bödeker, 'Thomas Abbt, Patriot, Bürger und bürgerliches Bewußtsein,' in *Bürger und Bürgerlichkeit im Zeitalter der Aufklärung*, ed. R. Vierhaus (Heidelberg, 1981): 221–53. Z. Batscha, 'Thomas Abbts politische Philosophie,' in *'Despotismus von jeder Art reizt nur zur Widersetzlichkeit.' Die Französische Revolution in der deutschen Popularphilosophie*, ed. Z. Batscha (Frankfurt, 1989): 126–68. H. E. Bödeker, 'Thomas Abbt (1738–1766),' *Aufklärung* 4 (1989):

103–105. B. W. Redekop, 'Thomas Abbt and the Formation of an Enlightened German "Public",' *Journal of the History of Ideas* 58 (1997): 81–103. Same, *Enlightenment and Community: Lessing, Abbt, Herder, and the Quest for a German Public* (Montreal, Kingston, 2000). [James Schmidt]

ACHENWALL, GOTTFRIED, b. Elbing (East Prussia), 1719; d. Göttingen, 1772. Philosopher and legal theorist. Studied at Jena, Halle, and Leipzig. In 1746 he lectured at Marburg, moving in 1748 to the University of Göttingen and was from 1753 professor of philosophy at Göttingen. He taught mainly history, statistics, and natural law. One of his most famous students was Georg Christoph Lichtenberg. A. is also known as 'the father of statistics'. He used that term in a lecture, entitled 'Notitia politica vulgo statistica' and in his *Staatsverfassung der heutigen vornehmsten europäischen Reiche und Völker im Grundrisse* of 1749. He understood it as a doctrine of the state (*Staatskunde*) and thought it should be a full account of the different parts of a state (including social, economic, and political aspects). His works (many of which went through many editions) are indispensable for understanding the natural law tradition in Germany. Most important works: *Prolegomena iuris natvralis: in usum auditorum; curatius exarata et nunc primum separatim edita* (1758); *Die Staatsklugheit nach ihren ersten Grundsätzen entworfen* (1761 and 1779); *Staatsverfassung der heutigen vornehmsten Europäischen Reiche im Grundrisse* (1790–8).

Secondary Sources: G. Achilles, *Die Bedeutung und Stellung von Gottfried Achenwall in der Nationalökonomie und der Statistik* (Bern, 1906). H.-H. Solf, *Gottfried Achenwall: sein Leben und sein Werk* (Göttingen, 1938). J. Hruschka, *Das deontologische Sechseck bei Gottfried Achenwall im Jahre 1767: zur Geschichte der deontischen Grundbegriffe in der Universaljurisprudenz zwischen Suarez und Kant* (Göttingen, 1986). [Manfred Kühn]

ALEMBERT, JEAN LE ROND D' b. Paris 1717; d. Paris 1783. Mathematician, physicist, and *philosophe*. Educated at the Collège des Quatre-Nations and trained in law in Paris, d'Alembert made his name as a mathematician and mathematical physicist during the 1740s as a member of the Académie des Sciences. In the *Traité de dynamique* (1743) he formulated 'd'Alembert's principle', which was extended to fluid motion in *Traité de l'équilibre et du mouvement des fluides* (1744). His *Réflexions sur la cause générale des vents* (1747) won the Prussian Academy's prize. While d'Alembert continued to publish prolifically on a wide range of issues in mathematics, physics, astronomy, and other sciences for the rest of his life, he also became a leading *philosophe*, especially when appointed co-editor with Diderot of the *Encyclopédie* (1747). He wrote the famous *Discours préliminaire* to the *Encyclopédie* (1751) in which he set out the epistemological basis for the work in Part 1 and then, in Part 2, gave an *histoire raisonnée* of the sciences, ending with a tree of knowledge that strongly invoked Bacon. While d'Alembert in his scientific and philosophical work declared his allegiance to 'sensationalism', the form given to Locke's ideas by French thinkers such as Condillac, he also retained clear elements of Cartesianism, and the balance and relationship between the two impulses is a matter of debate. D'Alembert also wrote a large number of articles for the *Encyclopédie*, not only on mathematical and scientific subjects but also on cultural matters, including one on Geneva (1757) with a plea for a theatre in the city that provoked Rousseau's *Lettre à d'Alembert*. He associated with Voltaire's anti-clericalism and when the license for the *Encyclopédie* was revoked, d'Alembert resigned his editorship (1758). His election as Secrétaire Perpétuel of the Académie Française (1754) was important in securing the *philosophes* a place in the Establishment. It was also a position from which he developed the genre of the *éloge* in his *Histoire des membres de l'Académie Française* (1785–7). Having published *Elémens de musique théorique et pratique suivant les principes de M. Rameau* (1752), he followed up with five volumes of *Mélanges de philosophie, d'histoire et de littérature* (1753–67), which contain studies of a wide variety of subjects, including the *Essai sur les Elémens de philosophie* (in vol. 4) and a further *Eclaircissemens* to this work (in vol. 5), both of which develop the article 'Elémens des sciences' in the *Encyclopédie*. Also of importance is his significantly paradoxical plea for the *philosophe*'s social independence in *Essai sur la société des gens de lettres avec les grands* (1753). There are several *Oeuvres* (18 vols., Paris, 1805; 5 vols., Paris, 1821; Paris, 1887), none of them complete.

Secondary Sources: J. Bertrand, *D'Alembert* (1889). M. Muller, *Essai sur la philosophie de Jean d'Alembert* (1926). R. Grimsley, *Jean d'Alembert* (1963). T. L. Hankins, *Jean d'Alembert: Science and Enlightenment* (1970). D. Essar, 'The Language Theory, Epistemology, and Aesthetics of Jean Le Rond d'Alembert', *Studies on Voltaire*, 159 (1976). M. Sides, 'Rhetoric on the Brink of Banishment: D'Alembert on Rhetoric in the *Encyclopédie*', *Rhetoric* 3 (1983):11–124. [Knud Haakonssen]

ARBUTHNOT, JOHN b. Arbuthnot (Scotland), 1667; d. London, 1735. Mathematician, physician and satirist. MA, Marischal College, Aberdeen, 1685; MD, St. Andrews University, 1696. His first publications, *On the Laws of Chance* (1692), *An Essay on the Usefulness of Mathematical Learning* (1701), and 'An Argument for Divine Providence' (*Philosophical Transactions*, 1710) reflect his acquaintance with early probability theory and Newtonianism. *The History of John Bull* (1712) and collaboration with Jonathan Swift and Alexander Pope on *The Memoirs of... Martinus Scriblerus* (1741) acquired him a reputation as a satirist. He wrote on medicine and ancient numismatics as well as a Pascalian poem, *Know Thyself* (1734).

Secondary Sources: G. A. Aiken, *The Life and Works of John Arbuthnot* (Oxford, 1892). L. M. Beattie, *John Arbuthnot, Mathematician and Satirist* (Cambridge, 1935). C. Condren, *Satire, Lies, and Politics: The Case of Dr. Arbuthnot* (New York, NY, 1997). [Dario Perinetti]

BALGUY, JOHN b. Sheffield, 1686; d. Harrogate, 1748. Moral philosopher and Anglican divine. Educated at St. John's College, Cambridge; school-master, private tutor, Anglican minister. Wrote in defence of Clarke's moral philosophy, attacking Shaftesbury in *A Letter to a Deist* (anon., 1726), Hutcheson in *The Foundation of Moral Goodness* (anon., 1728), and Tindal in *A Second Letter to a Deist* (anon., 1731). See further *Divine Rectitude* (anon., 1730); *The Law of Truth* (anon., 1733), and *A Collection of Tracts Moral and Theological* (1734).

Secondary Sources: F. C. Beiser, *The Sovereignty of Reason: The Defense of Rationality in the Early English Enlightenment* (Princeton, NJ, 1996): 307–19. I. Rivers, *Reason, Grace, and Sentiment. A Study of the Language of Religion in England 1660–1780*, 2 vols. (Cambridge, 1991, 2000): vol. 2: chapter 3. [Knud Haakonssen]

BANKS, JOSEPH b. London, 1743; d. Isleworth, England, 1820. Botanist, explorer, statesman of science. The botanical fruits of his epochal voyage on the *Endeavour*, 1768–71, under the command of James Cook, secured his scientific reputation which led to his election as President of the Royal Society in 1778, a post he held until his death. He was a promoter of science rather than one who advanced science through his own publications. His journal – *The Endeavour Journal of Joseph Banks, 1768–1771*, ed. J. C. Beaglehole (2 vols., Sydney, 1962) – provides a vivid impression of the impact of the Pacific in the age of the Enlightenment.

Secondary Sources: H. Carter, *Sir Joseph Banks, 1743–1820* (London, 1988) and *Sir Joseph Banks (1743–1820): A Guide to Biographical and Bibliographical Sources* (Winchester, 1987). [John Gascoigne]

BARBEYRAC, JEAN b. Béziers, France, 1674; d. Groningen, Netherlands, 1744. Natural lawyer, man of letters. A Huguenot refugee who studied in Lausanne, Geneva, Berlin, and Frankfurt a.d. Oder, B. was professor of ancient languages at the 'Collège français' in Berlin 1697–1710. During this time he annotated and translated Pufendorf into French (*Le droit de la nature et des gens*, 1706; *Les devoirs de l'homme et du citoyen*, 1707), and this secured him the highest reputation as a natural lawyer. The translations were re-edited throughout the century, and his annotations were included in English, Latin, and German translations. 1710–17 B. was professor of law and history at the Academy of Lausanne and was Rektor there 1714–17. Together with Jean-Pierre de Crousaz (Lausanne) and Jean-Alphonse Turrettini (Geneva), he combated Calvinist orthodoxy. He became a member of the Academy of Sciences in Berlin 1713 and in 1717 professor of public and private law at the University of Groningen, where he died. He rejected Leibniz' critique of Pufendorf: see appendix to 4th (1718) and later editions of *Les devoirs*. An annotated edition of Grotius' *De jure belli ac pacis* (1720) is followed by a French translation (1724). In *Traité sur la morale des pères de l'église* (1728) he defended his introduction to *Le droit de la nature et des gens* against the critique of Dom Demi Cueillier. Finally, B. published an annotated translation of Richard Cumberland: *Traité philosophique des loix naturelles (1744)*. There is a collection of shorter works: *Ecrits de droit et de morale*, ed. S. Goyard-Fabre (Paris, 1996), and three of them are translated in: Samuel Pufendorf, *The Whole Duty of Man, According to the Law of Nature*, eds. I. Hunter and D. Saunders, with Two Discourses and a Commentary by Jean Barbeyrac, trans. D. Saunders (Indianapolis, IN, 2003).

Secondary Sources: 'Mémoire sur la Vie et sur les Ecrits de Mr. Jean Barbeyrac, écrit par lui-même' (autobiography), in *Ecrits de droit et de morale*, 81–92. P. Meylan, *Jean Barbeyrac (1674–1744) et les débuts de l'enseignement du droit dans l'ancienne académie de Lausanne* (Lausanne, 1937). S. Othmer, *Berlin und die Verbreitung des Naturrechts in Europa: Kultur- und sozialgeschichtliche Studien zu Jean Barbeyracs Pufendorf-Übersetzungen und eine Analyse seiner Leserschaft* (Berlin, 1970). S. Zurbuchen, *Naturrecht und natürliche Religion: Zur Geschichte des Toleranzbegriffs von Samuel Pufendorf bis Jean-Jacques Rousseau* (Würzburg, 1991). T. Hochstrasser, 'Conscience and Reason: The Natural Law Theory of Jean Barbeyrac', in *The Historical Journal* 36.2 (1993): 289–398. H. Rosenblatt, *Rousseau and Geneva: From the First Discourse to the Social Contract, 1749–62* (Cambridge, 1997): 88–158. J. B. Schneewind, *The Invention of Autonomy: A History of Modern Moral Philosophy* (Cambridge, 1998): 250–9. [Simone Zurbuchen]

Basedow, Johann Bernhard b. Hamburg, 1724; d. Magdeburg, 1790. Educationist and theologian. Educated at the universities of Leipzig and Kiel. After a period as a tutor in Holstein he became Professor of Morals and Rhetoric (1753), and later of Theology, at the Danish Ritter-akademie in Sorø. He first came to prominence for his eudaimonistic, utilitarian philosophy as expressed in his *Practische Philosophie für alle Stände, ein weltbürgerlich Buch ohne Anstoss für irgend eine Nation und Kirche* (1758). Criticism from orthodox theologians led to his being transferred to the *Gymnasium* at Altona. Here he continued his project of removing the non-rational elements from Christian teaching, notably in *Philalethie: Neue Aussichten in die Wahrheiten und Religion der Vernunft bis in die Grenzen der glaubwürdigen Offenbarung dem denkenden Publico eröffnet* (1764). Basedow's fame rests on his all-embracing programme for school education which incorporated illustrated textbooks for different stages of childhood along with aids for teachers and parents. He was influenced by Rousseau, particularly in stressing the importance of learning from nature and experience. However he adapted Rousseau in a free and eclectic manner to suit, ideally, a system of public, non-confessional education along the lines of La Chalotais. His first major educational enterprise was *Vorstellung an Menschenfreunde und vermögende Männer über Schulen, Studien und ihren Einfluss in die öffentliche Wohlfahrt, mit einem Plane eines Elementarbuchs der menschlichen Erkenntnis* (1768). In 1771 he was invited by the Prince of Anhalt-Dessau to advise on education. He published *Das Methodenbuch für Väter und Mütter der Familie und Völker* (1770); *Agathokrator, oder von Erziehung künftiger Regenten* (1771); and his most comprehensive text, the

Elementarwerk (1774). He founded the Philanthropin in Dessau in 1774, which became a model for Enlightenment thinking and practice in education, attracting other educationists such as Campe and Trapp and earning the praise of Kant. A collection of his educational work appears in *Ausgewählte pädagogische Schriften*, ed. A. Reble (Paderborn, 1965).

Secondary Sources: G. Hahn, *Basedow und sein Verhältnis zu Rousseau* (Leipzig, 1885). A. Pinloche, *La réforme de l'éducation en Allemagne au dix-huitième siècle: Basedow et le philanthropisme* (Paris, 1889). W. Finzel-Niederstadt, *Lernen und Lehren bei Herder und Basedow* (Frankfurt am Main, 1986). C. Kersting, *Die Genese der Pädagogik im 18. Jahrhundert: Campes 'Allgemeine Revision' im Kontext der neuzeitlichen Wissenschaft* (Weinheim, 1992). H. Lempa, *Bildung der Triebe: Der deutsche Philanthropismus, 1768–1788* (Turku, 1993). [Geraint Parry]

BAUMEISTER, FRIEDRICH CHRISTIAN b. Großkörner (at Gotha), 1709; d. Görltz, 1785. Studied philosophy in Jena and Wittenberg. Became director of the gymnasium in Görlitz in 1736 and wrote a number of textbooks, propagating Wolffian metaphysics. Baumeister, like Baumgarten, belonged to the second generation of Wolffians. The most important works: *Philosophia definitiva* (1735); *Institutiones philosophiae rationalis methodo Wolfii conscriptae* (1735); *Institutiones metaphysicae, ontologiam, cosmologiam, psychologiam, theologiam denique naturalem complexae, methodo Wolfii adornatae* (1738 and 1751); *Historia doctrinae de mundo optimo* (1741).

Secondary Sources: H. W. Arndt, 'Vorwort,' *Philosophia definitiva* (Hildesheim, 1978 – reprint of the Wien and Wittenberg 1775 edition). [Manfred Kühn]

BAUMGARTEN, ALEXANDER GOTTLIEB b. Berlin, 1714; d. Frankfurt an der Oder, 1762. Following studies at University of Halle, he became professor of philosophy at Frankfurt an der Oder (from 1740 to his death) and one of the most effective transmitters of Wolffian philosophy through his *Metaphysica* (1739), *Ethica* (1740), and *Acroasis logica in Christianum L. B. de Wolff* (1762). Under the pseudonym 'Aletheophilus', he authored the weekly, *Philosophische Briefe* (1741), addressed principally to women. In *Meditationes philosophicae de nonnullis ad poema pertinentibus* (1735) and *Aesthetica* (2 vols., 1750 and 1758), he founded aesthetics as a science of clear but indistinct cognition afforded by the senses, the perfection of which is beauty. The *Aesthetica*'s concentration on cognition supposedly inferior to reason indirectly calls the Wolffian hierarchy of cognitive faculties into question. Writings on aesthetics and related subjects are reprinted with translations in *Philosophische Betrachtungen über einige Bedingungen des Gedichtes*, trans. H. Paetzold (Hamburg, 1983); *Reflections on Poetry*, trans. K. Aschenbrenner and W. Holther (Berkeley, CA, 1954); *Theoretische Aesthetik*, trans. H. R. Schweizer (Basel, 1973); *Texte zur Grundlegung der Aesthetik*, trans. H. R. Schweizer (Hamburg, 1983).

Secondary Sources: E. Cassirer, *Die Philosophie der Aufklärung* (Halle, 1932): 368–482. B. Croce, 'Rileggendo *L'Aesthetica* del Baumgarten', *La Critica* 31 (1933): 2–19. A. Nivelle, *Kunst- und Dichtungstheorien zwischen Aufklärung und Klassik* (Berlin, 1960). U. Franke, *Kunst als Erkenntnis: Die Rolle der Sinnlichkeit in der Ästhetik des Alexander Gottlieb Baumgarten* (Wiesbaden, 1972). H. R. Schweizer, *Ästhetik als Philosophie der sinnlichen Erkenntnis* (Basel, 1973). M. Gregor, 'Baumgarten's *Aesthetica*', *Review of Metaphysics* 37 (1983): 357–85; D. Dumouchel, 'A. G. Baumgarten et la naissance du discours esthétique', *Dialogue* 30 (1991): 473–501; H. Parret, 'De Baumgarten à Kant: sur la beauté', *Revue Philosophique de Louvain* 90 (1992): 317–43. [Daniel Dahlstrom]

BAXTER, ANDREW b. Aberdeen, c. 1686; d. Whittinghame, East Lothian, 1750. Educated at King's College, Aberdeen; peripatetic tutor, employed in later life mostly in the family of Hay of Drummelzier. *Some Reflections on a late Pamphlet called, The State of the Moral World Considered* (1732) challenged William Dudgeon's deism. *An Enquiry into the Nature of the Human*

Soul (1733) argued the necessity of spiritual agency from the *vis inertiae* of matter, against the different metaphysical assumptions of Locke and Berkeley; a separate *Appendix* (1750) criticized Colin MacLaurin's understanding of Newtonianism. *Matho* (1740), a tutorial dialogue on natural philosophy and metaphysics, was posthumously revised (1765) by another hand. Sequels to all three works were left in manuscript, *The Evidence of Reason in Proof of the Immortality of the Soul* reaching posthumous publication in 1779.

Secondary Sources: James McCosh, *The Scottish Philosophy* (London, 1875): 42–9. [M. A. Stewart]

Bayle, Pierre b. Carla, 1647; d. Rotterdam, 1706. Born into poor but intellectually vibrant Protestant family in the Pyrenees. Attended elementary school but then educated by father and self until sent to protestant Academy in Puylaurens (1768). Disappointed by the Academy, since he was much older and brighter than the rest of the students, left for a Jesuit college after three months. In 1669 converted to Catholicism but converted back in 1670 after defending his MA thesis and secretly fleeing Toulouse. Quickly departed for Geneva, as relapsing from Catholicism was punished by banishment. Lacking funds, became tutor to son of the Comte de Dohna at Coppet. Slipped back into France in 1674 and with help of his friend Jacques Basnage secured small posts and then in 1675 won competition for Philosophy chair at the Academy of Sedan (where he first met Pierre Jurieu). In 1681 the Academy was abolished by Louis XIV as a prelude to the revocation of the already diminished Edict of Nantes. Departed for Rotterdam when offered the chair of philosophy and history in the École Illustre of the Walloon community. Published *Lettre sur la Comète* in 1682 and revised it as *Pensées diverses sur la Comète* in 1683. The work met with some acclaim and included Bayle's scandalous argument that a perfectly moral atheist was possible. First of many works of Protestant controversy appeared the *Critique générale de l'histoire du calvinisme de M. Maimbourg* (1682), which was burned the following year by the public hangman in Paris. In 1684 began editing and writing countless book reviews for his monthly *Nouvelles de la République des Lettres*, which ceased publication in 1687. In 1685 brother Jacob seized by French authorities – since Pierre did little to hide his identity as author of *Critique générale* – and died in captivity. *Commentaire Philosophique*, one of the major early modern arguments for tolerationism, appeared in 1686–88 and initiated a long polemical battle with Jurieu. In 1696 published the enormously popular *Dictionnaire historique et critique*, one of the major works of scholarship, imagination, and argument of this or any time. It was expanded in the second edition (1702), but the standard edition (Amsterdam, 1730) includes posthumous notes and other additions – Pierre Bayle and Pierre Desmaizeaux, *Dictionnaire historique et critique*, 5th edn., with life of the author, ed. Des Maizeaux (Amsterdam, 1740). Two English translations of the *Dictionnaire* were available in the eighteenth century (1710 and 1734). From 1703 to his death serially published *Réponse aux Questions d'un provincial*, the final section of which appears posthumously as did *Entretiens de Maxime et Thémiste*. Bayle was the premier sceptic between Montaigne (whose work he knew nearly by heart) and Hume (whom he deeply influenced). His work was engaged by most every important philosopher of the eighteenth century, and the *Dictionnaire* was a central touchstone for enlightened intellectuals. Characteristic doctrines associated with Bayle include skeptical fideism (the latter controversially), tolerationism, the natural basis of morality, and, more generally, the independence of rational inquiry from theology.

Secondary Sources: G. W. Leibniz, *Essais de théodicée* (1710). *Pierre Bayle, le Philosophe de Rotterdam*, ed. P. *Dibon* (Paris, 1959). C. B. Brush, *Montaigne and Bayle: Variations on the Theme of Skepticism* (The Hague, 1966). É. Labrousse, *Bayle* (Oxford, 1983). T. Lennon, *Reading Bayle* (Toronto, 1999). [Aaron Garrett]

Beattie, James b. Laurencekirk, Kincardineshire, Scotland, 1735; d. Aberdeen, 1803. Poet, public moralist, and Common Sense philosopher. Educated at Marischal College, Aberdeen (graduated 1753); schoolmaster at Fordoun and Aberdeen 1753–60; professor of Moral Philosophy and Logic at Marischal College, 1760–93. His philosophy was largely derived from Thomas Reid's Common Sense realism which Beattie in the *Essay on the Nature and Immutability of Truth* (1770) aimed at Hume's scepticism. The performance gave the author instant national – and some international – fame, clerical favour, and a royal pension. It was closely followed by *The Minstrel* (Bk. I, 1771; Bk. II, 1774), a large poem, shaped in Spenser's stanzas, on the edifying theme of the rise and progress of poetical genius. There followed more poetry and collections of essays on moral, aesthetic, and religious topics: *Essay on Poetry and Music as they affect the Mind* (1776); *An Essay on Laughter and Ludicrous Composition* (1779); *Dissertations, Moral and Critical*, 1783; *Evidences of the Christian Religion* (1786); and the significant epitome of his academic lectures, *Elements of Moral Science* (2 vols., 1790–3). There is now a facsimile collection of *The Works of James Beattie*, with Introductions by R. J. Robinson, 10 vols. (London, 1996).

Secondary Sources: W. Forbes, *Life and Writings of Beattie* (Edinburgh, 1806). N. Phillipson, 'James Beattie and the Defence of Common Sense', in *Festschrift für Rainer Grünter*, ed. B. Fabian (Heidelberg, 1978): 145–54. P. Morère, *L'Oeuvre de James Beattie: tradition et perspectives nouvelles* (Paris, 1980). P. B. Wood, *The Aberdeen Enlightenment: The Arts Curriculum in the Eighteenth Century* (Aberdeen, 1993): 119–29. J. A. Harris, *Of Liberty and Necessity: The Free-Will Debate in Eighteenth-Century British Philosophy* (Oxford, 2005): ch. 6. [Knud Haakonssen]

Beccaria, Cesare b. Milan, 1738; d. Milan, 1794. Legal reformer and political economist. Studied in the Jesuit Collegio dei Nobili (Parma), with great success particularly in mathematics, and got his doctorate in Law in Pavia (1758). He attended the Accademia dei Trasformati in Milan (1758–61) but followed Pietro Verri when he left to found the Accademia dei Pugni (Academy of Fisticuffs), an informal circle of young reform-enthusiasts. From 1764 to 1766 he wrote articles for the journal of the Accademia dei Pugni, *Il caffé*, the most important organ of the Italian Enlightenment. After the great success of his major work, *Dei delitti e delle pene* (1764), he went to Paris in 1766 and met the *philosophes*. He refused the invitation of Catherine the Great to direct the reform of Russian law and became professor of political economy in Milan (1768–72), where he also held a wide variety of public offices from 1771 until his death. An edition of the works is in progress: *Edizione nazionale delle opere di Cesare Beccaria*, eds. L. Firpo and G. Francioni (Milano, 1984–).

Secondary Sources: G. Zarone, *Etica e politica nell'utilitarismo di Cesare Beccaria* (Naples, 1971). F. Venturi, *Italy and the Enlightenment* (London, 1972): 154–64. M. T. Maestro, *Cesare Beccaria and the Origins of Penal Reform* (1973). H. L. A. Hart, *Essays on Bentham* (Oxford, 1982): ch. 2. G. Francioni, 'La prima edizione del *Dei delitti e delle pene*', *Studi settecenteschi* 5 (1984): 131–73. R. Bellamy, Introduction, in Beccaria, *On Crimes and Punishments and Other Writings*, ed. R. Bellamy, trans. R. Davies et al. (Cambridge, 1995), ix–xlix. [Luca Fonnesu]

Bentham, Jeremy b. London, February 15, 1748; d. London, June 6, 1832. Legal reformer and secular utilitarian. A remarkably precocious child, B. attended Westminster School (1755–60) and then, at 12, Queen's College, Oxford (BA 1763, MA 1766), where he heard William Blackstone. He was admitted to Lincoln's Inn 1763 and to the bar 1769. In 1768–9 B. read (among others) Priestley, Beccaria, Helvétius and the *philosophes*, leading him to adopt the principle of utility. Over the next 15 years B. lived a sedate life on a small pension, writing prodigiously. In 1776 he published an anonymous criticism of Blackstone, *A Fragment on Government*, to some furor. In 1781 B. became friends with Lord Shelburne, who encouraged an interest in constitutional reform, and B. grew radical during the 1780s. In 1785–8 he visited his brother Samuel in Russia and wrote *A Defense of Usury* (1787), *An Introduction to the Principles of Morals and Legislation* (1789; initially printed in 1780), and the *Panopticon Papers*. In 1790 he drafted a constitutional plan for revolutionary France and criticised the National Assembly's juridical reforms: *The Principles of Juridical Procedure*. Inspired by the reformer John Howard, B. and his brother energetically, but to little effect, pursued prison reform with the *Panopticon: or the Inspection House* (1791). With his father's death B. acquired wealth for his reform work, and in the same year, 1792, he was made an honorary *citoyen* of France. As the Terror progressed, B. became more and more critical of the Revolution. B.'s philosophy is characterized by a hard-nosed application of the principle of utility to a wide range of matters in a deeply reformist and even radical spirit which flourished in the new century. *The Works of Jeremy Bentham*, ed. J. Bowring, 11 vols. (Edinburgh, 1843); *The Collected Works of Jeremy Bentham*, eds. J. H. Burns, J. R. Dinwiddy, and F. Rosen (London, 1968–81; Oxford, 1983–) (each volume with separate editor), includes *The Correspondence of Jeremy Bentham* (1971–).

Secondary Sources: Elie Halevy, *La Formation du radicalisme philosophique*, 3 vols. (Paris, 1901–4); translated as *The Growth of Philosophic Radicalism*, trans. M. Morris (London, 1928). C. W. Everett, *The Education of Jeremy Bentham* (New York, 1931). D. G. Long, *Bentham on Liberty* (Toronto, 1977). G. J. Postema, *Bentham and the Common Law Tradition* (Oxford, 1986). J. E. Crimmins, *Secular Utilitarianism: Social Science and the Critique of Religion in the Thought of Jeremy Bentham* (Oxford, 1990). [Aaron Garrett]

Bergk, Johann Adam b. Hainichen/Sachsen, 1769; d. Leipzig, 1834. Philosopher and publicist. Professor of philosophy and jurisprudence at University of Leipzig. Defended the French Revolution in *Untersuchungen aus dem Natur-, Staats- und Völkerrechte, mit einer Kritik der neuesten Konstitution der französischen Republik* (1796). Published commentaries on Kant, *Briefe über Immanuel Kant's Metaphysische Anfangsgründe der Rechtslehre* (1797) and *Reflexionen über I. Kant's Metaphysische Anfangsgründe der Tugendlehre* (1798). Translated Beccaria (1798) and wrote a treatise of punishment, *Die philosophie des peinlichen Rechtes* (1802), a treatise on critical reading, *Die Kunst, Bücher zu lesen* (1799), and accounts of his travels.

Secondary Sources: J. Garber, 'Liberaler und demokratischer Republikanismus. Kants *Metaphysik der Sitten* und ihre radikaldemokratische Kritik durch J. A. Bergk,' in *Die demokratische Bewegung in Mitteleuropa im ausgehenden 18. und frühen 19. Jahrhundert. Ein Tagungsbericht*, eds. O. Büsch, W. Grabet al. (Berlin, 1980), 251–89. R. Bledsoe, 'Harnessing Autonomous Art: Enlightenment and Aesthetic Education in Johann Adam Bergk's *Die Kunst, Bücher zu Lesen*,' *German Life and Letters* 53:4 (2000): 470–86. [James Schmidt]

Berkeley, George b. Kilkenny, Ireland, 1685; d. Oxford, 1753. Educated at Trinity College, Dublin (1700–4), elected fellow in 1707, senior fellow 1717; ordained deacon in the Church of Ireland in 1709, priest 1710. Between 1713 and 1720 he was absent in England and on the Continent, establishing literary contacts in London, functioning as chaplain to a diplomatic mission to Sicily during which he probably met Malebranche in Paris, and for three years travelling as tutor to the son of his university's vice-chancellor. He was appointed dean of Derry in 1724, holding the post *in absentia* for ten years. Four were spent in London, planning a missionary college in Bermuda to educate colonial settlers and Native Americans from the American mainland. He sailed with an advance party to Rhode Island in 1728, establishing a settlement from which the college might be launched, but returned in 1731 after the British government reneged on a promise of funds. In 1734 he resettled in Ireland as Bishop of Cloyne. Berkeley's earliest documented interests were in natural history and mathematics. He published a Latin textbook,

Arithmetica absque algebra aut Euclide demonstrata (London, 1707), with other mathematical items. Early notebooks reflect his wrestlings with the metaphysics of Cartesian and Newtonian science, and pieces unpublished in his lifetime show an early engagement with Locke's epistemology. *An Essay towards a New Theory of Vision* (Dublin, 1709), of lasting importance in the psychology of perception, laid the foundations for the full immaterialism of *A Treatise concerning the Principles of Human Knowledge* (Dublin, 1710). He contributed to contemporary political and moral debate in *Passive Obedience* (Dublin, 1712). In London, he reissued his philosophy in popular form as a contest between the established new philosophy and his own in *Three Dialogues between Hylas and Philonous* (1713), contributed essays to *The Guardian* (1713–14) against the growing tide of freethinking, and compiled *The Ladies Library* (1714) to better women's education, social standing, and knowledge of religion. While travelling he wrote *De motu* (London, 1721), presenting natural philosophy in a way consistent with immaterialism. *An Essay towards Preventing the Ruin of Great Britain* (London, 1721) was a call for moral regeneration in reaction to the South Sea Bubble. In Rhode Island he composed *Alciphron* (London, 1732), a defence of theism and immaterialism against deism and freethinking. These targets he pursued further after his return in revised editions of earlier publications and in a controversial attack, in *The Analyst* (London, 1734), on the logic of Newton's theory of fluxions. Most of his late writings from *The Querist* (Dublin, 1735–7) to *A Word to the Wise* (Dublin, 1749) were concerned with Irish economic reform. *Siris* (Dublin, 1744) sought to reconcile medicine with metaphysics, explaining the curative value of tar water on cosmical principles. Eighteenth-century interest in Berkeley's thought was greatest in Scotland and the colonial colleges. His ideas received dispassionate coverage in Chambers' *Cyclopaedia* (1728) and some English periodicals. Outside a small circle of friends, his most fervent Irish supporter was Richard Kirwan, FRS (1733–1812).

Collected Works: *The Works of George Berkeley, Bishop of Cloyne*, eds. A. A. Luce and T. E. Jessop, 9 vols. (Edinburgh, 1948–57).

Secondary Sources: B. Percival, *Berkeley and Percival* (London, 1914). A. A. Luce, *The Life of George Berkeley, Bishop of Cloyne* (Edinburgh, 1949). D. Berman, *George Berkeley: Idealism and the Man* (Oxford, 1994). M. A. Stewart, 'Berkeley, George', *Oxford Dictionary of National Biography* (Oxford, 2004). H. M. Bracken, *The Early Reception of Berkeley's Immaterialism 1710–1733*, rev. edn. (The Hague, 1965). A. A. Luce, *Berkeley and Malebranche* (Oxford, 1934, 1967). P. J. Olscamp, *The Moral Philosophy of George Berkeley* (The Hague, 1970). I. C. Tipton, *Berkeley: The Philosophy of Immaterialism* (London, 1974). C. J. McCracken, *Malebranche and British Philosophy* (Oxford, 1983). *Essays on Berkeley*, eds. J. Foster and H. M. Robertson (Oxford, 1985). A. C. Grayling, *Berkeley: The Central Arguments* (London, 1986). K. P. Winkler, *Berkeley: An Interpretation* (Oxford, 1989). M. Atherton, *Berkeley's Revolution in Vision* (Ithaca, NY, 1990). P. Walmsley, *The Rhetoric of Berkeley's Philosophy* (Cambridge, 1990). R. G. Muehlmann, *Berkeley's Ontology* (Indianapolis, IN, 1992). D. M. Jesseph, *Berkeley's Philosophy of Mathematics* (Chicago, IL, 1993). C. G. Caffentzis, *Exciting the Industry of Mankind: George Berkeley's Philosophy of Money* (Dordrecht, 2000). [M. A. Stewart]

Bernoulli, Daniel b. Groningen, 1700; d. Basel, 1782. Mathematician who with his father and rival Johann (1667–1748) began the process of extending the mathematical methods of Newton to phenomena such as fluid flow and elasticity. His *Hydrodynamica* (1738, trans. with Johann's *Hydraulics*, New York, NY, 1968), is chiefly known for 'Bernoulli's principle', that in a moving fluid pressure decreases as speed increases. His investigation of the St. Petersburg paradox in probability led him to introduce the concept of diminishing utility of money, crucial in modern economics; the relevant paper of 1738 is translated in *Econometrica* 22 (1954): 23–36. *Werke* (Basel, 1982–) in progress.

Secondary Sources: H. Straub, 'Bernoulli, Daniel', *Dictionary of Scientific Biography*, 16 vols. (New York, NY, 1970–80) 2: 36–46. E. A. Fellmann and J. O. Fleckenstein, 'Bernoulli, Johann I'., *Dictionary of Scientific Biography*, 2: 51–5. J. Dutka, 'On the St. Petersburg paradox', *Archive for History of Exact Sciences* 39 (1988): 13–39. [James Franklin]

Bilfinger, Georg Bernhard b. Cannstatt, Württemberg, Germany, 1693; d. Stuttgart, 1750. Philosopher, natural scientist, theologian. Studied theology, philosophy, and mathematics at the universities of Tübingen and Halle, where he became a disciple of Christian Wolff. Was extraordinary professor of philosophy at the University of Tübingen 1719–23; 1723–5 professor of mathematics and moral philosophy at the *Collegium illustre*; 1725–31 at the Academy of Sciences in St. Petersburg, concentrating on physics and mathematics; thereafter recalled to Tübingen as professor of theology by Duke Eberhard Ludwig of Württemberg. The University recommended that he not lecture on Wolff's philosophy, which he had earlier defended. In 1735 he became a member of the secret council in Stuttgart and was later appointed president of the *Consistorium*. His main philosophical works are: *Specimen doctrinae veterum Sinarum moralis et politicae* (repr. in Wolff, *Werke*, III.55), *De harmonia animi et corporis humani, maxime praestabilita, ex mente illustris Leibnitii, commentatio hypothetica* (1723; repr. in Wolff, *Werke*, III.21), *Commentatio philosophica de origine et permissione mali, praecique moralis* (1724), *Dilucidationes de Deo, anima humana, mundo et generalioribus rerum affectibus* (1725; repr. in Wolff, *Werke*, III.18).

Secondary Sources: J. Kintrup, *Das Leib-Seele-Problem in Georg Bernhard Bilfingers Buch De harmonia animi et corporis humani, maxime praestabilita, ex mente illustris Leibnitii, commentatio hypothetica (1723) in der geschichtlichen und philosophischen Zusammenschau*, (Münster, 1974). [Simone Zurbuchen]

Blair, Hugh b. 1718 in Edinburgh; d. Edinburgh. 1800. Man of letters and clergyman. Educated at the University of Edinburgh (MA 1739), Blair was licensed to preach in 1741 and thereafter had a highly successful career as a minister in Edinburgh and, from 1762, as the first Regius Professor of Rhetoric and Belles Lettres at the University there. Blair was a central figure in the 'Moderate' party in the Church of Scotland and, consequently, in the Scottish Enlightenment. Co-founder of the first *Edinburgh Review* (1755–6), Blair's main claim to fame was his promotion of the Ossianic poems, especially in *Critical Dissertation on the Poems of Ossian* (1763) in which he articulates a particularly clear formulation of the emotivist theory of the origins of language and a balanced compromise between primitivism and progressive notions of social development. The sentimentalist idea of the mind is also important in the rhetorical and aesthetic theories developed in the eclectic and highly influential *Lectures on Rhetoric and Belles Lettres* (1783) and many of his no less popular *Sermons* (5 vols. 1777–1801).

Secondary Sources: J. Hill, *An Account of the Life and Writings of Hugh Blair, D. D.* (Edinburgh, 1807). R. M. Schmitz, *Hugh Blair* (New York, NY, 1948). W. S. Howell, *Eighteenth-Century British Logic and Rhetoric* (Princeton, NJ, 1971). R. B. Sher, *Church and University in the Scottish Enlightenment: The Moderate Literati of Edinburgh* (Edinburgh, 1985). T. P. Miller, *The Formation of College English. Rhetoric and Belles Lettres in the British Cultural Provinces* (Pittsburgh, PA, 1997), ch. 8. [Knud Haakonssen]

Blumenbach, Johann b. Gotha, Thuringia (Germany) 1752; d. Göttingen 1840. Theoretician of medicine and natural history. Educated Gymnasium Ernestinum (completed 1769), Universities of Jena and Göttingen (MD 1775). Curator of Göttingen natural history collection, *professor extraordinarius* (1776), *professor ordinarius* and director of the medical faculty of the university

(1816). Member of *Königliche Societät der Wissenschaften zu Göttingen* (permanent secretary 1812) and numerous foreign societies. Became one of the most influential scientific figures of the late eighteenth and early nineteenth centuries. His works ranged over physical anthropology: *De generis humani varietate nativa liber* (Göttingen, 1776); English edition in *The Anthropological Treatises of Johann Friederich Blumenbach* (London, 1840); natural history: *Handbuch der Naturgeschichte* (12 editions, 1779–1830); comparative anatomy: *Handbuch der vergleichenden Anatomie* (1805); earth history: *Beyträge zur Naturgeschichte* (1806, 1811); medical theory: *Institutiones physiologiae* (1786); English edition, *Elements of Physiology* (1795). As a theoretician, he articulated modern conception of human race, defining five human races (*Caucasian, Mongolian, Malay, Ethiopian, American*). Blumenbach's rejection of preformationism led to his *Bildungstrieb* theory, assuming the organization of the embryo from vital material under the action of a teleologically directed force: *Ueber den Bildungstrieb* (1781); English translation of the 2nd edn., *An Essay on Generation* (1792). This concept was used by Kant (*Kritik der Urteilskraft*) as the primary example of a regulative vital force. Blumenbach's many students created a generation of important theoretical workers in the life sciences. No standard edition of his works.

Secondary Sources: T. Lenoir, *The Strategy of Life* (Chicago, 1992). J. L. Larson, *The Science of Living Form from Linnaeus to Kant* (Baltimore, MD, 1994). R. Richards, 'Kant and Blumenbach on the *Bildungstrieb*: A Historical Misunderstanding', *Studies in History and Philosophy of the Biological and Biomedical Sciences* 31 (2000): 11–32. P. R. Sloan, 'Preforming the Categories: Eighteenth-Century Generation Theory and the Biological Roots of Kant's A-Priori', *Journal of the History of Philosophy* 40 (2002): 229–53. [Phillip R. Sloan]

Bodmer, Johann Jakob b. Greifensee, Zürich, 1698; d. Zürich, 1783. Moralist, historian, art critic, poet, translator. 1725–31 administrator, 1731–75 professor of Helvetic history at the *Collegium Carolinum*, Zürich; 1747 member of the General Council of the city. 1721–23 he and J. J. Breitinger edited *Discourse der Mahlern*, the first moral weekly in German, modelled after Addison's *Spectator*. They entered into a controversy with Johann Christoph Gottsched about poetry, and B.'s main contributions in this field are *Critische Abhandlung von dem Wunderbaren in der Poesie* (1740) and *Critische Betrachtungen über die poetischen Gemählde der Dichter* (1741). Here he justified his interest in English literature, having translated Milton's *Paradise Lost* into German (1732), and in German poetry of the middle ages. As a critic of art, initiator of a new kind of Swiss historiography (together with J. J. Breitinger: *Helvetische Bibliothek*, 1735–41; *Historische und Critische Beiträge zu der Historie der Eidgenossen*, 1739), and as founder of reform societies, he aimed at a moral and political reform. Besides transmitting these ideas to his disciples (J. H. Füssli, J. K. Lavater, J. H. Pestalozzi), he also expressed them in political dramas composed towards the end of his life (*Schweizerische Schauspiele*, ed. A. M. Debrunner, St. Ingbert, 1998).

Secondary Sources: *Johann Jakob Bodmer: Denkschrift zum CC. Geburtstag* (Zurich, 1900) (contains a bibliography of his works). W. Bender, *J. J. Bodmer und J. J. Breitinger* (Stuttgart, 1973). A. M. Debrunner, *Das güldene schwäbische Alter: Johann Jakob Bodmer und das Mittelalter als Vorbildzeit im 18: Jahrhundert* (Würzburg, 1996). [Simone Zurbuchen]

Boerhaave, Hermann b. Voorhout, Netherlands, 1668; d. Leiden, 1738. Physician, botanist, and chemist. Graduated from the University of Leiden in philosophy in 1690, followed by a medical degree from the academy of Harderwijk in 1693. Devoted himself to teaching medicine at Leiden, where he was appointed as professor of medicine and botany in 1709. His duties included supervising the university's famed botanical gardens, and the task of properly cataloguing them prompted his interest in an effective system of classification – hence his early enthusiasm for the work of Linné. He also continued studies in clinical medicine. He became professor of chemistry in 1718, achieving a European-wide reputation with well-attended lectures. These promoted experimental methods through the use of exact quantitative measurements. Eclectic in nature, his lectures and the influential textbooks based on them – which included *Institutiones medicae* (1707) and *Elementa chemiae* (1724) – drew on Cartesian matter theory but also helped popularise the work of Boyle and Newton. His voluminous correspondence was edited by G. Lindeboom (2 vols., Leiden, 1959).

Secondary Sources: [W. Burton], *An Account of the Life and Writings of Herman Boerhaave* (London, 1743). G. Lindeboom, *Bibliographia Boerhaaviana* (Leiden, 1959). G. Lindeboom, *Boerhaave: The Man and His Work* (London, 1968). J. Christie, 'Historiography of Chemistry in the Eighteenth Century: Herman Boerhaave and William Cullen', *Ambix* 41 (1994): 4–19. [John Gascoigne]

Boileau-Despréaux, Nicolas b. Paris 1636; d. Paris 1711. Poet, critic, translator. Studied law at Paris, became an advocate, but on death of his father in 1657 he became prosperous enough to devote his life to literature. Collection of *Satires* grew from 1666-ed. to 1698-ed. 1674 saw *l'Art poétique*, the first four songs of the mock-heroic poem *Le lutrin* (which influenced Alexander Pope; last two songs 1683), and the translation of Longinus' *On the Sublime*. Royal historiographer in 1677, member of the Académie française 1684. The first nine *Reflexions critiques sur quelques passages de Longin* published 1694, the last three in 1713 in *Oeuvres diverses du sieur Boileau-Despréaux*. *Oeuvres complètes de Boileau*, ed. C. H. Boudhors, 7 vols. (Paris, 1932–43). *Oeuvres complètes*, ed. F. Escal (Paris, 1966).

Secondary Sources: G. Lanson, *Boileau* (Paris, 1892). D. Mornet, *Nicolas Boileau* (Paris, 1941). R. Bray, *Boileau, l'homme et l'oeuvre* (Paris, 1942). J. Brody, *Boileau and Longinus* (Geneva, 1948). Pierre Clarac, *Boileau* (Paris, 1964). J. E. White, Jr., *Nicolas Boileau* (New York, 1969). G. Pocock, *Boileau and the Nature of Neo-Classicism* (Cambridge, 1980). [Hans Aarsleff]

Böhmer, Justus Henning b. Hannover, 1674; d. Halle, 1749. Jurist, representative of the *Usus Modernus Pandectarum* and major author of works on Protestant ecclesiastical law. Educated 1693–8 at the universities of Jena, Rinteln, and Halle. Professor of jurisprudence at Halle from 1701. Appointed chancellor of the duchy of Magdeburg by the Prussian king 1743. Became *Ordinarius* of the faculty of law in Halle in the same year. In his works on Protestant church law Böhmer used Canon Law and historical argument to lay the foundations of Protestant church law. Important examples of his approach are the *Jus parochiale* (1701) or his main work, the *Jus ecclesiasticum protestantium, Usus modernus, juris canonici juxta . . . decretalium ostendens* (5 vols., 1717–37), of which the *Institutiones juris canonici* (1738) is a condensed version. He also wrote works on ecclesiastical history and the *Corpus iuris canonici*, as well as an *Introductio in ius publicum universale* (1710).

Secondary Sources: R. Stintzing/ E. Landsberg, *Geschichte der deutschen Rechtswissenschaft*, Abt. III.1, (Leipzig, 1898): 145–50. H. Rüping, *Die Naturrechtslehre des Christian Thomasius und ihre Fortbildung in der Thomasius-Schule*, (Bonn, 1968): 115–17. H. Schnizer, 'J. H. Boehmer und seine Lehre von der media via zur Interpretation der kanonischen Quellen des gemeinen Rechts', *Zeitschrift der Savigny-Stiftung für Rechtsgeschichte (Kanonistische Abteilung)* 93 (1976): 383–93. C. Link, *Herrschaftsordnung und bürgerliche Freiheit* (Vienna/ Cologne/ Graz, 1979): 42–4, 50 ff. and *passim*. W. Rütten, *Das zivilrechtliche Werk J. H. Böhmers. Ein Beitrag zur Methode des usus modernus pandectarum* (Tübingen, 1982). [Thomas Ahnert]

Bonnet, Charles b. Geneva, 1720; d. Geneva, 1793. Naturalist and founding father of modern biology. Deaf from childhood and almost blind from youth, Bonnet nevertheless became one of the great experimenters, as well as theoreticians. He discovered parthenogenesis, which for him supported preformationism; he formulated clearly the idea of the chain of being; applied the experimental method of the naturalist to the human mind; and subscribed to perfectibilism. Much of his work was contributions to the Académie des Sciences to which he was elected in 1741. Major works include *Traité d'insectologie* (1745); *Essai de psychologie* (1754); *Essai analytique sur les facultés de l'âme* (1760); *Considérations sur les corps organisés* (1761); *Contemplation de la nature* (1764); *La palingénésie philosophique* (1769); *Recherches philosophiques sur les preuves du christianisme* (1770); *Oeuvres d'histoire naturelle et de philosophie*, 8 vols. (1779–81). *The Correspondence Between Albrecht von Haller and Charles Bonnet*, ed. O. Sontag (Bern, Stuttgart, 1983). *Science Against the Unbelievers: The Correspondence of Charles Bonnet and Needham 1768–1788*, eds. R. Mazzolini and S. A. Toe (Oxford, 1986).

Secondary Sources: J. Trembley, *Mémoire pour servir à l'histoire de la vie et des ouvrages de M. Ch. Bonnet* (Bern, 1794). R. Savioz, *La philosophie de Charles Bonnet de Genève* (Paris, 1948). L. Anderson, 'Charles Bonnet's Taxonomy and Chain of Being', in *Journal of the History of Ideas* 37 (1976): 45–58. J. Marx, *Charles Bonnet contre les Lumières* (Oxford, 1976). L. Anderson, *Charles Bonnet and the Order of the Known* (Dordrecht, 1982). J. O'Neal, *The Authority of Experience: Sensationist Theory in the French Enlightenment* (University Park, PA, 1996). [Knud Haakonssen]

Boscovich, Roger Joseph b. Dubrovnik, 1711; d. Milan, 1787. Serbian-Italian Jesuit and scientific polymath, professor of mathematics and astronomer in Italy, later Director of Optics for the French Navy. His principal philosophical work, *Theoria philosophiae naturalis* (Vienna, 1758, trans. as *A Theory of Natural Philosophy*, Cambridge, MA, 1966), presented an atomic theory of matter in which the atoms were point particles surrounded by force fields that were alternately attractive and repulsive, depending on the distance from the atom. The theory is a classic case of philosophical speculation providing ideas useful for science, since nineteenth-century field and atomic theories followed the general lines of Boscovich's theory.

Secondary Sources: Z. Markovic, 'Boškovic', *Dictionary of Scientific Biography*, 16 vols. (New York, NY, 1970–8) 2: 326–32. *Roger Joseph Boscovich S. J., F. R. S., 1711–1787*, ed. L. L. Whyte (London, 1961), which includes a list of Boscovich's writings. J. Agassi, *Faraday as a Natural Philosopher* (Chicago, 1971), ch. 4. *The Philosophy of Science of Ruder Boškovic*, ed. I. Macan (Zagreb, 1987). Other recent work listed in *Isis Cumulative Bibliography* 1986–95. [James Franklin]

Bourguet, Louis b. Nîmes, France, 1678; d. Neuchâtel, Switzerland, 1742. Polymath with writings in archeology, geology, philosophy, Biblical scholarship, and mathematics. A correspondent of Leibniz. Entered College of Zurich in 1688. Professor of Philosophy and Mathematics at Neuchâtel in 1731. Sought to integrate aspects of Leibnizian philosophy with issues in natural science. Main philosophical work *Lettres philosophiques sur la formation des sels et des crystaux* (Amsterdam, 1729). No edition of collected works.

Secondary Sources: F. Ellenberger, 'Louis Bourguet', *Dictionary of Scientific Biography: Supplement*, vol. 15 (1978): 52–9. O. Rieppel, '"Organization" in the *Lettres philosophiques* of Louis Bourguet compared to the writings of Charles Bonnet', *Gesnerus* 44 (1987): 125–32. [Phillip R. Sloan]

Breitinger, Johann Jakob b. Zürich, Switzerland, 1701; d. Zürich, 1776. Theologian, art critic. 1731 professor of Hebrew, 1745 professor of Greek at the *Collegium Carolinum* in Zürich. As friend and collaborator of J. J. Bodmer he participated in a controversy about poetry with J. G. Gottsched. His main contributions to esthetics are *Critische Abhandlung von der Natur, den Absichten und dem Gebrauche der Gleichnisse*, ed. J. J. Bodmer (1740), and *Critische Dichtkunst* (1740). He co-edited several works with J. J. Bodmer.

Secondary Sources: W. Bender, *Johann Jakob Bodmer und Johann Jakob Breitinger* (Stuttgart, 1973). A. Wetterer, *Publikumsbezug und Wahrheitsanspruch: der Widerspruch zwischen rhetorischem Ansatz und philosophischem Anspruch bei Gottsched und den Schweizern* (Tübingen, 1981). [Simone Zurbuchen]

Brucker, Johann Jakob b. Augsburg, 1696; d. Augsburg, 1770. Lutheran theologian, historian of philosophy. Studied theology (1715–20) in Jena under Johann Franz Budde (Buddeus), whose brother C. F. Budde encouraged Brucker to write a history of philosophy, which he did while headmaster of the *Lateinschule* and pastor in Kaufbeuren. In the *Historia Critica Philosophiae*, published in five volumes between 1742 and 1744, B. rejected neo-Platonism and Scholasticism and praised Socrates, Aristotle, Melanchthon, and Budde. The best philosophical school was Eclecticism, selecting the best opinions from the different philosophical schools thus reflecting independent, critical thought. He also described Christian religion as the best philosophy for communicating the thoughts of the wisest men, directing the reader towards critical thought and correcting the will, thus serving the kingdom of God. Elected to the Prussian Academy of Sciences (1731), to the *Deutsche Gesellschaft* in Leipzig (1736), doctor in theology (1741), pastor in Augsburg 1744 until his death.

Secondary Sources: K. Alt, *Jakob Brucker; ein Schulmeister des 18. Jahrhunderts*, (Kaufbeueren, 1926). M. Longo, 'Storia 'Critica' della Filosofia e primo illuminismo: Jakob Brucker', in *Storia delle Storie generali della Filosofia*, ed. G. Santinello. vol. 2: *Dall'età cartesiana a Brucker*, (Brescia, 1979): 527–634. M. Albrecht, *Eklektizismus: Eine Begriffsgeschichte mit Hinweisen auf die Philosophie- und Wissenschaftsgeschichte* (Stuttgart-Bad Cannstatt, 1994): 545–50. *Jacob Brucker (1696–1770): Philosoph und Historiker der europäischen Aufklärung*, eds. W. Schmidt-Biggemann and T. Stammen (Berlin, 1998). [Thomas Ahnert]

Budde, Johann Franz; also Buddeus, b. Anclam (Pommern), 1767; d. Gotha, 1729. Studied in Wittenberg (MA 1768) and became adjunct of the faculty of philosophy. Later he taught at Jena, Koburg, and Halle. Embroiled in the dispute between Pietists and Wolffians at Halle through *Bedenken über die Wolffianische Philosophie* (1724), which provoked Wolff to respond. Budde was not really a Pietist; he tried to mediate between Orthodox Lutheranism and Pietism just as much as between philosophy and theology. His most important works: *Elementa philosophiae practicae* (1697); *Elementa philosophiae instrumentalis e. theoreticae*, 2 vols. (1703); *Institutiones theologiae moralis* (1711) (German translation, 1719); *Historia ecclesiastica Veteris Testamanti ab orbe condito usque ad Christum natum*, 2 parts (1715 and 1718); *Theses theologicae de atheismo et superstitione*, 1716 (German 1717, French 1740); *Institutiones theologicae dogmaticae*, 1723; *Historische und theologische Einleitung in die vornehmsten Religionsstreitigkeiten* (1724 and 1728).

Secondary Sources: W. Kümmel, *Die unio cum Deo als ethisches Zentralprinzip im Luthertum, insbes: bei Baier und Budde* (Dissertation, Greifswald, 1917). A. F. Stolzenburg, *Die Theologie des Johann Franciscus Budde und des Christoph Matthäus Pfaff* (1926; repr. Aalen, 1979), F. Nüssel, *Bund und Versöhnung: Zur Begründung der Dogmatik bei Johann Franz Buddeus* (Göttingen, 1996). [Manfred Kühn]

Buffon, George Louis LeClerc, Comte de b. 1707 Montbard (Côte d'Or), France; d. Paris, 1788. Leading French *philosophe*, natural philosopher, scientific administrator, early anthropologist. Educated at Jesuit Collège de Godrans in Dijon (law), Université de Angers (1726–8, medicine, mathematics). Travels in Italy and southern France from 1728–30 first interested him in issues of geology. Admitted to the Académie des Sciences (1734) for his work on probability theory. As *Intendant* of the King's Garden in Paris, 1739 until his death, he was one of the primary scientific administrators of French Enlightenment science. Early publications: translations of Stephen Hales' *Vegetable Staticks* (1735), Newton's *Fluxions* (1740). His monumental *Histoire naturelle, générale et particulière avec la description du cabinet du roi* (1749–67 in 14 vols.; *Histoire naturelle des oiseaux*, 1770–83 in 9 vols.; *Suppléments*, 1774–89, 7 vols.) included reflections on the historical changes in lineages of organisms, the naturalistic creation of the earth and solar system; and an alternative solution to the embryological formation of organisms in opposition to the reigning preformationist theory. Also offered reflections on significant philosophical issues of his day, including epistemology, probability theory, and the role of mathematics in natural philosophy. His historical form of natural history contrasted with that of his contemporary, Linnaeus. *Epoques de la nature* (*Supplément*, vol 5, 1788) was a grand synthesis of historical cosmology with the natural history of earth and living forms, a model for similar reflections on the history of nature by Johann Herder, Johann Blumenbach, Jean Baptiste Lamarck, and Georges Cuvier. Standard edition: *Imprimerie royale* edition (1749–88) with the Daubenton anatomical articles. Most complete recent edition with correspondence: *Oeuvres complètes de Buffon*, ed. J.-L. Lannessan, 14 vols. (Paris, 1884–5). Most accessible collection of writings: *Buffon: Oeuvres philosophiques*, ed. J. Piveteau (Paris, 1954). Translation of several early writings: *From Natural History to the History of Nature*, eds J. Lyon and P. R. Sloan (Notre Dame, IN, 1981).

Secondary Sources: *Buffon 88*, eds. J. Gayon et al. (Paris, 1992). J. Roger, *Buffon: A Life in Natural History*, trans. S. Bonnefoi (Ithaca, NY, 1997). J. Roger, *The Life Sciences in Eighteenth Century French Thought*, trans. R. Ellrich (Stanford, CA, 1997). E. Spary, *Utopia's Garden: French Natural History from Old Regime to Revolution* (Chicago, IL, 2000). [Phillip R. Sloan]

Burke, Edmund b. Dublin, 1729; d. Beaconsfield, 1797. Anglo-Irish statesman and political theorist. Educated at Trinity College Dublin (BA 1748), Burke read law at the Middle Temple from 1750 but seems not to have practised law. After an early career as a man of letters, among other things editing the *Annual Register*, Burke became a life-long Whig politician, Member of Parliament, holding minor government offices. One of the most powerful political orators England has known, his onslaught on the French Revolution secured him a lasting reputation as one of history's main conservative thinkers. *A Vindication of Natural Society* (1756), a satire on Bolingbroke, attracted little attention, but *Philosophical Enquiry into the Origin of our Ideas of the Sublime and Beautiful* (1757) established Burke's name and set out one of the few themes which more or less consistently bind together an *oeuvre* dominated by the requirements of politics. In a variety of contexts, Burke argued for the limitations on reason in the guidance of life, and the basis for this was his adherence to a sensationist epistemology and sentimentalist view of morals, politics, and aesthetics. The early work set out in particular the last topic and is notable for its elaboration of contemporary hedonistic ideas and for its understanding of the sublime in terms of fear and horror. Emphasis on the limitations of reason was minted into distrust of government and hence into appreciation of free socio-economic agency (especially *Thoughts and Details on Scarcity*, 1795, publ. 1800). On the same basis, Burke provided a traditionalist defence of Whig constitutional principles in criticism of executive encroachments (*Thoughts on the Causes of the Present Discontents*, 1770); and in continuation hereof, he defended the American revolution against what he saw as such transgression (*Letter to the Sheriffs of Bristol*, 1777). The most significant manifestation of Burke's strictures on rationalism was his vehement rejection of revolutionary changes of government and society on 'speculative', a priori principles, such as those of the French revolutionaries and their British followers, especially Richard Price, whose *Discourse on the Love of our Country* (1789) provoked Burke to write *Reflections on the Revolution in France* (1790), which again led to further polemics of importance: *An Appeal from the New to the Old Whigs* (1791); *A Letter to a Member of the National Assembly* (1791); *Letters on a Regicide Peace* (1792–5). *The Works of the Right Honourable Edmund Burke*, 6 vols. (1854–6). *The Correspondence of Edmund Burke*, ed. T. W. Copeland, 10 vols. (Cambridge, 1958–78). *Writings and Speeches of Edmund Burke*, ed. P. Langford et al. (in progress, Oxford, 1981–).

Secondary Sources: W. B. Todd, *A Bibliography of Edmund Burke* (Godalming, 1982). C. I. Gandy and P. J. Stanlis, *Edmund Burke: A Bibliography of Secondary Studies to 1982* (New York, 1983). L. W. Cowie, *Edmund Burke 1729–1797: A Bibliography* (Westport, CT, 1994). C. B. Cone, *Edmund Burke and the Nature of Politics*, 2 vols. (Lexington, KY, 1957). F. P. Lock, *Edmund Burke*, vol. 1 (Oxford, 1998). A. Cobban, *Edmund Burke and the Revolt against the Eighteenth Century* (New York, NY, 1929). C. Parkin, *The Moral Basis of Burke's Political Thought* (Cambridge, 1956). P. J. Stanlis, *Edmund Burke and the Natural Law* (Ann Arbor, MI, 1958). R. R. Fennessy, *Burke, Paine, and the Rights of Man: A Difference of Political Opinion* (The Hague, 1963). B. T. Williams, *The Problem of Burke's Political Philosophy* (Oxford, 1967). F. O'Gorman, *Edmund Burke: His Political Philosophy* (London, 1973). J. R. Dinwiddy, 'Utility and Natural Law in Burke's Thought: A Reconsideration', *Studies in Burke and His Time* 16 (1974–5): 105–28. I. Kramnick, *The Rage of Edmund Burke* (New York, NY, 1979). M. Freeman, *Edmund Burke and the Critique of Political Radicalism* (Oxford, 1980). C. B. Macpherson, *Burke* (Oxford, 1981). J. G. A. Pocock, Introduction, in Burke, *Reflections on the Revolution in France*, ed. Pocock (Indianapolis, IN, 1987). S. K. White, *Edmund Burke: Modernity, Politics, and Aesthetics* (Thousand Oaks, CA, 1994). J. C. D. Clark, Introduction, in Burke, *Reflections on the Revolution in France*, ed. Clark (Stanford, CA, 2001). [Knud Haakonssen]

Burlamaqui, Jean-Jacques b. Geneva, 1694; d. Geneva, 1748. Natural lawyer. Studied law and philosophy at the Academy of Geneva and was admitted advocate in 1716. Was elected 1730 to the General Council, 1740 to the more important Small Council of the city. He was professor of civil and natural law at the Academy 1723–40 when he retired due to ill health, having become famous as an excellent teacher. He published the first part of a great treatise, the *Principes du droit naturel* in 1747. A friend used his lecture notes to complete the unfinished treatise about civil law, the *Principes du droit politique* (1751). The two treatises soon appeared together under the title *Principes* or *Elémens du droit naturel et politique*. A new and enlarged edition of this work was published in 1764: *Principes du droit naturel et politique*, 3 vols. Translations into English by Thomas Nugent: *The Principles of Natural Law in which the True Systems of Morality and Civil Government Are Established* (1748); *The Principles of Politic Law* (1752); *The Principles of Natural and Politic Law* (1763).

Secondary Sources: L. Baulacre, 'Eloge historique de Mr. Burlamaqui', published as an appendix to the 1764 edn. of the *Principes du droit naturel*. B. Gagnebin, *Burlamaqui et le droit naturel* (Geneva, [1944]). A. Dufour, *Le mariage dans l'école romande du droit naturel au XVIIIe siècle* (Geneva, 1976). S. Zurbuchen, *Naturrecht und natürliche Religion* (Würzburg, 1991) ch. 5. K. Haakonssen, *Natural Law and Moral Philosophy: From Grotius to the Scottish Enlightenment* (Cambridge, 1996): 336–40. H. Rosenblatt, *Rousseau and Geneva: From the First Discourse to the Social Contract, 1749–62* (Cambridge, 1997): 88–158. [Simone Zurbuchen]

Burnett, James, Lord Monboddo b. Monboddo, Scotland, 1714; d. Edinburgh, 1799. Philosopher and judge. Educated at Aberdeen, Edinburgh, and Groningen. Passed the civil law examination at Edinburgh (admitted to Faculty of Advocates 1737) and practised thirty years until becoming an ordinary lord of session, and thus Lord Monboddo (1767). Edinburgh social fixture and member of the Select Society. Attempted to revive ancient philosophy against Hume and others. Authored a vast, idiosyncratic Platonist system emphasizing nature as rationally ordered, and criticizing materialism. A founding figure in historical linguistics, argued that language was artificial arising after communication through gesture, and co-evolving with society. As part of this theory developed an extensive anthropology, in which he claimed that orangutans were a species of man. His main works are *Of the Origin and Progress of Language*, 6 vols. (1773–92) and *Antient Metaphysics*, 6 vols. (1779–99).

Secondary Sources: W. Knight, *Lord Monboddo and Some of His Contemporaries* (London, 1900). O. Sherwin. 'A Man with a Tail – Lord Monboddo,' *Journal of the History of Medicine* 23 (1958), 435–67. E. L. Cloyd, *James Burnett: Lord Monboddo* (Oxford, 1972). A. Verri, *Lord Monboddo: Dalla Metafisica all'antropologia* (Ravenna, 1975). R. Wokler, 'Apes and Races in the Scottish Enlightenment: Monboddo and Kames on the Nature of Man', in *Philosophy and Science in the Scottish Enlightenment*, ed. P. Jones (Edinburgh, 1988). Lieve Jooken, *Lord Monboddo and Adam Smith on the Origin and Development of Language* (Louvain-La-Neuve, 1994). Same, *The Linguistic Conceptions of Lord Monboddo (1714–1799): A study of Theories on the Origin, Evolution and Nature of Languages in the Scottish Enlightenment* (Leuven, 1996). Catherine Hobbs, *Rhetoric on the Margins of Modernity: Vico, Condillac, Monboddo* (Carbondale, IL, 2002). [Aaron Garrett]

Butler, Joseph b. Wantage, 1692; d. Bath, 1752. Anglican divine and philosopher. Born into a dissenting family. Educated at Tewkesbury and then Oxford after subscribing to the established church. While still at Tewkesbury sent two objections to Samuel Clarke's *Boyle Lectures* which Clarke responded to, initiating a long correspondence. Took Oxford degree in 1718 and in 1719 began to preach at Rolls Chapel, where he delivered sermons, some of which were published as *Fifteen Sermons* (1726). In 1733 became chaplain to the Lord Chancellor, Charles Talbot, and took his Doctor of Law Degree. In 1736 appointed Clerk of the Closet of Queen Caroline and published the *Analogy of Religion . . . To Which are Added two Brief Dissertations: I. Of Personal Identity II. Of the Nature of Virtue* – a dominant work of British theology throughout the eighteenth and nineteenth centuries. After Caroline's death appointed Bishop of Bristol (1738). While in Bristol published some of his sermons as *Six Sermons Preached on Publick Occasions* (1749). George II designated him Clerk of Closet and offered him the position of Archbishop of Canterbury, which he declined. Appointed Bishop of Durham in 1750. Today best known for his arguments against hedonism and his criticism of Locke's theory of personal identity.

Secondary Sources: C. D. Broad, *Five Types of Ethical Theory* (London, 1930). A Duncan-Jones, *Butler's Moral Philosophy* (Harmondsworth, 1952). N. J. Sturgeon, 'Nature and Conscience in Butler's Ethics', *Philosophical Review* (1976) (85): 316–56. A. O. Rorty, 'Butler on Benevolence and Conscience', *Philosophy* 53 (1978): 171 –184. T. Penelhum, *Butler* (London, 1985). E. C. Mossner, *Bishop Butler and the Age of Reason* (Bristol, 1990). *Joseph Butler's Moral and Religious Thought*, ed. C. Cunliffe (Oxford, 1992). [Aaron Garrett]

Campbell, Archibald b. Edinburgh, 1691; d. St. Andrews, 1756. Moral philosopher and divine. Educated at Edinburgh and Glasgow, professor of church history at St. Andrews (1730). His first book, setting out a theory of morals based on self-love but critical of Mandeville, as well as of Hutcheson, was fraudulently published by Alexander Innes as his own, *Aretē-logia, or An Inquiry into the Original of Moral Virtue* (1728). Campbell re-published the work without Innes' notes, *An Inquiry into the Original of Moral Virtue . . .* (1733). His theological works, in part directed against Tindal, include *The Miracles of Jesus Vindicated* (1729); *A Discourse Proving that the Apostles were no Enthusiasts* (1730); *The Necessity of Revelation* (1739). He was charged with Pelagianism and warned by the General Assembly of the Church of Scotland (1735).

Secondary Sources: J. Hunter, *An Examination of Mr. Campbell's Principles . . .* (Edinburgh, 1731). A. Moncrieff, *An Enquiry into the Principle, Rule, and End of Moral Actions . . .* (Edinburgh, 1735). L.Turco, 'Sympathy and moral sense: 1725–40', *British Journal for the History of Philosophy* 7 (1999): 79–101. [Knud Haakonssen]

Campbell, George b. Aberdeen, 1719; d. Aberdeen, 1796. Common sense philosopher and divine. Educated in arts at Marischal College and in divinity at Marischal and at King's College, Aberdeen. Minister in the Church of Scotland; Principal of Marischal (1759) and professor of divinity ib. (1771). Active in the Aberdeen Philosophical Society (with Reid, Gregory, Beattie, Gerard, Dunbar, et al.). Developed common-sense arguments about the reliability of sensory evidence, of testimony, etc., to combat Hume on miracles, *A Dissertation on Miracles* (1762), and about the mental faculties as basis for a Baconian theory of inquiry after and presentation of knowledge, *The Philosophy of Rhetoric*, 2 vols. (1776). Also translated the Gospels; *Lectures on Ecclesiastical History and ... on Systematic Theology* were published posthumously, 2 vols. (1800).

Secondary Sources: G. S. Keith, 'Some Account of the Life and Writings of Dr. George Campbell', in Campbell, *Lectures on Ecclesiastical History*, Vol. 1. W. S. Howell, *Eighteenth-Century British Logic and Rhetoric* (Princeton, NJ, 1971): 577–612. H. L. Ulman, 'Thought and language in George Campbell's *Philosophy of Rhetoric*', in *Aberdeen and the Enlightenment*, eds. J. J. Carter and J. H. Pittock (Aberdeen, 1987): 270–6. T. P. Miller, *The Formation of College English: Rhetoric and Belles Lettres in the British Cultural Provinces* (Pittsburgh, PA, 1997): ch. 7. J. M. Suderman, *Orthodoxy and Enlightenment: George Campbell in the Eighteenth Century* (Montreal, Que., and Kingston, Ont., 2001) [Knud Haakonssen]

Campe, Joachim Heinrich b. Deensen in Braunschweig-Wolfenbüttel, 1746; d. Braunschweig, 1818. Educationist. Educated at Helmstedt and Halle. Tutor to the von Humboldt family, including briefly Wilhelm and Alexander. In 1776 he joined Basedow's Dessau Philanthropin but because of disagreements left abruptly after less than a year. He opened his own institute in Hamburg in 1777 but retired from it in 1782 to devote himself to writing, editing, and entrepreneurial activity in the sphere of education. He advised on reform of the Braunschweig school system, but the proposals were defeated by conservative opposition. He founded and owned the Braunschweigische Schulbuchhandlung and helped make the state a center for liberal educational publishing. Campe travelled with Wilhelm von Humboldt to Paris in the first months of the French Revolution. His open sympathy for revolutionary ideas resulted in his being granted honorary French citizenship in 1792.

Campe's fame rested largely on his many widely translated writings for children, notably *Robinson der Jüngere* (1779); *Theophron oder Der erfahrne Rathgeber für die unerfahrne Jugend* (1778); *Ein Gegenstück zum Theophron der erwachsenern weiblichen Jugend gewidmet* (1789); *Die Entdeckung von Amerika* (1781–2); *Väterlicher Rath für meine Tochter* (1789). In education, apart from his voluminous reviewing and entrepreneurship, his major achievement was editing the *Allgemeine Revision des gesammten Schul-und Erziehungswesen von einer Gesellschaft praktischer Erzieher*, 16 vols. (1785–92), which collected together books, articles, translations, and commentaries representative of the educational reform movement.

Secondary Sources: L. Fertig, *Campes politische Erziehung: Eine Einführung in die Pädagogik der Aufklärung* (Darmstadt, 1977). C. Kersting, *Die Genese der Pädagogik im 18. Jahrhundert. Campes 'Allgemeine Revision' im Kontext der neuzeitlischen Wissenschaft* (Weinheim, 1992); *Visionäre Lebensklugheit – Joachim Heinrich Campe in seiner Zeit (1746–1818)*, ed. H. Schmidt (Wiesbaden, 1996). [Geraint Parry]

Carmichael, Gershom b. London, 1672; d. Glasgow, 1729. Moral philosopher. Educated at Edinburgh, regent at St. Andrews (1693) then at Glasgow (1694, changed to professor of moral philosophy 1727). Published a logic text combining Arnauld and Nicole with Locke, *Breviuscula introductio ad logicam* (1720); an important edition of Pufendorf's *De officio hominis et civis* with extensive notes and appendices, using Grotius and Locke for a theory of rights (1718, important rev. ed. 1724); and a work on reformed scholastic theology, *Synopsis theologiae naturalis* (1729). *Natural Rights on the Threshold of the Scottish Enlightenment: The Writings of Gershom Carmichael.* Trans. M. Silverthorne, eds. J. Moore and M. Silverthorne (Indianapolis, IN, 2002).

Secondary Sources: J. McCosh, *The Scottish Philosophy; Biographical, Expository, Critical, from Hutcheson to Hamilton* (London, 1875), 36–42. J. Veitch, 'Philosophy in the Scottish Universities', *Mind* 2 (1877): 74–91, 207–34. J. Moore and M. Silverthorne, 'Gershom Carmichael and the Natural Jurisprudence Tradition in Eighteenth-Century Scotland', in *Wealth and Virtue: The Shaping of Political Economy in the Scottish Enlightenment*, eds. I. Hont and M. Ignatieff (Cambridge, 1983), 73–87. Same, 'Natural Sociability and Natural Rights in the Moral Philosophy of Gershom Carmichael', in *Philosophers of the Scottish Enlightenment*, ed. V. Hope (Edinburgh, 1984), 1–12. Same, 'Protestant Theologies, Limited Sovereignties: Natural Law and Conditions of Union in the German Empire, the Netherlands and Great Britain', in *A Union for Empire: Political Thought and the British Union of 1707*, ed. J. Robertson (Cambridge, 1995), 171–97. [Knud Haakonssen]

Clarke, Samuel b. Norwich, 1675; d. London, 1729. Latitudinarian divine, rationalist moral philosopher, Newtonian metaphysician. Educated at Caius College, Cambridge (BA 1695, MA 1698), where he already in 1697 published a popular Latin translation of Rohault's Cartesian physics-textbook with a plethora of Newtonian annotations. Held a succession of preferments, including chaplain to Queen Anne, but never rose to the top in the Church because of suspicions of his orthodoxy, especially the appearance of Arianism. He was, however, considered a leading philosopher, close to Newton and the latter's successor, William Whiston, and was in correspondence with most of the well-known philosophers of his time. His two Boyle Lectures (1704, 1705) were published as the immensely influential, *A Demonstration of the Being and Attributes of God; more particularly in Answer to Mr. Hobbes, Spinoza, and their Followers* (1705) and *A Discourse concerning the Unchangeable Obligations of Natural Religion, and the Truth and Certainty of the Christian Revelation* (1706). Newton asked him to translate the *Opticks* into Latin (1706). His controversies with Anthony Collins and others over the nature of the soul and freedom resulted in, *A Letter to Mr. Dodwell; wherein all the Arguments of his Epistolary Discourse against the Immortality of the Soul are particularly answered* (1706, followed by 'second', 'third', and 'fourth' defences, 1707 and 1708), further, *Remarks on a Book* [by Collins] *entituled A Philosophical Enquiry concerning Human Liberty* (1717), and *Letters to Dr. Clarke concerning Liberty and Necessity . . . with the Doctor's Answers . . .* (1717). A theological exchange with Bishop Butler was appended to the 4th edn. of the *Demonstrations* (1716). In 1712 *The Scripture Doctrine of the Trinity* led to controversy over C.'s alleged Arianism, including an investigation by Parliament. C.'s promise not to publish more on the topic was honoured in the breach. C. was a member of Queen Caroline's circle of intellectuals; at the instigation of the Queen, C. undertook a significant exchange with Leibniz over the nature of space and time, published with a critique of Collins on determinism, *A Collection of Papers, which passed between . . . Mr. Leibnitz, and Dr. Clarke, in the years 1715 and 1716, relating to the Principles of Natural Philosophy and Religion* (1717). Sermons and theological works are included in *The Works of Samuel Clarke*, ed. B. Hoadly, 4 vols. (1738).

Secondary Sources: W. Whiston, *Historical Memoirs of the Life of Dr. Samuel Clarke* (London, 1730). B. Hoadly, 'Account of the Life, Writings and Character of the Author' prefaced *The Works*, vol. 1 (1738). J. E. Le Rossignol, *The Ethical Philosophy of Samuel Clarke* (Leipzig, 1892). J. P. Ferguson, *The Philosophy of Dr. Samuel Clarke and Its Critics* (New York NY, 1974). W. R. Rowe, *The Cosmological Argument* (Princeton, NJ, 1975). J. P. Ferguson, *An Eighteenth-Century Heretic: Dr. Samuel Clarke* (Kineton, 1976). M. C. Jacob, *The Newtonians and the English Revolution 1689–1720* (Ithaca, NY, 1976). R. Attfield, 'Clarke, Collins and Compounds', *Journal of the History of Philosophy* 15 (1977): 45–54. L. Stewart, 'Samuel Clarke, Newtonianism and the Factions of Post-Revolutionary England', *Journal of the History of Ideas* 42 (1981): 53–71. S. Shapin, 'Of Gods and Kings: Natural Philosophy and Politics in the Leibniz-Clarke Disputes', *Isis* 72 (1981): 187–215. H. Ducharme, 'Personal Identity in Samuel Clarke', *Journal of the History of Philosophy* 24 (1986): 359–83. W. L. Rowe, 'Causality and Free Will in the Controversy between Collins and Clarke', *Journal of the History of Philosophy* 25 (1987): 51–67. E. Vailati, 'Clarke's Extended Soul', *Journal of the History of Philosophy* 28 (1990): 213–28. E. Khamara, 'Hume "versus" Clarke on the Cosmological Argument', *Philosophical Quarterly* 42.166 (1992): 34–55. E. Vailati, *Leibniz and Clarke: A Study of Their Correspondence* (New York NY, 1997). [Knud Haakonssen]

Collins, Anthony b. Isleworth, 1676; d. Essex, 1729. Freethinker and close friend and correspondent of Locke and Des Maizeaux. Born into wealthy landed family. Studied at Eton, Cambridge and Middle Temple (although not called to bar). In 1707 initiated famous controversy with Samuel Clarke on the immateriality and immortality of the soul in *A Letter to the Learned Mr. Henry Dodwell.* In same year published first of a number of works defending authority of reason in questions of religion, *An Essay concerning the Use of Reason, in Propositions whereof the Evidence is Human Testimony.* His position on unaided use of reason was further strengthened in the controversial *A Discourse of Free-Thinking* (1713), occasioning attacks from Bentley and Swift. Became treasurer for Essex in 1718. Works include *A Philosophical Inquiry concerning Human Liberty* (1717), *A Discourse of the Grounds and Reasons of the Christian Religion* (1724), and *A Dissertation on Liberty and Necessity* (1729).

Secondary Sources: J. O'Higgins, *Anthony Collins: The Man and His Works* (The Hague, 1970). D. Berman. 'Anthony Collins: Aspects of his Thoughts and Writings,' *Hermathena*, 119 (1975): 49–70. W. R. Rowe 'Causality and Free Will in the Controversy between Collins and Clarke', *Journal of the History of Philosophy* 25 (1987): 1–67. [Aaron Garrett]

Condillac, Etienne Bonnot de b. Grenoble, 1714; d. Lailly near Orleans, 1780. Philosopher, educator, historian, economist. The youngest child in a large family that had recently gained wealth and entered the nobility of the robe. Jean-Jacques Rousseau was tutor to the sons of the eldest brother; another brother was the moralist and historian the abbé de Mably. Attended the Jesuit college at Lyon in the early 1730s; 1733–8 studied theology and philosophy in Paris at the seminary of Saint-Sulpice and at the Sorbonne; entered the priesthood in 1741, became an abbé, but is said to have celebrated mass only once in his life. Attended the Paris salons, met Rousseau, Diderot, d'Alembert, and other *philosophes*. Published *Essai sur l'origine des connaissances humaines* anonymously 1746 with the help of Diderot. 1747 submitted essay on philosophy of Leibniz for prize set by Prussian Academy to which he was elected 1749 when he also published *Traité des systèmes* anonymously but as 'author of the Essai'. Though not a contributor, he clearly influenced the *Encyclopédie.* 1754 published *Traité des sensations* under his own name and 1755 *Traité des animaux*, with material from the prize essay of 1747. 1758–67 resided in Italy as tutor to the Prince of Parma, grandson of Louis XV. Elected to the *Académie française* 1768. 1775 publication in sixteen volumes of the *Cours d'études pour l'instruction du Prince de Parme*, containing *Grammaire, De l'Art d'écrire, De l'Art de raisonner, De l'Art de penser, Histoire ancienne, Histoire moderne*; often reprinted and translated, parts of the *Cours* became vastly influential. 1776 publication of *Le commerce et le gouvernement considérés rélativement l'un à l'autre.* 1780 publication of *La logique*, written at the request of the education authorities in Poland, influential and often reprinted. The late *La langue des calculs* remained unfinished. The first collected and still the most complete edition: *Oeuvres complètes*, 23 vols. (1798; at least 6 further editions in the following thirty years); *La Langue des calculs* published here for the first time. *Oeuvres philosophiques*, ed. G. Le Roy, 3 vols. (Paris, 1947–51). This contains substantial parts of the *Histoire ancienne*, the *Histoire moderne,*

Le Commerce et le Gouvernement, some correspondence, and, in Vol. 3, the first publication of *Dictionnaire des synonymes. Condillac. Lettres inédites à Gabriel Cramer*, ed. G. Le Roy (Paris, 1953); the first publication of the prize essay of 1747: *Condillac, Les monades*, ed., with an important introduction, L. L. Bongie, *Studies on Voltaire and the Eighteenth Century* 187 (1980); *Essai sur l'origine*, ed. C. Porset (Paris, 1973), with an essay by Jacques Derrida, 'L'archéologie du frivole;' *La Langue des calculs* (critical edn.), eds. A.-M. Chouillet and S. Auroux (Lille, 1981); *Traité des animaux* with an important introduction by F. Dagognet (Paris, 1987); *La Logique/Logic*, parallel French and English translation, introduction by W. R. Albury (New York, NY, 1980); *Essay on the Origin of Human Knowledge*, trans. and ed. H. Aarsleff (Cambridge, 2001). A new, complete edition (21 vols.) of Condillac, including the entire correspondence is in preparation.

Secondary Sources: Introduction in *Oeuvres philosophiques* (Le Roy edn.); comprehensive bibliography in same (3: 567–74). *Corpus Condillac (1714–1780)*, ed. J. Sgard et al. (Geneva, 1981) has biography, catalog of correspondence, listing of manuscripts, detailed bibliography. *Condillac et les problèmes du langage*, ed. J. Sgard (Geneva, 1982). N. Rousseau, *Connaissance et langage chez Condillac* (Geneva, 1986). G. Lanson, 'Les idées littéraires de Condillac', in Lanson, *Études d'histoire littéraire* (Paris, 1930), 210–23. G. Le Roy, *La psychologie de Condillac* (Paris, 1937). G. Madinier, 'Les Orientations psychologiques et réflexives de la pensée de Condillac', in *Madinier, Conscience et mouvement. Étude sur la philosophie française de Condillac à Bergson* (Paris, 1938), 1–38. P. Meyer, *E. B. de Condillac. Ein Wegbereiter der ökonomischen Theorie und des liberalen Gedankens* (Zürich, 1944). P. Salvucci, *Condillac filosofi della communità umana* (Milan, 1961). D. Baradeu, 'Le 'calcul' logique de Condillac', *Revue philosophique de la France et de l'étranger* 93 (1968), 337–60. J. Largeault, *Enquête sur le nominalisme* (Paris, 1971), 204–29. W. R. Albury, *The Logic of Condillac and the structure of French Chemical and Biological Theory* (Diss., Johns Hopkins, 1972). J. Dagen, *L'histoire de l'esprit humain dans la pensée française de Fontenelle à Condorcet* (Paris, 1977), 95–108. L. Guerci, *Condillac storico. Storia e politica nel Cours d'études pour l'instruction du prince de Parme* (Milan and Naples, 1978). E. McNiven Hine, *A Critical Study of Condillac's Traité des systèmes* (The Hague, 1979). H. Aarsleff, *From Locke to Saussure* (Minneapolis, MN, 1982). J. Derrida, *The Archeology of the Frivolous*, trans. J. P. Leavey, Jr. (Lincoln, NE, 1987). M. Beretta, *The Enlightenment of Matter: The Definition of Chemistry from Agricola to Lavoisier* (Nantucket, MA, and Uppsala, 1993). A. Becq, *Genèse de l'esthétique française moderne. De la raison classique à l'imagination créatrice 1680–1814* (Paris, 1994), 444–64. S. Bouquet, *Introduction à la lecture de Saussure* (Paris, 1997), 214–45. *Condillac et L'Essai sur l'origine des connaissances humaines*, ed. J.-C. Pariente and M. Pecharman; special issue of *Revue de Métaphysique et de Morale* 1 (1999). [Hans Aarsleff]

Condorcet, Jean-Antoine-Nicolas Caritat, marquis de b. Rifemont, 1743; d. Bour-la-Reine, 1794. Philosopher, mathematician, statesman. Born into the nobility, educated at Jesuit school in Reims (1754–8) and at the University of Paris (1758–60), where he studied mathematics and physics at the College of Navarre. His *Essai sur le calcul intégral* (1765) and *Mémoire sur le problème des trois corps* (1767) won him election to the Academy of Sciences in 1769 and the support of d'Alembert, who introduced him into the salon of Julie de Lespinasse, a meeting-place for contributors to the *Encyclopédie*. Wrote pamphlets in support of Turgot's reform policies (1774–6). Elected assistant secretary of the Academy of Sciences in 1773 and permanent secretary in 1776; elected to the French Academy in 1782. Advocated the use of statistical procedures to resolve political questions in *Essai sur l'application de l'analyse à la probabilité des décisions rendues à la pluralité des voix* (1785). Supported reforms strengthening provincial assemblies but opposed the convocation of *Estates General*, arguing its demands would be reactionary and anarchic. During the Revolution, served in the Legislative Assembly (1791) and Convention (1792), where he was an energetic opponent of slavery and supporter of equality for women. After the King's attempted escape, supported republican form of government. Drafted the 'Girondin Constitution'; opposed

Jacobin constitution plan of 1793 and their purge of the Convention. To avoid arrest, went into hiding, where he wrote the *Esquisse d'un Tableau des progrès de l'Esprit humain* (1795), a defense of the ideals of the Enlightenment. Captured in March 1794; found dead in his cell two days later. Standard edition: *Oeuvres*, eds. A. C. O'Connor and F. Arago, 12 vols. (Paris, 1847–9).

Secondary Sources: A. Koyré, 'Condorcet', *Journal of the History of Ideas*, 9 (1948): 131–152. R. Reichardt, *Reform und Revolution bei Condorcet: Ein Beitrag zur späten Aufklärung in Frankreich* (Bonn, 1973). K. M. Baker, *Condorcet: From Natural Philosophy to Social Mathematics* (Chicago, IL, 1975). [James Schmidt]

Cooper, Anthony Ashley – see Shaftesbury

Craig (or Craige), John b. Hoddam, Scotland, 1662–3?; d. London, 1731. Mathematician and theologian. Studied in Edinburgh under David Gregory and his mathematical skills earned him the friendship of Robert Hooke, Edmond Halley, and Isaac Newton. Craig helped develop calculus and introduced Leibnizian notation in England; see *Methodus figurarum lineis rectis et curvis comprehensarum quadraturas determinandi* (1685); *Tractatus mathematicus de figurarum curvilinearum quadraturis & locis geometricis* (1693); also *De calculo fluentium* (1718). He held ecclesiastical office in the see of Salisbury under the patronage of the latitudinarian bishop Gilbert Burnet and is mostly known for his *Theologiae Christianae Principia Mathematica* (1699), an eccentric attempt to provide a mathematical calculus of the diminishing rate of historical evidence and of the expectations of a future life.

Secondary Sources: R. Nash, *John Craige's Mathematical Principles of Christian Theology* (Carbondale, IL, 1991; containing the best available English translation of the *Principia*). [Dario Perinetti]

Crusius, Christian August b. Leuna, Saxony, Germany, 1715; d. Leipzig, 1775. Philosopher and theologian. Studied at Leipzig and became Professor of Philosophy there (1744), then of Theology (1750). Criticized the Wolffian philosophy from a pietist standpoint. Some emphasise his importance for Kant's philosophical development. His main philosophical works, published 1744–49, include: *Anweisung, Vernünftig zu Leben* (Leipzig, 1744); *Entwurf der nothwendigen Vernunft-Wahrheiten* (Leipzig, 1745); *Weg zur Gewißheit und Zuverläßigkeit der menschlichen Erkenntnis* (Leipzig, 1747); *Anleitung, über natürliche Begebenheiten ordentlich und vorsichtig nachzudenken*, 2 vols. (Leipzig, 1749). In later years he concentrated on theology. *Die Philosophischen Hauptwerke*, ed. G. Tonelli, 4 vols. (Hildesheim 1964–5).

Secondary Sources: C. Festner, *Christian August Crusius als Metaphysiker* (Halle, 1892). A. von Seitz, *Die Willensfreiheit in der Philosophie des Christian August Crusius* (Würzburg, 1899). M. Wundt, *Kant als Metaphysiker*, (Stuttgart, 1924): 60–81. H. Heimsoeth, *Metaphysik und Kritik bei Chr. Aug. Crusius* (Berlin, 1926). M. Wundt, *Die Deutsche Schulphilosophie im Zeitalter der Aufklärung* (Tübingen, 1945): 254–64. G. Tonelli, 'La Question des bornes de l'entendement humain au XVIII siècle', *Revue de métaphysique et de morale* 64 (1959): 396–427. L. W. Beck, *Early German Philosophy* (Cambridge, MA, 1969): 394–402. M. Kuehn, *Scottish Common Sense in Germany, 1768–1800: A Contribution to the History of Critical Philosophy* (Kingston and Montreal, 1987): 264–9. J. B. Schneewind, *The Invention of Autonomy* (Cambridge, 1998): 431–56). [Udo Thiel]

Cuvier, Georges b. Montbéliard, Württemberg, Germany, 1769; d. Paris, 1832. Leading natural historian of early nineteenth century. Education: Caroline University (Stuttgart 1784–8; natural history, administration). Main formulator of theory of geological catastrophism. Positions:

Muséum national d'histoire naturelle in 1795; chair of comparative anatomy (1803–32). Later Director of the *Muséum* and reorganizer of French education under Napoleon. Main works: *Recherches sur les Ossemens fossiles de quadrupèdes*, 4 vols. (Paris, 1812); *La Regne animale*, 4 vols. (Paris, 1817); *Histoire des progrès des sciences naturelles*, 4 vols. (Paris, 1828). No edition of collected works.

Secondary Sources: D. Outram, *Georges Cuvier: Vocation, Science, and Authority in Post-Revolutionary France* (Manchester, 1984). M. Rudwick, *Georges Cuvier, Fossil Bones, and Geological Catastrophes* (Chicago, IL, 1997). [Phillip R. Sloan]

DAUBENTON, LOUIS-JEAN-MARIE b. Montbard (Côte d'Or) France, 1716; d. Paris, 1800. Comparative anatomist, natural historian, mineralogist. Education: Dijon, Paris, Reims (MD 1741). Collaborated with Buffon on the first series of the *Histoire naturelle, générale et particulière* (1749–67). *Démonstrateur* of the King's natural history cabinet at the *Jardin du roi*. Admitted to the *Académie des sciences* 1744. At Revolution, instrumental in developing the new reorganizational plan that transformed the *Jardin du roi* into the *Muséum national d'histoire naturelle*. Held first chair of mineralogy.

Secondary Sources: P. L. Farber, 'Buffon and Daubenton: Divergent Traditions Within the *Histoire naturelle*', *Isis* 66 (1975): 63–74. E. Spary, *Utopia's Garden: French Natural History from Old Regime to Revolution* (Chicago, IL, 2000). [Phillip R. Sloan]

DESAGULIERS, JOHN THEOPHILUS b. La Rochelle, France, 1683; d. London, 1744. Popular experimenter and lecturer, whose lectures to the Royal Society and the London public popularised Newtonian science. His lectures, summarised in *A System of Experimental Philosophy, Prov'd by Mechanicks* (London, 1719) and *A Course of Experimental Philosophy* (London, 1734–44), covered ingenious machines, heat, optics, elasticity, and electricity. They provided a way of coming to know science that was an alternative to the rigid mathematical demonstrations of Newton. Other works include *The Newtonian System of the World the Best Model of Government* (London, 1728). His work on masonic constitutions, ritual, and symbolism helped make Freemasonry an ally of the English Enlightenment.

Secondary Sources: A. R. Hall, 'Desaguliers', *Dictionary of Scientific Biography*, 4: 43–6. D. C. Lee, *Desaguliers of no. 4 and His Services to Free-Masonry* (London, 1932). C. Poni, 'The Craftsman and the Good Engineer: Technical Practices and Theoretical Mechanics in J. T. Desaguliers', *History and Technology* 10 (1993): 215–32. [James Franklin]

DES MAIZEAUX, PIERRE b. Paillat, Puy-de-Dôme, Auvergnes, 1673; d. London, 1745. Journalist, editor, translator. The Huguenot family fled to Switzerland after the Revocation of the Edict of Nantes 1685. Intended for the ministry, he changed his mind during studies at the Academy in Geneva (1695–9). He met LeClerc and Bayle in Holland in 1699, then he went to England and developed close contacts with deist and free-thinking circles around Saint Evremond and Anthony Collins, publishing an attack on clerical power and deceit, the *Lettre d ún Gentilhomme de la Cour de Saint Germain* of 1710 (translated as *A Letter from a Gentleman at the Court of St. Germain* the same year). He was Bayle's and Saint Evremond's biographer and edited their works. In 1720 elected Fellow Member of the Royal Society of London. A record of his literary correspondence is in the MSS collections of the British Library.

Secondary Sources: J. Almagor, *Pierre Des Maizeaux (1673–1745), Journalist and English Correspondent for Franco-Dutch Periodicals, 1700–1720* (Amsterdam and Maarsen, 1980). J. H. Broome, 'Pierre Des Maizeaux, Journaliste. Les Nouvelles litteraires de Londres entre 1700 et 1740', *Revue de littérature comparée* 29 (1955):184–204. Same, 'Bayle's biographer, Pierre Des Maizeaux', *French*

Studies 9 (1955): 1–17. Same, 'Une collaboration: Anthony Collins et Desmaizeaux', *Revue de littérature comparée* 30 (1956): 161–79. D. C. Potts, 'Desmaizeaux and Saint-Evremond's text', *French Studies* 19 (1965): 239–51. [Thomas Ahnert]

Diderot, Denis b. Langres, Frances, 1713; d. Paris, 1784. Philosopher, encyclopedist, writer, critic. Educated by the Jesuits at Langres, Diderot studies theology at Paris 1732–5; in 1743 marries against his father's wishes, visits the salons, meets Rousseau and Condillac, assists in the translation of Robert James's *Medicinal Dictionary* (1743); translates Shaftesbury on virtue and merit (1745); in 1746 *Pensées philosophiques*, his first original work, is condemned to be burned; by mid-1740s begins planning, with d'Alembert, the *Encyclopédie*, completed in 1772 with the publication of the eleven volumes of plates. Writes in a great variety of genres – plays, novels, controversy, esthetics, philosophy, much of it published posthumously. His contributions to Grimm's *Correspondence littéraire, philosophique et critique* circulated only in manuscripts outside France, including his reports on the biennial exhibition of paintings in Paris, the so-called *Salons*, which inaugurate modern art criticism. In the winter of 1773–4 Diderot visits Catherine the Great at St. Petersburg at her invitation; his political counsel is not appreciated, but on his advice Catherine acquires the three large collections of paintings that create the greatness of the Hermitage museum. *Oeuvres complètes*, eds. J. Assézat and M. Tourneaux, 20 vols. (Paris, 1857–79) is now superseded by: *Oeuvres complètes*, eds. H. Dieckmann, J. Proust, J. Varloot, et al. (Paris, 1975–); *Oeuvres complètes*, ed. R. Lewinter, 15 vols. (Paris,1969–73); *Oeuvres*, ed. L. Versini, 5 vols. (Paris, 1994–7). *Corréspondance*, eds. G. Roth and J. Varloot, 16 vols. (Paris, 1955–70). *Oeuvres philosophiques*, ed. P. Vernière (Paris, 1955); *Oeuvres esthétiques*, ed. P. Vernière (Paris, 1959), *Oeuvres romanesques*, ed. P. Vernière (Paris, 1962), *Oeuvres politiques*, ed. P. Vernière (Paris, 1963), *Mémoires pour Catherine II*, ed. P. Vernière (Paris, 1966). François Hemsterhuis, *Lettre sur l'homme et ses rapports*, ed. Diderot, new ed. Georges May (New Haven, CT, 1964); Diderot, *Salons*, eds. J. Seznec and Jean A., 2nd edn., 3 vols., (Oxford, 1975–83). Diderot, *Ecrits sur la musique*, ed. B. Durand-Sendrail (Paris, 1987). In English: J. H. Mason, *The Irresistible Diderot* (London, 1982); Diderot, *Political Writings*, trans. and eds. J. H. Mason and R. Wokler (Cambridge, 1992).

Secondary Sources: Two series are dedicated to the study of Diderot: *Diderot Studies*, annually (Geneva) and *Recherches sur Diderot et sur l'Encyclopédie* (Paris, 1986–). M. Tourneux, *Diderot et Cathérine II* (Geneva, 1970 [1899]). F. Venturi, *La Jeunesse de Diderot*, trans. J. Bertrand (Paris, 1939). Y. Belaval, *L'Esthétique sans paradoxe* (Paris, 1950). H. Dieckmann, *Inventaire du fonds Vandeul et inédits de Diderot* (Geneva, 1951). J. R. Smiley, 'A list of Diderot's Articles for Grimm's *Correspondance littéraire*', *Romanic Review* 42 (1951): 189–97. L. Crocker, *Two Diderot Studies, Ethics and Esthetics* (Baltimore, MD, 1952). A. Vartanian, *Diderot and Descartes* (Princeton, 1953). R. Mortier, *Diderot et l'Allemagne (1750–1850)* (Paris, 1954). J. Seznec, *Essais sur Diderot et l'antiquité* (Oxford, 1957). H. Dieckmann, *Cinq leçons sur Diderot* (Geneva, 1959). J. Proust, *Diderot et l'Encyclopédie* (Paris, 1995 [1962]). A. M. Wilson, 'The Development and Scope of Diderot's Political Thought', *Studies on Voltaire and the Eighteenth Century*, 27 (1963), 1871–1900. R. Trousson, 'Diderot et l'antiquité grecque', *Diderot Studies* 6 (1964): 215–45. Same, 'Diderot et Homère', *Diderot Studies* 8 (1966): 185–216. Same, 'Diderot helléniste', *Diderot Studies* 12 (1969): 141–326. M.-L. Roy, *Die Poetik Diderots* (Munich, 1966). J. Roger, *Les sciences de la vie dans la pensée française du XVIIIe siècle*, 2nd edn. (Paris, 1971): 585–682. A. M. Wilson, *Diderot* (New York, NY, 1972). H. Dieckmann, *Diderot und die Aufklärung* (Stuttgart, 1972). J. Chouillet, *La formation des idées esthétiques de Diderot* (Paris, 1973). G. May, *Diderot et Baudelaire, critiques d'art* (Geneva, 1973). J. Chouillet, *Diderot*, (Paris, 1977). E. M. Bukdahl, *Diderot, critique d'art*, 2 vols. (Copenhagen, 1980–2). G. Bremner, *Order and Chance, The Pattern of Diderot's Thought* (Cambridge, 1983). J. Chouillet, *Diderot, poète de l'énergie* (Paris, 1984). D. Johnson, 'Corporality and Communication: The Gestural Revolution of Diderot, David and the "Oath of the Horatii"', *Art Bulletin* 71 (March 1989): 92–112. *Denis Diderot*, ed. J. Schlobach (Darmstadt, 1992). B. Durand-Sendrail, *La musique de Diderot, essai sur le hiéroglyphe musical* (Paris, 1994). W. E. Rex, *Diderot's Counterpoints: The Dynamics of Contrariety in His Major Works* (Oxford, 1998). [Hans Aarsleff]

Dohm, Christian Konrad Wilhelm von b. Lemgo (Lippe), 1751; d. Pustleben bei Nordhausen, 1820. Civil servant, man of letters. Studied theology (1769) and jurisprudence (1770) in Leipzig, then jurisprudence and statistics at Göttingen (1774). Founded journal *Deutsche Museum* with Boje, 1775. Professor of statistics and cameral and fiscal sciences at the Carolinum at Kassel from 1776; Prussian military councilor from 1779. Active in the *Mittwochsgesellschaft*, a secret society of 'Friends of Enlightenment', including many important figures in the Berlin Enlightenment. Contact with Moses Mendelssohn inspired his influential treatise on Jewish emancipation, *Über die bürgerliche Verbesserung der Juden* (Berlin, 1781–3). In diplomatic service 1786–1810.

Secondary Sources: W. Gronau, *Christian Wilhelm von Dohm nach seinem Wollen und Handeln: ein biographischer Versuch* (Lemgo, 1824). R. Liberles, 'Dohm's Treatise on the Jews: A Defense of the Enlightenment', *Leo Baeck Institute Year Book* 33 (1988): 29–42. [James Schmidt]

Du Bos, Jean-Baptiste b. Beauvais, 1670; d. Paris, 1742. Writer on esthetics, historian, scholar. BA Sorbonne 1691. Contributor to *Menagiana, ou, Bons mots, rencontres agréables, pensées judicieuses et observations curieuses, de M. Ménage* (Amsterdam, 1693). *Histoire des quatre Gordiens, prouvée et illustrée par les médailles* (Paris, 1695). As reward for diplomatic work around 1700 made commendatory abbot of Notre-Dame de Ressons in 1723. Publishes *Les Interêts de l'Angleterre mal-entendus dans la présente guerre* (Amsterdam, 1703); *Histoire de la ligue faite à Cambray* (Paris, 1709; translated into English and Italian). Visits London in 1698, meets, among others, Gilbert Burnet, Richard Bentley, and especially John Locke, with introduction from Locke's friend and correspondent Nicolas Thoynard. In lively correspondence and exchange of books with Locke over the next five years. Corresponding with Pierre Bayle, Du Bos is among the first to see final proofs of Pierre Coste's French translation of Locke's *Essay* and becomes an early advocate of Locke's philosophy on the Continent. Elected to the *Académie française* in 1720; permanent secretary from 1722. In 1734 publishes his chief historical work, *Histoire critique de l'établissement de la Monarchie française dans les Gaules*, 3 vols. (Amsterdam 1734). *Réflexions critiques sur la poésie et sur la peinture* published anonymously in 2 vols. 1719; augmented and rearranged in 3 vols. (1733); with author's name in 1740; 7th ed. 1770; Dutch, German, and English translations in quick succession. Part 3 of *Réflexions* 'On the theatrical performances of the ancients' was translated into German by Gotthold Ephraim Lessing (1755; Part 3 of his *Theatralische Biliothek*, 2 vols. (Berlin, 1754–8).

Secondary Sources: J. le Rond d'Alembert, 'Eloge de Jean Baptiste Du Bos' in *Oeuvres philosophiques, historiques et littéraires*, 18 vols. (Paris, 1805): 9: 395–410. M. Braunschvig, *L'Abbé Du Bos. Rénovateur de la critique au XVIIIe siècle (1670–1742)* (Toulouse, 1904). A. Lombard, *La Querelle des anciens et des modernes. Du Bos* (Neuchatel, 1908); lists Du Bos's writings. Same, *L'Abbé Du Bos, un initiateur de la pensée moderne, 1670–1742* (Paris, 1913). Same, *La Correspondance de l'Abbé Du Bos (1670–1742)* (Paris, 1913). E. Teuber, 'Die Kunstphilosophie des abbé Dubos', *Zeitschrift für Aesthetik und Kunstgeschichte* 17 (1924): 361–410. G. Bonno, 'Une amitié Franco-Anglaise du XVIIe siècle: John Locke et l'Abbé Du Bos (avec 16 lettres inédites de Du Bos à Locke)', *Revue de littérature comparée* 24 (1950): 481–520. Same, 'Les rélations épistolaires de Locke avec Du Bos', in Bonno, *Les Rélations intellectuelles de Locke avec la France* (University of California Publications in Modern Philology 38, no. 2 (1955), 37–264). E. Caramaschi, 'Du Bos et Voltaire', *Studies on Voltaire and the Eighteenth Century* 10 (1959): 113–236. E. Migliorini, 'Du Bos', *Studi sul pensiero estetico del settecento. Crousaz, Du Bos, Batteux, Diderot* (Florence, 1966), 149–232. B. Munteano, *Constantes dialectiques en littérature et en histoire* (Paris, 1967): 297–374, 139–71, 219–34. W. Folkierski, *Entre le classicisme et le romantisme. Etude sur l'esthétique et les esthéciens du XVIIIe siècle* (Paris, 1969). J.-B. Barrère, *L'idée de goût de Pascal à Valéry* (Paris, 1972), esp. 67–80. P. Jones, *Hume's Sentiments. Their Ciceronian and French Context* (Edinburgh, 1982), 93–106. A. Becq, *Genèse de l'esthétique française moderne. De la raison classique à l'imagination créatrice 1680–1814* (Paris, 1994). [Hans Aarsleff]

Du Chatelet, Gabrielle-Émilie le Tonnelier de Breteuil, Marquise de, b. Paris, 1706; d. Lunéville, 1749. Leading female *philosophe* and commentator on science. Home educated. Mistress and close friend of Voltaire (1733–49); collaborated with him on dissemination of Newtonian physics, including his *Élémens de la philosophie de Newton* (1738). Made her own anonymous synthesis of Leibnizian and Newtonian mechanics (*Institutions de Physique*, 1740) and the only French translation of Newton's *Principia* (posthumous, 1759).

Secondary Sources: J. Zinsser, 'Translating Newton's "Principia": The Marquise du Chatelet's Revisions and Additions for a French Audience', *Notes and Records of the Royal Society of London* 55 (2001): 227–45. L. Janik, 'Searching for the Metaphysics of Science', *Studies on Voltaire and the Eighteenth Century* 201 (1982): 85–113. [Phillip R. Sloan]

Duncan, William b. Aberdeen, 1717; d. Aberdeen, 1760. Educated at Marischal College, Aberdeen, and professor of natural philosophy there (appointed 1752). Author of the popular *Elements of Logick* (first in Robert Dodsley's *The Preceptor*, 2 vols., London, 1748, vol. 2), which combined Lockean theory of knowledge with syllogistic logic.

Secondary Sources: W. S. Howell, *Eighteenth-Century British Logic and Rhetoric* (Princeton, NJ, 1971): 331–61. [Knud Haakonssen]

Eberhard, Johann August b. Halberstadt, Germany, 1739; d. Halle/Saale, 1809. Theologian, popular philosopher and one of the last defenders of the Leibniz-Wolffian school of philosophy; very much influenced by Alexander Gottlieb Baumgarten and Moses Mendelssohn. Studied theology and philosophy at the University of Halle (1756–9); private tutor (1759–63), then co-rector and preacher in Halberstadt. In Berlin from 1766 and friends with Mendelssohn and Nicolai; 1768 preacher; 1778 Professor of Philosophy at Halle after Georg Friedrich Meier. Became known for his first publication, *Neue Apologie des Sokrates oder Untersuchung von der Seligkeit der Heiden* (Berlin, 1772), a criticism of basic elements of Christianity from a neological position. His main philosophical work was *Allgemeine Theorie des Denkens und Empfindens* (Berlin, 1776). Later argued that Kant's first *Kritik* was not original, its true elements being already in the work of Leibniz. Kant responded sharply in *Über eine Entdeckung, nach der alle neue Kritik der reinen Vernunft durch eine ältere entbehrlich gemacht werden soll* (Königsberg, 1790). E. edited the two main organs of anti-Kantian rationalism, *Philosophisches Magazin*, 4 vols. (Halle, 1788–92) and *Philosophisches Archiv*, 2 vols. (Berlin, 1792–5). His many publications include a translation of Bentham's *Defence of Usury* (Halle, 1788).

Secondary Sources: F. Nicolai, *Gedächtnißschrift auf Johann August Eberhard* (Berlin, Stettin, 1810). A. Richter, 'Eberhard, J. A.', *Allgemeine Deutsche Biographie* (Berlin 1877) 5: 569–71. *The Kant-Eberhard Controversy*, ed. H. Allison (Baltimore, MD, 1973). M. Gawlina, *Das Medusenhaupt der Kritik: Die Kontroverse zwischen Immanuel Kant und Johann August Eberhard* (Berlin, New York, NY, 1996). I. Kant, *Der Streit mit Johann August Eberhard*, ed. M. Lauschke (Hamburg, 1998). *Johann August Eberhard (1739–1809): Ein streitbarer Geist an den Grenzen der Aufklärung*, ed. G. Haßler (Halle, 2000). [Heiner F. Klemme]

Edwards, Jonathan b. East Windsor, CT, 1703; d. Princeton, NJ, 1758. Theologian and philosopher, educated at Yale (graduated 1720 and 1722), was a minister in New York and a tutor at Yale before he took over the parish of his grandfather in Northampton, MA, in 1727. The parishioners dismissed him for his stern teaching in 1748, and he became a missionary minister in Stockbridge, MA, until 1757 when he was appointed President of the College of New Jersey (later Princeton). Edwards was an active participant in the revivalism of the Great Awakening in the 1740s and a central figure in the formulation of eighteenth-century Puritan doctrine. He interpreted the Calvinist notion of the dependency of nature, including humanity, upon God in terms of an idealism somewhat like that of Berkeley. While upholding the unfreedom of the will against Arminianism, he thought of freedom in terms of personhood. And he fused neo-platonic and moral-sense ideas in his theological ethics. His main works are: *A Treatise Concerning Religious Affections* (1746); *Freedom of the Will* (1754); *Original Sin* (1758); *The Nature of True Virtue* (1765). Some of the most important ideas were first put forth in sermons. *Works*, ed. S. E. Dwight, 10 vols. (New York NY, 1829–30); *Works*, ed. P. Miller, in progress (New Haven, CT, 1957–).

Secondary Sources: G. M. Marsden, *Jonathan Edwards: A Life* (New Haven, CT, 2003). P. Miller, *Jonathan Edwards* (New York, NY, 1949). R. A. Delattre, *Beauty and Sensibility in the Thought of Jonathan Edwards* (New Haven, CT, 1968). N. Fiering, *Jonathan Edwards' Moral Thought and Its British Context* (Chapel Hill, NC, 1981). Sang Hyun Lee, *The Philosophical Theology of Jonathan Edwards* (Princeton, NJ, 1988). J. E. Smith, *Jonathan Edwards: Puritan, Preacher, Philosopher* (Notre Dame, IN, 1993). L. Chai, *Jonathan Edwards and the Limits of Enlightenment Philosophy* (Oxford, 1998). [Knud Haakonssen]

Eilschov, Frederik Christian b. Rynkeby, Funen, Denmark, 1725; d. Copenhagen, 1750. Magister in philosophy at the University of Copenhagen 1746. An eclectic Wolffian, he wanted a popularly accessible philosophy in the vernacular and made an influential contribution to Danish philosophical terminology – written in Latin: *Cogitationes de scientiis vernacula lingua docendis cum specimine terminologiae vernaculae* (Copenhagen, 1747). His main works, *Philosophiske Skrifter* (Copenhagen, 1747) and *Philosophiske Breve* (Copenhagen, 1748), consist of essays on a wide range of issues, including the morality of eating meat, the inclusion of animals in the moral realm, the centrality of providence to religion, Pythagoras, time, and much else. Writing in 'the manner of Fontenelle', whom he had translated, he argued for the equality of male and female intellect in *Fruentimmer Philosophie i tre Samtaler* (Copenhagen, 1749).

Secondary Sources: C. H. Koch, 'Man's Duties to Animals: A Danish Contribution to the Discussion of the Rights of Animals in the Eighteenth Century', *Danish Yearbook of Philosophy* 13 (1976), 11–28. [Knud Haakonssen]

Enfield, William b. Sudbury, Suffolk, 1741; d. Norwich, 1797. Dissenting divine. Educated at Daventry dissenting academy; tutor at Warrington Academy (1770–83) and minister to dissenting congregations in Warrington and Norwich. Translated and abridged Johann Jakob Brucker, *The History of Philosophy . . . drawn up from Brucker's 'Historia critica philosophiae'*, 2 vols. (1791) and wrote textbooks in natural philosophy and elocution as well as devotional and biographical works.

Secondary Sources: M. F. Fitzpatrick, 'Enfield, William' in *The Dictionary of Eighteenth-Century British Philosophers*, eds. J. W. Yolton, J. V. Price, and J. Stephens, 2 vols. (Bristol, 1999). K. Haakonssen, 'Introduction', in Enfield, *The History of Philosophy* (facsim. of 4th edn., Bristol, 2001). [Knud Haakonssen]

ENGEL, JOHANN JAKOB b. Parchim (Mecklenburg), 1741; d. Parchim, 1802. Educator, publicist, and theater director. Studied theology in Rostock and Bützow (with Tetens), then theology, philosophy, and languages at Leipzig, 1765. Professor of moral philosophy and fine arts at the Joachimsthal Gymnasium, Berlin, from 1776; director of the Royal Theater from 1787; tutor to Alexander and Wilhelm von Humboldt, and to Crown Prince Frederick William (III), tuition published as *Fürstenspiegel* (1798). Wrote on acting, *Ideen zu einer Mimik* (Berlin, 1785–86). Edited three-volume *Der Philosoph für die Welt* (1775–1800), a collection of stories, philosophical dialogues, allegories, character studies, and letters by Eberhard, Garve, Mendelssohn, and others, which provided a forum for philosophy beyond the confines of the university. Active in the *Mittwochsgesellschaft*, a secret society of 'Friends of Enlightenment', including many important figures in the Berlin Enlightenment. Standard edition: *J. J. Engels Schriften*, 11 vols. (Berlin, 1801–6).

Secondary Sources: C. Blatter, *Johann Jakob Engel (1741–1802): Wegbereiter der modernen Erzählkunst* (Bern, 1993). D. Bachmann-Medick, *Die ästhetische Ordnung des Handelns. Moralphilosophie und Ästhetik in der Popularphilosophie des 18. Jahrhunderts* (Stuttgart, 1989): 78–161. J. van der Zande, 'In the Image of Cicero: German Philosophy between Wolff and Kant', *Journal of the History of Ideas* 56:3 (July 1995): 419–42. [James Schmidt]

EULER, LEONHARD b. Basel, 1707; d. St. Petersburg, 1783. The most prolific mathematician ever, and the leading mathematician and mathematical physicist of the mid-eighteenth century. His most explicitly philosophical work, *Lettres à une Princesse d'Allemagne sur divers sujets de physique et de philosophie* (St Petersburg, 1768–72; trans. as *Letters of Euler on Different Subjects in Natural Philosophy*, New York, NY, 1833, repr. New York, 1975) is at once a book on popular science and a polemic against the atheist version of the Enlightenment. It discusses free-will, monads, scepticism, and other philosophical issues in a way designed to demonstrate the harmony of science and traditional Christianity. Its treatment of the problem of evil, for example, approves Leibniz's best of all possible worlds theory, but with a special emphasis on free will. The work also popularised the circle diagrams in logic later known as 'Venn diagrams'. Euler's *Opera Omnia* (Berlin-Göttingen-Leipzig-Heidelberg, 1911–) is largely complete.

Secondary Souces: A. P. Youschkevitch, 'Euler', *Dictionary of Scientific Biography*, 4: 467–84. Various introductory essays in Euler's *Opera Omnia*. C. Truesdell, *Essays in the History of Mechanics* (Berlin, 1968), ch. 2. R. Calinger, 'Euler's First St. Petersburg Years (1727–1741)', *Historia Mathematica* 23 (1996), 121–66. [James Franklin]

FEDER, JOHANN GEORG HEINRICH b. Schornweißbach, Germany, 1740; d. Hannover, 1821. Philosopher, psychologist and leading figure of German 'popular philosophy'; sometimes called the German Locke. Studied Wolffian philosophy in Erlangen (1757–60); doctorate 1765, with the thesis *Homo natura non ferus*; professor of metaphysics and Hebrew (later logic) at the Casimirianum in Coburg; professor in Göttingen (1768–97); director of the Georgianum and the Royal Library in Hannover (1797–1811). Worked on metaphysics, logic, psychology, ethics, pedagogic, and much else. He introduced Adam Smith's *Wealth of Nations* to the German audience. His critical revision of Garve's review of Kant's *Kritik der reinen Vernunft* in *Göttingische Anzeigen von gelehrten Sachen* (1782) aroused much controversy and marked the beginning of his public disregard. His textbooks were widely used at high schools and universities as late as the 1790s. Main works: *Grundriß der philosophischen Wissenschaften nebst der nöthigen Geschichte* (Coburg, 1767); *De sensu interno* (Göttingen, 1768); *Der neue Emil oder von der Erziehung nach bewährten Grundsätzen* (Erlangen, 1768); *Logik und Metaphysik nebst der philosophischen Geschichte im Grundrisse* (Göttingen, Gotha, 1769), *Lehrbuch der praktischen Philosophie* (Göttingen, Gotha,

1770); *Untersuchungen über den menschlichen Willen, dessen Naturtriebe, Veränderlichkeit, Verhältnisse zur Tugend und Glückseligkeit, und die Grundregeln, die menschlichen Gemüther zu erkennen und zu regieren*, 4 vols. (Göttingen, Lemgo, 1779–93); *Institutiones logicae et metaphysicae* (Göttingen, 1781); *Über Raum und Caussalität zur Prüfung der Kantischen Philosophie* (Göttingen, 1787); *Philosophische Bibliothek*, ed. with C. Meiners, 4 vols. (Göttingen, 1788–93).

Secondary Sources: *J. G. H. Feder's Leben, Natur und Grundsätze*, ed. C. A. L. Feder (Leipzig, Hannover, Darmstadt, 1825). L. W. Beck, *Early German Philosophy: Kant and his Predecessors* (Cambridge, MA, 1969). W. C. Zimmerli, '"Schwere Rüstung" des Dogmatikers und "anwendbare Eklektik"', *Studia Leibnitiana* 15 (1983), 58–71. K. Röttgers, 'J. G. H. Feder – Beitrag zu einer Verhinderungsgeschichte eines deutschen Empirismus', *Kant-Studien* 75 (1984), 420–41. G. Gawlick and L. Kreimendahl, *Hume in der deutschen Aufklärung* (Stuttgart-Bad Cannstatt, 1987). M. Kuehn, *Scottish Common Sense in Germany, 1768–1800* (Kingston, Montreal, 1987). R. Brandt, 'Kant und Feder', *Kant-Studien* 80 (1989), 249–64. [Heiner F. Klemme]

FÉNELON – see page 1236.

FERGUSON, ADAM b. Logierait, Perthshire, Scotland 1723; d. St. Andrews, 1816. Moral philosopher and philosophical historian of civil society. Educated at St. Andrews (MA 1742) and Edinburgh (divinity studies); chaplain to the 'Black Watch' regiment 1745–54; tutor and secretary in the household of Lord Milton, 1756–8; Librarian of the Faculty of Advocates 1758–9; professor of natural philosophy (1759–64) then of pneumatics and moral philosophy (1764–85) at Edinburgh. Ferguson was prominent in Edinburgh Enlightenment circles, a member of the Select Society, involved in the foundation of the Poker Club and the Royal Society of Edinburgh, etc. He was an energetic advocate of the moral and civic values of a voluntary militia and of the theatre: see the anonymous *Reflections Previous to the Establishment of a Militia* (1756); *The Morality of Stage-Plays* (1757); and *The History of the Proceedings in the Case of Margaret, commonly called Peg, only lawful Sister to John Bull, Esq.* (1760; authorship disputed by a modern editor: *Sister Peg: A pamphlet hitherto unknown by David Hume*, ed. D. R. Raynor, Cambridge, 1982). In both of his professorships he produced textbooks: *Of Natural Philosophy. For the Use of Students in the College of Edinburgh* (n.d.); *Analysis of Pneumatics and Moral Philosophy. For the Use of Students in the College of Edinburgh* (1766); and *Institutes of Moral Philosophy. For the Use of Students in the College of Edinburgh* (1769). It was, however, *An Essay on the History of Civil Society* (1767) that secured him lasting fame. He criticized Richard Price and the American revolution in *Remarks on a Pamphlet lately Published by Dr. Price, Intitled, Observations on the Nature of Civil Liberty . . .* (1776) and secured a position as secretary to the Carlisle Commision (1778), which sought a settlement with the Americans. He produced *The History of the Progress and Termination of the Roman Republic* (1783) as well as a major work based upon his lectures, *Principles of Moral and Political Science* (1792). In retirement he wrote but did not publish, a large number of miscellaneous essays, now in *Collection of Essays*, ed. Y. Amoh (Kyoto, 1996); one essay published as 'Of the principles of moral estimation: A discourse between David Hume, Robert Clerk, and Adam Smith': An unpublished ms. by Adam Ferguson', ed. E. C. Mossner in *Journal of the History of Ideas* 21 (1960): 223–32. See *The Correspondence of Adam Ferguson*, ed. V. Merolle and K. Wellesley, introd. by J. B. Fagg, 2 vols. (London, 1995).

Secondary Sources: J. Small, *Biographical Sketch of Adam Ferguson* (Edinburgh, 1864). W. C. Lehmann, *Adam Ferguson and the Beginning of Modern Sociology* (New York, NY and London, 1930). D. Kettler, *The Social and Political Thought of Adam Ferguson* (Columbus, OH, 1965). Editor's Introduction in Ferguson, *An Essay on the History of Civil Society*, ed. D. Forbes (Edinburgh, 1966). J. Robertson, *The Scottish Enlightenment and the Militia Issue* (Edinburgh, 1985).

F. Oz-Salzberger, *Translating the Enlightenment: Scottish Civic Discourse in Eighteenth-Century Germany* (Oxford, 1995). [Knud Haakonssen]

Feuerbach, Paul Johann Anselm von b. Hainichen, Saxony, Germany, 1775; d. Frankfurt am Main, 1833. Legal philosopher, law reformer, public servant and magistrate. Studied philosophy (graduated 1795), then law (graduated 1799) in Jena. Taught law at Jena 1799–1801, at Kiel 1802–4, and at Landshut 1804–6; public servant in the Bavarian government 1806–14; judge in Bamberg 1814–17 and in Ansbach 1817–33. The main eighteenth-century works of philosophical content are: *Kritik des natürlichen Rechts als Propädeutik zu einer Wissenschaft des natürlichen Rechts* (Altona, 1796); *Anti-Hobbes oder über die Grenzen der höchsten Gewalt und das Zwangsrecht der Bürger gegen den Oberherrn*, (Gießen, 1797); *Philosophisch-juridische Untersuchungen über das Verbrechen des Hochverrats* (Erfurt, 1798).

Secondary Sources: G. Radbruch, *Paul Johann Anselm Feuerbach: Ein Juristenleben* (3rd edn., Göttingen, 1969). H.-U. Stühler, *Die Diskussion um die Erneuerung der Rechtswissenschaft von 1780–1815* (Berlin, 1978): 196–221. G. Hartung, *Die Naturrechtsdebatte. Geschichte der Obligatio vom 17. bis 20. Jahrhundert* (Freiburg [Breisgau], 1998), 209–26. [Knud Haakonssen]

Fichte, Johann Gottlieb b. Rammenau, Lusatia, 1762; d. Berlin, 1814. Philosopher. Plucked from rural poverty by a nobleman who sponsored him at a ducal boarding school in Saxony (1774–80) and at the theological faculties of Jena, Wittenberg, and Leipzig (1780–4); tutor in Zürich, Leipzig, and Danzig. Converted to Kantianism by *Kritik der reinen Vernunft* in 1790. His anonymous *Versuch einer Kritik aller Offenbarung* (1792) applied critical philosophy to religion so successfully that it was at first attributed to Kant himself. Defended the French Revolution in his controversial *Beiträge zur Berichtigung der Urteile des Publikums über die französische Revolution* (1793). Lectures at Jena from 1794 enjoyed considerable success and influenced Jena romanticism. *Begriff der Wissenschaftslehre* (1794) and *Grundlage der gesammelten Wissenschaftslehre* (1794–95) articulated his system of philosophy as a completion of the Kantian system, a view Kant rejected in a public letter in 1799. *Einige Vorlesungen über die Bestimmung des Gelehrten* (1794) provided a popular introduction to his system. Elaborated moral and political implications of the system in *Grundlage des Naturrechts nach Principien der Wissenschaftslehre* (1796–7) and *Das System der Sittenlehre nach den Principien der Wissenschaftslehre* (1798). Long suspect to authorities because of radical political views, he was dismissed from Jena on charges of atheism in 1799; his defense of academic freedom only added to his fame. *Die Bestimmung des Menschen* (1800) elaborated the broader implications of his moral philosophy for a general audience, he outlined his views on economic policy in *Der geschlossene Handelsstaat* (1800), and his *Reden die deutschen Nation* (1808) helped rally public opinion against Napoleon. Briefly taught at Erlangen and Königsberg, then at newly established University of Berlin from 1810 until his death from typhus in 1814. The first edition of his works (edited by his son): *Sämmtliche Werke*, ed. I. H. Fichte, 8 vols. (Berlin, 1845). New critical edition: *Gesamtausgabe der Bayerischen Akademie der Wissenschaften*, eds R. Lauth, H. Jacob, and H. Gliwitsky (Stuttgart-Bad Cannstatt, 1964–).

Secondary Sources: I. H. Fichte, *J. G. Fichte's Leben und litterarischer Briefwechsel* (Sulzbach, 1830–1). K. Fischer, *Fichtes Leben, Weke, und Lehre* (Heidelberg, 1892). X. Léon, *Fichte et son temps*, 2 in 3 vols. (Paris 1922–7). A. J. La Vopa, *Fichte: The Self and the Calling of Philosophy, 1762–1799* (Cambridge, 2001). M. Gueroult, *L'évolution et la structure de la doctrine de la science chez Fichte* (Paris, 1930). G. A. Kelly, *Idealism, Politics, and History* (Cambridge, 1969), 179–285. D. Henrich, 'Fichte's Original Insight', *Contemporary German Philosophy* 1 (1982): 15–53. K. Ameriks, 'Kant, Fichte, and Short Arguments to Idealism', *Archiv für Geschichte der Philosophie* 72 (1990): 63–85. *Fichte. Historical Contexts/Contemporary Controversies*, eds. D. Breazeale and T. Rockmore (Atlantic Highlands, NJ, 1994). [James Schmidt]

Filangieri, Gaetano b. Napoli, 1752; d. Vico Equense, 1788. Jurist and economic theorist. Studied Law at the University of Naples, was prominent in Enlightenment circles there, and showed sympathy for Freemasonry. His life's work was the monumental, unfinished *Scienza della legislazione*, 4 vols. (1780–8). *Opere*, ed. P. Villari, 3 vols. (Florence, 1864–76); *La scienza della legislazione*, eds V. Frosini and F. Riccobono, 2 vols. (Rome, 1984).

Secondary Sources: B. Constant, *Commentaire sur l'ouvrage de Filangeri*, 2 vols. (Paris, 1822–4). S. Cotta, *Gaetano Filangieri e il problema della legge* (Turin, 1954). M. T. Maestro, 'Filangieri and his Science of Legislation', *Transactions of the American Philosophical Society* 66 (1976), 1–76. *Filangieri e l'illuminismo europeo*, ed. A. Villani (Naples, 1991). [Luca Fonnesu]

Fontenelle, Bernard Le Bovier de b. Rouen 1657; d. Paris 1757. Proto-*philosophe* and academician par excellence. Fontenelle was educated by Jesuits and took a law degree but lived as a man of letters. In the seventeenth century, he published a large amount of poetry, plays, and operas, nearly all fiascos quickly forgotten. His revival of Lucian in *Nouveaux dialogues des morts* (1683) was more substantial, and the *Entretiens sur la pluralité des mondes* (1686) was very successful as a piece of popular science; in a series of elegant dialogues, the philosopher instructs a lady in the ancient and modern astronomical systems and engages in speculations about the earth being just one of several inhabited planets. He took the modernist side in the dispute of ancients and moderns (*Digression sur les Anciens et les Modernes* 1687). Some of Fontenelle's most important and influential work was on historical method and its application to religious history with strongly critical implications for Christianity; especially, *Histoire des oracles* 1687; *Relation de l'île de Bornéo* 1686; *De l'origine des fables* 1724; and *Sur l'histoire* 1758. Having moved to Paris, Fontenelle became a prominent figure in the salons world, was elected to the Académie Française in 1691, and became Sécrétaire Perpétuel of the Académie des Sciences in 1699. In the latter position, he published an annual account of the work of the Academy, *Histoire de l'Académie des Science*; the first volume is prefaced with a manifesto of his philosophy of science (1702), and these works also carried Fontenelle's *éloges* of the academicians who had died during the year, a novelty of immense importance and continued by d'Alembert. *Œuvres completes*, ed. A. Niderst, 9 vols. (Paris 1989–2001).

Secondary Sources: L. Maigron, *Fontenelle, l'homme, l'oeuvre, l'influence* (Paris, 1906). J.-R. Carré, *La philosophie de Fontenelle, ou le sourire de la raison* (Paris, 1932). J. W. Cosentini, *Fontenelle's Art of Dialogue* (New York, NY, 1952). L. Marsak, 'Bernard de Fontenelle: The Idea of Science in the French Enlightenment', *Transactions of the American Philosophical Society*, n.s. 49, pt. 7 (1959): 1–64. A. Niderst, *Fontenelle à la recherche de lui-même* (Paris, 1972). C. Paul, *Science and Immortality: The Eloges of the Paris Academy of Science 1699–1791* (Berkeley, CA, 1980). [Knud Haakonssen]

Fordyce, David b. Broadford, Aberdeenshire, 1711; drowned at sea, 1751. Moral philososopher, educator. Educated at Marischal College, Aberdeen (MA 1728) and Northampton Academy, he qualified for the ministry before returning as regent to Marischal College in 1742. His anonymous *Dialogues concerning Education* (1745–8), a popular work on moral improvement in the Shaftesbury tradition, led to a commission for the highly successful *Elements of Moral Philosophy*, first published in Dodsley's *Preceptor*, vol. 2. (1748) and frequently reprinted. This addresses 'the Science of Manners or Duty, which it traces from Man's Nature and Condition' and 'the Art of being virtuous and happy', and gives an important role to sympathy. It was reissued posthumously under the author's name (1754; French trans. 1756, German, 1757) and in an anonymous abridgement in the *Encyclopaedia Britannica*, 1st edn. (Edinburgh, 1771). Further works on the inculcation of virtue appeared posthumously, one for preachers and one for young persons: *Theodorus: A Dialogue concerning the Art of Preaching* (1752); *The Temple of Virtue. A Dream* (1757).

Secondary Sources: P. Jones, 'The Scottish Professoriate and the Polite Academy, 1720–46', in *Wealth and Virtue*, eds. I. Hont and M. Ignatieff (Cambridge, 1983), at 108–11. I. Rivers, *Reason, Grace and Sentiment*, 2 vols. (Cambridge, 1991–2000), 2: 181–4, 194–5. [M. A. Stewart]

Forster, Johann Georg Adam b. Nassenhuben, Polish Prussia, 1754; d. Paris, 1794. Traveller, writer, and Jacobin. Educated in St. Petersburg (1765) and Warrington Academy (1768–70). Accompanied father, Johann Reinhold, on Captain Cook's second expedition (1772–5). Published his account of voyage leading to conflicts with Cook, his supporters, and admiralty (1777). Left for Germany and given academic appointments at Kassel (1778) and Vilna (1784), then librarian at Mainz (1792). Mainz's representative to national convention of Paris (1793). Important works include, *A Voyage Round the World* (1777), *Ansichten vom Niederrhein* (1791–2), and essays on race ('Noch etwas über die Menschenrasse' [1776]), art ('Die Kunst und das Zeitalter' [1789]), and politics ('Über die Beziehung der Staatskunst auf das Glück der Menscheit' [1793]).

Secondary Sources: T. Sain, *Georg Forster* (New York, NY, 1972). T. Strack, 'Philosophical Anthropology on the Eve of Biological Determinism: Immanuel Kant and Georg Forster on the Moral Qualities and Biological Characteristics of the Human Race', *Central European History* 29:3 (1996): 285–308. *Georg-Forster-Studien*, eds. H. Dippel and H. Scheuer (Berlin/Kassel, 1997). A. Schwarz, *Georg Forster (1754–1794): Zur Dialektik von Naturwissenschaft, Anthropologie, Philosophie und Politik* (Mainz, 1998). [Aaron Garrett]

Franklin, Benjamin b. Boston MA, 1706; d. Philadelphia, PA, 1790. Printer, writer, scientist, and inventor. With little formal education (although later given honorary doctorates by St. Andrews and Oxford) Franklin made himself the central American intellectual of the eighteenth century first through printing and writing newspapers and periodicals, then through his inventions, scientific investigations, and role in leading and creating civic institutions. A fulcrum of the American Revolution and later the main conduit of America's political relations with France (serving as minister plenipotentiary) as well as the French Enlightenment. Philosophical works include *A Dissertation on Liberty and Necessity, Pleasure and Pain* (1725), and *Experiments and Observations on Electricity* (1751).

Secondary Sources: I. Bernard Cohen, *Benjamin Franklin's Science* (Cambridge, 1990). [Aaron Garrett]

Fréret, Nicolas b. Paris, 1668; d. Paris, 1749. Historian, philosopher and prominent member of *Académie des Inscriptions et Belles-Lettres*. Among his countless dissertations, three are noteworthy for the polemic they generated. *Réflexions générales sur l'étude des anciennes histoires et sur le degré de certitude des différentes preuves historiques* (1724, publ. 1729) is a heated discussion of historical scepticism. *Défense de la Chronologie fondée sur les monuments de l'histoire ancienne, contre le système chronologique de Newton* (publ. 1758) defended chronology based on monuments and testimonies of ancient cultures against Newton's mathematical approach. *Lettre de Thrasibule à Leucippe* (1722) is a well-known clandestine manuscript on atheism (publ. 1766). The main works: *Mémoires Académiques* (Paris, 1996); critical edition of the *Lettre de Thrasibule à Leucippe* by S. Landucci (Florence, 1996).

Secondary Sources: Louis-Antoine, comte de Bougainville, 'Eloge de M. Fréret', *Mémoires de l'Académie des Inscriptions et Belles-Lettres* 23 (1756): 314–37. M. Walkenaer, *Rapport fait à l'Académie des Inscriptions et Belles-Lettres au Sujet des Manuscrits Inédits de Fréret* (Paris, 1850). R. Simon, *Nicolas Fréret, Académicien* (Geneva, 1961). C. Borghero, *La certezza e la storia: cartesianesimo, pirronismo e conoscenza storica* (Milan, 1983), 357–90. *Nicolas Fréret, légende et vérité: Colloque des 18 et*

19 octobre 1991, Clermont-Ferrand, eds. C. Grell and C. Volpilhac-Auger (Oxford, 1994). [Dario Perinetti]

Friedrich II, King of Prussia (1740–1786) b. Berlin, 1712; d. Potsdam, 1786. Early interest in art and literature led to considerable friction with his militaristic and authoritarian father, Frederick-William I, culminating in attempted escape to England (1730) and subsequent imprisonment. After his 1733 marriage to Elizabeth of Brunswick-Bevern (from whom he quickly separated) he was permitted his own court at Rheinsberg, where he studied French literature and philosophy, wrote *Considérations sur l'etat présent du corps politique de l'Europe* (1738), *Anti-Machiavel* (1739), and began an extended correspondence with Voltaire. As king, he pursued territorial expansion, beginning with Silesia in 1740 and continuing with unexpected victories against a coalition of French, Austrian, Swedish, and Russian forces in 1756. Domestically he favored religious toleration, legal and penal reforms, and the improvement of commerce and industry. He cultivated the friendship of leading figures in the French Enlightenment, including Voltaire, d'Alembert, La Mettrie, Maupertuis. A pupil of the composer Quantz, he was a talented flautist and amateur composer. Standard edition of his works: *Oeuvres de Frédéric le Grand*, ed. J. D. E. Preuss, 30 vols. (Berlin, 1846–57).

Secondary Sources: J. G. Zimmermann, *Fragmente über Friedrich den Grossen zur Geschichte seines Lebens, seiner Regierung, und seines Charakters* (Leipzig, 1790). J. D. E. Preuss, *Friedrich der Grosse. Eine Lebensgeschichte*, 5 vols., (Berlin, 1832–4). T. Carlyle, *History of Friedrich II of Prussia*, 6 vols. (London, 1858–65). E. Zeller, *Friedrich der Grosse als Philosoph* (Berlin, 1886). G. Ritter, *Friedrich der Grosse; ein historisches Profil* (London, 1936 [trans. 1968]). P. Gaxotte, *Frèdèric II* (Paris, 1938 [trans. 1942]). G. P. Gooch, *Frederick the Great: The Ruler, the Writer, the Man* (London, 1947). [James Schmidt]

Galiani, Ferdinando b. Chieti, 1728; d. Naples, 1787. Economic theorist, Neapolitan diplomat, and statesman. As Neapolitan Embassy Secretary in Paris (1757–69) he was a member of d'Holbach's circle and was a close friend of Diderot and Madame d'Epinay. His most important works are, *Della moneta* (1751), *Dialogues sur le commerce des blés* (1770), and *Doveri dei prìncipi neutrali* (about questions of international order, 1782). *Opere*, eds. F. Diaz and L. Guerci (Milan, Naples, 1975).

Secondary Sources: C. Larrère, *L'Invention de l'économie au xviiie siècle* (Paris, 1992), 249–68. D. Gordon, *Citizens without Sovereignty: Equality and Sociability in French Thought, 1670–1789* (Princeton, NJ, 1994): 215–25. P. Amodio, *Il disincanto della ragione e l'assolutezza del bonheur: studio sull'abate Galiani* (Naples, 1997). [Luca Fonnesu]

Garve, Christian b. Breslau, Germany, 1742; d. Breslau, 1798. Moral philosopher, translator, and 'popular philosopher'. Studied with Alexander Gottlieb Baumgarten in Frankfurt an der Oder (1762), then Halle after Baumgarten's death (1763, MA 1766), then Leipzig until 1767. Professor of Philosophy in Leipzig (1770–2) but forced by ill health to resign and return to Breslau. Known for his ambition to write essays as well as Hume did. The original version of Feder's review of Kant's *Kritik der reinen Vernunft* stemmed from him. Frederick the Great initiated his translation of Ciceros *De Officiis* (1783; with Garve's *Abhandlung über die menschlichen Pflichten*), important for Kant's *Grundlegung zur Metaphysik der Sitten*. Similarly *Abhandlung über die Verbindung der Moral mit der Politik* (1788; French trans. 1789) was significant for Kant's 'Über den Gemeinspruch: Das mag in der Theorie richtig sein, taugt aber nicht für die Praxis' and *Zum ewigen Frieden*. Other translations include works by Adam Ferguson, Edmund Burke, Alexander Gerard, John MacFarlan, William Paley, Adam Smith, and Aristotle. Main works: *Versuche über verschiedene Gegenstände aus der Moral, der Litteratur und dem gesellschaftliche Leben*, 5 vols.

(1792–1802); *Vermischte Aufsätze*, 2 vols. (1796, 1800); *Eigene Betrachtungen über die allgemeinsten Grundsätze der Sittenlehre* (1798). *Gesammelte Werke* (including correspondence), ed. K. Wölfel, 16 vols. (Hildesheim, New York, NY, 1985–2000). *Aphorismen aus dem Nachlass*, ed. A. Kosenina (Hannover, 1998).

Secondary Sources: G. Schulz: 'Christian Garve und Immanuel Kant. Gelehrten-Tugenden im 18. Jahrhundert', *Jahrbuch der Schlesischen Friedrich-Wilhelm-Universität zu Breslau* 5 (1960): 123–88. M. Stolleis, *Staatsraison, Recht und Moral in philosophischen Texten des späten 18. Jahrhunderts* (Bodenheim, 1972). A. Viviani, 'Christian Garve-Bibliographie', *Wolfenbütteler Studien zur Aufklärung* 1 (1974): 306–27, and 2 (1975): 328–30; G. Gawlick and L. Kreimendahl, *Hume in der deutschen Aufklärung* (Stuttgart-Bad Cannstatt, 1987). D. Bachmann-Medick, *Die ästhetische Ordnung des Handelns. Moralphilosophie und Ästhetik in der Popularphilosophie des 18. Jahrhunderts* (Stuttgart, 1989). C. Altmayer, *Aufklärung als Popularphilosophie* (St. Ingbert, 1992). F. Oz-Salzberger, *Translating the Enlightenment. Scottish Civic Discourse in Eighteenth-Century Germany* (Oxford, 1995). J. van der Zande, 'The Microscope of Experience: Christian Garve's Translation of Cicero's *De Officiis* (1783)', *Journal of the History of Ideas* 59 (1998): 75–94. [Heiner F. Klemme]

GENTZ, FRIEDRICH VON b. Breslau, 1764; d. Vienna, 1832. Publicist and statesman. Educated at the Joachimsthal Gymnasium (Berlin); studied law in Königsberg, where he was influenced by Kant. Initially supported French Revolution but repelled by events of August and September 1792. Translated Burke's *Reflections on the Revolution in France* (1793) as well as works by Mallet du Pan and Mounier. Founded the *Neue deutsche Monatsschrift* and the *Historisches Journal*, both important venues for political analysis and debate. Left Berlin in 1802 for Vienna, where he wrote polemics against Napoleon. Secretary and confidant to Metternich from 1812. Secretary to the Congress of Vienna (1814–15). First edition of his works: *Ausgewählte Schriften*, ed. W. Weick (1836–8); new edition, *Gesammelte Schriften* (Hildesheim, 1997–).

Secondary Sources: P. Reiff, *Friedrich Gentz, An Opponent of the French Revolution and Napoleon* (Urbana-Champaign, IL, 1912). P. R. Sweet, *Friedrich von Gentz* (Madison, WI, 1941). G. Mann, *Secretary of Europe* (New Haven, CT, 1946). [James Schmidt]

GERARD, ALEXANDER b. Chapel of Garioch, Aberdeenshire, 1728; d. Old Aberdeen, 1795. Educated under Fordyce at Marischal College, Aberdeen (MA 1744), he formed early ties with Reid and George Campbell, participating in the development of the 'common sense' philosophy, and was later active in the Aberdeen Philosophical Society. From 1750 he held a succession of appointments at Marischal College, rising to be professor of divinity (1760), and transferred to the same position at King's College in 1771. He was public apologist for the curricular reforms of 1753, publishing *Plan of Education in the Marischal College and University of Aberdeen, with the Reasons of it* (Aberdeen, 1755). *An Essay on Taste* (London, 1759), a prize-winning essay submitted to the Select Society of Edinburgh to which was later (1780) added a section on the standard of taste, presents a more detailed account of the aesthetic sense than Hutcheson's and finds greater scope for the theory of association. In *An Essay on Genius* (London, 1774), where genius is sharply differentiated from ability and the intellectual powers are investigated from a distinctive angle, the associationism takes a Humean form. *Dissertations on the Genius and Evidences of Christianity* (Edinburgh, 1766) includes a practical application of the 'common sense' canons to historical evidence. *A Compendious View of the Evidences of Natural and Revealed Religion* (London, 1828), lecture notes completed by his son and successor, Gilbert, contains extensive citation of liberal dissenters. Minor writings include a response to Hume on the clerical character.

Secondary Sources: *A Biographical Dictionary of Eminent Scotsmen*, eds. R. Chambers and T. Thomson (Glasgow, 1855), 2: 429–33. M. Green, 'Gerard's *Essay on Taste*', *Modern*

Philology 41 (1943), 45–58. P. B. Wood, *The Aberdeen Enlightenment* (Aberdeen, 1993). [M. A. Stewart]

GIANNONE, PIETRO b. Ischitella, 1676; d. Turin, 1748. Historian and jurist. Educated in Naples; Doctor of Law. *Dell' istoria civile del regno di Napoli*, 4 vols. (1723), deals with the relationship between church and state in the history of Naples and was a work of considerable European influence (Montesquieu, Voltaire, Gibbon). He was excommunicated and fled Naples, first to Vienna, then Geneva, but he was caught in Savoy and imprisoned in Turin until his death. He wrote another attack on the church, *Il triregno ossia del regno del cielo, della terra e del papa* (1735), and an *Autobiografia*, published posthumously. *Opere*, eds. S. Bertelli and G. Ricuperati (Milan, Naples, 1971).

Secondary Sources: G. Ricuperati, *L'esperienza civile e religiosa di P. Giannone* (Milan, Naples, 1970). L. Mannarino, *Le mille favole degli antichi: Ebraismo e cultura europea nel pensiero religioso di Pietro Giannone* (Florence, 1999). J. G. A. Pocock, *Barbarism and Religion*, vol. 2: *Narratives of Civil Government* (Cambridge, 1999), 29–71. [Luca Fonnesu]

GIBBON, EDWARD b. Lime Grove, Putney, 1737; d. London, 1794. Philosophical historian. Educated, unhappily, at Oxford, and then, to counter his conversion to Catholicism, he was sent to Lausanne in 1753 to be tutored by the Calvinist minister Daniel Pavilliard. He returned to England in 1758 and published his first important work three years later, *Essai sur l'étude de la littérature*. In 1764 on a visit to Rome G. hatched a plan to write the history of imperial Rome which, after other, abortive projects, was begun in 1773. Volume 1 of the *Decline and Fall of the Roman Empire* appeared in 1776, volumes 2 and 3 in 1781, and volumes 4 through 6 in 1788. The subject of virulent polemics due to his perceived anti-Christian stance, G. defended the *Decline* with a masterful *Vindication* (1779). G. was MP for Liskeard (1774–80) and Lymington (1781–3). His *Memoirs* were edited and published posthumously in 1796. He was celebrated throughout Europe as the greatest historian of the age. There is no collected works; the main editions are: *The History of the Decline and Fall of the Roman Empire*, ed. D. J. Womersley, 3 vols. (London, 1994); *The English Essays of Edward Gibbon*, ed. P. B. Craddock (Oxford, 1972); *Miscellaneous Works*, ed. Lord Sheffield, 5 vols. (London, 1814); *The Autobiographies of Edward Gibbon*, ed. J. Murray (London, 1896); *The Letters of Edward Gibbon*, ed. J. E. Norton, 3 vols. (London, 1956).

Secondary Sources: J. E. Norton, *A Bibliography of the Works of Edward Gibbon* (Oxford, 1940). Arnoldo Momigliano, 'Gibbon's Contribution to Historical Method', *Historia* 2 (1954), 45–63. *Religious Scepticism: Contemporary Responses to Gibbon*, ed. D. J. Womersley (Bristol, 1997). J. G. A. *Pocock, The Enlightenments of Edward Gibbon*, 1737–1764 (Cambridge, 1999–). [Aaron Garrett]

GOTTSCHED, JOHANN CHRISTOPH b. Königsberg (Kaliningrad), 1700; d. Leipzig, 1766. Literary critic and Wolffian philosopher. Educated at Königsberg; professor of philosophy and logic at Leipzig (1734–66). Modified Wolffian metaphysics in *Erste Gründe der gesamten Weltweisheit* (1734), translated Leibniz's *Theodicée* (1744), composed influential grammar and pronunciation texts, and edited several literary journals. Author of the tragedy *Sterbende Cato* (1732), he extended Wolffian principles to criticism in *Versuch einer critischen Dichtkunst vor die Deutschen* (1729), pressing successfully for reforms of German poetry and theater along French classicist lines. Famously criticized by Swiss critics, Bodmer and Breitinger, later Lessing and Goethe. *Ausgewählte Schriften*, eds. J. Birke et al., 12 vols. (Berlin, 1968–87).

Secondary Sources: D. Dahlstrom, 'Die Aufklärung der Poesie', *Zeitschrift für Ästhetik und allgemeine Kunstwissenschaft* 31:1 (1986): 139–68. [Daniel Dahlstrom] 'sGravesande, Willem Jacob b. 'sHertogenbosch, Netherlands, 1688; d. Leiden, 1742. Physicist and natural philosopher. Law degree from University of Leiden, 1707. Spent 1715 in England; became a member of the Royal Society and acquainted with Newton. As professor of mathematics and astronomy at the University of Leiden (1717) his lectures were principally based on Newtonian principles but devotion to experiment brought with it a certain philosophical eclecticism. The range of apparatus used in his popular lectures is apparent in the important textbook based on them, *Physices elementa mathematica, experimentis confirmata. Sive introductio ad philosophiam Newtonianam* (1720, 1721). From 1734 he was also professor of philosophy and lectured on philosophy in general rather than specifically natural philosophy as hitherto; see his textbook, *Introductio ad Philosophiam, Metaphysicam et Logicam* (1736). *Oeuvres Philosophiques et Mathématiques de Mr. G. J. 'sGravesande* (1774), edited with a memoir by J. Allamand.

Secondary Sources: P. Brunet, *Les physiciens hollandais et la méthode expérimentale en France au XVIIIe siècle* (Paris, 1926). [John Gascoigne]

Grimm, Friedrich Melchoir b. Regensberg 1723; d. Gotha, 1809. Diplomat and journalist. Graduated University of Leipzig (1746); frequented literary circles in Paris and became a friend of Diderot. Reader for the duke of Saxe-Gotha, secretary to the duke d'Orléans, and, after 1776, ambassador to France for the duke of Saxe-Gotha, for whom he traveled on diplomatic missions in central and eastern Europe. Lover of the noted salonnière Louise d'Epinay from 1753 until her death in 1783; with her edited the *Correspondence littéraire* (1753–73 [critical edition: Paris, 1877–82]), a newsletter which kept European courts abreast of discussions in Parisian salons and circulated a number of significant manuscripts by Diderot and others. Left Paris during the Revolution and, after 1795, served as Catherine the Great's minister to Lower Saxony.

Secondary Sources: Edmond Henri Adolphe Scherer, *Melchior Grimm, L'homme de lettres, le factotum, le diplomate* (Paris, 1887 [Reprint: 1968]). [James Schmidt]

Gundling, Nicolaus Hieronymus b. Kirchensittenbach in Middle Franconia, 1671; d. Halle, 1729. Jurist. Son of a pastor, studied theology in Altdorf, Jena, and Leipzig, and, from 1699, law at Halle where he became professor of philosophy (1705) and jurisprudence (1707) and *Konsistorialrat*. He wrote *Dissertatio de statu naturali Hobbesii* (1706), *Politica seu prudentia civilis ratione connexa, exemplis illustrata* (in: *Gundlinigiana*, 45. Stück, 1732) and *Ausführlicher Discours über den jetzigen Zustand der europäischen Staaten* (1733/4).

Secondary Sources: R. Stintzing/ E. Landsberg, *Geschichte der deutschen Rechtswissenschaft* Abt. III, 1 (Leipzig, 1898): 122–5. H. Rüping, *Die Naturrechtslehre des Christian Thomasius und ihre Fortbildung in der Thomasius-Schule* (Bonn, 1968): 70–4. N. Hammerstein, *Ius und Historie* (Göttingen, 1972): 203–67. M. Mulsow, 'Gundling versus Buddeus: Competing Models for the History of Philosophy', in *History and the Disciplines: The Reclassification of Knowledge in Early Modern Europe*, ed. D. R. Kelley (Rochester, 1997), 103–25. [Thomas Ahnert]

Haller, Albrecht von b. Bern, 1708; d. Bern, 1777. Medical scientist, poet. Studied medicine and science at Tübingen (1724–5) and Leiden (1725–7), MD 1727. After visiting London and Paris, practised medicine in Bern; professor of anatomy, botany, and surgery at Göttingen 1736–53 where he founded his reputation as a leading anatomist and physiologist. Main works of this period: *Icones anatomicae* (1743–54), *Primae lineae physiologiae* (1747), *De partibus corporis humani sensibilibus et irritabilibus* (1752), and descriptions of the flora of Switzerland. He promoted communication in the republic of letters by founding *Gesellschaft der Wissenschaften in Göttingen* (1751), by publishing the *Göttinger Gelehrte Anzeigen*, and by his extensive correspondence. Returning to Berne (1753), he held several political offices and continued his scientific activities and international correspondence. In the Bernese and Swiss context his early poems about Switzerland (*Versuch schweizerischer Gedichte*, 1732) as well as his political novels (*Usong*, 1771; *Alfred, König der Angelsachsen*, 1773, *Fabius and Cato*, 1774) are important. Parts of his correspondence with some 1,200 persons have been edited. A CD-ROM with a complete inventory of printed and unpublished work is being constructed.

Secondary Sources: J. G. Zimmermann, *Das Leben des Herrn von Haller* (Zürich, 1755). L. Hirzel, 'Introduction' to *Albrecht von Hallers Gedichte*, ed. L. Hirzel (Frauenfeld, 1882). K. S. Guthke, *Haller und die Literatur* (Göttingen, 1962). R. Toellner, *Albrecht von Haller. Über die Einheit im Denken des Universalgelehrten* (Wiesbaden, 1971). H. Balmer, *Albrecht von Haller* (Bern, 1977). *Albrecht von Haller 1708–1777. Zehn Vorträge gehalten am Berner Haller-Symposion vom 6. bis 8. Oktober 1977* (Basel, 1977). M. T. Monti, *Catalogo del Fondo Haller della biblioteca Nazionale Braidense di Milano*, 13 vols. (Milan, 1983–94). Same, *Congettura ed esperianza nella fisiologia die Haller. La riforma dell' anatomia animata e il sistema della generazione* (Florence, 1990). U. Boschung, *Albrecht von Haller in Göttingen, 1736–1753* (Bern, 1994). [Simone Zurbuchen]

HAMANN, JOHANN GEORG b. Königsberg (Kaliningrad), 1730; d. Münster, 1788. Philosophical man of letters. Close friend of Herder and Jacobi, dubbed *Magus im Norden*, he was a major force behind the *Sturm und Drang* movement in Germany, thanks to several cryptic, Pietist-inspired writings that aimed at disestablishing an overestimation of human capacities, especially, reason. Studied at Königsberg, including lectures by Knutzen and Rappolt; tutor and representative of a trading firm. On a business trip to London in 1757, he studied Hume and underwent a religious conversion that stamped his life's work. Returning to Königsberg in 1759, he presented Socrates as Jesus' – and not the Enlightenment's – forerunner in the successful *Sokratisiche Denkwürdigkeiten für die lange Weile des Publicums zusammengetragen von einem Liebhaber der langen Weile* (1759). *Aesthetica in nuce*, published in *Kreuzzüge des Philologen* (1762), attacked biblical scholars' failure to recognize the poetic nature of scripture and interpretation. Worked as toll-collector in Königsberg (1767–87) and maintained a scandalous but happy 'marriage of conscience'. *Golgotha und Schlebemini!* (1784) lampoons Mendelssohn's plea for distinguishing natural and civil orders. *Metakritik der Purismus der Vernunft* (1784; published posthumously, 1800) criticizes the 'transcendental superstition' of Kant's allegedly prelinguistic logic. *Sämtliche Werke*, ed. J. Nadler, 6 vols. (Vienna, 1949–57); translations with commentary in J. C. O'Flaherty, *Hamann's Socratic Memorabilia* (Baltimore, MD, 1967) and G. G. Dickson, *Johann Georg Hamann's Relational Metacriticism* (Berlin, 1995).

Secondary Sources: Comprehensive bibliography in F. Blanke and K. Gründer, *Johann Georg Hamanns Hauptschriften Erklärt*, vols. 1–2, 4–5, 7 (Gütersloh, 1956–63). R. Unger, *Hamann und die Aufklärung*, 2 vols. (Jena, 1911). J. C. O'Flaherty, *Johann Georg Hamann* (Boston, MA, 1979). [Daniel Dahlstrom]

HARRIS, JAMES b. Salisbury, 1709; d. Salisbury, 1780. Aristotelian critic of Locke and empiricism; writer on the philosophy of art and grammar. Educated at Salisbury grammar school, Wadham College, Oxford (1726), and Lincoln's Inn. On his father's death he became independent, returned to Salisbury and devoted his life to study and writing, deeply inspired by Greek and Latin literature. MP for Christchurch, 1761 until his death. 1763–65 commissioner of the admiralty and of the treasury. Main works: *Three Treatises, the First concerning Art, the Second concerning Music, Painting and Poetry, the Third concerning Happiness* (1744); *Hermes: or, a Philosophical Inquiry concerning Language and Universal Grammar* (1751); *Philosophical Arrangements* (1775); *Philological Inquiries*, 2 vols. (1781); all in his, *Miscellanies*, 5 vols. (1775–92). *The Works of James Harris, with an account of his life and character, by his son the Earl of Malmesbury*, 2 vols. (1810).

Secondary Sources: W. Knight, *Lord Monboddo and Some of His Contemporaries* (New York, NY and London, 1900) (nine letters between Harris and Monboddo). O. Funke, *Englische Sprachphilosophie im späteren 18. Jahrhundert* (Bern, 1934). N. Chomsky, *Cartesian Linguistics* (New York, NY, 1966). L. Lipking, 'James Harris, Samuel Johnson, and the Idea of True Criticism', in *The Ordering of the Arts in Eighteenth-Century England* (Princeton, NJ, 1970): 86–105. J. Malek, 'Art as Mind Shaped by a Medium: The Significance of James Harris: A Discourse on Music, Painting and Poetry', in *Texas Studies in Literature and Language* 12 (1970), 231–39. A. Joly, 'Introduction' to *Hermès ou recherches philosophiques sur la grammaire universelle*, trans. F. Thurot (Paris: an IV [1796], reissue ed. by A. Joly, Geneva, 1972). J. L. Subbiondo, 'The Semantic Theory of James Harris; A Study of Hermes', in *Historiographia Linguistica* 3 (1976): 275–91. K. D. Uitti, 'James Harris' *Hermes* in the Context of Revolutionary France: The Translations and Commentaries of François Thurot', in *Essays on the Age of Enlightenment in Honor of Ira O. Wade*, ed. J. Macary (Geneva, 1977), 329–45. P. Bergheaud, 'De James Harris à John Horne Tooke. Mutations de l'analyse du langage en Angleterre dans la deuxième moitié du XVIIIe siècle', in *Historiographia Linguistica* 6 (1979): 15–45. C. T. Probyn, *The Sociable Humanist. The Life and Works of James Harris 1709–1780. Provincial and Metropolitan Culture in Eighteenth-Century England* (Oxford, 1991). [Hans Aarsleff]

Hartley, David baptized Luddenden, England, 1705; d. Bath, 1757. Philosopher, psychologist, physician. Graduated BA Jesus College, Cambridge 1726 and MA 1729. After brief career as grammar school master, practiced medicine in Bury St. Edmunds, London, and Bath. Decisively influenced by John Gay. First in *Conjecturae quaedam de sensu, motu et idearum generatione* (1746) and then in *Observations on Man, his Frame, his Duty, and his Expectations* (1749) presented a materialist theory of mind built on pains and pleasures transmitted via vibrations in the brain. In the second part of the *Observations* developed a moral theory and rational theology anchored by a supremely benevolent deity. Also wrote numerous medical tracts. Friend of Butler's, admired by Coleridge and Priestley and considered a founding figure of modern psychology.

Secondary Sources: J. Priestley, *Hartley's Theory of the Human Mind on the Principle of Association of Ideas* (London, 1775). W. Hazlitt, *An Essay on the Principles of Human Action: Being an Argument in Favour of the Natural Disinterestedness of the Human Mind. To Which are Added, Some Remarks on the Systems of Hartley and Helvetius* (London, 1805). M. E. Webb, 'A New History of Hartley's Observations on Man', *Journal of the History of the Behavioral Sciences* 24 (1988): 202–11. R. Marsh, 'The Second Part of Hartley's System', *Journal of the History of Ideas*, 20 (1959): 264–73. R. K. Webb, 'Perspectives on David Hartley', *Enlightenment and Dissent* 17 (1998): 17–47. R. C. Allen, *David Hartley on Human Nature* (Albany, NY, 1999). [Aaron Garrett]

Hegel, Georg Wilhelm Friedrich b. Stuttgart, 1770; d. Berlin, 1831. Philosopher. Studied theology at Tübingen, 1788–93, where his classmates included Hölderlin and Schelling; while tutoring in Bern and Frankfurt, wrote series of manuscripts (first published in 1907 as *Hegels theologische Jugendschrifte*) contrasting Christianity with Greek antiquity. Joined Schelling at Jena in 1800, where they edited *Kritisches Journal der Philosophie* (1801–3), an important journal in the development of idealism. Criticized Fichte in his *Differenz des Fichteschen und Schellingschen Systems der Philosophie* (1801), published important articles in *Kritisches Journal* on faith and knowledge ('Glauben und Wissen,' 1802) and natural right theories ('Über die wissenschaftlichen Behandlungsarten des Naturrechts,' 1802–3) and *Phänomenologie des Geistes* (1807), a wide-ranging work intended as introduction to his philosophical system. With the closing of the university in the wake of Napoleon's victory at Jena, briefly edited a newspaper in Bamberg and led a classical gymnasium in Nüremberg. Published *Wissenschaft der Logik* in two volumes (1812–13 and 1816). Professor of philosophy at Heidelberg (1816–18), where he published *Enzyklopädie der philosophischen Wissenschaften im Grundrisse* (1817), consisting of logic, philosophy of nature, and philosophy of spirit. At the University of Berlin 1818–31, where lectures on aethetics, the philosophy of history, the philosophy of religion, and the history of philosophy (eventually published in the first edition of his works) secured his fame. Published *Grundlinien der Philosophie des Rechts* (1821). Died in cholera epidemic, 1831. First edition of his works: *Werke*, 17 vols. (Berlin, Duncker and Humblot, 1832–45). Subsequent, uncompleted editions now supplanted by *Sämtliche Werke, neue kritische Ausgabe* (Hamburg, 1968–) and *Werke in zwanzig Bänden*, eds. E. Moldenhauer and K. M. Michel 20 vols. (Frankfurt am Main, 1971), a revised version of the 1832–45 edition of the works.

Secondary Sources: K. Rosenkranz, *Georg Wilhelm Friedrich Hegels Leben* (Berlin, 1844). W. Dilthey, *Die Jugendgeschichte Hegels* (Berlin, 1806). T. Haering, *Hegel, sein Wollen und sein Werk* (Leipzig and Berlin, 1929–38). H. S. Harris, *Hegel's Development: Toward the Sunlight, 1770–1801* (Oxford, 1972); same, *Hegel's Development: Night Thoughts, Jena 1801–1806* (Oxford, 1983); same, *Hegel's Ladder* (Indianapolis, IN, 1997). T. Pinkard, *Hegel: A Biography* (Cambridge, 2000). H. Marcuse, *Reason and Revolution: Hegel and the Rise of Social Theory* (Oxford, 1942). D. Henrich, *Hegel im Kontext* (Frankurt am Main, 1967). J. d'Hondt, *Hegel secret: Recherches sur les sources cachées de la pensée de Hegel* (Paris, 1968). J. Hyppolite, *Genesis and Structure of Hegel's Phenomenology of Spirit* (Evanston, IL, 1974). J. Ritter, *Hegel and the French Revolution* (Cambridge, MA, 1982). L. P. Hinchman, *Hegel's Critique of the Enlightenment* (Gainesville, FL, 1984). L. Dickey, *Hegel: Religion, Economics, and the Politics of Spirit 1770–1807* (Cambridge, 1987). N. Waszek, *The Scottish Enlightenment in Hegel's Account of 'Civil Society'* (Dordrecht, 1988). [James Schmidt]

Helvétius, Claude Adrien b. Paris, 1715; d. Paris, 1771. Born into a wealthy family with royal connections. Studied at Jesuit college of Louis-le-Grand, became a member of Académie de Caen (1737), and, through Queen's influence, tax farmer (1738). He retired from his profitable tax farming in 1748. Became Queen's *maitre d'hotel*, married and moved to Voré in 1751, wintering in Paris and frequenting the clubs and suppers of the *Philosophes*. His major work, *De l'esprit* (1758) was passed by the censor with the help of his friend Le Roy and published with royal approval. The uproar over this work was one of the main dramas of the French Enlightenment with countless condemnations: from the Queen (who took away his sinecure), the Pope, the Spanish Inquisitor, the Sorbonne, the *Parlement* (who condemned the work to be burned), and many others. Was forced to write numerous retractions and very few of the *Philosophes* came to his aid. Despite this, and with the moderating influence of the King, he found literary celebrity and was warmly received in England (1764) and by Frederick the Great in Prussia. Other important works include an allegorical poem *Le bonheur* (1772) and *De l'homme* (1773). Philosophically, he was a sensationist emphasizing the malleability and perfectibility of the human mind through stimulus and education.

Secondary Sources: W. Hazlitt, *An Essay on the Principles of Human Action* (London, 1805). A. Keim, *Helvétius, sa vie et son oeuvre* (Paris, 1907). D. W. Smith, *Helvétius: A Study in Persecution* (Oxford, 1965). J. H. Bloch, 'Rousseau and Helvetius on Innate and Acquired Traits: The Final Stages of the Rousseau-Helvetius Controversy', *Journal of the History of Ideas* 40 (1979): 21–41. [Aaron Garrett]

Herder, Johann Gottfried b. Mohrungen (Morag, Poland), 1744; d. Weimar, 1803. Prolific writer, educator, and churchman. Influenced by his friend, Hamann, propounded the uniqueness and irreducible unity of history, literature, and language in a trio of writings published during his tenure as a court preacher in Bückeberg: *Abhandlung über den Ursprung der Sprache* (1772), a highly eclectic argument for the distinctively human and self-reflective development of language;

Auch eine Philosophie der Geschichte zur Bildung der Menschheit (1774), a parody of Enlightenment pretensions regarding the progress of history; and essays on Ossian and Shakespeare in *Von deutscher Art und Kunst* (1773), the manifesto of the so-called *Sturm und Drang*. In 1776 became chief pastor, court preacher, and director of schools in Weimar, his final residence. Published a significant collection of *Volkslieder* (1778–9), an intepretation of the Hebrew bible in *Vom Geist der ebräischen Poesie* (1782–83), and a philosophical treatment of the concept of God in *Gott, einige Gespräche* (1787). In an attempt to account for the entire development of human cultures in continuity with natural history and natural conditions he published the four-part *Ideen zur Philosophie der Geschichte der Menschheit* (1784–91). In the final decade of his life he produced a commentary on the contemporary scene and prospects for humanity in *Briefe zu Beförderung der Humanität* (1793–97) and a two-volume polemic against Kant (his former teacher) in *Verstand und Erfahrung. Eine Metakritik zur Kritik der reinen Vernunft* (1799). The standard and most complete edition is *Sämtliche Werke*, ed. B. Suphan, 33 vols. (Berlin, 1877–1913).

Secondary Sources: R. T. Clark, *Herder: His Life and Thought* (Berkeley, CA, 1955). W. Koepke, *Johann Gottfried Herder* (Boston, MA, 1987). F. M. Barnard, *Self-Direction and Political Legitimacy: Rousseau and Herder* (Oxford, 1988). M. Morton, *Herder and the Poetics of Thought* (University Park, PA, 1989). R. E. Norton, *Herder's Aesthetics and the European Enlightenment* (Ithaca, NY, 1991). C. Taylor, 'The Importance of Herder', in *Isaiah Berlin: A Celebration*, eds. E. Margalit and A. Margalit (Chicago, IL, 1991). *Herder und die Philosophie des deutschen Idealismus*, ed. M. Heinz (Amsterdam, 1997). [Daniel Dahlstrom]

HERZ, MARKUS b. Berlin, 1747; d. Berlin, 1803. Physician and philosopher; correspondent of Mendelssohn and Kant. Educated in the strict Talmudic tradition of his Jewish family. Studied medicine and 'humaniora' (including philosophy) at Königsberg (1766–70) and Berlin (1770; doctorate 1774). Made titular Professor of Philosophy by Frederick the Great (1787). His main philosophical work, *Betrachtungen aus der spekulativen Weltweisheit* (1771; modern ed. Hamburg, 1990), is based on his official response to Kant's inaugural dissertation (1770) on the 'forms and principles of the sensible and intelligible world'. *Versuch über den Geschmack und die Ursachen seiner Verschiedenheiten* (1776) is a work on aesthetics. Puts forward the ideal of a 'philosophical physician' in his medical writings, *Briefe an Aerzte*, 2 vols. (1777). Other philosophically relevant medical writings include his *Versuch über den Schwindel* (1786). His correspondence with Kant is in *Kants Gesammelte Schriften*, Ak: 10–12. His correspondence with Mendelssohn is in *Moses Mendelssohns Gesammelte Schriften*, ed. G. B. Mendelssohn (Leipzig, 1863), vol. 5.

Secondary Sources: E. Flatow, 'Markus Herz, ein Vorkämpfer der bewußten Psychotherapie vor 150 Jahren', *Deutsche Medizinische Wochenschrift* 54 (1928): 1220–1. D. Bourel, 'Moses Mendelssohn, Markus Herz und die Akademie der Wissenschaften zu Berlin', *Mendelssohn-Studien* 4 (1979): 223–34. B. Ibing: *Markus Herz. Arzt und Weltweiser im Berlin der Aufklärung. Lebens-und Werkbeschreibung*. (Diss. Münster, 1984). [Udo Thiel]

HEYDENREICH, KARL HEINRICH b. Stolpen, Saxony, 1764; d. Burgwerben, 1801. Philosopher and poet. Educated at the famous Thomasschule and the university in Leipzig (1782–5); Professor of Philosophy there 1787–97; was forced to leave his professorship and died without means. Influenced by Spinoza and *Sturm und Drang* in his youth, he became a convinced Kantian. His audience at Leipzig included Friedrich Freiherrr von Hardenberg (Novalis). His main works are *System der Ästhetik* (1790) and *System des Naturrechts nach kritischen Prinzipien* (1794–5). Other works include *Grundsätze der Kritik des Lächerlichen mit Hinsicht auf das Lustspiel* (1797), *Betrachtungen über die Philosophie der natürlichen Religion*, 2 vols. (1790–1), *Briefe über den Atheismus*

(1796), *Psychologische Entwickelung des Aberglaubens und der damit verknüpften Schwärmerey* (1798), *Über den Selbstmord* (1796), *Vesta. Kleine Schriften zur Philosophie des Lebens*, 5 vols. (1798–1801). His collected poems were edited posthumously by his brother (1802).

Secondary Sources: K. G. Schelle, *Karl Heinrich Heydenreichs Charakteristik als Menschen und Schriftsteller* (Leipzig, 1802). P. Schlüter, *Karl Heinrich Heydenreichs System der Ästhetik* (Halle, 1939). [Heiner F. Klemme]

Hissmann, Michael b. Hermannstadt (Sibui), Transsylvania, 1752; d. Göttingen, 1784. Radical materialist philosopher; translator of Condillac and Priestley. Studied philosophy at Erlangen and Göttingen from 1772; MA 1776; extraordinary professor at Göttingen 1782; full professor 1784. His main philosophical work is *Psychologische Versuche, ein Beytrag zur esoterischen Logik*, (1777). Editor of *Magazin für die Philosophie und ihre Geschichte*, 4 vols. (1778–83). Other philosophical writings include: *Anleitung zur Kenntniß der auserlesenen Literatur in allen Theilen der Philosophie* (1778), and *Briefe über Gegenstände der Philosophie* (1778).

Secondary Sources: M. Dessoir, *Geschichte der Neueren Deutschen Psychologie* (Berlin, 1902), 211–14. O. Finger, *Von der Materialität der Seele. Beitrag zur Geschichte des Materialismus und Atheismus im Deutschland der zweiten Hälfte des 18. Jahrhunderts* (Berlin, 1961), 35–51, 86–97. U. Thiel, 'Varietries of Inner Sense. Two Pre-Kantian Theories', *Archiv für Geschichte der Philosophie* 79 (1997): 58–79. [Udo Thiel]

Hoadly, Benjamin b. Westerham, Kent, 1676; d. Chelsea, 1761. Latitudinarian divine. Educated at St. Catharine Hall, Cambridge (BA 1696, MA 1699) and Fellow and Tutor there (1697 and 1699). Ordained 1701; DD (Lambeth, 1715). Miscellaneous clerical calls before becoming, in succession, Bishop of Bangor (1716), Hereford (1721), Salisbury (1723), and Winchester (1734); chaplain to George I (1715). Wrote prodigiously on principles that made Richard Price put him next to Sidney, Locke, and Milton. See esp. *A Defence of the Reasonableness of Conformity to the Church of England* (1703); *The Measures of Submission to the Civil Magistrate, Consider'd* (1706); *Some Considerations Humbly Offered to . . . the Bishop of Exeter* (1709); *The Original and Institution of Civil Government* (1710); *Several Discourses concerning the Terms of Acceptance with God* (1711); *A Preservative against the Principles and Practices of the Non-jurors both in Church and State* (1716); *The Common Rights of Subjects Defended and the Nature of the Sacramental Test Consider'd* (1719); *A Plain Account of the Nature and End of the Sacrament of the Lord's Supper* (1735); *The Repeal of the Corporation and Test Acts* (1736). The standard edn.: *The Works of Benjamin Hoadly*, ed. J. Hoadly, 3 vols. (1773).

Secondary Sources: L. Stephen, *History of English Thought in the Eighteenth Century*, 2 vols. (1876; New York, 1962), ch. 10, secs. 31–40, vol. 2: 132–41. N. Sykes, 'Benjamin Hoadly, Bishop of Bangor', in *The Social and Political Ideas of some English Thinkers of the Augustan Age A. D. 1650–1750*, ed. F. J. C. Hearnshaw (London, 1928): 112–56. R. Browning, *The Political and Constitutional Ideas of the Court Whigs* (Baton Rouge, LA, 1982), ch. 3. [Knud Haakonssen]

Holbach, Paul-Henri Thiry, Baron d' b. Edesheim, Germany (Palatinate), 1723; d. Paris, 1789. Radical materialist, disseminator of technical and scientific knowledge, chemist. Studied at Leiden, settled in Paris 1749, soon came into a large inheritance leaving him free to pursue his interests and to host the lavish weekly dinners at which he entertained the encyclopedists; contributed some four hundred entries to Diderot's and d'Alembert's *Encyclopédie*; translated some thirty works from English and German into French, including works by John Toland and Thomas Hobbes. *Le Christianisme devoilé* (1767); *Système de la nature. Ou des lois du monde physique et du monde moral* (1770), abbreviated as *Le Bon sens* (1770), ed. with notes by Diderot

(1821); *La politique naturelle* (1773); *Le système social* (1773); *La Morale universelle* (1776). *Oeuvres philosophiques*, ed. J. P. Jackson, in progress (Paris, 1998–).

Secondary Sources: J. Vercruysse, *Bibliographie déscriptive des écrits du baron d'Holbach* (Paris, 1971). V. W. Topazio, *D'Holbach's Moral Philosophy; Its Background and Development* (Geneva, 1956). E. Callot, *La philosophie de la vie au XVIIIe siècle, etudiée chez Fontenelle, Montesquieu, Maupertuis, La Mettrie, Diderot, d'Holbach, Linné* (Paris, 1965): 317–68. F. E. Manuel, *The Eighteenth Century Confronts the Gods* (New York, 1967), esp. 228–41. P. Nivelle, *D'Holbach et la philosophie scientifique au XVIIIe siècle* (Paris, 1967). John Lough, *Essays on the 'Encyclopédie' of Diderot and d'Alembert* (London, 1968): 110–229. A. C. Kors, *D'Holbach's Coterie: An Enlightenment in Paris* (Princeton, NJ, 1976). [Hans Aarsleff]

Home, Henry, Lord Kames b. Eccles, Berwickshire, Scotland, 1696; d. Edinburgh, 1782. Jurist, philosopher, Enlightenment 'improver'. Studied law privately in Edinburgh; admitted to the Faculty of Advocates, 1723; in practice in Edinburgh; judge in the Court of Session, 1752, in the High Court of Justiciary, 1763. Member of government boards managing the Scottish economy; broker of patronage for men of letters (Smith, Millar, Reid, and, unsuccessfully, Hume); and a central figure in cultural and improving clubs and societies in Edinburgh. His *Essays* led to heresy-charges, along with Hume. In a vast *oeuvre* encompassing agriculture, horticulture, legal history and case-studies, anthropology, pedagogy, aesthetics, metaphysics, theology, ethics, politics and jurisprudence, the philosophically most relevant works are: *Essays on the Principles of Morality and Natural Religion* (1751; important revisions, 1758, 1779); 'Of the Laws of Motion', in *Essays and Observations, Physical and Literary. Read Before a Society in Edinburgh and Published by Them.* Vol. 1, eds. David Hume and Alexander Monro I. (Edinburgh, 1754): 1–69; [anon] *Objections against the Essays on Morality and Natural Religion Examined* (1756 [with Robert Wallace and Hugh Blair?]); *Historical Law Tracts*, 2 vols. (1758); *Principles of Equity* (1760); *Introduction to the Art of Thinking* (1761); *Elements of Criticism*, 3 vols. (1762); *Sketches of the History of Man*, 2 vols. (1774); *Loose Hints upon Education, Chiefly Concerning the Culture of the Heart* (1781).

Secondary Sources: J. Boswell, 'Materials for Writing the Life of Lord Kames [c. 1778–1782]', in *Private Papers of James Boswell from Malahide Castle*, eds. G. Scott and F. A. Pottle, 18 vols. (Mt. Vernon, NY, 1928–34), vol. 15. W. Smellie, *Literary and Characteristical Lives of John Gregory, MD, Henry Home, Lord Kames, David Hume, Esq. and Adam Smith, LLD* (Edinburgh, 1800). A. F. Tytler, *Lord Woodhouselee, Memoirs of the Life and Writings of the Honourable Henry Home of Kames, . . . ,* 2 vols. (2nd rev. edn., Edinburgh, 1814). J. Ramsay of Ochtertyre, *Scotland and Scotsmen in the Eighteenth Century*, 2 vols. (Edinburgh, London, 1888). *The Correspondence of Thomas Reid*, ed. P. B. Wood (Edinburgh, 2002). A. E. McGuinness, *Henry Home, Lord Kames* (New York, NY, 1970). W. C. Lehmann, *Henry Home, Lord Kames and the Scottish Enlightenment: A Study in National Character and in the History of Ideas* (The Hague, 1971). I. S. Ross, *Lord Kames and the Scotland of His Day* (Oxford, 1972). D. F. Norton, *David Hume: Common-Sense Moralist, Sceptical Metaphysician* (Princeton, NJ, 1982). J. Cairns, 'Institutional Writings in Scotland Reconsidered', *Journal of Legal History* 4 (1983): 76–117. D. Lieberman, 'The Legal Needs of a Commercial Society: The Jurisprudence of Lord Kames', in *Wealth and Virtue: The Shaping of Political Economy in the Scottish Enlightenment*, eds. I. Hont and M. Ignatieff (Cambridge, 1983), 203–34. D. M. Walker, *The Scottish Jurists* (Edinburgh, 1985), 220–47. R. Wokler, 'Apes and Races in the Scottish Enlightenment: Monboddo and Kames on the Nature of Man', in *Philosophy and Science in the Scottish Enlightenment*, ed. P. Jones (Edinburgh, 1988), 145–68. D. Lieberman, *The Province of Legislation Determined: Legal Theory in Eighteenth-Century Britain* (Cambridge, 1989). [Knud Haakonssen]

Humboldt, Alexander von b. Berlin, 1769; d. Berlin, 1859. Geographer, geophysicist. During 1790s conducted zoological and mineralogical studies, including *Über die unterirdischen Gasarten* (1799). From 1799 to 1804 undertook Caribbean expeditions, evaluated by him and an international body of scientists in *Voyage aux régions équinoxiales du nouveau continent*, 36 vols. (1805–34). In Paris, composed *Ansichten der Natur* (1808). Following an 1829 scientific expedition to Siberia – source of *Asie centrale*, 3 vols. (1843) – settled in Berlin, working for the government and helping establish world-wide observatories of geomagnetism and other terrestrial forces. Gave a popular account of universe's structure in *Kosmos*, 4 vols. (1845–58). Standard edition: *Gesammelte Werke*, 12 vols. (Berlin, 1988).

Secondary Sources: H. Beck, *Alexander von Humboldt*, 2 vols. with extensive bibliography (Wiesbaden, 1959–61). O. Kraetz, *Alexander von Humboldt* (Munich, 2000). [Daniel Dahlstrom]

Humboldt, Wilhelm von b. Potsdam, 1767; d. Tegel, 1835. Statesman, philosopher of language, humanist educator, and friend of Friedrich Wolf, Schiller, and Goethe. In 'Ideen zu einem Versuch, die Grenzen der Wirksamkeit des Staates zu bestimmen' (partially: *Berlinische Monatschrift*, 1792; complete: Breslau, 1851), he argued for the state to protect but not patronize its citizens. As Prussia's Minister of Education, he reformed elementary education, founded University of Berlin (1809), and promoted the idea of general education (*allgemeine Bildung*), cultivation of all a person's powers via study of antiquity and languages. Investigated language as a holistic, dynamic, cultural phenomenon, as basic as reason to human beings, in numerous works, including *Über das vergleichende Sprachstudium in Beziehung auf die verschiedenen Epochen der Sprachentwicklung* (1822); *Über das Entstehen der grammatischen Formen und ihren Einfluß auf die Ideenentwicklung* (1825); and *Über die Verschiedenheit des menschlichen Sprachbaus und ihren Einfluß auf die geistige Entwicklung des Menschengeschlechts* (1836; also introduction to *Über die Kawi-Sprache*, 3 vols., 1836–39). Standard edition: *Gesammelte Schriften*, 17 vols. (Berlin, 1903–36).

Secondary Sources: P. Sweet, *Wilhelm von Humboldt: A Biography*, 2 vols. (1978–9). T. Borsche, *Wilhelm von Humboldt* (Munich, 1990). [Daniel Dahlstrom]

Hume, David b. Edinburgh, 1711; d. Edinburgh, 1776. He entered Edinburgh University at ten, pursuing a course dominated by the classical languages. He was introduced to natural philosophy at college, but in other branches of literature and philosophy was largely self-taught, skimping a subsequent legal training in order to study the classical moralists and, later, British and French thinkers. Stoic and mystic writers induced in him a nervous crisis at eighteen, after which he developed a strongly experiential emphasis in his philosophy. An essay on chivalry survives from the transitional period. In 1734, after brief employment with a Bristol merchant, he settled to three years' study and writing in France, returning from La Flèche in 1737 with *A Treatise of Human Nature* in draft. Books I–II were published after revision in January 1739 and Book III, after correspondence and disagreements with Francis Hutcheson, in 1740. Two promotional pamphlets, *An Abstract of a Book lately Published* (1740) and *A Letter from a Gentleman to his Friend in Edinburgh* (ed. Henry Home, Lord Kames, 1745), important for later scholarship, were virtually unknown in Hume's lifetime. In 1741–2 he sought to promote a more popular persona with two volumes of *Essays Moral and Political*, combining light journalism with serious pieces, particularly some historically informed essays on politics. Disappointed with the reception of the *Treatise*, he changed his literary strategy, but temporary employment as a tutor and travels as a military and diplomatic secretary between 1745 and 1748 disrupted his writing. In *Philosophical Essays* (later *An Enquiry*) *concerning Human Understanding* (1748) and *An Enquiry concerning the Principles of Morals* (1751), Hume revised some of the substance of Books I and III of the *Treatise*, giving it new applications and reducing the psychological detail. *Political Discourses* (1752) marked a shift of interest to political economy. Attempts to secure him university appointments in 1744–5 and 1751–2 met with clerical opposition, but from 1752 to 1757 he was Keeper of the Advocates' Library at Edinburgh. This enabled him to research his greatest narrative work, the *History of England* (6 vols., 1754–62). From 1753 on, the *Essays* and *Enquiries* were promoted as parts of an integrated, frequently revised collection, *Essays and Treatises on Several Subjects*, on which his philosophical reputation for long depended. Into this was absorbed *Four Dissertations* (1757), a collection dogged by controversy over Hume's attitude to religion. His *Dialogues concerning Natural Religion*, largely written in 1751, appeared posthumously (1779). From 1763 to 1768 he was employed in government service, first at the British embassy in Paris, then in London as Undersecretary for the Northern Department, after which he retired to Edinburgh. He made contact with the *philosophes* and physiocrats of Paris, but an attempt to befriend and give British hospitality to Rousseau ended in bitterness and recrimination. In Scotland he was on intimate terms with many in the clubs and learned societies of Edinburgh and Glasgow, but only with Adam Smith did he have a lasting intellectual rapport. Much of the sharp criticism he attracted in his lifetime and posthumously was religiously motivated and ephemeral. More moderate critics, from the leaders of 'common sense' philosophy in Scotland to Kant and his contemporaries in Germany, had a stronger influence both on philosophical opinion and on the perception and interpretation of Hume's philosophy well into the next century. His political, economic, and historical writing was less the victim of fashion. There is a wealth of posthumous biographical anecdote, all of it untrustworthy.

Collected works: *The Philosophical Works of David Hume*, eds. T. H. Green and T. H. Grose, 4 vols. (London, 1874–5); *The Clarendon Edition of the Works of David Hume: The Philosophical Works*, general eds. T. L. Beauchamp, D. F. Norton, M. A. Stewart, in progress, 9 vols. (Oxford, 1998–).

Secondary Sources: J. Y. T. Greig, *David Hume* (London, 1931). E. C. Mossner, *The Life of David Hume*, 2nd edn. (Oxford, 1980). M. A. Stewart, 'The Dating of Hume's Manuscripts', in *The Scottish Enlightenment*, ed. P. B. Wood (Rochester, NY, 2000), 267–314. T. H. Huxley, *Hume* (London, 1887). N. Smith, 'The Naturalism of Hume', *Mind* 14 (1905): 149–73, 335–47. C. W. Hendel, *Studies in the Philosophy of David Hume*, (1925; 2nd edn. Indianapolis, IN, 1963). A. Leroy, *La critique et la religion chez David Hume* (Paris, 1930). J. Laird, *Hume's Philosophy of Human Nature* (London, 1932). *David Hume: Dialogues concerning Natural Religion*, ed. N. K. Smith, 2nd edn. (Edinburgh, 1945). J. Passmore, *Hume's Intentions* (1952; 3rd edn. London, 1980). L. L. Bongie, *David Hume, Prophet of the Counter-Revolution* (Oxford, 1965). R. F. Anderson, *Hume's First Principles* (Lincoln, NE, 1966). P. S. Árdal, *Passion and Value in Hume's Treatise* (Edinburgh, 1966; 2nd edn. 1989). D. Forbes, *Hume's Philosophical Politics* (Cambridge, 1975). T. Penelhum, *Hume* (London, 1975). J. L. Mackie, *Hume's Moral Theory* (London, 1980). D. Miller, *Philosophy and Ideology in Hume's Political Thought* (Oxford, 1981). J. J. Richetti, *Philosophical Writing: Locke, Berkeley, Hume* (Cambridge, MA, 1983), ch. 4. J. P. Wright, *The Sceptical Realism of David Hume* (Manchester, 1983). D. W. Livingston, *Hume's Philosophy of Common Life* (Chicago, IL, 1984). R. Fogelin, *Hume's Scepticism in the Treatise of Human Nature* (London, 1985). D. F. Norton, 'Hume, Atheism, and the Autonomy of Morals', in *Hume's Philosophy of Religion*, ed. M. Hester (Winston-Salem, NC, 1986), 97–144. J. C. A. Gaskin, *Hume's Philosophy of Religion*, 2nd edn. (London, 1988). N. Phillipson, *Hume* (London, 1989). G. Strawson, *The Secret Connexion: Causation, Realism and David Hume* (Oxford, 1989). M. A. Box, *The Suasive Art of David Hume* (Princeton, NJ, 1990). *Studies in the Philosophy of the Scottish Enlightenment*, ed. M. A. Stewart (Oxford, 1990). K. E. Yandell, *Hume's 'Inexplicable Mystery': His Views on Religion* (Philadelphia, PA,

1990). A. Baier, *A Progress of Sentiments: Reflections on Hume's Treatise* (Cambridge, MA, 1991). I. Rivers, *Reason, Grace, and Sentiment*, 2 vols. (Cambridge, 1991–2000), 2: 238–329. *The Cambridge Companion to Hume*, ed. D. F. Norton (Cambridge, 1993). *Hume and Hume's Connexions*, eds. M. A. Stewart and J. P. Wright (Edinburgh, 1994). D. Garrett, *Cognition and Commitment in Hume's Philosophy* (New York, NY, 1996). S. P. Foster, *Melancholy Duty: The Hume-Gibbon Attack on Christianity* (Dordrecht, 1997). J. A. Herdt, *Religion and Faction in Hume's Moral Philosophy* (Cambridge, 1997). M. Frasca-Spada, *Space and the Self in Hume's Treatise* (Cambridge, 1998). *Early Responses to Hume*, ed. J. Fieser, 10 vols. (Bristol, 1999–2003). *Feminist Interpretations of David Hume*, ed. A. J. Jacobson (University Park, PA, 2000). D. Owen, *Hume's Reason* (Oxford, 2000). T. Penelhum, *Themes in Hume: The Self, the Will, Religion* (Oxford, 2000). S. Buckle, *Hume's Enlightenment Tract* (Oxford, 2001). D. Townsend, *Hume's Aesthetic Theory* (London, 2001). *Reading Hume on Human Understanding*, ed. P. Millican (Oxford, 2002). J. Moore, 'Utility and Humanity: The Quest for the Honestum in Cicero, Hutcheson and Hume', *Utilitas* 14 (2002): 365–86. *The Reception of David Hume in Europe*, ed. P. H. Jones (London, forthcoming). *Impressions of Hume*, eds. M. Frasca-Spada and P. Kail (Oxford, 2005). *The Blackwell Companion to Hume*, ed. E. S. Ratcliffe (Oxford, 2005). [M. A. Stewart]

HUTCHESON, FRANCIS b. Drumalig, nr. Saintfield, County Down, Ireland 1694; d. Dublin, 1746. Moral philosopher. Educated at dissenting academy in Killyleagh, County Down, and at Glasgow University in Arts and Divinity (1710–17). Though licensed as a probationer for the Presbyterian ministry (1719), he chose to keep a dissenting academy in Dublin which he ran until elected professor of moral philosophy at Glasgow, a post he held until his death (1730–46). In Dublin he was part of the intellectual circle around the Whig leader Robert Molesworth who was close to Shaftesbury. It was in this milieu that he produced his most original works, *An Inquiry into the Original of our Ideas of Beauty and Virtue* (1725) and *An Essay on the Nature and Conduct of the Passions and Affections. With Illustrations upon the Moral Sense* (1728). These works were accompanied by important polemical articles in *The London Journal* (1724, 1725) and the *Dublin Weekly Journal* (1725–6). The call to Glasgow occasioned an inaugural lecture, *De naturali hominum socialitate oratio inauguralis* (1730). In his Glasgow position Hutcheson became an influential figure for the 'moderate literati', so central to the Scottish Enlightenment, and gained the power to thwart Hume's academic ambitions. He intervened in the debate about patronage in the Church, *Considerations on Patronage, Addressed to the Gentlemen of Scotland* (1735) and with his colleague, James Moor, he translated Marcus Aurelius, *Meditations* (1742). In 1737 he was charged by the Presbytery of Glasgow with breaching the Westminster Confession but the case was not brought to conclusion. Late in his career, Hutcheson published several textbooks which may, however, in part derive from his time in Dublin: *Philosophiae moralis institutio compendiaria* (1742, rev. edn. 1744; influential English trans., not by Hutcheson, 1747: *Short Introduction to Moral Philosophy*); *Metaphysicae synopsis* (1742); and *Logicae compendium* (posthum. 1756). An attempt at a synoptic work was ready in the late 1730s but was only published posthumously: *A System of Moral Philosophy*, 2 vols. (1755). *Collected Works and Correspondence*, gen. ed. K. Haakonssen (Indianapolis, IN, 2003–).

Secondary Sources: William Leechman, 'Account of the Life, Writings, and Character of the Author', in Hutcheson, *System of Moral Philosophy*, vol. 1. W. R. Scott, *Francis Hutcheson: His Life, Teaching and Position in the History of Philosophy* (Cambridge, 1900). D. D. Raphael, *The Moral Sense* (Oxford, 1947), ch. 2. C. Robbins, ''When It Is that Colonies May Turn Independent': An Analysis of the Environment and Politics of Francis Hutcheson' (1954), in *Absolute Liberty: A Selection of the Articles and Papers of Caroline Robbins*, ed. B. Taft (Hamden, CT, 1982). W. Frankena, 'Hutcheson's Moral Sense Theory' *Journal of the History of Ideas* 16 (1955): 356–75. P. Kivy, *The Seventh Sense: A Study of Francis Hutcheson's Aesthetics* (New York, NY, 1976; 2nd edn., Oxford, 2003). D. F. Norton, 'Francis Hutcheson in America', *Studies in Voltaire and the Eighteenth Century* 154 (1976): 1547–68. W. Leidhold, *Ethik und Politik bei Francis Hutcheson* (Stuttgart, 1983). K. P. Winkler, 'Hutcheson's Alleged Realism', *Journal of the History of Philosophy* 23 (1985): 174–94. D. F. Norton, 'Hutcheson and Moral Realism', ib.: 397–418. J. Moore, 'The Two Systems of Francis Hutcheson: On the Origins of the Scottish Enlightenment', in *Studies in the Philosophy of the Scottish Enlightenment*, ed. M. A. Stewart (Oxford, 1990), 37–59. *Francis Hutcheson: A Supplement to Fortnight*, ed. D. Smyth (Belfast, 1992). T. Mautner, Introduction, in F. Hutcheson, *On Human Nature*, ed. T. Mautner (Cambridge, 1993), 3–87. J. Moore, 'Hume and Hutcheson', in *Hume and Hume's Connections*, eds. M. A. Stewart and J. P. Wright (Edinburgh, 1995), 23–57. J. Bishop, 'Moral Motivation and the Development of Francis Hutcheson's Philosophy', *Journal of the History of Ideas* 57 (1996): 277–95. K. Haakonssen, *Natural Law and Moral Philosophy: From Grotius to the Scottish Enlightenment* (Cambridge, 1996), ch. 2. J. Moore, 'Hutcheson's Theodicy: The Argument and the Contexts of *A System of Moral Philosophy*', in *The Scottish Enlightenment. Essays in Reinterpretation*, ed. P. B. Wood (Rochester, NY, 2000): 239–66. P. J. E. Kail, 'Hutcheson's Moral Sense: Skepticism, Realism and Secondary Qualities', *History of Philosophy Quarterly* 18 (2001): 57–77. M. Brown, *Francis Hutcheson in Dublin, 1719–30. The Crucible of His Thought* (Dublin, 2002). J. Moore, 'Unity and Humanity: The Quest for the *Honestum* in Cicero, Hutcheson, and Hume', *Utilitas* 14 (2002): 365–86. [Knud Haakonssen]

Iselin, Isaak b. Basel, Switzerland, 1728; d. Basel, 1782. Philosopher of history and politics. Having studied law and philosophy at the Universities of Basel and Göttingen, he became secretary (Ratschreiber) of the republic of Basel (1756). Influenced by J. J. Bodmer and A. v. Haller, he advocated a republican concept of politics: *Philosophische und patriotische Träume eines Menschenfreundes* (1755). Growing opposition to Rousseau and critical reception of Montesquieu's *De l'ésprit des lois* led to several revisions of this work (in *Vermischte Schriften*) and to the *Philosophische und politische Versuche* (1760) and culminated in *Über die Geschichte der Menschheit* (1764), a cautiously optimistic philosophy of history. I. was a co-founder of the *Helvetic Society*, the first national reform society in Switzerland. He published numerous articles in the *Allgemeine Deutsche Bibliothek* (1766–79), maintained a vast network of correspondence, and collaborated with and promoted I. B. Basedow's ideas of 'philanthropic' education. His reception of the French physiocrats, documented in the *Versuch über die gesellige Ordnung* (1772), led to the influential journal *Ephemeriden der Menschheit* (1776–8, 1780–2, continued by W. G. Becker until 1786) that was modelled on the physiocrats' *Ephémerides du citoyen*. *Träume eines Menschenfreundes* (1776) is a revised summary of his main works. No standard edition available. *Profile der Aufklärung: Friedrich Nicolai-Isaak Iselin, Briefwechsel (1767–82)*, ed. H. Jacob-Friesen (Bern, Haupt, 1997).

Secondary Sources: U. Im Hof, *Isaak Iselin. Sein Leben und die Entwicklung seines Denkens bis zur Abfassung der 'Geschichte der Menschheit' von 1764*, 2 vols. (Basel, 1947). U. Im Hof, *Isaak Iselin und die Spätaufklärung* (Bern, 1967). D. Brühlmeier, 'Isaak Iselin and the Call for Civic Virtue: A Model of Swiss Republicanism', in *Revolution and Enlightenment in Europe*, ed. T. O'Hagan (Aberdeen, 1991), 69–79. F. Oz-Salzberger, *Translating the Enlightenment: Scottish Civic Discourse in Eighteenth-Century Germany* (Oxford, 1995), 169–89. [Simone Zurbuchen]

Jacobi, Friedrich Heinrich b. Düsseldorf, 1743; d. Munich, 1819. Man of letters, businessman, public servant. Educated in Geneva, where he became acquainted with Bonnet and French and Scottish thought. A friend of Hamann and Lavater, he joined Goethe and Herder in opposing the Enlightenment but rejected what he regarded as their Spinozism. Between 1775 and 1779 he published installments of two philosophical novels, later published as *Eduard Allwills Briefsammlung* (1792) and *Woldemar* (1794). Thanks to his *Über die Lehre des Spinoza, in Briefen an Herrn*

Moses Mendelssohn (1785) and *Friedrich Heinrich Jacobi wider Mendelssohns Beschuldigungen betreffend die Briefe über die Lehre des Spinoza* (1786), he entered a heated exchange – catalyst of the *Pantheismusstreit* – with Mendelssohn over Lessing's alleged Spinozism. In the anti-Kantian dialogue, *David Hume über den Glauben oder Idealismus und Realismus* (1787), he defended his faith-based realism and a conception of self and thought founded upon community, history, and feelings. Though his writings influenced reactions against Kant's philosophy, his criticism of idealism also led to polemics with German idealists, notably in *Jacobi an Fichte* (1799) and *Von den Göttlichen Dingen und ihrer Offenbarung* (1811). Standard, complete edition: *Werke*, eds. J. F. Köppen and C. J. F. Roth, 6 vols. (Leipzig, 1812–25, repr. Darmstadt, 1968).

Secondary Sources: Comprehensive bibliography in *The Main Philosophical Writings and the Novel Allwill*, trans. and ed. G. di Giovanni (Montreal and Kingston, 1994). G. W. F. Hegel, 'Glauben und Wissen, oder die Reflexionphilosophie der Subjektivität, in der Vollständigkeit ihrer Formen, als Kantische, Jacobische, und Fichtesche Philosophie', *Kritische Journal* 11.1 (1802): 3–413. G. Baum, *Vernunft und Erkenntnis. Die Philosophie F. H. Jacobis* (Bonn, 1969). *F. H. Jacobi: Philosoph und Literat der Goethezeit*, ed. K. Hammacher (Frankfurt am Main, 1971). [Daniel Dahlstrom]

JEFFERSON, THOMAS b. Shadwell, Virginia, 1743; d. Monticello, Virginia, 1826. Political theorist, amateur scientist, plantation owner, 3rd President of the United States. Educated at the College of William and Mary, then studied and practiced law and was elected to House of Burgesses in 1768. His career as the major American theorist of rights began with 'A Summary View of the Rights of British America' (1774). After election to second Continental Congress (1775), he drafted the Declaration of Independence (1776), followed by the 'Virginia Statute of Religious Freedom', the archetypical American statement on religious freedoms (1777, passed in 1786). *Notes on the State of Virginia* (1787) engaged with the French Enlightenment including Buffon's disparagement of New World flora and fauna. He was Governor of Virginia (1779–81), trade commissioner and minister to France (1784–9), Secretary of State (1790–3), Vice President (1797–1801), and President (1801–9). Many major contributions to American intellectual life include foundation of the University of Virginia, a remarkable book collection that became the core of the Library of Congress, and his promotion of scientific culture and invention. He and Franklin were the major conduits of the French and Scottish Enlightenment in America. Much of his thought is in his correspondence: *The Papers of Thomas Jefferson*, eds. J. P. Boyd, C. T. Cullen, and J. Catanzariti (Princeton, NJ, 1950–). *The Writings of Thomas Jefferson*, ed. P. L. Ford, 10 vols. (New York, NY, 1892–9). *The Writings of Thomas Jefferson*, eds. A. L. Lipscomb and A. E. Bergh, 20 vols. (Washington, DC, 1903–4).

Secondary Sources: D. Malone, *Jefferson and his Time*, 6 vols. (Boston, MA, 1948–81). *Thomas Jefferson: A Comprehensive, Annotated Bibliography of Writings about Him, 1826–1997*, ed. F. Shuffelton, (online at http://etext.lib.virginia.edu/jefferson/bibliog). A. Koch, *The Philosophy of Thomas Jefferson* (New York, NY, 1943). E. T. Martin, *Thomas Jefferson: Scientist* (New York, NY, 1952). G. Wills, *Inventing America: Jefferson's Declaration of Independence* (New York, NY, 1978). R. Ferguson 'Mysterious Obligation: Jefferson's Notes on the State of Virginia' in *Law and Letters in American Culture* (Cambridge, MA, 1984): 34–58. C. A. Miller, *Jefferson and Nature: An Interpretation* (Baltimore, MD, 1988). G. W. Sheldon, *The Political Philosophy of Thomas Jefferson* (Baltimore, MD, 1991). [Aaron Garrett]

JENYNS, SOAME b. London, 1704; d. London, 1787. Literary man and MP (1742–80). Educated at St. John's College, Cambridge (1722–5). Three works are of philosophical interest, *Free Inquiry into the Nature and Origin of Evil* (1757) (cf. Johnson's review in his *Literary Magazine*), *A View of the Internal Evidence of the Christian Religion* (1776), and *Disquisitions on Several Subjects* (1782).

Standard collection, including poetry and political writings: *Works*, 4 vols. (London, 1790) with biographical memoir by the editor, C. Nalson Cole.

Secondary Sources: R. Rompkey, *Soame Jenyns* (Boston, MA, 1984). [Knud Haakonssen]

Justi, Johann Heinrich Gottlob von b. Brücken near Sangerhausen, Thüringen; d. in prison, 1771. Writer and cameralist. Educated at the university of Wittenberg. His teacher in jurisprudence was Augustin Leyser (1683–1752). In 1744 he defended his doctoral dissertation *De fuga militiae*. It remains unclear whether he continued his studies in Göttingen, Jena, or Leipzig. Made his living as writer and as editor of a journal. In 1747 he won the famous prize contest about the doctrine of the monads launched by the Prussian Academy of Sciences. He argued that the Leibnizian doctrine of monads was unfounded. From 1750 to 1753 he was professor of German eloquence in Vienna. He also taught courses on financial, commercial, fiscal, cameral, and mining affairs. In 1755 he was appointed police commissioner (*Ober Policey-Commisarius*) in Göttingen and later elected Royal British mining councillor (Bergrat). At the same time as J. S. Pütter (1725–1807) and J. J. Schmauss (1690–1757) he taught state economy and natural history at the university of Göttingen (1755–7). Around 1760 he settled in Berlin. In 1765 he was appointed mining captain responsible for the general supervision of mining and metallurgy in the Prussian States. Accused of embezzlement of public money in 1768, he was imprisoned. His work comprises more than 60 independent publications. His most important works are *Staatswirthschaft*, 2 vols. (1755; reprint of the 2nd edn. [1758] 1963) and *Grundsätze der Policeywissenschaft* (1756; reprint of the 3rd edn. [1782] 1969). They belong to the most influential textbooks (*Lehrbücher*) exposing the new science of cameralism.

Secondary Sources: J. Brückner, *Staatswissenschaften, Kameralismus und Naturrecht* (Munich, 1977). V. Bauer, *Hofökonomie. Der Diskurs über den Fürstenhof in Zeremonialwissenschaft, Hausväterliteratur und Kameralismus* (Vienna, 1997). F. Frensdorff, *Über das Leben und die Schriften des Nationalökonomen J. H. G. von Justi* (Göttingen, 1903; reprint 1970). M. Obert, *Die naturrechtliche 'politische Metaphysik' des Johann Heinrich Gottlob von Justi (1717–1771)* (Frankfurt am Main, 1992). K. Tribe, *Governing Economy. The Reformation of German Economic Discourse 1750–1840* (Cambridge, 1988). [Simone Zurbuchen]

Kames, Lord – see Home, Henry

Kant, Immanuel b. Königsberg, 1724; d. Königsberg, 1804. Educated at Collegium Fridericianum, a pietist school in Königsberg, and studied philosophy at the University of Königsberg. Private tutor; 1755, lecturer at the University of Königsberg; fifteen years later, professor of Logic and Metaphysics there. During this time, he wrote a number of smaller works that secured him a solid reputation, most importantly: *Allgemeine Naturgeschichte und Theorie des Himmels*; *Principiorum primorum cognitionis metaphysicae nova dilucidatio* (*A New Elucidation of the First Principles of Metaphysical Cognition*); *Metaphysica cum geometria iunctae usus in philosophia naturalis, cuius specimen I. continet monadologiam physicam* (*Physical Monadology*); *Die falsche Spitzfindigkeit der vier syllogistischen Figuren erwiesen*; *Der einzig mögliche Beweisgrund zu einer Demonstration des Daseins Gottes*; *Versuch den Begriff der negativen Größen in die Weltweisheit einzuführen*; *Untersuchungen über die Deutlichkeit der Grundsätze der natürlichen Theologie und der Moral*; *Beobachtungen über das Gefühl des Schönen und Erhabenen*; *Träume eines Geistersehers, erläutert durch Träume der Metaphysik*. In 1770 Kant published his Inaugural Dissertation *De mundi sensibilis atque intelligibilis forma et principiis* (*On the Form and Principles of the Sensible and the Intelligible World*), in which he for the first time gave a glimpse of what his mature philosophy would look like. After a period of relative silence that lasted more than ten years – during which he worked hard on the development of what later became known as his critical philosophy – he published *Kritik der reinen Vernunft* (1781); *Prolegomena zu einer jeden künftigen Methaphysik* (1783); *Grundlegung zur Metaphysik der Sitten* (1785); *Metaphysische Anfangsgründe der Naturwissenschaft* (1786); *Kritik der praktischen Vernunft* (1788); *Kritik der Urtheilskraft* (1790); *Die Religion innerhalb der Grenzen der bloßen Vernunft* (1792); *Metaphysische Anfangsgründe der Rechtslehre* (1797); and *Metaphysische Anfangsgründe der Tugendlehre* (1797). These are the works for which he is famous today and for which he will continue to be known as long as philosophy is done. The best collected edition: *Immanuel Kant, Gesammelte Schriften, Akademieausgabe* (Berlin, 1902–). *The Cambridge Edition of the Works of Immanuel Kant*, eds. P. Guyer and A. W. Wood (Cambridge, 1992–) offers the best English translations. Kant's work can be seen as addressing three main questions: What can I know? What shall I do? And, What can I hope for? His answer to the first question is that we can know only what we encounter in experience. He means to show not only that the speculations of philosophers in the past and present about the true nature of reality are highly questionable and based on invalid arguments as well as insufficient evidence, but also that the only true metaphysics is about the conditions that make experience possible. These conditions are essentially connected with three human faculties, the senses, the understanding, and reason, each of which has specific 'forms'. The senses are characterised by the forms of space and time. Though we cannot but experience things spatially and temporally, this does not mean that things themselves are in space and time. Indeed, they can be neither spatial nor temporal just because space and time are forms of our senses ('intuition'). The forms of the understanding (the 'categories') are valid only with respect to the materials given in the senses. They are independent of experience and precede experience, that is, a priori, and allow us to think about the world, but only about the world of experience. In his ethical theory Kant is an intellectualist or rationalist and opposed to any kind of eudaimonism. Central in this account is the 'categorical imperative' that enjoins us to ask whether the maxim of our action can be universalised. Maxims have moral worth only if they can be so universalised. Kant's philosophy of religion is clearly influenced by the enlightenment view that religion amounts ultimately to a primitive (meaning, a more simple and more easily understandable) form of morality. *Kritik der Urtheilskraft* is an attempt to show that there are a priori forms even in teleological and aesthetic contexts that often are understood as simply having to do with feeling.

Secondary Sources: M. Kuehn, *Immanuel Kant: A Biography* (Cambridge, 2001). E. Cassirer, *Kant's Leben und Lehre* (1918), trans. J. Haden (New Haven, CT and London, 1981). N. Kemp Smith, *A Commentary on Kant's 'Critique of Pure Reason'* (London, 1918). H. J. Paton, *Kant's Metaphysic of Experience: A Commentary on the First Half of the Kritik der reinen Vernunft* (London, 1936). L. W. Beck, *A Commentary on Kant's Critique of Practical Reason* (Chicago, IL, 1960). H.-J. de Vleeschauwer, *The Development of Kantian Thought: The History of a Doctrine*, trans. A. R. C. Duncan (London, 1962). M. J. Gregor, *Laws of Freedom: A Study of Kant's Method of Applying the Categorical Imperative in the Metaphysik der Sitten* (Oxford, 1963). P. Guyer, *Kant and the Claims of Taste* (Cambridge, MA, 1979). K. Ameriks, *Kant's Theory of Mind: An Analysis of the Paralogisms of Pure Reason* (Oxford and New York, NY, 1982). H. E. Allison, *Kant's Transcendental Idealism: An Interpretation and Defense* (New Haven, CT and London, 1986). P. Guyer, *Kant and the Claims of Knowledge* (Cambridge, 1987). O. O'Neill, *Constructions of Reason: Explorations of Kant's Practical Philosophy* (Cambridge, 1989). R. L. Velkley, *Freedom and the End of Reason: On the Moral Foundation of Kant's Critical Philosophy* (Chicago, IL, 1989). H. E. Allison, *Kant's Theory of Freedom* (Cambridge, 1990). M. Friedman, *Kant and the Exact Sciences* (Cambridge, MA, 1992). W. Kersting, *Wohlgeordnete Freiheit. Immanuel Kants Rechts- und Staatsphilosophie* (2nd edn. Frankfurt am Main, 1993). A. Quinton, 'The Trouble with Kant', *Philosophy* 72 (1997): 5–18. *Kant's Groundwork of the Metaphysics of Morals: Critical Essays*, ed. P. Guyer (Lanham, MD, 1998). A. W. Wood, *Kant's Ethical Thought* (Cambridge, 1999). H. E. Allison, *Kant's*

Theory of Taste: A Reading of the Critique of Aesthetic Judgment (Cambridge, 2001). [Manfred Kühn]

King, William b. County Antrim, 1650; d. Dublin, 1729. Anglican Archbishop of Dublin and philosophical theologian. King attended Trinity College Dublin (BA 1670, MA 1673, DD 1689) where he left Presbyterianism for the Anglican Church, rising through the ranks while spiritedly engaged in polemics, with Catholics, Presbyterians and fellow Anglicans. K. was elected Dean of St. Patrick's in 1689, and as de facto leader of the Anglican community – and outspoken Jacobite opponent – twice imprisoned. After the victory of William III and the Revolution Settlement, K. became Bishop of Derry (1791) and Archbishop of Dublin (1703). He was a member of the Dublin Philosophical Society and, like his friend William Molyneux, spread philosophical and scientific culture and Irish nationalism in the Protestant community. *De Origine Mali* (1702), a celebrated providentialist theodicy, influenced many, including Hutcheson and Pope, and led to further polemics, most notably by Pierre Bayle. John Gay's introduction to William Law's English translation, *An Essay on the Origin of Evil* (1731) is considered a foundational text of utilitarianism. K. developed some of his ideas in *Divine Predestination and Foreknowledge* (1709).

Secondary Sources: *Archbishop King's Sermon on Predestination*, ed. A.Carpenter (Dublin, 1976). P. O'Regan, *Archbishop William King (1650–1729) and the Constitution in Church and State* (Dublin, 2000). J. Moore, 'Hutcheson's Theodicy: The Arguments and the Contexts of *A System of Moral Philosophy*', in *The Scottish Enlightenment: Essays in Reinterpretation*, ed. P. B. Wood (Rochester, NY, 2000). [Aaron Garrett]

Klein, Ernst Ferdinand b. Breslau, 1744; d. Berlin, 1810. Jurist and legal theorist. Studied law with Christian Wolff's disciple Daniel Nettelbladt at Halle; practiced law in Breslau. Called to Berlin in 1781, where he served in Prussian justice department and collaborated with Carl Gottlieb Svarez on the *Allgemeines Landrecht*, a major project of enlightened legal reform. Active in the *Mittwochsgesellschaft*, a secret society of 'Friends of Enlightenment' whose membership included many important figures in the Berlin Enlightenment. *Freyheit und Eigenthum* (1790), his commentary on the deliberations in the French National Assembly was cast in the form of a series of dialogues between members of the society. Left Berlin in 1791 to assume directorship at Halle. Returned in 1800 as Upper Court Councillor. His writings include *Grundsätze des gemeinen deutschen und preussischen peinlichen Rechts* (1796); *Grundsätze der natürlichen Rechtswissenschaft* (1797); along with essays on law and politics for a lay audience in the *Berlinische Monatsschrift*, a journal linked to the *Mittwochsgesellschaft*.

Secondary Sources: E. Hellmuth, 'Ernst Ferdinand Klein: Politische Reflexionen im Preußen der Spätaufklärung', in *Aufklärung als Politisierung – Politisierung der Aufklärung*, eds. H. E. Bödeker and U. Hermann (Hamburg, 1987): and E. Hellmuth, 'Ernst Ferdinand Klein (1744–1810)', *Aufklärung* 2 (1987): 121–3. [James Schmidt]

Knutzen, Martin b. Königsberg, 1713; d. Königsberg, 1751. Studied philosophy, mathematics, and physics in Königsberg from 1728; MA with *Dissertatio metaphysica de aeternitate mundi impossibili* (1733); in 1734 Professor extraordinary for Logic and Metaphysics. Like his teacher Schultz, he taught a combination of pietism and Wolffianism, but British empirism (Locke) also had impact on him. Believed in the immateriality of the soul and tried to prove that Leibniz' thesis of pre-established harmony was wrong; instead he argued that the body has a physical impact on the soul (*influxus physicus*). Kant studied with Knutzen from 1740 and tutored other students on subjects covered in the latter's lectures. His main works are: *Systema causarum efficientium seu commentatio philosophica de commercio mentis et corporis per influxum physicum explicando* (2nd edn. 1745);

Philosophischer Beweis von der Wahrheit der christlichen Religion (1740); *Philosophische Abhandlung von der immateriellen Natur der Seele* (1744, in Latin 1741); *Vernünftige Gedanken von den Cometen* (1744); *Elementa philosophiae rationalis seu logicae cum generalis tum specialioris mathematica methodo demonstrata* (1747).

Secondary Sources: B. Erdmann, *Martin Knutzen und seine Zeit* (Leipzig, 1876). L. Cramer, ' Kants rationale Psychologie und ihre Vorgänger', *Vierteljahresschrift für wissenschaftliche Philosophie und Soziologie* 39, NF 14 (1915): 1–37, 201–51. F. Holz,'Knutzen, Martin', *Neue Deutsche Biographie* 12 (Berlin, 1980): 231–32. H.-J. Waschkies, *Physik und Physikotheologie des jungen Kant* (Amsterdam, 1987). *Die Schule Immanuel Kants*, ed. H. F. Klemme (Hamburg, 1994). A. Laywine, 'Martin Knutzen', *Routledge Encyclopedia of Philosophy*, ed. E. Craig, Vol. 5 (London, 1998): 287–89. [Heiner F. Klemme]

LAGRANGE, JOSEPH LOUIS b. Turin, 1736; d. Paris, 1813. French-Italian mathematician and theoretical physicist. Driven by a reductionist vision of freeing the science of mechanics from metaphysical assumptions, he attempted a grand synthesis that reduced mechanics to geometry (mentioning forces as little as possible), and then reduced geometry to algebra. His work in algebra initiated group theory, the first part of modern abstract algebra. His complete works were published as *Oeuvres de Lagrange*, 14 vols. (Paris, 1867–92).

Secondary Sources: J. Itard, 'Lagrange', *Dictionary of Scientific Biography* 7: 559–73. C. Truesdell, *Essays in the History of Mechanics* (Berlin, 1968), ch. 2. C. G. Fraser, 'Lagrange's Analytical Mathematics, Its Cartesian Origins and Reception in Comte's Positive Philosophy', *Studies in History and Philosophy of Science* 21 (1990): 234–56. T. Christidis, 'Philosophical and Mathematical Premises to the Development of Mechanics of Lagrange', *Nonlinear Analysis* 30 (1997): 2107–12. [James Franklin]

LAMARCK, JEAN-BAPTISTE-PIERRE-ANTOINE DE MONET DE b. Bazentin, Picardy (France) 1744; d. Paris, 1829. Botanist, invertebrate zoologist, early evolutionist. Educated Jesuit College, Amiens; military officer 1761–68; some medical study in Paris. Member of the *Académie royale des sciences*. In his first major work, *Flore françoise* (3 vols., 1778), he developed a serial classification of the plants and a method of identification by dichotomous keys. Became an understudy of Buffon at the Paris *Jardin du roi*. With the reorganization of the *Jardin* as the *Muséum national d'histoire naturelle* in 1793, he obtained the new chair of *Vers*. From this position he began a major reorganization of the miscellaneous groups of 'bloodless' animals into the 'animals without vertebrae', using a similar principle of linear classification to that which he previously employed in botany. In *Muséum* lectures of 1800, he first put forth his claim that the serial ordering of forms from simple to complex was also their historical order of genesis by derivation, the basis of his transformist theory, first developed in his *Recherches sur l'organisation des corps vivans* (1802, and expanded in his *Philosophie zoologie* (1809). Defined many of the main groups of invertebrates currently recognized (*Histoire naturelle des animaux sans vertèbres* [1st edn., 1815–22]). His transformism was opposed by his colleague Georges Cuvier. Best known for his use-disuse mechanism of evolutionary transformism.

Secondary Sources: R. Burhardt, Jr., *The Spirit of System: Lamarck and Evolutionary Biology* (Cambridge, MA, 1977). P. Corsi *The Age of Lamarck* (Berkeley, CA, 1988; extensively revised as *Lamarck: Genèse et enjeux du transformisme, 1770–1830* [Paris, 2001]). *Jean-Baptiste Lamarck*, ed. G. Laurent (Paris, 1997). [Phillip R. Sloan]

LAMBERT, JOHANN HEINRICH b. Mühlhausen, Alsace, 1728; d. Berlin, 1777. Physicist, mathematician, philosopher, and astronomer; never studied at a university. Tutor to a Swiss family

(1748–58); went to Berlin (1764) and became a member of the Academy of Science (1765). Made a number of scientific discoveries. Influenced by Locke and Wolff, he tried to introduce the standards of mathematics into philosophy through conceptual analysis and the deductive method. His main philosophical works are: *Neues Organon oder Gedanken über die Erforschung und Bezeichnung des Wahren und dessen Unterscheidung vom Irrthum und Schein*, 2 vols. (Leipzig, 1764) and *Anlage zur Architectonic, oder Theorie des Einfachen und Ersten in der philosophischen und mathematischen Erkenntniß*, 2 vols. (Riga, 1771). Other works: *Cosmologische Briefe über die Einrichtung des Weltbaus* (Ausgburg, 1761); *Deutscher gelehrter Briefwechsel*, ed. J. Bernoulli, 5 vols. (Berlin, 1787); *Abhandlung vom Criterium veritatis*, ed. K. Bopp (Berlin, 1915); *Über die Methode, die Metaphysik, Theologie und Moral richtiger zu beweisen*, ed. K. Bopp (Berlin, 1918); *Philosophische Schriften*, ed. H.-W. Arndt, 9 vols. (Hildesheim 1965–9); *Texte zur Systematologie und zur Theorie der wissenschaftlichen Erkenntnis*, ed. G. Siegwart (Hamburg, 1988); *Neues Organon*, ed. G. Schenk (Berlin, 1990).

Secondary Sources: L. W. Beck, *Early German Philosophy: Kant and His Predecessors* (Cambridge, MA, 1969): 402–12. M. Steck, *Bibliographia Lambertiana* (Hildesheim, 1970). C. J. Scriba, 'Johann Heinrich Lambert', *Dictionary of Scientific Biography*, ed. C. C. Gillispie, Vol. 8 (New York, NY, 1973): 595–600. G. Wolters, *Basis und Deduktion: Studien zur Entstehung und Bedeutung der Theorie der axiomatischen Methode bei J. H. Lambert (1728–1777)* (Berlin and New York, NY, 1980). F. Todesco, *Riforma della metafisica e sapere scientifico: Saggio su J. H. Lambert (1728–1777)* (Milan, 1987). *Lambert-Index*, ed. N. Hinske, 4 vols. (Stuttgart-Bad Cannstatt, 1983–7). G. L. Schiewer, *Cognitio symbolica: Lamberts semiotische Wissenschaft und ihre Diskussion bei Herder, Jean Paul und Novalis* (Tübingen, 1996). G. Zoeller, 'Johann Heinrich Lambert', *Routledge Encyclopedia of Philosophy*, ed. E. Craig, Vol. 5 (London, 1998): 350–2. [Heiner F. Klemme]

La Mettrie, Julien Offray de b. Saint-Malo, France, 1709; d. Potsdam, 1751. Physician, physiologist, philosopher. Born in a prosperous family, studied medicine in Paris 1728–33, at Rheims, and at Leiden under Hermann Boerhaave, whose works he later made known in French translation. Served as army doctor 1743–6. The materialism of his *Histoire naturelle de l'âme* (1745) caused a scandal, and he sought exile in Holland, 1747, but *L'homme machine* (1748) forced him to move on to Berlin at the invitation of Frederick II. *L'homme plante* (1748); *Sur l'origine des animaux* (1750); *Discours sur le bonheur* (1750); *Système d'Epicure* (1750). *Oeuvres philosophiques* (1751); *Oeuvres philosophiques*, 2 vols. (1774, repr. Hildesheim/New York, NY, 1970); *Oeuvres philosophiques*, 3 vols. (Berlin and Paris, 1796).

Secondary Sources: R. Bossier, *La Mettrie, médecin, pamphlétaire et philosophe (1709–1751)* (Paris, 1931). *La Mettrie's 'L'Homme Machine'. A Study in the Origins of an Idea*, ed. A. Vartanian (Princeton, NJ, 1960). E. Callot, *La philosophie de la vie au XVIIIe siècle, etudiée chez Fontenelle, Montesquieu, Maupertuis, La Mettrie, Diderot, d'Holbach, Linné* (Paris, 1965) 195–244. A. Thomson, *Materialism and Society in the Mid-Eighteenth Century: La Mettrie's 'Discours préliminaire'* (Geneva, 1981). K. A. Wellman, *La Mettrie: Medicine, Philosophy, and Enlightenment* (Durham, NC, 1992). A. Thomson, Introduction in, La Mettrie, *Machine Man and Other Writings*, trans. and ed. A. Thomson (Cambridge, 1996). C. Morilhat, *La Mettrie, un matérialisme radical* (Paris, 1997). U. P. Jauch, *Jenseits der Maschine: Philosophie, Ironie und Ästhetik bei Julien Offray de la Mettrie (1709–1751)* (Munich, 1998). [Hans Aarsleff]

Lange, Johann Joachim b. Gardelegen, 1670; d. Halle, 1744. Theologian and philosopher. Educated in Leipzig, Erfurt, and Halle, he was strongly influenced by Christian Thomasius and by the pietist August Hermann Francke. As professor of theology in Halle from 1709, he was, along with Buddeus, one of the main opponents of Christian Wolff. His main works are *Medicina mentis* (1704) and *Causa Dei et religionis naturalis adversum atheismum* (1723; reprinted in Wolff, *Werke*, III.17 (Hildesheim and New York, NY, 1984).

Secondary Sources: M. Wundt, *Die deutsche Schulphilosophie im Zeitalter der Aufklärung* (Hildesheim, 1945), 75–82. B. Bianco, 'Libertà e fatalismo. Sulla polemica tra Joachim Lange e Christian Wolff', *Verifiche* 15 (1986): 43–89 (German trans. in *Halle. Aufklärung und Pietismus*, ed. N. Hinske. Heidelberg, 1989: 111–55). [Luca Fonnesu]

LAPLACE, PIERRE-SIMON, MARQUIS DE b. Beaumont-en-Auge, France, 1749; d. Paris, 1827. The leading mathematical physicist of the century after Newton. He held great power over the official world of science and higher education in the Napoleonic era. Briefly Minister of the Interior under Napoleon, he was made a marquis after the Restoration. His philosophical influence resulted from popularizations of his work for a generally educated audience, *Exposition du système du monde* (1796) and *Essai philosophique sur les probabilités* (1814; *A Philosophical Essay on Probabilities*, New York, NY, 1995). His work on celestial mechanics showed how the solar system could be stable, and so needed no God to occasionally rewind it; it also bequeathed to philosophy a seductive picture of a deterministic universe whose future would be inferable exactly by an infinitely powerful intelligence. In probability theory, he largely founded statistical inference or 'inverse probability', the inferring of causes from events. *Oeuvres complètes*, 14 vols. (Paris, 1878–1912).

Secondary Sources: C. C. Gillispie, *Pierre-Simon Laplace, 1749–1827: A Life in Exact Science* (Princeton, NJ, 1997): [James Franklin]

LAVATER, JOHANN KASPAR b. 1741, Zürich; d.1801, Zürich. Protestant pastor and founder of physiognomics. Pastor of St Peter's Church in Zürich apart from a period at Basel, where he was exiled for objecting to the violence of the French Directory. As part of his quest to demonstrate the effects of the divine in human affairs he devoted himself to the study of human features as instances of the way in which the spirit interacted with the body. The result of his investigations was his *Physiognomische Fragmente zur Beförderung der Menschenkenntnis und Menschenliebe*, 4 vols. (1775–8), a work that attracted much notice throughout Europe.

Secondary Sources: G. Luginbühl-Weber, *Johann Kaspar Lavater, Charles Bonnet, Jacob Bennelle: Briefe, 1768–1790. Ein Forschungsbetrag zur Aufklärung in der Schweiz*, 2 vols. (Bern, 1997). G. Brooks and R. Johnson, 'Johann Caspar Lavater's "Essays on physiognomy"', *Psychological Reports* 46 (1980): 3–20. L. P. d'Amico, 'L'antropologia di Lavater e Gall nella 'Fenomenologia dello spirito" in *La Storia della Filosofia come Sapere Critico: Studi Offerti a Mario Dal Pra*, 446–56. M. Shortland, 'Skin Deep: Barthes, Lavater and the Legible Body', *Economy and Society* 14 (1985): 273–312. J. Stemmler, 'The Physiognomical Portraits of Johann Caspar Lavater', *Art Bulletin* 75 (1993): 151–68. K. Flavell, 'Mapping Faces: National Physiognomies as Cultural Prediction', *Eighteenth-Century Life* 18 (1994): 8–12. [John Gascoigne]

LAVOISIER, ANTOINE-LAURENT b. Paris 1743; d. Paris, 1794. Chemist, physiologist, geologist, public official. Educated at *Collège de Quatre Nations*, with degree in law (1763). Early interest in geology and minerology and early work in chemistry began from this work in minerology. Member of *Académie royale des sciences*. Became the primary architect of the 'Chemical Revolution' of the late eighteenth century that commenced with his inquiries into combustion and the chemistry of gases. This eventually led to his discovery of the elemental nature of oxygen gas and the nature of air in a series of landmark papers between 1772–7. Initiated a major transformation of physiology in collaborative work with Pierre-Simon Laplace (1781–3), using an ice calorimeter in which they worked out quantitative relations between respiration, combustion, the transformation of gases, and heat production. Main reform of chemical nomenclature commenced with the collaborative *Méthode de nomenclature chimique* (Paris, 1787; English translation, London, 1788). His best-known work the *Traité élémentaire de chimie* (Paris, 1789, English translation, Edinburgh, 1790). Executed by guillotine during the Terror for his work as a member of the Farmers-general.

Secondary Sources: H. Guerlac, *Lavoisier: The Crucial Year* (New York, NY, 1990). A. Donovan, *Antoine Lavoisier: Science, Administration, and Revolution* (Oxford, 1993). *Lavoisier in European Context*, eds. B. Bensaude-Vincent and F. Abbri (Canton, MA, 1995). J. P. Poirier, *Lavoisier, Chemist, Biologist, Economist* (Philadelphia, PA, 1996). F. L. Holmes, *Antoine Lavoisier, the Next Crucial Year, or the Sources of His Quantitative Method in Chemistry* (Princeton, NJ, 1998). [Phillip R. Sloan]

LAW, EDMUND b. Cartmel, Lancashire, 1703; d. Carlisle, 1787. Anglican divine, Lockean protagonist. Educated at St. John's College, Cambridge (BA 1723, MA 1727, DD 1754); ordained in 1727, he held several ecclesiastical positions before becoming Master of Peterhouse (1756), Knightsbridge Professor of Moral Philosophy at Cambridge (1764), and Bishop of Carlisle (1769). In association with Daniel Waterland, John Gay, and other Cambridge men who rejected the ideas of Samuel Clarke, he combined Lockean epistemology with religious utilitarianism, the latter deriving from William King whose *De origine mali* (1702) he translated with extensive notes as *An Essay on the Origin of Evil*, with a 'Prefatory Dissertation' by John Gay (1731). More systematic presentations were *Enquiry into the Ideas of Space, Time, Immensity, and Eternity* (1734), *Considerations on the State of the World with Regard to the Theory of Religion* (1745), *Defence of Mr. Locke's Opinions concerning Personal Identity* (1769), and *Considerations of the Propriety of Religious Subscription* (anon., 1774). These works have been reprinted, with introduction by V. Nuovo (Bristol, 1997). Law issued an edition of *The Works of John Locke* (1777).

Secondary Sources: W. Paley, *A Short Memoir of Life of Edmund Law, D. D., Bishop of Carlisle* (London, 1800). J. Stephens, 'Edmund Law and His Circle at Cambridge: Some Philosophical Activity of the 1740s', in *The Philosophical Canon in the 17th and 18th Centuries. Essays in Honour of John W. Yolton*, eds. G. A. J. Rogers and S. Tomaselli (Rochester, NY, 1996), 163–73. B. W. Young, *Religion and Enlightenment in Eighteenth-Century England: Theological Debates from Locke to Burke* (Oxford, 1998): 53–6, 106–12. [Knud Haakonssen]

LAW, WILLIAM b. Kings Cliffe, Northamptonshire, 1686; d. Kings Cliffe, 1761. High-Church divine turned Boehmenian mystic. Educated at Emmanuel College, Cambridge (BA 1708, MA 1712), Fellow there (1711), suspended as a Jacobite (1713). Family tutor, then private literary man. He attacked Hoadly in *Three Letters to the Bishop of Bangor* (1717–19); he asserted humanity's goodness, against Mandeville, in *Remarks upon a Late Book, Entituled, The Fable of the Bees* (1724); and he maintained the insufficiency of reason, against Tindal, in *The Case of Reason, or Natural Religion, Fairly and Fully Stated* (1731). Had a significant output of devotional works. He became a disciple of Jacob Boehme in the 1740s and '50s. *The Works*, 9 vols. (London, 1762–85).

Secondary Sources: J. H. Overton, *William Law, Non-Juror and Mystic: A Sketch of His Life, Thought and Character* (London, 1881). A. K. Walker, *William Law: His Life and Thought* (London, 1973). B. W. Young, 'William Law and the Christian Economy of Salvation', *The English Historical Review* 109 (1994): 308–22. Same, *Religion and Enlightenment in Eighteenth-Century England. Theological Debates from Locke to Burke* (Oxford, 1998): ch. 4. [Knud Haakonssen]

LE CLERC, JEAN b. Geneva, 1657; d. Amsterdam, 1736. Arminian theologian, journalist, philosopher, ecclesiastical historian. Educated in Geneva. Tutor to son of the Grenoble Counsellor de la Pierre (1678). Admitted to Holy Orders in Geneva and spent year at the academy in Saumur where he read R. Simon's *Histoire Critique du Vieux Testament* and developed interest in Arminianism. Went to London 1682 but failed to find a suitable position, mainly because of his religious heterodoxy. He became professor of Hebrew, philosophy, and humanities, and later of ecclesiastical history, at the college of the Arminians in Amsterdam under the aegis of Philipp van Limborch and taught there for the next 27 years. In 1685 he met Locke in exile in the Dutch Republic, and they remained in close contact. Is known in particular for his engagement with Simon's biblical criticism (see *Sentimens de quelques theologiens de Hollande sur l'histoire critique du Vieux Testament composée par R. Simon de l'Oratoire* [1685]) and as founder of a literary journal, the *Bibliothèque universelle & historique* (1686), entitled *Bibliothèque choisie* from 1703 and *Bibliothèque ancienne & moderne* from 1714. His correspondence up to 1732 has been edited by M. Sina: *Jean Le Clerc. Epistolario*, 4 vols. (Florence, 1987–97).

Secondary Sources: A. Barnes, *Jean Le Clerc et la République des lettres* (Paris, 1938). S. A. Golden, *Jean Le Clerc* (New York, NY, 1972). R. Colie, *Light and Enlightenment* (Cambridge, 1957). R. Voeltzel, 'Jean Le Clerc (1657–1736) et la critique biblique' in *Religion, érudition et critique a la fin du XVIIe siècle at au début du XVIII*^e^ (Paris, 1968): 3–52. H. Bots, 'Jean Le Clerc as Journalist of the *Bibliothèques*. His contribution to the spread of English learning on the European continent', in *English Literature, History and Bibliography: Festschrift for Professor F. A. Birrell*, eds. G. A. M. Janssens and F. G. A. M. Aarts (Amsterdam, 1984). G. N. M. Wijngaards, *De 'Bibliothèque choisie' van Jean Le Clerc (1657–1736). Een Amsterdams Geleerdentijdschrift uit de Jaren 1703 tot 1713* (Amsterdam and Maarsen, 1986). M. C. Pitassi, *Entre croire et savoir: le problème de la méthode critique chez Jean Le Clerc* (Leiden, 1987). [Thomas Ahnert]

Leibniz, Gottfried Wilhelm b. Leipzig, 1646; d. Hanover, 1716. Philosopher, mathematician, scientist, jurist, theologian, historian, librarian, court counsellor. Attended university at Leipzig (1661–6), Jena (summer 1663) and Altdorf (1666–7), earning degrees in philosophy and law. After declining the offer of a professorship in Altdorf (1667) he moved to Nuremberg. He left in the autumn of 1667 for the Netherlands, but was halted in Mainz by an outbreak of plague. This unexpected stay brought him into contact with Johann Christian von Boineburg, the former chief minister of the Elector of Mainz, Johann Philipp von Schönborn. Through the mediation of Boineburg he entered into the service of Schönborn. In March 1672 he was sent to Paris on a diplomatic mission. The period spent in Paris (1672–6), together with the visits to London (1673 and 1676) and Holland (1676), put the young German in contact with the most prestigious and advanced philosophical, scientific, and mathematical circles in Europe. In 1673 he was elected fellow of the Royal Society on the strength of his work in physics and his prototype of a mechanical calculator. As early as 1675, at the end of the Parisian period, he discovered the infinitesimal calculus independently of Newton. However, he was forced to give up his ambitions of being appointed to a research post attached to the French *Académie des Sciences*. Reluctantly he accepted a post as court councillor and librarian at Hanover, starting his service at the court of Duke Johann Friedrich of Brunswick-Lüneburg in December 1676. For the following forty years of his life, he remained in the service of the various branches of the Brunswick family, alternating his presence at the courts of Hanover, Wolfenbüttel, Brunswick, Celle, and Berlin. His main duties included the direction of two major libraries, legal and diplomatic advice, the supervision of the drainage of water from the Harz mines, and the reconstruction of the whole history of the Guelf family, of which the House of Brunswick was a branch. For this latter task he undertook massive archival research and a three-year tour of southern Germany, Austria, and Italy (1687–90). He worked intensively toward the creation of a number of academies of sciences and was appointed president of those of Berlin (1700), Dresden (1704), and Vienna (1713). In Vienna, after visits in 1700 and 1708, he spent almost two further years from December 1712 to September 1714. The last two years of his life were spent in Hanover, to which he was finally recalled from Vienna by news of the accession of the Elector of Hanover Georg Ludwig to the English throne. But at his arrival he discovered that the court had already left, leaving him behind. During the seventy years of his life, Leibniz corresponded with over a thousand learned men and women. It was mainly through these personal contacts and through some three hundred publications, most in the form of journal articles and reviews, that he was known to his contemporaries. These publications included: *Dissertatio de Arte Combinatoria* (1666), 'Nova methodus pro maximis et minimis' (1684), 'Meditationes de cognitione, veritate et Ideis' (1684), 'Brevis demonstratio erroris memorabilis cartesii' (1686), 'De primae philosophiae emendatione, et de notione substantiae' (1694), 'Specimen dynamicum' (1695), 'Système nouveau de la nature et de la communication des substances' (1695), 'De ipsa natura' (1698), and *Essais de theodicée* (1710). This, however, is only the tip of an enormous iceberg. Other key works such as the 'Discours de métaphysique' (1686), the *Nouveaux essais sur l'entendement humain* (1703–5), the 'Principes de la nature et de la grace, fondés en raison' (1714), and the 'Monadologie' (1714), remained unpublished during his life. The ongoing standard edition (*Sämtliche Schriften und Briefe*, edited by the German Academy of Sciences, series 1–7, Berlin, 1923–) will eventually run to some 80 large volumes. The current major edition of his philosophical writings is *Die Philosophischen Schriften von Gottfried Wilhelm Leibniz*, ed. C. I. Gerhardt, 7 vols. (Berlin, 1875–90; repr. Hildesheim, 1960–1).

Secondary Sources: G. E. Guhrauer, *Gottfried Wihelm Freiherr von Leibnitz. Eine Biographie*, 2 vols., 2nd edn. (Breslau, 1846). E. Aiton, *Leibniz: A Biography* (Bristol and Boston, 1985). E. Bodemann, *Der Briefwechsel des Gottfried Wilhelm Leibniz* (Hanover, 1889). E. Bodemann, *Die Leibniz-Handschriften* (Hanover, 1895). E. Ravier, *Bibliographie des oeuvres de Leibniz* (Paris, 1937). P. Schrecker, 'Une bibliographie de Leibniz', *Revue philosophique de la France et de l'étranger* 63 (1938): 324–46. *Leibniz-Bibliographie. Die Literature über Leibniz bis 1980*, eds. K. Müller and A. Heinekamp, 2nd edn. (Frankfurt am Main, 1984). *Leibniz-Bibliographie. Die Literature über Leibniz 1981–1990*, eds. K. Müller and A. Heinekamp (Frankfurt am Main, 1996; updated annually in the journal *Studia Leibnitiana* 1991–9; titles published since 1998 are listed on the Internet). B. Russell, *A Critical Exposition of the Philosophy of Leibniz* (Cambridge, 1900). L. Couturat, *La logique de Leibniz* (Paris, 1901). E. Cassirer, *Leibniz's System in seinen wissenschaftlichen Grundlagen* (Marburg, 1902). G. Grua, *Jurisprudence universelle et théodicée selon Leibniz* (Paris, 1953). G. H. R. Parkinson, *Logic and Reality in Leibniz's Metaphysics* (Oxford, 1965). B. Mates, *The Philosophy of Leibniz. Metaphysics and Language* (New York, NY and Oxford, 1986). R. C. Sleigh, Jr., *Leibniz and Arnauld: A Commentary on Their Correspondence* (New Haven, CT, 1990). M. Mugnai, *Leibniz' Theory of Relations* (Stuttgart, 1992). R. M. Adams, *Leibniz: Determinist, Theist, Idealist* (New York, NY and Oxford, 1994). *The Cambridge Companion to Leibniz*, ed. N. Jolley (Cambridge, 1995). D. Rutherford, *Leibniz and the Rational Order of Nature* (Cambridge, 1995). [Maria Rosa Antognazza]

LELAND, JOHN b. Wigan Lancashire, 1691; d. Dublin, 1766. Divine. MA at Glasgow University in 1734 and DD at King's College, Aberdeen, in 1739. A dissenting minister, he became pastor of two congregations in Dublin, where he remained until his death. Distinguished himself for his writings against Deism and in defence of the Christian revelation. These include *An Answer to a Late Book [by Matthew Tindal] Intituled, 'Christianity as Old as the Creation'* (1733) and, most notably, his extensive critical account of the Deist controversy in Britain, *A View of the Principal Deistical Writers that Have Appeared in England in the Last and Present Century*, 3 vols. (1754–6). A four-volume collection of writings was published two years after his death: *Discourses on Various Subjects. . . . With a Preface, Giving Some Account of the Life, Character, and Writings of the Author* (London, 1768–9).

Secondary Sources: 'A Life' by Isaac Weld in *Discourses on Various Subjects*. J. Hunt, *Religious Thought in England*, 3 vols. (London, 1870–3), 2: 459–61. R. E. Sullivan, *John Toland and the Deist Controversy* (Cambridge, MA, 1982). R. L. Emerson, 'Latitudinarianism and the English Deists', in J. A. L. Lemay, *Deism, Masonry, and the Enlightenment* (Newark, DE, 1987), 19–48. [Maria Rosa Antognazza]

Lessing, Gotthold Ephraim b. Kamenz, Oberlausitz, 1729; d. Braunschweig, 1781. Most illustrious German playwright and critic before Goethe and Schiller. After study of theology and literature at University of Leipzig, he moved to Berlin where he collaborated closely with Mendelssohn. Introduced Germans to a new tragic genre with his *Miß Sara Sampson: Ein bürgerliches Trauerspiel* (1757). With a controversial reading of Aristotelian catharsis and Shakespeare as his paradigm, he opposed French classicism in *Briefe, die neueste Literatur betreffend* (1759–65) and challenged the mixing of pictorial and verbal arts in *Laokoön oder über die Grenzen der Malerei und Poesie* (1766). He then produced a successful comedy *Minna von Barnhelm* (1767) and *Hamburgische Dramaturgie*, 2 vols. (1767–9), fruit of his work at the new 'Nationaltheater' from 1767 to 1769. His next and final move was to Wolfenbüttel where, while librarian for the Duke, he completed the dramas *Emilia Galotti* (1772) and his paean to religious tolerance, *Nathan der Weise* (1779). He also published deist fragments that incited a bitter polemic with religious thinkers. In *Eine Parabel* and *Axiomata* (both 1778) he argued that Christianity's trenchancy lies in its revealed content, not the evangelists' reliability. While claiming in *Über den Beweis des Geistes und der Kraft*, (anon., 1777) that history's accidental truths can never establish reason's necessary truths, he construed religious belief as part of humanity's maturation in *Die Erziehung des Menschengeschlechts* (1780). Standard editions, *Sämtliche Schriften*, eds. K. Lachmann and F. Muncker, 23 vols. (Leipzig, 1886–1924); *Werke*, 7th edn., ed. K. Balser, 5 vols. (Berlin, 1975); *Werke*, eds. K. Eibl and H. G. Göpfert, 8 vols. (Munich, 1970–9).

Secondary Sources: W. Oehlke, *Lessing und seine Zeit*, 2 vols., 2nd edn. (Munich, 1929). K. S. Guthke, *Gotthold Ephraim Lessing*, 3rd edn. (Stuttgart, 1979). W. Barner et al., *Lessing: Epoche – Werk -Wirkung*, 4th edn. (Munich, 1981). M. Kommerell, *Lessing und Aristoteles: Untersuchung über die Theorie der Tragödie*, 5th edn. (Frankfurt am Main, 1984). [Daniel Dahlstrom]

Linné (also Linnaeus), Carl von b. Södra Råshult, Småland, Sweden, 1707; d. Uppsala, Sweden, 1778. Botanical and zoological systematiser. Studied medicine in Lund and Uppsala, where he began his lifetime mission, a system of classification for the study of natural history the key to which, the new theory of plant sexuality, he had devised as early as 1730. In 1735, following trips to Lapland and central Sweden, he travelled to the Netherlands to obtain his MD at the University of Harderwijk. In the Netherlands until 1738 he established contact with the wider European scientific world and promoted the system of classification published in *Systema naturae* (1735). Securing a chair of medicine at Uppsala (1741) enabled him to promote the study of natural history as a popular teacher and keeper of the botanical garden. *Philosophia botanica* (1751) developed further the application of his system of classification and *Species plantarum* (1753) provided an inventory of much of the then known flora with 8,000 specimens from around the world. He also continued to expand *Systema naturae*, which dealt with animal as well as plant specimens, the definitive tenth edition (1758–9) running to 1,384 pages. All his works were informed by a physio-theology which assumed a basic order in Nature since it was the creation of an omnipotent Deity.

Secondary Works: T. Fries, *Linné*, 2 vols. (Stockholm, 1903). *Linnaeus: The Man and his Work*, ed. T. Frängsmyr (Canton, MA, 1994). L. Koerner, *Linnaeus: Nature and Nation* (Cambridge, MA, 1999). J. Hulth, *Bibliographia Linnaeana* (Uppsala, 1907). B. Soulsby, *A Catalogue of the Works of*

Linnaeus (London, 1933). *Contemporary Perspectives on Linnaeus*, ed. J. Weinstock (Lanham, MD, 1985). [John Gascoigne]

Locke, John b. Wrington, Somerset, 1632; d. Oates, Essex, 1704. Metaphysician, moral and political philosopher, philosopher of education, economic theorist, theological polemicist, medical doctor, intellectual in politics, and public servant. Educated at Westminster School 1647–52, Christ Church, Oxford 1652–8 (BA 1656, MA 1658). Remained at Christ Church as Student (life-fellow; position withdrawn 1684 by King), studying medicine for years, worked closely with Thomas Sydenham, friend of Boyle; deeply influenced by Descartes and esp. Gassendi, in later 1660s; elected Fellow of the Royal Society 1668. Early conservatism shown in two works only published three centuries later, *Two Tracts on Government* (1660 and 1661; ed. P. Abrams, 1967) and lectures on the law of nature delivered as Censor of Moral Philosophy at Christ Church in 1664 (*Essays on the Law of Nature*, ed. W. v. Leyden, 1954; and as *Questions concerning the Law of Nature*, ed. R. Horwitz, J. Strauss Clay, D. Clay, 1990). In 1667 he joined the household of Anthony Ashley Cooper (from 1672 1st Earl of Shaftesbury) as physician and political adviser. Was member of Council of Trade in 1672 when Shaftesbury was Lord Chancellor. This association saw a drastic change in L.'s political views, and already in 1667 Locke wrote an essay defending toleration (see Locke, *Political Essays*, ed. M. Goldie, 1997). Like Algernon Sidney and James Tyrrell, he wrote against royal absolutism as presented by Sir Robert Filmer. Exact date of *Two Treatises of Government* still disputed but nearly certainly 1680–3. After Shaftesbury's death in exile in Holland in 1683, Locke followed him there later that year. Established wide contacts among the Dutch Arminians and other liberal Protestants, esp. after revocation of Edict of Nantes (1685). Being excluded from active politics, Locke wrote *Essay concerning Human Understanding* and *Epistola de tolerantia*. After the Revolution, he could return to England in 1689, immediately publishing *Epistola* and the *Two Treatises of Government*, both anonymously. The *Essay* was published under his name at the end of the year. Deeply involved in economic and monetary policies of new government, served on the Board of Trade; literary results: *Some Considerations of the Consequences of the Lowering of Interest and Raising the Value of Money* (1692) and *Further Considerations concerning Raising the Value of Money* (1695). Locke's writings on colonial matters published posthumously (Locke, *Works*, 1823 edn., vol. 10). His defence of religious toleration extended in polemics: *A Second Letter concerning Toleration* (1690) and *A Third Letter for Toleration* (1692). In 1693 appeared *Some Thoughts concerning Education* and in 1695 *The Reasonableness of Christianity*. Accused of Socinianism, Locke defended himself in *A Vindication of the Reasonableness of Christianity* (1695) and *A Second Vindication of the Reasonableness of Christianity* (1697). All his works, except the *Essay*, remained anonymous during his life. Posthumously appeared *A Paraphrase and Notes on the Epistles of St. Paul* (1705–7); the fifth edn. of the *Essay* with significant revisions (1706); *Posthumous Works of Mr. Locke* (1706), containing *Of the Conduct of the Understanding* and *An Examination of P. Malebranche's Opinion of Seeing All Things in God*. Old standard edition: *The Works of John Locke*. New edn., corrected, 10 vols. (London, 1823). New edn. in progress: *The Clarendon Edition of the Works of John Locke*, gen. ed. M. A. Stewart (Oxford, 1975–). This includes *The Correspondence of John Locke*, ed. E. S. de Beer, 9 vols. (1976–92).

Secondary Sources: J. Le Clerc, *Éloge historique de feu Mr. Locke par Mr. Jean Le Clerc*, in *Bibliotheque choisie*, VI (1705), and in *Oeuvres diverses . . .* (1710); English trans. *The Life and Character of* Mr. J. Locke (London, 1706). P. King, *The Life of John Locke with Extracts from his Correspondence, Journals, and Commonplace Books*, new edn., 2 vols. (London, 1824). M. Cranston, *John Locke: A Biography* (London, 1957). P. Long, *A Summary Catalogue of the Lovelace Collection of the Papers of John Locke in the Bodleian Library* (Oxford, 1959). J. R. Harrison and P. Laslett, *The Library of John Locke* (Oxford, 1965). R. Hall and R. Woolhouse, *Eighty Years of Locke Scholarship: A Bibliographical Guide* (Edinburgh, 1983). J. W. Yolton, *John Locke and the Way of Ideas* (London, 1956). C. B.

Macpherson, *The Political Theory of Possessive Individualism. Hobbes to Locke* (Oxford, 1962). K. Dewhurst, *John Locke (1632–1704): Physician and Philosopher: A Medical Biography* (London, 1963). M. Seliger, *The Liberal Politics of John Locke* (London, 1968). J. Dunn, *The Political Thought of John Locke* (Cambridge, 1969). J. W. Yolton, *Locke and the Compass of Human Understanding* (London, 1970). J. W. Yolton, *John Locke and Education* (New York, NY, 1971). J. L. Mackie, *Problems from Locke* (Oxford, 1976). J. Tully, *A Discourse on Property: John Locke and His Adversaries* (Cambridge, 1980). K. I. Vaughn, *John Locke: Economist and Social Scientist* (Chicago, IL, 1980). J. Colman, *John Locke's Moral Philosophy* (Edinburgh, 1983). R. Ashcraft, *Revolutionary Politics and Locke's Two Treatises of Government* (Princeton, NJ, 1986). R. Ashcraft, *Locke's Two Treatises of Government* (London, 1987). W. M. Spellman, *John Locke and the Problem of Depravity* (Oxford, 1988). M. Ayers, *Locke*, 2 vols. (London, 1991). P. Schouls, *Reasoned Freedom: John Locke and the Enlightenment* (Ithaca, NY, 1992). A. J. Simmons, *The Lockean Theory of Rights* (Princeton, NJ, 1992). I. Harris, *The Mind of John Locke: A Study in Political Theory in Its Intellectual Setting* (Cambridge, 1993). A. J. Simmons, *On the Edge of Anarchy: Locke, Consent, and the Limits of Society* (Princeton, NJ, 1993). *The Cambridge Companion to Locke*, ed. V. Chappell (New York, NY, 1994). J. Marshall, *John Locke: Resistance, Religion, and Responsibility* (Cambridge, 1994). G. Sreenivasan, *The Limits of Lockean Rights in Property* (New York, NY, 1995). N. Wolterstorff, *John Locke and the Ethics of Belief* (Cambridge, 1996). *John Locke and Christianity: Contemporary Responses to the Reasonableness of Christianity*, ed. V. Nuovo (Bristol, 1997). G. Yaffe, *Liberty Worth the Name: Locke on Free Agency* (Princeton, NJ, 2000). J. Waldron, *God, Locke, and Equality: Christian Foundations in Locke's Political Thought* (Cambridge, 2002). W. R. Ott, *Locke's Philosophy of Language* (Cambridge, 2004). [Knud Haakonssen]

LOMONOSOV, MIKHAIL VASILYEVICH b. Mishaninskaya, Russia, 1711; d. St. Petersburg, 1765. Chemist, poet and educational reformer, the main figure in the introduction of Western scientific and philosophical thought to Russia. After studying in Marburg under Christian Wolff, he spent most of his mature life working with the St. Petersburg Academy of Sciences. He developed speculative atomic theories of chemical reactions and of heat, which extended those of Boyle; some of these are translated in *Mikhail Vasil'evich Lomonosov on the Corpuscular Theory* (Cambridge, MA, 1970). Although the data then available did not permit the testing of such theories, he instituted quantitative chemical experiments of the kind that would eventually underpin atomic theories. His dominant influence on education allowed him to reform Russian grammar and scientific terminology. Only notes survive of his main projected philosophical work, on the unity of nature. His complete works were published as *Pohoe sobranie sochineny* (Moscow and Leningrad, 1950–9).

Secondary Souces: G. S. Vasetskii, *Lomonosov's Philosophy*, trans. D. Fidlon (Moscow, 1968). B. M. Kedrov, 'Lomonosov', *Dictionary of Scientific Biography*, 7: 467–72. [James Franklin]

LOSSIUS, JOHANN CHRISTIAN b. Liebstadt near Weimar, 1743; d. Erfurt, 1813. Materialist philosopher. His later thought has agnostic and subjectivist features, tending towards Kantian views at times. Studied at Jena, Professor of Philosophy at Erfurt in 1770, Professor of Theology in 1772. His most important early works are *Physische Ursachen des Wahren* (1775, i.e., 1774) and *Unterricht der gesunden Vernunft* (1776). His later views are present in *Neues Philosophisches Reallexikon oder Wörterbuch der gesamten Philosophischen Wissenschaften* (1803).

Secondary Sources: G. Zart, *Einfluss der Englischen Philosophen seit Bacon auf die Deutsche Philosophie des 18. Jahrhunderts* (Berlin, 1881): 156–66. O. Finger, *Von der Materialität der Seele. Beitrag zur Geschichte des Materialismus und Atheismus im Deutschland der zweiten Hälfte des 18. Jahrhunderts* (Berlin, 1961), 68–85. M. Kuehn, *Scottish Common Sense in Germany, 1768–1800: A*

Contribution to the History of Critical Philosophy (Kingston and Montreal, 1987), 86–102. [Udo Thiel]

LUDOVICI, JAKOB FRIEDRICH b. Wacholzhagen near Treptow in Pomerania, 1671; d. Gießen, 1723. Jurist. Studied law in Stargard, Königsberg, and, finally, Halle: *Lizentiat* (1700), professor *extraordinarius* (1701), doctoral degree (1702), professor *ordinarius* (1711); and in 1716 he was made a royal Prussian aulic councillor. In 1721 he moved to Gießen on becoming privy councillor as well as vice-chancellor and *Professor Juris primarius* at the university there. Among his works are textbooks on feudal law, criminal procedure, civil procedure, the law of Justinian's *Digest*, and natural law, such as the *Delineatio historiae juris divini, naturalis et positivi universalis* (1701). Also published *Untersuchung des Indifferentismi Religionum* (1700). His son Jacob published his father's *Doctrinae juris naturae juridice considerata* in 1724, together with a short description of his father's life.

Secondary Sources: J. C. Adelung and H. W. Rotermund, *Fortsetzung und Ergänzung zu Christian Gottlieb Jöchers allgemeinem Gelehrten-Lexico*, vol. 4 (Bremen, 1813), cols 64–70. R. Stintzing and E. Landsberg, *Geschichte der deutschen Rechtswissenschaft* Abt. III.1 (Leipzig, 1898), 135–6. [Thomas Ahnert]

MABLY, GABRIEL BONNOT DE b. Grenoble, 1709; d. Paris, 1785. Revolutionary republican political philosopher and philosophical historian. Elder brother of Condillac. Attended Jesuit college and seminary and became a subdeacon in 1735 but never advanced in the church. Secretary to Cardinal Tencin and involved in high level diplomacy but abruptly left the Cardinal's service in 1747. Subsequently retired to a life of letters where he wrote many important works including *Parallèle des Romains et des François* (1740), *Le droit public de l'Europe* (1746), *Observations sur les Grecs* (1749), *Observations sur les Romains* (1751), *Des droits et devoirs du citoyen* (1758), *Entretiens de Phocion* (1763), *Observations sur l'Histoire de France* (1765), *Doutes proposées aux philosophes economistes* (1768), and a famous set of letters to John Adams, *Observations sur les government et les lois des États Unis d'Amérique* (1784). After his death an intellectual hero of the French Revolution, despite his many criticisms of the mainstream French Enlightenment and hatred of Voltaire. His writings are collected in *Collection complète des oeuvres*, 15 vols. (Paris, 1794–5; facsim., ed. G. Arnaud, Aalen, 1977).

Secondary Sources: T. Schleich, *Aufklärung und Revolution: Die Wirkungsgeschichte Gabriel Bonnot de Mablys in Frankreich (1740–1914)* (Stuttgart, 1981). K. M. Baker. 'A Script for a French Revolution: The Political Consciousness of the abbé Mably', *Eighteenth-Century Studies* 14 (1981): 235–63. J. K. Wright, *A Classical Republican in Eighteenth-Century France: The Political Thought of Mably* (Stanford, CA, 1997). [Aaron Garrett]

MACKINTOSH, SIR JAMES b. Aldourie, Inverness-shire, Scotland, 1765; d. London, 1832. Radical critic of Burke, turned Whig constitutionalist historian, *Edinburgh Reviewer*, in India service, MP. Educated at King's College, Aberdeen (1780–4) and Edinburgh (medical studies 1784–7); subsequently he studied law in London (called to the bar 1795). Philosophically he became a disciple of Dugald Stewart. Gained early fame attacking Burke's *Reflections* in the philosophically eclectic *Vindiciae Gallicae: A Defence of the French Revolution and Its English Admirers* (1791). He reneged his French sympathies in *A Discourse on the Study of the Law of Nature and Nations* (1799), republished in *The Miscellaneous Works of the Right Honourable Sir James Mackintosh*, ed. R. J. Mackintosh, 3 vols. (London, 1846), Vol. 1, and in *Vindiciae Gallicae and Other Writings on the French Revolution*, ed. D. Winch (Indianapolis, IN, 2006). Became Recorder at Bombay, Whig MP, and Professor of Law and Politics at the East India College at Hayleybury. His main philosophical work was *Progress of Ethical Philosophy* (1830), the first history of the subject in English.

Secondary Sources: *Memoirs of the Life of... Sir James Mackintosh*, ed. R. J. Mackintosh, 2 vols. (London, 1836). P. O'Leary, *Sir James Mackintosh, the Whig Cicero* (Aberdeen, 1989). J. Rendall, 'Scottish Orientalism: From Robertson to James Mill', *Historical Journal*, 25 (1982): 43–69. S. Collini, D. Winch, and J. Burrow, *That Noble Science of Politics: A Study in Nineteenth-Century Intellectual History* (Cambridge, 1983) ch. 1. K. Haakonssen, *Natural Law and Moral Philosophy: From Grotius to the Scottish Enlightenment* (Cambridge, 1995), ch. 8. [Knud Haakonssen]

MAIMON, SOLOMON b. Nieswiecz, Lithuania, 1754; d. Nieder-Siegesdorf, Silesia, 1800. After early Talmudic education and study with Mendelssohn, came to renown with sceptical criticisms of Kant's philosophy in *Versuch über die Transzendentalphilosophie mit einem Anhang über die symbolische Erkenntnis und Anmerkungen* (1790). Challenging Kant's transcendental deduction of categories and its dualist epistemological premises, he argued that perception is the product of a preconscious categorial synthesis of 'differentials' of sensations. The idea of a thing-in-itself, he insisted, can only be a regulative scientific ideal. In *Versuch einer neuen Logik oder Theorie des Denkens, nebst angehängten Briefen des Philaletes an Aenesidemus* (1794), he developed a logic for 'real' – not merely 'formal' – thought, based upon a Leibnizian-inspired 'principle of determinability'. Also critical of Kant's ethics, he identified the pleasurable feeling of one's own dignity as the motivation of moral action in *Kritische Untersuchungen über den menschlichen Geist: oder, Das höhere Erkenntniß- und Willensvermögen* (1797). Published an autobiography, *Lebensgeschichte* (1792/93). *Gesammelte Werke*, ed. V. Verra, 7 vols. (Hildesheim, 1965).

Secondary Sources: S. H. Bergman, *The Philosophy of Solomon Maimon* (Jerusalem, 1967). A. Engstler, *Untersuchungen zum Idealismus Solomon Maimons* (Stuttgart-Bad Canstatt, 1990). [Daniel Dahlstrom]

MANDEVILLE, BERNARD (DE) b. Rotterdam, 1670; d. Hackney, 1733. Polemicist and doctor. From a long line of physicians, studied at Erasmian School and then Leiden where he was awarded a doctorate in philosophy in 1689 and medicine in 1691. Following political troubles in Rotterdam his father was banished in 1693, and the younger Mandeville moved to London where he practiced medicine, specializing in psychological maladies, and published satirical fables and verse. In 1705 wrote a satirical poem entitled the 'Grumbling Hive', which in 1714 was expanded with commentary as his best-know work, the *Fable of the Bees*. Published proto-feminist dialogue the *Virgin Unmask'd* and a number of articles in the *Female Tatler*. In 1711 produced a pioneering work of psychology, *A Treatise of the Hypochondriack and Hysterick Passions*, in dialogue form. In 1723 published a further expanded version of the *Fable* and became a *successe de scandale*, twice presented before the King's Bench by the Middlesex Jury as a public nuisance, and attacked in print by many, including Francis Hutcheson and Bishop Berkeley. Enjoyed the friendship of Lord Macclesfield – the Lord Chancellor between 1718–24 – so likely never under serious threat. Continued to expand the *Fable of the Bees* (Part II, 1729) and to publish a steady stream of works including pamphlets on the legalization of prostitution (*A Modest Defence of Publick Stews* [1724]), and penal reform (*An Enquiry into the causes of the Frequent Executions at Tyburn* [1725]), *An Enquiry into the Origin of Honour* [1732], and his response to Berkeley, *A Letter to Dion* [1732]. Throughout his rich *oeuvre* emphasized the hypocrisy of moralizing elites in society and the inescapability of private vices for the public benefits of prosperity.

Secondary Sources: F. B. Kaye, 'Introduction' to *The Fable of the Bees* (Oxford, 1924, 2 vols; repr. Indianapolis, IN, 1988). H. Monro, *The Ambivalence of Bernard Mandeville* (Oxford, 1975). M. M. Goldsmith, *Private Vices, Public Benefits. Bernard Mandeville's Political and Social Thought*

(Cambridge, 1985). E. J. Hundert, *The Enlightenment's 'Fable': Bernard Mandeville and the Discovery of Society* (Cambridge, 1995). [Aaron Garrett]

MAUPERTUIS, PIERRE-LOUIS MOREAU DE b. Saint-Malo, France, 1698; d. Basel, Switzerland, 1759. Scientist, mathematician, philosopher. Early proponent of Newtonian physics, visits London 1728, becomes fellow of the Royal Society. 1736–7 leads expedition to Lapland to test Newton's claim that the earth is flattended toward the poles. Elected to *Académie française* 1743. Appointed president of the Berlin Academy by Frederick II in 1746. Invigorates the Academy, but later years are marked by wounding controversy and illness. *Réflexions philosophiques sur l'origine des langues et la signification des mots* (1740; date revised from 1748 by Beeson; see below); *Vénus physique* (1746); *Essai de philosophie morale* (1749); *Essai de cosmologie* (1750); *Essai sur la formation des corps organisés* (1754; in *Oeuvres* 1756 under title *Système de la nature*); *Lettre sur le progrès des sciences* (1752). *Oeuvres* (1752), in 2 vols. (1753), in 4 vols. (1756 and 1768). *Maupertuis et ses correspondants. Lettres inédites du Grand Frédéric*, ed. A. le Sueur (Geneva, 1971 [1896]); *Maupertuis, le savant et le philosophe. Présentation des extraits*, ed. E. Callot (Paris, 1964). *Maupertuis, Turgot et Maine de Biran sur l'origine du langage*, ed. R. Grimsley (Geneva, 1971).

Secondary Sources: P. Brunet, *Maupertuis*, 2 vols. (Paris, 1929; Vol. 1: *Étude biographique*, Vol. 2: *L'oeuvre et sa place dans la pensée philosophique du XVIIIe siècle*). B. Glass, 'Maupertuis, Pioneer of Genetics and Revolution', in *Forerunners of Darwin 1745–1859*, eds. B. Glass et al. (Baltimore, MD, 1959): 51–83. L. Velluz, *Maupertuis* (Paris, 1969). J. Roger, *Les sciences de la vie dans la pensée française du XVIIIe siècle*, 2nd edn. (Paris, 1971), 468–87. G. Tonelli, *La pensée philosophique de Maupertuis: son milieu et ses sources*, ed. C. Cesa (Hildesheim, 1987). D. Beeson, *Maupertuis: An Intellectual Biography* (Oxford, 1992) (with full bibliography). M. Valentin, *Maupertuis, un savant oublié* (Rennes, 1998). *Pierre-Louis Moreau de Maupertuis. Eine Bilanz nach 300 Jahren*, ed. H. Hecht (Berlin, 1999). [Hans Aarsleff]

MEIER, GEORG FRIEDRICH b. Ammendorf near Halle, 1718; d. Halle, 1777. Reformist Wolffian. Studied philosophy and theology at Halle. Doctorate 1739, extraordinary Professor of Philosophy at Halle in 1746, full Professor in 1748. His philosophy is often described as a 'reformed Wolffianism'. Followed Wolff and Baumgarten to a large extent but was also influenced by Locke and empiricist thought. Unlike Wolff, he emphasised epistemological issues and pointed out the limits of human understanding, for example, in *Betrachtungen über die Schranken der menschlichen Erkenntnis* (1775). Published works on metaphysics and logic but is best known for his aesthetics which is dependent on Baumgarten but stresses the importance of sensibility: *Anfangsgründe aller schönen Künste und Wissenschaften*, 3 vols. (1748–50). Other important writings: *Metaphysik* 4 vols. (1755–9); *Vernunftlehre* (1752); *Gedanken über die Religion* (1749); *Philosophische Sittenlehre*, 5 vols. (1753–61); *Versuch einer allgemeinen Auslegungskunst* (1757; modern ed. Hamburg, 1996); *Theoretische Lehre von den Gemühtsbewegungen überhaupt* (1744); *Gedancken von Schertzen* (1744). *Georg Friedrich Meier, Frühe Schriften zur ästhetischen Erziehung der Deutschen in 3 Teilen*, eds. H.-J. Kertscher and G. Schenk, 3 vols. (Halle/Saale, 1999–2001). Kant used Meier's short *Auszug aus der Vernuftlehre* (1752) for his lectures on logic (see *Kant's Gesammelte Schriften*, Ak 16, ed. E. Adickes, 1924).

Secondary Sources: S. G. Langen, *G. F. Meier* (Halle, 1778). E. Bergmann, *Die Begründung der deutschen Aesthetik durch A. G. Baumgarten und G. F. Meier* (Leipzig, 1911). J. Schaffrath, *Die Philosophie des Georg Friedrich Meier. Ein Beitrag zur Geschichte der Aufklärungsphilosophie* (Eschweiler, 1940). L. P. Wessel, Jr., 'G. F. Meier and the Genesis of Philosophical Theodicies of History in 18th-Century Germany', *Lessing Yearbook* 12 (1981): 63–84. U. Möller, *Rhetorische Überlieferung und Dichtungstheorie im frühen 18.Jahrhundert: Studien zu Gottsched, Breitinger und*

G. Fr. Meier (Munich, 1983). G. Gawlick, 'G. F. Meiers Stellung in der Religionsphilosophie der deutschen Aufklärung', in *Zentren der Aufklärung I: Halle: Aufklärung und Pietismus*, ed. N. Hinske (Heidelberg, 1989), 157–76. G. Schenk, *Leben und Werk des Halleschen Aufklärers Georg Friedrich Meier* (Halle, 1994). U. Dierse, 'Nachträge zu G. F. Meiers Religionsphilosophie', in *Aufklärung und Skepsis. Festschrift für Günther Gawlick*, ed. L. Kreimendahl (Stuttgart-Bad Cannstatt, 1995), 33–46. R. Pozzo, *Georg Friedrich Meiers 'Vernunftlehre'* (Stuttgart-Bad Cannstatt, 2000). [Udo Thiel]

Meiners, Christoph b. Warstarde near Otterndorf in Hadeln, Germany 1747; d. Göttingen, 1810. Philosopher and historian. Gymnasium in Bremen from 1763, student at Göttingen 1767–70, extraordinary professor in Göttingen 1772, full professor 1775. Strongly influenced by British philosophers such as Locke, Shaftesbury, and Hutcheson. In his most important philosophical work, the anonymous *Revision der Philosophie* (1772) he proposed that philosophy should be based on empirical psychology. His writings on psychology include: *Kurzer Abriß der Psychologie zum Gebrauche seiner Vorlesungen* (1773). 'Psychologisches Fragment über die Verschiedenheiten des innern Bewußtseins', in *Vermischte Philosophische Schriften*, 3 vols. (Leipzig, 1775–6), 2: 3–44; *Grundriß der Seelenlehre* (1786). Co-edited the anti-Kantian journal *Philosophische Bibliothek* (1788–91). Among his philosophically relevant historical writings are: *Grundriß der Geschichte aller Religionen* (1785); *Geschichte und Theorie der schönen Wissenschaften* (1787).

Secondary Sources: G. Zart, *Einfluss der Englischen Philosophen seit Bacon auf die Deutsche Philosophie des 18. Jahrhunderts* (Berlin, 1881), 150–3. U. Thiel, 'Varieties of Inner Sense: Two pre-Kantian Theories', *Archiv für Geschichte der Philosophie* 79 (1997): 58–79. S. Vetter, *Wissenschaftlicher Reduktionismus und die Rassentheorie von Christoph Meiners. Ein Beitrag zur Geschichte der verlorenen Metaphysik in der Anthropologie* (Mainz, 1997). [Udo Thiel]

Mendelssohn, Moses b. Dessau, 1729; d. Berlin, 1786. Jewish philosopher and man of letters at the center of the German Enlightenment. Together with his close friends, Nicolai and Lessing, he became a principal contributor to leading journals of criticism in Germany from the 1750s through the 1770s. His *Philosophische Schriften* (1761, 1771, 1777) contains influential reflections on the nature of sentiments, beauty, and sublimity, especially in the context of art, within a metaphysical framework shaped by a distinctive interpretation of the thought of Leibniz, Spinoza, and Wolff. His reputation as a thinker spread when his essay 'Abhandlung über die Evidenz in den metaphysischen Wissenschaften' (1764) won a contest staged by the Prussian Academy of Sciences (beating out an essay by Kant). In *Schreiben an den Herrn Diaconus Lavater zu Zürich* (1770), he delivers a measured response to Lavater's infamous challenge to refute or embrace the arguments made for Christianity in Bonnet's *La palingénésie philosophique* (1769). In addition to numerous translations of books of the Hebrew bible, he also produced a popular reconstruction of the Platonic dialogue and arguments for immortality in *Phaedo: oder, Über die Unsterblichkeit der Seele* (1767), a plea for political and religious tolerance of conscience in *Jerusalem: oder, Über religiöse Macht und Judenthum* (1783), and his mature epistemological and metaphysical treatise, *Morgenstunden: oder, Vorlesungen über das Daseyn Gottes* (1785). In the final five years of his life, he became embroiled in the so-called 'pantheism controversy' with Jacobi over the nature of Lessing's Spinozism. *An die Freunde Lessings* (1786) is a final attempt to set the record straight. *Gesammelte Schriften* (Berlin, 1929–; repr. Stuttgart-Bad Canstatt, 1971–).

Secondary Sources: A. Altmann, *Moses Mendelssohn: A Biographical Study* (University, AL, 1973). A. Arkush, *Moses Mendelssohn and the Enlightenment* (Albany, NY, 1994). Editor's Introduction, in Mendelssohn, *Philosophical Writings*, trans. and ed. D. Dahlstrom (Cambridge, 1997). [Daniel Dahlstrom]

Merian, Johann Bernhard b. Liestall near Basle, 1723; d. Berlin, 1807. Eclectic philosopher who played a major role in the *Académie Royale des Sciences et des Belles-Lettres* in Berlin. Studied philology and philosophy at the University of Basle and received his doctorate in 1740. In 1750 became a member of the Class for Speculative Philosophy of the Berlin Academy; director of the Class for *Belles-Lettres* in 1771, and permanent Secretary of the Academy from 1797. Translated Hume into French and published numerous papers in the Academy's *Mémoires*, including: 'Mémoire sur l'apperception de sa propre existence', *Histoire de l'Académie Royale des Sciences et Belles Lettres. Année 1749* (1751): 416–41; in the same volume: 'Mémoire sur l'apperception considerée relativement aux idées, ou, sur l'existence des idées dans l'âme', 442–77; 'Sur le principe des indiscernables', same: *Année 1754* (1756): 383–98; 'Parallèle de deux principes de psychologie' same: *Année 1757* (1759): 375–91; *Discours sur la métaphysique* (1765); 'Sur le phénoménisme de David Hume', *Mémoires de l'Académie Royale des Sciences et Belles-Lettres depuis l'avènement de Frédéric Guillaume II au thrône* (1792/3): 417–37; 'Parallèle historique de nos deux philosophies nationales', same (1797). In the 1770s he published a series of essays on the Molyneux problem in the *Mémoires* of the Berlin Academy. There is a modern edition of these essays: *Sur le Problème de Molyneux*, ed. F Markovits (Paris, 1984).

Secondary Sources: F. Ancillon, 'Éloge historique de J. B. Mérian', *Abhandlungen der Königlichen Akademie der Wissenschaften zu Berlin* (Berlin, 1810): 52–90. U. Thiel, 'Between Wolff and Kant: Merian's Theory of Apperception', *Journal of the History of Philosophy* 34 (1996): 213–32. J. Häseler, 'Johann Bernhard Merian – ein Schweizer Philosoph an der Berliner Akademie', *Schweizer im Berlin des 18. Jahrhunderts*, eds. M. Fontius and Helmut Holzhey (Berlin, 1996): 217–30. Bernard L. Baertschi, 'La conception de la conscience développée par Mérian', in ibid., 231–48. J. C. Laursen, 'Swiss Anti-Skeptics in Berlin', in ibid., 261–81. J. C. Laursen and R. H. Popkin, 'Hume in the Prussian Academy: Jean Bernard Mérian's "On the Phenomenalism of David Hume"', *Hume Studies* 23 (1997): 153–91. [Udo Thiel]

Meslier, Jean b. Mazerny (France), 1664; d. Etrepigny, 1729. *Curé* and clandestine anti-Christian polemicist. Educated in the seminar of Reims, he led an uneventful life as parish priest. A materialist interpretation of Cartesianism was the basis for a strong attack on Christianity in his massive clandestine *Mémoire des pensées et sentiments de M. J.* (1718–29) (often known as his 'Testament'), partially published as *Extrait* by Voltaire (1762). Also developed a communist, agrarian utopia. *Oeuvres complètes*, eds. J. Deprun, R. Desné, and A. Soboul, 3 vols. (Paris, 1970–2).

Secondary Sources: M. Dommanget, *Le curé Meslier* (Paris, 1965). *Études sur le curé Meslier*, ed. A. Soboul (Paris, 1966). *Le curé Meslier et la vie intellectuelle, religieuse et sociale à la fin du XVIIème siècle*, ed. R. Desné (Reims, 1980). [Luca Fonnesu]

Middleton, Conyers b. Yorkshire, 1683; d. Hildersham, near Cambridge, 1750. Divine and man of letters. Entered Trinity College, Cambridge, in 1700 (BA 1702, MA 1707); fellow there 1706. In 1717 he was made DD and, in 1721, the 'Protobibliothecarius' of the university library. During 1724–5 he travelled to Italy, staying mostly in Rome. In 1731 he was appointed first Woodwardian Professor of Geology. Throughout his life involved in fiery controversies, especially with Richard Bentley 1709–26. Especially significant was his contribution to the debate on the interpretation of Scripture and on miracles (in particular *A Free Inquiry into the Miraculous Powers, which Are Supposed to Have Subsisted in the Christian Church*, 1749), together with his attack on Roman Catholicism (*A Letter from Rome, Shewing an Exact Conformity Between Popery and Paganism*, 1729). Most of his works are included in *The Miscellaneous Works of the Late... Conyers Middleton*, 2nd edn., 5 vols. (London, 1755).

Secondary Sources: L. Stephen, *History of English Thought in the Eighteenth Century*, 3rd edn. 2 vols. (London, 1902), 1: 253–76. [Maria Rosa Antognazza]

MILLAR, JOHN b. Shotts, Lanarkshire, Scotland, 1735; d. Millheugh, 1801. Legal theorist and philosophical historian. Educated in Arts and Law at Glasgow; tutor in the household of his mentor Lord Kames (two years in the 1750s); admitted to the Faculty of Advocates (1760); Professor of Law at Glasgow (1761–1801). The ablest of Adam Smith's students, he developed the latter's science of a legislator in sociological and historical directions: *Observations concerning the Distinction of Ranks in Society* (1771, significantly rev. 2nd edn. 1773). In *An Historical View of the English Government* (1787), he wrote Whig history philosophically sobered up by the influence of Hume and Smith (much expanded as, *An Historical View of the English Government from the Settlement of the Saxons in Britain to the Revolution in 1688. To which are subjoined some Dissertations Connected with the History of the Government from the Revolution to the Present Time*, 3rd edn., eds. J. Craig and J. Mylne, 4 vols., Edinburgh, 1803; modern edn. Indianapolis, IN, 2006). See also *Letters of Crito, on the Causes, Objects, and Consequences of the Present War* (1796. Anonymous); *Letters of Sidney, on Inequality of Property, to which is added, A Treatise of the Effects of War on Commercial Prosperity* (1796. Anonymous, possibly written by Millar's student, John Craig).

Secondary Sources: J. Craig, 'An Account of the Life and Writings of the Author', in Millar, *The Origin of the Distinction of Ranks, or An Inquiry into the Circumstances which give rise to Influence and Authority in the Different Members of Society*, 4th edn. (1806) ed. A. Garrett (Indianapolis, IN, 2006). D. Forbes, ''Scientific' Whiggism: Adam Smith and John Millar', *Cambridge Journal* 7 (1953–4): 643–70. W. C. Lehmann, *John Millar of Glasgow, 1735–1801: His Life and Thought and His Contributions to Sociological Analysis* (Cambridge, 1960). J. W. Cairns, '"Famous as a School for Law, as Edinburgh . . . for Medicine": Legal Education in Glasgow, 1761–1801', in *The Glasgow Enlightenment*, eds. A. Hook and R. B. Sher (Edinburgh, 1994): 133–59. K. Haakonssen, *Natural Law and Moral Philosophy: From Grotius to the Scottish Enlightenment* (Cambridge, 1995), ch. 5. [Knud Haakonssen]

MONBODDO – see BURNETT, JAMES

MONTESQUIEU, CHARLES LOUIS DE SECONDAT BARON DE b. La Brède, 1689; d. Paris, 1755. Historian, jurist, and philosopher. Born to the baronies of Montesquieu and la Brède and nobility of the robe, he was educated at the Oratorian Collège de Jouilly and, in law, at the University of Bordeaux and afterwards in Paris, where he became acquainted with Père Desmolets and Nicolas Fréret and married a protestant woman. In 1716 inherited the family estates and the office of *president à mortier* of the Parliament of Bordeaux which he filled until 1725. For the rest of his life he was a man of letters, often dividing his time between the Paris salons-world and his estate. He wrote assiduously both for the Bordeaux academy and for his Paris audience on scientific, moral, political, and legal issues; *Lettres Persanes*' (1721) critical view of French mores was a major success. From 1728 to 1731 M. traveled in Italy, Austria, Hungary, Switzerland, Germany and England, where he stayed for two years. *Considérations sur les causes de la grandeur des Romains et de leur décadence* presented a new approach to historical causation, explaining historical facts by social causes rather than personal motivation. Such 'structural' explanation of social phenomena is characteristic for his magnum opus, *De l'esprit des lois* (1748). The virulent reaction of both Jansenists and Jesuits was met by M. in *Défense de l'Esprit des lois* (1750), but his work was still put on the Index. *De l'esprit* was of fundamental importance to social, political, and historical thought and had a major influence on the *philosophes*, Hume, Ferguson, Smith,

Madison, and many others. It is now considered not only as a major text in the history of political philosophy but also as a pioneering work in sociology. Until the completion of the new critical edition (Oxford, 1998–) the best scholarly edition of the complete works is *Oeuvres Complètes de Montesquieu*, ed. A. Masson, 3 vols. (Paris, 1950–5).

Secondary Sources: J. d'Alembert, 'Éloge de M. le Président de Montesquieu', in *Encyclopédie*, 5: iii–xviii (1755). R. Shackleton, *Montesquieu: A Critical Biography* (London, 1961). L. Desgraves, *Chronologie critique de la vie et des Œuvres de Montesquieu* (Paris, 1998). D. de Tracey, *Commentaire sur l'Esprit des lois de Montesquieu* (Paris, 1819). É. Durkheim, *Quid secundatus politicae scientiae instituendae contulerit* (Bordeaux, 1892). J. Starobinski, *Montesquieu par lui-même* (Paris, 1953). L. Althusser, *Montesquieu, la politique et l'histoire* (Paris, 1959; trans. 1971). R. Aron, *Les étapes de la pensée sociologique* (Paris, 1967; trans. 1968). T. L. Pangle, *Montesquieu's Philosophy of Liberalism* (1973). M. Hulliung, *Montesquieu and the Old Régime* (1976). M. Richter, *The Political Theory of Montesquieu* (1977). L. Desgraves, *Montesquieu* (Paris, 1986). G. Benrekassa, *Montesquieu: La liberté et l'histoire* (Paris, 1987). J. Shklar, *Montesquieu* (Oxford, 1987). A. M. Cohler, *Montesquieu's Comparative Politics and the Spirit of American Constitutionalism* (Lawrence, KS, 1988). S. Goyard-Fabre, *Montesquieu: la nature, les lois, la liberté* (Paris, 1993). J. Ehrard, *L'esprit des mots: Montesquieu en lui-même et parmi les siens* (Geneva, 1998). B. Binoche, *Introduction à De l'esprit des lois de Montesquieu* (Paris, 1998). [Dario Perinetti]

MORITZ, KARL-PHILIPP b. Hamelin, 1757; d. Berlin, 1793. Writer. Studied theology at Erfurt; taught in Dessau and Berlin, where he was professor of ancient art (1789) and member of the Prussian Academy (1791). Trip to England resulted in *Reisen eines Deutschen in England im Jahr 1782* (1783; English translation, 1795); joined Goethe in Weimar and accompanied him on Italian journey, recounted in *Reisen eines Deutschen in Italien in den Jahren 1786 bis 1788* (1792). His 1785 *Berlinische Monatsschrift* essay 'Versuch einer Vereinigung aller schönen Künste und Wissenschaften unter dem Begriff des in sich selbst Vollendeten', argued for the 'autonomy' of aesthetic experience. Best known for novel *Anton Rieser* (1785–90), a pioneering contribution to the genre of *Bildungsroman*. *Werke*, ed. H. Günther (Frankfurt am Main, 1981).

Secondary Sources: M. Boulby, *Karl Philipp Moritz: At the Fringe of Genius* (Toronto, 1979). H. J. Schrimpf, *Karl Philipp Moritz* (Stuttgart, 1980). M. L. Davies, 'Karl Philipp Moritz's *Erfahrungsseelenkunde*: Its Social and Intellectual Origins', *Oxford German Studies* 16 (1985), 13–35. J. M. Hess, *Reconstituting the Body Politic: Enlightenment, Public Culture, and the Invention of Aesthetic Autonomy* (Detroit, 1999). [James Schmidt]

MURATORI, LODOVICO ANTONIO b. Vignola (Modena), 1672; d. Modena, 1750. Historian and man of letters. Educated in philosophy, theology and law, he was a librarian in the Ambrosian Library, then a priest, and finally archivist and librarian in Modena from 1700. He had diplomatic tasks and corresponded with Leibniz (1711). Founded the historiography of medieval Italy with *Rerum italicarum scriptores* (1723–38) and *Antiquitates italicae Medii Aevi* (1738–42); he wrote on literature and aesthetics in *Della perfetta poesia Italiana* (1706); also *De Paradiso* (1738) and *Della forza della fantasia umana* (1740). *Opere*, eds. G. Falco and F. Forti, 2 vols. (Milan and Naples, 1964).

Secondary Sources: S. Bertelli, *Erudizione e storia in Lodovico Antonio Muratori* (Naples, 1960). F. Venturi, *Settecento riformatore: Da Muratori a Beccaria* (Turin, 1969). E. Pattaro, *Il pensiero giuridico di L. A. Muratori tra metodologia e politica* (Milan, 1974). G. De Martino, *Muratori filosofo: ragione filosofica e coscienza storica in L. A. Muratori* (Naples, 1996). [Luca Fonnesu]

Musschenbroek, Petrus van b. Leiden, Netherlands, 1692; d. Leiden, 1761. Experimental physicist. Studied at Leiden (MD 1715, doctorate in philosophy 1719). As professor at Utrecht (1723–40) and Leiden (1740–61) he promoted both the Newtonian and experimental philosophies in the manner of his close friend, 'sGravesande. The textbooks based on his lectures, such as *Institutiones physicae* (1748) and the posthumously published *Introductio ad philosophiam naturalem* (1762), were widely used throughout Europe. His electrical experiments culminated in the invention of the 'Leyden jar', the first capacitor.

Secondary Sources: D. Bierens De Haan, *Bibliographie Néerlandaise Historique-Scientifique* (Rome, 1883). C. Pater, 'Petrus van Musschenbroek (1692–1761): A Dutch Newtonian', *Janus* 64 (1977): 77–87. [John Gascoigne]

Nettelbladt, Daniel b. Rostock, 1719; d. Halle, 1791. Jurist and Wolffian philosopher. Studied first theology, then law at Rostock, Marburg, and Halle (doctor of law 1744). Full professor of jurisprudence in Halle and royal Prussian privy aulic councillor 1746. Royal privy councillor 1756. Author of *Systema elementare jurisprudentiae naturalis* (1749), *Historie der demonstrativischen Rechtsgelehrtheit, von ihrem Anfang bis auf das Jahr 1745* (1754).

Secondary Sources: R. Stintzing and E. Landsberg, *Geschichte der deutschen Rechtswissenschaft*, Abt. III.1 (Leipzig, 1898), 288–99. K. Nörr, *Naturrecht und Zivilprozeß* (Tübingen, 1976). J. Schröder, *Wissenschaftstheorie und Lehre der 'praktischen Jurisprudenz'* (Frankfurt am Main, 1979). E. Hellmuth, *Naturrechtsphilosophie und bürokratischer Werthorizont* (Göttingen, 1985), 27–110. [Thomas Ahnert]

Nicolai, Friedrich b. Berlin, 1733; d. Berlin, 1811. Writer, critic, and publisher, closely associated with proponents of German Enlightenment in Berlin. *Briefe über den itzigen Zustand der schönen Wissenschaften in Deutschland* (1755) brought him into contact with Lessing and Mendelssohn, with whom he conducted the celebrated *Briefe über das Trauerspiel* (1756–7). He founded the journal *Bibliothek der schönen Wissenschaften und der freyen Künste* (1757) and, together with Mendelssohn and Lessing, *Briefe, die neueste Literatur betreffend* (1759–67), which gave way to the *Allgemeine deutsche Bibliothek* (1766–96). Emphasizing the cultural and social utility of philosophy and letters, he satirized and parodied pietistic and *Sturm und Drang* authors (including the early Goethe) in *Das Leben und die Meinungen des Herrn Sebaldus Nothanker* (1774–6) and *Freuden des jungen Werthers* (1775). He also contested Kantian and post-Kantian developments in works like *Leben und Meinungen Sempronius Grundiberts, eines deutschen Philosophen* (1798). *Sämtliche Werke, Briefe, Dokumente: kritische Ausgabe mit Kommentar*, eds. P. M. Mitchell et al. (Berlin, 1991–).

Secondary Sources: P. J. Becker et al., *Friedrich Nicolai: Leben und Werk* (Berlin, 1983). U. Schneider, *Friedrich Nicolais Allgemeine deutsche Bibliothek* (Wiesbaden, 1995). [Daniel Dahlstrom]

Paine, Thomas b. Thetford (Norfolk) 1737; d. New York, NY, 1809. International revolutionary, radical writer, political theorist, and journalist. Largely self-educated, Paine turned to journalism and writing after a career as stay-maker and excise man. He was part of the radical circle around the publisher Joseph Johnson in London, where he met Benjamin Franklin, whose letter of recommendation helped Paine settle as a writer and eventually a public official in America (1774). He played an important role in the American Revolution and published the widely read *Common Sense* (1776) in support of American independence and republicanism. Returned to England in 1787, where he was charged with seditious libel upon the publication of part two of his most famous work, *The Rights of Man* (1791–2), but escaped to live in exile in France, where he served in the National Assembly before falling afoul of the Jacobins and being put in prison for a year. Wrote a deist attack on Christianity, *The Age of Reason* (1794–5); returned to America in 1802, where he died in 1809. The standard edition of Paine's work is *The Complete Writings of Thomas Paine*, ed. P. S. Foner, 2 vols. (New York, NY, 1945).

Secondary Sources: M. D. Conway, *The Life of Thomas Paine*, 2 vols. (New York, NY, 1892). A. O. Aldridge, *Man of Reason: The Life of Thomas Paine* (London, 1960). M. Philp, *Paine* (Oxford, 1989). E. Foner, *Tom Paine and Revolutionary America* (Oxford, 1976). G. Claeys, *Thomas Paine: Social and Political Thought* (Boston, MA, 1989). J. Fruchtman, *Thomas Paine and the Religion of Nature* (Baltimore, MD, 1993); *Thomas Paine: Apostle of Freedom* (New York, NY, 1994). J. Keane, *Tom Paine: A Political Life* (London, 1995). B. Kuklick, Introduction, in Paine, *Political Writings* (Cambridge, 2000). [Åsa Söderman]

Paley, William b. Peterborough, 1743; d. Lincoln, 1805. Anglican divine and moral philosopher. Educated Christ's College, Cambridge (1759–63), was a fellow there (1766–75) and held a succession of preferments ending as archdeacon of Carlisle (1782). Active in anti-slave trade campaign. His *Principles of Moral and Political Philosophy* (1785), based on his lectures, is a lucid culmination of a century's development of Christian utilitarianism and had lasting impact as a textbook (fifteen life-time editions). His *Horae Paulinae, or the Truth of the Scripture History of St. Paul . . .* (1790), *A View of the Evidences of Christianity* (1794), and *Natural Theology; or Evidence of the Existence and Attributes of the Deity collected from the Appearances of Nature* (1802) had similar success. Of several collections, see esp. *The Works of William Paley, D. D.*, ed. E. Paley, 7 vols. (London, 1825).

Secondary Sources: G. W. Medley, *Memoirs of William Paley, D. D.* (Sunderland, 1809). E. Paley, 'Account of the Life and Writings of the Author', in Paley, *Works*. M. L. Clarke, *Paley: Evidences for the Man* (Toronto, 1974). D. L. Le Mahieu, *The Mind of William Paley: A Philosopher of His Age* (Lincoln, NE, 1976). T. P. Schofield, 'A Comparison of the Moral Theories of William Paley and Jeremy Bentham', *The Bentham Newsletter*, 11 (1987): 4–22. J. E. Crimmins, 'Religion, Utility and Politics: Bentham versus Paley', in *Religion, Secularization and Political Thought: Thomas Hobbes to J. S. Mill*, ed. J. E. Crimmins (London and New York, NY, 1990), 130–52. A. M. C. Waterman, *Revolution, Economics and Religion: Christian Political Economy, 1798–1833* (Cambridge, 1991), 113–50. V. Nuovo, 'Rethinking Paley'. *Synthese* 91 (1992): 29–51. [Knud Haakonssen]

Pestalozzi, Johann Heinrich b. Zürich, Switzerland, 1746; d. Brugg, Switzerland, 1827. Educationist. Educated at Collegium Carolinum. Member of reformist society in Zürich. Was strongly influenced by Rousseau's *Émile*, although he was later to express reservations about its impractical approach. In 1771 he started an experimental farm at the Neuhof which was turned into an educational and industrial enterprise teaching poor children to manage their own work. It failed in 1780. P. began to publish political, philosophical, and educational works, notably *Die Abendstunde eines Einsiedlers* (1779–80), *Ueber Gesetzgebung und Kindermord* (1783), and his first popular book, *Lienhard und Gertrud. Ein Buch für's Volk* (4 vols., 1781–7), a novel portraying an ideal village community, family life, and education. P. made two major revisions of *Lienhard und Gertrud*. The evolution of morality is the subject of *Meine Nachforschungen über den Gang der Natur in der Entwicklung des Menschengeschlechts* (1797). He returned to active teaching by establishing an Institute, first at Stanz in 1797, then Burgdorf, and finally, and most famously, at Yverdon in 1805. Financial, personal, and organisational problems, which dogged all of Pestalozzi's enterprises, led to its closure in 1825, and plans for a mixed agricultural and industrial school for the very poor at Neuhof had to be abandoned. Nevertheless Yverdon became a centre of pilgrimage for reformist educators throughout Europe and a renowned teacher-training establishment.

There is no single comprehensive statement of Pestalozzi's educational philosophy, the core of which was the development of the child's capacities. His international celebrity rested on *Wie Gertrud ihre Kinder lehrt, ein Versuch den Müttern Anleitung zu geben, ihre Kinder selbst zu unterrichten, in Briefen* (1801). Other significant writings include *Pestalozzi's Brief an einen Freund über seinen Aufenthalt in Stanz* (1799); *Mémoire über Armenversorgung mit spezieller Rücksicht auf Neuenburg (Armenerziehungs-Anstalten)* (1807); *Rede von Pestalozzi an sein Haus an seinem zwei und siebenzigsten Geburtstage, den 12. Jänner 1818* (1818); and *Pestalozzi's Schwanengesang* (1826). The major edition of the writings is *Pestalozzi: Sämtliche Werke*, ed. A. Buchenau et al., 28 vols. (Berlin and Zürich, 1927–76). A translation of a selection of Pestalozzi's work is to be found in *Pestalozzi's Educational Writings* (London, 1912).

Secondary Sources: K. Silber, *Pestalozzi: The Man and His Work* (London, 1960, rev. edn. 1976). E. Spranger, *Pestalozzi's Denkformen* (3rd edn., Heidelberg, 1966). A. Rang, *Der politische Pestalozzi* (Frankfurt, 1967). M. Heafford, *Pestalozzi: His Thought and Its Relevance Today* (London, 1967). F. Delekat, *Johann Heinrich Pestalozzi: Mensch, Philosoph, Politiker und Erzieher* (3rd edn., Heidelberg, 1968). A. Stein, *Pestalozzi und die Kantische Philosophie* (2nd edn., Darmstadt, 1969). M. Soëtard, *Pestalozzi ou la naissance de l'éducateur* (Bern, 1981). P. Stadler, *Pestalozzi: Geschichtliche Biographie*, 2 vols. (Zurich, 1988). D. Tröhler, *Philosophie und Pädagogik bei Pestalozzi* (Bern, 1988). H. Dräger, *Pestalozzis Idee von der Einheit der Erziehung. Pädagogik, Andragogik, Politik* (Frankfurt am Main, 1992). F.-P. Hager, *Pestalozzi und Rousseau: Pestalozzi als Vollender und als Gegner Rousseaus* (Bern, 1995). [Geraint Parry]

Platner, Ernst b. Leipzig, 1744; d. Leipzig, 1818. Professor of medicine from 1770, professor of philosophy from 1801 until his death, in Leipzig. Adopted Leibniz's conception of nature as an expression of immaterial forces but substituted reciprocity for its pre-established harmony in *Philosophische Aphorismen nebst einigen Anleitungen zur philosophischen Geschichte* (1776–82). Challenging Kant's philosophy in later editions and *Lehrbuch der Logik und Metaphysik* (1795), he combined logic with psychology, countenanced metaphysics, and increasingly emphasized ethics' priority. A prolific writer, his other major works include: *Neue Anthropologie für Ärzte und Weltweise. Mit besonderer Rücksicht auf Physiologie, Pathologie, Moralphilosophie und Aesthetik* (1772–4), *Gespräche über den Atheismus* (1794), and a collection of thirty-four previously published questions of medicine in *Opuscula academica* (1824).

Secondary Sources: A. Koenina, *Ernst Platners Anthropologie und Philosophie* (Wurzburg, 1989). [Daniel Dahlstrom]

Pouilly, Louis-Jean Lévesque de b. Reims 1691; d. Paris, 1750. Philosopher and member of the *Académie des Inscriptions*. Studied philosophy and literature in Paris. His *Dissertation sur l'incertitude de l'histoire des premiers siècles de Rome* (1723) launched a debate on the merits of historical scepticism. A friend of Nicolas Fréret and Lord Bolingbroke, he met Newton in England and probably hosted the young David Hume at Reims. His most important contribution was *Théorie des sentimens agréables* (1736). The posthumous edition of the *Théorie* (Paris, 1774) contains some of his other writings.

Secondary Sources: P. de Saulx, *Éloge historique de M. Lévesque de Pouilly, lieutenant des habitans de la ville de Reims* (Reims, 1751). J.-V. Genet, *Étude sur la vie, l'administration et les travaux littéraires de L.-J. Lévesque de Pouilly*, in *Travaux de l'Académie nationale de Reims* 64–7 (1881): 1–201. C. Borghero, 'Pirronismo storico, tradizione Romana e teoria della conoscenza storica in un dibattito settecentesco all'Academie des Inscriptions', *Filosofia* 32 (1981): 175–210. J. S. Spink, 'Lévesque de Pouilly et David Hume', *Revue de littérature comparée* 56 (1982), 157–75. [Dario Perinetti]

PRICE, RICHARD b. Tynton, Llangeinor, Glamorgan, 1723; d. London, 1791. Dissenting minister, philosopher, political and social theorist. Educated at dissenting academies, esp. Moorfields Academy, London; minister at Newington Green and at Gravel Pit, Hackney. Price's main contribution to philosophy is *A Review of the Principal Questions in Morals* (1758), one of the sharpest formulations of eighteenth-century rationalism in ethics. His Real Whig principles developed in a radical direction from the 1760s when he began criticizing the politics of the national debt, esp. in *An Appeal to the Public on the Subject of the National Debt* (1772); and his ideas on freedom of theoretical inquiry and religious practice, political participation and self-determination, and patriotism, were brought out in sympathetic responses to the American Revolution and the first phase of the French Revolution, see esp. *Observations on the Nature of Civil Liberty* (1776); *Additional Observations on Civil Liberty* (1777) (together as *Two Tracts on Civil Liberty*, 1778); *Observations on the Importance of the American Revolution* (1784); and *A Discourse on the Love of our Country* (1789). His millennialist perspective on these events is further underlined in *The Evidence for a Future Period of Improvement in the State of Mankind* (1787). Pioneering work in probability and actuarial theory resulted in *Observations on Reversionary Payments* (1771). See also *Four Dissertations* (1767), *Sermons*, ed. W. Morgan (1816), and *The Correspondence of Richard Price*, eds. D. O. Thomas and W. B. Peach, 3 vols. (Cardiff and Durham, NC, 1983–94).

Secondary Sources: W. Morgan, *Memoirs of the Life of the Rev. Richard Price, DD, FRS* (London, 1815). R. Thomas, *Richard Price: Philosopher and Apostle of Liberty* (Oxford, 1924). C. B. Cone, *Torchbearer of Freedom: The Influence of Richard Price on Eighteenth-Century Thought* (Lexington, KY, 1952). *A Bibliography of the Works of Richard Price*, eds. D. O. Thomas, J. Stephens, and P. A. L. Jones (Aldershot, 1993). H. Laboucheix, *Richard Price: Théoricien de la Révolution Américain, le philosophe et le sociologue, le pamphlétaire et l'orateur* (Paris, 1970; Eng. trans. Oxford, 1982). W. D. Hudson, *Reason and Right: A Critical Examination of Richard Price's Moral Philosophy* (London, 1970). 'Editor's Introduction', in Price, *A Review of the Principal Questions in Morals*, ed. D. D. Raphael, rev. edn. (Oxford, 1974), xiv–lii. D. O. Thomas, *The Honest Mind: The Thought and Work of Richard Price* (Oxford, 1977). D. O. Thomas, Introduction, in R. Price, *Political Writings* (Cambridge, 1991), vii–xxvii. I. Rivers, *Reason, Grace, and Sentiment. A Study of the language of Religion and Ethics in England, 1660–1780*, 2 vols. (Cambridge, 1991–2000), 2: *Shaftesbury to Hume*, ch. 3. [Knud Haakonssen]

PRIESTLEY, JOSEPH b. Leeds, 1733; d. Northumberland, Pennsylvania, 1804. Philosopher, scientist, minister, writer, and reformer in politics and religion. Primarily self-educated, also at Dissenting Academy of Daventry (1752). Decisively influenced by Hartley and Collins. On leaving Daventry taught language and preached (ordained 1762). Gained notoriety as a scientist; through Price's assistance took post as librarian to Earl of Shelburne (1772–80), in whose service he discovered dephlogisticated air (oxygen) (1774). After leaving Shelburne became minister to the New Meeting at Birmingham (1780–91), helped found the Unitarian Society, and defended principles of the French Revolution. In 1791 a mob burned New Meeting, his house, and much else. Succeeded Price as morning preacher at Hackney (1791), then followed sons to America (1794), where he spent his last years. Among chief writings in his enormous, diverse *oeuvre* are: *The History and Present State of Electricity with Original Experiments* (1767), *An Essay on the First Principles of Government* (1768) *Experiments and Observations on Different Kinds of Air* (1774–86), *An Examination of . . . Reid . . . Beattie . . . and . . . Oswald* (1774), *Hartley's Theory of the Human Mind* (1775), *Disquisitions Relating to Matter and Spirit* (1777), *A Free Discussion of Materialism and Philosophical Necessity* (an exchange with Richard Price, 1778), *Letters to a Philosophical Unbeliever* (1780–2), *An History of the Corruptions of Christianity* (1782), *Memoirs of Dr. Joseph Priestley to the Year 1795 Written by Himself with a Continuation to the Time of His Decease by his Son, Joseph*

Priestley (1806). Collected edn.: *The Theological and Miscellaneous Works*, ed. J. T. Rutt, 25 vols. in 26 (London, 1817–32; facsim. New York, NY, 1972).

Secondary Sources: J. G. McEvoy, 'Joseph Priestley, Aerial Philosopher: Metaphysics and Methodology in Priestley's Chemical Thought from 1762 to 1781', *Ambix* 25.1 (1978): 1–54; 25.2 (1978): 93–116; 25.3 (1978): 153–75; 25.4 (1979): 16–38. I. Kramnick, 'Eighteenth-Century Science and Radical Social Theory: The Case of Joseph Priestley's Scientific Liberalism', *Journal of British Studies* 25 (1986): 1–30. J. Graham, 'Revolutionary Philosopher: The Political Ideas of Joseph Priestley (1733–1804)', *Enlightenment and Dissent* 8 (1989): 43–68 and 9 (1990): 14–46. A. Saunders, 'The State as Highwayman: From Candour to Rights' in *Enlightenment and Religion: Rational Dissent in Eighteenth-Century Britain* (Cambridge, 1996). R. Schofield *The Enlightenment of Joseph Priestley: A Study of His Life and Works from 1733 to 1773* (University Park, PA, 1997). [Aaron Garrett]

Réaumur, René-Antoine Ferchault de b. La Rochelle, France, 1683; d. St.-Julien-du-Terroux, France, 1757. Scientific researcher on a wide range of applied and biological topics, notably industrial chemistry and animal physiology. Such fields presented difficulties for the mathematized Newtonian science that appeared to be carrying all before it. His work on the ability of simple animals to regenerate severed limbs fascinated philosophers, who wondered whether a materialist theory of biology could explain such a phenomenon. His very detailed research on bees established the crucial role of the queen in bee society. Writings include *Histoire de fourmi* (*The Natural History of Ants*, unpubl. manuscript, trans. W. M. Wheeler, 1926); *L'Art de convertir le fer forgé en acier* (1722); *Mémoires pour servir a l'histoire des insectes*, 6 vols. (Amsterdam, 1734–42).

Secondary Sources: *La vie et l'oeuvre de Réaumur* (Paris, 1962). J. R. Gough, 'Réaumur', *Dictionary of Scientific Biography*, 11: 327–35. V. P. Dawson, *Nature's Enigma: The Problem of the Polyp in the Letters of Bonnet, Trembley and Réaumur* (Philadelphia, PA, 1987). C. E. Dinsmore, *A History of Regeneration Research* (Cambridge, 1991). [James Franklin]

Reid, Thomas b. Strachan, Kincardineshire, Scotland 1710; d. Glasgow 1796. Leading proponent of Common Sense philosophy. Educated at Marischal College, Aberdeen, 1722–31; presbytery clerk and librarian at Marischal, 1731–36; minister of New-Machar, 1737–51. As regent at King's College, Aberdeen, 1751–64, Reid taught the full arts curriculum (see his graduation *Orations*). He was heavily involved in the cultural life of Aberdeen, notably as co-founder and leading light in the Aberdeen Philosophical Society ('The Wise Club') in which he presented much of *An Inquiry into the Human Mind, on the Principles of Common Sense* (1764) and where he influenced John Gregory, David Skene, George Campbell, Alexander Gerard, James Beattie, et al. In 1764 he succeeded Adam Smith as professor of moral philosophy at the University of Glasgow, strongly supported by his friend, Lord Kames, with whom he had a philosophically interesting correspondence and to whose *Sketches of the History of Man* (1774) he contributed 'A Brief Account of Aristotle's Logic'. With the translation to a specialised professorship, he developed his philosophy in greater detail, partly through his teaching, partly in contributions to the Glasgow College Literary Society. Reid retired from teaching in 1780 and wrote up major parts of his philosophical thought in *Essays on the Intellectual Powers of Man* (1785) and *Essays on the Active Powers of Man* (1788). All his life he participated in physical sciences, was a fine mathematician, and a keen political and economic speculator. On all these subjects, and more, he wrote prodigiously but did not publish, except for a token of his late involvement in the political upheavals of the 1790s ('Observations on the Dangers of Political Innovation', 1794, in *Practical Ethics*, 277–99). Reid was influential, especially in France and America, in the first half of the nineteenth century. The old standard edition is *The Works of Thomas Reid, D. D. . . . with*

Selection from His Unpublished Letters, ed. W. Hamilton (Edinburgh, 1846). A 10-vol. critical edition including correspondence and extensive selections from the Nachlass is in progress: *The Edinburgh Edition of Thomas Reid*, gen. ed. K. Haakonssen (Edinburgh, 1995–). A forerunner for this edition is, *Practical Ethics; Being Lectures and Papers on Natural Religion, Self-Government, Natural Jurisprudence and the Law of Nations*, ed. K. Haakonssen (Princeton, NJ, 1990). Other ms. material is in *The Philosophical Orations of Thomas Reid delivered at Graduation Ceremonies in King's College Aberdeen, 1753, 1756, 1759, 1762*, ed. W. R. Humphries (Aberdeen, 1737); trans. S. D. Sullivan, ed. D. D. Todd (Carbondale, IL, 1989); 'Cura Prima. Of Common Sense', ed. D. F. Norton, in L. Marcil-Lacoste, *Claude Buffier and Thomas Reid: Two Common Sense Philosophers* (Kingston and Montreal, 1982); 'Thomas Reid on Adam Smith's Theory of Morals', ed. J. C. Stewart-Robertson and D. F. Norton, in *Journal of the History of Ideas* 41 (1980), 381–98 and 45 (1984), 309–21.

Secondary Sources: D. Stewart, *Account of the Life and Writings of Thomas Reid*, in Dugald Stewart, *Collected Works*, ed. W. Hamilton (Edinburgh, 1854–60) vol. 10. J. McCosh, *The Scottish Philosophy, Biographical, Expository, Critical, from Hutcheson to Hamilton* (Edinburgh, 1875), ch. 26. H. Sidgwick, 'The Philosophy of Common Sense', *Mind*, n.s. 4 (1895), 145–158. A. Campbell Fraser, *Thomas Reid* (Edinburgh, 1898). J. Priestley, *An Examination of Dr. Reid's Inquiry into the Human Mind* (London, 1774). D. D. Raphael, *The Moral Sense* (Oxford, 1947). S. A. Grave, *The Scottish Philosophy of Common Sense* (Oxford, 1960). D. F. Norton, 'From Moral Sense to Common Sense: An Essay on the Development of Scottish Common Sense Philosophy, 1700–1765' (PhD, University of California at San Diego, 1966). G. E. Davie, *The Social Significance of the Scottish Philosophy of Common Sense* (Dow Lecture, University of Dundee, Dundee, 1973). *The Philosophy of Thomas Reid*, in *The Monist* 61 (1978). *Thomas Reid: Critical Interpretations*, eds. S. F. Barker and T. L. Beauchamp (Philadelphia, PA, 1976). D. Schulthess, *Philosophie et sens commun chez Thomas Reid (1710–1796)* (Berne, 1983). P. B. Wood, 'Thomas Reid, Natural Philosopher: A Study of Science and Philosophy in the Scottish Enlightenment' (PhD, University of Leeds, 1984). J. W. Yolton, *Perceptual Acquaintance: From Descartes to Reid* (Oxford, 1984). M. Kuehn, *Scottish Common Sense in Germany, 1768–1800: A Contribution to the History of Critical Philosophy* (Kingston and Montreal, 1987). *The Philosophy of Thomas Reid*, eds. M. Dalgarno and E. Matthews (Dordrecht, 1989). N. Daniels, *Thomas Reid's Inquiry: The Geometry of Visibles and the Case for Realism* (Stanford, CA, 1989). R. D. Gallie, *Thomas Reid and 'the Way of Ideas'* (Dordrecht, 1989). K. Lehrer, *Thomas Reid* (London, 1989). W. L. Rowe, *Thomas Reid on Freedom and Morality* (Ithaca, NY, 1991). P. B. Wood, *The Aberdeen Enlightenment: The Arts Curriculum in the Eighteenth Century* (Aberdeen, 1993). J. W. Manns, *Reid and His French Disciples: Aesthetics and Metaphysics* (Leiden, 1994). K. Haakonssen, *Natural Law and Moral Philosophy: From Grotius to the Scottish Enlightenment* (Cambridge, 1996), ch. 6. P. J. Diamond, *Common Sense and Improvement: Thomas Reid as Social Theorist* (Frankfurt am Main, 1998). N. Wolterstorff, *Thomas Reid and the Story of Epistemology* (Cambridge, 2001). *The Philosophy of Thomas Reid. A Collection of Essays*, eds. J. Haldane and S. Read (Malden, MA, Oxford, 2003). *The Cambridge Companion to Thomas Reid*, eds. T. Cuneo and R. van Woudenberg (Cambridge, 2004). G. Yaffe, *Manifest Activity: Thomas Reid's Theory of Action* (Oxford, 2004). [Knud Haakonssen]

Reimarus, Hermann Samuel b. Hamburg, 1694; d. Hamburg, 1768. Philosopher and Deist. Studied theology, philosophy, and philology in Jena (1714–16) and Wittenberg (1716–20); travelled through Holland and England (1720–21); taught in Wittenberg; from 1723 principal at the high school in Wismar; Professor of oriental languages at the Academic Gymnasium in Hamburg. His writings were influenced by Johann Franz Buddeus, Christian Wolff, and English Deism (especially John Toland). Tried to prove in *Die vornehmsten Wahrheiten der natürlichen Religion* (1754) the wisdom and goodness of nature; the only miracle ever is the creation of the world. In the *Allgemeine Betrachtungen über die Triebe der Thiere, hauptsächlich über ihre Kunst-Triebe* (1760) he gave anti-cartesian animal psychology its foundation. In his *Vernunftlehre, als eine Anweisung zum richtigen Gebrauche der Vernunft in der Erkenntniß der Wahrheit* (1756) he contributed significantly to hermeneutics and the theory of probability. He is author of the so-called *Wolfenbütteler Fragmente* (1774–7) postnumously published by Lessing. Modern editions: *Vernunftlehre*, ed. F. Loetzsch (Munich, 1979); *Kleine gelehrte Schriften*, ed. W. Schmidt-Biggemann (Göttingen, 1994).

Secondary Sources: H. S. Reimarus, *Handschriftenverzeichnis und Bibliographie*, ed. W. Schmidt-Biggemann (Göttingen, 1979). D. F. Strauß, *Hermann Samuel Reimarus und seine Schutzschrift für die vernünftigen Verehrer Gottes* (Leipzig, 1862); *Hermann Samuel Reimarus (1694–1768) ein 'bekannter Unbekannter' der Aufklärung in Hamburg* (Göttingen, 1973). *Logik im Zeitalter der Aufklärung: Studien zur 'Vernunftlehre' von Hermann Samuel Reimarus*, eds. W. Walter and L. Borinski (Göttingen, 1980). *Unzeitgemäße Hermeneutik. Verstehen und Interpretation im Denken der Aufklärung*, ed. A. Bühler (Frankfurt am Main, 1994). W. Alexander, 'Pluraque credimus, paucissima scimus. Zur Diskussion über philosophische und hermeneutische Wahrscheinlichkeit in der ersten Hälfte des 18. Jahrhunderts', *Archiv für Geschichte der Philosophie* 78 (1996), 130–65. P. Stemmer, *Weissagung und Kritik. Eine Studie zur Hermeneutik bei Hermann Samuel Reimarus* (Göttingen, 1997). [Heiner F. Klemme]

Reinhard, Adolf Friedrich von b. Altstreliz,1726; d. Wetzlar, 1783. Civil servant and man of letters. Studied law in Thorn and theology in Halle and was a supporter of pietism and of the philosophy of Christian August Crusius. His *La système de Mr. Pope sur la perfection du monde comparé à celui de Mr. Leibniz* (1755; German trans. 1757), a critique of the philosophy of Pope, Leibniz, and Wolff, won first prize at the Academy of Sciences in Berlin. He became professor of law at the University of Bützow in 1770. Engaged in extensive polemics against Lessing, Herder, Wieland, Klopstock, and, disastrously for him, Goethe. His *Kritische Sammlungen zur neuesten Geschichte der Gelehrsamkeit* (founded 1744) was a counterpart to the *Deutsche Allgemeine Bibliothek* of Berlin.

Secondary Sources: *Allgemeine Deutsche Biographie*, vol. 28 (Leipzig, 1889), 35–6. S. Pott, *Reformierte Morallehren und deutsche Literatur von Jean Barbeyrac bis Christoph Martin Wieland* (Tübingen, 2002). [Luca Fonnesu]

Reinhold, Karl Leonhard b. Vienna, 1757; d. Kiel, Germany 1823. Post-Kantian philosopher. Jesuit education 1772–3; studied philosophy and theology at the college of the Barnabites from 1773 and later taught philosophy there. He moved to Weimar in 1783, converted to Protestantism, and became a contributor to Wieland's *Teutscher Merkur*. Was Professor of Philosophy at Jena from 1787–94, and at Kiel from 1794 until his death. He supported Kant's critical philosophy in his early *Briefe über die Kantische Philosophie* (first in the *Teutscher Merkur*, 1786–7, in bookform, 1790–2). His most important works are *Versuch einer neuen Theorie des menschlichen Vorstellungsvermögens* (1789); *Beyträge zur Berichtigung bisheriger Missverständnisse der Philosophen* (1790–4); and *Ueber das Fundament des philosophischen Wissens* (1791). In the *Versuch* he attempted to provide Kantian transcendental philosophy with a meta-critical foundation. This work is regarded as important not only for its critique of Kant but also for paving the way to Fichte and, indirectly, to German Idealism. He changed his position several times. Briefly a follower of Fichte, he developed his own system based on a philosophy of language. These later writings include: *Versuch einer Kritik der Logik aus dem Gesichtspunkt der Sprache* (1806); *Grundlegung einer Synonymik für den allgemeinen Sprachgebrauch in den philosophischen Wissenschaften* (1812). Early letters in *Karl Leonhard Reinhold Korrespondenzausgabe. Band 1: Korrespondenz 1773–1788*, eds. R. Lauth, E. Heller and K. Hiller (Stuttgart-Bad Cannstatt, 1983).

Secondary Sources: A. von Schönborn, *Karl Leonhard Reinhold. Eine annotierte Bibliographie* (Stuttgart-Bad Cannstatt, 1991). E. Reinhold, *Karl Leonhard Reinhold's Leben und litterarisches Wirken* (Jena, 1825). M. Selling, *Studien zur Transzendentalphilosophie I. Karl Leonhard Reinholds Elementarphilosophie in ihrem problemgeschichtlichen Zusammenhang* (Lund, 1938). A. Klemmt, *Karl Leonhard Reinholds Elementarphilosophie. Eine Studie über den Ursprung des deutschen Idealismus* (Hamburg, 1958). A. Klemmt, 'Die philosophische Entwicklung Karl Leonhard Reinholds nach 1800', *Zeitschrift für philosophische Forschung* 15 (1961): 79–101, 250–77. *Philosophie aus einem Prinzip. K. L. Reinhold*, ed. R. Lauth (Bonn, 1974). D. Breazeale, 'Between Kant and Fichte: Karl Leonhard Reinhold's 'Elementary Philosophy', *Review of Metaphysics* 35 (1981–2): 785–821. F. C. Beiser, *The Fate of Reason. German Philosophy from Kant to Fichte* (Cambridge, MA, 1987), 226–65. D. Henrich, 'Die Anfänge der Theorie des Subjekts (1789)', in *Zwischenbetrachtungen im Prozeß der Aufklärung*, eds. A. Honneth et al. (Frankfurt am Main, 1989), 106–70. M. Bondeli, *Das Anfangsproblem bei Karl Leonhard Reinhold* (Frankfurt am Main, 1995). K. Y. Kim, *Religion, Moral und Aufklärung. Reinholds philosophischer Werdegang* (Frankfurt and New York, NY, 1996). M. Frank, *Unendliche Annäherung. Die Anfänge der philosophischen Chromantik* (Frankfurt, 1997), 152–427. K. Ameriks, *Kant and the Fate of Autonomy. Problems in the Appropriation of the Critical Philosophy* (Cambridge, 2000): 81–160. [Udo Thiel]

Rousseau, Jean-Jacques b. Geneva 1712; d. Ermenonville 1778. Rousseauvian. The son of a watchmaker, Rousseau received no formal education but was apprenticed to an engraver until he ran away. 1728–40 his life was dominated by Mme. de Warens with whom he lived at Annency and Chambéry, interrupted by a stay in Turin, where he converted to Catholicism (consequently forfeiting his Genevan citizenship) and briefly attended a seminary. Having set his mind to become a writer while with Mme. de Warens, he became a tutor for the Mably family in Lyons, 1741–2, where he also met Mably's brother, the Abbé de Condillac. From 1742 to the mid '50s, Rousseau lived mainly in Paris, except for 1743–4 when he was secretary to the French ambassador in Venice. Vainly promoting such works as a new system of musical notation, his opera *Le Devin du village*, eventually staged 1752, his comedy *Narcisse*, finally performed 1752, and his poems, he lived mainly by tutoring and transcribing music. His friend Diderot commissioned articles on music from him for the *Encyclopédie*, and he achieved overnight literary fame across Europe with his *Discours sur les sciences et les arts* (1751), which won the prize of the Academy of Dijon for which it had been entered anonymously. He failed to win the Academy's next competition but his entry, *Discours sur l'origine et les fondements de l'inégalité parmi les hommes* (1755), was to prove his classic contribution to philosophical anthropology. Through an acute analysis of civilization's deformation of human nature, he held culture responsible for mankind's fall, which he tried to explain historically as an alternative to the Augustinian doctrine of original sin. A closely associated *Essai sur l'origine des langues* begun around this period but largely drafted a few years later was only published posthumously (1781); and his *Discours sur l'économie politique*, introducing his concept of the general will, appeared in vol. 5 of the *Encyclopédie* in 1755. In 1756 R. moved to the estate of a protectress and friend of Diderot, Mme. d'Epinay, where he lived in relative seclusion in the cottage *The Hermitage* with Thérèse Levasseur, whom he had met in Paris and who was to be his lifelong partner (from 1768, wife), bearing him five children, every one abandoned to a religious orphanage as soon as it was born. Having visited Geneva in 1754 and, after reconverting to Calvinism and reclaiming his citizenship, he continued to champion his ideal of that city as heir to a stern classical Roman republicanism, as he had done already in the two *Discours*. In *Lettre à d'Alembert* (1758) he applied his criticism of the arts in an attack on d'Alembert's proposal for a Genevan theatre, and this was the culmination of R.'s estrangement from the circle of Parisian *philosophes*. One of the most successful novels of the eighteenth century and a major source for R.'s moral psychology, *Julie, ou la Nouvelle Héloïse* appeared in

1761, succeeded the following year by the most influential work on education of the modern era, *Émile*, and by his attempt at a political solution to the moral problem of civilization's corruption, namely the doctrine that sovereignty could be legitimate only when it was based on the collective general will of all citizens, as articulated in his *Contrat social*. The latter two works were publicly condemned and burned in Geneva, *Émile* also in France, and both countries issued arrest warrants for the author, who sought exile in Neuchâtel (1763–5), then subject to the king of Prussia. With *Lettres de la montagne* (1764) he intervened in the Genevan constitutional controversy he had reinvigorated; and he drafted a *Projet de constitution pour la Corse* (published 1861). He also began his *Confessions* (published in two parts 1782 and 1789), a tour de force of candid self-analysis but to the work's critics a profoundly insightful study of self-deception. Apprehensive about his safety, he took refuge in England 1765–7, helped by David Hume; but the clashing temperaments of the two philosophers and Rousseau's mounting paranoia in this period led to one of the century's most celebrated quarrels. For the rest of his life, Rousseau lived in France, first in disguise but from 1770 openly and, as it transpired, largely ignored by the authorities. Along with other political thinkers, he was invited to advise on a new constitution for Poland and his *Considérations sur le gouvernement de Pologne* (1771 but only published 1782) reasserted the ideal of participatory citizenship set out in *Contrat social*. At the same time, he began a tortured and tortuous apologia, *Dialogues: Rousseau juge de Jean-Jacques* (published posthumously). He also deepened his botanical studies and continued composing music. A life's work devoted to interpreting humanity through authorial self-analysis ended – some would say culminated – with the meditations Rousseau was still drafting when he died, *Les Rêveries du promeneur solitaire*, in the tranquillity of its prose very different in character from the *Dialogues* and one of the chief sources of literary romanticism. His autobiographical and later political works and much other unpublished material appeared in *Collection complète des oeuvres de J. J. Rousseau* (Geneva, 1782). The modern standard edition of the works is *Oeuvres complètes*, eds. B. Gagnebin, M. Raymond, et al., 5 vols. (Paris 1959–99), and of the correspondence, *Correspondance complète*, ed. R. A. Leigh, 52 vols. (Geneva and Banbury 1965–89). A comprehensive translation is in progress, *Collected Works*, eds. R. D. Masters and C. Kelly (Hanover, NH, and London, 1990–).

Secondary Sources: R. Grimsley, *Jean-Jacques Rousseau, a Study in Self-Awareness* (Cardiff, 1961; 2nd edn. 1969). L. Crocker, *Jean-Jacques Rousseau: The Quest (1712–1758)* (New York, 1968); *Jean-Jacques Rousseau: The Prophetic Voice (1758–1778)* (New York, 1973). M. Cranston, *Jean-Jacques: The Early Life and Work of Jean-Jacques Rousseau 1712–1754* (Chicago, IL, 1982); *The Noble Savage: Jean-Jacques Rousseau 1754–1762* (Chicago, IL, 1991); *The Solitary Self: Jean-Jacques Rousseau in Exile and Adversity* (Chicago, IL, 1997). P.-M. Masson, *La Religion de J.-J. Rousseau*, 3 vols. (Paris, 1916). E. Cassirer, 'Das Problem Jean-Jacques Rousseau', *Archiv für Geschichte der Philosophie* 41 (1932): 177–213 and 479–513; English translation: *The Question of Jean-Jacques Rousseau*, trans. P. Gay (New York, NY, 1954). A. Cobban, *Rousseau and the Modern State* (London, 1934, 2nd ed. 1964). C. W. Hendel, *Jean-Jacques Rousseau: Moralist*, 2 vols. (London, 1934). A. O. Lovejoy, 'Rousseau's Supposed Primitivism', in *Essays on the History of Ideas* (Baltimore, MD, 1948). P. Burgelin, *La Philosophie de l'existence de J.-J. Rousseau* (Paris, 1950). R. Derathé, *Jean-Jacques Rousseau et la science politique de son temps* (Paris, 1950). J. W. Chapman, *Rousseau – Totalitarian or Liberal?* (New York, NY, 1956). J. Starobinski, *Jean-Jacques Rousseau: La transparence et l'obstacle* (Paris, 1957; rev. edn. 1970; English translation, Chicago IL, 1988). J. Derrida, *De la grammatologie* (Paris, 1967). R. D. Masters, *The Political Philosophy of Rousseau* (Princeton, NJ, 1968). J. N. Shklar, *Men and Citizens: A Study of Rousseau's Social Theory* (Cambridge, 1969). M. Duchet, *Anthropologie et histoire au siècle des lumières* (Paris, 1971). B. Baczko, *Rousseau: Solitude et communauté* (Paris, 1974). V. Goldschmidt, *Anthropologie et politique: Les principes du système de Rousseau* (Paris, 1974). A. Levine, *The Politics of Autonomy* (Amherst, MA, 1976). P. Riley, *Will and Political Legitimacy: A Critical Exposition of Social Contract Theory in Hobbes, Locke, Rousseau, Kant, and Hegel* (Cambridge, MA, 1982).

P. Coleman, *Rousseau's Political Imagination: Rule and Representation in the Lettre à d'Alembert* (Geneva, 1984). J. Miller, *Rousseau: Dreamer of Democracy* (New Haven, CT, 1984). J. Schwartz, *The Sexual Politics of Jean-Jacques Rousseau* (Chicago, IL, 1984). P. Riley, *The General Will Before Rousseau: The Transformation of the Divine into the Civic* (Princeton, NJ, 1986). C. Kelly, *Rousseau's Exemplary Life. The Confessions as Political Philosophy* (Ithaca, NY, 1987). R. Wokler, *Rousseau on Society, Politics, Music, and Language: An Historical Interpretation of his Early Writings* (New York, NY, 1987). A. M. Melzer, *The Natural Goodness of Man: On the System of Rousseau's Thought* (Chicago, IL, 1990). Z. Trachtenberg, *Making Citizens. Rousseau's Political Theory of Culture* (New York, NY, 1993). M. Hulliung, *The Autocritique of Enlightenment. Rousseau and the Philosophes* (Cambridge, MA, 1994). R. Wokler, *Rousseau* (Oxford, 1995, 2nd edn. 2001). H. Rosenblatt, *Rousseau and Geneva: From the First Discourse to the Social Contract, 1749–1762* (Cambridge, 1997). T. O'Hagan, *Rousseau* (London, 1999). C. Kelly, *Rousseau as Author: Consecrating One's Life to the Truth* (Chicago, IL, 2003). [Knud Haakonssen]

Rüdiger, Andreas b. Rochlitz, Germany, 1673; d. Leipzig, 1731. Pietist theologian, philosopher, and physician. Studied 1692–96 in Halle (Saale), where he became private tutor to the family of his teacher Christian Thomasius; studied theology in Jena (1696–7) and jurisprudence and medicine in Leipzig (MA 1700, medical doctor 1703); practiced medicine in Halle (1707–12) and taught in Leipzig. Was a declared opponent of the Leibniz-Wolffian school and of the mathematical method; advanced the theory of 'influxus physicus' and Thomasius' practical philosophy. Sometimes considered to be the most philosophical of the early Thomasians, he influenced Christian August Crusius, the main opponent of Wolffianism. His writings include: *Philosophia synthetica methodo mathematicae aemula comprehensa* (1707); revised versions: *Institutiones eruditionis* (1711) and *Philosophia pragmatica* (1723); *De sensu veri et falsi* (1709); *Anweisung zur Zufriedenheit* (1721); *Die Klugheit zu leben und zu herrschen* (1722).

Secondary Sources: W. Carls, *Andreas Rüdigers Moralphilosophie* (Halle, 1894). H. Schepers, *Andreas Rüdigers Methodologie und ihre Voraussetzungen: Ein Beitrag zur Geschichte der deutschen Schulphilosophie im XVIII. Jahrhundert* (Köln, 1959). L. W. Beck, *Early German Philosophy: Kant and his Predecessors* (Cambridge, MA, 1969). [Heiner F. Klemme]

Rutherforth, Thomas b. Papworth, Cambridgeshire, 1712; d. Albins, Essex, 1771. Philosopher and theologian. Educated at St. John's College, Cambridge; fellow there 1733 to 1752. He was a popular teacher of natural philosophy; his soundly Newtonian lectures were published as *A System of Natural Philosophy* (1748). He also was an influential teacher of moral philosophy; those lectures were published as the *Institutes of Natural Law* (1754–6) – a work which draws heavily on Grotius but also outlines a largely utilitarian conception of morality. Earlier, in *An Essay on the Nature and Obligations of Virtue* (1744), he had offered a critique of other dominant schools of moral philosophy in Britain at the time, chiefly the views of Mandeville and Hutcheson's concept of a moral sense.

Secondary Sources: J. Gascoigne, *Cambridge in the Age of the Enlightenment: Science, Religion and Politics from the Restoration to the French Revolution* (Cambridge, 1989), passim. P. N. Miller, *Defining the Common Good: Empire, Religion, and Philosophy in Eighteenth-Century Britain* (Cambridge, 1994), 142–9. [John Gascoigne]

Schelling, Friedrich Wilhelm Joseph von b. Leonberg, 1775; d. Bad Rogaz, 1854. Philosopher. Educated at cloister school in Bebenhausen and Tübingen Seminary (1790), where his classmates included Hegel and Hölderlin. Influenced by Fichte's writings, began elaborating his own philosophical system in *Über die Möglichkeit einer Form der Philosophie überhaupt* (1794), *Vom*

Ich als Princip der Philosophie (1795), *Briefe über Dogmatismus und Kritizismus* (1795), *Neue Deduction des Naturrechts* (1796), *Ideen zu einer Philosophie der Natur* (1797), and *Von der Weltseele* (1798). After serving as a tutor, moved to Jena, where, with Goethe's support, he became professor of philosophy (1798–1803) and wrote *System des transzendentalen Idealismus* (1800), *Darstellung meines Systems der Philosophie* (1801), *Bruno oder über das göttliche und natürliche Prinzip der Dinge* (1802), *Philosophie der Kunst* (1802–3), *Über das Wesen der philosophischen Kritik überhaupt* (1802) and, joined by Hegel, edited *Kritisches Journal der Philosophie* (1801–3), an important journal in the development of idealism. During this period, he played a central role in the development of Jena Romanticism, maintaining close contact with Ludwig Tieck, Novalis, and Friedrich and A. W. Schlegel, whose wife Caroline he married in 1803, after Schlegel moved to Berlin and granted her a divorce. Moved to university of Würzburg in 1803, then to Munich in 1806, where he served as associate of the Academy of Sciences, secretary of the Academy of the Arts, and secretary of the philosophical section of the Academy of Sciences, while lecturing at Stuttgart and Erlangen (1820–7). Appointed to the Berlin Academy and lectured at the university 1841–5. His Berlin lectures were published after his death as *Einleitung in die Mythologie, Philosophie der Mythologie* and *Philosophie der Offenbarung* in *Sämmtliche Werke*, ed. K. F. A. von Schelling, 14 vols. (Stuttgart and Augsburg, 1856–61). New critical edition: *Historisch-kritische Ausgabe* (Stuttgart, 1976–).

Secondary Sources: X. Tilliette, *Schelling: une philosophie en devenir*, 2 vols (Paris, 1970). W. Schulz, *Die Vollendung des deutschen Idealismus in der Spätphilosophie Schellings* (Pfullingen, 1975). A. White, *Schelling: An Introduction to the System of Freedom* (New Haven, CT, 1983). W. Marx, *The Philosophy of F. W. J. Schelling: History, System, and Freedom* (Bloomington, IN, 1985). A. Bowie, *Schelling and Modern European Philosophy* (London, 1993). [James Schmidt]

Schiller, Joseph Christoph Friedrich von b. Marbach, Würtemberg, 1759; d. Weimar, 1805. Poet, dramatist, historian. Compelled in 1773 by Karl Eugen, Duke of Würtemberg to study law at military school near Ludwigsburg, then medicine in Stuttgart (1775–80). Influenced by Rousseau, wrote drama *Die Räuber* (1777–8), an enormous success at its first production in Mannheim (1782). Forbidden by Karl Eugen to write further plays, he fled to Mannheim, then to Thuringia. Wrote dramas *Fiesko* (1783), *Kabale und Liebe* (1784); established the journal *Thalia* (1785–91). Moved to Leipzig in 1785 and then to Dresden, where he wrote *Don Carlos* (1787). Journeyed to Weimar in 1787 and began friendship with Goethe. Professor of history at Jena, 1789–99, where he wrote a history of the Thirty Year's War. Established journal *Die Horen* (1794). Lectured on aesthetics, and published *Über Anmut und Würde* (1793), *Briefe über die ästhetische Erziehung des Menschen* (1795), and *Über naïve und sentimentalische Dichtung* (1795–6/1800), which explore issues in Kant's aesthetics. Wrote dramas *Wallenstein* (1798–9), *Maria Stuart* (1800), *Die Jungfrau von Orleans* (1801), *Die Braut von Messina* (1803), and *Wilhelm Tell* (1804) as well as considerable body of poetry. *Sämtliche Schriften*, ed. K. Goedeke (Stuttgart, 1867–76). Critical edition: *Werke. Nationalausgabe*, eds. L. Blumenthal and B. von Weise (1943–67).

Secondary Sources: W. Vulpius, *Schiller Bibliographie 1893–1958* (Weimar, 1959). R. D. Miller, *Schiller and the Ideal of Freedom* (Harrogate, 1959). D. Regin, *Freedom and Dignity: The Historical and Philosophical Thought of Schiller* (The Hague, 1965). D. Henrich, 'Beauty and Freedom: Schiller's Struggle with Kant's Aesthetics', in *Essays in Kant's Aesthetics*, eds. T. Cohen and P. Guyer (Chicago, IL, 1982). L. Sharpe, *Friedrich Schiller: Drama, Thought and Politics* (Cambridge, 1991). [James Schmidt]

Schlegel, Karl Wilhelm Friedrich von b. Hannover, 1772; d. Dresden, 1829. Prime mover of German Romanticism. After extolling ancient poetry in 'Über das Studium der Griechischen

Poesie', *Die Griechen und Römer* (1797), he repudiated neoclassicism in 'Kritische Fragmente', *Lyceum der schönen Künste* (1797), and *Athenaeum* (1798–1800) in favor of an incomplete (hence, ironic) expression of a Christian, modern, and amorous longing for the infinite. Also composed the controversial novel, *Lucinde* (1799) and the stimulus to study India: *Über Sprache und Weisheit der Inder* (1808). Lecturing while serving the Viennese court, he construed 'romantic' as the ideal of all – not only modern – poetry in *Geschichte der alten und neuen Literature* (1815) and defended Catholicism in *Philosophie des Lebens* (1828) and *Philosophie der Geschichte* (1829). *Kritische Friedrich-Schlegel-Ausgabe*, eds. E. Behler et al., 35 vols. (Munich, 1979).

Secondary Sources: F. Imle, *Friedrich von Schlegels Entwicklung von Kant zum Katholicismus* (Paderborn, 1927). G. Hendrix, *Das politische Weltbild Friedrich Schlegels* (Bonn, 1962). W. Weiland, *Der junge Friedrich Schlegel oder die Revolution in der Frühromantik* (Stuttgart, 1968). K. Peter, *Idealismus als Kritik. Friedrich Schlegels Philosophie der unvollendeten Welt* (Stuttgart, 1973). F. C. Beiser, *Enlightenment, Revolution, and Romanticism* (Cambridge, MA, 1992), chap. 10. Editor's Introduction in *The Early Political Writings of the German Romantics*, trans. and ed. F. C. Beiser (Cambridge, 1996). [Daniel Dahlstrom]

SCHLEIERMACHER, FRIEDRICH DANIEL ERNST b. Breslau 1768; d. Breslau 1834. Theologian and philosopher. Schooled in the pietism of the Moravian Brethren (Herrnhutter), Schleiermacher studied theology and philosophy at the University of Halle, became a tutor and pastor, and was from 1796 a member of the early Romantic circles in Berlin. He was professor of theology at Halle 1804–7 and was founding professor of theology at the new Berlin University from 1810. While most of Schleiermacher's work belongs to the nineteenth century, his first book, *Über die Religion. Reden an die Gebildeten unter ihren Verächtern* (1799), had its roots in the Spinozist, or pantheistic, controversy in the Berlin Enlightenment. Commonly taken as a radical break with rationalistic and naturalistic forms of religion, the work's idea of religion as an expression of emotion extends expressivist ideas of culture which Herder had derived from Condillac and helped make central to the Romantic movement. *Reden* was matched by *Monologen* (1800), and *Grundlinien einer Kritik der bisherigen Sittenlehre* (1803) was aimed at Kant and Fichte. *Sämmtliche Werke*, 31 vols. (Berlin, 1835–64).

Secondary Sources: W. Dilthey, *Das Leben Schleiermachers* (Berlin 1870; enlarged edn., 2 vols., Berlin, 1970). B. A. Gerrish, *A Prince of the Church: Schleiermacher and the Beginnings of Modern Theology* (Philadelphia, PA, 1985). R. B. Brandt, *The Philosophy of Schleiermacher: The Development of His Theory of Scientific and Religious Knowledge* (New York, NY, 1941). E. Herms, *Herkunft, Entfaltung und erste Gestalt des Systems der Wissenschaften bei Schleiermacher* (Gütersloh, 1974). A. L. Blackwell, *Schleiermacher's Early Philosophy of Life: Determinism, Freedom, and Phantasy* (Chico, CA, 1982). K. Nowak, *Schleiermacher und die Frühromantik: Eine Literaturgeschichtliche Studie zum romantischen Religionsverständnis und Menschenbild am Ende des 18. Jahrhunderts in Deutschland* (Göttingen, 1986). G. Meckenstock, *Deterministische Ethik und kritische Theologie: Die Auseinandersetzung des frühen Scheliermacher mit Kant und Spinoza 1789–1794* (Berlin, 1988). R. Crouter, Introduction in Schleiermacher, *On Religion: Speeches to its Cultured Despisers*, ed. R. Crouter (Cambridge, 1996), xi–xlv. [Knud Haakonssen]

SCHLÖZER, AUGUST LUDWIG VON b. Gaggstedt/Hohenlohe-Kirchberg, 1735; d. Göttingen, 1809. Historian. Studied theology and oriental languages at Wittenberg and Göttingen; tutor in Sweden (1755–9), Russia (1761–7), where he was appointed by Catherine II to the St. Petersburg Academy. Returned to Göttingen, where he became professor of history. His writings include *Schwedische Biographie* (1760–8); *Allgemeine Nordische Geschichte* (1771); *Weltgeschichte im Auszuge*

(1785); and *Allgemeines Statsrecht und Statsverfassungslehre* (1793). Edited the important political journal *Staatsanzeigen*, 15 vols. (1782–93).

Secondary Sources: F. Furst, *August Ludwig von Schlözer, ein deutscher Aufklärer im 18. Jahrhundert* (Heidelberg, 1928). W. Hennies, *Die politische Theorie August Ludwig von Schlözers zwischen Aufklärung und Liberalismus* (Munich, 1985). [James Schmidt]

Schulze, Gottlob Ernst b. Schloss Heldrungen, Germany, 1761; d. Göttingen, 1833. Philosopher; known as Aenesidemus-Schulze. Studied in Wittenberg (Magister, 1783); deacon and associate of the philosophical faculty (1786); Professor of Philosophy in Helmstedt (1788–1810), then in Göttingen. Schopenhauer was an early student in Göttingen. Is mainly known for *Aenesidemus oder über die Fundamente der von dem Hrn. Reinhold in Jena gelieferten Elementar-Philosophie* (1792); he tried to show that Kant and Reinhold had not refuted Hume and Berkeley; Reinhold's 'proposition of consciousness' cannot be the foundation of philosophy because it presupposes the law of contradiction. Philosophical works include: *Grundriss der philosophischen Wissenschaften* (1788–90); *Einige Bemerkungen über Kants philosophische Religionslehre* (1795); *Kritik der theoretischen Philosophie* (1801); *Leitfaden der Entwicklung der philosophischen Prinzipien des bürgerlichen und peinlichen Rechts* (1813); *Encyklopädie der philosophischen Wissenschaften* (1814); *Philosophische Tugendlehre* (1817); *Über die menschliche Erkenntnis* (1832).

Secondary Sources: H. Wiegershausen, *Aenesidemus-Schulze, der Gegner Kants, und seine Bedeutung im Neukantianismus* (Berlin, 1910). F. C. Beiser, *The Fate of Reason* (Cambridge, MA, 1987). M. Frank, 'Einleitung', G. E. Schulze, *Aenesidemus* (Hamburg, 1996), ix–lxxxii. *The Skeptical Tradition around 1800*, eds. J. van der Zande, R. H. Popkin (Dordrecht, 1998). [Heiner F. Klemme]

Semler, Johann Salomo b. Saalfeld, 1725; d. Halle, 1791. Rationalist historian of theology. Studied classics, history, philosophy, mathematics, and especially theology at Halle. Influenced by Sigmund Jacob Baumgarten, a 'Wolffian' theologian. Professor in Altdorf 1751, a year later in Halle. Most notable works: *Zusätze zu Baumgartens Evangelischer Glaubenslehre*, 3 vols. (1759–60); *Unterricht von Auslegung der heiligen Schrift* (1759); an edition of Baumgarten's *Untersuchung Theologischer Streitigkeiten* (1762–4); *Geschichte der Religionspartheyen* (1766); *Vorbereitung zur theologischen Hermeneutik* (1760–9); *Zur Revision der kirchlichen Hermeneutik und Dogmatik* (1788); *Letztes Glaubensbekenntnis über natürliche und christliche Religion*, ed. C. G. Schütz (1792). Very critical of traditionalism, he is by some considered founder of the historical-critical method of biblical exegesis. But he also opposed radical enlightenment theology and defended the Frederick William II censorship edicts.

Secondary Sources: G. Hornig, *Die Anfänge der historisch-kritischen Theologie* (1961), 249–87. G. Hornig, *Johann Salomo Semler. Studien zu Leben und Werk des Hallenser Aufklärungstheologen* (Tübingen, 1996). H.-E. Hess, *Theologie und Religion bei Semler* (Augsburg, 1974). [Manfred Kühn]

Shaftesbury, Anthony Ashley Cooper, Earl of b. London, February 26, 1671; d. Naples, February 15, 1713. Shaftesbury's grandfather was leader of the Whig opposition in the Exclusion Crisis and one of its main casualties. Along with his secretary, John Locke, he was exiled in 1682 and died a year later. The future Third Earl was tutored by Locke and attended Winchester School following Locke's exile. After a quiet youth – with the Continental tour 1687–9 – he was MP for Poole 1695–98 and associated with young radical whigs, including Molesworth, Toland, and Andrew Fletcher. He resigned his seat because of his health and moved to Rotterdam for a year, meeting Bayle and Le Clerc. In 1699 *An Inquiry concerning Virtue* (composed a number of years earlier) was published by Toland, likely without S.'s knowledge. After another brief

Rotterdam sojourn (1703–4), he married in 1707, and published a series of important works: 'A Letter Concerning Enthusiasm' (1708), 'Sensus Communis' (1709), 'The Moralists' (1709), 'Soliloquy' (1710). All of these, *An Inquiry*, and 'Miscellaneous Reflections' were incorporated into his masterwork, the *Characteristicks of Men, Manners, Opinions, Times* (1711). He moved to Naples because of declining health and wrote the 'Historical Draught', revised the *Characteristicks*, adding plates engraved according to precise instructions (these appeared posthumously in 1715), and began a 'Second Characters'. One of the most influential philosophers of the eighteenth century, S. offered a stew of ancient sources, Renaissance hermeticism, deist naturalized theology, refutations of Hobbesian egoism, Cambridge-Platonist influenced criticisms of Lockean empiricism, aestheticized 'moral sense' theory, and a naturalized and civic minded virtue ethics all draped in his eloquent, diverse, and playful style. Shaftesbury was criticized by many – most notably Mandeville and Berkeley – and was a leading inspiration for many Enlightenment figures, including Diderot, Voltaire, Lessing, Mendelssohn, Herder, Hutcheson, and Hume. *Characteristicks of Men, Manners, Opinions, Times*, ed. P. Ayres, 2 vols. (Oxford, 1999). Same work, ed. D. Den Uyl, 3 vols. (Indianapolis, IN, 2001) includes reproductions of the plates. *Second Characters or the Language of Forms*, ed. B. Rand (Cambridge, 1914). *Complete Works, Selected Letters and Posthumous Writings*, with German translation, trans. and eds. G. Hemmerich, W. Benda, et al. (Stuttgart-Bad Cannstatt, 1981–).

Secondary Sources: L. Jaffro, 'Bibliographie des études relatives à Anthony Ashley Cooper, troisième Comte de Shaftesbury (1671–1713)' (published online at http://www-philo.univ-paris1.fr/Jaffro/ Shaftesbury.htm,1998–). B. Rand, *The Life, Unpublished Letters and Philosophical Regimen of Anthony, Earl of Shaftesbury* (London, 1900). S. Grean, *Shaftesbury's Philosophy of Religion and Ethics* (Athens, OH, 1967). R. Voitle, *The Third Earl of Shaftesbury, 1671–1713* (Baton Rouge, LA, 1984). L. Klein, *Shaftesbury and the Culture of Politeness* (Cambridge, 1994). S. Darwall, *The British Moralists and the Internal 'Ought'* (Cambridge, 1995), ch. 7. L. Jaffro, *Ethique de la communication et art d'écrire. Shaftesbury et les Lumières anglaises* (Paris, 1998). L. E. Klein, editor's Introduction, in Shaftesbury, *Characteristics of Men, Manners, Opinions, Times* (Cambridge, 1999). I. Rivers, *Reason, Grace, and Sentiment. A Study of the Language of Religion and Ethics in England, 1660–1780*, vol. 2: *Shaftesbury to Hume* (Cambridge, 2000). D. Grossklaus, *Natürliche Religion und aufgeklärte Gesellschaft: Shaftesburys Verhältnis zu den Cambridge Platonists* (Heidelberg, 2000). K. P. Winkler, ' "All Is Revolution in Us": Personal Identity in Shaftesbury and Hume,' *Hume Studies* 26.1 (2000): 3–40. *Il Gentleman filosofo. Nuovi saggi su Shaftesbury*, eds. G. Carabelli and P. Zanardi (Padua, 2000). [Aaron Garrett]

Sieyès, Emmanuel-Joseph b. Fréjus, France, 1748; d. Paris, 1836. Catholic priest, politician and political theorist. Educated at the *séminare de Saint-Sulpice*, he was ordained in 1772 and became vicar-general and chancellor of the diocese of Chartres (1780). His most well-known work, the pamphlet *Qu'est-ce que le tiers état?* (1789), made him a central figure in the States General. This work was followed by *Essai sur les privilèges* (1789) and an argument for freedom of religion, *Discours sur la liberté des cultes* (1791). On his motion, the delegates of the third estate proclaimed themselves a national assembly and in the National Convention he supported the execution of the king, but after the rise of the Jacobins he was only intermittently in the forefront of politics until he was elected to the Directory and was part of Bonaparte's coup (1799). He was an important administrator and legal expert under the *Directoire*, but with Napoleon's fall he was banished until the July Revolution in 1830. *Oeuvres de Sieyes*, 3 vols. (Paris, 1990; reprint of the 1789–94 edn.).

Secondary Sources: K. M. Baker, 'Sieyès', in: *Dictionnaire critique de la Révolution française*, eds. F. Furet and M. Ozouf (Paris, 1988), 334–45. B. Baczko, 'The Social Contract of the French:

Sieyès and Rousseau', *Journal of Modern History* 60 (1988): 89–123. P. Bastid, *Sieyès et sa pensée*, revised edn. (Paris, 1970). J.-D. Bredin, *Sieyès. La clé de la Révolution française* (Paris, 1988). M. G. Forsyth, *Reason and Revolution: The political Thought of the Abbé Sieyes* (New York, NY, 1987). T. Hafen, *Staat, Gesellschaft und Bürger im Denken von Emmanuel Joseph Sieyès* (Bern, 1994). P. Pasquino, *Sieyès et l'invention de la constitution en France* (Paris, 1998). W. H. Sewell, *A Rhetoric of Bourgeois Revolution: The Abbé Sieyès and What is the The Third Estate* (Durham, 1994). Editor's Introduction in Sieyès, *Political Writings*, trans. and ed. M. Sonenscher (Indianapolis, IN, 2003). [Simone Zurbuchen]

Smith, Adam b. Kirkcaldy, Fife, Scotland 1723; d. Edinburgh, 1790. Moral philosopher and political economist. Educated at Glasgow University under Francis Hutcheson (1737–40) and at Balliol College, Oxford, through self-study (1740–6). Free-lance public lecturer on rhetoric, philosophical history, and jurisprudence in Edinburgh (1748–51), then professor at Glasgow (1751–2 in logic, 1752–64 in moral philosophy). During this period, he published the Preface and Dedication to William Hamilton's *Poems on Several Occasions* (1748 and 1758); a review of Johnson's *Dictionary* and brief survey of recent continental thought, most importantly Rousseau's *Second Discourse*, both in the first *Edinburgh Review* (1755 and 1756); and in 1759 appeared *The Theory of Moral Sentiments* which had grown out of his Glasgow lectures. An importantly revised second edition appeared in 1761 (as did 'Dissertation on the origin of languages', in *Philological Miscellany*, Vol. 1) and a considerably changed sixth edition in 1790. As travelling tutor to the Duke of Buccleuch during the latter's European tour (1764–6), he had the opportunity of becoming acquainted with many of the leading French *philosophes* and physiocrats, thus securing further impulses and information for the study of political economy he had begun. Thereafter Smith worked on *The Wealth of Nations* (1776), mainly in seclusion at his mother's house in Kirkcaldy (1767–73) and in London, where he cultivated political and literary connections, for instance, through Johnson's 'The Club' and the Royal Society (fellow 1767). On the death of David Hume (1776), the epistolary eulogy for his close friend and mentor (published with Hume's *My Own Life*, 1777) brought him much controversy. From 1778 until his death, he was Commissioner of Customs in Edinburgh, where he was a central member of the intelligentsia and instrumental in the founding of the Oyster Club and the Royal Society of Edinburgh. He never completed to his satisfaction a couple of major book-projects meant to complement the works already published, and he destroyed all manuscripts shortly before his death, except for the *Essays on Philosophical Subjects* (posthumously published, 1795). His over-all system of thought may be discernible through the student-notes from his lectures, published during the last century. He issued the *Wealth of Nations* in four more editions of which the second (1778) is particularly important. Both of his major works were widely translated in his lifetime. The standard edition of works, manuscripts, correspondence and student-notes: *The Works and Correspondence of Adam Smith*, 6 vols. (Oxford, 1976–87).

Secondary Sources: D. Stewart, 'Account of the Life and Writings of Adam Smith LL.D.', (1793) in D. Stewart, *Collected Works*, ed. Sir W. Hamilton, 11 vols. (Edinburgh, 1854–60), 10: 1–98. J. Rae, *Life of Adam Smith* (1895; repr. with additional material by Jacob Viner, New York, 1965). W. R. Scott, *Adam Smith as Student and Professor* (Glasgow, 1937). R. H. Campbell and A. S. Skinner, *Adam Smith* (London, 1982). I. S. Ross, *The Life of Adam Smith* (Oxford, 1995). *A Critical Bibliography of Adam Smith*, gen. ed. K. Tribe (London, 2002). T. D. Campbell, *Adam Smith's Science of Morals*, (London, 1971). *Essays on Adam Smith*, eds. A. S. Skinner and T. Wilson (Oxford, 1975). D. Winch, *Adam Smith's Politics: An Essay in Historiographic Revision* (Cambridge, 1978). A. S. Skinner, *A System of Social Science: Papers Relating to Adam Smith* (Oxford, 1979). K. Haakonssen, *The Science of a Legislator: The Natural Jurisprudence of David Hume and Adam Smith* (Cambridge, 1981). *Adam Smith: Critical Assessements*, ed. J. C. Wood, 4 vols. (London,

1983–4). D. D. Raphael *Adam Smith* (Oxford, 1985). R. F. Teichgraeber, *'Free Trade' and Moral Philosophy: Rethinking the Sources of Adam Smith's Wealth of Nations* (Durham, NC, 1986). *Adam Smith: International Perspectives*, eds. H. Mizuta and C. Sugiyama (New York, 1993). V. Brown, *Adam Smith's Discourse: Canonicity, Commerce and Conscience* (London, 1994). K. Haakonssen, *Natural Law and Moral Philosophy: From Grotius to the Scottish Enlightenment* (Cambridge, 1996), ch. 4. D. Winch, *Riches and Poverty: An Intellectual History of Political Economy in Britain, 1750–1834* (Cambridge, 1996). C. Griswold, *Adam Smith and the Virtues of Enlightenment* (Cambridge, 1998). *Adam Smith's Library Catalogue*, ed. H. Mizuta (Oxford, 2000). E. Rothschild, *Economic Sentiments: Adam Smith, Condorcet, and the Enlightenment* (Cambridge, MA, 2001). G. Vivenza, *Adam Smith and the Classics. The Classical Heritage in Adam Smith's Thought* (Oxford, 2001). J. R. Otteson, *Adam Smith's Marketplace of Life* (Cambridge, 2002). P. Force, *Self-Interest Before Adam Smith: A Genealogy of Economic Science* (Cambridge, 2003). M. Biziou, *Adam Smith et l'origine du liberalisme* (Paris, 2003). S. Fleischacker, *On Adam Smith's Wealth of Nations. A Philosophical Commentary* (Princeton, NJ, 2004). L. Montes, *Adam Smith in Context* (Basingstoke, Hampshire, 2004). *The Cambridge Companion to Adam Smith*, ed. K. Haakonssen (Cambridge, 2005). [Knud Haakonssen]

Spalding, Johann Joachim b. Tribsees (Swedish Pommern), 1714; d. Berlin, 1804. Philosophical theologian. Educated in Rostock and Greifswald, he became a Lutheran pastor in Lassahn and Barth (1749–64). He befriended Christian Wolff in Halle and was influenced by Butler, Hutcheson, Shaftesbury, Lavater, and, later, Baumgarten. He was a court preacher, provost, and head of the consistory in Berlin 1764–1788, when he resigned in protest against the Wöllner edicts. Was prominent in 'neology' and a member of the *Montagsclub* and the *Mittwochsgesellschaft*. His *Bestimmung des Menschen* (1748) reached thirteen editions by 1794. Other important works: *Gedanken über den Werth der Gefühle im Christentum* (1761); *Ueber die Nutzbarkeit des Predigtamtes und deren Beförderung* (1772); *Religion, eine Angelegenheit des Menschen* (1796); and *Lebensbeschreibung* (1804). *Johann Joachim Spalding: Kritische Ausgabe*, ed. A. Beutel (Tübingen, 2001–).

Secondary Sources: J. Schollmeier, *Johann Joachim Spalding. Ein Beitrag zur Theologie der Aufklärung* (Gütersloh, 1967). B. Bianco, ''Vernünftiges Christentum'. Aspects et problèmes de la néologie allemande au XVIIIème siècle', *Archives de philosophie* 46 (1983), 179–218. H. Adler, 'Die Bestimmung des Menschen: Spaldings Schrift als Ausgangspunkt einer offenen Anthropologie', *Das achtzehnte Jahrhundert* 18 (1994): 125–37. J. H. Zamito, *Kant, Herder, and the Birth of Anthropology* (Chicago, IL, 2002). [Luca Fonnesu]

Stäudlin, Karl Friedrich b. Stuttgart, 1761, d. Göttingen, 1826. Theologian, historian, eclectic philosopher. Studied theology at the Tübinger Stift (1779–84); private tutor, also in England; 1790 professor of Theology at the University of Göttingen. Influential as historian of scepticism, moral philosophy, and the church. Following discussions about the relationship between Kant's critical philosophy and Christianity, he later advocated a rationalistic version of supernaturalism. Kant dedicated *Streit der Fakultäten* (1798) to him. His original historical works are still of interest today, especially *Geschichte und Geist des Skepticismus, vorzüglich in Rücksicht auf Moral and Religion* (1794) and *Geschichte der Moralphilosophie* (1822). Other works: *Beiträge zur Philosophie und Geschichte der Religion und Sittenlehre überhaupt und der verschiedenen Glaubensarten und Kirchen insbesondere* (1797–9), *Universalgeschichte der christlichen Kirche* (1806), *Geschichte der Vorstellungen der Lehre vom Selbstmorde* (1824), and *Geschichte des Rationalismus und Supernaturalismus vornehmlich in Beziehung auf das Christenthum* (1826).

Secondary Sources: *Zur Erinnerung an D. Carl Friedrich Stäudlin (. . .) seine Selbstbiographie nebst einer Gedächtnispredigt von Herrn Sup. D. Ruperti*, ed. J. T. Hemsen (Göttingen, 1826). C. W. T.

Blackwell, 'Skepticism as a Sect, Skepticism as a Philosophical Stance: Johann Jakob Brucker versus Carl Friedrich Stäudlin', *The Skeptical Tradition around 1800*, eds. J. van der Zande and R. H. Popkin (Dordrecht, 1998), 343–63. J. C. Laursen, 'Skepticism and the History of Moral Philosophy: The Case of Carl Friedrich Stäudlin', in *The Skeptical Tradition around 1800*, 365–78. [Heiner F. Klemme]

Stewart, Dugald b. Edinburgh, 1753; d. Edinburgh, 1828. Moral philosopher. Studied at the University of Edinburgh (1765–9) with Adam Ferguson and at Glasgow (1771–2) with Thomas Reid. Professor of mathematics, first conjointly with then in succession to his father, at Edinburgh, 1775–85; professor of moral philosophy at Edinburgh after Ferguson, 1785–1820 (1810–20 conjointly with Thomas Brown). Was enormously influential in his own time, thanks to his popular lectures and his numerous works – and the prominence of his students: the founders of the *Edinburgh Review*, literary men as different as Sir Walter Scott and James Mill, sons of the Whig grandees, foreign luminaries, such as Benjamin Constant, etc. Stewart was also immensely popular in France and America for a couple of generations. Main works: *Elements of the Philosophy of the Human Mind*, 3 vols. (1792, 1814, 1827); *Account of the Life and Writings of Adam Smith, LL.D.* (1794); *Outlines of Moral Philosophy* (1793); *Account of the Life and Writings of William Robertson, D. D.* (1801); *Account of the Life and Writings of Thomas Reid, D. D., F. R. S. E.* (1802); *Philosophical Essays* (1810); *Biographical Memoirs of Adam Smith, LL.D., William Robertson, D. D., Thomas Reid, D. D.* (1811); *Dissertation: Exhibiting the Progress of Metaphysical, Ethical, and Political Philosophy, since the Revival of Letters in Europe* (Parts 1 and 2 in the *Encyclopedia Britannica*, 1815 and 1821; separate publication with considerable additions in *Works*, 1: 1854); *The Philosophy of the Active and Moral Powers of Man* (1828). *Lectures on Political Economy* (in *Works*, vols. 8–9, 1855–6). The standard edition is, *The Collected Works of Dugald Stewart*, ed. Sir W. Hamilton, 11 vols. (Edinburgh, 1854–60; facsim. with an Introduction by K. Haakonssen, Bristol, 1994).

Secondary Sources: J. Veitch, 'Memoir of Dugald Stewart', in Stewart, *Works*, 10: i–cxv. S. A. Grave, *The Scottish Philosophy of Common Sense* (Oxford, 1960). D. Winch, 'The System of the North: Dugald Stewart and His Pupils', in S. Collini, D. Winch and J. Burrow, *That Noble Science of Politics. A Study in Nineteenth-Century Intellectual History* (Cambridge, 1983), 25–61. P. B. Wood, 'The Hagiography of Common Sense: Dugald Stewart's Account of the Life and Writings of Thomas Reid', in *Philosophy, Its History and Historiography*, ed. A. J. Holland (Dordrecht, 1985), 305–22. B. Fontana, *Rethinking the Politics of Commercial Society: The 'Edinburgh Review' 1802–1832* (Cambridge, 1985). R. B. Sher, 'Professors of Virtue: The Social History of the Edinburgh Moral Philosophy Chair in the Eighteenth Century', in *Studies in the Philosophy of the Scottish Enlightenment*, ed. M. A. Stewart (Oxford, 1990), 87–126. K. Haakonssen, *Natural Law and Moral Philosophy. From Grotius to the Scottish Enlightenment* (Cambridge, 1995), chs. 7–9. P. Wood, 'Introduction: Dugald Stewart and the Invention of "the Scottish Enlightenment"', in *The Scottish Enlightenment: Essays in Reinterpretation*, ed. P. Wood (Rochester, NY, 2000): 1–35. [Knud Haakonssen]

Sulzer, Johann Georg b. Winterthur, Switzerland, 1720; d. Berlin, 1779. Popular philosopher and man of letters. Studied theology in Zürich (1736–39); private tutor in Zürich (1740) and Magdeburg (1743); curate (1741); professor of mathematics at the Joachimsthaler Gymnasium (1747) and later (1765) professor at the newly founded Ritterakademie (*École militaire*) in Berlin; from 1750 member of the Berlin Royal Academy. Influenced in particular by Wolff. Is widely known for *Allgemeine Theorie der schönen Künste* (1771–4), an encyclopedia of general aesthetics and the theory and practice of literature and arts. Believed that the source of beauty lies in the perceiving subject and regarded music as the expression of passion. Edited the German translation of Hume's *Philosophical Essays concerning Human Understanding* (1755), expressing the hope that the Scottish sceptic might awaken German philosophers from their dogmatic slumber. Other philosophical works: *Die schönen Künste in ihrem Ursprung, ihrer wahren Natur und besten Anwendung betrachtet* (1772); *Vermischte philosophische Schriften* (1773–81); *Pädagogische Schriften*, ed. W. Klinke (Langensalza, 1922).

Secondary Sources: *Johann George Sulzer's Lebensbeschreibung, von ihm selbst aufgesetzt*, eds. J. B. Merian and F. Nicolai (1809). J. Dobai, *Die bildenden Künste in Johann Georg Sulzers Ästhetik* (Winterthur, 1978). *Schweizer im Berlin des 18. Jahrhunderts*, eds. M. Fontius and H. Holzhey (Berlin, 1996). [Heiner F. Klemme]

Svarez, Carl Gottlieb b. Schweidnitz, 1746; d. Berlin, 1798. Jurist and civil servant. Studied natural law at Frankfurt an der Oder. As Privy Justice and Upper Tribunal Councillor he collaborated with Ernst Ferdinand Klein on the *Allgemeines Landrecht* (1794), a major project of enlightened legal reform. Active in the *Mittwochsgesellschaft*, a secret society of 'Friends of Enlightenment' whose membership included many important figures in the Berlin Enlightenment. Gave lectures on natural law to Prussian crown prince Frederick William III (1790–1). *Gesammelte Schriften* (Stuttgart, 1996–).

Secondary Sources: A. F. Stolzel, *Carl Gottlieb Svarez. Ein Zeitbild aus der zweiten Hälfte des achtzehnten Jahrhunderts* (Berlin, 1885). G. Birtsch, 'C. G. Svarez: Mitbegründer des preussischen Gesetzesstaates', in *Geschichte und politisches Handeln. Studien zum europäischen Denken der Neuzeit. Zum Gedenken an Theodor Schieder, 1908–1984*, ed. P. Alter (Stuttgart, 1985): 85–101. [James Schmidt]

Tetens, Johann Nicolaus b. Tetenbüll, Schleswig, 1736; d. Copenhagen, 1807. German empiricist philosopher. Studied at Rostock and Copenhagen. Professor of Philosophy at Kiel 1776 to 1789. From 1789 to 1807 Tetens was a financial official in Copenhagen. In *Ueber allgemeine und speculativische Philosophie* (1775) Tetens criticized traditional rationalist metaphysics. His major work *Philosophische Versuche über die menschliche Natur und ihre Entwicklung* (1777) examined the origin and structure of human knowledge. Several commentators have emphasised the importance of Tetens to the development of Kant's philosophy.

Secondary Sources: W. Uebele, *Johann Nicolaus Tetens nach seiner Gesamtentwicklung betrachtet mit besonderer Berücksichtigung des Verhältnisses zu Kant* (Berlin, 1911). A. Seidel, *Tetens' Einfluß auf die Philosophie Kants* (Würzburg 1932). L. W. Beck, *Early German Philosophy* (Cambridge, MA, 1969), 412–25. J. Barnouw, 'The Philosophical Achievement and Historical Significance of Johann Nicolas Tetens', *Studies in Eighteenth-Century Culture* 9 (1979): 301–35. H. V. Rappard, *Psychology as Self-knowledge: The Development of the Concept of the Mind in German Rationalistic Psychology and Its Relevance Today* (Assen, 1979), 49–83. M. Kuehn, *Scottish Common Sense in Germany, 1768–1800: A Contribution to the History of Critical Philosophy* (Kingston and Montreal, 1987), 119–40. C. Hauser, *Selbstbewusstsein und personale Identität. Positionen und Aporien ihrer vorkantischen Geschichte. Locke, Leibniz, Hume und Tetens* (Stuttgart-Bad Cannstatt, 1994), 124–51. [Udo Thiel]

Thomasius (Thomas), Christian b. Leipzig, 1655; d. Halle, 1728. Founding figure of the German Enlightenment, 'eclectic' philosopher, natural lawyer, reformer in university and society. Son of the philosopher Jacob Thomasius. Educated under prominent Pufendorf-critic V. Alberti in Leipzig (MA 1672) and Frankfurt an der Oder (doctorate in law 1679). Advocate in Leipzig 1679–86. Lectured on Grotius and Pufendorf at Leipzig 1682–90, promoting teaching in German (1687). Forced to leave Leipzig (Saxony) 1690; transferred to Halle and was instrumental in foundation of Prussian state university there (1694), a model for German Enlightenment universities.

Direktor (president) of University for life from 1710. Thomasius was the most important follower of Pufendorf. In the 1680s he worked to complete Pufendorf's voluntarist program in ethics and politics, mainly in *Institutiones jurisprudentiæ divinæ* (1688; prefaced by important autobiographical account, 'Dissertatio prooemialis'; German trans. 1709). This was followed by ever deeper and more detailed analysis of human life as an economy of the passions and an account of culture, including morals, politics, and law, as conventional means of controlling the passions. This largely deleted the normative function of natural law and replaced it with a programme of historical and empirical accounts of the conventions of life. It is in this connection that Thomasius distinguishes between *justum*, *honestum*, and *decorum*. The main works in this development: *Introductio ad philosophiam aulicam* (1688; German trans. *Einleitung zur Hof-Philosophie*, 1710), *Scherz- und ernsthafte, vernünftige und einfältige Gedanken über allerhand nützliche Bücher und Fragen* ['Monatsgespräche'] (1688–90), *Einleitung zu der Vernunft-Lehre* (1691), *Ausübung der Vernunft-Lehre* (1691), *Einleitung zu der Sitten-Lehre* (1692), *Ausübung der Sitten-Lehre* (1696), *Fundamenta juris naturae et gentium ex sensu communi deducta* (1705; German trans. 1709). Thomasius continued to publish prodigiously; of philosophical interest are especially, *Paulo plenior historia juris naturalis* (1719), works on church and state, and several of his more than 100 dissertations and scores of essays dealing with issues in moral enlightenment and law reform (bigamy, witchcraft, torture, heresy, adultery, etc.).

Secondary Sources: 'Briefe von Pufendorf', ed. K. Varrentrap, *Historische Zeitschrift* 70, N. F. 34 (1893): 1–51 and 193–232. E. Gigas, *Briefe Samuel Pufendorfs an Christian Thomasius (1687–1693)* (Munich and Leipzig, 1897). W. Bienert, *Der Anbruch der christlichen deutschen Neuzeit dargestellt an Wissenschaft und Glauben des Christian Thomasius* (Halle, 1934). E. Bloch, 'Christian Thomasius, ein deutscher Gelehrter ohne Misere', in *Naturrecht und menschliche Würde* (Frankfurt am Main, 1953). R. Lieberwirth, *Christian Thomasius. Sein wissenschaftliches Lebenswerk* (Weimar, 1955). H. Rüping, *Die Naturrechtslehre des Christian Thomasius und ihre Fortbildung in der Thomasius-Schule* (Bonn, 1968). F. M. Barnard, 'The "Practical Philosophy" of Christian Thomasius', *Journal of the History of Ideas* 32 (1971): 221–46. W. Schneiders, *Naturrecht und Liebesethik. Zur Geschichte der praktischen Philosophie im Hinblick auf Christian Thomasius* (Hildesheim and New York, NY, 1971). G. Schubart-Fikentscher, *Christian Thomasius. Seine Bedeutung als Hochschullehrer am Beginn der deutschen Aufklärung* (Berlin, 1977). F. Battaglia, *Christiano Thomasio. Filosofo e giurista* (Bologna, 1982). F. M. Barnard, 'Fraternity and Citizenship: Two Ethics of Mutuality in Christian Thomasius', *Review of Politics* 50 (1988): 582–602. *Christian Thomasius 1655–1728. Interpretationen zu Werk und Wirkung. Mit einer Bibliographie*, ed. W. Schneiders (Hamburg, 1989). *Christian Thomasius (1655–1728). Neue Forschungen im Kontext der Frühaufklärung*, ed. F. Vollhardt (Tübingen, 1997). F. Grunert, *Normbegründung und politische Legitimität. Zur Recths- und Staatsphilosophie der deutschen Frühaufklärung*, Tübingen, 2000. T. Hochstrasser, *Natural Law Theories in the Early Enlightenment* (Cambridge, 2000), ch. 3. I. Hunter, 'Christian Thomasius and the Desacralization of Philosophy', *Journal of the History of Ideas*, 61 (2000): 1–16. I. Hunter, *Rival Enlightenments: Civil and Metaphysical Philosophy in Early Modern Germany* (Cambridge, 2001), ch. 5. M. Kühnel, *Das politische Denken von Christian Thomasius. Staat, Gesellschaft, Bürger* (Berlin, 2001). P. Schröder, *Naturrecht und absolutistisches Staatsrecht. Eine vergleichende Studie zu Thomas Hobbes und Christian Thomasius* (Berlin, 2001). K.-G. Lutterbeck, *Staat und Gesellschaft bei Christian Thomasius und Christian Wolff. Eine historische Untersuchung in systematischer Absicht* (Stuttgart-Bad-Cannstatt, 2002). [Knud Haakonssen]

THOMPSON, BENJAMIN (COUNT RUMFORD) b. Woburn, MA, 1753; d. Auteuil, France, 1814. Physicist. Largely self-educated, fled to England during the American Revolution, eventually joining the court of the elector of Bavaria. His experiments there on boring of cannons led him to a vibratory theory of heat in contrast to the generally accepted caloric or fluid theory.

The Complete Works of Count Rumford, ed. G. Ellis, 4 vols. (Boston, MA, 1870–5) includes a memoir.

Secondary Sources: S. Brown, *Benjamin Thompson, Count Rumford* (Cambridge, MA, 1979). S. Goldfarb, 'Rumford's Theory of Heat: A Reassessment', *British Journal for the History of Science* 10 (1977): 25–36. J. Sokolow, 'Count Rumford and Late Enlightenment Science, Technology, and Reform', *Eighteenth Century* 21 (1980): 67–86. [John Gascoigne]

THÜMMIG, LUDWIG PHILIPP b. Helmbrechts bei Kulmbach, 1697; d. Kassel, 1728. Philosopher, natural scientist, populariser of Wolff's philosophy. Studied philosophy under Christian Wolff in Halle (*magister* 1721). Professor of philosophy 1723 but forced to leave Halle together with Wolff the same year by Pietist opposition. Professor of philosophy at the *Collegium Carolinum* in Kassel (1724), where he also taught astronomy and mathematics from 1727. His main work, *Institutiones philosophiae Wolfianae, in usus academicos adornatae* (1725–6) is the first compendium of Wolff's philosophy. The first volume contains logic, metaphysics (and its subdivisions, ontology, cosmology, psychology and theology), experimental philosophy, and *Philosophia naturalis*; the second *Philosophia practica universalis*, natural law (divided into ethical and political natural law), ethics, economics, and politics.

Secondary Sources: M. Wundt, *Die deutsche Schulphilosophie im Zeitalter der Aufklärung* (Tübingen, 1945): 212–14. [Thomas Ahnert]

TIEDEMANN, DIETRICH b. Bremervörde, 1748, d. Marburg, 1803. Philosopher. Professor in Marburg from 1786. Influenced by Locke and other British thinkers, though he also knew Leibniz well. He denied the existence of innate ideas, trying to derive knowledge from reflection and the external sense. Accordingly, he was critical of Kant and is today mainly known as an 'anti-Kantian'. But his 'precritical' writings are of great interest for the understanding of the origins of the discipline of psychology in Germany. Main works: *Versuch einer Erklärung des Ursprungs der Sprache* (1772); *System der Stoischen Philosophie* (1776); *Untersuchungen über den Menschen* (1777–8); *Griechenlands erste Philosophie* (1780); *Theaetet oder Über das menschliche Wissen* (1794); *Idealistische Briefe* (1798); *Geist der spekulativen Philosophie von Thales bis Berkeley*, 6 vols. (1791–7).

Secondary Sources: F. J. M. Vonk and W. J. M. Tummers, 'Dietrich Tiedemann (1748–1803): Philosophische und empirisch-psychologische Aspekte der Spracherwerbsforschung im 18. Jahrhundert', in *Beiträge zur Geschichte der Sprachwissenschaft*, Vol. 1 (1991): 97–118. U. Thiel, 'Varieties of Inner Sense. Two Pre-Kantian Theories', *Archiv für Geschichte der Philosophie* 79 (1997): 58–79. [Manfred Kühn]

TINDAL, MATTHEW b. Bere Ferris, Devonshire, 1657; d. Coldbath Fields, London, 1733. Deist philosopher and lawyer. Educated at Oxford; law fellow at All Souls 1678; admitted advocate at Doctors' Commons 1685. *The Rights of the Christian Church asserted against the Romish and all other Priests who claim an Independent Power over it* (1706) caused a stir. His most famous book, destined to become one of the classic works of English deism, *Christianity as Old as the Creation, or the Gospel a Republication of the Religion of Nature* (1730) was attacked and discussed in dozens of writings and exercised a crucial influence on French and German deism. Other works: *An Essay Concerning the Laws of Nations and the Rights of Sovereigns* (1694); *An Essay concerning Obedience to the Supreme Powers* (1694); and *An Essay concerning the Power of the Magistrate and the Rights of Mankind in Matters of Religion* (1697).

Secondary Sources: E. Curll, *Memoirs of the Life and Writings of Matthew Tindall, LL.D.* (London, 1733). Anon., *The Religious, Rational, and Moral Conduct of Matthew Tindal, LL. D.* (London,

1735). J. Hunt, *Religious Thought in England* (London, 1871), ch. 2: 432–62. N. L. Torrey, *Voltaire and the English Deists* (New Haven, CT, 1930): 104–29. H. G. Reventlow, *The Authority of the Bible and the Rise of the Modern World* (London, 1984): 321–7, 374–83. [Maria Rosa Antognazza]

Toland, John b. Inishowen peninsula, Donegal, Ireland, 1670; d. Putney, London, 1722. Deist philosopher, historian, and man of letters. Raised as a Catholic, he converted to Protestantism at sixteen. Educated at Glasgow (1687–90), MA from Edinburgh 1690, then studied two years in Leiden. His most famous work and a pioneering manifesto of Deism, *Christianity not Mysterious: Or, a Treatise shewing, That there is Nothing in the Gospel Contrary to Reason, Nor Above it: And that no Christian Doctrine can be properly call'd a Mystery* (1696), aroused fiery replies, most notably Bishop Edward Stillingfleet's *Vindication of the Doctrine of the Trinity* (1697). His subsequent career was characterised by a flurry of pamphlets and a wandering search for patronage especially in quarters favourable to freethinking. Amongst other places he found a hearing at the courts of Hanover and Berlin. His *Letters to Serena* (1704), in which he claimed that force or motion is essential to matter, were addressed to Sophie Charlotte, queen of Prussia. *A Collection of Several Pieces of Mr. John Toland, Now First Publish'd from His Original Manuscripts: With some Memoirs of His Life and Writings*, ed. P. Des Maizeaux, 2 vols. (London, 1726).

Secondary Sources: A life is included in Des Maizeaux's collection. G. Carabelli, *Tolandiana: materiali bibliografici per lo studio dell'opera e della fortuna di John Toland* (Florence, 1975). R. E. Sullivan, *John Toland and the Deist Controversy* (Cambridge, MA, 1982). S. H. Daniel, *John Toland: His Methods, Manners and Mind* (Kingston, Ont., 1984). 'John Toland (1670–1722) et la crise de la conscience européenne', ed. G. Brykman, *Revue de synthèse* 116 (1995). *John Toland's Christianity Not Mysterious. Text, Associated Works and Critical Essays*, eds P. McGuinness, A. Harrison, and R. Kearney (Dublin, 1997). J. Champion, *Republican Learning: John Toland and the Crisis of Christian Culture, 1696–1722* (Manchester, 2003). [Maria Rosa Antognazza]

Tooke, John Horne b. London, 1736; d. Wimbledon, 1812. Political radical; linguistic philosopher. Born John Horne, he added Tooke as a tribute to his friend and benefactor William Tooke. After Eton and St. John's College, Cambridge (BA 1758), he read law at the Inner Temple, but was ordained on his father's insistence (1760) and became a popular preacher in London; he resigned his living in 1773. Tried for seditious libel in 1777, for high treason in 1795. In 1771 founded the 'Constitution Society', from 1780 called 'The Society for Constitutional Information'. Admired as lively conversationalist and associate of some of the prominent intellects of his time. *The Petition of an Englishman* (1765); *The Controversial Letters of John Wilkes, Esq., The Rev. John Horne, and their Principal Adherents* (1771); *A Letter to John Dunning, Esq.* (1778); *A Letter on Parliamentary Reform containing the Sketch of a Plan* (2nd edn. 1782); *A Letter to the Editor of the Times* (1807); *ΕΠΕΑ ΠΤΕΡΟΕΝΤΑ, or the Diversions of Purley* (1786; Vol. 2, 1805; many later editions).

Secondary Sources: J. Gurney, *The Trial of John Horne Tooke for High Treason*, 2 vols. (London, 1795). D. Stewart, 'On the Tendency of some Late Philological Speculations', in D. Stewart, *Philosophical Essays* (1810). L. Hunt, 'Horne Tooke' in *Political and Occasional Essays*, eds. L. H. Houtchens and C. W. Houtchens (New York, NY, 1962), 134–41 (obit. from *The Examiner*, April 5, 1812). A. Stephens, *Memoirs of John Horne Tooke*, 2 vols. (London, 1813). W. Hazlitt, 'The Late Mr. Horne Tooke' in his *The Spirit of the Age* (1825). M. C. Yarborough, *John Horne Tooke* (New York, NY, 1926). H. Aarsleff, *The Study of Language in England* (Princeton, NJ, 1983 [1967]): 44–104. O. Smith, *The Politics of Language 1791–1819* (Oxford, 1984): 110–53. J. C. McKusick, 'Coleridge and Horne Tooke,' in *Coleridge's Philosophy of Language* (New Haven, CT, 1986): 33–52. D. Rosenberg, ''A New Sort of Logick and Critick': Etymological Interpretation in Horne Tooke's *Diversions of Purley*,' in *Language, Self, and Society: A Social History of Language*, eds. P. Burke and R. Porter (Cambridge, 1991) 300–29. P. Lamarre, 'John Horne Tooke and the Grammar of Political Experience,' in *Philological Quarterly* 77 (1998): 187–207. C. Bewley and D. Bewley, *Gentleman Radical: A Life of John Horne Tooke 1736–1812* (London, 1998). See also Bergheaud 1979 listed under James Harris, Secondary Sources. [Hans Aarsleff]

Turgot, Anne Robert Jacques b. Paris, 1727; d. Paris 1781. Studied theology at the *Séminaire de Saint-Sulpice* and at the Sorbonne. After a brief clerical career as prior associated with the Sorbonne (1749–51), was in public administration until 1761 when he became *intendant* of the impoverished province of Limoges. In 1774 he became, briefly, Minister of Marine and then Comptroller General of Finance until 1776 when opposition at court, in *parlements*, and in the Church led to his dismissal. His works consist mostly of fragments and plans, including early pieces on history and progress; *Recherches sur les causes des progrès et de la décadence des sciences et des arts ou Réflexions sur l'histoire des progrès de l'esprit humain* (1749, unfinished); *Discours sur les avantages que l'établissement du christianisme a procurés au genre humain*; and *Tableau philosophique des progrès successifs de l'esprit humain* (both 1750). There were plans for a work on political geography (*Plan d'un ouvrage sur la géographie politique*) and for two discourses on universal history (*Plan de deux discours sur l'histoire universelle*), which contain the most complete account of his philosophy of history. He became acquainted with the leading *économistes* J.-C. Vincent de Gournay and François Quesnay and turned towards economic matters, experimenting with economic reforms in Limoges and engaging David Hume and Adam Smith in discussion. *Réflexions sur la formation et la distribution des richesses*, written 1766, first published 1769–70 in the *Ephémerides du citoyen*, the journal of the French physiocrats, advocated free trade, especially in corn, and demanded a new system of taxation. The main opponent of the theory of free trade was abbé Fernando Galiani (*Dialogues sur le commerce des blés*), and as a policy, liberalisation of corn was unpopular and cost T. his ministerial position. In 1778 he wrote the *Réflexions sur la situation des Américains des Etats Unis* in a letter to R. Price. *Oeuvres de Turgot et documents le concernant*, ed. G. Schelle, 5 vols. (Paris, 1919–23). C. Henry edited the *Correxpondance inédite de Condorcet et Turgot 1770–1779* (Paris, 1883; repr. Geneva, 1970). Modern translations: *Turgot on Progress, Sociology, and Economics*, trans. and ed. R. L. Meek (Cambridge, 1973); *Turgot, Le Ricchezze, il Progresso e la storia universale*, ed. R. Finzi (Turin, 1978); *Turgot über die Fortschritte des menschlichen Geistes*, eds J. Rohbeck and L. Steinbrügge (Frankfurt am Main, 1990).

Secondary Sources: M. J. A. N. de Condorcet, 'Vie de M. Turgot', in *Oeuvres*, eds. A. Condorcet, O'Connor, and F. Arago (Paris 1847–9), Vol. 5. Dupont de Nemours, 'Mémoires sur la vie et les ouvrages de Turgot', in *Oeuvres de M. Turgot* (Paris 1808–11), Vol. 1. P. D. Groenewegen, 'Turgot's Place in the History of Economic Thought: A Bicentenary Estimate', *History of Political Economy* 115 (1983): 611–15. R. L. Meek, 'Smith, Turgot, and the "Four Stages" Theory', *History of Political Economy* 3 (1971): 9–27. C. Morilhat, *La prise de conscience du capitalisme: économie et philosophie chez Turgot* (Paris, 1988). J.-P. Poirier, *Turgot: laissez-faire et progrès social* (Paris, 1999). A. Vauban, *Turgot: From Absolutism to Constitutionalism in Eighteenth-Century France* (New York, NY, 1967). [Simone Zurbuchen]

Turnbull, George b. Alloa, Scotland, 1698; d. The Hague, 1748. Scottish moral philosopher turned Anglican clergyman. Educated in Arts and Divinity at Edinburgh from 1711 (MA 1721); Regent at Marischal College, Aberdeen, 1721–7 (see his graduation theses: *De scientiae naturalis cum philosophia morali conjunctione*, 1723; *De pulcherrima mundi cum materialis tum rationalis constitutione*, 1726); travelling tutor; BCL (Oxford, 1733); ordained in the Church of England (1739); chaplain to the Prince of Wales (1741); priest at Drumachose, County Derry (1742–8). In Edinburgh he was a member of the Rankenian Club and of the circle of liberal students critical of Calvinist orthodoxy and authoritarian government in church and state. Through his travels, he became well acquainted with continental thought. He became close to prominent latitudinarians (Birch, Sykes, Hoadly, Warburton, Rundle) and wrote in criticism of the deists and in defence of the scientific foundation of morality, religion and art; see especially *A Philosophical Enquiry concerning the Connexion betwixt the Doctrine and Miracles of Jesus Christ*, by Philanthropos (pseud.) (1731); *Christianity neither False nor Useless, tho' not as Old as the Creation: Or, An Essay to prove the Usefulness, Truth, and Excellency of the Christian Religion* (1732); *An Impartial Inquiry into the Moral Character of Jesus Christ: Wherein He is considered as a Philosopher*, by Philalethes (pseud.) (1740); *The Principles of Moral Philosophy* (1740); *Christian Philosophy* (1740) (this and the previous work also issued together as a 2-vol. work, 1740; modern edn. Indianapolis, IN, 2005); *A Treatise on Ancient Painting* (1740); *Observations upon Liberal Education* (1742; modern edn. Indianapolis IN, 2003). Turnbull tried to combine humanistic neo-republicanism with modern natural jurisprudence in extensive notes to his translation of Heineccius' *A Methodical System of Universal Law*, 2 vols. (1741; modern edn. Indianapolis, IN, 2006) and in a work appended to that translation, *A Discourse upon the Nature and Origine of Moral and Civil Laws* (1740). See also *Education for Life: Correspondence and Writings on Religion and Practical Philosophy by George Turnbull*, eds. M. A. Stewart and P. B. Wood (Indianapolis, IN, 2007).

Secondary Sources: D. F. Norton, 'George Turnbull and the Furniture of the Mind', *Journal of the History of Ideas* 35 (1975): 701–16. J. C. Stewart-Robertson, 'The Well-Principled Savage, or the Child of the Scottish Enlightenment', *Journal of the History of Ideas* 42 (1981): 503–25. M. A. Stewart, 'Berkeley and the Rankenian Club', in *George Berkeley: Essays and Replies*, ed. D. Berman (Dublin, 1986), 25–45. C. Gibson-Wood, 'Painting as Philosophy: George Turnbull's *Treatise on Ancient Painting*', in *Aberdeen and the Enlightenment*, eds. J. J. Carter and J. H. Pittock (Aberdeen, 1987), 189–98. M. A. Stewart, 'George Turnbull and Educational Reform', in ib., 95–103. K. A. B. Mackinnon, 'George Turnbull's Common Sense Jurisprudence', in ib., 104–10. P. B. Wood, *The Aberdeen Enlightenment: The Arts Curriculum in the Eighteenth Century* (Aberdeen, 1993). K. Haakonssen, *Natural Law and Moral Philosophy: From Grotius to the Scottish Enlightenment* (Cambridge, 1996), ch. 2. [Knud Haakonssen]

Vattel, Emer de b. Couvet, Neuchâtel, 1714; d. 1767, Neuchâtel. Natural lawyer, philosopher, diplomat. Studied at the University of Basel and at the academy of Geneva. He defended Leibniz and Wolff against accusations of atheism in *Défense du système Leibnitien* (1741) and laid foundations of natural law in *Essai sur le fondement du droit naturel*, in *Le Loisir philosophique* (Geneva [in fact: Dresden], 1747). He was in the diplomatic service of Saxony, stationed in Bern, 1747–58 when he became a Privy Councillor. His main work, *Le droit des gens, ou principes de la loi naturelle, appliqués à la conduite et aux affaires des nations et des souverains*, 2 vols. (1758) was modelled after Wolff's *Jus naturae* and *Jus gentium* but introduced a number of significant changes that he justified in the *Questions de droit naturel* (1762). Aimed, like his friend and correspondent, Jean Henry Samuel Formey, the secretary of the Academy of Sciences in Berlin, at popularizing Wolff's philosophy. The standard edition of his main work is *Le droit des gens ou principes de la loi naturelle*, with English translation by C. G. Fenwick, 3 vols. (Washington, DC, 1916).

Secondary Sources: J. J. Manz, *Emer de Vattel. Eine Würdigung* (Zurich, 1971). F. S. Ruddy, *International Law in the Enlightenment: The background of E. de Vattel's Le Droit des Gens* (Dobbs Ferry, NY, 1975). F. G. Whelan, 'Vattel's Doctrine of the State', in *History of Political Thought* 9 (1988), 59–90. N. G. Onuf, *The Republican Legacy in International Thought* (Cambridge, 1998), 58–84. S. Zurbuchen, 'Die schweizerische Debatte über die Leibniz-Wolffsche Philosophie und ihre Bedeutung für Emer von Vattels philosophischen Werdegang', in *Reconceptualizing Nature, Science, and Aesthetics*, eds. P. Coleman et al. (Geneva, 1998), 91–113. [Simone Zurbuchen]

Vauvenargues, Luc de Clapiers, Marquis de b. Aix-en-Provence, France, 1715, d. Paris, 1747. Moral philosopher, critic. Of poor but noble family, he pursued a military career until illness forced him to live as an impoverished literary man in Paris. His general outlook was Stoic and a reaction against Augustinianism and the largely Epicurean stance of La Rochefoucauld. *Introduction à la connaissance de l'espirt humain, suivie de réflexions et maximes* (1746); *Oeuvres complètes de Vauvenargues*, ed. H. Bonnier, 2 vols. (Paris, 1968); *Oeuvres complètes*, ed. J.-P. Jackson (Paris, 2000).

Secondary Sources: C.-A. Sainte-Beuve, *Causeries du Lundi*, (8 Nov 1850; 24 Aug, 31 Aug, 7 Sept 1852). M. Wallas, *Luc de Clapiers. Marquis de Vauvenargues* (Cambridge, 1928). F. Vial, *Une philosophie et une morale du sentiment, Luc de Clapiers marquis de Vauvenargues* (Paris, 1938). [Hans Aarsleff]

Vico, Giambattista b. Naples, 1668; d. Naples, 1744. Philosopher, rhetorician, historian and jurist. Studied philosophy, literature, and law and was professor of rhetoric at the University of Naples 1699–1739. After the inaugural discourse, *De nostri temporis studiorum ratione* (1708, publ. 1709), his first noteworthy work, *De antiquissima Italorum sapientia* (1710), argues, against Descartes, that truth is only predicable of what is man-made (*verum ipsum factum*), a metaphysical perspective developed in *De universi juris*, 1720–1, and in his most famous work *Principi di una scienza nuova intorno alla natura delle nazione* (1725, 1730, and 1744). This last work gives the final metaphysical twist to the principle from 1710: if truth is only predicable of man-made things, true science can only be about man-made objects, especially, human institutions. Among less known writings are rhetorical dissertations, a medical treatise, an autobiography, *Vita di Giambattista Vico scritta da se medesimo* (1725–8), and *De mente heroica* (1732). Vico was almost completely isolated from the major trends of the Enlightenment. *Opere*, eds. G. Gentili and F. Nicolini, 7 vols. (Bari, 1911–40). *Opere* (Bologna, Naples, 1982–).

Secondary Sources: F. Nicolini, *La giovinezza di Giambattista Vico: Saggio biografico* (Naples, 1932). B. Croce and F. Nicolini, *Bibliografia Vichiana, accresiuta e rielaborata da Fausto Nicolini* (Naples, 1947). The 'Bollettino del Centro di Studi Vichiani' updates regularly the bibliography of Vico. S. Caianiello, 'Catalogo Vichiano Internazionale', *Studi vichiani* 30 (2000). R. Crease, *Vico in English* (Brunswick, NJ, 1978). B. Croce, *La Filosofia di Giambattista Vico* (Bari, 1911; trans. R. G. Collingwood, London, 1913). F. Nicolini, *Commento Storico alla Seconda Scienza Nuova*, 2 vols. (Rome, 1978). D. P. Verene, *Vico's Science of Imagination* (Ithaca, NY, 1981). L. Pompa, *Vico: A Study of the 'New Science'*, 2nd edn. (Cambridge, 1990). I. Berlin, *Three Critics of the Enlightenment: Vico, Hamann, Herder* (Princeton, NJ, 2000). [Dario Perinetti]

Voltaire, pseud. for François-Marie Arouet b. Paris, 1694; d. Paris, 1778. *Philosophe*, historian, playwright, and satirist. Studied at a Jesuit college and excelled in Latin poetry and rhetoric. He gave up legal studies for literature and became part of Parisian salons and libertine circles, displaying wit and provocative satire. The latter earned him exile in the provinces (1716) and a year in the Bastille (1717–18), where he began the epic poem *La Henriade* (1728). A quarrel with a nobleman sent him back to the Bastille and then to England (1726–8), which proved fruitful for his philosophical education. Strong influences from Locke, Newton, Swift, and Pope provided the materials for *Letters concerning the English Nation* (1733; in French as *Lettres sur les Anglais* later same year; expanded 1734 as *Les lettres philosophiques*). Here he defends English sensationalism in epistemology, a Newtonian vision of man's place in the universe (continued in *Éléments de la philosophie de Newton*, 1738), and the English political system as a model for political and religious tolerance. The book was burned and banned in France. Smart investments made V. a rich and independent man of letters. For ten years (1734–44) he stayed with his mistress Mme du Châtelet at Cirey, studying science with her and writing several tragedies. Under the patronage of Mme de Pompadour, he became historiographer of France (1745); he was elected to the Académie française (1746); and he accepted the invitation of Frederick the Great to come to Berlin (1750), an experiment that ended after a satirical onslaught on the President of the Berlin Academy of Science, Maupertuis (1753). He eventually ended up in Switzerland, acquiring the estate of Ferney, near Geneva, where he spent the rest of his life. While in Berlin he produced *Siècle de Louis XIV* (1751), which became one of the most important philosophical histories of the Enlightenment, *Micromegas* (1752), and *Défense de Lord Bolingbroke: Essai philosophique* (1752). Some of his most important contributions to philosophy of history and his many articles for the *Encyclopédie* followed the Berlin period. The *Essai sur les mœurs* (1756), a world history after Charlemagne, exchanged the providentialism of his immediate predecessor, Bossuet, for an entirely naturalistic, though progressivist, account which was further defended in the entry 'Histoire' in the *Encylopédie* and elaborated in *La Philosophie de l'histoire* (1764, later added as introduction to *Essai sur les mœurs*), which attempted a universal history from a naturalistic perspective. A string of works from the years at Ferney deepened V.'s Enlightenment agenda, promoting political and religious toleration (including his defence of Calas, a protestant merchant unjustly condemned for murdering his own son, and many other interventions in judicial matters), attacking revealed religion, arguing for penal reform, popularizing philosophy in the service of public life, and a great deal more: *Traité sur la tolerance* (1762); *Dictionnaire philosophique* (1764); *Quéstions sur les miracles* (1765); *Commentaires sur le livre des délits et des peines* (1766); *Prix de la justice et de l'humanité* (1778). Perhaps most famous of all was, and is, his attack on Leibniz's and Pope's philosophical optimism in *Candide* (1759). Ferney became an Enlightenment centre from which V. conducted a vast correspondence with enlightened Europe, gave advice to rulers, and received a stream of intellectual tourists. The old standard edition, *Œuvres complètes* (ed. L. Moland, Paris 1877–85), is being replaced by the critical edition from the Voltaire foundation, *The Complete Works of Voltaire* (Geneva and Toronto, 1968–).

Secondary Sources: F. A. Spear and E. Kreager, *Bibliographie analytique des écrits relatifs á Voltaire 1966–1990* (Oxford, 1992). J. M. Goulemot, A. Magnan and D. Masseau, *Inventaire Voltaire* (Paris, 1995). G. Bengesco, *Voltaire: Bibliographie de ses œuvres*, 4 vols. (Paris, 1882). J. Malcom, *Table de la Bibliographie de Voltaire par Bengesco* (Geneva, 1953). M.-M. H. Barr, *A Century of Voltaire Study: A Bibliography of Writings on Voltaire, 1825–1925* (New York, NY, 1929) and *Quarante années d'études voltairiennes: Bibliographie analytique des livres et articles sur Voltaire, 1926–1965* (Paris, 1968). M.-M. Harel, *Voltaire: Recueil des particularités curieuses de sa vie & de sa mort* (Porrentruy, 1781). T. Duvernet, *La vie de Voltaire* (Geneva, 1786). M. J. A. N. Condorcet, *Vie de Voltaire* [Kiehl], 1789). G. Desnoirterres, *Voltaire et la société française au XVIIIe siècle*, 8 vols. (Paris, 1867–76, reprint, 1967). G. Lanson, *Voltaire* (Paris, 1906). T. Bergner, *Voltaire: Leben und Werk eines streitbaren Denkers: Biographie* (Berlin, 1976). T. Besterman, *Voltaire* (3rd edn., Oxford 1976). P. Lepape, *Voltaire le conquérant: Naissance des intellectuals au siècle des Lumières* (Paris, 1994). *Voltaire en son temps*, ed. R. Pomeau, 2 vols. (Oxford and Paris, 1995). R. Pomeau, *La religion de Voltaire* (Paris, 1956). A. Delattre, *Voltaire l'impétuex* (Paris, 1957). R. Pomeau, *Politique de Voltaire* (Paris, 1963). P. Gay, *Voltaire's Politics* (New York, NY, 1965). A. O. Aldridge, *Voltaire and the Century of Light* (Princeton, NJ, 1975). G. Waterlot, *Voltaire: Le procureur des lumières* (Paris, 1996). *Voltaire et ses combats: Actes du congrès international, Oxford-Paris, 1994*, eds. U. Kölving and C. Mervaud (Oxford, 1997). B. L. Knapp, *Voltaire Revisited* (New York, NY, 2000). [Dario Perinetti]

Walch, Johann Georg b. Meiningen, 1693; d. Jena, 1775. Church historian, theologian, and philosopher. The son of a *Generalsuperintendent* in the Lutheran church, he studied theology, philosophy, and history in Leipzig (*magister* 1713). 1718 professor of philosophy and of antiquities, 1721 of poetry, 1724 of theology, in Jena. He wrote *Einleitung in die Philosophie* (1730) and *Philosophisches Lexikon* (1726), which reflects the influence of A. Rüdiger, C. Wolff, and J. F. Buddeus. Best known for *Historische und theologische Einleitung in die Religionsstreitigkeiten der evangelisch-lutherischen Kirche*, 5 vols. (1733–9), he also published *Historia critica Latinae linguae* (1716), *Historia ecclesiastica novi Testamenti variis observationibus illustrata* (1744), *Introductio in philosophiam universam* (1738), and *Einleitung in die christliche Moral* (1757).

Secondary Sources: J. E. J. Walch, *Leben und Charakter des wohlseeligen Herrn Kirchenraths D. Johann Georg Walch* (Jena, 1777). H. Leube, *Orthodoxie und Pietismus* (Bielefeld, 1975), *passim*. E. W. Zeeden, *The Legacy of Luther* (London, 1954), 110–7. F. Boltin, 'Johann Georg Walch (1693–1775). *Historiae logicae*' in *Dall' età cartesiana a Brucker*, eds F. Boltin, M. Longo and G. Piaia (Brescia, 1979), 415–21. [Thomas Ahnert]

Waterland, Daniel b. Walesby, Lincolnshire, 1683; d. Windsor, 1740. Cambridge theologian. Educated at Magdalene College, Cambridge (DD 1717), and Fellow then Master there (1704, 1713); Archdeacon of Middlesex (1730). Based on extensive scholarship and with an empirical attitude derived from Locke, he upheld Trinitarianism against Samuel Clarke, especially in *A Vindication of Christ's Divinity* (1719), criticized Clarke's rationalism in *A Dissertation upon the Argument A Priori for Proving a First Cause* (anon., appended to Edmund Law's *Enquiry into the Ideas of Space, Time, Immensity and Eternity*, 1734), and assailed Tindal's deism in *Scripture Vindicated; in Answer to a Book, intituled, Christianity as Old as the Creation* (1730) and in *Christianity Vindicated against Infidelity: A Second Charge deliver'd to the Clergy of the Archdeaconry of Middlesex* (1732).

Secondary Sources: R. T. Holtby, *Daniel Waterland 1683–1740: A Study in Eighteenth-Century Orthodoxy* (Carlisle, 1966). [Knud Haakonssen]

Watson, Richard b. Heversham, Westmoreland, 1737; d. 'Calgarth Park', Westmoreland, 1816. Whig political theorist, liberal churchman, popular chemist. Educated at Trinity College, Cambridge (BA 1759, MA 1762), professor of chemistry (1764–73) then Regius professor of Divinity (1771–1816) at Cambridge. Held several church appointments and became Bishop of Llandaff (1782–1816). Much of the political thought, including support for the American revolutionaries, is in sermons and tracts: *An Answer to the 'Disquisitions on Government and Civil Liberty'* (1782, against Soame Jenyns); *Sermons . . . and Tracts* (1788) (and see, *A Collection of Theological Tracts*, 6 vols. [1785]); *Miscellaneous Tracts*, 2 vols. (1815). There are answers to Gibbon, *An Apology for Christianity* (1776); and to Paine, *An Apology for the Bible* (1796); the chemical work, *Chemical Essays*, 5 vols. (1781–7); and the important memoirs, *Anecdotes of the Life of Richard Watson, Bishop of Llandaff* (1817).

Secondary Sources: R.W.D. Fenn, 'Richard Watson, a Reappraisal', *Journal of the Historical Society of the Church of Wales* 15 (1965). T. J. Brain, 'Richard Watson and the Debate on Toleration in the Eighteenth Century', *The Price-Priestley Newsletter* 2 (1978) [Knud Haakonssen]

Watts, Isaac b. Southhampton, 1674; d. London, 1748. Dissenting minister and hymn-writer. Educated at Stoke Newington dissenting academy (1690–4); minister in London from 1698 and private tutor. In a vast *oeuvre*, the philosophical works are the popular textbooks, *Logick, or the Right Use of Reason in the Inquiry after Truth* (1724) and *The Improvement of the Mind; or A Supplement to the Art of Logic* (1741), plus *Philosophical Essays on Various Subjects* (1733).

Secondary Sources: T. Milner, *The Life, Times and Correspondence of the Rev. Isaac Watts, D. D.* (London, 1834). A. P. Davis, *Isaac Watts: His Life and Works* (London, 1948). [Knud Haakonssen]

WHISTON, WILLIAM b. Norton, England, 1667; d. Lyndon, England, 1752. Mathematician and religious controversialist. Succeeded Newton as Lucasian professor of mathematics at Cambridge, and followed Newton, too, in an obsessive and detailed interest in Scriptural interpretation. His explanations of the stories of Genesis and the Flood in terms of natural phenomena such as comets were presented in *A New Theory of the Earth* (1696) and *Astronomical Principles of Religion, Natural and Revealed* (1717). They provided a different style of reconciliation between science and religion from that offered by Deism, which tended to ignore rather than reinterpret Scripture. Whiston's religious ideas progressively diverged from the consensus of his day, and he was deprived of his Cambridge chair for doubting the divinity of Christ.

Secondary Souces: M. Farrell, *William Whiston* (New York, 1981). J. E. Force, *William Whiston: Honest Newtonian* (Cambridge, 1985). P. Harrison, 'Newtonian Science, Miracles and the Laws of Nature', *Journal of the History of Ideas* 56 (1995): 531–53. [James Franklin]

WIELAND, CHRISTOPH MARTIN b. Biberach, Germany, 1733; d. Weimar, 1813. Prolific writer, translator, and editor. Departing from the religious enthusiasm of early works written in Tübingen and Zurich, such as *Empfindungen eines Christen* (1757), he wrote the popular coming-of-age novel, *Geschichte des Agathon* (1766–7) and translated Shakespeare, *Theatralische Werke* (8 vols., 1762–6), while director of the chancellery at Biberach. A professor of philosophy at Erfurt (1769–72), his final move was to Weimar, where he translated ancient authors (for example, Plato, Horace, Cicero), edited *Der teutsche Merkur* (68 vols., 1773–89), and composed novels in which Greek antiquity serves as a vehicle of criticism, for instance, *Geschichte der Abderiten* (1781) and *Aristipp und einige seiner Zeitgenossen* (Leipzig, 1800/02). The standard edition: reprint of the 1794–1811 edn. of *Sämtliche Werke*, 14 vols. (Hamburg, 1984).

Secondary Sources: S.-A. Jørgensen, et al., *Christoph Martin Wieland: Epoche, Werk, Wirkung* (Munich, 1994). [Daniel Dahlstrom]

WOLFF, CHRISTIAN b. Breslau 1679; d. Halle 1754. Universal metaphysician. Acquainted already in school with the usual textbook Aristotelianism and with the Jesuits' version of Thomism, but also with Descartes and von Tschirnhausen, Wolff studied in Jena (1699 to 1703) but took his degrees at Leipzig, *magister* in 1702 and doctor in 1703 with the dissertation *Philosophica practica universalis, mathematica methodo conscripta*. From 1703 he was a Privatdozent in Leipzig until he, in 1707, accepted a call to a chair in mathematics at the new University of Halle. Gradually, and apparently against considerable opposition from the pietistic establishment as well as in fierce competition with his rival, Christian Thomasius, Wolff branched out from mathematics to physics, logic, metaphysics, and moral philosophy. In keeping with the modern face of the University, Wolff lectured in German and transformed his lectures into a German text-book system of the whole of philosophy, all titles beginning *Vernünfftige Gedancken von* . . . : . . . *den Kräfften des menschlichen Verstandes* (1713), . . . *Gott, der Welt, und der Seele des Menschen* (1720), . . . *der Menschen Thun und Lassen* (1720), . . . *dem gesellschaftlichen Leben der Menschen* (1721), . . . *den Wirkungen der Natur* (1723), . . . *den Absichten der natürlichen Dingen* (1723), . . . *dem Gebrauche der Theile in Menschen, Thiere und Pflantzen* (1725). These works had a tremendous influence and, together with many other works, several in Latin, they earned Wolff a national and international reputation (for example, fellowships in the Royal Society and the Berlin Academy). It became a major scandal when the Prussian government tried to muzzle Wolff for arguing that the moral life had a universal foundation independent of confessional religion. Years of tension with the pietists reached a climax when Wolff, in a public lecture at the end of his office as pro-rector of the University in 1722, suggested that the ancient Chinese managed at least as well as those graced with the Christian revelation in founding morality, and that Confucius was a teacher who, like

Moses for the Jews, Christ for the Christians, and Muhammed for the Moslems, inculcated an independently established morality (*Oratio de Sinarum philosophia practica*, 1726). After a ferocious pen-fight in which the main charge against Wolff was that of Spinozistic determinism, the pietists, led by Joachim Lange, won over the King, Friedrich Wilhelm I, who apparently was brought to fear the social consequences of necessitarianism. Dismissed and ordered to leave the country within 48 hours, on pain of death, Wolff took up a standing offer of a professorship at Marburg (1723), where he continued teaching his system and, more importantly, reworked it in Latin, a task that was unfinished when he died, despite the appearance of some 30 quarto volumes. This enormous work was more than a re-writing for an international audience of the earlier German works, especially as far as the practical philosophy is concerned. Both the German and the Latin series certainly move from 'logic' or general theory of knowledge, through metaphysics to practical philosophy, but, in addition to significant rearrangements of the components of metaphysics (ontology, cosmology, empirical and rational psychology, natural theology), there are important developments in the Latin version of practical philosophy. With all these and many more works, as well as large numbers of students, Wolff established himself as the foremost German philosopher of the age, receiving honours and offers of professorial chairs from several countries as well as from other German states. It is, therefore, not surprising that Frederick the Great wanted him back to Prussia, which he got in 1740, the year of his ascension to the throne. Wolff returned to Halle, was made curator of all Prussian universities, Chancellor of Halle, and, in 1745, a Baron. All of Wolff's works have been published in a two-part facsimile edition, with a third part comprising a large number of related publications: *Gesammelte Werke* (Hildesheim, 1964–): Abteilung I: *Deutsche Schriften*, 24 vols.; Abteilung II: *Lateinische Schriften*, 38 vols.; Abteilung III: *Ergänzungsreihe: Materialien und Dokumente*, in progress.

Secondary Sources: C. Wolff, *Biographie* (*Werke* I.10; includes Wolff's autobiography plus biographies by Baumeister and Gottsched); *Briefe von Christian Wolff aus den Jahren 1719–1753. Ein Beitrag zur Geschichte der Kaiserlichen Academie der Wissenschaften zu St. Petersburg* (St. Petersburg, 1860; in *Werke* I.16). G. Biller, 'Die Wolff-Diskussion 1800 bis 1982. Eine Bibliographie', in *Christian Wolff 1679–1754*, ed. W. Schneiders (Hamburg, 1983): 321–45. E. Zeller, 'Wolffs Vertreibung aus Halle; der Kampf des Pietismus mit der Philosophie', *Preußische Jahrbücher*, 10 (1962): 47–72. P. Petersen, *Geschichte der aristotelischen Philosophie im protestantischen Deutschland* (Leipzig, 1921): 425–72. O. Nippold, Introduction, in Wolff, *Jus gentium methodo scientifica pertractatum*, [with English translation], 2 vols. (Oxford, London, 1934). M. Campo, *Cristiano Wolff e il razionalismo precritico*, 2 vols. (Milan, 1939). M.Wundt, *Die deutsche Schulphilosophie im Zeitalter der Aufklärung* (Tübingen, 1945): 122–264. R. J. Blackwell, 'Christian Wolff's Doctrine of the Soul', *Journal of the History of Ideas*, 22 (1961): 339–54. M. Thomann, *La pensée politique de l'absolutisme éclairé* (Strassburg, 1969). C. A. Corr, 'Christian Wolff and Leibniz', *Journal of the History of Ideas*, 36 (1975): 241–362; 'Christian Wolff's distinction between empirical and rational psychology', *Studia Leibnitiana*, Suppl. Vol. 14 (1975): 195–215. T. Frängsmyr, 'Christian Wolff's Mathematical Method and Its Impact on the Eighteenth Century', *Journal of the History of Ideas*, 36 (1975): 653–68. H.-M. Bachmann, *Die naturrechtliche Staatslehre Christian Wolffs* (Berlin, 1977). M. Casula, 'Die Beziehungen Wolff-Thomas-Carbo in der Metaphysica latina: Zur Quellengeschichte der Thomas Rezeption bei Christian Wolff', *Studia Leibnitiana*, 9 (1979): 98–123. *Christian Wolff als Philosoph der Aufklärung in Deutschland*, eds. H.-M. Gerlach, G. Schenk, B. Thaler (Halle an der Saale, 1980). *Christian Wolff 1679–1754. Interpretationen zu seiner Philosophie und deren Wirkung*, ed. W. Schneiders (Hamburg, 1983). E. Stipperger, *Freiheit und Institution bei Christian Wolff (1679–1754). Zum Grundrechtsdenken in der deutschen Hochaufklärung* (Frankfurt am Main, 1984). C. Schröer, *Naturbegriff und Moralbegründung. Die Grundlegung der Ethik bei Christian Wolff und deren Kritik durch Immanuel Kant* (Stuttgart, 1988). J. Ching and W. G. Oxtoby, 'Introduction', in *Moral Enlightenment: Leibniz and Wolff on China* (Nettetal, 1992). B. Winiger, *Das rationale Pflichtenrecht Christian Wolffs. Bedeutung und Funktion der transzendentalen, logischen und moralischen Wahrheit im systematischen und theistischen Naturrecht Wolffs* (Berlin, 1992). C. Schwaiger, *Das Problem des Glücks im Denken Christian Wolffs* (Stuttgart-Bad Cannstatt, 1995). G. Gawlick and L. Kreimendahl, 'Einleitung', in Wolff, *Discursus praeliminaris de philosophia in genere/Einleitende Abhandlung über Philosophie im Allgemeinen*, eds. Gawlick and Kreimendahl (Stuttgart-Bad Cannstatt, 1996). K.-G. Lutterbeck, *Staat und Gesellschaft bei Christian Thomasius und Christian Wolff. Eine historische Untersuchung in systematischer Absicht* (Stuttgart-Bad Cannstatt, 2002). K. Haakonssen, 'German Natural Law', in *Cambridge History of Eighteenth-Century Political Thought*, eds. M. Goldie and R. Wokler (Cambridge, 2006). [Knud Haakonssen]

WOLLASTON, WILLIAM b. Coton-Clanford, Staffordshire, 1660; d. London, 1724. Moral philosopher. Educated at Sidney Sussex College, Cambridge (1674–81). Schoolmaster until 1688, then independent scholar. Extensive biblical and Jewish scholarship, all destroyed by author. Sole publication, the best-selling *The Religion of Nature Delineated* (1724; private printing 1722). Manuscript autobiography in J. and J. B. Nichols, *Illustrations of the Literary History of the Eighteenth Century*, 8 vols. (London, 1817–58).

Secondary Sources: J. Clarke (Dean of Salisbury), Memoir appended to 6th edn. of Wollaston's work (London, 1738). C. G. Thompson, *The Ethics of William Wollaston* (Boston, MA, 1922). A. Altmann, 'William Wollaston: English Deist and Rabbinic Scholar', in Altmann, *Studies in Religious Philosophy and Mysticism* (London, 1969), 210–45. [Knud Haakonssen]

WOLLSTONECRAFT, MARY b. London 1759; d. London, 1797. Radical writer, educationalist, novelist, journalist, and polemicist. Self-educated, she briefly ran a school before joining the Rational Dissenters around Richard Price in Newington Green, becoming a protégé of the publisher Joseph Johnson and was from 1788 writing for his *Analytical Review. A Vindication of the Rights of Men* (1790) was the first printed response to Edmund Burke's *Reflections on the Revolution in France* and was published anonymously; a revised edition appeared under her own name within a month. In *A Vindication of the Rights of Woman* (1792), her most famous work, she argued for a radical revision of educational policy and for extending the rights of men also to women. *Letters Written during a Short Residence in Sweden, Norway, and Denmark* (1796), her most popular work, won her the admiration of William Godwin, whom she married in 1797. She died later that year giving birth to Mary Wollstonecraft Shelley, author of *Frankenstein, or, The Modern Prometheus. Works*, eds. J. Todd and M. Butler (7 vols., London, 1989).

Secondary Sources: J. Todd, *Mary Wollstonecraft: An Annotated Bibliography* (New York, NY, 1976); W. Godwin, *Memoirs of the Author of A Vindication of the Rights of Woman* (London, 1798); C. Tomalin, *The Life and Death of Mary Wollstonecraft* (rev. edn., London, 1992); G. Kelly, *Revolutionary Feminism: The Mind and Career of Mary Wollstonecraft* (London, 1992); V. Sapiro, *A Vindication of Political Virtue: The Political Theory of Mary Wollstonecraft* (Chicago, IL, 1992); *The Cambridge Companion to Mary Wollstonecraft*, ed. C. L. Johnson (Cambridge, 2002); B. Taylor, *Mary Wollstonecraft and the Feminist Imagination* (Cambridge, 2003). [Åsa Söderman]

WOOLSTON, THOMAS b. Northampton, c.1668; d. London, 1733. Philosopher and man of letters. Educated at Sidney Sussex College, Cambridge, 1685, BA 1689, MA 1692; elected to fellowship of his College 1691; BD 1699. Expelled from Sidney Sussex 1724. His reading of Origen led to thesis that scripture should be interpreted allegorically. With *Moderator between an Infidel and an Apostate* (1725) he involved himself in the Deist controversy between Anthony Collins and Edward Chandler, sympathizing with Collins. His six *Discourse[s] on the Miracles of our Saviour* (1727–9) met strong clerical opposition and a storm of replies; coupled with the unrepentant attitude manifested in *Mr. Woolston's Defence of his Discourses on the Miracles* (1729–30), they earned him a sentence of fines and imprisonment.

Secondary Sources: Thomas Stackhouse, *The Life of Mr. Woolston. With an Impartial Account of His Writings* (London, 1733). W. H. Trapnell, *Thomas Woolston: Madman and Deist* (Bristol, 1994). [Maria Rosa Antognazza]

Zedler, Johann Heinrich b. Breslau, 1706; d. Leipzig, 1751. Publisher of the main encylopedic reference work of the German Enlightenment. Following apprenticeships with booksellers in Breslau and Hamburg, he established his own publishing business, first in Freiberg (Saxony) in 1726, then in Leipzig 1727. The work for which he is best known, the *Große und vollständige Universal-Lexikon aller Wissenschaften und Künste, welche bißhero durch menschlichen Verstand und Witz erfunden und verbessert worden* appeared in 64 volumes between 1732 and 1754. Due to financial difficulties, his publishing house was taken over by the Leipzig merchant Johann Heinrich Wolff in 1738.

Secondary Sources: G. Quedenbaum, *Der Verleger und Buchhändler Johann Heinrich Zedler 1706–1751* (Hildesheim and New York, NY, 1977). B. Kossmann, 'Deutsche Universallexika des achtzehnten Jahrhunderts', *Börsenblatt für den deutschen Buchhandel* 84 (1968): 2947–68. [Thomas Ahnert]

Fénelon, Francois de Salignac de la Mothe b. Perigord 1651; d. Cambrai 1715, Churchman, mystic, writer on education and political theory. Educated at the University of Cahors and the Sorbonne and ordained in 1675, Fénelon was first a Paris preacher who wrote the important *Dialogues sur l'éloquence* (published posthumously 1718). 1678–88 he ministered to recently converted French Protestants, especially young girls; against this background he wrote *Traité de l'éducation des filles* (1687). In 1689, he became tutor to the duc de Bourgogne, grandson of Louis XIV, for whom he wrote – but only later published – *Fables* (1701), *Dialogues des morts composées pour l'éducation d'un prince* (1712), and his heroic poem *Les aventures de Télémaque, fils de Ulysse* (1699), one of the most popular works of the eighteenth century. In 1695, he became Archbishop of Cambrai. However, he was captivated by Quetism's ideal of entire self-alienation in the love of God, a doctrine so dangerous to traditional notions of divine reward and punishment (no self, no interest) that his erstwhile mentor, Bossuet, turned against him; he was dismissed from his tutorship, his *Explication des maxims des saints sur la vie interieur* (1697) was condemned by the Pope, and he was ordered to reside in Cambrai, which he did for the rest of his life. One of the great correspondents of the age, Fénelon also wrote influential works on theology (*Démonstration de l'existence de Dieu*, 1712–18), aesthetics (*Lettre à l' Académie française*, 1714, publ. 1716), and politics. In the posthumously published works, *Lettre à Louis XIV* (*c.* 1694), *Directions pour la conscience d'un roi*, and (with the duc de Beauvilliers) *Tables de Chaunes*, he spelled out ideas present already in the fables and in *Télémaque* (which had been published without Fénelon's permission), namely a critical analysis of contemporary luxury and despotism and a utopian solution based on the Old Testament with touches of More. *Oeuvres de Fénelon*, ed. M. Aimé-Martin, 3 vols. (Paris, 1835); *Oeuvers*, ed. J. Le Brun, 2 vols. (Paris, 1983–8); *Correspondence de Fénelon*, ed. J. Orcibal, vols. 1–5 (Paris, 1972–6), vols. 6–17 (Geneva, 1987–99).

Secondary Sources: L. F. Bausset, *Histoire de Fénelon*, 3 vols. (Paris, 1809). M. Aimé-Martin, 'Vie de Fénelon', in *Oeuvres de Fénelon*. P. Janet, *Fénelon: His Life and Work*, trans. V. Lenliette (London, 1941). J.-L. Gore, *L'itinéraire de Fénelon: Humanisme et spiritualité*, 2 vols. (Paris, 1957). W. S. Howell, Introduction, in Fénelon, *Dialogues on Eloquence*, ed. and trans. W. S. Howell (Princeton, NJ, 1951). R. Spaemann, *Reflexion und Spontanietät. Studien über Fénelon* (Stuttgart, 1963). H. Hillenaar, *Fénelon and the Jesuits* (The Hague, 1967). H. Gouhier, *Fénelon philosophe* (Paris, 1977). J. H. Davis, *Fénelon* (Boston, MA, 1979). P. Riley Introduction, in Fénelon, *Telemachus, Son of Ulysses*, ed. and trans. P. Riley (Cambridge, 1994). [Knud Haakonssen]

BIBLIOGRAPHY

The bibliography is a compilation of works cited and is divided into two parts, Bibliography: Before 1800 (*B1*) and Bibliography: After 1800 (*B2*). *B1* contains works published prior to 1800 or those whose authors published mainly before 1800. *B2* contains works after 1800 or those whose authors published mainly after 1800. The bibliography lists only editions quoted or mentioned in contributors' chapters; it does not include the literature of the Biobibliographical Appendix.

Multiple editions of a work, even if revised, may all be entered as one entry, but with indications of each edition by place of publication and year. Where two places of publication with same year of publication are listed, this may refer to two separate editions of the work. In such cases the year is repeated for the respective publication place: one edition with two publication places is listed as Place and Place, Year, whereas separate editions are listed as Place, Year; Place Year.

Please also refer to Methods of Reference and Abbreviations (p. xi).

B1. BIBLIOGRAPHY: BEFORE 1800

Anonymous. *Aenesidemus. See* Schulze.

Anonymous. *De l'éducation publique*. Amsterdam, 1762.

Anonymous. *De tribus impostoribus. See* Anonymous. *Traité de trois imposteurs.*

Anonymous. *L'âme matérielle: ouvrage anonyme*, ed. A. Niderst. Paris, 1969.

Anonymous. *L'esprit de Spinosa. See* Anonymous. *Traité des trois imposteurs.*

Anonymous. *L'examen de la religion*, in *L'Evangile de la raison*. London [i.e., Netherlands], 1764.

Anonymous. *Le militaire philosophe. See* d'Holbach.

Anonymous. "Observations on the University of Oxford". *Gentleman's Magazine* 50 (1780): 119–20, 277–8.

Anonymous. "On Charles White's Account of the Regular Gradation in Man". *Monthly Review* 33 (1800): 360–4. Reprinted in *Race: The Origins of An Idea, 1760–1850*, ed. H. F. Augstein. Bristol, 1996, pp. 51–5.

Anonymous. *Parité de la vie et de la mort: La 'Réponse' du médecin Gaultier*, ed. O. Bloch. Paris and Oxford, 1993.

Anonymous. *Q. D. B. V. de Scepticorum praecipuis hypothesibus, secundum constitutionem Fridericianum, praeside Georgio Paschio*. Cologne, 1704.

Anonymous. Rev. of Hume's *Treatise. Bibliothèque raisonnée des ouvrages des savans de l'Europe* 14 (1740): 328.
Anonymous. Rev. of Hume's *Treatise. Nouvelle Bibliothèque* 6 (July 1740): 291–316.
Anonymous. Rev. of Hume's *Treatise. Nouvelle Bibliothèque* 7 (September 1740): 44–63.
Anonymous. Rev. of Samuel Stanhope Smith's *An Essay on the Causes of the Variety . . .* ', *Monthly Review*, 80 (1789): 184–5; in *Race: The Origins of An Idea*, ed. H. F. Augstein. Bristol, 1966, pp. 56–7.
Anonymous. *Some Thoughts Concerning the Argument à Priori; Occasion'd by Mr. Knowles's Discourse Entitled the 'Existence and Attributes of God not Demonstrable à Priori'*. London, 1748.
Anonymous. *Theophrastus redivivus* (1659?). Eds. G. Canziani and G. Paganini. Florence, 1981.
Anonymous. *Traité des trois imposteurs*. Part 2 of Anonymous, *La vie et l'esprit de Mr. Benoit Spinoza*. (1719).
Anonymous. *Traité des trois imposteurs* (1721, 1768, 1777), in *Traité des trois imposteurs, manuscript clandestine du début du XVIIIe siècle (éd. 1777)*, ed. P. Rétat. Saint-Étienne, 1973. Trans. in Anderson, *The Treatise of the Three Impostors* (see *B2*).
Anonymous. *Two Dissertations concerning Sense, and The Imagination. With an Essay on Consciousness*. London, 1728; repr. with German trans. (*Pseudo-Mayne: Über das Bewusstsein 1728*), trans. and ed. R. Brandt, Hamburg, 1983.
Abbt, Thomas. *Vom Tode für das Vaterland* [1761], in *Vermischte Werke*. Berlin and Stettin, 1772–81; facsim. 6 in 3 vols., Hildesheim, 1978, vol. 1.
Abbt, Thomas. *Zweifel über die Bestimmung des Menschen* [1764], in Mendelssohn, *Gesammelte Schriften*, vol. 6.i.
Abernethy, John. *Discourses concerning the Being and Natural Perfections of God*. Dublin, 1740.
Abernethy, John. *Discourses concerning the Perfections of God; in which his Holiness, Goodness, and Other Moral Attributes, are Explained and Proved*. Dublin, 1742.
Adams, John. *Curious Thoughts on the History of Man; Chiefly Abridged from the Celebrated Works of Lord Kames, Lord Monboddo, Dr Dunbar and the Immortal Montesquieu*. London, 1789; repr., ed. A. E. Jacoby, Bristol, 1994.
Adams, William. *An Essay on Mr. Hume's Essay on Miracles* [1752]. London, 1754.
Addison, Joseph, and Richard Steele. *Selections from The Tatler and The Spectator*, ed. R. J. Allen. New York, NY, 1966.
Addison, Joseph, and Richard Steele. *The Spectator*, 8 vols. London, 1771.
[Aldrich, Henry]. *Artis logicæ compendium*. Oxford, 1691.
Alembert, Jean le Rond d'. *Discours préliminaire de l'Encyclopédie* [1751]. Paris, 1894; in *Oeuvres* (Geneva, 1967), vol. 1, pp. 99–114.
Alembert, Jean le Rond d'. "Discours préliminaire", in *Encyclopédie*, ed. D. Diderot, vol. 1, pp. i–xlv.
Alembert, Jean le Rond d'. *Encyclopédie. See*, Diderot.
Alembert, Jean le Rond d'. *Essai sur les éléments de philosophie . . . avec les éclaircissemens . . .* [1759–67], in *Oeuvres*, vol. 1.
Alembert, Jean le Rond d'. *Essai sur la société des gens de letters avec les grands* (1753), in *Oeuvres*, vol. 4.
Alembert, Jean le Rond d'. *Essai sur les éléments de philosophie ou Sur les principes des connaisances humaines*. Amsterdam, 1759; facsim, ed. C. Kintzler, Paris, 1986; in *Melanges de littérature, d'histoire, et de philosophie*, 5 vols., Amsterdam, 1759–67, vols. 4–5.
Alembert, Jean le Rond d'. "Introduction au *Traité de dynamique*", in *Oeuvres*, vol. 1, pp. 391–406.
Alembert, Jean le Rond d'.*Oeuvres*, 5 vols. Paris, 1821–2; repr. Geneva, 1967.

Alembert, Jean le Rond d'. *Preliminary Discourse to the Encyclopedia of Diderot*, trans. R. N. Schwab and W. E. Rex. Indianapolis, IN, 1963.

Alembert, Jean le Rond d'. *Traité de dynamique*, 2nd edn. Paris, 1758.

Alison, Archibald. *Essays on the Nature and Principles of Taste* [1790]. New York, NY, 1854.

Allestree, Richard. *The Ladies Calling*. Oxford, 1673.

Ancillon, Johann Peter Friedrich. "Dialogue entre Berkeley et Hume", in *Mémoires de l'Académie royale, proceedings for 1796*, Berlin, 1799, pp. 86–127.

Ancillon, Johann Peter Friedrich. "Essai sur le scepticisme", in *Mélanges de litterature et de philosophie*, 2 vols., Paris, 1809, vol. 2, pp. 3–70.

[Anderson, George]. *An Estimate of the Profit and Loss of Religion, Personally and Publicly Stated*. Edinburgh, 1753.

Anderson, George. *A Remonstrance against Lord Viscount Bolingbroke's Philosophical Religion*. Edinburgh, 1756.

André, Yves-Marie. *Essai sur le beau* [1731]. Paris, 1770.

Annet, Peter. *Collection of the Tracts of a certain Free Enquirer*, London, c. 1750.

Annet, Peter. *David, ou L'histoire de l'homme selon le coeur de Dieu*, trans. P.-H. T. d'Holbach. London [i.e., Amsterdam], 1768.

Annet, Peter. *The Resurrection of Jesus Considered*; in *Answer to the Tryal of the Witnesses*, 3rd edn. London, 1745.

Annet, Peter. *Supernaturals Examined: in Four Dissertations on Three Treatises*. London, n.d.

Anselm of Canterbury. *Proslogion*, in *Patrologia Latina*, ed. J.-P. Migne, 221 in 222 vols. Paris, 1844–91, vol. 158.

Aquinas, Thomas. *Summa theologiae*, Blackfriars Edition, ed. T. Gilby. New York, NY and London, 1964–81, vol. 28.

Arbuthnot, John. *An Essay Concerning the Effects of Air on Human Bodies*. London, 1733; 1751.

Argens, Jean Baptiste de Boyer, marquis d'. *Correspondence entre Prosper Marchand et le marquis d'Argens*, ed. S. Larkin. Oxford, 1984.

Argens, Jean Baptiste de Boyer, marquis d'. *Lettres juives*. The Hague, 1738.

Argens, Jean Baptiste de Boyer, marquis d'. *Mémoires secrets de la république des Lettres*. Amsterdam, 1738.

Aristotle. *The Complete Works*, ed. J. Barnes, 2 vols. Princeton, NJ, 1984.

Arnauld, Antoine, and Pierre Nicole. *The Art of Thinking: Port-Royal Logic*, trans. J. J. Dickoff and P. P. James. Indianapolis, IN, 1964.

Arnauld, Antoine, and Pierre Nicole. *Logic, or The Art of Thinking*, trans. J. Ozell. London, 1717; modern edn., trans. and ed. J. V. Buroker, Cambridge, 1996.

Arnauld, Antoine, and Pierre Nicole. *La logique, ou L'art de penser*. Paris, 1662; modern edn., eds. P. Clair and F. Girbal, Paris, 1965.

Arthur, Archibald. *Discourses of Theological and Literary Subjects*. Glasgow, 1803.

Astell, Mary. *A Fair Way with the Dissenters and their Patrons*. London, 1704.

Astell, Mary. *Reflections upon Marriage* (1700, 3rd edn., 1706), in *Political Writings*, ed. P. Springborg, Cambridge, 1996.

Astell, Mary. *A Serious Proposal to the Ladies for the Advancement of their True and Greatest Interest*, 3rd edn., 1696, in *The First English Feminist: Reflections Upon Marriage and other writings by Mary Astell*, ed. B. Hill. New York, NY, 1986.

Augustine. *De libero arbitrio*, in *Patrologia Latina*, ed. J.-P. Migne, 221 in 222 vols. Paris, 1844–91, vol. 32.

Azpilcueta (Navarro), Martín. *Comentario resolutorio de usuras*. Salamanca, 1556.

Bacon, Francis. *The Advancement of Learning*. London, 1605.

Bacon, Francis. *The Essayes, or Counsels, Civill and Morall* (1625), in *Works*, vol. 6.

Bacon, Francis. *New Atlantis* (1629), in *Works*, vol. 3.
Bacon, Francis. *Novum organum* [1620], in *The Physical and Metaphysical Works*, ed. J. Devey. London, 1891.
Bacon, Francis. *Of the Advancement of Learning*, in *Works*, vol. 3.
Bacon, Francis. *Preparative Towards a Natural and Experimental History: Aphorisms on the Composition of the Primary History*, in *Works*, vol. 4.
Bacon, Francis. *Works*, eds. J. Spedding, R. L. Ellis, and D. D. Heath, 14 vols. London, 1857–74.
Bailly, Jean Sylvain. *Histoire de l'astronomie moderne*, 3 vols. Paris, 1779–82.
Balfour, James. *A Delineation of the Nature and Obligation of Morality*. Edinburgh, 1753; repr. Bristol, 1989.
Balguy, John. *The Foundation of Moral Goodness: or A further Inquiry into the Original of our Idea of Virtue*. London, (Pt 1) 1728; (Pt 2) 1729; facsim., New York, NY, 1976.
Balguy, Thomas. *Divine Benevolence Asserted; and Vindicated from the Objections of Ancient and Modern Sceptics*. London, 1781.
Ballantyne, John. "On the Being of a God", in J. Brown ed., *Theological Tracts*, vol. 2, pp. 37–53 (*B2*).
Barre, François Poulain de la. *De l'égalité des deux sexes* [1673]. Paris, 1984.
Basedow, Johann Bernhard. *Agathokrator: oder Von Erziehung Künftiger Regenten*. Leipzig, 1771.
Basedow, Johann Bernhard. *Das Elementarwerk: Ein Geordneter Vorrath aller nöthigen Erkenntnis. Zum Unterrichte der Jugend*, Dessau, 1774.
Basedow, Johann Bernhard. *Das Methodenbuch für Väter und Mütter der Familien und Völker...* 2nd edn., Leipzig, 1771.
Batteux, Charles. *Les beaux-arts réduits à un même principe* (1746), ed. J.-R. Mantion. Paris, 1989.
Baumeister, Friedrich Christian. *Historia doctrinae recentius controversiae de mundo optimo exposit.* Leipzig, 1741.
Baumgarten, Alexander Gottlieb, *Aesthetica acrodinatica*, 2 vols., Frankfurt a. d. Oder, 1750–8; facsim. Hildesheim, 1961.
Baumgarten, Alexander Gottlieb. *Meditationes philosophicae de nonnullis ad poema pertinentibus: Reflections on Poetry* [1735], trans. K. Aschenbrenner and W. B. Holther. Berkeley, CA, 1954.
Baumgarten, Alexander Gottlieb. *Metaphysica* [1739], 4th edn., Halle, 1757; Halle 1779; facsim. Hildesheim, 1982.
Baumgarten, Alexander Gottlieb. *Metaphysik*, trans. G. F. Meier. Halle, 1766; 2nd edn., Halle, 1783.
Baumgarten, Alexander Gottlieb. *Reflections on Poetry. See Meditationes philosophicae...*
Baxter, Andrew. *An Enquiry into the Nature of the Human Soul; wherein the Immateriality of the Soul is Evinced from the Principles of Reason and Philosophy*. Edinburgh, 1733; 2nd edn. in 2 vols., London, 1737; facsim. ed. G. Vesey, Bristol, 1990.
Bayle, Pierre. *Commentaire philosophique sur ces paroles de Jesus-Christ, Contrain-les d'entrer; où l'on prouve... qu'il n'y a rien de plus abominable que de faire des Conversions par la Contrainte*, in *Oeuvres diverses* (1965), vol. 2, pp. 355–496.
Bayle, Pierre. *The Dictionary Historical and Critical of Mr. Peter Bayle*, trans. P. Des Maizeux, 5 vols. London, 1734–8.
Bayle, Pierre. *Dictionnaire historique et critique*, 2 vols. Rotterdam, 1697; 2nd edn., 3 vols., Rotterdam, 1702; 4th edn., 4 vols., Amsterdam, 1730; 5th edn., 5 vols., Amsterdam, 1734; 5th edn., 4 vols., Amsterdam, 1740.
Bayle, Pierre. *Dissertation* [1680], in *Oeuvres diverses*, vol. 4.
Bayle, Pierre. *Ecrits sur Spinoza*, eds. F. Charles-Daubert and P.-F. Moreau. Paris, 1983.

Bayle, Pierre. *Historical and Critical Dictionary: Selections*, trans. R. H. Popkin. Indianapolis, IN, 1965.
Bayle, Pierre. *Lettre à M. L. A. D. C., où il est prouvé par plusieurs raisons tirées de la philosophie [et] de la theologie que les comètes ne sont point le presage d' aucum malheur.* Cologne, 1682.
[Bayle, Pierre]. *Lettre sur le comète.* Rotterdam, 1682.
Bayle, Pierre. *Nouvelles lettres de Mr. P. Bayle*, 2 vols. The Hague, 1739.
Bayle, Pierre. *Oeuvres diverses* [(The Hague, 1727–31)], ed. E. Labrousse, 5 in 6 vols. Hildesheim, 1964–2001.
Bayle, Pierre. *Pensées diverses sur la comète* [1682]. Rotterdam, 1683.
Bayle, Pierre. *Philosophical Commentary*, trans. A. G. Tannenbaum. New York, NY, 1987.
Bayle, Pierre. *Reponse aux questions d'un provincial*, 5 vols. [Rotterdam], 1703–6.
Bayle, Pierre. *Systême de philosophie*, in *Oeuvres diverses*, vol. 4.
Beattie, James. *An Essay on the Nature and Immutability of Truth, in Opposition to Sophistry and Scepticism.* Edinburgh, 1770 (repr. Bristol, 2000); London, 1773; Edinburgh, 1776.
Beausobre, Louis de. *Le Pyrrhonisme raisonnable.* Berlin, 1755.
Beauzée, Nicolas. *See Encyclopédie méthodique* (see Serials and Collective Works p. 1293).
Beauzée, Nicolas. *Grammaire générale*, 2 vols. Paris, 1767; facsim. Stuttgart-Bad Cannstatt, 1974.
Beccaria, Cesare. *Edizione Nazionale delle opere di Cesare Beccaria*, ed. L. Firpo. Milan, 1984–.
Beccaria, Cesare. *On Crimes and Punishments and other Writings*, ed. R. Bellamy. Cambridge, 1995.
Beccaria, Cesare. *Richerche intorno alla natura dello stile*, eds. L. Firpo, G. Francioni, and G. Gaspari, in *Edizione Nazionale delle opere di Cesare Beccaria*, vol. 2, *Scritti filosofici e letterari* (Milan, 1984).
Benezet, Anthony. *A Short Account of that Part of Africa, Inhabited by the Negroes.* Philadelphia, PA, 1762.
Bentham, Edward. *An Introduction to Logick, Scholastick and Rational.* Oxford, 1773.
Bentham, Edward. *An Introduction to Moral Philosophy.* Oxford, 1745; 2nd edn., 1746.
Bentham, Edward. *Reflections upon the Nature and Usefulness of Logick.* Oxford, 1740, 2nd edn., retitled *Reflexions upon Logick*, 1755.
Bentham, Edward. *Reflexions upon Logick.* See *Reflections upon the Nature and Usefulness of Logick.*
Bentham, Jeremy. "Anarchical Fallacies", in *Bentham's Political Thought*, ed. B. Parekh, New York, NY, 1973.
Bentham, Jeremy. *Chrestomathia.* London, 1816; in *Works*, ed. J. Bowring, vol. 8.
Bentham, Jeremy. *The Collected Works*, eds. J. H. Burns et al. London, 1968–82; Oxford, 1983–.
Bentham, Jeremy. *A Comment on the Commentaries and A Fragment of Government*, eds. J. H. Burns and H. L. A. Hart, in *Works* (eds. Burns et al., 1977).
Bentham, Jeremy. *Essay on Logic*, in *Works* (ed. Bowring), vol. 8.
Bentham, Jeremy. *A Fragment on Government* [1776], in *Works* (eds. Burns et al.), vol. 3.
Bentham, Jeremy. *An Introduction to the Principles of Morals and Legislation* [1789], eds. J. H. Burns and H. L. A. Hart, in *Works* (eds. Burns et al., London, 1970).
Bentham, Jeremy. *Works*, ed. J. Bowring, 11 vols. Edinburgh, 1843.
Bentley, Richard. *A Confutation of Atheism from the Origin and Frame of the World.* London, 1692.
Bentley, Richard. *The Folly and Unreasonableness of Atheism.* London, 1693.
Bergk, Johann Adam. *Briefe über Kants metaphysische Anfangsgründe der Rechtslehre.* Leipzig, Gera, 1797.
Bergk, Johann Adam. *Untersuchungen aus dem Natur-, Staats- und Völkerrechte, mit einer Kritik der neuesten Konstitution der französischen Republik.* n.p., 1796.
Berkeley, George. *Alciphron, or the Minute Philosopher* (1732), in *Works*, vol. 3 (1950).
Berkeley, George. *The Analyst* (1734), in *Works*, vol. 4 (1951).
Berkeley, George. *De Motu* (1721), in *Works*, vol. 4 (1951).

Berkeley, George. *An Essay Towards a New Theory of Vision* (1709), in *Works*, vol. 1 (1948).

Berkeley, George. *An Essay towards Preventing the Ruin of Great Britain* [1721], in *Works*, vol. 6 (1953).

[Berkeley, George]. *George Berkeley's Manuscript Introduction*, ed. B. Belfrage. Oxford, 1987.

Berkeley, George. *Passive Obedience* [1712], in *Works*, vol. 6 (1953).

Berkeley, George. *Philosophical Commentaries* [1707–8], in *Works*, vol. 1 (1948).

Berkeley, George. *Siris* (1744), in *Works*, vol. 5 (1953).

Berkeley, George. *The Theory of Vision . . . Vindicated and Explained* [1733], in *Works*, vol. 1 (1948).

Berkeley, George. *Three Dialogues between Hylas and Philonous* [1713], in *Works*, vol. 2 (1949).

Berkeley, George. *A Treatise concerning the Principles of Human Knowledge* [1710], in *Works*, vol. 2 (1949).

Berkeley, George. *Works*, eds. A. A. Luce and T. E. Jessop, 9 vols. Edinburgh, 1948–57.

Bernoulli, Daniel. *Hydrodynamica, sive De viribus et motibus fluidorum commentarii*. Strasbourg, 1738.

Biberg, Isac J. *De Oeconomia naturæ*. Uppsala, 1749.

Bilfinger, Georg Bernhard. *Dilucidationes philosophicae de Deo, anima humana, mundo et generalibus rerum affectionibus*. Frankfurt, 1737.

Black, Joseph. *Lectures on the Elements of Chemistry, Delivered in the University of Edinburgh*, ed. J. Robison, 2 vols. Edinburgh, 1803.

Blackburne, Francis. *A Short Historical View of the Controversy Concerning an Intermediate State and the Separate Existence of the Soul between Death and the General Resurrection*. London, 1765; 2nd edn. 1772.

Blackstone, William. *Commentaries on the Laws of England*, 4 vols. London, 1765–9; Chicago, IL, 1979.

Blair, Hugh. *Critical Dissertation on the Poems of Ossian, Son of Fingal*. London, 1763.

Blair, Hugh. *Lectures on Rhetoric and Belles Lettres* [Edinburgh, 1783], ed. H. F. Harding, 2 vols. Carbondale, IL, 1965.

Blount, Charles. *Anima mundi: or An Historical Narration of the Opinions of the Ancients concerning Mans Soul after this Life, according to Unenlightened Nature*. Amsterdam, 1678.

Blount, Charles. *Great is Diana of the Ephesians: or The Original of Priestcraft and Idolatry, and of the Sacrifices of the Gentiles*. London, 1680.

Blount, Charles. *Miracles no Violations of the Laws of Nature*. London, 1683.

Blumenbach, Johann Gottfried. *Beyträge zur Naturgeschichte*, 2 vols. Göttingen, 1806–11.

Blumenbach, Johann Gottfried. *De generis humani varietate nativa* [1770], 3rd edn. Göttingen, 1795.

Bodin, Jean. *The Six Books of a Commonweale* [trans. 1606], trans. R. Knolles. Cambridge, 1962.

Bodin, Jean. *Les six livres de la république*. Paris, 1576.

Bodmer, Johann Jacob. *Kritische Betrachtungen über die poetischen Gemälde der Dichter*. Zurich, 1741; facsim. Frankfurt, 1971.

Boerhaave, Hermann. *Institutiones medicae*. Leiden, 1708.

Böhmer, Justus Henning. *Dissertatio iuridica de cauta Iudaeorum tolerantia* [1708]. Halle, 1723.

Boileau, Nicolas. *L'art poétique*, in *Oeuvres diverses*. Paris, 1674.

Boileau, Nicholas. *The Art of Poetry*, trans. W. Soames. London, 1683.

Bolingbroke, Henry St. John, Lord. "Fragments or Minutes of Essays", in *Works* (ed. Malet), vol. 5.

Bolingbroke, Henry St. John, Lord. *Historical Writings*, ed. I. Kramnick. Chicago, IL, 1972.

Bolingbroke, Henry St. John, Lord. *Letters on the Study and Use of History* [1735–6], 2 vols. London, 1752.

Bolingbroke, Henry St. John, Lord. *Works*, 4 vols. Philadelphia, PA, 1841.

Bolingbroke, Henry St. John, Lord. *Works*, ed. D. Malet, 5 vols. London, 1754.
Bonnet, Charles. *Essai analytique sur les facultés de l'âme*. Copenhagen, 1760.
Bonnet, Charles. *Essai de psychologie*. London, 1755.
Bonnet, Charles. *La palingénésie philosophique, ou Idées sur l'état passé et sur l'état futur des etres vivants*. Geneva, 1769.
Boscovich, Roger Joseph. *Theoria philosophiae naturalis*. Vienna, 1758; Venice, 1763.
Boscovich, Roger Joseph. *Theoria philosophiae naturalis/A Theory of Natural Philosophy*, (Latin-English from Venice, 1763 edn.), trans. J. M. Child. Chicago, IL, 1922.
Bossuet, Jacques Bénigne. *Discours sur l'histoire universelle* [1681], in *Oeuvres*, vol. 1.
Bossuet, Jacques Bénigne. *Discourse on Universal History*, trans. E. Forster, ed. O. Ranum. Chicago, IL, 1976.
Bossuet, Jacques Bénigne. *Oeuvres de Bossuet*, 4 vols. Paris, 1841.
Bott, Thomas. *Morality, Founded in the Reason of Things, and the Ground of Revelation*. London, 1730.
Bougeant, Guillaume-Hyacinthe. *Amusement philosophique sur le langage des bestes*. Paris, 1739.
Boulainvilliers, Henri de. *État de la France*. London, 1737.
Boulainvilliers, Henri de. *Oeuvres complètes*, ed. R. Simon, 2 vols. The Hague, 1973–5.
Boullier, David Renaud. *Essai philosophique sur l'âme des bêtes* [1728], (2nd edn.). Amsterdam, 1737; Paris, 1985.
Bourguet, Louis. "Mémoire sur la théorie de la terre", in *Lettres philosophiques sur la formation des sels et des cristaux*. Amsterdam, 1729.
Bramah, Joseph. *A Letter to the Rt. Hon. Sir James Eyre*... London, 1797.
Bramhall, John. *A Defence of True Liberty from Ante-cedent and Extrinsecall Necessity*... London, 1655.
Breitinger, Johann Jacob. *Critische Abhandlung von der Natur, den Absichten und dem Gebrauche der Gleichnisse*. Zurich, 1740; facsim. Stuttgart, 1967.
Briefe die neueste Litteratur betreffend, ed. Friedrich Nicolai. Berlin and Stettin, 1759–67.
Brissot de Warville, Jean-Pierre. *De la Vérité, ou Méditations sur les moyens de parvenir à la vérité dans toutes les connaissances humaines* [1782]. Neufchâtel, 1792.
Britannicus, Scepticus (pseud.). *An Investigation of the Essence of the Deity; with a Word or two by way of Postscript, to the Professors of Deism, in Refutation of their Doctrine, that the Bible is not the Word of God*. London, 1797.
Brown, John. *On the Female Character and Education: A Sermon Preached*... *at the Anniversary Meeting of*... *the Asylum for Deserted Female Orphans*. London, 1765.
Brown, John. *Thoughts on Civil Liberty, on Licentiousness and Faction*. Newcastle upon Tyne, 1765.
Browne, Peter. *The Procedure, Extent, and Limits of Human Understanding*. London, 1728.
Browne, Peter. *Things Divine and Supernatural Conceived by Analogy with Things Natural and Human*. London, 1733.
Brucker, Johann Jakob. *Historia critica philosophiae*, 4 in 5 vols. Leipzig, 1742–4; 2nd edn., 6 vols., Leipzig, 1762.
Brucker, Johann Jakob. *Historia philosophica doctrinae de ideis*. Augsburg, 1723.
Bruno, Giordano. *Spaccio della bestia triomphante*. Paris [i.e., London], 1584.
Budde, Johann Franz. *Doctrinæ orthodoxæ de origine mali contra recentiorum quorundam hypotheses modesta assertio*. Jena, 1712.
Budde, Johann Franz. *Theses theologicae de atheismo et superstitione variis observationibus illustratae et in usum recitationum academicarum editae/Lehrsätze von der Atheisterey und dem Aberglauben mit gelehrten Anmerckungen erläutert*, (Latin/German edn.). Jena, 1717.
Buffier, Claude. *Elémens de métaphysique*. Paris, 1725.

Buffier, Claude. *Traité des premières véritéz et de la source de nos jugements ou L'on examine le sentiment des philosophes sur les premiers notions des choses*. Paris, 1724.

Buffon, Georges-Louis Leclerc, comte de. *Discours sur la manière d' étudier et de traiter l'histoire naturelle*. Paris, 1749.

Buffon, Georges-Louis Leclerc, comte de. *Les époques de la nature*, ed. J. Roger. Paris, 1962.

Buffon, Georges-Louis Leclerc, comte de. "Essai d'arithmétique morale", in *Oeuvres philosophiques*, also in *Histoire naturelle: Supplément*, in *Oeuvres* (Imprimerie Royale edn.), vol. 2, pp. 46–148.

Buffon, Georges-Louis Leclerc, comte de. *From Natural History to the History of Nature: Readings from Buffon and His Critics*, trans. and eds. J. Lyon and P. R. Sloan. Notre Dame, IN, 1981.

Buffon, Georges-Louis Leclerc, comte de. *Histoire naturelle, générale et particulière*, 14 vols. Paris, 1749–67; 36 vols., Paris, 1749–1804; selections in *Oeuvres philosophique* (ed. Piveteau).

Buffon, Georges-Louis Leclerc, comte de. *Oeuvres complètes*, ed. M. le comte de Lacepède, 26 vols. Paris, 1825–8.

Buffon, Georges-Louis Leclerc, comte de. *Oeuvres complètes*, ed. M. Flourens, 12 vols. Paris, 1853–5.

Buffon, Georges-Louis Leclerc, comte de. *Oeuvres complètes* (Imprimerie Royale edn.), 44 vols. Paris, 1749–1804.

Buffon, Georges-Louis Leclerc, comte de. *Oeuvres philosophiques*, ed. J. Piveteau. Paris, 1954.

Burdy, Samuel. *The Life of the late Reverend Philip Skelton, with some curious Anecdotes* [1792], ed. N. Moore. Oxford, 1914.

Burgersdijk, Franco. *Institutionum logicarum libri duo*. Leiden, 1626.

Burke, Edmund. *Correspondence*, ed. T. H. Copeland, 10 vols. Cambridge, 1958–78.

Burke, Edmund. *A Philosophical Enquiry Into the Origin of Our Ideas of the Sublime and Beautiful* [1757], 2nd edn. London, 1759; modern edn., ed. A. Phillips, Oxford, 1990.

Burke, Edmund. *Reflections on the Revolution in France* [1790], ed. C. C. O'Brien. New York, NY, 1986; ed. J. G. A. Pocock, Indianapolis, IN, 1987.

Burke, Edmund. *Reflections on the Revolution in France* [1790], in *Writings and Speeches*, ed. P. Langford. 9 vols., Oxford, 1981–97, vol. 8: *The French Revolution* (1989), ed. L. G. Mitchell.

Burlamaqui, Jean-Jacques. *Principes du droit naturel et politique*, 2 vols. Geneva, 1747–51.

Burlamaqui, Jean-Jacques. *The Principles of Natural and Politic Law*, trans. T. Nugent, 2 vols. London, 1747–8; 2nd edn., 1763.

Burnet, Thomas. *A Demonstration of True Religion*, 2 vols. London, 1726.

Burnet, Thomas. *Telluris theoria sacras*. London, 1681.

Burnett, James (Lord Monboddo). *Antient Metaphysics. Volume Third Containing the History and Philosophy of Men*. London, 1784.

Burnett, James (Lord Monboddo). *Of the Origin and Progress of Language*, 3 vols. Edinburgh, 1773–6; 2nd edn., 6 vols., Edinburgh, 1774–92.

Burrow, Robert. *Civil Society and Government Vindicated from the Charge of being Founded on, and Preserv'd by, Dishonest Arts*. London, 1723.

Butler, Joseph. *The Analogy of Religion, Natural and Revealed, to the Constitution and Course of Nature* [1736], in *Works* (ed. Gladstone), vol. 2; in *Works* (ed. Bernard), vol. 2.

Butler, Joseph. *Dissertation of Personal Identity* (1736), 2 vols., in *Works* (ed. Gladstone), vol. 1, pp. 317–25.

Butler, Joseph. *Dissertation of the Nature of Virtue* (1736), in *Works* (ed. Gladstone), vol. 1.

Butler, Joseph. *Fifteen Sermons Preached at the Rolls Chapel* (1726), 2 vols., in *Works* (ed. Bernard), vol. 1.

Butler, Joseph. *Three Sermons upon Human Nature, with A Dissertation on the Nature of Virtue*. Cambridge, 1834.

Butler, Joseph. *Works*, ed. W. E. Gladstone, 2 vols. Oxford, 1896.

Butler, Joseph. *Works*, ed. J. H. Bernard, 2 vols. London, 1900.

Calvin, John. *Institutes of the Christian Religion*, trans. F. L. Battles, ed. J. T. McNeill, 2 vols. London, 1961.

Campbell, Archibald. *Aretē-Logia, or, An Enquiry into the Original of Moral Virtue*. Westminster, 1728.

Campbell, Archibald. *The Necessity of Revelation*. London, 1739.

Campbell, George. *Lectures, Sermons and Dissertations*, ed. D. Sonheim, 3 vols. Bristol, 2001.

Campbell, George. *A Dissertation on Miracles: Containing an Examination of the Principles Advanced by David Hume, Esq. in An Essay on Miracles*. Edinburgh, 1762.

Campbell, George. *The Philosophy of Rhetoric*, 2 vols. London, 1776.

Campe, Joachim Heinrich, ed. *Allgemeine Revision des gesammten Schul- und Erziehungswesens von einer Gesellschaft praktischer Erzieher*. 16 vols. Hamburg, 1785–92.

Campe, Joachim Heinrich. *Väterlicher Rath für meine Tochter: Ein Gegenstück zum Theophron. Der erwachsenern weiblichen Jugend gewidmet* [1789]. Frankfurt, 1790.

Camper, Pierre. *Dissertation physique. Sur les différences réelles que présentent les traits du visage chez les hommes de différents pays et de différents ages; Sur le beau qui caractérise les statues antiques et les pierres gravées. Suivie de la proposition d'une nouvelle méthode pour déssiner toutes sortes de têtes humaines avec la plus grande sûreté* [1790], trans. D. B. Q. D'Isjonval. Utrecht, 1791.

Cantillon, Richard. *Essai sur la nature du commerce en général*. London, 1755.

Carmichael, Gerschom. *Breviuscula introductio ad logicam*, 2nd edn., Edinburgh, 1722.

Carmichael, Gerschom. *Natural Rights on the Threshold of the Scottish Enlightenment: The Writings of Gershom Carmichael*, trans. M. Silverthorne, eds. J. Moore and M. Silverthorne. Indianapolis, IN, 2002.

Carmichael, Gerschom, ed., S. Pufendorf. *De officio hominis et civis, juxta legem naturalem, libri duo*. Glasgow, 1718.

Carnot, Lazare. *Réflexions sur la métaphysique du calcul infinitésimal*. Paris, 1797.

[Carroll, William?]. *Remarks upon Mr. Clarke's Sermons, Preached at St. Paul's against Hobbs, Spinoza, and Other Atheists*. London, 1705.

Castel, Charles-Irénée, Abbé de Saint-Pierre. *Ouvrages de politique*, 16 vols. Rotterdam, 1733–41.

Cavendish, Henry. "Experiments to determine the Density of the Earth". *Philosophical Transactions of the Royal Society of London* (1798): 469–526.

Cesalpino, Andrea. *De plantis libri xvi*. Florence, 1583.

Chaise, Nicolas Filleau de la. "Traité qu'il y a des demonstrations d'une autre espece & aussi certaines que celles de la geometrie", in *Pensées de M. Pascal sur la religion et sur quelques autres sujets*, ed. B. Pascal, Amsterdam, 1688.

Chalotais, Louis-René de Caradeuc de la. *Essai d'éducation nationale ou Plan d'études pour la jeunesse*. Paris, 1763.

Chambers, Ephraim. *Cyclopaedia: Or, an Universal Dictionary of Arts and Sciences*, 2 vols. London, 1728.

Chambers, Ephraim. *Cyclopaedia; or, an Universal Dictionary of Arts and Sciences . . . With the Supplement and Modern Improvements Incorporated in One Alphabet*, ed. A. Rees, 5 vols. London, 1786–8.

Champs, Jean des. *Cours abrégé de la philosophie wolffienne, en forme de lettres*, 2 vols. Amsterdam and Leipzig, 1743–7; facsim. Hildesheim, 1991.

Chandler, Samuel. *A Vindication of the Christian Religion, in Two Parts*. London, 1725.

Chapone, Hester. *Letters on the Improvement of the Mind Addressed to a Young Lady*. Dublin, 1773; Brookfield, VT, 1996.

Charron, Pierre. *De la Sagesse* [1601]. Geneva, 1777.

Châtelet, Gabrielle-Émilie Le Tonnelier de Breteuil, du. *Institutions de physique*. Paris, 1740; 2nd edn., 1742.

Châtelet, Gabrielle-Émilie Le Tonnelier de Breteuil, du. *Les lettres de la marquise du Châtelet*, ed. T. Besterman, 2 vols. Geneva, 1958.

Cherbury, Edward, Lord Herbert of. *De veritate*, trans. and ed. M. H. Carré. Bristol, 1937.

Cheyne, George. *Philosophical Principles of Religion, Natural and Revealed*. London, 1715; 5th edn., 1736.

Chladenius, Johann Martin. *Allgemeine Geschichtswissenschaft: worinnen der Grund zu einer neuen Einsicht in allen Arten der Gelahrheit gelegt wird*. Leipzig, 1752.

Chladenius, Johann Martin. *Vernünftige Gedanken von dem Wahrscheinlichen und desselben gefährlichen Missbrauche*, trans. U. G. Thorschmid. Leipzig, 1748.

Chubb, Thomas. *The Ground and Foundation of Morality Considered*. London, 1745.

Cicero. *Orator*, trans. H. M. Hubbell. Cambridge, MA, 1939.

Cicero. *De oratore*, trans. E. W. Sutton and H. Rackham, 2 vols. Cambridge, MA, 1942.

Clap, Thomas. *The Annals or History of Yale-College, in New-Haven, in the Colony of Connecticut, from the First Founding thereof, in the Year 1700, to the Year 1766*. New Haven, CT, 1766.

Clap, Thomas. *An Essay on the Nature and Foundation of Moral Virtue and Obligation: Being a Short Introduction to the Study of Ethics, for the Use of the Students of Yale-College*. New Haven, CT, 1765.

[Clarke, John] [d. 1757]. *A Defence of Dr. Clarke's Demonstration of the Being and Attributes of God, wherein is particularly Consider'd the Nature of Space, Duration, and Necessary Existence*. London, 1732.

Clarke, John [d. 1734]. *The Foundation of Morality in Theory and Practice Considered*. York, 1726.

[Clarke, John] [d. 1757]. *A Second Defence of Dr. Clarke's Demonstration of the Being and Attributes of God*. London, 1733.

[Clarke, John] [d. 1757]. *A Third Defence of Dr. Clarke's Demonstration of the Being and Attributes of God, being a Vindication of the Two Former Defences*. London, 1734.

Clarke, Joseph. *Dr. Clarke's Notions of Space Examin'd. In Vindication of the Translator of Archbishop King's 'Origin of Evil'*. London, 1733.

Clarke, Joseph. *A Farther Examination of Dr. Clarke's Notions of Space; with Some Considerations on the Possibility of Eternal Creation*. Cambridge, 1734.

[Clarke, Samuel, and Leibniz, Gottfried Wilhelm]. *A Collection of Papers, which passed between the Late Learned Mr. Leibniz and Dr. Clarke in the Years 1715 and 1716: Relating to the Principles of Natural Philosophy and Religion*. London, 1717.

Clarke, Samuel. *A Demonstration of the Being and Attributes of God: More Particularly in Answer to Mr. Hobbs, Spinoza, and their Followers*. London, 1705; facsim. Stuttgart-Bad Cannstatt, 1964.

Clarke, Samuel. *A Discourse concerning the Being and Attributes of God, the Obligations of Natural Religion, and the Truth and Certainty of the Christian Revelation*. London, 1706; 10th edn., 1749.

Clarke, Samuel. *A Discourse Concerning the Unchangeable Obligations of Natural Religion and the Truth and Certainty of the Christian Revelation*. London, 1706.

Clarke, Samuel. *A Fourth Defense of an Argument made use of in a Letter to Mr. Dodwel, to prove the Immateriality and Natural Immortality of the Soul*. London, 1708.

Clarke, Samuel. "Letters to Dr. Clarke concerning Liberty and Necessity, from a Gentleman of the University of Cambridge, with the Doctor's Answers to them", in *A Collection of Papers, which passed between the Late Learned Mr. Leibniz and Dr. Clarke in the Years 1715 and 1716: relating to the Principles of Natural Philosophy and Religion*. London, 1717.

Clarke, Samuel. *Letters Written, in MDCCXXV, to the Rev. Dr. Samuel Clarke, relating to an Argument Advanced by the Doctor, in his Demonstration of the Being and Attributes of God, in Proof of the Unity of the Deity: with the Doctor's Answers*. London, 1745.

Clarke, Samuel. *Remarks upon a Book, entitled, A Philosophical Enquiry concerning Human Liberty* [1717], 4 vols., in *Works*, vol. 4.

Clarke, Samuel. *Several Letters to the Reverend Dr. Clarke, from a Gentleman in Glocestershire, relating to the First Volume of the Sermons Preached at Mr. Boyle's Lecture; with the Dr.'s Answers Thereunto.* London, 1716.

Clarke, Samuel. *A Third Defense of an Argument made use of in a Letter to Mr. Dodwel, to prove the Immateriality and Natural Immortality of the Soul. In a Letter to the Author of the Reflexions on Mr. Clark's Second Defense.* London, 1708.

Clarke, Samuel. *Works*, ed. B. Hoadly, 4 vols. London, 1738.

Coleridge, Samuel Taylor. *The Collected Works of Samuel Taylor Coleridge*, multiple editors. London, Princeton, NJ, 1969–.

Coleridge, Samuel Taylor. "Lecture on the Slave-Trade" [1795], eds. L. Patton and P. Mann, in *Works/Lectures 1795 on Politics and Religion*, vol. 1 (1971).

C[olliber], S[amuel]. *An Impartial Enquiry into the Existence and Nature of God.* London, 1718; 3rd edn., 1735.

Collier, Arthur. *Clavis universalis or a New Inquiry after Truth.* London, 1713.

Collins, Anthony. *An Answer to Mr. Clark's Third Defence of his Letter to Mr. Dodwell.* London, 1708.

[Collins, Anthony]. *A Discourse of Free-Thinking, occasion'd by the Rise and Growth of a Sect call'd Free-Thinkers.* London, 1713; facsim. w. parallel German trans., ed. G. Gawlick; Stuttgart-Bad Cantstatt, 1965.

[Collins, Anthony]. *A Discourse of the Grounds and Reasons of the Christian Religion.* London, 1724.

[Collins, Anthony]. *An Essay concerning the Use of Reason in Propositions, the Evidence whereof depends upon Human Testimony.* London, 1707.

Collins, Anthony. *A Philosophical Inquiry concerning Human Liberty.* London, 1717; repr. (3rd edn. 1735), ed. J. Priestley, Birmingham, 1790; facsim. Bristol, 1990.

[Collins, Anthony]. *Priestcraft in Perfection.* London, 1710.

Collins, Anthony. *Scheme of Literal Profecy Considered.* London, 1726.

[Collins, Anthony]. *A Vindication of the Divine Attributes, in some Remarks on his Grace the Archbishop of Dublin's Sermon intituled Divine Predestination and Foreknowledg consistent with the Freedom of Man's Will.* London, 1710.

Condillac, Étienne Bonnot de. *Condillac, lettres inédites à Gabriel Cramer*, ed. G. Le Roy. Paris, 1953.

Condillac, Étienne Bonnot de. *Cours d'étude pour l'instruction du prince de Parme* [1775], in *Oeuvres phil.*, vol. 1.

Condillac, Étienne Bonnot de. *Essai sur l'origine des connaissances humaines* [1746], 3 vols., in *Oeuvres phil.*, vol. 1.

Condillac, Étienne Bonnot de. *Essai sur l'origines des connaissances humaines* [1746], ed. C. Porset. Paris, 1973.

Condillac, Étienne Bonnot de. *An Essay on the Origin of Human Knowledge*, trans. and ed. H. Aarsleff. Cambridge, 2001.

Condillac, Étienne Bonnot de. *Grammaire* [1775], in *Oeuvres phil.*, vol. 1.

Condillac, Étienne Bonnot de. *La langue des calculs* [1798], in *Oeuvres phil.*, vol. 2.

Condillac, Étienne Bonnot de. *L'art de penser* [1775], in *Oeuvres phil.*, vol. 1.

Condillac, Étienne Bonnot de. *L'art d'écrire*, in *Oeuvres phil.*, vol. 1.

Condillac, Étienne Bonnot de. *La logique* [1780], in *Oeuvres phil.*, vol. 2.

Condillac, Étienne Bonnot de. *La Logique – Logic* [1780], parallel text edn., trans. W. R. Albury. New York, NY, 1980.

Condillac, Étienne Bonnot de. *Oeuvres complètes*, ed. A. F. Théry, 12 vols. Paris, 1821–2.

Condillac, Étienne Bonnot de. *Oeuvres philosophiques*, ed. G. Le Roy, 3 vols. Paris, 1947–51.

Condillac, Étienne Bonnot de. *Traité des animaux* [1755], in *Oeuvres phil.*, vol. 1; ed. F. Dagognet. Paris, 1987.

Condillac, Étienne Bonnot de. *Traité des sensations*, 2 vols. London, 1754; in *Oeuvres complètes*, vol. 3; and in *Oeuvres phil.*, vol., 1.

Condillac, Étienne Bonnot de. *Treatise on the Sensations*, trans. G. Carr. London, 1930.

Condillac, Étienne Bonnot de. *Traité des sistêmes, où l'on en démêle les inconvéniens et les avantages.* The Hague, 1749.

Condorcet, Marie-Jean-Antoine-Nicolas de Caritat, marquis de. *Discours sur les sciences mathématiques*, in *Oeuvres*, vol. 1.

Condorcet, Marie-Jean-Antoine-Nicolas de Caritat, marquis de. *Esquisse d'un tableau historique des progrès de l'esprit humain.* Paris, 1795; facsim. Hildesheim, 1982.

Condorcet, Marie-Jean-Antoine-Nicolas de Caritat, marquis de. *Essai sur l'application de l'analyse à la probabilité des décisions rendues à la pluralité des voix.* Paris, 1785.

Condorcet, Marie-Jean-Antoine-Nicolas de Caritat, marquis de. *De l'influence de la révolution de l'Amérique sur l'Europe*, in *Oeuvres*, vol. 8, pp. 1–113.

Condorcet, Marie-Jean-Antoine-Nicolas de Caritat, marquis de. *Lettres d'un citoyen des Etats-Unis à un Français sur les affaires présentes*, in *Oeuvres*, vol. 9, pp. 95–123.

Condorcet, Marie-Jean-Antoine-Nicolas de Caritat, marquis de. *Oeuvres*, eds. A. C. O'Connor and F. Arago, 12 vols. Paris, 1847–9; facsim. Stuttgart-Bad Canstatt, 1968.

Condorcet, Marie-Jean-Antoine-Nicolas de Caritat, marquis de. *Rapport et projet de décret sur l'organisation générale de l'instruction publique présentés à l'Assemblée Nationale, au nom du Comité d'Instruction Publique.* Paris, 1792.

Condorcet, Marie-Jean-Antoine-Nicolas de Caritat, marquis de. *Réflexions sur l'esclavage des nègres* [published under the pseudonym Schwartz]. Paris, 1788.

Condorcet, Marie-Jean-Antoine-Nicolas de Caritat, marquis de. *Selected Writings*, ed. K. M. Baker. Indianapolis, IN, 1976.

Condorcet, Marie-Jean-Antoine-Nicolas de Caritat, marquis de. *Sketch for a Historical Picture of the Progress of the Human Mind*, trans. J. Barraclough. London, 1955.

Condorcet, Marie-Jean-Antoine-Nicolas de Caritat, marquis de. "Sur l'admission des femmes au droit de cité" [1790], in *Oeuvres*, vol. 10.

Condorcet, Marie-Jean-Antoine-Nicolas de Caritat, marquis de. *Tableau général de la science qui a pour objet l'application du calcul aux sciences politiques et morales* [1793], in *Oeuvres*, vol. 1, pp. 539–73.

Cook, James. *A Voyage to the Pacific Ocean; undertaken by Command of His Majesty, for Making Discoveries in the Northern Hemisphere: Performed under the Direction of Captains Cook, Clerke, and Gore, in the Years 1776, 1777, 1778, 1779, and 1780.* 4 vols., London, 1784.

Cooper, Myles. *Ethices compendium, in usum collegiorum Americanorum, emendatius editum; cui accedit Methodus argumentandi Aristotelica.* New York, NY, 1774.

Cooper, Thomas. *Philosophical Writings of Thomas Cooper*, ed. U. Thiel, 3 vols. Bristol, 2001 (facsim.).

Cooper, Thomas. *Tracts Ethical, Theological and Political* [London, 1789], in *Philosophical Writings of Thomas Cooper*, vol. 1.

Courdin, J. *Observations philosophiques sur la réforme de l'éducation publique.* Montpellier, 1792.

[Coyer, G. F.]. *Plan d'éducation publique.* Paris, 1770.

Craig, John. *Craig's Rules of Historical Evidence; from Joannis Craig, 'Theologiae Christianae principia mathematica.* s-Gravenhage, 1964.

Craig, John. *Theologiae christianae principia mathematica.* London, 1699.

Crousaz, Jean Pierre de. *Commentaire sur la traduction en vers de M. l'abbé du Resnel de l'Essai de M. Pope sur l'homme*. Geneva, 1738.
Crousaz, Jean Pierre de. *Examen de 'l'Essai de M. Pope sur l'homme'*. Lausanne, 1737.
Crousaz, Jean Pierre de. *Examen du pyrrhonisme ancien et moderne*. The Hague, 1733.
Crousaz, Jean-Pierre de. *Traité du beau*. Amsterdam, 1715; facsim. Geneva, 1970.
Crusius, Christian August. *Anweisung vernünftig zu leben* [1744], in *Hauptwerke*, vol. 1.
Crusius, Christian August. *Ausführliche Abhandlung von dem rechten Gebrauche und der Einschränkung des sogenannten Satzes vom zureichenden oder besser determinierenden Grunde*, 2nd edn. Leipzig, 1766.
Crusius, Christian August. *Dissertatio philosophica de usu et limitibus principii rationis determinantis, vulgo sufficientis* [Leipzig, 1743], eds. S. Carboncini and R. Finster, in *Die philosophischen Hauptwerke*, vol. 4.1 (1987).
Crusius, Christian August. *Entwurf der nothwendigen Vernunft-Wahrheiten, wiefern sie den zufälligen entgegen gesetzet werden*. Leipzig, 1745; also in *Hauptwerke*, vol. 2.
Crusius, Christian August. *Epistola ad Jo. Ern. L. B. ab Hardenberg de summis, rationis principiis, speciatim de principio rationis determinantis* [Leipzig, 1753], eds. S. Carboncini and R. Finster, in *Die philosophischen Hauptwerke*, vol. 4.1 (1987).
Crusius, Christian August. *Die philosophischen Hauptwerke* [Leipzig, 1744–7], eds. G. Tonelli, S. Carboncini and R. Finster. Hildesheim, 1964–.
Crusius, Christian August. *Weg zur Gewßheit und Zuverlässigkeit der menschlichen Erkenntniß*. Leipzig, 1747.
Cudworth, Ralph. *A Treatise concerning Eternal and Immutable Morality*. London, 1731; facsim. New York, NY, 1976.
Cudworth, Ralph. *The True Intellectual System of the Universe*. London, 1678.
Cuentz. *Essai d'un système nouveau concernant la nature des êtres spirituels Neuchatel*, 1742.
Cumberland, Richard. *De legibus naturae disquisitio philosophica*. London, 1672.
Cumberland, Richard. *A Treatise of the Laws of Nature*, trans. J. Maxwell. London, 1727; ed. J. Parkin, Indianapolis IN, 2005.
Cuvier, Georges. "Prospectus", in *Dictionnaire des sciences naturelles . . . par plusieurs professeurs du Jardin du Roi . . .* 60 vols., Strasbourg and Paris, 1816–30, vol. 1.
Cuvier, Georges. *Recherches sur les ossemens fossiles de quadrupèdes*. Paris, 1812.
Dalton, John. *A New System of Chemical Philosophy*, 2 in 3 vols. Manchester, 1808, 1810, 1827.
Darwin, Erasmus. *Zoonomia; or, the Laws of Organic Life*, 2 vols. Dublin, 1800.
Dean, Richard. *An Essay on the Future Life of Brute Creatures*, 2 vols. London, 1768.
Defoe, Daniel. *Conjugal Lewdness: Or, Matrimonial Whoredom*, London, 1727.
Defoe, Daniel. *The Family Instructor*, 2 vols. London, 1715–18.
Defoe, Daniel. *The Life and Strange Surprizing Adventures of Robinson Crusoe*, London, 1719.
Defoe, Daniel. *More Short-Ways with the Dissenters*. London, 1704.
Dennis, John. *The Advancement and Reformation of Modern Poetry* [1701]. London, 1701; facsim. New York, NY, 1971.
D'Epinay, Madame. *Les Conversations d'Émilie* [1773], ed. R. Davis. Oxford, 1996.
Derham, William. *Physico-Theology: or, A Demonstration of the Being and Attributes of God, from the Works of Creation*. London, 1713.
Desaguliers, John. *A Course of Experimental Philosophy*, 2 vols. London, 1734–44.
Desaguliers, John. *A System of Experimental Philosophy Prov'd by Mechanicks*. London, 1719.
Descartes, René. *Descartes: Selected Philosophical Writings*, trans. J. Cottingham, R. Stoothoff and D. Murdoch. Cambridge, 1988.
Descartes, René. *Discours de la méthode pour bien conduire sa raison, et chercher la vérité dans les sciences*, Leiden, 1637; in *Oeuvres phil.*, vol. 1; in *Oeuvres* (eds. Adam and Tannery), vol. 6.

Descartes, René. *Discourse on the Method of Rightly conducting one's Reason and seeking the Truth in the Sciences*, in *Phil. Writings*, vol. 1.

Descartes, René. *Meditationes de prima philosophia*. Paris, 1641.

Descartes, René. *Meditations on First Philosophy*, in *Phil. Writings*, vol. 2; in *Descartes: Selected Phil. Writ.*

Descartes, René. *Le monde de René Descartes ou traité de la lumière*, in *Oeuvres* (1897–1910), vol. 11.

Descartes, René. *Oeuvres*, eds. C. Adam and P. Tannery, 11 vols. Paris, 1897–1910; 12 vols. Paris, 1964–76.

Descartes, René. *Oeuvres philosophiques*, ed. F. Alquié, 3 vols. Paris, 1963–73.

Descartes, René. *Les passions de l'âme*. Paris, 1649.

Descartes, René. *The Passions of the Soul*, in *Phil. Writings*, vol. 1.

Descartes, René. *The Philosophical Writings of Descartes*, trans. J. Cottingham, R. Stoothoff, and D. Murdoch, 3 vols. Cambridge, 1984–91.

Descartes, René. *Principia philosophiæ*. Amsterdam, 1644.

Descartes, René. *Principles of Philosophy* [1644], in *Phil. Writings*, vol. 1; trans. V. R. Miller and R. P. Miller, Dordrecht, 1983.

Descartes, René. *Recherche de la vérité*, in *Oeuvres* (1964–76), vol. 10.

Deutsche Akademie der Wissenschaften zu Berlin. *Miscellanea Berolinensia ad incrementum scientiarum ex scriptis Societati Regiae scientiarum exhibitis edita*. Berlin, 1710.

Diderot, Denis. *Les bijoux indiscrets* [1748], in *Oeuvres complètes* (eds. Assézat and Tourneux), vol. 4.

Diderot, Denis. "Commentaire inédit", in F. Hemsterhuis, *Lettre sur l'homme et ses rapports, avec le commentaire inedit de Diderot*, ed. G. May, Paris, 1772, facsim. New Haven, CT, 1964.

Diderot, Denis. *A Diderot Pictorial Encyclopedia of Trades and Industry*. ed. C. C. Gillespie. 2 vols. New York, NY, 1959.

Diderot, Denis. *Diderot's Selected Writings*, trans. D. Coltman, ed. L. G. Crocker. New York, NY, 1966.

Diderot, Denis. *Early Philosophical Works*, trans. and ed. M. Jourdain. Chicago, IL, 1916; facsim. New York, NY, 1972.

Diderot, Denis. *De l'interpretation de la nature* [1753], in *Oeuvres phil.* (ed. Vernière, 1956).

Diderot, Denis. *Introduction aux grandes principes, ou Réception d'un philosophie*, in *Oeuvres complètes* (eds. J. Assézat and Tourneux), vol. 2.

Diderot, Denis. *Lettre sur les aveugles* [1749], in *Oeuvres phil.* (ed. Vernière, 1956), in *Oeuvres complètes* (eds. Dieckmann et al.), vol. 4 (1978).

Diderot, Denis. *Lettre sur les sourds et muets* [1751], ed. J. Chouillet, in *Oeuvres complètes* (eds. Dieckmann et al), vol. 4 (1978).

Diderot, Denis. *Oeuvres*, ed. L. Versini, 5 vols. Paris, 1994–7.

Diderot, Denis. *Oeuvres complètes*, eds. H. Dieckmann, J. Fabre, and J. Proust, Paris, 1975–.

Diderot, Denis. *Oeuvres complètes [de] Diderot*, ed. R. Lewinter. Paris, 1969.

Diderot, Denis. *Oeuvres complètes de Diderot*, eds. J. Assézat and M. Tourneux, 20 vols. Paris, 1875–7.

Diderot, Denis. *Oeuvres philosophiques*, ed. P. Vernière. Paris, 1956; 1964.

Diderot, Denis. *Pensées philosophiques*, in *Oeuvres phil.*

Diderot, Denis. *Pensées philosophiques. Addition aux Pensées philosophiques. Lettre sur Les aveugles. Additions à la Lettre sur les aveugles. Supplément au Voyage de Bougainville*, ed. A. Adam. Paris, 1972.

Diderot, Denis. *Pensées sur l'interprétation de la nature*. Paris, 1753.

Diderot, Denis. *Political Writings*, trans. and eds. J. H. Mason and R. Wokler. Cambridge, 1992.

Diderot, Denis. *Principes philosophiques sur la matière et le movement*, in *Oeuvres phil.*

Diderot, Denis. *Rameau's Nephew and Other Works*, trans. J. Barzun and R. Bowen. Indianapolis, IN, 1964.

Diderot, Denis. *Refutation suivie de l'ouvrage d'Helvétius intitulé l'Homme*, in *Oeuvres complètes* (eds. J. Assézat and Tourneux), vol. 2; *Oeuvres,* ed. Laurent Versini, 5 vols. (Paris: Robert Laffont, 1994–7), vol. 1, *Philosophie.*

Diderot, Denis. *La religieuse* [1780], in *Oeuvres complètes* (eds. Assézat and Tourneux), vol. 5.

Diderot, Denis. *Le rêve d'Alembert*, in *Oeuvres phil.*, also in *Oeuvres complètes* (eds. Dieckmann et al.), vol. 17 (1987).

Diderot, Denis. *Salon de 1767*, in *Oeuvres complètes* (eds. Dieckmann et al.), vol. 16 (1990).

Diderot, Denis. Supplément au Voyage de Bougainville, ou Dialogue entre A. et B. [1798], in *Oeuvres phil.*

Diderot, Denis. *Sur les femmes*, in *Oeuvres complètes* (eds. Assézat and Tourneux), vol. 2.

Diderot, Denis. "Sur les génie", in *Oeuvres esthétiques*, ed. P. Vernière, Paris, 1968.

Diderot, Denis, and Jean le Rond d'Alembert, eds. *Encyclopédie ou Dictionnaire raisonné des sciences, des arts et des métiers, par une société de gens de lettres.* 17 vols. Paris, 1751–65; 28 vols., Paris, 1751–72; 35 vols., Paris and Amsterdam, 1751–80 (facsim. 5 vols., New York, NY, 1969).

Ditton, Humphry. *A Discourse Concerning the Resurrection of Jesus Christ.* London, 1712.

Doddridge, Philip. *A Course of Lectures on the Principal Subjects in Pneumatology, Ethics, and Divinity.* London, 1763.

Dodsley, Robert. *The Preceptor*, 2 vols. London, 1748.

[Dodwell, Henry]. *Christianity not Founded on Argument.* London, 1741.

Dohm, Christian Wilhelm von. *Über die bürgerliche Verbesserung der Juden*, 2 vols. Berlin, 1781–3.

Du Bos, Jean-Baptiste. *Critical Reflections on Poetry, Painting, and Music.* Trans. T. Nugent, 3 vols. London, 1748; New York, 1978.

Du Bos, Jean-Baptiste, Abbé. *Réflexions critiques sur la poésie et sur la peinture* [1719], 3 vols. Dresden, 1760; 7th edn., 3 vols., Paris, 1770 (facsim. Geneva and Paris, 1982).

Du Marsais, César Chesneau. *Examen de la religion ou Doutes sur la religion dont on cherche l'éclaircissement de bonne foi*, ed. G. Mori. Oxford, 1998.

[Du Marsais, César Chesneau]. *Le Philosophe*, in *Nouvelles libertés de penser.* Amsterdam and Paris, 1743.

Duclos, Charles Pinot. *Considérations sur les mœurs de ce siècle* [1749]. Paris, 1751.

Dudgeon, William. *A Catechism Founded upon Experience and Reason: Collected by a Father for the Use of his Children. To which is prefixed, An Introductory Epistle to a Friend, concerning Natural Religion* [1739], in *The Philosophical Works of Mr. William Dudgeon.* n.p., 1765.

[Dudgeon, William]. *The Necessity of some of the Positive Institutions of Ch——ty consider'd, in a Letter to the Minister of Moffat.* London, 1731.

Duff, William. *An Essay on Original Genius; and Its Various Modes of Exertion in Philosophy and the Fine Arts, Particularly in Poetry.* London, 1767; facsim. Gainesville, FL, 1964.

Dunbar, James. *Essays on the History of Mankind in Rude and Cultivated Ages* (2nd edn.). London, 1781.

Duncan, William. *Elements of Logick.* London, 1748; 5th edn., 1764.

Dundas, John. *State of the Processes Depending against Mr. John Simson Professor of Divinity in the University of Glasgow; Setting forth the Proceedings of the Presbytery of Glasgow, General Assembly, and Committees thereof.* Edinburgh, 1728.

Eberhard, Johann August. *Allgemeine Theorie des Denkens und Empfindens.* Berlin, 1776; repr. Brussels, 1968.

Eberhard, Johann August. "Vorbericht", in Alexander Gottlieb Baumgarten, *Metaphysik*, trans. G. F. Meier, 2nd ed., Halle, 1783.
Edelmann, Johann Christian. *Sämtliche Schriften in Einzelausgaben*, ed. W. Grossmann. Stuttgart, 1969–, vol. 10 (1974).
Edwards, Jonathan. "Remarks on the Essays on the Principles of Morality and Natural Religion, in a letter to a minister of the Church of Scotland", in *The Works of Jonathan Edwards/Freedom of the Will*, ed. P. Ramsey, New Haven, CT, 1957–, vol. 1.
[Ellys, Anthony]. *Remarks on an Essay concerning Miracles, published by David Hume, Esq; amongst his Philosophical Essays*. London, 1752.
Encyclopédie méthodique: Grammaire literature, see p. 1293.
Estratto della letteratura Européa, see p. 1293.
Euler, Leonhard. *Briefe an eine deutsche Prinzessinn über verschiedene Gegenstände aus der Physik und Philosophie*, 2 vols. Leipzig, 1769.
Euler, Leonhard. *De Curvis elasticis*. Lausanne and Geneva, 1774.
Euler, Leonhard. *Elements of Algebra*. London, 1797.
Euler, Leonhard. *Histoire de l'Académie Royale des Sciences et des Belles-Lettres, 1748*. Berlin, 1750.
Euler, Leonhard. *Introductio in analysin infinitorum*, in *Opera omnia*, Ser. 1, vol. 8.
Euler, Leonhard. *Introduction to Analysis of the Infinite*, trans. J. D. Blanton. New York, NY, 1988.
Euler, Leonhard. "The Koenigsberg Bridges". *Scientific American* 189.1 (1953): 66–70. Repr. in *The World of Mathematics*, ed. J. R. Newman, 4 vols. (New York, NY, 1956), vol. 1, pp. 573–80.
Euler, Leonhard. "Leonard Euler's Elastic Curves", trans. W. A. Oldfather, C. A. Ellis and D. M. Brown. *Isis* (1933): 72–160.
Euler, Leonhard. *Letters of Euler on Different Subjects in Natural Philosophy. Addressed to a German Princess*, trans. H. Hunter, eds. D. Brewster and J. Griscom, 2 in 1 vols. New York, NY, 1975 (facsim. of 1833 edn.).
Euler, Leonhard. *Letters . . . to a German Princess on Different Subjects in Physics and Philosophy*, trans. H. Hunter, 2 vols. London, 1795.
Euler, Leonhard. *Lettres à une princesse d'Allemagne sur divers sujets de physique & de philosophie* [1768–72], in *Opera Omnia*, Ser. III, vol. 11.
Euler, Leonhard. *Mechanica sive motus scientia analytice exposita*, 2 vols. St. Petersburg, 1736.
Euler, Leonhard. *Methodus inveniendi lineas curvas* [1744], in *Opera omnia*, ser. I, vol. 24.
Euler, Leonhard. *Opera omnia*, eds. F. Rudio, A. Krazer and P. Stäckel. Leipzig, 1911–.
[Euler, Leonhard]. *Réflexions sur l'espace et le temps*, in *Histoire de l'Académie Royale des Sciences et des Belles-Lettres*, 1748. Berlin, 1750.
Euler, Leonhard. *Solutio problematis ad geometriam situs pertinentis*, in *Opera omnia*, ser. I, vol. 7.
Euler, Leonhard. *Specimen de usu observationum in mathesi pura* [1761], in *Opera omnia*, ser. I, vol. 2.
Euler, Leonhard. *Vollständige Anleitung zur Algebra* [1770], ed. H. Weber, in *Opera omnia*, vol. 1.
Feder, Johann Georg Heinrich. *Untersuchungen über den menschlichen Willen: dessen Naturtriebe, Verschiedenheiten, Verhältniss zur Tugend und Glückseligkeit und die Grundregeln, die menschlichen Gemüther zu erkennen und zu regieren*, 2 vols. Göttingen, 1779–82; 4 vol., 1779–93.
Feijoo, Benito Gerónimo. "Color etiópico", in *Teatro crítico universal, ò Discursos varios en todo género de materias, para desengaño de errores comunes*, 9 vols, Madrid, 1726–40, vol. 7.
The Female Tatler, see p. 1293.
Fénelon, François de Salignac de La Mothe-. *Les Aventures de Télémaque*. Paris, 1699.
Fénelon, François de Salignac de La Mothe-. *Démonstration de l'existence de Dieu*, ed. J. Deprun, in J. Meslier, *Oeuvres complètes*, vol. 3.
Fénelon, François de Salignac de La Mothe-. *Dialogues on Eloquence*, trans. W. S. Howell. Princeton, 1951.

Fenelon, François de Salignac de la Mothe-. *Dialogues sur l'eloquence en general, et sur celle de la chaire en particulier.* Paris, 1718.
Fénelon, François de Salignac de La Mothe-. *De l'éducation des filles* 1687, in *Oeuvres*, vol. 1.
Fénelon, François de Salignac de La Mothe-. *Fénelon on Education*, trans. H. C. Barnard. Cambridge, 1966.
Fénelon, François de Salignac de La Mothe-. *Oeuvres*, ed. J. Le Brun, 2 vols. Paris, 1983–7.
Ferguson, Adam. *An Essay on the History of Civil Society*. Edinburgh, 1767; ed. F. Oz-Salzberger, Cambridge, 1995.
Ferguson, Adam. *Principles of Moral and Political Science: Being Chiefly a Retrospect of Lectures Delivered in the College of Edinburgh*, 2 vols. Edinburgh, 1792.
Feuerbach, Paul Johann Anselm. *Anti-Hobbes, oder Über die Gränzen der höchsten Gewalt und das Zwangsrecht der Bürger gegen den Oberherrn*. Giessen, 1797.
Fichte, Johann Gottlieb. *Fichte und Forberg: Die philosophischen Schriften zum Atheismusstreit*, ed. F. Medicus. Leipzig, 1910.
Fichte, Johann Gottlieb. *Gesamtausgabe der Bayerischen Akademie der Wissenschaften*, eds. R. Lauth and H. Jacob. Stuttgart-Bad Cantstatt, 1962–.
Fichte, Johann Gottlieb. *Grundlage der gesammten Wissenschaftslehre als Handschrift für seine Zuhörer* [1794], 8 vols., in *Werke*, vol. 1; in *Gesamtausgabe*, I.2.
Fichte, Johann Gottlieb. "Recension des Aenesidemus" [1792], in *Werke*, vol. 1.
Fichte, Johann Gottlieb. *Reden an die deutsche Nation*. Berlin, 1807–8.
Fichte, Johann Gottlieb. *Sämmtliche Werke*, ed. I. H. Fichte, 8 vols. Berlin, 1845–6.
Fichte, Johann Gottlieb. *Die Schriften zu J. G. Fichte's Atheismus-Streit*, ed. H. Lindau. Munich, 1912.
Fichte, Johann Gottlieb. *Science of Knowledge, with the First and Second Introductions*, trans. and eds. P. Heath and J. Lachs. Cambridge, 1982.
Fichte, Johann Gottlieb. "Über den Grund unseres Glaubens an eine göttliche Weltregierung". *Philosophisches Journal* 8 (1798): 1–20.
Fichte, Johann Gottlieb. *Vergleichung des vom Hrn Prof. Schmid aufgestellten Systems mit der Wissenschaftslehre*, in *Gesamtausgabe*, vol. 1.
Fichte, Johann Gottlieb. *Versuch einer Kritik aller Offenbarung* [1792], in *Werke*, vol. 5.
Fichte, Johann Gottlieb. *Versuch einer neuen Darstellung der Wissenschaftslehre* [1797], in *Werke*, vol. 1.
Fichte, Johann Gottlieb. "Zurückforderung der Denkfreiheit von den Fürsten Europens," in *Gesamtausgabe*, vol. 1.
Fichte, Johann Gottlieb. *Zweite Einleitung in die Wissenschaftslehre* [1797], in *Werke*, vol. 1 (1845).
Fiddes, Richard. *A General Treatise of Morality, Form'd upon the Principles of Natural Reason only . . . in Answer to two Essays lately Published in The Fable of the Bees*. London, 1724.
Fiddes, Richard. *Theologia Speculativa: or, The First Part of a Body of Divinity under that Title. Wherein are Explain'd the Principles of Natural and Reveal'd Religion*. London, 1718.
Fieser, James, ed. *Early Responses to Hume's Writings on Religion*. 2 vols. Bristol, 2001.
Fleetwood, William. *An Essay on Miracles*. London, 1701.
Fontenelle, Bernard le Bovier de. *Dialogues des morts* (1683), in *Oeuvres* (ed. Depping), vol. 2.
Fontenelle, Bernard le Bovier de. *Entretiens sur la pluralité des mondes* [1686], ed. R. Shackleton. Oxford, 1955; in *Oeuvres complètes*, vol. 2.
Fontenelle, Bernard le Bovier de. *Histoire des oracles* (1686), in *Oeuvres complètes*, vol. 2.
Fontenelle, Bernard le Bovier de. *Oeuvres complètes* (repr. of Paris, 1818 edn.), ed. G.-B. Depping, 3 vols. Geneva, 1968.
Fontenelle, Bernard le Bovier de. *Oeuvres de Fontenelle*, 8 vols. Paris, 1790–2.

Fontenelle, Bernard le Bovier de. *De l'origine des fables* (1723), in *Oeuvres complètes*, vol. 2.
Fontenelle, Bernard le Bovier de. "Préface sur l'utilité des mathématiques et de la physique et sur les travaux de l'Académie des Sciences" [1699], in *Oeuvres complètes*, vol. 1.
Fontenelle, Bernard le Bovier de. "Sur l'instinct", in *Oeuvres de Fontenelle*, vol. 5.
[Fontenelle, Mirabeau, Du Marsais]. *Nouvelles libertés de penser.* Amsterdam and Paris, 1743.
Forberg, Friedrich C. "Entwicklung des Begriffes der Religion". *Philosophisches Journal* 8 (1798): 21–46; in J. G. Fichte, *Fichte und Forberg: Die philosophischen Schriften zum Atheismusstreit.*
Fordyce, David. *Dialogues concerning Education*, 2 vols. London, 1745–8.
Fordyce, David. *The Elements of Moral Philosophy*. London, 1754.
Forge, Louis de la. *Traité de l'esprit de l'homme . . . suivant les principes de René Descartes.* Paris, 1666.
Formey, Jean Henri Samuel. Rev. of Hume's *Philosophische Versuche über die menschliche Erkenntnis*, trans. J. G. Sulzer. *Nouvelle Bibliothèque germanique* 19, 20, 21 (1756, 1757): 78–109, 311–32; 57–86, 268–96; 65–81.
Formey, Jean Henri Samuel. *La belle Wolfienne*, 6 vols. The Hague, 1741–53; facsim. Hildesheim, 1983.
Formey, Jean Henri Samuel. *Histoire abregée de la philosophie.* Amsterdam, 1760.
Formey, Jean Henri Samuel. *Kurzgefassete Historie der Philosophie* [in French, 1760]. Berlin, 1763.
Formey, Jean Henri Samuel. *Le triomphe de l'évidence.* Berlin, 1740.
Forster, Georg. "Leitfaden zu einer künftigen Geschichte der Menschheit," ed. S. Scheibe, in *Werke* (1958–), vol. 8.
Forster, Johann Georg. "Noch etwas über die Menschenraßen" [1786], in *Werke* (1958–), vol. 8.
Forster, Johann Georg. *A Voyage round the World*, 2 vols. London, 1777.
Forster, Johann Georg. *Werke*, 4 vols. Frankfurt, 1967–70.
Forster, Johann Georg. *Werke: Sämtliche Schriften, Tagesbücher, Briefe*. Berlin, 1958–.
Forster, Joseph. *Two Essays: The One on the Origin of Evil; the Other on the Foundation of Morality.* Newcastle upon Tyne, 1734.
Francke, August Hermann. *Schriften über Erziehung und Unterricht*, ed. K. Richter. Berlin, 1871.
Franklin, Benjamin. *Experiments and Observations on Electricity*, 3 vols. London, 1751–4.
Franklin, Benjamin. *Papers*, eds. L. W. Labaree and W. J. Bell. New Haven, CT, 1959–.
Franklin, Thomas. *A Sermon Preached in . . . the Asylum for Female Orphans.* London, 1768.
Frederick II. *L'anti-Machiavel ou Essai de critique sur le Prince de Machiavel.* The Hague, 1740.
Fréret, Nicolas. *Lettre de Thrasybule à Leucippe*, ed. S. Landucci. Florence, 1986.
Fréret, Nicolas. *Mémoires académiques.* Paris, 1996.
Furneaux, Philip. *An Essay on Toleration: With a Particular View to the Late Application of the Protestant Dissenting Ministers to Parliament.* London, 1773; also in Goldie (ed.), *The Reception of Locke's Politics*, vol. 5, pp. 355–85.
Furneaux, Philip. *Letters to the Honourable Mr. Justice Blackstone, concerning His Exposition of the Act of Toleration, and Some Positions Relative to Religious Liberty, in his Celebrated Commentaries on the Laws of England* (2nd edn., 1773), in *The Palladium of Conscience, or the Foundation of Religious Liberty displayed, asserted, and established, agreeable to its true and genuine Principles.* Philadelphia, PA, 1774.
Gabler, Johann Philipp. "De iusto discrimine theologiae biblicae et dogmaticae . . . Oratio 1787", in *Opuscula Academica*, eds. T. A. Gabler and J. G. Gabler, 2 vols., Ulm, 1831, vol. 2.
Garat, Dominique-Joseph. *Mémoires historiques sur la vie de M. Suard, sur ses écrits, et sur le XVIIIe siècle.* Paris, 1820.
Garve, Christian. *Uebersicht der vornehmsten Principien der Sittenlehre, von dem Zeitalter des Aristoteles an bis auf die unsre Zeiten.* Breslau, 1798.

Gastrell, Francis. *The Certainty of the Christian Revelation, and the Necessity of Believing it, Established.* London, 1699.

Gastrell, Francis. *The Christian Institutes: or, The Sincere Word of God. Being a Plain and Impartial Account of the Whole Faith and Duty of a Christian. Collected out of the Writings of the Old and New Testament: Digested under Proper Heads, and Delivered in the Words of Scripture.* London, 1707.

Gatterer, Johann Christoph. "Abhandlungen vom Standort und Gesichtpunct des Geschichtsschreibers oder der deutsche Livius". *Allgemeine historische Bibliothek* 5 (1768): 3–17.

Gaultier (of Niort), *Parité de la vie et mort: La 'Réponse' du médecin Gaultier*, ed. O. Bloch. Paris and Oxford, 1993.

Gautier, Henri. *Nouvelles conjectures sur le globe de la terre.* Paris, 1721.

Gay, John. "Preliminary Dissertation concerning the Fundamental Principle of Virtue or Morality", in W. King, *An Essay on the Origin of Evil*, pp. xi–xxxiii.

Geddes, Alexander. *Critical Remarks on the Hebrew Scriptures: corresponding with a new Translation of the Bible.* London, 1801.

Geddes, Alexander, trans. *The Holy Bible, or the Books accounted Sacred by Jews and Christians.* London, 1792–7.

Genlis, Stéphanie Félicité. *Adèle et Théodore, ou Lettres sur l'éducation.* Paris, 1782.

Gentz, Friedrich von. "Politische Abhandlungen", in E. Burke, *Betrachtungen über die Französische Revolution. Nach dem Englischen des Herrn Burke . . . mit einer Einleitung, Anmerkungen, politischen Abhandlungen und einem critischen Verzeichniss der in England über diese Revolution erschienenen Schriften*, 2 vols., Berlin, 1793, vol. 2.

Gerard, Alexander. *Dissertations on Subjects relating to the Genius and the Evidences of Christianity.* Edinburgh, 1766.

Gerard, Alexander. *An Essay on Genius* [1774], ed. B. Fabian. Munich, 1966.

Gerard, Alexander. *An Essay on Taste* [1759], 3rd edn. Edinburgh, 1780; facsim. Gainesville, FL, 1963.

[Gerard, Alexander]. *Plan of Education in the Marischal College and University of Aberdeen, with the Reasons of it.* Aberdeen, 1755.

Gerard, Alexander, and Gilbert Gerard. *A Compendious View of the Evidences of Natural and Revealed Religion.* London, 1828.

Gibbon, Edward. *Essai sur l'étude de littérature.* London, 1762.

Gibbon, Edward. *The History of the Decline and Fall of the Roman Empire*, 6 vols. London, 1776–1788.

Gibbon, Edward. *Memoirs of My Life*, ed. B. Radice. London, 1984.

Gildon, Charles. *The Deist's Manual: or A Rational Enquiry into the Christian Religion.* London, 1705.

Girard, Gabriel. *Vrais principes de la langue françoise.* Paris, 1747.

Girtanner, Christoph. *Über das Kantische Prinzip für Naturgeschichte. Ein Versuch diese Wissenschaft philosophisch zu behandeln.* Göttingen, 1796.

Gisborne, Thomas. *An Enquiry into the Duties of the Female Sex.* London, 1797.

Gisborne, Thomas. *An Enquiry into the Duties of Men in the Higher and Middle Classes of Society in Great Britain.* London, 1794.

[Glover, Phillips]. *The Argument A Priori concerning the Existence and Perfections of God, and its Importance to Virtue and true Religion, Stated and Consider'd.* London, 1737.

Goclenius, Rudolph. *Lexicon philosophicum.* Frankfurt, 1613.

Godwin, William. *An Enquiry Concerning Political Justice*, in *Political and Philosophical Writings*, vol. 3.

Godwin, William. *Political and Philosophical Writings of William Godwin*, ed. M. Philp, 7 vols. London, 1993.

Goethe, Johann Wolfgang von. *Briefwechsel zwischen Goethe und F. H. Jacobi*, ed. M. Jacobi. Leipzig, 1846.

Goldie, Mark, ed. *The Reception of Locke's Politics*. 6 vols. London, 1999.

Gottsched, Johann Christoph. *Erste Gründe der gesammten Weltweisheit darinn alle philosophische Wissenschaften in ihrer natürlichen Verknüpfung abgehandelt werden* [1734]. Leipzig, 1756.

Gottsched, Johann Christoph. *De optimismi macula: diserte nuper Alexandro Popio*. Leipzig, 1753.

Gottsched, Johann Christoph. *Versuch einer critischen Dichtkunst vor die Deutschen*. (Leipzig, 1730).

Gouges, Olympe de. "Déclaration des Droits de la Femme, Dédiée à la Reine", in *Oeuvres*.

Gouges, Olympe de. *Oeuvres*, ed. B. Groult. Paris, 1986.

Gowan (Goveanus), Thomas. *Ars sciendi, sive Logica novo methodo disposita et novis praeceptis aucta*. London, 1681.

Gracian, Baltasar. *Oráculo manual y arte de prudencia*. Huesca, 1647; facsim. Saragossa, 2001.

Gravesande, Willem Jacob 's. *An Explanation of the Newtonian Philosophy in Lectures read to the Youth of the University of Leyden*, trans. E. Stone. London, 1741.

Gravesande, Willem Jacob 's. *Mathematical Elements of Natural Philosophy, confirmed by Experiments* [1720–1], 6th edn, trans. J. Desaguliers, 2 vols. London, 1747.

Gravesande, Willem Jacob 's. *Nova theoria lucis et colorum*. n.p., 1746.

Gravesande, Willem Jacob 's. *Physices elementa mathematica, experimentis confirmata: Sive, Introductio ad philosophiam newtonianam*. Leiden, 1720–1.

Gregory, George. *A Dictionary of Arts and Sciences*, 2 vols. London, 1806–7.

Gregory, John. *A Father's Legacy to His Daughters*. London and Edinburgh, 1774.

Gretton, Phillips. *A Review of the Argument a Priori, in Relation to the Being and Attributes of God: In Reply to Dr. Clarke's Answer to a Seventh Letter concerning that Argument, Printed at the End of the Last Edition of his Boyleian Lectures*. London, 1726.

Grimm, Friedrich Melchior et al. *Correspondance littéraire, philosophique et critique*, ed. M. Tourneux, 16 vols. Paris, 1877–82.

Grotius, Hugo. *De iure belli ac pacis*. Paris, 1625; facsim. of 1646 edn., trans. F. W. Kelsey, 2 vols, Oxford, 1925.

Grotius, Hugo. *De veritate religionis Christianae*. Leiden, 1627.

Grotius, Hugo. *On the Truth of the Christian Religion*, trans. S. Patrick. London, 1680.

Grotius, Hugo. *On the Truth of the Christian Religion*, trans. J. Clarke. London, 1711.

Grotius, Hugo. *The Rights of War and Peace, in three books*, trans. anonymous, ed. J. Barbeyrac, 3 vols. London, 1738; re-ed. R. Tuck, Indianapolis, IN, 2005.

Grove, Henry. *System of Moral Philosophy*, 2 vols. London, 1749.

Grove, Henry. *Wisdom the First Spring of Action in the Deity. A Discourse in which among other things, the Absurdity of God's being Acted upon by Natural Inclinations, and of an Unbounded Liberty, is Shewn. The Moral Attributes of God are Explain'd. The Origin of Evil is Consider'd. The fundamental Duties of Natural Religion are Shewn to be Reasonable, &c.* London, 1734.

Guénée, Antoine, Abbé de. *Letters of certain Jews to Monsieur Voltaire*, trans. P. Lafanu. Dublin, 1777.

Guénée, Antoine, Abbé de. *Lettres de quelques juifs portugais et allemands, à M. de Voltaire: Avec des réflexions critiques*. Lisbon [in fact, Paris], 1769.

Hales, Stephen. *La statique des végétaux et l'analyse de l'air*..., trans. G.-L. L. Buffon. Paris, 1735.

Hales, Stephen. *Vegetable Staticks and Analysis of the Air*. London, 1727.

Hall, William. *The New Royal Encyclopedia*, 3 vols. London, [1788].

Haller, Albrecht von. *Elemens de physiologie*, trans. P. Tarin. Paris, 1752.

Haller, Albrecht von. *Primae lineae physiologiae*. Göttingen, 1747.

Haller, Albrecht von. *Prüfung der Sekte die an allem zweifeln*. Göttingen, 1751.

Haller, Albrecht von. "Über den Ursprung des Übels", in *Gedichte*, ed. L. Hirzel, Bibliothek älterer Schriftwerke der deutschen Schweitz, 3, Frauenfeld, 1882.

Halley, Edmund. "An Estimate of the Degrees of the Mortality of Mankind, Drawn from Curious Tables of Births and Funerals at the City of Breslaw; with an Attempt to Ascertain the Price of Annuities Upon Lives. By Mr. E. Halley, R. S. S". *Philosophical Transactions of the Royal Society of London* 17 (1693): 596–610.

Halyburton, Thomas. *Essay concerning the Reason of Faith* with *Natural Religion Insufficient; and Reveal'd Necessary to Man's Happiness in his Present State: or, A Rational Enquiry into the Principles of the Modern Deists*. Edinburgh, 1714.

Halyburton, Thomas. *Memoirs of the Life of the Reverend Mr. Thomas Halyburton*. Edinburgh, 1714.

Halyburton, Thomas. *Natural Religion Insufficient and Reveal'd Necessary to Man's Happiness in his Present State: or, A Rational Enquiry into the Principles of the Modern Deists*. Edinburgh, 1714.

Hamann, Johann Georg. "Aesthetica in nuce: A Rhapsody in Cabalistic Prose", [1762] in *Eighteenth Century German Criticism*, ed. T. J. Chamberlain, New York, NY, 1992.

Hamann, Johann Georg. *Hamann's Schriften*, ed. F. Roth, 8 (in 9) vols. Berlin, 1821–43.

Hamann, Johann Georg. *Socratic Memorabilia, Compiled for the Boredom of the Public by a Lover of Boredom: With a Double Dedication to Nobody and to Two* [1759], trans. J. O. Flaherty. Baltimore, MD, 1967.

Hamann, Johann Georg. *Sokratische Denkwürdigkeiten für die lange Weile des Publicums zusammengetragen von einem Liebhaber der langen Weile. Mit einer doppelten Zuschrift an Niemand und an Zween*. Amsterdam (in fact Königsberg), 1759; in *Sokratische Denkwürdigkeiten. Aesthetica in nuce*, ed. S.-A. Jørgensen, Stuttgart, 1968.

Hamilton, Alexander, Jay, John, and Madison, James. *The Federalist, or The New Constitution*. New York, 1965.

Hamilton, Hugh. *An Attempt to Prove the Existence and Absolute Perfection of the Supreme Unoriginated Being, in a Demonstrative Manner* [Dublin, 1784], in *Works*, vol. 2.

Hamilton, Hugh. *Works*, 2 vols. London, 1809.

Harrington, James. *The Commonwealth of Oceana* [1656], in *The Political Works*, ed. J. G. A. Pocock. Cambridge, 1977.

Harris, John. *Lexicon Technicum, or, An Universal English Dictionary of Arts and Sciences*, 2 vols. London, 1704–10.

Hartley, David. *Observations on Man, his Frame, his Duty and his Expectations*, 2 vols. London, 1749; 1801; 1810; 6th edn., 1834; facsim. Hildesheim, 1967.

Harvard College. *Catalogus librorum bibliothecae collegii Harvardini*. Boston, MA, 1723.

Hays, Mary. *Appeal to the Men of Great Britain in Behalf of Women*. London, 1798.

Hayter, Thomas. *Remarks on Mr. Hume's Dialogues concerning Natural Religion*. Cambridge, 1780.

Heath, Benjamin. *An Essay Towards a Demonstrative Proof of the Divine Existence, Unity and Attributes: To Which is Premised a Short Defence of the Argument Commonly Called A Priori*. London, 1740.

Hegel, Georg Wilhelm Friedrich. *Early Theological Writings*, trans. T. M. Knox. Chicago, IL, 1948.

Hegel, Georg Wilhelm Friedrich. *Faith and Knowledge or the Reflective Philosophy of Subjectivity in the Complete Range of Its Forms as Kantian, Jacobian, and Fichtean Philosophy*, trans. W. Cerf and H. S. Harris. Albany, NY, 1977.

Hegel, Georg Wilhelm Friedrich. *Fragmente über die Positivität der christlichen Religion (1795–6)*, in *Frühe Studien*.

Hegel, Georg Wilhelm Friedrich. *Fragmente über Volksreligion und Christentum* [1793–4], in *Frühe Studien*.

Hegel, Georg Wilhelm Friedrich. *Frühe Studien und Entwürfe, 1787–1800*, ed. I. Gellert. Berlin, 1991.

Hegel, Georg Wilhelm Friedrich. *Der Geist des Christentums und sein Schicksal* [1798–1800], in *Werke*, vol. 1.

Hegel, Georg Wilhelm Friedrich. *Glauben und Wissen oder Die Reflexionsphilosophie der Subjektivität in der Vollständigkeit ihrer Formen als Kantische, Jacobische und Fichtesche Philosophie* [1802], in *Werke*, vol. 2.

Hegel, Georg Wilhelm Friedrich. *Grundlinien der Philosophie des Rechts*. Berlin, 1821.

Hegel, Georg Wilhelm Friedrich. *Lectures on the History of Philosophy*, trans. E. S. Haldane and F. H. Simson, 3 vols. London, 1892–6.

Hegel, Georg Wilhelm Friedrich. *Lectures on the Philosophy of Religion*, trans. R. F. Brown, P. C. Hodgson, and J. M. Stewart. Berkeley, CA, 1984.

Hegel, Georg Wilhelm Friedrich. *The Logic of Hegel*, trans. W. Wallace. Oxford, 1892.

Hegel, Georg Wilhelm Friedrich. *Phänomenologie des Geistes* [1806], ed. J. Hoffmeister. Hamburg, 1952.

Hegel, Georg Wilhelm Friedrich. *Theologische Jugendschriften* [1793–1800], ed. H. Nohl. Tübingen, 1907.

Hegel, Georg Wilhelm Friedrich. *Volksreligion und Christentum* (Fragmente), in *Hegels Theologische Jugendschriften*.

Hegel, Georg Wilhelm Friedrich. *Vorlesungen über die Beweise vom Dasein Gottes* [1829], ed. G. Lasson. Leipzig, 1930.

Hegel, Georg Wilhelm Friedrich. *Vorlesungen über die Geschichte der Philosophie* [1833–6], in *Werke*, vols. 18–20; in *Vorlesungen*, eds. P. Garniron and W. Jaeschke, vols. 6–9, Hamburg, 1983–6.

Hegel, Georg Wilhelm Friedrich. *Vorlesungen über die Philosophie der Religion*, 2 vols. Berlin, 1832.

Hegel, Georg Wilhelm Friedrich. *Werke*, eds. E. Moldenhauer and K. M. Michel, 20 vols. Frankfurt am Main, 1969–72.

Hegel, Georg Wilhelm Friedrich. *Die Wissenschaft der Logik*, in *Enzyklopädie der philosophischen Wissenschaften im Grundrisse*. Heidelberg, 1817; 2nd edn. 1827; 3rd edn. 1830.

Helvétius, Claude-Adrien. *De l'esprit*. Paris, 1758; facsim., ed. F. Chatelet. Verviers, 1973.

Helvétius, Claude-Adrien. *De l'esprit or, Essays on the Mind and Its Several Faculties*, trans. anon. London, 1759.

Helvétius, Claude-Adrien. *De l'homme, de ses facultés intellectuelles et de son éducation* [1772], 2 vols. London, 1773; in *Oeuvres*, vol. 5.

Helvétius, Claude-Adrien. *Oeuvres complètes*, 5 vols. London (i.e., Amsterdam), 1781.

Helvétius, Claude-Adrien. *A Treatise on Man, his Intellectual Faculties and his Education*, 2 vols., trans. W. Hooper. London, 1810.

Herbert, Edward. *See* Cherbury.

Herder, Johann Gottfried. *Abhandlung über den Ursprung der Sprache*. Berlin, 1772; ed. U. Gaier, in *Werke* (ed. Bollacher), vol. 1 (1985), pp. 695–810; in *Werke* (ed. Pross), vol. 2 (1987), pp. 251–357.

Herder, Johann Gottfried. *Älteste Urkunde des Menschengeschlechts*, 2 vols. Riga, 1774–6.

Herder, Johann Gottfried. *Auch eine Philosophie der Geschichte* [1774], in *Werke* (ed. Suphan), vol. 5, pp. 475–593.

Herder, Johann Gottfried. *Critical Forests: First Grove*, in *Eighteenth Century German Criticism*, ed. T. J. Chamberlain. New York, NY, 1992.

Herder, Johann Gottfried. *Einige Gespräche über Spinozas System*. Gotha, 1800 (2nd edn. of *Gott: einige Gespräche*).

Herder, Johann Gottfried. *Fragmente*. See *Über die neuere Deutsche Literatur*.

Herder, Johann Gottfried. *Frühe Schriften 1764–1772*, ed. U. Gaier, in *Werke* (ed. Bollacher), vol. 1 (1985).

Herder, Johann Gottfried. *God: Some Conversations* [1787], trans. F. H. Burkhardt, 1940.

Herder, Johann Gottfried. *Gott: einige Gespräche* [1787], in *Werke* (ed. Suphan), vol. 16.

Herder, Johann Gottfried. *Ideas for a Philosophy of the History of Mankind*, trans. F. M. Barnard, in *J. G. Herder on Social and Political Culture*, ed. F. M. Barnard, Cambridge, 1969.

Herder, Johann Gottfried. *Ideen zur Philosophie der Geschichte der Menschheit*, 4 vols. Riga/Leipzig, 1784–91; in *Werke* (ed. Bollacher), vol. 6 (1989).

Herder, Johann Gottfried. *Kritische Wälder, oder, Betrachtungen, die Wissenschaft und Kunst des Schönen betreffend, nach Massgabe neuerer Schriften* [1769], in *Werke* (ed. Suphan), vol. 3 (1878).

Herder, Johann Gottfried. *Outlines of a Philosophy of the History of Man*, trans. T. O. Churchill. London, 1800.

Herder, Johann Gottfried. *Reflections on the Philosophy of History of Mankind*, trans. T. O. Churchill, ed. F. E. Manuel. Chicago, IL, 1968.

Herder, Johann Gottfried. *Sämmtliche Werke*, ed. B. L. Suphan, 33 vols. Berlin, 1877–1913; facsim. Hildesheim, 1967.

Herder, Johann Gottfried. "Über die ersten Urkunden des menschlichen Geschlechts: Einige Anmerkungen", ed. R. Smend, in *Werke* (ed. Bollacher), vol. 5: *Schriften zum Alten Testament* (1993).

Herder, Johann Gottfried. *Über die neuere deutsche Literatur. Fragmente*, in *Werke* (ed. Pross), vol. 1 (1984).

Herder, Johann Gottfried. *Verstand und Erfahrung. Eine Metakritik zur Kritik der reinen Vernunft*, in *Werke* (ed. Suphan), vol. 21.

Herder, Johann Gottfried. *Werke*, ed. W. Pross. Munich, 1984–.

Herder, Johann Gottfried. *Werke*, ed. M. Bollacher, 10 vols. Frankfurt am Main, 1985–2000.

Herz, Marcus. *Betrachtungen aus der spekulativen Weltweisheit* [1771], ed. E. Conrad et al. Hamburg, 1990.

Hey, John. *Heads of a Course of Lectures in Divinity*. Cambridge, 1783.

Hey, John. *Lectures in Divinity*. Cambridge, 1796.

Heydenreich, Karl Heinrich. *System des Naturrechts nach kritischen Principien: Erster Theil*. Leipzig, 1795.

Hildrop, John. *Free Thoughts upon the Brute-Creation: In Two Letters to a Lady*, in *The Miscellaneous Works of John Hildrop*, 2 vols., London, 1754, vol. 1.

Hissmann, Michael. *Psychologische Versuche*. Göttingen, 1777.

Hoadly, Benjamin. *Bishop Hoadly's Refutation of Bishop Sherlock's Arguments against a Repeal of the Test and Corporation Acts, Wherein the Justice and Reasonableness of such a Repeal are Clearly Evidenced*. London, 1787.

Hoadly, Benjamin. *The Nature of the Kingdom, or Church, of Christ. A Sermon Preach'd Before the King at the Royal Chapel at St. James's, on Sunday March 31, 1717*. London, 1717; also in Goldie (ed.), *The Reception of Locke's Politics*, vol. 5, pp. 145–55.

Hobbes, Thomas. *The Collected Works*, ed. W. Molesworth, 12 vols. London, 1839–45; facsim. London, 1992.

Hobbes, Thomas. *Leviathan*, ed. R. Tuck. Cambridge, 1991.

Hobbes, Thomas. *Leviathan, or The Matter, Forme and Power of a Commonwealth Ecclesiasticall and Civill* [1651], in *Works*, vol. 3.

Hog, James. *A Letter to a Gentleman concerning the Interest of Reason in Religion*. Edinburgh, 1716.

Hog, James. *Memoirs . . . Written by himself, in a Testamentary Memorial*. Edinburgh, 1798.

Holbach, Paul-Henri Thiry, baron d'. *Le bon sens du curé Meslier, suivi de son testament*. Paris, 1833.

Holbach, Paul-Henri Thiry, baron d'. *Christianisme dévoilé ou, Examen des principes et des effets de la religion Chrétienne*. London, 1756.

Holbach, Paul-Henri Thiry, baron d'. *Le militaire philosophe, ou, Difficultés sur la religion proposées au R. P. Malebranche, prêtre de l'Oratoire, par un ancien officier*. London [i.e., Amsterdam], 1768.

Holbach, Paul-Henri Thiry, baron d.' *La morale universelle, ou les devoirs de l'homme fondés sur sa nature*, 3 vols. Paris, 1795–6.

Holbach, Paul-Henri Thiry, baron d'. *The System of Nature, or The Laws of the Moral and Physical World*, 2 vols. London, 1817.

Holbach, Paul-Henri Thiry, baron d'. *Système de la nature, ou Des loix du monde physique et du monde moral*, 2 vols. [London], 1770; ed. Diderot, Paris, 1821 (facsim., ed. Y. Belaval, 2 vols., Hildesheim, 1996).

Holbach, Paul-Henri Thiry, baron d'. *Théologie portative ou dictionnaire abrégé de la Religion Chrétienne*. London [i.e., Amsterdam], 1768.

Home, Henry. *See* Kames, Henry Home, Lord.

Hooker, Richard. *Of the Laws of Ecclesiastical Polity*, 8 bks. London, 1593–1662.

[Hooper, George]. "A Calculation of the Credibility of Human Testimony". *Philosophical Transactions of the Royal Society of London* 21 (1699): 359–65.

Höpfner, Ludwig Julius Friedrich. *Naturrecht des einzelnen Menschen, der Gesellschaften und der Völker*, 3rd edn. Giessen, 1785.

Hoppius, Christian. *Anthropomorpha*. Uppsala, 1760.

Houtteville, Claude-François. *La Vérité de la religion chrétienne prouvée par les faits*. Paris, 1722.

Howard, George S. *The New Royal Cyclopaedia, and Encyclopaedia or Complete, Modern and Universal Dictionary of Arts and Science*, 3 vols. London, 1796–1802.

Huet, Pierre-Daniel. *Demonstratio evangelica ad serenissimum delphinum*. Paris, 1679.

Huet, Pierre-Daniel. *Traité philosophique de la foiblesse de l'esprit humaine*. Amsterdam, 1723.

Humboldt, Wilhelm von. *On Language. The Diversity of Human Language Structure and its Influence on the Mental Development of Mankind*. Trans. P. Heath, introd. H. Aarsleff. Cambridge, 1988.

Hume, David. *An Abstract of a Book lately Published: Entituled, A Treatise of Human Nature*. London, 1740.

Hume, David. *An Abstract of a Treatise of Human Nature* [1740], eds. J. M. Keynes and P. Sraffa. Cambridge, 1938.

Hume, David. *The Clarendon Edition of the Works*, eds. T. L. Beauchamp, D. F. Norton and M. A. Stewart. Oxford, 1998–.

Hume, David. *Dialogues concerning Natural Religion* [1779], ed. N. Kemp Smith. Oxford, 1935; 2nd edn. London, 1947; ed. J. V. Price in *The Natural History of Religion and Dialogues concerning Natural Religion*, eds. A. W. Colver and J. V. Price, Oxford, 1976.

Hume, David. "Early Memoranda". *See* Mossner (*B2*).

Hume, David. *An Enquiry concerning Human Understanding* [1748], ed. T. L. Beauchamp, in *The Clarendon Edition of the Works of David Hume* (2000).

Hume, David. *An Enquiry concerning the Principles of Morals* [1751], ed. T. L. Beauchamp, in *The Clarendon Edition of the Works of David Hume* (1998).

Hume, David. *Essays Moral and Political*. Edinburgh, 1741 (2nd edn., Edinburgh 1742); vol. 2, Edinburgh, 1742; Edinburgh and London, 1748.

Hume, David. *Essays, Moral, Political, and Literary*, ed. E. F. Miller. Indianapolis, IN, 1987.

Hume, David. *Histoire naturelle de la religion*, trans. J. B. Merian. Amsterdam, 1759.

Hume, David. *The History of England: From the Invasion of Julius Caesar to the Revolution in 1688* [1754–62], 8 vols. London, 1778; 6 vols. Indianapolis, IN, 1983.

Hume, David. *A Letter from a Gentleman to his Friend in Edinburgh* [1745], eds. E. C. Mossner and J. V. Price. Edinburgh, 1967.

Hume, David. *The Letters of David Hume*, ed. J. Y. T. Greig, 2 vols. Oxford, 1932.

Hume, David. *The Natural History of Religion* [1757], in *Philosophical Works*, vol. 4, pp. 309–63; ed. A. W. Colver in *The Natural History of Religion and Dialogues Concerning Natural Religion*, eds. A. W. Colver and J. V. Price, Oxford, 1976.

Hume, David. *New Letters of David Hume*, eds. R. Klibansky and E. C. Mossner. Oxford, 1954.

Hume, David. *The Philosophical Works*, eds. T. H. Green and T. H. Grose, 4 vols. London, 1882; Facsim. Aalen 1954.

Hume, David. *Philosophische Versuche über die menschliche Erkenntniss, von David Hume, Ritter. Als dessen vermischter Schriften Zweyter Theil. Nach der zweyten vermehrten Ausgabe aus dem Englischen übersetzt und mit Anmerkungen des Herausgebers begleitet*, trans. and ed. J. G. Sulzer. Hamburg, Leipzig, 1755.

Hume, David. *Political Essays*, ed. K. Haakonssen. Cambridge, 1994.

Hume, David. *A Treatise of Human Nature* [1739–40], eds. D. F. Norton and M. J. Norton, in *The Clarendon Edition*, 2006.

Hunt, Jeremiah. *Sermons*, 4 vols. London, 1748.

Hunter, John. *Essays and Observations on Natural History, Anatomy, Physiology, and Geology*, 2 vols. London, 1861.

Hutcheson, Francis. *The Collected Works*, ed. B. Fabian, 7 vols. Hildesheim, 1969–71.

Hutcheson, Francis. *An Essay on the Nature and Conduct of the Passions and Affections. With Illustrations on the Moral Sense*. London, 1728 (facsim. Menston, 1972 and in *Works*, vol. 2: 1971); 3rd edn., 1742 (facsim. Gainsville, FL, 1976); ed. A. Garrett, Indianapolis, IN, 2002.

Hutcheson, Francis. *Illustrations on the Moral Sense*, ed. B. Peach. Cambridge, MA, 1971.

Hutcheson, Francis. *Inaugural Lecture on the Social Nature of Man* [1730], in *On Human Nature: Reflections on our Common Systems of Morality and On the Social Nature of Man*, ed. T. Mautner. Cambridge, 1993.

Hutcheson, Francis. *An Inquiry into the Original of Our Ideas of Beauty and Virtue; in Two Treatises*. London and Dublin, 1725; 3rd edn., London, 1729; 4th edn., London, 1738; ed. W. Leidhold, Indianapolis, IN, 2004.

Hutcheson, Francis. *Letters . . . concerning the true Foundation of Virtue and Moral Goodness*. London, 1735.

[Hutcheson, Francis]. *Logicae compendium*. Glasgow, 1756.

[Hutcheson, Francis]. *Metaphysicae synopsis*. Glasgow, 1742; 2nd edn.: *Synopsis metaphysicae*, [Glasgow], 1744.

Hutcheson, Francis. *Philosophiae moralis institutio compendiaria, ethices et jurisprudentiae naturalis elementa complectens, libris III*. Glasgow, 1742; 2nd edn., 1744.

Hutcheson, Francis. *Reflections on the Common Systems of Morality*, in *On Human Nature: Reflections on Our Common Systems of Morality and On the Social Nature of Man*, ed. T. Mautner. Cambridge, 1993.

Hutcheson, Francis. *A Short Introduction to Moral Philosophy*. Glasgow, 1747.

[Hutcheson, Francis]. *Synopsis metaphysicae. See Metaphysicae synopsis*.

Hutcheson, Francis. *A System of Moral Philosophy*. London, 1755; in *Works*, vol. 1.

Hutton, James. *Theory of the Earth, with Proofs and Illustrations*, 3 vols. Edinburgh, 1785; 2nd edn., 1795 (vols. 1 and 2); 1899 (vol. 3).

Huygens, Christiaan. *Traité de la lumière*. Leiden, 1690.

Iselin, Isaak. *Über die Geschichte der Menschheit*. Basel, 1786; facsim. Hildesheim, 1976.

Itard, Jean. *De l'éducation d'un homme sauvage; ou, Des premiers développemens physiques et moraux du jeune sauvage de l'Aveyron*. Paris, 1801. Translation in L. Malson and J. Itard, *Wolf Children. The Wild Boy of Aveyron*, trans. E. Fawcett, P. Ayrton, and J. White, London, 1972.

Jackson, John. *An Address to Deists, being a Proof of Reveal'd Religion from Miracles and Prophecies: In answer to a book, entitled, The Resurrection of Jesus consider'd by a Moral Philosopher*. London, 1744.

Jackson, John. *Calumny no Conviction; or, A Vindication of the Plea for Human Reason*. London, 1731.

Jackson, John. *A Defense of a Book entitled The Existence and Unity of God; Prov'd from his Nature and Attributes: Being a farther Vindication of Dr. Clarke's Demonstration of the Being and Attributes of God*. London, 1735.

Jackson, John. *The Existence and Unity of God; Proved from his Nature and Attributes: Being a Vindication of Dr. Clarke's Demonstration of the Being and Attributes of God*. London, 1734.

Jacobi, Friedrich Heinrich. *Briefwechsel*, eds. M. Brüggen and S. Sudhof, et al. Stuttgart, 1981–.

Jacobi, Friedrich Heinrich. *David Hume über den Glauben, oder Idealismus und Realismus*. Breslau, 1787; in *Werke*, vol. 2.

Jacobi, Friedrich Heinrich. *Spinoza Büchlein nebst Replik und Duplik*, ed. F. Mauthner. Munich, 1912.

Jacobi, Friedrich Heinrich. *Über die Lehre des Spinoza in Briefen an den Herrn Moses Mendelssohn* [1785], ed. M. Lauschke. Hamburg, 2000.

Jacobi, Friedrich Heinrich. *Werke*, eds. F. von Roth and F. Köppen, 6 vols. Leipzig, 1812–25; Darmstadt, 1968.

Jaucourt, chevalier Louis de. "Egalité", in *Encyclopédie*, eds. D. Diderot and J. d' Alembert, vol. 5.

Jefferson, Thomas. *A Bill for Establishing Religious Freedom*, in *The portable Thomas Jefferson*, ed. M. D. Peterson. New York, NY, 1975.

Jefferson, Thomas. *Notes on the State of Virginia* [1787], ed. W. Peden. Chapel Hill, NC, 1955.

Jefferson, Thomas. *Writings*. New York, NY, 1984.

Jennings, John. *Logica in usum juventutis academicae*. Northampton, 1721.

Jenyns, Soame. *A Free Inquiry Into the Nature and Origin of Evil* (2nd edn.). London, 1757; repr. New York, NY, 1976.

Johnson, Samuel [1709–84]. *A Dictionary of the English Language*, 2 vols. London, 1755; facsim. New York, NY, 1967.

Johnson, Samuel [1696–1772]. *Elementa Philosophica: Containing chiefly Noetica, or Things relating to the Mind or Understanding: and Ethica, or Things relating to Moral Behaviour*. Philadelphia, PA, 1752.

Johnson, Samuel [1696–1772]. *The Elements of Philosophy*, 3rd edn. London, 1754.

Johnson, Samuel [1696–1772]. *Ethices elementa. Or The first principles of moral philosophy: And especially that Part of it which is called Ethics*. Boston, MA, 1746.

Johnson, Samuel [1709–84]. *Rasselas, Prince of Abyssinia* [1759], in *Works*, vol. 3, pp. 299–442.

Johnson, Samuel [1709–84]. Review of Soame Jenyns, *A Free inquiry into the Nature and Origin of Evil*, in Johnson, *Works* (1825), vol. 6, pp. 47–76.

Johnson, Samuel [1709–84]. *A Review of A Free Enquiry into the Nature and Origin of Evil*, in *Works*, vol. 8, pp. 23–61.

Johnson, Samuel [1709–84]. *Works*, ed. A. Murphy, 12 vols. London, 1792; 11 vols. (Oxford and London, 1825).

Johnson, Thomas, ed. S. Pufendorf. *De officio hominis et civis*. Cambridge, 1735.

Johnson, Thomas. *Quaestiones philosophicae*. Cambridge, 1734; 2nd edn., 1735; 3rd edn., 1741.

Jussieu, Antoine-Laurent de. *Genera plantarum ... secundum ordines naturales disposita ...* Paris, 1789.

Justi, Johann Heinrich Gottlob von. *Gesammelte Politische und Finanzschriften über wichtige Gegenstände der Staatskunst, der Kriegswissenschaften und des Cameral- und Finanzwesens*, 3 vols. Copenhagen, 1761–4.

Justi, Johann Heinrich Gottlob von. *Die Natur und das Wesen der Staaten als Grundwissenschaft der Staatskunst, der Policey und aller Regierungswissenschaft, desgleichen als die Quelle aller Gesetze*. Berlin/Stettin/Leipzig, 1760.

Kames, Henry Home, Lord. *Elements of Criticism* [1762], 2 vols. Edinburgh, 1774; London, 1824.

Kames, Henry Home, Lord. *Essays on the Principles of Morality and Natural Religion*. Edinburgh, 1751 (facsim. New York, NY, 1983); 2nd edn. Edinburgh, 1758.

Kames, Henry Home, Lord. *The Gentleman Farmer*, 4th edn. Edinburgh, 1798.

Kames, Henry Home, Lord. *Loose Hints upon Education*. Edinburgh, 1781.

Kames, Henry Home, Lord. *Sketches of the History of Man* [1774], 4 vols. Edinburgh, 1788.

Kant, Immanuel. *Allgemeine Naturgeschichte und Theorie des Himmels* [1755], in *Ak*, vol. 1, pp. 215–368.

Kant, Immanuel. *Anthropologie in pragmatischer Hinsicht* [1798], in *Ak*, vol. 7, pp. 117–333.

Kant, Immanuel. *Anthropology from a Pragmatic Point of View*, trans. and ed. M. J. Gregor. The Hague, 1974.

Kant, Immanuel. "Beantwortung der Frage: Was ist Aufklärung?", in *Ak*, vol. 8, pp. 33–42.

Kant, Immanuel. *Beobachtungen über das Gefühl des Schönen und Erhabenen* [1764], in *Ak*, vol. 2, pp. 243–56.

Kant, Immanuel. *The Cambridge Edition of the Works*, eds. P. Guyer and A. W. Wood. Cambridge, MA, 1992–.

Kant, Immanuel. *Concerning the Form and Principles of the Sensible and Intelligible World*, in *Works/Theoretical Philosophy, 1755–1770*, trans. D. Walford and R. Meerbote (1992), pp. 373–416.

Kant, Immanuel. *Concerning the Ultimate Ground of the Differentiation of Directions in Space*, in *Works/Theoretical Philosophy, 1755–1770*, trans. D. Walford and R. Meerbote (1992), pp. 361–72.

Kant, Immanuel. *The Conflict of the Faculties*, trans. M. J. Gregor and R. Anchor, in *Works/Religion and Rational Theology* (1996), pp. 233–327.

Kant, Immanuel. *Correspondence*, trans. and ed. A. Zweig, in *Works* (1999).

Kant, Immanuel. *Critique of the Power of Judgment*, trans. P. Guyer and E. Matthews, ed. P. Guyer, in *Works* (2000).

Kant, Immanuel. *Critique of Practical Reason*, trans. and ed. M. J. Gregor, in *Works/Practical Philosophy* (1996), pp. 133–271.

Kant, Immanuel. *Critique of Pure Reason*, trans. and eds. P. Guyer and A. W. Wood, in *Works* (1998).

Kant, Immanuel. "Einige Bemerkungen zu Ludwig Heinrich Jakobs Prüfung der Mendelssohn'schen *Morgenstunden*", in *Ak*, vol. 8, pp. 149–55.

Kant, Immanuel. *Der einzig mögliche Beweisgrund zu einer Demonstration des Daseins Gottes* [1763], in *Ak*, vol. 2, pp. 65–163.

Kant, Immanuel. *Die falsche Spitzfindigkeit der vier syllogistischen Figuren erwiesen* [1762], in *Ak*, vol. 2, pp. 45–61.

Kant, Immanuel. *The False Subtlety of the Four Syllogistic Figures Demonstrated by M. Immanuel Kant*, in *Works/Theoretical Philosophy 1755–1770*, pp. 85–105.

Kant, Immanuel. *Gedanken von der wahren Schätzung der lebendigen Kräften* [1747], in *Ak*, vol. 1, pp. 1–181.

Kant, Immanuel. *Gesammelte Schriften*, ed. Deutsche Akademie der Wissenschaften zu Berlin. Berlin, 1902–.

Kant, Immanuel. *Groundwork of The Metaphysics of Morals*, trans. and ed. M. J. Gregor, in *Works/Practical Philosophy* (1996), pp. 37–108.

Kant, Immanuel. *Grundlegung zur Metaphysik der Sitten* [1785], in *Ak*, vol. 4, pp. 385–463.
Kant, Immanuel. "Idee zu einer allgemeinen Geschichte in weltbürgerlicher Absicht" [1784], in *Ak*, vol. 8, pp. 15–31.
Kant, Immanuel. *Inquiry concerning the Distinctness of the Principles of Natural Theology and Morality*, in *Works/Theoretical Philosophy, 1755–1770*, pp. 243–86.
Kant, Immanuel. *Jäsche Logik* [1800], in *Ak*, vol. 9, pp. 1–150.
Kant, Immanuel. *Kant on Education*, trans. A. Churton, London, 1899.
Kant, Immanuel. *Kant's Latin Writings: Translations, Commentaries and Notes*, trans. L. W. Beck, et al. New York, NY, 1986.
Kant, Immanuel. *Kritik der praktischen Vernunft* (1788), in *Ak*, vol. 5, pp. 1–163.
Kant, Immanuel. *Kritik der reinen Vernunft* (1781; 2nd edn. 1787), in *Ak*, vols. 3 and 4.
Kant, Immanuel. *Kritik der Urtheilskraft* [1790], in *Ak*, vol. 5.
Kant, Immanuel. *Lectures on Ethics*, trans. P. Heath, eds. P. Heath and J. B. Schneewind, in *Works* (1997).
Kant, Immanuel. *Lectures on Logic*, trans. and ed. J. M. Young, in *Works* (1992).
Kant, Immanuel. *Lectures on Metaphysics*, trans. and eds K. Ameriks and S. Naragon, in *Works* (1997).
Kant, Immanuel. *Lectures on the Philosophical Doctrine of Religion*, trans. A. W. Wood, in *Works/Religion and Rational Theology* (1996), pp. 335–451.
Kant, Immanuel. *Logik Blomberg*, in *Ak*, vol. 24, pp. 7–301.
Kant, Immanuel. "De Medicina corporis, quae philosophorum est" [1786 or 1788], in *Ak*, vol. 15, pp. 939–53.
Kant, Immanuel. "Menschenkunde" (1781/2), in *Vorlesungen über Anthropologie*, in *Ak*, vol. 25.2, pp. 849–1203.
Kant, Immanuel. *Metaphysical Foundations of Natural Science*, trans. M. Friedman, in *Works/Theoretical Philosophy after 1781* (2002), pp. 181–270.
Kant, Immanuel. *The Metaphysics of Morals*, trans. M. J. Gregor, in *Works/Practical Philosophy* (1991), pp. 353–603.
Kant, Immanuel. *Metaphysik der Sitten* (1797–8), in *Ak*, vol. 6.
Kant, Immanuel. *Metaphysische Anfangsgründe der Naturwissenschaft* [1786], in *Ak*, vol. 4, pp. 467–565.
Kant, Immanuel. *De mundi sensibilis atque intelligibilis forma et principiis* (1770), in *Ak* (1770), vol. 2, pp. 385–419.
Kant, Immanuel. "Muthmaßlicher Anfang der Menschengeschichte" [1786], in *Ak*, vol. 8, pp. 107–23.
Kant, Immanuel. *Neuer Lehrbegriff der Bewegung und Ruhe*, in *Ak*, vol. 2, pp. 13–25.
Kant, Immanuel. *A New Elucidation of the First Principles of Metaphysical Cognition*, trans. and eds. D. Walford and R. Meerbote, in *Works/Theoretical Philosophy 1755–1770*, pp. 1–45.
Kant, Immanuel. *Observations on the Feelings of the Beautiful and Sublime*, trans. J. T. Goldthwaite. Berkeley, CA, 1960.
Kant, Immanuel. "Of the Different Human Races", trans. J. M. Mikkelsen, in *The Idea of Race*, eds. R. Bernasconi and T. Lott, Indianapolis, IN, 2000, pp. 8–26.
Kant, Immanuel. *On History*, trans. L. W. Beck. Indianapolis, IN, 1963.
Kant, Immanuel. "On the Common Saying: That May Be Correct in Theory, but It Is of No Use in Practice", trans. and ed. M. J. Gregor, in *Works/Practical Philosophy*, pp. 273— 309.
Kant, Immanuel. *On the Form and Principles of the Sensible and the Intelligible World* [*Inaugural Dissertation*] [1770], in *Works/Theoretical Philosophy 1755–1770*, pp. 373–416.
Kant, Immanuel. *On the Miscarriage of all Philosophical Trials in Theodicy*, trans. G. di Giovanni, in *Works/Religion and Rational Theology* (1996), pp. 19–37.

Kant, Immanuel. "On the Use of Teleological Principles in Philosophy", in *Race*, ed. R. Bernasconi, Malden, MA and Oxford, 2001, pp. 37–56.

Kant, Immanuel. *The Only Possible Argument in Support of a Demonstration of the Existence of God*, in *Works/Theoretical Philosophy 1755–1770*, pp. 107–201.

Kant, Immanuel. *Opus postumum*, in *Ak*, vol. 21–2.

Kant, Immanuel. *Philosophische Religionslehre* [1817], in *Ak*, vol. 28, pp. 993–1126.

Kant, Immanuel. *Practical Philosophy*, trans. and ed. M. J. Gregor, in *Works* (1996).

Kant, Immanuel. *Principiorum primorum cognitionis metaphysica nova dilucidatio* [1755], in *Ak*, vol. 1, pp. 391–410.

Kant, Immanuel. *Prolegomena to Any Future Metaphysics that Will Be Able to Come Forward as Science*, trans. G. Hatfield, in *Works/Theoretical Philosophy after 1781*, eds. H. Allison and P. Heath (2002), pp. 29–169.

Kant, Immanuel. *Prolegomena zu einer jeden künftigen Metaphysik, die als Wissenschaft wird auftreten können* (1783), in *Ak*, vol. 4, pp. 253–383.

Kant, Immanuel. *Recensionen von I. G. Herders Ideen zur Philosophie der Geschichte der Menschheit*, in *Ak*, vol. 8, pp. 43–66.

Kant, Immanuel. *Reflexionen zur Optimismus*, nos. 3703–5, in *Ak*, vol. 17, pp. 229–39.

Kant, Immanuel. *Religion and Rational Theology*, trans. and eds. A. W. Wood and G. di Giovanni, in *Works* (1996).

Kant, Immanuel. *Die Religion innerhalb der Grenzen der bloßen Vernunft* [1793], in *Ak*, vol. 6, pp. 1–202.

Kant, Immanuel. *Religion within the Boundaries of Mere Reason*, trans. G. di Giovanni, in *Works/Religion and Rational Theology* (1996), pp. 39–215.

Kant, Immanuel. *Der Streit der Fakultäten* [1798], in *Ak*, vol. 7, pp. 1–116.

Kant, Immanuel. *Theoretical Philosophy after 1781*, trans. G. Hatfield et al., eds. H. Allison and P. Heath, in *Works* (2002).

Kant, Immanuel. *Theoretical Philosophy, 1755–1770*, trans. and eds D. Walford and R. Meerbote, in *Works* (1992).

Kant, Immanuel. *Toward Perpetual Peace*, trans. M. J. Gregor, in *Works/Practical Philosophy* (1996), pp. 311–51.

Kant, Immanuel. "Über das Miszlingen aller philosophischen Versuche in der Theodicee" (1791), in *Ak*, vol. 8, pp. 255–71.

Kant, Immanuel. "Über den Gebrauch teleologischer Principien in der Philosophie" [1788], in *Ak*, vol. 8, pp. 157–84.

Kant, Immanuel. "Über den Gemeinspruch: Das mag in der Theorie richtig sein, taugt aber nicht für die Praxis", in *Ak*, vol. 8, pp. 273–313.

Kant, Immanuel. *Über Pädagogik*, in *Ak*, vol. 9, pp. 437–99.

Kant, Immanuel. *Universal Natural History and Theory of the Heavens*, trans. and ed. S.L. Jaki, Edinburgh, 1981.

Kant, Immanuel. *Untersuchung über die Deutlichkeit der Grundsätze der natürlichen Theologie und Moral* (1764), in *Ak*, vol. 2, pp. 273–301.

Kant, Immanuel. "Versuch einiger Betrachtungen über den Optimismus" (1759), in *Ak*, vol. 2, pp. 27–35.

Kant, Immanuel. "Versuch über die Krankheiten des Kopfes" [1764], in *Ak*, vol. 2, pp. 257–72.

Kant, Immanuel. "Von dem ersten Grunde des Unterschieds der Gegenden im Raume" [1768], in *Ak*, vol. 2, pp. 375–83.

Kant, Immanuel. "Von den verschiedenen Racen der Menschen" [1775], in *Ak*, vol. 2, pp. 427–443.

Kant, Immanuel. *Vorlesungen über Metaphysik* (1770–80), in *Ak*, vol. 28, pp. i–ii and 29.

Kant, Immanuel. *M. Immanuel Kants Nachricht von der Einrichtung seiner Vorlesungen in dem Winterhalbenjahre von 1765–1766*, in *Ak*, vol. 2, pp. 303–13.

Kant, Immanuel. "Was heisst: Sich im Denken orientiren?" [1786], in *Ak*, vol. 8, pp. 131–47.

Kant, Immanuel. "What Does It Mean to Orient Oneself in Thinking?" in *Works/Religion and Rational Theology*, pp. 1–18.

Kant, Immanuel. *Wiener Logik*, in *Ak*, vol. 24, pp. 787–940.

Kant, Immanuel. *Zum ewigen Frieden* [1795], in *Ak*, vol. 8, pp. 341–86.

Keill, John. *An Examination of Dr. Burnet's Theory of the Earth, Together with Some Remarks on Mr. Whiston's New Theory of the Earth*. Oxford, 1698.

Kenrick, William. *The Whole Duty of Woman*. London, 1753.

King, William. *An Essay on the Origin of Evil*, trans. E. Law. London, 1731, revised edns. 1732, 1739, 1758, 1781.

King, William. *A Great Archbishop of Dublin, William King, D. D., 1650–1729. His Autobiography, Family, and a Selection from His Correspondence*, ed. C. S. King. London, 1906.

King, William. *De origine mali*. Dublin, 1702.

Kippis, Andrew. *Biographia Britannica*, 2nd edn. London, 1780.

Kirwan, Richard. *See (B2)*.

Klein, Ernst Ferdinand. *Freyheit und Eigenthum*. Berlin, 1790.

Knight, William Petty. "An Extract of Two Essays in Political Arithmetick concerning the Comparative Magnitudes, etc. of London and Paris by Sr. William Petty Knight. R. S. S". *Philosophical Transactions of the Royal Society of London* 16 (1686–92).

Knowles, Thomas. *The Existence and Attributes of God not Demonstrable a Priori; in Answer to the Arguments of the Learned Dr. Clarke, and his Followers*. Cambridge, 1746.

Knowles, Thomas. *The Scripture-Doctrine, of the Existence and Attributes of God, As Manifested by the Works of Creation and Providence: In Twelve Sermons, to Which is Prefixed a Preface, In Answer to a Late Pamphlet, Intitled, "Some Thoughts concerning the Argument à Priori"*. Cambridge, 1750.

Knox, Vicesimus. *Liberal Education: or, A Practical Treatise on the Methods of Acquiring Useful and Polite Learning*, 3rd edn. London, 1781.

La Mettrie, Julien Offray de. *Discours sur le bonheur* [1748], ed. J. F. Falvey. Banbury, 1975.

La Mettrie, Julien Offray de. *Histoire naturelle de l'âme*. The Hague, 1745.

La Mettrie, Julien Offray de. *L'homme machine*. Leiden, 1748 [1747]; in *Oeuvres* (Berlin), vol. 1.

La Mettrie, Julien Offray de. *Machine Man and Other Writings*, trans. and ed. A. Thomson. Cambridge, 1996.

La Mettrie, Julien Offray de. *Man a Machine; and, Man a Plant (L'Homme machine; L'Homme plante)* [1748], trans. R. A. Watson and M. Rybalka, ed. J. Leiber. Indianapolis, IN, 1994.

La Mettrie, Julien Offray de. *Oeuvres philosophiques*, 2 vols. Berlin, 1774 (facsim. Hildesheim, 1988); 3 vols., Amsterdam. 1774.

La Mettrie, Julien Offray de. *Traité de l'âme* [1750; previously publ. as *Histoire naturelle de l'âme*], ed. T. Verbeek. Utrecht, 1988.

La Mettrie, Julien Offray de. *Traité de la vie heureuse par Sénèque avec un Discours du traducteur sur le même sujet* [known posthumously as *Discours sur le bonheur*]. Amsterdam, 1748.

La Mothe Le Vayer, François. *Du peu de certitude qu'il y a dans l'histoire* [1668], in *Oeuvres*, 7 in 14 vols. Dresden, 1757, vol. 5.2.

Laclos, Choderlos de. *Les liaisons dangereuses, ou Lettres recueillies dans une société & publiées pour l'instruction de quelques autres*, 4 in 2 vols. Amsterdam, 1782.

Lafitau, Joseph-François. *Moeurs des sauvages ameriquains comparées aux moeurs des premiers temps*. Paris, 1724.

Lafond, Joseph Sigaud de, ed. *Elémens de physique théorique et expérimentale*. 4 vols. Paris, 1777.

Lagrange, Joseph-Louis de. *Mécanique analytique* [1788], in *Oeuvres*, vols. 11–12.

Lagrange, Joseph-Louis de. *Oeuvres*, eds. J.-A. Serret and G. Darboux, 14 vols., 1867–92; facsim. 14 vols. in 10. Hildesheim, 1973.
Lagrange, Joseph-Louis de. "Réflexions sur la résolution algébrique des équations" [1770–1], in *Oeuvres*, vol. 3, pp. 203–421.
Lagrange, Joseph-Louis de. *Théorie des fonctions analytiques*. Paris, 1797; rev. edn. in *Oeuvres*, vol. 5.
Lamarck, Jean Baptiste Pierre Antoine de Monet de. *Flore françois, ou, description succinte [sic] de toutes les plantes qui croissent naturellement en France, disposée selon une nouvelle méthode d'analyse, & à laquelle on a joint la citation de leurs vertus les moins équivoques en médecine, & de leur utilité dans les arts*. Paris, 1788.
Lamarck, Jean Baptiste Pierre Antoine de Monet de. *Histoire naturelle des animaux sans vertèbres*. Paris, 1815–22.
Lamarck, Jean Baptiste Pierre Antoine de Monet de. *Philosophie zoologique, ou Exposition des considérations relative à l'histoire naturelle des animaux*. Paris, 1809.
Lambert, Anne-Thérèse de Marguenat de Courcelles, marquise de. *D'avis d'une mère à sa fille*, in *Oeuvres*, pp. 95–150.
Lambert, Anne-Thérèse de Marguenat de Courcelles, marquise de. *Avis d'une mère à son fils*, in *Oeuvres*, pp. 43–150.
Lambert, Anne-Thérèse de Marguenat de Courcelles, marquise de. *Oeuvres*, ed. R. Granderoute. Paris, 1990.
Lambert, Anne-Thérèse de Marguenat de Courcelles, marquise de. "Réflexions nouvelles sur les femmes", in *Oeuvres*, pp. 213–37.
Lambert, Johann Heinrich. "Abhandlung vom Criterium veritatis", ed. K. Bopp *Kantstudien* Ergänzungsheft 36 (1915).
Lambert, Johann Heinrich. *Anlage zur Architectonik, oder Theorie des Einfachen und des Ersten in der philosophischen und mathematischen Erkenntni*, 2 vols. Riga, 1771; facsim. in *Philossophische Schriften*, ed. H. W. Arndt, 10 vols. Hildesheim, 1965, vol. 3.
Lambert, Johann Heinrich. *Cosmological Letters on the Arrangement of the World-Edifice*, trans. S. L. Jaki. Edinburgh, 1976.
Lambert, Johann Heinrich. *Kosmologische Briefe über die Einrichtung des Weltbaues*. Augsburg, 1761.
Lambert, Johann Heinrich. *Neues Organon, oder Gedanken über die Erforschung und Bezeichnung des Wahren und dessen Unterscheidung vom Irrtum und Schein*, 2 vols. Leipzig, 1764; repr. Berlin, 1990.
Lambert, Johann Heinrich. "Theorie der Parallellinien", in F. Engel and P. Stäckel, *Die Theorie der Parallellinien von Euklid bis auf Gauss*, Leipzig, 1895, pp. 152–207.
Lambert, Johann Heinrich. "Über die Methode die Metaphysik, Theologie und Moral richtiger zu beweisen". *Kantstudien* Ergänzungsheft 42 (1918).
Lamy, Bernard. *La rhétorique, ou l'art de parler*, 4th edn. Amsterdam, 1699.
Lamy, Guillaume. *Discours anatomiques*, Paris, 1675, new ed. by A. M. Belgrado, Oxford and Paris, 1996.
Laplace, Pierre Simon, marquis de. *Exposition du systême du monde*, 2nd edn. Paris, 1796.
Laplace, Pierre Simon, marquis de. *Mémoire sur la chaleur. See* Lavoisier and Laplace.
Laplace, Pierre Simon, marquis de. *Oeuvres complètes*, 14 vols. Paris, 1878–1912.
Laplace, Pierre Simon, marquis de. *Philosophical Essay on Probabilities*, trans. F. W. Truscott and F. L. Emory. New York, NY, 1951.
Lavoisier, Antoine. *Méthode de nomenclature chimique*. Paris, 1787.
Lavoisier, Antoine. *Traité élémentaire de chimie*, 2 vols. Paris, 1789; facsim. Brussels, 1965.
Lavoisier, Antoine, and Pierre Simon marquis de Laplace. *Mémoire sur la chaleur* [1780]. Paris, 1920.

Law, Edmund. *Considerations on the State of the World with Regard to the Theory of Religion*. Cambridge, 1745.

Law, Edmund. *A Defence of Mr. Locke's Opinion concerning Personal Identity*. Cambridge, 1769.

Law, Edmund. *An Enquiry into the Ideas of Space, Time, Immensity, and Eternity*. Cambridge, 1734.

Law, William. *The Case of Reason, or Natural Religion, Fairly and Fully Stated, in Answer to a Book Entitled Christianity as Old as the Creation*. London, 1731.

Le Cat, Claude Nicolas. *Traité de la couleur de la peau humaine en général et de celle des nègres en particulier, et de la métamorphose d'une de ces couleurs en l'autre, soit de naissance, soit accidentellement*. Amsterdam, 1765.

Le Clerc, Jean. Rev. of Sextus Empiricus. *Bibliothèque ancienne et moderne* 14 (1720): 1–113.

Le Clerc, Jean. Rev. of Huet's *Traité*. *Bibliothèque ancienne et moderne* 18 (1722): 455–65.

[Le Mercier de la Rivière, P. P. F. J. H.]. *De l'instruction publique; ou Considérations morales et politiques sur la nécessité, la nature et la source de cette instruction*. Stockholm, 1775.

Lee, Henry. *Anti-Scepticism: or, Notes Upon each Chapter of Mr. Lock's Essay Concerning Humane Understanding, With an Explication of all the Particulars of which he Treats, and in the same Order*. London, 1702.

Leechman, William. "The Preface, giving some Account of the Life, Writings, and Character of the Author", in F. Hutcheson, *A System of Moral Philosophy* (1755).

Leibniz, Gottfried Wilhelm. *Annotatiunculae subitaneae ad Tolandi librum de Christianismo Mysteriis carente* [8 August 1701], in *Opera omnia*, vol. 5.

Leibniz, Gottfried Wilhelm. *Briefwechsel zwischen Leibniz und Christian Wolff*, ed. C. I. Gerhardt. Halle, 1860.

[Leibniz, Gottfried Wilhelm, and Clarke, Samuel]. *A Collection of Papers, which passed between the Late Learned Mr. Leibnitz and Dr. Clarke in the Years 1715 and 1716: Relating to the Principles of Natural Philosophy and Religion*. London, 1717.

Leibniz, Gottfried Wilhelm. *Commentatiuncula de judice controversiarum* [c. 1669–70], in *Sämtliche Schriften*, Reihe 6, vol. 1.

Leibniz, Gottfried Wilhelm. *Defensio trinitatis contra Wissowatium* [c. 1669], in *Sämtliche Schriften*, Reihe 6, vol. 1.

Leibniz, Gottfried Wilhelm. "Denkschrift über den Zweck und Nutzen einer zu gründenden Sozietät der Wissenschaften zu Berlin", in *Politische Schriften*, vol. 2.

Leibniz, Gottfried Wilhelm. *Dialogus inter theologum et misosophum* [c. 1678–9], in *Sämtliche Schriften*, Reihe 6, vol. 4.

Leibniz, Gottfried Wilhelm. *Discours de métaphysique*, in *Phil. Schriften*, vol. 4.

Leibniz, Gottfried Wilhelm. *Discours de métaphysique et Correspondence avec Arnauld*, ed. G. Le Roy. Paris, 1970.

Leibniz, Gottfried Wilhelm. *Discourse on Metaphysics and Related Writings*, trans. and eds. R. N. D. Martin and S. Brown. Manchester, 1988.

Leibniz, Gottfried Wilhelm. *Elementa juris naturalis* [c. 1670–1671)], in *Sämtliche Schriften*, Reihe 6, vol. 2.

Leibniz, Gottfried Wilhelm. "Epistola ad Wagnerum, De Vi activa Corporis, de Animâ, de Animâ Brutorum", in *Opera Omnia*, vol. 2.

Leibniz, Gottfried Wilhelm. *Essais de théodicée sur la bonté de Dieu, la liberté de l'homme et l'origine du mal* [1710], in *Phil. Schriften*, vol. 6.

Leibniz, Gottfried Wilhelm. *Jugement sur les Oeuvres de M. le comte de Shaftsbury*, in *Opera omnia*, vol. 5.

Leibniz, Gottfried Wilhelm. *Lehr-Sätze über die Monadologie*, trans. H. Köhler, Frankfurt a.d. O., Leipzig, Jena, 1720.

Leibniz, Gottfried Wilhelm. *The Leibniz–Arnauld Correspondence*, trans. and ed. H. T. Mason. Manchester, 1967.
Leibniz, Gottfried Wilhelm. *The Leibniz–Clarke Correspondence, together with Extracts from Newton's "Principia" and "Opticks"*, ed. H. G. Alexander. Manchester, 1956.
Leibniz, Gottfried Wilhelm. *Meditationes de cognitione, veritate et ideis* [1684], in *Sämtliche Schriften*, Reihe 4, vol. 4.
Leibniz, Gottfried Wilhelm. *Monadologie* [1714, publ. 1840], ed. H. Herring. Hamburg, 1956; ed. É. Boutroux, Paris, 1970.
Leibniz, Gottfried Wilhelm. *Monadology*, in *Philosophical Papers and Letters*, trans. and ed. L. E. Loemker, 2 vols., Chicago, IL, 1956; 2nd edn. in 1 vol., Dordrecht, 1970.
Leibniz, Gottfried Wilhelm. *Monita quaedam ad Samuelis Pufendorfii Principia* (1789), in *Opera omnia*, vol. 4.
Leibniz, Gottfried Wilhelm. *New Essays on Human Understanding*, trans. and eds. P. Remnant and J. Bennett. Cambridge, 1981.
Leibniz, Gottfried Wilhelm. *De non violando principio contradictionis in Divinis contra Honoratum Fabri* [c. 1685], in *Sämtliche Schriften*, Reihe 6, vol. 4.
Leibniz, Gottfried Wilhelm. *Nouveaux essais sur l'entendement humain* [1765], eds. A. Robinet and H. Schepers, in *Sämtl. Schriften*, Reihe 6, vol. 6.
Leibniz, Gottfried Wilhelm. *Novissima Sinica* [1697], in *Writings on China*.
Leibniz, Gottfried Wilhelm. "Observations on the Book concerning 'The Origin of Evil'", in *Theodicy: Essays*, pp. 405–32.
Leibniz, Gottfried Wilhelm. *On Nature Itself, or On the Inherent Force and Actions of Created Things* [1698], trans. and ed. L. Loemker, in *Philosophical Papers* (1969), pp. 498–508.
Leibniz, Gottfried Wilhelm. *Opera omnia: Nunc primum collecta, in classes distributa*, ed. L. Dutens, 6 vols. Geneva, 1768 (facsim. Hildesheim, 1989); 1789.
Leibniz, Gottfried Wilhelm. "Opinion on the Principles of Pufendorf", in *Political Writings*.
Leibniz, Gottfried Wilhelm. *Opuscules et fragments inédits de Leibniz, extraits des manuscrits de la Bibliothèque royale de Hanovre*, ed. L. Couturat. Paris, 1903.
Leibniz, Gottfried Wilhelm. *Philosophical Essays*, trans. and eds. R. Ariew and D. Garber. Indianapolis, IN, 1989.
Leibniz, Gottfried Wilhelm. *Philosophical Papers and Letters*, trans. and ed. L. E. Loemker, 2 vols. Chicago, IL, 1956; 2nd edn. in 1 vol., Dordrecht, 1969.
Leibniz, Gottfried Wilhelm. *Philosophical Writings*, ed. G. H. R. Parkinson. London, 1973.
Leibniz, Gottfried Wilhelm. *Philosophische Abhandlungen*, in *Phil. Schriften*, vol. 6, pp. 607–23.
Leibniz, Gottfried Wilhelm. *Die philosophischen Schriften*, ed. C. I. Gerhardt, 7 vols. Berlin, 1875–90.
Leibniz, Gottfried Wilhelm. *Political Writings*, 2nd edn., trans. and ed. P. Riley. Cambridge, 1988.
Leibniz, Gottfried Wilhelm. *Politische Schriften*, ed. H. H. Holz, 2 vols. Frankfurt am Main, 1966–7.
Leibniz, Gottfried Wilhelm. *Principes de la nature et de la grace fondés en raison*. Paris, 1714; in *Phil. Schriften*, vol. 6.
Leibniz, Gottfried Wilhelm. *Principes de la nature et de la grace fondés en raison et Principes de la philosophie ou Monadologie*, ed. A. Robinet. Paris, 1954.
Leibniz, Gottfried Wilhelm. *The Principles of Nature and of Grace, Based on Reason* [1714], in *Selections*, ed. P. Wiener. New York, NY, 1951.
Leibniz, Gottfried Wilhelm. *The Principles of Philosophy, or, the Monadology*, in *Philosophical Essays*, pp. 213–25.

Leibniz, Gottfried Wilhelm. "Prospectus" (of the later *Protogaea*) [1693], in *Histoire de l'Académie Royale des Sciences, Année MDCCVI* . . . Paris, 1707, pp. 10–11.

Leibniz, Gottfried Wilhelm. *Protogaea: De l'aspect primitif de la terre et des traces d'une histoire très ancienne que renferment les monuments mêmes de la nature* (Latin and French text), trans. B. de Saint-Germain, ed. J.-M. Barrande. Toulouse, 1993.

Leibniz, Gottfried Wilhelm. "Raisons que M. Jaquelot m'a envoyées pour justifier l'argument contesté de des-Cartes qui doit prouver l'existence de Dieu, avec mes reponses" [20 November 1702], in *Phil. Schriften*, vol. 3, pp. 443–7.

Leibniz, Gottfried Wilhelm. *Rechtsphilosophisches aus Leibnizens ungedruckten Schriften*, ed. G. Mollat. Leipzig, 1885.

Leibniz, Gottfried Wilhelm. "Remarques sur la lettre de M. Arnauld", in *Phil. Schriften*, vol. 2, pp. 37–47.

Leibniz, Gottfried Wilhelm. "Remarques sur le Livre de l'origine du mal, publié depuis peu en Angleterre", in *Phil. Schriften*, vol. 6, pp. 400–36.

Leibniz, Gottfried Wilhelm. "Remarques sur le livre d'un antrinitaire anglois", in Maria Rosa Antognazza, "Inediti leibniziani sulle polemiche trinitarie", *Rivista di Filosofia neo-scolastica* 83/4 (1991): 525–550.

Leibniz, Gottfried Wilhelm. *De rerum originatione radicali* [1697], in *Phil. Schriften*, vol. 7.

Leibniz, Gottfried Wilhelm. *Sämtliche Schriften und Briefe*, ed. der Deutschen Akademie der Wissenschaften zu Berlin. Berlin, 1923–.

Leibniz, Gottfried Wilhelm. *Specimen inventorum de admirandis naturae Generalis arcanis*, in *Phil. Schriften*, vol. 7.

Leibniz, Gottfried Wilhelm. *Textes inédits d'après les manuscrits de la bibliothèque provinciale de Hanovre*, ed. G. Grua, 2 vols. Paris, 1948.

Leibniz, Gottfried Wilhelm. *Theodicy: Essays on the Goodness of God, the Freedom of Man and the Origin of Evil*, trans. E. M. Huggard, ed. A. Farrer. London, 1951; La Salle, IL, 1985.

Leibniz, Gottfried Wilhelm. *Writings on China*, trans. D. J. Cook and J. Henry Rosemont. Chicago and La Salle, IL, 1994.

Leland, John. *The Advantage and Necessity of the Christian Revelation shewn from the State of Religion in the Ancient Heathen World: especially with respect to the Knowledge and Worship of the one true God: a Rule of Moral Duty: and a State of Future Rewards and Punishments*, 2 vols. London, 1764.

Leland, John. *A View of the Principal Deistical Writers that have Appeared in England in the last and present Century*, 2 vols. and suppl., London, 1754–6 (vol. 1, 2nd edn., 1755); 3rd edn., 2 vols., 1757.

Leslie, Charles. *A Short and Easie Method with the Deists*. London, 1698.

Lessing, Gotthold Ephraim. *Des Andreas Wissowatius Einwürfe wider die Dreieinigkeit*, in *Werke*, vol. 7: *Theologiekritische Schriften I und II*.

Lessing, Gotthold Ephraim. *Die Erziehung des Menschengeschlechts*. Berlin, 1780; in *Sämtliche Schriften*, vol. 13, pp. 413–36; in *Werke* (eds. Eibl and Göpfert), vol. 8, pp. 489–510.

Lessing, Gotthold Ephraim. *Laokoön, order, Über die Grenzen der Mahlerey und Poesie*. Berlin, 1766.

Lessing, Gotthold Ephraim. *Laocoön: An Essay on the Limits of Painting and Poetry*, trans. E. A. McCormick. Indianapolis, IN, 1962.

Lessing, Gotthold Ephraim. *Lessing's Education of the Human Race*, trans. J. D. Haney. New York, NY, 1908.

Lessing, Gotthold Ephraim. *Nathan der Weise*, in *Werke* (ed. Balser), vol. 2, pp. 5–158.

Lessing, Gotthold Ephraim. *Sämtliche Schriften*, eds. K. Lachmann and F. Muncker, 23 vols. Leipzig, 1886–1924.

Lessing, Gotthold Ephraim. *Theologiekritische Schriften I und II* (1976), in *Werke* (eds. Eibl and Göpfert), vol. 7.

Lessing, Gotthold Ephraim. *Theologiekritische Schriften III; Philosophische Schriften* (1979), in *Werke* (eds. Eibl and Göpfert), vol. 8.

Lessing, Gotthold Ephraim. *Über den Beweis des Geistes und der Kraft*. Braunschweig, 1777; in *Werke* (eds. Eibl and Göpfert), vol. 8.

Lessing, Gotthold Ephraim. *Über die Entstehung der geoffenbarten Religion*, in *Werke* (eds. Eibl and Göpfert), vol. 7.

Lessing, Gotthold Ephraim. *Werke*, eds. K. Eibl and H. G. Göpfert, 8 vols. Munich, 1970–9.

Lessing, Gotthold Ephraim. *Werke*, 7th edn., ed. K. Balser, 5 vols. Berlin, 1975.

Leyser, Polycarp [IV]. *Apparatus literarius singularia nova anecdota rariora ex omnis generis eruditione depromens studio Societatis Colligentium*. Wittenberg, 1717.

l'Herminier, Nicolas. *Summa theologiae*, 8 vols. Paris, 1718–19.

Linnaeus. *See* Linné.

Linné, Carl von. *Oratio de telluris habitabilis incremento*. Leiden, 1744.

Linné, Carl von. *Praelectiones in ordines naturales plantarum*, eds. J. C. Fabricius and P. D. Giseke. Hamburg, 1792.

Linné, Carl von. *Systema naturae, sive, regna tria naturae systematice proposita per classes, ordines, genera, & species*. Leiden, 1735; 10th edn., 1758.

Locke, John. *The Clarendon Edition of the Works of John Locke*, ed. P. H. Nidditch. Oxford, 1975–.

Locke, John. *The Correspondence of John Locke*, ed. E. S. De Beer, in *The Clarendon Edition* (1976–).

Locke, John. *Discourse on Miracles*, in *Writings on Religion*, ed. V. Nuovo (2002).

Locke, John. *The Educational Writings*, ed. J. L. Axtell. Cambridge, 1968.

Locke, John. *Epistola de Tolerantia – A Letter on Toleration*, trans. J. W. Gough, ed. R. Klibansky. Oxford, 1968.

Locke, John. *An Essay Concerning Human Understanding*, ed. P. H. Nidditch, in *The Clarendon Edition* (1975).

Locke, John. *Essays on the Law of Nature* [written in 1663], trans. and ed. W. von Leyden. Oxford, 1954.

Locke, John. *An Examination of P. Malebranche's Opinion of Seeing All Things in God*, in *Posthumous Works of Mr. John Locke*, London, 1706, pp. 141–213; in *Works* (1810), vol. 9, pp. 209–55.

Locke, John. *Herrn Johann Locks Unterricht von Erziehung der Kinder, aus dem Englischen: nebst Herrn von Fénelon . . . Gedancken von Erziehung der Töchter, aus dem Frantzösischen übersetzet*, trans. G. Olearius. Leipzig, 1708.

Locke, John. *Letter concerning Toleration* [1689], trans. W. Popple, ed. M. Montuori. The Hague, 1963.

Locke, John. "Of Ethick in General", in Peter King, *The Life of John Locke* (see *B2*).

Locke, John. *Of the Conduct of the Understanding*. London, 1706.

Locke, John. *The Reasonableness of Christianity as delivered in the Scriptures* [1695], in *Works* (1801), vol. 7, pp. 1–158; ed. J. C. Higgins-Biddle, in the *Clarendon Edition* (1999).

Locke, John. *Some Thoughts Concerning Education* [1693], eds. J. W. Yolton and J. S. Yolton, in *The Clarendon Edition* (1989).

Locke, John. *Two Treatises of Government* [1690], ed. P. Laslett. Cambridge, 1967.

Locke, John. *A Vindication of the Reasonableness of Christianity*. London, 1695.

Locke, John. *Works*, 10 vols. London, 1810; 1823 (facsim. Aalen, 1963).

Locke, John. *Works*, 10th edn., 10 vols. London, 1801.

Locke, John. *Writings on Religion*, ed. V. Nuovo. Oxford, 2002.

Logan, John. *Elements of the Philosophy of History*. Edinburgh, 1781; facsim. Bristol, 1995.

[Long, James]. *An Enquiry into the Origin of the Human Appetites and Affections* [1747], facsim., in *Four Early Works on Motivation*, ed. P. McReynolds. Gainesville, FL, 1969.

Longin (Cassius Longinus) (attributed). *Traité du sublime* (1st century AD), trans. N. Boileau-Despréaux. Paris, 1674.

Lowman, Moses. *An Argument to Prove the Unity and Perfections of God a Priori*. London, 1735.

Lucian. [*Works*], 8 vols. Cambridge, MA, 1913–67.

Ludovici, Carl Günther. *Dissertatio de ratione philosophandi in genere*. Leipzig, 1730.

Lyttelton, George. *Observations on the Conversion and Apostleship of St. Paul, in a Letter to Gilbert West, Esq*. London, 1747.

Mably, Gabriel Bonnot de. *De la législation ou principes des lois*, in *Collection complète des oeuvres*, 15 vols. Paris, 1794–5, vol. 9, pp. 385–423; facsim., ed. G. Arnaud, Aalen, 1977.

Macaulay (Graham), Catharine. *Letters on Education with Observations on Religious and Metaphysical Subjects*. London, 1790; repr. London, 1996.

Machiavelli, Nicolo. *The Prince* [1532], trans. G. Bull. Harmondsworth, 1981.

Mackenzie, Henry. *Notebooks 1763–1827*, in *Literature and Literati. The Literary Correspondence and Notebooks of Henry Mackenzie*, ed. H. W. Drescher, 2 vols. Frankfurt am Main, 1989 and 1999, vol. 2.

Mackintosh, James. *Dissertation on the Progress of Ethical Philosophy, chiefly during the Seventeenth and Eighteenth Centuries* [1830], 2nd edn. Edinburgh, 1837.

Maclaurin, Colin. *An Account of Sir Isaac Newton's Philosophical Discoveries*. London, 1748.

Maclaurin, Colin. *A Treatise of Fluxions*. Edinburgh, 1742.

[Madelaine, L. Philipon de la]. *Vues patriotiques sur l'éducation du peuple, Tant des villes que de la campagnes, Avec beaucoup de notes interessantes*. Lyon, 1783.

Madison, James. *Declaration of Rights and Form of Government of Virginia*, in *Papers*, vol. 1.

Madison, James. "Memorial and Remonstrance against Religious Assessments", in *Papers*, vol. 8, pp. 298–304.

Madison, James. *Papers*, eds. W. T. Hutchinson and W. M. E. Rachal, 17 vols. Chicago, IL, 1962–91.

Maillet, Benoît de. *Telliamed or Conversations Between an Indian Philosopher and a French Missionary on the Diminution of the Sea*, trans. and ed. A. V. Carozzi. Urbana, IL, 1968.

Maillet, Benoît de. *Telliamed, ou Entretiens d'un philosophe indien avec un missionaire françois sur la diminution de la mer*. [Amsterdam], [1748].

Maimon, Salomon. *Lebensgeschichte*, ed. J. Fromer. Munich, 1911.

Maimon, Salomon. "Über die ersten Gründe des Naturrechts" [1795], in *Gesammelte Werke*, ed. V. Verra, 7 vols. Hildesheim, 1965–76, vol. 6.

Malebranche, Nicolas. *Discourse on Metaphysics* [1688], trans. W. Doney. New York, NY, 1980.

Malebranche, Nicolas. *Entretiens sur la métaphysique et sur la religion*. Rotterdam, 1688.

Malebranche, Nicolas. *Oeuvres*, ed. G. Rodis-Lewis, 2 vols. Paris, 1979.

Malebranche, Nicolas. *Oeuvres complètes*, ed. A. Robinet, 22 vols. Paris, 1958–84.

Malebranche, Nicolas. *De la recherche de la vérité* [1674–5], ed. G. Rodis-Lewis, in *Oeuvres compl.*, vols. 1–3 (1962).

Malebranche, Nicolas. *The Search after Truth*, trans. T. M. Lennon and P. J. Olscamp. Columbus, OH, 1980.

Malthus, Thomas Robert. *An Essay on the Principle of Population as It Affects the Future Improvement of Society: With Remarks on the Speculations of Mr. Godwin, M. Condorcet, and Other Writers*. London, 1798; 1803.

Malynes, Gerald De. *A Treatise of the Canker of Englands Common Wealth*. London, 1601; facsim., Amsterdam, 1977.

Mandeville, Bernard. *Aesop Dress'd: or A Collection of Fables Writ in Familiar Verse*. London, 1704.

Mandeville, Bernard. *By a Society of Ladies: Essays in The Female Tatler* [1709–10], ed. M. M. Goldsmith. Bristol, 1999.

Mandeville, Bernard. *An Enquiry into the Causes of the Frequent Executions at Tyburn*. London, 1725.
Mandeville, Bernard. *An Enquiry into the Origin of Honour, and the Usefulness of Christianity in War*. London, 1732; facsim. London, 1971.
Mandeville, Bernard. *The Fable of the Bees: or, Private Vices, Publick Benefits* [1714], 2nd edn. London, 1723; 6th edn. London, 1732; ed. F. B. Kaye, 2 vols., Oxford, 1924; facsim. Indianapolis, IN, 1988.
Mandeville, Bernard. *Free Thoughts on Religion, the Church, and National Happiness*. London, 1720; 1729 (facsim. Stuttgart and Bad Cannstatt, 1969).
[Mandeville, Bernard]. *A Modest Defence of Publick Stews: or, An Essay Upon Whoring as it is now Practis'd in These Kingdoms* [1724], ed. R. I. Cook. Los Angeles, CA, 1973.
Mandeville, Bernard. *The Virgin Unmask'd: or Female Dialogues Betwixt an Elderly Maiden Lady and her Niece on Several Diverting Discourses on Love Marriage, Memoirs and Morals of the Times*. London, 1709.
Marais, Matthieu. *Journal et Mémoires*, ed. M. de Lescure, 4 vols. Paris, 1863–8.
Marchand, Prosper. *See* Argens, Jean Baptiste de Boyer, marquis d'.
Marsden, William. *History of Sumatra*. London, 1783.
Mather, Cotton. *The Christian Philosopher*. London, 1721.
Mather, Cotton. *Manuductio ad Ministerium: Directions for a Candidate of the Ministry*. Boston, MA, 1726.
Mather, Cotton. *Ornaments for the Daughters of Zion. Or, The Character and Happiness of a Vertuous Woman*. Cambridge, MA, 1691.
Maupertuis, Pierre-Louis Moreau de. *Discours sur les différentes figures des astres* [1742], in *Oeuvres*, vol. 1.
Maupertuis, Pierre-Louis Moreau de. *Dissertation physique à l'occasion du nègre blanc*. Leiden, 1744.
Maupertuis, Pierre-Louis Moreau de. *Essai de cosmologie* [1750], in *Oeuvres*, vol. 1.
Maupertuis, Pierre-Louis Moreau de. *Essai de philosophie morale* [1749], in *Oeuvres*, vol. 1.
Maupertuis, Pierre-Louis Moreau de. *Oeuvres*. Lyon, 1768; Berlin, 1758 (facsim., ed. G. Tonelli, Hildesheim, 1965–74).
Maupertuis, Pierre-Louis Moreau de. *Réflexions philosophiques sur l'origine des langues, et la signification des mots*. Paris, 1748.
Maupertuis, Pierre-Louis Moreau de. *Système de la nature*. Berlin, 1754.
Maupertuis, Pierre-Louis Moreau de. *Vénus physique*. The Hague, 1745.
Maxwell, John. *Discourse concerning God; Wherein the Meaning of His Name, His Providence, the Nature and Measure of His Dominion are consider'd. To which is subjoined a translation of Sir Isaac Newton's General Scholium*. London, 1715.
[Mayne, Zachary]. *Essay on Consciousness*. *See* Anonymous *Two Dissertations concerning Sense*.
Meier, Georg Friedrich. *Anfangsgründe aller schönen Wissenschaften*, 3 vols. Halle, 1754–9; facsim. Hildesheim, 1976.
Meier, Georg Friedrich. *Auszug aus der Vernunftlehre*. Halle, 1752.
Meier, Georg Friedrich. *Vernunftlehre* [1752]. Halle, 1762.
Meier, Georg Friedrich. *Versuch einer allgemeinen Auslegungskunst*. Halle, 1757; Düsseldorf, 1965.
Meiners, Christoph. *Grundriss der Geschichte der Menschheit*. Lemgo, 1785.
Meiners, Christoph. *Untersuchungen über die Verschiedenheiten der Menschennaturen*, 3 vols. Tübingen, 1811–15.
Mémoires de Trévoux. *See* Anonymous, *Mémoires pour l'histoire des sciences et des beaux-arts*.
Mendelssohn, Moses. Rev. of Edmund Burke's *A Philosophical Enquiry into the Origin of our Ideas of the Sublime and Beautiful*, in *Bibliothek der schönen Wissenschaften und der freyen Künste* II.2 (1759): 290–1. 2nd edn., 1762.

Mendelssohn, Moses. *Anmerkungen zu Abbts freundschaftlicher Correspondenz* [1782], in *Gesammelte Schriften*, vol. 6.1, pp. 27–65.

Mendelssohn, Moses. "Betrachtung über die Ungleichheit und Geselligkeit der Menschen", in *Gesammelte Schriften*, vol. 2, pp. 133–40.

Mendelssohn, Moses. *Bibliothek der schönen Wissenschaften. See Serials.*

Mendelsohn, Moses. "Die Bildsäule", in *Schriften zur Philosophie, Aesthetik und Apologetik*, ed. M. Brasch, 2 vols. Leipzig, 1880, pp. 231–46.

Mendelssohn, Moses. *Briefe über die Empfindungen* (Berlin, 1755).

Mendelssohn, Moses. *An die Freunde Lessings: Ein Anhang zu Herrn Jacobi, Briefwechsel über die Lehre des Spinoza* [1786], in *Gesammelte Schriften*, vol. 3.2, ed. L. Strauss (1974), pp. 179–218.

Mendelssohn, Moses. "Gedanken von der Wahrscheinleichkeit", in *Vermischte Abhandlungen und Urtheile über das Neueste aus Gelehrsamkeit* (Berlin, 1756): 3–26. Republished as "Ueber die Wahrscheinleichkeit".

Mendelssohn, Moses. *Gesammelte Schriften: Jubiläumsausgabe*, eds. F. Bamberger and A. Altmann. Stuttgart and Bad Cannstatt, 1971–.

Mendelssohn, Moses. *Jerusalem oder über religiöse Macht und Judentum* (1783), in *Gesammelte Schriften*, vol. 8: *Schriften zum Judentum II*, pp. 99–204.

Mendelssohn, Moses. *Morgenstunden* [Berlin, 1785], ed. L. Strauss, in *Gesammelte Schriften*, vol. 3.2 (1974), pp. 1–175.

Mendelssohn, Moses. *Orakel, die Bestimmung des Menschen betreffend* [1763], in *Gesammelte Schriften*, vol. 6.1 (1981).

Mendelssohn, Moses. *Phaedon oder über die Unsterblichkeit der Seele* [1767]. Hamburg, 1979; in *Gesammelte Schriften*, vol. 2, pp. 5–128.

Mendelssohn, Moses. *Philosophical Writings*, trans. and ed. D. Dahlstrom. Cambridge, 1997.

Mendelssohn, Moses. *Philosophische Gespräche*, ed. F. Bamberger, in *Gesammelte Schriften*, vol. 1 (1971).

Mendelssohn, Moses. *Philosophische Schriften*. Berlin, 1761; 2nd edn., Berlin, 1771; in *Gesammelte Schriften*, vol. 1 (1971).

Mendelssohn, Moses. "Pope ein Metaphysiker!" [Danzig, 1755], in *Gesammelte Schriften*, vol. 2, eds. F. Bamberger and L. Strauss (1972).

Mendelssohn, Moses. Preface [1782] to Menasseh Ben Israel, *Rettung der Juden*, in *Schriften zum Judentum, II*, in *Gesammelte Schriften*, vol. 8, pp. 3–25.

Mendelssohn, Moses. *Schriften zur Philosophie, Aesthetik und Apologetik*, ed. M. Brasch, 2 vols. Leipzig, 1880; facsim. Hildesheim, 1968.

Mendelssohn, Moses. "Sendschreiben an Lessing, 2. Jenner 1756", in *Gesammelte Schriften*, vol. 2, pp. 83–96.

Mendelssohn, Moses. *Ueber das Erhabene und Naive in den schönen Wissenschaften*, in *Schriften zur Philosophie, Aesthetik und Apologetik*, vol. 2.

Mendelssohn, Moses. "Ueber die Frage: was heiszt aufklären?" [1784], in *Gesammelte Schriften*, vol. 6.1, pp. 113–19.

Mendelssohn, Moses. "Ueber die Wahrscheinlichkeit" in Mendelssohn, *Philosophische Schriften* (Berlin, 1761); translated as "On Probability", in Mendelssohn, *Philosophical Writings*, pp. 233–50.

Mendelssohn, Moses. "Zu Rousseaus *Discours sur l'origine et les fondements de l'inégalité parmi les hommes*", in *Gesammelte Schriften*, vol. 2, eds. F. Bamberger and L. Strauss (1972).

Merian, Johann Bernhard. *Mémoire sur l'apperception de sa propre existence*, in *Histoire de l'Académie Royale des Sciences et Belles Lettres (Année 1749)*. Berlin, 1751.

Merian, Johann Bernhard. "Sur le Phénoménisme de David Hume," in *Mémoires de l'Académie royale des sciences et belles-lettres depuis l'avénement de Fréderic Guillaume II au thrône*, Berlin, 1792–3, pp. 417–37.

Merian, Johann Bernhard. "Ueber die Apperzeption seiner eignen Existenz". *Magazin für die Philosophie und ihre Geschichte*, ed. M. Hissmann, 1 (1778): 89–132.

Meslier, Jean. *Mémoire des pensées et des sentiments*, in *Oeuvres complètes*, vol. 1.

Meslier, Jean. *Oeuvres complètes*, eds. J. Deprun, R. Desné and A. Soboul, 3 vols. Paris, 1970–2.

Meslier, Jean. *Testament*, in *Oeuvres*, vol. 2, pp. 149–525.

Michaëlis, Johann David. *A Dissertation on the Influence of Opinions on Language and of Language on Opinions*. London, 1769.

Middleton, Conyers. *A Free Enquiry into the Miraculous Powers, which are Supposed to have Subsisted in the Christian Church, from the earliest Ages through several successive Centuries*. London, 1749.

Millar, John. *The Origin of the Distinction of Ranks; or An Inquiry into the Circumstances which give rise to Influence and Authority, in the Different Members of Society*. Edinburgh, 1771, 3rd edn. London, 1781.

Mirabeau, Honoré Gabriel Riquetti comte de. *Aux Bataves sur le Stathoudérat*. [Amsterdam], 1788.

Mirabeau, Honoré Gabriel Riquetti comte de. *De la monarchie prussienne sous Frédéric le Grand*, 7 vols. London, 1788.

Mirabeau, Victor de Riquetti, marquis de. *Philosophie rurale*. *See* Quesnay.

Mole, Thomas. *The Foundation of Moral Virtue Consider'd*. London, 1732.

Mole, Thomas. *The Foundation of Moral Virtue Re-Consider'd*. London, 1733.

Monboddo, *See* Burnett.

Montaigne, Michel de. *The Complete Essays* (1580–8), trans. M. A. Screech, London, 1991.

Montesquieu, Charles de Secondat de. *Considerations on the Causes of the Greatness of the Romans and Their Decline*, trans. D. Lowenthal. Ithaca, NY, 1968.

Montesquieu, Charles de Secondat de. *Considérations sur les causes de la grandeur des Romains et de leur décadence*. Amsterdam, 1734; in *Oeuvres*, vol. 2.

Montesquieu, Charles de Secondat de. *De L'esprit des lois*. Paris, 1748; rev. edn. Paris, 1757; in *Oeuvres*, vol. 2.

Montesquieu, Charles de Secondat de. *Essai sur les causes qui peuvent affecter les esprits et les caractères*, in *Oeuvres*, vol. 2, pp. 39–68.

Montesquieu, Charles de Secondat de. "An Essay on the Causes that May Affect Men's Minds and Characters", trans. M. Richter. *Political Theory* 4.2 (1976): 139–62.

Montesquieu, Charles de Secondat de. *Lettres persanes*, 2 vols. Amsterdam, 1721; also in *Oeuvres*, vol. 1.

Montesquieu, Charles de Secondat de. *Oeuvres complètes*, ed. R. Caillois, 2 vols. Paris, 1949–51.

Montesquieu, Charles de Secondat de. *Persian Letters* [1721], trans. and ed. C. J. Betts. Harmondsworth, 1973.

Montesquieu, Charles de Secondat de. *The Spirit of the Laws*, trans. and eds. A. M. Cohler, B. C. Miller and H. S. Stone. Cambridge, 1989.

Montesquieu, Charles-Louis de Secondat de. "De la manière gothique", in *Voyages de Montesquieu*, 2 vols., Bourdeaux, 1894–6, pp. 367–75.

Montucla, Jean Étienne. *Histoire des mathématiques*, ed. J. de la Lande, 4 vols. Paris, 1799–1802; facsim., ed. C. Naux, Paris, 1968.

More, Henry. *Enchiridion ethicum, praecipua moralis philosophiae rudimenta complectens*. London and Cambridge, 1667.

Moreri, Louis. *Le grand dictionnaire historique ou Le mélange curieux de l'histoire sacrée et profane*. Lyon, 1674.

Moritz, Karl Philipp. "On the Concept of That Which Is Perfect in Itself", in *Eighteenth Century German Criticism*, ed. T. J. Chamberlain, New York, NY, 1992.

Moritz, Karl Philipp. *Schriften zur Ästhetik und Poetik*, ed. H. J. Schrimpf. Tübingen, 1962.

Morton, Charles. *Compendium Physicae* [1687]. Boston, MA, 1940.

Moyle, Walter. *An Essay upon the Constitution of the Roman Government*, in *Works*, 2 vols. London, 1726, vol. 1, pp. 3–148.

Mun, Thomas. *England's Treasure by Forraign Trade*. London, 1664.

Muratori, Lodovico Antonio. *Delle forze dell'intendimento umano, o sia il Pirronismo confutato, trattato . . . opposto al libro del preteso Monsignore Huet*. Venice, 1745.

Musschenbroek, Petrus van. *The Elements of Natural Philosophy*, trans. J. Colson. London, 1744.

Newton, Isaac. *Four Letters from Sir Isaac Newton to Doctor Bentley; containing some Arguments in Proof of a Deity*. London, 1756.

Newton, Isaac. *The Mathematical Principles of Natural Philosophy*, trans. A. Motte. London, 1729. Modern edn. trans. I. B. Cohen and A. Whitman. Berkeley, CA, 1999.

Newton, Isaac. *La Méthode des fluxions, et des suites infinies*, trans. G.-L. L. Buffon. Paris, 1740.

Newton, Isaac. *Optice, sive de reflexionibus, refractionibus, inflexionibus, et coloribus lucis, libri tres*. London, 1706; 1719.

Newton, Isaac. *Opticks: or, A Treatise of the Reflections, Refractions, Inflections and Colours of Light*, London, 1704; 2nd edn. London, 1718; 3rd edn., 1721; 4th edn., 1730.

Newton, Isaac. *Philosophia naturalis principia mathematica*, London, 1687; 2nd edn., Cambridge, 1713; 3rd edn., London, 1726.

Newton, Isaac. "Quadratura curvarum" [1704], in D. E. Smith, *A Source Book in Mathematics*, New York, NY, 1929, pp. 614–18.

Newton, Isaac. "Quadratura curvarum", in *Opticks, or A Treatise of . . . Light, Also Two Treatises of the Species and Magnitude of Curvilinear Figures*. London, 1704, pp. 165–211.

Newton, Isaac. *Two Treatises of the Quadrature of Curves, and Analysis by Equations of an Infinite Number of Terms, Explained*, trans. John Stewart. London, 1745.

Newton, Richard. *Rules and Statutes for the Government of Hertford College, in the University of Oxford: With observations on Particular Parts of them, Shewing the Reasonableness thereof*. London, 1747.

Nicholls, William. *The Duty of Inferiours towards their Superiours, in Five Practical Discourses*. London, 1701.

Nicolai, Friedrich. See *Briefe die neueste Litteratur betreffend* (p. 1292).

Nieuwentyt, Bernard. *The Religious Philosopher: or, The Right Use of Contemplating the Works of the Creator*, trans. J. Chamberlayne. London, 1718–19.

Nollet, Jean-Antoine. *Leçons de physique expérimentale*, 6 vols. Paris, 1743–8.

Norris, John. *Christian Blessedness: or, Discourses upon the Beatitudes of our Lord and Saviour Jesus Christ. To which are added, Reflections upon a late Essay concerning Human Understanding*. London, 1690.

Norris, John. *An Essay towards the Theory of the Ideal or Intelligible World*, 2 vols. London, 1701–4.

Nye, Stephen. *Considerations on the Explications of the Doctrine of the Trinity, By Dr. Wallis, Dr. Sherlock, Dr. S[ou]th, Dr. Cudworth, and Mr. Hooker; as also on the Account given by those that say, the Trinity is an Unconceivable and Inexplicable Mystery*. London, 1693.

Oldfield, Joshua. *An Essay towards the Improvement of Reason in the Pursuit of Learning, and Conduct of Life*. London, 1707.

Orton, Job. *Memoirs of the Life, Character and Writings of the late Reverend Philip Doddridge, DD*. Shrewsbury, 1766.

Oswald, James. *An Appeal to Common Sense in Behalf of Religion*, 2 vols. Edinburgh, 1766–72.

Oswald, John. *The Cry of Nature; or, an Appeal to Mercy and Justice, on Behalf of the Persecuted Animals*. London, 1791.
Paine, Thomas. *Political Writings*, ed. B. Kuklick. Cambridge, 1989.
Paine, Thomas. *The Rights of Man, Part I* [1791], in *Political Writings*, pp. 49–143.
Paley, William. *Horae Paulinae, or, The Truth of the Scripture History of St. Paul Evinced, by a Comparison of the Epistles which bear his Name, with the Acts of the Apostles, and with one another*. London, 1790.
Paley, William. *Natural Theology*. London, 1802; also in *Works*, 7 vols., London, 1825, vol. 5.
Paley, William. *The Principles of Moral and Political Philosophy*. London, 1785; 4th edn., Dublin, 1788; repr., ed. D. L. Le Mahieu, Indianapolis, IN, 2002.
Paley, William. *A View of the Evidences of Christianity*, 3 vols. London, 1794.
Pascal, Blaise. *Les pensées* (1670), ed. P. Sellier. Paris, 1991.
Pascal, Blaise. *Pensées and Other Writings*, trans. H. Levi, ed. A. Levi. Oxford, 1995.
Pauw, Cornelius de. *Recherches philosophiques sur les Américains ou Mémoires intéressant pour servir à l'histoire de l'espèce humaine*, 2 vols. Berlin, 1768–9; expanded edn. 3 vols. (in 2) London, 1771. 3 vols. London, 1771.
Pennington, Sarah. *An Unfortunate Mother's Advice to Her Absent Daughters*. London, 1761.
Perrault, Charles. *Parallèle des anciens et des modernes en ce qui regarde les arts et les sciences*. Paris, 1690; Munich, 1964.
Pestalozzi, J. H. *How Gertrude Teaches Her Children: An Attempt to Help Mothers to Teach their own Children*, trans. L. E. Holland and F. C. Turner. London, 1904.
Pestalozzi, J. H. *Leonard and Gertrude*, trans. E. Channing. Boston, MA, 1885.
Pestalozzi, J. H. *Lienhard und Gertrud: Ein Buch für das Volk* [1781], in *Sämtliche Werke*, vols. 2–3.
Pestalozzi, J. H. *Mémoire über Armenversorgung mit spezieller Rücksicht auf Neuenburg (Armenerziehungs-Anstalten)* [1807], in *Sämtliche Werke*, vol. 20, pp. 73–192.
Pestalozzi, J. H. *Pestalozzi's Educational Writings*, eds. J. A. Green and F. A. Collie. London, 1912.
Pestalozzi, J. H. "Rede an sein Haus an seinem zwei und siebenzigsten Geburtstage den 12. Jänner 1818" [1818], in *Sämtliche Werke*, vol. 25.
Pestalozzi, J. H. *Sämtliche Werke*, eds. A. Buchenau, E. Spranger and H. Stettbacher, 29 vols. Zurich, 1927–96.
Pestalozzi, J. H. *Wie Gertrud ihre Kinder Lehrt. Ein Versuch den Müttern Anleitung zu geben, ihre Kinder selbst zu unterrichten, in Briefen* [1801], in *Sämtliche Werke*, vol. 13, pp. 181–389.
Le philosophe. See [Du Marsais].
Philostratus (the Athenian). *The Two First Books, of Philostratus, concerning the Life of Apollonius of Tyaneus*, ed. C. Blount. London, 1680.
Pico della Mirandola, Giovanni. *Oratio de hominis dignitate* [1486], Latin and Italian parallel edn., ed. E. Garin. Pordenone, 1994.
Pico della Mirandola, Giovanni. *Oration on the Dignity of Man*, in *Renaissance Philosophy*, trans. and eds. A. B. Fallico and H. Shapiro, 2 vols. New York, NY, 1967, vol. 1.
Pinto, Isaac de. *Apologie pour la nation Juive: Réflexions critiques sur le premier chapitre du viie tome des oeuvres de M. Voltaire*. Amsterdam, 1762; also in Guénée, *Lettres de quelques Juifs portugais et allemands à M. Voltaire avec des réflexions critiques, &c.*
[Platner, Ernst]. *Philosophische Aphorismen nebst einer Anleitung zur philosophischen Geschichte*, 2 vols. Leipzig, 1776–82.
Playfair, J. "On the Arithmetic of Impossible Quantities". *Philosophical Transactions of the Royal Society of London* 68 (1778): 318–43.
Plot, Robert. *The Natural History of Oxfordshire: Being an Essay toward the Natural History of England*. Oxford, 1677.
Pope, Alexander. *An Essay on Man* [1732–34], in *Poetical Works*, ed. H. Davis. Oxford, 1966.

Pope, Alexander. *An Essay on Man: The Design*, in *The Poems of Alexander Pope*, ed. M. Mack. New Haven, CT, 1952.

Pope, Alexander. *Epistles to Several Persons (Moral Essays)*, ed. F. W. Bateson, New Haven, CT, 1951.

Pouilly, Louis Jean Lévesque de. "Dissertation sur l'incertitude de l'Histoire des quatre premiers siècles de Rome. Par M. de Pouilly", in *Mémoires de littérature tirés des registres de l'Académie Royale des inscriptions et belles lettres: Depuis l'année M. DCCXVIII. jusques & compris l'année M. DCCXXV*, Paris, 1729.

Prévost, Antoine François d'Exiles, ed. *Histoire générale des voyages, ou, Nouvelle collection de toutes les relations de voyages qui ont été publiées jusqu'à présent*. 20 vols. Paris, 1746–70.

Price, Richard. "Dissertation IV. On the Importance of Christianity, the Nature of Historical Evidence, and Miracles" [1767], in *Four Dissertations*, London, 1768, facsim. Bristol, 1990.

Price, Richard. *A Free Discussion of the Doctrines of Materialism and Philosophical Necessity in a Correspondence between Dr. Price and Dr. Priestley*. London, 1778.

Price, Richard. *A Review of the Principal Questions in Morals* [1758], ed. D. D. Raphael. Oxford, 1974.

Price, Richard. *Two Tracts on Civil Liberty, the War with America, and the Debts and Finances of the Kingdom* [1778], in *Political Writings*, ed. D. O. Thomas. Cambridge, 1991.

Priestley, Joseph. *A Course of Lectures on Oratory and Criticism*. London, 1777; facsim. Menston, 1969.

Priestley, Joseph. *Disquisitions relating to Matter and Spirit*. London, 1777.

Priestley, Joseph. *The Doctrine of Philosophical Necessity Illustrated* [1777], in *The Theological and Miscellaneous Works*, vol. 3, sect. 1, pp. 447–540.

Priestley, Joseph. *An Essay on a Course of Liberal Education for Civil and Active Life*. London, 1765.

Priestley, Joseph. *An Essay on the First Principles of Government, and on the Nature of Political, Civil, and Religious Liberty including Remarks on Dr. Brown's Code of Education* (2nd edn., 1771), in *Theological and Miscellaneous Works*, vol. 22, pp. 3–144.

Priestley, Joseph. *An Examination of Dr. Reid's Inquiry into the Human Mind on the Principles of Common Sense, Dr. Beattie's Essay on the Nature and Immutability of Truth and Dr. Oswald's Appeal to Common Sense in Behalf of Religion*. London, 1774; also in *Theological and Miscellaneous Works*, vol. 3.

Priestley, Joseph. *A Free Discussion of the Doctrines of Materialism and Philosophical Necessity . . . to which are added . . . Introduction . . . and Letters . . . on his Disquisitions Relating to Matter and Spirit*. London, 1778.

Priestley, Joseph. *Institutes of Natural and Revealed Religion*, 3 vols. London, 1772–4.

Priestley, Joseph. *Letters to a Philosophical Unbeliever, Part I*. Bath and London, 1780; 2nd edn., Birmingham and London, 1787; *Part II*. Birmingham and London, 1787; *Part III*. Philadelphia, PA, 1795.

Priestley, Joseph. *Miscellaneous Observations Relating to Education. More especially, as it respects the Conduct of the Mind. To Which is Added, An Essay on a course of Liberal Education for Civil and Active Life*. Cork, 1780.

Priestley, Joseph. *Priestley's Writings on Philosophy, Science and Politics*, ed. J. A. Passmore. New York, NY, 1965.

Priestley, Joseph. *Reflections on Death: A Sermon on Occasion of the Death of the Rev. Robert Robinson*, in *Theological and Miscellaneous Works*, vol. 15, pp. 404–19.

Priestley, Joseph. *The Theological and Miscellaneous Works*, ed. J. T. Rutt, 25 in 26 vols. London, 1817–32; facsim. New York, NY, 1972.

Primatt, Humphrey. *A Dissertation on the Mercy and Sin of Cruelty to Brute Animals*. London, 1776; facsim. Bristol, 2000.

Pufendorf, Samuel. *Les devoirs de l'homme et du citoien*, 4th edn., trans. and ed. J. Barbeyrac, 2 vols. Amsterdam, 1718.

Pufendorf, Samuel. *Le droit de la nature et des gens, ou Système général des principes les plus importans de la morale, de la jurisprudence, et de la politique* (2nd edn.), trans. and ed. J. Barbeyrac, 2 vols. Amsterdam, 1712.

Pufendorf, Samuel. *The Divine Feudal Law: or, Covenants with Mankind, Represented*, trans. T. Dorrington (1703), ed. S. Zurbuchen. Indianapolis, IN, 2002.

Pufendorf, Samuel. *De habitu religionis christianae ad vitam civilem*. Bremen, 1687; facsim. Stuttgart and Bad Cannstatt, 1972.

Pufendorf, Samuel. *De jure naturae et gentium libri octo* [1672] (facsim. of 1688 edn.), trans. and eds. C. H. Oldfather and W. A. Oldfather, 2 vols. Oxford, 1934.

Pufendorf, Samuel. *De officio hominis et civis*. Lund, 1673.

Pufendorf, Samuel. *Eris Scandica*. Frankfurt am Main, 1686.

Pufendorf, Samuel. *The Law of Nature and Nations*, 5th edn., trans. B. Kennet. London, 1749.

Pufendorf, Samuel. *On the Duty of Man and Citizen according to Natural Law*, ed. J. Tully, trans. M. Silverthorne. Cambridge, 1991.

Pufendorf, Samuel. *Of the Nature and Qualification of Religion in Reference to Civil Society*, trans. J. Crull (1698), ed. S. Zurbuchen. Indianapolis, IN, 2002.

Pufendorf, Samuel. *The Whole Duty of Man, According to the Law of Nature*, trans. A. Tooke (1691), ed. I. Hunter and D. Saunders; with Two Discourses and a Commentary by Jean Barbeyrac, trans. D. Saunders. Indianapolis, IN 2003.

Quesnay, François. *Le tableau économique*. n.p., 1758.

Quesnay, François, and Victor Riquetti, marquis de Mirabeau. *Philosophie rurale*. Amsterdam, 1763.

Quintilian. *The Orator's Education*, trans. H. E. Butler, 4 vols. Cambridge, MA, 1969–79.

Radicati, Alberto, conte di Passerano. *Dissertation sur la mort*. Paris, 1819.

Radicati, Alberto, conte di Passerano. *A Philosophical Dissertation upon Death: Composed for the Consolation of the Unhappy*, trans. J. Morgan. London, 1732.

Ray, John. *Synopsis methodica animalium quadrupedum et serpentini generis*. London, 1693.

Ray, John. *Synopsis methodica avium & piscium*, ed. W. Derham. London, 1713.

Ray, John. *The Wisdom of God Manifested in the Works of Creation*. London, 1691.

Reid, Thomas. *A Brief Account of Aristotle's Logic* [1774], in *Philosophical Works*, vol. 2; in *Thomas Reid on Logic . . .*

Reid, Thomas. *The Correspondence of Thomas Reid*, ed. P. B. Wood. Edinburgh, 2002.

Reid, Thomas. "An Essay on Quantity" [1748], in *Philosophical Works*, pp. 715–19.

Reid, Thomas. *Essays on the Active Powers of Man* [1788], in *Philosophical Works*, vol. 2.

Reid, Thomas. *Essays on the Intellectual Powers of Man*. Edinburgh, 1785; eds. D. R. Brookes and K. Haakonssen, Edinburgh, 2002.

Reid, Thomas. *An Inquiry into the Human Mind on the Principles of Common Sense* [1764], ed. D. R. Brookes. Edinburgh, 1997.

Reid, Thomas. *Lectures on the Fine Arts* [1774], ed. P. Kivy. The Hague, 1973.

Reid, Thomas. *Lectures on Natural Theology* [1780], ed. E. H. Duncan. Washington, DC, 1981.

Reid, Thomas. *Thomas Reid on Logic, Rhetoric, and the Fine Arts: Papers on the Culture of the Mind*, ed. A. Broadie. Edinburgh, 2005.

Reid, Thomas. *The Philosophical Orations of Thomas Reid*, ed. D. D. Todd. Carbondale, IL, 1989.

Reid, Thomas. *Philosophical Works*, ed. W. Hamilton, 2 in 1 vols., 8th edn., Edinburgh, 1895; facsim. Hildesheim, 1983.

Reid, Thomas. *Practical Ethics: Being Lectures and Papers on Natural Religion, Self-Government, Natural Jurisprudence, and the Law of Nations*, ed. K. Haakonssen. Princeton, NJ, 1990.

Reid, Thomas. *Thomas Reid on the Animate Creation: Papers on the Life Sciences*, ed. P. B. Wood. Edinburgh, 1995.

Reimarus, Hermann Samuel. *Allgemeine Betrachtungen über die Triebe der Thiere, hauptsächlich über ihre Kunsttrieb*. Hamburg, 1760.

Reimarus, Hermann Samuel. *Apologie oder Schutzschrift für die vernünftigen Verehrer Gottes* [c. 1750], ed. G. Alexander, 2 vols. Frankfurt am Main, 1972.

Reimarus, Hermann Samuel. *Die Vernunftlehre*, 2 vols. Hamburg, 1766; facsim. Munich, 1979.

Reimmann, Jakob Friedrich. *Historia universalis atheismi et atheorum falso et merito suspectorum*. Hildesheim, 1725; facsim. Stuttgart and Bad Cannstatt, 1992.

Reinhard, Adolf F. "Le sistème de Pope sur la perfection du monde comparé avec celui de Mr. Leibnitz, avec un examen de l'optimisme", in *Dissertations sur l'optimisme*. Berlin, 1755.

Reinhold, Karl Leonhard. *Briefe über die kantische Philosophie* [1786–7], 2 vols. Leipzig, 1790–2.

Reinhold, Karl Leonhard. *The Foundation of Philosophical Knowledge*, trans. G. di Giovanni and H. S. Harris, in G. di Giovanni and H. S. Harris (eds.), *Between Kant and Hegel*, pp. 54–103 (see *B2*).

Reinhold, Karl Leonhard. *Über das Fundament des philosophischen Wissens*. Jena, 1791; 1794.

Reinhold, Karl Leonhard. *Über das Fundament des philosophischen Wissens / Über die Möglichkeit der Philosophie als strenge Wissenschaft* [1791]. Hamburg, 1978.

Reinhold, Karl Leonhard. *Versuch einer neuen Theorie des menschlichen Vorstellungsvermögens*. Prague and Jena, 1789.

Rivarol, Antoine. *Discours sur l'universalité de la langue française* [1784]. Paris, 1936.

Robertson, William. *History of America*, 2 vols. Edinburgh, 1777; in *Works*, 8 vols. London, 1827, vol. 6.

Robertson, William. *The History of the Reign of the Emperor Charles V*, 3 vols. London, 1769.

Robertson, William. *The History of Scotland, during the Reigns of Queen Mary and of King James VI. till His Accession to the Crown of England*, 2 vols. London, 1759.

Robertson, William. *The Progress of Society in Europe: A Historical Outline from the Subversion of the Roman Empire to the Beginning of the Sixteenth Century* (1769), ed. F. Gilbert. Chicago, IL, 1972.

Robespierre, Maximilien de. *Sur les rapports des idées religieuses et morales avec les principes républicains, et sur les fêtes nationales*, in *Oeuvres*, 11 vols. Paris, 1910–67, vol. 10, pp. 442–65.

Robinet, Jean-Baptiste-René. *De la nature*, 3 vols. Amsterdam, 1763–6.

Röhr, Werner, ed. *Appellation an das Publikum: Dokumente zum Atheismusstreit um Fichte, Forberg, Niethammer, Jena 1798/99*. Leipzig, 1987.

Rousseau, Jean-Jacques. *The Collected Writings of Rousseau*, eds. C. Kelly and R. D. Masters. Hanover, NH and London, 1992–.

Rousseau, Jean-Jacques. *Collection complète des oeuvres de J. J. Rousseau*. Geneva, 1782.

Rousseau, Jean-Jacques. *Les confessions* [1782], in *Oeuvres*, vol. 1, pp. 1–656.

Rousseau, Jean-Jacques. *The Confessions, and, Correspondence, including the Letters to Malesherbes*, trans. C. Kelly, eds. C. Kelly, R. D. Masters and P. G. Stillman, in *Collected Writings*, vol. 5.

Rousseau, Jean-Jacques. *Considérations sur le gouvernement de Pologne et sur sa réformation projettée* [1782], in *Oeuvres*, vol. 3, pp. 951–1041.

Rousseau, Jean-Jacques. *Du contrat social ou Principes du droit politique*. Amsterdam, 1762; in *Oeuvres*, vol. 3, pp. 347–470.

Rousseau, Jean-Jacques. *Discours sur l'origine et les fondements de l'inégalité parmi les hommes* [1755], in *Oeuvres*, vol. 3, pp. 109–223.

Rousseau, Jean-Jacques. *Discours sur les sciences et les arts* [1751], in *Oeuvres*, vol. 3, pp. 1–102.

Rousseau, Jean-Jacques. *Discourse on the Origin and Foundation of Inequality Among Men*, in *The Discourses*, pp. 113–222.

Rousseau, Jean-Jacques. *The Discourses and Other Early Political Writings*, trans. and ed. V. Gourevitch. Cambridge, 1997.

Rousseau, Jean-Jacques. *Émile or On Education*, trans. A. Bloom. New York, NY, 1979; Harmondsworth, 1991.

Rousseau, Jean-Jacques. *Émile ou De l'éducation* [1762], in *Oeuvres*, vol. 4, pp. 239–868.

Rousseau, Jean-Jacques. *Essai sur l'origine des langues*, in *Traités sur la musique*, Geneva, 1781.

Rousseau, Jean-Jacques. *Essai sur l'origine des langues où il est parlé de la mélodie et de l'imitation musicale*, ed. J. Starobinski. Paris, 1990.

Rousseau, Jean-Jacques. *The Government of Poland*, trans. and ed. W. Kendall. Indianapolis, IN, 1985.

Rousseau, Jean-Jacques. *Julie, ou la nouvelle Héloïse*, 6 vols. Amsterdam, 1761.

Rousseau, Jean-Jacques. "Letter from J. J. Rousseau to M. de Voltaire", in *The Discourses*, pp. 232–46.

Rousseau, Jean-Jacques. *Letters on the Elements of Botany, Addressed to a Lady*, ed. T. Martyn. London, 1785.

Rousseau, Jean-Jacques. *Lettre à Christophe de Beaumont* [1763], in *Oeuvres*, vol. 4, pp. 925–1028.

Rousseau, Jean-Jacques. *Lettre à M. d'Alembert sur son article Genève dans le VIIe volume de l'Encyclopédie, et particulièrement sur le projet d'établir un Théatre de Comédie en cette ville* [1758], in *Oeuvres*, vol. 5, pp. 1–125.

Rousseau, Jean-Jacques. *Lettre à de Franquières* [1769], in *Oeuvres*, vol. 4, pp. 1133–47.

Rousseau, Jean-Jacques. *Lettre de J. J. Rousseau à Monsieur de Voltaire* [1756; publ. 1759], in *Oeuvres*, vol. 4, pp. 1059–75.

Rousseau, Jean-Jacques. *Lettres écrits de la montagne* [1764], in *Oeuvres*, vol. 3, pp. 683–897.

Rousseau, Jean-Jacques. *Lettres élémentaires sur la botanique*. Paris, 1789.

Rousseau, Jean-Jacques. *Oeuvres complètes*, eds. B. Gagnebin and M. Raymond, 5 vols. Paris, 1959–95.

Rousseau, Jean-Jacques. *Of the Social Contract or Principles of Political Right*, in *The Social Contract and Other Later Political Writings*, trans. and ed. V. Gourevitch. Cambridge, 1997.

Rousseau, Jean-Jacques. *Politics and the Arts: Letter to M. d'Alembert on the Theatre*, trans. and ed. A. Bloom. Ithaca, NY, 1968.

Rousseau, Jean-Jacques. "Preface" to *Narcissus*, in *The Discourses*, pp. 92–106.

Rousseau, Jean-Jacques. "Preface" to *Narcisse*, in *Oeuvres*, vol. 2, pp. 959–74.

Rousseau, Jean-Jacques. *Les Rêveries du promeneur solitaire* [1777–78], in *Oeuvres*, vol. 1, pp. 993–1099.

Rousseau, Jean-Jacques. *Rousseau juge de Jean-Jacques* [1772], in *Oeuvres*, vol. 1, pp. 657–992.

Rousseau, Jean-Jacques. *The Social Contract and Discourses*, trans. G. D. H. Cole, revised by J. H. Brumfitt and J. C. Hall. London, 1973.

Rüdiger, Andreas. *Institutiones eruditionis, seu philosophia synthetica*, 1711.

Rüdiger, Andreas. *De sensu veri et falsi*, 2nd edn. Leipzig, 1722.

Ruffini, Paolo. *Teoria generale delle equazioni in cui si dimostra impossibile la soluzione algebraica delle equazioni generali di grado superiore al quarto*. Bologna, 1799.

Rush, Benjamin. "Observations Intended to Favour a Supposition that the Black Color (As it is Called) of Negroes is Derived from the Leprosy". *American Philosophical Society Transactions* 4 (1799): 289–97.

Rush, Benjamin. *Thoughts upon Female Education, Accommodated to the Present State of Society, Manners, and Government in the United States of America* [1787], in F. Rudolph (ed.), *Essays on Education*, pp. 25–40 (see *B2*).

Rutherforth, Thomas. *The Credibility of Miracles Defended against the Author of Philosophical Essays*. Cambridge, 1751.

Rutherforth, Thomas. *An Essay on the Nature and Obligations of Virtue*. Cambridge, 1744.
Rutherforth, Thomas. *Institutes of Natural Law*, 2 vols. Cambridge, 1754–6; 2nd edn. 1774.
Rutherforth, Thomas. *A System of Natural Philosophy, being a Course of Lectures in Mechanics, Optics, Hydrostatics and Astronomy*, 2 vols. Cambridge, 1748.
Saccheri, Girolamo. *Euclides vindicatus*, (parallel Latin-English text), trans. and ed. G. B. Halstead. Chicago, IL, 1920.
Sade, Donatien Alphonse François, marquis de. "Cent onze notes pour la Nouvelle Justine", in *Oeuvres*, vol. 3.
Sade, Donatien Alphonse François, marquis de. *Oeuvres*, ed. M. Delon. Paris, 1990–.
Sade, Donatien Alphonse François, marquis de. *Oeuvres complètes*, eds. A. Le. Brun and J.-J. Pauvert, 15 vols. Paris, 1986–91.
Sade, Donatien Alphonse François, marquis de. *La philosophie dans le boudoir*, 2 vols. London 1795.
Schelling, Friedrich Wilhelm Joseph. *Erster Entwurf eines System der Naturphilosophie*. Jena, 1799.
Schelling, Friedrich Wilhelm Joseph. *Fernere Darstellungen aus dem System der Philosophie*, in *Werke* (ed. Schröter), Suppl. 1, pp. 385–575.
Schelling, Friedrich Wilhelm Joseph. *Ideen für eine Philosophie der Natur*. Leipzig, 1797.
Schelling, Friedrich Wilhelm Joseph. *On the History of Modern Philosophy*, trans. A. Bowie. Cambridge, 1994.
Schelling, Friedrich Wilhelm Joseph. *Vorlesungen über die Methode des akademischen Studiums*, in *Werke* (ed. Schröter), vol. 3, pp. 229–374.
Schelling, Friedrich Wilhelm Joseph. *Werke*, ed. M. Schröter, 12 vols. Munich, 1927–59.
Schelling, Friedrich Wilhelm Joseph. *Zur Geschichte der neueren Philosophie. Münchener Vorlesungen*. Berlin, 1986.
Schiller, Friedrich. *On the Aesthetic Education of Man*, trans. E. Wilkinson and L. A. Willoughby. Oxford, 1967.
Schiller, Friedrich. *Über die ästhetische Erziehung des Menschen in einer Reihe von Briefen*, in *Werke*, ed. A. Kurtscher, 10 vols. Berlin, 1907, vol. 8.
Schlegel, Friedrich von. "Versuch über den Begriff des Republikanismus", [1796] in *Kritische Friedrich Schlegel-Ausgabe*, ed. E. Behler, Paderborn, 1958–, vol. 7, pp. 11–25.
Schleiermacher, Friedrich. *Der christliche Glaube*. Berlin, 1821–2.
Schleiermacher, Friedrich. *On Religion: Speeches to its Cultured Despisers*, trans. J. Oman, ed. R. Otto. New York, NY, 1958.
Schleiermacher, Friedrich. *Reden über die Religion an die Gebildeten unter ihren Verächtern* [1799], ed. G. C. B. Pünjer. Brunswick, 1879.
Schlözer, August Ludwig von. *Allgemeines StatsRecht und StatsVerfassungsLere*. Göttingen, 1793.
[Schulze, Gottlob Ernst]. *Aenesidemus oder Über die Fundamente der von dem Herrn Professor Reinhold in Jena gelieferten Elementarphilosophie. Nebst einen Vertheidigung des Skepticismus gegen die Anmassungen der Vernunftkritik*. [Helmstädt], 1792; ed. A. Liebert, Berlin, 1911.
Schulze, Gottlob Ernst. *Kritik der theoretischen Philosophie*, 2 vols. Hamburg, 1801.
Scott, James. *General Dictionary of Arts and Sciences*, 2 vols. London, 1765–6.
Scott, William. *Hugonis Grotii De jure belli ac pacis librorum III compendium, annotationibus et commentariis selectis illustratum*. Edinburgh, 1707.
[Sergeant, John]. *The Method to Science*. London, 1696.
Sergeant, John. *Solid Philosophy Asserted . . . with Reflexions on Mr. Locke's Essay concerning Human Understanding*. London, 1697.

Sextus Empiricus. *Les Hipotiposes ou institutions Pirroniennes . . . en trois livres*, trans. C. Huart. Amsterdam, 1725; London, 1735.
Sextus Empiricus. *Opera graece et latine*, ed. J. A. Fabricius. Leipzig, 1718.
Shaftesbury, Anthony Ashley Cooper, Earl. *Characteristicks of Men, Manners, Opinions, Times*, 3 vols. London, 1711; ed. J. M. Robertson, 2 vols., London, 1900; repr. 2 in 1 vols. Indianapolis, IN, 1964.
Shaftesbury, Anthony Ashley Cooper, Earl. *Complete Works, Selected Letters and Posthumous Writings: in English with parallel German translation*, trans. and eds. G. Hemmerich and W. Benda. Stuttgart and Bad Cannstatt, 1981–.
Shaftesbury, Anthony Ashley Cooper, Earl. "An Inquiry concerning Virtue or Merit" [1699], in *Characteristicks of Men, Manners, Opinions, Times* (ed. Robertson), vol. 1.
Shaftesbury, Anthony Ashley Cooper, Earl. *The Life, Unpublished Letters, and Philosophical Regimen of Anthony, Earl of Shaftesbury*, ed. B. Rand. London, 1900.
Shaftesbury, Anthony Ashley Cooper, Earl. *Miscellaneous Reflections*, in *Works*, vol. 1.
Shaftesbury, Anthony Ashley Cooper, Earl. "The Moralists: A Philosophical Rhapsody" [1709], in *Characteristicks of Men, Manners and Opinions, Times*, vol. 2; in *Works*, vol. 2.
[Shaftesbury, Anthony Ashley Cooper, Earl]. Preface, in B. Whichcote, *Select Sermons*. London, 1698.
Shaftesbury, Anthony Ashley Cooper, Earl. *Soliloquy: Or, Advice to an Author*, in *Works*, vol. 1; in *Characteristicks of Men, Manners, Opinions, Times*, vol. 1.
Sharp, Granville. *Extract from a Representation of the Injustice and Dangerous Tendency of Tolerating Slavery, or Admitting the least Claim of Private Property in the Persons of Men in England*. London, 1769.
Sherlock, Thomas. *Bishop Sherlock's Arguments against a Repeal of the Corporation and Test Acts, Wherein Most of the Pleas Advanced in a Paper now Circulating, Styled the Case of Protestant Dissenters . . . Are Discussed*. London, 1787.
Sherlock, Thomas. *The Tryal of the Witnesses of the Resurrection of Jesus*. London, 1729.
Shirley, John. *The Illustrious History of Women, or, A Compendium of the Many Virtues that Adorn the Fair Sex*. London, 1686.
Sieyès, Emmanuel Joseph. *Qu'est ce que le Tiers Etat?* Paris, 1789.
Sieyès, Emmanuel Joseph. *What is the Third Estate?*, trans. M. Blondel, ed. S. E. Finer. London, 1963.
Skelton, Philip. *Ophiomaches, or Deism Revealed*, 2 vols. London, 1749.
Smellie, William, ed. *Encyclopaedia Britannica or, a Dictionary of Arts and Sciences, Compiled upon a New Plan*. 3 vols. Edinburgh, 1771.
Smellie, William. *The Philosophy of Natural History*, 2 vols. Edinburgh, 1790–9.
Smith, Adam. "Considerations concerning the first formation of languages, and the different genius of original and compounded languages", in *The Philological Miscellany*, vol. 1, London, 1761, 440–79; and in Adam Smith, *Lectures on Rhetoric and Belles Lettres*, ed. J. C. Bryce, in *Works* (1983).
Smith, Adam. *The Correspondence of Adam Smith*, eds. E. C. Mossner and I. S. Ross, in *Works* (1977).
Smith, Adam. *Essays on Philosophical Subjects*, eds. W. P. D. Wightman and J. C. Bryce, in *Works* (1980).
Smith, Adam. *Glasgow Edition of the Works and Correspondence*, 7 vols. Oxford, 1976–2001.
Smith, Adam. *An Inquiry into the Nature and Causes of the Wealth of Nations* [1776], eds. R. H. Campbell, A. S. Skinner, and W. B. Todd, 2 vols., in *Works* (1976).
Smith, Adam. *Lectures on Jurisprudence*, eds. R. L. Meek, D. D. Raphael and P. G. Stein, in *Works* (1978).

Smith, Adam. *Lectures on Rhetoric and Belles Lettres*, ed. J. C. Bryce, in *Works* (1983).
Smith, Adam. *The Theory of Moral Sentiments* [1759], eds. D. D. Raphael and A. L. Macfie, in *Works* (1976).
Smith, Samuel Stanhope. *An Essay on the Causes of the Variety of Complexion and Figure in the Human Species. To which are added, animadversions on certain remarks made on the first edition of this essay, by Mr. Charles White ... Also, strictures on Lord Kaim's discourse on the original diversity of mankind.* [1787], 2nd edn., New Brunswick, NJ, 1810. Modern edition by W. Jordan. Cambridge, 1965.
Smith, William. *Discourses on Several Public Occasions*. Philadelphia, PA, 1759; (2nd edn., 1762) ed. T. R. Adams, commentary by T. Woody, Philadelphia, PA, 1951.
Smith, William. *A General Idea of the College of Mirania: with a sketch of the method of teaching science and religion, in the several classes*. New York, NY, 1753.
[Smith, William]. "Philomathes", *Some Thoughts on Education: With Reasons for Erecting a College in This Province, and Fixing the Same in the City of New-York*. New York, NY, 1752.
Smith, William, and Thomas Peirson. "Some reflexions on education, with a modest scheme for augmenting schoolmasters livings. Humbly offered to the impartial consideration of the publick". *Scots Magazine* (Oct. 1750): 488–92.
Soemmering, Samuel Thomas. *Ueber die körperliche Verschiedenheit des Negers vom Europäer*. Frankfurt am Main, 1785.
Sonnenfels, Joseph von. *Grundsätze der Polizey, Handlung und Finanzwissenschaft*, 2 vols. Vienna, 1768.
Spalding, Johann Joachim. *Spaldings Bestimmung des Menschen (1748) und Wert der Andacht (1755)*, ed. H. Stephan. Giessen, 1908.
Spener, Philipp Jakob. *Pia desideria*. Frankfurt am Main, 1675.
Spinoza, Baruch de. *Ethica ordine geometrico demonstrata*. n.p., 1677.
Spinoza, Baruch de. *Ethics* [1677], trans. S. Stirling, ed. S. Feldman. Indianapolis, IN, 1992.
Spinoza, Baruch de. *Tractatus theologico-politicus*, Hamburg, 1670.
Sprat, Thomas. *History of the Royal Society*. London, 1667; facsim. St. Louis, MO, 1959.
Staël, Germaine de. *De l'influence des passions sur le bonheur des individus et des nations* [1796], in *Oeuvres*, 17 vols. Geneva, 1967, vol. 1.
Staël, Germaine de. *Lettres sur les écrits et le caractère de J.-J. Rousseau* [1788], in *Oeuvres complètes*, 17 vols. Paris, 1820–1, vol. 1.
Stanley, Thomas. *History of Philosophy*, 4 vols. London, 1655–62; 2nd edn., 1687.
Stäudlin, Carl Friedrich. *Der Geschichte und Geist des Skepticismus, vorzüglich in Rücksicht auf Moral und Religion*, 2 vols. Leipzig, 1794.
Stebbing, Henry. *A Defence of Dr. Clarke's Evidence of Natural and Revealed Religion*. London, 1731.
Stebbing, Henry. *An Essay concerning Civil Government, Consider'd as It Stands Related to Religion, wherein the Magistrate's Right to Support and Encourage True Religion by Human Laws Is Asserted, against the Modern Pleaders of an Absolute, Unrestrained Toleration*. London, 1724.
Steele, Richard. *See* Addison.
Stegmann, Joachim, the Elder. *De judice et norma controversiarum fidei Libri II*. "Eleutheropoli", 1644.
Stephens, William. *An Account of the Growth of Deism in England*. London, 1696.
Steuart, James. *An Inquiry into the Principles of Political Oeconomy* [1767], ed. A. S. Skinner, 2 vols. Edinburgh, 1966.
Stewart, Dugald. "Account of the Life and Writings of Adam Smith LL. D.", in *Works*, vol. 10; in A. Smith, *Essays on Philosophical Subjects*, eds. W. P. D. Wightman and J. C. Bryce, pp. 269–351.
Stewart, Dugald. *Collected Works*, ed. W. Hamilton, 11 vols. Edinburgh and London, 1854–60; facsim., ed. K. Haakonssen. Bristol, 1994.

Stewart, Dugald. *Dissertation Exhibiting the Progress of Metaphysical, Ethical and Political Philosophy since the Revival of Letters in Europe* [Edinburgh, 1815–21], in *Works*, vol. 1.
Stewart, Dugald. *Elements of the Philosophy of the Human Mind* [1792–1827], in *Works*, vol. 2–4.
Stewart, Dugald. *Histoire Abrégée des sciences metaphysiques, morales et politiques depuis la renaissance des lettres*, trans. J. A. Buchon. Paris, 1820.
Stewart, Dugald. *Outlines of Moral Philosophy*. Edinburgh, 1793; in *Works*, vol. 2.
Stewart, Dugald. *Philosophical Essays* (1810), in *Works*, vol. 5.
Stewart, Dugald. *The Philosophy of the Active and Moral Powers of Man*. Edinburgh, 1828.
Stillingfleet, Edward. *The Bishop of Worchester's Answer to Mr. Locke's Letter*. London, 1697; facsim. in Edward Stillingfleet, *Three Criticisms of Locke*, Hildesheim and New York, NY, 1987.
Stillingfleet, Edward. *A Letter to a Deist, in Answer to Several Objections against the Truth and Authority of the Scriptures*. London, 1677.
Stillingfleet, Edward, ed. *The Oracles of Reason*. London, 1693.
Stillingfleet, Edward. *Origines sacrae*. London, 1662.
Stillingfleet, Edward. *Three Criticisms of Locke*. London, 1697–8; facsim. Hildesheim and New York, NY, 1987.
Sturm, Johann Christoph. *Philosophia eclectica*. Altdorf, 1686.
Sturm, Johann Christoph. *Physica conciliatrix*. n.p., 1684.
Sturm, Johann Christoph. *Physica electiva sive hypothetica*, 2 vols. Nürnberg, 1697–1722.
Suárez, Francisco. *De legibus ac Deo legislatore*, in *Selections from Three Works*, trans. G. L. Williams, A. Brown, and J. Waldron. Oxford, 1944.
Sulzer, Johann Georg. *Allgemeine Theorie der schönen Künste*, 2 vols. Leipzig, 1771–4.
Süssmilch, Johann Peter. *Versuch eines Beweises, dass die erste Sprache ihren Ursprung nicht vom Menschen, sondern allein vom Schoepfer erhalten habe*. Berlin, 1766.
Svarez, Carl Gottlieb. *Vorträge über Recht und Staat*, eds. H. Conrad and G. Kleinheyer. Cologne, 1960.
Swinden, Jan van. *Positiones physicae*, 2 vols. Harderwijk, 1786.
Sykes, Arthur Ashley. *A Brief Discourse concerning the Credibility of Miracles and Revelation*. London, 1742.
Tatham, Edward. *The Chart and Scale of Truth*, 2 vols. Oxford, 1790.
Taylor, John. *An Examination of the Scheme of Morality Advanced by Dr. Hutcheson*. London, 1759.
Taylor, John. *A Sketch of Moral Philosophy: or, An essay to demonstrate the principles of virtue and religion, upon a new, natural, and easy plan*. London, 1760.
Templer, John. *Idea theologiae Leviathanis*. London, 1673.
Tennemann, Wilhelm Gottfried. *Geschichte der Philosophie*, 12 vols. Leipzig, 1798–1819.
Tetens, Johann Nicolas. *Philosophische Versuche über die menschliche Natur und ihre Entwicklung*, in *Werke*.
Tetens, Johann Nicolas. *Die philosophischen Werke*, 2 vols. Leipzig, 1777; facsim. Hildesheim, 1979.
Tetens, Johann Nicolas. *Über den Ursprung der Sprache und der Schrift*. Berlin, 1772.
Tetens, Johann Nicolas. *Über die allgemeine speculativische Philosophie*, 1775.
The Spectator. *See* Addison.
Thomas, Antoine-Léonard. *Essai sur le caractère, les moeurs, et l'esprit des femmes dans les différens siècles*. Paris, 1772.
Thomasius, Christian. *Ausgewählte Werke*, ed. W. Schneiders. Hildesheim, 1993–.
Thomasius, Christian. *Aussübung der Vernunftlehre, oder: Kurze, deutliche und wohlgegründete Handgriffe, wie man in seinem Kopffe aufräumen .... solle*. Halle, 1691; facsim. Hildesheim and New York, NY, 1998.
Thomasius, Christian. *Ausübung der Sittenlehre*. Halle, 1696; facsim. Hildesheim and New York, NY, 1999.

Thomasius, Christian. *Discours von der Freyheit der itzigen Zeiten gegen die vorigen*, in *Aus der Frühzeit der deutschen Aufklärung: Christian Thomasius und Christian Weise*, ed. F. Brüggemann (*see B2*).

Thomasius, Christian. *Einleitung zur Sittenlehre*. Halle, 1692; facsim. Hildesheim and New York, NY, 1995.

Thomasius, Christian. *Einleitung zur Vernunftlehre*. Halle, 1691; facsim. Hildesheim and New York, NY, 1998.

Thomasius, Christian. *Erörterung der Juristischen Frage: Ob Ketzerey ein straffbares Verbrechen sey?* [1705], in *Ausgewählte Werke*, vol. 23: *Auserlesene deutsche Schriften, Erster Teil*, pp. 210–307.

Thomasius, Christian. *Fundamenta juris naturae et gentium*. Halle, 1705.

Thomasius, Christian. *Institutiones iurisprudentiae divinae*. Leipzig, 1688.

Thomasius, Christian. *Introductio ad philosophiam aulicam*. Leipzig, 1688; facsim. Hildesheim, 1993.

Thompson, Benjamin, Count Rumford. "An Inquiry Concerning the Source of Heat which Is Excited by Friction". *Philosophical Transactions of the Royal Society of London* 88 (1798): 80–102.

Thümmig, Ludwig Philipp. *Institutiones philosophiae Wolfianae*, eds. J. École, et al., in *Wolff: Werke*, Abt III, vol. 19:1 (1982).

Tillotson, John. *Works*, ed. R. Barker, 3 vols. London, 1728.

Tindal, Matthew. *An Address to the Inhabitants of the two Great Cities of London and Westminster; in relation to a pastoral Letter said to have been written by the Bishop of London to the People of his Diocese*. London, 1729.

Tindal, Matthew. *Christianity as Old as the Creation or, The Gospel, a Republication of the Religion of Nature*. London, 1730; facsim. Stuttgart and Bad Cannstatt, 1967.

Tindal, Matthew. *An Essay concerning the Power of the Magistrate, and the Rights of Mankind, in Matters of Religion*. London, 1697.

Tindal, Matthew. *A Letter to the Reverend Clergy of both Universities concerning the Trinity and the Athanasian Creed*. London, 1694.

Tindal, Matthew. *The Reflections on the XXVIII Propositions touching the Doctrine of the Trinity, in A Letter to the Clergy, &c.* n.p., 1695.

Tindal, Matthew. *The Rights of the Christian Church Asserted, against the Romish and all other Priests who Claim an Independent Power over It*, Part I. London, 1706.

Todd, Janet, ed. *Female Education in the Age of Enlightenment*. 6 vols. London, 1996.

Toland, John. *Adeisidaemon, sive Titus Livius, a Superstitione vindicatus*. The Hague, 1709.

Toland, John. *Anglia Libera: or The Limitation and Succession of the Crown of England Explain'd and Asserted*. London, 1701.

Toland, John. *Christianity not Mysterious. Text, Associated Works, and Critical Essays*, eds. P. McGuinness, A. Harrison and R. Kearney. Dublin, 1997.

Toland, John. *Christianity not Mysterious: or, A Treatise Shewing, that there is Nothing in the Gospel Contrary to Reason, nor above it: And that no Christian Doctrine Can Be Properly Call'd a Mystery*. London, 1696; facsim. Stuttgart and Bad Cannstatt, 1964.

Toland, John. "Clidophorus, or, Of the Exoteric and Esoteric Philosophy", in *Tetradymus*.

Toland, John. *Letters to Serena*. London, 1704; repr. ed. G. Gawlick, Stuttgart and Bad Cannstatt, 1964.

Toland, John. *Nazarenus: or Jewish, Gentile and Mahometan Christianity* [1718], ed. J. Champion. Oxford, 1999.

Toland, John. *Pantheisticon: or, The Form of Celebrating the Socratic Society* [1720], trans. London, 1751.

Toland, John. *Reasons for Naturalizing the Jews in Great Britain and Ireland/Gründe für die Einbürgerung der Juden in Großbritannien und Irland* [1714], trans. and ed. H. Mainusch. Stuttgart, 1965.

Toland, John. *The State-Anatomy of Great Britain. Containing a Particular Account of its Several Interests and Parties, their Bent and Genius*... (Pt 1, 4th edn.; Pt 2, 2nd edn.). London, 1717.

Toland, John. *Tetradymus*. London, 1720.

Tooke, John Horne. *Epea ptepoenta, or, The Diversions of Purley*, 2 vols. London, 1786 and 1805.

Tournefort, Joseph Pitton de. *Élémens de botanique, ou, Méthode pour connoître les plantes*, 3 vols. Paris, 1694.

Tournemine, René Joseph. *Reflexions sur l'athéisme*, ed. J. Deprun, in J. Meslier, *Oeuvres complètes*, vol. 3.

Trenchard, John. *The Natural History of Superstition*. London, 1709.

Trotter [Cockburn], Catharine. *Remarks upon the Principles and Reasonings of Dr. Rutherforth's Essay on the Nature and Obligations of Virtue: in Vindication of the Contrary Principles and Reasonings*. London, 1747.

Trotter [Cockburn], Catharine. *Remarks upon some Writers in the Controversy Concerning the Foundation of Moral Virtue and Moral Obligation* (1743), in *The Works of Mrs. Catharine Cockburn, Theological, Moral, Dramatic, and Poetical*, 2 vols. London, 1751.

Tucker, Abraham. *The Light of Nature Pursued* [1768], 4 vols. Cambridge, MA, 1831.

Turgot, Anne-Robert-Jacques. *Lettre au Docteur Price sur les constitutions américaines*, in *Oeuvres*, vol. 5, pp. 532–40.

Turgot, Anne-Robert-Jacques. *Oeuvres de Turgot, et documents le concernant, avec biographie et notes*, ed. G. Schelle, 5 vols. Paris, 1913–23.

Turgot, Anne-Robert-Jacques. *Plan de deux discours sur l'histoire universelle* [1751], in *Oeuvres*, vol. 1, pp. 275–323.

Turgot, Anne-Robert-Jacques. *Première Lettre à un grand vicaire* [1753], in *Oeuvres*, vol. 1, pp. 387–91.

Turgot, Anne-Robert-Jacques. *Turgot on Progress, Sociology and Economics*, trans. and ed. R. L. Meek. London, 1973.

[Turnbull, George]. *Christianity neither False nor Useless, tho' not as Old as the Creation: or, an Essay to prove the Usefulness, Truth, and Excellency of the Christian Religion*. London, 1732.

[Turnbull, George]. *A Philosophical Enquiry concerning the Connexion betwixt the Doctrines and Miracles of Jesus Christ* [1731], 3rd edn. London, 1739.

[Turner, Matthew]. *Answer to Dr. Priestley's Letters to a Philosophical Unbeliever*. London, 1782; repr. Bristol, 1996.

Tyson, Edward. *The Anatomy of a Pygmy Compared with that of a Monkey, an Ape, and a Man: With an Essay concerning the Pygmies*... *of the Antients* [*Orang-outang, sive homo sylvestris*, 1699], 2nd edn. London, 1751.

Vaillant, Paul. *Catalogue of Books in Most Languages and Faculties*. London, 1745.

Vandermonde, A.-T. "Remarques sur les problèmes de situation", in *Histoire de l'Académie Royale des Sciences, 1771*. Paris, 1774, pp. 566–74.

Vattel, Emerich de. *Défense du système Leibnitien contre les objections et les imputations de Mr. De Crousaz, contenues dans l'Examens de L'Essai sur l'Homme de Mr. Pope: où l'on a joint la Réponse aux objections de Mr. Roques*. Leiden, 1741.

Vico, Giambattista. *Autobiografia*, in *Opere*, vol. 5.

Vico, Giambattista. *The Autobiography of Giambattista Vico*, trans. M. H. Fisch and T. G. Bergin. Ithaca, NY, 1944.

Vico, Giambattista. *De antiquissima italorum sapientia ex linguae latinae originibus eruenda*, 3 vols. Naples, 1710.

Vico, Giambattista. *Institutiones oratoriae*, ed. G. Crifò (Naples, 1989).

Vico, Giambattista. *De nostri temporis studiorum ratione* [1709], in *Opere*, vol. 1.

Vico, Giambattista. *De universi iuris: uno principio, et fine uno*. Naples, 1720–1.

Vico, Giambattista. *The New Science* [rev. trans. of 3rd edn., 1744], trans. T. G. Bergin and M. H. Fisch. Ithaca, NY, 1948; (abridged) 1970; (unabridged) 1984.

Vico, Giambattista. *On the Ancient Wisdom of the Italians*, in *Selected Writings*.

Vico, Giambattista. *On Method in Contemporary Fields of Study*, in *Selected Writings*.

Vico, Giambattista. *On the Most Ancient Wisdom of the Italians* [1710], trans. L. M. Palmer. Ithaca, NY, 1988.

Vico, Giambattista. *Opere*, eds G. Gentile and F. Nicolini, 8 in 9 vols. Bari, 1914–41.

Vico, Giambattista. *Princípi di scienza nuova d'intorno alla comune natura delle nazioni*. Naples, 1747; in *Opere*, vol.

Vico, Giambattista. *Princípi di una scienza nuova intorno alla natura della nazioni*. Naples, 1725, rev. 1744.

Vico, Giambattista. *Selected Writings*, trans. and ed. L. Pompa. Cambridge, 1982.

Vico, Giambattista. *Universal Right*, trans. and eds. G. A. Pinton and M. Diehl. Amsterdam/Atlanta, GA, 2000.

Virey, Julien-Joseph. *Histoire naturelle de genre humain, ou, recherches sur les principaux fondements physiques et moraux, precedées d'un discours sur la nature des êtres organiques*, 3 vols. Paris, 1800–1.

Voltaire, François Marie Arouet de. *Avis public sur les parricides imputés aux Calas et aux Sirven*, in *Oeuvres complètes* (ed. Besterman), vol. 38, pp. 400–34.

Voltaire, François Marie Arouet de. *Candide ou L'optimisme*. Paris and Geneva, 1759.

Voltaire, François Marie Arouet de. *Collection complette des oeuvres de M. de Voltaire*, 30 vols. (Geneva, 1768–77).

Voltaire, François Marie Arouet de. *The Complete Works. See Les oeuvres complètes/The Complete Works*.

Voltaire, François Marie Arouet de. *Correspondence*, ed. T. Besterman, 107 vols. Geneva, 1953–65.

Voltaire, François Marie Arouet de. *Dictionnaire philosophique* [1752], eds. J. Benda and R. Naves. Paris, 1954; in *Oeuvres complètes* (ed. Moland), vols. 17ff; ed. C. Mervaud, in *Oeuvres complètes* (ed. Besterman), vols. 35–36.

Voltaire, François Marie Arouet de. *Dictionnaire philosophique portatif*. London [i.e., Geneva], 1764.

Voltaire, François Marie Arouet de. *Éléments de la philosophie de Newton*. London [i.e., Paris]; Amsterdam, 1738; in *Oeuvres complètes* (ed. Moland), vol. 22, pp. 403–7.

Voltaire, François Marie Arouet de. *The Elements of Sir Isaac Newton's Philosophy*, trans. J. Hanna. London, 1738.

Voltaire, François Marie Arouet de. *Essai sur les moeurs et l'esprit des nations* [1756], in *Oeuvres* (ed. Beuchot), vols. 15–18; in *Oeuvres complètes* (ed. Besterman), vol. 11.

[Voltaire, François Marie Arouet de]. *Extrait des sentimens de Jean Meslier, adressés à ses paroissiens, sur une partie des abus et des erreurs en général et en particulier*. Geneva, 1762.

Voltaire, François Marie Arouet de. *Histoire de la guerre de 1741* [1756]. Paris, 1971.

Voltaire, François Marie Arouet de. *Histoire de Jenni, ou le sage et l'athée*, in *Oeuvres complètes* (ed. Besterman), vol. 60, pp. 223–320.

Voltaire, François Marie Arouet de. *Homélie sur l'athéisme* [1767], in *Oeuvres complètes* (ed. Moland), vol. 26, pp. 315–29.

Voltaire, François Marie Arouet de. *Homélies prononcées à Londres en 1765*, in *Oeuvres complètes* (ed. Besterman), vol. 43, pp. 331–57.

Voltaire, François Marie Arouet de. *Homélies prononcées à Londres en 1765 dans une assemblée particulière*. Geneva, 1767.

Voltaire, François Marie Arouet de. *Letters concerning the English Nation*, ed. N. Cronk. Oxford, 1994.

Voltaire, François Marie Arouet de. *Letters on England*, trans. L. Tannock. Harmondsworth, 1980.

Voltaire, François Marie Arouet de. *Lettres philosophiques, ou Lettres sur les Anglais*. Amsterdam [i.e., Rouen], 1734; ed. G. Lanson, 2 vols, Paris, 1915; rev. edn., A-M Rousseau. Paris, 1964.

Voltaire, François Marie Arouet de. *Oeuvres*, ed. A. J. Q. Beuchot, 72 vols. Paris, 1829–40.

Voltaire, François Marie Arouet de. *Oeuvres complètes*, ed. L. Moland, 52 vols. Paris, 1877–85.

Voltaire, François Marie Arouet de. *Les Oeuvres complètes/The Complete Works*, ed. T. Besterman. Geneva/Toronto/Oxford, 1968–.

Voltaire, François Marie Arouet de. *Philosophical Dictionary*, trans. and ed. T. Besterman. Harmondsworth, 1971.

Voltaire, François Marie Arouet de. *Poème sur le désastre de Lisbonne*, in *Poèmes sur la religion naturelle, et sur la destruction de Lisbonne*. Paris, 1756.

Voltaire, François Marie Arouet de. "Remarques sur le bon sens ou Idées naturelles opposées aux idées surnaturelles" [1774], in *Oeuvres complètes* (ed. Moland), vol. 31, pp. 151–60.

Voltaire, François Marie Arouet de. *Siècle de Louis XIV*. Berlin, 1751.

Voltaire, François Marie Arouet de. *Traité de metaphysique* [1734], ed. H. A. Temple Patterson. Manchester, 1937; in *Oeuvres complètes* (ed. Moland), vol. 22, pp. 189–230.

Voltaire, François Marie Arouet de. *Traité sur la tolerance* [1763], in *L'Affaire Calas et autres affaires*, ed. J. van den Heuvel, Paris, 1975; ed. J. Renwick, in *Oeuvres complètes* (ed. Besterman), vol. 56 C.

Voltaire, François Marie Arouet de. *Treatise on Tolerance*, trans. B. Masters, ed. S. Harvey. Cambridge, 2000.

Voltaire, François Marie Arouet de. *Un chrétien contre six juifs ou Réfutation d'un livre intitulé Lettres de Quelques Juifs Portugais, Allemands, et Polonais*, in *Oeuvres complètes* (ed. Besterman), vol. 8.

[Vroesen Jan]. *L'esprit de Spinosa*, 1719.

Wallace, George. *A System of the Principles of the Law of Scotland*. Edinburgh, 1760.

Wallace, Robert. *The Regard due to Divine Revelation, and to Pretences to it, Considered*. London, 1731.

Wallace, Robert. *A Reply to a Letter directed to the Minister of Moffat, concerning the Positive Institutions of Christianity*. London, 1732.

Warburton, William. *The Alliance between Church and State, or, The Necessity and Equity of an Established Religion and a Test-Law demonstrated from the Essence and End of Civil Society, upon the Fundamental Principles of the Law of Nature and Nations*. London, 1736; also in Goldie (ed.), *The Reception of Locke's Politics*.

Warburton, William. *The Divine Legation of Moses*, 3 vols. London, 1738–41.

Warburton, William. *The Divine Legation of Moses Demonstrated, on the Principles of a Religious Deist, From the Omission of the Doctrine of a Future State of Reward and Punishment in the Jewish Dispensation*, 2nd edn., 2 vols. in 3. London, 1738–42.

Warburton, William. *Essai sur les hiéroglyphes des Egyptiens, ou l'on voit l'origine et les progrès du langage et de l'écriture, l'antiquité des sciences en Egypte, et l'origine du culte des animaux*, trans. M.-A. L. des Malpeines, 1744; Paris, 1977.

Warburton, William. *A Vindication of Mr. Pope's Essay on Man, from the Misrepresentations of Mr. de Crousaz . . . in Six Letters*. London, 1740.

[Waterland, Daniel]. *Advice to a Young Student, with a Method of Study for the Four First Years*, 2nd edn. London and Cambridge, 1730, reset as a third edition (Cambridge, 1760; n.p., 1761); "Second edition Corrected" (Oxford, 1755) later in *Works*, vol. 6.

[Waterland, Daniel]. "A Dissertation upon the Argument a Priori for Proving the Existence of a First Cause. In a Letter to Mr. Law", in E. Law, *An Enquiry into the Ideas of Space, Time, Immensity, and Eternity*.

Waterland, Daniel. *Works*, 10 vols. in 11, ed. W. Van Mildert. Oxford, 1823.

Watts, Isaac. *Logick: or, The Right Use of Reason in the Enquiry after Truth.* London, 1724; London 1725.

Webster, Noah. *On the Education of Youth in America.* Boston, MA, 1790; in *Essays on Education*, ed. F. Rudolph, pp. 41–78 (*see* B2).

Wesley, John. *Works*, 14 vols. London, 1872; facsim. Grand Rapids, MI, 1958.

West, Gilbert. *Observations on the History and Evidence of the Resurrection of Jesus Christ.* London, 1747.

Whiston, William. *A New Theory of the Earth, From Its Original, to the Consummation of All Things.* London, 1696.

Whitby, Daniel. *Ethices compendium in usum academicæ juventutis.* London, 1684.

White, Charles. *An Account of the Regular Gradation in Man, and in Different Animals and Vegetables; and from the Former to the Latter.* London, 1799.

Whitehead, John. *Materialism Philosophically Examined, Or, the Immateriality of the Soul Asserted and Proved, on Philosophical Principles.* London, 1778; repr. Bristol, 1992.

Wilcke, H. C. D. *De Politia naturae.* Uppsala, 1760.

Wilkins, John. *Of the Principles and Duties of Natural Religion.* London, 1675.

Winckelmann, Johann Joachim. *Geschichte der Kunst des Alterthums* [1764], in *Werke*, vol. 1.

Winckelmann, Johann Joachim. *Werke*, 2 vols. Stuttgart, 1847.

[Winkopp, Peter A.]. *Geschichte der Böhmischen Deisten nebst freimüthigen Bemerkungen über die Grundsäzze und Duldung der Deisten.* Leipzig, 1785.

Wissowatius, Andreas. *Religio rationalis seu de rationis judicio, in controversiis etiam theologicis, ac religiosis, adhibendo, tractatus.* [Amsterdam], 1685.

Witherspoon, John. *Lectures on Moral Philosophy* [1800–1], ed. V. L. Collins. Princeton, NJ, 1912.

Witherspoon, John. *The Selected Writings of John Witherspoon*, ed. T. Miller. Carbondale and Edwardsville, IL, 1990.

Witherspoon, John. *Works*, 4 vols. Philadelphia, PA, 1800–1.

Wolff, Christian. *Der Anfangsgründe aller Mathematischen Wissenschaften erster Theil, welcher einen Unterricht von der Mathematischen Lehr-Art, die Rechenkunst, Geometrie, Trigonometrie und Bau-Kunst in sich enthält* [1710], ed. P. Hoffmann, in *Werke*, Abt. 1, vol. 12 (1973).

Wolff, Christian. *Anmerckungen über die vernünfftigen Gedancken von Gott, der Welt und der Seele des Menschen* [1724] (facsim. repr. of 4th edn, 1740), ed. C. A. Corr, in *Werke*, Abt. I, vol. 3 (1983).

Wolff, Christian. *Ausführliche Nachricht von seinen eigenen Schriften, die er in deutscher Sprache von den verschiedenen Theilen der Welt-Weisheit ans Licht gestellet.* Frankfurt, 1726.

Wolff, Christian. *Christian Wolffs eigene Lebensbeschreibung*, ed. H. Wuttke. Leipzig, 1841.

Wolff, Christian. *Discursus praeliminaris de philosophia in genere.* Frankfurt and Leipzig, 1728.

Wolff, Christian. *Discursus praeliminaris de philosophia in genere/Einleitende Abhandlung über Philosophie im allgemeinen*, trans. and eds G. Gawlick and L. Kreimendahl. Stuttgart and Bad Cannstatt, 1996.

Wolff, Christian. *Gesammelte Werke*, ed. J. École. Hildesheim, 1962–; 3 *Abteilungen*: Abt. I, Deutsche Werke; Abt II, Lateinische Werke; Abt. III, Materialien und Dokumente.

Wolff, Christian. *Grundsätze des Natur- und Völckerrechts* [1754], ed. M. Thomann, in *Werke*, Abt. I, vol. 19.

Wolff, Christian. *Horae subsecivae Marburgenses* (Frankfurt/Leipzig, 1729–41), ed. J. École, in *Werke*, Abt. II, vol. 34.1–3.

Wolff, Christian. *Jus naturae, methodo scientifica pertractatum*, ed. M. Thomann, 8 vols., in *Werke*, Abt. II, vol. 17–24.

Wolff, Christian. *Logic, or Rational Thoughts on the Powers of the Human Understanding, with their Use and Application in the Knowledge and Search of Truth.* London, 1770.

Wolff, Christian. *Oratio de Sinarum philosophia practica*, in *Fasces Prorectorales Successori Traderet* (Frankfurt a. M., 1726).

Wolff, Christian. *Oratio de Sinarum philosophia practica/Rede über die praktische Philosophie der Chinesen* (1721), trans. and ed. M. Albrecht. Hamburg, 1985; English translation in Julia Ching and Willard G. Oxtoby, *Moral Enlightenment: Leibniz and Wolff on China* (Nettetal, 1992).

Wolff, Christian. *Philosophia prima, sive Ontologia, methodo scientifica pertractata* [1730] (facsim. of 2nd edn., Frankfurt, 1736), ed. J. École, in *Werke*, Abt. II, vol. 3 (1962).

Wolff, Christian. *Philosophia rationalis sive logica* (facsim. of 3rd edn. rev., Frankfurt, 1740), ed. J. École, in *Werke*, Abt. II, vol. 1.1–3 (1962).

Wolff, Christian. *Preliminary Discourse on Philosophy in General*, trans. R. J. Blackwell. Indianapolis, IN, 1963.

Wolff, Christian. *Psychologia empirica* [1732] (Frankfurt, 1738), in *Werke*, Abt. II, vol. 5 (1968).

Wolff, Christian. *Psychologia rationalis methodo scientifica pertractata* (Frankfurt and Leipzig, 1740 edn.), in *Werke*, Abt. II, vol. 6 (1972).

[Wolff, Christian]. Review of Leibniz, *Théodicée*, in *Acta Eruditorum*, March, 1711, pp. 110–21, and April 1711, pp. 159–68.

Wolff, Christian. *Theologia naturalis, methodo scientifica pertractata* [1736] (Frankfurt and Leipzig, 1739; Halle 1741), ed. J. École, in *Werke*, Abt. II, vol. 7.1–2 (1978), 8 (1980).

Wolff, Christian. *Vernünfftige Gedancken von dem gesellschafftigen Leben der Menschen und insonderheit dem gemeinen Wesen* (Frankfurt and Leipzig, 1736), ed. H. W. Arndt, in *Werke*, Abt. I, vol. 5 (1975).

Wolff, Christian. *Vernünfftige Gedancken von den Kräfften des menschlichen Verstandes und ihrem richtigen Gebrauche in Erkänntnis der Wahrheit* [1713], ed. H. W. Arndt, in *Werke*, Abt. I, vol. 1.

Wolff, Christian. *Vernünfftige Gedancken von der Menschen Thun und Lassen, zur Beförderung ihrer Glückseligkeit* (4th edn., 1733), ed. H. W. Arndt, in *Werke*, Abt. I, vol. 4 (1976).

Wolff, Christian. *Vernünfftige Gedancken von Gott, der Welt und der Seele des Menschen, auch allen Dingen überhaupt* [1719–20] (facsim. repr. of 11th edn., 1757), ed. C. A. Corr, in *Werke*, Abt. I, vol. 2 (1983).

Wolff, Christian. "Von den Regenten, die sich der Weltweisheit befleißigen, und von den Weltweisen, die das Regiment führen", in *Werke*, vol. 21.1–6 (*Gesammelte kleine philosophische Schriften*).

Wollaston, William. *The Religion of Nature Delineated* [1722]. London, 1738.

Wollstonecraft, Mary. *Thoughts on The Education of Daughters*. London, 1787.

Wollstonecraft, Mary. *A Vindication of the Rights of Men: in a Letter to the Right Honourable Edmund Burke : Occasioned by His Reflections on the Revolution in France; and, A Vindication of the Rights of Woman: With Strictures on Political and Moral Subjects*, eds. D. L. Macdonald and K. Scherf. Peterborough, Ont., 1997.

Wollstonecraft, Mary. *Vindication of the Rights of Woman*, ed. M. B. Kramnick. Harmondsworth, 1975.

Wollstonecraft, Mary. *Vindication of the Rights of Woman, With Strictures on Political and Moral Subjects*. London, 1792.

Woodward, John. *An Essay toward a Natural History of the Earth and Terrestrial Bodies*. London, 1695.

Woolston, Thomas. *A Discourse on the Miracles of our Saviour, in view of the Present Controversy between Infidels and Apostates*. London, 1727.

Woolston, Thomas. *A Second Discourse on the Miracles of our Saviour, in view of the Present Controversy between Infidels and Apostates*. London, 1727.

Woolston, Thomas. *Mr. Woolston's Defence of his Discourses on the Miracles of our Saviour. Against the Bishops of St. David's and London, and his other Adversaries*, 2 vols. London, 1729–30.
Wright, Thomas. *An Original Theory or New Hypothesis of the Universe, Founded upon the Laws of Nature*, 1750 edn., facsim., ed. M. A. Hoskin. London, 1971.
Wynne, John. *An Abridgment of Mr. Locke's Essay Concerning Humane Understanding*. London, 1696.
[Yale College]. *A Catalogue of the Library of Yale-College in New-Haven*. New London, CT, 1743.
Young, Edward. *The Complaint, or: Night Thoughts on Life, Death and Immortality*. York, 1742–4.
Young, Edward. *Conjectures on Original Composition* [1759], ed. E. J. Morley. Manchester, 1918.
Young, Matthew. *An Analysis of the Principles of Natural Philosophy*. Dublin, 1800.
Zedler, Johann Heinrich. *Grosses vollständiges Universal-Lexikon aller Wissenschaften und Künste*, 64 vols. Halle and Leipzig, 1732–50.
Zedlitz, Karl Abraham Freiherr von. "Vorschläge zur Verbesserung des Schulwesens in den Königlichen Ländern". *Berlinische Monatschrift* 2 (1778): 97–115.
Ziegra, Christian, ed. *Sammlung der Streitschriften ueber die Lehre von der besten Welt und verschiedene damit verknuepfte wichtige Wahrheiten*. Rostock-Wismar, 1759.
Zimmermann, Eberhard August Wilhelm von. *Geographische Geschichte des Menschen, und der allgemein verbreiteten vierfüssigen Thiere: nebst einer hieher gehörigen zoologischen Weltcharte*. Leipzig, 1778–83.

Manuscript Material

Anonymous. *L'examen de la religion*. Landsdowne. 414, British Library, London.
Anonymous. *Le livre des trois imposteurs*. Add. Mss. 12064, British Library, London; Amsterdam, 1719.
Bowman, Walter. Papers. National Library, Florence. N. A. 1197.
Brissot de Warville, Jean-Pierre. *Pyrrhon*, Unpublished manuscript. Archives nationales. Paris. 446/AP/21.
Carmichael, Gerschom. Lecture dictates on metaphysics, pneumatology and natural theology. New College collection. Dr Williams's Library, London.
Carmichael, Gerschom. *Gershom Carmichael's Account of His Teaching Method*, 1712. GUL 43170, Glasgow University Library.
Drummond, Collin, and William Law. Drummond and Law dictates. MSS 3938, 183. National Library of Scotland, Edinburgh.
Kames, Henry Home, Lord. Papers. National Archives of Scotland, Edinburgh. GD24/1/548.

Serials and Collective Works

Acta Eruditorum. Leipzig, 1682–1731.
Allgemeine Deutsche Bibliothek, ed. F. Nicolai, Kiel, 1766–92.
Annual Review. 7 vols. London, 1803–7.
Berlinische Monatsschrift. 28 vols. Berlin, 1783–96.
Bibliothèque britannique. 25 vols. The Hague, 1733–47.
Bibliothèque raisonnée. 52 vols. Amsterdam, 1728–53.
Bibliothek der schönen Wissenschaften und der freyen Künste, eds. F. Nicolai, M. Mendelssohn and C. F. Weisse, 12 vols, Leipzig, 1757–65.
Briefe, die neueste Litteratur betreffend, ed. F. Nicolai, Berlin, 1759–65.
Dictionnaire de l'Académie française. 2 vols. Paris, 1694; 5th edn. 1798.
Edinburgh Review. 2 vols. Edinburgh, 1755.
Encyclopædia Britannica. 1st edn., ed. W. Smellie, 3 vols. Edinburgh, 1771.
Encyclopædia Britannica. 3rd edn., 15 vols. Edinburgh, 1788–97.

Encyclopédie méthodique. Grammaire et littérature. eds. N. Beauzée and J.-F. Marmontel, 3 vols. Paris, 1782–6.

English Encyclopaedia. 10 vols. London, 1802.

The English Cyclopedia: A New Dictionary of Universal Knowledge, ed. C. Knight. 27 vols. London, 1754–72.

Estratto della letteratura europea, ed. F. B. de Felice, Berne and Yderdon (i.e., Milan and Brescia), 1758–66.

The Female Tatler, London, 1709–10; modern edition by F. Morgan, London and Rutland, VT, 1992.

Göttingische Anzeigen von Gelehrten Sachen. Göttingen, 1753–1801.

Historisches Wörterbuch der Philosophie, see Ritter, Joachim et al. (*B2*).

Il Caffè, Milan, 1764–6.

Journal littéraire, The Hague, 1713–37.

Literary Journal, Dublin, 1744–49.

Mémoires de l'Académie royale des sciences et belles-lettres depuis l'avénement de Frédéric Guillaume III au trone, Berlin, 1792–1807.

Mémoires pour l'histoire des sciences et des beaux-arts (Mémoires de Trévoux), Paris, 1701–67.

Nouvelle Bibliothèque germanique. 26 vols. Amsterdam, 1746–60.

Nouvelles de la République des Lettres, eds. P. Bayle, et al., Amsterdam, 1684–1718.

The Present State of the Republic of Letters. London, 1728–1736. *Science in Context*, see (*B2*).

B2. BIBLIOGRAPHY: AFTER 1800

Aarsleff, Hans. *From Locke to Saussure: Essays on the Study of Language and Intellectual History.* Minneapolis, MN, 1982.

Aarsleff, Hans. "Introduction", in E. B. de Condillac, *Essay on the Origin of Human Knowledge*, pp. xi–xxxviii (*B1*).

Aarsleff, Hans. "Introduction", in W. von Humboldt, *On Language: The Diversity of Human Language-Structure and its Influence on the Mental Development of Mankind* (*B1*).

Aarsleff, Hans. "Locke's Influence", in *The Cambridge Companion to Locke*, ed. V. Chappell. Cambridge, 1994, pp. 252–289.

Aarsleff, Hans. "Origin of Universal Languages". *Language and Society* 6 (1977): 281–8.

Aarsleff, Hans. "Review Essay". *Anthropological Linguistics* 43 (2001): 491–507.

Aarsleff, Hans. "The Rise and Decline of Adam and His *Ursprache* in Seventeenth-Century Thought", in *The Language of Adam/Die Sprache Adams*, ed. A. P. Coudert. Wolfenbüttel, 1999, pp. 277–95.

Aarsleff, Hans. *The Study of Language in England 1780–1860.* London, 1983.

Abanime, P. Emeka. "Voltaire as an Anthropologist: The Case of the Albino". *Studies on Voltaire and the Eighteenth Century* 143 (1975): 85–104.

Adams, Geoffrey. *The Huguenots and French Opinion, 1685–1787: The Enlightenment Debate on Toleration.* Waterloo, Ont., 1991.

Adams, Marilyn McCord, and Robert Merrihew Adams, eds. *The Problem of Evil.* Oxford, 1990.

Adams, Robert M. *Determinist, Theist, Idealist.* Oxford, 1994.

Adickes, Erich. *Kant als Naturforscher*, 2 vols. Berlin, 1924–5.

Adickes, Erich. *Kants Ansichten über Geschichte und Bau der Erde.* Tübingen, 1911.

Ainslie, Donald. "Scepticism about Persons in Book II of the *Treatise*". *Journal of the History of Philosophy* 37 (1999): 469–492.

Aiton, Eric John. *The Vortex Theory of Planetary Motions.* London, 1972.

Albrecht, Michael. *Eklektik: Eine Begriffsgeschichte mit Hinweisen auf die Philosophie- und Wissenschaftsgeschichte.* Stuttgart and Bad Cannstatt, 1994.

Albrecht, Michael. *Kants Antinomie der praktischen Vernunft.* Hildesheim, 1978.

Aldridge, Alfred Owen. *Benjamin Franklin and Nature's God*. Durham, NC, 1967.
Allen, David Elliston. "Natural History in Britain in the Eighteenth Century". *Archives of Natural History* 20 (1993): 333–47.
Allen, David Elliston. *The Naturalist in Britain: A Social History*. London, 1976.
Allen, Richard C. *David Hartley on Human Nature*. Albany, NY, 1999.
Allison, Henry E. *Kant's Transcendental Idealism: An Interpretation and Defense*. New Haven, CT, 1983.
Almagor, Joseph. *Pierre Des Maizeaux (1673–1745), Journalist and English Correspondent for Franco-Dutch Periodicals, 1700–1720*. Amsterdam and Maarssens, 1989.
Althusser, Louis. *Montesquieu, la politique et l'histoire*. Paris, 1959.
Altmann, Alexander. "Gewissensfreiheit und Toleranz. Eine begriffsgeschichtliche Untersuchung", in *Die trostvolle Aufklärung: Studien zur Metaphysik und politischen Theorie Moses Mendelssohns*, pp. 245–75.
Altmann, Alexander. *Die trostvolle Aufklärung, Studien zur Metaphysik und politischen Theorie Moses Mendelssohns*. Stuttgart and Bad Cannstatt, 1982.
Ameriks, Karl. *Kant and the Fate of Autonomy: Problems in the Appropriation of the Critical Philosophy*. Cambridge, 2000.
Ameriks, Karl. *Kant's Theory of Mind: An Analysis of the Paralogisms of Pure Reason*. Oxford, 1982.
Anderson, Abraham. *The Treatise of the Three Impostors and the Problem of Enlightenment. A New Translation of the 'Traité des trios imposteurs' (1777 edition)*, Lanham, MD, 1997.
Anderson, P. J. *Fasti academiae Mariscallanae Aberdonensis*, 3 vols. Aberdeen, 1889–98.
Andrewes, William J. H., ed. *The Quest for Longitude*. Cambridge, MA, 1996.
Anellis, I. H. "Theology against Logic: The Origins of Logic in Old Russia". *History and Philosophy of Logic* 13 (1992): 15–42.
Aner, Karl. *Die Theologie der Lessingzeit*. Halle, 1929.
Angehrn, Emil. "Der Begriff des Glücks und die Frage der Ethik". *Philosophisches Jahrbuch* 92 (1985): 35–52.
Angelelli, Ignacio. "The Techniques of Disputation in the History of Logic". *The Journal of Philosophy* 67 (1970): 800–15.
Annan, Noel. *Our Age, Portrait of a Generation*. London, 1990.
Antognazza, Maria-Rosa. "The Defence of the Mysteries of the Trinity and the Incarnation: An Example of Leibniz's 'Other' Reason". *British Journal for the History of Philosophy* 9/2 (2001): 283–309.
Antognazza, Maria-Rosa. "Inediti leibniziani sulle polemiche trinitarie". *Rivista di filosofia neoscolastica* 83 (1991): 525–50.
Antognazza, Maria-Rosa. "Die Rolle der Trinitäts- und Menschenwürdigungsdiskussion für die Entstehung von Leibniz' Denken". *Studia Leibnitiana* 26 (1994): 56–75.
Antognazza, Maria-Rosa. *Trinità e Incarnazione: il rapporto tra filosofia e teologia rivelata nel pensiero di Leibniz*. Milan, 1999.
Appel, Toby. *The Cuvier-Geoffroy Debate: French Biology in the Decades Before Darwin*. New York, NY, 1987.
Ariès, Philippe. *Centuries of Childhood*, trans. R. Baldick. London, 1962.
Ariès, Philippe. *L'Enfant et la vie familiale sous l'ancien régime*. Paris, 1960.
Arkush, Allan. *Moses Mendelssohn and the Enlightenment*. Albany, NY, 1994.
Arndt, Hans Werner. *Methodo scientifica pertractatum. Mos geometricus und Kalkülbegriff in der philosophischen Theoriebildung des 17. und 18. Jahrhunderts*. Berlin, 1971.
Arnold, Günter. "Das schaffhauser Urmanuskript der 'Ältesten Urkunde des Menschengeschlechts' und sein Verhältnis zur Druckfassung", in *Bückeburger Gespräche über Johann Gottfried Herder 1988*, ed. B. Poschman. Rinteln, 1989.

Ashworth, E. J. "Locke on Language". *Canadian Journal of Philosophy* 14 (1984): 45–73.
Ashworth, William. "Emblematic Natural History of the Renaissance", in *The Cultures of Natural History*, eds. N. Jardine, J. Secord, and E. Spary, pp. 17–37.
Ashworth, William. "Natural History and the Emblematic World View", in *Reappraisals of the Scientific Revolution*, eds. D. C. Lindberg and R. S. Westman. Cambridge, 1990, pp. 303–32.
Atherton, Margaret. *Berkeley's Revolution in Vision*. Ithaca, NY, 1990.
Atiyah, P. S. *The Rise and Fall of Freedom of Contract*. Oxford, 1979.
Atkinson, R. F. "Hume on Mathematics". *Philosophical Quarterly* 10 (1960): 127–37.
Atlas, Samuel. *From Critical to Speculative Idealism: The Philosophy of Solomon Maimon*. The Hague, 1964.
Atran, Scott. *Cognitive Foundations of Natural History*. Cambridge, 1990.
Attfield, Robin. *God and the Secular: A Philosophical Assessment of Secular Reasoning from Bacon to Kant*. Cardiff, 1978.
Aubery, Pierre. "Montesquieu et les Juifs". *Studies on Voltaire and the Eighteenth Century* 87 (1972): 87–99.
Augstein, H. F., ed. *Race: The Origins of An Idea, 1760–1850*. Bristol, 1996.
Austen, Jane. *Pride and Prejudice* (1813), ed. R. W. Chapman. Oxford, 1988.
Austin, John. *Lectures on Jurisprudence, or The Philosophy of Positive Law*, 5th edn., ed. R. Campbell, 2 vols. London, 1885.
Ayers, Michael. *Locke*, 2 vols. London, 1991.
Bacharach, Armand. *Shaftesburys Optimismus und sein Verhältnis zum Leibnizschen*. Thann, 1912.
Bachelard, Suzanne. *Les polémiques concernant le principe de moindre action au XVIIIe siècle*. Paris, 1961.
Bachmann, Hanns-Martin. *Die naturrechtliche Staatslehre Christian Wolffs*. Berlin, 1977.
Baczko, Bronislaw, ed. *Une éducation pour la démocratie*. Paris, 1982.
Baeumler, Alfred. *Das Irrationalitätsproblem in der Ästhetik und Logik des 18. Jahrhunderts bis zur Kritik der Urteilskraft*. Darmstadt, 1974.
Baier, Annette. "Hume, the Women's Moral Theorist?", in *Moral Prejudices: Essays on Ethics*. Cambridge, MA, 1994, pp. 51–75.
Bailyn, Bernard. *Education in the Forming of American Society: Needs and Opportunities for Study*. New York, NY, 1972.
Bailyn, Bernard. *The Ideological Origins of the American Revolution*. Cambridge, 1967.
Baker, Keith Michael. *Condorcet: From Natural Philosophy to Social Mathematics*. Chicago, IL, 1975.
Balázs, Eva H., et al., eds. *Beförderer der Aufklärung in Mittel- und Osteuropa. Freimaurer, Gesellschaften, Clubs*. Berlin, 1979.
Bantock, G. H. *Studies in the History of Educational Theory*, 2 vols. London, 1980–4; vol. 1: *Artifice and Nature*, 1350–1765, vol. 2: *The Minds and the Masses, 1760–1980*.
Barber, Kenneth F., and Jorge J. E. Gracia, eds. *Individuation and Identity in Early Modern Philosophy. Descartes to Kant*. Albany, NY, 1994.
Barber, W. H. *Leibniz in France, from Arnauld to Voltaire: A Study in French Reactions to Leibnizianism 1670–1760*. Oxford, 1955.
Barfoot, Michael. "Hume and the Culture of Science in the Early Eighteenth Century", in *Studies in the Philosophy of the Scottish Enlightenment*, ed. M. A. Stewart, pp. 151–90.
Barlow, Richard Burgess. *Citizenship and Conscience: A Study in the Theory and Practice of Religious Toleration in England during the Eighteenth Century*. Philadelphia, PA, 1962.
Barnouw, Jeffrey. "The Philosophical Achievement and Historical Significance of Johann Nicolaus Tetens". *Studies in Eighteenth-Century Culture* 9 (1979): 301–35.

Barth, Hans-Martin. *Atheismus und Orthodoxie: Analysen und Modelle christlicher Apologetik im 17. Jahrhundert*. Göttingen, 1971.

Baum, Manfred. "Methode, transzendentale", in *Historisches Wörterbuch der Philosophie*, vol. 5 (1980), pp. 1375–8.

Baumgart, Peter. "Karl Abraham Freiherr von Zedlitz", in *Berlinische Lebensbilder. Wissenschaftspolitik in Berlin*, ed. W. Ribbe. Berlin, 1987.

Beaglehole, J. C. "Eighteenth Century Science and the Voyages of Discovery". *New Zealand Journal of History* 3 (1969): 107–23.

Beales, Derek. "Social Forces and Enlightened Policies", in *Enlightened Absolutism: Reform and Reformers in Later Eighteenth Century Europe*, ed. H. M. Scott. London, 1990, pp. 37–53.

Beck, Lewis White. *Early German Philosophy: Kant and His Predecessors*. Cambridge, MA, 1969.

Beck, Lewis White. "From Leibniz to Kant", in *The Age of German Idealism*, eds. R. C. Solomon. and K. M. Higgins. London, 1993, pp. 5–39.

Becker, George. "Pietism's Confrontation with Enlightenment Rationalism: An Examination of Ascetic Protestantism and Science". *Journal for the Scientific Study of Religion* 30 (1991): 139–58.

Becq, Annie. *Genèse de l'esthétique française 1680–1814*. Paris, 1994.

Bedini, Silvio A. *Thomas Jefferson, Statesman of Science*. New York, NY, 1990.

Beiser, Frederick C. *Enlightenment, Revolution and Romanticism: The Genesis of Modern German Political Thought, 1790–1800*. Cambridge, MA, 1992.

Beiser, Frederick C. *The Fate of Reason: German Philosophy from Kant to Fichte*. Cambridge, MA, 1987.

Belaval, Yvon. *Études leibniziennes: de Leibniz à Hegel*. Paris, 1976.

Bellah, Robert N. "The Revolution and Civil Religion", in *Religion and the American Revolution*, ed. J. C. Brauer. Philadelphia, PA, 1976, pp. 55–73.

Benitez, M. "Eléments d'une sociologie de la littérature clandestine: lecteurs et éditeurs de Telliamed", in *De bonne main. La communication manuscrite au XVIIIe siècle*, ed. F. Moureau. Paris, 1993, pp. 71–96.

Benitez, Miguel. *La face cache des Lumières. Recherches sur les manuscripts philosophiques clandestines de l'âge classique*. Oxford and Paris, 1994.

Benitez, Miguel. "Matériaux pour un inventaire des manuscrits philosophiques clandestins des XVIIe et XVIIIIe siècles". *Rivista di storia della filosofia* 3 (1988): 501–31.

Beretta, Marco. *The Enlightenment of Matter. The Definition of Chemistry from Agricola to Lavoisier*. Canton, MA, 1993.

Bergeal, Catherine. *Protestantisme et tolérance en France au XVIIIe siècle. De la Révocation à la Révolution, 1685–1789*. Carrières-sous-Poissy, 1988.

Berghahn, Klaus L. *Grenzen der Toleranz: Juden und Christen im Zeitalter der Aufklärung*. Vienna, 2000.

Berkvens-Stevelinck, Christine. *Prosper Marchand: la vie et l'oeuvre 1678–1756*. Leiden, 1987.

Berlin, Isaiah. *Against the Current: Essays in the History of Ideas*. London, 1979.

Berlin, Isaiah. "The Counter-Enlightenment", in *Against the Current: Essays in the History of Ideas*, pp. 1–24.

Berlin, Isaiah. "The Magus of the North". *New York Review of Books* 40.17 (1993): 64–71.

Berman, David. "Anthony Collins: Aspects of His Thought and Writings". *Hermathena* 119 (1975): 49–70.

Berman, David. "David Hume and the Suppression of 'Atheism'". *Journal of the History of Philosophy* 21 (1983): 375–87.

Berman, David. "Deism, Immortality, and the Art of Theological Lying", in *Deism, Masonry, and the Enlightenment: Essays Honoring Alfred Owen Aldridge*, ed. J. A. L. Lemay. Newark, DE, 1987, pp. 61–78.

Berman, David. "Disclaimers as Offence Mechanisms in Charles Blount and John Toland", in *Atheism from the Reformation to the Enlightenment*, eds. M. Hunter and D. Wootton. Oxford, 1992, pp. 255–72.
Berman, David. *George Berkeley. Idealism and the Man*. Oxford, 1994.
Berman, David. *A History of Atheism in Britain: From Hobbes to Russell*. London, 1988; London, 1990.
Berman, David. "The Theoretical/Practical Distinction as Applied to the Existence of God from Locke to Kant". *Trivium* 12 (1977): 92–108.
Bernasconi, Robert. "Who Invented the Concept of Race? Kant's Role in the Enlightenment Construction of Race", in *Race*, ed. R. Bernasconi. Malden, MA and Oxford, 2001, pp. 11–36.
Berti, Silvia. "The First Edition of the *Traité des trois imposteurs* and Its Debt to Spinoza's *Ethics*", in *Atheism from the Reformation to the Enlightenment*, eds. M. Hunter and D. Wootton. Oxford, 1992, pp. 183–220.
Besterman, Theodore. "Voltaire et le désastre de Lisbonne: ou, La mort de l'optimisme". *Studies on Voltaire and the Eighteenth Century* 2 (1956): 7–24.
Bianco, Bruno. "'Vernünftiges Christentum': Aspects et problèmes d'interpretation de la néologie allemande du XVIIIe siècle". *Archives de philosophie* 46 (1983): 179–218.
Biggs, Norman L., E. Keith Lloyd, and Robin J. Wilson. *Graph Theory 1736–1936*. Oxford, 1976.
Binoche, Bertrand. *Les trois sources des philosophies de l'histoire: (1764–1798)*. Paris, 1994.
Birtsch, Günter. "Religions- und Gewissensfreiheit in Preussen von 1780 bis 1817". *Zeitschrift für Historische Forschung* 11 (1984): 177–204.
Blackall, Eric A. *The Emergence of German as a Literary Language 1770–1775*. Cambridge, 1959.
Blackwell, Constance. "Diogenes Laërtius's 'Life of Pyrrho' and the Interpretation of Ancient Scepticism in the History of Philosophy – Stanley through Brucker to Tennemann", in *Scepticism and Irreligion in the Seventeenth and Eighteenth Centuries*, eds. R. H. Popkin and A. Vanderjagt, pp. 324–57.
Blanckaert, Claude. "J. J. Virey, observateur de l'homme (1800–1825)", in *Julien-Joseph Virey: naturaliste et anthropologue*, eds. C. Benichou and C. Blanckaert. Paris, 1988, pp. 97–182.
Blanckaert, Claude, et al., eds. *Le muséum au premier siècle de son histoire*. Paris, 1997.
Blettermann, Petra. *Die Universitätspolitik August des Starken 1694–1733*. Cologne, 1990.
Bloch, Jean H. *Rousseauism and Education in Eighteenth-Century France*. Oxford, 1995.
Bloch, Jean H. "Women and the Reform of the Nation", in *Women and Society in Eighteenth-Century France: Essays in Honour of John Stephenson Spink*, eds. E. Jacobs, et al.
Bloch, Olivier, ed. *Le matérialisme du XVIII siècle et la littérature clandestine: actes de la table ronde des 6 et 7 juin 1980*. Paris, 1982.
Bloch, Olivier, ed. *Spinoza au XVIIIe siécle*, Paris, 1990.
Blumenfeld, David. "Leibniz's Theory of the Striving Possibles". *Studia Leibnitiana* 5 (1973): 163–73.
Bobro, Marc. "Is Leibniz's Theory of Personal Identity Coherent?" *The Leibniz Review* 9 (1999): 117–129.
Bobro, Marc. *Self and Substance in Leibniz*. Dordrecht and Boston, 2004.
Bödeker, Hans Erich. "Journals and Public Opinion: The Politicization of the German Enlightenment in the Second Half of the Eighteenth Century", in *The Transformation of Political Culture*, ed. E. Hellmuth, pp. 423–45.
Bödeker, Hans Erich. "'Menschenrechte' im deutschen publizistischen Diskurs vor 1789", in *Grund- und Freiheitsrechte von der ständischen zur spätbürgerlichen Gesellschaft*, ed. G. Birtsch. Göttingen, 1987, pp. 392–433.

Bödeker, Hans Erich, and Ulrich Herrmann, eds. *Aufklärung als Politisierung – Politisierung der Aufklärung*. Hamburg, 1987.

Bois, Pierre-André. "Engagement maçonnique et engagement révolutionnaire: Les droits de l'homme comme 'Religion de l'humanité' d'après Knigge". *Francia* 16 (1989): 99–113.

Bolam, C. G., et al. *The English Presbyterians: From Elizabethan Puritanism to Modern Unitarianism*. London, 1968.

Bongie, Lawrence L. *David Hume, Prophet of the Counter-Revolution*. Oxford, 1965.

Bonnel, Roland, and Catherine Rubinger, eds. *Femmes savantes et femmes d'esprit: Women Intellectuals of the French Eighteenth Century*. New York, NY, 1994.

Bonwick, Colin. *English Radicals and the American Revolution*. Chapel Hill, NC, 1977.

Borghero, Carlo. *La Certezza e la Storia: Cartesianesimo, Pirronismo e Conoscenza Storica*. Milan, 1983.

Borghero, Carlo. "Dal 'Génie' all' 'Esprit'. Fisico e morale nelle considérations", in *Storia e ragione*, ed. A. Postigliola. Naples, 1987, pp. 251–76.

Bos, H. J. M. "Differentials, Higher-Order Differentials and the Derivative in the Leibnizian Calculus". *Archive for History of Exact Sciences* 14 (1974): 1–90.

Bos, H. J. M. "Mathematics and Rational Mechanics", in *The Ferment of Knowledge: Studies in the Historiography of Eighteenth-Century Science*, eds. G. S. Rousseau and R. Porter. Cambridge, 1980.

Bowen, James. *The Modern West: Europe and the New World*, in *A History of Western Education*, 3 vols. London, 1972–81, vol. 3.

Boyd, William. *The Educational Theory of Jean Jacques Rousseau*. London, 1911.

Boyer, Carl B. *The History of the Calculus and Its Conceptual Development: The Concepts of the Calculus*. New York, NY, 1959 (first published as *Concepts of the Calculus*, 1949).

Bracken, Harry M. "Bayle's Attack on Natural Theology: The Case of Christian Pyrrhonism", in *Scepticism and Irreligion in the Seventeenth and Eighteenth Centuries*, eds. R. H. Popkin and A. Vanderjagt, pp. 254–66.

Bracken, Harry M. "Philosophy and Racism". *Philosophia* 8 (1978): 241–60.

Bradley, James E. *Religion, Revolution, and English Radicalism: Nonconformity in Eighteenth-Century Politics and Society*. Cambridge, 1990.

Brandes, Ernst. *Betrachtungen über das weibliche Geschlecht und dessen Ausbildung in dem geselligen Leben*, 3 vols. Hannover, 1802.

Brandes, Ernst. *Ueber das Du und Du zwischen Eltern und Kindern*. Hannover, 1809.

Brands, Hartmut. *'Cogito ergo sum': Interpretationen von Kant bis Nietzsche*. Freiburg, 1982.

Brandt, Reinhard. *D'Artagnan und die Urteilstafel: Über ein Ordnungsprinzip der europäischen Kulturgeschichte*. Munich, 1998.

Brandt, Reinhard. "Beobachtungen zur gedanklichen und formalen Architektonik Humescher Schriften". *Archiv für Geschichte der Philosophie* 72 (1990): 47–62.

Brandt, Reinhard. "Raum und Zeit in der 'Transzendentalen Ästhetik' der Kritik der reinen Vernunft", in *Rehabilitierung des Subjektiven: Festschrift für Hermann Schmitz*, eds. M. Großheim and H.-J. Waschkies. Bonn, 1993, pp. 441–58.

Brandt, Reinhard. *Rousseaus Philosophie der Gesellschaft*. Stuttgart, 1973.

Braun, Lucien. *Histoire de l'histoire de la philosophie*. Paris, 1973.

Breazeale, Daniel. "Fichte on Skepticism". *Journal of the History of Philosophy* 29 (1991): 427– 53.

Breger, Herbert. "Symmetry in Leibnizian Physics", in *The Leibniz Renaissance: International Workshop . . . 1986*. Florence, 1989, pp. 23–42.

Briggs, Robin. "The Académie Royale des Sciences and the Pursuit of Utility". *Past and Present* 131 (1991): 38–88.

Broadie, Alexander, ed. *The Cambridge Companion to the Scottish Enlightenment*. Cambridge, 2003.

Broberg, Gunnar. "Homo Sapiens: Linnaeus's Classification of Man", in *Linnaeus: The Man and His Work*, ed. T. Frängsmyr. Berkeley, CA, 1983.

Brockliss, L. W. B. "The European University in the Age of Revolution 1789–1850", in *The History of Oxford University*, ed. T. H. Aston, 8 vols. Oxford, 1984–2000, vol. 6: *Nineteenth Century Oxford*, pt. I, eds. M. G. Brock and M. C. Curthoys. Oxford, 1997, 77–133.

Brockliss, L. W. B. *French Higher Education in the Seventeenth and Eighteenth Centuries: A Cultural History*. Oxford, 1987.

Brockliss, L. W. B. "Philosophy teaching in France 1600–1740". *History of Universities* 1 (1981): 131–68.

Brogi, Stefano. *Il cerchio dell'universo: Libertinismo, Spinozismo e filosofia della natura in Boulainvilliers*. Florence, 1993.

Brogi, Stefano. *Teologia senza verità. Bayle contro i 'rationaux'*. Milan, 1998.

Bronson, W. C. *The History of Brown University*. Providence, RI, 1914.

Brook, Andrew. *Kant and the Mind*. Cambridge, 1994.

Brooke, John H. *Science and Religion: Some Historical Perspectives*. Cambridge, 1991.

Brougham, Henry, Lord. *A Discourse of Natural Theology*. London, 1835.

Brown, Alice. *The Eighteenth-Century Feminist Mind*. Brighton, 1987.

Brown, John, ed. *Theological Tracts*. 3 vols. Edinburgh, 1853–4.

Brown, Sanborn C. *Count Rumford on the Nature of Heat*. New York, NY, 1967.

Brown, Thomas. *Lectures on the Philosophy of the Human Mind*, 2 vols. Edinburgh, 1820.

Browne, Janet. *The Secular Ark: Studies in the History of Biogeography*. New Haven, CT, 1983.

Brüggemann, Fritz, ed. *Aus der Frühzeit der deutschen Aufklärung: Christian Thomasius und Christian Weise*. Leipzig, 1938.

Brühlmeier, Daniel. *Die Rechts- und Staatslehre von Adam Smith und die Interessentheorie der Verfassung*. Berlin, 1988.

Brunet, Pierre. *Maupertuis*, 2 vols. Paris, 1929.

Brunet, Pierre. *Les physiciens Hollandais et la méthode expérimentale en France au XVIIIe siecle*. Paris, 1926.

Brunner, O., W. Conze, and R. Koselleck, eds. *Geschichtliche Grundbegriffe. Historisches Lexikon zur politisch-sozialen Sprache in Deutschland*. 8 vols. Stuttgart, 1972–97.

Bryce, R. "Paolo Ruffini and the Quintic Equation". *Symposia Mathematica* 27 (1986): 169–85.

Brykman, Geneviève. *Berkeley: Philosophie et apologétique*, 2 vols. Paris, 1984.

Brykman, Geneviève. *Berkeley et le voile des mots*. Paris, 1993.

Büchel, Gregor. *Geometrie und Philosophie*. Berlin, 1987.

Buchholz, Stephan. "Christian Thomasius: Zwischen Orthodoxie und Pietismus – Religionskonflikte und ihre literarische Verarbeitung", in *Christian Thomasius, 1655–1728. Interpretationen zu Werk und Wirkung*, ed. W. Schneiders, pp. 248–55.

Buckle, Stephen. *Natural Law and the Theory of Property: Grotius to Hume*. Oxford, 1991.

Buckley, Michael J. *At the Origins of Modern Atheism*. New Haven, CT, 1987.

Buickerood, J. G. "The Natural History of the Understanding: Locke and the Rise of Facultative Logic in the Eighteenth Century". *History and Philosophy of Logic* 6 (1985): 157–90.

Buickerood, J. G. "*Two Dissertations concerning Sense, and the Imagination. With an Essay on Consciousness* (1728): A Study in Attribution". *1650–1850: Ideas, Aesthetics, and Inquiries in the Early Modern Era* 7 (2002): 51–86.

Burgelin, Pierre. "L'Éducation de Sophie". *Annales de la societé J-J Rousseau* 35 (1959–62): 113–37.

Burgelin, Pierre. *La philosophie de l'existence de J-J Rousseau*. Paris, 1952.

Burns, R. M. *The Great Debate on Miracles: From Joseph Glanvill to David Hume*. Lewisburg, PA and London, 1981.

Burtt, Shelley. *Virtue Transformed: Political Argument in England, 1688–1740*. Cambridge, 1992.
Bury, J. B. *The Idea of Progress: An Inquiry into Its Origin and Growth*. London, 1920.
Buschmann, Cornelia. "Die philosophischen Preisfragen und Preisschriften der Berliner Akademie der Wissenschaften im 18. Jahrhundert", in *Aufklärung in Berlin*, ed. W. Förster. Berlin, 1989, pp. 165–228.
Butts, Robert E. "Rules, Examples and Constructions: Kant's Theory of Mathematics". *Synthese* 47 (1981): 257–88.
Butts, Robert E., and John W. Davis, eds. *The Methodological Heritage of Newton*. Oxford, 1970.
Cairns, David. "Natural Theology", in *A Handbook of Christian Theology*, eds. M. Halverson and A. A. Cohen. New York, NY, 1958, pp. 249–56.
Cajori, Floridan. "Frederick the Great on Mathematics and Mathematicians". *American Mathematical Monthly* 34 (1927): 122–30.
Campbell, T. D. *Adam Smith's Science of Morals*. London, 1971.
Canovan, Margaret. "Rousseau's Two Concepts of Citizenship", in *Women in Western Political Philosophy*, eds. E. Kennedy and S. Mendus. Brighton, 1987, pp. 78–105.
Cantor, Geoffrey N. "Berkeley's *The Analyst* Revisited". *Isis* 75 (1984): 668–83.
Cantor, Geoffrey N. *Optics after Newton: Theories of Light in Britain and Ireland, 1704–1840*. Manchester, 1983.
Canzoni, G., ed. *Filosofia e religione nella letteratura clandestina*. Milan, 1994.
Carayol, Elisabeth. *Thémiseul de Saint-Hyacinthe, 1684–1746*. Oxford, 1984.
Carboncini, Sonia. "Die thomasianisch-pietistische Tradition und ihre Fortsetzung durch Christian August Crusius", in *Christian Thomasius, 1655–1728: Interpretationen zu Werk und Wirkung*, ed. W. Schneiders. Hamburg, 1989, pp. 287–304.
Carboncini, Sonia. *Transzendentale Wahrheit und Traum: Christian Wolffs Antwort auf die Herausforderung durch den Cartesianischen Zweifel*. Stuttgart-Bad Cannstatt, 1991.
Cardwell, D. S. L. "Science, Technology and Industry", in *The Ferment of Knowledge: Studies in the Historiography of Eighteenth-Century Science*, eds. G. S. Rousseau and R. Porter, ch. 12.
Carozzi, Albert V. "Introduction", in de Maillet, *Telliamed or Conversations Between an Indian Philosopher and a French Missionary on the Diminution of the Sea (B1)*.
Carré, Jean Raoul. *La philosophie de Fontenelle ou Le sourire de la raison*. Paris, 1932; Geneva, 1970.
Carré, Jean Raoul. *Réflexions sur l'anti-Pascal de Voltaire*. Paris, 1935.
Carrithers, David. "The Enlightenment Science of Society", in *Inventing Human Science: Eighteenth-Century Domains*, eds. C. Fox, R. Porter, and R. Wokler, pp. 232–70.
Carrithers, David. "Montesquieu's Philosophy of History". *Journal of the History of Ideas* 47 (1986): 61–80.
Casini, Paolo. "Buffon et Newton", in *Buffon 88: Actes du Colloque international 1988*, ed. J. Gayon, pp. 299–308.
Cassirer, Ernst. *Das Erkenntnisproblem in der Philosophie und Wissenschaft der neueren Zeit*, 3 vols. Darmstadt, 1974, vol. 1.
Cassirer, Ernst. *Kant's Life and Thought*, trans. J. Haden. New Haven, CT, 1981.
Cassirer, Ernst. *Die Philosophie der Aufklärung*. Tübingen, 1932.
Cassirer, Ernst. *The Philosophy of the Enlightenment*, trans. F. C. A. Koelln and J. P. Pettegrove. Princeton, NJ, 1951.
Cassirer, Ernst. *The Platonic Renaissance in England*, trans. J. P. Pettegrove. Austin, TX, 1953.
Cassirer, Ernst. *The Question of Jean-Jacques Rousseau*, trans. P. Gay. New Haven, CT, 1989.
Casula, Mario. "Die historische Entwicklung der Frage: Ob die Materie denken kann? Von F. Suarez bis P. J. G. Cabanis. Ein Beitrag zur Einführung in die philosophische Problematik der künstlichen Intelligenz". *Filosofia oggi* 12 (1989): 407–62.
Cavallar, Georg. *Pax Kantiana. Systematisch-historische Untersuchung des Entwurfs "Zum ewigen Frieden" (1795) von Immanuel Kant*. Vienna, 1992.

Chamley, P. E. "The Conflict between Montesquieu and Hume. A Study of the Origins of Adam Smith's Universalism", in *Essays on Adam Smith*, eds. A. S. Skinner and T. Wilson. Oxford, 1975.

Champion, Justin *The Pillars of Priestcraft Shaken: The Church of England and Its Enemies, 1660–1730*. Cambridge, 1992.

Champion, Justin. "Toleration and Citizenship in Enlightenment England: John Toland and the Naturalization of the Jews, 1714–1753", in *Toleration in Enlightenment Europe*, eds. O. P. Grell and R. Porter, pp. 133–56.

Chappell, Vere. "Locke's Theory of Ideas", in *The Cambridge Companion to Locke*, ed. V. Chappell. Cambridge, 1994, pp. 26–55.

Chappell, Vere. "The Theory of Ideas", in *Essays on Descartes' Meditations*, ed. A. Oksenberg Rorty. Berkeley, CA, 1986, pp. 177–98.

Charles-Daubert, Françoise. "Les Traités des trois imposteurs aux XVIIe et XVIIIe siècles", in *Filosofia e religione*, ed. G. Canzoni. Milan, 1994, pp. 291–336.

Chartier, Roger, Dominique Julia, and Marie-Madeleine Compère. *L'éducation en France du XVIe au XVIIIe siècle*. Paris, 1976.

Chateau, Jean. *Jean-Jacques Rousseau: sa philosophie de l'éducation*. Paris, 1962.

Cherchi, Gavina. *Pantheisticon: Eterodossia e dissimulazione nella filosofia di John Toland*. Pisa, 1990.

Cheyney, Edward Potts. *History of the University of Pennsylvania, 1740–1790*. Philadelphia, PA, 1940.

Chisick, Harvey. *The Limits of Reform in the Enlightenment: Attitudes toward the Education of the Lower Classes in Eighteenth-Century France*. Princeton, NJ, 1981.

Chouillet, Jacques. *Diderot poète de l'énergie*. Paris, 1984.

Chouillet, Jacques. *La formation des idées esthétiques de Diderot*. Paris, 1973.

Christ, Kurt. *Jacobi und Mendelssohn: Eine Analyse des Spinozastreits*. Würzburg, 1988.

Christensen, Thomas. "Music Theory as Scientific Propaganda: The Case of d'Alembert's *Elémens de musique*". *Journal of the History of Ideas* 50.3 (1989): 409–27.

Ciafardone, Raffaele. "Von der Kritik an Wolff zum vorkritischen Kant: Wolff-Kritik bei Rüdiger und Crusius", in *Christian Wolff, 1679–1754*, ed. W. Schneiders, pp. 289–305.

Claesges, Ulrich. *Geschichte des Selbstbewusstseins: der Ursprung des spekulativen Problems in Fichtes Wissenschaftslehre von 1794–1795*. The Hague, 1974.

Clarke, Desmond. *Occult Powers and Hypotheses*. Oxford, 1989.

Cleve, James van. *Problems from Kant*. Oxford, 1999.

Coady, C. A. J. *Testimony: A Philosophical Study*. Oxford, 1992.

Cobban, Alfred. *Edmund Burke and the Revolt against the Eighteenth Century: A Study of the Political and Social Thinking of Burke, Wordsworth, Coleridge, and Southey*. London, 1960.

Cochrane, Eric W. *Tradition and Enlightenment in the Tuscan Academies 1690–1800*. Chicago, IL, 1961.

Cohen, Claudine. *Le destin du mammouth*. Paris, 1994.

Cohen, Hermann. *Kants Begründung der Ethik*. Berlin, 1877.

Cohen, I. Bernard. *Benjamin Franklin's Science*. Cambridge, MA, 1990.

Cohen, I. Bernard. *Franklin and Newton: An Inquiry into Speculative Newtonian Experimental Science and Franklin's Work in Electricity as an Example thereof*. Philadelphia, PA, 1956.

Cohen, Patricia C. *A Calculating People: The Spread of Numeracy in Early America*. Chicago, IL, 1982.

Coleman, Dorothy P. "Is Mathematics for Hume Synthetic *a priori*?" *Southwestern Journal of Philosophy* 10.2 (1979): 113–26.

Coleman, W. "Providence, Capitalism and Environmental Degradation". *Journal of the History of Ideas* 37 (1976): 27–44.

Coleridge, Samuel Taylor. *Lectures, 1818–19: On the History of Philosophy*, ed. J. R. de J. Jackson, in *Works*, vol. 8. (B1).
Collingwood, R. G. *The Idea of History*. New York, NY, 1956.
Columbia University. *A History of Columbia University 1754–1904*. New York, NY, 1904.
Compayré, Gabriel. *Histoire critique des doctrines de l'éducation en France depuis le seizième siècle*, 2 vols. Paris, 1879.
Comte, Auguste. *Cours de philosophie positive*. Paris, 1830–42.
Conant, James B., ed. *Harvard Case Histories in Experimental Science*. Cambridge, MA, 1966.
Conant, James B. "The Overthrow of the Phlogiston Theory: The Chemical Revolution of 1775–89", in *Harvard Case Histories in Experimental Science*, ed. J. B. Conant, pp. 67–115.
Conant, James B. *Science and Common Sense*. New Haven, CT, 1951.
Conant, James B. *Thomas Jefferson and the Development of American Public Education*. Berkeley and Los Angeles, CA, 1962.
Cook, Harold. "Physicians and Natural History", in *The Cultures of Natural History*, eds. N. Jardine, J. Secord and E. Spary, pp. 91–105.
Cook, Margaret G. "Divine Artifice and Natural Mechanism: Robert Boyle's Mechanical Philosophy of Nature". *Osiris* 16 (2001): 133–50.
Copleston, Frederick. *A History of Philosophy*, 9 vols. London, 1946–74.
Cormack, Lesley B. "'Good Fences Make Good Neighbors': Geography as Self-Definition in Early Modern England". *Isis* 82 (1991): 639–61.
Corr, Charles A. "Christian Wolff and Leibniz". *Journal of the History of Ideas* 36 (1975): 241–62.
Corsi, Pietro. *The Age of Lamarck*, trans. J. Mandelbaum. Berkeley, CA, 1988.
Costello, William T. *The Scholastic Curriculum at Early Seventeenth-Century Cambridge*. Cambridge, MA, 1958.
Crahay, Roland, ed. *La tolérance civile*. Brussels, 1982.
Craig, Edward. *The Mind of God and the Works of Man*. Oxford, 1987.
Crane, R. S. "The Houyhnhnms, the Yahoos and the History of Ideas", in *Reason and the Imagination: Studies in the History of Ideas 1600–1800*, ed. J. A. Mazzeo, pp. 231–53.
Crawford, Donald W. *Kant's Aesthetic Theory*. Madison, WI, 1974.
Creed, John Martin, and John Sandwith Boys Smith, eds. *Religious Thought in the Eighteenth Century, Illustrated from Writers of the Period*. Cambridge, 1934.
Cremin, Lawrence A. *American Education: The Colonial Experience, 1607–1783*. New York, NY, 1970.
Cremin, Lawrence A. *American Education: The National Experience, 1783–1876*. New York, NY, 1980.
Crimmins, James E. "John Brown and the Theological Tradition of Utilitarian Ethics". *History of Political Thought* 14 (1983): 523–50.
Crimmins, James E. "Religion, Utility and Politics: Bentham versus Paley", in *Religion, Secularization and Political Thought. Thomas Hobbes to J. S. Mill*, ed. J. E. Crimmins. London, 1989, pp. 130–52.
Crimmins, James E. "'The Study of True Politics': John Brown on Manners and Liberty". *Studies on Voltaire and the Eighteenth Century* 241 (1986): 65–86.
Croce, Benedetto. *La filosofia di Giambattista Vico*. Bari, 1911.
Crocker, Lester G. "The Discussion of Suicide in the Eighteenth Century". *Journal of the History of Ideas* 13 (1952): 47–72.
Crombie, Alexander. *Natural Theology*, 2 vols. London, 1829.
Crombie, A. C., ed. *Scientific Change. Historical Studies in the Intellectual, Social and Technical Conditions for Scientific Discovery and Technical Invention, From Antiquity to the Present*. London, 1963.

Crugten-André, Valérie van. *Le "Traité sur la tolérance de Voltaire": Un champion des Lumières contre le fanatisme*. Paris, 1999.

Cumming, Ian. *Helvetius, His Life and Place in the History of Educational Thought*. London, 1955.

Cuneo, Terence, and René van Woudenberg, eds. *The Cambridge Companion to Reid*. Cambridge, 2003.

Cunningham, Andrew. "The Culture of Gardens", in *The Cultures of Natural History*, eds. N. Jardine, J. Secord and E. Spary, pp. 38–56.

Curley, Edwin. "Leibniz on Locke on Personal Identity", in *Leibniz. Critical and Interpretive Essays*, ed. M. Hooker. Manchester, 1982, pp. 302–26.

Dagognet, François. "L'Animal selon Condillac", in Condillac, *Traité des animaux*, 1987, pp. 9–131 (*B1*).

Daniels, Norman. *Thomas Reid's 'Inquiry': The Geometry of Visibles and the Case for Realism*. Stanford, CA, 1989.

Darnton, Robert. *The Corpus of Clandestine Literature in France, 1769–1789*. New York, NY, 1995.

Darwall, Stephen. *The British Moralists and the Internal 'Ought': 1640–1740*. Cambridge, 1995.

Darwall, Stephen. "Obligation and Motive in Hume's Ethics". *Nous* 27 (1993): 415–48.

Darwin, Charles. *The Autobiography of Charles Darwin 1809–82*, ed. N. Barlow. London, 1958.

Dascal, Marcelo. "La razon y los mysterios de la fe segun Leibniz". *Revista latino-americana de filosofia* 1 (1975): 193–226.

Daston, Lorraine. *Classical Probability in the Enlightenment*. Princeton, NJ, 1988.

Daumas, Maurice. "Precision of Measurement and Physical and Chemical Research in the Eighteenth Century", in *Scientific Change: Historical Studies in the Intellectual, Social and Technical Conditions for Scientific Discovery and Technical Invention, From Antiquity to the Present*, ed. A. C. Crombie, pp. 418–30.

Davies, Catherine Glyn. *'Conscience' as Consciousness. The Idea of Self-Awareness in French Philosophical Writing from Descartes to Diderot*. Oxford, 1990.

Davis, James Herbert. *Fénelon*. Boston, MA, 1979.

De Jong, W. R. "How Is Metaphysics as a Science Possible? Kant on the Distinction between Philosophical and Mathematical Method". *Review of Metaphysics* 49 (1995): 235–74.

de la Fontainerie, F., ed. *French Liberalism and Education in the Eighteenth Century: The Writings of La Chalotais, Turgot, Diderot and Condorcet on National Education*. New York, NY, 1932.

Deggau, Hans-Georg. *Die Aporien der Rechtslehre Kants*. Stuttgart, 1983.

Demarest, W. H. S. *A History of Rutgers College, 1766–1924*. New Brunswick, NJ, 1924.

Denzer, Horst. *Moralphilosophie und Naturrecht bei Samuel Pufendorf: Eine geistes- und wissenschaftsgeschichtliche Untersuchung zur Geburt des Naturrechts aus der praktischen Philsophie*. Munich, 1972.

Deppermann, Klaus. *Der hallesche Pietismus und der preussische Staat unter Friedrich III. (I.)*. Göttingen, 1961.

Deprun, Jean. "Meslier philosophe", in J. Meslier, *Oeuvres complètes*, vol. 1, pp. lxxxi–c (*B1*).

Deprun, Jean. "Sade philosophe", in de Sade, *Oeuvres*, ed. M. Delon (*B1*).

Deprun, Jean. "Sade et le rationalisme des Lumières". *Raison présente* 55 (1980): 17–29.

Derathé, Robert. *Jean-Jacques Rousseau et la science politique de son temps*. Paris, 1988.

Derrida, Jacques. *The Archeology of the Frivolous: Reading Condillac* [1973], trans. J. P. Leavey, Jr. Lincoln, NE, 1987.

Desautels, Alfred R. *Les Mémoires de Trévoux et le mouvement des idées au XVIIIe siècle, 1701–1734*. Rome, 1956.

Dessoir, Max. *Geschichte der neueren deutschen Psychologie*. Berlin, 1902.

Dettlebach, Michael. "Introduction", in A. von Humboldt, *Cosmos: A Sketch of a Physical Description of the Universe*, trans. E. C. Otté, 2 vols. Baltimore, MD, 1997, vol. 2.

Dhombres, Jean G., and Patricia Radelet-de Grave. "Contingence et nécessité en mécanique". *Physis* 28 (1991): 35–114.

di Giovanni, George, and H. S. Harris, eds. *Between Kant and Hegel: Texts in the Development of Post-Kantian Idealism*. Albany, NY, 1985.

Dickey, Laurence. *Hegel: Religion, Economics, and the Politics of Spirit, 1770–1807*. Cambridge, 1987.

Dieckmann, Herbert. "Diderot's Conception of Genius". *Journal of the History of Ideas* 2 (1941): 151–82.

Dieckmann, Herbert. *Le Philosophe: Texts and Interpretation*. St. Louis, MO, 1948.

Diggins, John P. *The Lost Soul of American Politics: Virtue, Self-Interest, and the Foundations of Liberalism*. Chicago, IL, 1986.

Dilthey, Wilhelm. *Selected Works*, eds. R. A. Makkreel and F. Rodi. Princeton, NJ, 1985–.

Dilthey, Wilhelm. "Three Epochs of Modern Aesthetics and Its Present Task (1892)", in *Selected Works*, vol. 5: *Poetry and Experience* (1985), pp. 175–222.

Dippel, Horst. *Germany and the American Revolution, 1770–1800: A Sociohistorical Investigation of Late Eighteenth-Century Political Thinking*, trans. B. A. Uhlendorf. Wiesbaden, 1978.

Dix-huitièmè siècle, 24 (1992): "Le matérialisme des Lumières".

Domecq, Jean-Philippe. "La Fête de l'Etre suprême et son interprétation". *Esprit* 154 (1989): 91–125.

Domenech, Jacques. *L'Éthique des lumières: les fondements de la morale dans la philosophie française du XVIIIe siècle*. Paris, 1989.

Donovan, Arthur. *Philosophical Chemistry in the Scottish Enlightenment: The Doctrines and Discoveries of William Cullen and Joseph Black*. Edinburgh, 1975.

Douay-Soublin, Françoise. "La rhétorique en Europe à travers son enseignement", in *Histoire des idées linguistiques*, ed. S. Auroux, 2 vols. Liège, 1992, vol. 2, pp. 467–507.

Dreitzel, Horst. "Zur Entwicklung und Eigenart der 'Eklektischen Philosophie'". *Zeitschrift für Historische Forschung* 18 (1991): 281–343.

Duchesneau, François. *La physiologie des lumières: empirisme, modèles et theories*. The Hague, 1982.

Duchet, Michèle. *Anthropologie et histoire au siècle des lumières*. Paris, 1995.

Dulac, Georges. "Un nouveau La Mettrie à Pétersbourg: Diderot vu par l'Académie impériale des Sciences". *Recherches sur Diderot et sur l'Encyclopédie* 16 (1994): 19–44.

Dülmen, Richard van. *The Society of the Enlightenment: The Rise of the Middle Class and Enlightenment Culture in Germany*, trans. A. Williams. Cambridge, 1992.

Dumitriu, Anton. *History of Logic*, 4 vols. Tunbridge Wells, 1977.

Duris, Pascal. *Linné et la France, 1780–1850*. Geneva, 1993.

Dürr, Karl. *Die Logistik J. H. Lamberts*. Zurich, 1945.

Düsing, Klaus. "Kant und Epikur". *Allgemeine Zeitschrift für Philosophie* (1976): 39–58.

Düsing, Klaus. "Das Problem des höchsten Gutes in Kants praktischer Philosophie". *Kant-Studien* 62 (1971): 5–42.

Duso, Giuseppe. *Il contratto sociale nelle filosofia politica moderna*. Milan, 1993.

Eco, Umberto. *The Search for the Perfect Language*, trans. J. Fentress. Oxford, 1995.

École, Jean. *La métaphysique de Christian Wolff*, in Wolff, *Werke*, Abt. III, vol. 12.1–2 (*B1*).

Ehrard, Jean. *L'Idée de nature en France dans la première moitié du XVIII siècle*. Paris, 1970.

Ellenberger, François. "A l'aube de la géologie moderne: Henri Gautier (1660–1737)". *Histoire et nature* 7 (1975): 3–58; *Histoire et nature* 9–10 (1976–7): 3–142.

Ellenberger, François. "Louis Bourguet", in *Dictionary of Scientific Biography: Supplement*, ed. C. C. Gillispie, vol. 15, pp. 52–9.

Ellenberger, François. "Les sciences de la terre avant Buffon: bref coup d'oeil historique", in *Buffon 88: Actes du Colloque international 1988*, ed. J. Gayon.

Emerson, Roger L. "Conjectural History and Scottish Philosophers". *Historical Papers/Communications historiques* (1984): 63–90.
Emerson, Roger L. "Science and Moral Philosophy in the Scottish Enlightenment", in *Studies in the Philosophy of the Scottish Enlightenment*, ed. M. A. Stewart, pp. 11–36.
Engfer, Hans-Jürgen. *Philosophie als Analysis: Studien zur Entwicklung philosophischer Analysiskonzeptionen unter dem Einfluss mathematischer Methodenmodelle im 17. und frühen 18. Jahrhundert.* Stuttgart and Bad Cannstatt, 1982.
Engfer, Hans-Jürgen. "Zur Bedeutung Wolffs für die Methodendiskussion der deutschen Aufklärungsphilosophie", in *Christian Wolff, 1679–1754*, ed. W. Schneiders, pp. 48–65.
Erb, Peter C., ed. *Pietists: Selected Writings*. New York, NY, 1983.
Evans, Arthur William. *Warburton and the Warburtonians: A Study in Some Eighteenth-Century Controversies*. London, 1932.
Evans, Robert Rees. *Pantheisticon: The Career of John Toland*. New York, NY, 1991.
Ezell, Margaret J. M. "John Locke's Images of Childhood: Early Eighteenth Century Responses to *Some Thoughts Concerning Education*". *Eighteenth-Century Studies* 17 (1983–4): 139–55.
Fabian, Gerd. *Beitrag zur Geschichte des Leib-Seele-Problems (Lehre von der prästabilierten Harmonie und vom psychophysischen Parallelismus in der Leibniz-Wolffschen Schule)*. Langensalza, 1926.
Farber, Paul L. "Buffon's Concept of Species". *Journal of the History of Biology* 5 (1972): 259–84.
Fauvel, John, and Jeremy J. Gray, eds. *The History of Mathematics: A Reader*. Basingstoke, 1987.
Feingold, M. "The Ultimate Pedagogue: Franco Petri Burgersdijk and the English Speaking Academic Learning", in *Franco Burgersdijk (1590–1635): Neo-Aristotelianism in Leiden*, eds. E. P. Bos and H. A. Krop. Amsterdam, 1993, pp. 151–65.
Ferguson, J. P. *The Philosophy of Dr. Samuel Clarke and its Critics*. New York, NY, 1974.
Ferrari, Jean. "Kant, lecteur de Buffon", in *Buffon 88: Actes du Colloque international 1988*, ed. J. Gayon, pp. 155–63.
Ferrarin, Alfredo. "Construction and Mathematical Schematism: Kant on the Exhibition of a Concept in Intuition". *Kant-Studien* 86 (1995): 131–74.
Ferrarin, Alfredo. *Hegel and Aristotle*. Cambridge, 2001.
Ferrier, James Frederick. *Institutes of Metaphysics: The Theory of Knowing and Being*. Edinburgh, 1854; in *Philosophical Works*, 3 vols., eds. A. Grand and E. L. Lushington, Edinburgh, 1875.
Fertig, Ludwig. *Campes politische Erziehung: eine Einführung in die Pädagogik der Aufklärung*. Darmstadt, 1977.
Fetscher, Iring. *Rousseaus politische Philosophie: Zur Geschichte des demokratischen Freheitsbegriffs*. Frankfurt am Main, 1978.
Fiering, Norman. *Moral Philosophy in Seventeenth Century Harvard: A Discipline in Transition*. Chapel Hill, NC, 1981.
Finlen, Paula. "Courting Nature", in *The Cultures of Natural History*, eds. N. Jardine, J. Secord and E. Spary, pp. 57–74.
Finster, Reinhardt. "Zur Kritik von Christian August Crusius an der Theorie der einfachen Substanzen bei Leibniz und Wolff". *Studia Leibnitiana* 18 (1986): 72–82.
Finzel-Niederstadt, Wiltraut. *Lernen und Lehren bei Herder und Basedow*. Frankfurt am Main, 1986.
Fiorillo, Vanda. *Tra egoismo e socialità: il giusnaturalismo de Samuel Pufendorf*. Naples, 1992.
Fitzpatrick, M. "Heretical Religion and Radical Political Ideas in late Eighteenth-Century England", in *The Transformation of Political Culture: England and Germany in the Late Eighteenth Century*, ed. E. Hellmuth. Oxford, 1990.
Fitzpatrick, Martin. "Reflections on a Footnote: Richard Price and Love of Country". *Enlightenment and Dissent* 6 (1987): 41–58.
Fitzpatrick, Martin. "Toleration and Truth". *Enlightenment and Dissent* 1 (1982): 3–31.

Fleckenstein, Joachim Otto. "Introduction", in L. Euler, *Opera omnia*, Ser. 3, vol. 5. (*B1*).

Fleischmann, Hector. *La Guillotine en 1793*. Paris, 1908.

Flew, Antony. *Hume's Philosophy of Belief*. New York, NY, 1961.

Flower, Elizabeth, and Murray G. Murphey. *A History of Philosophy in America*, 2 vols. New York, NY, 1977.

Fogelin, Robert J. "Hume and Berkeley on the Proofs of Infinite Divisibility". *Philosophical Review* 97 (1988): 47–69.

Fogelin, Robert J. *Hume's Skepticism in the Treatise of Human Nature*. London, 1985.

Fonnesu, Luca. "Der Optimismus und seine Kritiker im Zeitalter der Aufklärung". *Studia Leibnitiana* 26 (1994): 131–62.

Fontius, M. "Littérature clandestine et pensée allemande", in *Le Matérialisme du XVIII siècle et la littérature clandestine*, ed. O. Bloch, pp. 251–62.

Forbes, Duncan. *Hume's Philosophical Politics*. Cambridge, 1975.

Formigari, Lia. *Language and Experience in Seventeenth-Century British Philosophy*. Amsterdam and Philadelphia, PA, 1988.

Forschner, Maximilian. *Rousseau*. Freiburg, 1977.

Foster, John, and Howard Robinson, eds. *Essays on Berkeley: A Tercentennial Celebration*. Oxford, 1985.

Foucault, Michel. *Discipline and Punish: The Birth of the Modern Prison*, trans. A. Sheridan. Harmondsworth, 1991.

Fox, Christopher. "How to Prepare a Noble Savage: The Spectacle of Human Science", in *Inventing Human Science: Eighteenth Century Domains*, eds. C. Fox, R. Porter and R. Wokler, pp. 1–30.

Fox, Christopher. *Locke and the Scriblerians: Identity and Consciousness in Early Eighteenth-Century Britain*. Berkeley, CA, 1988.

Fox, Christopher, Roy Porter, and Robert Wokler, eds. *Inventing Human Science: Eighteenth-Century Domains*. Berkeley, CA, 1995.

Fox, R. *The Caloric Theory of Heat*. Oxford, 1971.

France, Peter. *Rhetoric and Truth in France: Descartes to Diderot*. Oxford, 1972.

Frängsmyr, Tore. "The Mathematical Philosophy", in *The Quantifying Spirit in the 18th Century*, eds. T. Frängsmyr, J. L. Heilbron, and R. E. Rider, pp. 27–44.

Frängsmyr, Tore, John L. Heilbron, and Robin E. Rider, eds. *The Quantifying Spirit in the 18th Century*. Berkeley, CA, 1990.

Frank, Manfred. *'Unendliche Annäherung': Die Anfänge der philosophischen Frühromantik*. Frankfurt, 1997.

Franklin, James. "Achievements and Fallacies in Hume's Account of Infinite Divisibility". *Hume Studies* 20 (1994): 85–101.

Frasca-Spada, Marina. "Compendious Footnotes", in *Books and the Sciences in History*, eds. M. Frasca-Spada and N. Jardine. Cambridge, 2000, pp. 171–99.

Frasca-Spada, Marina, and Peter Kail, eds. *Impressions of Hume*. Oxford, 2005.

Freeman, Michael. *Edmund Burke and the Critique of Political Radicalism*. Oxford, 1980.

Freyer, Johannes. *Geschichte der Geschichte der Philosophie im achtzehnten Jahrhundert*. Leipzig, 1912.

Friedman, Michael. *Kant and the Exact Sciences*. Cambridge, MA, 1992.

Frost, Alan. "The Pacific Ocean: The Eighteenth Century's 'New World'". *Studies on Voltaire and the Eighteenth Century* 152 (1976): 779–822.

Fueter, Eduard. *Geschichte der neueren Historiographie*. Munich and Berlin, 1936.

Fuller, Reginald C. *Alexander Geddes 1737–1802: Pioneer of Biblical Criticism*. Sheffield, 1984.

Fumaroli, Marc. *L'Age de l'éloquence; Rhétorique et 'res literaria' de la Renaissance au seuil de l'époque classique*. Geneva, 1980; Paris, 1994.
Fumaroli, Marc, ed. *Histoire de la rhétorique dans l'Europe moderne*. Paris, 1999.
Gale, George. "On what God Chose: Perfection and God's Freedom". *Studia Leibnitiana* 8 (1976): 69–87.
Garber, Daniel, and Michael Ayers, eds. *The Cambridge History of Seventeenth-Century Philosophy*. 2 vols. Cambridge, 1998.
Garber, Jörn. "Liberaler und demokratischer Republikanismus. Kants Metaphysik der Sitten und ihre radikaldemokratische Kritik durch J. A. Bergk", in *Mitteleuropa im ausgehenden 18. und frühen 19. Jahrhundert*, eds. O. Büsch and W. Grab. Berlin, 1980.
Garber, Jörn. "Nachwort", in *Revolutionäre Vernunft. Texte zur jakobinischen und liberalen Revolutionsrezeption in Deutschland, 1798–1810*, ed. J. Garber. Kronberg/Ts, 1974.
Gascoigne, John. *Cambridge in the Age of the Enlightenment*. Cambridge, 1989.
Gascoigne, John. "The Eighteenth-Century Scientific Community: A Prosopographical Study". *Social Studies of Science* 25 (1995): 575–81.
Gascoigne, John. "Mathematics and Meritocracy: The Emergence of the Cambridge Mathematical Tripos". *Social Studies of Science* 14 (1984): 547–84.
Gascoigne, John. "A Reappraisal of the Role of the Universities in the Scientific Revolution", in *Reappraisals of the Scientific Revolution*, eds. D. C. Lindberg and R. S. Westman. Cambridge, 1990, pp. 251–20.
Gaskin, J. C. A. "Hume's Attenuated Deism". *Archiv für Geschichte der Philosophie* 65 (1983): 160–73.
Gaskin, J. C. A. *Hume's Philosophy of Religion*. London, 1988.
Gauss, Carl Friedrich. *Werke*, 12 vols. Göttingen, 1863–1929.
Gawlick, Günter. "Cicero and the Enlightenment". *Studies on Voltaire and the Eighteenth Century* 25 (1963): 657–82.
Gawlick, Günter. "Die ersten deutschen Reaktionen auf A. Collins' 'Discourse of Free-Thinking' von 1713", in *Eklektik, Selbstdenken, Mündigkeit*, ed. N. Hinske. Hamburg, 1986, pp. 11–25.
Gawlick, Günther, and Lothar Kreimendahl. *Hume in der deutschen Aufklärung. Umrisse einer Rezeptionsgeschichte*. Stuttgart and Bad Cannstatt, 1987.
Gawthrop, Richard L. *Pietism and the Making of Eighteenth-Century Prussia*. Cambridge, 1993.
Gay, Peter, ed. *Deism: An Anthology*. Princeton, NJ, 1968.
Gay, Peter. *The Enlightenment: An Interpretation*, 2 vols. New York, NY, 1977.
Gayon, Jean, ed. *Buffon 88: Actes du Colloque international 1988*. Paris, 1992.
Gayon, Jean. "L'Individualité de l'espèce: une thèse transformiste?", in *Buffon 88: Actes du Colloque international 1988*, ed. J. Gayon, pp. 475–89.
Gegenheimer, Albert F. *William Smith: Educator and Churchman 1727–1803*. Philadelphia, PA, 1943.
Genet-Varcin, E., and Jacques Roger. "Bibliographie de Buffon", in G.-L. L. Buffon, *Oeuvres philosophiques*, ed. J. Piveteau, pp. 513–75 (*BI*).
Geras, Norman, and Robert Wokler, eds. *The Enlightenment and Modernity*. Basingstoke, Hamps./London/New York, NY, 2000.
Gerbi, Antonello. *The Dispute of the New World: The History of a Polemic, 1750–1900*, trans. J. Moyle. Pittsburgh, PA, 1973.
Gerhardt, Volker. *Kants Entwurf "Zum Ewigen Frieden", Eine Theorie der Politik*. Darmstadt, 1995.
Gierke, Otto. *Johannes Althusius und die Entwicklung der naturrechtlichen Staatstheorien*. Breslau, 1902.

Gildin, Hilail. *Rousseau's Social Contract: The Design of the Argument*. Chicago, IL, 1983.
Gillespie, N. C. "Divine Design and the Industrial Revolution". *Isis* 81 (1990): 214–29.
Gillispie, Charles C., ed. *Dictionary of Scientific Biography*. 16 vols. New York, NY, 1970–80.
Gillispie, Charles C., ed. *Lazare Carnot, Savant: A Monograph Treating Carnot's Scientific Work*. Princeton, NJ, 1971.
Gillispie, Charles C. *Science and Polity in France at the End of the Old Regime*. Princeton, NJ, 1980.
Giuliani, Alessandro. "Vico's Rhetorical Philosophy and the New Rhetoric", in *Giambattista Vico's Science of Humanity*, eds. G. Tagliacozzo and D. P. Verene. Baltimore, MD, 1976, pp. 31–46.
Godley, A. D. *Oxford in the Eighteenth Century*. London, 1908.
Godson, Susan H., et al. *The College of William and Mary: A History*, 2 vols. Williamsburg, VA, 1993.
Gohau, Gabriel. "La 'Théorie de la terre', de 1749'", in *Buffon 88: Actes du Colloque international 1988*, ed. J. Gayon, pp. 343–520.
Goldgar, Anne. *Impolite Learning. Conduct and Community in the Republic of Letters*. New Haven, CT and London, 1995.
Goldie, Mark. "The Civil Religion of James Harrington", in *Languages of Political Theory in Early Modern Europe*, ed. A. Pagden. Cambridge, 1987, pp. 197–222.
Goldschmidt, Victor. *Anthropologie et politique: les principes du système de Rousseau*. Paris, 1974.
Goldstick, D. "Why Is There Something Rather than Nothing?" *Philosophy and Phenomenological Research* 40 (1979–80): 265–71.
Goldstine, Herman Heine. *A History of the Calculus of Variations from the 17th through the 19th Century*. New York, NY, 1980.
Gordon, Ann Dexter. *The College of Philadelphia, 1749–1779: Impact of an Institution*. Dissertation, University of Wisconsin-Madison, 1975.
Gordon, Daniel. *Citizens without Sovereignty: Equality and Sociability in French Thought (1670–1789)*. Princeton, NJ, 1994.
Gordon, Daniel. "Introduction: Postmodernism and the French Enlightenment", in *Postmodernism and the Enlightenment: New Perspectives in Eighteenth-Century French Intellectual History*, ed. D. Gordon, pp. 1–6.
Gordon, Daniel. "On the Supposed Obsolescence of the French Enlightenment", in *Postmodernism and the Enlightenment: New Perspectives in Eighteenth-Century French Intellectual History*, ed. D. Gordon, pp. 201–21.
Gordon, Daniel, ed. *Postmodernism and the Enlightenment: New Perspectives in Eighteenth-Century French Intellectual History*. New York, NY and London, 2001.
Gotterbarn, Donald. "Kant, Hume and Analyticity". *Kant-Studien* 65 (1974): 274–83.
Goyard-Fabre, Simone. *L'Interminable querelle du contrat social*. Ottawa, 1983.
Goyard-Fabre, Simone. *Kant e le problème du droit*. Paris, 1971.
Grabiner, Judith V. *The Calculus as Algebra: J.-L. Lagrange, 1736–1813*. New York, NY, 1990.
Gracyk, Theodore. "Rethinking Hume's Standard of Taste". *The Journal of Aesthetics and Art Criticism* 52 (1994): 169–182.
Graham, Jenny. "Revolutionary Philosopher: The Political Ideas of Joseph Priestley (1733–1804)". *Enlightenment and Dissent* 8 (1989): 43–68; 9 (1990): 14–46.
Grant, Alexander. *The Story of the University of Edinburgh during its First Three Hundred Years*, 2 vols. London, 1884.
Grattan-Guinness, Ivor. "Berkeley's Criticism of the Calculus as a Study in the Theory of Limits". *Janus* 56 (1969): 215–27.

Grattan-Guinness, Ivor. *The Development of the Foundations of Mathematical Analysis from Euler to Riemann*. Cambridge, MA, 1970.

Grau, K. J. *Die Entwicklung des Bewusstseinsbegriffes im XVII. und XVIII. Jahrhundert*. Halle, 1916; Hildesheim and New York, 1981.

Gray, Jeremy. *Ideas of Space: Euclidean, Non-Euclidean and Relativistic*, 2nd edn. Oxford, 1989.

Grean, Stanley. *Shaftesbury's Philosophy of Religion and Ethics: A Study in Enthusiasm*. Athens, OH, 1967.

Greenberg, John L. *The Problem of the Earth's Shape from Newton to Clairaut: The Rise of Mathematical Science in the Eighteenth Century and the Fall of 'Normal' Science*. Cambridge, 1995.

Greenberg, Robert. "The Content of Kant's Logical Function of Judgment". *History of Philosophy Quarterly* 11 (1994): 375–92.

Greene, John L. *The Death of Adam: Evolution and Its Impact on Western Thought*. Ames, IA, 1959.

Grell, Ole Peter, and Roy Porter, eds. *Toleration in Enlightenment Europe*. Cambridge, 2000.

Gres-Gayer, Jacques M. *Théologie et pouvoir en Sorbonne: La faculté de théologie de Paris et la bulle Unigenitus 1714–1721*. Paris, 1991.

Grice-Hutchinson, Marjorie, ed. *The School of Salamanca: Readings in Spanish Monetary Theory 1544–1605*. Oxford, 1952.

Grimm, Gerald. "Die Staats-und Bildungskonzeption Joseph von Sonnenfels' und deren Einfluss auf die österreichische Schul-und Bildungspolitik im Zeitalter des aufgeklärten Absolutismus", in *Staat und Erziehung in Aufklärungsphilosophie und Aufklärungszeit*, eds. F.-P. Hager and D. Jedan. Bochum, 1993, pp. 53–66.

Grossman, Mordecai. *The Philosophy of Helvetius, with Special Emphasis on the Educational Implications of Sensationalism*. New York, NY, 1926.

Grossmann, Walter. "Religious toleration in Germany, 1684–1750". *Studies on Voltaire and the Eighteenth Century* 201 (1982): 115–41.

Grua, Gaston. *Jurisprudence universelle et théodicée selon Leibniz*. Paris, 1953.

Grüsser, O. J. "Quantitative Visual Psychophysics during the Period of European Enlightenment". *Documenta Ophthalmologica* 71 (1989): 93–111.

Guerlac, Henry. *Antoine-Laurent Lavoisier: Chemist and Revolutionary*. New York, NY, 1975.

Guerlac, Henry. *Newton on the Continent*. Ithaca, NY, 1981.

Guerlac, Henry. "Where the Statue Stood: Divergent Loyalties to Newton in the Eighteenth Century", in *Aspects of the Eighteenth Century*, ed. E. R. Wasserman. Baltimore, MD, 1965, pp. 317–34.

Guicciardini, Niccolò. *The Development of Newtonian Calculus in Britain, 1700–1800*. Cambridge, 1989.

Gurr, John Edwin. *The Principle of Sufficient Reason in Some Scholastic Systems, 1750–1900*. Milwaukee, WI, 1959.

Guthke, Karl S. "Zur Religionsphilosophie des jungen Albrecht von Haller". *Filosofia* 17 (1966): 638–49.

Guttenplan, Samuel, ed. *Mind and Language*. Oxford, 1975.

Guyer, Paul. "Kant on Apperception and a priori Synthesis". *American Philosophical Quarterly* 17 (1980): 205–12.

Guyer, Paul. *Kant and the Claims of Taste*. Cambridge, MA, 1979.

Guyer, Paul. *Kant and the Experience of Freedom*. Cambridge, 1993.

Haakonssen, Knud. "Divine/Natural Law Theories in Ethics", in *The Cambridge History of Seventeenth-Century Philosophy*, eds. D. Garber and M. Ayers, vol. 2, pp. 1317–57.

Haakonssen, Knud, ed. *Enlightenment and Religion: Rational Dissent in Eighteenth-Century Britain*. Cambridge, 1996.

Haakonssen, Knud. "From Natural Law to the Rights of Man: A European Perspective on American Debates", in *A Culture of Rights. The Bill of Rights in Philosophy, Politics, and*

Law – 1791 and 1991, eds. M. J. Lacey and K. Haakonssen. Cambridge and New York, NY, 1991, pp. 19–61.

Haakonssen, Knud. "German Natural Law", in *Cambridge History of Eighteenth-Century Political Thought*, eds. M. Goldie and R. Wokler. Cambridge, forthcoming.

Haakonssen, Knud. "Introduction", in W. Enfield, *The History of Philosophy from the Earliest Periods: Drawn up from Brucker's "Historia critica philosophiæ"*, 2 vols. Bristol, 2001.

Haakonssen, Knud. "The Moral Conservatism of Natural Rights", in *Natural Law and Civil Sovereignty: Moral Right and State Authority in Early Modern Political Thought*, eds. I. Hunter and D. Saunders. Basingstoke, 2002, pp. 27–42.

Haakonssen, Knud. *Natural Law and Moral Philosophy: From Grotius to the Scottish Enlightenment.* Cambridge, 1996.

Haakonssen, Knud. "Protestant Natural Law Theory: A General Interpretation" in *New Essays on the History of Autonomy. A Collection Honoring J. B. Schneewind*, eds. N. Brender and L. Krasnoff. Cambridge, 2004, pp. 92–109.

Haakonssen, Knud. "Reason and Will in the Humanities", in *Is There a Human Nature?* ed. L. S. Rouner. Notre Dame, IN, 1997, pp. 63–77.

Haakonssen, Knud. *The Science of a Legislator: The Natural Jurisprudence of David Hume and Adam Smith.* Cambridge, 1981.

Haakonssen, Knud. "The Structure of Hume's Political Theory", in *The Cambridge Companion to Hume*, ed. D. F. Norton, pp. 182–221.

Haakonssen, Lisbeth. *Medicine and Morals in the Enlightenment: John Gregory, Thomas Percival, and Benjamin Rush.* Amsterdam and Atlanta, GA, 1997.

Hacking, Ian. *The Emergence of Probability: A Philosophical Study of Early Ideas about Probability, Induction and Statistical Inference.* London, 1975.

Hacking, Ian. *The Taming of Chance.* Cambridge, 1990.

Hakfoort, Caspar. "Newton's Optics: The Changing Spectrum of Science", in *Let Newton Be!*, ed. J. Fauvel et al., Oxford, 1988, pp. 81–99.

Halevy, Elie. *The Growth of Philosophic Radicalism*, trans. M. Morris. London, 1928.

Hammermayer, Ludwig. "Akademiebewegung und Wissenschaftsorganisation – Formen, Tendenzen und Wandel in Europa während der zweiten Hälfte des 18. Jahrhunderts", in *Wissenschaftspolitik in Mittel- und Osteuropa. Wissenschaftsliche Gesellschaften, Akademien und Hochschulen im 18. und beginnenden 19. Jahrhundert*, eds. E. Amburger, M. Ciesla and L. Sziklay. Berlin, 1976.

Hammermayer, Ludwig. *Geschichte der Bayerischen Akademie der Wissenschaften 1759–1807*, 2 vols. Munich, 1983.

Hammerstein, Notker. *Aufklärung und katholisches Reich. Untersuchungen zur Universitätsreform und Politik katholischer Territorien des Heiligen Römischen Reichs deutscher Nation im 18. Jahrhundert.* Berlin, 1977.

Hammerstein, Notker. "Göttingen, eine deutsche Universität im Zeitalter der Aufklärung", in *Die Universität in Alteuropa*, eds. A. Patschovsky and H. Rabe. Konstanz, 1994, pp. 169–82.

Hammerstein, Notker. *Ius und Historie. Ein Beitrag zur Geschichte des historischen Denkens an deutschen Universitäten im späten 17. und im 18. Jahrhundert.* Göttingen, 1972.

Hammerstein, Notker. "Die Universitätsgründungen im Zeichen der Aufklärung", in *Beiträge zu Problemen deutscher Universitätsgründungen der frühen Neuzeit*, eds. P. Baumgart and N. Hammerstein. Nendeln, 1978, pp. 263–98.

Hankins, Thomas L. "Eighteenth-Century Attempts to Resolve the Vis Viva Controversy". *Isis* 56 (1965): 281–97.

Hankins, Thomas L. *Jean d'Alembert: Science and the Enlightenment.* Oxford, 1970.

Hankins, Thomas L. *Science and the Enlightenment*. Cambridge, 1985.
Hanks, Lesley. *Buffon avant l'Histoire naturelle*. Paris, 1966.
Harari, Josué V. "D'une raison à l'autre: le dispositif Sade". *Studies on Voltaire and the Eighteenth Century* 230 (1985): 273–82.
Harnack, Adolf von. *Geschichte der Königlich-Preussischen Akademie der Wissenschaften zu Berlin*, 3 in 4 vols. Berlin, 1900.
Harrison, Jonathan. *Hume's Theory of Justice*. Oxford, 1981.
Harrison, Ross. *Bentham*. London, 1983.
Hartmann, Fritz, and Rudolf Vierhaus, eds. *Der Akademiegedanke im 17. und 18. Jahrhundert*. Bremen and Wolfenbüttel, 1977.
Häseler, Jens. "Réfugiés français à Berlin lecteurs de manuscrits clandestins", in *Filosofia e religione Nella Letteratura Clandestina*, ed. G. Canzoni, pp. 373–85.
Hassinger, Erich. "Wirtschaftliche Motive und Argumente für religiöse Duldsamkeit im 16. und 17. Jahrhundert". *Archiv für Reformationsgeschichte* 49 (1958): 226–45.
Hauser, Christian. *Selbstbewußtsein und personale Identität*. Stuttgart, 1994.
Havens, George R. "The conclusion of Voltaire's *Poème sur le désastre de Lisbonne*". *Modern Language Notes* 56 (1941): 422–6.
Havens, George R. "Voltaire's pessimistic revision of the conclusion of his *Poème sur le désastre de Lisbonne*". *Modern Language Notes* 44 (1929): 489–92.
Hazard, Paul. *The European Mind: The Critical Years, 1680–1715*. New Haven, CT, 1953.
Hazard, Paul. "Le problème du mal dans la conscience européenne du dix-huitième siècle". *Romanic Review* 32 (1941): 147–70.
Hazlitt, William. *Complete Works*, eds. P. P. Howe, et al., 21 vols. London, 1930–4.
Hazlitt, William. *An Essay on the Principles of Human Action: Being an Argument in Favour of the Natural Disinterestedness of the Human Mind. To Which are Added, Some Remarks on the Systems of Hartley and Helvetius*. London, 1805; repr. Gainesville FL, 1969.
Hazlitt, William. *The Spirit of the Age* (1825), in *Complete Works*, vol. 11.
Heafford, Michael. *Pestalozzi: His Thought and Its Relevance Today*. London, 1967.
Hegel, Georg Wilhelm Friedrich. *See* (*B1*).
Heilbron, J. L. *Elements of Early Modern Physics* Berkeley, CA, 1984.
Heilbron, J. L. "Introductory essay", in *The Quantifying Spirit in the 18th Century*, eds. T. Frängsmyr, J. L. Heilbron, and R. E. Rider, pp. 1–23.
Heilbron, J. L. "The Measure of Enlightenment", in *The Quantifying Spirit in the 18th Century*, eds. T. Frängsmyr, J. L. Heilbron, and R. E. Rider, pp. 207–42.
Heimann, P. M., and J. E. McGuire. "Newtonian Forces and Lockean Powers: Concepts of Matter in Eighteenth-Century Thought". *Historical Studies in the Physical Sciences* 3 (1971): 233–306.
Heinekamp, Albert. *Gottfried Wilhelm Leibniz*, 2 vols. Munich, 1992.
Heinekamp, Albert, and André Robinet, eds. *Leibniz: Le meilleur des mondes: Table ronde 1990*. Stuttgart, 1992.
Hellmuth, Eckhart, ed. *The Transformation of Political Culture: England and Germany in the Late Eighteenth Century*. Oxford, 1990.
Henderson, G. D. *Chevalier Ramsay*. London, 1952.
Henrich, Dieter. "Die Anfänge der Theorie des Subjekts (1789)", in *Zwischenbetrachtungen im Prozeß der Aufklärung. Jürgen Habermas zum 60. Geburtstag*, eds. A. Honneth, C. Offe, and A. Wellmer. Frankfurt, 1989, pp. 106–170.
Henrich, Dieter. "The Concept of Moral Insight", trans. M. Kuehn, in D. Henrich, *The Unity of Reason. Essays on Kant's Philosophy*, ed. R. Velkley. Cambridge, MA, 1994.
Henrich, Dieter. *Fichtes ursprüngliche Einsicht*. Frankfurt am Main, 1967.

Henrich, Dieter. "Hutcheson und Kant", *Kant-Studien*, 49 (1957–8): 49–69.

Henrich, Dieter. "The Identity of the Subject in the Transcendental Deduction", in *Reading Kant*, eds. E. Schaper and W. Vossenkuhl. Oxford, 1989, pp. 250–80.

Henrich, Dieter. "Über Kant's früheste Ethik". *Kant-Studien* 54 (1963): 404–31.

Henriques, Ursula. *Religious Toleration in England 1787–1833*. London, 1961.

Herman, Barbara. "Training to Autonomy: Kant and the Question of Moral Education", in *Philosophers on Education: New Historical Perspectives*, ed. A. Oksenburg Rorty. London, 1998, pp. 255–72.

Herrick, James A. *The Radical Rhetoric of the English Deists: The Discourse of Skepticism, 1680–1750*. Columbia, SC, 1997.

Herrmann, Ulrich, ed. *"Das pädagogische Jahrhundert": Volksaufklärung und Erziehung zur Armut im 18. Jahrhundert in Deutschland*. Basel, 1981.

Herschel, John Frederick William. *A Preliminary Discourse on the Study of Natural Philosophy*. London, 1830; facsim., ed. M. Partridge. New York, NY, 1966.

Hertzberg, Arthur. *The French Enlightenment and the Jews*. New York, NY, 1968.

Heyd, Michael. *Between Orthodoxy and the Enlightenment: Jean-Robert Chouet and the Introduction of Cartesian Science in the Academy of Geneva*. The Hague, 1983.

Hildebrandt, Kurt. "Kant's Verhältnis zu Leibniz in der vorkritischen Periode". *Zeitschrift für philosophische Forschung* 8 (1954): 3–29.

Hill, John Spencer, ed. *Imagination in Coleridge*. London, 1978.

Hills, Richard L. *Power From Steam: A History of the Stationary Steam Engine*. Cambridge, 1989.

Hinrichs, Carl. *Preußentum und Pietismus: Der Pietismus in Brandenburg-Preußen als religiös-soziale Reformbewegung*. Göttingen, 1971.

Hinsch, Werner. *Erfahrung und Selbstbewusstsein: zur Kategoriendeduktion bei Kant*. Hamburg, 1986.

Hinske, Norbert. "Mendelssohns Beantwortung der Frage: Was ist Aufklärung? oder Über die Aktualität Mendelssohns'", in *Ich handle mit Vernunft . . . Moses Mendelssohn und die europäische Aufklärung*, ed. N. Hinske. Hamburg, 1981, pp. 85–117.

Hinske, Norbert, ed. *Was ist Aufklärung? Beiträge aus der Berlinischen Monatsschrift*. Darmstadt, 1990.

Hinske, Norbert. "Zwischen fortuna und felicitas: Glücksvorstellungen im Wandel der Zeiten". *Philosophisches Jahrbuch* 85 (1975): 317–30.

Hintikka, Jaakko. "Kant's Theory of Mathematics Revisited", in *Essays on Kant's Critique of Pure Reason*, eds. J. N. Mohanty and R. W. Shahan. Norman, OK, 1982, pp. 201–15.

Hirsch, Emanuel. *Geschichte der neuern evangelischen Theologie: im Zusammenhang mit den allgemeinen Bewegungen des europäischen Denkens*, 5 vols. Gütersloh, 1949–54; 2nd edn., 1960.

Hirschman, Albert O. *The Passions and the Interests: Political Arguments for Capitalism before Its Triumph*. Princeton, NJ, 1977.

Hirzel, L., ed. *Wieland und Martin und Regula Künzli: ungedruckte Briefe*. Leipzig, 1891.

Hochstrasser, T. J. "Conscience and Reason: The Natural Law Theory of Jean Barbeyrac". *Historical Journal* 32 (1993): 289–308.

Hochstrasser, T. J. *Natural Law Theories in the Early Enlightenment*. Cambridge, 2000.

Hodges, Michael, and John Lachs. "Hume on Belief". *The Review of Metaphysics* 30 (1976): 3–18.

Höffe, Otfried, ed. *Immanuel Kant: Zum Ewigen Frieden*. Berlin, 1995.

Hofstadter, Richard, and Wilson Smith, eds. *American Higher Education: A Documentary History*. 2 vols. Chicago, IL, 1961.

Holmes, Geoffrey. *The Trial of Dr. Sacheverell*. London, 1973.

Hont, Istvan. "The Language of Sociability and Commerce: Samuel Pufendorf and the Theoretical Foundations of the 'Four-Stages Theory'", in *The Languages of Political Theory in Early-Modern Europe*, ed. A. Pagden. Cambridge, 1987, pp. 253–76.

Hoppen, K. T. *The Common Scientist in the Seventeenth Century: A Study of the Dublin Philosophical Society 1683–1708*. London, 1970.

Hornig, Gottfried. "Perfektibilität: Eine Untersuchung zur Geschichte und Bedeutung dieses Begriffs in der deutschsprachigen Literatur". *Archiv für Begriffsgeschichte* 24 (1980): 221–57.

Horstmann, Rolf-Peter. "What Is Wrong with Kant's Categories, Professor Hegel?", in *Proceedings of the 8th International Kant Congress*, ed. H. Robinson, pp. 1005–15.

Hoskin, Michael Anthony. *William Herschel and the Construction of the Heavens*. London, 1963.

Hostler, John. *Leibniz's Moral Philosophy*. London, 1975.

Houston, J. *Reported Miracles: A Critique of Hume*. Cambridge, 1994.

Houston, J., ed. *Thomas Reid: Context, Influence, and Significance*. Edinburgh, 2004.

Howell, Wilbur Samuel. "The Declaration of Independence and Eighteenth-Century Logic". *William and Mary Quarterly* 3rd ser., 18 (1961): 463–84.

Howell, Wilbur Samuel. *Eighteenth-Century British Logic and Rhetoric*. Princeton, NJ, 1971.

Hruschka, Joachim. "The Greatest Happiness Principle and Other Early German Anticipations of Utilitarian Theory". *Utilitas* 3 (1991): 165–77.

Hübener, Wolfgang. "Sinn und Grenzen des Leibnizschen Optimismus". *Studia Leibnitiana* 10 (1978): 222–46.

Humphrey, David C. *From King's College to Columbia, 1746–1800*. New York, NY, 1976.

Humphreys, Ted B. "The Historical and Conceptual Relations between Kant's Metaphysics of Space and Philosophy of Geometry". *Journal of the History of Philosophy* 11 (1973): 483–512.

Hunter, Ian. "The Morals of Metaphysics: Kant's Groundwork as Intellectual Paideia". *Critical Inquiry* 28.4 (2002): 908–29.

Hunter, Ian. *Rival Enlightenments: Civil and Metaphysical Philosophy in Early Modern Germany*. Cambridge, 2001.

Hunter, Michael, and David Wootton, eds. *Atheism from the Reformation to the Enlightenment*. Oxford, 1992.

Hunting, Claudine. "The Philosophes and Black Slavery: 1748–1765", in *Race, Gender, and Rank: Early Modern Ideas of Humanity*, ed. M. C. Horowitz. Rochester, NY, 1992, pp. 17–30.

Hurlbutt, Robert H. *Hume, Newton and the Design Argument*. Lincoln, NB, 1965.

Immerwahr, John. "Hume's Revised Racism". *Journal of the History of Ideas* 53 (1992): 481–6.

Irmscher, Hans Dietrich. "Nachwort", in J. G. Herder, *Abhandlung über den Ursprung de Sprache*, ed. H. D. Irmscher, Stuttgart, 1966.

Ishiguro, Hidé. *Leibniz's Philosophy of Logic and Language*. Cambridge, 1990.

Israel, Jonathan I. *Radical Enlightenment. Philosophy and the Making of Modernity 1650–1750*. Oxford, 2001.

Jack, M. R. "Religion and Ethics in Mandeville", in *Mandeville Studies: New Studies in the Art and Thought of Dr. Bernard Mandeville (1670–1733)*, ed. I. Primer, pp. 34–42.

Jacob, Margaret C. *The Radical Enlightenment: Pantheists, Freemasons and Republicans*. London, 1981.

Jacob, Margaret C. "Scientific Culture in the Early English Enlightenment", in *Anticipations of the Enlightenment in England, France and Germany*, eds. A. C. Kors and P. J. Korshin. Philadelphia, PA, 1987, ch. 6.

Jacobs, Eva, et al., eds. *Woman and Society in Eighteenth-Century France: Essays in Honour of John Stephenson Spink*. London, 1979.

James, D. G. *The Life of Reason: Hobbes, Locke, Bolingbroke*. London, 1949.

James, E. D. "Faith, Sincerity and Morality: Mandeville and Bayle", in *Mandeville Studies: New Studies in the Art and Thought of Dr. Bernard Mandeville (1670–1733)*, ed. I. Primer, pp. 43–65.

James, Susan. *Passion and Action: The Emotions in Seventeenth-Century Philosophy*. Oxford, 1997.

Janik, Linda G. "Searching for the Metaphysics of Science: The Structure and Composition of Madame Du Châtelet's *Institutions de Physique*, 1737–1740". *Studies on Voltaire and the Eighteenth Century* 201 (1982): 85–113.

Jankovic, Vladimir. *Reading the Skies: A Cultural History of English Weather, 1650–1820*. Chicago, IL, 2000.

Jardine, Nicholas, James Secord, and Emma Spary, eds. *The Cultures of Natural History*. Cambridge, 1996.

Jenkinson, Sally L. "Two Concepts of Tolerance: Why Bayle Is Not Locke". *The Journal of Political Philosophy* 4 (1996): 302–22.

Jentsch, W. "Christian Wolff und die Mathematik seiner Zeit", in *Christian Wolff als Philosoph der Aufklärung in Deutschland*, eds. H.-M. Gerlach, G. Schenk and B. Thaler. Halle, 1980, pp. 173–80.

Jesseph, Douglas M. *Berkeley's Philosophy of Mathematics*. Chicago, IL, 1993.

Jimack, P. D. *Rousseau: Emile*. London, 1983.

Jimack, P. D. "The Paradox of Sophie and Julie: Contemporary Response to Rousseau's Ideal Wife and Ideal Mother", in *Women and Society in Eighteenth-Century France: Essays in Honour of John Stephenson Spink*, eds. E. Jacobs, et al., pp. 162–65.

Jodl, Friedrich. *Geschichte der Ethik in der neueren Philosophie*, 2 vols. Stuttgart, 1882–9.

Johnson, Samuel. *Samuel Johnson, President of King's College, His Career and Writings*, eds. H. Schneider and C. Schneider, 4 vols. New York, NY, 1929.

Jolley, Nicholas. *Leibniz and Locke. A Study of the New Essays on Human Understanding*. Oxford, 1984.

Jolley, Nicholas. *The Light of the Soul: Theories of Ideas in Leibniz, Malebranche, and Descartes*. Oxford, 1990.

Jones, K. G. "The Observational Basis for Kant's Cosmogony". *Journal for the History of Astronomy* 2 (1971): 29–34.

Jones, Mary Gwladys. *The Charity School Movement: A Study of Eighteenth Century Puritanism in Action*. Cambridge, 1938.

Jones, Matthew L. "Descartes's Geometry as Spiritual Exercise". *Critical Inquiry* 28.1 (2001): 40–71.

Jones, Peter, ed. *The "Science of Man" in the Scottish Enlightenment. Hume, Reid and Their Contemporaries*. Edinburgh, 1989.

Jones, Vivien, ed. *Women in the Eighteenth Century*. London, 1990.

Jones, W. P. "The Vogue of Natural History in England, 1750–1770". *Annals of Science* 2 (1937): 332–56.

Kates, Gary. *The Cercle Social: the Girondins and the French Revolution*. Princeton, NJ, 1985.

Kawashima, K. "La participation de Madame du Châtelet à la querelle sur les forces vives". *Historia scientiarum* 40 (1990): 9–28.

Keller, Pierre. *Kant and the Demands of Self-Consciousness*. Cambridge, 1998.

Kelley, B. M. *Yale: A History*. New Haven, CT, 1974.

Kelley, Donald R. *The Descent of Ideas: The History of Intellectual History*. Aldershot, 2002.

Kelley, Donald R. *Faces of History: Historical Inquiry from Herodotus to Herder*. New Haven, CT, 1998.

Kemp, Betty. *Sir Francis Dashwood: An Eighteenth-Century Independent*. London, 1967.

Keohane, Nannerl O. *Philosophy and the State in France: The Renaissance to the Enlightenment*. Princeton, NJ, 1980.
Kersting, Christa. "La dottrina del duplice contratto nel diritto naturale Tedesco". *Filosofia politica*, 8 (1994): 409–37.
Kersting, Christa. *Die Genese der Pädagogik im 18. Jahrhundert: Campes 'Allgemeine Revision' im Kontext der neuzeitlichen Wissenschaft*. Weinheim, 1992.
Kersting, Wolfgang. "Der Kontraktualismus im deutschen Naturrecht", in *Das Europäische Naturrecht im ausgehenden 18. Jahrhundert*, eds. D. Klippel and O. Dann. Hamburg, 1994, pp. 90–110.
Kersting, Wolfgang. "Die Logik des kontraktualistischen Arguments", in *Der Begriff der Politik*, ed. V. Gerhardt. Stuttgart, 1990, pp. 216–37.
Kersting, Wolfgang. *Niccolò Machiavelli*. Munich, 1988.
Kersting, Wolfgang. *Die politische Philosophie des Gesellschaftsvertrags*. Darmstadt, 1994.
Kersting, Wolfgang. *Thomas Hobbes*. Hamburg, 1992.
Kersting, Wolfgang. *Wohlgeordnete Freiheit: Immanuel Kants Rechts- und Staatsphilosophie*. Frankfurt am Main, 1993.
Kieffer, Bruce. "Herder's Treatment of Süssmilch's Theory of the Origin of Language in the *Abhandlung über den Ursprung der Sprache*: A Re-Evaluation". *The Germanic Review* 53 (1978): 96–105.
Kilcullen, John. *Sincerity and Truth: Essays on Arnauld, Bayle, and Toleration*. Oxford, 1988.
King, Peter. *The Life of John Locke, with Extracts from His Correspondence, Journals, and Commonplace Books*, 2 vols. London, 1830.
Kintzler, Catherine. *Condorcet, l'instruction publique et la naissance du citoyen*. Paris, 1984.
Kirwan, Richard. *Logick; or, An Essay on the Elements, Principles, and different Modes of Reasoning*. London, 1807.
Kirwan, Richard. *Metaphysical Essays, containing the Principles and Fundamental Objects of that Science*. London, 1809.
Kirwan, Richard. "Remarks on some Sceptical Positions in Hume's Enquiry concerning Human Understanding and his Treatise of Human Nature". *Transactions of the Royal Irish Academy* 8 (1801): 157–201.
Kivy, Peter. "Recent Scholarship and the British Tradition: A Logic of Taste – The First Fifty Years", in *Aesthetics: A Critical Anthology*, eds. G. Dickie, R. Sclafani, and R. Roblin. New York, NY, 1989, pp. 626–46.
Klemme, Heiner F. *Kants Philosophie des Subjekts. Systematische und entwicklungsgeschichtliche Untersuchungen zum Verhältnis von Selbstbewusstsein und Selbsterkenntnis*. Hamburg, 1996.
Klemmt, A. *Karl Leonhard Reinholds Elementarphilosophie*. Hamburg, 1958.
Kline, M. "Euler and Infinite Series". *Mathematics Magazine* 56 (1983): 307–14.
Klippel, Diethelm. "Naturrecht als politische Theorie: Zur politischen Bedeutung des deutschen Naturrechts im 18. und 19. Jahrhundert", in *Aufklärung als Politisierung – Politisierung der Aufklärung*, eds. H. E. Bödeker and U. Herrmann, Hamburg, 1987, pp. 267–93.
Klippel, Diethelm. *Politische Freiheit und Freiheitsrechte im deutschen Naturrecht des 18. Jahrhunderts*. Paderborn, 1976.
Klossowski, Pierre. "Sade, or the Philosopher-Villain". *Substance* 50 (1986): 5–25.
Knight, Isabel F. *The Geometric Spirit: The Abbé de Condillac and the French Enlightenment*. New Haven, CT, 1968.
Knight, William Angus, ed. *Lord Monboddo and Some of His Contemporaries*. London, 1900.
Knudsen, Jonathan. "The Historicist Enlightenment", in *What's Left of Enlightenment?: A Postmodern Question*, eds. K. M. Baker and P. H. Reill. Stanford, CA, 2001, pp. 39–49.
Koerner, Lisbet. "Carl Linnaeus in His Time and Place", in *Cultures of Natural History*, eds. N. Jardine, J. Secord and E. Spary, pp. 145–62.

König, Helmut, ed. *Schriften zur Nationalerziehung in Deutschland am Ende des 18. Jahrhunderts*. Berlin, 1954.

Kors, Alan Charles. "The Atheism of d'Holbach and Naigeon", in *Atheism from the Reformation to the Enlightenment*, eds. M. Hunter and D. Wootton, pp. 273–300.

Kors, Alan Charles. *Atheism in France, 1650–1729*. Princeton, NJ, 1990, vol. 1: *The Orthodox Sources of Disbelief* [all published].

Kors, Alan Charles. *D'Holbach's Coterie. An Enlightenment in Paris*. Princeton, NJ, 1976.

Kors, Alan Charles. "Skepticism and the Problem of Atheism in Early-Modern France", in *Scepticism and Irreligion in the Seventeenth and Eighteenth Centuries*, eds. R. H. Popkin and A. Vanderjagt, pp. 185–215.

Koyré, Alexandre. "Hypothèse et expérience chez Newton". *Bulletin de la Societé française de philosophie* 50 (1956): 59–79.

Kra, Pauline. *Religion in Montesquieu's "Lettres persanes"*. Geneva, 1970.

Kramnick, Isaac. *Republicanism and Bourgeois Radicalism: Political Ideology in Late Eighteenth-Century England and America*. Ithaca, NY, 1990.

Kraus, Andreas. "Die Bedeutung der deutschen Akademien des 18. Jahrhunderts für die historische und naturwissenschaftliche Forschung", in *Der Akademiegedanke im 17. und 18. Jahrhundert*, ed. F. Hartmann and R. Vierhaus, pp. 139–70.

Krieger, Leonard. *The Politics of Discretion: Pufendorf and the Acceptance of Natural Law*. Chicago, IL, 1965.

Krieger, Martin. *Geist, Welt und Gott bei Christian August Crusius. Erkenntnistheorisch-psychologische, kosmologische und religionsphilosophische Perspektiven im Kontrast zum Wolffschen System*. Würzburg, 1993.

Kristeller, Paul Oskar. "The Modern System of the Arts", in *Problems in Aesthetics*, ed. M. Weitz. London, 1970.

Kubrin, David. *Providence and the Mechanical Philosophy: The Creation and Dissolution of the World in Newtonian Thought. A Study of the Relations of Science and Religion in Seventeenth Century England*, PhD thesis, Cornell University, 1968.

Kuehn, Manfred. "David Hume and Moses Mendelssohn". *Hume Studies* 21 (1995): 197–220.

Kuehn, Manfred. *Kant: A Biography*. Cambridge, 2001.

Kuehn, Manfred. "Kant's Transcendental Deduction: A Limited Defense of Hume", in *New Essays on Kant*, ed. B. den Ouden. New York, NY, 1987, pp. 47–82.

Kuehn, Manfred. *Scottish Common Sense in Germany, 1768–1800: A Contribution to the History of Critical Philosophy*. Kingston and Montreal, 1987.

Kuhfuss, Walter. *Mässigung und Politik: Studien zur politischen Sprache und Theorie Montesquieus*. Munich, 1975.

Kuhlemann, Frank-Michael. *Modernisierung und Disziplinierung: Sozialgeschichte des preussischen Volksschulwesens 1794–1872*. Göttingen, 1992.

Kulstad, Mark. *Leibniz on Apperception, Consciousness, and Reflection*. Munich, 1991.

La Vopa, Anthony J. *Grace, Talent and Merit: Poor Students, Clerical Careers and Professional Ideology in Eighteenth-Century Germany*. Cambridge, 1988.

Labrousse, Elisabeth. *Bayle*, trans. D. Potts. Oxford, 1983.

Labrousse, Elisabeth. "La méthode critique chez Pierre Bayle et l'histoire". *Revue internationale de philosophie de Bruxelles* 11 (1957): 450–66.

Labrousse, Elisabeth. *Pierre Bayle*, 2 vols. The Hague, 1963–4, vol. 2: *Pierre Bayle: Hétérodoxie et rigorisme*, 2nd edn. Paris, 1996.

Lachterman, David Rapport. *The Ethics of Geometry*. New York, NY, 1989.

Laird, John. *Hume's Philosophy of Human Nature*. London, 1932.

Land, Stephen K. *From Signs to Propositions. The Concept of Form in Eighteenth-Century Semantic Theory*. London, 1974.

Landucci, Sergio. *La teodicea nell'età cartesiana*. Naples, 1986.

Lange, Ulrich. "Teilung und Trennung der Gewalten bei Montesquieu". *Der Staat* 19 (1980): 213–34.

Langer, Claudia. *Reform nach Prinzipien: Untersuchungen zur politischen Theorie Immanuel Kants*. Stuttgart, 1986.

Larson, James L. "An Alternative Science, Linnæan Natural History in Germany, 1770–1790". *Janus* 66 (1979): 267–83.

Larson, James L. *Interpreting Nature: The Science of Living Form from Linnaeus to Kant*. Baltimore, MD, 1994.

Larson, James L. "Not without a Plan: Geography and Natural History in the Late Eighteenth Century". *Journal of the History of Biology* 19 (1986): 447–88.

Larson, James L. *Reason and Experience: The Representation of Natural Order in the Work of Carl von Linné*. Berkeley, CA, 1971.

Latour, Bruno. *Science in Action*. Cambridge, MA, 1987.

Laudan, L. L. "Thomas Reid and the Newtonian Turn of British Methodological Thought", in *The Methodological Heritage of Newton*, eds. R. E. Butts and J. W. Davis, pp. 103–31.

Lauer, Quentin. *Hegel's Concept of God*. Albany, NY, 1982.

Launay, Michel. Introduction, in J.-J. Rousseau, *Émile, ou L'éducation*. Paris, 1966.

Laurent, Pierre. *Pufendorf et la loi naturelle*. Paris, 1982.

Laursen, John C. "Kant in the History of Scepticism", in *John Locke und/and Immanuel Kant: Historische Rezeption und gegenwärtige Relevanz*, ed. M. P. Thompson. Berlin, 1991, pp. 254–68.

Laursen, John C. *The Politics of Skepticism in the Ancients, Montaigne, Hume and Kant*. Leiden, 1992.

Le Ru, Véronique. *Jean le Rond d'Alembert philosophe*. Paris, 1994.

Leeuwen, Henry G. Van. *The Problem of Certainty in English Thought, 1630–1690*. The Hague, 1963.

Lehmann, William C. *John Millar of Glasgow 1735–1801*. Cambridge, 1960.

Leigh, R. A. *Rousseau and the Problem of Tolerance in the Eighteenth Century: A Lecture Delivered in the Taylor Institution Oxford*. Oxford, 1979.

Lempa, Heikki. *Bildung der Triebe: Der deutsche Philanthropismus 1768–1788*. Turku, 1993.

Lennon, Thomas M. *The Battle of the Gods and Giants: The Legacies of Descartes and Gassendi, 1655–1715*. Princeton, NJ, 1993.

Lessnoff, Michael. *Social Contract*. Houndmills, 1986.

La Lettre clandestine. Bulletin d'information sur la literature philosophique clandestine de l'âge classique, Nos:. 1–3 1992–4.

Levie, Dagobert de. "Patriotism and Clerical Office: Germany 1761–1773". *Journal of the History of Ideas* 14 (1953): 622–27.

Levine, Joseph M. *The Autonomy of History: Truth and Method from Erasmus to Gibbon*. Chicago, IL, 1999.

Lewes, George Henry. *A Biographical History of Philosophy*, 4 in 2 vols. London, 1845.

Lewis, C. I. *A Survey of Symbolic Logic*, 2nd corr. edn. New York, NY, 1960.

Lewis, C. S. *Studies in Words*. Cambridge, 1960.

Leyden, Wolfgang von. "Locke and Nicole: Their Proofs of the Existence of God and their Attitude towards Descartes". *Sophia* [Padua].16 (1948): 41–55.

Lichtenstein, Erich. *Gottscheds Ausgabe von Bayles Dictionnaire*. Heidelberg, 1915.

Lindau, Hans, ed. *Die Schriften zu J. G. Fichte's Atheismus-Streit*. Munich, 1912.

Lindemann, Ruth. *Der Begriff der Conscience im französischen Denken*. Jena, 1938.

Link, Christoph. *Herrschaftsordnung und bürgerliche Freiheit: Grenzen der Staatsgewalt in der älteren deutschen Staatslehre*. Vienna, 1979.

Lipset, Seymour Martin, and David Riesman. *Education and Politics at Harvard*. New York, NY, 1975.

Lloyd, A. C. "The Self in Berkeley's Philosophy", in *Essays on Berkeley: A Tercentennial Celebration*, eds. J. Foster and H. Robinson, Oxford, 1985, pp. 187–209.

Lloyd, Genevieve. *The Man of Reason. "Male" and "Female" in Western Philosophy*. Minneapolis, MN, 1993.

Lock, F. P. *Burke's Reflections on the Revolution in France*. London, 1985.

Loewenich, Walther von. *Luther und Lessing*. Tübingen, 1960.

Loft, Leonore. "J.-P. Brissot and the Problem of Jewish Emancipation". *Studies on Voltaire and the Eighteenth Century* 278 (1990): 465–75.

Lokken, Roy N. "Discussions of Newton's Infinitesimals in Eighteenth-Century Anglo-America". *Historia Mathematica* 7 (1980): 141–55.

Long, Douglas. *Jeremy Bentham's Idea of Liberty in Relation to His Utilitarianism*. Toronto, 1977.

Longley, P. M. *Hume's Logic: Ideas and Inference*. PhD thesis, University of Minnesota, 1968.

Longuenesse, Beatrice. *Kant and the Capacity to Judge*. Princeton, NJ, 1997.

Lorenz, Stefan. *De mundo optimo. Zu Leibniz' Theodizee und ihrer Rezeption in Deutschland, 1710–1791*. Stuttgart, 1997.

Lorenz, Stefan. "Skeptizismus und natürliche Religion: Thomas Abbt und Moses Mendelssohn in ihrer Debatte über Johann Joachim Spaldings *Bestimmung des Menschen*", in *Moses Mendelssohn und die Kreise seiner Wirksamkeit*, eds. M. Albrecht, E. J. Engel, and N. Hinske, Tübingen, 1994, pp. 113–33.

Lovejoy, Arthur O. *The Great Chain of Being: A Study of the History of an Idea*. Cambridge, MA, 1936.

Lovejoy, Arthur O. "Kant and Evolution", in *Forerunners of Darwin 1745–1859*, eds. B. Glass, O. Temkin, and W. L. Strauss, Jr. Baltimore, MD, 1959.

Löwith, Karl. "Die beste aller Welten und das radikal Böse im Menschen", in *Sämtliche Schriften*, vol. 3: *Wissen, Glaube und Skepsis: zur Kritik von Religion und Theologie* (1985), pp. 275–97.

Löwith, Karl. *Sämtliche Schriften*, eds. K. Stichweh and M. B. de Launay, 9 vols. Stuttgart, 1981–8.

Lowrie, Walter. *Kierkegaard*. London, 1938.

Luce, A. A. *Berkeley and Malebranche. A Study in the Origin of Berkeley's Thought*, 2nd edn. Oxford, 1967.

Luke, Timothy W. "On Nature and Society: Rousseau versus the Enlightenment". *History of Political Thought* 5 (1984): 211–43.

Lundgren, A. "The Changing Role of Numbers in Eighteenth-Century Chemistry", in *The Quantifying Spirit in the 18th Century*, eds. T. Frängsmyr, J. L. Heilbron, and R. E. Rider, pp. 256–66.

Luporini, Luigi. *L'Ottimismo di Jean-Jacques Rousseau*. Florence, 1982.

Lütgert, Wilhelm. *Die Erschütterung des Optimismus durch das Erdbeben von Lissabon 1755*. Gütersloh, 1901.

Lüthe, Rudolf. *David Hume: Historiker und Philosoph*. Freiburg, 1991.

Lüthje, Hans. "Christian Wolff's Philosophiebegriff". *Kant-Studien* 30 (1926): 39–66.

Lütterfelds, Wilhelm. "Zum undialektischen Begriff des Selbstbewusstseins bei Kant und Fichte". *Wiener Jahrbuch für Philosophie* 8 (1975): 7–38.

Lützen, J. "Euler's Vision of a General Partial Differential Calculus for a Generalized Kind of Function". *Mathematics Magazine* 56 (1983): 299–306.

Lyon, John, and Phillip Sloan, eds. *From Natural History to the History of Nature: Readings from Buffon and His Critics*. Notre Dame, IN, 1981.
Macaulay, Thomas. "Mill's Essay on Government: Utilitarian Logic and Politics", [1829] in *Utilitarian Logic and Politics*, eds. J. Lively and J. C. Rees. Oxford, 1978, pp. 97–129.
MacIntosh, J. J. "Locke and Boyle on Miracles and God's Existence", in *Robert Boyle Reconsidered*, ed. M. Hunter. Cambridge, 1994, pp. 193–214.
MacLean, John. *History of the College of New Jersey*, 2 vols. Philadelphia, PA, 1877.
Maclear, James Fulton. "Isaac Watts and the Idea of Public Religion". *Journal of the History of Ideas* 53 (1992): 25–45.
MacLeod, Christine. *Inventing the Industrial Revolution: The English Patent System, 1600–1800*. Cambridge, 1988.
Maehle, Andreas-Holger. *Kritik und Verteidigung des Tierversuchs: Die Anfänge der Diskussion im 17. und 18. Jahrhundert*. Stuttgart, 1992.
Mahoney, John L. Introduction, in W. Duff, *An Essay on Original Genius*, (1964 edn.) (*B1*).
Mainusch, Herbert. Introduction, in J. Toland, *Reasons for Naturalizing the Jews in Great Britain and Ireland/Gründe für die Einbürgerung der Juden in Großbritannien und Ireland*. Stuttgart, 1965 (*B1*).
Makkreel, Rudolf A. "The Confluence of Aesthetics and Hermeneutics in Baumgarten, Meier, and Kant". *The Journal of Aesthetics and Art Criticism* 54 (1996): 65–75.
Makkreel, Rudolf A. *Imagination and Interpretation in Kant: The Hermeneutical Import of the 'Critique of Judgment'*. Chicago, IL, 1990.
Makkreel, Rudolf A. "Kant and the Interpretation of Nature and History". *Philosophical Forum* 21 (1989–90): 169–81.
Man, Paul de. *Allegories of Reading: Figural Language in Rousseau, Nietzsche, Rilke and Proust*. New Haven, CT, 1979.
Marcil-LaCoste, Louise. *Claude Buffier and Thomas Reid: Two Common-Sense Philosophers*. Kingston and Montreal, 1982.
Marcolungo, Ferdinando L. "Wolff e il problema del metodo", in *Werke*, Abt. III, vol. 31: *Nuovi studi sul pensiero di Christian Wolff*, eds. S. Carboncini and L. C. Madonna (Hildesheim, 1992), pp. 11–37.
Marienstras, Elise. *Nous, le peuple: les origines du nationalisme américain*. Paris, 1988.
Marshall, Paul. *A Kind of Life Imposed on Man: Vocation and Social Order from Tyndale to Locke*. Toronto, 1996.
Marshall, Peter J., and Glyndwr Williams. *The Great Map of Mankind: Perceptions of New Worlds in the Age of Enlightenment*. London and Cambridge, MA, 1982.
Martin, Jane. *Reclaiming a Conversation. The Ideal of the Educated Woman*. New Haven, CT, 1985.
Martin, Raymond, and John Barresi. *Naturalization of the Soul: Self and Personal Identity in the Eighteenth Century*. London and New York, NY, 2000.
Mason, Haydn Trevor. *Pierre Bayle and Voltaire*. London, 1963.
Mason, Haydn Trevor. "Voltaire and Manichean Dualism". *Studies on Voltaire and the Eighteenth Century* 26 (1963): 1143–60.
Mason, M. G. "How John Locke Wrote *Some Thoughts Concerning Education, 1693*". *Paedagogica Historica* 1.2 (1961): 244–90.
Mason, M. G. "The Literary Sources of John Locke's Educational Thoughts". *Paedagogica Historica* 5.1 (1965): 65–108.
Masters, Roger D. *The Political Philosophy of Rousseau*. Princeton, NJ, 1968.
Mattick, Paul, Jr. "Beautiful and the Sublime: Gender Totemism in the Constitution of Art". *The Journal of Aesthetics and Art Criticism* 48 (1990).

Maxwell, Constantia. *A History of Trinity College Dublin, 1591–1892*. Dublin, 1946.
May, J. A. *Kant's Concept of Geography and Its Relation to Recent Geographical Thought*. Toronto, 1970.
Mayr, Otto. "Adam Smith and the Concept of the Feedback System". *Technology and Culture* 12 (1977): 1–22.
Mazzeo, J. A., ed. *Reason and the Imagination: Studies in the History of Ideas 1600–1800*. New York, NY, 1962.
McCalman, Iain. "New Jerusalems: Prophecy, Dissent and Radical Culture in England, 1786–1830", in *Enlightenment and Religion: Rational Dissent in Eighteenth-Century Britain*, ed. K. Haakonssen, Cambridge, 1996 pp. 312–35.
McClellan, James E., III. *Science Reorganized: Scientific Societies in the Eighteenth Century*. New York, NY, 1985.
McClelland, Charles E. *State, Society, and University in Germany, 1700–1914*. Cambridge, 1980.
McCormick, Donald. *The Hell-Fire Club: The Story of the Amorous Knights of Wycombe*. London, 1958.
McCracken, Charles J. *Malebranche and British Philosophy*. Oxford, 1983.
McCulloch, J. R., ed. *Early English Tracts on Commerce*. Cambridge, 1954.
McDowell, R. B., and D. A. Webb. *Trinity College Dublin, 1592–1952: An Academic History*. Cambridge, 1982.
McGuinness, Philip, Alan Harrison, and Richard Kearney, eds. *See* John Toland (*B1*).
McGuire, James E. "Boyle's Conception of Nature". *Journal of the History of Ideas* 33 (1972): 523–42.
McGuire, J. E. "Force, Active Principles and Newton's Invisible Realm". *Ambix* 15 (1986): 154–208.
McIntyre, Jane L. "Personal Identity and the Passions". *Journal of the History of Philosophy* 27 (1989): 545–57.
McKenna, A., ed. *La litterature clandestine*. Oxford and Paris, 1996.
McKenna, A. "Le Marquis d'Argens et les manuscrits clandestins", in *Le Marquis de Argens*, ed. J. L. Vissière, pp. 111–40.
McLachlan, H. *English Education under the Test Acts*. Manchester, 1931.
McMahon, Darrin M. *Enemies of the Enlightenment: The French Counter-Enlightenment and the Making of Modernity*. Oxford, 2001.
McRae, Robert. *Leibniz: Perception, Apperception and Thought*. Toronto, 1976.
McReynolds, Paul. "Introduction", in *Four Early Works on Motivation*, ed. P. McReynolds. Gainesville, FL, 1969.
Medick, Hans. *Naturzustand und Naturgeschichte der bürgerlichen Gesellschaft: Die Ursprünge der bürgerlichen Sozialtheorie als Geschichtsphilosophie und Sozialwissenschaft bei Samuel Pufendorf, John Locke und Adam Smith*. Göttingen, 1973.
Medicus, Fritz, ed. *Fichte und Forberg: Die philosophischen Schriften zum Atheismusstreit*. Leipzig, 1910.
Meek, Ronald L. *The Economics of Physiocracy: Essays and Translations*. London, 1962.
Mehta, Uday Singh. *The Anxiety of Freedom: Imagination and Individuality in Locke's Political Thought*. Ithaca, NY, 1992.
Meinecke, Friedrich. *Die Entstehung des Historismus*, 4th edn. Munich, 1965.
Meinecke, Friedrich. *Historism: The Rise of a New Historical Outlook*, trans. J. E. Anderson. London, 1972.
Meinel, C. "*Artibus Academicis Inserenda*: Chemistry's Place in Eighteenth and Early Nineteenth Century Universities". *History of Universities* 7 (1988): 89–115.

Meli, D. B. "The Emergence of Reference Frames and the Transformation of Mechanics in the Enlightenment". *Historical Studies in the Physical and Biological Sciences* 23 (1993): 301–35.
Melnick, Arthur. *Space, Time, and Thought in Kant*. Dordrecht, 1989.
Melton, James Van Horn. *Absolutism and the Eighteenth-Century Origins of Compulsory Schooling in Prussia and Austria*. Cambridge, 1988.
Melzer, Arthur M. *The Natural Goodness of Man. On the System of Rousseau's Thought*. Chicago, IL, 1990.
Menozzi, Daniele. "Il dibattito sulla tolleranza nella chiesa italiana della seconda metà del Settecento", in *La Tolérance civile*, ed. R. Crahay, pp. 161–79.
Merlan, Philip. "Hamann et les dialogues de Hume". *Revue de métaphysique et de morale* 59 (1954): 285–9.
Merlan, Philip. "Hume and Hamann". *Personalist* 32 (1951): 111–18.
Merleau-Ponty, Jacques. "Situation et rôle de l'hypothèse cosmogonique dans la pensée cosmologique de Laplace". *Revue d'histoire des sciences et leurs applications* 29 (1976): 21–49.
Mijnhardt, Wijnand W. "The Dutch Enlightenment: Humanism, Nationalism and Decline", in *The Dutch Republic in the Eighteenth Century: Decline, Enlightenment, and Revolution*, eds. M. C. Jacob and W. W. Mijnhardt, Ithaca, NY, 1992, pp. 197–223.
Mijuskovic, Ben Lazare. *The Achilles of Rationalist Arguments: The Simplicity, Unity and Identity of Thought and Soul from the Cambridge Platonists to Kant. A Study in the History of an Argument*. The Hague, 1974.
Mill, James. *Analysis of the Phenomena of the Human Mind* (1829), 2 vols. London, 1878.
Mill, James. "An Essay on Government", in *Encyclopaedia Britannica*, 5th edn. Edinburgh, 1820.
Mill, James. *History of British India* [1817], 6 in 4 vols. New York, NY, 1968.
Mill, James. *Selected Economic Writings*, ed. D. Winch. London and Edinburgh, 1966.
Mill, John Stuart. *A System of Logic Ratiocinative and Inductive, Being a Connected View of the Principles of Evidence and the Methods of Scientific Investigation*. London, 1843.
Mill, John Stuart. *Utilitarianism* [1863], ed. R. Crisp. Oxford, 1999.
Miller, David. *Philosophy and Ideology in Hume's Political Thought*. Oxford, 1981.
Miller, David. "The Revival of the Physical Sciences in Britain, 1815–1840". *Osiris* 2nd ser., 2 (1986): 107–34.
Miller, Jim. *Rousseau: Dreamer of Democracy*. New Haven, CT, 1984.
Minerbi Belgrado, Anna. *Paura e ignoranza: studi sulla teoria della religione in d'Holbach*. Florence, 1983.
Mizuta, Hiroshi. *Adam Smith's Library: A Supplement to Bonar's Catalogue with a Checklist of the Whole Library*. Cambridge, 1967.
Mohr, Georg. *Das Sinnliche Ich: innerer Sinn und Bewusstsein bei Kant*. Würzburg, 1991.
Möller, Horst. *Aufklärung in Preussen: Der Verleger, Publizist und Geschichtsschreiber Friedrich Nicolai*. Berlin, 1974.
Möller, Horst. "Enlightened Societies in the Metropolis: The Case of Berlin", in *The Transformation of Political Culture*, ed. E. Hellmuth, pp. 219–33.
Momigliano, Arnaldo. "Ancient History and the Antiquarian", in *Studies in Historiography*. New York, NY, 1966, pp. 1–39.
Monk, Samuel. *The Sublime. A Study of Critical Theories in XVIII-Century England*. Ann Arbor, MI, 1960.
Monréal-Wickert, Irene. *Die Sprachforschung der Aufklärung im Spiegel der grossen französischen Enzyklopädie*. Tübingen, 1977.
Montgomery, T. H. *A History of the University of Pennsylvania from its Foundation to AD 1779*. Philadelphia, PA, 1900.

Moore, C. A. "Shaftesbury and the Ethical Poets in England, 1700–1760". *Proceedings of the Modern Language Association* 31 (1916): 264–325.
Moran, Francis. "Pongos and Men in Rousseau's *Discourse on Inequality*". *Review of Politics* 57 (1995): 641–64.
Moreau, Paul. *L'éducation morale chez Kant*. Paris, 1988.
Mori, Gianluca. *Bayle philosophe*. Paris, 1999.
Mori, Gianluca. *Introduzione a Bayle*. Rome, 1996.
Mori, Gianluca. "Per l'attributazione a Du Marsais dell' 'Examen de la religion'". *Atti e memorie dell' Academia Toscana di Scienze e Lettere La Colombaria* 48 (1993): 257–333.
Mori, Gianluca. *Tra Descartes a Bayle: Poiret e la teodicea*. Bologna, 1990.
Morison, E. *Three Centuries of Harvard 1636–1936*. Cambridge, MA, 1937.
Morris, W. E. "Hume's Scepticism about Reason". *Hume Studies* 15 (1989): 39–60.
Morsy, Zaghloul, ed. *Thinkers on Education*. 4 vols. Paris, 1995.
Mortier, Roland. "L'Athéisme en France au XVIIIe siècle: progrès et résistances". *Problèmes d'histoire du christianisme* 16 (1986): 45–62.
Mortier, Roland. *Diderot en Allemagne*. Geneva and Paris, 1986.
Mortier, Roland. "The 'Philosophes' and Public Education". *Yale French Studies* 40 (1968): 62–76.
Mossner, Ernest Campbell. "Hume's Early Memoranda, 1729–1740: The Complete Text". *Journal of the History of Philosophy* 9 (1948).
Mulholland, Leslie A. *Kant's System of Rights*. New York, NY, 1990.
Munteano, Basil. *Constantes dialectiques en littérature et en histoire*. Paris, 1967.
Munzel, G. Felicitas. *Kant's Conception of Moral Character: The 'Critical' Link of Morality, Anthropology, and Reflective Judgement*. Chicago, IL, 1999.
Myers, Richard. "Christianity and Politics in Montesquieu's 'Greatness and Decline of the Romans'". *Interpretation* 17 (1989–90): 223–38.
Nadler, Steven M. *Arnauld and the Cartesian Philosophy of Ideas*. Manchester and Princeton, NJ, 1989.
Nadler, Steven M. *Malebranche and Ideas*. New York, NY, 1992.
Nash, Richard. *John Craige's Mathematical Principles of Christian Theology*. Carbondale, IL, 1991.
Neiman, Susan. *The Unity of Reason: Rereading Kant*. Oxford, 1994.
Nelson, J. S., Allan Megill, and Donald N. McCloskey, eds. *The Rhetoric of the Human Sciences: Language and Argument in Scholarship and Public Affairs*. Madison, WI, 1987.
Neugebauer, Wolfgang. *Absolutistischer Staat und Schulwirklichkeit in Brandenburg-Preussen*. Berlin, 1985.
Neuhouser, Frederick. *Fichte's Theory of Subjectivity*. Cambridge, 1990.
Newman, Rosemary. "Hume on Space and Geometry". *Hume Studies* 7 (1981): 1–31.
Nicolson, Marjorie, and N. M. Mohler. "The Scientific Background to Swift's Voyage to Laputa", in M. Nicolson, *Science and Imagination*, Ithaca, NY, 1956, pp. 110–54.
Niderst, A. "Fontenelle et la littérature clandestine", in *Filosofia e religione nella letteratura clandestine*, ed. G. Canzoni. Milan, 1994, pp. 161–73.
Nivelle, Armand. *Kunst- und Dichtungstheorien zwischen Aufklärung und Klassik*. Berlin, 1971.
Noll, Mark A. *Princeton and the Republic 1768–1822*. Princeton, NJ, 1989.
Norton, David Fate, ed. *The Cambridge Companion to Hume*. Cambridge, 1993.
Norton, David Fate. *David Hume: Common-Sense Moralist, Sceptical Metaphysician*. Princeton, NJ, 1982.
Norton, David Fate. "Francis Hutcheson in America". *Studies on Voltaire and the Eighteenth Century* 151–5 (1976): 1547–68.

Norton, David Fate. "Hume, Atheism, and the Autonomy of Morals", in *Hume's Philosophy of Religion*, ed. M. Hester. Winston-Salem, NC, 1986, pp. 97–144.

Norton, David Fate. "Hume, Human Nature, and the Foundations of Morality", in *The Cambridge Companion to Hume*, ed. D. F. Norton, 1993, pp. 148–81.

Norton, David Fate. "Reid's Abstract of the Inquiry into the Human Mind", in *Thomas Reid: Critical Interpretations*, eds. S. F. Barker and T. L. Beauchamp. Philadelphia, PA, 1976, pp. 125–132.

Norton, Robert E. *Herder's Aesthetics and the European Enlightenment*. Ithaca, NY, 1991.

Nový, Lubos. *Origins of Modern Algebra*, trans. J. Tauer. Leiden, 1973.

Noxon, James. *Hume's Philosophical Development: A Study of His Methods*. Oxford, 1973.

Nuchelmans, Gabriel. *Judgment and Proposition from Descartes to Kant*. Amsterdam, 1983.

O'Brien, Charles. "Ideas of Religious Toleration in the Time of Joseph II: A Study of the Enlightenment among Catholics in Austria". *Transactions of the American Philosophical Society* 59.7 (1969): 5–76.

O'Brien, Charles. "Jansenists and Civil Toleration in France, 1775–1778: Le Paige, Guidi and Robert de Saint-Vincent", in *La tolérance civile*, ed. R. Crahay, pp. 183–93.

Oestreich, Gerhard. *Neostoicism and the Early Modern State*, trans. D. McLintock, eds. B. Oestreich and H. G. Koenigsberger. Cambridge, 1982.

Ogonowski, Zbigniew. "Le 'Christianisme sans mystères' selon John Toland et les sociniens". *Archiwum historii filozofii i mysli spolecznej* 12 (1966): 205–23.

Ogonowski, Zbigniew. "Leibniz und die Sozinianer", in *Theatrum Europaeum: Festschrift für Elida Maria Szarota*, ed. R. Brinkmann, Munich, 1982, pp. 385–408.

O'Higgins, James. *Anthony Collins, the Man and His Works*. The Hague, 1970.

Olaso, Ezequiel de. *Escepticismo e ilustracion: La crisis pirronica de Hume y Rousseau*. Valencia, Venezuela, 1981.

Olaso, Ezequiel de. "The Two Scepticisms of the Savoyard Vicar", in *The Sceptical Mode in Modern Philosophy: Essays in Honor of Richard H. Popkin*, eds. R. A. Watson and J. E. Force. Dordrecht, 1988, pp. 43–59.

Oldfield, J. R. *Popular Politics and British Anti-Slavery: The Mobilisation of Public Opinion Against the Slave Trade 1787–1807*. Manchester, 1995.

Olson, Mancur. *The Logic of Collective Action: Public Goods and the Theory of Groups*. Cambridge, MA, 1971.

Olson, R. G. "Scottish Philosophy and Mathematics 1750–1830". *Journal of the History of Ideas* 32 (1971): 29–44.

Olson, Richard G. "Tory-High Church Opposition to Science and Scientism in the Eighteenth Century: The Works of John Arbuthnot, Jonathan Swift and Samuel Johnson", in *The Uses of Science in the Age of Newton*, ed. J. G. Burke. Berkeley, CA, 1983, pp. 171–204.

O'Neill, Eileen. "Comments on Tuana", in *Teaching New Histories of Philosophy*, ed. J. B. Schneewind, Princeton, NJ, 2005.

O'Neill, Eileen. "Influxus Physicus", in *Causation in Early Modern Philosophy: Cartesianism, Occasionalism and Preestablished Harmony*, ed. S. Nadler. University Park, PA, 1993, pp. 27–55.

Oschlies, Wolf. *Die Arbeits-und Berufspädagogik August Hermann Franckes, 1663–1727: Schule und Leben im Menschenbild des Hauptvertreters des Halleschen Pietismus*. Witten, 1969.

Otto, Rüdiger. *Studien zur Spinozarezeption in Deutschland im 18. Jahrhundert*. Frankfurt am Main, 1994.

Owen, Richard. *The Hunterian Lectures in Comparative Anatomy, May-June 1837*, ed. P. R. Sloan. Chicago, IL and London, 1992.

Owen, Robert. *An Outline of the Rational System of Society*. London, 1830.

Oz-Salzberger, Fania. *Translating the Enlightenment: Scottish Civic Discourse in Eighteenth-Century Germany*. Oxford, 1995.

Paganini, Gianni. "Signes, imagination et mémoire. De la psychologie de Wolff à l'*Essai* de Condillac". *Revue des sciences philosophiques et théologiques* 72 (1988): 287–300.

Palladini, Fiammetta. *Samuel Pufendorf discepolo di Hobbes: per una reinterpretazione del giusnaturalismo moderno*. Bologna, 1990.

Palladini, Fiammetta, and Gerald Hartung, eds. *Samuel Pufendorf und die europäische Frühaufklärung*. Berlin, 1996.

Palmer, R. R. *The Improvement of Humanity. Education and the French Revolution*. Princeton, NJ, 1985.

Pangle, Lorraine Smith, and Thomas L. Pangle. *The Learning of Liberty: The Educational Ideas of the American Founders*. Lawrence, KS, 1993.

Pangle, Thomas L. *Montesquieu's Philosophy of Liberalism: A Commentary on the Spirit of the Laws*. Chicago, IL, 1973.

Pangle, Thomas L. *The Spirit of Modern Republicanism: The Moral Vision of the American Founders and the Philosophy of Locke*. Chicago, IL, 1988.

Parkinson, G. H. R. and S. G. Shanker, general eds. *Routledge History of Philosophy*, 10 vols. London, 1993–9.

Parry, Geraint. "Learning to be Men, Women and Citizens", in *The Cambridge Companion to Rousseau*, ed. P. Riley. Cambridge, 2001, pp. 247–71.

Parry, Geraint. "Thinking One's Own Thoughts: Autonomy and the Citizen", in *Rousseau and Liberty*, ed. R. Wokler. Manchester, 1995, pp. 99–120.

Passmore, John. "Descartes, the British Empiricists and Formal Logic". *Philosophical Review* 62 (1953): 545–53.

Passmore, John. "Enthusiasm, Fanaticism and David Hume", in *The "Science of Man" in the Scottish Enlightenment. Hume, Reid and their Contemporaries*, ed. P. Jones, pp. 85–107.

Passmore, John. *Hume's Intentions*. Cambridge, 1968.

Passmore, John. "The Malleability of Man in Eighteenth-Century Thought", in *Aspects of the Eighteenth Century*, ed. E. R. Wasserman. Baltimore, MD, 1965, pp. 21–46.

Passmore, John. *The Perfectibility of Man*. London, 1970.

Paul, Charles B. *Science and Immortality: The Eloges of the Paris Academy of Sciences, 1699–1791*. Berkeley and Los Angeles, CA, and London, 1980.

Payne, Harry C. *The Philosophes and the People*. New Haven, CT, 1976.

Peabody, Sue. *"There Are No Slaves in France": The Political Culture of Race and Slavery in the Ancien Régime*. Oxford, 1996.

Peaden, Catherine Hobbs. "Condillac and the History of Rhetoric". *Rhetorica* 11 (1993): 136–56.

Pears, David. *Hume's System: An Examination of the First Book of his Treatise*. Oxford, 1990.

Peccato, Piero. "Note sul carteggio Condillac-Cramer". *Belfagor* 26 (1971): 83–95.

Pedersen, Olaf. "Tradition and Innovation", in *Universities in Early Modern Europe*, ed. H. de Ridder-Symoens, pp. 480–7.

Penelhum, Terence. "Hume on Personal Identity". *Philosophical Review* 64 (1955): 571–89.

Perelman, Chaïm, and Lucie Olbrechts-Tyteca. *The New Rhetoric: A Treatise on Argumentation*, trans. J. Wilkinson and P. Weaver. Notre Dame, IN, 1969.

Perelman, Chaïm, and Lucie Olbrechts-Tyteca. *La nouvelle rhétorique: traité de l'argumentation*. 2 vols., Paris, 1958.

Pérez-Ramos, Antonio. *Francis Bacon's Idea of Science and the Maker's Knowledge Tradition*. Oxford, 1988.

Perkins, Jean A. *The Concept of the Self in the French Enlightenment*. Geneva, 1969.

Perrett, Roy W. *Death and Immortality*. Dordrecht, 1987.

Perry, Thomas W. *Public Opinion, Propaganda and Politics in Eighteenth-Century England: A Study of the Jew Bill of 1753*. Cambridge, MA, 1962.

Peters, W. S. "Johann Heinrich Lamberts Konzeption einer Geometrie auf einer imaginären Kugel". *Kant-Studien* 53 (1961): 51–67.

Peursen, Cornelis Anthonie van. "Ars inveniendi im Rahmen der Metaphysik Christian Wolffs", in *Christian Wolff, 1679–1754: Interpretationen zu seiner Philosophie und deren Wirkung*, ed. W. Schneiders, pp. 66–88.

Peursen, Cornelis Anthonie van. "Christian Wolff's Philosophy of Contingent Reality". *Journal of the History of Philosophy* 25 (1987): 69–82.

Phillips, Mark Salber. *Society and Sentiment: Genres of Historical Writing in Britain 1740–1820*. Princeton, NJ, 2000.

Philp, Mark. "Enlightenment, Toleration and Liberty". *Enlightenment and Dissent* 9 (1990): 47–62.

Piau-Gillot, Colette. "Le discours de Jean-Jacques Rousseau sur les femmes, et sa réception critique". *Dix-huitième siècle* 13 (1981): 317–33.

Pickering, Samuel F., Jr. *John Locke and Children's Books in Eighteenth-Century England*. Knoxville, TN, 1981.

Pinloche, A. *La réforme de l'éducation en Allemagne au dix-huitième siècle: Basedow et le philanthropinisme*. Paris, 1889.

Pippin, Robert B. "Fichte's Contribution". *Philosophical Forum* 19 (1987–8): 74–96.

Pocock, J. G. A. "Enlightenment and Counter-Enlightenment, Revolution and Counter-Revolution; A Eurosceptical Enquiry". *History of Political Thought* 20 (1999): 125–39.

Pocock, J. G. A. "Enthusiasm: The Antiself of Enlightenment", in *Enthusiasm and Enlightenment in Europe, 1650–1850*, eds. L. E. Klein and A. J. La Vopa. San Marino, CA, 1998, pp. 7–28.

Pocock, J. G. A. Introduction, in J. Harrington, *The Political Works*, ed. J. G. A. Pocock, Cambridge, 1977.

Pocock, J. G. A. *The Machiavellian Moment*. Princeton, NJ, 1975.

Poland, Burdette C. *French Protestantism and the French Revolution: A Study in Church and State, Thought and Religion, 1685–1815*. Princeton, NJ, 1957.

Pollock, Linda A. *Forgotten Children: Parent-Child Relations from 1500 to 1900*. Cambridge, 1983.

Polya, George. *Mathematics and Plausible Reasoning*, 2 vols. Princeton, NJ, 1954.

Pomeau, René. *La religion de Voltaire*. Paris, 1969.

Pons, Georges. *Gotthold Ephraim Lessing et le christianisme*. Paris, 1964.

Popkin, Richard H. "Berkeley in the History of Scepticism", in *Scepticism in the Enlightenment*, eds. R. H. Popkin, E. de Olaso, and G. Tonelli, pp. 173–86.

Popkin, Richard H. "Berkeley and Pyrrhonism", in *The Skeptical Tradition*, ed. M. Burnyeat. Berkeley and Los Angeles, CA, 1983, pp. 377–96.

Popkin, Richard H. "Condorcet, Abolitionist", in *Condorcet Studies I*, ed. L. C. Rosenfield. Atlantic Heights, NJ, 1984.

Popkin, Richard H. "Condorcet's Epistemology and His Politics", in *Knowledge and Politics: Case Studies in the Relationship between Epistemology and Political Philosophy*, eds. M. Dascal and O. Gruengard, Boulder, CO, 1989, pp. 111–24.

Popkin, Richard H. *The History of Scepticism from Erasmus to Spinoza*. Berkeley and Los Angeles, CA, 1979.

Popkin, Richard H. "Hume and Turgot and Condorcet", in *Condorcet Studies II*, ed. D. Williams. New York, NY, 1987, pp. 47–62.

Popkin, Richard H. *Isaac la Peyrère (1596–1676): His Life, Work and Influence*. Leiden, 1987.

Popkin, Richard H. "Kierkegaard and Scepticism", in *Kierkegaard. A Collection of Critical Essays*, ed. J. Thompson. Garden City, NY, 1972.

Popkin, Richard H. "New Views on the Role of Skepticism in the Enlightenment". *Modern Language Quarterly* 53 (1992): 279–97.

Popkin, Richard H. "Scepticism in the Enlightenment". *Studies on Voltaire and the Eighteenth Century* 24–7 (1963): 1321–45.

Popkin, Richard H. "Scepticism with Regard to Reason in the 17th and 18th Centuries", in *The Philosophical Canon in the 17th and 18th Centuries*, eds. G. A. J. Rogers and S. Tomaselli. Rochester, NY, 1996, pp. 33–48.

Popkin, Richard H. "Skepticism and the Study of History", in *David Hume: Philosophical Historian*, eds. D. F. Norton and R. H. Popkin. Indianapolis, IN, 1965, pp. ix–xxxi.

Popkin, Richard H. "Sources of Knowledge of Sextus Empiricus in Hume's Time". *Journal of the History of Ideas* 53 (1993): 137–41.

Popkin, Richard H. *The Third Force in Seventeenth-Century Thought*. Leiden, 1992.

Popkin, Richard H., Ezequiel de Olaso, and Giorgio Tonelli, eds. *Scepticism in the Enlightenment*. Dordrecht, 1997.

Popkin, Richard H., and Arjo Vanderjagt, eds. *Scepticism and Irreligion in the Seventeenth and Eighteenth Centuries*. Leiden, 1993.

Popper, Karl. *Objective Knowledge. An Evolutionary Approach*. Oxford, 1972.

Porset, Charles, ed. *Varia linguistica*. Bordeaux, 1970.

Porter, Roy, and Mikulas Teich, eds. *The Enlightenment in National Context*. Cambridge, 1981.

Posy, Carl J., ed. *Kant's Philosophy of Mathematics: Modern Essays*. Dordrecht, 1992.

Pott, Martin. *Aufklärung und Aberglaube: Die deutsche Frühaufklärung im Spiegel ihrer Aberglaubenskritik*. Tübingen, 1992.

Pott, Martin. "Thomasius' philosophischer Glaube", in *Christian Thomasius, 1655–1728. Interpretationen zu Werk und Wirkung*, ed. W. Schneiders, pp. 223–47.

Powell, C. Thomas. *Kant's Theory of Self-Consciousness*. Oxford, 1990.

Prauss, Gerold. *Kant und das Problem der Dinge an sich*. Bonn, 1974.

Primer, Irwin, ed. *Mandeville Studies: New Studies in the Art and Thought of Dr. Bernard Mandeville (1670–1733)*. The Hague, 1975.

Pulte, Helmut. *Das Prinzip der kleinsten Wirkung und die Kraftkonzeptionen der rationalen Mechanik*. Stuttgart, 1989.

Puster, Rolf W. *Britische Gassendi-Rezeption am Beispiel John Lockes*. Stuttgart and Bad Cannstatt, 1991.

Quetelet, Lambert Adolphe Jacques. *Sur l'homme, et le developpement de ses facultés, ou, Essai de physique sociale*. Paris, 1835.

Quine, Willard Van Orman. "Two Dogmas of Empiricism", in *From a Logical Point of View*, 2nd edn. Cambridge, MA, 1980.

Raeff, Marc. *The Well-Ordered Police State: Social and Institutional Change through Law in the Germanies and Russia, 1600–1800*. New Haven, CT, 1983.

Railton, Peter. "Pluralism, Determinacy, and Dilemma". *Ethics* 102. (1992): 720–42.

Rashed, R. *Condorcet: mathématique et société*. Paris, 1974.

Redekop, Benjamin W. "Reid's Influence in Britain, Germany, France, and America", in *The Cambridge Companion to Reid*, eds. T. Cuneo and R. van Woudenberg. Cambridge, 2004, pp. 313–39.

Redwood, John. *Reason, Ridicule and Religion: The Age of Enlightenment in England 1660–1750*. London, 1976.

Rée, Jonathan. "The Vanity of Historicism". *New Literary History* 22 (1991): 961–83.

Rée, Jonathan, Michael Ayers, and Adam Westoby, eds. *Philosophy and Its Past*. Brighton, 1978.
Reeds, Karen M. *Botany in Medieval and Renaissance Universities*. New York, NY and London, 1991.
Reich, Klaus. *The Completeness of Kant's Table of Judgements*, trans. J. Kneller and M. Losonsky. Stanford, CA, 1992.
Reid-Maroney, Nina. *Philadelphia's Enlightenment, 1740–1800*. Westport, CT, 2001.
Reif, Mary. *Natural Philosophy in Some Early-Seventeenth-Century Scholastic Textbooks*, 1962. PhD thesis, St. Louis University, 1962.
Reill, Peter Hanns. *Vitalizing Nature in the Enlightenment*. Berkeley, CA, and Los Angeles, CA, 2005.
Reill, Peter Hanns. *The German Enlightenment and the Rise of Historicism*. Berkeley, CA, 1975.
Reill, Peter Hanns. "The History of Science, the Enlightenment and the History of 'Historical Science' in Germany". *Beiträge zur Geschichtskultur* 5 (1991): 214–31.
Reinalter, Helmut, ed. *Der Josephinismus: Bedeutung, Einflüsse und Wirkungen*. Frankfurt am Main, 1993.
Reinhold, Meyer. "The Quest for 'Useful Knowledge' in Eighteenth-Century America". *Proceedings of the American Philosophical Society* 119 (1975): 108–32.
Rétat, Pierre. *Le Dictionnaire de Bayle et la lutte philosophique au XVIIIe siècle*. Paris, 1971.
Rétat, Pierre. "Meslier et Bayle: un dialogue cartésien et occasionaliste autour de l'athéisme", in *Le Curé Meslier et la vie intellectuelle, religieuse et sociale à la fin du 17e et au début du 18e siècle*, ed. R. Desné. Reims, 1980, pp. 497–516.
Rethwisch, Conrad. *Der Staatsminister Freiherr v. Zedlitz und Preussens höheres Schulwesen im Zeitalter Friedrich des Grossen*, 2nd edn. Berlin, 1886.
Rex, Walter. *Essays on Pierre Bayle and Religious Controversy*. The Hague, 1965.
Ricken, Ulrich. *Grammaire et philosophie au siècle des lumières*. Lille, 1978.
Ricken, Ulrich. *Linguistics, Anthropology and Philosophy in the French Enlightenment: Language Theory and Ideology*, trans. R. E. Norton. London, 1994.
Ricken, Ulrich, et al., ed. *Sprachtheorie und Weltanschauung in der europäischen Aufklärung*. Berlin, 1990.
Ricuperati, G. *L'esperienza civile e religiosa di Pietro Giannone*. Milan, 1970.
Ridder-Symoens, Hilde de, ed. See Rüegg, Walther.
Rider, R. E. *Mathematics in the Enlightenment: A Study of Algebra, 1685–1800*. PhD Thesis, University of California, Berkeley, CA, 1980.
Riley, Patrick. *Kant's Political Philosophy*. Totowa, NJ, 1983.
Risse, Wilhelm. *Bibliographia logica*, 4 vols. Hildesheim, 1965.
Risse, Wilhelm. *Die Logik der Neuzeit*, 2 vols. Stuttgart and Bad Cannstatt, 1964–70.
Ritschl, Albrecht. *Geschichte des Pietismus*, 3 vols. Bonn, 1880–96.
Ritter, Joachim, Karlfried Gründer, and Gottfried Gabriel, eds. *Historisches Wörterbuch der Philosopie*. 11 vols. Basel and Darmstadt, 1971–.
Ritterbush, Philip C. *Overtures to Biology: The Speculations of Eighteenth-Century Naturalists*. New Haven, CT, 1964.
Rivers, Isabel. *The Defence of Truth through the Knowledge of Error: Philip Doddridge's Academy Lectures*. London, 2003.
Rivers, Isabel. *Reason, Grace, and Sentiment: A Study of the Language of Religion and Ethics in England 1660–1780*, 2 vols. Cambridge, 1991–2000.
Rivers, Isabel. "Responses to Hume on Religion by Anglicans and Dissenters". *Journal of Ecclesiastical History* 52 (2001): 675–95.
Roberts, R. H., and J. M. M. Good, eds. *The Recovery of Rhetoric: Persuasive Discourse and Disciplinarity in the Social Sciences*. Bristol, 1993.

Robinson, Hoke, ed. *Proceedings of the 8th International Kant Congress in Memphis*. Milwaukee, WI, 1995.
Robson, David W. *Educating Republicans*. Westport, CT, 1985.
Roche, Daniel. "La diffusion des lumières. Un exemple: l'Académie de Châlons-sur Marne". *Annales: Économies, Sociétés, Civilisations* 19 (1964): 887–922.
Roche, Daniel. "Natural History in the Academies", in *The Cultures of Natural History*, eds. N. Jardine, J. Secord and E. Spary, pp. 127–44.
Roche, Daniel. *Le siècle des lumières en province: académies et académiciens provinciaux, 1680–1789*, 2 vols. Paris, 1978.
Rodis-Lewis, Geneviève. *Le Problème de l'inconscient et le Cartésianisme*. Paris, 1950.
Roe, Shirley A. *Matter, Life and Generation: Eighteenth-Century Embryology and the Haller-Wolff Debate*. Cambridge, 1981.
Roger, Jacques. *Buffon: A Life in Natural History*, trans. S. L. Bonnefoi. Ithaca, NY and London, 1997.
Roger, Jacques. *Buffon: Un philosophe au Jardin du Roi*. Paris, 1989.
Roger, Jacques. *The Life Sciences in Eighteenth-Century French Thought*, trans. R. Ellrich, ed. K. R. Benson, 1997.
Rogers, G. A. J., and Sylvana Tomaselli, eds. *The Philosophical Canon in the 17th and 18th Centuries*. Rochester, NY, 1996.
Roller, Duane. "The Early Development of the Concepts of Temperature and Heat", in *Harvard Case Histories in Experimental Science*, ed. J. B. Conant, pp. 119–214.
Romani, Roberto. *National Character and Public Spirit in Britain and France, 1750–1914*. Cambridge, 2002.
Römer, Ruth. *Sprachwissenschaft und Rassenideologie in Deutschland*, 2nd edn. Munich, 1989.
Roncaglia, Gino. "*Cum Deus Calculat* – God's Evaluation of Possible Worlds and Logical Calculus". *Topoi* 9.1 (1990): 83–90.
Rosa, Mario. "Encyclopédie, 'Lumieres' et tradition au 18e siècle en Italie'". *Dix-huitième siècle* 4 (1972): 109–68.
Rosenfeld, Boris Abramovic. *A History of Non-Euclidean Geometry: Evolution of the Concept of a Geometric Space*, trans. A. Shenitzer. New York, NY, 1988.
Ross, David. *Kant's Ethical Theory: A Commentary on the Grundlegung zur Metaphysik der Sitten*. Oxford, 1954.
Rossi, Paolo. *The Dark Abyss of Time: The History of the Earth & the History of Nations from Hooke to Vico*, trans. L. G. Cochrane. Chicago, IL, 1984.
Rössner, Lutz. *Pädagogen der englischen Aufklärungsphilosophie des 18. Jahrhunderts*. Frankfurt am Main, 1988.
Rotta, Graziella. *La 'Idea Dio': Il pensiero religioso di Fichte fino all'Atheismusstreit*. Genoa, 1995.
Röttgers, Kurt. "Dialektik IV: Die Dialektik von Kant bis zur Gegenwart", in *Historisches Wörterbuch der Philosophie*, ed. J. Ritter et al., vol. 2 (1972), pp. 184–9.
Rousseau, G. S., and Roy Porter, eds. *The Ferment of Knowledge: Studies in the Historiography of Eighteenth-Century Science*. Cambridge, 1980.
Rousseau, Nicolas. *Connaissance et langage chez Condillac*. Geneva, 1986.
Rowe, William L. *The Cosmological Argument*. Princeton, NJ, 1975.
Roy, Marie-Louise. *Die Poetik Denis Diderots*. Munich, 1966.
Royer-Collard, Pierre-Paul. *Les fragments philosophiques de Royer-Collard*, ed. A. Schimberg. Paris, 1913; in T. Reid, *Oeuvres complètes*, 6 vols., trans. T. Jouffroy, Paris, 1828–36.
Rudolf A. Makkreel. *Imagination and Interpretation in Kant: The Hermeneutical Import of the "Critique of Judgment"*. Chicago, 1990.

Rudolph, Frederick, ed. *Essays on Education in the Early Republic.* Cambridge, MA, 1965.
Rüegg, Walther, general ed. *A History of the University in Europe*, in progress; Vol. 2: *Universities in Early Modern Europe*, ed. H. de Ridder-Symoens. Cambridge, 1996.
Ruestow, Edward G. *Physics at Seventeenth- and Eighteenth-Century Leiden: Philosophy and the New Science in the University*. The Hague, 1973.
Russell, Bertrand. *A History of Western Philosophy*. New York, NY, 1945.
Ryle, Gilbert. *The Concept of Mind*. London, 1949.
Saage, Richard. "August Ludwig Schlözer als politischer Theoretiker", in *Vertragsdenken und Utopie: Studien zur politischen Theorie und zur Sozialphilosophie der frühen Neuzeit*, Frankfurt am Main, 1989, pp. 142–91.
Sachs, H., M. Stiebitz, and R. J. Wilson. "An Historical Note: Euler's Königsberg Letters". *Journal of Graph Theory* 12 (1988): 133–9.
Saine, Thomas P. *The Problem of Being Modern, or the German Pursuit of Enlightenment from Leibniz to the French Revolution*. Detroit, MI, 1997.
Saine, Thomas P. "Who's Afraid of Christian Wolff?", in *Anticipations of the Enlightenment in England, France, and Germany*, eds. A. C. Kors and P. J. Korshin, Philadelphia, PA, 1987, pp. 102–33.
Sala, Giovanni B. *Kant und die Frage nach Gott, Gottesbeweise und Gottesbeweiskritik in den Schriften Kants*. Berlin, 1990.
Sala, Giovanni B. "Wohlerhalten und Wohlergehen". *Theologie und Philosophie* 68 (1993): 182–207, 368–98.
Sampson, Ronald Victor. *Progress in the Age of Reason*. London, 1956.
Sandweg, Jürgen. *Rationales Naturrecht als revolutionäre Praxis. Untersuchungen zur "Erklärung der Menschen- und Bürgerrechte" von 1789*. Berlin, 1972.
Santinello, Giovanni, ed. *Models of the History of Philosophy*, Dordrecht, 1993–, vol. 1: *From Its Origins in the Renaissance to the "Historia Philosophica"*, (English) eds. C. W. T. Blackwell and P. Weller (all published).
Santinello, Giovanni, ed. *Storie delle storie generali della filosofia*. 5 vols. Brescia and Padua, 1979–2004.
Sauder, Gerhard. "Bayle-Rezeption in der deutschen Aufklärung". *Deutsche Vierteljahresschrift. für Literaturwissenschaft und Geistesgeschichte. Sonderheft* (1975): 83–104.
Say, Jean-Baptiste. *Traité d'economie politique*. Paris, 1803.
Scaglione, Aldo. "Direct vs. Inverted Order: Wolff and Condillac on the Necessity of the Signs and the Interrelationship of Language and Thinking". *Romance Philology* 33 (1980): 496–501.
Scattola, Merio. *La nascità della scienze dello stato: August Ludwig Schlözer (1735–1809) e le discipline politiche del settecento tedesco*. Milan, 1994.
Schaffer, S. "'The Great Laboratories of the Universe': William Herschel on Matter Theory and Planetary Life". *Journal for the History of Astronomy* 11 (1980): 81–111.
Schaffer, S. "Natural Philosophy and Public Spectacle in Eighteenth-Century Science". *History of Science* 21 (1983): 1–43.
Scheele, Meta. *Wissen und Glaube in der Geschichtswissenschaft: Studien zum historischen Pyrrhonismus in Frankreich und Deutschland*. Heidelberg, 1930.
Scheffler, Samuel. *Human Morality*. Oxford, 1992.
Scheffler, Samuel. "Leibniz on Personal Identity and Moral Personality". *Studia Leibnitiana* 8 (1976): 219–40.
Schelling, Friedrich Wilhelm Joseph. *See* (*B1*).
Schepers, Heinrich. "Andreas Rüdigers Methodologie und ihre Voraussetzungen: Ein Beitrag zur Geschichte der deutschen Schulphilosophie im 18. Jahrhundert". *Kantstudien Ergänzungsheft* 78 (1959): 117–25.

Schepers, Heinrich. "Zum Problem der Kontingenz bei Leibniz: Die beste der möglichen Welten ", in *Collegium Philosophicum. Studien Joachim Ritter zum 60. Geburtstag*, ed. E.-W. Böckenförde (Basel, 1965), 1965, pp. 326–50.

Schiebinger, Londa. *The Mind Has No Sex? Women in the Origins of Modern Science*. Cambridge, MA, 1989.

Schlaich, Klaus. "Der rationale Territorialismus: Die Kirche unter dem staatsrechtlichen Absolutismus um die Wende vom 17. zum 18. Jahrhundert". *Zeitschrift der Savigny-Stiftung für Rechtsgeschichte* 85 (1968): Kanonistische Abt. 269–340.

Schleiermacher, Friedrich. *See* (*B1*).

Schlüter, Gisela. *Die französische Toleranzdebatte im Zeitalter der Aufklärung: Materiale und formale Aspekte*. Tübingen, 1992.

Schmid, Heinrich. *The Doctrinal Theology of the Evangelical Lutheran Church*, 3rd edn., trans. C. A. Hay and H. E. Jacobs. Philadelphia, PA, 1899; repr. Minneapolis, MN, 1961.

Schmidt, James. "Introduction: What Is Enlightenment? A Question, Its Context, and Some Consequences", in *What Is Enlightenment? Eighteenth-Century Answers and Twentieth-Century Questions*, ed. J. Schmidt, pp. 1–44.

Schmidt, James. "Inventing the Enlightenment: Anti-Jacobins, British Hegelians, and the *Oxford English Dictionary*". *Journal of the History of Ideas* 64 (2003): 421–43.

Schmidt, James. "What Enlightenment Project?" *Political Theory* 28.6 (2000): 734–57.

Schmidt, James, ed. *What Is Enlightenment? Eighteenth-Century Answers and Twentieth-Century Questions*. Berkeley, CA, 1996.

Schmidt-Biggemann, Wilhelm. "New Structures of Knowledge", in *Universities in Early Modern Europe*, ed. H. de Ridder-Syemoens, pp. 489–529.

Schmidt-Biggemann, Wilhelm, and Theo Stammen, eds. *Jacob Brucker (1696–1770): Philosoph und Historiker der europäischen Aufklärung*. Berlin, 1998.

Schmitt, Charles B. "The Rise of the Philosophical Textbook", in *The Cambridge History of Renaissance Philosophy*, eds. C. B. Schmitt, Q. Skinner, and Eckhard Kessler. Cambridge, 1988, pp. 792–804.

Schmitt, Charles B. "Towards a Reassessment of Renaissance Aristotelianism". *History of Science* 11 (1973): 159–93.

Schmucker, Josef. *Die Ursprünge der Ethik Kants in seinen vorkritischen Schriften und Reflexionen*. Meisenheim am Glan, 1961.

Schneewind, J. B. *The Invention of Autonomy: A History of Modern Moral Philosophy*. Cambridge, 1998.

Schneewind, J. B., ed. *Moral Philosophy from Montaigne to Kant*. 2 vols. Cambridge, 1990.

Schneewind, J. B., ed. *Teaching New Histories of Philosophy*. Princeton, NJ, 2004.

Schneider, Herbert, and Carol Schneider. *See* Johnson, Samuel *Samuel Johnson* . . .

Schneider, U. J. *Philosophie und Universität. Historisierung der Vernunft im 19. Jahrhundert*. Hamburg, 1998.

Schneider, U. J. "The Teaching of Philosophy at German Universities in the Nineteenth Century". *History of Universities* 12 (1993): 197–338.

Schneider, U. J. *Die Vergangenheit des Geistes: Eine Archäologie der Philosophiegeschichte*. Frankfurt am Main, 1990.

Schneiders, Werner, ed. *Christian Thomasius, 1655–1728: Interpretationen zu Werk und Wirkung*. Hamburg, 1989.

Schneiders, Werner, ed. *Christian Wolff, 1679–1754: Interpretationen zu seiner Philosophie und deren Wirkung*. Hamburg, 1983.

Schneiders, Werner. "Gottesreich und gelehrte Gesellschaft: Zwei politische Modelle bei G. W. Leibniz", in *Der Akademiegedanke im 17. und 18. Jahrhundert*, eds. Hartmann and Vierhaus, pp. 47–61.

Schneiders, Werner. *Naturrecht und Liebesethik: Zur Geschichte der praktischen Philosophie im Hinblick auf Christian Thomasius*. Hildesheim, 1971.

Schneiders, Werner. "Die Philosophie des aufgeklärten Absolutismus". *Der Staat* 24 (1985): 383–406.

Schochet, Gordon J. "John Locke and Religious Toleration", in *The Revolution of 1688: Changing Perspectives*, ed. L. G. Schwoerer. Cambridge, 1992, pp. 147–64.

Schofield, Robert E. "The Industrial Orientation of Science in the Lunar Society of Birmingham", in *Science, Technology and Economic Growth in the Eighteenth Century*, ed. A. E. Musson. London, 1972, pp. 136–47.

Schofield, Robert E. *Mechanism and Materialism: British Natural Philosophy in an Age of Reason*. Princeton, NJ, 1970.

Schollmeier, Jonathan. *Johann Joachim Spalding: Ein Beitrag zur Theologie der Aufklärung*. Gütersloh, 1967.

Schottlaender, Rudolf. "Die verkannte Lehre Condillacs vom Sprachursprung". *Beiträge zu romanischen Philologie* 8 (1969): 158–65.

Schouls, Peter A. "The Cartesian Methods of Locke's *Essay Concerning Human Understanding*". *Canadian Journal of Philosophy* 4 (1974–5): 579–601.

Schouls, Peter A. *The Imposition of Method: A Study of Descartes and Locke*. Oxford, 1980.

Schouls, Peter A. *Reasoned Freedom: John Locke and Enlightenment*. Ithaca, NY, 1992.

Schoute, C. Louise Thijssen. "La diffusion européenne des idées de Bayle", in *Pierre Bayle, le philosophe de Rotterdam*, ed. P. Dibon. Paris, 1959, pp. 150–95.

Schreyer, Rüdiger. "Condillac, Mandeville, and the Origin of Language". *Historiographia linguistica* 5 (1978): 15–43.

Schröder, Winfried. *Spinoza in der deutschen Frühaufklärung*. Würzburg, 1987.

Schröder, Winfried. "Spinoza im Untergrund: Zur Rezeption seines Werkes in der 'littérature clandestine'", in *Spinoza in der europäischen Geistesgeschichte*, eds. A. Delf, J. H. Schoeps, and M. Walther. Berlin, 1994, pp. 142–61.

Schröder, Winfried. *Ursprünge des Atheismus: Untersuchungen zur Metaphysik- und Religionskritik des 17. und 18. Jahrhunderts*. Stuttgart-Bad Cannstatt, 1998.

Schulthess, Daniel. "L'École écossaise et la philosophie d'expression française: le role de Pierre Prevost (Geneva 1751–1839)". *Annales Benjamin Constant* 18–19 (1996): 97–105.

Schulthess, Daniel. "L'Impact de la philosophie écossaise sur la dialectique enseignée à Genève: un cours latin inédit (1793–1794) de Pierre Prevost," in *Nomen Latinum. Mélanges de langue, de litterature et de civilisation latines offerts au professeur André Schneider*, ed. D. Knoepfler. Geneva, 1997, pp. 383–90.

Schultze, Harald. *Lessings Toleranzbegriff: Eine theologische Studie*. Göttingen, 1969.

Schwartz, Joel. *The Sexual Politics of Jean-Jacques Rousseau*. Chicago, IL, 1984.

Science in Context, 4 (1991): 223–447 (symposium on style in science).

Selbach, Ralf. *Staat, Universität und Kirche: Die Institutionen- und Systemtheorie Immanuel Kants*. Frankfurt, 1993.

Sell, A. P. F. "Philosophy in the Eighteenth-Century Dissenting Academies in England and Wales". *History of Universities* 11 (1992): 75–122.

Sgard, Jean, ed. *Condillac et les problèmes du langage*. Geneva, 1982.

Sgard, Jean, ed. *Dictionnaire des Journalistes*. Paris, 1999.

Shackleton, Robert. "The Encyclopédie and Freemasonry", in *The Age of Enlightenment: Studies presented to Theodore Bestermann*, eds. W. H. Barber, et al. Edinburgh and London, 1967, pp. 223–37.

Shackleton, Robert. *Montesquieu: A Critical Biography*. London, 1961.

Shapin, Steven, and Simon Schaffer. *Leviathan and the Air Pump*. Princeton, NJ, 1985.

Shapiro, Barbara J. *A Culture of Fact: England, 1550–1720*. Ithaca, NY and London, 2000.

Shapiro, Barbara J. *Probability and Certainty in Seventeenth-Century England: A Study of the Relationships between Natural Science, Religion, History, Law, and Literature*. Princeton, NJ, 1983.

Shaver, Robert. "Grotius on Scepticism and Self-Interest". *Archiv für Geschichte der Philosophie* 78 (1996): 27–47.

Shell, Susan Meld. *The Rights of Reason: A Study of Kant's Philosophy and Politics*. Toronto, 1980.

Sher, Richard B. *Church and University in the Scottish Enlightenment. The Moderate Literati of Edinburgh*. Edinburgh, 1985.

Sher, Richard B. "Professors of Virtue", in *Studies in the Philosophy of the Scottish Enlightenment*, ed. M. A. Stewart, pp. 87–126.

Sheridan, Geraldine. *Nicolas Lenglet Dufresnoy and the Literary Underworld of the Ancien Régime*. Oxford, 1989.

Sherry, D. "The Logic of Impossible Quantities". *Studies in History and Philosophy of Science* 22 (1991): 37–62.

Sheynin, O. B. "J. H. Lambert's Work on Probability". *Archive for History of Exact Sciences* 7 (1970–1): 244–56.

Sheynin, O. B. "On the Prehistory of Probability". *Archive for History of Exact Sciences* 12 (1974): 97–141.

Shklar, Judith. *Men and Citizens: A Study of Rousseau's Social Theory*. Cambridge, 1969.

Shklar, Judith. "Montesquieu and the New Republicanism", in *Machiavelli and Republicanism*, eds. G. Bock, Q. Skinner and M. Viroli, Cambridge, 1990, pp. 265–79.

Shortland, Michael. "'On the Connexion of the Physical Sciences': Classification and Organization in Early Nineteenth-Century Science". *Historia Scientiarum* 41 (1990): 545–73.

Sides, M. "Rhetoric on the Brink of Banishment: d'Alembert on Rhetoric in the *Encyclopédie*". *Rhetorik* 3 (1982): 111–24.

Sidgwick, Henry. *Outlines of the History of Ethics for English Readers*. London, 1886.

Silber, John R. "Kant's Conception of the Highest Good as Immanent and Transcendent". *Philosophical Review* 68 (1959): 469–92.

Silber, Kate. *Pestalozzi*, 4th edn. London, 1976.

Sillem, Edward A. *George Berkeley and the Proofs of the Existence of God*. London, 1957.

Simon, Brian. *The Two Nations and the Educational Structure, 1780–1870*. London, 1974.

Simon, Julia. "Natural Freedom and Moral Autonomy: Émile as Parent, Teacher and Citizen". *History of Political Thought* 16 (1995): 21–36.

Sina, Mario. *L'anti-Pascal di Voltaire*. Milan, 1970.

Sina, Mario. *L'Avvento della ragione. 'Reason' e 'above reason' dal razionalismo teologico inglese al deismo*. Milan, 1976.

Sina, Mario. "L'Illuminismo francese", in *Storia della Filosofia Moderna*, ed. S. Vanni Rovighi, 1981, pp. 382–6.

Sinopoli, Richard S. *The Foundations of American Citizenship: Liberalism, the Constitution, and Civic Virtue*. New York, NY, 1992.

Skinner, Andrew S. *A System of Social Science: Papers Relating to Adam Smith*. Oxford, 1979.

Skinner, Andrew S., and Thomas Wilson, eds. *Essays on Adam Smith*. Oxford, 1975.

Skoczylas, Anne. *Mr Simson's Knotty Case*. Montreal, 2001.

Sloan, Phillip R. "From Logical Universals to Historical Individuals: Buffon's Conception of Biological Species", in *Histoire du concept d'espèce dans les sciences de la vie*, eds. J. Roger and J.-L. Fischer. Paris, 1987, pp. 101–40.

Sloan, Phillip R. "The Gaze of Natural History", in *Inventing Human Science. Eighteenth-Century Domains*, eds. C. Fox, R. Porter, and R. Wokler, pp. 112–51.

Sloan, Phillip R. "L'Hypothétisme de Buffon: sa place dans la philosophie des sciences du dix-huitième siècle", in *Buffon 88: Actes du Colloque international 1988*, ed. J. Gayon, pp. 207–22.

Sloan, Phillip R. "The Idea of Racial Degeneracy in Buffon's *Histoire Naturelle*", in *Studies in Eighteenth Century Culture: Racism in the Eighteenth Century*, ed. H. Pagliaro. Cleveland, OH, 1973, pp. 293–321.

Sloan, Phillip R. "John Locke, John Ray and the Problem of the Natural System". *Journal of the History of Biology* 5 (1972): 1–53.

Sloan, Phillip R. "Preforming the Categories: Eighteenth-Century Generation Theory and the Biological Roots of Kant's A-Priori". *Journal of the History of Philosophy* 40 (2002): 229–253.

Smith, Crosbie. "'Mechanical Philosophy' and the Emergence of Physics in Britain: 1800–1850", *Annals of Science* 33 (1976): 3–29.

Smith, David Eugene, and Jekuthiel Ginsburg. *History of Mathematics in America Before 1900*. Chicago, IL, 1934.

Smith, G. C. "Thomas Bayes and Fluxions". *Historia Mathematica* 7 (1980): 379–88.

Smith, J. W. Ashley. *The Birth of Modern Education: The Contribution of the Dissenting Academies, 1660–1800*. London, 1954.

Snyders, Georges. *La pédagogie en France aux XVIIe et XVIIIe siècles*. Paris, 1965.

Soëtard, Michel. *Pestalozzi ou La naissance de l'éducateur: Étude sur l'évolution de la pensée et de l'action du pédagogue suisse (1746–1827)*. Bern, 1981.

Sommer, Manfred. "Kant und die Frage nach dem Glück", in *Die Frage nach dem Glück*, ed. G. Bien. Stuttgart and Bad Cannstatt, 1978, pp. 131–45.

Southgate, Beverley C. "'Beating down Scepticism': The Solid Philosophy of John Sergeant", in *English Philosophy in the Age of Locke*, ed. M. A. Stewart, pp. 281–315.

Spary, Emma. *Utopia's Garden: French Natural History from Old Regime to Revolution*. Chicago, IL, 2000.

Specht, Rainer. "Gassendi Analogien in Lockes Theorie des sinnlichen Wissens". *Philosophisches Jahrbuch* 100 (1993): 267–281.

Spellman, W. M. *John Locke and the Problem of Depravity*. Oxford, 1988.

Spink, John S. *French Free Thought from Gassendi to Voltaire*. London, 1960.

Spurlock, Janis. "What Price Economic Prosperity? Public Attitudes to Physiocracy in the Reign of Louis XVI". *British Journal for Eighteenth Century Studies* 9 (1986): 183–96.

Stafford, Barbara Maria. *Artful Science: Enlightenment, Entertainment and the Eclipse of Visual Science*. Cambridge, MA, 1994.

Stafleu, Frans. *Linnaeus and the Linnaeans: the Spreading of Their Ideas in Systematic Botany, 1735–1789*. Utrecht, 1971.

Stanlis, Peter J. *Edmund Burke and the Natural Law*. Ann Arbor, MI, 1958.

Stein, K. Heinrich von. *Die Entstehung der neueren Ästhetik*. Stuttgart, 1886; facsim. Hildesheim, 1964.

Steinbrügge, Lieselotte. *The Moral Sex: Woman's Nature in the French Enlightenment*, trans. P. E. Selwyn. Oxford, 1995.

Steiner, David M. *Rethinking Democratic Education: The Politics of Reform*. Baltimore, MD, 1994.

Stephen, Leslie. *The History of English Thought in the Eighteenth Century*, 2 vols. London, 1876. 3rd edn., 2 vols. London, 1902.

Stephens, John. "Edmund Law and His Circle at Cambridge", in *The Philosophical Canon in the 17th and 18th Centuries*, eds. G. A. J. Rogers and S. Tomaselli. Rochester, NY, 1996, pp. 163–73.

Stewart, Larry. *The Rise of Public Science: Rhetoric, Technology and Natural Philosophy in Newtonian Britain, 1660–1750*. Cambridge, 1992.

Stewart, M. A. "An Early Fragment on Evil", in *Hume and Hume's Connexions*, eds. M. A. Stewart and J. P. Wright, pp. 160–70.

Stewart, M. A., ed. *English Philosophy in the Age of Locke*. Oxford, 2000.

Stewart, M. A. "Hume's Historical View of Miracles", in *Hume and Hume's Connexions*, eds. M. A. Stewart and J. P. Wright. Edinburgh, 1994, pp. 171–200.

Stewart, M. A. "Hume's Intellectual Development", in *Impressions of Hume*, eds. M. Frasca-Spada and P. Kail.

Stewart, M. A. *Independency of the Mind in Early Dissent*. London, 2004.

Stewart, M. A. "Rational Religion and Common Sense", in *Thomas Reid: Context and Significance*, ed. J. Houston.

Stewart, M. A. "Religion and Rational Theology", in *The Cambridge Companion to the Scottish Enlightenment*, ed. A. Broadie. Cambridge, 2003, pp. 31–59.

Stewart, M. A. "Stillingfleet and the Way of Ideas", in *English Philosophy in the Age of Locke*, ed. M. A. Stewart, pp. 245–280.

Stewart, M. A., ed. *Studies in the Philosophy of the Scottish Enlightenment*. Oxford, 1990.

Stewart, M. A., and John P. Wright, eds. *Hume and Hume's Connexions*. Edinburgh, 1994 and University Park, PA, 1995.

Stewart, Philip. "Science and Superstition: Comets and the French Public in the Eighteenth Century". *American Journal of Physics* 54 (1986): 16–24.

Stewart-Robertson, J. C., and David Fate Norton. "Thomas Reid on Adam Smith's Theory of Morals". *Journal of the History of Ideas* 45 (1984): 309–321.

Stichweh, Rudolf. *Der frühmoderne Staat und die europäische Universität: Zur Interaktion von Politik und Erziehungssystem im Prozess ihrer Ausdifferenzierung (16–18. Jahrhundert)*. Frankfurt am Main, 1991.

Stigler, Stephen M. *Statistics on the Table: The History of Statistical Concepts and Methods*. Cambridge, MA, 1999.

Stoeffler, F. E. *The Rise of Evangelical Pietism*, 2nd edn. Leiden, 1971.

Stolzenberg, Jürgen. *Fichtes Begriff der Intellektuellen Anschauung: die Entwicklung in der Wissenschaftslehre von 1793/94 bis 1801/2*. Stuttgart, 1986.

Stolzenberg, Jürgen. "Selbstbewußtsein: Ein Problem der Philosophie nach Kant. Zum Verhältnis Reinhold-Hölderlin-Fichte". *Revue internationale de philosophie* 197 (1996): 461–82.

Stove, D. C. "The Nature of Hume's Skepticism", in *McGill Hume Studies*, eds. D. F. Norton, N. Capaldi, and W. L. Robison. San Diego, CA, 1979, pp. 203–25.

Strack, Thomas. "Philosophical Anthropology on the Eve of Biological Determinism: Immanuel Kant and Georg Forster on the Moral Qualities and Biological Characteristics of the Human Race". *Central European History* 29 (1996): 285–308.

Strawson, Galen. "Hume on Himself", in *Exploring Practical Philosophy: From Action to Values*, eds. D. Egonsson, et al. Aldershot, 2001, pp. 69–94.

Strawson, Peter F. *The Bounds of Sense: An Essay on Kant's Critique of Pure Reason*. London, 1966.

Strong, Tracy B. *Jean-Jacques Rousseau: The Politics of the Ordinary*. Thousand Oaks, CA and London, 1994.

Stroud, Barry. *Hume*. London, 1977.

Stroup, Alice. *A Company of Scientists: Botany, Patronage and Community at the Seventeenth-Century Parisian Royal Academy of Sciences*. Berkeley, CA, 1990.

Stroup, John. *The Struggle for Identity in the Clerical Estate: Northwest German Protestant Opposition to Absolutist Policy in the Eighteenth Century*. Leiden, 1984.

Stückrath, Jörn. "Der junge Herder als Sprach- und Literaturtheoretiker – ein Erbe des französischen Aufklärers Condillac?," in *Sturm und Drang. Ein literaturwissenschaftliches Studienbuch*, ed. W. Hinck. Frankfurt am Main, 1978, pp. 81–96.

Sturma, Dieter. *Kant über Selbstbewusstsein: zum Zusammenhang von Erkenntniskritik und Theorie des Selbstbewusstseins*. Hildesheim, 1985.
Styazhkin, N. I. *History of Mathematical Logic from Leibniz to Peano*. Cambridge, MA, 1969.
Suchting, W. A. "Euler's 'Reflections on Space and Time'". *Scientia* 104 (1969): 270–8.
Suderman, Jeffrey M. *Orthodoxy and Enlightenment: George Campbell in the Eighteenth Century*. Montreal and Kingston, 2001.
Sullivan, Robert E. *John Toland and the Deist Controversy: A Study in Adaptations*. Cambridge, MA, 1982.
Sutherland, L. S., and L. G. Mitchell, eds. *The Eighteenth Century*, in *The History of the University of Oxford*, 8 vols. Oxford, 1984–2000, vol. 5 (1986).
Swerdlow, Noel M. "Montucla's Legacy: The History of the Exact Sciences". *Journal of the History of Ideas* 54 (1993): 299–328.
Swinburne, R. G. "The Argument from Design". *Philosophy* 43 (1968): 199–212.
Taber, John. "Fichte's Emendation of Kant". *Kant-Studien* 75 (1984): 442–59.
Tarcov, Nathan. *Locke's Education for Liberty*. Chicago, IL, 1984.
Taylor, Charles. "The Importance of Herder", in *Isaiah Berlin, a Celebration*, eds. E. Margalit and A. Margalit. London, 1991, pp. 40–63.
Temkin, Owsei. "German Concepts of Ontogeny and History around 1800". *Bulletin of the History of Medicine* 24 (1950): 227–46.
Thackray, Arnold. *Atoms and Powers: An Essay on Newtonian Matter-Theory and the Development of Chemistry*. Cambridge, MA, 1970.
Theis, Robert. *Gott, Untersuchung zur Entwicklung des theologischen Diskurses in Kants Schriften zur theoretischen Philosophie bis hin zum Erscheinen der Kritik der reinen Vernunft*. Stuttgart and Bad Cannstatt, 1994.
Thiel, Udo. Rev. of Hauser, *Selbstbewußtsein und personale Indentität*. *Das Achtzehnte Jahrhundert* 19 (1995): 243–5.
Thiel, Udo. "Between Wolff and Kant: Merian's Theory of Apperception". *Journal of the History of Philosophy* 34 (1996): 213–32.
Thiel, Udo. "Cudworth and Seventeenth-Century Theories of Consciousness", in *The Uses of Antiquity*, ed. S. Gaukroger. Dordrecht, 1991, pp. 79–99.
Thiel, Udo. "'Epistemologism' and Early Modern Debates about Individuation and Identity". *British Journal for the History of Philosophy* 5 (1997): 353–72.
Thiel, Udo. "Hume's Notions of Consciousness and Reflection in Context". *British Journal for the History of Philosophy* 2 (1994): 75–115.
Thiel, Udo. Introduction, in T. Cooper, *Philosophical Writings of Thomas Cooper*, vol. 1, pp. v–xix (*B1*).
Thiel, Udo. "Kant's Notion of Self-Consciousness in Context", in *Kant und die Berliner Aufklärung*, eds. V. Gerhardt, R. Horstmann, and R. Schumacher, 5 vols., Berlin, 2001, vol. 2, pp. 468–76.
Thiel, Udo. "Leibniz and the Concept of Apperception". *Archiv für Geschichte der Philosophie* 76 (1994): 195–209.
Thiel, Udo. "Locke and Eighteenth-Century Materialist Conceptions of Personal Identity." *The Locke Newsletter* 29 (1998): 59–83.
Thiel, Udo. *Lockes Theorie der personalen Identität*. Bonn, 1983.
Thiel, Udo. "Personal Identity", in *The Cambridge History of Seventeenth-Century Philosophy*, eds. D. Garber and M. Ayers, 2 vols., Cambridge, 1998, vol. 1, pp. 868–912.
Thiel, Udo. "Varieties of Inner Sense. Two Pre-Kantian Theories". *Archiv für Geschichte der Philosophie* 79 (1997): 58–79.
Thomas, D. O. *The Honest Mind: The Thought and Work of Richard Price*. Oxford, 1977.

Thomson, Ann. *Barbary and Enlightenment: European Attitudes towards the Maghreb in the 18th Century*. Leiden and New York, NY, 1987.

Thomson, Ann. "Joseph Morgan et le monde islamique". *Dix-huitème siècle* 27 (1995): 349–63.

Thomson, Ann. "La litterature clandestine et la circulation des idées antireligieuses dans la première moitié du XVIIIe siècle", in *L'encyclopédie, Diderot, l'esthétique: mélanges en homage à Jacques Chouillet*, eds. S. Auroux, D. Bourel, and C. Porset. Paris, 1991, pp. 297–304.

Thomson, Ann. *Materialism and Society in the Mid-Eighteenth Century: La Mettrie's Discours Preliminaire*. Geneva and Paris, 1981.

Thomson, Ann. "La Mettrie et la littérature clandestine", in *Le Matérialisme du XVIII siècle et la littérature clandestine*, ed. O. Bloch. Paris, 1982, pp. 235–44.

Tiles, Mary. *Mathematics and the Image of Reason*. London, 1991.

Tilling, L. "Early Experimental Graphs". *British Journal for the History of Science* 8 (1975): 193–213.

Tipton, I. C. "Ideas in Berkeley and Arnauld". *History of European Ideas* 7 (1986): 575–85.

Tipton, I. C., ed. *Locke on Human Understanding*. Oxford, 1977.

Todesco, Fabio. *Riforma della metafisica e sapere scientifico: saggio zu J. H. Lambert (1728–1777)*. Milan, 1987.

Tonelli, Giorgio. "Kant und die antiken Skeptiker", in *Studien zu Kants philosophischer Entwicklung*, ed. H. Heimsoeth. Hildesheim, 1967, pp. 93–123.

Tonelli, Giorgio. "La necessité des lois de la nature au XVIIIe siècle et chez Kant en 1762". *Revue d'histoire des sciences et leurs applications* 12 (1959): 225–41.

Tonelli, Giorgio. *La pensée philosophique de Maupertuis: son milieu et ses sources*, ed. C. Cesa. Hildesheim, 1987.

Tonelli, Giorgio. "The Philosophy of D'Alembert: A Sceptic beyond Scepticism". *Kant-Studien* 67 (1976): 353–71.

Tonelli, Giorgio. "Pierre-Jacques Changeux and Scepticism in the French Enlightenment". *Studia Leibnitiana* 6.1 (1974): 106–26.

Tonelli, Giorgio. *Poesia a pensiero in Albrecht von Haller*. Turin, 1961.

Tonelli, Giorgio. "La question des bornes de l'entendement humain au XVIIIe siècle et la genèse du criticisme kantien, particulièrement par rapport au problème de l'infini". *Revue de métaphysique et de morale* (1959): 396–427.

Tonelli, Giorgio. "Der Streit über die mathematische Methode in der Philosophie in der ersten Hälfte des 18: Jahrhunderts und die Entstehung von Kants Schrift über die 'Deutlichkeit' ". *Archiv für Philosophie* 9 (1959): 37–66.

Tonelli, Giorgio. "Tetens, Johann Nicolaus", in *The Encyclopedia of Philosophy*, ed. P. Edwards, 8 vols., New York, NY, 1972.

Tonelli, Giorgio. "The 'Weakness' of Reason in the Age of Enlightenment". *Diderot Studies* 14 (1971): 217–44.

Totok, Wilhelm. "Leibniz als Wissenschaftsorganisator", in *Leibniz – sein Leben – sein Wirken – seine Welt*, eds W. Totok and C. Haase. Hanover, 1966, pp. 293–320.

Totok, Wilhelm. "Theodizee bei Leibniz und Lessing", in *Beiträge zur Wirkungs- und Rezeptionsgeschichte von Gottfried Wilhelm Leibniz*, ed. A. Heinekamp. Stuttgart, 1986, pp. 177–87.

Trapnell, William H. *Thomas Woolston: Madman and Deist*. Bristol, 1994.

Treash, Gordon. "Introduction", in I. Kant, *Der einzig mögliche Beweisgrund zu einer Demonstration des Daseins Gottes/The One Possible Basis for a Demonstration of the Existence of God*, ed. G. Treash. Lincoln, NE, 1994.

Tribe, Keith. *Governing Economy: The Reformation of German Economic Discourse 1750–1840*. Cambridge, 1988.

Trouille, Mary. "Eighteenth-Century Amazons of the Pen: Stephanie de Genlis & Olympe de Gouges", in *Femmes savantes et femmes d'esprit: Women Intellectuals of the French Eighteenth Century*, eds. R. Bonnel and C. Rubinger, pp. 341–70.

Trouille, Mary. "La Femme Mal Mariée: Mme D'Epinay's Challenge to Julie and Émile". *Eighteenth-Century Life* 20 (1996): 42–66.

Trudeau, Richard J. *The Non-Euclidean Revolution*. Boston, MA, 1987.

Truesdell, Clifford A. "Early Kinetic Theories of Gases", in *Essays in the History of Mechanics*, Berlin, 1968, pp. 272–304.

Truesdell, Clifford A. Introduction, in L. Euler, *Rational Mechanics*, in *Opera omnia*, ser. 2, vol. 11.

Truesdell, Clifford A. "A Program toward Rediscovering the Rational Mechanics of the Age of Reason". *Archive for History of Exact Sciences* 1 (1960–2): 3–36.

Truesdell, Clifford A. "Whence the Law of Moment of Momentum?," in *Mélanges Alexandre Koyré*, 2 vols., 1964, vol. 1: *L'aventure de la science*, pp. 588–612.

Tschackert, P. "Stäudlin", in *Allgemeine Deutsche Biographie*, 56 vols., Leipzig, 1875–1912, vol. 35, pp. 516–20.

Tsugawa, Albert. "David Hume and Lord Kames on Personal Identity". *Journal of the History of Ideas* 22 (1961): 398–403.

Tuana, Nancy. "The Forgetting of Gender and the New Histories of Philosophy", in *Teaching New Histories of Philosophy*, ed. J. B. Schneewind. Princeton, NJ, 2004.

Tubach, Frederic C. "Perfectibilité: der zweite Diskurs Rousseaus und die deutsche Aufklärung". *Études germaniques* 15 (1960): 144–51.

Tuck, Richard. "Grotius, Carneades, and Hobbes". *Grotiana* 4 (1983): 43–62.

Tuck, Richard. "The 'Modern' Theory of Natural Law", in *The Languages of Political Theory in Early-Modern Europe*, ed. A. Pagden. Cambridge, 1987, pp. 99–119.

Tucker, Louis T. *Puritan Protagonist: President Thomas Clap of Yale College*. Chapel Hill, NC, 1962.

Tully, James. *An Approach to Political Philosophy: Locke in Contexts*. Cambridge, 1993.

Tully, James. *A Discourse on Property: John Locke and His Adversaries*. Cambridge, 1980.

Turner, James G. "The Properties of Libertinism", in *'Tis Nature's Fault: Unauthorized Sexuality during the Enlightenment*, ed. R. P. Maccubbin. Cambridge, 1987, pp. 75–87.

Turton, Thomas. *Thoughts on the Admission of Persons without Regard to their Religious Opinions to Certain Degrees in the Universities of England*. Cambridge, 1834; 2nd edn., 1835.

Twynam, Ella. *Peter Annet, 1693–1769*. London, 1938.

Ueberweg, Friedrich. *Grundriss der Geschichte der Philosophie* [1863], 12th edn., 5 vols. Berlin, 1923–8.

Uglow, Jenny. *The Lunar Men: The Friends who Made the Future*. London, 2002.

Urbach, Peter. *Francis Bacon's Philosophy of Science*. La Salle, IL, 1987.

Vaihinger, Hans. *Kommentar zu Kants Kritik der reinen Vernunft*, 2nd ed., 2 vols. Stuttgart, 1922.

Vailati, Ezio. Introduction, in Samuel Clarke, *A Demonstration of the Being and Attributes of God. And other Writings*, ed. E. Vailati. Cambridge, 1998, pp. ix–xxxvi.

Vailati, Ezio. "Leibniz's Theory of Personal Identity in the *New Essays*". *Studia Leibnitiana* 17 (1985): 36–43.

Valeri, Mark. "Church and State in America from the Great Awakening to the American Revolution", in *Church and State in America, a Bibliographical Guide: The Colonial and Early National Periods*, ed. J. F. Wilson, pp. 115–50.

Vanni Rovighi, Sofia. *La filosofia e il problema di Dio*. Milan, 1986.

Vanpaemel, G. *Echo's van een wetenschappelijke revolutie: De mecanistische natuurwetenschap aan de Leuvense Artesfaculteit (1650–1797)*. Brussels, 1986.

Vartanian, Aram. "Quelques réflexions sur le concept d'âme dans la littérature clandestine", in *Le Matérialisme du XVIII siècle et la littérature clandestine*, ed. O. Bloch. Paris, 1982, pp. 149–65.
Venn, John. *Symbolic Logic*, 2nd. rev. edn. London, 1894; repr. New York, NY, 1971.
Venturi, Franco. *Jeunesse de Diderot (1713–53)*, trans. J. Bertrand. Paris, 1939.
Venturi, Franco. *Saggi sull' Europa illuminista 1: Alberto Radicati di Passerano*. Turin, 1954.
Venturi, Franco. *Settecento riformatore*. 5 vols. Turin, 1969–1997.
Venturi, Franco. *Utopia and Reform in the Enlightenment*. Cambridge, 1970.
Verene, Donald. *Vico's Science of Imagination*. Ithaca, NY, 1981.
Vernière, Paul. *Spinoza et la pensée française avant la révolution*, 2 vols. Paris, 1954.
Vickers, Brian. *In Defence of Rhetoric*. Oxford, 1988.
Vickers, Brian, ed. *Rhetoric Revalued*. Binghamton, NY, 1982.
Vickers, Brian. "Rhetorical and Anti-Rhetorical tropes: On Writing the History of *Elocutio*". *Comparative Criticism* 3 (1981): 105–32.
Vienne, Jean Michel. "Malebranche and Locke: The Theory of Moral Choice, a Neglected Theme", in *Nicolas Malebranche: His Philosophical Critics and Successors*, ed. S. Brown. Assen and Maastricht, 1991, pp. 94–108.
Viguerie, Jean de. *Une oeuvre d'éducation sous l'Ancien Régime: les Pères de la doctrine chrétienne en France et en Italie 1592–1792*. Paris, 1976.
Vincenti, Luc. *Éducation et liberté: Kant et Fichte*. Paris, 1992.
Vissière, J. L., ed. *Le Marquis d'Argens*. Aix-en-Provence, 1990.
Vlachos, Georges. *La pensée politique de Kant: métaphysique de l'ordre et dialectique du progrés*. Paris, 1954.
Vleeschauwer, H. J. de. *La déduction transcendentale dans l'oeuvre de Kant*, 2 vols. Paris, 1934.
Völkel, Markus. *'Pyrrhonismus Historicus' und 'Fides Historica': Die Entwicklung der deutschen historischen Methodologie unter dem Gesichtpunkt der Skepsis*. Frankfurt am Main, 1987.
Vorländer, Karl. *Geschichte der Philosophie*, 2 vols. Leipzig, 1903.
Voss, J. "Die Akademien als Organisationsträger der Wissenschaften im 18. Jahrhundert". *Historische Zeitschrift* 231 (1980): 43–74.
Vyverberg, Henry. *Human Nature, Cultural Diversity, and the French Enlightenment*. Oxford, 1989.
Wade, Ira O. *The Clandestine Organization and Diffusion of Philosophic Ideas in France from 1700 to 1750*. Princeton, NJ, 1938.
Waldron, Jeremy. "Locke: Toleration and the Rationality of Persecution," in *A Letter Concerning Toleration in Focus*, eds. J. Horton and S. Mendus, London, 1991, pp. 98–124.
Wallace, William. "Traditional Natural Philosophy", in *The Cambridge History of Renaissance Philosophy*, eds. C. Schmitt, Q. Skinner, and E. Kessler, Cambridge, 1988, pp. 201–35.
Waniek, Erdmann. "Karl Philipp Moritz's Concept of the Whole in his 'Versuch einer Vereinigung . . . ' (1785)." *Studies in Eighteenth-Century Culture* 12 (1983), ed. H. C. Payne.
Waring, Edward Graham, ed. *Deism and Natural Religion: A Source Book*. New York, NY, 1967.
Waszek, N. *The Scottish Enlightenment and Hegel's Account of 'Civil Society'*. Dordrecht, 1988.
Watson, R. A., and J. E. Force, eds. *The High Road to Pyrrhonism*. San Diego, CA, 1980.
Watts, Ruth. "Joseph Priestley and Education". *Enlightenment and Dissent* 2 (1983): 83–100.
Waxman, Wayne. *Hume's Theory of Consciousness*. Cambridge, 1994.
Waxman, Wayne. *Kant's Model of the Mind*. Oxford, 1991.
Weber, Max. *The Protestant Ethics and the Spirit of Capitalism*, trans. T. Parsons, ed. R. H. Tawney. New York, NY, 1958.
Wedberg, Anders. *A History of Philosophy*, 3 vols. Oxford, 1982–4.

Weinrich, Harald. "Literaturgeschichte eines Weltereignisses: Das Erdbeben von Lissabon", in *Literatur für Leser: Essays und Aufsätze zur Literaturswissenschaft*, Munich, 1986, pp. 74–90.
Weiser, Christian F. *Shaftesbury und das deutsche Geistesleben*. Leipzig, 1916.
Wells, G. A. "Condillac, Rousseau and Herder on the Origin of Language". *Studies on Voltaire and the Eighteenth Century* 230 (1985): 235–46.
Wenzel, Hans. *Naturrecht und materiale Gerechtigkeit*. Göttingen, 1962.
Wenzel, Hans. *Die socialitas als oberstes Prinzip der Naturrechtslehre Samuel Pufendorfs*. Heidelberg, 1930.
Wertenbaker, T. J. *Princeton 1746–1896*. Princeton, NJ, 1946.
West, Shearer. "Libertinism and the Ideology of Male Friendship in the Portraits of the Society of Dilettanti". *Eighteenth-Century Life* 16 (1992): 76–104.
Whaley, Jochim. "A Tolerant Society? Religious Toleration in the Holy Roman Empire, 1648–1806", in *Toleration in Enlightenment Europe*, eds. O. P. Grell and R. Porter, pp. 175–95.
Whelan, Frederick G. *Order and Artifice in Hume's Political Philosophy*. Princeton, NJ, 1985.
Whelan, Ruth. *The Anatomy of Superstition: A Study of the Historical Theory and Practice of Pierre Bayle*. Oxford, 1989.
White, Morton. *The Philosophy of the American Revolution*. New York, NY, 1978.
White, Morton. *Philosophy, The Federalist, and the Constitution*. New York, NY, 1987.
Whyte, Lancelot L., ed. *Roger Joseph Boscovich, SJ, FRS, 1711–1787: Studies of His Life and Work on the 250th Anniversary of His Birth*. London, 1961.
Wilkinson, E. M. *Johann Elias Schlegel: A German Pioneer in Aesthetics*. Darmstadt, 1973.
Willey, Basil. *The Eighteenth-Century Background: Studies on the Idea of Nature in the Thought of the Period*. London, 1940.
Williams, Howard. *Kant's Political Philosophy*. New York, NY, 1983.
Williams, Howard, ed. *Kant's Political Philosophy*. Cardiff, 1992.
Wilson, Fred. "Substance and Self in Locke and Hume", in *Individuation and Identity*, eds. Barber and Garcia, pp. 155–99.
Wilson, John F., ed. *Church and State in America, a Bibliographical Guide: The Colonial and Early National Periods*. New York, NY, 1986.
Wilson, Margaret D. "Leibniz: Self-Consciousness and Immortality in the Paris Notes and After". *Archiv für Geschichte der Philosophie* 58 (1976): 335–52.
Winch, Donald. *Adam Smith's Politics: An Essay in Historiographic Revision*. Cambridge, 1978.
Winkler, Kenneth P. "'All is Revolution in Us': Personal Identity in Shaftesbury and Hume". *Hume Studies* 26 (2000): 3–40.
Winkler, Kenneth P. *Berkeley: An Interpretation*. Oxford, 1989.
Winterbourne, Anthony. *The Ideal and the Real: An Outline of Kant's Theory of Space, Time and Mathematical Construction*. Dordrecht, 1988.
Wittgenstein, Ludwig. *Philosophical Grammar*, trans. A. Kenny, ed. R. Rhees. Berkeley, CA, 1978.
Wittgenstein, Ludwig. *Philosophical Investigations*, trans. G. E. M. Anscombe. Cambridge, MA, 1997.
Wittgenstein, Ludwig. *Zettel*, trans. G. E. M. Anscombe, eds. G. E. M. Anscombe and G. H. von Wright. Oxford, 1967.
Wocjik, Jan. *Robert Boyle and the Limits of Reason*. Cambridge, 1997.
Wokler, Robert. "Anthropology and Conjectural History in the Enlightenment", in *Inventing Human Science: Eighteenth-Century Domains*, eds. C. Fox, R. Porter and R. Wokler, pp. 31–52.
Wolters, Gereon. *Basis und Deduktion: Studien zur Entstehung und Bedeutung der Theorie der axiomatischen Methode bei J. H. Lambert (1728–1777)*. Berlin, 1980.

Wolzendorff, Kurt. *Staatsrecht und Naturrecht in der Lehre vom Widerstandsrecht des Volkes gegen rechtswidrige Ausübung der Staatsgewalt: Zugleich ein Beitrag zur Entwicklungsgeschichte des modernen Staatsgedankens*. Breslau, 1916.

Womersley, David. *Gibbon and the 'Watchmen of the Holy City': The Historian and His Reputation, 1776–1815*. Oxford, 2002.

Wood, Allen W. *Hegel's Ethical Thought*. Cambridge, 1990.

Wood, Allen W. *Kant's Rational Theology*. Ithaca, NY, 1978.

Wood, Gordon. *The Creation of the American Republic*. Chapel Hill, NC, 1969.

Wood, Paul B. *The Aberdeen Enlightenment: The Arts Curriculum in the Eighteenth Century*. Aberdeen, 1993.

Wood, Paul B. "The Natural History of Man in the Scottish Enlightenment". *History of Science* 27 (1989): 89–123.

Wood, Paul B. "Science and the Pursuit of Virtue in the Aberdeen Enlightenment", in *Studies in the Philosophy of the Scottish Enlightenment*, ed. M. A. Stewart, pp. 127–49.

Woolhouse, Roger S. "Locke's Theory of Knowledge", in *The Cambridge Companion to Locke*, ed. V. Chappell. Cambridge, 1994, pp. 146–171.

Woolhouse, Roger S. *Descartes, Spinoza, Leibniz: The Concept of Substance in Seventeenth-Century Metaphysics*. London, 1993.

Wootton, David. "Hume's 'Of Miracles': Probability and Irreligion", in *Studies in the Philosophy of the Scottish Enlightenment*, ed. M. A. Stewart, pp. 191–229.

Wootton, David. "New Histories of Atheism", in *Atheism from the Reformation to the Enlightenment*, eds. M. Hunter and D. Wootton, pp. 13–53.

Wordsworth, Christopher. *Scholae Academicae: Some Account of Studies at the English Universities in the Eighteenth Century*. Cambridge, 1877; repr. London, 1968.

Wright, John P. "Hume's Criticism of Malebranche's Theory of Causation: A Lesson in the Historiography of Philosophy", in *Nicolas Malebranche: His Philosophical Critics and Successors*, ed. S. Brown, Assen and Maastricht, 1991, pp. 116–130.

Wundt, Max. *Die deutsche Schulphilosophie im Zeitalter der Aufklärung*. Tübingen, 1945; facsim. Hildesheim, 1964.

Wussing, Hans. *The Genesis of the Abstract Group Concept: A Contribution to the History of the Origin of Abstract Group Theory*, trans. A. Shenitzer. Cambridge, MA, 1984.

Wykes, David L. "The Contribution of the Dissenting Academy to the Emergence of Rational Dissent", in *Enlightenment and Religion: Rational Dissent in Eighteenth-Century Britain*, ed. K. Haakonssen. Cambridge, 1996, pp. 99–139.

Yeo, Richard. "A Solution to the Multitude of Books: Ephraim Chalmers's *Cyclopaedia* (1728) as 'the Best Book in the Universe'". *Journal of the History of Ideas* 64 (2003): 61–72.

Yolton, John W. *Locke and French Materialism*. Oxford, 1991.

Yolton, John W. *Locke: An Introduction*. Oxford, 1985.

Yolton, John W. *Perceptual Acquaintance from Descartes to Reid*. Minneapolis, MN, 1984.

Yolton, John W. "Schoolmen, Logic and Philosophy", in *The History of the University of Oxford*, eds. L. S. Sutherland and L. G. Mitchell, vol. 5: *The Eighteenth Century*, pp. 565–91.

Yolton, John W. *Thinking Matter: Materialism in Eighteenth-Century Britain*. Minneapolis, MN, 1983; Oxford, 1984.

Yolton, John W., John Valdimir Price, and J. N. Stephens, eds. *The Dictionary of Eighteenth-Century British Philosophers*. 2 vols. Bristol, 1999.

Yolton, John W., and Jean S. Yolton. Introduction, in J. Locke, *Some Thoughts Concerning Education*, eds. J. W. Yolton and J. S. Yolton, pp. 1–70 (*B1*).

Young, B. W. *Religion and Enlightenment in Eighteenth-Century England: Theological Debate from Locke to Burke*. Oxford, 1998.

Youschkevitch, A. P. "Lazare Carnot and the Competition of the Berlin Academy in 1786 on the Mathematical Theory of the Infinite", in *Lazare Carnot, Savant*, ed. C. C. Gillispie, pp. 149–68.

Zabeeh, Farhang. *Hume, Precursor of Modern Empiricism: An Analysis of His Opinions on Meaning, Metaphysics, Logic and Mathematics*. The Hague, 1960.

Zac, Sylvain. *Spinoza en Allemagne: Mendelssohn, Lessing et Jacobi*. Paris, 1989.

Zammito, John. *The Genesis of Kant's Critique of Judgment*. Chicago, IL, 1992.

Zammito, John. *Kant, Herder, and the Birth of Anthropology*. Chicago, IL, 2002.

Zande, J. van der, and Richard H. Popkin, eds. *The Skeptical Tradition around 1800: Skepticism in Philosophy, Science, and Society*. Dordrecht, 1998.

Zart, G. *Einfluss der englischen Philosophen seit Bacon auf die deutsche Philosophie des 18. Jahrhunderts*. Berlin, 1881.

Zupko, Ronald Edward. *Revolution in Measurement: Western European Weights and Measures Since the Age of Science*. Philadelphia, PA, 1990.

Zurbuchen, Simone. "Gewissensfreiheit und Toleranz: Zur Pufendorf-Rezeption bei Christian Thomasius", in *Samuel Pufendorf und die europäische Frühaufklärung*, eds. F. Palladini and G. Hartung, pp. 169–80.

Zurbuchen, Simone. *Naturrecht und natürliche Religion. Zur Geschichte des Toleranzbegriffs von Samuel Pufendorf bis Jean-Jacques Rousseau*. Würzburg, 1991.

Zurbuchen, Simone. "Republicanism and Toleration", in *Republicanism: A Shared European Heritage*, eds. M. van Gelderen and Q. Skinner, 2 vols. Cambridge, 2002, vol. 2, pp. 47–71.

Zurbuchen, Simone. "Samuel Pufendorf's Concept of Toleration", in *Difference and Dissent, Theories of Tolerance in Medieval and Early Modern Europe*, eds. C. J. Nederman and J. C. Laursen. Lanham, 1996, pp. 163–84.

INDEX NOMINUM

INDEX RERUM